SOURCES AND METHODS
LABOUR STATISTICS
VOLUME 1
CONSUMER PRICE INDICES

THIRD EDITION

SOURCES ET MÉTHODES
STATISTIQUES DU TRAVAIL
VOLUME 1
INDICES DES PRIX À LA CONSOMMATION

TROISIÈME ÉDITION

FUENTES Y METODOS
ESTADISTICAS DEL TRABAJO
VOLUMEN 1
INDICES DE LOS PRECIOS DEL CONSUMO

TERCERA EDICION

SOURCES AND METHODS
LABOUR STATISTICS
VOLUME 1
CONSUMER PRICE INDICES

Companion to the *Year Book*
and *Bulletin of Labour Statistics*

THIRD EDITION

SOURCES ET MÉTHODES
STATISTIQUES DU TRAVAIL
VOLUME 1
INDICES DES PRIX À LA CONSOMMATION

Complément de l'*Annuaire* et du *Bulletin*
des statistiques du travail

TROISIÈME ÉDITION

FUENTES Y METODOS
ESTADISTICAS DEL TRABAJO
VOLUMEN 1
INDICES DE LOS PRECIOS DEL CONSUMO

Complemento del *Anuario* y del *Boletín*
de Estadísticas del Trabajo

TERCERA EDICION

INTERNATIONAL LABOUR OFFICE   GENEVA
BUREAU INTERNATIONAL DU TRAVAIL   GENÈVE
OFICINA INTERNACIONAL DEL TRABAJO   GINEBRA

Copyright ©
International Labour Organisation 1992

Publications of the International Labour Office enjoy copyright under Protocol 2 of the Universal Copyright Convention. Nevertheless, short excerpts from them may be reproduced without authorisation, on condition that the source is indicated. For rights of reproduction or translation, application should be made to the Publications Branch (Rights and Permissions), International Labour Office, CH-1211 Geneva 22, Switzerland. The International Labour Office welcomes such applications.

ISBN 92-2-007340-4
(the set of 2 volumes)
ISSN 0084-3857

This volume:
ISBN 92-2-008487-2
ISSN 1014-9856

Third edition 1992

The designations employed in ILO publications, which are in conformity with United Nations practice, and the presentation of material therein do not imply the expression of any opinion whatsoever on the part of the International Labour Office concerning the legal status of any country, area or territory or of its authorities, or concerning the delimitation of its frontiers. The responsibility for opinions expressed in signed articles, studies and other contributions rests solely with their authors, and publication does not constitute an endorsement by the International Labour Office of the opinions expressed in them.
Reference to names of firms and commercial products and processes does not imply their endorsement by the International Labour Office, and any failure to mention a particular firm, commercial product or process is not a sign of disapproval.

ILO publications can be obtained through major booksellers or ILO local offices in many countries, or direct from ILO Publications, International Labour Office, CH-1211 Geneva 22, Switzerland. A catalogue or list of new publications will be sent free of charge from the above address.

Printed in Switzerland

Copyright ©
Organisation internationale du Travail 1992

Les publications du Bureau international du Travail jouissent de la protection du droit d'auteur en vertu du protocole n° 2, annexe à la Convention universelle pour la protection du droit d'auteur. Toutefois, de courts passages pourront être reproduits sans autorisation, à la condition que leur source soit dûment mentionnée. Toute demande d'autorisation de reproduction ou de traduction devra être adressée au Service des publications (Droits et licences), Bureau international du Travail, CH-1211 Genève 22, Suisse. Ces demandes seront toujours les bienvenues.

ISBN 92-2-007340-4
(le jeu de 2 volumes)
ISSN 0084-3857

Ce volume:
ISBN 92-2-008487-2
ISSN 1014-9856

Troisième édition 1992

Les désignations utilisées dans les publications du BIT, qui sont conformes à la pratique des Nations Unies, et la présentation des données qui y figurent n'impliquent de la part du Bureau international du Travail aucune prise de position quant au statut juridique de tel ou tel pays, zone ou territoire, ou de ses autorités, ni quant au tracé de ses frontières. Les articles, études et autres textes signés n'engagent que leurs auteurs et leur publication ne signifie pas que le Bureau international du Travail souscrit aux opinions qui y sont exprimées. La mention ou la non-mention de telle ou telle entreprise ou de tel ou tel produit ou procédé commercial n'implique de la part du Bureau international du Travail aucune appréciation favorable ou défavorable.

Les publications du Bureau international du Travail peuvent être obtenues dans les principales librairies ou auprès des bureaux locaux du BIT. On peut aussi se les procurer directement, de même qu'un catalogue ou une liste des nouvelles publications, à l'adresse suivante: Publications du BIT, Bureau international du Travail, CH-1211 Genève 22, Suisse.

Imprimé en Suisse

Copyright ©
Organización Internacional del Trabajo 1992

Las publicaciones de la Oficina Internacional del Trabajo gozan de la protección de los derechos de propiedad intelectual en virtud del protocolo 2 anexo a la Convención Universal sobre Derecho de Autor. No obstante, ciertos extractos breves de estas publicaciones pueden reproducirse sin autorización, a condición de que se mencione la fuente. Para obtener los derechos de reproducción o de traducción hay que formular las correspondientes solicitudes al Servicio de Publicaciones (Derechos de autor y licencias), Oficina Internacional del Trabajo, CH-1211 Ginebra 22, Suiza, solicitudes que serán bien acogidas.

ISBN 92-2-007340-4
(el juego de 2 volúmenes)
ISSN 0084-3857

Este volúmen:
ISBN 92-2-008487-2
ISSN 1014-9856

Tercera edición 1992

Las denominaciones empleadas, en concordancia con la práctica seguida en las Naciones Unidas, y la forma en que aparecen presentados los datos en esta publicación no implican juicio alguno por parte de la Oficina Internacional del Trabajo sobre la condición jurídica de ninguno de los países, zonas o territorios citados o de sus autoridades, ni respecto de la delimitación de sus fronteras. La responsabilidad de las opiniones expresadas en los artículos, estudios y otras colaboraciones firmados incumbe exclusivamente a sus autores, y su publicación no significa que la OIT las sancione.
Las referencias a firmas o a procesos o productos comerciales no implican aprobación alguna por la Oficina Internacional del Trabajo, y el hecho de que no se mencionen firmas o procesos o productos comerciales no implica desaprobación alguna.

Las publicaciones de la OIT pueden obtenerse en las principales librerías o en oficinas locales de la OIT en muchos países o pidiéndolas a: Publicaciones de la OIT, Oficina Internacional del Trabajo, CH-1211 Ginebra 22, Suiza, que también puede enviar a quienes lo soliciten un catálogo o una lista de nuevas publicaciones.

Impreso en Suiza   BAS

Important

● In order to enhance the usefulness of the *Year Book of Labour Statistics,* each issue will now be accompanied by a methodological volume of the series formerly entitled *Statistical Sources and Methods.*

● This series, which will in future be known as *Sources and Methods: Labour statistics,* provides methodological descriptions of the data published in the *Year Book* and *Bulletin of Labour Statistics.* Each volume covers different subjects according to the source of the data; gradually, all the subjects in the *Year Book* will be covered by a volume in this series.

● The methodological descriptions include information on the method of data collection, coverage, concepts and definitions, classifications, historical changes, technical references, etc. In each volume the information is presented by country under standard headings.

Important

● Afin de mettre en valeur l'utilité de l'*Annuaire des statistiques du travail,* chaque édition sera dorénavant accompagnée d'un volume méthodologique de la série intitulée précédemment *Sources et méthodes statistiques.*

● Cette série, qui s'appellera à l'avenir *Sources et méthodes: statistiques du travail,* fournit des descriptions méthodologiques des données publiées dans l'*Annuaire* et dans le *Bulletin des statistiques du travail.* Chaque volume traite de sujets différents suivant la source des données; progressivement, tous les sujets traités dans l'*Annuaire* seront couverts par un volume de cette série.

● Les descriptions méthodologiques contiennent des informations sur la méthode de collecte des donnée, la portée, les concepts et définitions, les classifications, les modifications apportées aux séries, les références techniques, etc. Dans chaque volume, les informations sont présentées par pays sous des rubriques standardisées.

Importante

● Con el fin de mejorar la utilidad del *Anuario de Estadísticas del Trabajo,* desde ahora cada edición irá acompañada de un volumen metodológico de la serie titulada anteriormente *Fuentes y Métodos Estadísticos.*

● Esta serie, que en lo sucesivo se llamará *Fuentes y Métodos: Estadísticas del trabajo,* proporciona las descripciones metodológicas de los datos que se publican en el *Anuario* y el *Boletín de Estadísticas del Trabajo.* Cada volumen abarca diferentes temas de acuerdo con la fuente de los datos; en forma gradual, todos los temas del *Anuario* quedarán cubiertos por un volumen de esta serie.

● Las descripciones metodológicas incluyen informaciones acerca del método de recolección de datos, el alcance, los conceptos y definiciones, las clasificaciones, los cambios históricos, las referencias técnicas, etc. En cada volumen, la información se presenta por país de acuerdo a encabezamientos estándar.

PREFACE

This third edition of Volume 1 of the series *Sources and Methods: Labour Statistics* is a revised and enlarged version of Volume 1 of the series Statistical Sources and Methods, published in 1987. Information about new developments and corrections which were received after June 1992 have been introduced into the database and can be forwarded by the ILO Bureau of Statistics upon request. The series comprises the following volumes:

Volume 1 Consumer price indices (Geneva, 1992).

Volume 2 Employment, wages and hours of work (establishment surveys) (Geneva, 1987).

Volume 3 Economically active population, employment, unemployment, wages and hours of work (household surveys) (Geneva, 1990).

Volume 4 Employment, unemployment, wages and hours of work (administrative records and related sources) (Geneva, 1989).

Volume 5 Total and economically active population, employment and unemployment (population censuses) (Geneva, 1990).

Volume 6 Household income and expenditure surveys (Geneva, 1992).

The present volume of this series provides methodological information on national series of consumer price indices. Further volumes will contain methodological information on total and economically active population, employment, unemployment, wages and hours of work, labour cost, occupational injuries, strikes and lock-outs, and household income and expenditure surveys.

The purpose of these volumes is to document the national practices used in the collection of various types of labour statistics in order to assist the users of these statistics in evaluating their quality and comparability, and their validity for the user's descriptive and analytical needs. *Sources and Methods: Labour Statistics* can consequently be seen as companion volumes to the various chapters of the ILO *Year Book of Labour Statistics* and of the *Bulletin of Labour Statistics*.

This volume was prepared by Ms. R. Fokianos of the ILO Bureau of Statistics.

Its computerised production was carried out by Mr. P. Cornu of the ILO Bureau of Statistics.

AVANT-PROPOS

Cette troisième édition du volume 1 de la série des *Sources et méthodes: statistiques du travail* est une version mise à jour et augmentée du volume 1 de la série des Sources et méthodes statistiques publié en 1987. Les informations concernant des faits nouveaux et les corrections reçues après juin 1992 ont été introduites dans la base de données et peuvent être transmises sur simple demande adressée au Bureau de statistique du BIT. La série comprend les volumes suivants:

Volume 1 Indices des prix à la consommation (Genève, 1992).

Volume 2 Emploi, durée du travail et salaires (enquêtes auprès des établissements) (Genève, 1990).

Volume 3 Population active, emploi, chômage et durée du travail (enquêtes auprès des ménages) (Genève, 1991).

Volume 4 Emploi, chômage, salaires et durée du travail (documents administratifs et sources assimilées) (Genève, 1989).

Volume 5 Population totale et population active, emploi et chômage (recensements de population) (Genève, 1990).

Volume 6 Enquêtes sur le revenu et les dépenses des ménages (en préparation).

Le présent volume fournit des informations méthodologiques des séries nationales des indices des prix à la consommation. Les autres volumes contiendront des informations méthodologiques sur la population totale et la population active, l'emploi, le chômage, la durée du travail, les salaires, le coût de la main-d'oeuvre, les lésions professionnelles, les grèves et les lock-out, les enquêtes sur le revenu et les dépenses des ménages.

Ces volumes ont pour but de renseigner sur les pratiques nationales appliquées pour établir différentes statistiques du travail et d'aider ainsi les utilisateurs de ces statistiques à en apprécier la qualité, la comparabilité et la validité pour leurs besoins descriptifs et analytiques. On peut donc voir dans les volumes *Sources et méthodes: statistiques du travail*, un complément aux diverses éditions de l'*Annuaire des statistiques du travail* et du *Bulletin des statistiques du travail* du BIT.

Ce volume a été préparé par Mme. R. Fokianos du Bureau de statistique du BIT.

La production informatique a été assurée par M. P. Cornu du Bureau de statistique du BIT.

PREFACIO

Esta tercera edición del volumen 1 de la serie de *Fuentes y métodos: estadísticas del trabajo* es una versión actualizada y ampliada del volumen 1 de la serie de Fuentes y Métodos Estadísticos publicada en 1987. Las informaciones adicionales y las correcciones que llegaron a la oficina después de junio de 1992 se introdujeron en la base de datos y los interesados pueden solicitarlas a la Oficina de Estadísticas de la OIT. La serie comprende los siguientes volúmenes:

Volumen 1 Indices de los precios del consumo (Ginebra, 1992).

Volumen 2 Empleo, salarios y horas de trabajo (encuestas de establecimientos) (Ginebra, 1990).

Volumen 3 Población económicamente activa, empleo, desempleo y horas de trabajo (encuesta de hogares) (Ginebra, 1992).

Volumen 4 Empleo, desempleo, salarios y horas de trabajo (registros administrativos y fuentes conexas) (Ginebra, 1989).

Volumen 5 Población total y población económicamente activa, empleo y desempleo (censos de población) (Ginebra, 1990).

Volumen 6 Encuestas de ingresos y gastos de los hogares (en preparación).

El presente volumen ofrece informaciones metodológicas de las series nacionales de índices de precios del consumo. Otros volúmenes abarcaron informaciones metodológicas sobre la población total y población activa, empleo, desempleo, horas de trabajo, salarios, costo de la mano de obra, lesiones profesionales, huelgas y cierres patronales, y encuestas de ingresos y gastos de los hogares.

El objetivo de estas publicaciones consiste en documentar las prácticas nacionales seguidas para recopilar los diferentes tipos de estadísticas del trabajo y ayudar a evaluar su calidad y comparabilidad, así como su adecuación a las necesidades descriptivas y analíticas de quienes las utilicen. Las *Fuentes y métodos: estadísticas del trabajo*, se pueden considerar por tanto como volúmenes que acompañan a las diversas ediciones del *Anuario de Estadísticas del Trabajo* y del *Boletín de Estadísticas del Trabajo* de la OIT.

La preparación del contenido de este volumen estuvo a cargo de la Sra. R. Fokianos, de la Oficina de Estadísticas de la OIT.

La elaboración computarizada estuvo a cargo del Sr. P. Cornu, de la Oficina de Estadísticas de la OIT.

CONTENTS

Introduction   1

Algeria (Algiers)   2

American Samoa (Pago-Pago)   2

Angola (Luanda)   3

Antigua and Barbuda   3

Argentina (Buenos Aires)   4

Australia   5

Austria   6

Bahamas   6

Bangladesh (Dhaka)   7

Barbados   7

Belgium   8

Belize   9

Bermuda   10

Bolivia (La Paz)   10

Botswana   11

Brazil   11

Brazil (Sao Paulo)   12

Brunei Darussalam   12

Bulgaria   13

Burkina Faso (Ouagadougou)   13

Burundi (Bujumbura)   14

Cameroon (Yaoundé, Africans)   14

Cameroon (Yaoundé, Europeans)   15

Canada   15

Cape Verde (Praya)   17

Cayman Islands   17

Central African Rep. (Bangui)   18

Chad (N'Djamena)   18

Chile   19

China   20

Colombia   20

Commonwealth of Independent States   21

Congo (Brazzaville, Africans)   22

Congo (Brazzaville, Europeans)   22

Cook Islands (Rarotonga)   23

Costa Rica (San José)   23

Côte d'Ivoire (Abidjan, Africans)   24

Côte d'Ivoire (Abidjan, Europeans)   24

Cyprus   24

Czechoslovakia   26

Denmark   26

Dominica   27

Dominican Republic   28

Ecuador   28

Egypt   29

El Salvador   30

Ethiopia (Addis Ababa)   30

Falkland Is. (Malvinas) (Stanley)   31

Fiji   31

Finland   32

France   34

French Guiana (Cayenne)   34

French Polynesia   35

Gabon (Libreville 1)   35

Gabon (Libreville 2)   36

Gambia (Banjul, Kombo St. Mary)   36

Germany 1   37

Germany 2   38

Ghana   38

Gibraltar   39

Greece   40

Greenland   40

Grenada   41

Guadeloupe   42

Guam   42

Guatemala   43

Guyana   43

Haiti   44

Honduras   44

Hong Kong   45

Hungary   46

Iceland (Reykjavik)   47

India (All India 1)   48

India (All India 2)   48

India (All India 3)   49

India (Delhi)   50

Indonesia   51

Iran, Islamic Rep. of   52
Iraq   52
Ireland   53
Isle of Man   54
Israel   55
Italy   56
Jamaica   56
Japan   57
Jordan   58
Kenya (Nairobi)   58
Kiribati (Tarawa)   59
Korea, Republic of   59
Kuwait   60
Lesotho   61
Liberia (Monrovia)   61
Luxembourg   62
Macau   63
Madagascar (Antananarivo)   64
Madagascar (Antananarivo, Europeans)   64
Malawi (Blantyre 1)   65
Malawi (Blantyre 2)   66
Malaysia   66
Mali (Bamako)   67
Malta   67
Martinique   68
Mauritius   69
Mexico   69
Montserrat   70
Morocco   70
Myanmar (Yangon)   71
Nepal   71
Netherlands   72
Netherlands Antilles   73
New Caledonia (Noumea)   73
New Zealand   74
Nicaragua (Managua)   76
Niger (Niamey, Africans)   76
Niger (Niamey, Europeans)   76
Nigeria 1   77
Nigeria 2   77
Niue   78
Norway   78

Pakistan   79
Panama (Panama City)   79
Papua New Guinea   80
Paraguay (Asunción)   81
Peru (Lima)   81
Philippines   82
Poland   83
Portugal   83
Puerto Rico   84
Qatar   85
Réunion   85
Romania   86
Rwanda (Kigali)   86
St. Helena   87
St. Lucia   87
St. Vincent and the Grenadines (St. Vincent)   88
Samoa   88
San Marino   89
Saudi Arabia 1   89
Saudi Arabia 2   90
Senegal (Dakar)   91
Seychelles   92
Sierra Leone (Freetown)   92
Singapore   93
Solomon Islands (Honiara)   94
South Africa   95
Spain   95
Sri Lanka (Colombo)   96
Sudan   96
Suriname (Paramaribo)   97
Swaziland (Mbabane-Manzini)   97
Sweden   98
Switzerland   99
Syrian Arab Republic (Damascus)   99
Tanzania (Tanganyika)   100
Thailand   100
Togo (Lomé)   101
Tonga   101
Trinidad and Tobago   102
Tunisia   103
Turkey   104

Uganda (Kampala) 105

United Kingdom 106

United States 107

Uruguay (Montevideo) 107

Vanuatu 108

Venezuela (Caracas) 108

Virgin Islands (British) 109

Yemen (Aden) 109

Yugoslavia 110

Zambia 110

Zimbabwe 111

TABLE DES MATIERES

Introduction   113
Afrique du Sud   114
Algérie (Alger)   114
Allemagne 1   115
Allemagne 2   116
Angola (Luanda)   117
Antigua-et-Barbuda   118
Antilles néerlandaises   118
Arabie saoudite 1   118
Arabie saoudite 2   120
Argentine (Buenos Aires)   121
Australie   122
Autriche   123
Bahamas   124
Bangladesh (Dhaka)   125
Barbade   125
Belgique   126
Belize   127
Bermudes   128
Bolivie (La Paz)   128
Botswana   129
Brésil   130
Brésil (Sao Paulo)   130
Brunéi Darussalam   131
Bulgarie   131
Burkina Faso (Ouagadougou)   132
Burundi (Bujumbura)   132
Cameroun (Yaoundé, Africains)   133
Cameroun (Yaoundé, Européens)   133
Canada   134
Cap-Vert (Praya)   135
Rép. centrafricaine (Bangui)   136
Chili (Santiago)   136
Chine   137
Chypre   137
Colombie   139
Communauté des Etats Indépendants   140
Congo (Brazzaville, Africains)   141
Congo (Brazzaville, Européens)   141
République de Corée   142
Costa Rica (San José)   142
Côte d'Ivoire (Abidjan, Africains)   143
Côte d'Ivoire (Abidjan, Européens)   143
Danemark   144
République dominicaine   145
Dominique   145
Egypte   146
El Salvador   147
Equateur   147
Espagne   148
Etats-Unis   149
Ethiopie (Addis-Abeba)   150
Fidji   150
Finlande   151
France   153
Gabon (Libreville 1)   154
Gabon (Libreville 2)   154
Gambie (Banjul, Kombo St. Mary)   155
Ghana   155
Gibraltar   156
Grèce   157
Grenade   157
Groenland   158
Guadeloupe   159
Guam   160
Guatemala   160
Guyana   161
Guyane française (Cayenne)   161
Haïti   162
Honduras   162
Hong-kong   163
Hongrie   164
Iles Caïmanes   165
Iles Cook (Rarotonga)   166
Iles Falkland (Malvinas) (Stanley)   166
Ile de Man   167
Iles Salomon (Honiara)   167
Iles Vierges (britanniques)   168

Inde (ensemble du pays 1)   168
Inde (ensemble du pays 2)   169
Inde (ensemble du pays 3)   170
Inde (Delhi)   171
Indonésie   172
Iran, Rép. islamique d'   173
Iraq   173
Irlande   174
Islande (Reykjavik)   176
Israël   177
Italie   178
Jamaïque   179
Japon   180
Jordanie   181
Kenya (Nairobi)   181
Kiribati (Tarawa)   182
Koweït   182
Lesotho   183
Libéria (Monrovia)   184
Luxembourg   185
Macao   186
Madagascar (Antananarivo)   187
Madagascar (Antananarivo, Européens)   187
Malaisie   188
Malawi (Blantyre 1)   189
Malawi (Blantyre 2)   190
Mali (Bamako)   190
Malte   191
Maroc   191
Martinique   192
Maurice   193
Mexique   194
Montserrat   194
Myanmar (Yangon)   195
Népal   195
Nicaragua (Managua)   196
Niger (Niamey, Africains)   196
Niger (Niamey, Européens)   197
Nigéria 1   197
Nigéria 2   198
Nioué   198
Norvège   199

Nouvelle-Calédonie (Nouméa)   199
Nouvelle-Zélande   200
Ouganda (Kampala)   202
Pakistan   203
Panama (ville de Panama)   204
Papouasie-Nouvelle-Guinée   205
Paraguay (Asunción)   205
Pays-Bas   206
Pérou (Lima)   207
Philippines   208
Pologne   209
Polynésie française   209
Porto Rico   210
Portugal   210
Qatar   211
Réunion   211
Roumanie   212
Royaume-Uni   213
Rwanda (Kigali)   214
Sainte-Hélène   215
Sainte-Lucie   215
Saint-Marin   216
Saint-Vincent-et-Grenadines (St. Vincent)   216
Samoa   217
Samoa américaines (Pago-Pago)   217
Sénégal (Dakar)   217
Seychelles   218
Sierra Leone (Freetown)   218
Singapour   219
Soudan   221
Sri Lanka (Colombo)   221
Suède   222
Suisse   223
Suriname (Paramaribo)   224
Swaziland (Mbabane-Manzini)   224
République arabe syrienne (Damas)   225
Tanzanie (Tanganyika)   225
Tchad (N'Djamena)   226
Tchécoslovaquie   227
Thaïlande   228
Togo (Lomé)   228

Tonga   229

Trinité-et-Tobago   230

Tunisie   231

Turquie   232

Uruguay (Montevideo)   233

Vanuatu   233

Venezuela (Caracas)   234

Yémen (Aden)   235

Yougoslavie   235

Zambie   235

Zimbabwe   236

CONTENIDO

Introducción   239

Alemania 1   240

Alemania 2   241

Angola (Luanda)   242

Antigua y Barbuda   242

Antillas Neerlandesas   243

Arabia Saudita 1   243

Arabia Saudita 2   244

Argelia (Argel)   245

Argentina (Buenos Aires)   246

Australia   247

Austria   249

Bahamas   249

Bangladesh (Dhaka)   250

Barbados   251

Bélgica   251

Belice   252

Bermudas   253

Bolivia (La Paz)   253

Botswana   254

Brasil   255

Brasil (Sao Paulo)   256

Brunéi Darussalam   256

Bulgaria   257

Burkina Faso (Ouagadougou)   257

Burundi (Bujumbura)   257

Cabo Verde (Praya)   258

Camerún (Yaundé, africanos)   258

Camerún (Yaundé, europeos)   259

Canadá   259

Rep. Centroafricana (Bangui)   261

Colombia   261

Comunidad de Estados Independientes   263

Congo (Brazzaville, africanos)   263

Congo (Brazzaville, europeos)   264

República de Corea   264

Costa Rica (San José)   265

Côte d'Ivoire (Abidjan, africanos)   266

Côte d'Ivoire (Abidjan, europeos)   266

Chad (N'Djamena)   267

Checoslovaquia   268

Chile (Santiago)   268

China   269

Chipre   270

Dinamarca   271

Dominica   272

República Dominicana   272

Ecuador   273

Egipto   273

El Salvador   275

España   275

Estados Unidos   276

Etiopía (Addis Abeba)   277

Fiji   277

Filipinas   278

Finlandia   279

Francia   281

Gabón (Libreville 1)   282

Gabón (Libreville 2)   282

Gambia (Banjul, Kombo St. Mary)   283

Ghana   283

Gibraltar   284

Granada   284

Grecia   285

Groenlandia   286

Guadalupe   287

Guam   288

Guatemala   288

Guayana Francesa (Cayena)   289

Guyana   289

Haití   290

Honduras   290

Hong Kong   291

Hungría   292

India (todo el país 1)   293

India (todo el país 2)   293

India (todo el país 3)   295

India (Delhi)   296

Indonesia 297
Irán, Rep. Islámica del 297
Iraq 298
Irlanda 298
Islandia (Reykiavik) 300
Islas Caimán 301
Islas Cook (Rarotonga) 302
Islas Malvinas (Falkland) (Stanley) 303
Isla de Man 303
Islas Salomón (Honiara) 304
Islas Vírgenes (Británicas) 304
Israel 305
Italia 306
Jamaica 306
Japón 307
Jordania 308
Kenya (Nairobi) 308
Kiribati (Tarawa) 309
Kuwait 309
Lesotho 310
Liberia (Monrovia) 311
Luxemburgo 311
Macao 313
Madagascar (Antananarivo) 313
Madagascar (Antananarivo, europeos) 314
Malasia 315
Malawi (Blantyre 1) 316
Malawi (Blantyre 2) 317
Malí (Bamako) 317
Malta 318
Marruecos 318
Martinica 319
Mauricio 319
México 320
Montserrat 321
Myanmar (Yangon) 321
Nepal 322
Nicaragua (Managua) 322
Níger (Niamey, africanos) 323
Níger (Niamey, europeos) 323
Nigeria 1 324
Nigeria 2 324

Niue 325
Noruega 325
Nueva Caledonia (Numea) 326
Nueva Zelandia 326
Países Bajos 329
Pakistán 329
Panamá (ciudad de Panamá) 330
Papua Nueva Guinea 331
Paraguay (Asunción) 332
Perú (Lima) 333
Polinesia Francesa 334
Polonia 334
Portugal 335
Puerto Rico 335
Qatar 336
Reino Unido 336
Reunión 338
Rumania 338
Rwanda (Kigali) 339
Samoa 340
Samoa Americana (Pago-Pago) 340
San Marino 340
San Vicente y las Granadinas (St. Vincent) 341
Santa Elena 341
Santa Lucía 342
Senegal (Dakar) 342
Seychelles 343
Sierra Leona (Freetown) 343
Singapur 344
República Arabe Siria (Damasco) 346
Sri Lanka (Colombo) 346
Sudáfrica 347
Sudán 347
Suecia 348
Suiza 349
Suriname (Paramaribo) 350
Swazilandia (Mbabane-Manzini) 350
Tailandia 351
Tanzanía (Tangañika) 352
Togo (Lomé) 352
Tonga 353

Trinidad y Tabago   354

Túnez   355

Turquía   356

Uganda (Kampala)   356

Uruguay (Montevideo)   357

Vanuatu   358

Venezuela (Caracas)   358

Yemen (Aden)   359

Yugoslavia   359

Zambia   360

Zimbabwe   360

INTRODUCTION

The present Volume 1 of *Sources and Methods: Labour Statistics* provides methodological descriptions of national consumer price indices published by the ILO in the 1992 editions of the *Year Book of Labour Statistics* and the *Bulletin of Labour Statistics*. It is a revised, enlarged and updated version of the second edition of *Statistical Sources and Methods* issued in 1987.

This volume contains descriptions of 171 consumer price series in respect of 157 countries. Most of the descriptions were prepared from the official replies from national statistical offices to a specifically designed questionnaire and/or from national publications on consumer price indices. In certain cases, the descriptions presented may relate only to new series published in the *Bulletin* pending the availability of annual averages to be published in a later issue of the *Year Book*.

The volume has two main purposes: (i) to provide basic information on the sources and methods used in each country in compiling the consumer price indices published by the ILO, so as to enhance their usefulness for different purposes; and (ii) to indicate the differences between the various national series with regard to their scope, coverage, sources of data, definitions, classifications, the treatment of selected special problems and the formula used for computation. The descriptions have been structured and presented using 14 standard headings for the different characteristics in order to facilitate comparisons. These headings are as follows.

Official title
The title of the consumer price index in the language used in official correspondence between the country and the ILO and, if necessary, its English translation.

Scope
Information is given on the periodicity of the series (monthly, quarterly, half-yearly or yearly); the types of household covered in terms of households within a given income or expenditure class or households of a specific size; the population groups covered, which may refer to the whole population or specific socio-economic groups such as industrial workers, non-manual employees, etc.; and the geographical areas covered, such as the whole country, urban centres, the capital city, specific towns or a group of towns.

Official base
The base year or period used in the original computation of the index, and its presentation in national publications.

Source of weights
The source(s) and the reference period of the weights used for the index, e.g. a household expenditure survey, national accounts, etc. If the reference period for the weights differs from the base period of the index, the adjustments made to the weights to take account of the price changes between the two periods are described.

If the weights were derived from a household expenditure survey, information is provided about the types of household, population groups and geographic areas covered, the duration of the survey, the reference period for expenditure data and the sample size. If the weights were obtained from the national accounts or other sources, the methods of deriving them are given, wherever possible. The criteria and the method used for selecting index items or for dealing with items not priced (imputation of weights) are also described.

Weights and composition
The number of items and the weights used to compute the index are given according to expenditure group. The term "item" is used here to mean the smallest grouping of goods and services for which a specific weight is given. For example, beef might be an item represented by several varieties such as round steak, sirloin steak, etc., for which separate weights are not available. The following major groups are distinguished: food; fuel and light; clothing; housing; and miscellaneous. However, if the national classification does not conform with the above groupings, the actual classification used by the country is given. Where possible, the approximate number of price quotations used for computing the index is indicated.

Household consumption expenditure
Household consumption expenditure is generally defined as the expenditure incurred by private households on consumer goods and services. It may refer to actual purchases or to actual consumption. The descriptions explain, wherever possible, the treatment of home-produced goods consumed by the household, home ownership, durable goods credit purchases, second-hand purchases, contributions to social insurance and pension funds, licence fees, insurance associated with specific consumer goods, health care, income and other direct taxes, life insurance payments, remittances, gifts and other similar disbursements.

Method of data collection
The methods used for selecting localities and outlets; the frequency with which prices are collected for different categories of goods and services; the treatment of discounts, sale prices, black-market prices, hire-purchase or credit terms, second-hand purchases, import prices and indirect taxes; the methods of collecting prices for different types of item (visits to outlets, mail questionnaires, official tariffs, actual purchases); and special techniques used for price collection in respect of such items as electricity, gas and water, medical care, education or transport and communication.

Housing
The methods used to obtain data on rents, as well as the treatment of owner-occupied dwellings. The treatment of disbursements such as rates, insurance, mortgage interest, repairs, etc., and the methods and frequency of collecting the data are indicated when information is available.

Specification of varieties
Specifications are the criteria used to describe precisely the variety being priced. These could be in terms of quality, make, brand, unit, etc. The procedure used to identify the varieties when there are no detailed and tight specifications is indicated.

Substitution, quality change, etc.
The appearance of a new product on the market, and the disappearance of an item or quality changes affect the index. The methods used by countries to deal with these problems are described briefly.

Seasonal items
If the index includes items such as fresh fruit and vegetables which experience seasonal fluctuations in their prices or availability, the procedures used to deal with these seasonal influences are briefly noted.

Computation
The price data for the different items included in the computation of the index are normally weighted in order to take into account the relative importance of each item with respect to total consumption expenditure. In most countries, the indices are computed in a derived form such as weighted arithmetic averages of price relatives for a selected number of representative items between the period under consideration and the base period, using one or other forms of Laspeyres' formula. The descriptions explain the exact methods used by the countries wherever these are known. A few countries use a Laspeyres' chain index with yearly links or Paasche's formula for computing their indices. These are indicated in the descriptions.

The methods of calculating the average prices and price relatives, as well as whether the index is computed directly or as an aggregation of local or regional indices, are also described.

Other information
Where available, complementary information is furnished concerning the publication by the country of various sub-groups of the index, or the computation of series for other population or income groups or other geographical areas.

Organisation and publication
The statistical authority responsible for computing and publishing the index, as well as the titles of the major current national publications in which the index appears, are given under this heading. Wherever possible, the titles and sources of national publications providing detailed methodological descriptions of the series are also indicated.

List of tables published by the ILO
A. *Year Book of Labour Statistics:*

Consumer Prices:

23 General indices
24 General indices, excluding shelter
25 Food indices
26 Fuel and light indices
27 Clothing indices
28 Rent indices

B. *Bulletin of Labour Statistics*.
  9A General indices
  9B Food indices

Remarks
As the original base period of the series varies between countries, a uniform base period has been adopted for the presentation of the data in ILO publications. Since 1986 this base period has been changed to the year 1980. (If data are available only for periods subsequent to 1980, the indices are generally shown with the first calendar year for which the figures are available as the base period and are printed in italics.) This operation involves no change in the weighting system used for the computation of the series.

Signs and symbols used
.	Not applicable
...	Not available
-	Nil or less than half of unit employed
(a)	Footnote to table

In the tables, decimal points are indicated by a full stop.

ALGERIA (ALGIERS)

Official title
Consumer Price Index (Indice des prix à la consommation).

Scope
The index is compiled monthly and relates to all households of all sizes and all socio-professional categories in Algiers.

Official base
1982 = 100.

Source of weights
The weights were derived from the results of a national household expenditure survey conducted between March 1979 and March 1980, covering a sample of 8,208 households throughout Algeria divided into six housing areas, five economic zones and 20 socio-professional categories. The index relates to all households (except for unmarried people) of all sizes and all socio-professional categories in the town of Algiers. The articles selected were taken from a census of varieties and services consumed by households conducted in 1982. The index covers 712 varieties selected on the basis of criteria such as annual expenditure, frequency of expenditure, use. The weights of the varieties are calculated on the basis of annual expenditure in 1979. The coverage rate of the index (in terms of expenditure on consumption) is 93 per cent.

Weights and composition

Major groups	Number of items	Weights	Approximate number of price quotations
Food	56	522.4	9,919
Clothing and footwear	59	70.6	709
Housing fuel and light	9	72.5	95
Furniture and furnishings	43	55.0	152
Medical care	26	26.5	6
Transport and communication	20	96.1	47
Education and recreation	20	42.3	28
Other goods and services	23	84.6	128
Total	256	1,000.0	11,084

Household consumption expenditure
The consumption expenditure taken into account to establish the weights includes the goods and services recorded during the survey on household expenditure. The following are excluded: investments, property owned, national insurance and pension fund contributions, trading licences, income tax and other direct taxes, insurance premiums, remission of funds, donations and similar payments.

Method of data collection
Price quotations are obtained periodically by agents in ten geographic sectors of the town of Algiers from a sample of outlets (public and private) in accordance with a survey programme established for each group of goods and services. Declared or posted prices are recorded. On average almost 450 varieties are investigated each month and approximately 11,000 prices are processed each month. Fresh fruit and vegetables and fresh fish are surveyed three times a week at ten public and private retail outlets (markets); meat, poultry and eggs are surveyed twice a month at 36 public and private retail outlets.
Prices for clothing are recorded every four months. Information regarding water, electricity, gas, education, transport and communications is obtained once a year and information concerning medical care is obtained twice a year.

Housing
The agents record the price of the rent plus additional expenses once a year for dwellings with three rooms, kitchen and bathroom; for the public sector they consult organisations responsible for managing buildings and for the private sector they consult households. The index for the "rent" group is obtained by combining the public sector index with the private sector index.
Owner-occupied dwellings are not taken into account in the computation of the index.

Specification of varieties
A census of varieties of goods and services consumed by households was conducted in 1982. On this basis of the results, almost 2,000 varieties were processed (specification, definition of the item, calculation of average price) for the index. Each article has detailed specifications and a description of the variety, the quality, the manufacture, the make, the unit, etc.

Substitution, quality change, etc.
Changes in the quality of an article and the appearance of new articles on the market are not taken into account in the computation of the index.

Seasonal items
Due to the seasonal nature of their marketing, fresh fruit and vegetables receive special treatment: using a monthly high-season basket, an index is calculated which compares the costs of the current month's basket with the cost for the same month in the reference year (1982). The base prices of the varieties in the basket are monthly as are the weights. The comparison of the indices of different months does not indicate a (relative) pure variation in prices, but the ratio between the variations of prices for each month.

Computation
The index is computed according to the Laspeyres formula as a weighted arithmetic average with fixed base, the weights corresponding to 1979.

Other information
At present a national index is computed by observing prices in a sample of 18 towns and villages. This has been calculated on a monthly basis since January 1989.

Organisation and publication
Office national des statistiques: "Statistiques" (quarterly) (Algiers).

AMERICAN SAMOA (PAGO-PAGO)

Official title
Retail Price Index.

Scope
Not available.

Official base
January - March 1974 = 100.

Source of weights
The weights used to compute the index were derived from import statistics.

Weights and composition
Not available.

Household consumption expenditure
Not available.

Method of data collection
Prices are collected each quarter from seven supermarkets, by agents.

Housing
Not available.

Specification of varieties
Not available.

Substitution, quality change, etc.
Not available.

Seasonal items
Seasonal fluctuations in the prices of certain items are taken into account by maintaining the closing prices for the previous season during the off season.

Computation
The index is computed according to the Laspeyres formula as a weighted arithmetic average with fixed base, using weights corresponding to the base period.

Other information
A new series (base October-December 1982 = 100) is now computed but the relevant methodological information was not available in the ILO at the time the present volume was published.

Organisation and publication
The index is compiled by the Economic and Planning Office (Fagotogo).

ANGOLA (LUANDA)

Official title
Indice de Preços no Consumidor da cidade de Luanda (Consumer Price Index - Luanda).

Scope
The index is computed monthly and relates to urban households in Luanda.

Official base
December 1990 = 100.

Source of weights
The weights and items were derived from a household expenditure survey conducted by UNICEF and the Instituto Nacional de Estatística from February to April 1990 in 16 districts of Luanda. The weights of items not selected for pricing were distributed over similar items within the sub-group.

Weights and composition

Major groups	Number of items	Weights	Approximate number of price quotations
Food and tobacco	85	74.07	4,200
Clothing and footwear	10	5.48	450
Housing (incl. fuel and light)	6	5.47	200
Furniture, household goods, repair and maintenance	26	4.67	1,065
Medical care	5	1.81	110
Transport and communications	7	3.92	35
Education and recreation	11	2.69	250
Other goods and services	10	1.89	410
Total	160	100.00	6,720

Household consumption expenditure
Consumption expenditure used to derive the weights relates to goods and services acquired during the period of the survey excluding investments, transfers, house purchase and extensive repairs, business expenses, etc.

Method of data collection
Prices are collected from 81 selected markets, retail outlets and service establishments in Luanda. Depending on the nature of the item, prices are ascertained each day (food items), week or month (newspaper, fuel, electricity). Until December 1991, prices for subsidised items sold to workers by means of a ration card were obtained as well as free market prices. The prices collected refer to those actually paid by consumers.

Housing
Not available.

Specification of varieties
Specifications for heterogeneous items are detailed, and given in terms of the quality, brand, model, size, unit of measure, etc. to ensure that the same item is priced over time. Homogeneous items need less specifications (e.g. white sugar: kg.).

Substitution, quality change, etc.
If a product is no longer available, a similar product to the original is substituted and a method of linking is used.

Seasonal items
Weights for seasonal items are not very important and relate to mangoes, pineapples and oranges. Seasonal fluctuations in the prices of these items are taken into account by maintaining the closing prices for the previous season during the off season.

Computation
The index is computed according to the Laspeyres formula as a weighted arithmetic average with fixed base, using weights corresponding to the period February to April 1990.
In computing item indices, price relatives for the current period and the base period are used. Relatives of average prices are calculated for those items with homogeneous varieties and averages of price relatives are used for those with heterogeneous varieties.

Other information
Detailed information on group and sub-group indices are also published for official market and free-market prices.

Organisation and publication
Instituto Nacional de Estatística: "Indice de Preços no Consumidor da Cidade de Luanda" (Luanda).
Idem: "Metodología do Indice de Preços no Consumidor de Luanda", serie A: Metodología No. 1 (November 1991).

ANTIGUA AND BARBUDA

Official title
Cost of Living Index.

Scope
The index is compiled monthly and relates to middle-class households with a monthly income of between 350 and 550 East Caribbean dollars in 1974, and with a monthly average family size of four to five members (including at least three adults).

Official base
1 January 1969 = 100.

Source of weights
The weights and items were based on a standard average monthly market basket derived from the results of various studies of consumption patterns of a cross-section of households of different sizes and incomes, conducted in 1974.

Weights and composition

Major groups	Number of items	Weights	Approximate number of price quotations
Food	43	46.5	...
Rent, fuel and light	4	28.8	...
Clothing and footwear	4	7.5	...
Transport	1	10.0	...
Personal and medical care, recreation, etc.	9	7.2	...
Total	61	100.0	...

Household consumption expenditure
Not available.

Method of data collection
For the period 1969-1973, prices were ascertained from various sources for 1 January and 1 July of each year. Since 1976, prices have been collected each month.

Housing
Not available.

Specification of varieties
Not available.

Substitution, quality change, etc.
Not available.

Seasonal items
Not available.

Computation
The index is compiled according to the Laspeyres formula as a weighted arithmetic average with fixed base, using weights corresponding to the base period.

Organisation and publication
Ministry of Planning, Development and External Affairs, Statistics Division: "Cost of Living Index" (Antigua).
Idem: "Cost of Living Index 1969-1974" (Antigua), Vol. I.

ARGENTINA (BUENOS AIRES)

Official title
Consumer Price Index (Indice de precios al consumidor).

Scope
The index is computed monthly and covers private households living in the Federal Capital and the 19 suburbs of the metropolitan area of Buenos Aires, excluding the 5 per cent of households with the highest per capita family income and single person households, given their different consumption patterns.

Official base
1988 = 100.

Source of weights
The weights and items were derived from a household expenditure survey conducted during the period July 1985 to June 1986 in the metropolitan area of Buenos Aires, among a sample of 2,745 expenditure units. For the purpose of the Survey, an expenditure unit was defined as one or more persons, related or not, contributing to and using the same budget, sharing food and living in the same dwelling.

Items and services paid for by households were chosen if they had a significant weight within each sub-group and were bought and sold with some degree of regularity and in sufficient quantities to allow price quotations to be obtained with adequate precision.

The weighting for the other items and services in the sub-group was assigned on the basis of similarity, or proportionally within the sub-group. Two items or services can be considered similar if one can be substituted for the other and if their change in price is comparable. Thus an article which has not been selected but which is similar to a selected article is given the weight of the latter, while the weight of other articles is spread proportionally throughout the sub-group.

Weights and composition

Major groups	Number of items	Weights	Approximate number of price quotations
Food	205	40.1	72,500
Clothing and footwear	111	9.4	7,900
Housing:			
Rent	1	2.3	400
Repairs and maintenance	13	2.0	800
Fuel, light and sanitary services	5	4.2	200
Household equipment	84	8.6	12,300
Medical care	31	7.2	1,600
Transport and communication	23	11.4	800
Education and recreation	61	8.9	4,800
Miscellaneous goods and services	23	5.9	4,700
Total	557	100.0	106,000

Household consumption expenditure
Consumption expenditure includes monetary expenditure by members of the household on items and services for individual consumption or for the entire household; the items and services produced by the household for its own consumption (own consumption and own supplying of food); and the items and services received as income in kind by members of the household. Expenditure on housing is registered as expenditure on repairs and maintenance of owner-occupied dwellings.

Method of data collection
The sample of retail outlets corresponding to residential areas was taken in two stages. First, 130 areas were selected (46 in the Federal Capital and 84 in the suburbs of the metropolitan area of Buenos Aires) as groups of retail outlets. Secondly, in each area, an outlet was selected in each class (department store, butcher's, haberdasher's, rotisserie, chandler's, ironmonger's, pharmacy, hairdresser's, stationer's etc.) from which prices are obtained twice a month.

Forty seven shopping centres were chosen, 21 in the Federal Capital and 26 in the suburbs of Buenos Aires; 140 sub-samples of stores were chosen from all the outlets in these centres, which are visited once a month.

In order to determine the number of respondents for each variety, the geographical area covered by the index and the variability of the price were taken into account. The sample of outlets is revised periodically in order to incorporate new marketing techniques and possible changes in the geographical distribution of the stores.

The prices of items and services are recorded every working day of the month, that is, the sample of outlets for a specific item or service is distributed throughout the working days of the month (excluding Saturdays, Sundays and holidays).

Most of the prices are recorded by means of personal contact, the telephone being used only for certain services for which quality does not often change and for which telephone surveys give a good response.

For services subject to state price control (electricity, gas, sanitary services, public transport, etc.); the days of the month when the price comes into force are used. The cash price is recorded for the various items and services.

Housing
Rent is treated differently because the respondents are the consumers themselves, i.e. the tenants, and not the leasers or owners of the dwellings. Rent quotations are obtained through a sample of rented dwellings; 25 per cent of the sample is renewed each quarter to avoid overburdening the informant, and also to try to cover the time when the contract is renewed. In total, the sample covers 624 dwellings which are divided into 6 rotation groups of 104 dwellings in each. The rental value of 416 dwellings is recorded each month.

Given the many possible interpretations of the term "rent", quotations are recorded for the following rented dwellings: occupied family dwellings, unfurnished flats, houses, apartments, permanent living quarters in residential hotels and leased property dwellings for which the rent is paid in national currency, dwellings in which the rent does not cover services, and rented dwellings that are not dependant on an employment relationship. The amount of rent is recorded as well as other data on the dwelling and the contract, which help to verify the declared value and to detect when there are changes in the quality of the dwelling.

Specification of varieties
For a precise definition of the "family shopping basket", a detailed description must be given of all characteristics determining the existence of different prices at a given moment, and the extent to which changes in these characteristics are imputed to price variations for practical purposes. Details of the variety are usually necessary for each respondent (make, model, size, etc.) to ensure the comparability of subsequent price quotations. Two kinds of definition have been adopted to specify items. First, for homogeneous varieties, equivalent products are quoted in the various outlets, enabling a significant average price to be calculated (butter, roast meat, eggs, oranges, chard, bar of soap, etc.). Secondly, for heterogeneous varieties corresponding to an incomplete specification, the description of the product is specific to the outlet. It is extremely useful to use heterogeneous varieties, e.g. for clothing, so as to reflect differences from one store to another and changes in fashion (footwear, clothes, television, education, rent, etc.).

Substitution, quality change, etc.
For changes in quality or respondents, or substitution of items, when overlapping price quotations are available, it is assumed that the relationship between the prices reflects the relationship between qualities and that linking is thus possible.

If there are no overlapping price quotations to compare quality, a quality adjustment is made in the price of the new variety so that it can be compared with the former.

Seasonal items
If a seasonal item temporarily disappears from the market, the price relative is based on the hypothesis that the price movement of this seasonal item would have been similar to the one registered for similar items.

Seasonal items include all items and services for which the quantity consumed and prices vary significantly throughout the year. Generally, it is fluctuations in supply (vegetables, fruit, etc.) or demand (winter and summer clothing, etc.) that lead to a temporary disappearance of the item.

Computation
The index is computed according to the Laspeyres formula as a weighted arithmetic average with fixed base, using weights corresponding to July 1985 to June 1986.

The indexes of each basic aggregate (minimum level of expenditure detail for which the weighting is constant) are estimated using a sample of prices from a specific group of items or services from an established group of outlets.

The method used to calculate the price relative of an item depends on whether it is considered a homogeneous or a heterogeneous variety. For homogeneous varieties, the price relatives for the current and previous periods are used. For heterogeneous varieties, the average of price relatives for the various outlets is used.

Supermarkets, department stores and other retail outlets are assigned weights according to their estimated retail sales volume. The weights are used to calculate the relatives of average prices or the averages of price relatives.

Other information
Detailed sub-groups are published (134). The index is published in a press release on the third working day of the month following the month to which the index corresponds.

Organisation and publication
Instituto Nacional de Estadística y Censos: "Estadística mensual" (Buenos Aires).

Idem: "Indice de precios al consumidor, Revisión base 1988 = 100, Sintesis metodológica".

AUSTRALIA

Official title
Consumer Price Index.

Scope
The index is compiled quarterly and covers all metropolitan employees' households. Employees' households are defined as those households which obtain at least three quarters of their total income from wages and salaries, but the top 10 per cent (in terms of income) of such households are excluded. Metropolitan means the eight capital cities of the Australian States and Territories.

Official base
Year ending June 1981 = 100.

Source of weights
The present weights are based on the 1984 household expenditure survey supplemented by information from a range of other statistics, such as those obtained from financial institutions and the 1986 Health Insurance Survey. Items are selected for pricing if they represent a significant amount of metropolitan household expenditure, if the prices can be associated with an identifiable and specific commodity or service and if they can be priced to constant quality. The price movements of items not priced are assumed to be represented by those of items priced and the weights of the items not priced are allocated to the priced items representing them.

Weights and composition

Major groups	Number of items (a)	Weights	Approximate number of price quotations (b)
Food	34	19.0	27,000
Tobacco and alcohol	4	8.2	11,200
Clothing and footwear	14	6.9	5,500
Housing:			
Rent of privately owned dwellings	1	4.1	8,200
Rent of Government-owned dwellings	1	0.4	5,600
Home ownership (mortgage interest charges, rates, repairs and maintenance and insurance)	4	9.6	22,000
Household equipment and operation:			
Fuel and light	3	2.4	100
Household appliances	1	1.5	900
Furniture and floor coverings	2	4.1	1,200
Household textiles	2	0.7	600
Other household goods and services	14	5.7	3,000
Postal and telephone services	2	1.5	200
Consumer credit	1	2.5	200
Health and personal care	6	5.6	3,800
Transport	7	17.0	5,600
Recreation and Education	11	10.8	5,500
Total	107	100.0	100,600

Note: (a) See below. (b) Per quarter.

(a) These figures represent the number of "expenditure classes" and not individual items priced. Each expenditure class consists of a selection of similar "items" e.g., the four expenditure classes in the Tobacco and alcohol group are: beer; wine; spirits; cigarettes and tobacco. Each of these classes covers a range of varieties of liquor or tobacco products.

Household consumption expenditure
Household consumption expenditure for the purpose of the index is defined as the actual expenditure on consumer goods and services during the weighting base period. It excludes notional expenditure, contributions to private superannuation and pension funds, income taxes and other direct taxes, life insurance payments, remittances and gifts, jewellery, legal services, club and trade union subscriptions and gambling. It includes income in kind, mortgage interest charges, consumer credit charges, optical services, motor car registration and licence fees, insurance associated with specific consumer goods, health care, local government rates and charges.

Method of data collection
Localities and outlets are selected on the basis of information from the population census, retail trade data and the local knowledge of the field collection officers. No point-of-purchase survey was carried out. Approximately 5,500 respondents in eight cities are approached for price data and about 100,000 price quotations are collected each quarter from supermarkets, department stores, footwear stores, restaurants, home delivery suppliers, other retail outlets, service establishments, etc. Prices for items such as rail fares, electricity, etc. are obtained from the authorities concerned. Prices are collected each week for fresh fruit and vegetables, each fortnight for fresh fish and each month for fresh meat, bread, cigarettes and tobacco, packaged alcohol and petrol. Prices for some important items are collected at the end of the quarter and dates of price changes are registered to enable average quarterly prices to be calculated. Prices for all other items are collected once a quarter, with the exception of local government rates and charges, seasonal clothing and lawn movers, for which prices are collected once a year. The prices used in the index are those that any member of the public would have to pay on the pricing day to purchase the specified good or service, including sales and excise taxes. Sale and discount prices and "specials" are reflected in the index so long as the items are of normal quality and are offered for sale in reasonable quantities. There is no general pricing date. Price collection is spread throughout the quarter.

Housing
Rent quotations are collected each quarter and are based on an extensive sample of privately-owned and government-owned dwellings. Home ownership costs are represented by actual outlays on repairs and maintenance, rates, insurance and mortgage interest charges.

Specification of varieties
The selection of the particular varieties of items to be priced is made after the analysis of data from manufacturers, importers and retailers. Brands and varieties are generally those which sell in greatest volume. On the basis of these data, detailed specifications are drawn up for each item to be priced, including such details as: brand name, model name, size, country of manufacture, and other necessary information to enable pricing to constant quality over time.

Substitution, quality change, etc.
Completely new products are introduced in the index at the time this is reviewed, approximately every four to five years. New varieties of existing products are introduced when they become significant in terms of that category of consumer expenditure. When a given type or quality disappears from the market, it is taken away from the index and, if warranted, a replacement is substituted using the linking procedure. With respect to quality changes, the main techniques adopted are: i) direct assessment of the value of the quality change with a corresponding adjustment to the price of the item concerned; ii) linking in new specifications.

Seasonal items
Price collection for fresh fruit and vegetables is extended to seasonal items not available throughout the year. In periods when particular seasonal items are not available, prices are imputed on the basis of movements in prices of those items that are available. Prices for seasonal clothing items are collected once a year in the relevant seasonal quarter. For the other quarter of the year, the price is held constant. No adjustment is made for seasonal fluctuations in item prices.

Computation
The index is computed quarterly according to the Laspeyres chain-linked formula with fixed base weights. Changes in the

weighting pattern and composition occur at approximately every five years.

The national index is calculated as a weighted average of the index numbers of the eight capital cities, using as weights the number of households of the index population group in each city.

Other information
A new series of Consumer Price Indices (base: year ending June 1990 = 100) is under preparation and will be published shortly.

Organisation and publication
Australian Bureau of Statistics: "Consumer Price Index" Catalogue No. 6401.0 quarterly (Canberra, ACT).

Actual prices of a selection of goods included in the CPI are published in: "Average Retail Prices of Selected Items, Eights Capital Cities", Catalogue No. 6403.0.

Idem: "A Guide to the Consumer Price Index", Cat. No. 6440.0, 1987.

Idem: "Review of the Consumer Price Index", Cat. No. 6450.0.

Idem: "The Australian Consumer Price Index; Concepts, Sources and Methods", Cat. No. 6461.0.

AUSTRIA

Official title
Consumer Price Index.

Scope
The index is compiled monthly and covers the whole country and all households without size or income limits.

Official base
1986 = 100.

Source of weights
The weights and items were derived from a household expenditure survey conducted during one month between March 1984 and February 1985, covering 6,599 households representing the whole population. The average monthly expenditure per household was 20,390 Schillings at the time of survey and the average household size 2.7. The weights were adjusted on the basis of data obtained from national accounts.

Weights and composition

Major groups	Number of items	Weights	Approximate number of price quotations
Food	149	23,268	...
Tobacco	79	2,512	...
Rent (incl. maintenance and repairs)	28	13,056	...
Fuel and light	13	5,405	...
Household equipement	41	7,582	...
Clothing and footwear	50	10,694	...
Cleaning materials	9	1,402	...
Personal and medical care	31	6,006	...
Education and recreation	85	14,302	...
Transport and communication	130	15,773	...
Total	615	100,000	50,000

Household consumption expenditure
Consumption expenditure for the purpose of the index refers to all money expenditure by the household on goods and services intended for consumption. It includes the consumer value of home-produced goods consumed by households. Contributions to social insurance and pension funds, purchase of dwellings, income taxes and other taxes, remittances and gifts are excluded.

Method of data collection
Prices are collected by agents on the second Wednesday of each month. Prices are obtained centrally for 328 items and regionally for the other 287 items from retail outlets, fixed market areas and service establishments representing usual shopping places in 20 towns. The prices used in the calculation of the index are the regular prices paid by consumers. Sale and discount prices are not taken into account.

Housing
Rent quotations are obtained from the quarterly results of the microcensus for 10,000 rented and owner-occupied dwellings. So as to facilitate housing cost comparisons, prices are calculated per square metre. The changes in rent quotations from one quarter to the next are distributed proportionately over each of the following three months.

Specification of varieties
The descriptions of the varieties are of a general nature, to enable price collectors to choose the type, quality, quantity, etc. of items with the highest volume of sales in each retail outlet for regular pricing.

Substitution, quality change, etc.
If the quality of an item changes, the base price is modified in proportion to the percentage change between the current and preceding months.

Seasonal items
Seasonal fluctuations in the prices of fresh fruit and vegetables are taken into account by varying items and item weights within monthly baskets of constant group weights.

Computation
The index is computed according to the Laspeyres formula as a weighted arithmetic average with fixed base, using weights corresponding to the base period. In computing item indices, the average of price relatives of the current and base periods are used. The national index represents the weighted arithmetic average of indices relating to 20 towns, the weights being proportional to the population of the each town according to the 1981 population census.

Organisation and publication
Oesterreichisches Statistisches Zentralamt: "Statistische Nachrichten" (Vienna).

Idem: "Verbraucherpreisindex, Revision 1987", Beiträge zur österreichischen Statistik, Heft 853, 1987.

BAHAMAS

Official title
Retail Price Index for New Providence.

Scope
The index is computed monthly and covers all private households in New Providence.

Official base
March - April 1987 = 100.

Source of weights
The weights and items were derived from a household expenditure survey conducted in 1983 throughout the island of New Providence, except for the extreme western and eastern ends of the island, among a sample of private households. If more than 0.001 per cent of the total household expenditure was spent on an item, that item was selected to be part of the "basket". The weights of items not chosen were aggregated and the sum was placed in the "other" category of that item group. The weights were not adjusted to take into account price changes between the survey and base periods.

Weights and composition

Major groups	Number of items	Weights	Approximate number of price quotations
Food	98	17.196	1,332
Clothing and footwear	20	6.647	294
Housing:			
Rent	2	5.213	39
Net rental value of owner occupied dwellings	3	13.435	7
Fuel and light	3	3.992	3
Maintenance and repairs	4	2.965	12
Furniture, furnishings and household equipment and operation	28	9.527	296
Medical care	8	3.263	118
Transport and communication	17	22.094	151
Education and recreation	25	12.792	221
Miscellaneous	15	2.878	287
Total	223	100.000	2,760

Household consumption expenditure
Included are house purchases, property insurance and taxes, accident and health insurance, and life insurance associated with professional activity.

Excluded are ordinary life insurance, savings, purchases of stocks and shares, the capital content of mortgage payments and repaymenta on bank loans.

Method of data collection
Prices for most items are collected by agents or through telephone contacts, from 208 retail outlets and service establishments. Prices for medical services and insurance are obtained by mail questionnaires. Prices are ascertained each month or quarter and generally refer to the first two weeks of the month. For all commodities and services, the prices or charges used for the Retail Price Index are those actually charged in cash transactions. Extra charges for credit are excluded and discounts are ignored. Listed prices are ignored if a retailer is regularly selling at prices other than those listed; temporary reductions are not taken into account.

Housing
Both furnished and unfurnished rented dwellings with one or two bedrooms are included. Rent quotations are obtained for 32 unfurnished and 7 furnished dwellings through personal visits or telephone contacts.

The value of home purchases, property insurance and property taxes is taken into account in the net rental value of owner-occupied dwellings.

Specification of varieties
In order to determine the item specifications, discussions were held with store managers as to which brands and sizes of a particular item generated the most sales.

Substitution, quality change, etc.
If a price change is caused by a quality change, the base price is changed in order to eliminate the price movement. A new item may be introduced in the index to replace an item that has disappeared from the market. Prices of both "new" and "old" items are noted in the same months to ensure that only price movements are recorded in the month of the change-over. If an item disappears temporarily, the last price collected is kept until the item reappears on the shelf. If, however, the item does not reappear after a certain length of time (say 3 months), substitution is necessary.

Seasonal items
There is no special treatment for the seasonal items in the index.

Computation
The index is computed according to the Laspeyres formula as a weighted arithmetic average with fixed base, using weights corresponding to 1983.

The price relative for each item is calculated by dividing the average price for the current period by the average price for the base period. The average price of an item is the simple arithmetic mean of the prices obtained for that item.

Other information
A Retail Price Index for Grand Bahama (base March 1974 = 100) is also computed and published by the Department of Statistics. However, the New Providence Retail Price Index is used as the national index.

Organisation and publication
Ministry of Finance, Department of statistics: "Retail Price Index" (Nassau).
Idem: "Quarterly Statistical Summary".
Idem: "Annual Review of Retail Prices".
Idem: "An explanation of the Retail Price Index".
Idem: "The revised index for New Providence".

BANGLADESH (DHAKA)

Official title
Middle-class cost of living index for government employees in Dhaka city.

Scope
The index is compiled monthly and covers middle-class households of government employees in Dhaka city.

Official base
1973-74 = 100.

Source of weights
The weights and items were derived from the household expenditure survey conducted in 1973-74, covering all households of all income groups. The index relates to middle-income group households in Dhaka with monthly income between 300 and 999 Taka at the time of the survey.

Weights and composition

Major groups	Number of items	Weights	Approximate number of price quotations
Food	77	62.74	...
Fuel and lighting	5	7.50	...
Housing and household items	24	11.85	...
Clothing, footwear, etc.	25	6.20	...
Miscellaneous	57	11.71	...
Total	188	100.00	...

Household consumption expenditure
Not available.

Method of data collection
Prices are collected by enumerators, from markets, selected retail stores and establishments each week, fortnight, month and quarter. The frequency of price collection depends on the nature of the item. Prices for electricity, gas, medical care, education and transport are collected from the respective service establishments. The prices used in the index are the open market prices for all items except rice for which both open and controlled prices are taken into account.

Housing
Rent quotations are obtained from a sample of 10 dwellings.

Specification of varieties
Not available.

Substitution, quality change, etc.
When an item is no longer available it is substituted by another item with approximately the same quality, and a linking method is used.

Seasonal items
Fresh fruit and vegetables are regarded as seasonal items, and are priced when they are available during the season. Closing prices for the previous season are maintained during the off season.

Computation
The index is computed according to the Laspeyres formula as a weighted arithmetic average with fixed base, using weights corresponding to the base period.

Other information
The Bangladesh Bureau of Statistics also calculates series for middle-income families in Khulna and Chittagong as well as for low- and high-income families in Dhaka.

Organisation and publication
Bangladesh Bureau of Statistics: "Monthly Statistical Bulletin of Bangladesh" (Dhaka).

BARBADOS

Official title
Index of Retail Prices.

Scope
The index is compiled monthly and covers the whole country. Households with monthly disposable income of 2,000 dollars or more are excluded from the index.

Official base
March 1980 = 100.

Source of weights
The weights and items were derived from the household budget survey conducted during the period 1 April 1978-31 March 1979. The survey covered a sample of 1,200 households. Items for the basket were selected on the basis of the percentage contribution which the items made to the total budget. Those items whose contribution was deemed to be insignificant were either left out altogether or grouped with related items and included as a group item.

Household consumption expenditure
This includes goods consumed by households, home produced goods for own use, home ownership, credit purchase. Social security contributions and compulsory pension payments are not treated as household consumption expenditure, nor is income tax.

Method of data collection
Prices are collected from 85 selected retail stores and estab-

Weights and composition

Major groups	Number of items	Weights	Approximate number of price quotations
Food	62	43.2	257
Alcoholic beverages and tobacco	7	8.4	36
Housing	9	13.1	26
Fuel and light	5	6.2	9
Household operations and supplies	24	9.6	96
Clothing and footwear	21	5.1	99
Transport	13	4.6	30
Personal and medical care	19	6.0	69
Education, recreation and miscellaneous	8	3.8	36
Total	168	100.0	658

lishments by the field staff of the Statistical Service. Most of the items are collected on the Wednesday nearest to the middle of each month. In the case of fruit, vegetables and fish, these prices are collected every Friday of the month. Quarterly price collections, which include telephone rates, water rates, laundry services, hairdressing rates, bus fares and taxi fares, are carried out in the middle month of each quarter.

The prices used in the index are the regular prices paid by any member of the general public. Discounts are taken only when they are given to all purchasers. Price reductions to special groups are not considered.

Housing
Data on house rent are collected only for government-owned housing units. Rent changes are taken into account when they occur, based on information supplied by the authorities.

Specification of varieties
The items collected must have clear and precise specifications, such as brand, unit, type quality and quantity.

Substitution, quality change, etc.
If a product is no longer available, it is substituted by another product with approximately the same quality, and a method of linking is used.

Seasonal items
The main seasonal item is locally-caught fish.

Computation
The index is computed according to Laspeyres formula as a weighted arithmetic average with fixed base, using weights corresponding to the base period.

The price relative for each item is calculated by dividing the sum of prices quoted for the current period by the sum of prices quoted for the previous period. The average price of an item is the simple arithmetic mean of the prices obtained for that item.

Organisation and publication
Statistical Service: "Monthly Digest of Statistics" (Bridgetown).
Idem: "The Barbados Economic Report".
Idem: "Monthly Statistical Bulletin".
Idem: "Economic and Financial Statistics".

BELGIUM

Official title
Indice des prix à la consommation (Consumer Price Index).

Scope
The index is compiled monthly and covers average households of the whole country.

Official base
1988 = 100.

Source of weights
The weights and items were derived from a household expenditure survey conducted during May 1987-May 1988 among 3,315 families of wage earners, salaried employees, non-active people and own-account workers.

Household consumption expenditure
Consumption expenditure for the purpose of the index includes almost all goods and services consumed by households. It also includes the imputed values of home-grown and home-produced goods and goods received as income in kind.

Weights and composition

Major groups	Number of items	Weights	Approximate number of price quotations (a)
Food	157	18.985	58,900
Tobacco	4	1.130	1,200
Clothing and footwear	46	8.580	9,600
Housing:			
Rent	2	7.175	-
Repairs, maintenance and water	10	6.155	-
Fuel and light	20	6.070	-
Furniture and household appliances	54	7.850	12,500
Medical care	17	4.900	2,100
Transport and communication	33	16.495	2,600
Education and recreation	39	8.355	5,900
Other goods and services	47	14.305	7,300
Total	429	100.000	102,300

Note: (a) Number of quotations collected by field agents, excluding quotations obtained by the central service.

Method of data collection
Prices of most items are collected by agents at retail outlets and service establishments in 65 towns and villages throughout the country. Price are collected each month between the 1st and the 20th for almost all items.

The prices collected are for cash purchases, inclusive of all taxes, by consumers who are not given any special treatment. Price reductions are taken into consideration from the first day of special offers if they last at least one day, provided the product is of good quality and is available in sufficient quantities. Prices of sale items are not taken into consideration.

Housing
Rent quotations are obtained for public and non-public housing in the country's 11 provinces. Data on rented public housing are collected from a number of registered public housing companies. Data on rent for non-public housing are obtained from a representative sample of 1,521 apartments and houses of various sizes. The sample is revised each month by replacing two dwellings with two new ones in order to take into account turnover in the rented housing market.

Specification of varieties
Specifications indicate in particular the choice of units used. In most cases definitions are rather flexible to allow for possible changes to be taken into consideration, but sufficiently strict to ensure continuity of data collection.

Substitution, quality change, etc.
With the approval of the central service, agents are given a certain leeway to replace an item which has disappeared, in accordance with the following guidelines. A shop of a given type must be replaced by an outlet of the same type. A given product should be replaced either by an equivalent product at the same shop, or by the same product at another shop.

For certain specific items for which samples have been derived (cars, non-public rents, third-party insurance for automotive vehicles and third-party family life insurance), the new item is chosen from a pre-defined list according to specific criteria. The new item is introduced in the average index as set by the other items of the same sub-group. An increase over the previous month's price is taken into account by assigning the same progression to the missing item as that of the average index of other items in its sub-group.

Seasonal items
Seasonal fluctuations in the prices of fresh flowers, fruit and vegetables are taken into account by changing the monthly composition of the items in the sub-group, the overall weight of which remains constant. The indices of certain seasonal items and services are calculated using the price of the corresponding month of the base period rather than the average price for the whole base period, the base prices being the result of the arithmetic average of prices in the corresponding month of 1987, 1988 and 1989.

Computation
The index is computed according to the Laspeyres formula as a weighted arithmetic average with fixed base, using weights corresponding to the base period.

Separate indices are calculated for 65 towns and villages. The price relative for each item and for each town or village is computed by dividing the average price by its base period price. The average price is the simple arithmetic mean of all prices collected. The 65 towns' or villages' indices are then weighted to arrive at the national index, the weights used being proportional to the population of each town or village as of 1 January 1988.

Other information
The general index is also published using the following bases: 1981 = 100; July 1974-June 1975 = 100; and 1971 = 100.

Organisation and publication
Ministère des Affaires économiques, Institut national de statistique: "Bulletin de statistique" (Brussels).
Idem: "Communiqué hebdomadaire".
Ministère des Affaires économiques, Administration du commerce, Service de l'indice: "Le nouvel indice des prix à la consommation; base 1988 = 100" (Brussels, 1991).

BELIZE

Official title
Consumer Price Index.

Scope
The index is compiled quarterly and relates to the whole country.

Official base
February 1980 = 100.

Source of weights
The weights and items were derived from a household expenditure survey conducted in Belize in 1980, covering 1,800 households in urban and rural areas.

Household consumption expenditure
Not available.

Method of data collection
Prices are collected during the third week of February, May, August and November, in markets, retail outlets and service establishments in six districts.

Housing
Not available.

Specification of varieties
No detailed specifications are used.

Substitution, quality change, etc.
When an item is missing, the price for the previous quarter is maintained.

Seasonal items
Not available.

Computation
The index is computed according to the Laspeyres formula as a weighted arithmetic average with fixed base, using weights corresponding to the base period.

Separate indices are first computed for the six districts. The national index is a weighted average of indices for the six districts, using weights proportionate to the population of each district.

Organisation and publication
Ministry of Economic Development, Central Statistical Office: "Belize Consumer Price Index (quarterly)" (Belmopan).

Weights and composition
Corozola

Major groups	Number of items	Weights	Approximate number of price quotations
Food	39	386	...
Cleaning products	5	33	...
Personal and medical care	9	71	...
Clothing and footwear	14	152	...
Rent, fuel and light	5	47	...
Furniture, furnishings and household equipment	12	107	...
Transport	8	89	...
Miscellaneous	15	115	...
Total	107	1,000	...

Orange Walk

Major groups	Number of items	Weights	
Food	39	378	...
Cleaning products	5	26	...
Personal and medical care	9	65	...
Clothing and footwear	14	117	...
Rent, fuel and light	5	62	...
Furniture, furnishings and household equipment	12	127	...
Transport	8	106	...
Miscellaneous	15	119	...
Total	107	1,000	...

Belize

Major groups	Number of items	Weights	
Food	39	394	...
Cleaning products	5	27	...
Personal and medical care	9	48	...
Clothing and footwear	14	116	...
Rent, fuel and light	5	122	...
Furniture, furnishings and household equipment	12	104	...
Transport	8	60	...
Miscellaneous	15	129	...
Total	107	1,000	...

Cayo

Major groups	Number of items	Weights	
Food	39	376	...
Cleaning products	5	30	...
Personal and medical care	9	46	...
Clothing and footwear	14	128	...
Rent, fuel and light	5	85	...
Furniture, furnishings and household equipment	12	127	...
Transport	8	85	...
Miscellaneous	15	123	...
Total	107	1,000	...

Stan Creek

Major groups	Number of items	Weights	
Food	39	481	...
Cleaning products	5	28	...
Personal and medical care	9	47	...
Clothing and footwear	14	121	...
Rent, fuel and light	5	79	...
Furniture, furnishings and household equipment	12	85	...
Transport	8	28	...
Miscellaneous	15	131	...
Total	107	1,000	...

Toledo

Major groups	Number of items	Weights	
Food	39	396	...
Cleaning products	5	39	...
Personal and medical care	9	53	...
Clothing and footwear	14	201	...
Rent, fuel and light	5	40	...
Furniture, furnishings and household equipment	12	102	...
Transport	8	43	...
Miscellaneous	15	126	...
Total	107	1,000	...

BERMUDA

Official title
Consumer Price Index.

Scope
The index is compiled monthly and covers about 87 per cent of all private households in Bermuda with incomes between 200 and 1,499 dollars per week in 1982.

Official base
January 1985 = 100.

Source of weights
The weights and items were derived from a household expenditure survey conducted in 1982, covering about 750 households with weekly incomes between 200 and 1,499 dollars at the time of the survey. The weights were not adjusted to take into account price changes between the survey and base periods.

Weights and composition

Major groups	Number of items	Weights	Approximate number of price quotations
Food	111	181	2,000
Rent	1	218	420
Clothing and footwear	37	60	200
Tobacco and alcohol	4	26	80
Fuel and light	2	45	2
Furniture, furnishings, household equipment and operations	52	147	450
Transport, foreign travel	15	171	85
Education, recreation and reading	17	84	115
Personal and medical care	9	68	400
Total	248	1,000	3,752

Household consumption expenditure
Consumption expenditure for the purpose of the index includes all cash or credit purchases for household consumption, plus current transfers made on a regular basis for items such as insurance and social security. Owner-occupied dwellings are included. Income taxes and other direct taxes, savings and investments, and repayments of loans and gifts are excluded.

Method of data collection
Prices are collected during personal visits of the staff of the Statistical Department to the various reporting outlets and, when necessary, prices are checked with supervisory staff at each outlet. Prices for food items, household supplies, tobacco and alcohol, personal care products, self-prescribed medicines and medical supplies are obtained each month from 11 of the largest supermarkets of the country. Quarterly price surveys are carried out for those items whose prices tend to change more slowly, such as motor cars, motorcycles, clothing and footwear, household appliances, prescribed drugs, etc. Prices are ascertained once a year for school fees, car insurance premiums, health insurance premiums and car licensing fees. When necessary, the pricing frequency is adjusted to keep abreast of rapidly changing circumstances.

Housing
Owner-occupied dwellings are taken into account in the calculation of the weight for the shelter component for the all-items index by making an assessment of their annual rental equivalence. However, for pricing purposes, changes in the cost of shelter are based purely on changes in monthly market rentals of a cross-section of rented properties. No attempt is made to monitor actual expenditures relating specifically to owner-occupied dwellings such as mortgage interest rates, repairs, or insurance, nor notional expenditures such as depreciation.

Specification of varieties
Particular varieties for pricing are selected within each sample outlet. The most popular brand, type or size (the volume seller) is selected for regular price collection on the advice of the outlet's management.

Substitution, quality change, etc.
When the quality of an item changes, a method of linking is used.

Seasonal items
No special account is taken of seasonal fluctuations in item prices.

Computation
The index is computed according to the Laspeyres formula as a weighted arithmetic average with fixed base, using weights corresponding to 1982.

Organisation and publication
Ministry of Finance, Department of Statistics: "Bermuda Annual Digest" (Hamilton).

Idem: "Bermuda Quarterly Digest of Statistics".

Idem: "Retail Price Index Reference Paper" (April 1986).

BOLIVIA (LA PAZ)

Official title
Indice de Precios al Consumidor (Consumer Price Index).

Scope
The index is compiled monthly and covers wage earners' and salaried employees' families in La Paz, with lower and middle incomes Paz.

Official base
1966 = 100.

Source of weights
The weights and items were derived from a household expenditure survey conducted in La Paz from the end of 1964 to the end of 1965 among a random sample of some 800 wage earners' and salaried employees' families with lower and middle incomes.

Weights and composition

Major groups	Number of items	Weights	Approximate number of price quotations
Food	66	51.30	...
Housing:			
Rent	1	7.41	...
Real estate taxes	1	1.25	...
Fuel and power	2	5.03	...
Household expenditure	32	5.18	...
Clothing and footwear	32	12.10	...
Miscellaneous	27	17.73	...
Total	161	100.00	...

Household consumption expenditure
This does not include savings, investments, taxes on rent or other direct taxes.

Method of data collection
Prices are collected by agents at 1,200 outlets and service establishments. Depending on the nature of the items, prices are ascertained weekly, monthly or annually. Food items and items falling under "Housing" are priced weekly. Information on fuel and clothing detergents is obtained weekly and on power each month. Prices used in the index calculation are the current prices paid at the selected outlets. Discounts and sale prices are not taken into consideration.

Housing
Data on rent are obtained monthly from a sample of 100 dwellings. Housing units occupied by their owners are not taken into consideration.

Specification of varieties
The specifications of items to be priced are given in terms of brand name, size, unit, quality, volume and weight.

Substitution, quality change, etc.
When an item disappears from the market, it is substituted by a similar item and its weight is maintained.

Seasonal items
Prices for the off season are assumed to follow the price movements of the other items in the sub-group.

Computation
The index is computed according to the Laspeyres formula as a weighted arithmetic average with fixed base, using weights corresponding to 1964-65. The index for an item is obtained using price ratios for the current and preceding periods.

Other information
Monthly and annual reports contain general indices, indices for groups and sub-groups and index variations from the previous month.

Organisation and publication
Instituto Nacional de Estadística, Departemento de Estadísticas Económicas, División de Precios: "Indice de Precios al Consumidor", (La Paz).
Idem: "Indice de Precios al Consumidor".

BOTSWANA

Official title
National Cost of Living Index.

Scope
The index is computed monthly and covers all households in urban and rural areas.

Official base
September 1985 = 100.

Source of weights
The weights and items were derived from the results of a household expenditure survey conducted during the latter part of 1978 and the first three quarters of 1979. It covered 915 urban households and 1,221 rural households in the four main towns and 13 villages with populations of more than 3,000 at the time of the 1971 census. Although the number of items and the weights were revised, the weights were not adjusted to take into account price changes between the survey period and September 1985.

In selecting the items for the index, attempts were made to ensure that each sub-group contained all the most important items in that sub-group as well as a selection of the items of lesser importance to represent all other items covered by that sub-group. Consequently, many of the items in the index were chosen not because they are themselves particularly important but because they represent a wide range of consumer goods.

Weights and composition

Major groups	Number of items (a)	Weights	Approximate number of price quotations
Food	48	36.65	2,970
Beverages and tobacco	7	3.43	270
Clothing and footwear	13	10.84	717
Rent, fuel, light, water	16	13.07	239
Household items and operation	24	13.70	1,069
Medical care	6	1.30	127
Transport and communications	18	10.54	129
Other goods and services	20	10.46	582
Total	152	100.00	6,103

Note: (a) Although national weights are not directly used in the computation of the index, they are given for reference purposes.

Household consumption expenditure
Consumption expenditure for the purpose of the index includes expenditure on cash and credit purchases of new and second-hand goods. It excludes income in kind and own-produced goods consumed by the household, life insurance premiums, pension and social security contributions.

Method of data collection
Prices are collected every month from representative retail outlets in selected towns and villages throughout the country, in particular in four urban areas, eight large villages and five small villages.

All types of shops are represented in the price collection exercise: large, medium and small. About 330 retail outlets are visited each month. Prices are collected by officers from Central Statistical Office in Gaborone who visit all the areas during the first two weeks of the month. About 6,100 price quotations are collected every month.

Domestic servants' wages are collected every three months in Gaborone. Some prices are ascertained through telephone calls. Discounts, sale prices and free-market prices for items which also have official prices are used whenever they exist. Only cash purchases are taken into account.

Price collection is carried out in accordance with the Statistics Act of 1976. This Act requires that respondents provide the data asked for but at the same time requires Central Statistics Office to treat the data as strictly confidential and not to reveal it to any person, organisation or other Government department outside Central Statistics Office.

Housing
Rent quotations are obtained from the Botswana Housing Corporation and from a quarterly survey conducted by the Central Statistics Office on the average private rent paid by tenants of one-room accommodation in Gaborone. However, the price quotes derived from these surveys are used for all urban areas, not just for Gaborone. The changes in rents in Gaborone are likely to give a reasonable indication of changes in the rest of the country. Owner-occupied housing is represented by the interest payable on land and repayments of loans for building materials.

Specification of varieties
Both detailed and broad specifications are used. For items with detailed specifications, the descriptions include the brand, make, quality, size, etc. For broadly specified items, general descriptions are given and store-specific items are selected.

Substitution, quality change, etc.
The item descriptions remain unchanged throughout the life of the index series. However, it may be necessary to make certain changes to the constituents and the item descriptions are amended accordingly. When this happens, a base price is imputed for the replacement item by assuming that its price increased from September 1985 at the same rate as that of the old item.

In this way, if a given shop has no stocks of the 250g pack of butter, no use is made of the price of the 500g pack. This is because it is not essential that a price is available for every item in every shop. Instead, all the price quotes for the 250g pack of butter from all shops within the same area are averaged and the average is compared with the base price for the item in that area. If a few shops do not have it in stock, this does not matter, provided at least one outlet in that area does have it in stock so as to provide an average price for it in that area. The following month the same item description for a 250g of butter appears on the questionnaire for that shop. This method assumes that the number of errors caused by pricing an item that does not exactly match the item description will be reduced.

Seasonal items
There is no special treatment for seasonal items.

Computation
The index is computed according to the Laspeyres formula as a weighted arithmetic average with fixed base, using weights corresponding to 1978-79.

The price relative for each item in each area is first calculated by dividing the average price for the current period by the average price for the base period. The relatives are then used to compute separate indices for low-, middle- and high-income group households in urban areas and for large and small villages in rural areas.

All-income group indices for the urban areas are calculated as the weighted averages of the three income group indices, taking into account the average consumption expenditure in urban areas. The national index is the weighted average of the urban and rural indices using the population of urban and rural areas as weights.

Other information
Major sub-group indices are published for this index. Separate all-items indices are also published for urban areas and rural areas.

New series relating to urban areas, rural areas and the whole country (base November 1991 = 100) are now computed, but the relevant methodological information was not available in the ILO at the time the present volume was published.

Organisation and publication
Central Statistics Office: "Statistical Bulletin" (Gaborone), (quarterly).
Idem: "Cost of living index 1985", November 1985.
Idem: "Consumer Price Statistics".

BRAZIL

Official title
Indice de Preços ao Consumidor Amplo - IPCA (Consumer Price Index).

Scope
The index is computed monthly and covers employees' house-

holds in all metropolitan areas of the country and with monthly incomes of between one and 40 times the minimum wage.

Official base
December 1990 = 100.

Source of weights
The weights and items were derived from a national household expenditure survey conducted between August 1974 and August 1975, covering a sample of 55,000 households with one to five members, in all metropolitan areas of the country. The weights were updated using the results of a household expenditure survey conducted from March 1987 to February 1988. They were not adjusted to take into account price changes between the survey and base periods.

Weights and composition
Not available.

Household consumption expenditure
Excluded from the weights is expenditure that increases savings, e.g. the purchase of a house, telephone etc.; direct taxes, real estate taxes, interest, insurances, debts paid off, credit card payments, reimbursement of loans, purchase of construction materials for improving dwellings; expenditure concerning birthdays, baptisms, weddings, carnivals, Christmas etc.; and owner-occupied dwellings. Durable goods are treated in the same way as other items and are taken into account in expenditure for the 12-month reference period. Credit purchases are taken as payments made during the reference period. Second-hand purchases of vehicles are included in the weights. Life insurance premiums are excluded.

Method of data collection
Depending on the item, prices are collected by agents once a month, quarter or year, from retail outlets or service establishments in 11 metropolitan areas. No mail questionnaires are sent. Certain tariffs fixed by the Government, e.g. for electricity, water, gas, transport and communication, are collected when they change. Data for medical care are collected every two months. Discounts are taken into account. All prices refer to those paid by consumers.

Housing
The sample of dwellings is obtained from a national survey of dwellings and is divided into 12 groups, and a different group is surveyed each month. Owner-occupied housing is not included in the weights.

Specification of varieties
There are detailed specifications for most items, describing the brand, packing, size, quality, unit of measurement, etc. For some items, only general specifications are provided.

Substitution, quality change, etc.
No account is taken of quality changes in items. New items appearing in the market are introduced when the specifications are revised. If an item disappears temporarily from the market, its price is imputed on the basis of the price movements of the other items in the sub-group.

Seasonal items
For items such as roots, vegetables and fruits, seasonal fluctuations are taken into account by using monthly items and monthly weights. The Paasche formula is used to calculate the index for seasonal items,

Computation
The index is computed according to the Laspeyres formula as a weighted arithmetic average with fixed base, using weights corresponding to March 1987-March 1988. Averages of price relatives between the current and previous periods are used to compute the indices.

To obtain the national index, metropolitan areas indices are first computed and combined, using weights based on the estimated current total expenditure of each metropolitan area.

Other information
The Fundaçao Instituto Brasileiro de Geografia e Estatística (IBGE) also calculates a National Consumer Price Index (INPC) and other indices (IPC) relating to households receiving one to eight times the monthly minimum wage.

Organisation and publication
Fundaçao Instituto Brasileiro de Geografia e Estatística (IBGE): "Indicadores" (Rio de Janeiro).

Idem: "Sistema Nacional de Indices de Preços ao Consumidor, Métodos de Cálculo", 1984.

Idem: "Estructura Básica de Ponderaçoes", 1983.
Idem: "Guia de campo para a Pesquisa de Especificaçao de Productos e Serviços", Janeiro 1980.
Idem: "Métodos para o Trabalho de Campo", 1983.
Idem: "Manual de Implantaçao", November 1979.
Idem: "Para compreender o INPC", 1981.

BRAZIL (SAO PAULO)

Official title
Indice de Preços ao Consumidor (Consumer Price Index).

Scope
The index is compiled monthly and relates to families with an annual income of between 451 and 1,353 cruzeiros in 1971.

Official base
December of the previous year = 100.

Source of weights
The weights and items were derived from a pilot survey conducted in May and June 1971 among middle-income families in São Paulo by the Institute of Economic Surveys of the University of São Paulo.

Weights and composition

Major groups	Number of items	Weights	Approximate number of price quotations
Food	143	435.3	...
Housing:			
Rent	1	86.3	...
Fuel, light, water, repairs, rates, domestic services, etc.	18	117.7	...
Cleaning materials	12	22.9	...
Clothing and footwear	7	64.0	...
Personal expenditures:			
Beverages and tobacco	11	54.3	...
Personal services	6	16.1	...
Culture and recreation	8	21.2	...
Health and personal care	17	21.9	...
Other expenditures	4	22.7	...
Transport	10	62.8	...
Medical care	7	52.8	...
Education	4	22.0	...
Total	248	1,000.0	

Household consumption expenditure
Not available.

Method of data collection
Prices are collected by agents each day for food items and each month for all other items, from 1,251 retail outlets and service establishments in São Paulo.

Housing
Not available.

Specification of varieties
Not available.

Substitution, quality change, etc.
Not available.

Seasonal items
Not available.

Computation
The index is a chain index (i.e. instead of comparing prices for the reference month with those for the base period, they are compared with those of the previous month), using a formula equivalent to the base-weighted arithmetic average.

Organisation and publication
Universidade de São Paulo, Instituto de Pesquisas Econômicas: "Indice de Preços ao Consumidor" (São Paulo).

Idem: "O actual Indice de Preços ao Consumidor - Custo de Vida da classe de renda familiar modal do Município de São Paulo", Relatório Preliminar No. 2.

BRUNEI DARUSSALAM

Official title
Consumer Price Index for Brunei Darussalam.

Scope
The index is compiled monthly, covering households of government employees with monthly expenditure between 300 and 2,099 dollars in 1977.

Official base
1977 = 100.

Source of weights
The weights and items were derived from a household expenditure survey carried out in 1977, covering government employees only. The weighting pattern of the index was based on households with expenditure between 300 and 2,099 dollars in 1977.

Weights and composition

Major groups	Number of items	Weights	Approximate number of price quotations
Food	42	4,507	...
Clothing and footwear	8	614	...
Housing:			
Rent	1	181	...
Minor repairs and maintenance	1	83	...
Fuel and utilities:			
Water, electricity and gas	1	215	...
Other fuel and light	1	20	...
Furniture, furnishings and household equipment and operations	8	831	...
Transport and communication	6	1,718	...
Education, recreation, entertainment and cultural services	8	893	...
Miscellaneous goods and services	8	938	...
Total	84	10,000	...

Household consumption expenditure
Consumption expenditure for the purpose of the index comprises almost all goods and services consumed by the index population. It excludes expenditure on land and buildings, life insurance premiums, savings and income taxes.

Method of data collection
Prices are collected from selected retail stores and establishments in Brunei-Muara District, which includes the capital, Bandar Seri Begawan. Information on prices for all the items is collected by personal visits to shopkeepers by officers of the Statistics Division of the Economic Planning Unit and by telephone calls.

Prices of fresh fish, fresh fruit and vegetables are collected every Saturday while prices of the remaining items are collected on a fixed date every month.

The prices used for the index are those actually charged in cash transactions. Extra charges for credit are excluded and discounts are also ignored unless given to all purchasers. Sale prices are taken into account if they cover the specified article and meet the comparability requirement.

Housing
Information on rent is obtained monthly with respect to a building containing flats with two bedrooms.

Specification of varieties
The specifications of items to be priced are given in terms of the brand name, unit, quality and size.

Substitution, quality change, etc.
When a particular item is no longer available on the market, the price of the nearest similar item available is substituted.

Seasonal items
Seasonal fresh food items are omitted from the index during their off season and their weights are distributed among the remaining items in the same group.

Computation
The index is computed according to the Laspeyres formula as a weighted arithmetic average with fixed base, using weights corresponding to the base period.

In computing item indices, price relatives for each variety in each outlet for the current and base periods are used. The simple arithmetic average of the price relatives for all varieties of an item yields the item index.

Organisation and publication
State Secretariat, Economic Planning Unit, Statistics Division: "Brunei Statistical Yearbook" (Bandar Seri Begawan).

Idem: "Consumer Price Index for Brunei, Base year 1977 = 100" (Bandar Seri Begawan, Jan. 1980).

BULGARIA

Official title
Indice des prix de détail d'Etat (State Retail Price Index).

Scope
Not available.

Official base
1960 = 100.

Source of weights
Weights are calculated on the basis of the value and quantity of goods and services sold or provided to the community, derived from retail trade statistics supplemented by family budget data.

Weights and composition
Not available.

Household consumption expenditure
Not available.

Method of data collection
Prices for most items are fixed by the authorities; they are uniform throughout the country except for certain items for which prices are fixed by area. Prices for fresh fruit and vegetables are collected on the 5th, 15th and 25th of each month from shops (state trade) distributed over 90 cities.

Housing
Rent quotations are obtained for dwellings of one or more rooms.

Specification of varieties
Not available.

Substitution, quality change, etc.
Not available.

Seasonal items
Not available.

Computation
The index is a chain index; it is calculated each year with yearly links, using the Paasche formula.

Other information
A new series is now computed but neither the data nor the relevant methodological information were available in the ILO at the time the present volume was published.

Organisation and publication
Central Statistical Office of the Council of Ministers: "Statistical Yearbook of the People's Republic of Bulgaria" (Sofia).

BURKINA FASO (OUAGADOUGOU)

Official title
Indice des prix à la consommation africaine (Consumer Price Index for African households).

Scope
The index is compiled monthly and published quarterly and relates to low-income households living in Ouagadougou.

Official base
July 1981 - June 1982 = 100.

Source of weights
The weights and items were derived from a household expenditure survey conducted in Ouagadougou during the 12 months of 1980. The survey covered a sample of 54 households with a monthly income ranging from 15,000 to 20,000 CFA francs at the time of the survey and an average household size of 4.54.

Household consumption expenditure
Household consumption expenditure for the purpose of the index comprises all expenditure by households for consumption. Goods and services received as income in kind and consumed by the households, contributions to social security and pension funds and payments for licence fees have not been taken into account.

Weights and composition

Major groups	Number of items	Weights	Approximate number of price quotations
Food	48	4,766	...
Clothing and footwear	8	441	...
Rent and building costs	5	515	...
Fuel, light and water	5	1,368	...
Household equipment	13	303	...
Health and medical care	8	518	...
Transport and communication	8	1,858	...
Education and recreation	4	231	...
Total	99	10,000	...

Method of data collection
Prices are collected by agents from the central market, retail outlets and service establishments in Ouagadougou. Prices for food items and beverages are obtained three times a month (including one direct purchase). Prices of other items which do not vary frequently are collected quarterly.

Housing
Rent quotations are obtained monthly. The cost of owner-occupied dwellings is represented by the price of building materials.

Specification of varieties
The specifications of items to be priced are given in detail.

Substitution, quality change, etc.
When an item is no longer available on the market, the last price quotation is maintained for six months before it is substituted by a similar item.

Seasonal items
Seasonal fluctuations in the prices of certain fresh food items are taken into account by pricing the items only when they are in season; during the off-season, the relevant item weights are assigned to replacement items.

Computation
The index is computed according to the Laspeyres formula as a weighted arithmetic average with fixed base, using weights corresponding to 1980.

Organisation and publication
Institut national de la statistique et de la démographie. Direction des études démographiques, Service des prix: "Indice des prix à la consommation africaine" (Ouagadougou).

Idem: "Bulletin d'information statistique et économique".

BURUNDI (BUJUMBURA)

Official title
Indice des prix à la consommation des ménages à Bujumbura (Consumer Price Index for households in Bujumbura).

Scope
The index is compiled monthly and covers all households in Bujumbura.

Official base
January 1980 = 100.

Source of weights
The weights and items were derived from a household expenditure survey conducted during 1978-79 among a sample of households in Bujumbura. One hundred and thirty items whose weights were among the most significant were retained for pricing.

Weights and composition

Major groups	Number of items	Weights	Approximate number of price quotations
Food	61	55.31	...
Clothing and footwear	19	13.21	...
Housing and household operation	23	16.70	...
Transport and recreation	8	10.80	...
Medical care and miscellaneous	19	3.98	...
Total	130	100.00	...

Household consumption expenditure
Consumption expenditure for the purpose of establishing the weights includes all goods and services purchased by the index population for their own use. It excludes income taxes, statutory contributions, investment expenditures and all insurance.

Consumption expenditure excludes: pension fund contributions, owner-occupied housing (only rented housing is included), the trade-in value of used goods, down-payments on the purchase of new goods, trading licences, fund transfers, gifts and other transfers, all taxes and insurance.

It includes: income in kind, second-hand purchases, durable goods, medical care, credit purchases (limited to disbursements made during the survey period).

Method of data collection
Prices are collected from about 34 selected retail stores, markets and service establishments by personal visits. Prices for food items such as starchy foods, fish, vegetables, fruit and some clothing items are obtained four times a week and for other items once a week. Prices for food items sold in market places are ascertained by weighing the items.

Housing
Rent data are obtained from selected rented dwellings with two rooms, a concrete floor and electricity. For owner-occupied dwellings, only the cost of repairs and maintenance is included in the index.

Specification of varieties
The specifications of items to be priced are given in detail in terms of the brand, quality, make and unit.

Substitution, quality change, etc.
If a product is no longer available in the outlet, a similar product to the original is substituted.

Seasonal items
Seasonal items such as fresh fruit and vegetables are not significant in the index, and no special treatment is therefore given for seasonal items.

Computation
The index is computed according to the Laspeyres formula as a weighted arithmetic average with fixed base, using weights corresponding to the period 1978-79.

Relatives of average prices are used to calculate item indices. Annual indices are the averages of the 12 monthly indices

Other information
A survey is currently being conducted in Bujumbura for the purpose of updating the base for computing the consumer price index.

Organisation and publication
Institut de statistiques et d'études économiques (ISTEEBU): "Bulletin mensuel des prix" (Bujumbura).

Idem: "Annuaire statistique".

Idem: "Bulletin trimestriel".

CAMEROON (YAOUNDE, AFRICANS)

Official title
Indice des prix de détail à la consommation des familles de condition moyenne - Familles "originaires" (Retail Consumer Price Index for Middle-Class Families - Cameroon Families).

Scope
The index is compiled monthly and relates to middle-class households with a monthly budget of about 21,900 CFA francs and an average composition of 4.15 consumption units in 1964-65.

Official base
1968 = 100.

Source of weights
The weights and items were derived from a household expenditure survey conducted in Yaoundé during the period 1964-65, among 764 Cameroon households representing all urban consumers. Only middle-class households with a monthly budget of about 21,900 CFA francs and an average composition of 4.15 consumption units were taken into account in the computation of the index.

Household consumption expenditure
Not available.

Weights and composition

Major groups	Number of items	Weights	Approximate number of price quotations
Food	50	336	...
Beverages and tobacco	11	103	...
Rent, fuel, light, water and domestic services	7	75	...
Furniture, furnishings and household equipment	16	71	...
Clothing and footwear	13	163	...
Transport	8	105	...
Personal and medical care	13	50	...
Recreation	4	51	...
Services and miscellaneous	10	46	...
Total	132	1,000	...

Method of data collection
Prices for most items are collected each month by agents or by mail questionnaire, from about 60 retail outlets and service establishments or from official documentation for those prices fixed by government authorities. In addition, certain food items are priced, through direct buying by agents on the 5th, 15th and 25th of each month in three public markets.

Housing
Rent quotations are obtained from reports submitted by a large real estate company.

Specification of varieties
Not available.

Substitution, quality change, etc.
Not available.

Seasonal items
Seasonal fluctuations in the prices of certain fruits are taken into account by pricing the items only when they are in season; during the off season, the relevant item weights are assigned to replacement items.

Computation
The index is computed according to the Laspeyres formula as a weighted arithmetic average with fixed base, using weights corresponding to 1964-65.

Organisation and publication
Direction de la statistique et de la comptabilité nationale: "Bulletin mensuel de statistique" (Yaoundé).

CAMEROON (YAOUNDE, EUROPEANS)

Official title
Indice des prix de détail à la consommation familiale - Familles "non originaires" (Retail Consumer Price Index for Non-Indigenous Families).

Scope
The index is compiled monthly and relates to European households with more than one person, in Yaoundé.

Official base
May 1966 = 100.

Source of weights
The weights and items were derived from a household expenditure survey conducted in Yaoundé from March to July 1965 among 91 European households with more than one person.

Household consumption expenditure
Not available.

Method of data collection
Prices are collected two to three times a month by agents from retail stores for food items, and by means of monthly questionnaires addressed to various outlets and service establishments for other items. Data for domestic servants' wages are obtained from the minimum wage scales fixed by the Government.

Housing
Rent is not included as an index item, nor is it taken into account in determining the weights.

Specification of varieties
Not available.

Weights and composition

Major groups	Number of items	Weights	Approximate number of price quotations
Food	50	373	...
Beverages and tobacco	13	133	...
Household operation (domestic services, water, gas, electricity and household equipment)	13	193	...
Clothing and footwear	6	36	...
Transport	7	65	...
Recreation	5	59	...
Personal and medical care	9	35	...
Services and miscellaneous	10	106	...
Total	113	1,000	...

Substitution, quality change, etc.
Not available.

Seasonal items
Not available.

Computation
The index is computed according to the Laspeyres formula as a weighted arithmetic average with fixed base, using weights corresponding to March-July 1965.

Organisation and publication
Direction de la statistique et de la comptabilité nationale: "Bulletin mensuel de statistique" (Yaoundé).

CANADA

Official title
Consumer Price Index.

Scope
The index is computed monthly and covers all private households (families and individuals) living in urban centres with 30,000 or more inhabitants.

Official base
1986 = 100.

Source of weights
The weights and items were derived from the 1986 family expenditure survey and the 1986 family food expenditure survey. These data correspond to the cost of the 1986 basket expressed in 1986 prices.

Weights and composition

Major groups	Number of items	Weights	Approximate number of price quotations
Food	213	18.05	550,000
Housing:			
Rented accommodation	3	7.75	170,000
Home ownership (including repairs and maintenance)	10	12.72	5,000
Other accommodation	5	1.38	1,000
Water, fuel and electricity	5	3.82	1,400
Other household operations	44	5.77	23,000
Furnishings and household equipment	67	4.88	15,000
Clothing and footwear	91	8.69	50,000
Transport	30	18.29	33,000
Health and personal care	35	4.20	62,000
Recreation, reading and education	95	8.84	35,000
Tobacco and alcohol	10	5.60	21,000
Total	608	100.00	(a) 966,400

Note: (a) Annual number of quotations.

Household consumption expenditure
The index takes into account only those goods and services that have a price that can be associated with a specific quantity and quality. Goods and services that are provided to the population by the government and paid for through the tax system are excluded, because the amount of taxes paid by an individual does not relate to any specific quantity or quality of public goods or services received by the individual.

Insurance is an area that necessitates a diversified approach. In some cases, the insurance can be associated with specific goods and services and is therefore included in the index. Insurance for homeowners and tenants and vehicle insurance are in this category, because the contract guarantees to replace or restore given goods. On the other hand, life and disability insurance are excluded because the payments stipulated in the insurance contract represent future purchasing power that cannot be identified with any specific set of goods or services.

Health services received by the population through the health insurance system are excluded, because the health insurance premiums do not reflect either the full value of the services rendered or a constant proportion of the value. Health services received by means of direct payment to the physician or hospital are likewise excluded, because the amounts paid for them are affected, in varying degrees, by government financing of medical care. On the other hand, medical supplies, pharmaceuticals and dental care are currently included, because the amounts of money paid for them relate to specific quantities and qualities of goods or services.

A special case for inclusion is made with regard to property taxes. While property taxes are not directly associated with specific goods or services obtained by homeowners, they are considered an integral part of the cost of owning and using a dwelling, and for this reason are included.

Method of data collection

The selection of cities and outlets in which prices are collected is judgemental, based on information from various sources, including market intelligence obtained from the Statistics Canada Regional Offices. Food prices are collected from both chain and independent food stores; clothing and home furnishings are priced in department stores and speciality shops; and automobile parts, in automotive speciality shops and garages. The outlet sample is designed primarily to include retail outlets with high sales volume. Prices of commodities such as bus, rail and air fares, hydro and gas rates, telephone charges and property taxes are collected from the appropriate local, regional or provincial authorities.

The frequency of price collection depends on the nature of the commodity. Some goods and services subject to frequent price change require frequent price collection. Prices for food commodities and gasoline, for example, are collected once a month. Most other commodities have monthly price collection. These include: household supplies, clothing, pharmaceuticals, personal care supplies, tobacco products, alcoholic beverages, rent, mortgage interest and new houses. The remaining commodities are characterised by less frequent price changes and, for this reason, their prices are collected at intervals longer than one month. Prices for furniture and household appliances are collected six times a year. Prices for automobiles, clothing services, personal care services, and newspapers are collected each quarter; automobile registration fees and property taxes are recorded once a year. However, additional price collections are carried out for these commodities when there is evidence of a significant price change between regular pricing dates, and, if required, changes are made to the regular pricing dates.

For most commodities, the price collection for a given month's index is carried out within a four-week period, starting from about the 20th of the previous month and ending in the middle of the given month.

Housing

Rents are collected using the framework of the Labour Force Survey of Statistics Canada. This survey is based on a statistical sample of approximately 54,000 owned and rented dwellings drawn from across the country. On average, 14,000 of them are rented dwellings located in the urban centres covered by the CPI. Once a dwelling in a given location enters the sample, data are collected during a period of six consecutive months. The sample is designed so that one-sixth is replaced each month. The information on rents relates to tenant-occupied dwellings, and is collected from the tenants. The treatment of owned accommodation is designed to measure the impact of price changes on a selection of costs specific to homeowners.

The following elements are included as homeowners' costs: the cost of homeowners' repairs, property taxes, the replacement cost of that amount of owner-occupied dwellings that is assumed to be used up, the cost of homeowners' insurance and mortgage interest cost.

Specification of varieties

The specification contains the detailed characteristics of the commodity and such information as the standard quantity, the unit of measure, the frequency of pricing and other instructions for price collectors. Frequently, one detailed description may be applicable to all of the outlets in which prices are collected.

In other cases, there is no single detailed description applicable to all of the outlets in which prices are collected; instead, the price collectors have to decide, within certain guide-lines, which particular commodity should be priced in specific outlets. The selection may differ between outlets, but remain unchanged within a given outlet, so long as the selected commodity satisfies the criteria of representativeness and of expected continuous availability.

Substitution, quality change, etc.

Specific action is taken regarding commodities that are out of stock in certain outlets. When a commodity is out of stock in a given outlet, but prices of similar commodities are observable in other outlets within the same urban-centre stratum, the price is imputed from the observed price movement in these other outlets. Otherwise, the last recorded price is retained, unless the last recorded price is a sale price (in which case the last regular price is used). However, if a non-seasonal commodity is out of stock in a given outlet for more that two consecutive periods, its price is no longer used in the calculation of the index, and the commodity is replaced by a similar one in the same outlet, or, if necessary, by the same or a similar commodity in a different outlet.

In many cases it is possible to collect prices of both the initial variety and of its replacement at a particular point of time. The ratio of these prices can be used as the price adjustment factor for quality change. The same technique is also applied when a given retail outlet replaces another outlet in the sample. This technique, sometimes referred to as splicing, is based on the implicit assumption that the difference in market prices between the two commodities (or the two outlets), as observed for a specific point of time, is entirely attributable to quality differences between these commodities (or between the services provided by these outlets).

Sometimes it is possible to make explicit quality adjustments to recorded prices, i.e. to assess the difference in worth between the new variety and the replaced one due to the variation in quality between them. In the case of relatively minor changes, the assessment may be derived from cost analysis or by comparing the respective retail market prices of added or deleted equipment or services.

Seasonal items

Some commodities are subject to seasonal variations in their supply. These include various fresh fruits and vegetables, such as strawberries and corn, that are only available in quantity for a few weeks or a few months every year. Other commodities are subject to seasonal variations in demand. These include many articles of clothing (e.g. bathing suits and winter coats) and most articles of sports and recreation equipment (e.g. bicycles and cross-country skis).

The practice for the treatment of seasonal items is to extrapolate the index for the seasonally priced item based on the index movement of continuously priced commodities in the group to which it belongs. For example, the February index for women's winter coats would be represented by the January index multiplied by the ratio of the February index to the January index for a women's wear aggregate. This aggregate, as well as all others used in seasonal imputation, excludes any basic groupings that are seasonally priced.

The carry-forward imputations are made for prices of items at the outlet level; the group imputations are made for price indexes at the basic grouping level. Where feasible, the group that is the source of the imputation is the group immediately above the targeted good in the primary classification. If there are no continuously priced basic groupings in that group, the group one level higher in the primary classification is used instead as the source group.

Computation

The index is computed according to the Laspeyres formula as a weighted arithmetic average with fixed basket, using weights corresponding to the base period.

First, monthly average prices are derived for each priced commodity, for each urban-centre stratum. Month-to-month price indexes are then calculated as ratios of the corresponding average prices in the given month and in the previous month. Price indexes on a time base other than the previous month are not calculated directly by comparing (dividing) average prices, but are derived by multiplying, up to the given month, all month-to-month indexes subsequent to the time base. If a given basic grouping is represented by more than one priced commodity, price indexes are first calculated for each of these priced commodities and then their weighted average forms the estimate of the price movement for the basic grouping.

The national index for Canada can be computed both as a fixed basket price index relating to the national 1986 basket, or as a weighted arithmetic average of corresponding price indices for all 82 urban centres.

Other information
With the introduction of the 1986 basket, 82 urban centres are represented by the CPI, grouped into 34 urban-centre strata and 10 provinces. However, consumer price indexes are published only for the following 18 urban centres: St. John's, Charlottetown-Summerside, Halifax, Saint John, Quebec, Montreal, Ottawa, Toronto, Thunder Bay, Winnipeg, Regina, Saskatoon, Edmonton, Calgary, Vancouver, Victoria, Whitehorse and Yellowknife.

Organisation and publication
Statistics Canada, Prices Division: "The Consumer Price Index" (Ottawa), Monthly, Catalogue No. 62-001, Bilingual (English and French).

Idem: "The Consumer Price Index reference paper: Updating based on 1986 expenditures", Catalogue No. 62-553, Bilingual (English and French).

CAPE VERDE (PRAYA)

Official title
Indice de preços no consumidor (Consumer Price Index).

Scope
The index is computed quarterly and relates to the whole population.

Official base
1983 = 100.

Source of weights
The weights and items were derived from a household expenditure survey conducted in 1983 in Praya.

Weights and composition

Major groups	Number of items	Weights	Approximate number of price quotations
Food and tobacco	83	...	...
Clothing and footwear	40	...	...
Fuel, electricity and water	4	...	...
Furniture and household equipment	9	...	...
Hygiene and personal care	5	...	...
Transport and communications	4	...	...
Total	145	...	...

Household consumption expenditure
Not available.

Method of data collection
Prices are collected from retail outlets and service establishments in Praya.

Housing
Rent is not included in the index.

Specification of varieties
Not available.

Substitution, quality change, etc.
Not available.

Seasonal items
Not available.

Computation
The index is computed according to the Laspeyres formula as a weighted arithmetic average with fixed base, using weights corresponding to the base period.

Other information
An index for St. Vincent is also calculated.

Organisation and publication
Direcçao general de Estatistica: "Indices de preços no consumidor, Praia 1984-1986", January 1987, Praya.

CAYMAN ISLANDS

Official title
Consumer Price Index.

Scope
The index is compiled four times a year, covering the months of March, June, September and December, and relates to all residents households in Grand Cayman and Cayman Brac.

Official base
September 1984 = 100.

Source of weights
The weights and items were derived from a household expenditure survey conducted during April 1983-March 1984 among 234 private households living in Grand Cayman and Cayman Brac. The average weekly expenditure per household was 440 dollars at the time of the survey and the average household size was 3.52 persons.

Weights and composition

Major groups	Number of items	Weights	Approximate number of price quotations
Food	282	206.43	590
Alcoholic drinks and and tobacco	56	31.46	133
Housing:			
Rent	13	67.58	13
Mortgage interest	1	36.98	3
Repairs and maintenance and house insurance	70	27.90	83
Fuel, light and water	16	45.01	24
Clothing and footwear	160	39.21	242
Furniture, furnishings and household equipment	200	57.85	222
Transport and communications	59	178.68	84
Education	29	24.35	32
Medical care	29	56.89	48
Recreation	93	178.90	115
Personal goods and services	82	48.76	130
Total	1,090	1000.00	1,719

Household consumption expenditure
Insurance associated with consumer goods and health costs is included. Business expenditure, gifts and income in kind used for household consumption are excluded.

Method of data collection
Prices are collected four times a year, in March, June, September and December, from supermarkets, larger retail outlets and service establishments in George Town and its immediate vicinity and on the island of Cayman Brac. Prices obtained by agents are collected on Tuesday, Wednesday or Thursday during the collection month. Prices for a number of items, such as electricity, gas, water, medical care, education, transport and communication, are collected centrally by the Statistics Unit, by telephone or postal questionnaires. The cost of loan repayments is allocated to major spending headings such as vehicles or furniture.

For all the goods and services priced, the prices used to calculate the index are those actually charged in cash transactions. Charges made for credit are excluded and discounts ignored unless they are available to everybody. List prices are also ignored if the shop is selling at other than the list price. Sale prices are only included when they represent a real price reduction and are not being used as an incentive to sell stale, damaged, shop-soiled or imperfect goods.

Housing
Specified houses and apartments with one, two or three bedrooms are priced each quarter, including some privately-owned and some government-owned. Interest payments are taken into account for owner-occupied dwellings.

Specification of varieties
As the index measures changes in prices, in formation is collected each quarter for exactly the same goods and services, in the same quantity at the same outlet. The items whose prices are recorded must remain constant throughout the period of the index. Loose specifications are used for clothing and furniture for which it is not possible to be more precise.

Substitution, quality change, etc.
A new item is spliced into the index if an old one is not avail-

able for three consecutive periods, using the ratio of the new item price over the old item price to estimate a proxy base price for the new item. Higher prices due to better quality are discounted in the index except when the quantity of a specific item is improved without any change to its description. New products are not picked up (except in the above) and need to wait for a revision of the index.

Proxy prices are calculated for a missing item using changes in prices actually collected for that item. If no other prices are available for an item, the average change for the three-digit group heading is used. All of these proxies can be changed by the statistician on inspection.

Seasonal items
No adjustments are made to seasonal fluctuations in item prices.

Computation
The index is computed according to the Laspeyres formula as a weighted arithmetic average with fixed base, using weights corresponding to April 1983-March 1984.

Prices are averaged within each five-digit item code. Grand Cayman and Cayman Brac averages are calculated separately and weighted together in proportion to their relative household expenditure.

Other information
The index is published in about the middle of the month following the reference month.

Sub-group indices are published for Food, Alcoholic drinks and tobacco, Housing, Clothing, Durable household equipment, Transport and communications, Education and medical expenses, and Personal goods and services.

Organisation and publication
Department of Finance and Development, Statistics Unit: "Annual Abstract of Statistics" (Grand Cayman).

Idem: "Annual Report of the Cayman Islands".

Idem: "Cayman Islands, A Guide to the new Consumer Price Index", February 1985.

CENTRAL AFRICAN REP. (BANGUI)

Official title
Indice des prix à la consommation (Consumer Price Index).

Scope
The index is compiled monthly and covers all urban households whose head is a wage earner or salaried employee residing in Bangui.

Official base
1981 = 100.

Source of weights
The weights and items were derived from a household expenditure survey conducted during 1975-76. The survey covered the whole country, divided into six regions representing the major geographical areas. The size of the sample was 1,530 budgetary units. The index relates to households in Bangui. The weights were not adjusted to take into account price changes between the survey period and 1981.

Weights and composition

Major groups	Number of items	Weights	Approximate number of price quotations
Food	76	705	585
Clothing and footwear	14	85	30
Manufactured products	43	76	61
Fuel and light	7	73	43
Services	20	61	33
Total	160	1,000	752

Household consumption expenditure
Consumption expenditure for the purpose of the index includes all goods and services purchased by the index population. It excludes income taxes, social security contributions, interest on debts, insurance premiums, the purchase or construction of housing, the purchase of furniture and furnishings, major expenditures for property maintenance, and products produced by the household for its own consumption.

Method of data collection
Prices are collected by specialised agents from a representative sample of 37 retail stores (large and small) for manufactured products, and from four markets for food. Prices for manufactures products are collected during the second week of each month, while those of food items are collected during the first and second weeks of each month. Unmarked prices in markets are ascertained by consulting the seller and by weighing the products. Prices for electricity, gasoline and gas are obtained from the relevant authorities and reflect the official price schedules.

Housing
Rent data are obtained once a month for dwellings with three rooms.

Specification of varieties
There are detailed specifications for each item, based on standard units of measurement (e.g. cup, bucket, bundle, bag, unit, litre, kilogramme, etc.).

Substitution, quality change, etc.
If a product is no longer available in an outlet, either an item similar to the original is substituted, or another item is chosen and assigned a fictitious base price.

Seasonal items
The prices of seasonal items are not adjusted.

Computation
The index is computed according to the Laspeyres formula as a weighted arithmetic average with fixed base, using weights corresponding to the period 1975-76. The average price is the simple arithmetic mean of prices observed at the various outlets.

Other information
A consumer price index for technical assistance families is also calculated by the Division de la statistiqiue.

Organisation and publication
Division de la statistique et des études économiques: "Lettres mensuelles de la statistique" (Bangui).

Idem: "Bulletin trimestriel".

Idem: "Annuaire statistique".

CHAD (N'DJAMENA)

Official title
Indice des prix à la consommation (Consumer Price Index).

Scope
The index is compiled monthly and covers households of employees in the public and private sectors residing in N'Djamena.

Official base
February 1988 = 100.

Source of weights
The weights and items were derived from a household expenditure survey conducted in N'Djamena in 1972, covering non-single public and private sector employees earning between 5,000 and 20,000 francs CFA at the time of the survey. The weights were adjusted to take into account price changes between the survey period and February 1988.

Weights and composition

Major groups	Number of items	Weights	Approximate number of price quotations
Food	67	5,902	...
Clothing	13	959	...
Household furnishings	18	277	...
Personal and medical care	16	401	...
Fuel and light	4	437	...
Construction materials	10	403	...
Vehicles	8	491	...
Tobacco	4	59	...
Housing	2	770	...
Personal services	4	93	...
Other services (incl. transport and travel)	9	208	...
Total	155	10,000	...

Household consumption expenditure
The consumer price index covers only expenditure categories

for which the sum paid is the result of a price (real or fictitious), applied to a quantity, and among these categories, those that correspond to household consumption.

It includes own-production and own-consumption (especially as regards agricultural products). These goods and services are estimated by assigning them fictitious or conventional prices (the market price in the nearest consumer market).

Rent and minor repairs to the dwelling (repair of adobe walls with cement) are included as consumer expenditure, but not the purchase of a dwelling, even with monthly payments, nor the addition of a room.

Also excluded are direct taxes, miscellaneous contributions and gambling. On the other hand, indirect taxes included in prices paid by consumers are included in the index.

In many households, certain family members are self-employed or own-account workers (agriculture, industry, crafts or trade). Any related supplies are obviously excluded from the household's final consumption expenditure. Also excluded from the monthly index is expenditure for which either there is no information on prices, or for which the prices noted do not conform strictly with the definition of the item considered.

Method of data collection
Prices are collected by agents twice a month from N'Djamena's two major markets. The prices of bulk products can only be determined after purchase and weighing to convert to a price per kilogramme. For certain items whose prices move very slowly (e.g. rent), prices are collected only once or twice a year. The prices collected are the asking prices in the markets surveyed, inclusive of taxes.

The asking price (quoted by the trader or artisan) differs from the average price actually paid by the consumer. The difference between these two prices is variable: it is lowest for furniture, clothing and household appliances, and highest for food. A similar difference is presumed to exist for cereals and non-food items in the index.

Housing
Not available.

Specification of varieties
Each of the 155 items is directly included in the index; in practice, for a given item in the index there may be a variety of homogeneous or heterogeneous items.

For a homogeneous variety, prices are generally similar. Thus, an average price (the average of the prices found in each of the survey outlets) makes sense. The index for the variety in N'Djamena is then equal to the average price relatives for this variety between the two periods. However, the current index uses the simple arithmetic average of the basic indices.

For a heterogeneous variety, products may differ considerably, and cannot necessarily substitute for each other. The concept of an average price therefore makes little sense. Nevertheless, it is possible for each product, e.g. three kinds of pants, to compute a basic index equal to the price relative of the product in an outlet in the base period. The index of the variety in N'Djamena is therefore equal to the simple arithmetic average of the basic indices.

Substitution, quality change, etc.
The inclusion in the index of a product whose price was not or could not be ascertained during the base period, poses no problem for homogeneous varieties since the concept of an average price for such varieties is valid. Problems arise for heterogeneous varieties, and several approaches are possible: (a) an item is no longer available and is therefore replaced by another which was on the market in the reference period; (b) the price of the new item may be estimated on the basis of proportionality, computed on the basis of a variable quantity (the "rule of three" method); (c) the price is linked to several of the product's characteristics. For simplicity, it is possible to focus on one of the characteristics and thereby use alternative (b). It is also possible, by using a so-called "econometric" formula, to shift from the product's characteristics to its value; this is the "regression" method.

Once incorporated into the index, the new product is considered to "replace", in whole or in part, one or more products in the index. This means integrating the new product in an existing category, through the creation of a variety.

Seasonal items
Not available.

Computation
The index is computed according the Laspeyres formula as a weighted arithmetic average with fixed base, using weights corresponding to 1972.

Organisation and publication
Direction de la statistique, des études économiques et démographiques: "Evolution des prix à la consommation dans la ville de N'Djamena".

Idem: "Indice des prix à la consommation 1983-1989", February 1990.

CHILE

Official title
Indice de precios al consumidor (Consumer Price Index).

Scope
The index is compiled monthly and covers all private households in Greater Santiago.

Official base
April 1989 = 100.

Source of weights
The weights and items were derived from a household expenditure survey, conducted between December 1987 and November 1988 in Greater Santiago, among a sample of around 5,500 households of all social groups. The basic criterion for the selection of goods and services to be included in the basket was that they should each account for at least 0.0325 per thousand of total household expenditure.

In addition, if a sub-group accounted for 0.0325 per thousand or more, but included no single item reaching this percentage, the goods which had the highest weights were selected.

Once the goods and services for a given sub-group were selected, the general approach was to distribute the sub-group's total weight proportionately among those items.

The weights of non-selected sub-groups were distributed proportionately among the selected goods of the corresponding group.

Weights and composition

Major groups	Number of items	Weights	Approximate number of price quotations
Food	137	32.98	...
Housing:			
Rent and repair	11	9.89	...
Fuel, light, water	6	6.40	...
Furniture, furnishings and household equipment	53	9.11	...
Clothing and footwear	64	8.44	...
Transport and communication	19	16.96	...
Other:			
Medical and personal care	32	5.15	...
Education and recreation	35	6.90	...
Tobacco	1	1.81	...
Other	10	2.37	...
Total	368	100.00	...

Household consumption expenditure
Consumption expenditure includes all goods and services purchased by households, excluding property (land, dwellings, etc.) and stocks, bonds, etc.

Consumption expenditure includes life insurance premiums, money orders, gifts and insurance premiums for consumer goods (dwelling, vehicles). It excludes benefits in kind, owner-occupied dwellings, social security and pension fund contributions, income tax and other direct taxes. For credit purchases, only payments actually made during the reference period are included.

Method of data collection
Prices are collected by agents from about 3,700 selected retail outlets and service establishments in the 28 areas of Greater Santiago. Food prices are collected once a week; prices for housing, clothing and others, once a month; and for medical care, once a quarter.

Supplementary surveys were carried out in order to determine the distribution of the total sample of data sources for each item among the various areas of Greater Santiago, in light of the different types of establishments selling such items. The first such survey covered over 6,000 retail establishments, and identified the most representative establishments in each area of Greater Santiago with respect to sale of the various items. It led to a classification of these establishments as regards the availability of items, sub-groups, groups and collections of items for sale.

The second survey was a point of purchase survey, covering a sample of around 1,000 private households. This survey revealed the communes and types of establishments with the most frequent sales and greater share of household expenditure in Greater Santiago.

Housing
Rent data are obtained each quarter.

Specification of varieties
Along with the definition of the basket, specifications of items to be priced were developed in as much detail as possible, including the quality, shape, size, weight, make and appearance of each item selected. This was based on data from the household expenditure survey, market studies and related methodological studies carried out recently for Greater Santiago, as well as INE experience in price monitoring.

Substitution, quality change, etc.
If an item is no longer available on the market, a similar item is substituted and a linking method is used. If a similar item does not exist, the weight is redistributed among the other items in the sub-group. If there is a quality change, a linking method is used.

Seasonal items
Not included in the index.

Computation
The index is computed according the Laspeyres formula as a weighted arithmetic average with fixed base, using weights corresponding to the base period.

The price relative for each item is calculated by dividing the average price for the current period by the average price for the base period. Average prices are the simple arithmetic averages of prices ascertained in the various points of sale.

Other information
Sub-indices are published for food, housing, clothing, transport and communication, and others.

Organisation and publication
Instituto Nacional de Estadísticas: "Indice de Precios al Consumidor" (Santiago).

Idem: "Informativo Estadístico".

Idem: "Indice de Precios al Consumidor. Base Abril 1989 = 100. Aspectos Metodologicos".

CHINA

Official title
Overall Staff and Workers' Cost of Living Index.

Scope
The index is computed once a year and covers staff and workers throughout the whole country.

Official base
1950 = 100.

Source of weights
The weights for calculating the general index are the actual value of sales and purchases based on the different prices.

Weights and composition
Not available.

Household consumption expenditure
Not available.

Method of data collection
Prices are collected in 140 cities and 230 country towns, and are the official list prices for state-owned establishments, free market (fair trade) prices, negotiated prices or the purchase prices of surplus farm produce and side-line products. Prices are collected for 450 items in the cities and 400 items in the country towns.

Housing
Not available.

Specification of varieties
A standard commodity is adopted for each item to be priced.

Substitution, quality change, etc.
Not available.

Seasonal items
Not available.

Computation
Not available.

Other information
The index is also published by region and on base preceding year = 100. Other indices are calculated for "Overall Residents" and for "Overall Farmers", also by region.

Organisation and publication
State Statistical Bureau: "Statistical Yearbook" (Beijing).

COLOMBIA

Official title
Indice de los precios del consumo - familias de ingresos bajos (Consumer price index - low-income group).

Scope
The index is computed monthly and covers urban households with low incomes.

Official base
December 1988 = 100.

Source of weights
The weights and items were derived from a household expenditure survey conducted between March 1984 and February 1985 among private households, which was used as the basis for defining the reference population of the index. Thus the consumer price index refers to a social group which is as wide as possible and sufficiently homogeneous in its consumption habits to constitute the reference population.

The reference population was defined as the total number of private households situated in the urban areas of 13 cities; single-person households and collective households were excluded because of their special consumption patterns, as well as very high-income households with widely varying consumption patterns (such exclusions account for 5 per cent of all households surveyed in each city).

Items were selected on the basis of the following criteria: the relative weight of the expenditure: at least 5 per cent within the group; frequency of acquisition observed: the item must be purchased by more than 30 per cent of households; the feasibility of identification, i.e. of observing prices and quantities purchased.

The weights were not adjusted to take account of price changes between 1984-1985 and 1988.

Weights and composition

Major groups	Number of items	Weights	Approximate number of price quotations
Food	77	42.58	2,540
Housing:			7,341
Rent	1	19.35	...
Fuel, light and water	5	4.82	...
Furniture, furnishings, cleaning products, household linen	28	7.14	...
Clothing	24	8.16	1,715
Medical care	13	3.30	1,037
Education and recreation	18	4.79	990
Transport and communication	12	4.03	420
Miscellaneous	16	5.84	1,039
Total	194	100.00	15,082

Household consumption expenditure
This includes only expenditure for the acquisition of goods and services for final consumption. The index therefore excludes expenditure on financial transactions, payment of taxes, fines, etc.

Following the exclusion of this expenditure, which is taken into account in the survey on incomes and expenditure but which does not correspond to the concept of consumption expenditure, the remaining expenditures were grouped together into categories according to production function and in line with the structure of the price index.

Income in kind consumed by the households is imputed to the expenditure on the relevant goods and services; owner-occupied housing is imputed to the weights of rent, but only rent data are collected. The purchase of used goods is treated as any other acquisition; social security contributions are considered as a deduction from income.

Method of data collection
Prices are collected by agents from retail outlets and service establishments. In addition, another kind of source is used for the "Rent" sub-group under the "Housing" major group: tenants are asked directly how much they pay for the rent of their housing.

Other sources include the municipal public undertakings which provide information on the rates applied for water, sewage, electricity and telephone services, and town halls which provide the decrees establishing the rates applicable on the urban transport system.

For food prices, the month is divided into three equal periods in which data are obtained from one-third of each group. Thus, although the sources are surveyed each month, prices are obtained in three periods throughout the month. Data are collected each month for items such as public services (water and sewage services, electricity and telephone) and airline tickets, the cost of which varies from month to month.

Where establishments provide data during visits by agents, prices are collected every month except for the following items:
- every two months for cleaning products, medicaments, personal hygiene items;
- quarterly for clothing, furniture, household appliances, school supplies;
- annually for school inscriptions, fees and texts.

These periodicities were established because of the relative variability of prices of goods and services over time.

For some items (gas, cooking paraffin, petrol for automobiles, lotteries and cinema admission in particular) prices are collected in the period in which the variation occurs.

The prices observed or collected are those paid by the consumer for goods or services on sale for cash in retail outlets at the time when the data are collected at the source establishment.

Housing
The data concerning rents are collected every four months but every month the index includes price variations for one-quarter of the sample with the remainder being included without variation.

House rent includes only the cost of the actual rent of private households. Data are collected by means of direct interview. Owner-occupied dwellings are not surveyed.

Specification of varieties
Once items have been selected, their qualities are defined as varieties, for which prices are to be collected periodically for each of the items. A study of the 13 index cities was carried out in January 1987 for this purpose, which established detailed specifications for the items. It was decided that the items selected in each of the sub-groups should:
- show a price evolution similar to that of the other items in the sub-group;
- be commonly consumed by households in the respective socio-economic stratum;
- offer reasonable guarantees of remaining on the market;
- be easily observable.

Substitution, quality change, etc.
If it is not possible to continue recording the price of a specification previously used, or if it is necessary to replace the source establishment, the "change of reference" procedure is used; this method enables variations in prices due to a change in the specification of the item or the source of information to be cancelled out. However, for the "clothing" sub-groups, in which the references and specifications are subject to many changes, each new element appearing in the collection of data is analysed to enable a decision to be taken regarding the validity of the price variation recorded.

Seasonal items
No special treatment is given to seasonal items.

Computation
The index for each city is computed according to the Laspeyres formula as a weighted arithmetic average with fixed base, using weights corresponding to March 1984-February 1985.

The index for an aggregate (sub-group, group, city, the whole country) is the weighted average of the elementary indices, with the weights used in the computation of the index corresponding to the structure of expenditure by low-income families in the various spatial units (13 cities) covered.

Other information
Other indices are computed for urban middle-income families (employees) and all families in the country (low and middle incomes) and for 13 cities separately (all families, low-income families, middle-income families).

Detailed sub-groups are published.

Organisation and publication
Departamento Administrativo Nacional de Estadística: "Boletín Mensual de Estadística" (Bogotá).

Idem: "Boletín Mensual de Estadística" (Bogotá) No. 433, April 1989 (for more detailed methodological information).

COMMONWEALTH OF INDEPENDENT STATES

Official title
General Consumer Price Index.

Scope
The index is computed quarterly and relates to all urban and rural families in all member States of the Commonwealth (CIS).

Official base
The base period of the index used in national publications is generally one year = 100.

Source of weights
The weights were derived from a family expenditure survey conducted during a whole of 1989, covering a sample of 90,000 families in the member States of the Commonwealth (CIS) living in urban and rural areas. The weights were not adjusted to take into account price changes between the survey period and the base period.

Weights and composition

Major groups	Number of items	Weights	Approximate number of price quotations
Food	58	35.168	...
Alcoholic beverages	4	9.620	...
Clothing and footwear	27	22.616	...
Furniture, household goods and appliances	11	11.805	...
Cleaning products, personal and medical care, tobacco, fuel, etc.	9	7.070	...
Services:			
Repairs, maintenance, and recreation	11	6.462	...
Transport and communication	2	3.346	...
Rent and rates	1	3.418	...
Other services	1	0.496	...
Total	124	100.000	...

Household consumption expenditure
All expenditure intended for consumption is covered, including gifts. All types of taxes or contributions, insurance premiums, income in kind, and owner-occupied housing are excluded.

Method of data collection
Statistical investigators collect prices in approximately 100,000 retail outlets and service establishments throughout the member States of the CIS.

Localities and outlets were selected on the basis of data on the volume and structure of commodity turnover. Price collection takes place seven to ten days before the end of each month. Data on medical care, communal services, transport and communications are obtained on a fixed day of the month. Trade-in goods at speculative prices are taken into account by collecting black-market prices at the end of each quarter. However, the interference in average prices caused by shortages of goods sold at more accessible, lower set prices through State outlets is not fully taken into consideration.

Housing
Not available.

Specification of varieties
Detailed specifications are given for each item, describing the

raw material used, quality and basic characteristics of the product.

Substitution, quality change, etc.
Quality changes are estimated during the price collection period at outlets. The price of the new quality is adjusted using a linking factor.

Seasonal items
No adjustment is made to seasonal fluctuations of item prices.

Computation
The index is computed according to the Laspeyres formula as a weighted arithmetic average with fixed base, using weights corresponding to 1989.

The general index for the Commonwealth of Independent States is an aggregate of local indices of the CIS member States, with weights corresponding to the employment structure, income levels and general turnover of goods.

Other information
In a number of member States, another CPI is calculated for a standard set of goods and services for a minimum subsistence level budget.

The data for Consumer Price Index described above were not yet available in the ILO at the time present volume was published.

Organisation and publication
Committee on Statistics: "Narodnoe Khozyaistvo" (National Economy).

Idem: "Sotsialnoe Razvitie" (Social Development).

Idem: "Statistical Bulletin" (Special issues).

CONGO (BRAZZAVILLE, AFRICANS)

Official title
Indice des prix à la consommation familiale africaine (Consumer Price Index for African families).

Scope
The index is compiled monthly and relates to African households in Brazzaville.

Official base
December 1977 = 100.

Source of weights
The weights and items were derived from a household expenditure survey conducted between July 1976 and July 1977 among 100 African households of all types in Brazzaville.

Weights and composition

Major groups	Number of items	Weights	Approximate number of price quotations
Food	70	58.6	1,035
Beverages and tobacco	10	3.4	59
Clothing, footwear and household linen	12	6.9	11
Housing, construction	17	10.1	17
Fuel, power and water	8	5.7	16
Hygiene and medical care	15	3.8	47
Transport, recreation	12	8.6	14
Miscellaneous	13	2.9	23
Total	157	100.0	1,222

Household consumption expenditure
This includes payments in kind and consumption of own-produced goods. Income tax is excluded.

Method of data collection
Prices for most items are collected each month by agents at markets, various retail outlets and service establishments. Prices of fresh food sold at markets are obtained twice a month. Data for power, water, transport, medical care and recreation are collected each quarter. Discounts and sale prices are not taken into consideration.

Housing
Data on rents are collected each quarter for a sample of 14 four-room housing units with electricity and a water tap on their lot, located in central neighbourhoods. Owner-occupied housing is not taken into consideration.

Specification of varieties
The specifications are given in great detail.

Substitution, quality change, etc.
If an item disappears from the market, its last price is used for three months at most; subsequently, the price of a similar item is taken and a correction factor is applied when computing the index.

Seasonal items
If an item disappears temporarily from the market, its last reported price is taken or it is replaced by a similar item.

Computation
The index is computed according to the Laspeyres formula as a weighted arithmetic average with fixed base, using weights corresponding to July 1976-July 1977.

The index for an item is obtained using the price ratios for the current and base periods. Average prices are the simple arithmetic averages of all prices collected.

Organisation and publication
Centre National de la statistique et des Etudes économiques: "Bulletin mensuel des statistiques" (Brazzaville).

Idem: "Annuaire statistique du Congo".

CONGO (BRAZZAVILLE, EUROPEANS)

Official title
Indice des prix à la consommation familiale européenne (Consumer Price Index for European families).

Scope
The index is compiled monthly and relates to European households in Brazzaville.

Official base
January 1964 = 100.

Source of weights
The weights and items were derived from a household expenditure survey conducted from February to March 1963 among a number of European households in Brazzaville.

Weights and composition

Major groups	Number of items	Weights	Approximate number of price quotations
Food	71	51.6	112
Household items and operations	18	6.9	24
Medical care	5	3.1	10
Clothing, footwear and household linen	13	7.7	15
Fuel, power and water	3	5.4	4
Domestic services	5	6.7	5
Miscellaneous	20	18.6	21
Total	135	100.0	191

Household consumption expenditure
This includes payments in kind and consumption of own-produced goods. Income tax is excluded.

Method of data collection
Prices for most items are collected each month by agents at various retail outlets and service establishments. Prices of fresh food sold at markets are obtained twice a month. Data for power, water and transport are collected each quarter. Discounts and sale prices are not taken into consideration.

Housing
Rent is not included in the index, nor is it taken into account in determining the weights.

Specification of varieties
The specifications are given in great detail.

Substitution, quality change, etc.
If an item disappears from the market, its last reported price is used for a maximum of three months; subsequently, the price of a similar item is taken and a correction factor is applied in computing the index.

Seasonal items
If an item disappears temporarily from the market, its last reported price is taken or it is replaced by a similar item.

Computation
The index is computed according to the Laspeyres formula as a weighted arithmetic average with fixed base, using weights corresponding to February-March 1963.

The index for an item is obtained using the price ratio for the current and base periods. Average prices are the simple arithmetic averages of all prices collected.

Organisation and publication
Centre National de la statistique et des Etudes économiques: "Bulletin mensuel des statistiques" (Brazzaville).
Idem: "Annuaire statistique du Congo".

COOK ISLANDS (RAROTONGA)

Official title
Retail Price Index.

Scope
The index is computed quarterly and relates to employees' households.

Official base
2nd quarter 1967 = 100.

Source of weights
The weights and items were derived from a household expenditure survey conducted in May 1967 among an ad hoc selection of employees' households (excluding agricultural workers) in which the head of the family had an average weekly income of between 4 and 20 Pounds at the time of the survey. (Of the 156 budgets analysed, the heads of 99 households received between 4 and 6 Pounds a week).

Weights and composition

Major groups	Number of items	Weights	Approximate number of price quotations
Food	76	58.4	...
Tobacco and alcohol	5	6.8	...
Housing	11	3.1	...
Household operation	51	9.6	...
Clothing and footwear	48	12.4	...
Transport	10	5.7	...
Miscellaneous	36	4.0	...
Total	237	100.0	...

Household consumption expenditure
Not available.

Method of data collection
Prices are collected by agents during the third and fourth weeks of February, May, August and November from five main shopping centres in Rarotonga.

Housing
Not available.

Specification of varieties
Not available

Substitution, quality change, etc.
Not available.

Seasonal items
Not available.

Computation
The index is computed according to the Laspeyres formula as a weighted arithmetic average with fixed base, using weights corresponding to the base period.

Other information
A new series (base June 1989 = 100) is now computed but the relevant methodological information was not available in the ILO at the time the present volume was published.

Organisation and publication
Statistical Office: "Quarterly Statistical Bulletin" (Rarotonga).
Government of Cook Islands: "Rarotonga Retail Price Index" (Rarotonga, 1967).

COSTA RICA (SAN JOSE)

Official title
Indice de precios para los consumidores de ingresos medios y bajos del área metropolitana de San José (Consumer Price Index for Middle- and Low-Income Group Families in the Metropolitan Area of San José).

Scope
The index is computed monthly and covers middle- and low-income group families living in the metropolitan area of San José.

Official base
1975 = 100.

Source of weights
The weights and items were derived from a household expenditure survey conducted in the metropolitan area of San José during 52 weeks in 1974, among a sample of 1,633 families with middle or low incomes, earning up to 5,499 colones in 1974. The weights were adjusted to take into account price changes between the survey period and 1975.

Weights and composition

Major groups	Number of items	Weights	Approximate number of price quotations
Food	59	40.76	1,845
Housing:			
Rent	1	12.30	106
Fuel, light and telephone	7	6.62	13
Cleaning materials, furniture and household equipment	24	8.19	510
Clothing and footwear	34	10.02	336
Miscellaneous:			
Personal and medical care	20	6.39	390
Education and recreation	10	9.23	92
Transport	3	6.50	28
Total	158	100.00	3,320

Household consumption expenditure
Consumption expenditure for the purpose of the index comprises all goods and services purchased for consumption by the index population. Credit purchase is considered only for the part paid in the reference period. Excluded is the value of used goods traded in to acquire new ones, but only the part actually paid is taken into account. Home ownership, contributions to social insurance and pension funds are excluded. Consumption from income in kind is taken into account.

Method of data collection
Prices for most items are collected by agents each month from retail outlets and service establishments. Prices for fresh fruit and vegetables are ascertained twice a week. Discounts, sale prices, black-market prices and second-hand purchases are excluded.

Housing
Rent quotations are obtained quarterly. No account is taken of owner-occupied dwellings.

Specification of varieties
Specifications for each item indicate major characteristics such as quality, weight, appearance, etc.

Substitution, quality change, etc.
If the quality of an item changes or a new item appears on the market, it is taken into account only when prices for two consecutive months are available.

Seasonal items
No account is taken of seasonality. Quantities remain fixed throughout the year.

Computation
The index is computed according to the Laspeyres formula as a weighted arithmetic average with fixed base, using weights corresponding to 1975.

Other information
Sub-group indices are published and item-indices can be made available.

A household income and expenditure survey was conducted in 1987-88 so as to up-date the base of the index.

Organisation and publication
Dirección General de Estadística y Censos: "Indices de Precios para los Consumidores de Ingresos Medios y Bajos del Area Metropolitana de San José" (San José).

COTE D'IVOIRE (ABIDJAN, AFRICANS)

Official title
Indice des prix à la consommation - Africains. (Consumer Price Index - Africans).

Scope
The index is compiled monthly and relates to African wage earners' and salaried employees' families of four or five persons, excluding families with more than three adults or more than one wage or salary earner.

Official base
February 1960 = 100.

Source of weights
The weights and items were derived from a household expenditure survey conducted in August-September 1956 among African wage earners' and salaried employees' families in Abidjan, and relate to African families of four or five persons, excluding families with more than three adults or more than one wage or salary earner.

Weights and composition

Major groups	Number of items	Weights	Approximate number of price quotations
Food	47	51.1	...
Rent	2	11.6	...
Fuel, light, water and soap	6	8.1	...
Clothing and footwear	12	8.4	...
Household goods	13	7.3	...
Services	9	8.5	...
Miscellaneous	11	5.0	...
Total	100	100.0	...

Household consumption expenditure
Not available.

Method of data collection
Prices for food, fuel and certain other items are collected daily from four important markets. Prices of other goods and services are obtained once a month.

Housing
Rent quotations refer to low-priced apartments with three rooms.

Specification of varieties
Not available.

Substitution, quality change, etc.
Not available.

Seasonal items
Not available.

Computation
The index is computed according to the Laspeyres formula as a weighted arithmetic average with fixed base, using weights corresponding to August-September 1956.

Other information
A new series relating to African households, in which the head of the household is either a wage earner, a qualified salaried employee or an artisan in Abidjan, is now computed (base August 1984-July 1985 = 100). The relevant methodological information was not available in the ILO at the time the present volume was published.

Organisation and publication
Ministère de l'Economie et des Finances, Direction de la statistique: "Bulletin mensuel de statistique" (Abidjan).

COTE D'IVOIRE (ABIDJAN, EUROPEANS)

Official title
Indice des prix à la consommation - Européens (Consumer Price Index - Europeans).

Scope
The index is compiled monthly and relates to European families of two or more persons in Abidjan.

Official base
1960 = 100.

Source of weights
The weights and items were derived from a household expenditure survey conducted in June 1961 among European families of two or more persons in Abidjan.

Weights and composition

Major groups	Number of items	Weights	Approximate number of price quotations
Food	57	50	...
Fuel, light and water	5	4	...
Clothing, footwear, household linen and various household equipment	28	8	...
Cleaning materials, personal hygiene and medical expenses	22	10	...
Domestic services	2	8	...
Miscellaneous	26	20	...
Total	140	100	...

Household consumption expenditure
Not available.

Method of data collection
Prices for all items are collected by agents from five markets, four large stores, and service establishments. Prices of local food, fuel and certain other items are collected each day; prices of imported food items are collected each week; and prices of all other items are collected at the end of each month.

Housing
Rent is not included in the index, nor was it taken into account in determining the weights.

Specification of varieties
Not available.

Substitution, quality change, etc.
Not available.

Seasonal items
Not available.

Computation
The index is computed according to the Laspeyres formula as a weighted arithmetic average with fixed base, using weights corresponding to June 1961.

Organisation and publication
Ministère de l'Economie et des Finances, Direction de la statistique: "Bulletin mensuel de statistique" (Abidjan).
Ministère des Finances, des Affaires économiques et du Plan, Direction de la statistique: Supplément trimestriel to the "Bulletin mensuel de statistique" (Abidjan), études et rapports No. 3, 1962.

CYPRUS

Official title
Retail Price Index.

Scope
The index is computed monthly and covers private households with an annual net income of 3,000 to 8,000 pounds in 1984-85, in urban areas.

Official base
1986 = 100.

Source of weights
The weights and items were derived from a household expendi-

ture survey conducted during March 1984-February 1985, covering a random sample of households residing in the Government Controlled Area. Urban and rural households of all classes were represented in the survey. For computing the weights, however, and on the recommendations of the Advisory Committee, only households residing in urban areas and with an annual income of 3,000 to 8,000 pounds were taken into account. This group covered 56.9 per cent of all urban households; the 22.9 per cent of household with very low incomes and the 20.2 per cent of households with high incomes were excluded. Households of foreign nationals and people living in institutions such as hospitals, old-aged homes etc. were excluded from the sample.

In all, 3,759 households constituting 2.5 per cent of all households were enumerated, 2,363 in urban and 1,396 in rural areas. However, the number of households that qualified for the computation of the weights was restricted to 1,346, i.e. those in urban areas and within the annual income group of 3,000 to 8,000 pounds. The weights were adjusted to take account of price changes between the survey period and 1986. The method of adjustment was based on the average price developments during the 12 months of 1986.

Weights and composition

Major groups	Number of items	Weights	Approximate number of price quotations
Food	98	3,206	2,226
Alcoholic beverages and tobacco	4	301	24
Household durable goods and supplies	52	679	342
Clothing and footwear	42	958	252
Transport and communication	36	1,930	76
Rent and housing	5	1,530	232
Fuel and light	4	208	9
Miscellaneous goods and services	72	1,188	397
All Items	313	10,000	3,558

Household consumption expenditure

The consumption expenditure used for deriving the weights corresponds to the SNA classification of household final consumption expenditure with the following amendments: (a) expenditure on lottery, gambling, horse race betting etc. was not included for the calculation of the weights, and (b) expenditure on motor vehicle circulation licences and driving licences was included for the calculation of weights.

Goods from own production were valued at wholesale prices and included in expenditure. For own-dwelling occupiers, an imputed rent was estimated and used in calculating the weights. Durable goods credit purchases were considered as normal purchases and the full price of the items was taken into account.

Second-hand purchases were also taken into account at the price bought. Trade-in of used goods and in part payment for new ones were only considered in the case of cars for which only the net difference between the used car and the new purchase was used in calculating expenditure on cars.

Contributions to social insurance and pension funds were excluded from the expenditure used for derivating the weights. Insurance associated with specific consumer goods was included. Expenditure on health care was included only if paid directly by a member of the household. Income taxes and other direct taxes, life insurance payments and other transfers of money to other households were also excluded. However, purchases of gifts given to other households were included.

Method of data collection

The criteria for selecting an item for price collection were: its availability on the retail market, its share in total expenditure and quality, unit of measurement, variety and other specifications being available. The weights of items not priced were distributed proportionately among similar items that are priced.

As no point-of-purchase survey was carried out, the outlets where price data are obtained were selected empirically so as to include a representative sample of stores from which the index population make their purchases. The outlets selected were restricted to the three largest towns, namely Nicosia, Limassol and Larnaca and prices are obtained from two outlets in each town for each type of commodity or service, by trained enumerators from the Department of Statistics and Research.

The price collection frequency varies according to the item. Prices for fresh fruit and vegetables are collected once a week (every Thursday) from the municipal market, while for other commodities prices are obtained once a month (on the Thursday closest to the 15th of the month). For price controlled items (such as fuel, electricity, telephone, water etc.) data are obtained from invoices issued by the organisations concerned.

The prices refer to the prices actually paid. As from 1991, discounts, sales and seasonal special offers have been taken into account. These are now held regularly twice a year, in February and in August-September and are regulated by a law which came into force in 1991. Black-market and credit terms are not taken into consideration. Import prices are reflected in the respective retail prices.

Housing

Rent quotations are obtained every two months from 200 dwellings, through mail questionnaires and by personal visits for those not replying by post. The sample of 200 dwellings covered by the rent data was randomly selected from Nicosia (98), Limassol (70) and Larnaca (32). The number of dwellings selected in each town was based on the population distribution. The sample selection was restricted to urban dwellings with a monthly rent of 30 to 100 Cyprus pounds as determined in the household expenditure survey. This group represented 77.5 per cent of all rented urban dwellings and excluded the 19.3 per cent of dwellings with very low rents and the 3.2 per cent with very high rents.

The rent index is computed as follows: first, an average rent per dwelling is calculated for each town; then a national average rent is obtained using the same weights as for all other items of the index (i.e. Nicosia 5, Limassol 3, Larnaca 2); finally, a price relative is calculated by dividing the current national average rent by the previous month's rent index to arrive at the current month's index.

Owner-occupied houses were taken into account in calculating the overall rent weight by estimating an imputed rent. In computing the rent index, only the rents actually paid are taken into account; the imputed rents are disregarded on the assumption that their evolution is similar to that of rent actually paid.

Specification of varieties

The goods and services priced are specified in detail, i.e. size, make, brand, quantity, quality, commercial presentation and other characteristics, so as to avoid variations of prices which might be brought about by a different quality, method of packing, model etc. Normally, the item specifications are the same for all outlets, but if this is not possible the relevant items are defined separately. Each month, the interviewers should use the same variety or report a change of type when it occurs.

Substitution, quality change, etc.

If quality changes take place, the relevant items are substituted for so that the price relative remains unchanged. New products are only introduced when a revision of the weights takes place, about once every five years. The disappearance of a given quality from the market is dealt with by substituting another similar product available on the market and the price relative is left unchanged. If the quality of the substitute product is not directly comparable with that of the previous product, an adjustment for quality is made.

A substitution is made by linking the prices of the new and old items, by taking a theoretical base price for the substitute item. For this, it is necessary to obtain prices for both the current and previous months.

Seasonal items

Fresh fruit and vegetables are treated as seasonal items. To overcome the seasonality problem, a different basket of fruit and vegetables was prepared for each month, on the basis of data obtained from all municipal wholesale markets. The weights allocated to the various kinds of fruit and vegetables are proportional to their total value of sales as recorded in the wholesale markets for a period of three years. The relevant sales for the years 1983, 1984 and 1985 were computed by combining the respective quantities for each item and then multiplying this by the retail prices that prevailed in the market during the base year, 1986.

In computing the fresh fruit and vegetables indices, the total weights are kept constant each month, but the variety of items and their respective weights vary from month to month, depending on their availability.

For items which are not sold during the whole year, such as heaters, summer and winter clothing and footwear, flowers, fresh fish etc., the last price recorded is repeated in the months these items are not available.

Computation
The index is computed according to the Laspeyres formula as a weighted arithmetic average with fixed base, using weights corresponding to the base period.

The index is directly computed at the national level. A weighted average price is computed for the three towns using weights, Nicosia 5, Limassol 3 and Larnaca 2, which approximately reflect their respective populations. The price relative is calculated by dividing the current average price by the previous month's average price and multiplying this by the previous month's price relative.

Other information
Major sub-group indices are published and as well as special sub-indices accordint to the economic origin of goods and services.

Organisation and publication
Ministry of Finance, Department of Statistics and Research: "Monthly Economic Indicators".

Idem: "Economic Report".

Idem: "Statistical Abstract".

Idem: "Labour Statistics".

Idem: "Methodology of the Retail Price Index", Series I, Report 4, November 1988 (Nicosia).

CZECHOSLOVAKIA

Official title
Consumer Price Index.

Scope
The index is compiled monthly and covers the whole population of the Czech Republic and the Slovak Republic.

Official base
January 1989 = 100.

Source of weights
The weights and items were derived from retail trade turnover. The weights relate to 1989.

Weights and composition

Major groups	Number of items	Weights	Approximate number of price quotations
Food	239	297.64	...
Public housing	79	105.63	...
Industrial goods:	500	450.77	...
Clothing	150	101.86	...
Footwear and leather	52	28.69	...
Other (incl. fuel)	248	320.22	...
Services (incl. rent, transport and communications)	233	145.96	...
Total	1,051	1,000.00	...

Household consumption expenditure
All monetary expenditure by households in state, co-operative and private shops for the purchase of food and industrial goods, expenditure in restaurants and public canteens, expenditure for services, including administrative, notarial, lawyers', judicial and local fees, and material and personal insurance.

Method of data collection
The items selected for price collection must currently be purchased by consumers, important from the point of view of consumers' expenditure and representative of certain groups of goods.

Most prices are collected by regional statisticians each month with respect to the 15th of the month, at selected shops and service establishments in all districts of the Czech Republic and the Slovak Republic.

For some items with prices fixed for a several years, the prices are recorded by the reporting unit at the beginning of each year. If a change of price occurs during the year, the unit reports the new price within five days. For instance, prices for electricity, gas, water, transport and communication are uniform throughout the country and are collected centrally.

Prices for fruit and vegetables are ascertained three times a month, on the 1st, 10th and 20th day of each month.

Health, medical care and education are provided free of charge. The fees for some items, e.g. language and music courses, are obtained from the appropriate service establishments.

The index is based on prices paid in state, co-operative and private trade for full-value goods; prices of second-hand goods are not included in the index.

Housing
The rent data for dwellings are determined on the basis of flat rates per square metre of floor space and rates for basic household equipment, e.g. cookers, space for storage of fuel, food, hygienic facility, electricity, water conduit and sewerage system, bathroom, washing line, cupboards, central heating, house cleaning and lift.

Rent quotations are obtained for flats of different sizes: one-room studio, one room with kitchen, two rooms with kitchen and three rooms with kitchen. Rents for flats are collected centrally (by decree of the central organisation). A decentralised rent inquiry is being prepared.

Changes in the costs of owner-occupied housing are represented in the index by the price trend of building materials and the prices for building work and housing maintenance.

Specification of varieties
The goods and services to be priced are specified in detail, i.e. size, make, brand, quantity, quality, etc. The quality description was established with the assistance of trade specialists.

Substitution, quality change, etc.
When a product is no longer available, it is substituted by another product of approximately the same quality. If the quality of the substitute product is not directly comparable with that of the previous product, adjustments for quality are made on the advice of the specialists from trade organisations. As a rule, insignificant differences in quality (e.g. of a fashionable character) are not taken into account.

Seasonal items
Fresh fruit and vegetables are not always on sale each month. A separate monthly basket is compiled comprising selected varieties currently on sale in the relevant month. The weights of the individual varieties of vegetables and fruit in these baskets are based on the average for the years 1985-1989. The sub-group index for vegetables and fruit is then computed using constant weights based on the percentage of total consumption expenditure.

Computation
The index is computed according to the Laspeyres formula as a weighted arithmetic average with fixed base, using weights corresponding to the base period.

The prices collected from the individual reporting units are used to calculate unweighed arithmetic averages. Separate indices are calculated for the Czech Republic and the Slovak Republic. The index for the whole country is the average of these two indices.

Other information
"Cost of living indices" for the main social groups of households, for low- and high-income household groups, and for households with one, two and three children are also computed and published.

Organisation and publication
Federal Statistical Office, Czech Statistical Office and Slovak Statistical Office: "Statistical Information" (Prague). - Development of price indices in consumer and production sphere (quick monthly information) - Development of consumer price indices (monthly information)

Idem: "Statistical Yearbook".

Idem: "Figures for Everybody".

DENMARK

Official title
Consumer Price Index.

Scope
The index is compiled monthly and covers total private consumption on Danish territory.

Official base
1980 = 100.

Source of weights
The weights were obtained from the 1987 national accounts statistics. Total household final consumption expenditure in the national accounts is divided into 63 groups. The breakdown of the expenditure within these groups is based on the more detailed information obtained from a household expenditure survey conducted in 1987, covering a sample of 2,232 private households. The weights were adjusted for price changes between 1987 and January 1991. If the expenditure for an article was negligible then its weight was distributed proportionately among the selected items within a sub-group. Total expenditure was thus distributed among the selected items before the relative weights were calculated.

Weights and composition

Major groups	Number of items	Weights	Approximate number of price quotations
Food	152	14.45	14,000
Beverages and tobacco	21	6.63	900
Rent and maintenance	13	21.46	(a) 150
Fuel and light	8	6.99	200
Clothing and footwear	60	5.71	1,300
Household goods	90	6.51	2,350
Medical care	12	1.79	(b) 100
Transport and communication	64	17.19	700
Education and recreation	64	9.47	1,800
Other goods and services	47	9.80	500
Total	531	100.00	22,000

Note: (a) Maintenance only, excl. semi-annual rent survey of sample of 4,200 rented dwellings. (b) Excl. special survey for medicine covering total range of products.

Household consumption expenditure
The concept of household consumption expenditure in the Danish national accounts is that of final consumption in the domestic market.

Method of data collection
Prices are collected monthly from approximately 1,500 private stores and local branches of chain stores and 270 establishments, trade organisations, etc.
Prices for 71 items, mainly food and beverages, are collected by interviewers from about 480 retail outlets in 34 municipalities. Prices for other foodstuffs, non-durable household goods, goods for personal care, etc. are collected from national or regional chain stores either from price lists or by direct reporting by questionnaire. Prices for the remaining items are collected through a monthly postal survey covering a varying number of shops throughout the country. The prices used in the index are the actual prices paid by any member of the public. Discounts and sales prices are taken into consideration when the quality and quantity of the product are according to specifications.

Housing
Rent data are obtained in April and October each year from a fixed sample of 4,200 rented dwellings throughout the country. New dwellings are included in the computation of the average rent. These are dwellings of a higher standard than the average dwelling in the stock. The problem of quality difference has to be solved somewhat arbitrarily because the rents are subject to control. The Danish approach at present is to measure the rent of new dwellings in relation to the rent of dwellings built in the last 3-year period. Briefly, the influence of new flats in the computation is similar to the influence of a separate index for new dwellings considered as a separate item. The weight for rent also includes the imputed rent for owner-occupied dwellings. The computation of imputed rents for owner-occupied housing is based on information on rents for rented flats.

Specification of varieties
Detailed specifications of the 345 items included in the postal survey are given according to brand name, size, unit and model, etc. In several cases the choice of brand and model is left to the individual shopkeeper, and once selected the brand name and model will be entered in the questionnaire form. The specification of items for price collection in local municipalities is less rigid, leaving the choice to the interviewers. Interviewers must use the same variety from one month to the next or report a change of type when this occurs.

Substitution, quality change, etc.
When a product is no longer available, it is replaced by a similar product, or its weight is added to another item or distributed within the sub-group. Quality changes in products are examined by consulting the dealers or manufacturers/importers. If the price change due to a quality change can be estimated, a correction will be made. Failing this, the price of the substituted product will be used in the computation before a price is available for two successive months. For motor cars, adjustments for changes in a model are based on the opinion of the consumer organisation and the importer/producer.

Seasonal items
Prices for fish (cod, plaice), fresh fruit (apples, oranges, grapes) are fresh vegetables are subject to seasonal adjustments.

Computation
The index is computed according to the Laspeyres formula as a weighted arithmetic average with fixed base, using weights corresponding to January 1991. Item indices are computed using relatives of average prices for many items and averages of price relatives for others. These average prices and the average of price relatives are weighted or simple arithmetic averages, depending on the nature of the price data. In the case of weighted averages, the weights are either the population of urban areas or are derived from figures of retail sales turnover.

Other information
In addition to the consumer price index, an index excluding taxes and subsidies is published: nettoprisindekset (the net price index).

Organisation and publication
Danmarks Statistik: "Statistiske Efterretninger" (Copenhagen).
Idem: "Nyt fra Danmarks Statistik" (newsletter).
Idem: "Statistik Manedsoversigt".
Idem: "Statistikservice: Prisstatistik".
Idem: "Statistik Arbog".
Idem: "Statistiske Efterretninger, Indkomst, forbrug og priser", no. 8, 1991.

DOMINICA

Official title
Retail Price Index.

Scope
The index is compiled monthly and relates to all private households throughout the country.

Official base
April 1964 = 100.

Source of weights
The weights and items were derived from a household expenditure survey conducted in 1961 among a random sample of 232 households representative of all households.

Weights and composition

Major groups	Number of items	Weights	Approximate number of price quotations
Food	51	56.9	...
Alcoholic drinks and tobacco	5	8.3	...
Housing:			
Rent	1	3.7	...
Maintenance and repairs	1	5.2	...
Fuel and light	3	5.4	...
Household and miscellaneous items	11	4.6	...
Clothing and footwear	12	9.5	...
Services	13	6.4	...
Total	97	100.0	...

Household consumption expenditure
Not available.

Method of data collection
Prices are collected in Roseau by agents during the third week of each month from three stores, one market and service establishments.

Housing
Rent quotations are obtained each month for one type of dwelling with two bedrooms.

Specification of varieties
Not available.

Substitution, quality change, etc.
Not available.

Seasonal items
No account is taken of seasonal fluctuations in prices.

Computation
The index is computed according to the Laspeyres formula as a weighted arithmetic average with fixed base, using weights corresponding to the base period.

Other information
A new series (base July 1984 = 100) is now computed but the relevant methodological information was not available in the ILO at the time the present volume was published.

Organisation and publication
Department of Economic Development and Planning, Statistical Division: "Annual Statistical Digest" (Roseau).

DOMINICAN REPUBLIC

Official title
Indice nacional de precios al consumidor (National Consumer Price Index).

Scope
The index is calculated monthly and covers households throughout the country, with monthly incomes of 50 to 600 pesos in 1976-77.

Official base
May 1976-April 1977 = 100.

Source of weights
The weights were derived from a household expenditure survey conducted during May 1976-April 1977 among a sample of 4,457 households of two or more persons, representing the whole population, with monthly incomes of 50 to 600 pesos at the time of the survey.

Weights and composition

Major groups	Number of items	Weights	Approximate number of price quotations
Food and tobacco	46	...	...
Housing:			
Rent and repairs	2	...	...
Fuel, light, water and telephone	7	...	...
Furniture and household items	8	...	...
Cleaning materials, etc.	9	...	...
Clothing and footwear	33	...	...
Miscellaneous:			
Personal and medical care	17	...	...
Education and recreation	6	...	...
Transport and communication	2	...	...
Total	130	...	...

Household consumption expenditure
Consumption expenditure for the purpose of the index comprises all goods and services which the reference households purchased for their own consumption. It also includes some expenditure on direct taxes, gifts and contributions, postage charges and mortgage payments for owner-occupied dwellings.

Method of data collection
The pricing frequency varies according to the item. For food, beverages and tobacco, prices are collected each day or week, according to the nature of item and outlet. For housing, clothing and miscellaneous items, prices are collected each week or month. In total, 4,300 outlets and service establishments are visited for pricing. Discounts are not taken into account.

Housing
Rent quotations are obtained from 604 dwellings; the estimated rent of owner-occupied dwellings, repair costs, payment of mortgages and monthly contributions (including insurance) are taken into account.

Specification of varieties
Each item to be priced is specified in terms of the most popular local name for the item, brand, size, weight, etc. There is a list of the information sources and specifications for each item for each city and rural area.

Substitution, quality change, etc.
Quality changes are reflected in the index using a linking method.

Seasonal items
No account is taken of seasonal fluctuations.

Computation
The index is computed according to the Laspeyres formula as a weighted arithmetic average with fixed base, using weights corresponding to the base period.

The price relative for each item is calculated by dividing the average price for the current period by the average price for the previous period.

Separate indices are compiled for rural and urban areas of each major region of the country. These indices are then weighted together to obtain separate rural and urban indices for the whole country. Finally, the urban and rural indices are weighted together to obtain the national index, the weights used being the consumption expenditures of the areas concerned.

Organisation and publication
Banco Central de la República Dominicana: "Boletín Mensual" (Santo Domingo).

Idem: "Metodología para el cálculo del índice de precios al consumidor en la República Dominicana 1982" (Santo Domingo).

ECUADOR

Official title
Indice de precios al consumidor - área urbana nacional (Consumer Price Index - National Urban Area).

Scope
The index is computed monthly and covers low- and middle-income group families in urban areas.

Official base
May 1978-April 1979 = 100.

Source of weights
The weights and items were derived from a household expenditure survey conducted between July 1975 and June 1976 in 12 towns with more than 10,000 inhabitants. The survey was conducted during 52 weeks among low- and middle-income group families. The weighting pattern was adjusted for price changes between 1976 and 1978-79.

Weights and composition

Major groups	Number of items	Weights	Approximate number of price quotations
Food	18	396.0	2,413
Housing:			
Rent	1	161.0	1,400
Fuel and light	1	29.6	47
Furniture, furnishings and household equipment	6	56.0	332
Clothing and footwear	5	107.7	1,060
Miscellaneous	8	249.7	1,354
Total	(a) 39	1,000.0	6,606

Note: (a) These are sub-groups representing between 150 and 170 items according to town.

Household consumption expenditure
Consumption expenditure comprises all disbursements made by the households for buying consumer goods and services. Income in kind and owner-occupied housing are taken into account in income and expenditure. Durable goods bought during the reference period are taken into account. For credit purchases, only the amount paid during the reference period is included in expenditure. Second-hand purchases are excluded. Social security taxes deducted from gross income are considered as consumption expenditure. Payments made during the reference period for insurance of consumer goods and for life insurance are included.

Method of data collection
The prices for certain food items of major consumption are ascertained weekly or fortnightly by direct buying in various markets. The prices of other items and services are obtained by investigators. All prices are those actually paid by the consumer, and include indirect taxes but exclude discount and sale

prices, second-hand purchases and import prices. Prices fixed by the authorities are taken into account only when they are actually paid by consumers.

Housing
Rent quotations are obtained from a sample of houses, apartments and rooms. Each month, a sixth of the sample is surveyed. A weighted arithmetic average is used for computing the index. No account is taken of owner-occupied dwellings.

Specification of varieties
The specifications of varieties relate to those items and services of major consumption and describe brand, dimension, weight, unit, etc.

Substitution, quality change, etc.
If an item disappears from the market, it is replaced by another with similar characteristics. If there is a quality change, the item is considered to be a new one and adjustments are made using the linking method.

Seasonal items
The choice of items included in the index has been made so as to ensure continuity of price collection throughout the year; however, if an item is not available on the market in certain months, the price quotation of the previous month is maintained.

Computation
The index is computed according to the Laspeyres formula as a weighted arithmetic average with fixed base, using weights corresponding to the base period.

Indices are calculated separately for each of the 12 towns according to the Laspeyres formula; the regional and national indices are computed using estimated population weights for 1979.

Organisation and publication
Instituto Nacional de Estadística y Censos: "Indice de Precios al Consumidor Area Urbana Nacional" (Quito).

EGYPT

Official title
Consumer Price Index - All Urban Population.

Scope
The index is compiled monthly covering all urban households throughout the country without limits as to size or income.

Official base
July 1986 - June 1987 = 100.

Source of weights
The weights and items were derived from a household expenditure survey conducted in 1981-1982 among a sample of 10,000 households. The items included in the index are based on their relative importance. The weights of items which are not included are allocated to the nearest item with the same price trend or among other items in the same sub-group. The weights were not adjusted to take into account price changes between the survey period and the base period.

Household consumption expenditure
Consumption expenditure for the purpose of the index is defined as the actual expenditure on consumer goods and services during the reference period. It excludes income taxes and other direct taxes, life insurance payments, internal and external transfers, instalments for commodities received out of the reference period, gifts and charity donations.

Method of data collection
Prices for most items are collected each month by the regional statistical offices. Prices of services and some manufactured goods are obtained each quarter. At least three outlets report for each commodity and service for each of the 26 cities. Of the 402 commodities and services, the prices of about 190 are collected centrally by the Prices Division. The prices used in the index are the prices actually paid. Controlled prices for rationed goods are taken into account.

Housing
The rent index is calculated periodically using the rents for newly established and demolished dwellings, since the rent of old dwellings is kept constant by the authorities.

Specification of varieties
Not available.

Weights and composition
Upper Egypt

Major groups	Number of items	Weights	Approximate number of price quotations
Food	141	576.2	...
Rent and water	4	77.4	
Fuel and light	9	38.3	...
Furniture, cleaning materials and domestic services	55	48.7	
Clothing and footwear	92	106.5	...
Medical care	42	23.9	...
Transport and communication	14	29.9	
Education and recreation	29	27.4	
Miscellaneous	16	71.7	
Total	402	1,000.0	...

Lower Egypt

	Number of items	Weights	
Food	141	575.5	...
Rent and water	4	72.0	
Fuel and light	9	37.6	...
Furniture, cleaning materials and domestic services	55	44.1	
Clothing and footwear	92	116.5	
Medical care	42	26.8	
Transport and communication	14	34.1	...
Education and recreation	29	25.0	...
Miscellaneous	16	68.4	...
Total	402	1,000.0	...

Canal Cities

	Number of items	Weights	
Food	141	567.2	
Rent and water	4	64.8	
Fuel and light	9	36.0	...
Furniture, cleaning materials and domestic services	55	59.9	
Clothing and footwear	92	106.5	
Medical care	42	23.1	...
Transport and communication	14	45.5	
Education and recreation	29	30.0	
Miscellaneous	16	67.0	
Total	402	1,000.0	...

Alexandria

	Number of items	Weights	
Food	141	559	...
Rent and water	4	59	...
Fuel and light	9	41	...
Furniture, cleaning materials and domestic services	55	47	...
Clothing and footwear	92	101	...
Medical care	42	26	...
Transport and communication	14	63	
Education and recreation	29	32	...
Miscellaneous	16	72	
Total	402	1,000	...

Cairo

	Number of items	Weights	
Food	141	520	...
Rent and water	4	59	
Fuel and light	9	34	...
Furniture, cleaning materials and domestic services	55	58	
Clothing and footwear	92	107	...
Medical care	42	32	...
Transport and communication	14	67	
Education and recreation	29	45	
Miscellaneous	16	78	...
Total	402	1,000	

Border lands

	Number of items	Weights	
Food	141	583.8	...
Rent and water	4	81.6	...
Fuel and light	9	40.7	...
Furniture, cleaning materials and domestic services	55	34.3	
Clothing and footwear	92	122.3	...
Medical care	42	12.9	...
Transport and communication	14	42.9	
Education and recreation	29	23.6	...
Miscellaneous	16	57.9	...
Total	402	1,000.0	...

Substitution, quality change, etc.
If an item is no longer available on the market, it is substituted by a similar item. The base price of the old item is adjusted by experts to take into account the change in quality.

Seasonal items
Fresh fruit and vegetables are treated as seasonal items. During the off season, the weights of these items are assigned to the other items in the same group.

Computation
The all-urban population index is computed as the weighted average of six separate indices relating to Cairo, Alexandria, Canal Zone, Upper Egypt, Lower Egypt and Border Land. The index for each town or group of towns is computed according to the Laspeyres formula as a weighted average of relatives formula. These indices are then weighted according to the population of each town or group of towns to arrive at the all-urban population index. The weights applied are 28.6 per cent for Cairo, 13.8 per cent for Alexandria, 4.7 per cent for Canal Zone, 25.5 per cent for Upper Egypt, 25.9 per cent for lower Egypt and 1.4 per cent for Border Land.

Other information
Separate indices are published for Cairo, Alexandria, Canal Zone, Upper Egypt, Lower Egypt and Border Land. An All Rural Population Index and separate indices for Upper Egypt and Lower Egypt are also published. Detailed sub-groups are published for all these series.

Organisation and publication
Central Agency for Public Mobilisation and Statistics, "Monthly Bulletin of Consumer Price Index", Cairo.

EL SALVADOR

Official title
Indice de precios al consumidor (Consumer Price Index).

Scope
The index is computed monthly and covers all middle-income urban households.

Official base
December 1978 = 100.

Source of weights
The weights and items were derived from a nationwide household expenditure survey conducted between August 1976 and July 1977 among 1,819 urban and 1,408 rural households. The weights relate to urban families of the middle-income group.

Weights and composition

Major groups	Number of items	Weights	Approximate number of price quotations
Food	56	42.78	...
Clothing and footwear	30	8.38	...
Housing:			
Rent	1	11.70	...
Water, telephone and domestic services	3	2.97	...
Fuel and light	7	3.87	...
Household utensils and linen	9	1.27	...
Household equipment	11	6.01	...
Cleaning materials	4	1.23	...
Miscellaneous:			
Medical care	7	2.54	...
Personal care	12	2.12	...
Education and recreation	10	8.69	...
Transport and communication	7	7.76	...
Tobacco	1	0.68	...
Total	158	100.00	...

Household consumption expenditure
Not available.

Method of data collection
Prices for most items and services are obtained by agents during the week containing the 15th of each month in the metropolitan area of San Salvador, Santa Ana and San Miguel. Some prices with uncertain quantity are ascertained through direct buying. Prices for fresh fruit and vegetables are collected during the first and third weeks of each month, those for clothing items, every two months and those for furniture, household equipment, medical and dental fees, each quarter.

Housing
Rent quotations are obtained in March and September of each year from 50 rented dwellings. No account is taken of owner-occupied dwellings.

Specification of varieties
Specifications of varieties are kept confidential and are detailed, taking into account the quality, make, brand, pattern, etc.

Substitution, quality change, etc.
If a change in the specifications of an item occurs, it is treated as a new item and the price relative calculated when the new item price is collected twice; the weight assigned to the new item remains unchanged. If the item is completely new, a special enquiry will show the relative importance of the item, and the weights will be redistributed over the other items in the sub-group concerned.

Seasonal items
If an item disappears temporarily from the market, it is assumed that the seasonal item varies in the same proportion as all other items in the same sub-group.

Computation
The index is computed according to the Laspeyres formula as a weighted arithmetic average with fixed base, using weights corresponding to August 1976-July 1977.

The price relative for each item is calculated by dividing the average price for the current period by the average price for the previous period. Average prices are simple arithmetic averages.

Organisation and publication
Ministerio de Economía, Dirección General de Estadística y Censos: "Boletín Estadístico" (San Salvador).

Ministerio de Planificación y Coordinación del Desarrollo Económico y Social, Unidad Investigaciones Muestrales: "Metodología para la construcción del Indice de precios al consumidor, base Diciembre 1978 = 100" (San Salvador, Nov. 1978).

ETHIOPIA (ADDIS ABABA)

Official title
Retail Price Index for Addis Ababa.

Scope
The index is compiled monthly and covers urban households with monthly incomes below 400 Birrs during 1963.

Official base
1963 = 100.

Source of weights
The original weights and items were derived from a household expenditure survey conducted in Addis Ababa in 1963 among a sample of about 600 households.

Weights and composition

Major groups	Number of items	Weights	Approximate number of price quotations
Food and tobacco	33	48.98	318
Rent	...	...	...
Fuel and light	4	10.23	42
Household items	3	4.37	33
Transport	3	4.52	30
Clothing and footwear	6	6.71	30
Personal and medical care	11	2.64	87
Reading and recreation	5	2.57	25
Other goods and services	9	5.43	36
Total	74	85.45	601

Household consumption expenditure
Consumption expenditure for the purpose of the index comprises all goods and services purchased for consumption by the index population. It also includes insurance associated with specific consumer goods and licence fees. Income tax, life insurance payments and savings are excluded.

Method of data collection
Prices are collected by the permanent staff of the Central Statistical Office from about 545 retail stores, open markets and service establishments.

Prices are collected each month for most of the items. Prices for durable consumer goods, clothing, transportation and miscellaneous items are collected once every three months.

The prices used to calculate the index are the retail prices actually paid. Sale and discount prices are not taken into account.

Housing
The index excludes rent.

Specification of varieties
All items covered by the consumer price survey are specified in considerable detail so that complications in the collection of data are avoided. The specifications describe the make, brand, unit, colour, physical state, etc., of each item included in the sample.

Substitution, quality change, etc.
If an item disappears from the market, it is either substituted by a similar item or the last price is kept until it reappears on the market.

Seasonal items
Retail prices of fish, meat, all kinds of fruits and vegetables, exercise books, pencils, umbrellas and rubber boots show seasonal variations, but no seasonal index is constructed nor are these items treated in a special way.

Computation
The index is computed according to the Laspeyres formula as a weighted arithmetic average with fixed base, using weights corresponding to the base period.

Organisation and publication
Central Statistical Office: "Statistical Abstract" (Addis Ababa).

FALKLAND IS. (MALVINAS) (STANLEY)

Official title
Retail Price Index.

Scope
The index relates to wage earners' families living in Stanley.

Official base
1 January 1971 = 100.

Source of weights
The weights and items were derived from a household expenditure survey conducted in 1971 among wage earners' families (small size) in Stanley.

Weights and composition

Major groups	Number of items	Weights	Approximate number of price quotations
Food	15	409	...
Beverages and tobacco	6	94	...
Clothing and footwear	64	128	...
Fuel and light	2	45	...
Furniture, furnishings and household appliances	24	54	...
Housing (mortgage interest, rates and repairs)	6	98	...
Cleaning materials	7	28	...
Personal and medical care	7	30	...
Stationery	2	27	...
Services	10	87	...
Total	143	1,000	...

Household consumption expenditure
Not available.

Method of data collection
Prices are collected by agents at the end of the last month of each quarter, from three retail outlets and service establishments in Stanley.

Housing
Rent is not included as as index item nor was it taken into account in determining the weights.

Specification of varieties
Not available.

Substitution, quality change, etc.
Not available.

Seasonal items
No adjustment is made to seasonal fluctuations in the item prices.

Computation
The index is computed according to the Laspeyres formula as a weighted arithmetic average with fixed base, using weights corresponding to the base period.

Other information
A new series (base 1 July 1989 = 100) is now computed but the relevant methodological information was not available in the ILO at the time the present volume was published.

Organisation and publication
Government Printing Office: "Falkland Islands Gazette" (Stanley).

FIJI

Official title
Consumer Price Index.

Scope
The index is computed monthly and covers urban households in six major urban centres.

Official base
1985 = 100.

Source of weights
The weights and items were derived from a household expenditure survey conducted from February 1983 to January 1984 among a sample of 4,402 households throughout Fiji. The index relates to 1,756 households in urban areas. The weights were not adjusted to take into account price changes between the survey period and the base period.

Weights and composition

Major groups	Number of items	Weights	Approximate number of price quotations
Food	103	339.3	...
Alcoholic drinks and tobacco	7	63.8	...
Housing (rent, rates, maintenance)	9	186.1	...
Fuel and light	3	48.7	...
Durable household goods	36	75.6	...
Clothing and footwear	32	63.1	...
Transport	15	112.9	...
Services	27	67.5	...
Miscellaneous	35	43.0	...
Total	267	1,000.0	...

Household consumption expenditure
Excluded are income tax, payments to savings and pension funds, life insurance premiums, house purchases and mortgage interest, subscriptions to unions and betting payments.

Method of data collection
Prices are collected during the middle of two weeks each month from centres in the Suva-Nausori area and the middle week from centres in Ba, Lautoka, Nadi and Labasa. As an index based on the consumption pattern of all urban dwellers in Fiji, the Suva-Nausori area was considered as representative of the central division, Labasa the northern division and centres in Ba, Lautoka and Nadi were considered as representative of in the western division. Together, the price changes in these areas are considered to be representative of price movements in all urban areas of Fiji.

The prices collected for the construction of the index are those charged in cash transactions. Price collectors visit each centre and personally note down the prices and weights of items displayed in shops. If the prices are not marked or are illegible, the investigators are instructed to obtain the information directly from supermarket managers or supervisors. Prices for items on "sale" or "specials" are recorded when they apply to items in the index, except when the price has been reduced due to damage, "shop-soiled" or any form of deterioration of the goods. The latter conditions reflect changes in the quality of the merchandise and price variations caused by quality differences are excluded from the index.

Officers of the Bureau of Statistics visit each pricing establishment personally to record prices. Information relating to services levied by the Government and statutory bodies is obtained directly from them. Consistency in terms of visiting the establishment at the same time and day of the week is maintained each month, especially at regional municipal markets where there can be considerable variation in prices between the morning and afternoon.

Food items for pricing purposes are divided into municipal market items and supermarket items. Items in supermarkets are well defined in terms of size and brand, and prices are read from the tags. With the market items, however, officers carry their own scales to weigh and price items. Generally, three samples of an item are taken from various vendors in the market and the average price per unit weight is later computed in the office. Markets are visited on Fridays and Saturdays at specified times in the morning. This is to capture normal prices for perishable goods which often deteriorate towards the end of the day when they are generally sold at reduced prices.

Cooking gas, white benzine and kerosene are priced from the usual pricing establishments while electricity tariffs obtained directly from the Fiji Electricity Authority are regularly checked for possible changes.

Housing
The major component of this section is rent. The sample was chosen from among the rented households identified during the expenditure survey, and represents a random selection of all rented households of Fiji citizens during 1983. Data on rental charges are collected each month along with prices for other items. On each visit, households are asked for any improvements to the houses and any increase in rent due to such improvements is adjusted for a change in quality. Other items, such as those used for maintenance, are priced in the usual way during visits to hardware shops each month.

Specification of varieties
An important consideration after the items were selected for the index was to decide which particular brand and what size of packet or how many brands of a particular item were to be priced. If a particular item was overwhelmingly popular, it was easy to choose this from the expenditure and brand details recorded by households in their weekly diaries issued during the survey. However, in many cases, additional details had to be obtained from distributors and supermarket supervisors before final selections could be made. The criteria for an item to be included in the index were that it should be representative, a "good-seller" and generally available in major centres throughout Fiji.

Substitution, quality change, etc.
If an item is not available, the price is generally repeated for three months and then a substitute is selected. Care is taken to ensure that the substitute item is as similar to the original as possible in terms of quality, size and end-use.

Seasonal items
For seasonal items such as fresh fruit and vegetables, the closing prices for the previous season are maintained during the off season.

Computation
The national urban index (for the main island of Fiji) is computed as the weighted average of three separate indices relating to the central, western and northern regions. Each regional index is computed according to the Laspeyres formula as a weighted arithmetic average with fixed base, using weights corresponding to February 1983-January 1984. The three regional indices are then combined into a national urban index according to the proportionate expenditure for each region, the proportions being 0.571 for the central region, 0.361 for the western region and 0.068 for the northern region.

To compute the item indices, the weighted average of price relatives between the current and base periods is used.

Other information
Major sub-group indices are published.

Organisation and publication
Bureau of Statistics, Suva: "Statistical News".

Idem: "Methodological Report on the Consumer Price Index (Base average 12 months 1985 = 100)", Parliamentary Paper No. 22 of 1988.

FINLAND

Official title
Consumer Price Index.

Scope
The index is computed monthly and covers all private households and all population groups throughout the country.

Official base
1985 = 100.

Source of weights
The weights and items were derived from a household expenditure survey conducted in 1985, covering all private households and all population groups throughout the country and lasting one year. 11,800 persons from different households in the target population were selected by geographically stratified sampling, using 25 strata. Of these, 8,200 households provided fully acceptable information. The overall response rate was thus 69.5 per cent. Nonresponse was highest among one-person households and in big cities. For some commodities, including alcohol, tobacco, sweets, lottery stakes and soft drinks, the consumption data were corrected using data from other sources.

The selection of items is based mainly on their importance, representativeness, availability and the extent of their use. The weight of an item does not always refer only to the relative contribution to consumption of that item, but can represent the combined consumption expenditure value of several items similar in nature and price behaviour for which prices are not collected.

Weights and composition

Major groups	Number of items	Weights	Approximate number of price quotations
Food	111	19	...
Beverages and tobacco	7	7	...
Clothing and footwear	51	6	...
Housing, fuel and light	9	19	...
Household furnishings, supplies and services	70	7	...
Health and medical care	10	3	...
Transport and communications	34	17	...
Free time, recreation and education	57	9	...
Other goods and services	54	13	...
Total	403	100	(a) 38,000

Note: (a) The number of price quotations does not include price quotations used in measuring housing items.

Household consumption expenditure
The definition of consumption expenditure used for deriving the weights is mainly the same as in the household survey, with a few exceptions. It includes only purchased commodities, i.e. the weights of the CPI do not include the values of self-produced goods, such as home-grown agricultural products, self-gathered berries and mushrooms and so on.

As a general rule, consumption expenditure is recorded using the acquisition principle, so that purchases on hire-purchase schemes and on credit plans (including durable goods credit purchases) are included in consumption before their payment (i.e. at the time of their purchase).

Included are receipts of goods and services and the value of gifts of goods received.

Excluded are gifts and assistance given to other households, such as gifts of money and goods, newspapers and periodicals, consumer durables, travel, maintenance allowance payments and damages paid directly to households.

Included are goods and services received as income in kind (on the basis of an employment contract or a life annuity or as assistance) and the value of gifts or goods received (e.g. dwelling, motorcar, meals).

Expenditures reimbursable under the Sickness Insurance Act, such as those for travel, medicines and health care services, and lottery stakes are recorded in net amounts, i.e. prizes won and reimbursements received were deducted.

For certain consumer commodities, income received from the sale of used goods was deducted from the purchase value of new goods. This applies to household appliances and transport equipment.

Certain items comparable to current transfers are counted as consumption expenditure because of the voluntary nature of the payments. These include compulsory fees and fines paid to government authorities, membership fees paid to non-profit institutions (churches, political parties, trade unions), indemnity insurance premia and interest payments on consumer credit (i.e. life and accident insurance premia, travel and travel goods insurance premia, third-party insurance premia, registration and licence fees, passports and visas, fines and other comparable compulsory fees, membership fees to labour market organisations, church tax, offertory payments, charitable contributions and the like, interest payments on study loans and interest payments on other consumer credits). Purchases of used goods are included in consumption expenditure in the same way as other purchased goods.

Excluded are income tax and other direct taxes and contributions to pension funds and social insurance schemes.

Motor insurance premia (for both compulsory motor third-party liability and motor vehicle insurance) are recorded in gross amounts.

Currency exchanges and the imputed housing benefit provided by owner-occupied dwellings are not included in consumption expenditure in the CPI.

Insurance associated with specific consumer goods is included. Among housing expenditure for owner-occupied dwellings, depreciation charges for wear and tear, maintenance costs and other fixed expenses are counted as consumption expenditure.

Method of data collection
The localities were selected using stratified random sampling (regional stratification). When the CPI base 1985=100 was revised, the samples were not revised; the sample of localities and the sample of outlets thus derived from 1983.

The largest population centres (urban areas) in the four major areas of Finland served as regional centre collection localities. The criteria for determining the number of localities to be selected in each major area were as follows: the size of the area's population, the disposable income of the area's population, total consumption expenditure in the area and the adequacy of the number of price data for computing a reliable index for the area.

Seventeen regional centre localities were selected. The outlets in these localities were selected by the interviewers in consultation with the CPI staff. Included were the biggest and the most popular outlets, and special attention was paid to the relative position occupied in the area by the outlets of different retailing chains and the extent that different speciality shops were represented. About 1,400 outlets were selected.

Price data collection for CPI items takes place mainly through visits by interviewers to outlets. In addition, for a small number of food and other perishable items, price data are collected from the price lists of the outlets concerned.

Price data are collected each month for food and other perishable items, household utensils, cleaning and washing preparations and other household supplies; every two months for consumer durables and certain categories of clothing; seasonally for certain other categories of clothing, fruit, vegetables and berries; each quarter or as needed for services and other items.

The data are collected between the 11th and the 17th of each month. The interviewers are instructed to collect the data randomly within the specified time period, so as to avoid collecting data always on the same weekday. The price data for (i) electricity, gas and water are collected from municipal electricity boards and water works; for (ii) medical care, from government health care authorities; for (iii) education and training from universities and the press, respectively; and for (iv) transport and communication centrally by the Central Statistical Office by telephone, from price lists, lists of official tariffs or brochures, or by visiting the enterprises concerned.

The main principle is that account is taken of retail prices and of any normal discounts on retail prices that are available to all persons. Normal sale prices are taken into account but cash discounts and hire purchase or credit terms are not.

Prices are only collected for new products (second-hand purchases are netted out in the weights).

Housing
For rented dwellings, the price movement of rents is measured by the movement of rents actually paid. The Central Statistical Office conducts a rent survey four times a year. Each year, the sample consists of about 24,000 rental dwellings. Rent information is requested from tenants using postal questionnaires.

The price movement of housing services provided by owner-occupied dwellings is measured by the price movement of various cost items, such as maintenance expenses and interest and depreciation charges.

For owner-occupied houses, maintenance costs cover repair, chimney-sweep services and waste management costs, ground rents, insurance premia, water charges and street tax. Interest expenditure on housing loans, whether conventional loans or low-interest government loans, are measured by the movement of the nominal interest rate. The price movement of the depreciation item is measured by the Central Statistical Office price index for old owner-occupied flats.

For owner-occupied flats, maintenance costs are measured by the price movement of maintenance charges and repair costs. Interest expenditure and depreciation deductions are measured in the same way as for owner-occupied houses. The weights of the different cost items for owner-occupied housing are derived from the Central Statistical Office household survey for 1985.

Specification of varieties
In developing the detailed specifications for the collection items, use was made of the expertise of different bodies (associations, organisations, trade, distributors, importers, manufacturers and enterprises) and of the CPI staff in the relevant subject areas. International price comparison experts (OECD) were also consulted.

Detailed specifications (quality specifications) were prepared for all collection items.

The specifications (product specifications) lay down the requirements which the items must meet. In many cases, the interviewer is free to select the final collection item as long as the selection takes place according to the set guide-lines. The specifications include the following: detailed quality specifications, size or size range, composition, material, etc.; and, for some items, a list of brand names accepted for price collection and instructions concerning the type of packaging used.

In some specifications, mainly for services, cars and car parts, the item is restricted to a strictly specified brand, product or service.

Substitution, quality change, etc.
If commodity qualities change, any price change solely due to the change in quality is always eliminated. Quality changes mainly concern differences in material, size, finish, service life, power, etc. between the old and the new commodity quality. Differences merely due to fashion or the country of manufacture are not treated as commodity quality changes. The assessment of quality changes always starts from the service the new and the old commodities provide to the consumer, i.e. from the point of view of the consumer, changes in production costs do not necessarily mean changes in quality.

Daily consumed goods are subject to few quality change adjustments because their prices relate to unit prices, i.e. prices per gramme or litre, and not to the price for per item. Any quality change adjustments to these commodities are made at the Central Statistical Office.

Regarding clothing items, household appliances, home electronics and other items on which price data are collected for the regional centres, a change in quality is at first evaluated by the interviewer after consulting the seller about quality differences between the old and the new commodities. The final decision is made at the Central Statistical Office, ensuring uniform treatment of quality changes throughout the country.

Seasonal items
The index includes items which are available (for sale) for only part of the year. Traditional items seasonally available are fresh potatoes and berries; similarly, certain clothing items, sports equipment, etc. are only intended for winter or summer use. Price data for items with seasonal variations are collected during the months they are sold (or purchased). During other months, their prices remain at the level of the last collection month, changing only when price collection is resumed.

Some commodities (e.g. fresh vegetables) are often sold at special prices when they are first introduced on the market or withdrawn from it. No prices are collected in such circumstances. For example, the price of domestic cucumbers is not included in the collection for the month of March.

Items with seasonal variations have the same weight throughout the year, as is the case for all items.

Computation
The index is computed according to the Laspeyres formula as a weighted arithmetic average with fixed base, using weights corresponding to the base period. The price relative for each item is computed by dividing the current price by the base price.

The price relative of an item for a major area is computed as the average (arithmetic mean) of the price relatives of products priced for the item in the major area. At the national level, the price relatives for the major areas are weighted according to the relative contribution of each major area to final consumption expenditure.

The index is computed by weighting the indices for the major areas according to the relative contribution of each major area to final consumption expenditure. Within each major area, the index is calculated by weighting the price relatives of items according to their relative contributions to the area's final consumption expenditure.

If price data are missing, the data for the previous reference period remain in effect. If no data have ever been recorded for a product, it is excluded from the index and has no influence on it. In case of faulty data, an attempt is made to obtain correct data through interviews. If this is not possible, the presumably correct data for the previous reference period remain in effect.

Other information
The CPI is published each month at the major-group level. General indices are also available for the following population groups: own-account farmers, all employees (management and upper-level salaried employees, other salaried employees, wage earners) and pensioners; for the following major areas: Metropolitan area of Helsinki, rest of southern Finland, Central Finland, Northern Finland; and for: one-person households, childless couples and families with children. A Net Price Index and a Tax Rate Index are also calculated.

Organisation and publication
Central Statistical Office of Finland: "Bulletin of Statistics" (Helsinki).

Idem: "Consumer Price Index 1985 = 100", Studies No. 144, 1988.

FRANCE

Official title
Indice des prix à la consommation des ménages urbains dont le chef est ouvrier ou employé (Consumer Price Index for Urban Households).

Scope
The index is compiled monthly and covers urban households of all sizes, in which the head of the household is a wage or salary earner.

Official base
1980 = 100.

Source of weights
The weights are revised at the beginning of each calendar year using the results of continuing family expenditure surveys conducted among 10,000 households and data on household accounts obtained from the system of national accounts. The weights used to compute the indices for a given year are based on the results of surveys carried out two years before and updated to December of the preceding year. The number of items and the weights used in 1992 are as follows:

Weights and composition

Major groups	Number of items	Weights	Approximate number of price quotations
Food	91	22.67	...
Clothing, footwear and household linen	59	8.36	...
Furniture, furnishings, household goods, cleaning materials, tobacco, etc.	82	25.64	...
Fuel and light	7	8.18	...
Housing:			
Rent	1	7.74	...
Water	1	0.76	...
Maintenance and repairs	3	1.22	...
Personal and medical care	12	6.14	...
Public transport and maintenance of vehicles	8	6.81	...
Other services (incl. restaurants, etc.)	32	12.48	...
Total	296	100.00	180,000

Household consumption expenditure
Home-produced goods and services, second-hand purchases, hospital services, social security contributions, used car insurance premiums, sea and air transport, veterinary services, goods and services for funerals and domestic services are not included in the index, but indirect taxes (VAT) are included.

Method of data collection
Prices are collected by agents from 30,000 retail outlets and service establishments in 108 urban centres with more than 2,000 inhabitants. They are collected monthly for most goods and services, quarterly for clothing and furnishings and twice a month for fresh products. Mail-order sales are not covered. The prices collected are those actually paid by consumers.

Housing
Rent quotations are obtained for all types of dwellings during the first month of a quarter, using a special household survey. Owner-occupied dwellings are excluded from the index.

Specification of varieties
Specifications are detailed. The price collector chooses the specific product for regular price collection in each retail outlet.

Substitution, quality change, etc.
If the quality of an item changes, either it is replaced by a similar item assuming that there is no price change, or the quality change is measured and isolated from the price change. New items are introduced only when their sales become important.

Seasonal items
Seasonal fluctuations in the prices of fresh products are taken into account by varying items and item weights within monthly baskets of constant group weights and by using a 12-month moving average.

Computation
The index is a chain index, in which the weights are changed at the beginning of each calendar year. The index for each month is first computed on base December of the preceding year = 100; the resulting index is then calculated on base 1980 = 100 (Laspeyres' chain index).

Other information
Detailed sub-groups and various other groups are published, as are consumer price index estimates for various social and occupational categories of heads of households (base 1970 = 100), and a series for greater Paris.

Organisation and publication
Institut national de la statistique et des études économiques (INSEE): "Bulletin mensuel de statistique" (Paris).

Idem: "Informations rapides".

Idem: "Pour comprendre l'indice des prix".

FRENCH GUIANA (CAYENNE)

Official title
Indice des prix à la consommation (Consumer Price Index).

Scope
The index is compiled monthly and relates to urban lower-income group households in Cayenne.

Official base
1980 = 100.

Source of weights
The weights and items were derived from a household expenditure survey conducted in 1969 in Cayenne and Kourou.

Weights and composition

Major groups	Number of items	Weights	Approximate number of price quotations
Food	...	50.0	...
Housing (incl. fuel, light and water)	...	19.5	...
Clothing and footwear	...	8.4	...
Hygiene, health and services	...	7.6	...
Transport and communications	...	6.1	...
Education and recreation	...	4.9	...
Other services	...	3.5	...
Total	...	100.0	...

Household consumption expenditure
Not available.

Method of data collection
Prices are collected by agents from 46 retail outlets and 15 service establishments. The frequency of price collection depends on the nature of the item. Prices for fruit and vegetables are ascertained each week, other food items are priced once a month. Prices for manufactured items and for services are collected quarterly. No account is taken of sale prices.

Housing
Rent quotations are obtained each quarter from one company specialising in renting dwellings (covering 1,840 dwellings).

Specification of varieties
For each item a list of varieties was given by INSEE. The pricing agents select the most appropriate variety, i.e. commonly sold and available for future pricing. The specification of the selected product is then noted in terms of the brand, make, quality and size, etc.

Substitution, quality change, etc.
If the quality of an item changes, it is considered as a new item. It is introduced in the index calculation only when it is available on the market for some months.

Seasonal items
Seasonal fluctuations in the prices of certain vegetables are taken into account by using moving averages in the computation of the index.

Computation
The index is computed according to the Laspeyres formula as a weighted arithmetic average with fixed base, using weights corresponding to the base period.

Organisation and publication
INSEE, Service régional de la Guyane: "Bulletin Mensuel de Statistique" (Cayenne).

Idem: "Annuaire de la Guyane".

FRENCH POLYNESIA

Official title
Indice des prix de détail à la consommation familiale (Retail Price Index).

Scope
The index is computed monthly and covers households of all categories.

Official base
December 1980 = 100.

Source of weights
The weights and items were derived from the results of a nation-wide household expenditure survey supplemented by import statistics. The survey was conducted over three and a half months during the second half of 1979 among a sample of 836 households of all categories.

Weights and composition

Major groups	Number of items	Weights	Approximate number of price quotations
Food	79	3,650	4,107
Manufactured items:			
Clothing, footwear and household linen	28	900	362
Furniture, furnishings and household equipment	25	922	508
Cleaning materials	13	522	785
Vehicles	6	916	87
Recreation and reading items	18	699	375
Fuel and light	5	862	6
Tobacco and other	6	279	60
Services:			
Rent, water	2	445	25
Maintenance and repairs	4	148	34
Personal and medical care	5	101	32
Transport and communication	11	390	46
Education, recreation, other	14	166	130
Total	216	10,000	6,557

Household consumption expenditure
Account was taken of goods produced by households. Second-hand and credit purchases and social security contributions were excluded, but insurance premiums for cars and motor cycles were included.

Method of data collection
Prices for most items are collected each month by investigators or by means of telephone inquiries, from 326 retail outlets and service establishments. Prices for food items and those for manufactured products of important consumption items are obtained from all 13 localities of the islands of Tahiti and Moorea. Prices for other items and services are collected in the urban areas of Tahiti (Papeete, Faaa, Pirae and Arne). Prices include indirect taxes.

Housing
Rent quotations are obtained four times a year for 22 dwellings.

Specification of varieties
A list of 2,160 specifications is used for price collection, giving details of the type, brand, weights, quality and country of origin for each item.

Substitution, quality change, etc.
If an item disappears from the market, it is substituted by a similar item and a linking method is used. No account is taken of minor quality change. If the quality change is significant, a linking method is used.

Seasonal items
Prices for fresh fruit, vegetables and fish are ascertained each week from markets in Papeete and Pirae and each month from the other retail outlets. A 12-month moving average is used to compute the final index.

Computation
The index is computed according to the Laspeyres formula as a weighted arithmetic average with fixed base, using weights corresponding to the base period.

Other information
A new series is now computed (base December 1988 = 100), but the relevant methodological information was not available in the ILO at the time the present volume was published.

Organisation and publication
Institut territorial de la statistique: "Te Avei'a" (Papeete).

Idem: "Journal officiel de la Polynésie Française".

GABON (LIBREVILLE 1)

Official title
Indice des prix à la consommation - africains (Consumer Price Index - Africans).

Scope
The index is compiled monthly and covers African families in Libreville in which the head of the household is a wage earner or salaried employee (public or private sector, including domestic services).

Official base
June 1975 = 100.

Source of weights
The weights and items were derived from a household expenditure survey conducted during 1968-69 in Libreville among 9,942 African families of which the head of the household was a wage earner or salaried employee in the public or private sector, including domestic services.

Weights and composition

Major groups	Number of items	Weights	Approximate number of price quotations
Food	57	547	...
Clothing and footwear	9	175	...
Housing:			
Rent and building materials	4	23	...
Fuel, light, water and soap	8	14	...
Household equipment	16	93	...
Personal and medical care	10	19	...
Transport	9	63	...
Recreation and miscellaneous	12	66	...
Total	125	1,000	...

Household consumption expenditure
Consumption expenditure for the purpose of the index comprises all goods and services purchased for consumption by the index population. It excludes income tax, gifts and charities, loans and repayments, purchase of house and dowries.

Method of data collection
Prices are collected by agents, during the second half of each month, from selected markets, retail shops and other commercial outlets.

The prices used in the index are the retail prices actually paid by consumers.

Housing
Not available.

Specification of varieties
The item specifications are given in terms of the brand, make, quality and unit.

Substitution, quality change, etc.
Not available.

Seasonal items
Seasonal fluctuations in prices are not taken into account in the index.

Computation
The index is computed according to the Laspeyres formula as a weighted arithmetic average with fixed base, using weights corresponding to 1968-69.

Organisation and publication
Présidence de la République, Direction générale de la statistique et des études économiques: "Bulletin mensuel de statistique" (Libreville).

For further methodological details, see:

Idem: "Changement de base de l'indice des prix à la consommation des ménages-type africains residant à Libreville".

GABON (LIBREVILLE 2)

Official title
Indice des prix à la consommation - Familles à revenu élevé (Consumer Price Index - High Income Group).

Scope
The index is compiled monthly and covers African households with a monthly income of more than 100,000 francs, CFA and non-African households in the public and private sectors with a monthly income of less than 100,000 francs, CFA during March and May 1969. The index relates to Libreville.

Official base
June 1972 = 100.

Source of weights
The weights and items were derived from a household expenditure survey conducted between March and May 1969 in Libreville among a sample of 156 high-income group households, composed of 20 African households whose head had a monthly income of more than 100,000 francs, CFA, and 59 non-African households in the public sector and 77 non-African households in the private sector, whose head had a monthly income of less than 100,000 francs, CFA, at the time of the survey.

Weights and composition

Major groups	Number of items	Weights	Approximate number of price quotations
Food	84	511	...
Household expenditure:			
Electricity, gas and water	3	56	...
Domestic services	3	65	...
Cleaning materials	7	21	...
Household equipment and household linen	10	32	...
Clothing and footwear	8	34	...
Hygiene and health	10	35	...
Transport and communication	10	123	...
Miscellaneous	20	123	...
Total	155	1,000	...

Household consumption expenditure
Consumption expenditure for the purpose of the index comprises all goods and services purchased for consumption by the index population. It excludes income tax, gifts and charities, loans and repayments, purchase of housing and rent.

Method of data collection
Prices of most items are collected by agents around the 25th of each month from major retail outlets, one market and service establishments in Libreville. Prices for fresh food items are ascertained once a week.

The prices used in the index are the retail prices actually paid.

Housing
Rent is not included in the index.

Specification of varieties
The specifications are given in terms of the brand, make, quality and unit.

Substitution, quality change, etc.
Not available.

Seasonal items
Seasonal fluctuations in prices are not taken into account in the index.

Computation
The index is computed according to the Laspeyres formula as a weighted arithmetic average with fixed base, using weights corresponding to March-May 1969.

Organisation and publication
Présidence de la République, Direction générale de la statistique et des études économiques: "Bulletin mensuel de statistique" (Libreville).

For further methodological details, see:

Ministère délégué à la Présidence de la République chargé du plan, du développement et de l'aménagement du territoire, Direction générale de la statistique et des études économiques: "Bulletin mensuel de statistique" (Libreville), No. 166-167, Jan.-Feb. 1973.

GAMBIA (BANJUL, KOMBO ST. MARY)

Official title
Consumer Price Index.

Scope
The index is compiled monthly and covers low-income group households with an annual income of up to 1,500 dalasis during August 1968 to August 1969. The index relates to Banjul, the capital city, and Kombo St. Mary.

Official base
1974 = 100.

Source of weights
The weights and items were derived from a household expenditure survey conducted from August 1968 to August 1969, covering 618 households in Banjul. The price changes between the survey period and the base period (1974) were not taken into account in the weights. The criteria for selecting items for the basket was that all expenditure items with 0.5 per cent or more of the market basket should be included.

Weights and composition

Major groups	Number of items	Weights	Approximate number of price quotations
Food	52	580	...
Clothing, footwear and household linen	12	175	...
Rent	42	51	...
Fuel and light	5	54	...
Miscellaneous (including personal and medical care, education, recreation, tobacco, etc.)	24	140	...
Total	135	1,000	...

Household consumption expenditure
Consumption expenditure for the purpose of the index comprises all goods and services purchased for consumption by the index population. Income tax, gifts and charities, religious and ceremonial functions such as births, funerals and marriages, loans, purchase and maintenance of motor vehicles for commercial use, life insurance, credits and savings are excluded.

Method of data collection
Prices are collected by the permanent staff of the Central Statistics Division from four market areas and 48 retail outlets and service establishments in Banjul and Kombo St. Mary.

Prices are ascertained each month for most of the items. For certain items with large price fluctuations, prices are collected each fortnight through direct buying.

For items such as electricity charges, doctors' fees, hairdressing, school fees, cinema tickets, dances, newspapers, taxi

fares, air fares, foreign air-letters and dry-cleaning and washing, prices are collected once a month.
The prices used in the index are the prices actually paid.

Housing
Rent data are collected in February, May, August and November for 42 rented dwellings. The sample is kept fixed except for occasional adjustments.

Specification of varieties
A detailed description of each item priced is provided to the price collectors.

Substitution, quality change, etc.
If a product is no longer available on the market, it is substituted by a similar product and a method of linking is used.

Seasonal items
Fresh fruit and vegetables are treated as seasonal items. During the off season, the weights of these items are assigned to the other items within the same group.

Computation
The index is computed according to the Laspeyres formula as a weighted arithmetic average with fixed base, using weights corresponding to August 1968-August 1969.
Price relatives of the current and base periods are used to compute item indices.

Organisation and publication
Ministry of Economic Planning and Industrial Development, Central Statistics Division: "Consumer Price Index" (Banjul).
President's Office, Central Statistics Division: "Proposals for a new series of Consumer Price Index Numbers for Banjul and Kombo St. Mary" (Banjul, nov. 1973).

GERMANY 1

Note: The description relates to the territory of the Federal Republic of Germany before 3.10.1990.

Official title
Preisindex für die Lebenshaltung aller privaten Haushalte (Consumer Price Index for All Private Households).

Scope
The index is computed monthly and covers all private households of German residents, excluding institutional households.

Official base
1985 = 100.

Source of weights
The weights and items were derived from a household expenditure survey conducted in 1983, covering about 55,000 private households with one or more members and with a net monthly income of up to 25,000 marks. The weights were updated to 1985 on the basis of the current budget survey of about 1,000 selected private households. The index relates to an average household size of 2.3 persons and an average household consumption expenditure of 3,105 marks per month in 1985. The weights of items not priced were allocated to the other items.

Weights and composition

Major groups	Number of items	Weights	Approximate number of price quotations
Food and tobacco	186	229.89	116,000
Clothing and footwear	77	69.47	31,000
Rent	5	177.77	13,000
Fuel and light	18	72.52	4,000
Furniture, furnishings and other household items	138	72.21	37,000
Transport and communication	81	144.03	14,000
Personal and medical care	55	40.99	15,000
Education and entertainment	147	83.71	29,000
Other goods and services	44	109.41	41,000
Total	751	1,000.00	300,000

Household consumption expenditure
Household consumption expenditure used for deriving the weights includes home ownership, licence fees, insurance associated with specific consumer goods, gifts and similar disbursements. Private contributions to life, social and old-age insurance are excluded. Also excluded are income in kind, credit purchases, second-hand purchases, income taxes and other direct taxes.

Method of data collection
Prices are collected by agents around the middle of each month in 118 municipalities and about 15,000 retail outlets and service establishments.
Prices applying uniformly to the whole country (e.g. prices for books and magazines, postal fees, air tariffs, prices of inclusive tours, insurance premiums) are determined centrally at regular intervals or according to the dates of change. The prices used to calculate the index are the retail prices actually paid by consumers (not list prices), including value-added tax and excise duties (e.g. mineral oil tax, tobacco tax) and other statutory charges (e.g. equalisation charges for electric power, storage contribution for mineral oil products). Discount prices are collected only if items correspond to regular items. No sale prices are used.

Housing
Rent quotations are obtained each quarter from all dwellings included in the sample (11,000 dwellings). In order to show monthly changes, however, every month one third of the dwellings (about 3,700) is included in the index.
Owner-occupied housing is taken into account in the weights. Its price movement is represented by the rent of rented dwellings.

Specification of varieties
The descriptions of the individual goods and services included in the survey are so extensive that, in each reporting unit, the varieties of goods which account for the greatest part of turnover can be selected for the reporting unit. The price collector records the exact descriptions of the varieties (brand, article, number, quantity, etc.) for each of the individual goods and services so that it is possible to check and ensure comparability over time.

Substitution, quality change, etc.
If there is a change of price-determining characteristics, calculations or estimates are made in consultation with the relevant experts in order to eliminate any non-genuine price changes. A change from one item to another is carried out when the old item is still important on the market and the new one already has sufficient market importance; in this case, a procedure that simply links the old price series to the new one is applied.

Seasonal items
Seasonal items available on the market for a short period only are not included in the index. Prices for items available during the whole year are taken into account in their full amount.

Computation
The index is computed according to the Laspeyres formula as a weighted arithmetic average with fixed base, using weights corresponding to the base period.
Unweighted average prices are first calculated for each municipality and "Land". The average of price relatives for the current and base periods are used to compute item indices. Indices for the eleven Länder are then weighted according to the population in each "Land" and combined to obtain the index for the whole country.

Other information
Separate series are calculated for:
a) four-person households of civil servants and salaried employees with high incomes;
b) four-person households of wage earners and salaried employees with middle incomes;
c) two-person households of pensioners and social assistance beneficiaries with low incomes;
d) a child under 18.

Organisation and publication
Statistisches Bundesamt: "Wirtschaft und Statistik" (Wiesbaden).
Idem: "Eilbericht und Monatsbericht der Fachserie 17, Reihe 7, Preise und Preisindizes für die Lebenshaltung".
Idem: "Wirtschaft un Statistik" (Nos 7/84 and 1/90) for further methodological details.

GERMANY 2

Official title
Preisindex für die Lebenshaltung aller Arbeitnehmerhaushalte (Consumer Price Index for all employee households).

Scope
The index is computed monthly and relates to all employee households in the five new Laender and Berlin (East).

Official base
1989 = 100.

Source of weights
The weights and items were derived from a household expenditure survey conducted in the five new Laender and Berlin (East). Data were collected each month from January to December 1989 from a representative sample of 2,600 households. The average family size was 2.87 persons.

Weights and composition

Major groups	Number of items	Weights	Approximate number of price quotations
Food and tobacco	187	385.9	19,000
Clothing and footwear	79	134.1	10,000
Rent, fuel and light	30	55.1	8,000
Furniture, household appliances and operation	138	119.1	15,000
Health and personal care	47	29.7	7,000
Transport and communications	68	124.0	7,500
Education, entertainment, leisure (excl. services of hotel and restaurant)	145	90.4	11,500
Personal goods and services of the lodging trade and other goods	44	61.7	4,000
Total	738	1,000.0	82,000

Note: (a) See below.

(a) For non-centrally covered positions, the following numbers of price quotations are generally collected per priced item: in cities of up to 20,000 inhabitants: 4; in cities of 20,000 to 100,000 inhabitants: 6; in cities of more than 100,000 inhabitants: 8. Exceptions are: rents: per housing society selected and regulated (uniform) prices: 1 price quotation.

Household consumption expenditure
For deriving the weights, expenditure for the payment of goods, services, contributions to property insurance and motor vehicle taxes of private households were recorded.

Money expenditure does not include contributions to old-age and social insurance. Health expenditure is included only in so far as costs were incurred by private persons. The major part of the costs (visits to the doctor, stays in hospital, prescribed pharmaceuticals and other applications and appliances) is borne by the public health insurance and therefore not taken into account in the weighting scheme. Income tax and other direct taxes were not treated as money expenditure, except for the motor vehicle tax which is included in the weighting scheme. Income in kind, money transfers, donations, contributions and similar payments were excluded. For credit purchases and the hire purchase of commodities, the full purchase price at the time of purchase was recorded. Sales and purchases of used goods are included, but not shown as separate positions in the index. Administrative fees, property insurance contributions are included (household - house and content - and other property insurances, motor insurance).

Method of data collection
A representative sample of 80 survey communities or cities was selected. The reporting units, where the prices are collected directly, are selected in the survey communities by the relevant staff on the basis of turnover size.

Prices are recorded around the middle of each month, by investigators, directly at the reporting units. For some goods (e.g. electricity, gas, water), the written price lists of the enterprises are used, and rents of dwellings are covered by means of questionnaires. Officially-fixed uniform tariffs (passenger transport by rail, postal tariffs) are collected centrally on the basis of the tariff lists. The current regular prices and the comparable prices for the preceding month are collected by the investigators at the reporting units. Individual prices are then grossed up to average prices for communities (simple arithmetic means of the prices for the respective month and of comparable prices for the previous month). Discount and sale prices are not recorded. Black-market prices, hire-purchase and credit terms are not collected.

Housing
Rent quotations are obtained for six types of dwellings. Data are collected non-centrally at monthly intervals by means of special survey questionnaires; they are included in the index calculation as average prices and price relatives. Owner-occupied dwellings and houses are not covered as yet.

Specification of varieties
The descriptions of the items to be priced are relatively general. The quality and unit of measurement are indicated, but not the brand.

The price collector selects the specific commodities according to their turnover size in co-operation with the reporting unit.

Substitution, quality change, etc.
If there is a quality change, the comparable price for the previous month is recorded and a base price adjustment is made using the quotient of the current price and the price for the previous month. If a covered item or quality disappears, a new one is selected and the quality change is then assessed as compared with the former priced item; on the basis of this evaluation, a comparable price is calculated for the new item or quality for the previous month.

Seasonal items
Seasonal items are covered in the same way as all other priced items, and included in the monthly index computation without adjustment.

Computation
The index is computed according to the Laspeyres formula as a weighted arithmetic average with fixed base, using weights corresponding to the base period.

The simple arithmetic mean is used up to the calculation of the Land average prices and the Land price relatives. To compute average prices and price relatives for the territory of the five new Laender as a whole, the Land average prices and Land price relatives are weighted according to the population of each Land. Annual averages for the main index and the major index groups are computed using the simple arithmetic mean of the monthly indices.

Other information
Indices are published for major groups, along with indices for other types of households. It is intended to publish indices according to the procedure followed in the Federal Republic (territory prior to 3 October 1990) beginning with the second half of 1991. An index revision will probably be made with the introduction of a new (all-German) base year (1991).

A new series (base July 1990-June 1991 = 100) is now computed but the relevant methodological information series was not available in the ILO at the time the present volume was published.

Organisation and publication
The index is computed by the Federal Statistical Office, Branch Office, Berlin, Alexanderplatz, and published by Statistisches Bundesamt: "Eilbericht und Monatsbericht der Fachserie 17, Reihe 7, Preise und Preisindizes für die Lebenshaltung (Wiesbaden)".

GHANA

Official title
Consumer Price Index Numbers (national).

Scope
The index is compiled monthly and covers urban and rural households.

Official base
1977 = 100.

Source of weights
The weights and items were derived from a national household expenditure survey conducted during March 1974-February 1975. When working out the weights, expenditure on items not included in the index were allocated to the selected items taking into account the close nature of the items, e.g. the total expenditure on vegetables was allocated to the selected vegetable items. Some expenditure was into two or more parts and allocated to different items, e.g. expenditure on prepared meals

was split and distributed among the principal components of the meal.

Weights and composition

Major groups	Number of items	Weights	Approximate number of price quotations
Food	71	49.2	...
Beverages and tobacco	21	6.2	...
Clothing and footwear	65	19.2	...
Rent, fuel and light	6	6.8	...
Furniture, furnishings, household equipment and operation	48	5.1	...
Medical care and health	8	1.8	...
Transport and communication	15	4.3	...
Education and recreation	10	5.5	...
Miscellaneous	6	1.9	...
Total	250	100.0	...

Household consumption expenditure
Consumption expenditure for the purpose of the index comprises all the important goods and services purchased for consumption by the index population. The imputed values of consumption goods used by households from their own production, interest rates, licence fees, etc., are excluded.

Method of data collection
Price data are collected from selected retail stores and market places in nine urban and 30 rural centres. Prices are collected twice a month, on dates that are as close as possible to the 8th and the 22nd of the month. The prices used in the index are those that any member of the public would have to pay on the pricing day to purchase the specified item or service.

Whenever the goods are available at the controlled prices at the selected outlets, such prices are reported and used. The enumerators are provided with weighing scales so that they can convert the prices for quantities sold in terms of traditional measures or heaps to prices for standard weights.

Housing
Rent data are collected from a random sample of 300 urban-household dwellings selected from the Municipal Assessment Registers. Every month, rents are collected from a third of the sample selected. By rotation, each sample dwelling is covered once every three months. All the sample households occupy rented units. Owner-occupied dwellings and rent-free quarters provided by employers are excluded. Data on electricity and water charges are also collected if such charges are not included in the rent.

Specification of varieties
For some items, more than one variety is selected, depending upon the importance of the item. The specifications of items to be priced are given according to the size, unit and in some cases the brand name.

Substitution, quality change, etc.
Not available.

Seasonal items
Not available.

Computation
The index is computed according to the Laspeyres formula as a weighted arithmetic average with fixed base, using weights corresponding to March 1974-February 1975.

The average prices of varieties are the simple arithmetic averages of all the price quotations obtained. The price relative for each variety of an item is calculated by dividing the average price for the current period by the average price for the base period. If two or more varieties are selected for an item, a simple arithmetic average of price relatives for the varieties represents the price relative for the item.

Separate indices are first compiled for rural and urban areas in each region of the country. The urban and rural indices for each region are then combined to obtain national urban or rural indices. The weighted average of the urban and rural indices is computed to arrive at the national index, using as weights the urban and rural household consumption expenditures.

Other information
The Central Bureau of Statistics calculatea and publishes separate consumer price indices for Accra City, urban areas and rural areas.

Organisation and publication
Central Bureau of Statistics: "Quarterly Digest of Statistics" (Accra).

Idem: "Consumer Price Index Numbers, A new series" (Oct. 1978).

GIBRALTAR

Official title
Index of Retail Prices.

Scope
The index is compiled monthly for the food group and quarterly for other groups. The index relates to all types of households permanently resident in Gibraltar.

Official base
October 1980 = 100.

Source of weights
The weights and items were derived from a household expenditure survey conducted between February 1979 and March 1980, covering about 221 sample households.

Weights and composition

Major groups	Number of items	Weights	Approximate number of price quotations
Food	104	330.67	...
Beverages and tobacco	9	59.56	...
Clothing and footwear	39	110.00	...
Durable household goods	26	100.42	...
Rent	12	125.90	...
Services	24	75.39	...
Transport and vehicles	17	133.29	...
Miscellaneous	44	64.77	...
Total	294	1,000.00	...

Household consumption expenditure
Consumption expenditure for the purpose of the index includes almost all important goods and services purchased for consumption by the index population. It excludes income taxes and other direct taxes, social insurance contributions, savings and investment, contributions to pension funds and betting.

Method of data collection
Prices are collected by agents during the few days of each month. Prices for food items are collected each month from about 30 retail outlets.

Price for other items are collected each quarter from up to five outlets for each item.

The prices used to calculate the index are the prices actually charged to the consumer.

Housing
Rent data are obtained from government-owned properties and from a sample of approximately 100 private dwellings.

Specification of varieties
The specifications of items to be priced are given in terms of brand, make, quality and size, etc.

Substitution, quality change, etc.
If a new item is substituted in the index, its price is collected for three months and an average base price is calculated.

Seasonal items
Seasonality does not generally affect tne availability of goods in Gibraltar.

Computation
The index is computed according to the Laspeyres formula as a weighted arithmetic average with fixed base, using weights corresponding to the base period.

Price relatives for the current and base periods are used in computing item indices.

Organisation and publication
The index is compiled by the Economic Planning and Statistics Office (Gibraltar).

Government Printer: "Gibraltar Gazette" (The all-item index is published quarterly and the food group index monthly).

GREECE

Official title
Consumer Price Index.

Scope
The index is compiled monthly and relates to urban centres.

Official base
1982 = 100.

Source of weights
The weights and items were derived from a household expenditure survey conducted in 1982 among a random sample of 3,725 households in urban centres of 10,000 inhabitants or more. The survey also covered semi-urban and rural areas. The weights of the items not priced are allocated to the priced items representing them.

Weights and composition

Major groups	Number of items	Weights	Approximate number of price quotations
Food	134	324.4	...
Alcoholic beverages, tobacco	8	36.5	...
Clothing and footwear	58	128.3	...
Housing (incl. fuel and light)	11	130.6	...
Household equipment	65	85.5	...
Personal and medical care	34	62.5	...
Education and recreation	37	87.4	...
Transport and communication	26	130.0	...
Other goods and services	13	14.8	...
Total	386	1,000.0	...

Household consumption expenditure
Consumption expenditure for the purpose of the index refers to all money expenditure (both in cash and on credit) by households on goods and services intended for consumption. For health and education, only the amounts actually paid by the consumers are taken into account. Imputed rents, direct taxes and contributions to insurance funds are excluded.

Method of data collection
Prices are collected by agents from 1,016 retail outlets and service establishments in 17 towns which were considered to be representative of price changes in all urban areas of the country (five towns for some clothing items and durable goods). For items whose prices are defined by the State, prices are taken from the official invoices. The frequency of price collection depends on the nature of the item, e.g. fresh fruit, vegetables, meat, fish, etc., are priced once a week. Prices for other items are collected each month. Prices collected once a week refer to Tuesday; prices collected once a month are obtained in such a way as to refer the whole month (e.g. they refer to the first five-day period for the first establishment, the second five-day period for the second establishment, etc.).

Generally, the prices used in the index are real "cash prices". Discounts are taken into consideration but "special offer" prices are not. If the price of a certain item differs from the official one, the latter is taken into account.

Housing
Rent quotations are obtained twice a year from a random sample of 600 dwellings. The monthly rents actually paid are taken into consideration. The rent index is obtained from the total rent expenditure for the current month as compared to the corresponding average monthly expenditure for the base year. The imputed rent of owner-occupied dwellings is not taken into consideration.

Specification of varieties
Item specifications were established through market research. Detailed specifications are given for each index item (e.g. technical characteristics, make, brand, weight, quality, variety, etc.).

Substitution, quality change, etc.
If a selected product is no longer available for pricing, it is substituted by a similar product. Quality differences between the old and new products are taken into account by using a fictitious base price for the new product.

Seasonal items
Seasonal fluctuations in the prices of fresh fruit and vegetables are taken into account by varying the item weights within the baskets of constant group weights. Other seasonal items, such as summer and winter clothing and footwear, are taken into account by maintaining the closing prices of the previous season during the off season.

Computation
The index is computed according to the Laspeyres formula as a weighted arithmetic average with fixed base, using weights corresponding to the base period.

Price relatives for each variety in each outlet are first calculated by dividing the current period price by the base period price. Simple arithmetic averages of these price relatives are then calculated for each city. These are weighted using city weights to obtain price relatives of varieties for the whole country. The simple arithmetic averages of these price relatives are then computed to arrive at item indices for the whole country.

Other information
The general index and nine group indices are published each month.

A new series (base 1988 = 100) is now computed but the relevant methodological information was not available in the ILO at the time the present volume was published

Organisation and publication
National Statistical Service of Greece: "Monthly Statistical Bulletin" (Athens).

Idem: "Statistical Yearbook of Greece".

GREENLAND

Official title
Consumer Price Index for Greenland.

Scope
The index is compiled twice a year and relates to resident households in towns and settlements in Greenland.

Official base
January 1981 = 100.

Source of weights
The weights were derived from the statistics of the supply of goods and services for private consumption for the year 1985. The sources were import statistics, sales from the Greenland Trade Company and, with regard to inland production and services, information collected from a sample of 195 private households in 1985. The weight for rent is based on information from the Danish Ministry for Greenland and local administration, as 60 per cent of the rented dwellings are publicly owned by the Greenland Home Rule or municipalities. For owner-occupied dwellings, the costs are calculated as rental equivalents. For energy items, the weights were derived from information from the Technical Organisation for Greenland. The weights were adjusted to take into account price changes between the survey year and January 1987, when the new weights were first applied.

The sample of items priced was adjusted for changes since the previous revision in 1977-78.

Weights and composition

Major groups	Number of items	Weights	Approximate number of price quotations
Food	139	18.62	1,129
Beverages	20	11.44	84
Tobacco	7	7.13	30
Gross rent (housing)	5	10.01	23
Fuel and light	7	5.40	7
Clothing and footwear	50	7.69	332
Furniture, household equipment, etc.	64	9.21	279
Medical Care	6	0.29	18
Transport	11	4.86	32
Communication	4	3.28	11
Trapping, fishing, etc.	16	2.99	56
Other hobbies and recreational expenses	32	12.47	110
Miscellaneous goods and services	32	6.61	231
Total	393	100.00	(a) 2,342

Note: (a) Excluding the rent survey.

Household consumption expenditure
Consumption is defined as the total private consumption of goods and services in Greenland. Income in kind is not included. Direct taxes are excluded. There are no contributions

to social insurances and pension funds. Health care is public and free of charge and is not included in the weighting system. Insurance fees associated with specific items such as houses(fire) and cars are included. Other insurances, subscriptions and similar disbursements, covering about 1.7 per cent of total consumption, are not included. Home ownership has an additional weight for property in Denmark.

Method of data collection
Prices are collected mainly by mailed questionnaires or from official tariffs. Prices for goods are obtained twice a year from the Greenland Trade Company (publicly owned by the Home Rule), six co-operative societies and about 50 private retailers. Public tariffs for electricity, water, heating, etc. are supplied by the Technical Organisation and the municipalities. Tariffs for services are received from seven municipalities, the Technical Organisation, an insurance company and a few other reporting units.

Price data refer to the first week in January and July. The prices used are the regular prices paid by any member of the public (i.e. market prices).

Housing
Rent is the gross rent inclusive of fees for water and the removal of refuse. As 60 per cent of dwellings are rented dwellings owned by the Greenland Home Rule or the municipalities, information on rent changes is collected from administrative sources. Rents for existing dwellings are regulated once a year in October, normally with a general percentage increase per square metre. For new dwellings, a supplementary calculation is based on the increase in building costs. Costs for owner-occupied dwellings do not normally change, as fees for water, the removal of refuse, etc. are dealt with separately. Supplementary information for new or purchased dwellings is collected and enters into the calculation based on the increase in building costs. Costs for maintenance are dealt with as separate items.

Specification of varieties
There are detailed specifications for each item, describing the quality, make, brand and unit.

Substitution, quality change, etc.
New products are only introduced in the index compilation if they are substitutes for existing products. Quality changes andthe disappearance of a given type or quality from the market are treated in the same way by using the method of "overlapping periods".

e.g. if a radio of a certain make and quality is sold until July 1984, the new model that replaces it was normally introduced on the market in advance. This means that the price for the new model can be linked to the index for July 1984 for the old model.

Seasonal items
There is no special treatment of seasonal items. Items subject to very large seasonal fluctuations are not included in the index.

Computation
The index is computed according to the Laspeyres formula as a weighted arithmetic average with fixed base, using weights corresponding to 1985.

Other information
Detailed sub-group indices are published for these series. Danmarks Statistik also computes a price index net of import duties called "Reguleringspristallet for Gronland". In general, this index is used for indexation purposes in private contracts. It was previously used for regulating wages and salaries but this practise has been discontinued.

Organisation and publication
Danmarks Statistik: "Nyt fra Danmarks Statistik" (Copenhagen).
Idem: "Statistike Efterretninger" (Serien om Faeroerne og Gronland) (Copenhagen).
Idem: "Statistik Aarbog".
Idem: "Statistik tiaarsoversigt".

GRENADA

Official title
Consumer Price Index.

Scope
The index is computed monthly and covers all households throughout the country.

Official base
1987 = 100.

Source of weights
The weights and items were derived from a household expenditure survey conducted in 1987 among a random sample of 900 households throughout the country. The weights of items not selected for pricing were either distributed over similar items within the sub-group or grouped together into a single other-category to be represented by the most important item within the other category.

Weights and composition

Major groups	Number of items	Weights	Approximate number of price quotations
Food, alcoholic drinks and tobacco:	149	...	569
Food	...	38.7	...
Alcoholic drinks and tobacco	...	2.0	...
Clothing and footwear	72	5.2	72
Rent, Household operations:	20	...	30
Rent	...	11.9	...
Household operations	...	5.4	...
Fuel and light, Furniture, furnishings and household equipment:	62	...	169
Fuel and light	...	3.9	...
Furniture, furnishings and household equipment	...	8.3	...
Transport	17	9.1	20
Personal and medical care	30	8.6	139
Education, recreation and reading	24	4.6	30
Miscellaneous	10	2.3	10
Total	384	100.0	1,039

Household consumption expenditure
Included are home-produced goods, gifts, life insurance payment, credit purchases. Excluded are income taxes and other direct taxes, interest on loans and bank charges, hire-purchase payments, donations and church contributions.

Method of data collection
Prices of fresh meat, fish, fruit and vegetables are collected each week, on Fridays in St. George's and on Saturdays in Grenville and Gouyave.

Supermarket products, clothing, household items, fuel and light, and personal care items are priced each month. Rent quotations, insurance payments, travel expenses, prices for transportation, entertainment and miscellaneous expenses are ascertained each quarter.

The prices of items collected each month or quarter are obtained during the last week of the current month, following a fixed order every day starting on Mondays with supermarkets, pharmacies, etc. Officers from the Statistical Department collect all prices by field visits, or in some instances by telephone; e.g. doctors' fees, telephone charges, electricity charges etc. In the fruit and vegetable markets where units of measurements vary, e.g. bundles, heaps and numbers, kitchen scales are used to estimate the price for a standard measure.

Sale prices are used if they become permanent; if the price of the commodity is returned to its original price at the end of the sale, it is not used. Hire-purchase prices and discount prices are not used. Second-hand goods are not priced because there are no established markets. No special treatment is given to import prices. The prices used are those at which consumers make their purchases at the specified outlets.

Housing
Rent quotations are obtained each quarter from a sample of two- and three-bedroom dwellings. The quotations used for rent are also taken to represent owner-occupied housing. The weights for owner-occupied housing are combined with those of rented dwellings.

Specification of varieties
The point-of-purchase survey was incorporated in the household expenditure survey, in which respondents were asked to indicate the outlets where they made their purchases.

The questionnaire provided information on the brand and type for each item purchased, from which the most popular brands were selected for pricing in the outlets chosen. Visits were made to the outlets and detailed specifications were obtained, including the quality, size, country of origin and variety.

Substitution, quality change, etc.
A quality change is not treated as an increase in price; instead, the last price of the "old" quality item is kept constant for three months and then a new quality item is introduced.

New products are included in the basket at the time a new household expenditure survey is taken, approximately once every five years.

If a given type or quality disappears from the market, the last price of the specified item is held constant for three months. If the item does not reappear in the fourth month, a similar item, whose price has been collected for the past three months, is then introduced into the index.

Seasonal items
Whenever a commodity is not available on the market for at least three weeks of a month, it is treated as being a seasonal item.

When fresh fish is not available on the market, the movement in the price of fresh meat is used.

All items in the fresh vegetables and starchy food group are considered as seasonal except onions, Irish potatoes, garlic, bananas and plantains. This group is treated in a different way from fresh fish since the items are generally not out of the market for more than three months. Therefore, the last available price is kept constant until the item returns to the market.

Except for bananas, fresh fruit are considered seasonal and are treated in the same way as fresh vegetables, except for oranges and grapefruits, for which concentrated juice is used as a substitute.

Computation
The index is computed according to the Laspeyres formula as a weighted arithmetic average with fixed base, using weights corresponding to the base period.

Prices are averaged using the simple arithmetic method; the relatives are obtained by dividing the current average price by the previous average price.

Other information
Detailed sub-group indices are published.

Organisation and publication
Ministry of Finance. Statistical Department, "Annual Abstract of Statistics", (St. Georges).

Government Printer "Government Gazette".

GUADELOUPE

Official title
Indice des prix à la consommation des ménages en milieu urbain (Consumer Price Index - Urban households).

Scope
The index is compiled monthly and relates to urban households.

Official base
April 1978 - March 1979 = 100.

Source of weights
The weights and items were derived from a household expenditure survey conducted from September to December 1972 in Basse-Terre and Pointe-à-Pitre. The results were extrapolated on the assumption that consumption patterns in France and Guadeloupe evolved in a similar way from 1972 to 1978.

Household consumption expenditure
Only direct purchases of consumer goods and services are taken into account. The following expenditure is excluded: investments designed to maintain or increase the value of property, and transfers (income tax, social security contributions, etc.) which include amounts deducted from the income of certain households for redistribution among others either directly (social security benefits) or in the form of services provided free of charge to households (services provided by the administration, education, road network, etc.).

Method of data collection
Prices for most items are collected each month by agents from markets, retail outlets and service establishments in Basse-Terre and Pointe-à-Pitre. Prices for fish, fresh fruit and vegetables are collected each week. When there are both official and free-market prices for the same item, account is taken only of

Weights and composition

Major groups	Number of items	Weights	Approximate number of price quotations
Food	66	34.39	...
Restaurants	8	2.34	...
Clothing and footwear	37	9.25	...
Housing:			
Rent	1	10.06	...
Maintenance and repairs	3	2.49	...
Furniture, furnishings and household equipment	24	6.02	...
Fuel, light and water	5	5.72	...
Personal and medical care and domestic services	14	6.80	...
Transport	19	16.34	...
Education and recreation	21	6.59	...
Total	198	100.00	3,500

the official prices, except for public transport (taxis and buses) for which median prices are calculated on the basis of the free-market prices. The index is then calculated using these median prices. Discounts and reductions are not taken into account. Sale prices are collected as though they were the usual prices.

Housing
Rent quotations are obtained twice a year for 99 rented dwellings of all kinds.

Specification of varieties
There are few specifications for homogeneous varieties; for heterogeneous varieties, the size, brand, model, etc., are specified.

Substitution, quality change, etc.
If the characteristics are exactly the same, the new item replaces the old one without breaking the series. If there is a difference in quality between the substitute article and the one it is replacing, linking is carried out so that only the part of the price variation that is caused by the normal evolution of prices is taken into account. For certain items of clothing, especially women's clothing, the most common quality characteristics are defined. The prices of all these items are then collected and the median price is used to calculate the index for this sub-group.

Seasonal items
Account is taken of seasonal fluctuations in the prices of fresh fruit, vegetables and fish by varying the items and their weights within the monthly "baskets" whose overall weights remain constant.

Computation
The index is computed according to the Laspeyres formula as a weighted arithmetic average with fixed base, using weights corresponding to the base period.

Organisation and publication
INSEE, Service départemental de la Guadeloupe: "Bulletin de statistique" (Basse-Terre).

Idem: "Les cahiers de l'INSEE - Dossier prix" (Basse-Terre, first quarter, 1979).

GUAM

Official title
Consumer Price Index.

Scope
The index is compiled quarterly and relates to households of all income groups.

Official base
1978 = 100.

Source of weights
The weights and items were derived from a consumer expenditure survey conducted in 1978 among a sample of 500 households representing all income groups.

Household consumption expenditure
Consumption expenditure for the purpose of the index includes almost all goods and services purchased by the index population, including medical services and recreational goods.

Method of data collection
Prices are collected by agents during the second month of each

Weights and composition

Major groups	Number of items	Weights	Approximate number of price quotations
Food	103	24.13	...
Housing	51	28.59	...
Clothing, footwear and upkeep	44	10.61	...
Transport	15	17.98	...
Medical care	13	4.75	...
Entertainment	15	5.07	...
Other goods and services	18	8.87	...
Total	259	100.00	1,200

quarter from approximately 120 groceries, department stores and other retail outlets and service establishments.

Housing
Rent quotations are obtained for dwellings with one to three bedrooms.

Specification of varieties
Not available.

Substitution, quality change, etc.
Not available.

Seasonal items
Seasonal items are not included in the index.

Computation
The index is computed according to the Laspeyres formula as a weighted arithmetic average with fixed base, using weights corresponding to the base period.

The price relative for each item is computed by dividing the average price for the current period by the average price for the base period.

Other information
Detailed sub-groups are published for this index.

Organisation and publication
Department of Commerce, Economic Research Centre, Cost of Living Office: "Quarterly Report on the Guam Consumer Price Index" (Agana).

Idem: "The Guam Consumer Price Index: 1978 Market Basket and Expenditure Weight Adjustment".

GUATEMALA

Official title
Indice de los precios al consumidor para la República de Guatemala - áreas urbanas (Consumer Price Index for the Republic of Guatemala - Urban Areas).

Scope
The index is computed monthly and covers all urban households.

Official base
March-April 1983 = 100.

Source of weights
The weights and items were derived from a national household expenditure survey conducted during November 1979-August 1981, covering a sample of 4,800 households in the central urban area and 2,678 households in the remaining urban areas of the country. A household comprises two or more persons sharing a family dwelling or part of one, and whose consumption of food and other goods is financed from the same budget. The weights were adjusted to take account of price changes between the survey period and March-April 1983.

Household consumption expenditure
Not available.

Method of data collection
The prices of food items are collected each week in the seven regions. Prices for furniture, clothing, water and fuel are obtained each month and those for medical care, education, reading material, recreation, transport and communication each quarter. Prices are collected by mail questionnaires from markets, supermarkets, retail outlets and service establishments in the seven urban regions.

Housing
Rent data are obtained each quarter, with 589 quotations for Guatemala city and 60 for the other regions. Owner-occupied housing is not taken into account in the index.

Weights and composition
Guatemala city

Major groups	Number of items	Weights	Approximate number of price quotations
Food	99	42.25	...
Rent, water, repairs and maintenance	6	9.94	...
Fuel and light	6	4.73	...
Furniture, household equipment and domestic services	24	7.82	...
Clothing and footwear	30	10.07	...
Medical care	7	2.71	...
Education	6	2.44	...
Transport and communications	17	11.59	...
Reading and recreation	7	4.20	...
Other goods and services	11	4.25	...
Total	213	100.00	...

Remaining urban areas

Food	91	57.27	...
Rent, water, repairs and maintenance	5	4.74	...
Fuel and light	5	7.92	...
Furniture, household equipment and domestic services	15	5.96	...
Clothing and footwear	27	10.35	...
Medical care	4	2.09	...
Education	4	0.98	...
Transport and communications	10	5.78	...
Reading and recreation	3	1.75	...
Other goods and services	7	3.16	...
Total	171	100.00	...

Specification of varieties
The specifications are based on consumer habits and take account of the variety, quality, brand and unit.

Substitution, quality change, etc.
If an item disappears permanently from the market, it is replaced by an item with the same characteristics. If a quality change occurs, the necessary adjustments are made using a linking method.

Seasonal items
Not available.

Computation
The index is computed according to the Laspeyres formula, as a weighted arithmetic average with fixed base, using weights corresponding to the base period.

The price relative for each item is computed by dividing the average price for the current period by the average price for the base period.

Organisation and publication
Ministerio de Economía, Dirección General de Estadística: "Informador Estadístico" (Guatemala).

Idem: "Anuario Estadístico".

Idem: "Metodología de los índices de precios al consumidor para la República de Guatemala, base marzo-abril de 1983 = 100" (March 1983).

GUYANA

Official title
Urban Consumer Price Index.

Scope
The index is compiled monthly and relates to Georgetown, New Amsterdam and Linden.

Official base
1970 = 100.

Source of weights
The weights and items were derived from a household expenditure survey conducted during 1969-70.

Household consumption expenditure
Not available.

Method of data collection
Prices for most items are collected around the 15th of each month from about 200 retail outlets, market stalls and service

Weights and composition

Major groups	Number of items	Weights	Approximate number of price quotations
Food and tobacco	86	42.5	...
Clothing and footwear	56	8.6	...
Housing:			
Fuel and light	5	5.2	...
Rent and water charges	5	21.4	...
Furniture, furnishings, household goods and services	7	2.9	...
Miscellaneous:			
Personal and medical care	21	7.2	...
Education and recreation	15	6.4	...
Transport and communication	8	4.8	...
Other expenses	2	1.0	...
Total	205	100.0	...

establishments in Georgetown, New Amsterdam and Linden. Prices for certain food items such as fresh fish, fruits and vegetables are ascertained each week.

Housing
Not available.

Specification of varieties
Not available.

Substitution, quality change, etc.
Not available.

Seasonal items
Not available.

Computation
The index is computed according to the Laspeyres formula as a weighted arithmetic average with fixed base, using weights corresponding to the base period.

Organisation and publication
The index is compiled by the Ministry of Economic Development, Statistical Bureau (Georgetown).

Government Georgetown: "Official Gazette".

Idem: "Household Consumer Expenditure Survey, 1969-1970, Part I" (Georgetown).

HAITI

Official title
Indice des prix à la consommation (Consumer Price Index - metropolitan area).

Scope
The index is compiled monthly and relates to urban households in the metropolitan area.

Official base
1980 = 100.

Source of weights
The weights and items were derived from a household expenditure survey conducted in 1976, covering households in both urban and rural areas. The expenditure of 747 households with two persons or more and an annual family income equivalent to at least 250 gourdes was used to calculate the weights for the index. The index covers urban households in the metropolitan area of Port-au-Prince, Delmas, Carrefour and Pétion-Ville. The weights were not adjusted to take into account price changes between the survey period and 1980.

Weights and composition

Major groups	Number of items	Weights	Approximate number of price quotations
Food	27	64.48	...
Clothing and footwear	15	3.16	...
Housing	6	11.71	...
Furniture and furnishings	16	5.75	...
Services	13	14.90	...
Total	77	100.00	...

Household consumption expenditure
Consumption expenditure for the purpose of the index comprises all goods and services purchased for consumption by the index population. It excludes income tax, payments to savings, insurance premiums, etc.

Method of data collection
Prices are collected by agents from selected retail outlets and service establishments. The frequency of price collection and the number of outlets selected depend on the nature of the item. Food items are priced three times a week (Tuesday, Thursday and Saturday) in the three main markets, and in supermarkets and selected groceries. Prices for clothing, furniture, furnishings and services are obtained during the first, second and third weeks of each month.

Housing
Rent quotations are obtained in the first month of each quarter from a sample of rented dwellings.

Specification of varieties
Not available.

Substitution, quality change, etc.
Not available.

Seasonal items
Not available.

Computation
The index is computed according to the Laspeyres formula as a weighted arithmetic average with fixed base, using weights corresponding to 1976.

Price relatives for varieties of each item are calculated by dividing the average price of the variety for the current period by its base period average price. Simple arithmetic averages of these relatives are then computed to arrive at item indices.

Organisation and publication
Département des finances et des affaires économiques, Institut Haïtien de statistique: "Bulletin trimestriel de statistique" (Port-au-Prince).

Ministère du plan, Institut Haïtien de statistique et d'informatique, Division des statistiques générales: "Indices des prix à la consommation, base 100 en 1980" (Port-au-Prince, June 1983).

HONDURAS

Official title
Indice General de Precios al Consumidor (Consumer Price Index).

Scope
The index is computed monthly and covers families from all urban areas with an annual income ranging between 3,000 to 12,000 lempiras during the period 1978-79.

Official base
1978 = 100.

Source of weights
The weights and items were derived from a nation-wide urban household expenditure survey conducted during the period January 1978-August 1979 among 5,328 households in 44 towns. The sample for the index covered 2,306 urban households with an annual income ranging between 3,000 to 12,000 lempiras at the time of the survey.

Weights and composition

Major groups	Number of items	Weights	Approximate number of price quotations
Food	64	41.214	7,968
Beverages and tobacco	7	3.790	133
Housing:			
Rent	1	13.202	164
Repairs	4	3.288	73
Household expenditure (including fuel and light)	19	9.611	190
Furniture and household equipment	13	4.510	520
Clothing and footwear	34	9.110	1,320
Personal and medical care	30	6.952	906
Transport	7	3.033	94
Education and recreation	10	5.290	184
Total	189	100.000	11,552

Household consumption expenditure
Not available.

Method of data collection
Prices are collected by agents in markets, retail outlets and service establishments in six towns throughout the country. Prices for food items are collected each Tuesday, those for educational services once a year, rent quotations, medical services and transport are obtained half-yearly. For about 150 items, prices are collected around the 15th of each month.

Housing
Rent quotations are obtained twice a year from a sample of 164 dwellings occupied by middle-income group families with living room, dining room, kitchen and at least two bedrooms.

Specification of varieties
The items covered by the survey are based on strict specifications.

Substitution, quality change, etc.
If an item disappears from the market, a similar item is substituted for pricing. No account is taken of quality change in item specifications.

Seasonal items
Items subject to seasonal fluctuations are not included in the index.

Computation
The index is computed according to the Laspeyres formula as a weighted arithmetic average with fixed base, the weights corresponding to the base period.

Average prices for each item in each city are simple arithmetic averages of prices obtained in each city. These average prices are then combined using area weights to arrive at average prices for regions. The average item price relatives for regions are calculated by dividing the regional average price for the current period by the regional average price for the base period. The national index is a weighted average of five urban regional indices (Central, North, South, East and West), using weights proportionate to expenditure shares of the regions as derived from the household expenditure survey.

Organisation and publication
Banco Central de Honduras, Departamento de Estudios Económicos: "Boletín Estadístico" (Tegucigalpa, D.C.).

Idem: "Indice de Precios al Consumidor" (monthly).

Idem: "Honduras en Cifras" (annual).

Idem: "Indice General de Precios al Consumidor, Base 1978 = 100, Metodología y Series Cronológicas" (November 1982).

HONG KONG

Official title
Consumer Price Index (A).

Scope
The index is compiled monthly and covers about 50 per cent of urban households in Hong Kong, with a monthly expenditure between 2,500 and 9,999 dollars during October 1989-September 1990.

Official base
October 1989-September 1990 = 100.

Source of weights
The weights were obtained from the household expenditure survey conducted from October 1989 to September 1990, covering all private households in the urban areas of Hong Kong, excluding seamen's households, and collective and rural households. Also excluded were households receiving public assistance and households absent from Hong Kong during the survey reference period. About 4,850 households were covered by the survey. The 12-month reference period was divided into 26 bi-weekly cycles. Each co-operating household was asked to take part in one cycle, during which all household members aged 12 and over were asked to record all expenditures incurred in the reference fortnight in specially-designed diary books. They were also asked to recall expenditures incurred in a reference quarter on selected infrequently-purchased items (such as motor cars, refrigerators and jewellery).

The criteria adopted for selecting items for price collection are as follows: (i) the weight of a selected item should not be so small that a significant change in the average price of the item has a negligible effect on the overall CPI; (ii) the items, in total, should represent practically the full consumption pattern of the households covered by the CPI; (iii) the number of items selected should be close to that for the old CPI series, so as to maintain continuity between the old and the new series. The weights of non-selected items were distributed proportionately among the selected items within the same group.

Weights and composition

Major groups	Number of items	Weights	Approximate number of price quotations
Food	387	41.2	...
Alcoholic drinks and tobacco (for home consumption)	16	2.45	...
Housing	26	20.56	...
Fuel and light	5	3.18	...
Clothing and footwear	113	4.56	...
Durable household goods	110	4.92	...
Transport and vehicles	52	7.20	...
Services	104	10.05	...
Miscellaneous	147	5.88	...
Total	960	100.00	40,000

Household consumption expenditure
Household expenditure refers to consumption expenditure on goods and services (including payments in kind), and does not include business expenses, remittance, betting, income tax, life insurance premiums of the endowment type, house mortgage payments, investments in properties and stocks and shares or various other payments of a savings nature. Generally, expenditure includes the payments actually made for goods and services during the reference period, irrespective of whether these goods and services were acquired or consumed during that period. However, for payments by credit card or on credit accounts, the amount of expenditure signed for during the reference period was recorded, but not the amount settled in the credit account bills received in that period. Some special cases were treated as follows:

Income in kind was counted as both income and expenditure to the household and included accommodation provided free or subsidised by employers, medical expenses and expenditure on petrol reimbursed by employers, and any allowance made for items obtained from employers at concessionary prices. The full retail value of such items was recorded as expenditure and the difference between the retail and concessionary prices was added to income. Fringe benefits such as free meals, free transport and free medical care were not recorded due to the practical difficulties in quantifying such benefits.

For owner-occupier households not paying rent, rent was imputed on the basis of the fair market values. This imputed rent was taken as both income and expenditure, using the rental equivalence approach.

For durable goods obtained on a hire-purchase (instalment credit) basis, the full cost of the item at the time of purchase was recorded as the expenditure rather than the down payment. Therefore, for hire purchases made during the reference period, the respondent was required to recall the cash price which he would have paid if he had purchased the item by one payment. By the same token, instalment payments made during the reference period for durable goods acquired before the reference period were not included.

Payments actually made for second-hand purchases were recorded as expenditure. Anything bought by part-exchange was recorded as the net amount of payment, plus the estimated amount allowed in part-exchange where this was quantifiable.

Licence fees, insurance for specific consumer goods and health care were treated as normal consumption expenditure. Contributions to social insurance and pension funds, income taxes and other direct taxes and life insurance payments were treated as non-consumption expenditure. Remittances, gifts and similar disbursements and cash contributions to other households were not treated as normal consumption expenditure. Gifts received were treated as normal consumer goods and included in household expenditure.

Method of data collection
Prices are obtained from selected outlets in the most populous urban areas, divided into 12 pricing districts. Prices are collected mainly by personal visits to selected outlets and sometimes by telephone. Prices are collected three times a week for all fresh food items, with the exception of fresh fruit, pork, beef, eggs and rice for which prices are obtained each week. Other

items are priced every month, two months, quarter or year. For certain items such as public transport, public house rents, water charges, petroleum and oil and vehicle licence fees, price changes are taken into account whenever they occur. The prices used in the index are the retail prices actually paid by consumers. Discount prices are accepted only if the items on discount are regular, up-to-date merchandise in good condition and are available for sale in reasonable quantities to all customers.

Housing
Rent quotations for private dwellings are collected through a monthly sample survey. Rent data are collected for both the current and previous months for all dwellings in the sample. The dwellings are then post-stratified according to floor area. The total rent paid by households in each stratum in both the current and previous months is then calculated and the relative change computed. These "rent relatives" for different strata are pooled to arrive at an aggregate index using a set of weights determined in the 1989-90 household expenditure survey, and then linked to the base period. Rent changes for government-subsidised dwellings are taken into account when they occur on the basis of the information supplied by the authorities concerned. For owner-occupied housing, the rental equivalence approach is adopted, whereby the cost of owner-occupied housing is assumed to move at the same rate as the rent for private rented dwellings. The rent relatives compiled for each stratum as described above are also aggregated using the weights for owner-occupied housing to arrive at a monthly index.

Specification of varieties
A store-specific pricing approach is used in which the items to be priced are only broadly defined. However, detailed specifications showing the variety, quality, make, brand, unit are recorded for each price quotation during the field interview. Interviewers ask the respondents in the sample outlets to specify the most populat varieties their outlets at that time, i.e. those with the largest sales volume. If the most popular varieties for the current month remain the same as those for the previous month, their prices in the current month are collected. Otherwise, some other more popular varieties are selected for the current month and their prices in both the current and previous months are collected for splicing purpose.

Substitution, quality change, etc.
A splicing method is used when the quality of an item changes. Prices for a new quality are collected for two consecutive months before it is incorporated into the CPI.

If the product is entirely new and cannot be classified under any item in the existing list of items for which prices are being collected, the price of that product will not be collected until the next CPI revision. On the other hand, if the product is only a new brand of an existing item, then a splicing method is used. If an item disappears from the market, the price of a similar item is collected as a substitute.

Seasonal items
Seasonal fresh food items are omitted from the index during their off season and their weights are distributed among the other items in the same group. For non-fresh food items, the last season's prices are kept constant until the next season.

Computation
The index is computed according to the Laspeyres formula as a weighted arithmetic average with fixed base, using weights corresponding to the base period. Two methods are used for computing item indices. For homogeneous items, price relatives are calculated by dividing the average price for the current period by the average price for the base period. Price relatives for other items are calculated for each variety in each outlet by dividing the average price for the current period by the average price for the previous period, and the average of these relatives is computed to arrive at the item indices.

Other information
In addition to the CPI (A), two other consumer price indices are published in Hong Kong on a monthly basis. One is the 1989-90 based Consumer Price Index (B) (CPI (B)), which is also compiled by the Census and Statistics Department of the Hong Kong Government. This index refers to households spending between 10,000 and 17,499 dollars a month during October 1989-September 1990, the period in which the 1989-90 Household Expenditure Survey was conducted. The other is the Hang Seng Consumer Price Index (Hang Seng CPI), which is compiled by the Hang Seng Bank, a private organisation. This index refers to households living in private housing, with an average monthly expenditure of between 17,500 and 37,499 dollars in 1989-90. The CPI (B) covers about 30 per cent of urban households in Hong Kong and the Hang Seng CPI about 10 per cent.

Organisation and publication
Census and Statistics Department, Consumer Price Index Section: "Consumer Price Index Report" (Hong Kong).

Idem: "Hong Kong Monthly Digest of Statistics" (Hong Kong).

HUNGARY

Official title
Indice des prix à la consommation (Consumer Price Index).

Scope
The index is compiled monthly and covers the whole country and the entire population.

Official base
The base period of the index shown in the national publications is the corresponding month of the previous year, the previous month and December of the previous year, taken as 100. The Hungarian Central Statistical Office chains these indices back to the base used for publication by the ILO.

Source of weights
The weights and items were derived from a household expenditure survey and are revised periodically. The survey covers a sample of 8,000 households. Each household keeps an expenditure diary providing information on detailed expenditures. Under-reporting of expenditure on certain items including expenditure on alcohol, tobacco, confectionery and meals taken outside the house is corrected using macro data.

Weights and composition

Major groups	Number of items	Weights	Approximate number of price quotations
Food	49	28	27,100
Beverages and tobacco	5	12	4,800
Fuel and light	8	5	1,100
Clothing and footwear	27	8	22,400
Services	34	15	13,200
Rent	2	5	400
Other	39	27	33,200
Total	164	100	102,200

Household consumption expenditure
Consumption expenditure for the purpose of the index includes almost all goods and services purchased by the index population. Television licences, repairs and an imputed rent of owner-occupied dwellings are included. Consumption in kind from own production or received free of charge, passenger car licences, consumer credit charges, life insurance and direct taxes, free health services and second-hand transactions (except second-hand cars) are excluded.

Method of data collection
Prices are obtained for about 1,800 individual items from the selected outlets and local authorities by 145 price collectors. Fruit and vegetable prices are obtained from selected markets and outlets. Special sale prices are taken into consideration.

Housing
Not available.

Specification of varieties
Individual articles are selected taking account of their most characteristic features. Within each of the specifications for manufactured items, prices are obtained for two or three of the best-selling lines chosen in consultation with the salespeople.

Substitution, quality change, etc.
Once a specific variety is selected, it is maintained as long as possible. However, the price collector is allowed to substitute a variety within the limits of the specifications. Other substitutions are controlled centrally; no adjustments are made on the basis of quality changes.

Seasonal items
Monthly calculations use variable monthly weights reflecting seasonal changes in availability within a fixed basket for seasonal food.

Computation
The index is compiled using the relatives of mean prices calcu-

lated for each item specified, omitting any missing observations. There are fixed annual weights for each social group and for each income bracket.

Other information
In national publications, the index is published on base 1980=100, previous year=100, corresponding period of the previous period=100, previous month=100 and December of the previous year=100.

Organisation and publication
Központi Statiszikai Hivatal (Central Statistical Office): "Statiszikai Havi Közlemények" (Monthly Bulletin of Statistics) (Budapest).

Idem: "Statiszikai Evkönyv" (Statistical Yearbook).

Idem: "Fogyasztói árindex fuzetek" (Consumer Price Index Booklet).

ICELAND (REYKJAVIK)

Official title
Cost of Living Index.

Scope
The index is compiled monthly and relates to households of all types (including those of civil servants) in Reykjavik.

Official base
May 1988 = 100.

Source of weights
The household expenditure survey on which the present Consumer Price Index is based was conducted from July 1985 to June 1986, covering the whole country. A random sample of households was selected from the National Register, regardless of size, occupation and domicile, but with an upper age limit of 70 years for the head of the household. When the new base was adopted, the household expenditure weights were adjusted for the time lag between the survey period and May 1988. This adjustment mainly concerned an increase in the ownership and use of passenger cars and in TV licences following the establishment of a private television channel partly financed by viewers' charges. The weights for items not priced are reflected by their closest substitutes among the priced items.

Weights and composition

Major groups	Number of items	Weights	Approximate number of price quotations
Food	269	20.6	2,933
Beverages and tobacco	32	4.4	245
Clothing and footwear	75	7.9	327
Rent, electricity and hot water for heating	59	16.2	59
Furniture and household equipment	99	7.4	371
Medical care	34	2.3	60
Transport and communications	46	18.9	158
Recreation and education	100	11.0	179
Other goods and services	80	11.3	358
Total	794	100.0	4,690

Household consumption expenditure
The household expenditure survey from which the weights are derived was intended to cover all types of expenditure. Income in kind was not covered in the household accounts, but was taken into account to some extent in the expenditure reports for the year (1985) and is thus partially reflected in the index. Home ownership is covered as the Icelandic owner-occupant ratio is estimated to be over 80 per cent. Expenditure on this category includes interest payments, depreciation, maintenance and insurance costs, real estate taxes, etc. Durable goods credit purchases, second-hand purchases and trade-ins were all covered in the household expenditure survey and used to determine the original weights. However, once adopted, the weights were all defined as relating new purchases, and therefore no account is taken of credit purchases or changes in consumer credit terms.

Social insurance is funded through the tax system in Iceland and not included in the index. Pension fund contributions are not covered; in Iceland, these are compulsory flat-rate deductions from wages and salaries.

Licence fees are included to the extent that these were reflected in the household expenditure survey; insurance associated with specific consumer goods, life insurance and remittances of various kinds are treated in the same way.

Health care expenditure is included to the extent that it is borne directly by patients or recipients. Income taxes and other direct taxes are not included.

Method of data collection
Outlets and other sources of price data for goods and services were selected mainly so as to provide an even geographic distribution throughout the capital region. Where applicable (mainly food stores), the outlets have also been given weights based on their estimated turnover. Prices are obtained from 322 retail outlets and service establishments.

For the majority of categories, prices are collected during the first week of each month. For certain seasonal expenditure (holiday travel abroad, domestic vacation or leisure expenditure, certain educational expenditure concentrated at the beginning of the school-year), prices are collected and adjusted less frequently.

Information on the prices of goods and private services is collected directly from sellers, either through visits to outlets by investigators or, mainly as regards certain service items, by telephone.

Information on service charges for public utilities is obtained either by direct communication with the utilities or from official tariffs, regulations, etc.

Electricity and geothermal water prices (heating and hot water) are computed as national averages. The Statistical Bureau obtains its information from the National Energy Authority that collects prices from all electricity and geothermal heating utilities in the country. Information on the medical care costs borne directly by patients or recipients is mainly based on official tariffs. Dentistry prices are based on tariffs published by the Dentists' Association.

Information on prices of educational items is obtained by both investigators and direct communication with establishments.

Transport and communication prices are collected both from official or published tariffs and by direct communication with establishments.

Prices are collected by trained personnel. As a rule, the same persons carry out the field work in each type of establishment, i.e. certain people collect price data on food and drink, others on clothing, etc.

As a rule, discounts are not included except for discounts for cash payments. Sale prices are not observed. Official prices are only included to the extent that it is certain that these are the real market prices.

If a difference emerges between official or regulated prices and market prices, the official prices are always discarded. No attempt is made to investigate the black market; in Iceland this would in any case almost exclusively extend to illegal goods or services such as narcotics, etc. Hire-purchase or credit terms are not covered. All price quotations are based on cash prices. Second-hand purchases are not included. Prices of imported goods are collected at the relevant outlets; consumers' own imports of goods are not specifically observed as they account for only a small fraction of all purchases.

Housing
Because of the high owner-occupant ratio in Iceland, rent is not treated as an index item. Home-ownership is covered as the Icelandic owner-occupant ratio is estimated to be over 80 per cent. Expenditure for this category includes interest payments, depreciation, maintenance and insurance costs, real estate taxes, etc.

Specification of varieties
Items for price collection were selected on the basis of the household expenditure survey which itemised in great detail the make, brand, unit and description of the merchandise, subject to certain revisions to correct for the time lag between the survey period and the adoption of the index. There are detailed specifications for each item that describe the variety, make, brand, unit, etc. selected as indicated above.

Substitution, quality change, etc.
Quality changes are not a major problem becaus of the detailed product specifications that are applied. If such changes are thought to be cause for concern, they are dealt with by a change in the specified brand or type. The appearance of a new product should be reflected in the household expenditure surveys that are carried out at least once every five years. However, new products are incorporated as they appear to the

extent that they fully replace products that were priced in the index. The disappearance of a product that was priced in the index is dealt with by replacing it by its closest substitute on the market.

Seasonal items
No adjustments are made for seasonality. In a few instances, the prices of certain seasonal services, mainly recreation expenditures, are collected at predetermined points in time and kept constant in the interval.

Computation
The index is computed according to the Laspeyres formula as a weighted arithmetic average with fixed base, using weights corresponding to the base period. Weighted arithment averages are used to calculate price averages. In most cases, the weights are based on estimated turnover or sales. Missing or faulty price data are generally dealt with by applying the average change for other products in the same group or sub-group.

The computation of the index is based on prices for the capital region, except for fuel, heat and light, for which prices are calculated as averages for the whole country. Annual averages are calculated as arithmetic averages of the monthly computations, in which the indices for the beginning of each month from February to December have equal weights but the index for the beginning of January and a specially estimated index for the end of December each have half of the monthly weights. This more or less equals a conversion of the beginning-of-the-month indices to mid-month indices.

Organisation and publication
Statistical Bureau of Iceland: "Hagtidindi" (Reykjavik).
Central Bank of Iceland: "Economic Statistics" (quarterly).

INDIA (ALL INDIA 1)

Official title
Consumer Price Index for Agricultural Labourers.

Scope
The index is compiled monthly and covers households of agricultural labourers (i.e. agricultural labourers employed for wages in the processes of crop production) and their dependants.

Official base
July 1960-June 1961 = 100.

Source of weights
The weights were derived from consumer expenditure data obtained through the Second Agricultural Labour Enquiry conducted from August 1956 to August 1957 and covering 7,800 households. The weights were not adjusted to take into account the difference in price levels between 1956-57 and 1960-61. Items selected for inclusion in the index are those which are relatively important in family spending, which have distinctive price movements and which are representative of a larger group of related items. Expenditure on items which could not be included was imputed to other items or groups.

Weights and composition

Major groups	Number of items	Weights	Approximate number of price quotations
Food	37	78.1	...
Fuel and light	4	8.0	...
Clothing, footwear and bedding	11	6.1	...
Miscellaneous	10	7.8	...
Total	62	100.0	...

Household consumption expenditure
Consumption expenditure for the purpose of the index comprises only goods and services which are relatively important in household expenditure. Expenditure on ceremonials and the cost of repairs to buildings and of land are not included.

Method of data collection
Retail prices are collected each month by the field staff of the National Sample Survey from shops and markets in 422 sample villages. The date of price collection is the first market day or the first Saturday every month. Whenever the selected items are available at fair-price shops, fair-price quotations are also obtained.

Housing
As expenditure on house rent is nil or negligible, it is excluded.

Specification of varieties
Detailed specifications of items to be priced were fixed for each of the 422 sample villages on the basis of information collected during a special inquiry conducted in these villages during July-September 1960.

Substitution, quality change, etc.
If possible, quality adjustments are made whenever the characteristics of a product are altered. The linking method is also used in some cases.

Seasonal items
Seasonal items are not included in the index.

Computation
The country-wide index is computed as the weighted average of the separate indices for agricultural labourers for 15 individual States (including groups of smaller States/Union Territories).

The index for each State is computed according to the Laspeyres formula as a weighted arithmetic average with fixed base, using weights corresponding to August 1956-August 1957. These indices are then weighted to obtain the country-wide index, using weights corresponding to the aggregate consumption expenditure of the population group represented by each State.

Organisation and publication
Ministry of Labour, Labour Bureau: "Indian Labour Journal" (Simla).
Ministry of Labour, Employment and Rehabilitation: "Indian Labour Journal" (Simla, Dec. 1962 and Oct. 1968).

INDIA (ALL INDIA 2)

Official title
Consumer Price Index for Urban Non-Manual Employees.

Scope
The index is computed monthly and covers families deriving the major part of their incomes from non-manual occupations in the non-agricultural sectors, living in 59 selected urban centres.

Official base
April 1984-March 1985 = 100.

Source of weights
The weights and items were derived from a household expenditure survey conducted during one year from July 1982 to June 1983 among a sample of 45,000 non-manual households living in 59 selected urban centres. The weights were not adjusted to take into account price changes between the survey and base periods. The weights of items excluded were imputed to items included in the weighting diagram, generally on the principle of similarity in their price trends. If imputation to any specific items was not considered suitable, imputation was made at the sub-group level.

Weights and composition

Major groups	Number of items (a)	Weights (b)	Approximate number of price quotations
Food and tobacco	...	...	...
Fuel and light	...	...	...
Housing	...	...	...
Clothing, footwear and bedding	...	...	...
Miscellaneous	...	...	...
Total	...	...	167,540

Note: (a) The number of items varies from 146 to 345 according to the centre. (b) The weights differ in each centre.

Household consumption expenditure
Expenditure on savings and investments such as life insurance premiums, pension contributions, debts repaid, interest, litigation, taxes (including road tax, municipal tax etc.), subscriptions to trade unions, ceremonies etc., gifts and charity, remittance to dependents, etc., were excluded from the weighting diagram because they mainly form non-consumption disbursements, and, although expenditure on remittance to dependents, ceremonies, etc., may have some consumption element, they are not priceable since they cannot be identified uniquely with a specific quantity of commodity or service.

Receipts in kind (whether received free or as concessions from employers or others) and gifts received were evaluated at prevailing market prices and the values were recorded as part of income and were also included in the respective expenditure blocks. For self-owned houses (home ownership) and concessional or free houses provided by employers or others, the rental values were imputed on the basis of prevailing rents in the locality for similar rented houses. No distinction was made between the treatment of durable and non-durable goods. However, since purchases of durable goods were infrequent, expenditure was recorded not only for the reference month but also for the reference year and the average monthly expenditure based on reference year values was used for deriving the weights. There was no difference in the treatment of first- and second-hand purchases. Expenditure for health care consisting of medicines purchased, doctors' services and related medical services and contributions to health schemes was included in the weighting diagram.

Method of data collection
The sample of markets and outlets popular with index families was selected through a market survey conducted during 1983 in each urban centre, using a suitable combination of purposive and random sampling methods.

Prices for all items are collected each month from markets, controlled shops, fair-price shops, consumer co-operative stores (including the super bazaars), other retail outlets and service establishments, by the Field Operations Division of the National Sample Survey Organisation, a permanent field organisation for conducting large scale surveys and the regular collection of statistical data.

The prices for different commodity groups are collected on fixed days of the week as far as possible so that comparisons between two quotations from the same outlet are not affected by difference in the timing of the collection. The choice of the days on which price data for a particular commodity group are to be collected is made, keeping in view the volume of transactions on different days of the week.

The prices reported are those paid for actual transactions, inclusive of sales tax and other such charges normally payable by the consumer and net of discounts or rebates commonly allowed. Illegal (black-market) prices, hire-purchase and credit terms, second-hand purchases and trade-in of used goods are not included in price collection. Import prices as such are not included in the price collection. They are rarely, if ever, included in the consumption of index families and, in addition, there are no separate outlets where these items are regularly and exclusively available.

Housing
Rent data are collected from a sample of rented dwellings through a continuous house rent survey conducted every six months. All the sample rented dwellings canvassed for the detailed house rent survey as a part of the 1982-83 household expenditure survey constituted the basic framework for the continuous house rent survey. These dwellings were distributed uniformly over the six months, July to December, as follows: dwellings canvassed from July 1982 to January 1983 are assigned to July, those canvassed from August 1982 to February 1983 assigned to August and so on. From the list assigned to a month, a sample of 14 rented dwellings per investigator was drawn after stratifying the dwellings into four strata according to the number of rooms. Data on rents are collected from sample dwellings assigned to different months at intervals of six months. The house-rent index is compiled from the house-rent data for six months to represent the average half-yearly change in house rent.

In addition to rented dwellings, owner-occupied and rent free dwellings are included in the overall house-rent index. The rent index calculated from the rent data for rented dwellings is used as a proxy for the rent index for owner-occupied dwellings.

The average of the rent relatives for the current six months is calculated over the immediately preceding six months for each of the rent quotations and the rent index is computed as a chain index. Average rent relatives are calculated for each stratum and the averages for the four strata are combined using the actual composition of owner-occupied and rented dwellings available from results of the household expenditure survey to derive the overall average rent relatives. The rent index for the rented and owner-occupied components is calculated as a chain index using the rent index for the previous six month period. The rent index for rent-free dwellings is fixed at 100 and the overall house-rent index is calculated on the basis of an index for rent-free dwellings and an index for owner-occupied and rented dwellings using as weights the proportion of households in the respective categories, available from the household expenditure survey.

Specification of varieties
Specifications for various items were established in sufficient detail with respect to quality, variety and other essential physical characteristics such as size, dimensions, material content etc., bearing in mind the prevalent conditions in different centres, to enable unambiguous identification.

The specifications for each commodity popular with index families were determined using both a market and a consumer level approach, and were earmarked for selected outlets for regular price collection.

Substitution, quality change, etc.
Procedures were laid down for cases in which a particular price quotation consisting of specifications of outlets is not available in the month. Substitute price quotations are then collected, either from reserve outlets for the same specifications or for comparable popular specifications, and the new quotations are linked to the old ones through the usual splicing techniques. Quality changes and the disappearance of old products are treated in the same way, to the extent that they reflect a change of specifications.

Seasonal items
Item coverage in the index for fruit and vegetables varies from month to month depending on their availability in the month. The following method is used for assigning weights to such seasonal items in the index: the sub-group weights for "fruit and vegetables" are calculated on the basis of average monthly expenditure covering all the items in the sub-groups. However, the individual item weights for the priced items in different months are calculated by distributing the weights of unpriced items to those of priced items on a pro-rata basis.

Computation
The index is computed according to the Laspeyres formula as a weighted arithmetic average with fixed base, using weights corresponding to July 1982-June 1983.

The index is computed directly for each of the centres. The All-India index is computed as the weighted average of the centre indices, using weights based on the estimated total household expenditure in the different centres, using the 1981 population census data and the 1982-83 household expenditure survey data.

Other information
Consumer price indices for industrial workers and for agricultural labourers are also computed by the Labour Bureau and published in the "Indian Labour Journal".

Organisation and publication
The index is computed by the Central Statistical Organisation, New Delhi and published in: "Monthly Abstract of Statistics".

Idem: "Statistical Abstract".

Labour Bureau, Simla: "Indian Labour Journal".

INDIA (ALL INDIA 3)

Official title
Consumer Price Index for Industrial Workers.

Scope
The index is computed monthly and covers industrial workers' families in 70 industrial centres throughout the country.

Official base
1982 = 100.

Source of weights
The weights and items were derived from a household expenditure survey conducted during one year in 1981-82 among 32,616 families of industrial workers in seven sectors (factories, mines, plantations, railways, public motor transport undertakings, electricity generating and distributing establishments, ports and docks) in 70 industrial centres. The weights were not adjusted to take into account price changes between the survey period and the base period.

The inclusion of items in the index basket depends upon the average expenditure on each item reported by the working class families in comparison with total consumption expenditure, and the number of families reporting expenditure. Items with a negligible reporting of expenditure are generally imputed to related items in the same sub-group.

Weights and composition

Major groups	Number of items	Weights	Approximate number of price quotations
Food	106	57.00	...
Tobacco, pan, supari, etc.	16	3.15	...
Housing	1	8.67	...
Fuel and light	10	6.28	...
Clothing, footwear and bedding	39	8.54	...
Miscellaneous	88	16.36	...
Total	260	100.00	...

Household consumption expenditure
The imputed value of income in kind, home ownership, gifts, etc. was used. For part-payments, only payments made the reference month were taken into account. Second-hand purchases and trade-in of used goods were excluded. Expenditure on social insurance, pension funds, licence fees, insurance of goods, direct taxes, life insurance, remittances, etc. were treated as non-consumption expenditure.

Method of data collection
Prices are collected for the different goods and services, including electricity, gas, medical care, education, transport and communication, by personal visits from state government employees to the most popular markets and retail outlets and to the controlled shops (fair-price shops) and service establishments. Prices are collected each week for price sensitive items. Prices of items such as cinema tickets, furniture, utensils, household appliances, transport, clothing and footwear, etc. are collected once in a month as their prices do not change frequently. The prices of items such as house-rent, school or college fees and school or college books are collected once every six months. All prices are collected on the fixed price collection day at the same point of time. Net prices are used in the index. Free-market and official prices (controlled prices) are used, combined in the ratio of supplies of average requirements through the two sources. Black-market prices, hire-purchase, second-hand purchase and import prices are not taken into account in the index computation.

Housing
Data are collected every six months for rented, rent-free and owner-occupied dwellings, including taxes, minor repairs and white-washing charges incurred by tenants, but excluding charges such as water, electricity, sweeper etc. The rent index is compiled using the chain base method, in which rent movements are compared with those of the last six months and not with the base period, as this method is better for taking into account the depreciation of housing. New houses are not included in the sample as it is felt that the relative movement of rents for new houses does not differ from that of old houses.

In the case of owner-occupied houses, rents for comparable rented dwellings are ascertained. If such houses are not available on the market, the owned houses' index is taken to be the same as that of rented houses.

Specification of varieties
Each item has been given fixed specifications including the variety, quality, make/brand and units etc. The specifications were established on the basis of local preference determined through market enquiries.

Substitution, quality change, etc.
If the prescribed quality of an article is not available, a substitute variety of equivalent or comparable quality is selected. The old variety is brought back to the price schedule if it reappears in the market. Adjustments are made for price differences due to quality differences of the substitute. When the substitute chosen differs in quality by as much as 100 per cent (or when the difference is difficult to assess), the price quotations for the new product are linked to those for the product replaced.

Seasonal items
The weights for the vegetables and fruit sub-group are kept constant in the food group, but monthly varying weights have been worked out for various items depending upon their availability. Weights of items not available in a month are imputed to related items.

Computation
The index is computed according to the Laspeyres formula as a weighted arithmetic average with fixed base, using weights corresponding to 1981-82.

Generally, a simple average of all prices reported in a month is used for each item. If more than one variety is priced for an item, a simple average of price relatives is calculated for the item.

Indices are computed directly at the centre level, but the All-India index is computed as a weighted average of all the centre indices, using centre weights are based on the product of average consumption expenditure per family and the number of families in each centre in 1981-82.

Other information
In addition to the consumer price index for industrial workers, two other series are published: consumer price indices for agricultural labourers and for urban non-manual employees. The former is computed by the Labour Bureau and published in the "Indian Labour Journal"; the latter is computed by the Central Statistical Organisation, New Delhi, and published in the "Monthly Abstract of Statistics" (New Delhi).

Organisation and publication
Ministry of Labour, Labour Bureau: "Indian Labour Journal" (Simla) (November 1988 and January 1989 issues for further methodological information).
Idem: "Indian Labour Year Book - Annual."
Idem: "Pocket Book of Labour Statistics - Annual."
Idem: "Indian Labour Statistics - Annual."

INDIA (DELHI)

Official title
Consumer Price Index for Industrial Workers.

Scope
The index is computed monthly and covers industrial workers families in Delhi.

Official base
1982 = 100.

Source of weights
The weights and items were derived from a household expenditure survey conducted during one year in 1981-82 among 648 industrial workers families of seven sectors namely factories, mines, plantations, railways, public motor transport undertakings, electricity generating and distributing establishments, ports and docks in 70 industrial centres. The index relates to industrial workers' families in Delhi. The weights were not adjusted to take into account price changes between the survey period and the base period. The inclusion of items in the index basket depends on the average expenditure reported by the working class families compared to total consumption expenditure and the number of families reporting expenditure. Items with negligible expenditure reported are generally imputed to related items in the same sub-group.

Weights and composition

Major groups	Number of items	Weights	Approximate number of price quotations
Food	61	50.71	524
Tobacco, pan, supari, etc.	8	2.35	56
Rent	1	14.02	21
Fuel and light	6	5.61	39
Clothing, footwear and bedding	15	12.53	31
Miscellaneous	39	14.78	143
Total	130	100.00	814

Household consumption expenditure
The imputed value was taken in the case of income in kind, home ownership, gifts etc. For part payments, only payments made during the reference month were taken into account. Second-hand purchases and trade-in of used goods were excluded. Expenditure on social insurance, pension funds, licence fees, insurance of goods, direct taxes, life insurance, remittances etc. were treated as non-consumption expenditure.

Method of data collection
Prices are collected by state government employees for the different goods and services including electricity, gas, medical care, education, transport and communication by personal visits to the most popular markets and retail outlets and to the con-

trolled shops (fair price shops) and service establishments. The frequency of price collection is weekly for price sensitive items. Prices of items such as cinema tickets, furniture, utensils, household appliances, transport, clothing and footwear, etc. are collected once a month as their prices do not change frequently. The prices of items such as house rent, school or college fees and school or college books are collected once in six months. All prices are collected on a fixed price collection day at the same point of time. Net prices are used in the index. Free-market and official prices (controlled prices) are taken by combining them in the ratio of supplies of average requirements through two sources. Black-market prices, hire-purchase, second-hand purchase and import prices are not taken into account in the index computation.

Housing
The costs of rented, rent-free and self-owned dwellings, including taxes, minor repairs and white-washing charges incurred by tenants, but excluding charges such as water, electricity, sweeper etc., are collected once every six months. The rent index is compiled using the chain base method, in which rent movements are compared with the last six month period and not with the base period, as this method takes better care of the depreciation aspect of housing. New houses are not included in the sample as it is felt that the relative movement of rents in new houses does not differ from that of old houses.

For owner-occupied houses, the rent for comparable rented dwellings is obtained. If such houses are not available on the market, the owned houses' index is taken to be the same as that of rented houses.

Specification of varieties
Each item was given fixed specifications, including the variety, quality, make, brand and units etc. Specifications were established on the basis of local preference determined through market enquiries.

Substitution, quality change, etc.
When the prescribed quality of an article is not available, a substitute variety of equivalent or comparable quality is selected. The old variety is brought back to the price schedule if it reappears in the market. Adjustments are made for price differences due to quality differences of the substitute. When the substitute chosen differs in quality by as much as 100 per cent (or when the difference is difficult to assess), the price quotations for the new product are linked to those for the product replaced.

Seasonal items
The weights of the vegetables and fruit sub-group are kept constant in the food group but monthly varying weights were calculated for various items depending on their availability. The weights of items not available in a month are imputed to related items.

Computation
The index is computed according to the Laspeyres formula as a weighted arithmetic average with fixed base, using weights corresponding to 1981-82.

Generally, a simple average of all prices reported in a month is used for each item. If more than one variety is priced for an item, a simple average of price relatives is calculated for the item.

All centre indices are computed directly but the All-India Index is computed as a weighted average of all the centre indices, using centre weights based on the product of average consumption expenditure per family and the number of families in each centre in 1981-82.

Other information
In addition to consumer price indices for industrial workers, two other series are published: Consumer Price Indices for Agricultural Labourers and Consumer Price Indices for Urban Non-Manual Employees. The former is computed by the Labour Bureau and published in its monthly "Indian Labour Journal"; the latter is being computed by the Central Statistical Organisation, New Delhi and published in its "Monthly Abstract of Statistics" (New Delhi).

Organisation and publication
Ministry of Labour, Labour Bureau: "Indian Labour Journal" (Simla) (November 1988 and January 1989 issues for further methodological information).

Idem: "Indian Labour Year Book - Annual."

Idem: "Pocket Book of Labour Statistics - Annual."

Idem: "Indian Labour Statistics - Annual."

INDONESIA

Official title
Combined Consumer Price Index of 27 capital cities of provinces.

Scope
The index is computed monthly and covers private households in the urban areas of 27 capital cities of provinces.

Official base
April 1988-March 1989 = 100.

Source of weights
The weights and items were derived from a cost-of-living survey conducted from July 1988 to June 1989 in 27 capital cities of provinces, covering a sample of 35,000 private households. Excluded from the survey were single-person households, those with more than 10 members, institutional households and illiterate households.

Weights and composition
Not available.

Household consumption expenditure
The consumption approach was used for food, beverages, tobacco and services and the delivery approach for calculating expenditure for all semi-durable and durable goods.

Imputed rent for owner-occupied and rent-free houses was calculated by applying the rent tariff applicable at that time. The amount imputed was taken as income to the household as well as expenditure. If the household occupied an official (company) house with rent less than the market value of rent, the amount of rent difference was taken as imputed income and the market value of the rent as expenditures. In addition, goods received free of charge and the goods purchased at low prices were valued at market price and classified as expenditure for these goods. The difference between the market values and low prices were included as household income.

The credit purchase of goods and services consumed during the reference period was classified as consumption expenditure on the goods and services concerned, and also as imputed income. Advance payments and instalments paid during the reference period were classified as non-consumption expenditure.

Non-consumption expenditure and other payments cover: income tax, vehicle taxes/ownership transfer costs, taxes on land and buildings, property tax, and radio and television contributions; savings, insurance premium payments, debts payment, interest payments, advance payments for goods purchase, loans to other parties, purchases of immovable goods (land, houses) including major repairs, the cost of parties, cost of religious or traditional events, money lost, etc.

Method of data collection
Prices are collected by central and local statistical agents from selected retail shops and establishments. Prices are collected each week, month or quarter.

The pricing day is Tuesday for weekly collection, the 15th of the month for monthly collection and the 10th to the 20th for quarterly collection. Data for electricity, gas, water and communications are obtained from the official tariffs.

The prices used to calculate the index are the retail prices actually paid by consumers.

Housing
Rent quotations are obtained in March and September each year from 16 types of dwellings, according to the condition of the building and its facilities. Owner-occupied housing was included in the calculation of the weights, but in the index the price changes are calculated from changes in the cost of housing materials and of wages of housing builders.

Specification of varieties
Detailed specifications are provided for each item included in the index, describing the variety, quality and brand.

Substitution, quality change, etc.
If there is a quality change for an item, the new quality is introduced only when prices are available for both the current and previous periods.

Seasonal items
There is no change of season, so all items are available the whole year round.

Computation
The index is computed according to the Laspeyres formula as a weighted arithmetic average with fixed base, using weights corresponding to the base period. The price relative for each item is computed by dividing the average price for the current period by the average price for the previous period. Average prices are simple arithmetic averages.

The combined indices are obtained by computing weighted price indices for each sub-group, major group and all items.

The index is an aggregation of the series for the different province capitals. The national index is calculated from the city series, using the number of households in the urban areas of each city as weights.

Other information
Separate indices are also computed and published for the 27 provincial capital cities.

Organisation and publication
Central Bureau of Statistics: "Monthly Statistical Bulletin" (Jakarta).

IRAN, ISLAMIC REP. OF

Official title
Consumer Price Index.

Scope
The index is compiled monthly and covers urban families with annual expenditure up to 4,700,000 rials in 1982-83.

Official base
21 March 1982-20 March 1983 = 100.

Source of weights
The weights and items were derived from a household expenditure survey conducted between March 1982 and March 1983, covering 15,000 urban families with annual expenditure up to 4,700,000 rials.

Weights and composition

Major groups	Number of items	Weights	Approximate number of price quotations
Food, beverages and tobacco	96	40.06	55,000
Other groups:	...	...	45,000
Clothing and footwear	42	8.07	...
Housing, fuel and power	25	26.20	...
House furnishings and household operations	41	7.24	...
Medical care	41	3.94	...
Transport and communication	22	8.14	...
Recreation, education and reading	16	1.60	...
Miscellaneous goods and services	20	4.75	...
Total	303	100.00	100,000

Household consumption expenditure
The consumption expenditure used for deriving the weights consists of the money value of all goods and services purchased during the base year by households for their consumption or given to other households. It includes the total value at purchase time of durable goods credit purchases, the value of income in kind (not received from other households), contributions to social insurance funds, licence fees, health care, insurance, life insurance payments and expenditure on gifts. It excludes remittances, direct taxes, contributions to pension funds and the value of home-produced and consumed goods.

Method of data collection
Prices for most items are collected by agents during the first 25 days of each month from retail outlets, supermarkets and service establishments in 80 cities. Discounts, sale prices and black-market prices are not used. For items with both official and free-market prices, a weighted average of prices is computed, using weights derived from the latest household expenditure survey.

Housing
Rent quotations are obtained each quarter from a sample of approximately 7,000 dwellings. The rental equivalence of owner-occupied dwellings is imputed by assuming that it has the same rate of change as the general index.

Specification of varieties
The specifications of items to be priced are given in terms of quality, unit and size, etc.

Substitution, quality change, etc.
Attempts are made to obtain the prices of goods with the same quality each month. If this is not possible, the nearest quality is priced. If a quality change is significant, quality adjustment or a linking method is used.

Seasonal items
When a seasonal item is absent from the market, its price is imputed by assuming that it has the same rate of change as the weighted average of the prices of other goods of the group.

Computation
The index is computed according to the Laspeyres formula as a weighted arithmetic average with fixed base, using weights corresponding to the base period.

The averages of matched prices are used for deriving price relatives in consecutive months. The necessary adjustments are made if prices are incorrect. Missing prices are substituted by prices from other similar cities. The index is computed on regional basis.

Other information
The main sub-groups are published. No other national series are computed.

Organisation and publication
Economic Statistics Department, Central Bank Markazi: "Economic Report and Balance Sheet" (Teheran).

IRAQ

Official title
Consumer Price Index.

Scope
The index is compiled monthly and relates to all urban households.

Official base
1973 = 100.

Source of weights
The weights and items were derived from a household expenditure survey conducted in 1971-72 in urban areas, among a sample of all types of households.

Weights and composition

Major groups	Number of items	Weights	Approximate number of price quotations
Food	80	49.73	...
Tobacco and alcohol	7	3.47	...
Clothing	73	8.20	...
Footwear	9	1.77	...
Household items	37	5.01	...
Fuel	7	4.01	...
Cleaning items and personal care	14	1.69	...
Education and recreation	5	1.72	...
Housing and household expenditure	2	15.62	...
Miscellaneous goods and services	2	8.78	...
Total	236	100.00	...

Household consumption expenditure
Not available.

Method of data collection
Prices are collected on the 3rd, 9th, 21st and 27th of each month from ten main markets in Baghdad and two main markets in other urban centres.

Housing
Rent quotations are obtained in March and September each year from 143 rented houses in Baghdad and 208 rented houses in the other governorates.

Specification of varieties
Not available.

Substitution, quality change, etc.
Not available.

Seasonal items
Not available.

Computation
The index is computed according to the Laspeyres formula as a weighted arithmetic average with fixed base, using weights corresponding to 1971-72.

Other information
A new series (base 1988 = 100) is now computed but the relevant methodological information was not available in the ILO at the time the present volume was published.

Organisation and publication
Ministry of Planning, Central Statistical Organisation: "Annual Abstract of Statistics" (Baghdad).
Idem: "Annual Abstract of Statistics".

IRELAND

Official title
Consumer Price Index.

Scope
The index is computed in February, May, August and November. It covers all private households in the country without size or income limits.

Official base
Mid-November 1989 = 100.

Source of weights
The weighting pattern is based on the best available estimates of the current average weekly expenditure on consumer goods and services by all households in the country. These estimates were derived almost entirely from the results of the large scale national household expenditure survey which was conducted during 1987 specifically for this purpose. The survey covered a national representative sample of 7,705 private households throughout the country. Fieldwork commenced in February 1987 and terminated in April 1988. The survey expenditure estimates, which related to the calendar year 1987, were updated to mid-November 1989 using the percentage changes between 1987 and mid-November 1989 in the prices of the individual items covered by the former index series. Accurate information was not available on any quantitative changes in the detailed pattern of household consumption during this two-year period; no adjustments were made for this.

The expenditure corresponding to unpriced varieties in the item category is either added directly to the weight of similar varieties considered to exhibit the same price trend or distributed proportionally over all the priced varieties.

Weights and composition

Major groups	Number of items	Weights	Approximate number of price quotations
Food (including meals out)	50	25.7528	12,700
Alcoholic beverages	3	11.7301	1,400
Tobacco	3	3.3382	400
Housing:			
Rent	1	1.5150	900
Mortgage interest	1	3.3864	2
Repair, decorations, water and house insurance	3	1.6098	400
Fuel and light	7	5.9012	800
Clothing and footwear	24	6.7229	4,300
Durable household goods	13	4.7146	4,200
Other goods (cleaning products, hygiene, sports and recreational goods, etc.)	20	5.8502	5,400
Transport	13	13.7488	1,400
Services and related expenditure	21	15.0850	5,600
Total	159	100.0000	39,000

Household consumption expenditure
The index covers all consumer goods and services for which private households incur expenditure. In addition to food, drink, clothing, footwear, etc., this includes house insurance, motor taxation and insurance, driving licences, subscriptions to clubs, societies, associations and trade unions, mortgage interest payments and credit purchase instalments. As a price index, the CPI cannot in practice embrace goods and services which either have no price or cannot be priced. For this reason, the following items of household expenditure are excluded from the index coverage: church and charity donations, ground rent, personal cash allowances, lottery and betting payments. Furthermore, since the CPI is based on the concept of household expenditure, the following non-purchased consumption items are also excluded: the value of own farm or garden produce consumed by households, social welfare and other benefits in kind, imputed rents of owner-occupied dwellings. Certain other items of expenditure are also outside the scope of the index even though they affect the living costs and budgets of many households, namely: life assurance premiums, pension contributions, mortgage capital repayments, repayments of other personal loans, capital expenditure on the outright purchase of a house or on major structural extensions and repairs, other forms of savings and investments, social insurance contributions and income tax.

Method of data collection
Prices are collected each quarter on the Tuesday nearest to the middle of February, May, August and November from about 3,000 retail outlets and service establishments in all towns with 10,000 or more inhabitants and a representative sample of smaller towns.

The total number of different varieties priced is 807. 403 varieties are priced locally. The remainder either involve a single enterprise (e.g. electricity, bus and rail services, post and telephone charges), relate to small groups of companies (e.g. domestic gas, fuel oil, etc.) or need not be comprehensively priced at the local level (e.g. fees for doctors, dentists and opticians, regular subscriptions). These are priced directly by the Central Statistics Office (CSO) in special postal and telephone inquiries.

The prices collected are those which are actually paid by the consumer in cash transactions. Estimates, averages or ranges of prices are not accepted. The price quotations include indirect taxes. Credit charges are ignored and discounts are also excluded unless given to everybody. Special offer and sale prices are accepted if they were operative on the pricing day, but price quotations for shop-soiled, damaged or sub-standard articles being sold at clearance prices are not accepted. List prices are not collected unless they are actually charged to the consumer.

Credit purchase payments for domestic appliances, acoustic appliances, motor cars and motor cycles are collected separately. Separate price indicators are used for interest payments and repayments of advances based on a fixed pattern of hire-purchase and credit sales agreements of varying ages. Price indicators based on current cash prices are used for the expenditure weight corresponding to the down-payment made on new agreements.

Housing
The CPI covers housing costs actually incurred. Specific account is taken of changes in the cost of the following housing items: rent (private and local authority); local authority service charges; house insurance (all dwellings); repairs and decorations (all dwellings); mortgage interest payments (dwellings owned with mortgage). The gross payment of mortgage interest (i.e. before deduction of income tax relief) is used for both weighting and pricing purposes. The capital element of mortgage payments is not included in the concept of household expenditure covered by the index as it relates to the acquisition of a valuable capital asset (i.e. the dwelling).

Changes in the average level of rents paid by local authority tenants are incorporated in the index each quarter. Calculations are based on details of the total number of such dwellings and the aggregate rents paid, obtained directly from each local administrative area. Changes in the level of rents charged in respect of privately-owned dwellings are also taken into account each quarter. A special direct rent inquiry is undertaken each quarter by CSO staff in the Dublin area and by the part-time private price collectors in the small provincial towns. Two longstanding postal inquiries addressed to small panels of landlords and tenants respectively continue to be conducted.

The actual housing costs of owner-occupied accommodation are covered (i.e. imputed rent is not taken into account). Changes in mortgage interest costs are based on a fixed pattern of building society and local authority mortgages of varying ages, amounts and interest rates. The capital element of mortgage repayment is not covered. Details of water charges are obtained once a year from local authorities.

The price indicator for house insurance is based on standard insurance rates for private dwellings and their contents as well as on appropriate indices for value updating. Prices for a representative selection of materials for home repairs and decorations are obtained each quarter by postal inquiry from a national panel of merchants.

Specification of varieties
Pricing procedures are based strictly on the principle that an identical quality or brand of each selected variety must be priced as far as possible in the same shop on each occasion. The specifications of selected varieties are of a general nature. These delineate a range of products (i.e. particular brands, qualities, sizes, etc.) from which individual price collectors are free initially (or on replacement) to choose a specific product for regular pricing. For example, in the present series, a selection of five varieties is listed under the item category toys, of which one is a model car. No further specifications are given and individual price collectors are free initially to select for regular pricing any of the different types of model cars available locally. The only restriction to their choice is that the particular model selected has to be popular, suitable for regular pricing (i.e. can be specified precisely) and likely to be available in the long term. Once chosen initially, individual price collectors are required to price the identical product on each successive occasion. Because of the interval between each such occasion and the possibility that different price collectors might be involved, the price booklets are specially designed so that the exact specification of each selected product is recorded to ensure that the identical set of articles is priced on each occasion as required.

Under these arrangements, the specific products priced by different price collectors for a particular variety are not the same. The method used ensures that the prices of a wide variety of brands and qualities are collected in different places and, as they reflect local tastes and preferences, are more representative of the price movements of the variety in question than would be the case if a single narrowly defined identical variety was priced everywhere.

Substitution, quality change, etc.
Substitution is made at the local level when discontinuities occur as a result of model and quality changes or if a product is in low supply or no longer in popular demand. Alternative popular articles are then introduced.

The price booklets are designed to allow the detailed specifications of the new products to be inserted. The particular discontinuity is restricted to a single price booklet and the relevant price is excluded from the index calculations until two consecutive quotations are again obtained for the substitute. Price collectors are also allowed to substitute a new article in place of any original product which is in low supply or no longer in popular demand locally. However, the price of a particular product is used in the compilation of the index only when two consecutive quarterly price quotations are available for it.

A change in a shop surveyed is also treated as a discontinuity and the prices for the particular products affected are not used in the index calculations until successive quarterly quotations are obtained from the same shop. The price booklets are designed so that the shop in which each particular product is priced is clearly identified. If a particular outlet can no longer be used (e.g. goes out of business, refuses to cooperate, etc.) the price collector replaces it with a similar popular shop in the same area.

An official of the CSO regularly visits all provincial price collectors to ensure that the pricing arrangements are adhered to. The CSO officials who survey prices in the Dublin area are instructed in the Office.

Seasonal items
The prices of some fresh food items, such as eggs, vegetables, fruit, etc., fluctuate seasonally in varying degrees due to market forces of supply and demand. Traditionally, the price changes for three items (i.e. eggs, potatoes and tomatoes) have been corrected for seasonality in the CPI because, when account is taken of their weights, their seasonal pattern could have a discernible impact on the index. As this could make it unduly difficult to distinguish underlying price trends, the seasonal price variations for these items continue to be excluded from the index. This is done using the X-11 Variant of the US Bureau of the Census Method 11 Seasonal Adjustment Program.

There are other index items whose prices tend to change regularly at the same time each year simply because they are levied annually at that time. These include are school and university fees, annual subscriptions to clubs and societies, etc. Items with a high duty content (drink and tobacco) are also affected in this fashion by budget changes. Price changes for these particular products and for other items with insignificant individual seasonal contributions are reflected in the CPI without adjustment. For this reason, seasonality is not fully excluded from the CPI.

Computation
The index is computed according to the Laspeyres formula as a weighted arithmetic average with fixed base, using weights corresponding to the base period.

National averages of the prices are first calculated for each sample variety. These averages are compiled in two stages. Simple arithmetic average prices are calculated within town size strata, then the strata average prices are combined into national averages using retail sales strata weights derived from the 1987 Census of Services. Department stores are segregated as a separate stratum so that their prices are incorporated in the national average with appropriate weighting. Complementary national average prices are recalculated for the preceding quarter using matched sets of quotations. The ratio of these directly comparable national average prices gives the estimated quarterly change in price. This is used to update the previous quarter's cost for the fixed quantity of each index variety to give the current quarter's cost for the constant basket. Indexes of price changes can then be derived directly for all items or any combination of them by dividing their total current cost by their corresponding cost in the base quarter.

Other information
Separate indices are calculated for the ten commodity groups distinguished in the former series, namely: Food; Alcoholic drink; Tobacco; Clothing and footwear; Fuel and light; Housing; Durable household goods; Other goods; Transport; Services and related expenditure. An additional index is also published for energy products covering fuel, light, petrol, motor diesel, motor gas (LPG) and motor oil. For continuity purposes, each of these series is also published on the former base mid-November 1982 = 100.

The next CPI updating should be completed in November 1996 based on the results of a 1994 large scale household expenditure survey.

Organisation and publication
Central Statistics Office: "Irish Statistical Bulletin" (Dublin).

Idem: "Consumer Price Index - Introduction of Updated series - Base: Mid-November 1989 as 100".

ISLE OF MAN

Official title
General Index of Retail Prices.

Scope
The index is compiled monthly covering all private households, excluding 3-4 per cent of the top income group and the lowest group receiving social assistance.

Official base
March 1976 = 100.

Source of weights
The weights and items were derived from the household expenditure survey conducted in 1976 among a random sample of households.

Weights and composition

Major groups	Number of items	Weights	Approximate number of price quotations
Food	...	244	...
Alcoholic beverages	...	82	...
Tobacco	...	53	...
Housing	...	104	...
Fuel and light	...	90	...
Durable household goods	...	66	...
Clothing and footwear	...	72	...
Transport and vehicles	...	134	...
Miscellaneous goods	...	64	...
Services	...	59	...
Meals outside home	...	32	...
Total	450	1,000	...

Household consumption expenditure
Consumption expenditure for the purpose of the index includes almost all goods and services purchased by the index popu-

lation. It excludes contributions to pension funds, income and other direct taxes, cash gifts and life insurance payments.

Method of data collection
Prices are collected from about 100 selected retail outlets and service establishments by agents, mail questionnaires or telephone enquiry. Price are collected each month on the Tuesday nearest to the middle of the month.

The prices used to calculate the index are the prices actually paid. Discounts and reduced prices available only to certain members of the public are not taken into account. Sale prices, special offers, etc., are taken into consideration if the product concerned is of the usual size and quality.

Housing
Rent data are obtained from a small number of representative dwellings.

Specification of varieties
The specifications of items to be priced are given in terms of brand, quality and size, etc.

Substitution, quality change, etc.
Account is taken of changes occurring in similar products in order to distinguish genuine price increases from changes in quality, and judgement is used to identify these.

Seasonal items
In the case of fresh fruit and vegetables, a fixed weight for the sub-group is distributed over item weights which vary each month.

Computation
The index is computed according to the Laspeyres formula as a weighted arithmetic average with fixed base, using weights corresponding to the base period.

Organisation and publication
Treasury's Economics Section: "Index of Retail Prices" (Douglas).
Idem: "Digest of Economic and Social Statistics".

ISRAEL

Official title
Consumer Price Index.

Scope
The index is compiled monthly and covers all families living in urban areas.

Official base
1987 = 100.

Source of weights
The weights and items were derived from a household expenditure survey conducted during June 1986-May 1987 among a representative sample of approximately 5,000 households with one or more members, living in 104 urban areas. The weights were adjusted to take into account price changes between the survey period and the base period.

Weights and composition

Major groups	Number of items	Weights	Approximate number of price quotations
Food (excl. fruit and vegetables)	270	16.51	7,000
Fruit and vegetables	90	6.42	17,000
Housing	5	16.46	(a)
Household maintenance (incl. fuel and light)	85	9.33	2,000
Furniture and household equipment	185	7.18	3,000
Clothing and footwear	190	7.20	12,000
Health	80	5.50	1,000
Education, culture and entertainment	260	12.01	3,000
Transport and postal charges	85	15.25	1,000
Miscellaneous	110	4.14	1,000
Total	1,355	100.00	47,000

Note: (a) See under Housing below.

Household consumption expenditure
This comprises the value of commodities and services received by the household, not including commodities related to investments or savings (e.g. purchase of a flat, vehicle, stocks etc.). Consumption is measured as the sum of payments which the household paid or undertook to pay. Consumption includes additional expenditure connected with purchases, e.g. interest, commission, transport fees or installation fees (if paid to the vendor).

Also included in consumption is the calculated value of depreciation and alternative interest on capital invested in housing or a vehicle, or a value for the use of housing or a vehicle not privately owned by the household and not paid for. The services of commodities and services received from employers are also included. Not included in consumption are payments on account for future purchases (for goods not yet received), debt repayments for past purchases and returned expenditures. Included are second-hand purchases and trade-in of used goods in part payment for new goods, where only the difference in value between the old and new good is considered as consumption; insurance associated with specific consumer goods and health insurance. Excluded is expenditure on direct taxes, social insurance, pension funds, life insurance, money-gifts and lotteries.

Method of data collection
The items are selected according to the value of expenditure in the household expenditure survey and the number of varieties that exist for the item. Items accounting for more than 0.1 per cent of household expenditure are priced separately. Items accounting for less then 0.1 per cent are priced separately only when no suitable items are available to represent their price movements. Expenditure for items not priced is transferred to similar items that can represent their price movements properly.

The sample size for the outlets was determined according to the weights of the group of items for an outlet and the variance between the price changes for each item in the group in the various outlets. The localities were sampled with probability proportional to size within geographical strata, size being the total household expenditure in the locality. Prices for most items are collected each month by agents, from 1,300 outlets. Prices for electricity, gas, water, medical care education and transport and communication etc. are collected by mail or telephone, from 600 reporting sources.

Prices are collected by 20 enumerators who transmit the data to field offices located in the three large cities, which transfer the data to the centre in Jerusalem. Discounts are recorded if they are offered to all purchasers. Sale prices are collected where applicable. Market prices are used, not official tariffs. Items are priced on the basis of cash purchases. Second-hand automobiles and owner-occupied houses are priced according to their local prices.

Prices for most items are collected to obtain a monthly average, by staggering the outlets into four groups, each priced in a different week.

Housing
Two panels of rental houses are priced in alternate months, and cover furnished or unfurnished dwellings.

The yearly expenditure on services supplied by owner-occupied dwellings is computed by including the depreciation of the dwelling over time, and the alternative interest on the capital invested in the dwelling.

In the current index, both new and second-hand dwellings which changed hands are priced. The prices are obtained from the forms used for purchase taxes and are supplied by the tax authorities. The data refers to about 3,000 to 4,000 dwellings in a quarter, in 25 urban localities. Data on the quality of the dwellings are used to prepare regression analysis, so that the index only reflects price changes.

Specification of varieties
General specifications are prepared for items. Detailed specifications for each item, e.g. the brand, make, quality, etc., are chosen by the enumerator for each outlet, and prices are collected each month for a specific variety.

Substitution, quality change, etc.
Large quality changes and substitutions are linked into the index, so that their introduction does not affect the price level. Small quality changes are considered as changes in price. Quality adjustments are made only in some special cases, when there are enough characteristics which can be measured.

Seasonal items
Prices of seasonal items are collected as long as they appear on the market. When they are no longer available, their prices are estimated on the basis of price movements of similar items.

When the seasonal item again appears its price is compared to the last month for which a price was available. Prior to 1988, changing weights were used for fresh fruit and vegetables.

Computation
The index is computed according to the Laspeyres formula as a weighted arithmetic average with fixed base, using weights corresponding to the base period.

The index for each item is calculated on the basis of price relatives. If no price is available for an item in an outlet, the price movement is estimated according to price movements in other outlets. If no price is available for the item from any outlet, the price movement of the item is estimated according to that of similar items.

Other information
In addition to the index for all urban families, price movements are calculated for "baskets" for families in the lower and upper deciles of the income distribution.

Organisation and publication
Central Bureau of Statistics: "Monthly Bulletin of Statistics" (Jerusalem).

Idem: "Price statistics Monthly" (Hebrew only).

Revision of consumer price index, published in "Price Statistics"

ITALY

Official title
National Consumer Price Index.

Scope
The index is computed monthly and covers all households in main towns in 93 provinces.

Official base
1990 = 100.

Source of weights
The weights were derived from consumption patterns and national accounts data for the two first quarters of 1989 and the two last quarters of 1990.

Weights and composition

Major groups	Number of items	Weights	Approximate number of price quotations
Food and tobacco	250	22.78	200,000
Clothing and footwear	57	10.83	20,000
Housing:	...	7.62	13,500
Rent	1	...	...
Maintenance and repairs	5	...	...
Fuel and light	7	...	...
Other groups:	...	...	50,000
Furniture and household utensils	76	10.58	...
Medical care	137	6.74	...
Transport and communication	168	13.46	...
Education and recreation	110	9.97	...
Other goods and services	96	18.02	...
Total	907	100.00	283,500

Household consumption expenditure
Consumption expenditure for the purpose of the index does not include income taxes, investment and savings, consumption from own production or the imputed rent of the owner-occupied dwellings.

Method of data collection
Prices are collected by agents in the provincial capitals of 93 provinces from approximately 26,300 retail stores and outlets (9,500 for food and 10,800 for other items) and from 6,000 service establishments.

Prices for fresh fish, potatoes, fruit and vegetables are collected on the 5th, 15th and 25th of each month, while those for other food items, clothing and personal services are ascertained around the 15th of each month. For the computation of the index, however, the prices on the 5th and 15th of the current month and the prices on the 25th of the previous month are taken. Price collection for household durable goods and the cost of some services is made on 5 February, 5 May, 5 August and 5 November. The prices used to calculate the index are the normal prices paid by consumers. Sale prices, discounts, hire-purchase or credit terms and second-hand purchases are not taken into account in the index, but sale prices for food items are collected if they last at least a month.

Housing
Rent quotations for 13,500 dwellings are obtained each quarter, on 5 January, 5 April, 5 July and 5 October.

Specification of varieties
Detailed specifications are provided for each item included in the market basket. A specification provides a complete description of the item, its brand, name or trade mark, type of packing, quantity or unit, etc.

Substitution, quality change, etc.
If a product is not available, a similar product to the original is substituted and a method of linking is used in the calculation.

Seasonal items
Fresh fruit, vegetables and flowers are treated as seasonal items. The composite index for seasonal items is obtained using the average price of the first 75 per cent of items listed in ascending order of their recorded prices. The seasonal items available in the market are intended to be interchangeable. Adjustments are made using a 13-month (current month and 12 previous months) moving average.

Computation
The index is computed according to the Laspeyres formula as a weighted arithmetic average with fixed base, using weights corresponding to the base period.

The index for each item in each town is the simple arithmetic average of all the basic indices for that item in that town. An average index for an item for each region is the weighted arithmetic average of all the indices obtained in that particular region.

The national index is the weighted arithmetic average of indices relating to 20 regions, using weights proportionate to the (urban) population of the regions as on 31 December 1989.

Other information
The Istituto Nazionale di Statistica also calculates and publishes a series of consumer price indices for wage earners and salaried employees.

Organisation and publication
Istituto Nazionale di Statistica, "Bollettino mensile di statistica" (Rome).

JAMAICA

Official title
Consumer Price Index.

Scope
The index is compiled monthly and covers households in urban and rural areas with an annual income of 24,000 dollars or less at the time of the survey.

Official base
January 1988 = 100.

Source of weights
The weights and items were derived from a household expenditure survey conducted in 1984 in urban and rural areas among households with an annual income of 24,000 dollars or less at the time of the survey. Item sub-groups representing less than 0.50 per cent of expenditure within a group in all regions were left out and their weights redistributed among the other sub-groups. The same selection criterion was applied to the items in each sub-group, exception for the Food and drink group, where the cut-off point for each item was 0.40 per cent.

Weights and composition

Major groups	Number of items	Weights	Approximate number of price quotations
Food	...	55.63	...
Fuel and household supplies	...	7.35	...
Rent and household operation	...	7.86	...
Furniture and furnishings	...	2.83	...
Medical care	...	6.97	...
Clothing and footwear	...	5.07	...
Transport	...	6.44	...
Miscellaneous	...	7.85	...
Total	...	100.00	...

Household consumption expenditure
Not available.

Method of data collection
Prices for most items are collected during the first weekend of each month from a fixed set of outlets throughout the island. Doctors' and dentists' fees are collected each quarter, school fees each term and health insurance once a year. Changes in the cost of telephone rates, water rates and bus fares are recorded when announced. The Institute's team of field officers are responsible for collecting the prices from various sources including supermarkets, department stores, footwear stores, restaurants, service stations, doctors and dentists, clubs, schools, hair-dressers and barbers. Items such as electricity and telephone charges are collected from the authorities concerned while information on rent is obtained from a sample of dwellings.

The outlets are visited each month by the agents. The respondent outlets are located in areas commonly used by the target group and are typical of the types of the outlets they patronise. They were not selected at random, but rather a purposive or judgement sample was selected in collaboration with the experienced field officers who have a very good knowledge of the area covered and general popularity of the stores with the target population. The outlets were chosen on the basis of volume of sales. The selection process was not restricted to larger establishments; small grocery shops and small stores within communities where people buy when they are out of stock are also included in the sample.

The prices charged for stale, damaged, shop-soiled or otherwise imperfect goods are ignored since they represent a departure from the given specifications. If illegal prices are charged openly to the groups covered by the index, they are taken into consideration.

Housing
Rent quotations are obtained each month from a sample of specific types of houses with regard to the number of bedrooms and other rooms. Household payments such as mortgage down payment, repayments and interest charges, and home insurance represent the user cost of owner-occupied dwellings, i.e. cash outlays are used as a proxy for the estimated rental value. The price index used to arrive at a quantum covers the rents of the representative categories of dwellings.

Specification of varieties
Items for which prices are collected are clearly specified to ensure that items of comparable quality are priced every month.

Substitution, quality change, etc.
A commodity or service maybe observed to be disappearing from the market and a new one entering it. If there is an overlap of price observations and a quality difference is evident, the following linking method is employed: a base period price is imputed for the new variety using price relatives for the current and base periods.

However, if the old and new varieties are of comparable quality, the price of the new one is taken and the difference in price treated as an increase or decrease. If the consumer has no choice but to buy the new variety, the difference in price is treated as a price change and not as payment for a higher or lower quality, even if there is a utility differential.

The appearance of truly new products (i.e. products not replacing any item in the index) which bring about significant readjustments to the consumer budget is rare; if this occurs, a revision of the index is necessary.

Seasonal items
No adjustment is made to seasonal fluctuations of item prices.

Computation
The index is computed according to the Laspeyres formula as a weighted arithmetic average with fixed base, using weights corresponding to 1984. The price relative for each item is calculated by dividing the average price for the current period by the average price for the base period. A weighted average of the three regional indices is calculated to obtain the all-island index.

Organisation and publication
Statistical Institute of Jamaica: "Consumer Price Index Monthly Bulletin" (Kingston).
Idem: "Consumer Price Index Monthly Report".
Idem: "Consumer Price Index - Annual Review".

JAPAN

Official title
Consumer Price Index.

Scope
The index is compiled monthly and covers households in the entire country, excluding one-person households and households mainly engaged in agriculture, forestry and fishing.

Official base
1990 = 100.

Source of weights
The weights were derived from a household expenditure survey conducted in 1990, covering approximately 8,000 households. The monthly weights of fresh food items (i.e. fresh fish, fresh vegetables and fresh fruit) were obtained from average expenditure data for 1989 and 1990. Index items were selected according to the relative importance of each item to the total consumption expenditure (0.01 per cent or more, in principle), representativeness of price movements and continuity of price data collection. The weights of items not priced were allocated to the priced items representing them.

Weights and composition

Major groups	Number of items	Weights	Approximate number of price quotations
Food	215	3,140	...
Housing	23	1,478	...
Fuel, light and water	6	553	...
Furniture and household utensils	60	444	...
Clothing and footwear	84	860	...
Medical care	23	312	...
Transport and communication	36	1,185	...
Education	13	466	...
Reading and recreation	69	1,115	...
Miscellaneous	32	446	...
Total	561	10,000	230,000

Household consumption expenditure
Consumption expenditure for the purpose of the index relates to disbursements for purchasing goods and services necessary for daily life and includes imputed rental values for owner-occupied housing. It excludes income tax, life insurance, social security payments, savings, securities, remittances, gifts, religious contributions and other non-consumption items.

Method of data collection
Prices for most items are collected through personal visits to selected outlets and service establishments in 167 cities, towns and villages. Official tariffs are used for items such as transport and postal services. Prices are surveyed on Wednesday, Thursday or Friday of the week which includes the 12th of each month. However, for 42 items of fresh fish, fresh vegetables and fresh fruit, prices are collected three times a month. Education fees are surveyed in April and September. The prices used in the index are the retail prices actually paid by consumers on the pricing day. Low prices due to bargain, clearance and discount sales, temporary abnormal prices, reduced prices for quantity purchases and prices of second-hand articles, etc., are excluded.

Housing
Rent quotations relate to privately owned houses and rooms and publicly owned houses. Data on rents of publicly owned houses are supplied each month by the agency managing them. Rent quotations for private houses are obtained according to structure and floor space through a survey conducted each month, covering all households in privately rented houses in the sampled districts. The rental equivalence approach (imputed rent) is used for the housing cost for owner-occupied dwellings.

Specification of varieties
Specifications of varieties are given in detail according to such characteristics as size, quality, brand and accessories so that the same items are constantly surveyed every month.

Substitution, quality change, etc.
If a selected product is no longer available for pricing, a product similar to the original is substituted. When the old and the new products are identical, the method of direct linking is used. Oth-

erwise, adjustments are made to the prices to take into account differences in volume or quality.

Seasonal items
The sub-group weights for seasonal items (i.e. fresh fish, fresh vegetables and fresh fruit) are fixed throughout the year. Each item in this sub-group is given the weight according to its relative importance which varies from month to month. The average prices for the latest on-season period are used for seasonal items other than fresh food during the off season.

Computation
The index is computed according to the Laspeyres formula as a weighted arithmetic average with fixed base, using weights corresponding to the base period.

Price relatives by item for each municipality are calculated and then averaged with the respective weights for each municipality, and average price relatives by items for the whole country are obtained. The average price relatives for the whole country are averaged with the respective item weights to obtain sub-group indexes. Major group indexes and the general index are calculated in a similar way from the sub-group index by using the respective group weights.

Other information
A "General index", "Ten major group index" and "Sub-group index" are compiled for 72 areas, i.e. the whole country, eight city groups, ten districts, four metropolitan areas, 47 cities with prefectural government, Kawasaki-shi and Kitakyushu-shi. "Commodity and service group index" and "Index by items" are compiled for the whole country and Ku-area of Tokyo. "Index by types of households", "Index by characteristics of items" and "Index computed by chain index method" are compiled for the whole country.

Organisation and publication
Management and Coordination Agency, Statistics Bureau: "Monthly Report on the Consumer Price Index".

Idem: "Annual Report on the Consumer Price Index".

JORDAN

Official title
Cost of Living Index.

Scope
The index is computed monthly and covers all urban and rural households in the Kingdom (East Bank).

Official base
1986 = 100.

Source of weights
The weights and items were derived from a household expenditure survey conducted during one year in 1986-87 among 2,357 households of all population groups in urban and rural areas.

The items were selected by sampling techniques according to the relative importance of each item.

Weights and composition

Major groups	Number of items	Weights	Approximate number of price quotations
Food	141	41.170	1,870
Clothing and footwear	65	7.454	1,394
Housing	55	28.092	1,445
Other goods and services	47	23.284	2,244
Total	208	100.000	6,953

Household consumption expenditure
This includes all expenditure by households during a complete year and income in kind consumed by households. It also includes the estimated rental value of owner-occupied housing.

Durable goods credit purchasea were treated as expenditure. Second-hand purchases and trade-in of used goods and in part payment for new ones were not taken in consideration. Contributions to social insurance and pension funds, licence fees, insurance associated with specific consumer goods, health care, income and other direct taxes, life insurance payments, remittances, gifts and similar disbursements deal with in accordance with the definitions in the national accounts.

Method of data collection
Prices are collected each month by agents in all capitals of governorates and districts in Jordan, taking in consideration the population density. Outlets are selected according to the number of items in the market basket. They should not be located near very high-income residential areas. Ten outlets are selected for each item. Prices for fresh fruit and vegetables are obtained on Tuesdays, four times a month. Prices for other food items are ascertained once a month, during the first week, clothing the second week and other goods and services the third and fourth weeks.

The prices are the regular prices on the market, whether they are official prices or not. Discounts, sale prices, black-market prices, hire-purchase and second-hand purchases are not included.

Housing
Rent quotations are obtained every six months for all types of dwellings. Owner-occupied housing is excluded from the index.

Specification of varieties
The specifications of items to be priced are obtained from traders and are given in terms of the variety, quality, make, brand, unit, country of production, etc.

Substitution, quality change, etc.
If a product is not available on the market, a similar product to the original is substituted.

Seasonal items
When an item is out of season, the missing price is imputed.

Computation
The index is computed according to the Laspeyres formula as a weighted arithmetic average with fixed base, using weights corresponding to the base period.

The average price of each item in the current month is first divided by the price in the base period to give the price relative.

The weighted price average for a locality is multiplied by the weight for the locality which is proportionate to its population size.

Organisation and publication
The index is compiled by the Department of Statistics (Amman).

Central Bank of Jordan: "Monthly Statistical Bulletin" (Amman).

KENYA (NAIROBI)

Official title
Consumer Price Index - Lower Income Group.

Scope
The index is compiled monthly and covers households in Nairobi with a monthly income of up to 1,999 shillings in 1982-83.

Official base
February-March 1986 = 100.

Source of weights
The weights and items were derived from a household expenditure survey conducted during 1982-83 in all urban centres. The sample comprised 1,648 households of low-, middle- and high-income groups. The index relates to low-income group households in Nairobi with a monthly income of up to 1,999 shillings at the time of the survey. The weights were not adjusted to take into account price changes between the survey period and February-March 1986.

Weights and composition

Major groups	Number of items	Weights	Approximate number of price quotations
Food	49	44.2	...
Beverages and tobacco	11	2.1	...
Clothing and footwear	34	5.0	...
Rent	1	25.0	...
Fuel, light and water	4	3.1	...
Furniture, furnishings, household equipment and operation	29	5.3	...
Health and personal care	18	3.0	...
Transport and communication	15	4.1	...
Education, recreation and entertainment	15	6.2	...
Miscellaneous goods and services	10	2.0	...
Total	186	100.0	...

Household consumption expenditure
Consumption expenditure for the purpose of the index comprises the goods and services purchased for consumption by the index population. It excludes income tax, payments to pension funds, savings, life insurance premiums, house purchases, subscriptions to trade unions and betting payments.

Method of data collection
Prices are collected by agents in markets, supermarkets, retail outlets and service establishments. Prices for food items are ascertained through direct purchase during the first week of each month. Those for non-durable household goods are obtained during the third week of each month and those for durable household goods and services are collected each quarter. The prices used in the index are the market prices actually paid by households.

Housing
Rent quotations are obtained once a year. During the months when no rent data are obtained, it is assumed that rents vary in the same proportion as all other items in the index. The imputed rent for owner-occupied housing is ascertained.

Specification of varieties
The specifications of items to be priced are given in detail, taking into account the popularity of the items and the continuity of price series. Specifications are given in terms of the brand, make, quality and size.

Substitution, quality change, etc.
If a product is no longer available on the market, another product is substituted. The base period price of the old product is adjusted according to the price ratio of the old and the substitute products. If there is a quality change, the item is treated as a new one and the same method is used.

Seasonal items
Seasonal fluctuations in item prices are taken into account by using monthly moving averages.

Computation
The index is computed according to the Laspeyres formula as a weighted arithmetic average with fixed base, using weights corresponding to the period 1982-83.
The relatives of average prices for the current and base periods are used to compute item indices. The average prices are the simple arithmetic means of all the price quotations obtained.

Other information
Along with the lower-income group index, the Central Bureau of Statistics publishes middle-income and upper-income group indices for Nairobi.

Organisation and publication
Ministry of Finance and Planning, Central Bureau of Statistics: "Kenya Statistical Digest" (Nairobi).
Idem: "On current and revised Kenyan Consumer Price Indices".

KIRIBATI (TARAWA)

Official title
Retail Price Index.

Scope
The index is compiled quarterly and relates to households in urban Tarawa.

Official base
October-December 1975 = 100.

Source of weights
The weights and items were derived from a household expenditure survey conducted over a six-week period from late August 1975 to early October 1975 among a sample of 61 households living in urban Tarawa, and from various records.

Household consumption expenditure
Not available.

Method of data collection
Prices are collected around the 15th of each month, by agents, from markets, retail outlets and service establishments in three main centres in urban Tarawa.

Housing
Not available.

Weights and composition

Major groups	Number of items	Weights	Approximate number of price quotations
Food	47	50.00	...
Beverages and tobacco	8	14.00	...
Clothing and footwear	15	8.00	...
Transport	15	8.00	...
Housing:			
Rent	4	1.01	...
Fuel and light	4	3.56	...
Maintenance and certain household equipment	13	2.93	...
Miscellaneous	22	12.50	...
Total	128	100.00	...

Specification of varieties
Not available.

Substitution, quality change, etc.
Not available.

Seasonal items
No adjustment is made for seasonal fluctuations in prices.

Computation
The index is computed according to the Laspeyres formula as a weighted arithmetic average with fixed base, using weights corresponding to the base period.

Organisation and publication
Ministry of Finance, Statistical Unit: "Quarterly Digest of Statistics" (Tarawa).

KOREA, REPUBLIC OF

Official title
All Cities Consumer Price Index.

Scope
The index is computed monthly and covers wage earners' and salaried employees' households in urban areas.

Official base
1985 = 100.

Source of weights
The weights and items were derived from a household expenditure survey conducted during one year in 1985 in 50 cities among about 3,700 private households, excluding households of farmers, fishermen, single persons and foreigners, and those whose income and expenditure were difficult to calculate. The index relates only to wage earners' and salaried employeesÁ households. The items selected are those that account for more than 1/10,000 of total household expenditure, which are representative of homogeneous commodity groups and are available for continuous survey. However, important items whose consumption is increasing are included even if they represent less than 1/10,000 of the total expenditure. The weights of items not priced are either distributed among similar items or proportionately distributed into similar groups.

Weights and composition

Major groups	Number of items	Weights	Approximate number of price quotations
Food	380.2	153	...
Housing	129.8	17	...
Fuel, light and water charges	76.1	9	...
Furniture and utensils	49.5	57	...
Clothing and footwear	77.7	45	...
Medical care	69.3	26	...
Education, reading and recreation	114.7	59	...
Transport and communication	64.6	16	...
Miscellaneous	38.1	29	...
Total	1000.0	411	...

Household consumption expenditure
Included are gifts and similar disbursements, durable goods credit purchase, second-hand purchases and trade-in of used goods and in part payment for new ones, insurance associated with specific consumer goods and license fees.
Excluded is non-consumption expenditure such as income taxes and other direct taxes, contributions to social insurance and

pension funds, remittances, health care, disbursements other than expenditure (e.g. life insurance payments), the rental value of owner-occupied housing and income in kind.

Method of data collection
The data are collected mainly through personal interview, but, for some items for which there is a single predominant price, prices are collected by telephone (36 items of electricity, gas, water, medical care, education, transport, communication, etc.).

Most of the items are priced three times a month (on the 5th, 15th and 25th) from about 2,600 retail outlets and service establishments in eleven cities, except house rents, which are collected each month, and admission fees for theatres and school fees, which are collected each quarter.

Although the reference date for the price survey is the 5th, 15th and 25th of the month, the reference day is replaced by the previous day if it falls on a Sunday, or is advanced by two days when it falls on a festival day. In particular, fresh vegetables and fish are surveyed at a fixed time of the day due to the fluctuation of prices. Prices quoted through discounts, sales, black market, credit-terms. second-hand purchases, etc. are excluded.

Housing
About 2,500 households from the sample of the family expenditure survey and the economically active population survey are surveyed each month to obtain data on rent. The cost of owner-occupied housing is excluded from the index.

Specification of varieties
Items are usually specified in detail in terms of their variety, prices, brands and taking into account their volume of sales.

Substitution, quality change, etc.
When considerable quality change arises, the following splicing method is used:

P'o = Po x (P't/Pt)

P'o: price of improved quality at assumed base period
Po: price of original quality at base period
P't: price of improved quality at time of replacement
Pt: price of original quality at time of replacement

If a new item appears on the market it is spliced into the sub-group to which it belongs, as follows:

P'o = (P't/I) x 100

P'o: price of new item at assumed base period
P't: price of new item at time of splice
I: sub-group index to which new item belongs

If a given type of quality disappears from the market and no replacement item is available, the weight is redistributed over the remaining items in the same sub-group.

Seasonal items
For seasonal items such as fresh fish, vegetables and fruit that are not available on the market during the off season, the last available prices are used for the index calculation until new prices are available.

Computation
The index is computed according to the Laspeyres formula as a weighted arithmetic average with fixed base, using weights corresponding to the base period.

The price relatives for each item in each city are calculated by dividing the average price for the current period by the average price for the base period. Average prices are simple arithmetic averages of prices obtained within each city. The item indices for eleven cities are then weighted to arrive at an item index for all cities.

Other information
Sub-indices for major items are published.

Organisation and publication
National Bureau of Statistics, Economic Planning Board, Bureau of Statistics: "Monthly Statistics of Korea" (Seoul).
Idem: "Annual Report on the Price Survey" (for further methodological information).

KUWAIT

Official title
Consumer Price Index Numbers.

Scope
The index is compiled monthly and comprises all private households including one-person households.

Official base
1978 = 100.

Source of weights
The weights and items were derived from the 1977-78 household budget survey.

Weights and composition

Major groups	Number of items	Weights	Approximate number of price quotations
Food	192	357.09	2,484
Beverages and tobacco	8	12.70	85
Clothing and footwear	67	99.55	323
Housing	14	187.03	25
Household goods and services	119	110.23	646
Transport and communication	73	152.91	105
Education and medical care	55	25.49	365
Other goods and services	72	55.00	291
Total	(a) 600	1,000.00	4,324

Note: (a) Varieties representing about 260 items.

Household consumption expenditure
Consumption expenditure for the purpose of the index comprises all the important goods and services purchased for consumption by the index population. It excludes income taxes, investment and savings, and other non-consumption expenditure.

Method of data collection
Price data are obtained from the relevant retail outlets which were chosen on the basis of the extent to which they are patronised by the consumers. The Ministry of Trade and Industry provides price quotations for all subsidised items.

Prices are collected by personal visits of trained staff members, once a month for most of the items, twice a month for fresh fruit and vegetables and each quarter for services. For services provided by government agencies such as transport, postal services, education, health, etc., the necessary changes are made as and when the rates are revised.

Housing
Rent quotations are provided by the Annual Survey of House Rents conducted by the Central Statistical Office.

Specification of varieties
Detailed specifications are provided for each item included in the market basket. A specification gives a complete description of the item, its brand name or trade mark, country of origin, type of packing, quantity or unit, etc. Only the important specifications for each item are included in the price index calculation.

Substitution, quality change, etc.
Quality changes are not taken into account. Every effort is made to secure price quotations for the same item-specifications for which base year prices are available to minimise the influence of quality changes on the index.

Seasonal items
Fresh fruit and vegetables are treated as seasonal items. Each month, a typical market seasonal basket is constructed for fresh fruit and vegetables. Prices are collected for all items in the basket and compared with the prices for the same month of the base year.

Computation
The index is computed according to the Laspeyres formula as a weighted arithmetic average with fixed base, using weights corresponding to the base period.

The price relative for each variety is calculated by dividing the price for the current period by the price for the base period. The index for an item is then calculated as an average of the variety price relatives. In the case of those items available at subsidised as well as free market prices, price relatives are obtained as weighted averages, weights being proportional to the quantities sold at subsidised and free market prices. Also, for some items which are not subsidised, weighted average price relatives are compiled by assigning weights to important varieties.

Other information
Detailed sub-group indices are published for 13 months.

Organisation and publication
Ministry of Planning, Central Statistical Office: "Monthly Price Index Number" (Kuwait).

Idem: "Consumer Price Index Number, Revised Series 1978 = 100, Scope and Method of Construction" (Kuwait).

LESOTHO

Official title
Consumer Price Index for Low-Income Households.

Scope
The index is compiled quarterly and covers all urban low-income group households.

Official base
April 1989 = 100.

Source of weights
The weights and items were derived from a household expenditure survey conducted between October 1986 and September 1987 among all population groups (excluding institutions) in all geographical areas.

The selection of sample units in this survey was based on a two-stage nationwide stratified sample covering 4,800 rural and 2,880 urban households. The nation was divided into districts and four aggro-ecological zones, with 24 strata in the rural areas and 14 strata in the urban areas, with three strata for Maseru alone. In urban Maseru, neighbourhoods were assigned to a high-, middle- or low-income strata on the basis of the external characteristics of dwellings in order to further improve the design. Sampling was proportional to size within each stratum. In the urban areas, eight households were selected each month as an optimum workload for each enumerator, and five households were selected in the rural areas as an optimum workload for each enumerator.

The index relates to low-income households comprising all households with a monthly income of less than 200 Maloti. The weights were not adjusted to take into account price changes between the survey period and April 1989.

The item selection criteria was based on total expenditure, and the weights for items not priced were spliced within the relevant groups and sub-groups when elementary aggregates were constructed.

Weights and composition

Major groups	Number of items	Weights	Approximate number of price quotations
Food and tobacco	108	76.3	552
Clothing and footwear	46	13.9	148
Gross rent, fuel and light	25	12.4	58
Furniture, furnishings and household operation	49	10.0	171
Transport and communication	16	3.9	32
Other goods and services	48	7.1	139
Total	292	100.0	1,100

Household consumption expenditure
Consumption expenditure is defined as in the national accounts. This means that some adjustments were made to the weights from the household expenditure survey. Consumption in kind and the imputed consumption expenditure on home-ownership were included in the weights.

Method of data collection
Prices are collected by agents in January, April, July and October from about 170 retail outlets and service establishments distributed over six towns. In Maseru, prices are collected on Monday to Friday in the first week of the survey month, and in the other towns, on Monday to Friday in the third week of the survey month. The prices used in the index are the prices actually paid. Discounts and sale prices are included if they are offered to the general public and not only to a selected group. Hire-purchase or credit terms, second-hand purchases and import prices are not used.

Housing
Rent quotations are obtained each quarter, and include rental charges and cost of repairs and redecoration. Owner-occupied dwellings are valued at the existing rental charges for similar types of housing.

Specification of varieties
The specifications include as many characteristics as are necessary for the different price collectors to obtain almost identical varieties in the different outlets. For example, they include the type, variety, name, origin, size, brand, packaging, etc. However, the price collector is free to choosing the product in the selected outlet.

Substitution, quality change, etc.
Substitutions are made with almost similar quality. If new products appear and prove popular on the market, they are ultimately spliced into the relevant group or item. If an item disappears from the market, a new substitute is selected.

Seasonal items
For seasonal items such as fresh fruit and vegetables that are not available on the market during the off season, the last available prices are used for the index calculation until new prices are available.

Computation
The index is computed according to the Laspeyres formula as a weighted arithmetic average with fixed base, using weights corresponding to October 1986-September 1987.

Price relatives are first calculated for each price quotation, variety and item using the price relatives for the current and previous periods.

Weighted indexes are calculated for sub-groups, main groups and all items with base, previous period = 100. They are then converted to base, April 1989 = 100.

Other information
Consumer price indices for all urban-all income groups is published as well as a series for Maseru high-income group.

Organisation and publication
Bureau of Statistics: "Statistical Reports - Consumer Price Index" (Maseru).

Idem: "Lesotho - Consumer Price Index".

LIBERIA (MONROVIA)

Official title
Consumer Price Index.

Scope
The index is compiled monthly and covers wage earners' and clerical employees' households of two or more persons and with a monthly income not exceeding 250 dollars during October-December 1963. The index relates to the capital city, Monrovia.

Official base
September-November 1964 = 100.

Source of weights
The weights and items were derived from a household expenditure survey conducted in Monrovia during October-December 1963 among a sample of wage earners' and clerical employees' households of two or more persons and with a monthly income not exceeding 250 dollars at the time of the survey. The weights were adjusted according to a limited expenditure survey conducted in June 1964 to take account of the time lag between the two surveys.

Weights and composition

Major groups	Number of items	Weights	Approximate number of price quotations
Food	32	34.4	...
Beverages and tobacco	6	5.7	...
Fuel and light	3	5.0	...
Rent	1	14.9	...
Clothing and footwear	14	13.8	...
Household goods and furniture	7	6.1	...
Health, personal care and services	9	11.4	...
Miscellaneous	7	8.7	...
Total	79	100.0	188

Household consumption expenditure
Consumption expenditure for the purpose of the index includes all goods and services purchased for consumption by the index population. It includes licence fees, health and legal services, entertainment and other services. Income in kind, credit purchases, life insurance, property insurance, income tax and personal property taxes are excluded.

Method of data collection
Prices are collected by agents from 18 stores, two markets and 14 service establishments.

Prices for food are collected twice a month. Prices for drinks and tobacco, fuel and light, clothing, household goods and furniture are ascertained once a month. Price data for medical care and school fees are collected once a year.

Items sold in non-standardised units, e.g. pile, each, bunch, etc. are weighted and then adjusted to conform to the base period weight.

The prices used to calculate the index are the retail prices actually paid by consumers. Discounts, sale and other abnormal prices are not taken into account.

Housing
Rent quotations are collected twice a year, in January and July, from about 100 dwellings. Owner-occupied housing is not included in the index.

Specification of varieties
Detailed specifications are provided for each item included in the index. Specifications provide a complete description of the item, its brand, size, unit of quantity material, trade mark, etc.

Substitution, quality change, etc.
If a product is no longer available on the market, a similar product to the original is substituted and a method of linking is used.

Seasonal items
Seasonal fluctuations in the prices of certain items are taken into account by maintaining the closing prices for the previous season during the off season.

Computation
The index is computed according to the Laspeyres formula as a weighted arithmetic average with fixed base, using weights corresponding to June 1964.

The relatives of average prices for the current and base periods are used to calculate item indices. Average prices are simple arithmetic means of all price quotations obtained.

A missing price for an item is dealt with by using the last price reported for the item.

Organisation and publication
National Planning Agency, Bureau of Statistics: "Statistical Newsletter" (Monrovia).
Idem: "Quarterly Statistical Bulletin".
Idem: "Economic Survey of Liberia".
Idem: "Results of the study related to the Consumer Price Index for Monrovia", Methodological Series No. 1 (1964).

LUXEMBOURG

Official title
Indice des prix à la consommation (Consumer Price Index).

Scope
The index is compiled monthly and covers all households in the country, except for those of self-employed workers in industry and services and of farmers.

Official base
1990 = 100.

Source of weights
The weights were derived from a household expenditure survey conducted between April 1986 and September 1987, covering 2,764 households representing the whole population. The index covers all households in the country, except for those of self-employed workers in industry and services and of farmers. The weights were not adjusted to take into account price changes between the survey period and 1990.

The items were selected according to their weight in household budgets, as well as their suitability for price observation over time.

The weights of items which were not included because of their small share in household expenditures were allocated to similar items. The value of items not included for political reasons (cigarettes, tobacco and hard liquor, and certain services closely linked to sliding wage scales) was discarded before the calculation of total consumption expenditure.

Household consumption expenditure
With a few major exceptions, the concept of "expenditure", i.e. only sums actually disbursed by the household during the period of observation, was used. The value of households' consumption of their own production and the rental value of owner-occupied dwellings were excluded.

On the other hand, the nonreimbursed portion of health care costs and employers' and workers' contributions for benefits in kind were included in computing the weights for health care expenditure.

In computing the weights for insurance services, the premium had to be separated from the amount corresponding to the price paid for the purchase of the insurance service itself. Over a long period, the difference between the premiums collected and benefits paid for covered risks represents the cost of the insurance service. The ten-year ratio between this difference and the total of premiums paid is considered as household expenditure on insurance. This method was used to determine the weights for the "insurance" item.

Weights and composition

Major groups	Number of items	Weights	Approximate number of price quotations
Food	91	205.2	2,175
Clothing and footwear	42	131.1	800
Housing, fuel and light	11	137.0	600
Furniture, furnishings and household equipment	39	100.8	700
Medical care	27	81.9	300
Transport and communications	24	148.6	275
Education and leisure	37	79.9	700
Other goods and services	32	115.5	850
Total	303	100.0	6,400

Method of data collection
Prices are collected each month by agents, from retail outlets, supermarkets and service establishments in the capital and other representative cities in other regions.

Prices for fresh fruit and vegetables, fish and flowers are obtained three times a month.

Official tariffs are obtained from the relevant national or local authorities for electricity, heating oil, water, medical care (medical and paramedical fees and hospital charges) and certain items under "Transport and Communications" (petrol, railway and bus services, postage, telephone). The price of the transaction (the total price) is always used in computing the index, regardless of the form of payment or the conditions for reimbursement by social security schemes (as regards health care expenditures).

Public education is free of charge. To the extent that certain representative items may not be free, the price paid by the consumer is used in computing the index.

Reduced prices, discounts and rebates are used in computing the index provided the products concerned are available to all consumers in substantial quantities for a period of at least one month, and have the same characteristics as the usual products.

Clearance sale prices are not used, since sales are limited by regulation to 15 days and, furthermore, do not meet the other conditions established for reduced prices.

The prices collected are those quoted on the index reference date, i.e. the first of the month, regardless of the form of payment agreed between buyer and seller.

Second-hand purchases and trade-in of used goods are not taken into account in the index.

The prices used are the final consumer prices to households. Intermediate prices, if any, are not taken into account.

Housing
The rent considered is the price paid by the renter for an unfurnished dwelling, net of service and other charges. The dwellings considered are generally representative of the overall population. No type of dwelling is excluded a priori.

Rent data are collected from individual renters twice a year, with one sixth of the sample surveyed each month. Rent data are collected by telephone (occasionally by mail). The rent index (two separate items: apartment rent and house rent) is the arithmetic average of specific indices computed for each dwelling in the two samples.

Owner-occupied dwellings are not included in the index (as regards expenditure items).

Specification of varieties
The specifications are detailed as regards variety, brand and model. They are the exclusive responsibility of the Service central de la statistique et des études économiques (STATEC) and are confidential.

Substitution, quality change, etc.
If there is a change in quality, either: the product's essential characteristics are unchanged, in which case any change in the price is reflected in the index without adjustment; or the change affects the product's essential characteristics, in which case the part of the price increase due to the quality change is neutralised. In practice, changes in quality are accompanied by changes in price, and it is therefore a question of determining whether the change in price corresponds to the change in quality in whole or in part. If necessary, a full or partial link is carried out.

In future, the goods and services basket will be reviewed every five years. In the interval, its composition remains constant. Nevertheless, if a new product comes on to the market and is widely consumed, it is incorporated in the index by a linking method as a representative variety of an item in the basket.

If an item or quality disappears from the market, it is replaced by another with similar characteristics, ideally in the same outlet. If the new variety is of the same brand and fills the same consumer needs, it is included in the index with account taken of any parallel price variation. If the new variety has basically different characteristics (including customer service), or if it carries another brand name, it is included in the index as a replacement using a linking method.

Seasonal items
Fresh fruit and vegetables have fixed weights: the composition of the representative baskets for each of these items varies each month, as do the weights for the different varieties covered. The computations for these items are based on a 12-month moving average.

Other seasonal items that are not available year-round remain in the index out of season, at the same price as was last quoted, pending their reappearance on the market.

Computation
The index is computed according to the Laspeyres formula as a weighted arithmetic average with fixed base 1990 = 100, using weights corresponding to 1986-87.

Price relatives for the current and base periods are used to compute item indices.

Other information
The general index, group indices, major sub-group indices and indices for several important items are published each month. All sub-group indices are available to the public on request.

Organisation and publication
The index is computed and published each month by the Service central de la statistique et des études économiques, in "Indicateurs rapides du STATEC, série A1, Indice des prix à la consommation" (Luxembourg).

Idem: "Cahier économique du STATEC no. 81, Le nouvel indice des prix à la consommation, Réforme de 1990/91".

Idem: "Note de conjoncture" (quarterly).

Idem: "Annuaire statistique".

MACAU

Official title
Indice de Preços no Consumidor (Consumer Price Index).

Scope
The index is computed monthly and covers households with an average monthly expenditure of 3,313 Pataca. It covers the peninsula of Macau (excluding the two islands of Taipa and Coloane).

Official base
October 1982-September 1983 = 100.

Source of weights
The weights and items were derived from a household expenditure survey conducted during one year in 1981-82 among a random sample of 1,560 households. The reference period for expenditure data for each household was two weeks. The weights were not adjusted to take into account price changes between the survey period and the base period.

The criteria and method of selecting items for price collection are based on the weights for items derived from the household expenditure survey, the popularity of the items and the possibility that they could be regularly and continuously priced over time. The weights of items not priced were are redistributed to similar items by either direct imputation or proportion.

Weights and composition

Major groups	Number of items	Weights	Approximate number of price quotations
Food	72	42.03	...
Alcoholic beverages and tobacco	4	2.22	...
Rent	-	-	-
Fuel and light	4	4.78	...
Household expenditure	8	1.63	...
Clothing and footwear	29	7.25	...
Durable goods	26	2.91	...
Miscellaneous goods	29	4.97	...
Transport	17	4.88	...
Services	35	8.14	...
Total	224	78.81	...

Household consumption expenditure
The definition of consumption expenditure used for deriving the weights covers all expenditure of households for the purchase goods and services. Since these payments were made at the moment of purchase, all consumption expenditure of households during the cycle was recorded.

Credit purchase was considered as expenditure only if they were paid for during the cycle. Goods and services received by the household as income in kind were valued at market prices. Rents were imputed for home ownership and free housing. Excluded were income and other direct taxes, mortgage, investment, betting, contribution to pension funds, life insurance, etc.

Method of data collection
Prices are collected by agents or postal questionnaires from markets, retail outlets and service establishments in all five localities. Fresh food prices are obtained each day and week, those for other food items each month. Each day, enumerators collect the prices for fresh food in the market early in the morning and then the prices for other goods and services according to the time schedule.

Prices for alcoholic drinks, tobacco, clothing, footwear, durable goods, miscellaneous goods are obtained every two months and those for the remaining items once every three or six months.

Sudden price changes of items such as gas, electricity, water, newspapers, etc. are recorded when they occur.

Discount and sale prices not exceeding 20 per cent are collected and used in the index calculation. Black-market prices, hire-purchase or credit terms, second-hand purchases and trade-in of used goods and in part payment for new goods are not taken into account.

The prices actually paid by consumers buying the items and services for the purpose of consumption are used.

Housing
The rent component is excluded from the index.

Specification of varieties
There are detailed specifications for each item, i.e. variety, quality, place of origin, brand, unit, size, packaging, etc. Prices are collected following the same specifications each month.

Substitution, quality change, etc.
In there are quality changes or a given type or quality disappears from the market, the following methods are used: either direct substitution using a linking method between the old item (variety) and the substitute item (variety) or recalculation of the price relative which is imputed in the existing sub-group.

Seasonal items
Clothing is divided into summer and winter clothing. In summer, the prices of summer clothes clothes are collected while those of winter clothes are kept constant, and vice versa in winter.

Computation
The index is computed according to the Laspeyres formula as a weighted arithmetic average with fixed base, using weights corresponding to 1981-82.

Other information
Sub-groups are published for food, housing, fuel and light, alco-

holic beverages and tobacco, clothing and footwear, durable goods, miscellaneous goods, transport and vehicles, services.

Organisation and publication
Direcçao de Servicios de Estatistica e Censos: "Indice de Preços no Consumidor" (Macau).

Idem: "Metodologia do Indice de Preços no Consumidor".

MADAGASCAR (ANTANANARIVO)

Official title
Indice des prix de détail à la consommation familiale malgache (Retail Price Index - Malagasy).

Scope
The index is compiled monthly and relates to Malagasy households in Antananarivo.

Official base
August 1971-July 1972 = 100.

Source of weights
The weights and items were derived from a household expenditure survey conducted from March 1968 to February 1969 among Malagasy households of all sizes and categories in Antananarivo.

The items used in computing the index are all items with a market value to which a specific unit and quality can be assigned and whose price over time is easy to observe. These items have a relative share in total expenditure that is equal to or higher than 0.05 per cent for the "Malagasy index".

Weights and composition

Major groups	Number of items	Weights	Approximate number of price quotations
Food	60	603.5	3,636
Fuel and light	8	91.4	140
Clothing and footwear	15	85.5	144
Household goods	3	4.1	56
Cleaning materials	5	20.3	292
Personal and medical care	20	38.6	988
Domestic services	1	18.2	1
Miscellaneous	19	138.4	390
Total	131	1,000.0	5,647

Household consumption expenditure
Own-consumption is taken into account in computing the weights. No account is taken of rent expenditure or owner-occupied housing. Expenditure on the following items is also excluded: durable goods, education, insurance other than for vehicles, contributions, gifts, income tax and other taxes, fines, transfers, personal goods and miscellaneous expenditure. Wages paid for domestic services (not taking account of benefits in kind) and the running expenses and insurance of private vehicles are included.

Method of data collection
Price observation is limited to a certain number of shops selected so as to correspond to the population covered by the index and to reflect the size of the reference population which makes its purchases there. The shops are selected empirically, taking account of the site, type or category of shop and of the distribution of the reference population. The number and the distribution of the shops vary according to the group of items.

The prices of food items and cleaning materials are collected in 20 shops in the town centre and in areas where there is quite a large Malagasy population.

The prices of certain food items such as poultry and fresh fruit and vegetables are obtained during the first, second and fourth weeks of each month by direct purchase by agents in two important weekly public markets. The prices of the other items are collected by means of questionnaires sent each month to some 40 retail shops and service establishments.

Data on domestic services are obtained once a year by means of a special survey of a sample of households. The list of these households is brought up to date every year by reference to the list of employers provided by the Caisse Nationale de Prévoyance Sociale (national social insurance fund).

Housing
Rent is not included as an index item, nor was it taken into account in determining the weights.

Specification of varieties
Items are specified and defined by the terms most familiar to tradespeople and buyers and which influence the price (type, quality, size, weight, country of origin, etc.). The method of acquiring the items is also one of the factors included in the specifications, and is provided on the basis of the behaviour of the reference households. For items that are not homogeneous, especially manufactured goods, the definitions are not strict but each shop is obliged to give the price for the same variety of item.

Substitution, quality change, etc.
If a shop closes down or changes its activity, a comparable substitute is sought, if possible in the same area.

If an item disappears from the market and an equivalent cannot be found, but a similar one has already been introduced in the index, the weight of the item that has disappeared is attributed to the similar item. If a similar item has not been introduced and a substitute cannot be found, its weight is distributed among the various items of the same group.

In most cases, the disappearance of an item leads to the appearance of a new one. Generally, therefore, there is a certain period when the prices of the two items can be collected and when the difference in quality and price can be evaluated so that the link does not conceal the real difference in price. The new item is not incorporated in the index until its sales volume has become fairly significant.

Seasonal items
Seasonal fluctuations in the prices of fresh fruit and vegetables are taken into account by shifting the monthly item weights within the constant group weights.

Computation
The index is computed according to the Laspeyres formula as a weighted arithmetic average with fixed base, using weights corresponding to March 1968-February 1969.

Organisation and publication
Ministère des Finances, Direction générale de la Banque de données de l'Etat: "Bulletin mensuel de statistique" (Antananarivo).

Idem: "Situation économique".

Direction générale du gouvernement, Direction de l'Institut national de la statistique et de la recherche économique: "L'établissement des nouveaux indices des prix de détail à la consommation familiale à Tananarive, base août 1971 à juillet 1972 = 100" (Antananarivo).

MADAGASCAR (ANTANANARIVO, EUROPEANS)

Official title
Indice des prix de détail à la consommation familiale européenne (Retail price index for European families).

Scope
The index is compiled monthly and relates to European families in Antananarivo.

Official base
August 1971-July 1972 = 100.

Source of weights
The weights and items were derived from a household expenditure survey conducted from May to June 1969 among European families of all sizes and categories in Antananarivo.

The items used in computing the index are all items with a market value to which a specific unit and quality can be assigned and whose prices can be easily observed over a period of time. These items have a relative share in the total expenditure that is equal to or higher than 0.03 per cent for the "European index".

Household consumption expenditure
Own-consumption was taken into account in computing the weights. No account was taken of rent expenditure or of owner-occupied housing.

Expenditure on the following items was also excluded: durable goods, education, insurance other than for vehicles, contributions, gifts, income tax and other taxes, fines, transfers, personal goods and miscellaneous expenditure. Wages paid for domestic services (not taking account of benefits in kind) and

Weights and composition

Major groups	Number of items	Weights	Approximate number of price quotations (a)
Food	105	451.6	7,110
Fuel and light	5	60.8	20
Clothing and footwear	20	76.2	508
Household goods	5	6.4	324
Cleaning materials	12	29.7	804
Personal and medical care	24	67.6	1,576
Domestic services	3	112.6	36
Miscellaneous	25	195.1	475
Total	199	1,000.0	10,853

Note: (a) Number of annual quotations.

the running expenses and insurance of private vehicles were included.

Method of data collection
Price observation is limited to a certain number of shops selected so as to correspond to the population covered by the index and to reflect the size of the reference population which makes its purchases there. The shops were selected empirically, taking account of the site, type or category of shop and of the distribution of the reference population. The number and distribution of the shops vary according to the group of items.

The prices of food items and cleaning materials are collected in 23 supermarkets and large grocery stores in town centres and in areas where there is quite a large European population.

The prices of certain food items such as fresh fruit and vegetables are obtained every six days by direct purchase of these items by agents in the major public market. The prices of the other items are collected by means of questionnaires sent each month to some 43 retail shops and establishments.

Data on domestic services are obtained once a year by means of a special survey of a sample of households. The list of these households is brought up to date every year by reference to the list of employers provided by the Caisse Nationale de Prévoyance Sociale (national social insurance fund).

Housing
Rent is not included as an index item, nor was it taken into account in determining the weights.

Specification of varieties
Items are specified and defined by the terms most familiar to tradespeople and buyers and which influence the price (type, quality, size, weight, country of origin, etc.). The method of acquiring the items is also one of the factors that appears in the specifications of the item and is provided on the basis of the behaviour of the reference households. For items that are not homogeneous, especially manufactured goods, the definitions are not strict but each shop is obliged to give the price for the same variety of item.

Substitution, quality change, etc.
If a shop closes down or changes its activity, a comparable substitute is sought, if possible in the same area.

If an item disappears from the market and an equivalent cannot be found, but a similar one has already been introduced in the index, the weight of the item that has disappeared is attributed to the similar item. If a similar item has not been introduced and a substitute cannot be found, its weight is distributed among the various items of the same group.

In most cases, the disappearance of an item leads to the appearance of a new one. Generally, therefore, there is a certain period when the prices of the two items can be collected and when the difference in quality and price can be evaluated so that the link does not conceal the real difference in price. The new item is not incorporated in the index until its sales volume has become fairly significant.

Seasonal items
Seasonal fluctuations in the prices of fresh fruit and vegetables are taken into account by shifting the month item weights within the constant group weights.

Computation
The index is computed according to the Laspeyres formula as a weighted arithmetic average with fixed base, using weights corresponding to May-June 1969.

Organisation and publication
Ministère des Finances, Direction générale de la Banque de données de l'Etat: "Bulletin mensuel de statistique" (Antananarivo).

Idem: "Situation économique".

Direction générale du gouvernement, Direction de l'Institut national de la statistique et de la recherche économique: "L'établissement des nouveaux indices des prix de détail à la consommation familiale à Tananarive, base août 1971-juillet 1972 = 100" (Antananarivo).

MALAWI (BLANTYRE 1)

Official title
Retail Price Index for Low-Income Group Families.

Scope
The index is compiled monthly and covers households in Blantyre with monthly expenditure below 100 kwachas during 1979-80.

Official base
1980 = 100.

Source of weights
The weights and items were derived from an urban household expenditure survey conducted in 1979-80 covering 4,000 households in Blantyre, Lilongwe, Zomba and Mzuzu. The index relates to low-income group families with monthly expenditure below 100 kwachas during the period of the survey.

Weights and composition

Major groups	Number of items	Weights	Approximate number of price quotations
Food	34	500	102
Beverages and tobacco	7	39	21
Clothing and footwear	24	154	72
Housing	14	108	42
Household operation	7	86	21
Transportation	8	48	8
Miscellaneous	14	65	42
Total	108	1,000	308

Household consumption expenditure
Consumption expenditure for the purpose of the index refers to all money expenditure by households on goods and services intended for consumption, including repayment of loans.

Income in kind and imputed rent of owner-occupied dwellings are excluded.

Method of data collection
Prices are collected by agents from markets, selected retail outlets and service establishments in Blantyre. For items sold in markets, prices are collected three times a month and for all other items, prices are ascertained on the Tuesday or Friday nearest the 15th of each month. Price quotations are used for all items, except for vegetables, fruit and fish, where prices are obtained by direct buying.

The prices used to calculate the index are the regular prices paid by any member of the public. Sale, discount and reduced prices are not used.

Housing
Rent and owner-occupied housing costs are not included in the index, nor were they taken into account in determining the weights.

Specification of varieties
Detailed specifications are given for each item, describing the variety, quality, make, brand and unit.

Substitution, quality change, etc.
When a product is no longer available, a similar product to the original is substituted and a method of linking is used.

Seasonal items
Prices of seasonal items are estimated during their off season.

Computation
The index is computed according to the Laspeyres formula as a weighted arithmetic average with fixed base, using weights corresponding to 1979-80.

At least three price quotations are obtained for each item to calculate average prices.

Other information
The National Statistical Office also compiles and publishes series relating to medium- and high-income group households in Blantyre and Lilongwe and to low- and medium-income group households in Zomba and Mzuzu. In addition, Blantyre and Lilongwe are combined to arrive at a composite index for the two cities.

Organisation and publication
National Statistical Office: "Monthly Statistical Bulletin" (Zomba).

MALAWI (BLANTYRE 2)

Official title
Retail Price Index for High-Income Group Families.

Scope
The index is compiled quarterly and covers households in Blantyre with monthly expenditure of 400 kwachas or more during 1979-80.

Official base
1980 = 100.

Source of weights
The weights and items were derived from a household expenditure survey conducted in 1979-80, covering 400 households in Blantyre with monthly expenditure of 400 kwachas or more during the survey period.

Weights and composition

Major groups	Number of items	Weights	Approximate number of price quotations
Food	49	203	147
Beverages and tobacco	14	76	42
Clothing and footwear	27	71	81
Housing	26	130	78
Household operation	12	108	36
Transportation	19	253	19
Miscellaneous	26	159	78
Total	173	1,000	481

Household consumption expenditure
Consumption expenditure for the purpose of the index refers to all money expenditure by households on goods and services intended for consumption, including repayment of loans.

Income in kind and imputed rent of owner-occupied dwellings are excluded.

Method of data collection
Prices are collected by agents from markets, selected retail outlets and service establishments in Blantyre. For most of the items, prices are obtained on the Tuesday or Friday nearest the 15th of each month. Prices of important food items are ascertained three times a month through direct buying in two market areas. Data for servants' wages are obtained from an annual inquiry. Data for other services are obtained from appropriate service establishments.

The prices used to calculate the index are the regular prices paid by any member of the public. Sale, discount and reduced prices are not used.

Housing
Rent and owner-occupied housing costs are not included in the index, nor were they taken into account in determining the weights.

Specification of varieties
Detailed specifications are given for each item, describing the variety, quality, make, brand and unit.

Substitution, quality change, etc.
If a product is no longer available, a similar product to the original is substituted and a method of linking is used.

Seasonal items
Prices for seasonal items are estimated during their off season.

Computation
The index is computed according to the Laspeyres formula as a weighted arithmetic average with fixed base, using weights corresponding to 1979-80.

At least three price quotations are obtained for each item to calculate average prices.

Other information
The National Statistical Office also compiles and publishes series relating to low- and medium-income group households in Blantyre and Lilongwe and to low- and medium-income group households in Zomba and Mzuzu. In addition, Blantyre and Lilongwe are combined to arrive at a composite index for the two cities.

Organisation and publication
National Statistical Office: "Monthly Statistical Bulletin" (Zomba).

MALAYSIA

Official title
Consumer Price Index.

Scope
The index is computed monthly and covers all private households in urban and rural areas.

Official base
1980 = 100.

Source of weights
The weights and items were derived from a household expenditure survey conducted in Peninsular Malaysia during the month of December 1980, covering about 3,000 private households, and from a household expenditure survey conducted in Sabah and Sarawak during six months from May to October 1982, covering about 3,000 private households. The weights were not adjusted to take into account price changes between the survey year and the base year, although the Peninsular Malaysia expenditure proportions were adjusted to reflect the situation in 1982. Items with relatively larger weights are selected for price collection. For items with weights but for which price collection is not possible, the weighted price relative of other items within the group or sub-group is used in the price relative for that item. The weights of items not selected are redistributed to selected items within the group.

Weights and composition

Major groups	Number of items	Weights	Approximate number of price quotations
Food	468	36.9	32,539
Beverages and tobacco	42	4.7	2,026
Clothing and footwear	96	4.8	2,053
Gross rent, fuel and light	46	18.7	1,017
Furniture, furnishings, household equipment and operation	170	5.8	5,676
Medical care	64	1.2	2,010
Transport and communication	119	16.0	499
Recreation, education and cultural services	105	6.4	863
Miscellaneous goods and services	139	5.5	5,414
Total	1,249	100.0	52,097

Household consumption expenditure
The expenditure data were collected using the acquisition approach, which requires that all household expenditure outlays on goods and services be recorded at the point in time the purchases were made. Goods on hire-purchase were considered to have been bought at the time when the hire-purchase contracts were signed, or, if there were no contracts, when the goods were delivered. In addition, the concept of household expenditure on goods and services used in the survey includes items purchased as well as those produced on own account and used in final consumption. Imputed rents of owner-occupied dwellings, consumption from own production or stocks, goods and services furnished to employees free of charge or at reduced rates, and goods received as wages in kind and gifts were included in the estimation of household expenditure. Purchases of goods and services by households from government bodies, including fees which are charged in respect of public hospitals, were also considered as consumption expenditure if there was a clear link between the payment and the acquisition of the services or goods and if the decisions to make such payment were voluntary. Income tax, social security contributions, compensation paid, compulsory fees and fines and remittances to other households, amounts invested or loaned, repayment of loans, additions to savings, gambling losses, cash grants and donations and free recreational and cultural services provided

to the population at large by the government were not considered as part of household consumption expenditure.

Method of data collection
Prices for all categories of goods and services are collected around the middle of each month by agents, from about 6,800 markets, retail outlets and service establishments in 103 price collection centres (localities) throughout Malaysia.

Discounted prices are taken as the normal selling prices. Sale prices are taken if the items are sold in sufficient quantities. Some items come under the control of the Supplies Act and frequently the recommended price for the item is widely publicised. It is possible that these items may be sold at free-market prices. The criteria for price collection is the normal selling price. If the respondent quotes the "official" price as the normal selling price, this price is recorded. Black-market prices do not arise. Only cash prices are taken; hire-purchase or credit terms prices are not considered. Second-hand purchases are not priced. Prices for imported items are taken inclusive of import duties and sales tax.

Housing
The rent survey is carried out each quarter in January, April, July and October. A panel of rented dwellings is interviewed by field enumerators. The total rent according to type of dwelling is first computed and this is linked to the previous rent relative by type-of-dwelling index. The linked type-of-dwelling index is then weighted using the type-of-dwelling weight to obtain the rent index.

Owner-occupied housing is not included in the index.

Specification of varieties
Specifications were developed by obtaining product specifications from manufacturers and producers. Both detailed and broad specifications are used. The descriptions for items with detailed specifications include the brand, grade, unit, make, quality, etc. General descriptions are given for broadly-specified items, and store-specific brands are selected.

Substitution, quality change, etc.
No attempt is made to quantify quality changes with changes in model for electrical appliances, motor vehicles or other products such as clothing. New products are linked to the index only if they are taken as substitutes. If a given type or quality disappears from the market, a close substitute is priced and linked.

Seasonal items
For items with strong seasonal fluctuations, current prices are used in the index calculations only in the months when they are in season. When they are out of season, index calculations are based on the average prices for the last season.

Computation
The index is computed according to the Laspeyres formula as a weighted arithmetic average with fixed base, using weights corresponding to the base period.

The price relative for each item for each price collection centre within the region is computed by dividing the average price for each centre by its base price. These price relatives are weighted by the centre weights to give the item price relatives; which are in turn weighted by the item weights to give the sub-group and overall indices. Unsubstantiated low or high prices are deleted and the previous price inserted. Missing prices are also inserted. The unsubstantiated prices are queried and the necessary action taken to accept or reject them.

The index is computed directly at the regional level. However, the index at the three-digit level for Malaysia is computed as a composite index taking into consideration the expenditure proportions of the three regions.

Other information
Indices for the nine major groups and the sub-groups of the Food index are published. Indices for the reclassification of goods in terms of Durables, Semi-durables, Non-durables and Services are also available.

Organisation and publication
Department of Statistics "Consumer Price Index for Malaysia" (Kuala Lumpur). A brief description of the methodology is given in this publication.

MALI (BAMAKO)

Official title
Indice des prix du groupe "Alimentation" - marchés de Bamako (Price Index for Food Items - markets of Bamako).

Scope
The index is compiled monthly and relates to households with at least four members, in Bamako.

Official base
1 July 1962 - 1 July 1963 = 100.

Source of weights
The weights were estimated from a pilot household expenditure survey conducted in March 1963 in Bamako among households with at least four members and from comparisons of weights used in the compilation of indices for other African countries with similar consumption patterns.

Weights and composition

Major groups	Number of items	Weights	Approximate number of price quotations
Food:			
Flour and starch	4	33.9	...
Seasoning	5	8.0	...
Fresh fruit and vegetables	5	9.1	...
Meat and fish	5	38.1	...
Milk, fats, miscellaneous	5	10.9	...
Total	24	100.0	...

Household consumption expenditure
Not available.

Method of data collection
Prices are collected by agents three or four times a month, from nine markets in Bamako.

Housing
Not available.

Specification of varieties
Not available.

Substitution, quality change, etc.
Not available.

Seasonal items
No adjustment is made for seasonal fluctuations in prices.

Computation
The index is computed according to the Laspeyres formula as a weighted arithmetic average with fixed base, using weights corresponding to March 1963.

Other information
Since 1988, a National Consumer Price Index (base July 1986 - June 1987 = 100) has been computed, covering the towns of Kayes, Sikasso and Bamako. This series is published in the "Year Book" and "Bulletin of Labour Statistics", but the relevant methodological information was not available in the ILO at the time the present volume was published.

Organisation and publication
Ministère du Plan, Direction nationale de la statistique et de l'informatique: "Bulletin mensuel de statistique" (Bamako).

MALTA

Official title
Retail Price Index.

Scope
The index is compiled monthly and covers employees' households.

Official base
1983 = 100.

Source of weights
The weights and items were derived from a household expenditure survey conducted in 1983, covering employees' households with two to six persons, not more than two full-time working members and the head of the household earning 23 and 40

pounds per week. Households of professional and own-account workers and pensioners were excluded.

Weights and composition

Major groups	Number of items	Weights	Approximate number of price quotations
Food	90	41.91	...
Beverages and tobacco	13	9.46	...
Clothing and footwear	37	10.57	...
Housing:			
Rent	2	1.90	...
Water charges	2	0.25	...
Maintenance and repairs	5	1.82	...
Fuel and light	5	3.14	...
Furniture, furnishings and household equipment	29	6.15	...
Transport and communication	13	9.93	...
Personal and medical care	33	5.55	...
Education and recreation	31	4.92	...
Other goods and services	14	4.40	...
Total	274	100.00	...

Household consumption expenditure
Fees for driving licence and motor car insurance premiums are excluded.

Method of data collection
Prices for most items are collected once a month by agents, from retail outlets and service establishments in 13 localities. Prices for fresh fruit, vegetables, meat and fish are ascertained three times a month. The prices used to calculate the index are the prices actually paid.

Housing
Rent quotations are obtained from an annual survey of 400 households living in rented dwellings. No account is taken of owner-occupied housing in the index.

Specification of varieties
Not available.

Substitution, quality change, etc.
If the quality of an item changes or an item appears on the market, a new series of prices is established.

Seasonal items
Seasonal fluctuations in the prices of certain items are taken into account by varying monthly item weights within constant group weights.

Computation
The index is computed according to the Laspeyres formula as a weighted arithmetic average with fixed base, using weights corresponding to the base period.

The national index is the average for the 13 localities.

Other information
Sub-groups are published for Food, beverages and tobacco, Clothing and footwear, Housing, Fuel and power, Furniture, furnishings and household equipment, Transport and communications, Personal care and health, Educational, entertainment and recreation, and Other goods and services.

A new series (base 1991 = 100) is now computed, but the relevant methodological information was not available in the ILO at the time the present volume was published.

Organisation and publication
Central Office of Statistics: "Quarterly Digest of Statistics" (Valletta).

Idem: "Annual Abstract of Statistics.".

Idem: "Report on Proposals for a New Index of Retail Prices - 1984".

MARTINIQUE

Official title
Indice des prix à la consommation (Consumer Price Index).

Scope
The index is compiled monthly and relates to urban households with average income and expenditure, but including only households whose head is a wage earner or salaried employee in the non-agricultural private and public sectors, excluding the armed forces.

Official base
1979 = 100.

Source of weights
The weights were calculated on the basis of data from various sources, such as administrative records and production and trade statistics, supplemented by private consumption expenditure patterns for France and Réunion.

Weights and composition

Major groups	Number of items	Weights	Approximate number of price quotations
Food	57	31.66	...
Clothing and footwear	24	8.79	...
Housing:			
Fuel and light	4	4.33	...
Rent	1	9.96	...
Furniture, household goods, maintenance and other services	25	10.83	...
Personal and medical care	12	8.58	...
Transport	12	16.44	...
Education and recreation	31	9.41	...
Total	166	100.00	...

Household consumption expenditure
Consumption expenditure for the purpose of the index comprises all the important goods and services purchased for consumption by the index population including expenditure on domestic and administrative services. It excludes direct taxes, building costs considered as investment, home-produced goods consumed by households, the value of owner-occupied dwellings, second-hand purchases, social security contributions and insurance premium payments.

Method of data collection
Prices are collected by agents from about 277 retail outlets, markets and service establishments in two main urban areas: Fort-de-France and Schoelcher. Prices are obtained each month for most items. Prices of fresh food, namely fish, fruit and vegetables, are ascertained twice a month from retail shops and weekly from market places. Prices for some items are ascertained every three months.

The prices used to calculate the index are the retail prices actually paid.

Housing
Rent quotations are obtained every six months from a sample of 144 rented dwellings in Fort-de-France and Schoelcher.

Specification of varieties
Broad specifications are given. The price collector chooses the most popular product in each retail outlet for regular price collection.

Substitution, quality change, etc.
If a product is no longer available, it is substituted by another product with approximately the same quality. If the quality of the substitute is not directly comparable with that of the old product, adjustments are made for quality changes whenever possible.

Seasonal items
Seasonal fluctuations in the prices of fresh fish, fruit and vegetables are taken into account by varying the items and item weights within monthly baskets of constant group weights.

Computation
The index is computed according to the Laspeyres formula as a weighted arithmetic average with fixed base.

Price relatives for the current and base periods are used to compute item indices. Relatives of average prices are calculated for most items, but for heterogeneous varieties, averages of price relatives are computed.

Other information
Detailed sub-groups are published for this series.

Organisation and publication
INSEE, Service régional de la Martinique, "Bulletin statistique de la Martinique" (Fort-de-France).

Idem: "Sélection mensuelle de statistiques".

INSEE, Service interrégional Antilles-Guyane: "L'indice des prix de la Martinique, base 100 en 1979; Méthodes, bilan 1979-1984 et perspectives", Les dossiers Antilles-Guyane (Fort-de-France, June 1985).

MAURITIUS

Official title
Consumer Price Index.

Scope
The index is computed monthly and covers all types of households, all population groups and all geographic areas.

Official base
July 1986-June 1987 = 100.

Source of weights
The weights and items were derived from a household expenditure survey conducted from July 1986 to June 1987 on a sample basis such that all types of households, all population groups and all geographic areas of Mauritius were represented in the selected sample of 4,320 households.

Items are selected on the basis of the survey. They must be commonly bought by Mauritian households, normally available for pricing in shops or markets and available for some years to come in order to ensure continuity. The weights of items which are not priced are simply redistributed over identical items of that commodity sub-group.

Weights and composition

Major groups	Number of items	Weights	Approximate number of price quotations
Food and beverages	76	419	1,964
Alcoholic beverages and tobacco	6	72	138
Clothing and footwear	37	84	275
Housing and household operation	53	135	525
(of which gross rent)	(3)	(24)	(180)
Medical care and health expenses	10	30	136
Transport and communication	11	93	94
Recreation, entertainment, education & cultural services	20	60	158
Miscellaneous goods and services	25	50	251
Total	241	1,000	3,566

Household consumption expenditure
Goods and services obtained free or produced for own consumption are valued at the market prices prevailing at the time they were reported in the household expenditure survey. Items which were excluded when determining the weights are: goods and services provided free by the government, such as medical services, medicinal products, education and books; imputed rents of owner-occupied dwellings; contributions to social insurance and pension funds; income tax and other direct taxes; debt repayments; outlays on betting and gambling; life insurance premiums, cash gifts and remittances. Licence fees associated with private household activities and insurance associated with specific consumer goods are included.

Method of data collection
A point-of-purchase survey was carried out during the 1986-87 household expenditure survey.

The localities for price data collection were chosen not only to represent both urban and rural regions, but also in relation to their importance as shopping centres. For urban regions, all five municipal council areas (Port-Louis, Rose Hill, Quatre Bornes, Vacoas and Curepipe) were selected, while for the rural regions at least one major village was selected in the North, South, East, West and centre of the island.

The collection of price data is carried out by the staff of the Central Statistical Office.

Once the localities and outlets are selected, the statistician identifies the different items and varieties available in the outlets of each locality, such that most goods and services in the basket are priced in every locality.

Perishable goods such as fresh vegetables, fresh fruits, fresh meat and fish are priced each week in markets on a specific day.

Prices for all other goods and services are collected every month in all localities during the period from the 12th to the 18th.

Official tariffs are referred to for electricity, water, bus fares and telephone charges.

The free-market prices which are actually paid by consumers are used. Discounts and sale prices are taken into account but irregular sales such as liquidation sales are ignored.

No account is taken of black-market prices, hire-purchase or credit terms, second-hand purchases or trade-in of used goods and in part payment for new ones, or import prices.

Housing
The item "rent" covers the rent actually paid by tenants excluding electricity, water and sewerage charges.

The rent index is computed each quarter in March, June, September and December from a survey of 180 households in rented accommodation. Of the 4,320 households covered by the 1986-87 household expenditure survey, 785 were living in rented accommodation. The sample of 180 was selected from these 785 households, systematically according to region and amount of rent paid. The survey of rented dwellings is undertaken using a special questionnaire.

Owner-occupied housing is not taken into account in the index. Data on rates and expenditure on maintenance and repairs were collected in the survey and these have been included in the index.

Specification of varieties
A representative sample of varieties or indicators are selected for each item, and are priced as available on the market. Detailed specifications regarding quality, make, brand, unit, etc. are then drawn up for every item or variety in each outlet and locality.

Substitution, quality change, etc.
Quality changes are difficult to quantify. Minor changes in quality are not taken into account. When the change is substantial, the older product is assumed to have disappeared and is substituted by the changed-quality product which is linked.

When new products appear on the market, their prices are collected for future use either when revising the basket of goods and services or when a substitute is needed due to the permanent disappearance of a product from the market.

When a product is no longer available, it is replaced by the nearest similar product on the market. The base price (fictitious) of this substitute is calculated in such a way that the current price relative of the substitute is the same as that of the product being replaced.

Seasonal items
Account is taken of the seasonal fluctuations of fresh vegetables by varying the items in that sub-group each month while keeping the overall weights constant. The vegetable index compares the cost of the basket for the current month with that for the same month of the base year.

Computation
The index is computed according to the Laspeyres formula as a weighted arithmetic average with fixed base, using weights corresponding to the base period.

Price averages are calculated only for fresh vegetables, fruit, fish and meat collected from different outlets. Average prices are simple arithmetic means of all price quotations obtained.

Prices relatives are calculated by dividing current prices by base prices. If different varieties are used for an item, the price relative is calculated for each variety and weighted averages of price relatives are computed to obtain item indices.

The prices collected are carefully scrutinised at various levels to eliminate faulty reporting. If price data are missing, the previous month's price is used.

Organisation and publication
Central Statistical Office: "Annual Digest of Statistics" (Rose Hill).

Ministry of Finance: "Government Gazette of Mauritius" (Rose Hill).

MEXICO

Official title
Indice nacional de precios al consumidor (National Consumer Price Index).

Scope
The index is computed monthly and covers all urban consumers of the country.

Official base
1978 = 100.

Source of weights
The weights and items were mainly derived from a national income and expenditure survey conducted in 1977.

Weights and composition

Major groups	Number of items	Weights	Approximate number of price quotations
Food and tobacco	141	37.39	60,000
Clothing and footwear	45	9.88	40,000
Housing	6	17.77	20,000
Furniture, furnishings and household equipment	34	6.21	5,000
Personal and medical care	28	5.81	4,000
Transport	17	11.25	4,000
Education and recreation	23	5.75	5,000
Other services	8	5.94	2,000
Total	302	100.00	140,000

Household consumption expenditure
Not available.

Method of data collection
Prices for food items and tobacco are collected each week. Prices for the other items are ascertained every two weeks. The prices used to compute the index refer to those actually paid by consumers: net and cash prices (including taxes, rates and discounts if the latter was in force at least more than half of the days included in the price collection period).

Housing
Rent quotations for the 35 towns included in the index are obtained from approximately 10,000 dwellings visited directly by agents.

Specification of varieties
Not available.

Substitution, quality change, etc.
If the specification of a product changes, the linking method is adopted. If an item disappears from the market, it is replaced by a similar item using the linking method and, if necessary, a quality adjustment is made so as to ensure the principle of constant quality.

Seasonal items
Seasonal fluctuations in the prices of certain items are taken into account by maintaining the closing price of the previous season during the off season.

Computation
The index is computed according to the Laspeyres formula as a weighted arithmetic average with fixed base, using weights corresponding to 1977.
Price relatives for each variety in each outlet are first calculated by dividing the average price for the current period by the average price for the base period. A simple arithmetic average of price relatives of varieties representing an item is then computed to arrive at an item index. Separate indices are calculated for the 35 towns. The national index is a weighted average of the indices for the 35 towns, the weights being proportional to the consumption expenditure of each town.

Organisation and publication
Banco de México, Subdirección de Investigación Económica: "Indicadores Económicos" (Mexico).

MONTSERRAT

Official title
Consumer Price Index.

Scope
The index is compiled monthly and relates to the whole population.

Official base
September 1982 = 100.

Source of weights
The weights and items were derived from a household expenditure survey conducted during two weeks in 1980 among a random sample of 400 households. The weights were not adjusted to take account of price changes between 1980 and 1982. The weights of items not included in the index were distributed among the items included.

Weights and composition

Major groups	Number of items	Weights	Approximate number of price quotations
Food	73	495	...
Alcoholic beverages and tobacco	9	46	...
Household goods	37	102	...
Gas, electricity, water	3	18	...
Rent	3	7	...
Clothing and footwear	43	179	...
Services and others	34	153	...
Total	202	1,000	...

Household consumption expenditure
This includes car licence fees and car insurance.
It excludes income tax, contributions to social insurance and pension funds, remittances, gifts and similar disbursements.

Method of data collection
Prices are collected on the 15th of each month by agents from selected retail outlets and service establishments in Plymouth.
The prices used to calculate the index are the retail prices paid. Discount and sale prices are not taken into account.

Housing
Rent quotations are obtained each month for three types of furnished dwellings. Owner-occupied housing is not included in the index.

Specification of varieties
The specifications of items to be priced are given in terms of the brand name, make, quality, unit and size, etc.

Substitution, quality change, etc.
No account is taken of quality changes.

Seasonal items
No account is taken of seasonal fluctuations in item prices.

Computation
The index is computed according to the Laspeyres formula as a weighted arithmetic average with fixed base, using weights corresponding to 1980.

Organisation and publication
Government of Montserrat, Statistics Office: "Montserrat Statistical Digest" (Plymouth).
Idem: "Cost of living report".

MOROCCO

Official title
Indice du coût de la vie (Cost of Living Index).

Scope
The index is compiled monthly and relates to low-income group families in eight major cities.

Official base
May 1972-April 1973 = 100.

Source of weights
The weights and items were derived from a household expenditure survey conducted in 1970-71 among low-income group families in eight major cities of the country.

Household consumption expenditure
Not available.

Method of data collection
Prices are collected by agents from retail outlets and service establishments in eight major cities. The frequency of price collection depends on the price variability of the item.

Housing
Data on rent are obtained each quarter from a sample of three- and four-room dwellings in moderately priced neighbourhoods.

Specification of varieties
The specifications describe the quality and brand name.

Substitution, quality change, etc.
If an item is temporarily unavailable on the market, its last price is used if the price of similar products has not varied significantly; otherwise, the estimated price of the product is based

Weights and composition

Major groups	Number of items	Weights	Approximate number of price quotations
Food	83	54.0	...
Tobacco	1	1.9	...
Housing:			
Rent	1	5.8	...
Maintenance and repairs	2	1.2	...
Fuel, light and water	7	3.0	...
Furniture and household linen	14	2.1	...
Household equipment	21	1.5	...
Clothing and footwear	34	8.5	...
Cleaning materials, personal and medical care	19	5.5	...
Transport and communication	12	6.9	...
Education, recreation and miscellaneous	16	9.6	...
Total	210	100.0	...

on the price changes of similar products. If an item has disappeared permanently, it is replaced by a similar one or, if there is none, by an item of differing quality. In this case, a linking factor is applied, which is based on the prices observed for both products (the one that has disappeared and the new one) during the same period, on comparative production costs, on a product equally satisfactory for the consumer or on the development of an econometric model to determine quality differences.

Seasonal items
Seasonal fluctuations in the prices of fresh fruit and vegetables are taken into account by shifting monthly item weights within constant group weights and by using a three-month moving average in computing the final index.

Computation
The index is computed according to the Laspeyres formula as a weighted arithmetic average with fixed base, using weights corresponding to 1970-71.

Other information
Separate indices are also published separately for Agadir, Casablanca, Fes, Kénitra, Marrakesh, Oujda, Rabat and Tetouan.

Organisation and publication
Premier Ministre, Secrétariat d'Etat au plan et au développement régional, Direction de la statistique: "Bulletin mensuel de statistiques" (Rabat).

Idem: "Bulletin méthodologique trimestriel", nouvelle série no. 3 (Rabat).

MYANMAR (YANGON)

Official title
Consumer Price Index at Yangon.

Scope
The index is compiled monthly and covers all households of all levels of income in 1978. The index relates to the capital city, Yangon.

Official base
1978 = 100.

Source of weights
The weights and items were derived from the household expenditure survey conducted in 1978, covering 1,200 households in 24 townships of the Yangon Division.

Weights and composition

Major groups	Number of items	Weights	Approximate number of price quotations
Food	43	64.42	...
Tobacco	2	3.74	...
Rent and repairs	3	3.82	...
Fuel and light	6	7.84	...
Clothing and footwear	9	8.04	...
Miscellaneous	17	12.14	...
Total	80	100.00	...

Household consumption expenditure
Consumption expenditure for the purpose of the index comprises all goods and services purchased for consumption by the population. It excludes income taxes, life insurance, gifts and expenditures for ceremonies.

Method of data collection
Prices are collected from the selected markets located in the area administered by Yangon City Development Committee.

Retail prices of commodities are collected each day while prices of commodities under control are obtained once a month.

School fees and transport costs are obtained once a year from the appropriate service establishments.

Housing
The weights for rent were obtained from the 1978 household expenditure survey. The rent index is held constant at 100.

Specification of varieties
Specifications of items to be priced are given in terms of the quality, brand name, size and unit, etc.

Substitution, quality change, etc.
If a product is no longer available on the market, it is substituted by a similar product and the base year price of the old product is revised.

Seasonal items
Adjustments are made for seasonal items such as fresh fruit and vegetables to eliminate seasonal fluctuations.

Computation
The index is computed according to the Laspeyres formula as a weighted arithmetic average with fixed base, using weights corresponding to the base period.

Other information
A new series relating to Yangon (base 1986 = 100) is now computed but the relevant methodological information was not available in the ILO at the time the present volume was published.

Organisation and publication
Central Statistical Organisation: "Selected Monthly Economic Indicators" (Yangon).

Idem: "Statistical Yearbook".

Idem: "Statistical Abstracts".

NEPAL

Official title
National Urban Consumer Price Index.

Scope
The index is computed monthly and covers private households in 13 urban areas.

Official base
Mid-July 1983 - mid-July 1984 = 100.

Source of weights
The weights and items were derived from a household expenditure survey conducted from mid-March 1984 to mid-February 1985 among 1,161 private households in urban areas. The index is designed to cover all non-institutional private households residing in urban areas, except one-person households, households composed of more than ten persons, households whose total consumption expenditure was less than 450 rupees or more than 3,500 rupees, households which derived more than 50 per cent of the value of their consumption expenditure from home production or sources other than the market place. The index covers 13 urban areas.

Weights and composition

Major groups	Number of items	Weights	Approximate number of price quotations
Food	...	62.63	...
Clothing	...	10.09	...
Footwear	...	1.72	...
Housing (incl. fuel, light and water)	...	12.66	...
Transport and communication	...	2.13	...
Personal and medical care	...	4.59	...
Education, reading and recreation	...	4.14	...
Tobacco	...	2.04	...
Total	...	100.00	...

Household consumption expenditure
Included is the total value of goods and services purchased,

home-produced goods and received free and as part of wage income and consumed, including the rental value of owner-occupied dwellings and free housing. Excluded are direct taxes, gifts and contributions, insurance premiums, occupational expenses, consumer debts, lottery tickets, money losses, expenditure on weddings, litigation expenses, etc.

Method of data collection
Prices are collected from about 700 retail stores and establishments by personal visits.

Prices are collected each week for fresh fruit and vegetables, each fortnight for fresh fish, milk and milk products, etc., and each month for clothing, fuel, etc. Prices for all other items are collected each quarter, except for education fees, physicians' fees, electricity charges and water charges, which are priced once a year.

The prices used in the index are those that any member of the public would have to pay on the pricing day to purchase the specified item or service, including sales and excise taxes.

The investigators collect prices from retail outlets on the cash payment basis. If the goods are not available on the free market, the prevailing black-market price is collected.

Housing
Rent data are collected each year through the house rent survey which covers about 448 households. No account is taken of owner-occupied housing in the index.

Specification of varieties
A number of market surveys were conducted in each sample town, mainly to select outlets and specifications for pricing. Each of the priced items in each of the selected centres is described in specifications which give the size, weight, materials used, workmanship and other qualitative and quantitative features.

Substitution, quality change, etc.
If a specific item is not available on the market, an appropriate substitution is made and the index is adjusted for the change in quality.

Seasonal items
For seasonal items such as fresh fish, fruit and vegetables that are not available on the market during the off season, the last available prices are used to calculate the index until new prices are available.

Computation
The index is computed according to the Laspeyres formula as a weighted arithmetic average with fixed base, using weights corresponding to the base period.

To obtain the national urban index, the three regional indices are combined, using regional weights based on the total urban population of each region.

Other information
Separate indices are published for the three regions: Urban Consumer Price Index for Kathmandu, Urban Consumer Price Index for Hills, Urban consumer Price index for Terai.

Organisation and publication
Publications: Nepal Rastra Bank, Research Department: "Main Economic Indicators".

NETHERLANDS

Official title
Price Index Numbers of Final Consumption Expenditure.

Scope
The index is compiled monthly. It covers households of wage earners and salaried employees, consisting of adults without children or with resident children without incomes, and whose family incomes in 1985 were below the wage limit for compulsory sickness benefit insurance. The index covers the whole country.

Official base
1985 = 100.

Source of weights
The weights and items were derived from the household expenditure survey conducted in 1985 among a sample of 962 households.

Weights and composition

Major groups	Number of items	Weights	Approximate number of price quotations
Food	234	21.3	...
Clothing and footwear	120	6.8	...
Medical care	5	11.4	...
Household goods	60	6.6	...
Rent, fuel and light	41	27.2	...
Transport and communication	49	11.4	...
Education and recreation	103	8.4	...
Other goods and services	78	6.9	...
Total	690	100.0	(a) ...

Note: (a) Every month an average number of 100,000 prices are collected (excluding rents, on which data are collected whenever there is a general rent increase).

Household consumption expenditure
Consumption expenditure for the purpose of the index comprises all consumer goods and services on which private households incur expenditure, including the purchases made from shops, department stores and other suppliers; payments for services of mechanics or craftsmen; spending in hotels, restaurants and cafés; payments for transportation and public amusements; payments for services of physicians, specialists, hospitals, pharmaceutical products and other medical care; payments for domestic services; the administrative costs of life insurance and pension funds; and spending on durable goods such as furniture, radio sets, etc. It excludes voluntary transfers by families to non-profit-making institutions; transfers within the household sector; compulsory transfers by households to the government and social insurance institutions; and savings in the form of premium payments for life insurance and pensions.

Method of data collection
Prices are collected each month on the Thursday of the week including the 15th, from selected outlets comprising market and street vendors, mobile shops, department stores, small, medium and large retail outlets, wholesalers and service establishments in 100 municipalities with over 10,000 inhabitants.

Prices are collected for about 1,200 items. Mail inquiries are used for a number of items (excluding house rent), which together account for about 38 per cent of the total weight. The prices collected are those actually paid by the consumer and include indirect taxes. Clearance sales are covered only when consumers can benefit without much difficulty and when they last for at least one week. Discounts given in cash at the time of purchase are deducted. Electricity, gas and water prices are collected from the relevant companies.

Housing
Rent data are collected by mail, mainly from house owners or administrators. Investigators collect rent data directly from the tenants of about three per cent of rented housing, as mail inquiry did not appear feasible for these cases. The rent inquiry takes place in 482 of the 702 municipalities in the Netherlands.

The purchase of dwellings by private individuals for their own use is not included in the index, but the services derived from these dwellings are considered to be part of family consumption. The value of such services is taken as corresponding to the rent of comparable rented dwellings.

Specification of varieties
There are very precise quality descriptions for all goods and services. Attention is paid to the weight, number, make, size, material (for clothing), etc.

Substitution, quality change, etc.
New products are included in the weighting scheme at the next change of base year. When an item disappears, another similar item is substituted and a linking method is used.

Seasonal items
The group weights for potatoes, fresh vegetables and fruit, flowers and indoor plants are kept constant each month. The monthly within-group weights of these groups are not those for the base year, but are based on an average ratio calculated over a number of years ending with the base year.

There are two baskets for seasonal clothing and footwear: one for the winter months and the other for the summer months. In March and September both baskets are included in the weighting scheme, each with half of the weight for this sub-group.

Computation
The index is computed according to the Laspeyres formula as a weighted arithmetic average with fixed base, using weights corresponding to the base period.

The price relative for each item is calculated by dividing the average price for the current period by the average price for the base period.

Organisation and publication
Centraal Bureau voor de Statistiek (Central Bureau of Statistics): "Maandstatistiek van de prijzen" (Monthly Bulletin of Price Statistics) (Voorburg).

Idem: "Statistisch bulletin" (Statistical Bulletin).

NETHERLANDS ANTILLES

Official title
Consumer Price Index.

Scope
The index is compiled monthly and relates to the whole population of Curaçao and Bonaire.

Official base
December 1984 = 100.

Source of weights
The weights and items were derived from a household expenditure survey conducted in 1981 among a sample of the whole population living in Curaçao and Bonaire.

Weights and composition

Major groups	Number of items	Weights	Approximate number of price quotations
Food	9	22.07	...
Beverages and tobacco	2	2.32	...
Clothing and footwear	2	8.68	...
Housing (incl. rent, fuel and light, and household expenditure)	5	18.76	...
Furniture, furnishings and household equipment	7	9.96	...
Medical care	1	2.16	...
Transport and communication	4	19.45	...
Education and recreation	5	5.95	...
Other (incl. personal care, insurance and other goods and services)	3	10.65	...
Total	(a) 38	100.00	...

Note: (a) Number of sub-groups.

Household consumption expenditure
Not available.

Method of data collection
Prices are collected from retail outlets and service establishments.

Housing
Not available.

Specification of varieties
Not available.

Substitution, quality change, etc.
Not available.

Seasonal items
Not available.

Computation
The index is computed according to the Laspeyres formula as a weighted arithmetic average with fixed base, using weights corresponding to 1981.

Other information
A new series (base October 1990 = 100) is now computed but the relevant methodological information was not available in the ILO at the time the present volume was published.

Organisation and publication
Central Bureau of Statistics: "Statistical Monthly Bulletin" (Willemstad).

NEW CALEDONIA (NOUMEA)

Official title
Indice des prix de détail à la consommation (Consumer Price Index).

Scope
The index is computed monthly and covers urban households of wage earners and salaried employees in the private and public sectors (excluding wage earners in agriculture).

Official base
August 1975 = 100.

Source of weights
The weights and items were derived from a household expenditure survey conducted in 1968-69 among households of different social classes and ethnic groups in urban, mining and rural areas (excluding Melanesians living in rural areas). The weights relate to wage earners and salaried employees in the private and public sectors (excluding wage earners in agriculture). The 1975 weights were obtained by extrapolation based on price changes between 1969 and the end of 1974.

Weights and composition

Major groups	Number of items	Weights	Approximate number of price quotations
Food	245	37.00	...
Manufactured items:			
Clothing, footwear and household linen	114	7.00	...
Fuel and light	4	7.00	...
Furnishings, household equipment and other items	174	20.50	...
Services:			
Rent, water, maintenance	14	15.70	...
Personal and medical care	24	3.30	...
Transport and communication	29	5.25	...
Education and recreation	10	1.15	...
Meals taken outside the home	6	2.00	...
Miscellaneous	20	1.10	...
Total	640	100.00	5,500

Household consumption expenditure
All money expenditure by households is included. Rent-free dwellings, owner-occupied dwellings, gifts, social security contributions, direct taxes and charges as well as consumption of own-produced commodities are excluded.

Method of data collection
Prices are collected between the 2nd and the 25th of each month, by agents, from approximately 250 retail outlets and service establishments in Nouméa. Prices for electricity (collected twice a year for a standard consumption), water, gas, transport, medical care, etc., are those fixed by rates or regulations. Clearance sales are not taken into account.

Housing
Rent quotations are obtained from 10 specialised agencies and relate to about 80 dwellings (mainly subsidised housing).

Specification of varieties
Detailed specifications of varieties for each item describe the quality, make, brand, unit, etc.

Substitution, quality change, etc.
If an item disappears from the market, it is replaced by a similar item using the linking method. If there is a quality change, the linking method is applied.

Seasonal items
Seasonal fluctuations in the prices of fresh fruit and vegetables are taken into account by maintaining the closing price from the preceding season during the off season and by using 12-month moving averages for computing the final index.

Computation
The index is computed according to the Laspeyres formula as a weighted arithmetic average with fixed base, using weights corresponding to the base period.

Organisation and publication
Direction territoriale de la statistique et des études économiques: "Indice des prix de détail, Nouvelle-Calédonie" (Nouméa).

NEW ZEALAND

Official title
Consumer Price Index.

Scope
The index is computed quarterly and covers all private New Zealand resident households. There are no exclusions on the grounds of geographical location, nor on the basis of income levels or occupational classifications.

Official base
October - December 1988 = 1000.

Source of weights
The prime data source used to derive the index expenditure weights is the Department of Statistics' household expenditure survey. This on-going survey provides comprehensive and detailed information on expenditure outlays made by private households throughout New Zealand. The sample size is approximately 4,500 households in a CPI-revision survey year.

The results were completed with data from other sources such as production and trade statistics, housing surveys and other public or private sources. The weighting pattern for the current index is based on expenditure on goods and services by private households for the year ended 31 March 1988. Expenditure for this period is then rated up to the December 1988 quarter price level, using the price movements of appropriate CPI commodities. The survey's target population is all New Zealand resident private households living in the two main islands of New Zealand except for very remote rural areas. New Zealand resident households are those in which the head of the household has lived in New Zealand for at least 12 months. 95 per cent of the overall population falls within this definition. The expenditure weights of all items covered by the index are allocated to priced commodities, either by direct (percentage) allocation to one or more commodities or on a pro rata basis to two or more commodities (sometimes a section, sub-group or group is nominated) or by a combination of these methods.

Weights and composition

Major groups	Number of items	Weights	Approximate number of price quotations (a)
Food	94	18.35	...
Housing:			
Rent	2	4.20	...
Home ownership costs	22	19.31	...
Household operations:			
Fuel and light	3	2.77	...
Furnishings and furniture	44	6.82	...
Household supplies, communication and services	27	6.20	...
Clothing and footwear	54	5.34	...
Transport	24	15.39	...
Miscellaneous:			
Alcoholic beverages and tobacco	8	9.72	...
Personal and medical care	42	4.90	...
Recreation, education and credit charges	32	7.00	...
Total	352	100.00	150,000

Note: (a) The number of price quotations for each item in the index is not available.

Household consumption expenditure
The consumer price index is designed as a statistical measure of the changing price levels of goods and services actually purchased in New Zealand by New Zealand private households. Accordingly, consumption from own production, goods received as income in kind and goods and services supplied free of charge are outside the scope of the index. Also considered to be outside the scope of the index are income tax (not being a payment for a service whose quality is subject to statistical measurement or control) and items that represent savings and investment rather than expenditure.

Certain areas of expenditure are excluded, not because they fall outside the conceptual coverage of the index, but because movements in prices cannot be satisfactorily measured, nor can they be adequately indicated by the price movements of any other related or associated commodities which could be priced, e.g. works of art, court fines, charitable donations, catering charges and pets.

An expenditure-commitment approach is used in the current index to weight owner-occupied housing. Under this approach the expenditure weight assigned to owner-occupied housing is the gross expenditure incurred by the index population in purchasing and constructing dwellings in the reference year, offset by the proceeds from housing sales.

In New Zealand, householders place great value on the security of tenure of their housing. It is therefore considered that purchase and construction of dwellings should be included in the regimen if the index is to be a relevant measure of the household population's actual price-paying experience.

The weight for other durable goods is also determined by an expenditure-commitment approach. The full cost of durable goods is taken into account at the time of purchase, regardless of when payment is actually made, or when the commodity is actually consumed. Charges for credit services for the purchase of durables are a separate commodity in the same section of the regimen.

The expenditure weight for most second-hand goods is added to that for new goods of the same class. Only the prices of new commodities are surveyed, as it is assumed that price movements of second-hand goods will be similar. The exceptions are second-hand cars and previously-occupied housing, which are separate commodities in the regimen.

The value of trade-ins and related sales are netted from purchases of equivalent commodities when calculating expenditure weights.

Life insurance payments and superannuation contributions are excluded because they represent savings rather than expenditure. House, mortgage repayment, house contents and motor vehicle insurance are included as separate commodities in the index regimen.

Licence fees and health-care services are included in the index regimen.

Method of data collection
Price surveys are carried out in 15 centres.

Outlets located in suburban shopping centres are currently included in the sample of index outlets at which food and non-food grocery prices are surveyed. Other commodities are priced mainly in the central shopping districts of urban areas, to reduce the travel costs of survey interviewers. Some outlets in the major suburban shopping areas are also surveyed, but as most suburban retail outlets are branches of central city outlets with common prices, widespread suburban pricing is not generally considered to be necessary.

Where commodity prices are surveyed by an interviewer, the outlets are currently selected using purposive sampling procedures. Prices are surveyed from a representative sample of outlets most commonly patronised by the index population. Prices from each outlet are given equal weights and averaged.

Probability sampling is used to select outlets for a variety of postal surveys such as those for dwelling rentals and solicitors' fees.

Fresh fruit and vegetable prices are surveyed each Friday in the 15 main and secondary urban areas. All other food commodities are price-surveyed on or around the 15th of each month in the same 15 urban areas. Prices of commodities in the Household supplies section of the index, except gardening supplies, are also surveyed each month, as are those of newspapers, electricity, gas, cigarettes and tobacco, alcohol and domestic air fares. Petrol prices are surveyed twice a month. All these commodities are also priced in the 15 urban areas.

The remaining index commodity prices that are surveyed by departmental field staff are collected each quarter, on or close to the 15th of the middle month of the quarter.

Surveys of prices for the Consumers Price Index are carried out, in general, by personal visits to retail outlets by full-time departmental field staff, based in the four main urban areas.

For some commodities, shelf prices may be unobtainable or inappropriate; e.g. some materials for home maintenance, motor mowers, carpets and upholstered furniture sometimes fall into this category, and in such cases the interviewer obtains the list price.

Quarterly postal price surveys are used for the following index commodities: housing rentals; expenses for the purchase and financing of home ownership; contractors' charges for home maintenance jobs; coal and firewood; household furniture removal; insurance premiums for dwellings, household contents, motor vehicles and medical care; health services; prescription charges; telephone charges; credit card charges; holiday accommodation; urban, suburban and long-distance bus and rail fares; sea travel; taxi fares; used cars; motor vehicle registration; automobile association membership; driving school fees; cinema and theatre admissions; admissions to sporting venues and events; sports club subscriptions; labour union dues; veterinary fees; music tuition fees; primary, secondary and tertiary educational tuition fees; kindergarten and child care fees; and magazine subscriptions.

Actual "ticket" prices are generally surveyed for the purpose of calculating the index. Discounts, to the extent that they reduce the "ticket" price of the surveyed commodity, are included. Informal, individually-negotiated discounts are not reflected in the index. Sale prices recorded during the normal course of price surveys are included in the index. There is no distinction between free-market and official prices. For technical reasons, illegal transactions are not covered by the index. Credit charges for new and used cars and hire purchase charges (other than for motor vehicles), are included in the present index in the same section as the related commodity. The method of pricing credit charges involves compounding the changes in the interest rate charged in respect of the loan with changes in the prices of the commodities for which the loans were raised. Except for used cars and previously-owned property, only the prices of new commodities are surveyed. Changes in import prices, to the extent that these influence the prices of surveyed commodities, are included in the index.

Factors determining the number of price quotations are:

a) The degree of similarity in the price movements of commodities in a particular grouping. If they have similar price movements, an accurate price-change indicator can be derived from a relatively small number of surveyed commodity prices.

b) The overall and relative importance of the commodities within the grouping. In general, the more important a grouping, the larger the number of commodities that will be price-surveyed.

c) If a single national price prevails for a commodity, only one price quote is required.

Housing

The types of dwellings covered by the rent data include: housing corporation houses and flats, local authority houses and flats, private houses and private flats. The number of rooms includes all types except bathrooms, separate toilets and laundries. All dwellings covered are unfurnished. Data are collected through a quarterly postal survey of landlords in the case of local authority and private dwellings. A complete census of Housing Corporation rentals is obtained.

Sections and previously-occupied houses and flats: property sales data for houses, flats and residential sections, processed at quarterly intervals by the government valuation agency, Valuation New Zealand, are used to prepare the property price inputs.

Construction of dwellings: the changing quarterly cost of constructing a dwelling (houses and flats) is measured using the data obtained from a sample of builders who provide prices for set plan house specifications.

Purchase of newly-constructed houses and flats: the house construction price series is combined with section-price movements to generate the price change indicator for the purchase of newly-constructed houses and flats.

Mortgage interest: This relates to the cost of borrowing the same average real amount of money to assist in the finance of a dwelling purchase as in the index base period. This is described as a "simple revaluation" method. Mortgage interest price-change calculation, therefore, involves the product of two separate indicators: (i) the change in the average interest rate paid on existing property mortgages; and (ii) the price change of dwelling property itself, as this is the appropriate price measure to ensure the purchasing power (or the real value of the borrowed finance) is kept unchanged (constant quality). Average interest rates paid on outstanding dwelling mortgages for the whole private household population are obtained from the Department's household expenditure survey. Quality control of the mortgage profile, the interest rates of which are measured in the household survey, is achieved through time-to-run stratification of the mortgage sample, each stratum having a fixed weight in the index. This practice was adopted on the assumption that the utility of a mortgage at any time is chiefly determined by the amount of money lent and the balance of the period of the loan.

Land agents' and conveyancing fees: Since scale fees were abandoned, the Department of Statistics has conducted quarterly postal surveys for both Land Agents' and Conveyancing Fees. A randomly-selected sample of each group is used. Real Estate Agents' and Conveyancing Fees are influenced by the value of the traded property. A change in the average fee paid on a fixed basket of traded properties can therefore arise either from a change in fees and/or from a change in property price levels. The questionnaires survey the fees for transactions relating to properties with specified purchase of sale prices. These prices are adjusted each quarter by changes in previously-occupied property prices.

Specification of varieties

If the most suitable price-change indicator for a particular commodity is a nationally-available item, a detailed, precise specification is given on a preprinted, price-survey questionnaire. Where different brands, sizes, qualities, etc. of a commodity can be sold in different regions of outlets, the specifications are left open at this stage. Where "open" specifications are used, the details are established at each outlet and are fixed for that outlet. This procedure ensures that the most appropriate item, in terms of consumer demand, is price-surveyed at each outlet.

Substitution, quality change, etc.

If a quality change occurs, an assessment is made of the dollar value of the difference in the quality between the old and new models and the price of the surveyed commodity is adjusted accordingly. New commodities with significant expenditures are added to the index regimen at the time of a revision, when it can be seen that they have become widely available, that they are likely to be a continuing feature of household expenditure and that they have price patterns which have been established free from high premiums for novelty or from scarcity value. Wherever possible, the same quantity and quality of a commodity is priced in each period, to ensure that only "pure price change" is incorporated in the index. The substitution of a priced commodity in the index is necessitated when that commodity is withdrawn from the market or when its price behaviour is no longer typical of the commodity grouping it represents. A quality adjustment is made whenever the replacement commodity is judged to be, in any degree, qualitatively or quantitatively different from its predecessor. In practice, this process involves assessing the dollar value of the difference between the two commodities and thereby calculating a scaling factor that will be applied to the prices surveyed for the replacement commodity. The scaling factor, known as a "quote weight", adjusts the price of the "new" commodity to one that would be charged, were the item of the same quality as the "old" commodity. If data are missing, the previous period's price is carried forward. After a predetermined time, if the data are still unavailable, a substitution is made for the priced commodity in question.

Seasonal items

Special treatment is applied to the fresh fruit and vegetables sub-group to allow for seasonal fluctuations in supply and price. The prices of seasonal sports club subscriptions, admission charges to seasonal sporting fixtures, salad lunches, oysters, vegetable and flower plants and seasonal clothing items are carried forward if they are unavailable in the current period. Peak and off-peak prices for international airfares are surveyed in each pricing period if available.

Computation

The index is computed according to the Laspeyres formula as a weighted arithmetic average with fixed base, using weights corresponding to the base period. The prices used to calculate the CPI (15 urban areas combined) are population-weighted averages of arithmetic-average prices from the 15 price-surveyed urban areas. The population weights represent the total estimated population for each urban area combined with that of the surrounding local authority areas assigned to it. The weights are derived from the most recent Census of Population (1986) and adjusted to take into account subsequent population changes.

Other information

Separate commodity group and sub-group indexes are published each quarter for (i) each of the three largest main urban areas (Auckland, Wellington and Christchurch), (ii) the three largest main urban areas combined, (iii) all North Island urban areas combined and all South Island urban areas combined, and (iv) New Zealand as a whole (15 main and secondary urban areas combined). Commodity section indexes are also published, but only for the 15 urban areas combined. In addition the group index for food and sub-group and section indexes are published each month for the same regional groupings as above.

Organisation and publication
Department of Statistics: "Key Statistics" (monthly) (Wellington).
Idem: "News Release" (quarterly).
Idem: "Hot off the Press" (Information Release).
Idem: "New Zealand Official Year Book".

NICARAGUA (MANAGUA)

Official title
Indice de precios al consumidor (Consumer Price Index).

Scope
The index is compiled monthly and covers households in Managua metropolitan area with monthly incomes ranging from 400 to 7,000 córdobas during May to October 1972.

Official base
December 1974 = 100.

Source of weights
The weights and items were derived from a household expenditure survey conducted in Managua between May and October 1972, among a sample of 330 families selected on the basis of the results of the Population and Housing Census of April 1971

Weights and composition

Major groups	Number of items	Weights	Approximate number of price quotations
Food and tobacco	81	43.07	...
Clothing and footwear	36	6.62	...
Housing (incl. rent, fuel, light, repairs, furniture, household operation, etc.)	34	24.74	...
Miscellaneous expenses:	31		
Personal and medical care	...	7.61	...
Education and recreation	...	6.13	...
Transport	...	11.61	...
Personal insurances	...	0.22	...
Total	182	100.00	...

Household consumption expenditure
Consumption expenditure for the purpose of the index refers to almost all money expenditure by households on goods and services intended for consumption. It includes the value of goods and services received as income in kind and home-produced goods consumed by households.

Method of data collection
Prices for fresh fruit and vegetables are ascertained between Tuesday and Friday each week through direct buying. Prices for other items and services are collected each month by agents, between Tuesday and Friday of the week which includes the 15th of the month, from selected markets, retail outlets and service establishments.

The prices used to calculate the index are the regular prices paid. Discount and sale prices are not taken into account.

Housing
Rent quotations are obtained for 33 dwellings throughout the city.

Specification of varieties
Specifications of items to be priced are given broadly so that substitutions can be made.

Substitution, quality change, etc.
When an item disappears from the market, it is substituted by a similar item and a linking method is used.

Seasonal items
Off-season prices for seasonal items are assumed to follow the price movements of the other items in the same sub-group. When the seasonal item reappears on the market, the ratio of the new price to the last price collected is calculated.

Computation
The index is computed according to the Laspeyres formula as a weighted arithmetic average with fixed base, using weights corresponding to May-October 1972.

In computing item indices, the relatives of average prices are calculated by dividing the average price for the current period by the average price for the previous period.

Other information
A new series (base October-December 1987 = 100) is now computed but the relevant methodological information was not available in the ILO at the time the present volume was published.

Organisation and publication
Oficina Ejecutiva de Encuestas y Censos: "Indice General de Precios al Consumidor de la Ciudad de Managua" (Managua).

NIGER (NIAMEY, AFRICANS)

Official title
Indice des prix à la consommation familiale africaine (African Consumer Price Index).

Scope
The index is compiled monthly and covers African families in Niamey.

Official base
July 1962-June 1963 = 100.

Source of weights
The weights and items were derived from a household expenditure survey conducted in Niamey from March 1961 to April 1962 among 317 African households.

Weights and composition

Major groups	Number of items	Weights	Approximate number of price quotations
Food	42	45	...
Clothing and footwear	9	10	...
Household operations (incl. fuel, light and water)	9	18	...
Miscellaneous	16	27	...
Total	76	100	...

Household consumption expenditure
Not available.

Method of data collection
Prices for food and other items are collected by agents twice a month from five retail stores and four times a month from one market. Quotations for certain public services are obtained every month from official tariffs.

Housing
Rent is not included as an index item, nor is it taken into account in determining the weights.

Specification of varieties
Not available.

Substitution, quality change, etc.
Not available.

Seasonal items
Prices for seasonal items are collected throughout the year. Average prices of these items are used to calculate the index.

Computation
The index is computed according to the Laspeyres formula as a weighted arithmetic average with fixed base, using weights corresponding to March 1961-April 1962.

Organisation and publication
Ministère du développement et de la coopération, Direction de la statistique: "Bulletin de statistique" (Niamey).

NIGER (NIAMEY, EUROPEANS)

Official title
Indice des prix à la consommation familiale européenne (European Consumer Price Index).

Scope
The index is compiled monthly and relates to European families in Niamey.

Official base
15 November-15 December 1964 = 100.

Source of weights
The weights and items were derived from a household expenditure survey conducted in Niamey from 15 November to 15 December 1964, by means of mail questionnaires addressed to a sample of households of French officials engaged in technical co-operation.

Weights and composition

Major groups	Number of items	Weights	Approximate number of price quotations
Food	78	46.1	...
Electricity, gas and water	3	11.1	...
Cleaning materials	10	2.5	...
Clothing, footwear and household linen	12	6.0	...
Domestic services	2	8.2	...
Miscellaneous	28	26.1	...
Total	133	100.0	...

Household consumption expenditure
Not available.

Method of data collection
Prices for food and other items are collected by agents twice a month from five retail stores and four times a month from one market.

Housing
Rent is not included as an index item, nor is it taken into account in determining the weights.

Specification of varieties
Not available.

Substitution, quality change, etc.
Not available.

Seasonal items
Prices for seasonal items are collected throughout the year. Average prices of these items are used to calculate the index.

Computation
The index is computed according to the Laspeyres formula as a weighted arithmetic average with fixed base, using weights corresponding to the base period.

Organisation and publication
Ministère du développement et de la coopération, Direction de la statistique: "Bulletin de statistique" (Niamey).

NIGERIA 1

Official title
Urban Consumer Price Index - All Income Groups.

Scope
The index is compiled monthly and covers households of all income groups in urban areas.

Official base
1975 = 100.

Source of weights
The weights and items were derived from a household expenditure survey conducted in 1974-75 in urban areas among households of all income groups.

Weights and composition
Not available.

Household consumption expenditure
Not available.

Method of data collection
The prices are collected by agents, from markets and local stores. The frequency of price collection for each item depends on the variability of its price, and ranges from daily (for food items) to monthly (for other items).

The prices used to calculate the index are the retail prices actually paid.

Housing
Not available.

Specification of varieties
The specifications of items to be priced are given in terms of brand, make, quality and size.

Substitution, quality change, etc.
If an item is not available, a similar item is substituted, and a linking method is used in the calculation. If this is not possible, the last recorded price of the item is repeated.

Seasonal items
Seasonal items such as fresh fruit and vegetables are priced only when they are in season.

Computation
The index is computed according to the Laspeyres formula as a weighted arithmetic average with fixed base, using weights corresponding to the period 1974-75.

Separate indices are first calculated for low-, middle- and high-income groups in each centre. The price relative for each item within each centre is computed by dividing the average price for the current period by the average price for the base period. Urban-centre indices are combined to obtain the index for all income groups in urban areas.

Other information
A new series is now computed for urban areas (base September 1985 = 100) but the relevant methodological information was not available in the ILO at the time the present volume was published.

Organisation and publication
Federal Office of Statistics: "Retail prices in selected centres and consumer price indices" (Lagos).

Idem: "Retail prices in selected centres and consumer price indices" (March 1978).

NIGERIA 2

Official title
Composite Consumer Price Index - Rural and Urban Areas.

Scope
The index is compiled monthly and covers households of all income groups in both urban and rural areas.

Official base
1975 = 100.

Source of weights
The weights and items were derived from a household expenditure survey conducted in 1974-75 in urban and rural areas among households of all income groups.

Weights and composition
Not available.

Household consumption expenditure
Not available.

Method of data collection
The prices are collected by agents, from markets and local stores. The frequency of price collection for each item depends on the variability of its price, and ranges from daily (for food items) to monthly (for other items).

The prices used to calculate the index are the retail prices actually paid.

Housing
Not available.

Specification of varieties
The specifications of items to be priced are given in terms of brand, make, quality and size.

Substitution, quality change, etc.
If an item is not available, a similar item is substituted and a linking method is used in the calculation. If this is not possible, the last recorded price of the item is repeated.

Seasonal items
Seasonal items such as fresh fruit and vegetables are priced only when they are in season.

Computation
The index is computed according to the Laspeyres formula as a weighted arithmetic average with fixed base, using weights corresponding to the period 1974-75.

Separate indices are first calculated for low-, middle- and high-income groups in each centre. The price relative for each item within a centre is computed by dividing the average price for the current period by the average price for the base period.

The national index is the weighted arithmetic average of the indices for urban and rural areas, and for low-, middle- and high-income group families. The weights used are proportionate to the population of the areas concerned.

Other information
A new series is now computed for urban and rural areas (base September 1985 = 100), but the relevant methodological information was not available in the ILO at the time the present volume was published.

Organisation and publication
Federal Office of Statistics: "Retail prices in selected centres and consumer price indices" (Lagos).
Idem: "Retail prices in selected centres and consumer price indices" (March 1978).

NIUE

Official title
Retail Price Index.

Scope
The index is compiled quarterly and covers all medium-income households in urban areas (Alofi town).

Official base
March quarter 1982 = 100.

Source of weights
The weights and items were derived in 1981 from a number of sources, including trade statistics, advice from the three major stores, government accounts and additional information provided by several government authorities.

Weights and composition

Major groups	Number of items	Weights	Approximate number of price quotations
Food	59	430	...
Alcoholic beverages and tobacco	6	115	...
Housing	9	50	...
Household operations	26	130	...
Clothing and footwear	13	50	...
Transport	12	175	...
Miscellaneous	12	50	...
Total	137	1,000	...

Household consumption expenditure
Consumption expenditure for the purpose of the index comprises all goods and services purchased for consumption by the index population. It excludes the purchase of new houses, air fares for permanent movement in or out of Niue, gifts and donations.

Method of data collection
Not available.

Housing
Not available.

Specification of varieties
The specifications of items to be priced are given in terms of brand, make, size and quality, etc.

Substitution, quality change, etc.
When an item is no longer available, a similar item or another item of the same sub-group is substituted.

Seasonal items
Not available.

Computation
The index is computed according to the Laspeyres formula as a weighted arithmetic average with fixed base, using weights corresponding to the base period.

In computing item indices, price relatives for the current and previous periods are used.

Other information
A new series (base January-March 1990 = 100) is now computed but the relevant methodological information was not available in the ILO at the time the present volume was published.

Organisation and publication
The index is compiled by the Development Planning Office, Statistics Unit (Alofi).
Treasurer Department: "Quarterly Abstract of Statistics" (Alofi).

NORWAY

Official title
Consumer Price Index.

Scope
The index is compiled monthly and covers all private households in the country.

Official base
1979 = 100.

Source of weights
The weights are calculated as the average expenditure shares obtained from the expenditure surveys conducted during the last three years. As from August 1991 the weights are obtained from 1988, 1989 and 1990 surveys. The selected items and weights are continuously revised. The following weights relate to August 1991-July 1992.

Weights and composition

Major groups	Number of items	Weights	Approximate number of price quotations
Food	241	152.1	27,910
Beverages and tobacco	45	36.0	1,360
Clothing and footwear	89	67.4	3,910
Housing (incl. repairs and maintenance)	29	215.4	1,930
Fuel and light	5	47.5	130
Furniture, furnishings and household equipment	113	81.5	5,180
Medical care and health expenses	25	23.3	120
Transport and communication	105	199.0	1,460
Education, recreation and entertainment	62	98.3	760
Miscellaneous goods and services	66	81.1	2,020
Total	780	1,001.6	44,780

Household consumption expenditure
Consumption expenditure for the purpose of the index comprises all goods and services purchased for consumption by the index population. The consumption expenditure for durable goods corresponds to the difference between expenses in connection with purchase of "new" goods and the sale of "old" goods. Payments on hire purchase are included, as are consumption of own-produced commodities and gifts received. It excludes direct taxes, savings and investment, personal loans, life insurance premiums, contributions to pension funds and gifts given away.

Method of data collection
Prices are collected by agents from about 1,400 selected retail stores and service establishments. Most of the items are priced on the 15th of each month. The prices used in the index are the regular prices paid by any member of the public.

Housing
Rent data are collected each quarter from about 1,800 dwellings.

Specification of varieties
The specifications of items to be priced are given in detail in terms of brand, make and size, etc.

Substitution, quality change, etc.
If a product is not available in the outlet, a similar product to the original is substituted.

Seasonal items
Seasonal fluctuations in the prices of certain fresh fruits, vegetables and fish are taken into account by using the average prices of the preceding season during the off season.

Computation
From August 1982, the index is a Laspeyres chain index with yearly links. The weights are changed in August each year. The monthly index is first computed by item for each area as the price change of the unweighted arithmetic mean of all the prices for an item. The average level of prices in the previous July is taken as 100. The monthly index for an item for the whole country is computed by weighting the price changes for

the various areas according to their relative share in the country's turnover.

Organisation and publication
Statistisk sentralbyrä (Central Bureau of Statistics): "Statistisk Mänedshefte (Monthly Bulletin of Statistics)" (Oslo).

PAKISTAN

Official title
Combined Consumer Price Index.

Scope
The index is compiled monthly and covers industrial, commercial and government employees in four monthly income groups: up to 1,000 rupees, 1,001 to 2,500 rupees, 2,501 to 4,500 rupees, and over 4,500 rupees. The index covers 25 important urban centres.

Official base
July 1980-June 1981 = 100.

Source of weights
The weights are based on the results of the household expenditure survey conducted in 1982 in 46 urban centres including 25 major urban centres, among a sample of 26,864 households. Index items were selected to be representative of the tastes, habits and customs of the people, easily recognisable and describable and unlikely to vary in quality.

Weights and composition

Major groups	Number of items	Weights	Approximate number of price quotations
Food and tobacco	176	49.90	...
Clothing and footwear	73	6.68	...
Rent	1	17.76	...
Fuel and light	15	5.62	...
Furniture and household equipment	38	2.34	...
Transport and communication	44	6.20	...
Education and recreation	44	3.50	...
Cleaning products and personal care	45	5.56	...
Miscellaneous	28	2.44	...
Total	464	100.00	(a) ...

Note: (a) There are about four quotations for each item from different shops in each shopping area.

Household consumption expenditure
Consumption expenditure for the purpose of the index comprises all the important goods and services purchased for consumption by the index population. It excludes non-consumption expenditure, house purchase, interest charges, jewellery and all forms of assets and liabilities.

Method of data collection
Field staff of the Federal Bureau of Statistics collect prices from market areas, selected retail stores and service establishments in 46 urban centres including 25 major cities. Prices are collected using four schedules. Prices of basic consumption goods and perishable food items such as meat, fish, eggs, vegetables, etc. are collected on the third Tuesday of each month. Prices of other items are collected each month.

The prices used in the index are prices at which retailers and service establishments sell their goods and services direct to consumers.

Housing
Current rent data are not available on a country-wise basis; changes in the price of input construction items are used as an indicator of rent trends.

Specification of varieties
Most of the specifications of items priced were defined by the Statistics Division of the Federal Bureau of Statistics. If it was not possible to establish specifications for certain items, the local best quality is used.

Substitution, quality change, etc.
The Statistics Division examines all proposals by the field staff for substitution when an item is not available at all or when it is not available according to the specification or unit. If the use of a substitute is accepted, it is introduced in the index by a method of linking.

Seasonal items
Seasonal items show a wide range of variation between in-season and off-season prices. To remove this variation, arrangements have been made in the programming for computating these indices to keep the prices of such items at zero in their off season.

Computation
The index is computed according to the Laspeyres formula as a weighted arithmetic average with fixed base, using weights corresponding to 1982. Weights for various cities provided by the household income and expenditure survey were used to compute city indices for three categories of employees and four income groups.

The national index is computed by using a combined set of weights that ignores the distinction between cities, occupational categories and income groups.

Organisation and publication
Federal Bureau of Statistics, Statistics Division: "Monthly Statistical Bulletin" (Karachi).

Idem: "Pakistan Key Economic Indicators".

Idem: "Consumer Price Index Numbers of Pakistan 1980-81 = 100".

PANAMA (PANAMA CITY)

Official title
Indice de precios al consumidor (Consumer Price Index).

Scope
The index is compiled monthly and relates to all private households of different income levels in Panama City.

Official base
1987 = 100.

Source of weights
The weights and items were derived from a household expenditure survey conducted in 1983-84 in Panama City among a sample of 1,070 families of different income levels.

The families were selected on the basis of a stratified random sample, consisting of a housing list reported in the population census of 1980, supplemented with a list of buildings constructed since the census; in other words, housing constituted the unit of selection and the family the unit of observation. The survey used the method of directly interviewing families. The data were gathered by means of a monthly form that examined in detail the expenditure and income of families and a daily diary that was used to obtain the daily expenditure and incomes during one week.

The weights were not adjusted to take into account price changes between the survey period and 1987.

Weights and composition

Major groups	Number of items	Weights	Approximate number of price quotations
Food	101	34.9	81
Clothing and footwear	38	5.1	34
Rent, fuel and light (1)	4	12.6	5
Furniture, furnishings, household equipment and maintenance	37	8.4	43
Personal and medical care	11	3.5	21
Transport and communications	10	15.1	24
Education and recreation	20	11.7	41
Other goods and services	23	8.7	26
Total	244	100.0	275

Note: (1) Excluding 109 dwellings throughout Panama City, for which rent quotations are obtained.

Household consumption expenditure
This refers to net expenditure, excluding sales of second-hand goods by families and the equivalent market value of these used goods; and trading-in as partial payment for the purchase of new goods.

It excludes contributions to social insurance and pension funds, insurance associated with specific consumer goods, income tax and other direct taxes. In computing the weights of the index, account is taken of life insurance payments, remittances, gifts and similar disbursements.

Method of data collection
Prices are regularly collected by means of direct visits to selected establishments carried out by staff using forms specifically designed for this purpose. The staff receive special training to carry out this work with precision and in the time required.

Prices are collected each month, except those of rents, maintenance, hairdressers, manicurists, air tickets and insurance companies which are gathered each quarter; those of domestic service and education are collected once a year.

The prices of goods and services, except those at the market, are collected in the first three weeks of each month; market prices are obtained on the Tuesday and Thursday of the second week of the month.

Selling-off prices are not taken into consideration when calculating the index. Sale prices are only included if the items are on sale for several weeks and if they are in good condition and part of the regular stock.

Housing
Rent quotations are obtained each quarter from 109 dwellings. Owner-occupied dwellings are not taken into account.

Specification of varieties
Once the items and services have been selected, a decision is taken on the specification which is defined as the detailed description of the characteristics of a good or service; these are decisive factors in establishing prices and include for example: quality, size, type of manufacture, model, style, etc. The specifications include indications usually sought by the purchasers and supplied by the sales persons. The aim of identifying the items is to guarantee that the index only shows price changes.

In order to facilitate the collection of prices on the basis of established criteria, there is a manual on the items in question and the specifications required for the work. Of course, it should be taken into account that not all items included in the index need to be so precisely defined.

Substitution, quality change, etc.
If changes occur in the specification of an item, substitutions are made in one of two ways:

(a) Direct comparison of prices: The substitute item is more or less of the same quality as the article eliminated, but a different brand. The prices of the two brands are directly compared and, if there is any change in price, this is reflected in the index.

(b) Relative linking: The new item may have the same utility or objective but differ in quality even though the price remains the same. These changes do not occur suddenly, but there is a period when the two items are on the market. Both items are valued at the same time and, when the price of the new item is available for two consecutive periods, the substitute item is linked to the index in such a way that the difference in prices between the two items is not reflected in the index. The price of the substitute item is compared with its price in the previous period, and the relative of this item is applied to the weighted price of the item that has been eliminated.

Seasonal items
In periods when it is impossible to obtain prices for a seasonal item, the relative of the prices corresponding to items in the same sub-group available throughout the year is taken; this is obtained by dividing the total of the weighted prices in the quarter under consideration by the total of the weighted prices in the previous period. The price of the seasonal item is calculated by multiplying the price for the previous period by the relative of the prices estimated for the period under consideration.

Computation
The index is computed according to the Laspeyres formula as a weighted arithmetic average with fixed base, using weights corresponding to 1983-84.

The price relative of each item is calculated by dividing the average price for the current period by the average price for the previous period.

Other information
Detailed sub-groups are published for the present series.

Organisation and publication
Dirección de Estadística y Censos: "Estadística Panameña" (Panama; March, June, September and December).

PAPUA NEW GUINEA

Official title
Consumer Price Index.

Scope
The index is compiled quarterly and relates to wage earners' households in urban areas. A wage earner's household is defined as one in which at least 50 per cent of its income comes from wages or salaries. "Urban" means areas with population of 2,000 or more in 1977.

Official base
1977 = 100.

Source of weights
The weights and items were derived from a household expenditure survey conducted between September 1975 and February 1976 among 501 wage earners' households in six urban areas of 2,000 or more inhabitants in 1977. The results were adjusted for price changes between the survey period and 1977. The following criteria were applied in choosing items for the index: (i) items with expenditure of not less than 0.05 per cent of total expenditure; (ii) representative of the wider group of related items to which they belong; and (iii) feasibility of collecting prices regularly.

Weights and composition

Major groups	Number of items	Weights	Approximate number of price quotations
Food	51	40.89	...
Beverages and tobacco	7	20.00	...
Clothing and footwear	16	6.17	...
Rent, fuel and light	4	7.19	...
Household equipment and operations	15	5.28	...
Transport and communication	11	12.96	...
Miscellaneous goods and services	20	7.51	...
Total	124	100.00	...

Household consumption expenditure
Consumption expenditure for the purpose of the index comprises all goods and services purchased for consumption by the index population. It excludes gambling, superannuation, savings, cash gifts, life insurance and income taxes.

Method of data collection
Prices are obtained from approximately 240 different outlets throughout the six urban areas by agents or postal questionnaires.

Fresh fruit, vegetables and betel-nut prices are priced each week in markets. Prices for other food items, non-food groceries, drinks and tobacco are collected each month; information on education fees is collected once a year and for all other goods and services once a quarter.

Prices are collected around the 15th of each month except for fresh fruit and vegetables for which prices are collected on Friday or Saturday each week.

The prices used to calculate the index are those which consumers have to pay on the pricing day. Discount or sale prices are used if they account for a significant volume of sales.

Housing
Rent data are collected from rented dwellings with one to four bedrooms.

Specification of varieties
The specifications of items to be priced are given in terms of the brand, make, quality, size and unit, etc.

Substitution, quality change, etc.
Special adjustments are made in order to ensure that the prices used reflect only price changes and not changes in the quality or quantity of a specification.

Seasonal items
No adjustments are made for seasonal variations.

Computation
The index is computed as a weighted average of six separate indices relating to Port Moresby, Lae, Rabaul, Madang, Goroka and Kieta/Arawa/Panguna. Each index is computed according to the Laspeyres formula as a weighted arithmetic average with fixed base, using weights corresponding to the base period. They are then weighted together to obtain the index for the six

urban areas combined, using weights proportional to the urban population of the towns.

Other information
Separate indices are also published for the six urban areas.

Organisation and publication
National Statistical Office: "Statistical Bulletin, Consumer Price Index" (Port Moresby).
Idem: "Statistical Bulletin, Consumer Price Indexes", March Quarter 1979, June Quarter 1979.
Idem: "Technical Note No. 4, Consumer Price Indexes (Base Year 1977), April 1980".

PARAGUAY (ASUNCION)

Official title
Indice de precios del consumo (Consumer Price Index).

Scope
The index is compiled monthly and covers families from every social and economic background within Greater Asunción.

Official base
1980 = 100.

Source of weights
The weights and items were derived from the results of a household expenditure survey conducted from September 1978 to September 1979 among a sample of 1,591 urban families of wage earners, salaried employees, professionals, retired persons, and single and married persons with or without a family. It excludes persons living in military and police facilities, hospitals, convents and other similar institutions. The average number of persons per family was 4.7. The index relates to families from every social and economic background within Greater Asunción. The amount of expenditure and the number of families were taken as the basis for pre-selecting items.

Weights and composition

Major groups	Number of items	Weights	Approximate number of price quotations
Food and tobacco	146	36.98	1,937
Housing:			725
Rent	1	15.47	...
Fuel and electricity	13	6.37	...
Furniture and household equipment	44	4.67	...
Cleaning materials	11	1.21	...
Clothing and footwear	99	8.99	972
Miscellaneous	231	26.30	2,074
Total	545	100.00	5,708

Household consumption expenditure
Not available.

Method of data collection
An average of 5,700 prices collected each month to calculate the variation in the price index. Outlets were selected according to the location of the shops where families purchased goods most often, with other representative shopping centres being added.

An average of ten outlets were selected for each item sold in retail outlets, markets, stores and supermarkets. Prices are collected in Asunción as follows: staple foods every week; other foods, housing expenditure and miscellaneous expenditure every month; clothing and related expenditure every two months. The price survey is carried out by employees of the Banco Central del Paraguay who are trained in the technical procedure of setting up index systems. Discounts are taken into account if they are a regular practice of the sales outlet, are available to all customers without exception, and are used in calculating the price relative compared to the price for the previous period with the corresponding discount. The marked price is normally collected if the commercial establishment does not grant discount on the item to all its customers. It is used in calculating the price relative compared with the marked price for the previous period. In the case of items for which official prices are fixed and which are sold on the free market at a price different from that stipulated by the Government, the prices on the free market are collected, as this is the amount spent by consumers. Black market prices are not collected, as the items on sale have no legal existence, although they do exist physically. Purchases on installments or on credit are not taken into account, only cash purchases are used. Second-hand purchases and the exchange of used goods in part payment for new goods are taken into account in national currency and at the price at which the seller is prepared to sell them. In other words, the prices paid by the consumer in acquiring a product are collected.

Housing
Regarding the items included under the heading of rent, the sub-group home ownership and rented housing includes only rented housing. The sample for the collection of prices of rented housing consists of 200 units divided into four groups of 50 units each, situated in different districts of Asunción. Each unit in each group is visited every four months on a rotating basis. For example, group 1 consists of 50 units in district A, for which rents are collected in January. These are used to calculate the price relative compared to the rents collected in September of the previous period, the other three groups remaining the same. Group 2 consists of another 50 units located in district B for which rents are collected in February. These are compared with the rents for the previous period, October, while the other groups remain the same. In March, the rents of group 3, consisting of 50 units in district C, are collected and compared with those collected in November, while the other groups remain the same. In April, the rents of group 4, consisting of 50 units in district D, are collected and compared with those of the previous December, while the other groups remain the same.

Specification of varieties
The information used in establishing the item specifications refers to the variety, quality and unit of measure used in calculating the price relative. Depending on the product, the brand, origin, weight and size are also included.

Substitution, quality change, etc.
If a certain type of product disappears from the market, its price relative is calculated on the basis of the other elements in the stratum to which it belongs. If the quality changes, the item may be substituted by another similar item without comparing prices at the time of substitution.

Seasonal items
The prices of seasonal items and their weights are kept constant during collecting periods in which they are not available on the market, and when they are available prices are collected and compared to those which were previously constant. This procedure is used in order to avoid excessive distortion of already distorted weights.

Computation
The index is calculated according to the Laspeyres formula, modified according to a fixed volume of consumption and varying weights. The index for each item is obtained using the price relatives for the current and previous periods.

Other information
The Banco Central del Paraguay also compiles a parallel consumer price index covering workers' families in Greater Asunción.

Organisation and publication
Banco Central del Paraguay: "Folleto Explicativo del Indice de Precios del Consumo, Año 1980", June 1988.
Idem: "Boletín Estadístico".
Idem: "Revista Ñemú Renda".
Dirección General de Estadística y Censos, Presidencia de la República: "Anuario Estadístico".

PERU (LIMA)

Official title
Indice de precios al consumidor (Consumer Price Index).

Scope
The index is calculated monthly and covers urban households whose head is a wage or salary earner with an average income. Households with a high or very low per capita income are excluded, as are one-person households.

Official base
1979 = 100.

Source of weights
Items were selected and weights determined on the basis of the results of a household expenditure survey carried out during 12 months between September 1977 and August 1978 and covering 1,985 households in the Lima metropolitan area.

The items were selected using the following criteria: relative importance within the sub-group, representative of price movements of similar items and continuously available. The value of expenditure on items not included in the basket was added to that of the selected items either: (a) directly, by assigning it to another item with similar characteristics, which was considered to be a substitute; or (b) indirectly, by distributing the cost proportionately among the other items in the sub-group.

Weights and composition

Major groups	Number of items	Weights	Approximate number of price quotations
Food and tobacco	75	38.09	23,386
Clothing and footwear	11	7.33	1,323
Rent, fuel, electricity	8	15.57	1,424
Furniture, household equipment, cleaning materials	36	6.98	1,589
Personal and medical care	8	2.64	417
Transport and communication	10	9.83	272
Education and recreation	12	7.40	592
Other goods and services	13	12.16	997
Total	173	100.00	30,000

Household consumption expenditure
Household consumption is defined as that part of expenditure on goods and services which is designed to satisfy the needs of the family, excluding the acquisition of housing and land, and all disbursements which may generate income for households. Home-produced goods and services consumed by the household are valued at market prices and included in household consumption. Thus, for example, household expenditure includes the imputed rent of owner-occupied housing. Account is also taken of all payments that do not involve double counting, for example the cost of car insurance provided the repair costs of insured vehicles are not included.

Method of data collection
The results of a special National Institute for Statistics (INE) survey were used to select the sample of outlets, on the basis of the number of points of sale and the number of street vendors in the area. The sample comprised 33 markets and four supermarkets. Commercial and service establishments were selected from commercial streets or zones in each district on the basis of their readiness to collaborate in the survey and the range of products available. Account was also taken of the large chains of supermarkets. The prices used to calculate the index are those paid by housewives in markets or by most consumers in establishments. The prices are recorded in supermarkets, retail outlets and service establishments. Items with prices that vary considerably, such as fresh produce (vegetables, tubers, roots, fruits, fish, greens) and those whose prices vary only very slightly but which are sold in large public markets (rice, sugar, edible oils and fats, etc.) are priced each week. Items with less varying prices, such as cereals, clothing, furniture, etc, are priced each month. Rents, property prices and municipal taxes are recorded twice a year. Public service charges are recorded periodically. Some prices are obtained by direct purchase in markets.

Housing
Data on house rents are obtained from a fixed sample of households covered by the survey.

Specification of varieties
The selection of a given variety under a heading depends on its importance within the category, the ease with which it can be defined and priced and its continued availability over time.

The articles selected in the household survey do not always have well defined characteristics, as regards trade marks, size, etc. In order to compile initial samples for the purpose of observation, the investigators visited the establishments in the sample, and noted in detail the characteristics of the items selected: name, trade mark, model, size or weight, etc. Where possible, the dealer was asked which brand of the particular variety he sold most of. The sample was then centrally controlled to ensure that the prices recorded correspond exactly to those appearing in the sample.

Substitution, quality change, etc.
For various reasons, (e.g. the season, absence of traders, discontinuity of items) it is not always possible to record prices for all items. The National Institute for Statistics solves this problem as follows: when a variety is homogeneous, an average price is used, calculated on the basis of the prices collected for other similar items during the period; when a variety is heterogeneous, the latest available price is maintained if it is certain that the item will reappear in the near future; if the item does not reappear after three months, it is replaced.

Seasonal items
Not available.

Computation
The index is computed according to the Laspeyres formula as a weighted arithmetic average with fixed base, using weights corresponding to September 1977-August 1978.

Price relatives of the current and previous periods are used to compute item indices. Relatives of average prices are calculated for homogeneous varieties, and averages of price relatives are used for heterogeneous varieties. Simple arithmetic averages are calculated in both cases.

Other information
A new series is now computed (base 1990 = 100), but the relevant methodological information was not available in the ILO at the time the present volume was published.

Organisation and publication
Instituto Nacional de Estadística: "Indice de Precios al Consumidor de Lima Metropolitana" (Lima).

Idem: "Indice de Precios al Consumidor de Lima Metropolitana, Metodología, dic. 1980" (Lima).

PHILIPPINES

Official title
Consumer Price Index for All-Income Households in the Philippines.

Scope
The index is compiled monthly and covers all households (urban and rural) in 72 provinces in the 13 regions.

Official base
1988 = 100.

Source of weights
The weights were derived from the results of the 1988 household expenditure survey covering a sample of 19,000 households. Items and services selected for regular pricing and outlets where these items are purchased are based on a commodity and outlet survey conducted in 1985 among a sample of 19,000 households. This approach ensures that only the items most commonly consumed by households are represented in the index.

Weights and composition

Major groups	Number of items	Weights	Approximate number of price quotations
Food and tobacco	198	58.5	...
Clothing and footwear	106	4.3	...
Housing and repairs	34	13.3	...
Fuel, light and water	15	5.4	...
Services	98	10.9	...
Miscellaneous	111	7.6	...
Total	562	100.0	(a) ...

Note: (a) There are generally six price quotations for each commodity or service.

Household consumption expenditure
Consumption expenditure for the purpose of the index covers only expenditure for family living consumption. It excludes residential, real estate and personal income taxes, gifts, contributions and assistance to others, life insurance, health and accident insurance, retirement and social security premiums, the value of services rendered by a family member to another family member and outlays not considered as expenditure for family living consumption. It includes the value of non-cash items of expenditure: own-produced foods consumed, payments in kind made by the family and imputed rent for owner-occupied houses or housing supplied free.

Method of data collection
The prices are collected through a price survey carried out in 72 provincial capitals and about 744 municipalities in the country. The municipalities were selected on the basis of the availability of commodities and items. The outlets were selected

according to the the volume of sales or turnover of the establishment, the consistency and completeness of the stock of commodities, the permanence of the outlet, the co-operativeness of the dealer and the convenience and accessibility of the outlet. Prices of unprocessed agricultural food items are collected by the Bureau of Agricultural Statistics, while prices of processed food items, beverages and tobacco, and price data for transportation and services and all other non-food items are obtained by the National Statistics Office.

The prices are obtained through personal interviews. In Metro Manilla, the National Capital Region, prices of unprocessed food items are collected on Monday, Wednesday and Friday each week, while prices of all processed food items, beverages and tobacco are collected on Friday or Saturday each week. All the other items are priced twice a month.

Only prevailing market prices are collected for the purpose of the index. Sale prices are not collected and prices of discounted items are not quoted.

Housing
Rent quotations are collected monthly. All rental rates are taken from the tenants. Owner-occupied housing is excluded.

Specification of varieties
The items to be priced are specified in great detail, including the grade, brand name, size number, quality, make, contents, weight and unit of measure.

Substitution, quality change, etc.
The items in the market basket are not changed until the base year is shifted. However, if an item disappears from the market, a substitution is made on the following basis: (a) the substitute must be of the same or almost the same quality as the lost item; (b) the substitute must be of the same price range or price level as the lost item.

Seasonal items
No special treatment is given to seasonal items. Generally, all the items in the market basket are available throughout the year.

Computation
The index is computed according to the Laspeyres formula as a weighted arithmetic average with fixed base, using weights corresponding to the base period.

The index is an aggregation of provincial indices: the provincial indices are first combined to give regional indices and then aggregated to give the index for the Philippines. All of these are weighted.

Other information
Indices are published for major groups, the current and the preceding month and for the different regions of the country.

Organisation and publication
National Statistics Office: "Monthly Statistical Bulletin" (Manila).
Idem: "Quarterly Journal of Philippine Statistics".
Idem: "Philippine Yearbook".

POLAND

Official title
Consumer Price Index.

Scope
The index is computed monthly and covers more than 90 per cent of the population.

Official base
The base period of the index used in the national publications is the corresponding period of the previous year taken as 100. The Central Statistical Office of Poland chains these indices back to the base used by the ILO for publication.

Source of weights
The weighting system was derived from a household expenditure survey.

Household consumption expenditure
Not available.

Method of data collection
Prices are collected between the 1st and 25th of each month by the staff of statistical offices in 307 regions, covering 281 towns. Prices are surveyed at 27,556 outlets of which 45 per cent are retail outlets, 5 per cent catering establishments and 50 per cent service establishments. Prices for food items are obtained three times a month and those of non-food items, condiments, alcoholic beverages and tobacco, twice a month.

Weights and composition

Major groups	Number of items	Weights	Approximate number of price quotations
Food	390	41.8	...
Alcoholic beverages	40	5.9	...
Non-food items	800	32.2	...
Services	220	20.1	...
Total	1,450	100.0	...

Housing
Not available.

Specification of varieties
Not available.

Substitution, quality change, etc.
Not available.

Seasonal items
Seasonal fluctuations in the prices of potatoes, vegetables and fruit are taken into account by varying monthly item weights within constant group weights.

Computation
The index is computed according to the Laspeyres formula as a weighted arithmetic average with fixed weights.

The price index for each item is calculated for the current period, compared to an average price of a base period. Individual price indices for a given item on a nationwide scale are computed as the geometric mean of individual price indices for the item in the respective regions. A group index for each elementary group is calculated as the geometric mean of individual price indices of items in the group; if there is only one item in a group, it is the price index for this item.

The group indices for the respective consumer goods and services are then calculated, and the final price index is obtained through successive aggregation and weighting.

Other information
The Central Statistical Office also publishes price indices for four socio-economic population groups: (1) employees, (2) farmers, (3) farmworkers and (4) retired persons and pensioners.

Organisation and publication
Glowny Urzad, Statistycznz (Central Statistical Office): "Statistical Bulletin" (Warsaw).

PORTUGAL

Official title
Indice de preços no consumidor - series A - Continente General (Consumer Price Index).

Scope
The index is compiled monthly and covers all urban and rural households.

Official base
1983 = 100.

Source of weights
The weights and items were derived from a household expenditure survey conducted from March 1980 to February 1981 among a random sample of 8,000 households. The weights were adjusted to reflect price changes between the survey period and 1983.

Household consumption expenditure
This includes goods produced by the household for its own consumption, as well as income in kind. It excludes direct taxes and statutory contributions, unless they can be considered as service fees (e.g. radio and television fees).

Method of data collection
Prices for food items, tobacco and everyday items are collected each day during the last full week of the month. The prices for other items or services are collected each quarter; they are divided into three groups and collected each month on a rotating basis. Education data are obtained once a year, and officially

Weights and composition

Major groups	Number of items	Weights	Approximate number of price quotations
Food	188	4,606	11,461
Clothing and footwear	73	1,014	5,980
Rent	...	(515)	...
Housing	75	1,261	3,876
Medical care	69	263	748
Transport and communications	41	1,382	847
Education and recreation	29	412	1,195
Tobacco	5	128	62
Other goods and services	31	419	1,286
Total	511	10,000	25,455

set tariffs are adjusted whenever they change. Prices are collected from 4,800 markets, supermarkets, retail outlets and services in 25 agglomerations. The prices used are those paid directly in the outlets. Special and promotional prices are not included.

Housing
Rent is not used in the monthly computation of the index, although it was taken into account in determining the weights. Rent data are collected by rotation during the second and third quarters of each year for 32,000 dwellings. The rent index is incorporated in the annual index once a year.

Specification of varieties
The characteristics of goods and services are described as fully as possible as regards quality and other physical characteristics, to ensure consistency of data from other establishments.

Substitution, quality change, etc.
If there is a change in quantity, a proportional adjustment coefficient is calculated. If there is a change in quality, the price is estimated by means of a quality coefficient. If there is a change of both quantity and quality, an econometric method is used. When a new item is introduced in the index, its base price is estimated by reference to the price trends of similar items.

Seasonal items
Seasonal variations in the prices of fresh fruit and vegetables are taken into account by varying the items and their weights within a monthly basket, whose overall weight remains constant and by using a 12-month moving average in the final computation of the index.

Computation
The index is computed according to the Laspeyres formula as a weighted arithmetic average with fixed base, using weights corresponding to the base period.

The relative price of each item is computed by dividing the average price for the current period by the average price for the base period. The general index for the continent is a weighted arithmetic average of indices, using as weights the population of each agglomeration, according the 1981 census.

Other information
The "A" series: Continent Général (published by the ILO) excludes rent; the annual average, including rent, is published by the Instituto nacional de estadistica in "Anuario estadistico" (Lisbon). The "B" series refers to the urban populations of Lisbon and Porto.

A new series for the Mainland and a National series (base 1991 = 100) are now computed but the relevant methodological information was not available in the ILO at the time the present volume was published

Organisation and publication
Instituto nacional de estadistica: "Annuario estadistico" (Lisbon).
Idem: "Boletim mensal de estadistica".

PUERTO RICO

Official title
Consumer Price Index for All Families.

Scope
The index is compiled monthly and covers all urban households including households of wage earners and salaried workers, self-employed workers, pensioners and unemployed persons. It excludes farm families, military personnel and persons in institutions.

Official base
1967 = 100.

Source of weights
The weights and items were derived from the household expenditure survey conducted in 1977, covering 2,017 households (1,360 urban and 657 rural households). The weights were based on the expenditure pattern of urban households. The items included in the index were selected according to their relative importance. The weights were adjusted to take into account price changes between the survey period and 1979.

Weights and composition

Major groups	Number of items	Weights	Approximate number of price quotations (a)
Food	110	30.40	366
Housing:			
Rent	1	2.00	(b)
Hotel rates	1	0.71	25
Owner-occupied housing	4	7.02	27
Furnishings and household operation	42	9.46	172
Fuel and light	5	5.11	8
Clothing and footwear	37	10.00	310
Transport	12	17.20	318
Medical care	19	5.10	165
Education and recreation	11	4.60	38
Other goods and services	16	8.40	71
Total	258	100.00	1,500

Note: (a) Number of establishments. (b) 2,000 rented dwellings.

Household consumption expenditure
Consumption expenditure for the purpose of the index includes all goods and services purchased for consumption by the index population. Insurance associated with specific goods and services such as vehicle insurance, tenants' and home-owner insurance and mortgage interest rates are included. It excludes personal life insurance, income taxes and personal property taxes.

Method of data collection
Prices are collected from about 1,500 selected retail stores and establishments in 11 municipalities by agents.

Most of the items are priced each month. Prices for lodging expenses, legal services, shoe repairs, plumbing services, hairdressers, medical care, transportation, etc. are collected each quarter. The prices used in the index are the regular prices paid by any member of the public. Sale items are also quoted.

Housing
The shelter element of housing comprises rent, lodging expenses and expenditures on owner-occupied housing. Rent data are collected quarterly from 2,343 (rented) dwellings. Under owner-occupied housing, data are collected for mortgage interest, repairs and maintenance.

Specification of varieties
Broad descriptions are given for the items to be priced. Different brands can be used in different outlets to represent an item so long as prices are collected for the same brand month after month. The specific item for pricing is selected on the basis of the sales information.

Substitution, quality change, etc.
If an item is no longer available, it is substituted by a similar item.

Seasonal items
Very few seasonal items are included in the index. Prices for fresh fruit are quoted when available in season and no adjustment is made.

Computation
The index is computed according to the Laspeyres formula as a weighted arithmetic average with fixed base, the weights corresponding to 1979. The index was linked in December 1979 to base 1967 = 100.

The price relative for each item is calculated by dividing the average price for the current period by the average price for the previous period. The average price of an item is the simple arithmetic average of all price quotations obtained for the particular item.

Other information
A Consumer Price Index for wage earners' families (base 1967 = 100) is also computed and published.

Organisation and publication
Departamento del Trabajo y Recursos Humanos: "Indice de precios al consumidor para todas las familias en Puerto Rico" (San Juan).
Idem: "Importancia relativa de los bienes y servicios de consumo en el índice de precios al consumidor para todas las familias en Puerto Rico" (June 1980).
Idem: "Articulos y servicios cuyos precios se recopilan para el índice de precios al consumidor de todas las familias y el revisado de familias obreras en Puerto Rico" (September 1980).

QATAR

Official title
Consumer Price Index Number.

Scope
The index is computed monthly and relates to Qatari and non-Qatari households.

Official base
1988 = 100

Source of weights
The weights and items were derived from a household expenditure survey conducted in the State of Qatar in 1988 among a sample of Qatari and non-Qatari households.

Weights and composition

Major groups	Number of items	Weights	Approximate number of price quotations
Food and tobacco	...	286.8	...
Clothing and footwear	...	106.3	...
Housing:			
Rent	...	78.5	...
Maintenance	...	23.2	...
Fuel, electricity, water	...	22.3	...
Furniture and furnishings	...	125.8	...
Transport and communication	...	193.3	...
Medical care	...	12.3	...
Education and recreation	...	76.4	...
Miscellaneous goods and services	...	75.1	...
Total	...	1,000.0	...

Household consumption expenditure
Not available.

Method of data collection
Not available.

Housing
Not available.

Specification of varieties
Not available.

Substitution, quality change, etc.
Not available.

Seasonal items
Not available.

Computation
The index is computed according to the Laspeyres formula as a weighted arithmetic average with fixed base, using weights corresponding to the base period.

Organisation and publication
Central Statistical Organisation: "Annual Statistical Abstract".
Idem: "Monthly Survey on Retail and Consumer Index".

REUNION

Official title
Indice des prix à la consommation des ménages urbains de condition moyenne (Consumer Price Index for Middle-Income Urban Households).

Scope
The index is computed monthly and covers middle-income households of all sizes living in Saint-Denis. Middle-income households are those whose head is a wage earner or salaried employee in the private or public sector.

Official base
1978 = 100.

Source of weights
The weights and items were determined from the results of a household expenditure survey undertaken in 1986 and 1987 covering the whole population of Réunion. The consumption used for determining the weights related only to urban households whose head was a wage earner or salaried employee.

Weights and composition

Major groups	Number of items	Weights	Approximate number of price quotations
Food	87	27.93	...
Clothing and footwear	49	8.60	...
Fuel and light	6	7.16	...
Rent	1	6.27	...
Other manufactured goods (furniture, furnishings and other household goods, cleaning materials, etc.)	75	35.32	...
Other services (transport, personal and medical care, etc.)	50	14.72	...
Total	268	100.00	8,000

Household consumption expenditure
Consumption expenditure for the purpose of the index comprises most of the payments for goods and services purchased for consumption by the index population. It includes medical care and vehicle repairs valued at the actual cost to the household, as well as car insurance premiums. It excludes direct taxes, building costs considered as investment, home-produced goods consumed by households, the value of owner-occupied dwellings and benefits in kind, which are non-consumption expenditure in terms of economic accounts.

Method of data collection
The price data are collected by the field staff of INSEE, Direction Régionale de la Réunion, from 224 retail outlets and service establishments in Saint-Denis.

The prices are those actually paid, but no account is taken of sale prices. Prices of meat, eggs, fresh fruit and vegetables are collected each week, rent data every three months and prices for other goods and services each monthly. The selection of outlets took into account the different types of areas in the town of Saint-Denis, of commerce (such as supermarkets, independent businesses, markets, etc.) and of purchasing habits.

Housing
Rent data are obtained through a quarterly survey of a sample of 284 rented dwellings.

Specification of varieties
The list of varieties is modified to take into account changes in consumption habits, which may be frequent in the case of food. Items are selected if they are representative of one of the 268 expenditure headings.

Substitution, quality change, etc.
Three methods are used to take into account quantity or quality changes in the items priced, the disappearance of old items or the appearance of new ones: (i) when the new item differs from the old one in terms of quantity only, the price is adjusted proportionately; (ii) when both its quality and quantity are different from those of the old one, a closely-related item is substituted on the assumption that the new item has the same past price trend as the old one; and (iii) the field staff themselves make on-the-spot estimates of the price differences resulting from a quality change.

Seasonal items
Account is taken of the seasonal fluctuations of fresh fruit and vegetables by varying the items in the sub-group each month while keeping the overall weights constant. The index compares the cost of the basket for the current month with that for the same month of the base year. The base price for a variety is the weighted annual average for the previous year, which is then used for each month.

Computation
Since January 1990, the index is a chain index in which the weights are changed each calendar year. The index for each month is first computed on base December of the previous year=100; the resulting index is then calculated on base 1978 = 100 (Laspeyres' chain index).

In computing item indices, price relatives for the current and base periods are used. Relatives of average prices are calculated for items with homogeneous varieties, and averages of price relatives are used for those with heterogeneous varieties.

Organisation and publication
INSEE, Service départemental de la Réunion: "Bulletin de statistiques" (Saint-Denis).

Idem: "L'indice des prix à la consommation des ménages urbains de condition moyenne"(document No. 33, Oct. 1980).

ROMANIA

Official title
Indice des prix à la consommation de la population (Consumer Price Index).

Scope
The index is compiled monthly and covers households throughout the country whose head is a wage earner, pensioner or farmer.

Official base
October 1990 = 100.

Source of weights
The weights and items were derived from a household expenditure survey conducted from January to December 1990 among 5,900 wage earner households, 2,700 farmer households, and 400 pensioner households.

Weights and composition

Major groups	Number of items	Weights	Approximate number of price quotations
Food	79	40.5	...
Non-food products	111	40.3	...
Services	51	19.2	...
Total	241	100.0	...

Household consumption expenditure
Consumption expenditure for the purpose of establishing weights includes all goods and services purchased from the public, co-operative, private and mixed sectors. It excluded the consumption of goods and services produced by the household, imputed rent for owner-occupied dwellings, taxes, fines, gambling, interest on loans, social security contributions, loans and fund remittances.

Method of data collection
Prices are collected by agents from markets, fairs, retail outlets, co-operatives and service establishments. The prices of food items are collected from markets on the 5th, 15th and 25th of each month. Data for rent, electricity, gas, water, heating oil, post, telecommunications and public transport are official tariffs and are collected once a month. The index takes into account discounts and free market prices for items which also have an official price and an import price, when the volume of sales is considerable.

Housing
Rent data for state-owned housing are obtained each month. Owner-occupied dwellings are not included in the index.

Specification of varieties
The specifications of items to be priced are detailed and describe technical characteristics, etc.

Substitution, quality change, etc.
If a product's quality changes, or if it disappears from the market, or if a new product comes on to the market, a base price is estimated by reference to the price trends of other items in the same sub-group.

Seasonal items
For seasonal items such as fresh fruit and vegetables and wool, use is made of a monthly basket whose overall weight remains constant.

Computation
The index is computed according to the Laspeyres formula as a weighted arithmetic average with fixed base, using weights corresponding to the base period.

Price relatives for the current and base periods are used to compute item indices. Average prices are the simple arithmetic averages of all prices observed.

Organisation and publication
Commission nationale de statistique, Division des statistiques des prix et tarifs: "Bulletin statistique des prix" (Bucarest).

Idem: "La méthodologie de construction de l'indice des prix à la consommation de la population".

RWANDA (KIGALI)

Official title
Indice des prix à la consommation (Consumer Price Index).

Scope
The index is computed monthly and covers households of wage earners in the public, semi-public and private sectors of the urban area of Kigali.

Official base
March-June 1982 = 100.

Source of weights
The weights and items were derived from a household expenditure survey conducted during March-June 1982 among households of wage earners in the public, semi-public and private sectors of the urban area of Kigali with a monthly income of 5,000 to 100,000 francs at the time of the survey.

Weights and composition

Major groups	Number of items	Weights	Approximate number of price quotations
All items:			
Food	105	34.90	...
Beverages and tobacco	22	9.30	...
Clothing and footwear	71	11.35	...
Household equipment	36	8.40	...
Medical care	37	1.70	...
Personal and other care	55	3.55	...
Housing	59	13.20	...
Transport	20	10.30	...
Recreation and leisure	12	1.20	...
Miscellaneous	24	6.10	...
Total	441	100.00	...

Household consumption expenditure
Consumption expenditure comprises: monetary consumer expenditure; presents given in kind; items bartered; and own-consumption (i.e. a household's production for its own consumption). The latter was taken into account indirectly because it could not be set apart in the the survey. The aim of the survey was not to determine final household expenditure but the weights for the various items of the index.

Income in kind was taken into account when computing the overall income of households surveyed and concerns free housing, free electricity and water, and free transport.

Owner-occupied dwellings, the trading-in of used goods and in payment for new goods were not taken into account at the time of the survey. Income tax and other direct taxes, and contributions to social insurance and pension funds were not taken into account. Although these items account for household expenditure, they are not consumer goods and it is difficult, if not impossible, to establish their prices. Life insurance payments were excluded from the index to avoid overlapping in the accounts, since insurance services are difficult to ascertain. For medical care, hospital expenditure is not included in the monthly consumer price index because of the lack of rapid information on the corresponding prices; only the costs of medical consultations in both the state and private health sectors (as well as the most commonly consumed medicine) were taken into account at the time of the survey. Remittances, gifts and similar disbursements were not included because no price is given to these. The purchase of durable goods, credit purchases and second-hand purchases were taken into account in the household expenditure survey.

Method of data collection
Prices are collected twice a month from all markets and the most representative retail outlets in the urban area of Kigali. The prices used to compute the index are the prices actually paid by the consumers.

Information on electricity, gas and water rates, medical consultation fees, school fees, transport and communication costs which are established by the Government are collected when the prices change.

Housing
Data on rents are obtained every month for four rented dwellings, of which two have two bedrooms and no electricity and two have two bedrooms and electricity. Owner-occupied dwellings are not taken into account.

Specification of varieties
These are specifications for imported and local items, as well as items imported but manufactured locally (raw materials imported).

Substitution, quality change, etc.
If there is a change in the quality of an item, and if it may be considered as new one and causes the old item to be discontinued, it is included. A fictitious base price is calculated by applying the percentage of increase of the former item.

Seasonal items
When a seasonal item is not available on the market, its price is maintained for a maximum of three months.

Computation
The index is computed according to the Laspeyres formula as a weighted arithmetic average with fixed base, using weights corresponding to the base period.

Organisation and publication
Banque Nationale du Rwanda: "Bulletin de la Banque Nationale du Rwanda" (Kigali).

Idem: "Rapport annuel sur l'évolution économique et monétaire du Rwanda".

ST. HELENA

Official title
Retail Price Index.

Scope
The index is computed quarterly and covers all households thgoughout the island.

Official base
November 1987 = 100.

Source of weights
The weights and items were derived from a household expenditure survey conducted in two stages, in October-November 1987 among a sample of 84 households and in April-May 1988 among a sample of 94 households. The average weekly household expenditure was about 74 pounds at the time of the survey. The results were checked against data from import statistics to amend the weights.

Weights and composition

Major groups	Number of items	Weights	Approximate number of price quotations
Food	75	44.6	75
Alcohol and tobacco	7	10.1	7
Housing (incl. rent and rates)	3	5.6	3
Fuel and light	5	5.1	5
Clothing and footwear	15	5.8	15
Household goods	13	7.3	13
Transport	10	11.6	10
Miscellaneous goods	15	7.9	15
Services	6	2.0	6
Total	149	100.0	149

Household consumption expenditure
Fees for driving licences and motor car insurance are included as well as housing loan repayments and land taxes, but life insurance premiums are excluded.

Method of data collection
Prices are collected by two agents from the Economic and Statistics Unit during two weekdays around the 20th of February, May, August and November from seven outlets in Jamestown.

Supplies in St. Helena depend on the arrival of the ship that calls about once every six weeks. If the price collection date is just before (under one week) the arrival of the ship, the collection date is put back so that the goods are available on the market. Controlled prices such as for water, electricity and land taxes, and for some building materials, are obtained through telephone calls to government departments. Discounts and sale prices are taken into account.

Housing
Rent quotations are obtained each quarter for the weekly rent of a government-owned three-bedroom dwelling. Owner-occupied housing is not treated explicitly.

Specification of varieties
Specifications include the type, size, brand and point of purchase. Price collection sheets span one year, so sharp deviations are easily identifiable.

Substitution, quality change, etc.
When an item is no longer available on the market, it is substituted by a similar item.

Seasonal items
No adjustments are made to the market prices.

Computation
The index is computed according to the Laspeyres formula as a weighted arithmetic average with fixed base, using weights corresponding to the base period.

Other information
Sub-group indices are published for Food, Alcohol and tobacco, Housing, Fuel and light, Clothing, Household goods, Transport, Miscellaneous goods and services. A low-income index is also computed but not published.

Organisation and publication
Economic and Statistics Unit: "Quarterly Statistical Review" (Jamestown).

Idem: "Statistical News".

ST. LUCIA

Official title
Consumer Price Index.

Scope
The index is computed monthly and relates to urban, sub-urban and rural households.

Official base
April 1984 = 100.

Source of weights
The weights were derived from household expenditure surveys conducted during September-November 1982 in the Castries Administration Area, the capital city of St. Lucia, among a sample of 170 urban, 157 sub-urban and 154 rural households. The weights were not adjusted to take into account price changes between the survey period and the base period.

Weights and composition

Major groups	Number of items	Weights	Approximate number of price quotations
Food	77	467.51	...
Beverages and tobacco	5	28.17	...
Clothing and footwear	16	64.97	...
Housing	7	135.34	...
Fuel and light	4	44.95	...
Furniture and household operation	11	57.71	...
Medical care	6	22.78	...
Transport and communication	10	63.48	...
Recreation	6	32.36	...
Miscellaneous	26	82.73	...
Total	168	1,000.00	...

Household consumption expenditure
The classification scheme conforms with the SNA classification of household final consumption expenditure.

Method of data collection
Prices are collected by agents once a month, on the second

Tuesday, from supermarkets, retail outlets and service establishments.

Electricity rates are obtained by mail questionnaires. Telephone and water rates are collected by telephone and other services by personal visits. Officers of the Statistics Office obtain item prices, brands, quality, unit, etc. from retail outlets. Prices of these "basket items" were collected over a period of four months and from the data collected the pricing outlets were selected.

Housing
Rent quotations for houses are collected every six months. No account is taken of owner-occupied housing in the index.

Specification of varieties
Each item has detailed specifications, such as the unit, brand, quality, etc.

Substitution, quality change, etc.
If an item disappears from the market, another item is selected and the weight remains the same but the base price is adjusted.

Seasonal items
Seasonal items are not included in the index.

Computation
The index is computed according to the Laspeyres formula as a weighted arithmetic average with fixed base, using weights corresponding to September-November 1982.

Other information
The index is calculated by the Government Statistical Department, Castries.

Organisation and publication
Government Printer: "The St.Lucia Gazette" (Castries).

ST. VINCENT AND THE GRENADINES (ST. VINCENT)

Official title
Index of Retail Prices.

Scope
The index is computed monthly and relates to the whole population in St.Vincent.

Official base
January 1981 = 100.

Source of weights
The weights and items were derived from a household expenditure survey conducted during six months beginning in November 1975 in the urban area and the rural areas of St. Vincent. The survey covered 164 households of all income groups. The average household size was 5.84 persons.

Weights and composition

Major groups	Number of items	Weights	Approximate number of price quotations
Food	88	597.9	...
Other groups:	130	402.1	...
Clothing and footwear	...	...	...
Housing, fuel and light	...	...	...
Furniture and household supplies	...	...	...
Medical care	...	...	...
Transport and communication	...	...	...
Education and recreation	...	...	...
Miscellaneous	...	...	...
Total	218	1,000.0	...

Household consumption expenditure
Not available.

Method of data collection
Prices are collected by agents from market areas, retail outlets, supermarkets and service establishments on the second Tuesday of each month.

Housing
Included under rent are a three-bedroom unfurnished house in the capital city and a three-bedroom unfurnished house in the rural area. Owner-occupied housing is not used in the index.

Specification of varieties
Not available.

Substitution, quality change, etc.
Not available.

Seasonal items
Not available.

Computation
The index is computed according to the Laspeyres formula as a weighted arithmetic average with fixed base, using weights corresponding to 1975-76.

Price relatives for the current and base periods are used to compute item indices.

Organisation and publication
Central Planning Division, Statistical Office: "Annual Digest of Statistics" (Kingstown).

Idem: "Retail Price Bulletin".

SAMOA

Official title
Consumer Price Index.

Scope
The index is compiled monthly and covers Samoan households throughout the country.

Official base
1980 = 100.

Source of weights
The weights and items were derived from the household expenditure survey conducted from August 1976 to July 1977, covering 1,560 households throughout the country. The weights were not adjusted to take account of price changes between the survey period and 1980.

Weights and composition

Major groups	Number of items	Weights	Approximate number of price quotations
Food	55	588	1,016
Clothing and footwear	16	42	168
Housing:			
Building materials	7	14	67
Kitchen utensils	7	26	96
Household linen	7	11	48
Fuel and light	5	50	24
Other	7	19	48
Transport and communication	9	90	37
Miscellaneous	24	160	96
Total	137	1,000	1,600

Household consumption expenditure
Consumption expenditure for the purpose of the index comprises all goods and services purchased for consumption by the index population. It excludes goods or services produced on own account and goods or services received as income in kind for household use.

Method of data collection
Prices are collected by statistical officers of the Department of Statistics from selected retail stores, markets and service establishments. Ten major stores were selected from the Apia urban area, seven from the rest of Upolu, six from Satelologa and seven from the rest of Savaii. As price movements in the rural areas are similar to those in the urban area, price collection is limited to the urban area.

Most prices are collected in the middle of each month. Prices for vegetables, fruit, nuts and fresh fish are obtained every Friday from the Apia urban area.

The prices used in the calculation of the index are the retail prices actually paid. Sale and discount prices are not taken into account.

Housing
Rent is excluded from the index. The housing index comprises building materials and furniture, kitchen utensils, linen, fuel and light and certain other items.

Specification of varieties
The specifications of items to be priced are given in detail in terms of brand, make, quality and size.

Substitution, quality change, etc.
When a product disappears from the market, it is substituted by

a similar product. Quality changes are adjusted as much as possible to the original quality required.

Seasonal items
In case of seasonal items such as fruit and vegetables which are not available on the market during the off season, the last available prices are used for calculating the index until the items can be priced again.

Computation
The index is computed according to the Laspeyres formula as a weighted arithmetic average with fixed base, using weights corresponding to August 1976-July 1977.

The price relative for each item is computed by dividing the average price for the current period by the average price for the base period. Average prices are simple arithmetic averages of all available price quotations.

Organisation and publication
Department of Statistics: "Quarterly Statistical Bulletin" (Apia).
Idem: "The Annual Abstracts".
Idem: "Monthly C.P.I. Release".
Idem: "Report on the Revised Consumer Price Index for Western Samoa, 1980 = 100".

SAN MARINO

Official title
Consumer Price Index.

Scope
The index is computed monthly and covers wage earner's and salaried employee's households in San Marino.

Official base
1985 = 100.

Source of weights
The weights were derived from the 1984 consumption patterns and national accounts data for Italy, adjusted for households in San Marino. The items for which prices are collected are those consumed by the majority of households.

Weights and composition

Major groups	Number of items	Weights	Approximate number of price quotations
Food and tobacco	86	30.92	...
Clothing and footwear	38	8.67	...
Rent, maintenance and repairs	3	4.97	...
Fuel and light	5	4.72	...
Other goods and services	150	50.72	...
Total	282	100.00	...

Household consumption expenditure
Consumption expenditure for the purpose of the index does not include income taxes, investment and savings, consumption from own production or the imputed rent of the owner-occupied dwellings.

Method of data collection
Prices are collected on the 15th of each month, using mailed questionnaires, from 50 retail outlets and service establishments distributed throughout the territory according to population size. Official tariffs fixed by the government are used for certain items and services. The prices used in to calculate the index are the normal prices paid by the consumers. Sale prices, discounts, hire-purchase or credit terms and second-hand purchases are not covered in the index.

Housing
Rent quotations are obtained twice a year for 47 privately rented dwellings.

Specification of varieties
Detailed specifications are provided for each item included in the market basket, comprising a complete description of the item, its brand, name or trade mark, type of packing, quantity or unit, etc.

Substitution, quality change, etc.
If a product is not available, a product similar to the original is substituted and a method of linking is used.

Seasonal items
typical seasonal market basket is constructed for these items for each of the twelve months.

Computation
The index is computed according to the Laspeyres formula as a weighted arithmetic average with fixed base, using weights corresponding to 1984.

The price relative for each item is calculated by dividing the average price for the current period by the average price for the previous period.

Other information
Detailed sub-group indices are published.

Organisation and publication
Centro Elaborazione dati e statistica: "Bolletino di statistica" (San Marino).

SAUDI ARABIA 1

Official title
Cost of Living Index (All Cities Index).

Scope
The index is compiled monthly and relates to Saudi and non-Saudi households in the following ten cities: Riyadh, Jeddah, Damman, Abha, Buraydah, Makkah, Medinah, Taif, Hofhuf and Tabuk.

Official base
1988 = 100.

Source of weights
The weights and items were derived from the 1985-86 household expenditure survey which lasted a full year. The reference period for reporting monthly expenditures for each household was one month. The survey was conducted in 15 cities, the 10 cities mentioned above and five smaller cities. All geographic regions were represented in the survey. The household sample was an area sample and the specific households were selected randomly. In all, approximately 15,000 households were initially surveyed. The weights used in the Cost of Living Index were a combination of cost (based on family expenditure data) and population. No national accounts data were used.

Items were selected for the Cost of Living Index using probability proportionate to size (PPS) methods, as well as random methods for certin items. Over 200 items are included in the item sample. The weights of those items not selected are imputed monthly by the movement of the group that the "Unpriced items" fall in.

Weights and composition

Major groups	Number of items	Weights	Approximate number of price quotations
Food	87	32.62	6,090
Housing (incl. fuel, light and water)	7	19.69	353
Clothing and footwear	29	8.40	725
Furniture and furnishings	36	9.38	900
Medical care	7	1.24	175
Transport and communication	8	17.30	200
Entertainment and education	15	2.95	375
Other expenditure	13	8.42	275
Total	202	100.00	(a) 9,093

Note: (a) See below.

(a) Judgement, based on past pricing experience, is used to determine the number of prices for each item. Seven prices are collected for each food item and five prices for each non-food item. More prices are obtained for food items because of their variations.

Household consumption expenditure
Consumption expenditure does not include taxes, insurances or owner-occupied housing.

Method of data collection
Retail stores and other outlets were selected from the results of a retail outlet survey. The Central Department of Statistics (CDS) collects seven prices for each food item in each city each month. Non-food items are priced every month, covering half the items in alternate months. Five prices are collected for most non-food items, except for items whose prices are set or controlled by the government. For example, prices for electricity, telephone charges, gasoline, etc. are held constant until

there is a price change. Price changes for these items are announced in the daily newspapers. Medical care prices are collected by visits to physicians offices or hospitals. Education prices are collected from a sample of schools in each of the ten cities. Transportation prices are collected by visits to the airline offices, bus companies, etc. Airline charges are for both domestic and international flights. For telephone charges, a combination of the basic service charge plus charges for long-distance calls are used.

In general, all prices are collected by personal visits by trained data collectors. Prices are collected randomly from the 1st to the 21st of the month. Data collectors are instructed to collect any given outlet's prices at approximately the same time each month so certain outlets may be priced around the 5th of the month, others are priced around the 20th, and so on. An outlet priced around the 5th of the month is not priced the following month around the 20th.

Data collectors are instructed to request the most common price of the item. If discounts are normally given, this is the price they record.

Sale prices are treated as any other price. The price is entered and, when calculated, would show a decrease from the previous regular price. A number of food staples are subsidised (official prices) and there are no lower prices than these. There are no black market prices.

Hire purchase or credit terms do not apply in Saudi Arabia (no items are leased in the index).

No second-hand goods are priced. Data collectors are instructed to price up-to-date merchandise available in saleable quantity.

Import prices are treated as any other prices. In Saudi Arabia, many items are imported. The data collectors identify the country of origin.

Housing
A detailed rent schedule is completed by the data collector and includes whether or not utilities are included in the rent, whether or not the rental unit has air conditioning, etc. Both villas and flats are priced. The rental sample in each city is divided into six panels with each panel being priced every six months. One-sixth of the price movement of rents in each city are applied to the rental cost-population weights. These are aggregated for all 10 cities and a Kingdom-wide rent index is calculated.

Owner-occupied housing is not priced in the housing component of the index.

Specification of varieties
The CDS has detailed specifications for all items in the index. These require the data collector to enter the variety, type, make, brand, serial number, and country of origin, etc. The data collector needs to enter as much information as possible so that he can price the same, or a comparable item, in the following pricing period.

Substitution, quality change, etc.
If an item is priced which has a different size or weight from the previous item, the price of the previous item is converted to a comparable weight so that an accurate comparison can be made. Because of the lack of data to adjust for most quality changes, no effort is made to adjust for these and new items are linked into the index.

The index is revised at five-year intervals. New products which enter the market between revisions are not priced but may be captured in the next consumer expenditure survey. If a new product enters the market for an item that is already being priced, the data collector does substitute it unless the previously priced item is not available and it is the closest available substitute.

If a given type of quality disappears from the market, as has occurred on occasion, the weight of the item is initially imputed by the movement of that group. If it is certain that the item will no longer be stocked or sold, instructions are sent to the computer centre to include the weight for that item in the weight of the unpriced items category. The unpriced items category is also imputed by the movement of prices for that specific group.

Seasonal items
Seasonal items are priced when they are available. For example, certain fruits and vegetables are very plentiful at certain times of the year. Prices, of course, are lower then. As the supply diminishes, prices rise. If data collectors are unable to price a given item, they enter on the price schedule that the item is unavailable and the item is not priced until it is again available in the market.

Computation
The index is computed according to the Laspeyres formula as a weighted arithmetic average with fixed base, using weights corresponding to the base period.

The relatives of average prices for the current and previous periods are used to calculate item indices. The index for all cities is an aggregate of the ten primary sampling units (PSU). A weight reflecting estimated current expenditure for the base period market basket is determined for each item, in each PSU. The population of each PSU is used to combine the weights of each item, in order to obtain the final weights for all cities.

Other information
Detailed sub-group indices and cities indices are also published. The Central Department of Statistics also publishes a Middle-Income Index.

Organisation and publication
Ministry of Finance and National Economy, Central Department of Statistics: "The Statistical Indicator" (Riyadh).
Idem: "Statistical Yearbook".
Idem: "Cost of Living Index".

SAUDI ARABIA 2

Official title
Cost of Living Index (Middle-Income Index).

Scope
The index is compiled monthly and covers middle-income group households with monthly expenditure between 2,500 and 10,000 riyals in the following ten cities: Riyadh, Jeddah, Damman, Abha, Buraydah, Makkah, Medinah, Taif, Hofhuf and Tabuk.

Official base
1988 = 100.

Source of weights
The weights and items were derived from the 1985-86 household expenditure survey which covered a full year. The reference period for reporting monthly expenditure for households was one month. The survey was conducted in 15 cities, the 10 cities mentioned above and five smaller cities. All geographic regions were represented in the survey. The household sample was an area sample and the specific households were selected randomly. In all, approximately 15,000 households were initially surveyed. The weights used in the Cost of Living Index were a combination of cost (based on family expenditure data) and population. No national accounts data were used.

Items were selected for the Cost of Living Index using probability proportionate to size (PPS) methods, or random methods for certain items. Over 200 items are included in the item sample. The weights of those items not selected are imputed monthly by the movement of the group that the "Unpriced items" fall in.

Weights and composition

Major groups	Number of items	Weights	Approximate number of price quotations
Food	85	37.66	5,950
Housing (incl. fuel, light and water)	8	21.11	353
Clothing and footwear	26	7.93	650
Furniture and furnishings	31	7.42	750
Medical care	7	1.13	175
Transport and communication	9	15.08	225
Entertainment and education	15	2.01	350
Other expenditure	13	7.66	300
Total	194	100.00	(a) 8,753

Note: (a) See below.

(a) Judgement, based on past pricing experience, is used to determine the number of prices for each item. Seven prices are collected for each food item and five for each non-food item. More prices are obtained for food items because of their variations.

Household consumption expenditure
Consumption expenditures does not include taxes, insurances or owner-occupied housing.

Method of data collection
Retail stores and other outlets were selected from the results of

a retail outlet survey. The Central Department of Statistics (CDS) collects seven prices for each food item in each city each month. Non-food items are priced every two months with half of the items alternately each month. Five prices are collected for most non-food items, except for items whose prices are set or controlled by the government. For example, prices for electricity, telephone charges, gasoline, etc. are held constant until there is a price change. Price changes for these items are announced in the daily newspapers. Medical care prices are collected by visits to physicians offices or hospitals. Education prices are collected from a sample of schools in each of the ten cities. Transportation prices are collected by visits to the airline offices, bus companies, etc. Airline charges are for both domestic flights and international flights. For telephone charges, a combination of the basic service charge plus charges for long-distance calls are used.

In general, all prices are collected by personal visits by trained data collectors. Prices are collected randomly from the 1st to the 21st of the month. Data collectors are instructed to collect any given outlet's prices at approximately the same time each month, so e.g. certain outlets may be priced around the 5th of the month and others around the 20th. An outlet priced around the 5th of the month would not be priced the following month around the 20th.

Data collectors are instructed to request the most common price of the item. If discounts are normally given, this is the price they record.

Sale prices are treated as any other price. The price is entered and, when calculated, shows a price decrease from the previous regular price. A number of food staples are subsidised (official prices) and there are no lower prices than these. There are no black market prices.

Hire purchase or credit terms do not apply in Saudi Arabia (no items are leased in the index).

No second-hand goods are priced. Data collectors are instructed to price up-to-date merchandise available in saleable quantity.

Import prices are treated as any other prices. In Saudi Arabia, many items are imported. The data collectors identify the country of origin.

Housing
A detailed rent schedule is completed by the data collector and includes whether or not utilities are included in the rent, whether or not the rental unit has air conditioning, etc. Both villas and flats are priced. The rental sample in each city is divided into six panels with each panel being priced every six months. One-sixth of the price movement of rents in each city are applied to the rental cost-population weights. These are aggregated for all 10 cities and a Kingdom-wide rent index is calculated.

Owner-occupied housing is not priced in the housing component of the index.

Specification of varieties
The CDS has detailed specifications for all items in the CLI. These require the data collector to enter the variety, type, make, brand, serial number, and country of origin, etc. The data collector needs to enter as much information as possible so that he can price the same, or a comparable item, in the following pricing period.

Substitution, quality change, etc.
If an item is priced which has a different size or weight from the previous item, the price of the previous item is converted to a comparable weight so that an accurate comparison can be made. Because of the lack of data to adjust for most quality changes, no effort is made to adjust for these and new items are linked into the index.

The CLI is revised at five-year intervals. New products which enter the market between revisions are not priced but may be captured in the next consumer expenditure survey. If a new product enters the market for an item that already is being priced, the data collector does not substitute to it unless the previously priced item is not available and it is the closest available substitute.

If a given type of quality disappears from the market, which has occurred on occasion, the weight of the item is firts simply imputed by the movement of that group. If it is certain that the item will no longer be stocked or sold, instructions are sent to the computer centre to include the weight for that item in the weight of the unpriced items category. The unpriced items category is also imputed by the movement of prices for that specific group.

Seasonal items
Seasonal items are priced when they are available. For example, certain fruits and vegetables are very plentiful at certain times of the year. Prices, of course, are lower then. As the supply diminishes, prices rise. If data collectors are unable to price a given item, they enter on the price schedule that the item is unavailable and the item is not priced until it is again available in the market.

Computation
The index is computed according to the Laspeyres formula as a weighted arithmetic average with fixed base, using weights corresponding to the base period.

The relatives of average prices for the current and base periods are used to compute item indices. The index for all cities is an aggregate of the ten primary sampling units (PSU). A weight reflecting estimated current expenditure for the base period market basket is determined for each item, in each PSU. The population of each PSU is used to combine the weights of each item, in order to obtain the final weights for all cities.

Other information
Detailed sub-group indices and cities indices are also published. The Central Department of Statistics also publishes an All-Cities Index.

Organisation and publication
Ministry of Finance and National Economy, Central Department of Statistics: "The Statistical Indicator" (Riyadh).

Idem: "Statistical Yearbook".

Idem: "Cost of Living Index".

SENEGAL (DAKAR)

Official title
Indice des prix à la consommation (Consumer Price Index).

Scope
The index is compiled monthly and relates to Senegalese households in Dakar with a monthly income of less than 100,000 CFA francs in 1960-61.

Official base
1967 = 100.

Source of weights
The weights and items were derived from a household expenditure survey conducted in Dakar in 1960-61 among Senegalese households with a monthly income of less than 100,000 CFA francs at the time of the survey.

Weights and composition

Major groups	Number of items	Weights	Approximate number of price quotations
Food	71	56.0	...
Clothing and footwear	22	11.9	...
Housing:			
Rent and repairs	5	8.7	...
Fuel, light and water	5	5.8	...
Household equipment	7	1.7	...
Personal and medical care and cleaning materials	14	4.0	...
Transport	9	5.4	...
Education, recreation, tobacco domestic services, etc.	18	6.5	...
Total	151	100.0	...

Household consumption expenditure
Not available.

Method of data collection
Prices for food items are collected weekly, by agents, from retail outlets and from six markets in Dakar. Prices for other items are obtained during the second half of each month. Quotations relating to service items are obtained from official tariffs. No account is taken of sale prices.

Housing
Rent data for recent dwellings with two rooms are obtained from a large real-estate company.

Specification of varieties
The specifications describe the variety, quality, make, brand, unit, etc.

Substitution, quality change, etc.
If an item disappears from the market, its price is used for a maximum of three months. The item is then replaced by a similar item for which a fictitious base price is calculated.

Seasonal items
Seasonal fluctuations in the prices of certain items are taken into account by maintaining the closing prices of the preceding season during the off season.

Computation
The index is compiled according to the Laspeyres formula as a weighted arithmetic average with fixed base, using weights corresponding to 1960-61.

Organisation and publication
Ministère de l'Economie, des Finances et du Plan, Direction de la prévision et de la statistique: "Note mensuelle sur les indices des prix de détail" (Dakar).

SEYCHELLES

Official title
Retail Price Index.

Scope
The index is compiled monthly and relates to households of all income groups throughout the country.

Official base
March 1986 = 100.

Source of weights
The weights and items were derived from a household expenditure survey conducted between 8 August 1983 and 5 August 1984 covering a sample of 969 households of all income groups living in the islands of Mahé, Praslin and La Digue.

Expenditure by all household members was recorded over a two-week period, and information was provided about the major purchases for the previous three months. The weights were not adjusted to take into account price changes between the survey period and 1986.

Weights and composition

Major groups	Number of items	Weights	Approximate number of price quotations
Fresh fish	1	5.16	...
Other food items	90	28.90	...
Alcoholic drinks and tobacco	9	18.74	...
Clothing and footwear	15	8.57	...
Rent and building costs	3	11.20	...
Fuel, light and water	7	7.44	...
Household goods	14	5.86	...
Personal care	16	1.63	...
Transport and communication	14	7.63	...
Other services and recreation	16	4.87	...
Total	185	100.00	...

Household consumption expenditure
Consumption expenditure for the purpose of the index includes almost all goods and services purchased for consumption by the index population. It includes car insurance, licence fees and imputed rent for owner-occupied dwellings. It excludes savings and investment, income taxes and other direct taxes.

Method of data collection
Prices for most items are collected each month by agents from 22 retail outlets and markets in Mahé and Praslin. Prices for services are obtained from their suppliers. Price data refer to the week including the 15th of the month. Fish prices are collected through direct buying five times a week. Prices of fruit and vegetables are obtained once a week.

The prices used to calculate the index are those actually charged to consumers. Official prices fixed by the government for items such as fruit and vegetables are also used in the index calculation.

Housing
Rent data are collected every three months, on a rotating basis, from a sample of 180 houses, comprising 20 per cent government houses and 80 per cent private houses.

Specification of varieties
The specifications of items to be priced are given in terms of the variety, quality, type of packaging, make, brand and unit.

Substitution, quality change, etc.
If a product is no longer available, a product similar to the original is substituted and a method of linking is used.

Seasonal items
The only seasonal item is fish and no adjustment is made.

Computation
The index is computed according to the Laspeyres formula as a weighted arithmetic average with fixed base, using weights corresponding to 8 August 1983-5 August 1984.
Price relatives are first calculated per item and per outlet, then the average is computed.

Organisation and publication
Ministry of Finance, Statistics Division: "Monthly Statistical Bulletin - Retail Price Index" (Victoria).

SIERRA LEONE (FREETOWN)

Official title
Consumer Price Index for Low-Income Families.

Scope
The index is compiled monthly and relates to low-income group households in Freetown, including Greater Freetown, with an average monthly total expenditure not exceeding 100 leones in 1976-77.

Official base
1978 = 100.

Source of weights
The weights and items were derived from a household expenditure survey conducted during April 1976-July 1977, among 576 private households in Freetown including Greater Freetown, with an average monthly expenditure not exceeding 100 leones in 1976-77. The weights were adjusted for price changes between the survey period and 1978.

Weights and composition

Major groups	Number of items	Weights	Approximate number of price quotations
Food	62	63.1	...
Tobacco and cola nuts	5	3.8	...
Housing:			
Rent	1	9.2	...
Rates and repairs	4	0.3	...
Fuel and light	6	6.9	...
Furniture, furnishings, and household goods	18	1.8	...
Clothing and footwear	31	5.4	...
Miscellaneous goods and services:			
Personal care	10	1.4	...
Medical care	11	1.6	...
Cleaning materials	6	1.9	...
Recreation	4	0.2	...
Reading and education	5	0.6	...
Transport and communication	7	3.5	...
Other expenses	2	0.3	...
Total	172	100.0	

Household consumption expenditure
Not available.

Method of data collection
Prices for most items are collected by agents from retail outlets. Prices for food items are collected from three major public markets. The frequency of price collection may be weekly, monthly or quarterly depending on the price variability of the individual item; most food items are priced once a week.

Housing
Rent quotations are obtained each quarter for 91 dwellings, while rates for communal services are obtained once a year.

Specification of varieties
The specifications of items to be priced are given in detail taking into account the popularity of the items. Specifications are given in terms of the brand, make, quality and size.

Substitution, quality change, etc.
If an item is no longer available, it is replaced by a similar item and a method of linking is used.

Seasonal items
For fresh fruit and vegetables, prices during the off season are assumed to follow the price movements of the other items included in the sub-group.

Computation
The index is computed according to the Laspeyres formula as a weighted arithmetic average with fixed base, using weights corresponding to the base period.
Price relatives for the current and previous periods are used to compute item indices.

Organisation and publication
Central Statistics Office: "Statistical Bulletin" (Freetown).
Idem: "Technical Report on Revision of Consumer Price Index for Freetown with base 1978 = 100" (August 1984).
Government Printing Department: "The Sierra Leone Gazette".

SINGAPORE

Official title
Consumer Price Index.

Scope
The index is computed monthly and covers households with monthly expenditure of between 500 and 4,999 dollars during 1987-1988.

Official base
September 1987-August 1988 = 100.

Source of weights
The weights and items were derived from a household expenditure survey conducted during September 1987-August 1988.

The spending pattern of households with monthly expenditure of between 500 and 4,999 Singapore was used to derive the weighting pattern. This group of households made up 90 per cent of the total number of households surveyed.

The survey covered the whole country and a representative sample of all private households with at least two persons in the main island of Singapore. One-person households and foreign resident households were outside the scope of the survey. Personal interviewing was used, and the survey was spread over a period of twelve months from September 1987 to August 1988. The first group of households was covered in the reference month September 1987 and the last group in August 1988. In the final analyses and tabulations, the records of 5,742 households were used.

The criteria for items to be selected were their relative importance, their price movements being typical of similar or related items and their priceability i.e. whether they are available for regular pricing. Items that are relatively insignificant, or have no meaningful quantitative units or whose specifications are not standardised, were excluded for pricing purposes, but are nevertheless indirectly represented by the selected similar or related items. Their shares of total expenditure were assigned to selected similar or related items.

Weights and composition

Major groups	Number of items	Weights	Approximate number of price quotations
Food	272	3,977	8,424
Clothing and footwear	65	570	382
Housing:	71	1,717	1,011
Rented accommodation	4	110	224
Owner-occupied accommodation	7	603	382
Repairs and maintenance	4	226	34
Fuel and light	8	456	42
Household durables	48	322	329
Transport and communication	38	1,450	255
Miscellaneous:	147	2,286	1,904
Education	34	500	322
Health	22	249	403
Recreation and entertainment	15	295	110
Alcoholic drinks and tobacco	12	282	175
Other goods and services	64	960	894
Total	593	10,000	11,976

Household consumption expenditure
Consumption expenditure used for deriving the weights refers to payments incurred for goods and services acquired by households during the survey month. For items purchased on credit, the amounts were recorded on the days the items were acquired. For items or goods withdrawn from own grocery shops or farms, the amounts imputed at current market value were recorded as expenditure. For large but infrequent expenditure, such as on consumer durables, vacation travel and major house repairs and renovations, householders were asked to record the expenditure with a recall period of 12 months ending with the survey month, and one-twelfth of such value was used as expenditure for that month. For the trade-in of used goods and in part payment for new ones, the net payment was used, i.e. the difference between the price of new item and the trade-in value of the old one. The same applied to second-hand purchases. Central Provident Fund contributions and other non-consumption payments such as income tax, loan repayments, properties, stocks and shares were excluded, as well as gifts. Licence fees, house insurance, and health care were considered as consumption expenditure, and the actual payments for such items were recorded.

Method of data collection
The frequency of pricing varies according to the price behaviour of the item. Items whose prices fluctuate frequently, such as perishable food items, are priced thee times a week at market stalls. Prices of provisions and sundries which do not fluctuate as often as those of perishable food items are collected each week. Prices for items with greater price stability, such as clothing, textiles, haircut services, tailoring charges, crockery and furniture are updated once a month. Changes in the prices of items such as Mass Rapid Transit, bus and taxi fares, cinema admission charges, utility charges, maintenance and conservancy charges for flats, government medical fees and school fees are incorporated in the index when they are revised.

Prices of perishable food items are collected on Tuesdays, Thursdays and Fridays, and those of provisions and sundries, every Wednesday. For the monthly surveys, prices normally refer to those as at 15th of the month.

Information pertaining to the places usually patronised by consumers for their marketing items, provisions and clothing was obtained from respondents during the household expenditure survey. This was used as a guide in the selection of outlets, supplemented by information from the Department's Survey of Wholesale and Retail Trades and Survey of Services from which a list of large outlets was drawn up for each type of commodity. Generally, the outlets selected for food items were mainly drawn from densely populated areas, particularly those in large public housing estates. For non-food items such as ready-made clothing and footwear, furniture, household equipment and appliances, prices are collected mainly from shopping centres which have a large concentration of retailers specialising in the respective items.

The prices of perishable food items from markets and those from provision shops and crockery shops are collected by personal visits, while prices of other items are obtained through mailed questionnaires. Electricity, gas and water tariffs are obtained directly from the Public Utilities Board. Medical care costs (hospitalization fees and medical treatment fees) are collected via postal questionnaires from both private and government hospitals and clinics. Education costs (tuition fees for every level of education) are obtained directly from the Ministry of Education, tertiary institutions and other private institutions. Transport and communication costs (prices of cars, motorcycles, petrol and other running costs) are obtained from the respective respondents in the retail trade. For public road transport, fares for buses and subways are supplied by the Singapore Bus Services and Mass Rapid Transit Corporation. Air fares are ascertained from the sales offices of selected airlines. Charges for postage and telephone rentals are collected from the Singapore Telecom.

At any one time, there are six field interviewers visiting the selected outlets. Four field interviewers go to the market every Tuesday, Thursday and Friday to collect prices of fish, vegetables, meat, fruits etc. On every Wednesday, they are assigned to visit the provision shops where prices of dried goods and sundries are obtained. Other items which require personal visits such as textiles, cooked food, ladies' clothing etc. are priced on Mondays.

Discounts or other sales promotion gimmicks are ignored. The prices of such items are not used in the calculation of index or average prices. Sale prices are included when they are genuine reductions and widely available, i.e. they become the predominant prices. Regarding hire-purchase and credit terms, only the prices charged in normal cash transactions are used.

The number of price quotations for an item depends on its relative importance, the volatility of its price and whether its price is controlled by a central agency.

Housing
Rent is the only item included under rent. Data on rents for public flats, private flats, bungalows, semi-detached, terrace houses and chophouses are collected each quarter in January, April, July and October. The selected households are divided into two groups and each group is surveyed only once in six months, i.e. one group is surveyed in January and July and the other group in April and October each year. There is no need to survey the same houses more frequently as most rented houses have fixed-rent contracts for one or two years. For the collection of rent data, postal questionnaires are sent to the selected households for their completion, stating the current rent, the rent paid six months ago, duration of the lease the tenant signed with the landlord and details of the furniture and consumer durables provided (if any). The rents for the various types of flats and houses have different weights in the Consumer Price Index. For each type of flat or house, an index is computed using the average of price relatives based on the rent data collected. The indices for all types of flat or house are then weighted to produce the overall rent index.

For owner-occupied accommodation, the rental equivalent approach is used, and the expected rental the owner would have to pay if he were the tenant was imputed by government assessors. The imputed rents of a sample of owner-occupied houses are ascertaining each quarter from the Valuation and Assessment Division of the Inland Revenue Department.

Specification of varieties
To ensure that price changes are not caused by quality changes, detailed specifications of the items are provided to assist the field interviewers or the retailers of the items, such as the brand, quality, material, size, unit of measurement and country of origin that clearly distinguishes it from those with similar generic descriptions. Such detailed specifications were first obtained when the field enquiries were carried out. For ladies' clothing items which change with fashions from time to time, in addition to the specifications required such as the design or art number, type of fabrics used, print (plain or floral), sizes and colours available, field officers also sketch the pattern of the items to enable the office staff to consider whether they are suitable for use.

Substitution, quality change, etc.
As far as possible, if the degree of quality change can be quantified, prices are adjusted accordingly. However, if the change in quality cannot be assessed, attempts are made to "replace" the old item by a new one, when both are available during an overlapping period.

When new products appear, a splicing method is adopted.

If a given type or quality disappears from the market, the Office is usually informed in advance either by the field interviewers or the respondents. Before the old item disappears from the market, the price of the nearest substitute is usually obtained for the overlapping period to enable the application of the technique of splicing price series. If the disappearance is sudden, price is usually assumed to remain unchanged for the month and immediate action is taken to introduce the nearest substitute.

Seasonal items
Most of the items selected in the Consumer Price Index basket are non-seasonal, i.e., their prices are usually available all the time. There are few seasonal items of importance.

Computation
The index is computed according to the Laspeyres formula as a weighted arithmetic average with fixed base, using weights corresponding to the base period.

Price averages are calculated for each distinct brand by summing the prices obtained and dividing by the total number of quotations. Price relatives are computed by taking the reference month's price divided by its corresponding base year price (average September 1987-August 1988). Missing prices are treated differently depending on the reason for the absence.

If the price of a particular brand from a particular outlet is not available, it is assumed not to have changed for the month. Missing prices due to the disappearance of item are linked to the price of the nearest substitute. Faulty price data or doubtful prices are usually clarified and reconfirmed with the respondents.

Other information
Broad components are published at the group and sub-group levels.

Organisation and publication
Department of Statistics: "Consumer Price Index, Singapore" - monthly CPI report.

Idem: "Monthly Digest of Statistics" (monthly). Monthly indices are published at the group and sub-group level for the last 24 months.

Idem: "Yearbook of Statistics" (annual). Annual indices are published for last 10 years.

Idem: "The consumer price index, Singapore, based on Household Expenditure Survey 1987-88".

SOLOMON ISLANDS (HONIARA)

Official title
Retail Price Index.

Scope
The index is compiled monthly and relates to households in Honiara whose head earned less than 4,000 dollars net per year in 1977.

Official base
October-December 1977 = 100.

Source of weights
The weights and items were derived from a household expenditure survey conducted in October-November 1977 in Honiara among households whose head earned less than 4,000 dollars net per year, at the time of the survey.

Weights and composition

Major groups	Number of items	Weights	Approximate number of price quotations
Food	76	47.0	...
Beverages and tobacco	8	9.5	...
Clothing and footwear	12	5.0	...
Transport	22	11.0	...
Housing (incl. rent, fuel and light, etc.)	14	15.5	...
Miscellaneous	33	12.0	...
Total	165	100.0	...

Household consumption expenditure
Not available.

Method of data collection
Prices are collected by agents between the 15th and 20th of each month from markets, retail outlets and service establishments in Honiara. Prices for fresh fruit and vegetables are ascertained each week.

Housing
Rent quotations are obtained for three government-owned and four private dwellings.

Specification of varieties
Not available.

Substitution, quality change, etc.
Not available.

Seasonal items
Seasonal fluctuations of item prices are taken into account by maintaining the closing prices of the previous season during the off season.

Computation
The index is computed according to the Laspeyres formula as a weighted arithmetic average with fixed base, using weights corresponding to the base period.

Other information
A new series relating to households in Honiara with annual earnings of less than 11,000 dollars from all sources in 1982 (base October-December 1984 = 100) is now computed, but the

relevant methodological information was not available in the ILO at the time the present volume was published.

Organisation and publication
Ministry of Finance, Statistics Office: "Statistical Bulletin" (Honiara).

SOUTH AFRICA

Official title
Consumer Price Index.

Scope
The index is computed monthly and relates to all population groups in 12 urban areas.

Official base
1985 = 100.

Source of weights
The weights and items were derived from a household expenditure survey conducted in November 1985.

Weights and composition

Major groups	Number of items	Weights	Approximate number of price quotations
Food	88	22.72	...
Drinks, alcoholic drinks and tobacco	8	2.84	...
Clothing and footwear	55	5.98	...
Housing:			
Rent	2	5.88	...
Home-owners' costs	7	13.91	...
Other (incl. water)	3	1.41	...
Fuel and light	6	2.44	...
Furniture and household equipment	29	4.72	...
Household operations	14	3.77	...
Medical care	5	2.56	...
Transport and communication	21	18.93	...
Education and recreation	21	4.96	...
Personal care	12	3.08	...
Miscellaneous	14	6.77	...
Total	285	100.00	...

Household consumption expenditure
Consumption expenditure includes car licence and registration fees, interest on loans, bank charges, life insurance premiums, endowment policies, annuities, mortgage debt insurance, membership fees for trade unions, staff and professional associations, legal and other fees for professional services.

Certain types of expenditure are not taken into account for the purposes of the Consumer Price Index, e.g. income tax, contributions to pension and provident funds.

Method of data collection
Prices are collected by postal questionnaires from a representative sample of retail outlets and service establishments in different areas, or from other organisations, associations or public bodies. Prices of vegetables and fruit are obtained from the Division of Agricultural Marketing Research of the Department of Agricultural Economics and Marketing, which collects prices each week.

For most other food items, as well as for clothing, fuel and washing and cleaning materials, prices are collected each month. Prices for furniture and equipment, personal care requisites, stationery, etc., prices are collected every three months. Certain price information is obtained once a year or as often as price changes occur.

Price information for all items except for fruit and vegetables refers to the first seven days of the relevant months.

Housing
Rent data are obtained for houses and apartments from the annual survey conducted by the Department of Statistics. Home-owner costs include interest payments, assessment rates, sanitary service, refuse removal, insurance of buildings, repairs and maintenance and other ownership costs.

Specification of varieties
Not available.

Substitution, quality change, etc.
Not available.

Seasonal items
No adjustment is made to seasonal fluctuations in item prices.

Computation
The index is computed according to the Laspeyres formula as a weighted arithmetic average with fixed base, using weights corresponding to 1985.

The index is computed as the weighted average of separate indices relating to 12 urban areas.

Other information
Series are also published separately for low-, middle- and high-income group families for all items excluding housing, for all items excluding food, for detailed sub-groups and separately for 12 urban areas.

A seasonally adjusted consumer price index and a pensioners' consumer price index for urban areas are also published.

A new series (base 1990 = 100) is now computed, but the relevant methodological information was not available in the ILO at the timet the present volume was published.

Organisation and publication
Central Statistical Service: "Bulletin of Statistics" (Pretoria).

SPAIN

Official title
Indice de precios de consumo (Consumer Price Index).

Scope
The index is compiled monthly and covers families of two or more persons, with annual incomes of between 322,575 and 2,000,000 pesetas at the time of the household expenditure survey (April 1980 to March 1981).

Official base
1983 = 100.

Source of weights
The weights and items were derived from a household expenditure survey conducted between April 1980 and March 1981 among a sample of 24,000 households throughout the country.

Weights and composition

Major groups	Number of items	Weights	Approximate number of price quotations
Food and tobacco	171	330	...
Clothing and footwear	56	87	...
Housing	24	186	...
Furnishings, household equipment and domestic services	56	74	...
Medical care	18	24	...
Transport and communication	26	144	...
Education and recreation	40	70	...
Other goods and services	37	85	...
Total	428	1,000	146,000

Household consumption expenditure
Consumption expenditure for the purpose of the index comprises all goods and services purchased for consumption by the index population. It includes consumption of own-produced goods, payments of insurance premiums and taxes for cars. It excludes direct and indirect taxes, special materials and expenditure concerning professional activities, gambling, veterinary care, loan interest payments and loan repayments, remittances, gifts and similar payments.

Method of data collection
Prices are collected by agents in market areas, supermarkets, other retail outlets and service establishments throughout the country. Prices for perishable food items are collected four times a month in certain important towns and twice a month in the other towns. Prices for durable goods are obtained once a month and those for electric household appliances once a quarter. Prices for fuel, electricity, tobacco and telephone charges, which are uniform throughout the country, are obtained from the Official Bulletin (Boletín Oficial del Estado).

Housing
Rent quotations are obtained once a month from a sample of 3,000 rented and 2,000 owner-occupied dwellings. Controlled rent prices are collected once a year and the value of free rent is obtained once a month.

Specification of varieties
The specifications of the varieties vary according to the item.

Generally, the description of variety takes into account the quality, brand and unit, but not the date of manufacture.

Substitution, quality change, etc.
If an item disappears from the market or the quality changes, it is substituted by a similar item. New items are introduced only when the index is revised.

Seasonal items
Seasonal fluctuations in the prices of fresh fruit and vegetables are taken into account by varying the items and item weights within baskets of constant group weights.

Computation
The index is computed according to the Laspeyres formula as a weighted arithmetic average with fixed base, using weights corresponding to the base period.

In computing item indices, the relatives of average prices are calculated by dividing the average price for the current period by the average price for the base period. Initially, the average prices are calculated as simple arithmetic averages for each primary sampling area unit. These average prices are then weighted using population weights to arrive at average prices for the whole country.

Other information
Major groups are published.

Organisation and publication
Instituto Nacional de Estadística: "Indice de Precios de Consumo - Boletín Informativo" (Madrid).

Idem: "Indicadores de coyuntura"

Idem: "Indice de precios de consumo, base 1983, Monografía Tecnica" (Madrid, 1985).

SRI LANKA (COLOMBO)

Official title
Consumer Price Index.

Scope
The index is compiled monthly and covers manual workers' families in Colombo.

Official base
1952 = 100.

Source of weights
The weights and items were derived from a household expenditure survey conducted in 1949-50, covering 455 manual workers' families in Colombo. The expenditure data obtained from this survey were revalued at 1959 prices to determine the weights.

Weights and composition

Major groups	Number of items	Weights	Approximate number of price quotations
Food	94	61.9	...
Fuel and light	4	4.3	...
Rent	1	5.7	...
Clothing, footwear and household linen	63	9.4	...
Miscellaneous	57	18.7	...
Total	219	100.0	...

Household consumption expenditure
Consumption expenditure for the purpose of the index includes all goods and services purchased for consumption by the index population. It excludes life insurance, property insurance, income tax and personal property taxes.

Method of data collection
Prices are collected each week by investigators from the Department of Census and Statistics from selected retail stores and establishments in the seven principal market areas in Colombo. Prices for most food items are ascertained through direct buying. Items sold in the open market and in co-operatives are priced. A weighted average of prices is calculated, with weights assigned in proportion to the estimated quantities sold in the two groups of stores.

The prices used in the index are the prices actually paid. Discount and sale prices are used. Hire-purchase or credit terms, second-hand purchase and trade-in of used goods are not collected.

Housing
Data on house rent are collected every three months for 148 working-class houses and from the assessment registers of the municipal authorities. Imputed rent is used for owner-occupied housing.

Specification of varieties
Detailed specifications are provided for each item included in the index. Specification provide a complete description of the item, its brand, country of origin, quality and unit.

Substitution, quality change, etc.
If a product is not available, a similar product to the original is substituted and a method of linking is used in the calculation.

Seasonal items
Fresh fruit and vegetables are regarded as seasonal items, which are priced when they are available during the season. The closing prices for the previous season are maintained during the off season.

Computation
The index is computed according to the Laspeyres formula as a weighted arithmetic average with fixed base, using weights corresponding to the expenditure data for 1949-50, revalued at 1959 prices.

Organisation and publication
The index is compiled by the Department of Census and Statistics (Colombo).

Department of Government Printing: "The Gazette of the Republic of Sri Lanka" (Colombo).

Government Publications Bureau: "A New Consumers' Price Index", Sessional Paper VI, 1953 (Colombo).

Idem: "Report of Committee to Revise the Cost of Living Index", Sessional Paper XI, 1959 (Colombo).

SUDAN

Official title
Retail Price Index.

Scope
The index is compiled monthly and covers households with six members and with an annual income of between 300 and 500 pounds in 1967-68.

Official base
January 1970 = 100.

Source of weights
The weights and items were derived from a household expenditure survey conducted in 1967-68 in Khartoum, Khartoum North and Omdurman, among a random sample of 1,500 households with six members and with an annual income of between 300 and 500 pounds.

Weights and composition

Major groups	Number of items	Weights	Approximate number of price quotations
Food and tobacco	31	66.5	...
Housing:			
Rent, fuel, light and water	5	12.4	...
Clothing and footwear	22	5.9	...
Miscellaneous	12	15.2	...
Total	70	100.0	...

Household consumption expenditure
Not available.

Method of data collection
Prices are collected from selected retail stores and service establishments in Khartoum, Khartoum North and Omdurman. Prices for most items are collected by agents on Thursday each week. Price data for electricity, gas, education and transportation are collected directly from the authorities. Costs of medical care are based on doctors' fees and the price of one selected medical product.

The prices used in the calculation of the index are the normal prices paid. Sale and discount prices are not taken into account.

Housing
Basic rent quotations come from a survey undertaken in De-

cember 1969. A rent survey is conducted only occasionally as rents do not change frequently.

Specification of varieties
Not available.

Substitution, quality change, etc.
Not available.

Seasonal items
The price quotations are the current prices, which are not adjusted for any seasonal fluctuations.

Computation
The index is computed according to the Laspeyres formula as a weighted arithmetic average with fixed base, using weights corresponding to the period 1967-68.

In computing item indices, the relatives of average prices for the current and base periods are used. Average prices are the simple arithmetic averages of the prices obtained from the three towns.

Other information
New series relating to low-, middle- and high-income group families are now computed (base January 1988 = 100), but the relevant methodological information was not available in the ILO at the time the present volume was published.

Organisation and publication
The index is compiled by the Department of Statistics (Khartoum). The figures published by the International Labour Office are received directly from the Department of Statistics, Khartoum. They do not appear in national publications.

SURINAME (PARAMARIBO)

Official title
Consumer Price Index.

Scope
The index is compiled monthly and covers households of wage earners and salaried employees with an annual income not exceeding 6,000 florins from April 1968 to March 1969. The index relates to the capital city, Paramaribo.

Official base
April 1968-March 1969 = 100.

Source of weights
The weights and items were derived from a household expenditure survey conducted from April 1968 to March 1969 in Paramaribo and its surroundings, covering 592 households of wage earners and salaried employees of three or more persons, with an annual income not exceeding 6,000 florins at the time of the survey. The index items were selected on the basis of two criteria: the items were important in household consumption and they were purchased by most of the households.

Weights and composition

Major groups	Number of items	Weights	Approximate number of price quotations
Food	92	39.9	1,252
Housing:			
Rent, water and electricity	3	9.5	3
Fuel	4	1.9	20
Furniture, furnishings and cleaning materials	36	12.3	400
Clothing and footwear	48	11.0	252
Other:			
Personal and medical care	23	6.2	251
Transport	5	9.5	10
Tobacco	2	1.3	46
Education and recreation	16	8.4	104
Total	229	100.0	2,338

Household consumption expenditure
Consumption expenditure for the purpose of the index comprises all goods and services purchased or received for consumption by the index population. It includes the value of goods and services received by households as income in kind, and home-produced goods consumed by households. It excludes income tax, social security contributions, repayment of loans, insurance premiums, gifts and contributions, betting and gambling, major improvements to the home and payments on mortgage principal, other investments, savings and interest on personal debts.

Method of data collection
Prices are collected by a team of interviewers from 125 selected retail stores and service establishments in Paramaribo and its surroundings. After 1969, new outlets were chosen and various goods and services were standardised. Prices for scarce goods and blackmarket prices are collected by interviewing 150 to 200 households per month. The price interviewers follow the prices of most of the items each month, between the first and the 30th of the month. The prices of fresh fruit and vegetables are collected three times a week (on Monday, Wednesday and Friday) in the Central Market and "vegetable markets" in Paramaribo and its surroundings. Fourteen price quotations are obtained for each item per day.

Specification of varieties
Detailed specifications are provided for each item included in the index. A specification provides a complete description of the item, its brand, name or trade mark, type of packing, quality, unit, etc.

Substitution, quality change, etc.
If an item disappears from the market, it is substituted by a similar item.

Seasonal items
Seasonal items are not included in the index.

Computation
The index is computed according to the Laspeyres formula as a weighted arithmetic average with fixed base, using weights corresponding to the base period.

Organisation and publication
Algemeen Bureau voor de Statistiek, "Prijsindexcijfers van de Gezinsconsumptie" (Paramaribo).

Stichting Planbureau: "Basis Budget van Consumptieve Huishouduitgaven in Paramaribo en Omgeving 1968-69" (Paramaribo).

SWAZILAND (MBABANE-MANZINI)

Official title
Retail Price Index "B".

Scope
The index is compiled monthly and relates to low-income wage earners' households in Mbabane and Manzini with an annual income of about 1,000 emalangeni in 1977.

Official base
January 1967 = 100.

Source of weights
The weights were derived from household expenditure data concerning low-wage families in Kenya, Rhodesia, the United Kingdom and South Africa.

Weights and composition

Major groups	Number of items	Weights	Approximate number of price quotations
Food:			
Fruit and vegetables	5	4.5	...
Other food	19	57.5	...
Beverages and tobacco	3	12.0	...
Fuel and light	4	6.0	...
Clothing and footwear	9	10.0	...
Other items	8	10.0	...
Total	48	100.0	...

Household consumption expenditure
Not available.

Method of data collection
Prices are obtained from four markets, and from retail outlets and service establishments in Mbabane and Manzini. A permanent staff member of the Central Statistical Office collects prices for all items except fruit and vegetables, for which prices are collected by agents.

Prices of fresh fruit and vegetables are ascertained on Tuesday each week and for the others around the 15th of each month. Price data for education, transportation and medical care are gathered by telephone.

The prices used to compute the index are the retail prices actually paid.

Housing
Rent is not included in the index, nor was it taken into account in determining the weights.

Specification of varieties
The goods and services to be priced are specified in detail, i.e. size, make, brand, quantity and quality.

Substitution, quality change, etc.
When an item is no longer available, it is substituted by another with approximately the same quality and a linking method is used.

Seasonal items
Not available.

Computation
The index is computed according to the Laspeyres formula as a weighted arithmetic average with fixed base, using weights corresponding to the base period.

Price relatives for the current and base periods are generally used to compute item indices, except for clothing and textiles, for which price relatives of the current and previous periods are used. In computing average prices, outlet prices in different localities are weighted according to retail sales turnover.

Other information
New series relating to low-, middle- and high-income group families are now computed (base September 1988 = 100), but the relevant methodological information was not available in the ILO at the time the present volume was published.

Organisation and publication
Central Statistical Office: "Swaziland Statistical News" (Mbabane).

SWEDEN

Official title
Consumer Price Index (Konsumentprisindex).

Scope
The index is compiled monthly and covers the whole population, both urban and rural.

Official base
1980 = 100.

Source of weights
The weights and items are revised at the beginning of each year. The weights for major groups are based on the Swedish National Accounts System: quarterly statistics for the first three-quarters of the preceding year supplemented by an estimate for the fourth quarter. Weights within groups are derived from the most recent sources, e.g. for food items, from surveys and estimates made by the Swedish National Agricultural Market Board. The weights for other items are derived from the latest household expenditure survey. The household expenditure survey covers all expenditure of private households in Sweden during one year.

Weights and composition

Major groups	Number of items	Weights	Approximate number of price quotations
Food	(1) 25 + 770	172	18,000
Alcoholic beverages	(a) (1) 15	32	(a) 500
Tobacco	(1) 25	21	1,200
Clothing	27	62	900-1,800
Footwear	10	13	650
Housing, fuel and electricity	(b)	270	(b)
Furniture and household equipment	(1) 39 + 60	65	3,300
Transport and communication	22	175	(2) 800
Recreation, entertainment and cultural services	50 + 20	98	2,100
Miscellaneous	(1) 33 + 30	92	(3) 2,800
Total	...	1,000	...

Note: (a) and (b) See below. (1) Sampled specified varieties. (2) Excluding price quotations and calculations for travelling. (3) Excluding calculations for medical care, dental services and medicine.

(a) Almost all items or varieties covered for wine, spirits and strong beer (weight 28). (b) See text below.

Household consumption expenditure
Consumption expenditure used for deriving the weights includes all private family consumption of goods and services inside the private sector, i.e. paid by households, including expenditure on certain capital goods (except land, own permanent house and weekend cottage).

The consumption costs for home ownership are included. Durable goods credit purchases are registered at the time of delivery. Second-hand purchases, trade-in of used goods and in part payment for new ones are not included in the index. Also excluded are financial transactions, such as life insurance, other social insurance, income tax and other direct taxes. Gifts are registered as consumption of given goods or services by the giver at the time of purchase. Income in kind is only a small part of Swedish private consumption. The value of income in kind is only estimated for food from surveys regularly published by the Swedish National Agricultural Market Board in their food statistics.

Method of data collection
Prices are collected around the 15th of each month by agents from a random sample of about 900 retail outlets and service establishments. A general interviewer organisation of about 200 persons is used for all countrywide interview surveys including price collection. The supervisors are centrally stationed in the SCB office keeping contact with the interviewers by telephone, letters and intermittent conferences. Food prices, except certain fresh food i.e. bread, fish vegetables and fruit, and other everyday commodities are collected each month from price lists applied in a random sample of approximately 60 shops. Once a year, in December, the prices of these commodities are collected from the shops by agents. These prices are only used for calculating the long-term link (see below). Postal questionnaires are used for rents, electricity and water. Telephone interviews are used for gasoline and cars. Data for medical care, transport and communication are obtained from official tariffs. The prices used in the index are the regular prices paid by any member of the public. Indirect taxes are included in the prices. Discounts on cash payments are deducted. Bargain prices during the price collection period are recorded. Black-market prices are irrelevant. Only cash prices are recorded; hire-purchase and credit terms are not included. Also excluded are second-hand purchases and the trade-in of used goods and in part payment for new ones and direct import purchases by households.

Housing
Rent surveys are carried out four times a year, in January, April, July and October, or when negotiated rents come into force, from a sample of 1,000 rented dwellings. Heating costs are included in the recorded total rent. A sample of newly-built apartments is included successively in the rent index calculations.

An owner-occupied housing index is calculated according to the cost development each month. All common house costs are included in the cost calculations, such as costs for interest, house insurance, water, garbage collection, chimney sweeping, tax on real estate, heating, electricity and house repairs, as well as depreciation. Interest costs are calculated on the total amount of capital defined in terms of the purchase price (by present owner). State grants to subsidise interests are deducted.

Specification of varieties
The item definitions are specified as far as possible. The price collector specifies each priced item more closely, so that the same article or service can be priced next time even by a new price collector. The specifications for certain food items and other goods purchased each day are given in detail, including the article reference number.

Substitution, quality change, etc.
Quality changes are judged as far as possible at the price-collection stage. Only the price difference for equivalent quality is recorded. For certain food and other everyday commodities, substitution is not normally permitted. For clothing, substitutions are made only between items with equivalent quality according to certain criteria. New products are normally introduced at the time of the annual examination of the selection of items. If possible, a given type or quality which disappears is replaced, otherwise, a non-response is reported.

Seasonal items
Winter clothes are priced only from September to March. The last recorded price is then used in the index calculations during the off season, April to August. Prices of certain items (pota-

toes, vegetables and fruit) are adjusted for seasonal variations. Seasonal quotients are computed for the prices of these items based on the seasonal prices for the three previous years.

Computation
The index is a chain with yearly links, with the weights changed for each link. Two different types of links (each link with December of the preceding year = 100) are used, i.e. a short-term link and a long-term link.

The short-term link is used for month from January to December. The long-term link is used only for yearly links from December to December.

The link for each month is firstly computed as a weighted arithmetic average of separate price relatives for items with prices in the previous December taken as 100. These results are then linked back by the long-term links through December of each preceding year to 1980.

Other information
A Net Price Index is also calculated, defined as an index in which the prices of consumer goods have been reduced by the sum of the indirect taxes which in different production stages constitute cost elements in the production of the final consumer goods. The prices are also adjusted by including certain subsidies.

The Basic Amount statistics are used to adjust basic pensions, supplementary pensions, governmental study loan, certain life-annuities and maintenance allowances.

Organisation and publication
Statistics Sweden: "Statistiska meddelanden", serie P14 och P15 (Statistical reports, Series P14 and P15) (Stockholm).

Idem: "Allmän Manadsstatistik" (Monthly Digest of Swedish Statistics).

Sveriges Officiella Statistik, Statistika Central Byrän (SCB): "Konsumentpriser och index beräkningar 1989" (Stockholm, 1990).

SWITZERLAND

Official title
Indice suisse des prix à la consommation (Consumer Price Index).

Scope
The index is computed monthly and covers employees' households throughout the country.

Official base
December 1982 = 100.

Source of weights
The weights and items were derived from a household expenditure survey conducted in 1981 among a sample of 442 employees' households throughout the whole country. Data on income and expenditure were collected each month from each sample household over a period of 12 months. The weighting pattern was adjusted for price changes between the middle of 1981 and the middle of 1982.

Weights and composition

Major groups	Number of items	Weights	Approximate number of price quotations
Food	127	21	73,300
Beverages and tobacco	22	5	27,700
Clothing and footwear	56	7	61,800
Rent	15	18	107,000
Fuel and light	13	5	2,600
Household equipment and maintenance	35	6	24,800
Transport and communication	58	14	5,300
Health and personal care	54	8	12,300
Education and recreation	33	16	19,500
Total	413	100	334,300

Household consumption expenditure
Consumption expenditure for the purpose of the index comprises all goods and services which employees' households purchase. It includes indirect taxes, insurance premiums associated with the use of motor vehicles, and radio and television licences. Consumption expenditure not included in the compilation of the index relates to items such as contributions to societies, gifts, fines, loan interest, business travel, personal effects such as jewellery, watches, bags, etc.

Method of data collection
Prices are collected from retail outlets and service establishments by local authority investigators or by means of mail questionnaires. The criterion for choosing an outlet is its local economic importance. Prices for most food items, fuel and petrol are ascertained during the first two weeks of each month in 48 towns (localities). Prices for other items are collected quarterly. Special prices are taken into account at the moment of the survey.

Housing
Rent quotations are obtained in May and November each year for 100,000 apartments with one to five rooms, in 87 localities. The different kinds of apartments (old, new and those built since the last quotation) are represented in the index in proportion to their respective numbers.

Specification of varieties
Each investigator can choose the most important specifications for each item in terms of turnover and adapt his selection as necessary according to market developments.

Substitution, quality change, etc.
Small quality changes are not taken into account. If there is an important quality change, the item is treated as a new one and the linking method is used. If an article is no longer available on the market and the consumer has to buy a substitute, the price of the substitute item is used for computing the index.

Seasonal items
Seasonal fluctuations in the prices of fresh fruit and vegetables are taken into account by varying the items and item weights within the monthly baskets with constant group weights.

Computation
The index is computed according to the Laspeyres formula as a weighted arithmetic average with fixed base, using weights corresponding to the base period.

Separate indices are first calculated for each price quotation in each individual outlet using averages of price relatives for the current and base periods.

The national index represents the weighted arithmetic average of indices relating to the different types of outlets and communes.

Other information
A new consumer price index is under preparation and will appear shortly. Detailed sub-group indices are published, as well as separate indices for 48 localities.

Organisation and publication
Département fédéral de l'intérieur, Office fédéral de la statistique: "L'indice suisse des prix à la consommation" (Berne).

Idem: "Communiqué de presse".

Département fédéral de l'économie publique, Office fédéral de l'industrie, des arts et métiers et du travail: "La Vie économique" (February 1983).

Idem: "La Vie économique, l'indice suisse des prix à la consommation", 89ème numéro spécial, 1977.

SYRIAN ARAB REPUBLIC (DAMASCUS)

Official title
Retail Price Index.

Scope
The index is compiled monthly and covers private households in Damascus.

Official base
1970 = 100.

Source of weights
The weights and items were derived from a household expenditure survey conducted in 1971-72.

Household consumption expenditure
Consumption expenditure for the purpose of the index comprises almost all important goods and services purchased by the index population.

Weights and composition

Major groups	Number of items	Weights	Approximate number of price quotations
Food and tobacco	74	488.2	...
Fuel and light	5	45.6	...
Rent	1	177.3	...
Furniture and household utensils	8	18.4	...
Cleaning materials	4	11.8	...
Durable goods	5	11.4	...
Household linen	4	9.5	...
Clothing and footwear	17	90.6	...
Transport	6	38.1	...
Personal and medical care	19	78.4	...
Education and recreation	7	30.7	...
Total	150	1,000.0	...

Method of data collection
Prices are collected by agents from selected retail outlets and service establishments. Prices for fruit and vegetables are collected each week and those for other items each month.
The prices used to calculate the index are the prices actually paid.

Housing
Rent data are collected for furnished and unfurnished rented dwellings. Owner-occupied housing is not included.

Specification of varieties
Item specifications are given in terms of quality, make, brand, unit, etc.

Substitution, quality change, etc.
No substitutions are made. If an item disappears from the market, its price and weight are both omitted from the index.

Seasonal items
Seasonal items are priced during the period they are available and omitted from the index during the off season.

Computation
The index is computed according to the Laspeyres formula as a weighted arithmetic average with fixed base, using weights corresponding to 1971-72.

Other information
Annual averages are published for Aleppo and for Damascus, for all items and sub-groups.

Organisation and publication
Office of the Prime Minister, Central Bureau of Statistics: "Statistical Abstract" (Damascus).

TANZANIA (TANGANYIKA)

Official title
National Consumer Price Index.

Scope
The index is compiled quarterly and covers all types of households and population groups in 20 urban centres in mainland Tanzania.

Official base
1977 = 100.

Source of weights
The weights and items were derived from a household expenditure survey conducted during one year from September 1976 to November 1977 among a sample of 6,042 households. Items with significant weights are priced. The weights of items not priced are excluded.

Household consumption expenditure
Consumption expenditure for the purpose of the index includes almost all important goods and services purchased by the index population. It excludes taxes, fines, gambling, money transfers, gifts, savings and investment, life insurance premiums and bride prices.

Method of data collection
Prices are collected in March, June, September and December from markets, retail outlets and service establishments in 20 urban centres. No point-of-purchase survey was carried out, but either all outlets are covered if there are only a few, or at least 50 per cent of them if there are many. Prices for items from markets, including fruit, vegetables, cereals and pulses, are obtained through direct purchase. Some prices are obtained from shops by mail questionnaires. Prices for electricity, water and communications are the official tariffs. The prices used to calculate the index are the regular free-market prices paid by consumers. Sale and discount prices are not taken into account. Black market prices are used if the items are available to all consumers.

Housing
Rent quotations are obtained each quarter by mail inquiry, for at least 30 dwellings occupied by low-income group families, 30 by middle-income group families and 30 by high-income group families, in each town. Owner-occupied housing not covered in the index.

Specification of varieties
Item specifications are given in terms of variety, quality, make, brand, unit etc.

Substitution, quality change, etc.
If an item disappears from the market or the quality of an item changes, a similar item is substituted for pricing.

Seasonal items
Seasonal items are priced when they are available and in season.

Computation
The index is computed according to the Laspeyres formula as a weighted arithmetic average with fixed base, using weights corresponding to the base period. Price relatives for the current and base periods are used to compute item indices. The national index is a weighted average of the indices relating to 20 towns, using weights proportional to the population of each town.

Organisation and publication
Ministry of Finance, Planning and Economic Affairs, Bureau of Statistics: "Quarterly Statistical Bulletin" (Dar-es-Salaam).
For further methodological detail, see: Ministry of Economic Affairs and Development Planning, Bureau of Statistics: "National Consumer Price Index" (October 1974).

Weights and composition

Major groups	Number of items	Weights	Approximate number of price quotations
Food	44	64.2	...
Drinks and tobacco	5	2.5	...
Rent	1	4.9	...
Fuel, light and water	6	7.6	...
Clothing and footwear	21	9.9	...
Furniture and utensils	18	1.4	...
Household operations	9	3.4	...
Personal and medical care	9	1.3	...
Recreation	5	0.7	...
Transport	12	4.1	...
Total	130	100.0	...

THAILAND

Official title
General Consumer Price Index.

Scope
The index is computed monthly and covers families living in urban areas, with two to ten persons, and with monthly expenditure of 4,000 to 10,000 bahts in 1986.

Official base
1986 = 100.

Source of weights
The weights and items were derived from a household socio-economic survey conducted in 1986 in the whole country covering a sample of all private non-institutional households. The items were selected on the basis of their relative importance in the household expenditure pattern, the degree to which a given item can represent the price changes of a larger group of items, the variability of price changes among the group in which an item was classified, the degree to which an item can be identified reliably by specification and the anticipated demand which would increase the relative importance of the item in the future. Expenditure for unpriced items which were similar to priced

items in terms of physical characteristics and use were added to the expenditure for the priced items. Expenditure for other unpriced items in a specific sub-group was distributed proportionately for each sub-group. All miscellaneous expenditure not classified in any sub-group was distributed proportionately to all priced items. The number of items and the weights used since 1991 are as follows:

Weights and composition

Major groups	Number of items	Weights	Approximate number of price quotations
Food	...	40.38	...
Housing:			
Shelter, Furniture and household appliances	...	24.76	...
Clothing and footwear	...	4.77	...
Medical and personal care	...	5.13	...
Transport and communication	...	8.94	...
Recreation and education	...	11.69	...
Tobacco and alcoholic beverages	...	4.33	...
Total	...	100.00	...

Household consumption expenditure
Consumption expenditure for the purpose of the index comprises the purchase of goods and services, the value of goods and services received as part of pay, received free, home produce and the rental value of owned home. It excludes direct taxes paid to the government, cash gifts and contributions, insurance premiums, purchase of lottery tickets and other forms of gambling, interest on debts and shares and all forms of assets and liabilities.

Method of data collection
Prices are collected by agents from market centres, retail outlets and service establishments in urban areas. Prices for food items are collected each week from at least four retail outlets in each market area. Prices for other items are collected during the week which includes the 15th of the month. Telephone charges, electricity, water rates, hospital charges, etc., are obtained from government agencies. The prices used in the index are those that any member of the public would have to pay on the pricing day.

Housing
The rental value of owner-occupied dwellings is added to the expenditure weight for rents. The price change is measured by the change from period to period in average rents paid. These are obtained each quarter from a sample of about 355 tenants.

Specification of varieties
The specifications describe the variety, quality, make, brand etc.

Substitution, quality change, etc.
If the characteristics of a product are altered, a method of linking is used. If an item disappears from the market, it is replaced by a similar item.

Seasonal items
No account is generally taken of seasonal fluctuations in item prices. For certain items, fluctuations are taken into account by maintaining the closing prices of the previous season during the off season.

Computation
The index is computed according to the Laspeyres formula as a weighted arithmetic average with fixed base, using weights corresponding to the base period.

In practice, however, the index is a monthly chain computation of base weights and price relatives for two consecutive periods. In this computation, the index for the previous month is updated to obtain the index for the current month.

The nationwide index is an aggregation of the regional series weighted by the population weight of each region.

Organisation and publication
The index is computed each month by the Ministry of Commerce, Department of Business Economics, Price Index Division (Bangkok). Idem: "Monthly Report Consumers Price Index".
Office of the Prime Minister, National Statistical Office: "Bulletin of Statistics" (Bangkok).

TOGO (LOME)

Official title
Indice des prix à la consommation (Consumer Price Index).

Scope
The index is compiled monthly and relates to private African households in Lomé.

Official base
1963 = 100.

Source of weights
The weights and items were derived from a household expenditure survey conducted from June 1964 to June 1965 among private African households in Lomé.

Weights and composition

Major groups	Number of items	Weights	Approximate number of price quotations
Food	53	47.9	...
Alcoholic drinks, tobacco and cola	12	10.6	...
Fuel, light and water	6	5.3	...
Household equipment and cleaning materials	13	2.8	...
Housing:			
Rent	1	2.9	...
Repairs	7	3.9	...
Clothing and footwear	16	7.7	...
Transport	4	3.5	...
Services	9	3.1	...
Miscellaneous	30	12.3	...
Total	151	100.0	...

Household consumption expenditure
Not available.

Method of data collection
Prices for all items are collected by agents, from the local market, main stores and service establishments. Prices for local food items are ascertained twice a week; those for all other items are obtained once a month.

Housing
Rent quotations are obtained from tax returns.

Specification of varieties
Not available.

Substitution, quality change, etc.
Not available.

Seasonal items
Not available.

Computation
The index is computed according to the Laspeyres formula as a weighted arithmetic average with fixed base, using weights corresponding to June 1964-June 1965.

Organisation and publication
Ministère du Plan, Direction de la statistique: "Bulletin mensuel de statistique" (Lomé).

Ministère des Finances, de l'Economie et du Plan, Direction de la statistique: "Prix-indices des prix et coût de la vie à Lomé. Indice des prix à la consommation familiale à Lomé, Base 100 en 1963".

TONGA

Official title
Consumer Price Index.

Scope
The index is compiled quarterly and covers all wage earners' households in Tongatapu.

Official base
1984 = 100.

Source of weights
The weights and items were derived from a household expenditure survey conducted in Tongatapu in 1984.

The weight of items excluded from the index are allocated to items that are included in two different ways:

- if the item excluded is closely related to an item included, the weight is added directly to that of the included item, i.e. the weight of the index item represents expenditure on both items. These are referred to as kindred items. For example, the weight given to orange also represents expenditure on orange sour, citron, lemons and mandarins.
- in most other cases, i.e. where an excluded item cannot reasonably be regarded as kindred to any one item included, the weight of the excluded item is distributed among a number of included items or all the items in a whole sub-group or group. For example, the weight for vacuum cleaners, excluded from the index, is distributed among the individual household appliance items.

In a few cases where it is not feasible to distribute the weight of an excluded item amongst other items, sub-groups or groups, the expenditure is excluded entirely from the weighting calculations. This is the same as if the weight had been distributed amongst all of the items in the whole CPI, i.e. it does not alter the relative weights of any of the items included.

Weights and composition

Major groups	Number of items	Weights	Approximate number of price quotations
Food	104	49.308	5
Housing	34	10.458	5
Household goods	60	13.316	5
Clothing and footwear	40	5.623	5
Transport	15	5.771	3
Tobacco, alcoholic beverages and Kava	6	6.987	5
Other goods and services	48	8.537	4
Total	307	100.000	32

Household consumption expenditure
Consumption expenditure for the purpose of the index excludes income taxes, rent, home ownership savings and business purchases.

Method of data collection
Prices are collected in Nuku'alofa and other centres on Tongatapu island as closely as possible to the middle of the mid-month of each quarter, i.e. the middle of February, May, August and November. Price collection is spread over a period because of the amount of work involved in making the personal visits. For fresh fruit and vegetables whose prices frequently vary substantially over short periods, prices are collected each fortnight during the quarter so as to provide a better representation of average prices during the quarter.

In selecting outlets for pricing, the large traders are first selected because they account for substantial proportions of sales and sell a wide range of goods. These are then supplemented by a sample of smaller outlets of various types to ensure that there is a balanced coverage for all items. For example, for an item such as tinned foods some small corner shops are selected both in and out of Nuku'alofa as well as the large supermarkets in Nuku'alofa.

Prices are not only collected from retail shops but also from a wide variety of businesses which sell consumer goods and services to the public, including fruit and vegetable markets, restaurants, hotels, motor vehicle dealers and service stations, electricity authority, taxi and bus operators, building contractors and various kinds of tradesmen, postal and telephone authority etc. Almost all of the information on retail prices is collected by means of personal visits by staff of the Statistics Department to the shops or other businesses concerned.

The CPI measures changes in actual transaction prices, i.e. the prices that consumers actually pay when they purchase goods or services. It takes into account all kinds of discounts, special offers, etc. as long as they relate to the goods and services specified and are available to all purchasers. It does not take account of discounted prices for damaged or shop-spoiled goods or special prices relating only to a sell-out of the last few items in stock.

The prices used in the CPI include retail sales tax, since this is part of the prices that consumers actually pay. Thus, any change in the rate of sales tax affects the movement in the CPI.

Housing
Rent is not included as an index item.

Specification of varieties
After determining the list of items to be included in the index, it is necessary to specify precisely which goods and services are to be priced regularly for the purpose of compiling the index numbers. Items described as "tea", "man's shirt", "bicycle" or "taxi fare" are defined sufficiently for the purpose of calculating weights but are not described in enough detail to permit consistent pricing. For "tea" the specification must state whether tea-bags or packet tea are to be priced, the size of package, etc. For a man's shirt, the specification must state whether it should have long sleeves or short sleeves, the type of material and so on. For a bicycle, the specification must indicate the type and size of bike, the accessories included, etc. For taxi fares, the length of journey to be priced is specified.

Consequently, for every item in the index, detailed item specifications are written down to guide the price collectors in obtaining prices for comparable goods and services in each successive quarter. For some index items, only one specification is priced but for others two or more specifications are priced.

Substitution, quality change, etc.
If a selected item is found to be temporarily out of stock, the usual practice is to continue using the last recorded price for the item until it becomes available again. If the item continues to be out of stock for several successive quarters (but is still expected to be restocked in the near future) a price may be imputed on the basis of changes in prices of other closely related items whose prices might be expected to change in a similar manner to that of the item not available. If an item becomes unavailable permanently the usual procedure is to replace it with a similar item. If a new model replaces the discontinued one this is substituted in the index. If nothing directly replaces the discontinued item another similar item is chosen as a substitute. In either case, the new item has to be introduced in the index in such a way that any difference in prices of the two items does not affect the level of the index. This is done by linking the two prices together. If the old and new items happen to be available at the same time splicing is a straightforward process.

However, if the old item simply disappeared without warning and a new item has then to be chosen, the process is not as simple. In that event, it is desirable in principle to obtain additional information before attempting to splice the two price series; ideally one should have a price for the new item for the last period in which the old item was available. In practice, this is often not possible and splicing has to be done on the assumption that the last price for the old item and the first price of the new item represent an appropriate price relationship between the two items.

Seasonal items
If a seasonal item, e.g. some kind of fruit or vegetable, is not available in a particular quarter, its weight is redistributed amongst other similar items until it becomes available again. This procedure has the same effect as imputing missing prices.

Computation
The index is computed according to the Laspeyres formula as a weighted arithmetic average with fixed base, using weights corresponding to the base period. For those items for which prices are collected from more than one outlet, and for items such as fresh fruit and vegetables which are priced more than once in each quarter, an average price for the item for the quarter is first calculated. Then the current quarter's price for each item is compared with the base year price for the same item in order to calculate a "price-relative".

Organisation and publication
Statistics Department: "The Annual Statistical Abstract" (Nuku'alofa).
Idem: "Consumer Price Index".

TRINIDAD AND TOBAGO

Official title
Index of Retail Prices.

Scope
The index is compiled monthly and covers households, with monthly income between 100 and 800 dollars in 1976.

Official base
September 1982 = 100.

Source of weights
The weights were obtained from the household expenditure sur-

vey carried out in 1975/76 and covering a sample of 2,493 households, including 1,618 households with a monthly income of between 100 and 800 dollars in 1976. The weights were not adjusted to take into account price changes between the survey period and the base period. Items with weights equal to or greater than 1 per 1000 were selected for inclusion in the index.

Weights and composition

Major groups	Number of items	Weights	Approximate number of price quotations
Food	94	351	...
Meals taken outside home	4	15	...
Alcoholic drinks and tobacco	6	47	...
Fuel and light	5	26	...
Rent and water	5	126	...
Maintenance and repairs	11	12	...
Furniture and household supplies	44	84	...
Services	5	14	...
Clothing and footwear	45	189	...
Transport	13	86	...
Education	6	25	...
Medical goods	8	25	...
Total	246	1,000	(a) ...

Note: (a) Where available three price quotations are collected for each item.

Household consumption expenditure
Consumption expenditure for the purpose of the index comprises all expenditure on goods and services for consumption, including insurance and mortgage interest rates relating to housing. Income in kind is included as income if received on a regular basis. Gifts and licence fees are also included. Excluded from the index are income taxes and other direct taxes, contributions to social insurance and pension funds, insurance associated with specific consumer goods, health care and life insurance payments.

Method of data collection
Prices of commodities and services are obtained from about 375 selected outlets. Localities were selected on the basis of expenditure and population and outlets chosen on the basis of field staff's knowledge. Collection of price data is the responsibility of the Chief, Census and Surveys Office, who has nine field officers visiting selected outlets periodically and collecting the required data. Prices of vegetables, fruit and meat are collected twice a month. Prices are collected each month for other food, drink and tobacco, and each quarter for clothing, house repairs and maintenance, meals out, rent, household supplies, services, transportation and medical services. Prices for fuel and light are collected part-monthly, part-quarterly. Price data on education are collected twice a year. Price collection starts on the second Wednesday of the month and continues for one week.

The prices used in the index are those that any member of the public would have to pay on the pricing day to purchase the specified good or service.

Sale prices are excluded unless they account for a large proportion of sales during the reference period. Black-market prices are taken into account if quoted by the retailer. Discount, hire-purchase or credit terms, and second-hand purchases are not included.

Housing
Rent data are collected each quarter from selected dwellings varying from one to three bedrooms. The total current rent data for a particular pricing area is expressed as a relative of the total base rent data of the respective area. The area relatives are combined into a final relative using the area weights. An imputed net rent for owner-occupied housing was obtained by taking a percentage of the market value of each unit, and this was added to rent paid in deriving the weights of the item. For the purpose of computing the index, only data from rented units are monitored.

Specification of varieties
There are detailed specifications of the brand, quality, unit etc., for the varieties selected for pricing.

Substitution, quality change, etc.
Whenever the characteristics of the products are altered, adjustments are made on base year prices. Obsolete items and items disappearing from the market are replaced by suitable new substitutes.

Seasonal items
Seasonal fresh food items are omitted from the index during their off-season and their weights are distributed among the remaining items in the same group.

Computation
The index is computed according to the Laspeyres formula as a weighted arithmetic average with fixed base, using weights corresponding to the base period.

Average prices of items for each area are first calculated as simple arithmetic averages of the price quotations. Separate price relatives of items for each area are then calculated by dividing the average price of the current period by the average price of the previous period. These price relatives are weighted together to arrive at national price relatives using area weights that are based on the population and retail sales data of the areas concerned.

Organisation and publication
Central Statistical Office: "The Index of Retail Prices 1982 - Statistical Studies and Papers", No. 10, 1984 (Port of Spain).

Government Printing: "Gazette of Trinidad and Tobago" (Port of Spain).

TUNISIA

Official title
Indice spécifique des prix à la consommation (Specific Consumer Price Index).

Scope
The index is computed monthly and covers urban households of employees with an annual expenditure of between 160 and 250 dinars per person in 1980.

Official base
1983 = 100.

Source of weights
The weights and items were derived from a household expenditure survey conducted in 1980. The weights were not adjusted to take account of changes in prices between the survey period and 1983.

Weights and composition

Major groups	Number of items	Weights	Approximate number of price quotations
Food	164	503	25,000
Housing:			
Rent and rates	2	33	64
Fuel and light	16	62	512
Furniture, household equipment and maintenance	60	78	1,924
Personal and medical care and cleaning materials	127	56	4,064
Transport	25	54	800
Clothing and footwear	91	101	2,910
Education, recreation and other	69	113	2,210
Total	554	1,000	37,484

Household consumption expenditure
Household consumption expenditure for calculating the index corresponds to the goods and services usually purchased by the urban population and includes credit purchases which are recorded in full. The following are excluded: income in kind, goods produced by households for their own consumption, rental value of owner-occupied housing, down payments for the purchase of new goods, the purchase of housing and land, national insurance and pension contributions, life insurance premiums, the cost of trading licences, insurance of specific consumer goods (apart from private vehicle insurance), direct taxes, remittances of funds, donations and similar payments.

Method of data collection
The prices are collected by agents at markets and from retail outlets and service establishments in the 16 largest towns in the country. The retail outlets selected in the towns are representative of all forms of trade in each type of quarter (medina, modern and outlying quarters). The price quotations are collected systematically at all supermarkets, at 55 markets, 322 groceries, 240 clothing shops and 785 service establishments. Public rates are recorded directly at the public services concerned. The price survey is conducted by means of direct con-

tacts using agents appointed on a permanent basis. In practice, there is one agent per district, with the exception of Tunis and Sfax where there are three and two agents respectively due to the size of these towns. The prices for most items are collected once a month at each retail outlet, apart from the prices of fresh fruit, vegetables and fish which are collected every day at the markets. This rate of collection means that two to three prices per variety can be obtained at the end of each month. The staggering of observations over the course of the month depends on the planning of visits to retail outlets. The daily average prices of fresh products are generally the prices recorded in the morning (from 10.00 to 12.00) at the markets. Clearance sales, reductions, hire purchase and credit purchases are not taken into account.

Housing
Rent quotations are obtained every six months from a sample of 2,000 tenants of apartments, villas and Arab houses, and include the monthly cost of the rent and, where appropriate, rates. The calculation of the rent index takes account of the size of each type of dwelling.

Owner-occupied dwellings are not covered in the index.

Specification of varieties
In order to follow the progress over a period of time of the price of the same good or service of similar quality so that any changes in price are pure price variations, the varieties are determined by the agents at each retail outlet and an indication is made of the make, the volume, the weight, etc.

Substitution, quality change, etc.
Varieties that have been under observation for a certain length of time may disappear from a certain retail outlet or from the market. The disappearance of a product is considered temporary until it passes the six-month mark, after which the disappearance is considered as final and a replacement is sought.

The substitution method differs according to the nature of the variety. In the case of heterogeneous varieties, the agent proceeds with the replacement in accordance with the retail outlet and changes the base price of the article in the shop if there is an appreciable difference in quality.

In the case of homogeneous varieties, if the replaceable variety is comparable to the one that has disappeared (only a different make), the agent is permitted to substitute it without altering the base price.

Seasonal items
Fresh products such as fruit, vegetables and fish are characterised by frequent price fluctuations, and also by variations in the volume of production, depending on the season. For this reason these products are not treated in the same way as the other ordinary varieties included in the index basket.

The index for fresh products is calculated by using the price ratios of the current month and of the same month during the base period. These indices are then weighted and moving averages are used in the computation of the final index.

Computation
The index is computed according to the Laspeyres formula as a weighted arithmetic average with fixed base, using weights corresponding to 1980.

First, simple average prices are calculated for each district in the case of homogeneous varieties, and simple average indices are calculated for each district in the case of heterogeneous varities. From the district to the regional level, the urban population of each district is used as the weight. From the regional to the national level, the weights used are in accordance with the structure of consumption expenditure in each region.

Other information
Detailed sub-groups are published in the "Bulletin mensuel de statistique" and also another national index: "Indice général des prix à la consommation familiale" (base 1983=100).

Organisation and publication
Institut national de la statistique: "Bulletin mensuel de statistique" (Tunis).

Idem: "Annuaire statistique de la Tunisie".

Idem: "Economie Tunisienne en chiffres".

TURKEY

Official title
Urban Areas Consumer Price Index.

Scope
The index is compiled monthly and relates to urban households with an average monthly income of 50,000 to 1,000,000 lira in 1987 in the five main urban regions of the country, Aegean and Marmara, Mediterranean, Central Anatolia, Black Sea and East and South-East Anatolia.

Official base
1987 = 100.

Source of weights
The weights and items were derived from a household expenditure survey conducted during January-December 1987 among 14,424 households of all socio-economic groups in a sample of 50 settlements with more than 20,000 inhabitants, representing the five main urban regions mentioned above and 16 cities.

Items most commonly consumed by households were selected to be used for the index calculation. The items in each group were place in descending order according to their shares in total consumption and their cumulative values were estimated. Items that constituted 85 to 90 per cent of total consumption in the group were selected to represent that group in the index. This ratio was 100 per cent in some groups and around 60 to 65 per cent in others.

Weights and composition

Major groups	Number of items	Weights	Approximate number of price quotations
Food	132	34.88	36,451
Clothing and footwear	62	12.80	18,727
Furniture, furnishings and household equipment	53	11.24	11,199
Medical and personal care	29	3.44	4,470
Transport and communication	23	6.48	1,278
Education and entertainment	33	5.01	3,748
Housing:	...	26.15	4,397
Rent	2	...	...
Fuel and light	8	...	...
Repairs and maintenance	5	...	...
Total	347	100.00	80,270

Household consumption expenditure
Actual and imputed consumption values were taken as the basis for calculating weights (income in kind used for household consumption, imputed rent for owner-occupied dwellings).

Consumption was taken as "purchasing" that is, as entering into the possession of a household. In general, the moment of purchase was used and delays in the delivery of goods were ignored. Except for purchases on an instalment basis, the act of purchasing wais regarded as complete when the goods entered into the possession of the household. For purchases on an instalment basis, the delivery of the goods was taken as the completion of the purchase. For "income in kind" the moment of entering into the possession of the household was taken as the basis.

Method of data collection
Prices are collected in 33 settlement areas by the personnel of the Price Statistics and Index Division of the State Institute of Statistics (SIS) in Ankara and by the staff of the SIS regional agencies.

Prices of the goods which do not show regional differences are collected centrally in order to prevent mistakes which could arise during separate collection, and to reduce the work load of regional agencies. For example, State hospitals, airlines, postal services, newspapers, telephone charges, encyclopedias, textbooks published by Ministry of Education, university fees, medicine, electricity, monopoly goods, etc. are covered centrally.

In the collection of monthly current prices, it was decided to collect the prices twice a month for all goods except fresh fruit and vegetables in order to be able to obtain all possible price changes. These prices are collected in the weeks which include the 10th and 20th. Since the prices of fresh fruit and vegetables show greater variability, their prices are collected once a week, i.e. four times a month.

The prices used in the index are the regular prices paid by any member of the public. Credit charges and discounts are ignored but sales are taken into consideration for clothing and fabrics.

Housing
Rents are evaluated as the real rents and the imputed rents of households. Therefore, not only the rents of the tenants, but also the imputed rents of owner-occupied dwellings are reflected in the index.

The houses for which rents are recorded in each settlement are chosen by taking into consideration the socio-economic structure and housing characteristics of the districts included in the samples in the 1987 Household Expenditure Survey which were occupied by households with an average monthly income of 50,000 to 1,000,000 lira.

Specification of varieties
The 347 items used for calculating the index were defined in each settlement area and when necessary they were redefined in detail on an establishment basis. The items are defined in such detail that even if different people are collecting the prices the same item can be priced.

Substitution, quality change, etc.
If a specified product is no longer available, it is replaced by a similar product or its weight is added to a similar item or distributed within the sub-group. New products are included in the weighting scheme at the next change of base year.

Seasonal items
For items showing seasonal variabitions in consumption, monthly variable weights are used. Fresh and dried fruit, vegetables, fish and poultry are the items showing monthly changes in consumption. Variable weights are used for these items since an item entering the index for a few months in a season leaves its place to another item the next season and it is not consumed by the same amount every month.

The weights were analysed on the basis of items. The decline in the weight of an early vegetable or fruit due to its underconsumption and the increase in its weight when its price falls and overconsumption occurs were studied and controlled with respect to each month.

Computation
The index is computed according to the Laspeyres formula as a weighted arithmetic average with fixed base, using weights corresponding to the base period.

The urban area consumer price index is calculated as the weighted average of the indices for the five urban regions, taking as weights the total consumption in each region.

Other information
The Consumer Price Index is generally updated every five years to reflect structural changes.

Separate indices are published for the five main urban regions and for 16 towns and for detailed sub-groups.

The indices are published in the Press Bulletin on the fourth day of the month following their calculation.

Organisation and publication
State Institute of Statistics: "Aylik Istatistik Bulteni" (Monthly Bulletin of Statistics) (Ankara).

Idem: "Wholesale and Consumer Price Indexes Monthly Bulletin", (January, February, March 1990).

UGANDA (KAMPALA)

Official title
Consumer Price Index.

Scope
The index is computed monthly and relates to all households with monthly expenditure of 100,000 shillings or less, living in Kampala and Entebbe.

Official base
December 1988 = 100.

Source of weights
The weights and items were derived from a household expenditure survey conducted from April 1989 to April 1990 among low- and middle-income group households with monthly expenditure of 100,000 shillings or less.

The criteria used in selecting items for price collection are: the item should have significant weight according to the survey, should be common to many households in the survey and should have specific quality, quantity and location. Due to limited resources, some items selected are not priced, although they have the above mentioned characteristics. The weights of two or more items were therefore combined, one of the items being expected to remain on the market, and these were selected to represent the others with combined weights. The items were combined in such a way that their price movement had the same trend and end use.

Weights and composition

Major groups	Number of items	Weights	Approximate number of price quotations
Food	29	50.8	...
Beverages and tobacco	7	6.3	...
Fuel and light	3	7.3	...
Transport	9	5.9	...
Clothing and footwear	12	5.5	...
Miscellaneous	14	8.5	...
Services (incl. rent, education and health)	15	15.7	...
Total	89	100.00	...

Household consumption expenditure
Not available.

Method of data collection
Six markets were selected for both Kampala city and Entebbe town. No scientific method was used to select these market places. The criteria used to choose them were their size and geographic distribution.

In each market, prices are collected for food, drinks and tobacco, fuel and power, clothing and footwear. Clinics and hospitals provide prices of medicaments and drugs as well as consultation fees. These were selected according to attendance rate of patients and geographic distribution. Schools, both primary and secondary, give charges for education and were chosen according to the number of pupils or students attending and by location. Transport companies and groups that are generally responsible for the bulk of this activity provide information on fare changes.

Prices of all items are collected every month except for education charges which are collected once every four months, i.e. once every academic term. The prices collected refer to the middle of the month in question and there is no special treatment for fruit and vegetables.

Prices for items that do not have standard measurements, especially those that are found in heaps and other items for which there are no standard weights are obtained through direct purchase. However, items for which prices are too high to fit the financial budget of the Statistics Department, are priced either by interview methods or are simply quoted.

The data for services are obtained by mail questionnaires.

Usually four people are involved in the price collection exercise. They are equipped with the same amount of money for each market, two weighing scales and a list of items to be priced. Most of the items are bought through the process of bargaining and then weighed, while for others prices are just quoted.

The prices actually paid by the consumer are collected, without excluding discounts, sale prices or black-market prices.

Housing
Rent quotations are obtained for selected apartments, boys' quarters, flats and bungalows in such a way that all social groups are represented.

Specification of varieties
Specifications describe the quantity, quality and market location.

Substitution, quality change, etc.
If the quality of an item changes considerably, a new quality is taken as a different item and as a close substitute for the old item. When a new commodity appears on the market, it is priced but not introduced in the index until enough data are available. When a commodity disappears from the market, the previous months' prices are used for a period of about two months, but if the situation persists it is replaced by a close substitute.

Seasonal items
Although consumer prices for are collected for seasonal items, so far no adjustment have been made for seasonal effects.

Computation
The index is computed according to the Laspeyres formula as a weighted arithmetic average with fixed base, using weights corresponding to the base period.

Price relatives of the current and previous periods are used to compute item indices.

Other information
The index will be revised on the basis of the final calculations of the household expenditure survey.

Organisation and publication
Ministry of Planning and Economic Development, Statistics Department: "Key Economic Indicators" (Entebbe).

Idem: "Statistical Bulletin No. CPI/1 Consumer Price Index Kampala (to September 1990)", Entebbe, October 1990.

UNITED KINGDOM

Official title
Retail Prices Index.

Scope
The index is computed monthly and covers the goods and services purchased by all households, apart from those in the top four per cent of the income distribution, and pensioner households deriving at least three-quarters of their income from state benefits. The index covers the whole of the United Kingdom.

Official base
January 1987 = 100.

Source of weights
The weights and items are revised at the beginning of February each year using the latest available results of the household expenditure survey. Generally the data for the year ending in June of the previous year are used to calculate the weights to be used from February of the next year. Adjustments are made to take account of this time lag when implementing new weights, on the assumption that expenditure on individual categories of goods and services will have changed in line with their price movements (not allowing for any increase or decrease in the volume of consumption).

All types of private household in the United Kingdom are covered in the survey, which is a continuous survey covering over 7,000 households in the course of a year, selected in such a way that every household has an equal chance of being included. Each household records its expenditure over a period of two weeks, and also provides information for a longer period about payments which are made relatively infrequently.

The number of items and weights used in 1992 are as follows:

Weights and composition

Major groups	Number of items	Weights	Approximate number of price quotations
Food	127	152	...
Meals taken outside home	4	47	...
Alcoholic drinks	9	80	...
Tobacco	4	36	...
Housing:			
Rent	2	35	...
Owner-occupiers' mortgage interest payments, insurance of dwellings, etc.	2	72	...
Repairs and maintenance	12	25	...
Rates and water	4	40	...
Fuel and light	11	47	...
Durable household goods and services	57	125	...
Clothing and footwear	66	59	...
Transport and vehicles	17	163	...
Miscellaneous goods	69	75	...
Services	10	44	...
Total	394	1,000	130,000

Household consumption expenditure
Consumption expenditure include income in kind, home-ownership costs, trade-in of used goods in part payment for new ones, licence fees, insurance associated with specific consumer goods and health care. Excluded are income taxes and other direct taxes, life insurance premiums, remittances, gifts and similar disbursements, contributions to social insurance and pension funds, savings and investments and charges for credit.

Method of data collection
The 180 localities where price are collected are selected so as to be a representative sample of the country as a whole. Within each area, a price collector familiar with local shopping facilities is given considerable discretion to select typical outlets, with broad guide-lines designed to ensure that each type of outlet is adequately represented.

- Prices are collected each month for all goods and most services.
- The index relates to a single day in each month, normally but not invariably the second Tuesday of each month.

  On the index day, most retail outlets used for price collection purposes are visited by officials of the Central Statistical Office. For some large supermarket chains charging the same prices in all their outlets, the Office obtains price lists centrally. Information for items such as electricity, gas, public transport fares, telephone and postal charges is collected from the head offices of the organisations concerned.
- A field organisation already exists for other unrelated purposes. Data are collected through Unemployment Benefit Offices which send forms each month to a central point.
- The prices used for the index are net of discounts, provided that they are available to all potential customers and/or financed by the seller.
- Sale prices are regarded as price reductions unless they are for goods of inferior quality to those whose prices were previously collected.
- Hire-purchase and credit terms are ignored.
- Second-hand prices and trade-in values are covered in principle, but in practice the only second-hand prices used are for motor cars.
- Imported goods are not separately distinguished.
- Price quotations for items with fixed prices (e.g. newspapers, postage, etc.) are collected singly from a central point.
- Price quotations for items with varying prices are collected from many retail outlets all over the United Kingdom; about 130,000 quotations are collected to cover 600 items. The number of quotations sought for specific items is broadly in line with their relative weights.

Housing
The index covers all types of dwelling which can normally be rented. Most such property is owned by local authorities who review their rents only in April and October-November. The relevant information is collected at these times by postal enquiry. The price indicator is the average rent charged, without deductions for any rebates or allowances received. Mortgage interest payments are included in the index as a proxy for the housing costs (other than rates, repairs, etc. which are separately covered) of owner-occupiers.

Specification of varieties
Specifications vary from product to product and year to year. Some brand names and specifications are currently included. The local collector selects the most representative brand of the specified item in each of the outlets visited.

Substitution, quality change, etc.
Price collectors have the opportunity to notify changes in quality, which are taken into account as far as possible when preparing the index. Items are reviewed each year to reflect changes in consumer taste and behaviour.

Seasonal items
Prices of seasonal items are collected when they are available. In general, the weights for seasonal items do not vary from month to month, but the relative weights attached to different varieties of fresh fruit and vegetables do vary in the course of the year (within a fixed total weight for fresh fruit and fresh vegetables) to reflect changes in consumption patterns.

Computation
The index is calculated as a Laspeyres' chain index with linking in January each year. Indices for individual varieties of fresh fruit and vegetables are combined using a Paasche-type formula. Depending on the item, price averages or price relatives are calculated. Missing or unusable price quotations are replaced by values imputed on the assumption that the actual prices have changed in line with those of items for which valid data have been collected elsewhere. The index is computed directly at the national level.

Other information
Since 1989, the Central Statistical Office has been responsible for collecting the current price data and computing the index.

A "Tax and price index" is also calculated and published by the Central Statistical Office.

Organisation and publication
Central Statistical Office: "Monthly Digest of Statistics" (London). Department of Employment: "Employment Gazette".

Idem: "A short guide to the Retail Price Index", published in the August 1987 issue of the "Employment Gazette".

UNITED STATES

Official title
Consumer Price Index for All Urban Consumers (CPI-U).

Scope
The index is computed monthly and covers about 80 per cent of the total noninstitutional population. Rural residents outside metropolitan areas, all farm residents, the armed forces and persons in institutions are excluded from the index.

Official base
1982-84 = 100.

Source of weights
The weights were derived from the consumer expenditure survey carried out during 1982-84, consisting of an interview survey and a diary survey. Approximately 5,000 consumer units were contacted each year for each type of survey. The consumer unit concept is based on the economic interdependencies within a housing unit and thus differs from the concepts of the family and the household. The expenditure weight for each item stratum is an estimate of total the expenditure by the index population for that item, calculated as the product of estimates of mean expenditures of consumer units and the number of consumer units.

Weights and composition

Major groups	Number of items	Weights	Approximate number of price quotations
Food and beverages	100	17.627	44,102
Housing	97	41.544	(c) 18,864
Clothing, footwear and upkeep	59	6.097	11,059
Transport	38	17.013	6,564
Medical care	15	6.689	4,483
Entertainment	30	4.357	2,800
Other goods and services	31	6.674	2,080
Total	(a) 370	(b) 100.000	89,952

Note: (a) Includes 23 unpriced items. (b) Relative importance for December 1991. (c) Includes 9,000 quotations for shelter.

Household consumption expenditure
Household consumption expenditure refers to all goods and services that people buy for their day-to-day living.

Method of data collection
The outlet sample is selected from a point-of-purchase survey conducted each year in about one-fifth of the urban areas included in the CPI. Consumer units are interviewed in each of the areas in which prices are collected. Respondents are asked for information on purchases of items within specific categories during a prescribed reference period. If a purchase has been made, the name and address of the outlet is recorded along with the cost for each transaction. The Bureau of Labor Statistics then selects a probability sample from these outlets for each expenditure category, using the expenditure at each outlet as a measure of size. This ensures an unbiased outlet sample with all types of establishments represented; the system also permits the estimation of variances and sampling error.

Prices of most goods and services are obtained through personal visit by the Bureau's trained representatives to approximately 21,000 retail establishments and 6,000 housing units. Mail questionnaires are used to obtain public utility rates, some fuel prices and prices for certain other items. Prices are collected in 85 urban areas across the country from retail outlets and service establishments. Prices of food, fuel and a few other items are obtained each month in all 85 locations. Other items and services are priced each month in the five largest metropolitan areas and every two months in the remaining areas. Food is priced throughout the month. The prices used to calculate the index are the regular cash prices in effect, including all taxes directly associated with the purchase and use of the items.

Housing
Information on rent is collected via the rent survey, covering a sample of about 60,000 housing units divided into six panels. Every month, one panel is priced and the panels are rotated so that the same units are priced every six months. The rental equivalence method is used to measure the cost of owner-occupied housing. The price of home repair materials purchased by tenants is included, as well as the rental values of owner-used vacation property. The shelter index is adjusted for the change in quality resulting from the effect of aging on rental housing, using the hedonic regression method.

Specification of varieties
Items for pricing are selected by the price collector within each sample outlet in proportion to their dollar volume of sales in the outlet, i.e. with probability proportional to size (the percentage of sales is the measure of size). The price collector prepares a detailed description of the selected item using a check-list developed by commoditiy specialists for each entry-level item. This outlet-specific specification is used to identify the item for pricing.

Substitution, quality change, etc.
Quality adjustments are made by the commodity specialist when substitution occurs. If quality adjustment is not possible, a linking method is used.

Seasonal items
Prices for seasonal items not currently available are imputed using standard imputation procedures.

Computation
The index is computed according to the Laspeyres formula as a weighted arithmetic average with fixed base, using weights corresponding to the base period.

Weighted price relatives for the current and previous periods are used to compute the item indices. The weights are based on the importance of the item, the outlet and the area, and on the number of other sampled price quotations.

The index for All Urban Consumers is an aggregation of data for the 85 primary sampling units where prices are collected. Weights reflecting estimated current expenditure for the base period market basket are determined for each item in each primary sampling unit. The market baskets are then weighted using the population represented by each primary sampling unit to obtain the All Urban item weights.

Organisation and publication
US Department of Labor, Bureau of Labor Statistics: "The CPI Detailed Report" (Washington, DC).

Idem: "The Consumer Price Index: The 1987 Revision, Report 736".

Idem: "The Consumer Price Index: BLS Handbook of Methods" Bulletin No. 2285, Chapter 19.

URUGUAY (MONTEVIDEO)

Official title
Indice de los precios del consumo (Consumer Price Index).

Scope
The index is compiled monthly and relates to middle-income households living in Montevideo.

Official base
December 1985 = 100.

Source of weights
The weights and items were derived from a household expenditure survey conducted in Montevideo during September 1982-August 1983 among a sample of 1,946 middle-income households. The weights were adjusted to take into account price changes between the survey period and December 1985.

Household consumption expenditure
Consumption expenditure for the purpose of the index comprises all acquisitions of goods and services for consumption during the reference period, including consumption from own-produced goods and income in kind received. The acquisition of durable goods other than owner-occupied houses is meas-

Weights and composition

Major groups	Number of items	Weights	Approximate number of price quotations
Food	84	39.91	...
Clothing and footwear	50	7.02	...
Housing	16	17.58	...
Furniture, household equipment and cleaning materials	19	6.36	...
Medical care	11	9.26	...
Transport and communication	9	10.38	...
Recreation	11	3.10	...
Education	8	1.30	...
Other expenditure (incl. personal care and tobacco)	13	5.09	...
Total	221	100.00	...

ured on the basis of payments made during the reference period. Gifts, indirect taxes, municipal rates and other expenditure related to the use of goods and services such as licence fees are also included. Excluded from the index are money transfers, income tax and other direct taxes, savings and gambling.

Method of data collection
Prices are collected from more than 400 retail outlets, markets and service establishments in Montevideo. Price data for most items are collected by agents visiting selected outlets periodically. The prices of items sold in market places are ascertained once a week. For items with centrally-fixed prices, such as milk, bread, electricity and public transport fares, prices are obtained directly from the relevant authorities and/or service establishments when changes occur.

The prices used in the index are those that any member of the public would have to pay on the pricing day to purchase the specified goods or services.

Housing
Rent data are collected each month from 12 selected house-renting agencies. Information for owner-occupied houses is obtained from the Mortgage Bank of Uruguay.

Specification of varieties
The specifications of varieties to be priced give in detail the brand name, description, unit and size.

Substitution, quality change, etc.
If an item disappears from an outlet, its price is imputed on the basis of items available in other outlets.

Seasonal items
Seasonal fluctuations in the prices of fresh fruit and vegetables are taken into account by varying items and item weights within monthly baskets of constant group weights.

Computation
The index is computed according to the Laspeyres formula as a weighted arithmetic average with fixed base, using weights corresponding to the base period.

The price relative for each item, calculated by dividing the average price for the current period by the average price for the base period, is used to calculate item indices.

Organisation and publication
Dirección general de Estadística y Censos: "Boletín mensual" (Montevideo).

Idem: "Indice de los precios del consumo, Metodología, Base Diciembre 1985".

VANUATU

Official title
Consumer Price Index - Low-Income Group Families.

Scope
The index is compiled quarterly and covers low-income group families living in urban areas, with monthly income of the head of the family of less than 20,000 FNH in 1975.

Official base
January-March 1976 = 100.

Source of weights
The weights and items were derived from a household expenditure survey conducted during the first quarter of 1975 among 220 households in Vila and in Santo (Luganville).

Weights and composition

Major groups	Number of items	Weights	Approximate number of price quotations
Food	...	45.8	...
Beverages and tobacco	...	10.1	...
Clothing and footwear	...	14.1	...
Rent, fuel, light and water	...	2.2	...
Furniture, furnishings, household goods and services	...	8.0	...
Transport and communication	...	9.8	...
Health, education and recreation	...	10.0	...
Total	...	100.0	...

Household consumption expenditure
Consumption expenditure for the purpose of the index comprises all goods and services purchased for consumption by the index population. It excludes income taxes, investments, savings and personal loans.

Method of data collection
Prices are collected around the middle of each month in Santo and around the middle of each quarter in Vila, from selected retail outlets and service establishments.

The prices used to calculate the index are the normal prices paid by consumers.

Housing
Not available.

Specification of varieties
Item specifications are given in terms of brand, make, quality and size.

Substitution, quality change, etc.
If an item is not available in an outlet, a similar item is substituted.

Seasonal items
Not available.

Computation
The index is computed according to the Laspeyres formula as a weighted arithmetic average with fixed base, using weights corresponding to the first quarter of 1975.

Price relatives for the current and previous periods are used to compute item indices.

Other information
A new series relating to all urban households in Vanuatu is now computed (base January-March 1990 = 100), but the relevant methodological information was not available in the ILO at the time the present volume was published.

Organisation and publication
National Planning and Statistics Office: "Statistical Bulletin" (Port Vila).

VENEZUELA (CARACAS)

Official title
Indice de precios al consumidor para el área metropolitana de Caracas. (Consumer Price Index for the Metropolitan Area of Caracas).

Scope
The index is compiled monthly and relates to all families in the metropolitan area of Caracas.

Official base
1984 = 100.

Source of weights
The weights and items were derived from a household expenditure survey conducted during 12 months from 1 November 1974 to 31 October 1975, covering all types of households in the metropolitan area of Caracas. Items were selected for pricing if they represented more than one per cent of total household expenditure. The price movements of items not priced are assumed to be represented by those of items priced and the weights of the items not priced are allocated to the priced items representing them. The weights were not adjusted to take into account price changes between the survey period and 1984.

Weights and composition

Major groups	Number of items	Weights	Approximate number of price quotations
Food and tobacco	180	30.83	...
Household operations (housing, fuel and light, furnishings, etc.)	59	29.64	...
Clothing and footwear	72	9.33	...
Miscellaneous	64	30.20	...
Total	375	100.00	...

Household consumption expenditure
Consumption expenditure for the purpose of the index comprises all goods and services purchased for consumption by the index population. It also includes the consumption of home grown and produced goods and income in kind received, social security and pension fund contributions, payments made to municipal authorities in connection with the use of goods and services, i.e. fees for motor vehicle registration, licence fees, etc.

Method of data collection
Prices are obtained each month by agents from 1,136 selected outlets, including market areas, supermarkets, retail stores and service establishments. The samples are distributed uniformly throughout the month. Prices for fresh fruit are collected three times from each selected outlet to obtain an average price per outlet. Official tariffs are used for electricity, gas and water and special inquiries are conducted for medical care, education, transport and communication.

The prices used in the index calculation are the prices actually charged in cash transactions. Prices of second-hand goods and black-market prices are not taken into account.

Housing
Rent quotations are obtained each month from a sample of rented dwellings (houses and apartments). The sample is distributed over 12 months, and approximately about 200 rented dwellings are visited each month. No account is taken of owner-occupied dwellings.

Specification of varieties
The specifications of items to be priced are given in detail, providing the brand name, description, unit and size, etc.

Substitution, quality change, etc.
If the quality of an item changes, it is considered as a new item. When this new item becomes relevant, it is included in the index as a variety of the sub-group investigated. If an item disappears from the market, it is substituted by a similar item.

Seasonal items
The index computation does not take into account seasonal fluctuations in item prices.

Computation
The index is computed according to the Laspeyres formula as a weighted arithmetic average with fixed base, using weights corresponding to 1 November 1974-31 October 1975.

Price relatives for each variety in each outlet in the current and previous periods are used to compute item indices. The simple arithmetic averages of these price relatives are calculated to yield item indices.

Organisation and publication
Banco Central de Venezuela, Departamento de Estadísticas de Precios: "Boletín Mensual" (Caracas).

VIRGIN ISLANDS (BRITISH)

Official title
Consumer Price Index.

Scope
The index is compiled monthly and covers middle-income households in the British Virgin Islands, with a monthly income of betwen 500 and 700 US dollars in September 1983.

Official base
March 1985 = 100.

Source of weights
The weights and items were derived from a household expenditure survey conducted in September 1983, covering a sample of 105 households of middle-income families, with a monthly income of between 500 and 700 US dollars in September 1983. The weights were not adjusted to take into account price changes between the survey period and March 1985.

Weights and composition

Major groups	Number of items	Weights	Approximate number of price quotations
Food and tobacco	133	400	...
Housing	11	206	...
Furniture	24	62	...
Clothing and footwear	23	115	...
Transport	12	114	...
Services	19	82	...
Miscellaneous	15	21	...
Total	237	1,000	...

Household consumption expenditure
This excludes contributions to social security, income tax, second-hand purchases and trade-in of used goods.

Method of data collection
Price data are collected by agents from 89 selected retail stores and establishments in the greater Road Town (capital) and Virgin Gorda. Most of the items are priced each month on the Thursday or Friday nearest to the 15th of the month. Prices for electricity, taxi fares, telephone and postage cost are collected each quarter or half a year. The prices used in the calculation of the index are the retail prices actually paid. Sale and discount prices are not taken into account.

Housing
Rent data are collected quarterly among rented dwellings with two bedrooms.

Specification of varieties
The specifications of items to be priced are given in detail, based on the results of the household expenditure survey, in terms of brand, make, quality and size.

Substitution, quality change, etc.
When a product disappears from the market, it is substituted by a similar product.

Seasonal items
No special treatment is given to seasonal items.

Computation
The index is computed according to the Laspeyres formula as a weighted arithmetic average with fixed base, using weights corresponding to September 1983. Price relatives for the current and previous periods are used to compute item indices.

Other information
Major sub-group indices are published.

Organisation and publication
Chief Minister's Office, Development Planning Unit: "Consumer Price Index Report" (Road Town).

YEMEN (ADEN)

Official title
Retail Price Index.

Scope
The index is computed annually and covers households in Aden.

Official base
1969 = 100.

Source of weights
The weights and items were derived from a household expenditure survey on government employees. The weights were revised later to take into account the changed expenditure pattern.

Household consumption expenditure
Not available.

Method of data collection
Prices are collected regularly on Monday and Tuesday of the second week of each month, in Aden.

Housing
Not available.

Weights and composition

Major groups	Number of items	Weights	Approximate number of price quotations
Food	48	508	...
Fuel, light and water	6	39	...
Rent	5	60	...
Clothing and footwear	24	90	...
Household supplies	13	40	...
Qat, tobacco and alcoholic drinks	3	100	...
Other expenses (health, personal care, transport, culture and recreation)	24	163	...
Total	123	1,000	...

Specification of varieties
To ensure that prices are comparable over time, the quality and quantity of items and services were defined carefully.

Substitution, quality change, etc.
Not available.

Seasonal items
Not available.

Computation
The index is computed according to the Laspeyres formula as a weighted arithmetic average with fixed base, using weights corresponding to the base period.

Organisation and publication
Central Statistical Organisation: "Statistical Yearbook" (Aden).

YUGOSLAVIA

Official title
Cost of Living Index.

Scope
The index is compiled monthly and relates to workers' and employees' families.

Official base
Indices appearing in national publications are computed on the basis of changes in average prices from the previous year; thus the index base changes each calendar year.

Source of weights
The weights and items are derived from the results of a permanent survey of income and expenditure conducted in more than 50 large towns and covering more than 2,000 workers' and employees' families with two adults and one or two children or dependent persons. The weights relating to 1979 are as follows:

Weights and composition

Major groups	Number of items	Weights	Approximate number of price quotations
Food	94	45.84	...
Beverages and tobacco	8	4.92	...
Housing:			
Rent	1	3.60	...
Maintenance and water	4	2.74	...
Fuel and light	9	5.62	...
Clothing and footwear	54	12.37	...
Household goods and services	36	6.88	...
Personal hygiene	17	3.58	...
Education and recreation	18	5.54	...
Transport and communication	9	8.91	...
Total	260	100.00	...

Household consumption expenditure
Not available.

Method of data collection
Prices for most items are collected each month by agents from about 3,500 retail outlets in 53 towns; prices for agricultural products are collected each fortnight.

Housing
Rent quotations are obtained from eight standard categories of dwellings in each of the 53 towns.

Specification of varieties
Not available.

Substitution, quality change, etc.
Not available.

Seasonal items
Seasonal fluctuations in the prices of fresh fruit and vegetables are taken into account by shifting monthly item weights within constant group weights.

Computation
The index is computed according to the Laspeyres formula as a weighted arithmetic average with fixed base, using weights corresponding to the base period. The index is obtained by successive weighting of arithmetic price averages, using weights based on the sales turnover for items sold in the different towns and republics where prices are collected and on the expenditure pattern of the families covered by the permanent survey.

Organisation and publication
Federal Statistical Institute: "Indeks" (Belgrade).

Idem: "Metodoloski Materyali", Nos. 122, 168 and 233.

ZAMBIA

Official title
Consumer Price Index for Low-Income Group Families.

Scope
The index is compiled monthly and covers urban households with monthly incomes less than 100 kwachas during 1974-75. The index reflects price changes in Lusaka, the Copperbelt, Kabwe and Livingstone.

Official base
1975 = 100 and 1985 = 100.

Source of weights
The weights and items were derived from a household expenditure survey conducted during March 1974-March 1975 in Lusaka, Ndola and Kitwe. The index relates to urban households with monthly income of less than 100 kwachas at the time of the survey.

Weights and composition

Major groups	Number of items	Weights	Approximate number of price quotations
Food and tobacco	74	680	459
Clothing and footwear	40	99	268
Fuel and light	25	106	87
Household goods, furnishings	25	44	208
Medical care	36	3	98
Transport and communication	11	22	16
Education and recreation	10	9	43
Other goods and services	63	37	244
Total	284	1,000	1,423

Household consumption expenditure
This excludes life insurance, income taxes and personal property taxes.

Method of data collection
A price survey is carried out around the 10th of each month by officers of the Central Statistical Office. Prices are obtained by personal visits to selected outlets within Lusaka, while mailed questionnaires are used for outlets and service establishments in the other towns. Some prices are ascertained through direct purchase. For items such as electricity, gas, water, transport and communication, official tariffs are used.

Prices for fresh fruit and vegetables are collected twice a month from the city centre market.

The prices used to calculate the index are the prices actually paid by consumers. Discount and sale prices are also taken into account.

Housing
Rent is not included in the index nor is the cost of owner-occupied housing.

Specification of varieties
The specifications of each item to be priced are given according to size, unit, brand name and quality.

Substitution, quality change, etc.
Quality changes are estimated on the basis of closely related

substitutes. Replacement items are introduced only when they become sufficiently important in the market.

Seasonal items
No adjustment is made to seasonal fluctuations of item prices.

Computation
The index is computed according to the Laspeyres formula as a weighted arithmetic average with fixed base, using weights corresponding to March 1974-March 1975.

The relatives of average prices for the current and base periods are used to compute item indices. The average prices are simple arithmetic averages of price quotations.

Other information
A consumer price index for High-Income Group Families (base 1975 = 100) is also computed.

Organisation and publication
Central Statistical Office: "Monthly Digest of Statistics" (Lusaka).

Idem: "Studies in Official Statistics - No. 3, Methods and Procedures used in Compiling Price Statistics".

ZIMBABWE

Official title
Consumer Price Index for Lower Income Urban Families.

Scope
The index is compiled monthly and relates to African households. Households of which the head is a pensioner, unemployed or self-employed are excluded, as are households with a monthly income of more than 250 dollars at the time of the survey. The four urban areas, Harare, Bulawayo, Mutare and Gweru are covered by the index.

Official base
1980 = 100.

Source of weights
The weights and items were derived from the results of the 1978-79 household expenditure survey, covering 250 households in Harare and 233 in Bulawayo. The weights were not adjusted to take into account price changes between the survey period and the base period.

Weights and composition

Major groups	Number of items	Weights	Approximate number of price quotations
Food	27	54.9	1,466
Beverages and tobacco	5	5.4	156
Clothing and footwear	25	6.6	496
Rent, fuel and light	4	18.4	87
Household goods	23	4.6	741
Transport	19	4.7	34
Miscellaneous	21	5.4	295
Total	124	100.0	3,275

Household consumption expenditure
The consumption of goods and services received as income in kind is not taken into account. Household consumption expenditure excludes direct taxes and savings such as life insurance premiums and payments to pension funds, and expenditure on gambling and donations.

Method of data collection
Prices are collected each month from selected retail stores and service establishments in the high density suburbs of Harare, Bulawayo, Mutare and Gweru. Outlets in the city centres are also covered.

Price collection is mostly carried out through mail questionnaires. In Bulawayo, Mutare and Gweru, the questionnaires are distributed and collected by officers of the Department of Community Services. In these areas, price data for fruit and vegetables are collected each quarter by means of interviews in the markets. In Harare, some of the price data for those items such as fruit and vegetables sold in markets are collected by staff of the prices section of the Central Statistical Office.

The prices used in the index are those that any member of the public would have to pay on the pricing day. Price data refer to the 8th of each month. Sale, black-market and discount prices are not taken into account.

Housing
Rent quotations are collected through a six-monthly survey of dwellings. The rent index is based on rent, including water and sewerage charges paid for various types of municipal housing. Housing repair costs are excluded from the major group "Rent" but are included in the "Miscellaneous" group.

Specification of varieties
For some items, mainly groceries, the brand and size are specified on the price collection forms. For the remaining items broad descriptions are given in the questionnaires by the Central Statistical Office. Different brands can be used in different outlets to represent an item so long as prices are collected for the same brand each month. The best-selling medium-priced article from a line or range is to be chosen.

Substitution, quality change, etc.
If an item is temporarily out of stock, the last price recorded is maintained until it is again available, or a substitute item is introduced, using the method of linking.

Seasonal items
Only fruit and vegetables are treated as seasonal items. A variable monthly weighting structure is used to allow for seasonal variations. The total weight for fruit and vegetables is kept constant.

Computation
The index is computed according to the Laspeyres formula as a weighted arithmetic average with base December 1981. The group indices are then converted to the base 1980 = 100 using certain conversion factors.

In computing item indices, price relatives for the current and previous periods are used. For most of the items, relatives of average prices are calculated; averages of price relatives are computed for a few items such as car spare parts.

Separate indices are first calculated for each of the four towns and these are then weighted according to the population of each town to arrive at the national index. The weights applied to the individual towns are Harare 56, Bulawayo 32, Gweru 6, and Mutare 6.

Other information
The Central Statistical Office also publishes a consumer price index for higher-income urban families (base 1980 = 100). In addition, an all-items index exclusive of sales tax and excise duty is also produced for both lower- and higher-income urban families.

Organisation and publication
Central Statistical Office: "Quarterly Digest of Statistics" (Harare).

Idem: "Monthly Supplement to the Digest of Statistics".

INTRODUCTION

Ce volume 1 des *Sources et méthodes: statistiques du travail*, donne des descriptions méthodologiques des séries nationales d'indices des prix à la consommation publiées par le BIT dans les éditions de 1992 de l'*Annuaire des statistiques du travail* et du *Bulletin des statistiques du travail*. Il s'agit d'une version revue, augmentée et mise à jour de la deuxième édition de *Sources et méthodes statistiques* publiée en 1987.

On trouvera ici des descriptions de 171 séries d'indices des prix à la consommation concernant 157 pays. La plupart de ces descriptions ont été préparées soit à partir des réponses officielles faites par les services statistiques nationaux à un questionnaire spécial, soit à partir de publications nationales sur les indices des prix à la consommation. Dans un certain nombre de cas, les descriptions présentées pourraient ne correspondre qu'à de nouvelles séries publiées dans le *Bulletin*, en attendant la mise à disposition des moyennes annuelles devant être publiées dans une version ultérieure de l'*Annuaire*.

L'objet du présent volume est double: i) fournir des informations sur les sources et les méthodes utilisées par les pays pour l'établissement des séries d'indices des prix à la consommation publiées par le BIT, de manière à en accroître l'utilité à différents égards; ii) signaler les différences existant entre les diverses séries nationales en ce qui concerne la portée, le champ d'application, les sources des données, les définitions, les classifications, le traitement de certains problèmes particuliers et la formule utilisée pour le calcul. Pour faciliter les comparaisons, les descriptions ont été organisées et présentées sous quatorze rubriques correspondant aux différentes caractéristiques. Ces rubriques sont les suivantes:

Dénomination officielle
La dénomination de l'indice des prix à la consommation dans la langue de correspondance officielle qu'utilise le pays avec le BIT et, s'il y a lieu, la traduction en français.

Portée
Des informations sont données sur la périodicité de la série (mois, trimestre, semestre ou année), les types de ménages couverts par catégorie de revenus ou de dépenses ou selon la taille du ménage; les groupes de population couverts, qui peuvent représenter l'ensemble de la population ou des groupes socio-économiques particuliers tels que les travailleurs de l'industrie, les salariés non manuels, etc., et la région géographique considérée (ensemble du pays, centres urbains, capitale du pays, villes ou groupes de villes particuliers, etc.).

Base originale
La période prise comme base par les services statistiques nationaux pour le calcul de l'indice et sa présentation dans les publications nationales.

Source des coefficients de pondération
Cette rubrique recouvre la ou les sources et la période de référence des coefficients de pondération utilisés pour le calcul de l'indice, par exemple les enquêtes sur les dépenses des ménages, la comptabilité nationale, etc. Si la période de référence des pondérations diffère de la période de base de l'indice, les ajustements apportés aux pondérations pour tenir compte de la durée différente des deux périodes sont décrits.

Lorsque les coefficients de pondération sont tirés d'une enquête sur les dépenses des ménages, des indications sont données sur les types de ménages, les groupes de population et la région géographique considérés, la durée de l'enquête, la période de référence correspondant aux dépenses et les dimensions de l'échantillon. Lorsque les coefficients de pondération sont tirés de la comptabilité nationale ou d'autres sources, les méthodes de calcul sont, si possible, indiquées. Les critères et la méthode utilisés pour choisir les articles ou pour traiter les articles pour lesquels les prix ne sont pas relevés (estimation des coefficients de pondération) sont également décrits.

Pondération et composition
Le nombre d'articles et les coefficients de pondération utilisés pour le calcul de l'indice sont présentés par groupe de dépenses. Un «article» s'entend ici du plus petit groupement de biens ou de services auquel un coefficient de pondération spécifique est affecté. Par exemple, la viande de boeuf peut constituer un article comprenant plusieurs variétés comme le romsteck, l'aloyau, etc. pour lesquelles des pondérations distinctes ne sont pas disponibles. Les principaux groupes sont les suivants: alimentation; combustible et éclairage; habillement; logement; divers. Lorsque les classifications ne correspondent pas aux groupes ci-dessus, c'est la classification utilisée par le pays qui est indiquée. Lorsque c'est possible, le nombre approximatif de prix relevés ayant servi au calcul de l'indice est indiqué.

Dépenses de consommation des ménages
On définit généralement les dépenses de consommation de ménages comme les dépenses consacrées par les ménages privés à des biens et services de consommation. Il peut s'agir en fait d'achats ou de consommation. Les descriptions expliquent, lorsque c'est possible, comment sont traités les biens produits à domicile et consommés par les ménages, la propriété du logement, les biens durables, les achats à crédit, les achats d'articles d'occasion, les cotisations à la sécurité sociale et aux caisses de retraite, les redevances, les assurances correspondant à certains biens de consommation, les dépenses de santé, les impôts sur le revenu et autres impôts directs, les primes d'assurance-vie, les envois d'argent, dons et autres débours.

Mode de relevé des prix
La méthode appliquée au choix des localités et des points de vente, la fréquence des relevés pour différentes catégories de biens et de services, le traitement des rabais, soldes, prix pratiqués au marché noir, achats en location-vente ou à crédit, achats d'articles d'occasion, prix d'articles d'importation, impôts indirects, la méthode des relevés de prix pour différents types d'articles (visite des points de vente, enquêtes par correspondance, tarifs officiels, achats) et les techniques spéciales appliquées aux relevés de prix correspondant à des articles comme l'électricité, le gaz et l'eau, les soins médicaux, l'éducation ou les transports et les communications.

Logement
Les méthodes utilisées pour obtenir des données sur les loyers et le mode de traitement des logements occupés par le propriétaire sont exposés. Le traitement des dépenses telles que taxes, assurances, intérêts hypothécaires, réparations, etc., et les méthodes et la fréquence de collecte des données sont indiqués lorsque des informations sont disponibles.

Spécification des variétés
Les spécifications sont les critères utilisés pour décrire avec précision la variété pour laquelle des prix sont relevés. Il peut s'agir de la qualité, du fabricant, de la marque, de l'unité, etc. La procédure utilisée pour identifier les variétés lorsqu'il n'existe pas de spécifications détaillées et précises est indiquée.

Substitution, changement de qualité, etc.
L'apparition d'un nouveau produit sur le marché, la disparition d'un article ou des changements de qualité ont des incidences sur l'indice. Les méthodes appliquées par les pays pour résoudre ces problèmes sont brièvement décrites.

Articles saisonniers
Les prix de certains articles comme les fruits et les légumes frais connaissent des fluctuations saisonnières. Diverses méthodes utilisées pour calculer les influences saisonnières sont mentionnées ici.

Calcul
Les prix des différents articles retenus pour le calcul de l'indice sont généralement pondérés pour tenir compte de l'importance relative de chaque article par rapport à l'ensemble des dépenses de consommation. Dans la plupart des pays, les indices sont calculés sous une forme dérivée telle que la moyenne arithmétique pondérée des rapports de prix pour un certain nombre d'articles représentatifs entre la période considérée et la période de base, en utilisant l'une des formes de la formule de Laspeyres. Lorsqu'elle est connue, la méthode exacte utilisée par les pays est décrite. Quelques pays utilisent un indice-chaîne de Laspeyres avec des raccordements annuels ou une formule de Paasche pour calculer leurs indices. Ils sont indiqués dans les descriptions.

Les méthodes de calcul des moyennes de prix et des rapports de prix sont décrites, et il est également indiqué si l'indice est calculé directement ou comme une agrégation d'indices locaux ou régionaux.

Autres informations
Si disponibles, des informations complémentaires sont fournies concernant la publication par le pays, de différents sous-groupes de l'indice, ou le calcul de séries pour d'autres groupes de population ou de revenus, ou pour d'autres zones géographiques.

Organisation et publication
Le service statistique chargé du calcul et de la publication de l'indice ainsi que les titres des principales publications nationales dans lesquelles l'indice est publié sont indiqués sous cette rubrique. Dans la mesure du possible, elle mentionne également les titres et les sources des publications nationales dans lesquelles ont paru des descriptions méthodologiques détaillées de la série.

Liste des tableaux publiés par le BIT
A. *Annuaire des statistiques du travail*:

Prix à la consommation:
- 23 Indices généraux
- 24 Indices généraux non compris l'habitation
- 25 Indices de l'alimentation
- 26 Indices du combustible et de l'éclairage
- 27 Indices de l'habillement
- 28 Indices du loyer

B. *Bulletin des statistiques du travail*:
- 9A Indices généraux
- 9B Indices de l'alimentation

Remarques
Comme la période de base originale des séries diffère selon les pays, une période de base uniforme a été adoptée dans les publications du BIT pour la présentation des données. Depuis 1986, cette période de base est l'année 1980 (lorsqu'on ne dispose de données que pour des périodes postérieures à 1980, les indices sont généralement présentés avec, pour période de base, la première année civile pour laquelle des chiffres sont disponibles et ils sont imprimés en italiques). Ces opérations n'impliquent aucune modification des systèmes de pondération utilisés pour le calcul de la série.

Signes et symboles utilisés

.	Ne s'applique pas
...	Pas disponible
-	Nul ou inférieur à la moitié de l'unité retenue
(a)	Note de bas de page.

Dans les tableaux, les unités et les décimales sont séparées par un point.

AFRIQUE DU SUD

Dénomination officielle
Consumer Price Index (Indice des prix à la consommation).

Portée
L'indice est calculé mensuellement et porte sur tous les groupes de population dans 12 régions urbaines.

Base originale
1985 = 100.

Source des coefficients de pondération
La valeur des coefficients de pondération et le choix des articles résultent d'une enquête sur les dépenses des ménages effectuée en novembre 1985.

Pondération et composition

Groupes principaux	Nombre d'articles	Pondération	Nombre approximatif de relevés de prix
Alimentation	88	22,72	...
Boissons, boissons alcoolisées et tabac	8	2,84	...
Habillement et chaussure	55	5,98	...
Logement:			
Loyer	2	5,88	...
Coût de l'habitat en propriété	7	13,91	...
Autres (y compris l'eau)	3	1,41	...
Combustible et éclairage	6	2,44	...
Mobilier et articles d'équipement ménager	29	4,72	...
Dépenses de ménage	14	3,77	...
Soins médicaux	5	2,56	...
Transports et communications	21	18,93	...
Instruction et loisirs	21	4,96	...
Soins personnels	12	3,08	...
Divers	14	6,77	...
Total	285	100,00	...

Dépenses de consommation des ménages
Les dépenses de consommation comprennent: permis et frais d'immatriculation automobile, intérêts sur prêts, frais bancaires, primes d'assurance-vie, polices d'assurance mixte, annuités, assurance prêts hypothécaires, cotisations aux syndicats, aux associations de personnel et professionnelles, honoraires pour services juridiques et autres. Certaines dépenses ne sont pas prises en compte dans l'indice des prix à la consommation. C'est ainsi que sont exclus, par exemple, l'impôt sur le revenu, les contributions aux caisses de retraite et de prévoyance.

Mode de relevé des prix
Les prix sont relevés au moyen de questionnaires adressés par correspondance à un échantillon représentatif de points de vente au détail et de prestataires de services de différentes zones ou à des organisations, associations ou services publics. Les prix des fruits et légumes sont fournis par la Division du marketing agricole du Département de l'économie et du marketing agricoles qui procède chaque semaine à leur relevé.

Pour la plupart des autres denrées alimentaires, de même que pour l'habillement, le combustible et les produits d'entretien, les prix sont relevés mensuellement. Ils sont relevés tous les trois mois pour les meubles et l'équipement, les soins personnels, la papeterie, etc. Certaines informations relatives aux prix sont obtenues annuellement ou aussi souvent que des changements de prix se produisent. Tous les relevés de prix, sauf ceux des fruits et légumes, se rapportent aux sept premiers jours du mois considéré. Pour les fruits et légumes, les relevés sont hebdomadaires.

Logement
Les données relatives au loyer des maisons et des appartements proviennent de l'enquête annuelle effectuée par le Département des statistiques. Le coût des logements en propriété comprend le paiement des intérêts, le taux de taxation, les services sanitaires, l'enlèvement des ordures, l'assurance des bâtiments, les réparations et l'entretien, ainsi que d'autres frais inhérents à la propriété.

Spécification des variétés
Pas disponible.

Substitution, changement de qualité, etc.
Pas disponible.

Articles saisonniers
Il n'est procédé à aucun ajustement des fluctuations saisonnières des prix des articles.

Calcul
L'indice est calculé selon la formule de Laspeyres, sous forme de moyenne arithmétique pondérée à base fixe, les coefficients de pondération correspondant à 1985.

Il s'agit de la moyenne pondérée d'indices séparés relatifs à 12 régions urbaines.

Autres informations
Cette série est également publiée séparément pour les groupes de ménages à revenu modeste, moyen et élevé, pour tous les articles à l'exclusion du logement, pour tous les articles à l'exclusion de l'alimentation, pour des sous-groupes détaillés, et séparément pour 12 régions urbaines.

Un indice des prix à la consommation ajusté sur une base saisonnière et un indice des prix à la consommation des retraités concernant les régions urbaines sont également publiés.

Une nouvelle série (base 1990 = 100) est maintenant calculée, mais les informations méthodologiques relatives à cette série n'étaient pas disponibles au BIT lors de la publication du présent Volume.

Organisation et publication
Central Statistical Service: «Bulletin of Statistics» (Prétoria).

ALGERIE (ALGER)

Dénomination officielle
Indice des prix à la consommation.

Portée
L'indice est calculé mensuellement et porte sur l'ensemble des ménages d'Alger, de toutes tailles et toutes catégories socio-professionnelles.

Base originale
1982 = 100.

Source des coefficients de pondération
Les coefficients de pondération ont été déterminés sur la base des résultats d'une enquête nationale sur les dépenses des ménages effectuée entre mars 1979 et mars 1980 auprès d'un échantillon de 8 208 ménages répartis sur l'ensemble du territoire algérien selon 6 secteurs d'habitat, 5 zones économiques et 20 catégories socio-professionnelles. L'indice se rapporte à l'ensemble des ménages de la ville d'Alger (célibataires exclus) de toutes tailles et toutes catégories socio-professionnelles. Les articles sélectionnés proviennent d'un recensement des variétés et services consommés par les ménages, effectué en 1982. L'indice se compose de 712 variétés sélectionnées sur la base de critères tels que la dépense annuelle, la fréquence de la dépense, l'utilité. Les pondérations des variétés sont calculées à partir des dépenses annuelles en 1979, données par l'enquête nationale sur la consommation des ménages. Le taux de couverture de l'indice (en termes de dépenses de consommation) est de 93%.

Pondération et composition

Groupes principaux	Nombre d'articles	Pondération	Nombre approximatif de relevés de prix
Alimentation	56	522,4	9 919
Habillement et chaussure	59	70,6	709
Logement, combustible et éclairage	9	72,5	95
Mobilier et ameublement	43	55,0	152
Soins médicaux	26	26,5	6
Transports et communication	20	96,1	47
Instruction et loisirs	20	42,3	28
Autres biens et services	23	84,6	128
Total	256	1 000,0	11 084

Dépenses de consommation des ménages
Les dépenses de consommation prises en compte pour établir les coefficients de pondération comprennent les biens et services recensés lors de l'enquête sur les dépenses des ménages. Sont exclus les dépenses d'investissements, le logement en propriété, les cotisations d'assurances sociales et de caisses de pensions, les patentes, les impôts sur le revenu et autres impôts directs, les versements au titre d'assurances sur la vie, les envois de fonds, dons et versements similaires.

Mode de relevé des prix
Les relevés de prix sont effectués périodiquement par des enquêteurs dans 10 secteurs géographiques de la ville d'Alger auprès d'un échantillon de points de vente (publics et privés) selon un programme d'enquêtes fixé pour chaque groupe de biens et services. Il s'agit de prix déclarés ou affichés. En moyenne, près de 450 variétés sont enquêtées mensuellement et 11 000 prix environ sont traités par mois. En particulier, les fruits et légumes frais ainsi que les poissons frais sont enquêtés 3 fois par semaine auprès de 10 points de vente (marchés) publics et privés; les viandes, volailles et oeufs le sont 2 fois par mois auprès de 36 points de vente publics et privés. Les prix des articles pour l'habillement sont relevés tous les 4 mois. Les données se référant à l'eau, l'électricité, le gaz, l'instruction, les transports et communications sont obtenues une fois l'an et celles des soins médicaux deux fois par an.

Logement
Les enquêteurs relèvent le prix du loyer et des charges une fois par an, pour des logements de trois pièces, cuisine et salle de bains, auprès des organismes chargés de la gestion des immeubles pour le secteur public et auprès des ménages pour le secteur privé. L'indice pour le groupe «loyer» est obtenu en combinant l'indice du secteur public et l'indice du secteur privé. Les logements occupés par leur propriétaire ne sont pas pris en compte dans le calcul de l'indice.

Spécification des variétés
En 1982, un recensement des variétés des biens et services consommés par les ménages a été effectué. Sur cette base, près de 2 000 variétés ont été traitées (spécification, définition de l'article, calcul de prix moyens) en vue de la composition de l'indice. Chaque article a des spécifications détaillées et décrit la variété, la qualité, la fabrication, la marque, l'unité, etc.

Substitution, changement de qualité, etc.
On ne tient pas compte dans le calcul de l'indice du changement de qualité d'un article ni d'un nouvel article apparaissant sur le marché.

Articles saisonniers
Les fruits et légumes frais, en raison du caractère saisonnier de leur commercialisation, subissent un traitement particulier: à partir d'un panier mensuel de pleine saison, il est calculé un indice brut, lequel indice compare les coûts du même panier (mensuel) du mois courant et du mois de même nom de l'année de référence (1982). Les prix de base des variétés du panier, ainsi que les pondérations, sont mensuels. La comparaison d'indices bruts de mois de noms différents indique, non pas une variation (relative) pure des prix, mais le rapport des variations de prix pour chacun des mois.

Calcul
L'indice est calculé selon la formule de Laspeyres, sous forme de moyenne arithmétique pondérée à base fixe, les coefficients de pondération correspondant à 1979.

Autres informations
Actuellement un indice national est calculé sur la base de l'observation des prix dans un échantillon de 18 villes et villages. Cet indice national est élaboré mensuellement depuis Janvier 1989.

Organisation et publication
Office national des statistiques: «Statistiques» (trimestriel) (Alger).

idem: «Données statistiques» (mensuel).

ALLEMAGNE 1

Remarque: La description se réfère au territoire de la République fédérale d'Allemagne avant le 3.10.1990.

Dénomination officielle
Preisindex für die Lebenshaltung aller privaten Haushalte (Indice des prix à la consommation pour l'ensemble des ménages privés).

Portée
L'indice est calculé mensuellement et porte sur tous les ménages privés de résidents allemands, à l'exception des personnes vivant dans des logements institutionnels.

Base originale
1985 = 100.

Source des coefficients de pondération
La valeur des coefficients de pondération et le choix des articles résultent d'une enquête sur les dépenses des ménages effectuée en 1983. Cette enquête portait sur environ 55 000 ménages privés composés d'une personne au minimum et disposant d'un revenu mensuel net inférieur ou égal à 25 000 DM. Les pondérations ont été mises à jour en 1985 au moyen d'une enquête relative au budget courant d'environ 1 000 ménages privés choisis au préalable. L'indice se rapporte à une taille moyenne des ménages de 2,3 personnes et à des dépenses de consommation moyennes de 3 105 DM par ménage et par mois en 1985. Les pondérations des articles non relevés sont reportées sur les articles restants.

Pondération et composition

Groupes principaux	Nombre d'articles	Pondération	Nombre approximatif de relevés de prix
Alimentation et tabac	186	229,89	116 000
Habillement et chaussure	77	69,47	31 000
Loyer	5	177,77	13 000
Combustible et éclairage	18	72,52	4 000
Mobilier, ameublement, et autres articles de ménage	138	72,21	37 000
Transports et communications	81	144,03	14 000
Soins personnels et médicaux	55	40,99	15 000
Instruction et loisirs	147	83,71	29 000
Autres biens et services	44	109,41	41 000
Total	751	1 000,00	300 000

Dépenses de consommation des ménages
Les dépenses de consommation prises en compte pour le calcul des coefficients de pondération comprennent les frais relatifs à la propriété immobilière, aux licences et aux primes d'assurance pour les biens spécifiques de consommation, ainsi que les dons et les déboursements du même type. Sont exclues les primes d'assurance vie, d'assurance sociale et d'assurance vieillesse. Sont également exclus les revenus en nature, les achats à crédit, les achats d'articles d'occasion, l'impôt sur le revenu et les autres impôts directs.

Mode de relevé des prix
Les prix sont relevés par des enquêteurs vers le milieu de chaque mois dans 118 municipalités et environ 15 000 magasins de détail et établissements de services.

Les prix applicables uniformément à l'ensemble du pays (livres et revues, tarifs postaux, tarifs aériens, voyages organisés, primes d'assurance) sont notés sous une forme centralisée à intervalles réguliers ou lorsqu'ils subissent un changement. Les prix ainsi relevés sont ceux que paient réellement les consommateurs (et non pas les prix de catalogue). Ils comprennent la taxe à la valeur ajoutée, les contributions indirectes (impôt sur les produits pétroliers, sur le tabac) et les autres taxes légales (taxes de péréquation sur le courant électrique, taxe de stockage des produits pétroliers). Les réductions ne sont relevées que si elles correspondent à des articles faisant l'objet d'une offre régulière. Les prix de soldes ne sont pas relevés.

Logement
Les données relatives au loyer sont obtenues trimestriellement pour la totalité des logements de l'échantillon (11 000 logements). Cependant, afin de pouvoir faire état des changements mensuels, le tiers de ces logements (environ 3 700) est inclus dans l'indice.

Les habitations occupés par leur propriétaire sont prises en compte par les coefficients de pondération. L'évolution des prix est représentée par les loyers des logements en location.

Spécification des variétés
La description des différents biens et services inclus dans l'enquête est assez large pour qu'il soit possible de tenir compte, dans chaque point de vente retenu, pour chaque article, de la variété dont la vente est la plus forte. L'enquêteur en note la désignation exacte (marque, nom de l'article, numéro, quantité, etc.) afin de pouvoir contrôler et assurer la comparabilité des prix dans le temps.

Substitution, changement de qualité, etc.
Lorsque survient un changement dans les caractéristiques pouvant influer sur le prix d'un article, il est procédé, avec l'aide des spécialistes responsables, à des calculs ou à des estimations destinées à éliminer les changements artificiels de prix. La substitution d'un article par un autre s'effectue lorsque l'importance commerciale de l'article le plus ancien est encore appréciable et que celle du nouvel article l'est déjà; dans ce cas, il est procédé à l'enchaînement simple de l'ancienne série de prix à la nouvelle.

Articles saisonniers
Les articles saisonniers qui ne sont disponibles sur le marché que pour une courte période ne sont pas inclus dans l'indice. Le prix des articles disponibles durant toute l'année est pris en compte pour la totalité de leur montant.

Calcul
L'indice est calculé selon la formule de Laspeyres sous forme de moyenne arithmétique pondérée à base fixe, les coefficients de pondération correspondant à la période de base.

Des prix moyens non pondérés sont tout d'abord calculés par municipalité et par «Land»; lors du calcul des indices par article on utilise la moyenne des rapports de prix de la période courante et de la période de base. Les indices concernant les onze Länder sont alors pondérés en fonction de la population respective de chaque «Land», puis combinés pour obtenir l'indice d'ensemble du pays.

Autres informations
Des séries séparées sont calculées pour:
a) les ménages de fonctionnaires et d'employés salariés disposant d'un revenu élevé et composés de 4 personnes;
b) les ménages de travailleurs salariés disposant d'un revenu moyen et composés de 4 personnes;
c) les ménages de retraités et d'assistés sociaux disposant d'un faible revenu et composés de 2 personnes;
d) les enfants de moins de 18 ans.

Organisation et publication
Statistisches Bundesamt: «Wirtschaft und Statistik» (Wiesbaden).

idem: «Eilbericht und Monatsbericht der Fachserie 17, Reihe 7, Preise and Preisindizes für die Lebenshaltung».

Pour de plus amples détails d'ordre méthodologique, voir:
idem: «Wirtschaft und Statistik» (nos. 7/84 et 1/90).

ALLEMAGNE 2

Dénomination officielle
Preisindex für die Lebenshaltung aller Arbeitnehmerhaushalte (Indice des prix à la consommation pour l'ensemble des ménages de salariés).

Portée
L'indice est calculé mensuellement et porte sur tous les ménages de salariés habitant les cinq nouveaux länder et Berlin-Est.

Base originale
1989 = 100.

Source des coefficients de pondération
La valeur des coefficients de pondération et le choix des articles résultent d'une enquête sur les dépenses des ménages effectuée dans les cinq nouveaux länder et Berlin-Est. Les données ont été rassemblées mensuellement, de janvier à décembre 1989, au sein d'un échantillon représentatif de 2 600 ménages. La taille moyenne des familles était de 2,87 personnes.

Pondération et composition

Groupes principaux	Nombre d'articles	Pondération	Nombre approximatif de relevés de prix
Alimentation et tabac	187	385,9	19 000
Habillement et chaussure	79	134,1	10 000
Loyer, combustible et éclairage	30	55,1	8 000
Mobilier, appareils et dépenses domestiques	138	119,1	15 000
Soins de santé et personnels	47	29,7	7 000
Transports et communications	68	124,0	7 500
Instruction et loisirs (à l'exclusion des services d'hôtel et restaurant)	145	90,4	11 500
Biens personnels et services des établissements, d'hébergement et autres biens	44	61,7	4 000
Total	738	1 000,0	82 000

Remarque: (a) Voir ci-après.

(a) Pour les articles dont les données ne sont pas couvertes par une enquête au niveau central, le nombre suivant de relevés de prix est généralement effectué, compte tenu des prix établis:
- dans les villes dont la population n'est pas supérieure à 20 000 habitants: 4;
- dans les villes de 20 000 à 100 000 habitants: 6;
- dans les villes de plus de 100 000 habitants: 8.

Les exceptions à cette règle sont les suivantes:
- loyers: par agences immobilières sélectionnées;
- prix régularisés (uniformes): un relevé de prix.

Dépenses de consommation des ménages
Pour le calcul des coefficients de pondération, ont été relevées les dépenses relatives aux paiements de biens, services, contributions à l'assurance immobilière et impôts sur les véhicules à moteur des ménages privés.

Les dépenses en espèces n'incluent pas les cotisations à l'assurance-pension et aux assurances sociales. Les frais de santé ne sont inclus que pour autant que leur coût est à la charge de personnes privées. La plus grande partie de ces coûts (visites médicales, séjours dans les hôpitaux, produits pharmaceutiques, traitements et appareils prescrits) sont du ressort du régime d'assurance-santé et il n'en est donc pas tenu compte dans les coefficients de pondération. L'impôt sur le revenu et autres impôts directs ne sont pas considérés comme des dépenses en espèces sauf en ce qui concerne la taxe sur les véhicules à moteur. Les revenus en nature, les transferts d'argent, les dons, contributions et paiements analogues sont exclus. Pour les achats à crédit et la location-vente de biens, le prix entier au moment de l'achat est relevé. La vente et l'achat d'articles usagés sont compris mais ne figurent pas en tant que position séparée dans l'indice. Les dépenses de caractère administratif, contributions à l'assurance sur les propriétés immobilières (logement et biens des ménages, autres assurances de type immobilier, assurances sur les véhicules à moteur) sont comprises.

Mode de relevé des prix
Un échantillon représentatif de 80 communautés ou villes ayant fait l'objet d'une enquête a été sélectionné. Dans l'enquête sur les collectivités, les unités où un relevé est effectué directement

sont sélectionnées par un personnel compétent, sur la base de l'importance de leur volume de ventes.

Les prix sont relevés par des enquêteurs vers le milieu de chaque mois directement auprès des unités concernées. Pour certains articles (par exemple, l'électricité, le gaz et l'eau) des listes de prix des entreprises sont utilisées et les loyers des habitations sont traités au moyen de questionnaires. Officiellement des tarifs fixes uniformes (transports des passagers par chemin de fer, tarifs postaux) sont relevés centralement à partir de barèmes. Les prix courants normaux et les prix comparables du mois précédent sont recueillis par les enquêteurs auprès des unités concernées. Chaque prix est alors calculé en chiffres bruts des prix moyens pratiqués par la collectivité (moyenne arithmétique simple des prix du mois respectif/prix comparables du mois précédent). Les rabais et les soldes ne sont pas relevés, et il en est de même des prix du marché noir, des prix d'achats en location-vente et à crédit.

Logement
Les relevés de loyers sont obtenus auprès de six types d'habitations. Les données sont recueillies à intervalles mensuels, sous une forme non centralisée, au moyen d'enquêtes, par formulaires spéciaux; elles figurent dans le calcul de l'indice en tant que prix moyens et rapports de prix. Les logements et maisons occupées en propriété ne sont pas encore inclus.

Spécification des variétés
La description des articles dont le prix doit être relevé n'a pas de caractère vraiment spécifique. La qualité et l'unité de mesure sont indiquées mais la marque n'est pas spécifiée. L'enquêteur sélectionne les biens spécifiques compte tenu de l'importance de leur chiffre de vente en coopération avec l'unité concernée.

Substitution, changement de qualité, etc.
Lorsqu'il y a changement de qualité, le prix comparable du mois précédent est relevé et un ajustement du prix de base est effectué: on utilise à cet effet le quotient du prix en cours et le prix antérieur du mois précédent. Si un article, ou une qualité, qui a jusqu'ici été relevé, disparaît du marché, un nouvel article est sélectionné et il est procédé à l'estimation des changements de qualité par rapport à l'ancien relevé de prix; à partir de cette évaluation, un prix comparable est calculé pour le mois précédent.

Articles saisonniers
Les articles saisonniers sont pris en compte comme tout article qui fait l'objet d'un relevé de prix et sont compris dans le calcul mensuel de l'indice, sans ajustement.

Calcul
L'indice est calculé selon la formule de Laspeyres, sous forme de moyenne arithmétique pondérée à base fixe, les coefficients de pondération correspondant à la période de base.

La moyenne arithmétique simple est utilisée pour le calcul des prix moyens du Land et des rapports de prix du Land. Pour le calcul des prix moyens et des rapports de prix du territoire de l'ensemble des cinq nouveaux länder, les prix moyens et les rapports de prix du Land sont pondérés, compte tenu du nombre d'habitants du Land respectif. Les indices annuels moyens de l'indice d'ensemble et des principaux groupes sont calculés par la moyenne arithmétique simple des indices mensuels.

Autres informations
Les indices sont publiés par groupes principaux et indices d'autres types de ménages. Depuis le deuxième semestre de 1991, des tentatives sont faites en vue de la publication d'indices, conformément aux modalités suivies sur le territoire de la République fédérale avant le 3 octobre 1990. Il sera probablement procédé à une révision de l'indice dans lequel sera introduite une nouvelle année de base (1991) pour l'ensemble de l'Allemagne.

Une nouvelle série (base juillet 1990 - juin 1991 = 100) est maintenant calculée mais les informations méthodologiques relatives à cette série n'étaient pas disponibles au BIT lors de la publication du présent Volume.

Organisation et publication
L'indice est calculé par la succursale de l'Office fédéral des Statistiques de Berlin, Alexander Platz, et publié par le Statistisches Bundesamt: «Eilbericht und Monatsbericht der Fachserie 17, Reihe 7, Preise und Preisindizes für die Lebenshaltung (Wiesbaden)».

ANGOLA (LUANDA)

Dénomination officielle
Indice de preços no consumidor da cidade de Luanda (Indice des prix à la consommation).

Portée
L'indice est calculé mensuellement et porte sur les ménages urbains de Luanda.

Base originale
Décembre 1990 = 100.

Source des coefficients de pondération
La valeur des coefficients de pondération et les choix des articles résultent d'une enquête sur les dépenses des ménages menée par l'UNICEF et l'Instituto Nacional de Estadistica de février à avril 1990 dans 16 districts de Luanda. Les coefficients de pondération des articles qui n'ont pas été retenus ont été répartis sur des articles similaires appartenant au même sous-groupe.

Pondération et composition

Groupes principaux	Nombre d'articles	Pondération	Nombre approximatif de relevés de prix
Alimentation et tabac	85	74,07	4 200
Habillement et chaussure	10	5,48	450
Logement (y compris combustible et éclairage)	6	5,47	200
Mobilier, articles de ménage, réparations et entretien	26	4,67	1 065
Soins médicaux	5	1,81	110
Transport et communication	7	3,92	35
Instruction et loisirs	11	2,69	250
Autres biens et services	10	1,89	410
Total	160	100,00	6 720

Dépenses de consommation des ménages
Les dépenses de consommation des ménages prises en compte pour le calcul des coefficients de pondération concernent les biens et services acquis au cours de la période de l'enquête à l'exclusion des investissements, transferts, achats de maisons et réparations importantes, dépenses de caractère commercial, etc.

Mode de relevé des prix
Les prix sont relevés auprès de 81 marchés, points de vente au détail et prestataires de service sélectionnés de Luanda. Les prix relevés tiennent compte de la nature des articles: quotidiennement (produits alimentaires), toutes les semaines ou tous les mois (journaux, combustible, électricité). Jusqu'à décembre 1991 les prix pour les articles subventionnés vendus aux travailleurs au moyen de cartes de rationnement étaient obtenus de même que les prix du marché libre. Les prix relevés sont ceux effectivement payés par les consommateurs.

Logement
Pas disponible.

Spécification des variétés
Les articles de caractère hétérogène font l'objet d'une spécification détaillée et sont fournis en fonction de la qualité, de la marque, du modèle, de la taille, de l'unité de mesure, etc. afin de s'assurer que le relevé porte sur le même article au cours des périodes successives. Les articles de caractère homogène nécessitent moins de spécifications (par exemple, sucre blanc, le kilo).

Substitution, changement de qualité, etc.
Lorsqu'un produit n'est plus en vente, il lui est substitué un autre produit d'une qualité analogue, auquel on applique la formule d'enchaînement.

Articles saisonniers
Les pondérations des articles saisonniers sont peu importantes et concernent les mangues, ananas et oranges. On tient compte des fluctuations saisonnières des prix de ces articles en maintenant, hors saison, le dernier prix de saison.

Calcul
L'indice est calculé selon la formule de Laspeyres sous forme de moyenne arithmétique pondérée à base fixe, les coefficients de pondération correspondant à la période février-avril 1990.

Dans le calcul des indices par article, les rapports de prix de la période en cours et de la période de base sont utilisés. Pour les variétés homogènes les rapports des prix moyens sont calculés et les moyennes de rapports de prix sont utilisées pour les variétés hétérogènes.

Autres informations
Des informations détaillées sur les indices par groupes et sous-groupes sont également publiées en ce qui concerne les prix du marché officiel et du marché libre.

Organisation et publication
Instituto Nacional de Estadistica: «Indice de preços no consumidor da Cidade de Luanda» (Luanda).

idem: «Metodologia do Indice de preços no consumidor de Luanda», serie A: metodologia No. 1 (novembre 1991).

ANTIGUA-ET-BARBUDA

Dénomination officielle
Cost of Living Index (Indice du coût de la vie).

Portée
L'indice est calculé mensuellement et porte sur les ménages de classe moyenne disposant d'un revenu mensuel compris entre 350 et 550 dollars des Caraïbes orientales en 1974 et composés en moyenne de quatre à cinq personnes (dont au moins trois adultes).

Base originale
1 janvier 1969 = 100.

Source des coefficients de pondération
Les coefficients de pondération et les articles sélectionnés ont été obtenus sur la base d'un «panier type» mensuel, déterminé à partir de différentes études effectuées en 1974 sur la structure de consommation d'une coupe transversale de ménages de tailles et de revenus différents.

Pondération et composition

Groupes principaux	Nombre d'articles	Pondération	Nombre approximatif de relevés de prix
Alimentation	43	46,5	...
Loyer, combustible et éclairage	4	28,8	...
Habillement et chaussure	4	7,5	...
Transports	1	10,0	...
Soins personnels et médicaux, loisir, etc.	9	7,2	...
Total	61	100,0	...

Dépenses de consommation des ménages
Pas disponible.

Mode de relevé des prix
Les prix pour la période 1969-1973 ont été déterminés, le 1er janvier et le 1er juillet de chaque année, auprès de sources diverses. A partir de 1976, les prix sont relevés mensuellement.

Logement
Pas disponible.

Spécification des variétés
Pas disponible.

Substitution, changement de qualité, etc.
Pas disponible.

Articles saisonniers
Pas disponible.

Calcul
L'indice est calculé selon la formule de Laspeyres, sous forme de moyenne arithmétique pondérée à base fixe, les coefficients de pondération correspondant à la période de base.

Organisation et publication
Ministry of Planning, Development and External Affairs, Statistics Division: «Cost of Living Index» (Antigua).
idem: «Cost of Living Index 1969-1974» (Antigua), Vol. I.

ANTILLES NEERLANDAISES

Dénomination officielle
Consumer Price Index (Indice des prix à la consommation).

Portée
L'indice est calculé mensuellement et porte sur toute la population de Curaçao et Bonaire.

Base originale
Décembre 1984 = 100.

Source des coefficients de pondération
Les coefficients de pondération et les articles sélectionnés ont été déterminés sur la base des résultats d'une enquête sur les dépenses des ménages effectuée en 1981 auprès d'un échantillon de l'ensemble de la population de Curaçao et Bonaire.

Pondération et composition

Groupes principaux	Nombre d'articles	Pondération	Nombre approximatif de relevés de prix
Alimentation	9	22,07	...
Boissons et tabac	2	2,32	...
Habillement et chaussure	2	8,68	...
Logement (y compris loyer, combustible et éclairage et dépenses de ménage)	5	18,76	...
Mobilier, ameublement et articles d'équipement ménager	7	9,96	...
Soins médicaux	1	2,16	...
Transports et communications	4	19,45	...
Instruction et loisirs	5	5,95	...
Autres (y c. soins personnels, assurances et autres biens et services)	3	10,65	...
Total	(a) 38	100,00	...

Remarque: (a) Nombre de sous-groupes.

Dépenses de consommation des ménages
Pas disponible.

Mode de relevé des prix
Les prix sont relevés auprès de points de vente au détail et de prestataires de services.

Logement
Pas disponible.

Spécification des variétés
Pas disponible.

Substitution, changement de qualité, etc.
Pas disponible.

Articles saisonniers
Pas disponible.

Calcul
L'indice est calculé selon la formule de Laspeyres, sous forme de moyenne arithmétique pondérée à base fixe, les coefficients de pondération correspondant à 1981.

Autres informations
Une nouvelle série (base octobre 1990 = 100) est maintenant calculée mais les informations méthodologiques relatives à cette série n'étaient pas disponibles au BIT lors de la publication du présent Volume.

Organisation et publication
Central Bureau of Statistics: «Statistical Monthly Bulletin» (Willemstad).

ARABIE SAOUDITE 1

Dénomination officielle
Cost of Living Index - All cities index (Indice du coût de la vie, indice toutes villes).

Portée
L'indice est calculé mensuellement et porte sur les ménages saoudiens et étrangers résidant dans les 10 villes suivantes: Riyadh, Jeddah, Damman, Abha, Buraydah, La Mecque, Médine, Taif, Hufuf et Tabuk.

Base originale
1988 = 100.

Source des coefficients de pondération
La valeur des coefficients de pondération et le choix des articles résultent d'une enquête sur les dépenses des ménages effectuée pendant toute une année. La période de référence du relevé mensuel des dépenses de chacun des ménages était d'un mois. L'enquête a été réalisée dans 15 villes du royaume, les 10 villes ci-dessus mentionnées et 5 villes plus petites.

Toutes les zones géographiques du royaume étaient représentées dans l'enquête. L'échantillon des ménages était un échantillon par zone et chacun des ménages a fait l'objet d'un choix aléatoire. Au total, 15 000 ménages environ ont été initialement couverts par l'enquête.

Pour les coefficients de pondération utilisés dans l'indice du coût de la vie, les coûts (ayant pour base les données relatives aux dépenses des ménages) et la population ont été combinés. Aucune donnée relative aux comptes nationaux n'a été utilisée.

Les articles figurant dans l'indice du coût de la vie, ont été sélectionnés en utilisant des méthodes de probabilité proportionnelles à leur importance, de même que des méthodes aléatoires pour les articles non sélectionnés en fonction de la méthode précédente. Au total, plus de 200 articles sont inclus dans l'échantillon. Les coefficients de pondération des articles non sélectionnés sont estimés chaque mois en tenant compte du mouvement des groupes auxquels appartiennent «les articles dont le prix n'est pas relevé».

Pondération et composition

Groupes principaux	Nombre d'articles	Pondération	Nombre approximatif de relevés de prix
Alimentation	87	32,62	6 090
Logement (y compris combustible, éclairage et eau)	7	19,69	353
Habillement et chaussure	29	8,40	725
Mobilier et ameublement	36	9,38	900
Soins médicaux	7	1,24	175
Transports et communications	8	17,30	200
Instruction et loisirs	15	2,95	375
Autres dépenses	13	8,42	275
Total	202	100,00	(a) 9 093

Remarque: (a) Voir ci-après.

(a) Un critère de jugement, fondé sur des expériences en matière de relevés de prix, sert à déterminer le nombre des prix de chaque article. Il est procédé au relevé de sept prix pour chaque produit alimentaire et de cinq prix pour chaque produit non alimentaire. En raison de leur variabilité les produits alimentaires font l'objet d'un plus grand nombre de relevés de prix.

Dépenses de consommation des ménages
Dans les dépenses de consommation, les impôts, assurances et logements occupés en propriété ne sont pas pris en compte.

Mode de relevé des prix
Des magasins et autres points de vente au détail ont été choisis sur la base des résultats d'une enquête portant sur les points de vente au détail. Les enquêteurs relèvent mensuellement sept prix pour chaque produit alimentaire dans chaque ville. Le prix des produits non alimentaires est établi sur une base bimensuelle pour la moitié des produits dont le prix est indiqué chaque mois. Les prix de la plupart des produits non alimentaires font l'objet de cinq relevés, à l'exception de ceux dont les prix sont établis ou contrôlés par le gouvernement. C'est ainsi que les prix de l'éclairage, des frais concernant le téléphone, l'essence, etc. sont considérés comme constants jusqu'à ce que se produise un changement de prix. Les changements de prix pour ces articles sont indiqués dans les journaux. Les coûts des soins médicaux sont recueillis à la suite de visites dans des cabinets médicaux ou des hôpitaux. Les coûts en matière d'instruction sont relevés auprès d'un échantillon d'écoles des dix villes figurant dans l'indice. Les prix des transports sont relevés à la suite de visites aux bureaux des compagnies aériennes, compagnies d'autobus, etc. Les tarifs aériens concernent aussi bien les vols nationaux qu'internationaux. Pour les frais de téléphone, le tarif forfaitaire de base est combiné avec le coût des appels à longue distance.

En général, tous les prix sont collectés à l'occasion de visites personnelles effectuées par des enquêteurs. Ils font l'objet d'un relevé effectué sur une base aléatoire du 1er au 21ème jour de chaque mois. Les enquêteurs sont chargés de relever tous les prix dans des points de vente déterminés, vers la même époque chaque mois, de façon à ce que les prix dans certains points de vente puissent être indiqués vers le 5 du mois et d'autres vers le 20 du même mois. Un point de vente dont les prix n'ont été relevés le cinquième jour du mois ne fera pas l'objet d'un relevé le 20 du mois suivant.

Les enquêteurs sont chargés de demander aux intéressés de fournir les prix les plus courants de l'article. En cas de rabais normalement accordés, ces prix sont relevés. Les soldes sont traitées exactement comme les autres prix. Le prix est inclus dans l'indice et, lors de son calcul, une diminution est indiquée par rapport au prix régulier précédent.

La liberté des prix existe en ce qui concerne certains produits pour lesquels des prix officiels sont également établis - un certain nombre de produits alimentaires bénéficient de subventions dans le royaume et il n'y a pas de prix inférieurs aux leurs. Il n'existe pas de prix au marché noir dans le royaume.

Les achats en location vente ou à crédit n'existent pas en Arabie Saoudite (l'indice ne comprend aucun article à ce sujet). En ce qui concerne les achats d'articles d'occasion et la reprise d'articles usagés en tant que paiement partiel d'un nouvel article, aucun prix n'est relevé. Les enquêteurs sont chargés de relever les prix actualisés des produits disponibles en quantités pouvant être vendues.

Les prix à l'importation sont traités comme n'importe quel autre prix. En Arabie Saoudite, de nombreux articles sont importés. Les enquêteurs identifient le pays d'origine des articles.

Logement
Un barème détaillé des loyers est mis au point par l'enquêteur. Il y est fait mention des équipements compris ou non dans le prix du loyer, de l'existence ou non de climatisation dans les logements loués. Le relevé des prix porte à la fois sur les villas et les appartements. L'échantillon des loyers de chaque ville est divisé en six groupes dont les prix sont établis tous les six mois. Un sixième des mouvements des prix des loyers de chaque ville est appliqué aux coefficients de pondération du coût du loyer - population. Une valeur globale est établie pour l'ensemble des dix villes et il est procédé au calcul d'un indice des loyers pour l'ensemble du royaume.

Au chapitre «Logement» de l'indice, ne figurent pas les logements occupés en propriété.

Spécification des variétés
Le CSD dispose de spécifications détaillées pour tous les articles inclus dans l'indice du coût de la vie. Pour l'établissement de ces spécifications, l'enquêteur introduit dans l'indice la variété, le type, la fabrication, le numéro de série et le pays d'origine, etc. Le plus grand nombre d'informations possible est nécessaire à l'enquêteur pour qu'il puisse relever le prix du même article ou d'un article comparable au cours de la période qui suit le relevé des prix.

Substitution, changement de qualité, etc.
Changements de qualité: lorsqu'il est procédé au relevé du prix d'un article dont la taille et le poids sont différents de l'article qu'il remplace, le prix de l'article précédent est converti en celui d'un article d'une pondération comparable afin qu'une comparaison précise puisse être effectuée. Etant donné le manque de données qui empêchent de prendre en compte la plupart des changements de qualité, on ne tient pas compte de ces derniers et les nouveaux articles font l'objet d'un enchaînement dans l'indice.

Apparition de nouveaux produits: l'indice du coût de la vie est révisé tous les cinq ans. Les prix des nouveaux produits qui font leur apparition sur le marché entre ces périodes quinquennales ne sont pas relevés, mais peuvent être captés lors de l'enquête suivante sur les dépenses de consommation. Lorsqu'un nouveau produit remplace sur le marché un article dont le prix est déjà relevé, l'enquêteur ne doit pas procéder à son remplacement sauf si l'article dont le prix est déjà relevé n'est pas disponible et s'il s'agit du produit de remplacement le plus voisin dont on dispose.

Disparition du marché d'un produit de qualité déterminée: cela s'avère parfois produit. Initialement, le coefficient de pondération de l'article est simplement estimé sur la base des mouvements du groupe auquel il appartient. S'il s'avère que l'article ne fera plus l'objet de stockage ou de vente, des instructions sont adressées au centre d'ordinateurs afin de combiner le coefficient de pondération de cet article dans le coefficient de la catégorie des articles dont les prix ne sont pas relevés. L'évaluation des articles entrant dans la catégorie de ceux dont les prix ne sont pas relevés est également fonction du mouvement des prix de ce groupe spécifique.

Articles saisonniers
Le relevé des prix des articles saisonniers a lieu lorsque ces derniers sont disponibles. C'est ainsi, par exemple, qu'il y a abondance de certains fruits et légumes à certaines périodes de l'année. Les prix de ces produits sont alors évidemment moins élevés. Les prix augmentent à mesure que l'offre diminue. Si les enquêteurs n'ont pas la possibilité de relever le prix d'un article déterminé, ils indiquent dans la liste des prix

que l'article n'est pas disponible et que son prix ne sera indiqué que lorsqu'il sera de nouveau disponible sur le marché.
Calcul
L'indice est calculé selon la formule de Laspeyres sous forme de moyenne arithmétique pondérée à base fixe, les coefficients de pondération correspondant à la période de base.

Pour le calcul des indices par article, on utilise le rapport des prix moyens de la période en cours et de la période précédente. L'indice toutes villes est un agrégat des dix unités primaires de sondage. On établit pour chaque article, dans chaque unité primaire de sondage, un coefficient de pondération reflétant les dépenses estimatives courantes, afférentes au panier du marché pendant la période de base. On a recours à la population de chaque unité primaire de sondage pour combiner les coefficients de pondération de chaque article afin d'obtenir les coefficients de pondération finaux pour toutes les villes.

Autres informations
Des indices détaillés relatifs aux sous-groupes, de même que des indices par ville sont publiés. Le Central Department of Statistics publie également un Indice des familles à revenu moyen.

Organisation et publication
Ministry of Finance and National Economy, Central Department of Statistics: «The Statistical Indicator» (Riyadh).
idem: «Statistical Yearbook».
idem: «Cost of Living Index».

ARABIE SAOUDITE 2

Dénomination officielle
Cost of Living Index - Middle Income Index (Indice du coût de la vie, revenu moyen).

Portée
L'indice est calculé mensuellement et porte sur les ménages à revenu moyen dont les dépenses mensuelles se situent entre 2 500 et 10 000 riyals saoudiens, résidant dans les villes suivantes: Riyadh, Jeddah, Damman, Abha, Buraydah, La Mecque, Médine, Taif, Hufuf et Tabuk.

Base originale
1988 = 100.

Source des coefficients de pondération
La valeur des coefficients de pondération et le choix des articles résultent d'une enquête sur les dépenses des ménages effectuée pendant une durée d'un an, en 1985-86. La période de référence du relevé des dépenses mensuelles de chacun des ménages était d'un mois. L'enquête a été réalisée dans 15 villes du royaume - les 10 villes mentionnées ci-dessus et 5 villes plus petites. Toutes les zones géographiques du royaume étaient représentées dans l'enquête. L'échantillon des ménages est un échantillon par zones et chaque ménage a été choisi au hasard. Au total, 15 000 ménages ont fait l'objet de l'enquête initiale.

Les coefficients de pondération utilisés dans l'indice du coût de la vie combinent le coût (sur la base des données relatives aux dépenses des familles) et la population. Aucune donnée relative aux comptes nationaux n'a été utilisée.

Les articles figurant dans l'indice du coût de la vie, ont été sélectionnés en utilisant des méthodes de probabilités proportionnelles à leur importance, de même que des méthodes aléatoires pour les articles non sélectionnés en fonction de la méthode précédente. Au total, plus de 200 articles sont inclus dans l'échantillon. Les coefficients de pondération des articles non sélectionnés sont estimés chaque mois en tenant compte du mouvement des groupes auxquels appartiennent «les articles dont le prix n'est pas relevé».

Dépenses de consommation des ménages
Dans les dépenses de consommation, les impôts, assurances et logements occupés en propriété ne sont pas pris en compte.

Mode de relevé des prix
Des magasins et autres points de vente au détail ont été choisis sur la base des résultats d'une enquête portant sur les points de vente au détail. Les enquêteurs relèvent mensuellement sept prix pour chaque produit alimentaire dans chaque ville. Le prix des produits non alimentaires est établi sur une base bimensuelle pour la moitié des produits dont le prix est indiqué chaque mois. Les prix de la plupart des produits non alimentaires font l'objet de cinq relevés, à l'exception de ceux dont les prix sont établis ou contrôlés par le gouvernement. C'est ainsi que les prix de l'éclairage, des frais concernant le téléphone, l'essence, etc. sont considérés comme constants jusqu'à ce que se produise un changement de prix. Les changements de prix pour ces articles sont indiqués dans les journaux. Les coûts des soins médicaux sont recueillis à la suite de visites dans des cabinets médicaux ou des hôpitaux. Les coûts en matière d'instruction sont relevés auprès d'un échantillon d'écoles des dix villes figurant dans l'indice. Les prix des transports sont relevés à la suite de visites aux bureaux des compagnies aériennes, compagnies d'autobus, etc. Les tarifs aériens concernent aussi bien les vols nationaux qu'internationaux. Pour les frais de téléphone, le tarif forfaitaire de base est combiné avec le coût des appels à longue distance.

Pondération et composition

Groupes principaux	Nombre d'articles	Pondération	Nombre approximatif de relevés de prix
Alimentation	85	37,66	5 950
Logement (y compris combustible, éclairage et eau)	8	21,11	353
Habillement et chaussure	26	7,93	650
Mobilier et ameublement	31	7,42	750
Soins médicaux	7	1,13	175
Transports et communications	9	15,08	225
Instruction et loisirs	15	2,01	350
Autres dépenses	13	7,66	300
Total	194	100,00	(a) 8 753

Remarque: (a) Voir ci-après.

(a) Un critère de jugement, fondé sur des expériences en matière de relevés de prix, sert à déterminer le nombre des prix de chaque article. Il est procédé au relevé de sept prix pour chaque produit alimentaire et de cinq prix pour chaque produit non alimentaire. En raison de leur variabilité les produits alimentaires font l'objet d'un plus grand nombre de relevés de prix.

En général, tous les prix sont collectés à l'occasion de visites personnelles effectuées par des enquêteurs. Ils font l'objet d'un relevé effectué sur une base aléatoire du 1er au 21ème jour de chaque mois. Les enquêteurs sont chargés de relever tous les prix dans des points de vente déterminés, vers la même époque chaque mois, de façon à ce que les prix dans certains points de vente puissent être indiqués vers le 5 du mois et d'autres vers le 20 du même mois. Un point de vente dont les prix ont été relevés le cinquième jour du mois ne fera pas l'objet d'un relevé le 20 du mois suivant.

Les enquêteurs sont chargés de demander aux intéressés de fournir les prix les plus courants de l'article. En cas de rabais normalement accordés, ces prix sont relevés. Les soldes sont traitées exactement comme les autres prix. Le prix est inclus dans l'indice et, lors de son calcul, une diminution est indiquée par rapport au prix régulier précédent.

La liberté des prix existe en ce qui concerne certains produits pour lesquels des prix officiels sont également établis - un certain nombre de produits alimentaires bénéficient de subventions dans le royaume et il n'y a pas de prix inférieurs aux leurs. Il n'existe pas de prix au marché noir dans le royaume.

Les achats en location vente ou à crédit n'existent pas en Arabie Saoudite (l'indice ne comprend aucun article à ce sujet).

En ce qui concerne les achats d'articles d'occasion et la reprise d'articles usagés en tant que paiement partiel d'un nouvel article, aucun prix n'est relevé. Les enquêteurs sont chargés de relever les prix actualisés des produits disponibles en quantités pouvant être vendues.

Les prix à l'importation sont traités comme n'importe quel autre prix. En Arabie Saoudite, de nombreux articles sont importés. Les enquêteurs identifient le pays d'origine des articles.

Logement
Un barème détaillé des loyers est mis au point par l'enquêteur. Il y est fait mention des équipements compris ou non dans le prix du loyer, de l'existence ou non de climatisation dans les logements loués. Le relevé des prix porte à la fois sur les villas et les appartements. L'échantillon des loyers de chaque ville est divisé en six groupes dont les prix sont établis tous les six mois. Un sixième des mouvements des prix des loyers de chaque ville est appliqué aux coefficients de pondération du coût du loyer - population. Une valeur globale est établie pour l'ensemble des dix villes et il est procédé au calcul d'un indice des loyers pour l'ensemble du royaume.

Au chapitre «Logement» de l'indice, ne figurent pas les logements occupés en propriété.

Spécification des variétés
Le CSD dispose de spécifications détaillées pour tous les articles inclus dans l'indice du coût de la vie. Pour l'établissement de ces spécifications, l'enquêteur introduit dans l'indice la variété, le type, la fabrication, le numéro de série et le pays d'origine, etc. Le plus grand nombre d'informations possible est nécessaire à l'enquêteur pour qu'il puisse relever le prix du même article ou d'un article comparable au cours de la période qui suit le relevé des prix.

Substitution, changement de qualité, etc.
Changements de qualité: lorsqu'il est procédé au relevé du prix d'un article dont la taille et le poids sont différents de l'article qu'il remplace, le prix de l'article précédent est converti en celui d'un article d'une pondération comparable afin qu'une comparaison précise puisse être effectuée. Etant donné le manque de données qui empêchent de prendre en compte la plupart des changements de qualité, on ne tient pas compte de ces derniers et les nouveaux articles font l'objet d'un enchaînement dans l'indice.

Apparition de nouveaux produits: l'indice du coût de la vie est révisé tous les cinq ans. Les prix des nouveaux produits qui font leur apparition sur le marché entre ces périodes quinquennales ne sont pas relevés, mais peuvent être captés lors de l'enquête suivante sur les dépenses de consommation. Lorsqu'un nouveau produit remplace sur le marché un article dont le prix est déjà relevé, l'enquêteur ne doit pas procéder à son remplacement sauf si l'article dont le prix est déjà relevé n'est pas disponible et s'il s'agit du produit de remplacement le plus voisin dont on dispose.

Disparition du marché d'un produit de qualité déterminée: cela s'est parfois produit. Initialement, le coefficient de pondération de l'article est simplement estimé sur la base des mouvements du groupe auquel il appartient. S'il s'avère que l'article ne fera plus l'objet de stockage ou de vente, des instructions sont adressées au centre d'ordinateurs afin de combiner le coefficient de pondération de cet article dans le coefficient de la catégorie des articles dont les prix ne sont pas relevés. L'évaluation des articles entrant dans la catégorie de ceux dont les prix ne sont pas relevés est également fonction du mouvement des prix de ce groupe spécifique.

Articles saisonniers
Le relevé des prix des articles saisonniers a lieu lorsque ces derniers sont disponibles. C'est ainsi, par exemple, qu'il y a abondance de certains fruits et légumes à certaines périodes de l'année. Les prix de ces produits sont alors évidemment moins élevés. Les prix augmentent à mesure que l'offre diminue. Si les enquêteurs n'ont pas la possibilité de relever le prix d'un article déterminé, ils indiquent dans la liste des prix que l'article n'est pas disponible et que son prix ne sera indiqué que lorsqu'il sera de nouveau disponible sur le marché.

Calcul
L'indice est calculé selon la formule de Laspeyres sous forme de moyenne arithmétique pondérée à base fixe, les coefficients de pondération correspondant à la période de base.

Pour le calcul des indices par article, on utilise le rapport des prix moyens de la période en cours et de la période précédente. L'indice toutes villes est un agrégat des dix unités primaires de sondage. On établit pour chaque article, dans chaque unité primaire de sondage, un coefficient de pondération reflétant les dépenses estimatives courantes, afférentes au panier du marché pendant la période de base. On a recours à la population de chaque unité primaire de sondage pour combiner les coefficients de pondération de chaque article afin d'obtenir les coefficients de pondération finaux pour toutes les villes.

Autres informations
Des indices détaillés relatifs aux sous-groupes, de même que des indices par ville sont publiés. Le Central Department of Statistics publie également un Indice du coût de la vie - indice toutes villes.

Organisation et publication
Ministry of Finance and National Economy, Central Department of Statistics: «The Statistical Indicator» (Riyadh).

idem: «Statistical Yearbook».

idem: «Cost of Living Index».

ARGENTINE (BUENOS AIRES)

Dénomination officielle
Indice des prix à la consommation (Indice de precios al consumidor).

Portée
L'indice est calculé mensuellement et porte sur l'ensemble des ménages privés résidant dans la capitale fédérale et les dix-neuf districts urbains composant la région métropolitaine de Buenos Aires, non compris le 5 pour cent des ménages ayant le revenu familial per capita le plus élevé et les ménages d'une personne, étant donné que leur structure de consommation particulière est différente des autres.

Base originale
1988 = 100.

Source des coefficients de pondération
Les coefficients de pondération et les articles sélectionnés ont été déterminés sur la base des résultats d'une enquête sur les dépenses des ménages effectuée entre juillet 1985 et juin 1986 dans la région métropolitaine de Buenos Aires auprès d'un échantillon de 2 745 unités de dépenses. Aux fins de l'enquête, une unité de dépenses est définie comme étant constituée par une ou plusieurs personnes ayant ou non des liens de parenté qui participent à la constitution et à l'utilisation d'un même budget, partagent les dépenses alimentaires et vivent dans le même logement.

Parmi tous les biens et services acquis par les ménages, on a retenu ceux qui avaient une pondération significative à l'intérieur de chaque sous-groupe. On a également tenu compte des biens et des services vendus et achetés avec un certain degré de régularité et en quantité suffisante de manière à obtenir des relevés de prix d'un niveau de précision adéquat.

Les pondérations correspondant aux autres biens et services du sous-groupe sont assignées par affinité ou proportionnellement à l'intérieur du sous-groupe. Deux biens ou services sont considérés comme analogues si l'on peut remplacer l'un par l'autre et si leur prix évoluent de façon similaire. De ce fait la pondération propre à un article non sélectionné mais semblable à un article sélectionné est attribuée à cet article sélectionné, tandis que la pondération correspondant aux autres articles est répartie proportionnellement à l'intérieur du sous-groupe.

Pondération et composition

Groupes principaux	Nombre d'articles	Pondération	Nombre approximatif de relevés de prix
Alimentation	205	40,1	72 500
Habillement et chaussures	111	9,4	7 900
Logement:			
Loyer	1	2,3	400
Entretien et réparations	13	2,0	800
Combustible, éclairage et services sanitaires	5	4,2	200
Equipement de ménage	84	8,6	12 300
Soins médicaux	31	7,2	1 600
Transports et communications	23	11,4	800
Instruction et loisirs	61	8,9	4 800
Divers biens et services	23	5,9	4 700
Total	557	100,0	106 000

Dépenses de consommation des ménages
Les dépenses de consommation comprennent les dépenses monétaires effectuées par les membres du ménage en biens et services pour leur consommation à titre individuel, ou pour la consommation de l'ensemble du ménage; les biens et services produits par le ménage pour sa consommation propre (autoconsommation alimentaire et auto-approvisionnement); les biens et services reçus à titre de rémunération en espèces par les membres du ménage. Les dépenses correspondant à l'entretien et à la réparation du logement du ménage sont inscrites dans les dépenses de logement.

Mode de relevé des prix
L'échantillon des points de vente correspondant à des zones résidentielles a été constitué en deux phases: la première en sélectionnant 130 zones de recensement (46 dans la capitale fédérale et 84 dans les districts qui composent la région métropolitaine de Buenos Aires) comme ensembles de points de vente; la seconde en sélectionnant dans chacune de ces zones un

point de vente de chaque catégorie (épicerie, boucherie, mercerie, rôtisserie, produits de nettoyage, quincaillerie, pharmacie, salon de coiffure, papeterie, etc.) dans lequel on relève les prix deux fois par mois.

En ce qui concerne les centres commerciaux, on a sélectionné 47 centres répartis comme suit: 21 dans la capitale fédérale et 26 dans les districts urbains de la région métropolitaine de Buenos Aires. A partir du total des points de vente appartenant à ces centres, on a sélectionné 140 sous-échantillons de fonds de commerce dont chacun fait l'objet d'une visite une fois par mois.

Afin de déterminer le nombre d'informateurs dans chaque catégorie, il a été tenu compte de la couverture géographique de l'indice et de la variabilité du prix. Il est prévu que l'échantillon des points de vente pourra faire l'objet de révisions périodiques afin d'incorporer les nouvelles formes de commercialisation, et les changements possibles dans la répartition géographique des fonds de commerce.

Les prix des biens et services sont relevés chaque jour ouvrable du mois. L'échantillon de points de vente pour un bien ou un service déterminé est donc réparti entre les jours ouvrables du mois. Sont donc exclus les samedis et les dimanches et les jours fériés. La plus grande partie des prix est relevée par la méthode de l'interrogatoire direct. Le téléphone n'est utilisé que pour certains services dont la qualité change rarement et pour lesquels les taux de réponses aux enquêtes téléphoniques sont élevés. Dans le cas des services dont les prix sont fixés par les pouvoirs publics (éclairage, gaz de ville, services sanitaires, transports publics, etc.) on retient dans le mois la date d'entrée en vigueur des prix. Le prix relevé pour les divers biens et services est le prix payé au comptant.

Logement
Le traitement spécial du logement locatif réside dans le fait que les informateurs ne sont pas les commerçants qui, dans ce cas, seraient les loueurs ou les propriétaires des logements, mais les consommateurs eux-mêmes, à savoir les locataires. Pour procéder au relevé des prix, on utilise un échantillon de logements locatifs. Cet échantillon est renouvelé par quart chaque trimestre pour ne pas fatiguer l'informateur, d'une part, et pour saisir la date de renouvellement du contrat, d'autre part. La taille de l'ensemble de l'échantillon est de 624 logements répartis en six groupes où une rotation de 104 logements est effectuée chaque mois; on surveille donc chaque mois la valeur locative de 416 logements.

A l'intérieur des nombreuses variantes du marché des locations on retient les prix des logements locatifs qui répondent aux conditions suivantes: logements familiaux habités; logements non meublés, maisons, appartements, hôtels résidence, locations payées dans la monnaie nationale, logements dans lesquels la location peut ne pas comprendre les services; et locations non liées à la relation de travail. En plus du montant des loyers, on recueille d'autres données sur le logement et sur le contrat qui permettent de contrôler la valeur déclarée et de connaître le moment où se produit un changement de qualité dans le logement.

Spécification des variétés
Pour une spécification précise des biens et des services du «panier de la ménagère», il est nécessaire de décrire en détail toutes les caractéristiques qui déterminent l'existence de prix différents à un même moment et les limites dans lesquelles les changements de ces caractéristiques sont imputables, pour des raisons pratiques, à des variations de prix. Chaque informateur pour les prix, a besoin d'une grande précision concernant la variété, (marque, modèle, dimension, etc.) afin de garantir la comparabilité des observations successives des prix. Pour la spécification des biens, on a opté pour deux types de définitions: la première, qualifiée de variété homogène, correspond au cas où le produit relevé dans des points de vente distincts est le même, permettant ainsi de calculer un prix moyen significatif (beurre, viande, oeufs, oranges, bettes, pains de savon, etc.); la seconde, qualifiée de variété hétérogène, correspond à une spécification incomplète, de telle sorte que la description du produit devra être précisée dans chaque point de vente. L'utilisation des variétés hétérogènes est d'une grande utilité, dans le cas par exemple de l'habillement, étant donné l'hétérogénéité entre commerces et variation de la mode (chaussures, vêtements, téléviseurs, «écolage», loyer, etc.)

Substitution, changement de qualité, etc.
En cas de changements de qualité, de changements d'informateurs et de substitution de biens, lorsqu'il existe des informations sur les prix pour l'ancien et le nouvel article, on assume que le rapport entre les prix reflète le rapport entre les qualités, et l'enchaînement est donc possible.

Lorsqu'il n'y a pas d'observations simultanées des prix pour comparer les qualités, le prix de la nouvelle variété est ajusté en fonction de la qualité, afin de la comparer à l'ancienne.

Articles saisonniers
Lorsqu'un article saisonnier disparaît temporairement du marché, on calcule le prix relatif en estimant que le mouvement du prix de l'article disparu aurait été similaire au mouvement du prix des articles comparables.

La dénomination d'articles saisonniers correspond à l'ensemble des biens ou services dont la quantité consommée et les prix montrent des variations significatives en cours d'année. Il s'agit en général de fluctuations de l'offre (légumes, fruits, etc.) ou de la demande (vêtements d'hiver, d'été, etc.) qui peuvent conduire à la disparition temporaire de l'article.

Calcul
L'indice est calculé selon la formule de Laspeyres sous forme de moyenne arithmétique pondérée à base fixe, les coefficients de pondération correspondant à la période juillet 1985 - juin 1986.

Les indices de chaque agrégat élémentaire (niveau minimum de précision sur les dépenses pour lesquelles les pondérations sont constantes) sont estimés en utilisant un échantillon de prix d'un groupe déterminé de biens ou de services à partir d'un ensemble établi de points de vente.

La méthode utilisée pour le calcul du prix relatif d'un bien varie selon qu'on le considère comme une variété homogène ou hétérogène. Dans le cas de variétés homogènes, on calcule les rapports de prix moyens de la période courante et de la période précédente. Pour les variétés hétérogènes, on utilise la moyenne des rapports de prix de divers points de vente.

Des pondérations sont attribuées aux supermarchés, aux grands magasins et autres points de vente au détail selon l'importance du volume des ventes. Ces pondérations sont utilisées pour calculer des rapports de prix moyens ou des moyennes des rapports de prix.

Autres informations
Des sous-groupes détaillés sont publiés (134). L'indice est publié par communiqué de presse le troisième jour ouvrable du mois qui suit celui correspondant à l'indice.

Organisation et publication
Instituto Nacional de Estadística y Censos: «Estadística mensual» (Buenos Aires).

idem: «Indice de precios al consumidor, Revisión base 1988 = 100, Sintesis metodológica».

AUSTRALIE

Dénomination officielle
Consumer Price Index (Indice des prix à la consommation).

Portée
L'indice est calculé trimestriellement et porte sur tous les ménages métropolitains de salariés. On entend par ménages de salariés ceux dont les salaires et traitements représentent au moins les trois quarts du revenu total, à l'exclusion du dixième d'entre eux qui se situent au sommet de l'échelle des revenus. Le terme «métropolitain» désigne les habitants des capitales des huit états ou territoires.

Base originale
Année terminant en juin 1981 = 100.

Source des coefficients de pondération
Ceux-ci se fondent sur l'enquête de 1984 relative aux dépenses des ménages, ainsi que sur les résultats de tout un éventail de données statistiques telles que celles fournies par des établissements financiers ou par l'enquête de 1986 sur les assurances maladies. On n'a retenu pour l'indice que des articles entrant pour une part significative dans les dépenses des ménages des huit villes, à condition que leurs prix puissent être mis en rapport avec un bien ou un service clairement identifiable et qu'ils correspondent à une qualité constante. On a considéré que le mouvement des prix des articles n'apparaissant pas à l'indice était représenté par ceux qui y figurent et que leurs coefficients de pondération sont les mêmes que ceux appliqués aux articles de l'indice qui les représentent.

Pondération et composition

Groupes principaux	Nombre d'articles (a)	Pondération	Nombre approximatif de relevés de prix (b)
Alimentation	34	19,0	27 000
Tabac et alcool	4	8,2	11 200
Habillement et chaussure	14	6,9	5 500
Logement:			
Loyer des habitations appartenant aux particuliers	1	4,1	8 200
Loyer des habitations appartenant au gouvernement	1	0,4	5 600
Habitations occupées par leur propriétaire (frais des intérêts hypothécaires, impôts locaux, réparations et entretien, assurance)	4	9,6	22 000
Equipement et dépenses de ménages:			
Combustible et éclairage	3	2,4	100
Equipement ménager	1	1,5	900
Mobilier, tapis, etc.	2	4,1	1 200
Linge de maison	2	0,7	600
Autres biens et services ménagers	14	5,7	3 000
Postes et téléphone	2	1,5	200
Crédit à la consommation	1	2,5	200
Soins personnels et médicaux	6	5,6	3 800
Transports	7	17,0	5 600
Instruction et loisirs	11	10,8	5 500
Total	107	100,0	100 600

Remarque: (a) Voir ci-après. (b) Par trimestre.

(a) Ces chiffres représentent le nombre de «classes de dépenses» et non d'articles considérés séparément dont les prix ont été relevés. Chacune de ces classes de dépenses consiste en une sélection «d'articles» identiques. Ainsi, dans le groupe des alcools, on trouve bières, vins, liqueurs, cigarettes et tabacs. Ces classes contiennent chacune un large choix de tabacs ou de boissons alcooliques.

Dépenses de consommation des ménages
Par dépenses de consommation au sens de l'indice, on entend les dépenses réelles que les intéressés effectuent pendant la période de référence pour se procurer services et biens de consommation. En sont exclus les dépenses virtuelles, les cotisations aux caisses de pension et de retraite privées, l'impôt sur le revenu et autres impôts directs, les primes d'assurance vie, les envois de fonds et les dons, la bijouterie, les frais d'avocat, les cotisations aux associations et syndicats, les dépenses de jeu. Sont retenus les éléments suivants: revenus en nature, frais des intérêts hypothécaires et des crédits à la consommation, frais d'opticien, immatriculation et impôts sur les automobiles, primes d'assurance liées à des biens de consommation précis, soins médicaux, impôts et taxes locaux.

Mode de relevé des prix
Les localités et points de vente retenus l'ont été en fonction de données empruntées aux recensements de population, aux statistiques du commerce de détail et à l'expérience personnelle des enquêteurs travaillant sur le terrain. Il n'est pas effectué d'enquête portant sur les points de vente. Près de 100 000 prix sont relevés chaque trimestre dans les huit villes de référence auprès d'environ 5 500 supermarchés, grands magasins, commerces de chaussures, restaurants, commerçants livrant à domicile, autres détaillants, établissements de services, etc. Les tarifs relatifs à des articles tels que les voyages en chemin de fer, l'électricité, etc. sont recueillis auprès des administrations compétentes. Les relevés sont effectués chaque semaine pour les fruits et légumes frais, deux fois par mois pour le poisson frais, mensuellement pour la viande fraîche, le pain, les cigarettes et le tabac, les alcools en bouteille et l'essence. Les prix de certains articles importants sont relevés à la fin du trimestre et les dates de changement des prix le sont également afin de calculer les prix trimestriels moyens. Pour tous les autres articles, on relève les prix une fois par trimestre à l'exception des taxes et impôts locaux, des vêtements de saison et des tondeuses à gazon, dont les prix sont relevés annuellement. Les prix retenus pour le calcul de l'indice sont ceux que paieraient le public au jour de relevé pour se procurer les biens ou les services concernés, taxes de vente et droits d'excise inclus. Le prix des articles soldés, les rabais et les prix «spéciaux» sont pris en compte dans l'indice dès lors que les articles correspondants sont de qualité normale et offerts en quantité raisonnable. Les relevés ne se font pas à date fixe, mais s'étalent sur la durée d'un trimestre.

Logement
Les données relatives au loyer sont obtenues trimestriellement sur un large échantillon de logements appartenant à des particuliers et au gouvernement. Quant aux logements occupés en propriété, c'est la valeur effective des frais de réparation et d'entretien, les impôts et les intérêts des prêts hypothécaires qui entrent en ligne de compte.

Spécification des variétés
Le choix des variétés d'articles à retenir pour les relevés de prix est arrêté après étude de renseignements fournis par les fabricants, les importateurs et les détaillants. Les marques et variétés retenues sont généralement celles qui se vendent le plus. En fonction de ces renseignements sont établies pour chaque article dont le prix est a relever, des spécifications détaillées, marque, nom du modèle, pays de fabrication et autres données nécessaires à l'élaboration de séries de prix temporelles répondant à une qualité constante.

Substitution, changement de qualité, etc.
Les produits entièrement nouveaux sont introduits dans l'indice au moment ou celui-ci est révisé, c'est-à-dire environ tous les quatre ou cinq ans. Les variétés nouvelles de produits existants y sont introduites lorsqu'elles viennent à constituer un élément appréciable de la catégorie de dépenses de consommation correspondante. Un type de produit ou une qualité qui disparaît du marché est retiré de l'indice et lorsque cela est justifié, remplacé par un article de substitution à l'aide de la formule d'enchaînement. En présence d'un changement de qualité, les principales techniques appliquées sont les suivantes: i) détermination directe de la valeur que représente le changement de qualité et correction correspondante du prix de l'article en question; ii) enchaînement d'une nouvelle spécification.

Articles saisonniers
Le prix des fruits et légumes frais qui ne sont pas disponibles toute l'année sont également relevés. Pendant les périodes où des articles saisonniers ne sont pas offerts, les prix de ceux-ci sont imputés sur la base du mouvement des prix des articles disponibles. Le prix des vêtements de saison est relevé une fois par an dans le trimestre correspondant à leur saison et est maintenu constant pendant les autres trimestres de l'année. Les fluctuations saisonnières des prix ne font pas l'objet d'ajustement.

Calcul
L'indice est calculé trimestriellement selon la formule chaîne de Laspeyres à coefficients de pondération fixes, mais la structure de la pondération et la composition sont remaniées tous les cinq ans environ. L'indice national est calculé sous la forme d'une moyenne des indices des huit villes principales du pays, pondérés par le nombre de ménages de référence de chaque ville.

Autres informations
Une nouvelle série d'indices des prix à la consommation (base année terminant en juin 1990 = 100) est actuellement en préparation et sera publiée prochainement.

Organisation et publication
Australian Bureau of Statistics: «Consumer Price Index», numéro de catalogue 6401.0, trimestriel, (Canberra, ACT).

Les prix effectifs d'un choix d'articles entrant dans le calcul de l'indice des prix à la consommation paraissent dans la revue «Average Retail Prices of Selected Items, Eight Capital Cities», numéro de catalogue 6403.0.

idem: «A Guide to the Consumer Price Index», numéro de catalogue 6440.0, 1987.

idem: «Review of the Consumer Price Index», numéro de catalogue 6450.0.

idem: «The Australian Consumer Price Index; Concepts, Sources and Methods», numéro de catalogue 6461.0.

AUTRICHE

Dénomination officielle
Indice des prix à la consommation.

Portée
L'indice est calculé mensuellement et porte sur l'ensemble du pays et sur tous les ménages sans limitation de taille ou de revenu.

Base originale
1986 = 100.

Source des coefficients de pondération
Les coefficients de pondération et les articles sélectionnés ont été déterminés sur la base des résultats d'une enquête sur les dépenses des ménages effectuée pendant un mois entre mars 1984 et février 1985 auprès de 6 599 ménages représentant l'ensemble de la population. Les dépenses mensuelles moyennes par ménage étaient, lors de l'enquête, de 20 390 Schillings et les ménages étaient composés, en moyenne, de 2,7 personnes. Les coefficients de pondération ont été corrigés d'après des données tirées des comptes nationaux.

Pondération et composition

Groupes principaux	Nombre d'articles	Pondération	Nombre approximatif de relevés de prix
Alimentation	149	23 268	...
Tabac	79	2 512	...
Loyer (y c. entretien et réparations)	28	13 056	...
Combustible et éclairage	13	5 405	...
Equipement ménager	41	7 582	...
Habillement et chaussure	50	10 694	...
Produits d'entretien et de nettoyage	9	1 402	...
Soins personnels et médicaux	31	6 006	...
Instruction et loisirs	85	14 302	...
Transports et communications	130	15 773	...
Total	615	100 000	50 000

Dépenses de consommation des ménages
Les dépenses de consommation prises en compte dans le calcul de l'indice comprennent tous les biens et services qu'un ménage acquiert moyennant finances pour les consommer. Elles comprennent aussi la valeur de consommation des biens produits et consommés par les ménages. En sont exclus les cotisations à l'assurance sociale et aux caisses de retraite, l'achat des logements, les impôts sur le revenu et à d'autres titres, les envois de fonds et les dons.

Mode de relevé des prix
Les relevés des prix sont effectués par des enquêteurs le deuxième mercredi de chaque mois. Les prix de 328 articles sont relevés centralement et ceux des autres 287 articles régionalement dans 20 villes auprès de points de vente au détail, de marchés fixes et de prestataires de services habituellement fréquentés par la clientèle. Les prix retenus pour l'indice sont les prix normaux payés par les consommateurs. Les prix des soldes et des rabais ne sont pas retenus.

Logement
Les données relatives au loyer sont obtenues à partir des résultats d'un microrecensement trimestriel auprès de 10 000 logements en location ou occupés par leur propriétaire. Pour faciliter la comparaison des dépenses affectées au logement, les calculs sont rapportés au mètre carré. Les changements observés dans les prix des loyers entre un trimestre et le suivant sont répartis proportionnellement entre les trois mois de ce dernier.

Spécification des variétés
La description des variétés est suffisamment générale pour permettre à l'enquêteur de choisir, pour ses relevés réguliers, le type, la qualité, la quantité, etc., d'un article donné le plus vendu dans chaque point de vente au détail.

Substitution, changement de qualité, etc.
Lorsque la qualité de l'article change, le prix de base est modifié proportionnellement à l'importance relative du changement, exprimé en pourcentage, entre le mois précédent et le mois courant.

Articles saisonniers
Il est tenu compte des fluctuations saisonnières des prix des fruits et légumes frais en variant les articles et leur coefficient de pondération à l'intérieur de «paniers» mensuels dont le coefficient de pondération d'ensemble demeure constant.

Calcul
L'indice est calculé selon la formule de Laspeyres sous forme de moyenne arithmétique pondérée à base fixe, les coefficients de pondération correspondant à la période de base. L'indice pour un article est obtenu en utilisant des moyennes des rapports de prix de la période courante et de la période de base. L'indice national est la moyenne arithmétique pondérée d'indices relatifs à 20 villes, les coefficients de pondération étant proportionnels à la population de chacune selon le recensement de 1981.

Organisation et publication
Oesterreichisches Statistisches Zentralamt: «Statistische Nachrichten» (Vienne).

idem: «Verbraucherpreisindex, Revision 1986», Beiträge zur österreichischen Statistik, Heft 853, 1987.

BAHAMAS

Dénomination officielle
Retail Price Index for New Providence (Indice des prix de détail pour New Providence)

Portée
L'indice est calculé mensuellement et porte sur l'ensemble des ménages privés habitant New Providence.

Base originale
Mars - avril 1987 = 100.

Source des coefficients de pondération
La valeur des coefficients de pondération et le choix des articles résultent d'une enquête sur les dépenses des ménages effectuée en 1983 dans l'ensemble de l'île de New Providence, à l'exception de ses régions extrêmes orientale et occidentale, auprès d'un échantillon de ménages privés. Si un article donné entre pour plus de 0,001 pour mille dans les dépenses totales des ménages, il est choisi pour faire partie du «panier». Les coefficients de pondération des articles non choisis ont été additionnés; la somme qui en résulte a été classée dans la catégorie «divers» du même groupe d'articles. Les coefficients de pondération n'ont fait l'objet d'aucun ajustement visant à prendre en compte les changements de prix survenus entre l'époque de l'enquête et la période de base.

Pondération et composition

Groupes principaux	Nombre d'articles	Pondération	Nombre approximatif de relevés de prix
Alimentation	98	17,196	1 332
Habillement et chaussure	20	6,647	294
Logement:			
Loyer	2	5,213	39
Valeur locative nette des logements occupés en propriété	3	13,435	7
Combustible et électricité	3	3.992	3
Entretien et réparations	4	2.965	12
Mobilier, ameublement et articles d'équipement ménager	28	9,527	296
Soins médicaux	8	3,263	118
Transports et communications	17	22,094	151
Instruction et loisirs	25	12.792	221
Divers	15	2,878	287
Total	223	100,000	2 760

Dépenses de consommation des ménages
Sont inclus dans l'indice les achats de logements, les assurances et impôts sur les propriétés, les assurances couvrant les accidents et les soins de santé, l'assurance-vie liée à l'activité professionnelle.

Sont exclus les assurances-vie ordinaires, l'épargne, les achats d'actions et de valeurs mobilières, la partie des versements hypothécaires qui correspond à l'amortissement du capital et le remboursement des prêts bancaires.

Mode de relevé des prix
Les prix de la plupart des articles sont relevés par des enquêteurs ou au moyen d'appels téléphoniques auprès de 208 points de vente au détail et établissements de services. Les prix des services médicaux et les primes d'assurance sont obtenus au moyen de questionnaires adressés par correspondance. Les prix sont relevés une fois par mois ou par trimestre, et correspondent généralement aux deux premières semaines du mois considéré.

Pour l'ensemble des biens et services, les prix et les tarifs utilisés dans l'Indice sont ceux effectivement pratiqués lors des transactions au comptant. N'entrent en ligne de compte ni les suppléments perçus pour les ventes à crédit, ni les rabais. Les prix de catalogue ne comptent pas si le détaillant pratique habituellement d'autres prix. Les rabais temporaires ne sont pas davantage pris en considération.

Logement
Sont retenus les logements en location meublés et non meublés. Il peut s'agir d'appartements d'une ou deux chambres.

Les données relatives aux loyers sont obtenues au moyen de visites à domicile ou d'appels téléphoniques auprès des locataires de 32 logements non meublés et 7 logements meublés.

La valeur d'achat des logements, les assurances et impôts sur les propriétés sont pris en compte pour l'estimation de la valeur locative nette des logements occupés en propriété.

Spécification des variétés
Afin de sélectionner les spécifications relatives aux articles, il a été procédé à des échanges de vues avec les dirigeants des magasins pour déterminer les marques et tailles de chaque variété faisant l'objet de la majeure partie des ventes.

Substitution, changement de qualité, etc.
Lorsqu'un changement de prix correspond à un changement de qualité, le prix de base est modifié afin de compenser le mouvement de prix. Un nouvel article peut être introduit dans l'indice pour remplacer un autre article ayant disparu du marché. Le relevé des prix des «anciens» et «nouveaux» articles est effectué dans des mois qui se chevauchent afin d'assurer que seuls les mouvements de prix sont enregistrés au cours du mois où est opérée la substitution. Lorsqu'un article disparaît temporairement, le dernier prix relevé est conservé jusqu'à sa réapparition en rayon. Toutefois, si l'article ne reparaît pas après un certain laps de temps (trois mois par exemple), une substitution est alors nécessaire.

Articles saisonniers
Les articles saisonniers ne font l'objet d'aucun traitement particulier dans l'indice.

Calcul
L'indice est calculé selon la formule de Laspeyres sous forme de moyenne arithmétique pondérée à base fixe, les coefficients de pondération correspondant à l'année 1983.

Le rapport de prix pour chaque article est calculé en divisant le prix moyen de la période en cours par le prix moyen de la période de base. Le prix moyen d'un article est la moyenne arithmétique simple des prix obtenus pour cet article.

Autres informations
Un indice des prix au détail (Base: mars 1974 = 100) est également calculé pour l'île de Grand Bahama, et publié par le Department of Statistics. Il est à noter, cependant, que l'Indice des prix au détail pour New Providence est utilisé en guise d'Indice national.

Organisation et publication
Ministry of Finance, Department of Statistics: «Retail Price Index» (Nassau).
idem: «Quarterly Statistical Summary».
idem: «Annual Review of Retail Prices».
idem: «An explanation of the Retail Price Index».
idem: «The Revised Index for New Providence».

BANGLADESH (DHAKA)

Dénomination officielle
Middle Class Cost of Living Index for Government Employees in Dhaka City (Indice du coût de la vie des fonctionnaires de la classe moyenne résidant à Dhaka).

Portée
L'indice est calculé mensuellement et porte sur les ménages de fonctionnaires de la classe moyenne résidant à Dhaka.

Base originale
1973-74 = 100.

Source des coefficients de pondération
La valeur des coefficients de pondération et le choix des articles résultent d'une enquête sur les dépenses des ménages menée au cours de la période 1973-74. L'enquête couvrait les ménages appartenant à tous les groupes de revenus. L'indice porte sur le groupe de ménages à revenu moyen résidant à Dhaka dont le revenu mensuel variait de 300 à 999 taka au moment de l'enquête.

Dépenses de consommation des ménages
Pas disponible.

Mode de relevé des prix
Les prix sont relevés par des enquêteurs toutes les semaines, quinzaines, mois ou trimestres auprès de marchés, commerces de détail et prestataires de services sélectionnés. La fréquence

Pondération et composition

Groupes principaux	Nombre d'articles	Pondération	Nombre approximatif de relevés de prix
Alimentation	77	62,74	...
Combustible et éclairage	5	7,50	...
Logement et équipement ménager	24	11,85	...
Habillement, chaussure, etc.	25	6,20	...
Divers	57	11,71	...
Total	188	100,00	...

des relevés dépend de la nature des articles. Les prix de l'électricité, du gaz, des soins médicaux, de l'instruction et du transport sont relevés auprès des établissements prestataires de ces services. Les prix retenus pour le calcul de l'indice sont ceux du marché libre pour tous les articles, excepté le riz pour lequel sont pris en compte les prix contrôlés aussi bien que ceux du marché libre.

Logement
Les données relatives au loyer sont obtenues auprès d'un échantillon de 10 logements.

Spécification des variétés
Pas disponible.

Substitution, changement de qualité, etc.
Lorsqu'un produit n'est plus en vente, il lui est substitué un autre produit, approximativement de la même qualité, auquel est appliquée la formule d'enchaînement.

Articles saisonniers
Les fruits et légumes frais sont réputés articles saisonniers. Les prix en sont relevés lorsqu'ils sont en vente pendant leur saison. Hors saison, les prix de clôture de la saison précédente sont appliqués.

Calcul
L'indice est calculé selon la formule de Laspeyres sous forme de moyenne arithmétique pondérée à base fixe, les coefficients de pondération correspondant à la période de base.

Autres informations
Le Bureau de statistiques du Bangladesh procède également au calcul de séries concernant les familles à revenus moyens résidant à Khulna et Chittagong et les familles à revenus modestes et élevés vivant à Dhaka.

Organisation et publication
Bangladesh Bureau of Statistics: «Monthy Statistical Bulletin of Bangladesh» (Dhaka).

BARBADE

Dénomination officielle
Index of Retail Prices (Indice des prix de détail).

Portée
L'indice est calculé mensuellement et porte sur l'ensemble du pays. Les ménages disposant d'un revenu mensuel d'au moins 2 000 dollars de la Barbade ont été exclus de l'indice.

Base originale
Mars 1980 = 100.

Source des coefficients de pondération
La valeur des coefficients de pondération et le choix des articles résultent d'une enquête sur les dépenses des ménages menée au cours de la période du 1er avril 1978 au 31 mars 1979. Cette enquête a porté sur un échantillon de 1 200 ménages. Les articles composant le panier ont été choisis selon leur part en pourcentage du budget total. Ceux dont la part a été insignifiante ont été soit écartés soit inclus dans des groupes d'articles connexes.

Dépenses de consommation des ménages
Elles comprennent les biens consommés par les ménages, les biens produits par les ménages pour leur propre consommation, la propriété du logement, les achats à crédit. Les cotisations à la sécurité sociale et les paiements des pensions obligatoires ne sont pas considérés comme dépenses de consommation des ménages; il en est de même de l'impôt sur le revenu.

Mode de relevé des prix
Les prix sont relevés par les enquêteurs du Service statistique

Pondération et composition

Groupes principaux	Nombre d'articles	Pondération	Nombre approximatif de relevés de prix
Alimentation	62	43,2	257
Boissons alcoolisées et tabac	7	8,4	36
Logement	9	13,1	26
Combustible et éclairage	5	6,2	9
Dépenses de ménage et fourniture	24	9,6	96
Habillement et chaussure	21	5,1	99
Transports	13	4,6	30
Soins personnels et médicaux	19	6,0	69
Instruction, loisirs et divers	8	3,8	36
Total	168	100,0	658

dans 85 magasins de vente au détail et établissements. Pour la plupart des postes de dépenses les relevés ont lieu le mercredi le plus proche du milieu de chaque mois. Pour les fruits, les légumes et le poisson, le relevé a lieu tous les vendredis du mois. Les relevés trimestriels qui comprennent les tarifs des communications téléphoniques, du service des Eaux, des blanchisseries, des salons de coiffure, des autobus et des taxis sont effectués dans le mois situé au milieu de chaque trimestre.

Les prix utilisés dans l'indice sont les prix normaux payés par le grand public. Les rabais n'entrent en ligne de compte que s'ils sont accordés à tous les acheteurs. Les réductions accordées à certains groupes ne sont pas retenues.

Logement
Les données relatives au loyer ne sont retenues que pour des unités de logement appartenant au gouvernement. Les changements du loyer sont pris en compte lorsqu'ils ont lieu sur la base d'informations fournies par les autorités.

Spécification des variétés
Les articles relevés doivent faire l'objet d'une spécification claire et précise: marque, unité employée, type, qualité et quantité.

Substitution, changement de qualité, etc.
Lorsqu'un produit disparaît, il est remplacé par un autre dont la qualité est approximativement la même et la formule d'enchaînement est appliquée.

Articles saisonniers
Le principal est le poisson pêché sur place.

Calcul
L'indice est calculé selon la formule de Laspeyres sous forme de moyenne arithmétique pondérée à base fixe, les coefficients de pondération correspondant à la période de base.

Le rapport de prix pour chaque article est calculé en divisant la somme des prix relevés pour la période en cours par la somme des prix pour la période précédente. Le prix moyen d'un article est la moyenne arithmétique simple des prix obtenus pour cet article.

Organisation et publication
Statistical Service: «Monthly Digest of Statistics» (Bridgetown).
idem: «The Barbados Economic Report».
idem: «Monthly Statistical Bulletin».
idem: «Economic and Financial Statistics».

BELGIQUE

Dénomination officielle
Indice des prix à la consommation.

Portée
L'indice est calculé mensuellement et porte sur les ménages moyens dans l'ensemble du pays.

Base originale
1988 = 100.

Source des coefficients de pondération
Les coefficients de pondération et les articles sélectionnés ont été déterminés sur la base des résultats d'une enquête sur les dépenses des ménages effectuée au cours de la période mai 1987 à mai 1988 auprès de 3 315 familles d'ouvriers, d'employés, de non-actifs et d'indépendants.

Dépenses de consommation des ménages
Les dépenses de consommation prises en considération pour

Pondération et composition

Groupes principaux	Nombre d'articles	Pondération	Nombre approximatif de relevés de prix (a)
Alimentation	157	18,985	58 900
Tabac	4	1,130	1 200
Habillement et chaussure	46	8,580	9 600
Logement:			
Loyer	2	7,175	-
Réparations, entretien et eau	10	6,155	-
Combustible, éclairage	20	6,070	-
Mobilier et appareils ménagers	54	7,850	12 500
Soins médicaux	17	4,900	2 100
Transports et communications	33	16,495	2 600
Instruction et loisirs	39	8,355	5 900
Autres biens et services	47	14,305	7 300
Total	429	100,000	102 300

Remarque: (a) Nombre de relevés effectués par les agents du Service extérieur, non compris les relevés effectués par le Service central.

l'établissement de l'indice comprennent presque tous les biens et services consommés par les ménages. Elles comprennent également les valeurs correspondant aux produits récoltés et élaborés à domicile et aux produits reçus en tant que revenu en nature.

Mode de relevé des prix
Les prix de la plupart des articles sont relevés par des enquêteurs auprès de points de vente au détail et de prestataires de services dans 65 localités réparties dans tout le pays. Les relevés de prix s'effectuent mensuellement entre le 1er et le 20 pour presque tous les articles.

Les prix à relever sont les prix, toutes taxes comprises, payés pour un achat au comptant par le consommateur qui ne bénéficie d'aucune condition particulière. La réduction de prix est prise en considération dès le premier jour de l'offre promotionnelle, si celle-ci dure au moins une journée, pour autant que le produit soit de bonne qualité et disponible en quantité suffisante. Les prix des articles en solde ne sont pas retenus.

Logement
Les données relatives au loyer sont obtenues pour des logements sociaux et non-sociaux dans les onze provinces du pays. Le loyer des logements sociaux effectivement loués est relevé auprès d'un certain nombre de sociétés agréées d'habitations sociales. Le loyer des logements non-sociaux est obtenu à partir d'un échantillon représentatif de 1 521 appartements et maisons de différentes tailles. Chaque mois, l'échantillon est renouvelé par l'introduction de deux nouveaux logements en remplacement de deux anciens et ce pour tenir compte du renouvellement du parc locatif.

Spécification des variétés
Les spécifications portent plus particulièrement sur le choix des unités utilisées. Dans la majorité des cas, les définitions sont assez souples pour permettre de tenir compte d'éventuelles modifications, mais suffisamment rigides pour garantir la continuité des relevés des prix.

Substitution, changement de qualité, etc.
L'enquêteur dispose de la liberté nécessaire, sous réserve de l'approbation du service central, pour opérer le remplacement d'un article disparu en respectant les directives suivantes: un magasin de type déterminé doit être remplacé par un point de vente du même type; un produit déterminé doit être remplacé soit par un produit équivalent dans le même magasin, soit par le même produit dans un autre magasin.

Pour certains articles spécifiques, pour lesquels des échantillons ont été constitués (voitures automobiles, loyers non-sociaux, assurances responsabilité civile pour véhicules automoteurs et assurance responsabilité civile vie familiale), le nouvel article est choisi parmi une réserve prédéterminée et en fonction de critères précis. Le nouvel article est introduit à l'indice moyen atteint par les autres articles du même sous-groupe. Une hausse par rapport au mois antérieur est prise en compte en attribuant à l'article disparu la même évolution que l'indice moyen des autres articles du même sous-groupe.

Articles saisonniers
Il est tenu compte des fluctuations saisonnières des prix des fleurs, fruits et légumes frais en variant la composition mensuelle des articles du sous-groupe, dont le coefficient de pondération d'ensemble demeure constant. Les indices de certains articles et services saisonniers sont calculés par rapport au

mois correspondant de la période de base et non pas par rapport à la moyenne de toute la période de base, les prix de base étant le résultat de la moyenne arithmétique des prix des mois correspondants de 1987, 1988 et 1989.

Calcul
L'indice est calculé selon la formule de Laspeyres, sous forme de moyenne arithmétique pondérée à base fixe, les coefficients de pondération correspondant à la période de base. Des indices séparés pour 65 localités sont calculés. Le rapport de prix pour chaque article et pour chaque localité est calculé en divisant le prix moyen de la période courante par le prix moyen de la période de base. Le prix moyen est la moyenne arithmétique simple de tous les prix relevés. Les indices des 65 localités sont ensuite pondérés afin d'obtenir l'indice national, les coefficients de pondération utilisés étant proportionnels à la population de chaque localité telle qu'elle ressort des données sur la population au 1er janvier 1988.

Autres informations
L'indice général est également publié sur base 1981 = 100, juillet 1974 - juin 1975 = 100 et 1971 = 100.

Organisation et publication
Ministère des Affaires économiques, Institut national de statistique: «Bulletin de statistique» (Bruxelles).
idem: «Communiqué hebdomadaire».
Ministère des Affaires économiques, Administration du commerce, Service de l'indice: «Le nouvel indice des prix à la consommation; base 1988 = 100» (Bruxelles, 1991).

BELIZE

Dénomination officielle
Consumer Price Index (Indice des prix à la consommation).

Portée
L'indice est calculé trimestriellement et porte sur l'ensemble du pays.

Base originale
Février 1980 = 100.

Source des coefficients de pondération
La valeur des coefficients de pondération et le choix des articles résultent d'une enquête sur les dépenses des ménages effectuée au Belize en 1980. Cette enquête portait sur 1 800 ménages habitant les zones urbaines et rurales.

Dépenses de consommation des ménages
Pas disponible.

Mode de relevé des prix
Les prix sont relevés pendant la troisième semaine des mois de février, mai, août et novembre sur les marchés, auprès des points de vente au détail et des établissements de service répartis dans six districts.

Logement
Pas disponible.

Spécification des variétés
Aucune spécification détaillée n'est utilisée.

Substitution, changement de qualité, etc.
Lorsqu'un article manque, le prix correspondant au trimestre précédent est maintenu.

Articles saisonniers
Pas disponible.

Calcul
L'indice est calculé selon la formule de Laspeyres, sous forme de moyenne arithmétique pondérée à base fixe, les coefficients de pondération correspondant à la période de base.
Des indices séparés sont d'abord calculés pour les six districts. L'indice national constitue une moyenne pondérée des chiffres relatifs aux indices des six districts, les coefficients de pondération étant proportionnels à la population de chaque district.

Organisation et publication
Ministry of Economic Development, Central Statistical Office: «Belize Consumer Price Index (quarterly)» (Belmopan).

Pondération et composition
Corozola

Groupes principaux	Nombre d'articles	Pondération	Nombre approximatif de relevés de prix
Alimentation	39	386	...
Produits de nettoyage	5	33	...
Soins personnels et médicaux	9	71	...
Habillement et chaussure	14	152	...
Loyer, combustible et éclairages	5	47	...
Mobilier, ameublement et articles d'équipement ménager	12	107	...
Transports	8	89	...
Divers	15	115	...
Total	107	1 000	...

Orange Walk

Alimentation	39	378	...
Produits de nettoyage	5	26	...
Soins personnels et médicaux	9	65	...
Habillement et chaussure	14	117	...
Loyer, combustible et éclairages	5	62	...
Mobilier, ameublement et articles d'équipement ménager	12	127	...
Transports	8	106	...
Divers	15	119	...
Total	107	1 000	...

Belize

Alimentation	39	394	...
Produits de nettoyage	5	27	...
Soins personnels et médicaux	9	48	...
Habillement et chaussure	14	116	...
Loyer, combustible et éclairages	5	122	...
Mobilier, ameublement et articles d'équipement ménager	12	104	...
Transports	8	60	...
Divers	15	129	...
Total	107	1 000	...

Cayo

Alimentation	39	376	...
Produits de nettoyage	5	30	...
Soins personnels et médicaux	9	46	...
Habillement et chaussure	14	128	...
Loyer, combustible et éclairages	5	85	...
Mobilier, ameublement et articles d'équipement ménager	12	127	...
Transports	8	85	...
Divers	15	123	...
Total	107	1 000	...

Stan Creek

Alimentation	39	481	...
Produits de nettoyage	5	28	...
Soins personnels et médicaux	9	47	...
Habillement et chaussure	14	121	...
Loyer, combustible et éclairages	5	79	...
Mobilier, ameublement et articles d'équipement ménager	12	85	...
Transports	8	28	...
Divers	15	131	...
Total	107	1 000	...

Toledo

Alimentation	39	396	...
Produits de nettoyage	5	39	...
Soins personnels et médicaux	9	53	...
Habillement et chaussure	14	201	...
Loyer, combustible et éclairages	5	40	...
Mobilier, ameublement et articles d'équipement ménager	12	102	...
Transports	8	43	...
Divers	15	126	...
Total	107	1 000	...

BERMUDES

Dénomination officielle
Consumer Price Index (Indice des prix à la consommation).

Portée
L'indice est calculé mensuellement et porte sur près de 87 pour cent de tous les ménages privés disposant, en 1982, d'un revenu de 200 à 1 499 dollars des Bermudes par semaine.

Base originale
Janvier 1985 = 100.

Source des coefficients de pondération
Les coefficients de pondération et le choix des articles résultent d'une enquête sur les dépenses des ménages effectuée en 1982. Cette enquête portait sur environ 750 ménages disposant à l'époque de l'enquête d'un revenu hebdomadaire situé entre 200 et 1 499 dollars des Bermudes. Aucun ajustement n'a été effectué pour prendre en compte les changements de prix survenus entre l'époque de l'enquête et la période de base.

Pondération et composition

Groupes principaux	Nombre d'articles	Pondération	Nombre approximatif de relevés de prix
Alimentation	111	181	2 000
Loyer	1	218	420
Habillement et chaussure	37	60	200
Tabac et alcool	4	26	80
Combustible et éclairage	2	45	2
Mobilier, ameublement, équipement et dépenses de ménage	52	147	450
Transports, voyages à l'étranger	15	171	85
Instructions, loisirs et lecture	17	84	115
Soins personnels et médicaux	9	68	400
Total	248	1 000	3 752

Dépenses de consommation des ménages
Les dépenses de consommation prises en compte dans le calcul de l'indice correspondent à la totalité des achats payés au comptant ou à crédit aux fins de consommation des ménages, plus les virements courants effectués périodiquement pour les assurances et la sécurité sociale. Les logements occupés en propriété sont inclus. Ne sont pas pris en compte l'impôt sur le revenu et autres impôts directs, l'épargne et les investissements, le remboursement d'emprunts et les dons.

Mode de relevé des prix
Les prix sont relevés par les fonctionnaires du département des statistiques, qui se rendent personnellement en différents points de vente fournissant des renseignements et, au besoin, ils sont vérifiés avec le personnel d'encadrement de chaque point de vente. Les prix des denrées alimentaires, de l'équipement de ménage, du tabac et de l'alcool, des produits de soins personnels, de l'automédication et des fournitures médicales sont obtenus mensuellement auprès de 11 des plus grands supermarchés du pays. Des enquêtes trimestrielles sur les prix sont effectuées pour les articles dont les prix ont tendance à changer plus lentement, comme les automobiles, les motocyclettes, l'habillement et la chaussure, les appareils ménagers, les médicaments prescrits, etc. Les prix sont relevés annuellement en ce qui concerne les frais de scolarisation, les primes d'assurance automobile, les primes d'assurance-maladie et les droits de mise en circulation de voitures automobiles. Au besoin, la fréquence des relevés est adaptée pour tenir compte de l'évolution rapide de l'environnement.

Logement
Lors du calcul des coefficients de pondération de la rubrique logement de l'indice général, les logements occupés en propriété sont pris en compte en utilisant la méthode d'équivalence locative annuelle. Cependant, aux fins du relevé des prix, les modifications du coût du logement sont exclusivement fondées sur les changements survenus sur le marché des loyers mensuels d'un échantillon représentatif de propriétés en location. En conséquence, aucune tentative n'est effectuée pour contrôler les dépenses réelles spécifiques aux logements occupés en propriété, comme le taux d'intérêt hypothécaire, les réparations ou les assurances, et pas davantage pour ce qui est des dépenses virtuelles, telle que la dépréciation.

Spécification des variétés
Des variétés déterminées pour le relevé sont sélectionnées dans chaque échantillon de point de vente. La marque, le type ou la taille (l'importance du vendeur) les plus en faveur sont choisis pour le relevé des prix, sur le conseil de la direction du point de vente.

Substitution, changement de qualité, etc.
Lorsque la qualité d'un article change, la méthode d'enchaînement est utilisée.

Articles saisonniers
Les fluctuations saisonnières des prix ne font pas l'objet d'ajustements.

Calcul
L'indice est calculé selon la formule de Laspeyres sous forme de moyenne arithmétique pondérée à base fixe, les coefficients de pondération correspondant à l'année 1982.

Organisation et publication
Ministry of Finance, Department of Statistics: «Bermuda Annual Digest» (Hamilton).

idem: «Bermuda Quaterly Digest of Statistics».

idem: «Retail Price Index Reference Paper» (avril 1986).

BOLIVIE (LA PAZ)

Dénomination officielle
Indice de Precios al Consumidor (Indice des prix à la consommation).

Portée
L'indice est calculé mensuellement et porte sur les ménages d'ouvriers et d'employés de la Paz à revenu modique et moyen.

Base originale
1966 = 100.

Source des coefficients de pondération
Le choix des articles et la valeur des coefficients de pondération résultent d'une enquête sur les dépenses des ménages effectuée à la Paz, au cours de la période fin 1964 - fin 1965, auprès d'un échantillon aléatoire d'environ 800 ménages d'ouvriers et d'employés à revenu modique et moyen.

Pondération et composition

Groupes principaux	Nombre d'articles	Pondération	Nombre approximatif de relevés de prix
Alimentation	66	51,30	...
Logement:			
Loyer	1	7,41	...
Impôts sur les biens fonds	1	1,25	...
Combustible et éclairage	2	5,03	...
Dépenses de ménage	32	5,18	...
Habillement et chaussure	32	12,10	...
Divers	27	17,73	...
Total	161	100,00	...

Dépenses de consommation des ménages
Dans ces dépenses sont exclus l'épargne, les investissements, l'impôt sur le revenu et autres impôts directs.

Mode de relevé des prix
Les prix sont relevés par des enquêteurs auprès de 1 200 points de vente et prestataires de service selon la nature des articles, toutes les semaines, tous les mois ou une fois par an. Le relevé des prix des denrées alimentaires et ceux relatifs au chapitre «Logement» ont lieu une fois par semaine. Les informations concernant le combustible et le savon pour lessive sont obtenues deux fois par mois, et celles pour l'éclairage, mensuellement. Les prix utilisés pour le calcul de l'indice sont ceux payés au moment de l'enquête dans les points de vente sélectionnés. Il n'est pas tenu compte du prix des marchandises vendues au rabais et de soldes.

Logement
Les relevés des loyers ont lieu tous les mois auprès d'un échantillon de 100 logements. Il n'est pas tenu compte des logements occupés en propriété.

Spécification des variétés
Les articles dont les prix doivent être enregistrés font l'objet d'une spécification qui indique leur marque, leur taille, l'unité employée, leur qualité, leur volume et leur poids.

Substitution, changement de qualité, etc.
Lorsqu'un article disparaît du marché, il lui est substitué un article analogue.

Articles saisonniers
Hors saison, les prix sont censés suivre les mêmes fluctuations que les autres articles compris dans le même sous-groupe.

Calcul
L'indice est calculé selon la formule de Laspeyres, sous forme de moyenne arithmétique pondérée à base fixe, les coefficients de pondération correspondant à la période 1964-65. L'indice par article est obtenu en utilisant les rapports de prix de la période en cours et de la période précédente.

Autres informations
Tant dans les publications mensuelles que dans les publications annuelles, on publie les indices pour groupes, sous-groupes et les variations relatives au mois précédent.

Organisation et publication
Instituto Nacional de Estadísticas Económicas, División de Precios: «Indice de Precios al Consumidor», Boletín mensual (La Paz).
idem: «Indice de Precios al Consumidor», Anuario.

BOTSWANA

Dénomination officielle
National Cost of Living Index (Indice national du coût de la vie).

Portée
L'indice est calculé mensuellement et porte sur l'ensemble des ménages des zones urbaines et rurales.

Base originale
Septembre 1985 = 100.

Source des coefficients de pondération
La valeur des coefficients de pondération et le choix des articles résultent d'une enquête sur les dépenses des ménages menée pendant la dernière partie de 1978 et les trois premiers trimestres de 1979. L'enquête a été effectuée auprès de 915 ménages urbains et 1 221 ménages ruraux des quatre principales villes et des 13 villages dont la population dépassait 3 000 habitants à l'époque du recensement de 1971. Bien que le nombre d'articles et les coefficients de pondération aient fait l'objet d'une mise à jour, les pondérations n'ont pas été ajustées pour tenir compte de l'évolution des prix entre le moment de l'enquête et septembre 1985.

Lors du choix des articles de l'indice, on a tenté de faire figurer à la fois, dans chaque sous-groupe, tous les articles les plus importants ainsi qu'un échantillon des articles de moindre importance pour représenter l'ensemble des autres articles de la catégorie. En conséquence, de nombreux articles de l'indice ont été choisis non pas en raison de leur importance particulière, mais parce qu'ils représentent un large éventail de biens de consommation.

Pondération et composition

Groupes principaux	Nombre d'articles (a)	Pondération	Nombre approximatif de relevés de prix
Alimentation	48	36,65	2 970
Boissons et tabac	7	3,43	270
Habillement et chaussure	13	10,84	717
Loyer, combustible, éclairage et eau	16	13,07	239
Equipement et dépenses des ménages	24	13,70	1 069
Soins médicaux	6	1,30	127
Transports et communications	18	10,54	129
Autres biens et services	20	10,46	582
Total	152	100,00	6 103

Remarque: (a) Bien qu'ils ne soient pas utilisés dans le calcul de l'index, les coefficients nationaux de pondération sont indiqués en guise de référence.

Dépenses de consommation des ménages
Les dépenses de consommation prises en compte dans le calcul de l'indice comprennent les achats au comptant et à crédit de biens neufs et d'occasion. En sont exclus les revenus en nature et les biens produits par les ménages pour leur propre consommation, les primes d'assurance-vie, les pensions et les cotisations à la sécurité sociale.

Mode de relevé des prix
Les prix sont relevés chaque mois auprès de commerces de détail représentatifs, situés dans des villes et villages sélectionnés de l'ensemble du pays, en particulier dans quatre zones urbaines, huit villages importants et cinq petits villages.

Tous les types de magasins (de grande, de moyenne ou de petite taille) sont représentés dans le relevé des prix. Au total, près de 330 points de vente différents sont visités tous les mois. Les prix sont relevés par les agents du Bureau central de statistiques de Gaborone, qui se rendent dans les régions concernées au cours des deux premières semaines de chaque mois. Un total d'environ 6 100 relevés de prix sont obtenus chaque mois.

Les salaires des employés de maison sont relevés tous les trois mois à Gaborone. Certains prix sont relevés à la suite d'appels téléphoniques. Lorsqu'il s'agit d'articles réglementés par des prix officiels, on utilise, le cas échéant, également les prix d'escompte, des soldes et du marché libre.

Seuls les achats au comptant sont pris en compte.

Le relevé des prix est effectué conformément à la Loi de 1976 sur les statistiques. Cette loi prescrit aux personnes interrogées de fournir les renseignements demandés, mais exige en même temps du Bureau central de statistiques qu'il fasse un usage strictement confidentiel des données et ne les révèle à aucune personne, organisation ou service étatique extérieurs au Bureau.

Logement
Les relevés sont obtenus auprès de la Botswana Housing Corporation, ainsi que par le biais d'une enquête effectuée tous les trois mois par le Bureau central de statistique sur les loyers privés moyens payés par les locataires de logements d'une pièce à Gaborone. Cependant, les relevés de prix obtenus à la suite de ces enquêtes seront utilisés pour toutes les zones urbaines, et pas simplement à Gaborone. Les changements du prix des loyers à Gaborone semblent constituer une indication raisonnable des modifications survenues dans le reste du pays. Les données sur les logements occupés par leur propriétaire sont représentées par les intérêts à payer pour le terrain et le remboursement des emprunts pour les matériaux de construction.

Spécification des variétés
On utilise des spécifications détaillées et des spécifications étendues. Les spécifications détaillées comprennent la marque, la fabrication, la qualité, les dimensions, etc., de l'article décrit. En ce qui concerne les spécifications étendues, des descriptions globales sont fournies et l'on doit sélectionner les articles spécifiques au magasin concerné.

Substitution, changement de qualité, etc.
Les descriptions des articles demeurent inchangées tant que les séries statistiques restent en vigueur. Cependant, il peut s'avérer nécessaire d'opérer certaines transformations sur les éléments et la description de l'article devra être modifiée en conséquence. Dans un tel cas, un prix de base est attribué à l'article de remplacement, en supposant que son prix a augmenté, depuis septembre 1985, au même rythme que le prix de l'ancien article.

D'après ce système, si un point de vente déterminé n'a pas en stock des plaquettes de beurre 250g, on n'utilise pas le prix d'une plaquette de 500g. En fait, il n'est pas indispensable que dans chaque magasin le prix de tous les articles soit indiqué. Il est procédé, dans la pratique, au calcul de la moyenne des prix de 250g de beurre dans tous les magasins de la même région. Cette moyenne est ensuite comparée au prix de base de l'article dans la même région. Si certains points de vente n'ont pas cet article en magasin, cela n'a pas d'importance - à condition que, dans la région, au moins un commerce en dispose afin que l'on puisse indiquer le prix moyen de l'article pour la région concernée. Au mois suivant, la même description d'article - pour 250g de beurre - figure au questionnaire du magasin en question. Il est à supposer que peut être ainsi réduit le nombre d'erreurs produit par le relevé du prix d'un article qui ne correspond pas exactement à sa description.

Articles saisonniers
Ils ne font l'objet d'aucun traitement particulier.

Calcul
L'indice est calculé selon la formule de Laspeyres sous forme de moyenne arithmétique pondérée à base fixe, les coefficients de pondération correspondant à la période 1978-79.

Le rapport de prix pour chaque article dans chaque région est d'abord calculé en divisant le prix moyen de la période courante par le prix moyen de la période de base. Ces rapports de prix sont ensuite utilisés pour calculer des indices séparés pour les ménages à revenu modique, moyen et élevé dans les zones urbaines ainsi que dans les villages importants et petits villages des zones rurales.

Les indices pour tous les groupes de revenu des zones urbaines se calculent par la moyenne pondérée des indices pour chacun des trois groupes, et en tenant compte de la moyenne des dépenses de consommation dans les zones urbaines. L'indice national est la moyenne pondérée d'indices urbains et ruraux, les coefficients de pondération correspondant à la population respective des zones urbaines et rurales.

Autres informations
Les indices des principales catégories sont publiés. Des indices généraux séparés pour les zones urbaines et rurales sont également publiés.

De nouvelles séries pour les zones urbaines, rurales et pour l'ensemble du pays sont maintenant calculées (base 1991 = 100), mais les informations méthodologiques relatives à ces séries n'étaient pas disponibles au BIT lors de la publication du présent volume.

Organisation et publication
Central Statistics Office: «Statistical Bulletin», (Gaborone) (trimestriel).

idem: «Cost of living index 1985», novembre 1985.

idem: «Consumer Price Statistics».

BRESIL

Dénomination officielle
Indice de Preços ao Consumidor Amplo - IPCA (Indice des prix à la consommation).

Portée
L'indice est calculé mensuellement et porte sur les ménages de salariés vivant dans toutes les agglomérations urbaines du pays et disposant d'un revenu mensuel compris entre un et 40 salaire(s) minimum(s).

Base originale
Décembre 1990 = 100.

Source des coefficients de pondération
Les coefficients de pondération et les articles sélectionnés résultent d'une enquête sur les dépenses des ménages réalisée dans l'ensemble du pays entre août 1974 et août 1975.

L'enquête portait sur un échantillon de 55 000 ménages de un à cinq membres, vivant dans toutes les agglomérations urbaines du pays. Les coefficients de pondération ont été mis à jour en utilisant les résultats d'une enquête sur les dépenses des ménages effectuée de mars 1987 à février 1988. Il n'a été effectué aucun ajustement des coefficients pour prendre en compte les changements de prix survenus entre la période de l'enquête et la période de base.

Pondération et composition
Pas disponible.

Dépenses de consommation des ménages
Dans le calcul des coefficients de pondération il n'est pas tenu compte des dépenses qui accroissent l'épargne, par exemple l'achat d'une maison, l'installation du téléphone, etc. Sont exclus les taxes directes, les taxes sur la propriété immobilière, les intérêts, les assurances, les dettes des amortissements, les cartes de crédit, remboursements de prêts, achats de matériaux de construction pour l'amélioration des logements. Sont également exclues les dépenses effectuées à l'occasion d'anniversaires, de baptêmes, de mariages, du carnaval, de Noël, etc. Il n'est pas non plus tenu compte des logements occupés en propriété. Les biens durables sont traités comme les autres articles et pris en compte dans les dépenses effectuées au cours des douze mois de la période de référence. Les achats à crédit sont considérés comme un paiement effectué au cours de la période de référence de l'enquête. L'achat de véhicules d'occasion est pris en compte. Les primes d'assurance-vie sont exclues du calcul.

Mode de relevé des prix
Les prix sont relevés par des agents tous les mois, tous les trimestres ou tous les ans selon les articles, auprès de points de vente au détail ou de prestataires de services dans onze agglomérations urbaines. Il n'est pas adressé de questionnaires par correspondance. Certains tarifs sont fixés par l'Etat, par exemple en ce qui concerne l'électricité, l'eau, le gaz, les transports et communications et peuvent être obtenus au moment de leur modification. Les données relatives aux soins médicaux sont relevées tous les deux mois. Les rabais sont pris en compte. Tous les prix sont ceux payés par les consommateurs.

Logement
Le prix des appartements est obtenu auprès d'un échantillon à partir d'une enquête nationale sur les logements, l'échantillon étant divisé en douze parties. L'enquête portant sur l'une d'entre elles a lieu chaque mois. Il n'est pas tenu compte des logements occupés en propriété.

Spécification des variétés
Les spécifications fournissent des précisions pour la plupart des articles ainsi qu'une description de la marque de l'empaquetage, de la taille, de la qualité, de l'unité de mesure, etc. Pour certains articles où cela n'est pas possible, les spécifications ne sont pas aussi complètes.

Substitution, changement de qualité, etc.
Il n'est pas tenu compte des changements de qualité des articles. Les articles qui font leur apparition sur le marché sont introduits dans le calcul lors de la révision des spécifications. Lorsqu'un article disparaît temporairement du marché, un prix lui est attribué compte tenu du mouvement des prix des autres articles du même sous-groupe.

Articles saisonniers
Pour des produits tels que les racines, les légumes et les fruits, il est tenu compte des fluctuations saisonnières en utilisant des articles et des coefficients de pondération mensuels. Pour le calcul de l'indice des articles saisonniers, la formule de Paasche est utilisée.

Calcul
L'indice est calculé selon la formule de Laspeyres, sous forme de moyenne arithmétique pondérée à base fixe, les coefficients de pondération correspondant à la période mars 1987-mars 1988.

Lors du calcul des indices, la moyenne des rapports des prix entre la période en cours et la période précédente est utilisée.

Pour obtenir l'indice national, les indices des zones urbaines sont tout d'abord calculés et combinés; les coefficients de pondération utilisés sont liés à l'estimation du total des dépenses courantes dans chaque zone urbaine.

Autres informations
La Fundaçao Instituto Brasileiro de Geografia e Estatística - IBGE - procède également au calcul d'un indice national des prix à la consommation (INPC) et d'autres indices (IPC) relatifs aux ménages disposant d'un salaire mensuel compris entre un et huit salaire(s) minimum(s).

Organisation et publication
Fundaçao Instituto Brasileiro de Geografia e Estatística (IBGE): «Indicadores» (Rio de Janeiro).

idem: «Sistema Nacional de Indices de Preços ao Consumidor, Métodos de Cálculo», 1984.

idem: «Estructura Básica de Ponderaçoes», 1983.

idem: «Guia de campo para a Pesquisa de Especificaçao de Produtos e Serviços», Janeiro 1980.

idem: «Métodos para o Trabalho de Campo», 1983.

idem: «Manual de Implantaçao», Novembre 1979.

idem: «Para compreender o INPC», 1981.

BRESIL (SAO PAULO)

Dénomination officielle
Indice de Preços ao Consumidor (Indice des prix à la consommation).

Portée
L'indice est calculé mensuellement et porte sur les familles disposant d'un revenu annuel compris entre 451 et 1 353 cruzeiros en 1971.

Base originale
Décembre de l'année précédente = 100.

Source des coefficients de pondération
Les coefficients de pondération et les articles sélectionnés ont

été déterminés sur la base des résultats d'une enquête pilote effectuée en mai et juin 1971 par l'Institut d'enquêtes économiques (Instituto de Pesquisas Econômicas) de l'Université de São Paulo auprès de familles à revenu moyen à São Paulo.

Pondération et composition

Groupes principaux	Nombre d'articles	Pondération	Nombre approximatif de relevés de prix
Alimentation	143	435,3	...
Logement:			
Loyer	1	86,3	...
Combustible, éclairage, eau, réparations, charges municipales, services domestiques, etc.	18	117,7	...
Produits d'entretien	12	22,9	...
Habillement et chaussure	7	64,0	...
Dépenses personnelles:			
Boissons et tabac	11	54,3	...
Services personnels	6	16,1	...
Instruction et loisirs	8	21,2	...
Santé et soins personnels	17	21,9	...
Autres dépenses	4	22,7	...
Transports	10	62,8	...
Soins médicaux	7	52,8	...
Instruction	4	22,0	...
Total	248	1 000,0	

Dépenses de consommation des ménages
Pas disponible.

Mode de relevé des prix
Les prix sont relevés par des enquêteurs, chaque jour pour les denrées alimentaires et mensuellement pour les autres articles, auprès de 1 251 points de vente au détail et prestataires de services à São Paulo.

Logement
Pas disponible.

Spécification des variétés
Pas disponible.

Substitution, changement de qualité, etc.
Pas disponible.

Articles saisonniers
Pas disponible.

Calcul
L'indice est un indice-chaîne (c'est-à-dire qu'au lieu de comparer les prix relevés pour le mois de référence avec ceux de la période de base, on les compare avec les prix relevés le mois précédent) calculé selon une formule équivalant à celle de la moyenne arithmétique pondérée à base fixe.

Organisation et publication
Universidade de São Paulo, Instituto de Pesquisas Econômicas: «Indice de Preços ao Consumidor» (São Paulo).

idem: «O actual índice de preços ao consumidor. Custo de vida da classe de renda familiar modal do Município de São Paulo», Relatório Preliminar No. 2.

BRUNEI DARUSSALAM

Dénomination officielle
Consumer Price Index for Brunei Darussalam. (Indice des prix à la consommation de Brunéi Darussalam).

Portée
L'indice est calculé mensuellement et porte sur les ménages de fonctionnaires dont les dépenses mensuelles se situaient entre 300 et 2 099 dollars de Brunéi en 1977.

Base originale
1977 = 100.

Source des coefficients de pondération
La valeur des coefficients de pondération et le choix des articles résultent d'une enquête sur les dépenses des ménages menée en 1977. L'enquête se bornait aux fonctionnaires. Le système de pondération de l'indice s'est fondé sur les ménages dont les dépenses mensuelles se situaient entre 300 et 2 099 dollars de Brunéi en 1977.

Dépenses de consommation des ménages
Les dépenses de consommation prises en compte dans le calcul de l'indice comprennent la quasi-totalité des biens et services

Pondération et composition

Groupes principaux	Nombre d'articles	Pondération	Nombre approximatif de relevés de prix
Alimentation	42	4 507	...
Habillement et chaussure	8	614	...
Logement:			
Loyer	1	181	...
Petites réparations et entretien	1	83	...
Combustibles et services:			
Eau, electricité et gaz	1	215	...
Autres dépenses de combustible et d'éclairage	1	20	...
Mobilier, ameublement, équipement et dépenses de ménage	8	831	...
Transports et communications	6	1 718	...
Instruction, loisirs et services culturels	8	893	...
Biens et services divers	8	938	...
Total	84	10 000	...

consommés par les ménages de référence. Elles excluent les dépenses relatives à l'achat de terres et de bâtiments, primes d'assurance vie, épargne et impôt sur le revenu.

Mode de relevé des prix
Les prix sont relevés dans des magasins de vente au détail et établissements choisis dans le district de Brunéi-Muara, qui comprend la capitale Bandar Seri Begawan. Les renseignements y relatifs sont relevés pour tous les articles soit par des visites des agents de la Statistics Division de l'Economic Planning Unit aux commerçants, soit par téléphone.

Les prix du poisson, des fruits et légumes frais sont relevés chaque samedi, tandis que les prix des autres articles le sont à date fixe chaque mois.

Les prix retenus pour le calcul de l'indice sont ceux effectivement payés au comptant. Sont exclus les suppléments perçus pour les ventes à crédit et les rabais qui ne sont pas consentis à tous les acheteurs. Les prix des soldes sont pris en compte s'ils portent sur l'article spécifié et satisfont à la condition de comparabilité.

Logement
Les renseignements relatifs aux loyers sont obtenus mensuellement dans un immeuble comprenant des appartements avec deux chambres à coucher.

Spécification des variétés
Les articles sont spécifiés par la marque, le nom, l'unité employée, la qualité et la taille.

Substitution, changement de qualité, etc.
Quand un article disparaît du marché, on prend le prix de celui qui est le plus analogue.

Articles saisonniers
Les aliments frais saisonniers sont omis hors saison et leurs coefficients de pondération sont répartis alors entre les autres articles du même groupe.

Calcul
L'indice est calculé selon la formule de Laspeyres sous forme de moyenne arithmétique pondérée à base fixe, les coefficients de pondération correspondant à la période de base.

L'indice pour un article est obtenu en utilisant les rapports de prix de la période courante et de la période de base. La moyenne arithmétique simple des rapports de prix de toutes les variétés d'un article donne l'indice pour un article.

Organisation et publication
State Secretariat, Economic Planning Unit, Statistics Division: «Brunei Statistical Yearbook» (Bandar Seri Begawan).

idem: «Consumer Price Index for Brunei, Base year 1977 = 100» (Bandar Seri Begawan, janv. 1980).

BULGARIE

Dénomination officielle
Indice des prix de détail d'Etat.

Portée
Pas disponible.

Base originale
1960 = 100.

Source des coefficients de pondération
Les pondérations sont calculées d'après la valeur et la quantité des biens et services vendus ou fournis à la communauté et déterminées sur la base d'informations tirées des statistiques sur le commerce de détail et de données relatives aux dépenses des ménages.

Pondération et composition
Pas disponible.

Dépenses de consommation des ménages
Pas disponible.

Mode de relevé des prix
Les prix pour la plupart des articles sont fixés par les autorités; ils sont uniformes pour l'ensemble du pays, sauf pour certains articles dont les prix sont établis pour chaque région. Les prix des fruits et légumes frais sont observés vers les 5, 15 et 25 de chaque mois auprès de points de vente (commerce d'Etat) répartis dans 90 villes.

Logement
Les données relatives au loyer sont obtenues pour des logements d'une à plusieurs pièces.

Spécification des variétés
Pas disponible.

Substitution, changement de qualité, etc.
Pas disponible.

Articles saisonniers
Pas disponible.

Calcul
L'indice est un indice-chaîne; il est calculé chaque année avec enchaînement annuel en utilisant la formule de Paasche.

Autres informations
Une nouvelle série est maintenant calculée mais ni les données ni les informations méthodologiques relatives à cette série n'étaient disponibles au BIT lors de la publication du présent Volume.

Organisation et publication
Central Statistical Office of the Council of Ministers: «Statistical Yearbook of the People's Republic of Bulgaria» (Sofia).

BURKINA FASO (OUAGADOUGOU)

Dénomination officielle
Indice des prix à la consommation africaine.

Portée
L'indice qui est calculé mensuellement et publié trimestriellement, porte sur les ménages à revenus modiques résidant à Ouagadougou.

Base originale
Juillet 1981 - juin 1982 = 100.

Source des coefficients de pondération
Les coefficients de pondération et les articles sélectionnés ont été déterminés sur la base des résultats d'une enquête sur les dépenses des ménages effectuée au cours des douze mois de 1980 à Ouagadougou. Cette enquête portait sur un échantillon de 54 ménages composés en moyenne de 4.54 personnes dont le revenu se situait entre 15 000 et 20 000 francs CFA par mois lors de l'enquête.

Pondération et composition

Groupes principaux	Nombre d'articles	Pondération	Nombre approximatif de relevés de prix
Alimentation	48	4 766	...
Habillement et chaussure	8	441	...
Loyer et frais de construction	5	515	...
Combustible, éclairage et eau	5	1 368	...
Equipement de ménage	13	303	...
Hygiène et soins médicaux	8	518	...
Transports et communications	8	1 858	...
Education et loisirs	4	231	...
Total	99	10 000	...

Dépenses de consommation des ménages
Les dépenses de consommation des ménages prises en compte dans le calcul de l'indice comprennent toutes les dépenses engagées par les ménages pour leur consommation. Il n'a pas été tenu compte des biens et services reçus sous la forme de revenus en nature et consommés par les ménages, des cotisations aux assurances sociales et caisses de pensions et des droits à payer pour l'obtention d'une patente.

Mode de relevé des prix
Les prix sont relevés par des enquêteurs sur le marché central et auprès de points de vente au détail et prestataires de services à Ouagadougou. Les prix des denrées alimentaires et des boissons sont obtenus trois fois par mois (dont une fois par achat direct) ceux des autres articles dont les prix ne varient pas fréquemment sont relevés une fois tous les trois mois.

Logement
Les données relatives au loyer sont obtenues mensuellement. Le coût des logements occupés par leur propriétaire est représenté par les prix des matériaux de construction.

Spécification des variétés
Les articles retenus font l'objet de spécifications.

Substitution, changement de qualité, etc.
Lorsqu'un article n'est plus disponible sur le marché, le dernier prix relevé est maintenu pendant six mois. Ensuite, l'article disparu est remplacé par un autre article similaire.

Articles saisonniers
Il est tenu compte des fluctuations saisonnières de certaines denrées alimentaires fraîches en ne retenant pas ces articles pour le calcul de l'indice lorsqu'ils sont hors de saison; les coefficients de pondération qui leur étaient attribués sont alors reportés sur des articles de remplacement.

Calcul
L'indice est calculé selon la formule de Laspeyres sous forme de moyenne arithmétique pondérée à base fixe, les coefficients de pondération correspondant à 1980.

Organisation et publication
Institut national de la statistique et de la démographie. Direction des études démographiques. Service des prix: «Indice des prix à la consommation africaine» (Ouagadougou).

BURUNDI (BUJUMBURA)

Dénomination officielle
Indice des prix à la consommation des ménages de Bujumbura.

Portée
L'indice est calculé mensuellement et porte sur tous les ménages de Bujumbura.

Base originale
Janvier 1980 = 100.

Source des coefficients de pondération
La valeur des coefficients de pondération et le choix des articles résultent d'une enquête sur les dépenses des ménages effectuée en 1978-79 auprès d'un échantillon de ménages à Bujumbura. Un choix de 130 articles, dont les coefficients de pondération étaient les plus importants, ont été retenus pour le calcul de l'indice.

Pondération et composition

Groupes principaux	Nombre d'articles	Pondération	Nombre approximatif de relevés de prix
Alimentation	61	55,31	...
Habillement et chaussure	19	13,21	...
Logement et dépenses de ménage	23	16,70	...
Transports et loisirs	8	10,80	...
Soins médicaux et divers	19	3,98	...
Total	130	100,00	...

Dépenses de consommation des ménages
Les dépenses de consommation prises en compte pour établir les coefficients de pondération correspondent aux achats de tous les biens et services effectués par les ménages de référence pour leur consommation.

Les éléments suivants ne sont pas considérés comme dépenses de consommation: cotisations à la sécurité sociale et aux caisses de pensions, logements en propriété (seules les logements en location sont prises en compte), reprise de biens usagés et arrhes pour l'achat de biens neufs, patentes, envois de fonds,

dépenses d'investissement, dons et versements similaires, impôts sur le revenu et tous les impôts et assurances.
Sont pris en compte les éléments suivants: revenu en nature, achats d'occasion, biens durables, soins médicaux, achats à crédit (seuls les remboursements effectués pendant la période de l'enquête sont inclus).

Mode de relevé des prix
Les prix sont relevés par des enquêteurs auprès d'environ 34 magasins de détail, marchés et prestataires de services sélectionnés. Les prix de certaines denrées alimentaires, telles que les farineux et féculents, les poissons, les fruits et légumes, ainsi que ceux de certains articles d'habillement, sont obtenus quatre fois par semaine; les prix des autres articles le sont une fois par semaine. Les prix des denrées alimentaires vendues sur les marchés s'obtiennent en pesant les produits.

Logement
Les données relatives au loyer sont obtenues pour des logements loués de deux pièces ayant l'électricité et un sol cimenté. Pour les logements occupés par leur propriétaire, seuls les frais de réparation et d'entretien sont inclus dans l'indice.

Spécification des variétés
Les articles dont les prix sont à relever font l'objet de spécifications portant sur la marque, la qualité, le nom et l'unité.

Substitution, changement de qualité, etc.
Lorsqu'un produit n'est plus en vente, un produit comparable lui est substitué.

Articles saisonniers
Les articles saisonniers, tels que fruits et légumes frais, ne sont pas significatifs dans l'indice et ne font pas l'objet d'ajustements.

Calcul
L'indice est calculé selon la formule de Laspeyres sous forme de moyenne arithmétique pondérée à base fixe, les coefficients de pondération correspondant à la période 1978-79.
Pour calculer les indices des articles, on utilise des rapports de prix moyens. Les indices annuels sont les moyennes des indices des 12 mois.

Autres informations
Une enquête pour actualiser la base de calcul de l'indice des prix à la consommation est actuellement en cours à Bujumbura.

Organisation et publication
Institut de statistiques et d'études économiques, (ISTEEBU): «Bulletin mensuel des prix», Bujumbura.
idem: «Annuaire statistique».
idem: «Bulletin trimestriel».

CAMEROUN (YAOUNDE, AFRICAINS)

Dénomination officielle
Indice des prix de détail à la consommation des familles de condition moyenne - Familles «originaires».

Portée
L'indice est calculé mensuellement et porte sur les ménages de classe moyenne ayant un budget mensuel d'environ 21 900 francs CFA et composés en moyenne de 4,15 unités de consommation en 1964-1965.

Base originale
1968 = 100.

Source des coefficients de pondération
Les coefficients de pondération et les articles sélectionnés ont été déterminés sur la base des résultats d'une enquête sur les dépenses des ménages effectuée en 1964-65 à Yaoundé auprès de 764 ménages camerounais représentatifs de l'ensemble des consommateurs urbains.

Dépenses de consommation des ménages
Pas disponible.

Mode de relevé des prix
Les prix pour la plupart des articles sont relevés une fois par mois soit par des enquêteurs, soit au moyen d'enquêtes par correspondance, auprès d'environ 60 points de vente au détail et prestataires de services ou à partir de la documentation officielle pour les prix fixés par les autorités gouvernementales.

Pondération et composition

Groupes principaux	Nombre d'articles	Pondération	Nombre approximatif de relevés de prix
Alimentation	50	336	...
Boissons et tabac	11	103	...
Loyer, combustible, éclairage, eau et services domestiques	7	75	...
Mobilier, ameublement et articles d'équipement ménager	16	71	...
Habillement et chaussure	13	163	...
Transports	8	105	...
Soins personnels et médicaux	13	50	...
Loisirs	4	51	...
Services et divers	10	46	...
Total	132	1 000	...

Certains articles d'alimentation font, de plus, l'objet d'achats par les enquêteurs les 5, 15 et 25 de chaque mois sur trois marchés publics.

Logement
Les données relatives au loyer font l'objet d'une enquête auprès d'une importante société immobilière.

Spécification des variétés
Pas disponible.

Substitution, changement de qualité, etc.
Pas disponible.

Articles saisonniers
Il est tenu compte des fluctuations saisonnières de certains fruits en ne retenant pas ces articles pour le calcul de l'indice lorsqu'ils sont hors de saison; les coefficients de pondération qui leur étaient attribués sont alors reportés sur des produits de remplacement.

Calcul
L'indice est calculé selon la formule de Laspeyres, sous forme de moyenne arithmétique pondérée à base fixe, les coefficients de pondération correspondant à la période 1964-65.

Organisation et publication
Direction de la statistique et de la comptabilité nationale: «Bulletin mensuel de statistique» (Yaoundé).

CAMEROUN (YAOUNDE, EUROPEENS)

Dénomination officielle
Indice des prix de détail à la consommation familiale - Familles «non originaires».

Portée
L'indice est calculé mensuellement et porte sur les ménages européens de plus d'une personne à Yaoundé.

Base originale
Mai 1966 = 100.

Source des coefficients de pondération
Les coefficients de pondération et les articles sélectionnés ont été déterminés sur la base des résultats d'une enquête sur les dépenses des ménages effectuée à Yaoundé de mars à juillet 1965 auprès de 91 ménages européens de plus d'une personne.

Pondération et composition

Groupes principaux	Nombre d'articles	Pondération	Nombre approximatif de relevés de prix
Alimentation	50	373	...
Boissons et tabac	13	133	...
Dépenses de ménage (services domestiques, eau, gaz, électricité de ménage)	13	193	...
Habillement et chaussure	6	36	...
Transports	7	65	...
Loisirs	5	59	...
Soins personnels et médicaux	9	35	...
Services et divers	10	106	...
Total	113	1 000	...

Dépenses de consommation des ménages
Pas disponible.

Mode de relevé des prix
Les prix sont relevés deux à trois fois par mois par des enquêteurs auprès de magasins de détail pour les denrées alimentaires et au moyen de questionnaires envoyés mensuellement à différents points de vente et prestataires de services en ce qui concerne les autres articles. Le montant des gages des domestiques est fondé sur les salaires minima fixés par les autorités gouvernementales.

Logement
Les dépenses relatives au loyer ne sont retenues ni dans le calcul de l'indice ni dans la détermination des coefficients de pondération.

Spécification des variétés
Pas disponible.

Substitution, changement de qualité, etc.
Pas disponible.

Articles saisonniers
Pas disponible.

Calcul
L'indice est calculé selon la formule de Laspeyres, sous forme de moyenne arithmétique pondérée à base fixe, les coefficients de pondération correspondant à la période mars - juillet 1965.

Organisation et publication
Direction de la statistique et de la comptabilité nationale: « Bulletin mensuel de statistique» (Yaoundé).

CANADA

Dénomination officielle
Consumer Price Index (Indice des prix à la consommation).

Portée
L'indice est calculé mensuellement et porte sur tous les ménages privés (familles et personnes seules) de 64 centres urbains comptant au moins 30 000 habitants.

Base originale
1986 = 100.

Source des coefficients de pondération
La valeur des coefficients de pondération et le choix des articles ont été déterminés sur la base des résultats de l'enquête sur les dépenses des ménages de 1986 et de l'enquête sur les dépenses alimentaire des ménages de 1986. Ces données correspondent au coût du panier de 1986 exprimé en prix de 1986.

Pondération et composition

Groupes principaux	Nombre d'articles	Pondération	Nombre approximatif de relevés de prix
Alimentation	213	18,05	550 000
Logement:			
Habitat en location	3	7,75	170 000
Habitat en propriété (y c. réparation et entretien)	10	12,72	5 000
Autre habitat	5	1,38	1 000
Eau, combustibles et électricité	5	3,82	1 400
Autres dépenses de ménage	44	5,77	23 000
Mobilier et articles d'équipement ménager	67	4,88	15 000
Habillement et chaussure	91	8,69	50 000
Transports	30	18,29	33 000
Santé et soins personnels	35	4,20	62 000
Loisirs, lecture et instruction	95	8,84	35 000
Tabac et alcool	10	5,60	21 000
Total	608	100,00	(a) 966 400

Remarque: (a) Nombre annuel de relevés.

Dépenses de consommation des ménages
L'indice ne tient compte que des biens et services dont le prix peut être lié à une quantité et à une qualité données et ne tient pas compte des biens et services offerts par le gouvernement et financés au moyen du régime fiscal, car il n'y a aucun rapport entre le montant d'argent versé en impôts par une personne et la quantité ou la qualité des biens ou des services publics que reçoit cette personne.

L'assurance est un domaine nécessitant une approche diversifiée. Dans certains cas, l'assurance peut être liée à des biens et services précis et, de ce fait, est prise en considération dans l'indice. L'assurance-logement, des propriétaires ou locataires, et l'assurance-automobile entrent dans cette catégorie puisque le contrat garantit le remplacement ou la remise en état de biens précis. En revanche, l'assurance-vie et l'assurance-invalidité sont exclues parce que les prestations prévues dans le contrat d'assurance représentent un pouvoir d'achat futur qui ne peut être lié à un ensemble spécifique de biens ou de services.

Les services de santé que reçoit la population par le biais du régime d'assurance-maladie sont exclus parce que les primes d'assurance-maladie ne reflètent ni la pleine valeur des services rendus ni une proportion constante de cette valeur. Les services de santé payés directement au médecin ou à l'hôpital sont également exclus, car le montant payé dépend, à des degrés divers, du financement des soins de santé par l'Etat. En revanche, les articles médicaux, les produits pharmaceutiques et les soins dentaires sont prix en compte dans l'indice puisque les sommes versées à ce titre correspondent à des quantités et à des niveaux de qualité précis de biens et de services.

L'inclusion des impôts fonciers constitue un cas particulier. Même si ces impôts ne sont pas liés directement à des biens ou des services précis obtenus par les propriétaires, on considère qu'ils font partie intégrante du coût de possession et d'utilisation d'un logement, ce qui explique leur inclusion.

Mode de relevé des prix
Le choix des villes et des points de vente où l'on relève des prix est fait au jugé: il est fondé sur des renseignements provenant de sources diverses, dont l'information sur les marchés fournie par les bureaux régionaux de Statistique Canada. On observe les prix des produits alimentaires à la fois dans les magasins à succursales et les magasins indépendants; l'observation des prix des vêtements et des articles d'ameublement se fait dans les grands magasins et dans les boutiques spécialisées; celle des prix des pièces d'automobiles se fait dans les magasins spécialisés et dans les garages. L'échantillon de points de vente est conçu surtout de façon à inclure les détaillants qui ont un fort volume de ventes. Les prix des produits comme les tarifs d'autobus, de train et d'avion, les tarifs d'électricité, de gaz et de téléphone et les impôts fonciers sont relevés auprès de l'administration locale, régionale ou provinciale compétente.

La fréquence des relevés de prix dépend de la nature du produit. Les biens et services dont les prix varient fréquemment nécessitent de fréquents relevés de prix. Par exemple, on observe les prix des produits alimentaires et de l'essence une fois par mois. Pour la plupart des autres produits, l'observation des prix se fait mensuellement. Ces produits comprennent les articles ménagers, l'habillement, les produits pharmaceutiques, les produits de soins personnels, les produits du tabac, les boissons alcoolisées, les loyers, les intérêts hypothécaires et les maisons neuves. Les autres produits se caractérisent par des variations de prix moins fréquentes; c'est pourquoi leurs prix sont observés à des intervalles plus longs qu'un mois. On relève les prix des appareils électroménagers et des meubles six fois par année. Les prix des automobiles, des services vestimentaires, des services de soins personnels et des journaux sont observés trimestriellement, les frais d'immatriculation d'automobiles et les impôts fonciers une fois par année. Nonobstant ce calendrier d'observation, on procède à d'autres relevés de prix pour ces produits lorsqu'on a des raisons de croire qu'il y a eu un changement de prix important entre les dates d'observation habituelles. Au besoin, on modifie alors les dates habituelles des relevés.

Logement
Les loyers sont relevés dans le cadre de l'Enquête sur la population active de Statistique Canada. Cette enquête est fondée sur un échantillon statistique de quelque 54 000 logements en propriété ou loués et répartis dans tout le pays. En moyenne, 14 000 de ces logements sont loués et sont situés dans les centres urbains visés par l'IPC. Dès qu'un logement dans une localité donnée est inclus dans l'échantillon, les données sont recueillies pendant six mois consécutifs. D'après le plan de sondage, un sixième de l'échantillon est remplacé chaque mois. Les renseignements sur les loyers se rapportent aux logements occupés par des locataires et sont recueillis auprès des locataires eux-mêmes.

Le traitement du logement en propriété est destiné à mesurer l'effet des variations de prix sur certaines catégories de coûts à la charge des propriétaires.

Les coûts à la charge des propriétaires inclus dans l'indice se composent des éléments suivants: le coût des réparations, les impôts fonciers, le coût de remplacement de la portion des logements occupés par leur propriétaire qui est censée être «usée», le coût d'assurance de propriétaire, et les coûts d'intérêts hypothécaires.

Spécification des variétés
La spécification précise en détail les caractéristiques du produit et donne des informations comme la quantité standard, l'unité de mesure, la fréquence des relevés de prix et d'autres renseignements à l'intention des enquêteurs.

Souvent, une seule description détaillée d'un produit peut être applicable à tous les points de vente où les prix du produit en question sont relevés.

Dans d'autres cas, une seule description détaillée ne peut s'appliquer à tous les points de vente où les prix sont relevés. Les enquêteurs doivent alors décider, suivant certaines règles, de quels produits en particulier ils doivent relever les prix dans des points de vente spécifiques. Le choix peut différer entre les points de vente, tout en restant inchangé dans un même point de vente, tant que les produits choisis satisfont aux critères de représentativité et de disponibilité continuelle attendue.

Substitution, changement de qualité, etc.
On prend des mesures particulières pour ce qui a trait aux produits qui sont épuisés dans certains points de vente. Lorsque ce cas se présente et qu'il est possible d'observer le prix de produits semblables dans d'autres points de vente de la même strate de centres urbains, le prix est imputé à partir du mouvement de prix observé dans ces autres points de vente. Autrement, on conserve le dernier prix consigné, à moins qu'il ne s'agisse d'un prix de vente en solde (auquel cas on utilise le dernier prix régulier inscrit). Cependant, si le stock d'un produit non saisonnier est épuisé dans un point de vente donné pendant plus de deux mois consécutifs, on cesse d'utiliser son prix dans le calcul de l'indice et on remplace le produit par un autre semblable dans le même point de vente ou, si nécessaire, par le même produit ou un produit semblable dans un autre point de vente.

Dans beaucoup de cas, on peut relever les prix de l'ancienne et de la nouvelle variété à un moment précis. Le rapport de ces prix peut ensuite servir de facteur de rajustement de prix pour le changement de qualité. On procède de la même façon lorsqu'un point de vente au détail donné en remplace un autre dans l'échantillon. Cette méthode, parfois dite de raccordement, repose sur l'hypothèse implicite que l'écart entre les valeurs marchandes des deux produits (ou entre deux points de vente) observées à un moment précis est entièrement attribuable à des différences de qualité entre ces produits (ou entre les services offerts à ces points de vente).

On peut parfois rajuster explicitement les prix observés en regard de la qualité, c'est-à-dire établir la différence de valeur entre l'ancienne et la nouvelle variété amenée par une différence de qualité entre elles. Lorsqu'il s'agit de modifications relativement mineures, on peut établir la différence de valeur par l'analyse des coûts ou en comparant les prix de vente au détail respectifs des accessoires ou services ajoutés ou supprimés.

Articles saisonniers
L'offre de certains produits varie selon la saison. C'est le cas notamment de divers fruits et légumes frais, tels que les fraises et le maïs qui ne sont disponibles en quantité que pendant quelques semaines ou quelques mois chaque année. Par ailleurs, des fluctuations saisonnières de la demande s'observent pour d'autres produits, notamment pour de nombreux articles d'habillement (p.ex., costumes de bain et manteaux d'hiver) et pour la plupart des articles de sport et de loisirs (p.ex., bicyclettes et skis de fond).

La nouvelle pratique consiste à extrapoler l'indice pour le bien faisant l'objet de relevés saisonniers à partir du mouvement de l'indice pour les produits du même groupe dont les prix sont relevés en permanence.

Par exemple, l'indice de février des manteaux d'hiver pour femmes représenterait l'indice de janvier multiplié par le ratio de l'indice de février à l'indice de janvier pour un agrégat de vêtements pour femmes. Cet agrégat, de même que tous les autres utilisés dans l'imputation saisonnière, ne comprend aucun groupe de base faisant l'objet de relevés saisonniers.

Les imputations par report étaient faites pour les prix des articles au niveau du point de vente; les imputations fondées sur le groupe sont faites pour les indices de prix au niveau du groupe de base. Dans la mesure du possible, le groupe servant pour l'imputation est celui qui se situe immédiatement au-dessus du produit visé dans la classification primaire. Si ce groupe ne comprend aucun groupe de base faisant l'objet de relevés continuels, on utilise à sa place le groupe qui se situe un cran plus haut dans la classification primaire.

Calcul
L'indice est calculé selon la formule de Laspeyres sous forme de moyenne arithmétique pondérée à base fixe, les pondérations correspondant à la période de base.

On calcule les prix mensuels moyens pour chaque produit observé dans chaque strate de centres urbains. On calcule alors des indices de prix d'un mois sur l'autre sous forme de ratios des prix moyens correspondants pour le mois donné et pour le mois précédent. Les indices de prix dont la base est autre que le mois précédent ne sont pas calculés directement par comparaison (division) des prix moyens mais par multiplication de tous les indices d'un mois à l'autre postérieurs à cette base jusqu'au mois donné. Si un groupe de base est représenté par plusieurs produits observés, on calcule d'abord les indices de prix pour chacun de ces produits observés et leur moyenne pondérée constitue l'estimation du mouvement de prix pour ce groupe de base.

L'indice national peut être calculé soit comme indice de prix à panier fixe relatif à la structure des dépenses familiales de 1986, soit comme moyenne arithmétique pondérée d'indices des prix correspondant à l'ensemble des 82 centres urbains.

Autres informations
Avec l'introduction du panier de 1986, l'IPC représente 82 centres urbains regroupés en 34 strates de centres urbains et 10 provinces. On publie toutefois des indices des prix à la consommation seulement pour les dix-huit centres urbains suivants: St. John's, Charlottetown-Summerside, Halifax, Saint John, Québec, Montréal, Ottawa, Toronto, Thunder Bay, Winnipeg, Regina, Saskatoon, Edmonton, Calgary, Vancouver, Victoria, Whitehorse et Yellowknife.

Organisation et publication
Statistique Canada, Division des prix: «L'indice des prix à la consommation» (Ottawa), mensuel, catalogue 62-001, bilingue (anglais et français).

idem: «Document de référence de l'indice des prix à la consommation, mise à jour fondée sur les dépenses de 1986», catalogue 62-553, bilingue (anglais et français).

CAP-VERT (PRAYA)

Dénomination officielle
Indice de preços no consumidor (Indice des prix à la consommation).

Portée
L'indice est calculé trimestriellement et porte sur l'ensemble de la population.

Base originale
1983 = 100.

Source des coefficients de pondération
La valeur des coefficients de pondération et le choix des articles résultent d'une enquête sur les dépenses des ménages effectuée en 1983 à Praia.

Pondération et composition

Groupes principaux	Nombre d'articles	Pondération	Nombre approximatif de relevés de prix
Alimentation et tabac	83	...	...
Habillement et chaussure	40	...	...
Combustible, électricité et eau	4	...	...
Mobilier et articles de ménage	9	...	...
Hygiène et soins personnels	5	...	...
Transports et communications	4	...	...
Total	145	...	...

Dépenses de consommation des ménages
Pas disponible.

Mode de relevé des prix
Les prix sont relevés auprès de points de vente au détail et prestataires de services à Praia.

Logement
Le loyer n'est pas compris dans l'indice.

Spécification des variétés
Pas disponible.

Substitution, changement de qualité, etc.
Pas disponible.

Articles saisonniers
Pas disponible.

Calcul
L'indice est calculé selon la formule de Laspeyres sous forme de moyenne arithmétique pondérée à base fixe, les coefficients de pondération correspondant à la période de base.

Autres informations
Un indice pour St. Vincent est également calculé.

Organisation et publication
Direcçao-geral de Estatistica: «Indices de preços no consumidor, Praia 1984-1986», janvier 1987, Praia.

REP. CENTRAFRICAINE (BANGUI)

Dénomination officielle
Indice des prix à la consommation.

Portée
L'indice est calculé mensuellement et porte sur tous les ménages urbains dont le chef est ouvrier ou employé résidant à Bangui.

Base originale
1981 = 100.

Source des coefficients de pondération
Les coefficients de pondération et les articles sélectionnés ont été déterminés sur la base des résultats d'une enquête sur les dépenses des ménages effectuée au cours de la période 1975-1976. L'enquête a porté sur l'ensemble du pays et les régions ont été réparties selon six secteurs géographiques importants. La taille de l'échantillon était de 1 530 unités budgétaires. L'indice se rapporte aux ménages résidant à Bangui. Les coefficients de pondération n'ont pas été ajustés pour tenir compte de l'évolution des prix entre la période de l'enquête et 1981.

Pondération et composition

Groupes principaux	Nombre d'articles	Pondération	Nombre approximatif de relevés de prix
Alimentation	76	705	585
Habillement et chaussure	14	85	30
Produits manufacturés	43	76	61
Combustible et éclairage	7	73	43
Services	20	61	33
Total	160	1 000	752

Dépenses de consommation des ménages
Les dépenses de consommation prises en compte dans le calcul de l'indice comprennent tous les biens et services consommés par les ménages de référence. En sont exclus l'impôt sur le revenu, les cotisations de la sécurité sociale, les intérêts payés pour les dettes, les primes d'assurances, les achats ou constructions d'immeubles, les achats de mobilier, les dépenses importantes pour l'entretien des immeubles et les biens produits par les ménages pour leur propre consommation.

Mode de relevé des prix
Les prix sont relevés par des enquêteurs spécialisés auprès d'un échantillon représentatif de 37 points de vente au détail (grands magasins, petits magasins) pour les produits manufacturés et sur quatre marchés pour les denrées alimentaires. Les prix des produits manufacturés sont recueillis au cours de la deuxième semaine de chaque mois et ceux des denrées alimentaires au cours de la 1ère et 2ème semaines de chaque mois. Les prix des produits non affichés sur les marchés sont obtenus en interrogeant les vendeurs et en procédant ensuite à la pesée. Les prix pour l'électricité, l'essence et le gaz sont des tarifs officiels et sont relevés auprès de l'administration concernée.

Logement
Les données relatives au loyer sont obtenues une fois par mois pour des logements de trois pièces.

Spécification des variétés
Il y a des spécifications détaillées pour chaque article. Les produits sont vendus en unités de vente telles que le tas, le seau, la botte, le sachet, l'unité, le litre, le kg, etc.

Substitution, changement de qualité, etc.
Il arrive que l'enquêteur se trouve dans l'impossibilité de retrouver, à la période courante, le produit retenu à la période de base. Dans ce cas, afin de maintenir la représentativité de l'échantillon, il est recommandé de choisir un produit similaire ou un autre produit proche, mais en recalculant un prix fictif de base.

Articles saisonniers
Les prix des articles saisonniers ne font l'objet d'aucun ajustement.

Calcul
L'indice est calculé selon la formule de Laspeyres, sous forme de moyenne arithmétique pondérée à base fixe, les coefficients de pondération correspondant à 1975-1976.

Le prix moyen est égal à la moyenne arithmétique simple des prix relevés aux différents points de vente.

Autres informations
La Division de la statistique calcule également un indice des prix à la consommation en milieu d'assistance technique.

Organisation et publication
Division de la statistique et des études économiques: «Lettres mensuelles de la statistique» (Bangui).
idem: «Bulletin trimestriel».
idem: «Annuaire statistique».

CHILI (SANTIAGO)

Dénomination officielle
Indice de precios al consumidor (Indice des prix à la consommation).

Portée
L'indice est calculé mensuellement et porte sur l'ensemble des ménages privés de la ville de Santiago et de ses environs.

Base originale
Avril 1989 = 100.

Source des coefficients de pondération
La valeur des coefficients de pondération et le choix des articles résultaient d'une enquête relative aux dépenses des ménages, menée entre décembre 1987 et novembre 1988 dans l'agglomération urbaine de Santiago, portant sur un échantillon d'environ 5 500 ménages appartenant à tous les groupes sociaux. Le critère fondamental pour déterminer les biens et services devant être inclus dans le «panier» consistait à sélectionner tous les produits dont la part dans les dépenses totales des ménages est supérieure ou égale à 0,0325 pour mille.

En outre, si la part d'un sous-groupe de biens ou de services s'est avérée supérieure ou égale à 0,0325 pour mille et si aucun article du même sous-groupe n'a atteint ce taux, le choix s'est porté sur le(s) bien(s) dont la pondération est la plus importante.

Une fois sélectionnés les biens et services représentant un sous-groupe donné, il a généralement été procédé à la répartition proportionnelle de la pondération totale du sous-groupe entre les différents biens concernés.

D'autre part, dans le cas des sous-groupes non sélectionnés, leur pondération a été répartie, d'une manière proportionnelle, sur les biens sélectionnés du groupe auquel est rattaché le sous-groupe concerné.

Dépenses de consommation des ménages
Ont été considérés comme biens de consommation tous les biens et services acquis par les ménages, à l'exception des immeubles (terrains, logements et autres) et des valeurs mobilières (actions, bons, lettres hypothécaires, etc.).

Sont compris les primes d'assurance-vie, les virements, dons et paiements des assurances portant sur les biens de consommation (logements, véhicules). Sont exclus les avantages perçus en espèces, la valeur des logements occupés en propriété, les cotisations à la sécurité sociale et aux caisses de retraite, l'impôt sur le revenu et les autres impôts directs. Pour les achats à crédit, sont prises en considération les dépenses effectuées au cours de la période de référence.

Mode de relevé des prix
Les prix sont relevés par des enquêteurs auprès d'environ 3 700 points de vente au détail et établissements de services

Pondération et composition

Groupes principaux	Nombre d'articles	Pondération	Nombre approximatif de relevés de prix
Alimentation	137	32,98	...
Logement :			
Loyer et réparations	11	9,89	...
Combustible, éclairage et eau	6	6,40	...
Ameublement et articles d'équipement ménager, etc.	53	9,11	...
Habillement et chaussure	64	8,44	...
Transports et communications	19	16,96	...
Divers :			
Soins personnels et médicaux	32	5,15	...
Instruction et loisirs	35	6,90	...
Tabac	1	1,81	...
Autres biens	10	2,37	...
Total	368	100,00	...

dans les 28 zones de la ville de Santiago et de ses environs (Grand Santiago). Les relevés ont lieu chaque semaine pour l'alimentation, chaque mois pour les groupes logement, habillement et divers, et une fois par trimestre pour les soins médicaux.

Le travail de répartition de l'échantillon total des sources d'information, déterminé pour chaque produit et pour les différentes communes et les divers secteurs géographiques du Grand Santiago, s'est appuyé sur deux enquêtes complémentaires, en tenant compte des divers types d'établissements dans lesquels les différents articles sont disponibles. La première de ces enquêtes consistait en un recensement de plus de 6 000 points de vente au détail. Dans le cadre de cette enquête, il a été procédé à l'identification des établissements les plus représentatifs en matière de vente des différents produits pour chacune des communes du Grand Santiago, ainsi qu'à l'élaboration d'une typologie de ces établissements en fonction de la disponibilité des biens, et des sous-groupes, groupes ou regroupements de biens destinés à la vente.

La seconde enquête, désignée sous le nom de «points d'achat», a porté sur un échantillon d'environ 1 000 ménages privés. Cette enquête, également effectuée au niveau communal, visait à identifier les communes et les types d'établissements dont la fréquence et l'importance dans les dépenses des ménages du Grand Santiago est la plus grande.

Logement
Les données relatives au loyer sont obtenues trimestriellement.

Spécification des variétés
Parallèlement à la constitution du panier, la description détaillée des biens et services spécifiques susceptibles de faire l'objet d'un suivi de leurs prix a été effectuée avec le maximum de précision. Ce travail consistait à définir la qualité, la forme, la taille, le poids, la marque et l'aspect concret des articles sélectionnés. A cet effet, il a été tenu compte des informations provenant de l'enquête sur les dépenses des ménages, ainsi que des études de marché, de travaux méthodologiques connexes réalisés pour le Grand Santiago à une date récente et de l'expérience acquise par l'INE en matière de suivi des prix.

Substitution, changement de qualité, etc.
Lorsqu'un article disparaît, il lui est substitué un autre article comparable et la méthode d'enchaînement est appliquée. S'il n'existe pas d'article comparable, le coefficient de pondération est réparti sur les autres articles du même sous-groupe. Pour les changements de qualité, on applique la formule d'enchaînement.

Articles saisonniers
Ils n'entrent pas dans l'indice.

Calcul
L'indice est calculé selon la formule de Laspeyres sous forme de moyenne arithmétique pondérée à base fixe, les coefficients de pondération correspondant à la période de base.

Le rapport de prix pour chaque article est calculé en divisant le prix moyen de la période en cours par le prix moyen de la période de base. Les prix moyens sont les moyennes arithmétiques simples de prix obtenus dans les différents points de vente.

Autres informations
Des sous-indices sont publiés pour les groupes suivants: Alimentation, Logement, Habillement, Transports et Communications, Divers.

Organisation et publication
Instituto Nacional de Estadísticas: «Indice de Precios al Consumidor» (Santiago).
idem: «Informativo Estadístico».
idem: «Indice de Precios al Consumidor, Base Abril 1989 = 100, Aspectos Metodológicos».

CHINE

Dénomination officielle
Overall Staff and Workers' Cost of Living Index. (Indice général du coût de la vie des employés et ouvriers).

Portée
L'indice est calculé une fois par an et porte sur les employés et ouvriers de l'ensemble du pays.

Base originale
1950 = 100.

Source des coefficients de pondération
La valeur effective des quantités vendues et achetées à différents prix sert à établir les coefficients de pondération retenus pour le calcul de l'indice général.

Pondération et composition
Pas disponible.

Dépenses de consommation des ménages
Pas disponible.

Mode de relevé des prix
Les relevés sont effectués dans 140 villes et 230 agglomérations rurales et portent sur les prix officiels des magasins de l'Etat, les prix du marché libre, les prix négociés et les prix d'achat des excédents agricoles et des produits secondaires. Ces relevés portent sur 450 articles dans les villes et 400 articles dans les agglomérations rurales.

Logement
Pas disponible.

Spécification des variétés
Le prix d'un produit normalisé est adopté pour chaque article.

Substitution, changement de qualité, etc.
Pas disponible.

Articles saisonniers
Pas disponible.

Calcul
Pas disponible.

Autres informations
L'indice est également publié par régions et sur la base de l'année précédente = 100. D'autres indices sont calculés pour les résidents et pour les agriculteurs, les deux également par régions.

Organisation et publication
State Statistical Bureau: «Statistical Yearbook» (Beijing).

CHYPRE

Dénomination officielle
Retail Price Index (Indice des prix de détail).

Portée
L'indice est calculé mensuellement et porte sur les ménages privés disposant d'un revenu annuel net de 3 000 à 8 000 livres chypriotes en 1984/85 et vivant en zone urbaine.

Base originale
1986 = 100.

Source des coefficients de pondération
La valeur des coefficients de pondération et le choix des articles résultent d'une enquête sur les dépenses des ménages menée de mars 1984 à février 1985, qui portait sur un échantillon aléatoire de ménages habitant les territoires contrôlés par le gouvernement. Les ménages urbains et ruraux, toutes catégories sociales confondues, étaient représentés dans l'enquête. Toutefois, pour le calcul des coefficients de pondération, et à la suite des recommandations du Comité consultatif, seuls les ménages habitant en zone urbaine et disposant d'un revenu annuel de 3 000 à 8 000 livres chypriotes ont été pris en compte.

Cette catégorie comprend 56,9 pour cent de l'ensemble des ménages urbains et, en même temps, 22,9 pour cent des ménages à très faibles revenus, tandis que sont exclus 20,2 pour cent des ménages à revenus plus élevés. Les ménages composés de ressortissants étrangers et de personnes vivant dans des institutions telles que hôpitaux, maisons de retraite, etc., ont été exclus de l'échantillon.

Au total, 3 759 ménages représentant 2,5 pour cent de l'ensemble des ménages ont été énumérés, dont 2 363 dans les zones urbaines et 1 396 dans les zones rurales. Cependant, le nombre de ménages pris en compte pour le calcul des coefficients de pondération a été réduit à 1 346. Il s'agissait des ménages habitant des zones urbaines et appartenant au groupe dont le revenu annuel était compris entre 3 000 et 8 000 livres chypriotes. Les pondérations ont été ajustées pour tenir compte de l'évolution des prix entre le moment de l'enquête et 1986. La méthode d'ajustement était fondée sur l'évolution moyenne des prix durant les 12 mois de 1986.

Pondération et composition

Groupes principaux	Nombre d'articles	Pondération	Nombre approximatif de relevés de prix
Alimentation	98	3 206	2 226
Boissons alcoolisées et tabac	4	301	24
Biens durables ménagers et fournitures ménagères	52	679	342
Habillement et chaussure	42	958	252
Transports et communications	36	1 930	76
Loyer et logement	5	1 530	232
Combustible et électricité	4	208	9
Biens et services divers	72	1 188	397
Total	313	10 000	3 558

Dépenses de consommation des ménages

Les dépenses de consommation utilisées pour l'obtention des coefficients de pondération correspondent à la classification SCN des dépenses finales de consommation des ménages, auxquelles il convient d'apporter les précisions suivantes: (a) les dépenses consacrées à la loterie, aux jeux d'argent, aux paris sur les courses de chevaux, etc. n'ont pas été incluses dans le calcul des coefficients de pondération; (b) les dépenses consacrées au permis de circuler pour les automobiles et au permis de conduire ont été incluses.

Les biens produits par les ménages ont été évalués aux prix de gros et inclus dans les dépenses. En ce qui concerne les logements occupés par leur propriétaire, un loyer a été estimé, puis utilisé dans le calcul des coefficients de pondération. Les achats à crédit de biens durables ont été considérés comme des achats courants et le prix total des articles concernés a été pris en compte.

Les achats d'occasion ont également été pris en compte au prix d'achat. Les échanges de biens usagés et les paiements partiels de nouvelles acquisitions n'ont été pris en considération que dans le cas des automobiles, où seule a été utilisée, pour le calcul des dépenses, la différence nette entre le prix d'une vieille voiture et celui d'une nouvelle. Les contributions à la sécurité sociale et aux fonds de pensions ont été exclus des dépenses utilisées pour obtenir les coefficients de pondération. Les assurances sur les biens de consommation spécifiques ont été incluses. Les dépenses consacrées aux soins de santé n'ont été incluses que si elles ont été payées directement par un membre du ménage considéré. Les impôts sur le revenu et autres impôts directs, les primes d'assurance-vie et autres transferts au bénéfice de ménages tiers ont également été exclus. Ont cependant été inclus les achats de cadeaux pour d'autres ménages.

Mode de relevé des prix

Les critères du choix d'un article pour le relevé des prix ont été les suivants: disponibilité sur le marché de détail, importance par rapport au total des dépenses, unité de mesure, qualité, variété et autres spécifications disponibles. En ce qui concerne les articles pour lesquels aucun prix n'est établi, l'ajustement de leur coefficient de pondération a été calculé proportionnellement à celui d'autres articles semblables pour lesquels des prix avaient effectivement été fixés.

Etant donné qu'aucune enquête n'a été menée sur les points d'achat, les magasins où s'effectue le relevé des prix ont été sélectionnés par des procédés empiriques, de manière à inclure un échantillon représentatif des commerces fréquentés par la population de l'indice. Les points de vente retenus ont été restreints aux trois plus grandes villes, à savoir Nicosie, Limassol et Larnaca. Les prix sont relevés, pour chaque type de bien ou de service, auprès de deux points de vente de chaque ville, par des enquêteurs spécialement formés du Department of Statistics and Research.

La fréquence des relevés de prix diffère selon les produits concernés. Pour les fruits et légumes frais, les relevés ont lieu une fois par semaine (tous les jeudis) au marché municipal, tandis que pour les autres articles les prix sont relevés une fois par mois (le jeudi le plus proche du 15 de chaque mois). Pour les articles dont le prix est contrôlé (tels que le combustible, l'électricité, le téléphone, l'eau, etc.) les données sont obtenues à partir des factures adressées par les organismes concernés.

Les prix retenus sont les prix réellement payés par les acheteurs. A partir de 1991, sont prises en compte les réductions, les soldes et les offres spéciales à caractère saisonnier. Ces campagnes commerciales se tiennent aujourd'hui régulièrement deux fois l'an, en février et en août/septembre. Elles sont réglementées par la loi entrée en vigueur en 1991. Les prix du marché noir et les prix à crédit ne sont pas pris en considération. Les prix d'importation sont répercutés sur les prix de détail des produits concernés.

Logement

Les données relatives au loyer sont obtenues tous les deux mois sur 200 logements, au moyen de questionnaires adressés par la poste ou de visites à domicile en cas de non-réponse. Les 200 logements de l'échantillon ont été tirés par sondage aléatoire effectué dans les villes de Nicosie (98), Limassol (70) et Larnaca (32). Le nombre de logements sélectionnés pour chaque ville a été déterminé en fonction de la répartition de sa population. Le choix de l'échantillon a été restreint aux logements urbains dont le loyer mensuel se situe entre 30 et 100 livres chypriotes, comme l'a montré l'enquête sur les dépenses des ménages. Ce groupe représente 77,5 pour cent du total des logements urbains en location. En sont exclus 19,3 pour cent des loyers à très bas prix et 3,2 pour cent des loyers les plus élevés.

La méthode de calcul de l'indice des loyers est la suivante: tout d'abord, le loyer moyen par logement est calculé pour chaque ville. On obtient ensuite un loyer national moyen en utilisant les mêmes coefficients de pondération que pour les autres articles de l'indice (c'est-à-dire 5 pour Nicosie, 3 pour Limassol, 2 pour Larnaca). Enfin, un rapport de prix est calculé en divisant le loyer national moyen du mois en cours par l'indice des loyers du mois précédent, ce qui permet d'obtenir l'indice du mois en cours.

Les logements occupés par leur propriétaire ont été pris en compte dans le calcul du coefficient de pondération global des loyers en leur attribuant un loyer estimé. Seuls les loyers effectivement payés sont pris en considération dans le calcul de l'indice des loyers, les loyers fictifs étant écartés en partant de l'hypothèse que leur évolution est semblable à celle des loyers effectifs.

Spécification des variétés

Les biens et services dont le prix est relevé font l'objet de spécifications détaillées, à savoir la taille, la fabrication, la marque, la quantité, la qualité, la présentation commerciale et autres caractéristiques, de manière à éviter les variations de prix qui pourraient être causées par des différences dans la qualité, l'emballage, le modèle, etc. La spécification des articles est, en principe, la même pour tous les points de vente, mais dans quelques cas les articles concernés sont définis séparément. Tous les mois, les enquêteurs doivent utiliser le même type de produit ou, le cas échéant, en notifier la modification.

Substitution, changement de qualité, etc.

Lorsque se produisent des changements en matière de qualité, les articles concernés sont substitués de manière à ce que les rapports de prix demeurent inchangés. L'introduction de nouveaux produits n'a lieu que lors des révisions des coefficients de pondération, environ tous les cinq ans. Il est tenu compte de la disparition du marché d'un certain type de qualité, la substitution étant effectuée par un autre produit similaire disponible sur le marché sans que soient modifiés les rapports de prix. Si la qualité du produit de substitution ne peut être directement comparée au premier produit, un ajustement de qualité est alors effectué.

La substitution est effectuée en enchaînant le prix du nouvel article à celui de l'ancien, un prix de base théorique étant fixé pour l'article substitué. Cette méthode rend nécessaire l'obtention du prix du mois en cours de même que celui du mois précédent.

Articles saisonniers
Les fruits et légumes frais sont considérés comme des articles saisonniers. Afin de résoudre les difficultés liées au caractère saisonnier de ces articles, il a été procédé à la composition d'un «panier» de fruits et de légumes différent pour chaque mois, sur la base de données obtenues auprès de tous les marchés municipaux de gros. Le coefficient de pondération attribué aux différents types de fruits et légumes est proportionnel à la valeur totale de leurs ventes, telles qu'elles ont été enregistrées sur les marchés de gros sur une période de trois années. En fait, les ventes relatives aux années 1983, 1984 et 1985 ont été calculées en combinant tout d'abord les quantités respectives de chaque article, puis en les multipliant par les prix de détail prévalant sur le marché pendant l'année de base 1986.

Il est à noter que, lors du calcul des indices relatifs aux fruits et légumes frais, les coefficients de pondération globaux sont maintenus chaque mois à un niveau constant alors que la variété et la pondération respective des articles sont modifiées chaque mois, en fonction de leur disponibilité. Pour ce qui est des articles qui ne sont pas en vente toute l'année durant, tels que les appareils de chauffage, les vêtements et les chaussures d'été ou d'hiver, les fleurs, le poisson frais, etc., le dernier prix enregistré est reporté pour les mois où ils ne sont pas disponibles.

Calcul
L'indice est calculé selon la formule de Laspeyres sous forme de moyenne arithmétique pondérée à base fixe, les coefficients de pondération correspondant à la période de base.

L'indice est calculé directement au niveau national. Un prix moyen pondéré est calculé pour chacune des trois villes principales, en utilisant les coefficients de pondération suivants: 5 pour Nicosie, 3 pour Limassol et 2 pour Larnaca, ces coefficients reflétant approximativement l'ordre de grandeur de leur population respective. Le rapport de prix est calculé en divisant le prix moyen du mois courant par celui du mois précédent et en multipliant le résultat par le rapport de prix du mois précédent.

Autres informations
Les principaux indices par sous-groupe sont publiés, ainsi que certains indices partiels spéciaux ventilés selon l'origine économique des biens et services.

Organisation et publication
Ministry of Finance, Department of Statistics and Research: «Monthly Economic Indicators».

idem: «Economic Report».

idem: «Statistical Abstract».

idem: «Labour Statistics».

idem: «Methodology of the Retail Price Index», Series I, Report 4, novembre 1988 (Nicosie).

COLOMBIE

Dénomination officielle
Indice de los precios del consumo - familias de ingresos bajos, (Indice des prix a la consommation - familles à revenu modique).

Portée
L'indice est calculé chaque mois et porte sur les ménages urbains à revenu modique.

Base originale
Décembre 1988 = 100.

Source des coefficients de pondération
Le choix des articles et la détermination des coefficients de pondération sont conformes aux résultats d'une enquête sur les dépenses des ménages effectuée de mars 1984 à février 1985, auprès de ménages privés servant à la population de référence de l'indice. De ce fait, l'indice des prix à la consommation porte sur un groupe social qui est le plus large possible tout en restant suffisamment homogène dans ses habitudes de consommation pour concourir à la définition de la population de référence. Aux fins de la présente étude, cette population de référence se définit comme l'ensemble des ménages privés résidant dans les zones urbaines de treize villes; en sont exclus les ménages d'une personne et les ménages collectifs, dont les habitudes de consommation sont très particulières, et les ménages aux revenus très élevés dont ces mêmes habitudes présentent une grande dispersion, le tout représentant 5 pour cent de la totalité des ménages recensés dans chaque ville.

Pour le choix des articles, les trois critères ci-après ont été retenus:

- poids relatif de la dépense correspondant à l'article: 5 pour cent ou plus des dépenses du groupe;
- fréquence d'acquisition observée: l'article doit être acheté par plus de 30 pour cent des ménages;
- possibilité d'identification, c'est-à-dire possibilité d'observer les prix et les quantités achetées.

Les coefficients de pondération n'ont pas été ajustés pour tenir compte des variations de prix entre 1984-85 et 1988.

Pondération et composition

Groupes principaux	Nombre d'articles	Pondération	Nombre approximatif de relevés de prix
Alimentation	77	42,58	2 540
Logement:			7 341
Loyer	1	19,35	...
Combustible, éclairage eau	5	4,82	...
Mobilier, ameublement, produits d'entretien, linge de maison	28	7,14	...
Habillement	24	8,16	1 715
Soins médicaux	13	3,30	1 037
Instruction et loisirs	18	4,79	990
Transports et communications	12	4,03	420
Divers	16	5,84	1 039
Total	194	100,00	15 082

Dépenses de consommation des ménages
Ne sont prises en compte que les dépenses qui correspondent à l'achat de biens et de services aux fins de consommation finale. Sont donc exclus de l'indice les dépenses afférentes à des opérations financières, le remboursement des dettes, les intérêts liés à l'usage de cartes de crédit, les impôts, amendes, etc. Une fois ôtées ces dépenses - qui sont prises en compte dans l'enquête sur les revenus et les dépenses, mais qui sont étrangères à la notion de dépenses de consommation - les autres dépenses sont regroupées en catégories conformes à la structure de l'indice des prix.

Les revenus en nature consommés par les ménages sont imputés aux dépenses des biens ou services respectifs; les logements occupés en propriété sont imputés à la pondération des loyers, mais seules les données relatives au loyer sont relevées. L'achat de biens usagés est traité comme toute autre acquisition; les cotisations à la sécurité sociale sont considérées comme une déduction du revenu.

Mode de relevé des prix
Les prix sont relevés par des enquêteurs auprès de points de vente au détail et de prestataires de services. Mais les établissements spécialisés dans la vente au détail ou la prestation de services ne sont pas les seules sources utilisées pour l'indice des prix à la consommation. Dans le cas des loyers par exemple, qui constituent un sous-groupe de la rubrique logement, les enquêteurs demandent directement au locataire combien il dépense à ce titre.

Comme autres sources d'information, il faut encore citer les entreprises de services publics municipaux, qui procurent aux enquêteurs les tarifs pratiqués pour l'adduction d'eau, le tout-à-l'égout, l'électricité et le téléphone. De même, les mairies communiquent les décrets qui fixent les tarifs des transports publics urbains.

Les prix des denrées alimentaires sont relevés avec une périodicité inférieure au mois: celui-ci est divisé en trois décades dans chacune desquelles l'enquêteur interroge un tiers des informateurs. Chaque mois, par conséquent, les informateurs sont interrogés une fois, alors que les prix sont relevés trois fois.

Sont relevés mensuellement des articles comme le prix des services publics (adduction d'eau, tout à l'égout, électricité, téléphone) et les tarifs des lignes d'aviation, à cause des variations que les uns et les autres présentent de mois en mois.

S'agissant de la visite des établissements informateurs, les prix y sont relevés chaque mois de l'année, à l'exception de certains articles qui font l'objet de relevés plus espacés:

- bimestriels pour les produits d'entretien, les médicaments, les produits d'hygiène corporelle;
- trimestriels pour l'habillement, le mobilier, l'électroménager, les fournitures scolaires;

- annuels pour le coût de l'inscription, de la pension et des livres dans les établissements scolaires.

Ces périodicités sont fixées en fonction de la variabilité relative dans le temps, du prix des biens et services considérés. Les prix de quelques articles - gaz de ville, gaz en bouteille, essence automobile, billets de loterie et de cinéma notamment - sont relevés dans la période où se produit la variation. Les prix observés ou relevés sont ceux que paie le consommateur pour un bien ou un service offert à la vente au détail et au comptant, au moment où l'enquêteur effectue sa visite dans l'établissement considéré.

Logement
Les données relatives au logement sont recueillies tous les quatre mois, mais les enquêteurs reportent chaque mois dans l'indice les variations de prix du quart de l'échantillon, les trois autres quarts y figurant sans variation.

Est seul pris en compte le prix des loyers proprement dit, et seuls sont considérés les logements privés. Les relevés se font par entrevue directe. Les logements occupés en propriété ne sont pas enquêtés.

Spécification des variétés
Une fois terminé le choix des articles, on en définit les différentes qualités, qui constitueront autant de variétés dont les prix seront à relever périodiquement pour chaque article. Il a été procédé, en janvier 1987, à une étude à cet effet dans les treize villes de l'indice; puis chacun des articles retenus a fait l'objet d'une spécification détaillée. Il avait été décidé en outre, comme condition essentielle, que les articles retenus dans chacun des sous-groupes devaient:

- présenter un évolution de prix comparable à celle des autres articles du sous-groupe;
- être habituellement consommés dans les ménages du groupe socio-économique considéré;
- présenter une garantie raisonnable de permanence sur le marché;
- être facilement observables.

Substitution, changement de qualité, etc.
Lorsqu'il n'est plus possible de relever le prix correspondant à une spécification figurant dans l'indice, ou quand il est nécessaire de remplacer l'établissement informateur, on procède à un «changement de référence», méthode qui permet d'annuler les variations de prix dues au changement de spécification ou de source. Toutefois, s'agissant des sous-groupes de l'habillement, dont les références et, en général, les spécifications, sont très changeantes, chaque nouveauté qui se présente à l'enquêteur fait l'objet d'une étude qui doit l'aider à décider de la validité de la variation de prix constatée.

Articles saisonniers
Ils ne font l'objet d'aucun traitement spécial.

Calcul
L'indice est calculé selon la formule de Laspeyres, sous forme de moyenne arithmétique pondérée à base fixe, les coefficients de pondération correspondant à la période mars 1984 à février 1985.

L'indice d'un agrégat (sous-groupe, ville, tout le pays) est la moyenne pondérée d'indices élémentaires, les pondérations utilisées correspondant à la structure des dépenses effectuées par les ménages à revenu modique des différents espaces retenus (en l'occurrence les treize villes).

Autres informations
D'autres indices sont calculés pour les familles urbaines à revenu moyen (employés), pour toutes les familles du pays (à revenus modiques et moyens), et pour chacune des treize villes (toutes familles, familles à revenu modique, familles à revenu moyen). Des indices de sous-groupes détaillés sont publiés.

Organisation et publication
Departemento Administrativo Nacional de Estadística: «Boletín Mensual de Estadística (Bogota)».

idem: «Boletín Mensual de Estadística» (Bogota), no 433, avril 1989 (pour de plus amples détails d'ordre méthodologique).

COMMUNAUTE DES ETATS INDEPENDANTS

Dénomination officielle
Indice général des prix à la consommation.

Portée
L'indice est calculé trimestriellement et porte sur toutes les familles urbaines et rurales de tous les Etats membres de la Communauté des Etats Indépendants (CEI).

Base originale
La période de base de l'indice utilisée dans les publications nationales est généralement une année = 100.

Source des coefficients de pondération
Les coefficients de pondération sont calculés à partir d'une enquête relative aux dépenses des familles effectuée tout au long de l'année 1989. L'échantillon était constitué par 90 000 familles vivant dans les zones urbaines et rurales des Etats membres de la Communauté des Etats Indépendants. Les pondérations n'ont pas été ajustées pour tenir compte de l'évolution des prix entre la période de l'enquête et la période de base.

Pondération et composition

Groupes principaux	Nombre d'articles	Pondé-ration	Nombre approximatif de relevés de prix
Alimentation	58	35,168	...
Boissons alcoolisées	4	9,620	...
Habillement et chaussure	27	22,616	...
Mobilier, articles et équipement de ménage	11	11,805	...
Produits d'entretien, soins personnels et médicaux, tabac, combustible, etc.	9	7,070	...
Services:			
Réparations, entretien, loisirs	11	6,462	...
Transports et communications	2	3,346	...
Loyer et taxes	1	3,418	...
Autres services	1	0,496	...
Total	124	100,000	...

Dépenses de consommation des ménages
Sont comprises toutes les dépenses de consommation, y compris les cadeaux. Tous les types d'impôts ou de contributions, primes d'assurances, revenus en nature et logements occupés en propriété sont exclus.

Mode de relevé des prix
Les enquêteurs procèdent au relevé des prix auprès d'approximativement 100 000 points de vente au détail et de prestataires de services dans l'ensemble du territoire des Etats membres de la Communauté des Etats Indépendants. Les localités et points de vente ont été sélectionnés sur la base des données relatives au volume et à la structure du chiffre d'affaires. Les relevés des prix ont lieu sept à dix jours avant la fin de chaque mois. Les données concernant les soins médicaux, les services communaux, les transports et communications sont obtenues mensuellement à jour fixe. Le commerce des marchandises à des prix spéculatifs est pris en compte lors du relevé des prix au marché noir à la fin de chaque trimestre. Cependant, il n'est pas pleinement tenu compte des interférences sur les prix moyens causées par la pénurie d'articles vendus à des prix fixes plus accessibles dans des points de vente officiels.

Logement
Pas disponible.

Spécification des variétés
Chaque article fait l'objet de spécifications détaillées portant sur la matière première utilisée, la qualité et les caractéristiques essentielles du produit.

Substitution, changement de qualité, etc.
Les changements de qualité sont pris en compte au cours de la période de relevés des prix dans les points de vente. Le prix de la nouvelle qualité est ajusté au moyen de la méthode d'enchaînement.

Articles saisonniers
Il n'est pas tenu compte des fluctuations saisonnières des prix.

Calcul
L'indice est calculé selon la formule de Laspeyres sous forme de moyenne arithmétique pondérée à base fixe, les coefficients de pondération correspondant à 1989.

L'indice général pour la Communauté des Etats Indépendants est un agrégat d'indices locaux des Etats membres de la Communauté, les coefficients de pondération correspondant à la structure de l'emploi, au niveau des revenus et à la rotation d'ensemble des marchandises.

Autres informations
Dans un certain nombre d'Etats membres de la Communauté, un autre indice des prix à la consommation est calculé pour une série de biens et de services normalisés pour des ménages disposant d'un budget de subsistance d'un niveau minimum.

Les données de la série d'indices des prix à la consommation décrite ci-dessus n'étaient pas disponibles au BIT lors de la publication du présent Volume.

Organisation et publication
Comité des statistiques: «Narodnoe Khozyaistvo» (Economie nationale).
idem: «Sotsialnoe Razvitie» (Développement social).
idem: «Bulletin statistique» (Questions spéciales).

CONGO (BRAZZAVILLE, AFRICAINS)

Dénomination officielle
Indice des prix à la consommation familiale africaine.

Portée
L'indice est calculé mensuellement et porte sur les ménages africains à Brazzaville.

Base originale
Décembre 1977 = 100.

Source des coefficients de pondération
Les coefficients de pondération et les articles sélectionnés ont été déterminés sur la base des résultats d'une enquête sur les dépenses des ménages africains effectuée de juillet 1976 à juillet 1977 à Brazzaville auprès de 100 ménages de toutes catégories.

Pondération et composition

Groupes principaux	Nombre d'articles	Pondération	Nombre approximatif de relevés de prix
Alimentation	70	58,6	1 035
Boissons et tabac	10	3,4	59
Habillement, chaussure et linge de maison	12	6,9	11
Logement, construction	17	10,1	17
Combustible, éclairage et eau	8	5,7	16
Hygiène et soins médicaux	15	3,8	47
Transport, loisirs	12	8,6	14
Divers	13	2,9	23
Total	157	100,0	1 222

Dépenses de consommation des ménages
Sont compris les paiements en nature et l'autoconsommation. L'impôt sur le revenu est exclu.

Mode de relevé des prix
Les prix de la plupart des articles sont relevés une fois par mois par des enquêteurs sur des marchés, auprès de différents points de vente au détail et prestataires de services. Les prix des denrées alimentaires fraîches vendues sur les marchés sont obtenus deux fois par mois. Les données relatives à l'électricité, l'eau, les transports, les soins médicaux et les loisirs sont recueillies une fois par trimestre. Il n'est pas tenu compte des rabais et des prix de soldes.

Logement
Les données relatives au loyer sont relevées trimestriellement auprès d'un échantillon de 14 logements de quatre pièces avec électricité et un robinet d'eau dans la parcelle, situés dans des quartiers centraux. Les logements occupés par leur propriétaire ne sont pas pris en compte.

Spécification des variétés
Les spécifications sont très détaillées.

Substitution, changement de qualité, etc.
Lorsqu'un article disparaît du marché, le dernier prix est répertorié pendant 3 mois au maximum; ensuite le prix d'un article similaire est relevé et, pour le calcul de l'indice, un facteur de correction est appliqué.

Articles saisonniers
Lorsqu'un article disparaît temporairement du marché on reporte le dernier prix relevé ou bien il est remplacé par un article similaire.

Calcul
L'indice est calculé selon la formule de Laspeyres, sous forme de moyenne arithmétique pondérée à base fixe, les coefficients de pondération correspondant à la période juillet 1976 - juillet 1977.

L'indice pour un article est obtenu en utilisant les rapports de prix de la période courante et de la période de base. Les prix moyens sont des moyennes arithmétiques simples de tous les relevés de prix.

Organisation et publication
Centre National de la statistique et des Etudes économiques: «Bulletin mensuel des statistiques» (Brazzaville).
idem: «Annuaire statistique du Congo».

CONGO (BRAZZAVILLE, EUROPEENS)

Dénomination officielle
Indice des prix à la consommation familiale européenne.

Portée
L'indice est calculé mensuellement et porte sur les ménages européens à Brazzaville.

Base originale
Janvier 1964 = 100.

Source des coefficients de pondération
Les coefficients de pondération et les articles sélectionnés ont été déterminés sur la base des résultats d'une enquête sur les dépenses des ménages effectuée de février à mars 1963 au moyen de questionnaires envoyés à un certain nombre de ménages européens de Brazzaville.

Pondération et composition

Groupes principaux	Nombre d'articles	Pondération	Nombre approximatif de relevés de prix
Alimentation	71	51,6	112
Articles et dépenses de ménage	18	6,9	24
Soins médicaux	5	3,1	10
Habillement, chaussure et linge de maison	13	7,7	15
Combustible, éclairage et eau	3	5,4	4
Services domestiques	5	6,7	5
Divers	20	18,6	21
Total	135	100,0	191

Dépenses de consommation des ménages
Sont compris les paiements en nature et l'autoconsommation. L'impôt sur le revenu est exclu.

Mode de relevé des prix
Les prix de la plupart des articles sont relevés une fois par mois par des enquêteurs auprès de différents points de vente au détail et prestataires de services. Les prix des denrées alimentaires fraîches vendues sur les marchés sont obtenus deux fois par mois. Les données relatives à l'électricité, l'eau et les transports sont recueillies une fois par trimestre. Il n'est pas tenu compte des rabais et des prix de soldes.

Logement
Les dépenses relatives au loyer ne sont retenues ni dans le calcul de l'indice ni dans la détermination des coefficients de pondération.

Spécification des variétés
Les spécifications sont très détaillées.

Substitution, changement de qualité, etc.
Lorsqu'un article disparaît du marché, le dernier prix est répertorié pendant 3 mois au maximum; ensuite le prix d'un article similaire est relevé et, pour le calcul de l'indice, un facteur de correction est appliqué.

Articles saisonniers
Lorsqu'un article disparaît temporairement du marché on reporte le dernier prix relevé ou bien il est remplacé par un article similaire.

Calcul
L'indice est calculé selon la formule de Laspeyres, sous forme de moyenne arithmétique pondérée à base fixe, les coefficients de pondération correspondant à la période février - mars 1963.

L'indice pour un article est obtenu en utilisant les rapports de prix de la période courante et de la période de base. Les prix moyens sont des moyennes arithmétiques simples de tous les relevés de prix.

Organisation et publication
Centre National de la statistique et des Etudes économiques: «Bulletin mensuel des statistiques» (Brazzaville).
idem: «Annuaire statistique du Congo».

REPUBLIQUE DE COREE

Dénomination officielle
All cities Consumer Price Index (Indice des prix à la consommation - toutes les villes).

Portée
L'indice est calculé mensuellement et porte sur les ménages d'ouvriers et d'employés habitant des zones urbaines.

Base originale
1985 = 100.

Source des coefficients de pondération
La valeur des coefficients de pondération et le choix des articles résultent d'une enquête sur les dépenses des ménages effectuée tout au long de l'année 1985, dans 50 villes, auprès de quelque 3 700 ménages privés, à l'exception des ménages d'agriculteurs et de pêcheurs, des ménages d'une personne, des ménages étrangers et des ménages dont les revenus et les dépenses sont difficiles à calculer. L'indice ne porte que sur les ménages d'ouvriers et d'employés. Les articles sélectionnés correspondent à plus de 1/10 000 du total des dépenses de ménage, représentent des groupes de produits de base homogènes et l'on peut en disposer pour une enquête suivie. Cependant, des articles d'une grande importance dont la consommation s'accroît sont compris même s'ils sont inférieurs à 1/10 000 dans l'ensemble des dépenses. La valeur des coefficients de pondération des articles dont le prix n'est pas relevé est répartie entre des articles similaires ou proportionnellement entre les groupes de même nature.

Pondération et composition

Groupes principaux	Nombre d'articles	Pondération	Nombre approximatif de relevés de prix
Alimentation	380,2	153	...
Logement	129,8	17	...
Combustible, éclairage et eau	76,1	9	...
Mobilier et articles de ménage	49,5	57	...
Habillement et chaussure	77,7	45	...
Soins médicaux	69,3	26	...
Instruction, lecture et loisirs	114,7	59	...
Transport et communication	64,6	16	...
Divers	38,1	29	...
Total	1000,0	411	...

Dépenses de consommation des ménages
Elles comprennent: les dons et dépenses analogues, l'achat à crédit de biens durables, les articles d'occasion, la reprise d'articles déjà usagés et le paiement partiel d'un nouvel article, les assurances liées à des biens de consommation spécifiques ainsi que les frais d'obtention de licences.
Sont exclues les dépenses ne concernant pas la consommation, telles que: l'impôt sur le revenu et autres impôts directs, les cotisations aux assurances sociales et aux fonds de retraite, les envois de fonds, les soins de santé, les versements autres que ceux effectués à titre de dépenses, par exemple le paiement des primes d'assurance-vie, la valeur locative des logements occupés en propriété et les revenus en nature.

Mode de relevé des prix
La méthode adoptée est essentiellement celle de l'entrevue personnelle. Cependant, certaines données relatives à des produits caractérisés par leur prix unique sont relevées à la suite d'entretiens téléphoniques (36 articles: électricité, gaz, eau, soins médicaux, instruction, transports, communications, etc.).
Le prix de la plupart des articles est établi trois fois par mois (le 5, le 15 et le 25 de chaque mois) à partir des données fournies par quelque 2 600 points de vente au détail et prestataires de services dans onze villes, à l'exception des locations d'appartements dont le relevé a lieu mensuellement, des places de théâtre et des frais scolaires dont le relevé est effectué tous les trimestres.
Bien que l'enquête relative aux prix soit effectuée le 5, le 15 et le 25 de chaque mois, ces dates sont remplacées le jour précédent lorsqu'elles tombent un dimanche; dans le cas d'un jour férié, elles sont déplacées deux jours avant. L'enquête portant sur les légumes et le poisson frais a lieu à heure fixe au cours de la même journée en raison de la fluctuation des prix. Ne sont pas retenus les prix des articles en réclame, en solde, vendus au marché noir, à crédit, ou d'occasion.

Logement
Les données relatives au logement sont obtenues mensuellement auprès d'environ 2 500 ménages extraits de l'échantillon de l'enquête sur les dépenses des familles et de celle portant sur la population active. N'entre pas dans l'indice le coût des logements occupés en propriété.

Spécification des variétés
Les articles font généralement l'objet de spécifications détaillées en raison de leur variété, prix, marque, et compte tenu du volume de leurs ventes.

Substitution, changement de qualité, etc.
Lorsqu'un changement considérable se produit en matière de qualité, la méthode d'enchaînement est utilisée comme suit:
P'o = Po × (P't/Pt)
P'o: prix de la qualité améliorée, à une période de base supposée
Po: celui de la qualité d'origine, à la période de base
P't: prix de la qualité améliorée, au moment du remplacement
Pt: celui de la qualité d'origine, au moment du remplacement
Lorsqu'un nouvel article fait son apparition sur le marché, il entre dans le sous-groupe auquel il appartient:
P'o = (P't/I) × 100
P'o: prix du nouvel article, à la période de base supposée
P't: prix du nouvel article, au moment de l'enchaînement
I: indice du sous-groupe, auquel le nouvel article appartient
Lorsqu'un type de qualité déterminée disparaît du marché et qu'aucun article de remplacement n'est disponible, le coefficient de pondération est réparti entre les autres articles du même sous-groupe.

Articles saisonniers
Pour les articles saisonniers comme le poisson, les légumes et les fruits frais absents du marché pendant la période horssaison, le prix retenu pour le calcul de l'indice est le dernier prix disponible aussi longtemps qu'on ne dispose pas d'un nouveau prix.

Calcul
L'indice est calculé selon la formule de Laspeyres sous forme de moyenne arithmétique pondérée à base fixe, les coefficients de pondération correspondant à la période de base.
Le rapport de prix de chaque article dans chaque ville est calculé en divisant le prix moyen de la période en cours par le prix moyen de la période de base. Les prix moyens représentent des moyennes arithmétiques simples des prix relevés dans chaque ville. Les indices pour un article dans 11 villes sont ensuite pondérés pour obtenir l'indice pour un article dans toutes les villes.

Autres informations
Des sous-indices sont publiés pour les articles les plus importants.

Organisation et publication
National Bureau of Statistics, Economic Planning Board, Bureau of Statistics: «Monthly Statistic of Korea» (Seoul).
idem: «Annual Report on the Price Survey» (pour de plus amples informations méthodologiques).

COSTA RICA (SAN JOSE)

Dénomination officielle
Indice de precios para consumidores de ingresos medios y bajos del área metropolitana de San José (Indice des prix à la consommation pour les familles à revenus moyens et modiques de la région métropolitaine de San José).

Portée
L'indice est calculé mensuellement et se rapporte aux familles à

revenus moyens et modiques résidant dans la région métropolitaine de San José.
Base originale
1975 = 100.
Source des coefficients de pondération
Les coefficients de pondération et les articles sélectionnés ont été déterminés sur la base des résultats d'une enquête sur les dépenses des ménages effectuée dans la région métropolitaine de San José pendant 52 semaines en 1974, auprès d'un échantillon de 1 633 ménages à revenus moyens et modiques, dont les gains ne dépassaient pas 5 499 colones en 1974. Les pondérations ont été ajustées pour tenir compte de l'évolution des prix entre la période de l'enquête et 1975.
Pondération et composition

Groupes principaux	Nombre d'articles	Pondération	Nombre approximatif de relevés de prix
Alimentation	59	40,76	1 845
Logement:			
Loyer	1	12,30	106
Combustible, éclairage et téléphone	7	6,62	13
Produit d'entretien, mobilier et articles de ménage	24	8,19	510
Habillement et chaussure	34	10,02	336
Divers:			
Soins personnels et médicaux	20	6,39	390
Instruction et loisirs	10	9,23	92
Transports	3	6,50	28
Total	158	100,00	3 320

Dépenses de consommation des ménages
Les dépenses de consommation des ménages correspondent aux biens et services consommés au moment de l'enquête. Les achats à crédit ne sont pris en compte que pour la partie payée pendant la période de référence. La valeur d'un article usagé utilisé comme reprise pour acquérir un nouvel article est exclue, mais seule la part effectivement payée est incluse. Le logement en propriété, les cotisations d'assurances sociales et de caisses de pensions ne sont pas pris en compte. La consommation du revenu en nature est prise en compte.
Mode de relevé des prix
Les prix de la plupart des articles sont relevés mensuellement par des enquêteurs auprès de points de vente au détail et de prestataires de services. Les prix des légumes et fruits frais sont relevés deux fois par semaine. Les rabais, les prix des soldes, les prix du marché noir et les achats d'occasion ne sont pas pris en compte.
Logement
Les loyers sont relevés chaque trimestre. Les logements occupés par leur propriétaire ne sont pas pris en compte.
Spécification des variétés
Les spécifications de chaque article indiquent les principales caractéristiques telles que qualité, poids, présentation etc.
Substitution, changement de qualité, etc.
Si la qualité d'un article change ou si un nouvel article apparaît sur le marché, il n'est pris en compte que lorsque les prix pour deux mois consécutifs sont disponibles.
Articles saisonniers
On ne tient pas compte de la saisonnalité. Les quantités restent fixes tout au long de l'année.
Calcul
L'indice est calculé sous forme de moyenne arithmétique pondérée à base fixe, les coefficients de pondération correspondant à 1975.
Autres informations
Les indices sont publiés au niveau du sous-groupe; les indices au niveau des articles peuvent être obtenus.

Une enquête sur les revenus et dépenses des ménages a été effectuée en 1987-88 pour actualiser la base de l'indice.
Organisation et publication
Dirección General de Estadística y Censos: «Indices de Precios para los Consumidores de Ingresos Medios y Bajos del Area Metropolitana de San José» (San José).

COTE D'IVOIRE (ABIDJAN, AFRICAINS)

Dénomination officielle
Indice des prix à la consommation (Africains).
Portée
L'indice est calculé mensuellement et porte sur les familles africaines d'ouvriers et d'employés composées de quatre ou cinq personnes, non compris les familles comprenant plus de trois adultes et plus d'un ouvrier ou d'un employé.
Base originale
Février 1960 = 100.
Source des coefficients de pondération
Les coefficients de pondération et les articles sélectionnés ont été déterminés sur la base des résultats d'une enquête sur les dépenses des ménages effectuée à Abidjan en août-septembre 1956 auprès de familles africaines d'ouvriers et d'employés composées de quatre ou cinq personnes; l'enquête n'a pas retenu les familles comprenant plus de trois adultes et plus d'un ouvrier ou employé.
Pondération et composition

Groupes principaux	Nombre d'articles	Pondération	Nombre approximatif de relevés de prix
Alimentation	47	51,1	...
Loyer	2	11,6	...
Combustible, éclairage, eau et savon	6	8,1	...
Habillement et chaussure	12	8,4	...
Biens d'équipement ménager	13	7,3	...
Services	9	8,5	...
Divers	11	5,0	...
Total	100	100,0	...

Dépenses de consommation des ménages
Pas disponible.
Mode de relevé des prix
Les prix des denrées alimentaires, du combustible et de certains autres articles sont relevés chaque jour sur quatre grands marchés. Les informations concernant les autres biens et services sont recueillies une fois par mois.
Logement
Les données relatives au loyer portent sur des appartements bon marché de trois pièces.
Spécification des variétés
Pas disponible.
Substitution, changement de qualité, etc.
Pas disponible.
Articles saisonniers
Pas disponible.
Calcul
L'indice est calculé selon la formule de Laspeyres, sous forme de moyenne arithmétique pondérée à base fixe, les coefficients de pondération correspondant à la période août - septembre 1956.
Autres informations
Une nouvelle série relative aux ménages africains dont le chef est ouvrier, employé qualifié ou artisan traditionnel à Abidjan (base août 1984-juillet 1985 = 100) est maintenant calculée. Les informations méthodologiques de cette série n'étaient pas disponibles au BIT lors de la publication du présent Volume.
Organisation et publication
Ministère de l'Economie et des Finances, Direction de la statistique: «Bulletin mensuel de statistique» (Abidjan).

COTE D'IVOIRE (ABIDJAN, EUROPEENS)

Dénomination officielle
Indice des prix à la consommation (Européens).

Portée
L'indice est calculé mensuellement et porte sur les familles européennes composées de deux personnes ou plus à Abidjan.

Base originale
1960 = 100.

Source des coefficients de pondération
Les coefficients de pondération et les articles sélectionnés ont été déterminés sur la base des résultats d'une enquête sur les dépenses des ménages effectuée à Abidjan en juin 1961 auprès de familles européennes composées de deux personnes ou plus.

Pondération et composition

Groupes principaux	Nombre d'articles	Pondération	Nombre approximatif de relevés de prix
Alimentation	57	50	...
Combustible, éclairage et eau	5	4	...
Habillement, chaussure, linge de maison et divers articles de ménage	28	8	...
Produits d'entretien, hygiène et soins médicaux	22	10	...
Services domestiques	2	8	...
Divers	26	20	...
Total	140	100	...

Dépenses de consommation des ménages
Pas disponible.

Mode de relevé des prix
Les prix pour l'ensemble des articles sont relevés par des enquêteurs sur cinq marchés, dans quatre grands magasins et auprès de certains prestataires de services. Les prix sont recueillis chaque jour pour les denrées alimentaires du pays, les articles du sous-groupe «Combustible» ainsi que pour certains autres articles et chaque semaine pour les denrées alimentaires importées; les prix des autres articles sont obtenus à la fin de chaque mois.

Logement
Les dépenses relatives au loyer ne sont retenues ni dans le calcul de l'indice ni dans la détermination des coefficients de pondération.

Spécification des variétés
Pas disponible.

Substitution, changement de qualité, etc.
Pas disponible.

Articles saisonniers
Pas disponible.

Calcul
L'indice est calculé selon la formule de Laspeyres, sous forme de moyenne arithmétique pondérée à base fixe, les coefficients de pondération correspondant à juin 1961.

Organisation et publication
Ministère de l'Economie et des Finances, Direction de la statistique: «Bulletin mensuel de statistique» (Abidjan).

Ministère des Finances, des Affaires économiques et du Plan, Direction de la statistique: Supplément trimestriel au «Bulletin mensuel de statistique» (Abidjan), Etudes et rapports No. 3, 1962.

DANEMARK

Dénomination officielle
Consumer Price Index (Indice des prix à la consommation).

Portée
L'indice est calculé mensuellement et porte sur l'ensemble de la consommation privée sur le territoire danois.

Base originale
1980 = 100.

Source des coefficients de pondération
Les coefficients de pondération ont été déterminés sur la base des statistiques des comptes nationaux de 1987. Dans les comptes nationaux, les dépenses totales de consommation finale des ménages sont réparties entre 63 groupes. La ventilation des dépenses à l'intérieur de ces groupes est fondée sur des informations plus détaillées tirées d'une enquête sur les dépenses des ménages effectuée en 1987 et portant sur un échantillon de 2 232 ménages privés. Les coefficients de pondération ont été ajustés pour tenir compte des changements de prix survenus entre 1987 et janvier 1991. Si la dépense effectuée pour l'achat d'un article était négligeable, son coefficient de pondération a été réparti proportionnellement sur les articles sélectionnés à l'intérieur d'un sous-groupe. L'ensemble des dépenses a donc été réparti sur les articles sélectionnés, avant le calcul des coefficients de pondération relatifs.

Pondération et composition

Groupes principaux	Nombre d'articles	Pondération	Nombre approximatif de relevés de prix
Alimentation	152	14,45	14 000
Boissons et tabac	21	6,63	900
Loyer et entretien	13	21,46	(a) 150
Combustible et éclairage	8	6,99	200
Habillement et chaussure	60	5,71	1 300
Biens d'équipement ménager	90	6,51	2 350
Soins médicaux	12	1,79	(b) 100
Transports et communications	64	17,19	700
Instruction et loisirs	64	9,47	1 800
Autres biens et services	47	9,80	500
Total	531	100,00	22 000

Remarque: (a) Entretien seulement, non compris une enquête semi-annuelle sur les loyers, portant sur un échantillon de 4 200 logements loués. (b) Non compris une enquête spéciale sur les médicaments couvrant l'ensemble de l'assortiment des produits.

Dépenses de consommation des ménages
Dans les comptes nationaux du Danemark, cette notion désigne la consommation finale sur le marché intérieur.

Mode de relevé des prix
Les prix sont relevés mensuellement auprès d'environ 1 500 commerces privés et succursales locales de chaînes de magasins et de 270 prestataires de services, organisations commerciales, etc.

Les prix de 71 articles, essentiellement des denrées alimentaires et des boissons, sont relevés par des enquêteurs auprès de 480 points de vente au détail situés dans 34 municipalités. Ceux des autres produits alimentaires, des biens d'équipement ménager non durables, des articles pour soins personnels, etc. sont relevés auprès de succursales de magasins multiples nationaux ou régionaux, soit à l'aide de listes de prix, soit de réponses à un questionnaire. Pour le reste, les prix des articles sont obtenus au moyen d'une enquête par correspondance effectuée tous les mois et portant sur un nombre variable de magasins répartis dans tout le pays. Les prix retenus pour le calcul de l'indice sont les prix que paie réellement le public. Les rabais et prix des soldes sont pris en compte lorsque la qualité et la quantité du produit ainsi offert sont conformes à la spécification qui lui correspond.

Logement
Les données relatives au loyer sont recueillies en avril et octobre de chaque année à partir d'un échantillon de 4 200 logements loués dans tout le pays. Il s'agit de logements d'une qualité supérieure à celle de la moyenne des logements sur le marché. Lorsque les loyers font l'objet d'un contrôle, toute solution au problème portant sur la différence de qualité présente un caractère quelque peu arbitraire. La méthode actuellement utilisée au Danemark consiste à évaluer le loyer d'un nouveau logement par rapport à celui d'un logement construit au cours de la dernière période triennale. En bref, l'incidence du loyer des nouveaux appartements sur le calcul est similaire à celle exercée par un indice séparé pour de nouveaux logements considérés en tant qu'articles à part. Le calcul de la valeur imputée du loyer des maisons occupées en propriété est fondé sur les informations relatives aux loyers des appartements loués.

Spécification des variétés
Un total de 345 articles visés par l'enquête par correspondance fait l'objet de spécifications détaillées portant sur le nom, la marque, la taille, l'unité, le modèle, etc. Le choix de la marque et du modèle est parfois laissé au commerçant, mais, une fois choisis, le nom, la marque et le modèle doivent figurer dans le questionnaire mensuel. Les articles dont les prix sont relevés par les municipalités font l'objet de spécifications moins strictes qui laissent une marge de choix à l'enquêteur. Mois après mois, celui-ci doit retenir la même variété ou signaler, le cas échéant, les changements de variétés.

Substitution, changement de qualité, etc.
Lorsqu'un produit n'est plus en vente, il est remplacé par un produit analogue ou son coefficient de pondération est ajouté à celui d'un autre article ou réparti dans le sous-groupe. Les changements de qualité des produits sont étudiés après consultation des négociants ou des fabricants/ importateurs. Lorsqu'une estimation du changement de prix imputable au changement de qualité est possible, il est procédé à une correction. Dans le cas contraire, il n'en est pas tenu compte pour le calcul du prix du produit de remplacement tant que l'on ne dispose pas d'un prix pour deux mois successifs. En ce qui concerne les voitures, les corrections apportées pour tenir compte des changements dans les modèles se fondent sur l'avis de l'association des consommateurs et de l'importateur/ producteur.

Articles saisonniers
Les prix du poisson (cabillaud, carrelet), des fruits frais (pommes, oranges, raisins) et des légumes frais donnent lieu à des corrections saisonnières.

Calcul
L'indice est calculé selon la formule de Laspeyres sous forme de moyenne arithmétique pondérée à base fixe, les coefficients de pondération correspondant à janvier 1991.

Les indices sont calculés en utilisant, pour beaucoup d'articles, des rapports de prix moyens, et pour d'autres, des moyennes de rapports de prix. Ces moyennes de prix ainsi que les moyennes de rapports de prix sont des moyennes arithmétiques simples ou pondérées selon la nature des prix relevés, les coefficients de pondération utilisés étant le nombre d'habitants des régions urbaines, ou découlant des données relatives au chiffre d'affaires du commerce de détail.

Autres informations
En plus de l'indice des prix à la consommation, il est procédé à la publication d'un indice qui exclut impôts et subventions: l'indice des prix nets.

Organisation et publication
Danmarks Statistik: «Statistiske Efterretninger» (Copenhague).
idem: «Nyt fra Danmarks Statistik» (bulletin).
idem: «Statistik Manedsoversigt».
idem: «Statistikservice: Prisstatistik».
idem: «Statistik Arbog».
idem: «Statistiske Efterretninger, Indkomst, forbrug og priser», No. 8, 1991.

REPUBLIQUE DOMINICAINE

Dénomination officielle
Indice nacional de precios al consumidor (Indice national des prix à la consommation).

Portée
L'indice est calculé mensuellement et porte sur les familles de tout le pays disposant d'un revenu mensuel compris entre 50 et 600 pesos dominicains en 1976/77.

Base originale
Mai 1976 - avril 1977 = 100.

Source des coefficients de pondération
La valeur des coefficients de pondération résulte d'une enquête sur les dépenses des ménages effectuée de mai 1976 à avril 1977 sur un échantillon de 4 457 ménages de deux ou plusieurs personnes représentatifs de l'ensemble de la population, dont le revenu mensuel était compris entre 50 et 600 pesos au moment de l'enquête.

Dépenses de consommation des ménages
Les dépenses de consommation prises en compte dans le calcul de l'indice correspondent aux achats de tous les biens et services effectués par les ménages de référence pour leur consommation et comprennent certaines dépenses relatives aux impôts directs, cadeaux, contributions, taxes postales et remboursements de prêts hypothécaires pour les logements occupés par leur propriétaire.

Mode de relevé des prix
La fréquence des relevés dépend de la nature des produits. Pour les articles du groupe «Alimentation, boissons et tabacs», les relevés sont en général quotidiens ou hebdomadaires selon le type d'article et la localité. Pour les groupes «Logement»,

Pondération et composition

Groupes principaux	Nombre d'articles	Pondération	Nombre approximatif de relevés de prix
Alimentation et tabac	46	...	...
Logement:			
Loyer et réparations	2	...	...
Combustible, éclairage, eau et téléphone	7	...	...
Mobilier et équipement ménager	8	...	...
Produits d'entretien etc.	9	...	...
Habillement et chaussure	33	...	...
Divers:			
Soins personnels et médicaux	17	...	...
Instruction et loisirs	6	...	...
Transports et communications	2	...	...
Total	130	...	...

«Habillement» et «Divers», ils sont hebdomadaires ou mensuels. Chaque relevé touche 4 300 établissements. Les prix de soldes ne sont pas retenus.

Logement
Les données relatives aux loyers sont relevées sur 604 habitations (cinq loyers par semaine). Sont pris en compte la valeur locative du logement, le coût des réparations, le remboursement des prêts hypothécaires, les charges mensuelles (assurances comprises).

Spécification des variétés
Chaque article fait l'objet d'une spécification portant sur les éléments suivants: nom sous lequel il est le plus connu localement, marque ou type, taille, poids, etc. Les enquêteurs disposent, pour chaque ville et chaque zone rurale, d'une liste des sources d'information et des spécifications de chaque article.

Substitution, changement de qualité, etc.
Les changements de qualité sont pris en compte dans le calcul de l'indice, au moyen d'une formule d'enchaînement.

Articles saisonniers
Les fluctuations saisonnières des prix ne font pas l'objet d'ajustements.

Calcul
L'indice est calculé selon la formule de Laspeyres sous forme de moyenne arithmétique pondérée à base fixe, les coefficients de pondération correspondant à la période de base.

Le rapport de prix pour chaque article est calculé en divisant le prix moyen de la période courante par le prix moyen de la période précédente.

Des indices séparés sont calculés pour les zones urbaines et rurales de chaque région principale du pays. Ces indices sont ensuite pondérés afin d'obtenir des indices urbains et des indices ruraux séparés pour l'ensemble du pays. Les indices urbains et ruraux sont finalement pondérés pour obtenir, l'indice national, les pondérations étant proportionnelles aux dépenses de consommation des régions concernées.

Organisation et publication
Banco Central de la República Dominicana: «Boletín Mensual» (Saint-Domingue).
Idem: «Metodología para el cálculo del Indice de Precios al Consumidor en la República Dominicana» (Saint-Domingue, 1982).

DOMINIQUE

Dénomination officielle
Retail Price Index (Indice des prix de détail).

Portée
L'indice est calculé mensuellement et porte sur tous les ménages privés du pays.

Base originale
Avril 1964 = 100.

Source des coefficients de pondération
Les coefficients de pondération et les articles sélectionnés ont été déterminés sur la base des résultats d'une enquête sur les dépenses des ménages effectuée en 1961 auprès d'un échantillon aléatoire de 232 ménages représentatif de l'ensemble des ménages.

Pondération et composition

Groupes principaux	Nombre d'articles	Pondération	Nombre approximatif de relevés de prix
Alimentation	51	56,9	...
Boissons alcoolisées et tabac	5	8,3	...
Logement:			
Loyer	1	3,7	...
Entretien et réparations	1	5,2	...
Combustible et éclairage	3	5,4	...
Articles de ménage et articles divers	11	4,6	...
Habillement et chaussure	12	9,5	...
Services	13	6,4	...
Total	97	100,0	...

Dépenses de consommation des ménages
Pas disponible.

Mode de relevé des prix
Les prix sont relevés à Roseau par des enquêteurs au cours de la troisième semaine de chaque mois dans trois magasins, sur un marché et auprès de prestataires de services.

Logement
Les données relatives au loyer sont obtenues mensuellement pour un type de logement composé de deux chambres à coucher.

Spécification des variétés
Pas disponible.

Substitution, changement de qualité, etc.
Pas disponible.

Articles saisonniers
Il n'est pas tenu compte des fluctuations saisonnières des prix.

Calcul
L'indice est calculé selon la formule de Laspeyres, sous forme de moyenne arithmétique pondérée à base fixe, les coefficients de pondération correspondant à la période de base.

Autres informations
Une nouvelle série (base juillet 1984 = 100) est maintenant calculée mais les informations méthodologiques relatives à cette série n'étaient pas disponibles au BIT lors de la publication du présent Volume.

Organisation et publication
Department of Economic Development and Planning, Statistical Division: «Annual Statistical Digest» (Roseau).

EGYPTE

Dénomination officielle
Consumer Price Index - All Urban Population (Indice des prix à la consommation - ensemble de la population urbaine).

Portée
L'indice est calculé tous les mois et porte sur tous les ménages urbains de l'ensemble du pays, sans limitations liées à la taille ou au revenu.

Base originale
Juillet 1986 - juin 1987 = 100.

Source des coefficients de pondération
La valeur des coefficients de pondération et le choix des articles résultent d'une enquête sur les dépenses des ménages effectuée en 1981-82 auprès d'un échantillon de 17 000 ménages. Les articles retenus pour le calcul de l'indice l'ont été en raison de leur importance relative dans la consommation des ménages concernés. Les pondérations des articles non retenus ont été réparties sur les articles qui présentaient la courbe des prix la plus proche, ou entre les autres articles de leurs sous-groupes respectifs. Aucun ajustement des coefficients de pondération n'a été effectué pour prendre en compte les changements de prix survenus entre l'époque de l'enquête et la période de base.

Dépenses de consommation des ménages
Au sens de l'indice, les dépenses des ménages sont définies comme les dépenses réelles consacrées aux biens et services de consommation durant la période de référence. Sont exclus l'impôt sur le revenu et les autres impôts directs, les primes d'assurance-vie, les transferts internes et externes, les versements relatifs aux produits livrés en dehors de la période de référence, les dons et les donations à titre caritatif.

Pondération et composition
Haute-Egypte

Groupes principaux	Nombre d'articles	Pondération	Nombre approximatif de relevés de prix
Alimentation	141	576,2	...
Loyer et eau	4	77,4	...
Combustible et éclairage	9	38,3	...
Mobilier, produits d'entretien et services à domicile	55	48,7	...
Habillement et chaussure	92	106,5	...
Soins médicaux	42	23,9	...
Transports et communications	14	29,9	...
Instruction et loisirs	29	27,4	...
Divers	16	71,7	...
Total	402	1 000,0	...

Basse-Egypte

Groupes principaux	Nombre d'articles	Pondération	Nombre approximatif de relevés de prix
Alimentation	141	575,5	...
Loyer et eau	4	72,0	...
Combustible et éclairage	9	37,6	...
Mobilier, produits d'entretien et services à domicile	55	44,1	...
Habillement et chaussure	92	116,5	...
Soins médicaux	42	26,8	...
Transports et communications	14	34,1	...
Instruction et loisirs	29	25,0	...
Divers	16	68,4	...
Total	402	1 000,0	...

Villes du Canal

Groupes principaux	Nombre d'articles	Pondération	Nombre approximatif de relevés de prix
Alimentation	141	567,2	...
Loyer et eau	4	64,8	...
Combustible et éclairage	9	36,0	...
Mobilier, produits d'entretien et services à domicile	55	59,9	...
Habillement et chaussure	92	106,5	...
Soins médicaux	42	23,1	...
Transports et communications	14	45,5	...
Instruction et loisirs	29	30,0	...
Divers	16	67,0	...
Total	402	1 000,0	...

Alexandrie

Groupes principaux	Nombre d'articles	Pondération	Nombre approximatif de relevés de prix
Alimentation	141	559	...
Loyer et eau	4	59	...
Combustible et éclairage	9	41	...
Mobilier, produits d'entretien et services à domicile	55	47	...
Habillement et chaussure	92	101	...
Soins médicaux	42	26	...
Transports et communications	14	63	...
Instruction et loisirs	29	32	...
Divers	16	72	...
Total	402	1 000	...

Le Caire

Groupes principaux	Nombre d'articles	Pondération	Nombre approximatif de relevés de prix
Alimentation	141	520	...
Loyer et eau	4	59	...
Combustible et éclairage	9	34	...
Mobilier, produits d'entretien et services à domicile	55	58	...
Habillement et chaussure	92	107	...
Soins médicaux	42	32	...
Transports et communications	14	67	...
Instruction et loisirs	29	45	...
Divers	16	78	...
Total	402	1 000	...

Territoires frontaliers

Groupes principaux	Nombre d'articles	Pondération	Nombre approximatif de relevés de prix
Alimentation	141	583,8	...
Loyer et eau	4	81,6	...
Combustible et éclairage	9	40,7	...
Mobilier, produits d'entretien et services à domicile	55	34,3	...
Habillement et chaussure	92	122,3	...
Soins médicaux	42	12,9	...
Transports et communications	14	42,9	...
Instruction et loisirs	29	23,6	...
Divers	16	57,9	...
Total	402	1 000,0	...

Mode de relevé des prix
Les prix de la plupart des articles sont relevés mensuellement par les offices statistiques régionaux. Les prix des services et

de certains produits manufacturés sont obtenus trimestriellement. Dans chacune des 26 villes couvertes par l'indice, chaque bien ou service doit être disponible dans au moins trois points de vente au détail. Parmi les 402 biens et services, les prix d'au moins 190 articles sont relevés centralement par le Département des prix. Les prix retenus dans le calcul de l'indice sont les prix effectivement payés par les consommateurs. Les prix contrôlés des produits rationnés sont pris en compte.

Logement
L'indice des loyers est calculé régulièrement en utilisant les chiffres relatifs aux logements démolis et ceux nouvellement construits, étant donné que le loyer des anciens logements est maintenu à un niveau constant par les autorités.

Spécification des variétés
Pas disponible.

Substitution, changement de qualité, etc.
Lorsqu'un article disparaît du marché, il est remplacé par un produit analogue. Le prix de base de l'ancien produit est corrigé par des spécialistes afin de prendre en compte le changement de qualité.

Articles saisonniers
Les fruits et légumes frais sont traités comme des articles saisonniers. Lorsque l'un d'eux n'est plus de saison, son coefficient de pondération est réparti sur les autres articles de son groupe.

Calcul
L'indice de l'ensemble de la population urbaine est la moyenne pondérée de six indices distincts: Le Caire, Alexandrie, Zone du Canal, Haute-Egypte, Basse-Egypte et Territoires frontaliers. Chacun de ces indices est calculé selon la formule de Laspeyres sous forme de moyenne pondérée des formules relatives. Après pondération par la population de la ville ou groupe de villes à laquelle ils se réfèrent, ils sont ensuite combinés pour former l'indice national. Les coefficients de pondération appliqués sont les suivants: 28.6% pour le Caire, 13.8% pour Alexandrie, 4.7% pour la Zone du Canal, 25.5% pour la Haute-Egypte, 25.9% pour la Basse-Egypte et 1.4% pour les Territoires frontaliers.

Autres informations
Des indices séparés sont publiés pour Le Caire, Alexandrie, la Zone du Canal, la Haute-Egypte, la Basse-Egypte et les Territoires frontaliers. L'indice pour la population rurale et des indices séparés pour la Haute-Egypte et la Basse-Egypte sont également publiés. Des sous-groupes sont publiés en détail pour toutes ces séries statistiques.

Organisation et publication
Central Agency for Public Mobilisation and Statistics: «Monthly Bulletin of Consumer Price Index» (Le Caire).

EL SALVADOR

Dénomination officielle
Indice de los precios al consumidor (Indice des prix à la consommation).

Portée
L'indice est calculé mensuellement et porte sur tous les ménages urbains à revenus moyens.

Base originale
Décembre 1978 = 100.

Source des coefficients de pondération
La valeur des coefficients de pondération et le choix des articles résultent d'une enquête sur les dépenses des ménages menée entre août 1976 et juillet 1977 auprès de 1 819 ménages urbains et 1 408 ménages ruraux. Les coefficients de pondération correspondent aux ménages urbains à revenus moyens.

Dépenses de consommation des ménages
Pas disponible.

Mode de relevé des prix
Les prix de la plupart des articles et services sont relevés au cours de la semaine incluant le 15 de chaque mois, par des enquêteurs qui opèrent dans la zone métropolitaine de San Salvador, Santa Ana et San Miguel. Quelques prix auxquels correspond une quantité incertaine sont établis par achat direct. Les relevés sont effectués les première et troisième semaines de chaque mois pour les fruits et légumes frais, tous les deux

Pondération et composition

Groupes principaux	Nombre d'articles	Pondération	Nombre approximatif de relevés de prix
Alimentation	56	42,78	...
Habillement et chaussure	30	8,38	...
Logement:			
Loyer	1	11,70	...
Eau, téléphone et services domestiques	3	2,97	...
Combustible et éclairage	7	3,87	...
Ustensiles et linge de maison	9	1,27	...
Equipement ménager	11	6,01	...
Produits d'entretien	4	1,23	...
Divers:			
Soins médicaux	7	2,54	...
Soins personnels	12	2,12	...
Instruction et loisirs	10	8,69	...
Transports et communications	7	7,76	...
Tabac	1	0,68	...
Total	158	100,00	...

mois pour les articles d'habillement et trimestriellement pour les meubles, l'équipement ménager et les soins médicaux et dentaires.

Logement
Les données relatives aux loyers sont obtenues en mars et septembre de chaque année sur un échantillon de 50 logements en location. Il n'est pas tenu compte des logements occupés par leur propriétaire.

Spécification des variétés
La spécification des variétés est traitée confidentiellement et prend en compte la qualité, le nom, la marque, le modèle, etc.

Substitution, changement de qualité, etc.
Lorsqu'un article fait l'objet d'un changement de spécification, il est traité comme un nouvel article, et le rapport de prix en est calculé après le deuxième relevé de prix de ce nouvel article, la pondération demeurant inchangée. A l'apparition d'un article entièrement nouveau, on en détermine, à l'aide d'une enquête spéciale, l'importance relative, et l'on remanie en conséquence les coefficients de pondération des autres articles du sous-groupe concerné.

Calcul
L'indice est calculé selon la formule de Laspeyres sous forme de moyenne arithmétique pondérée à base fixe, les coefficients de pondération correspondant à la période août 1976 - juillet 1977.
Le rapport de prix pour chaque article est calculé en divisant le prix moyen de la période courante par le prix moyen de la période précédente. Les prix moyens sont des moyennes arithmétiques simples.

Organisation et publication
Ministerio de Economía, Dirección General de Estadística y Censos: «Boletín Estadístico» (San Salvador).
Ministerio de Planificación y Coordinación del Desarollo Económico y Social, Unidad Investigaciones Muestrales: «Metodología para la construcción del índice de precios al consumidor, base Diciembre 1978 = 100» (San Salvador, nov. 1978).

EQUATEUR

Dénomination officielle
Indice de precios al consumidor - área urbana nacional (Indice des prix à la consommation, zones urbaines nationales).

Portée
L'indice est calculé mensuellement et porte sur les familles à revenu modeste et moyen des zones urbaines.

Base originale
Mai 1978 - avril 1979 = 100.

Source des coefficients de pondération
La valeur des coefficients de pondération et le choix des articles résultent d'une enquête sur les dépenses des ménages menée entre juillet 1975 et juin 1976 dans 12 villes de plus de 10 000 habitants. L'enquête, qui a duré 52 semaines, portait sur des familles à revenu modeste et moyen. On a corrigé le système de pondération pour tenir compte de l'évolution des prix entre 1976 et 1978-79.

Pondération et composition

Groupes principaux	Nombre d'articles	Pondération	Nombre approximatif de relevés de prix
Alimentation	18	396,0	2 413
Logement:			
Loyer	1	161,0	1 400
Combustible et éclairage	1	29,6	47
Mobilier, ameublement et articles d'équipement ménager	6	56,0	332
Habillement et chaussure	5	107,7	1 060
Divers	8	249,7	1 354
Total	(a) 39	1 000,0	6 606

Remarque: (a) Nombre de sous-groupes (entre 150 et 170 articles selon la ville).

Dépenses de consommation des ménages
Les dépenses de consommation comprennent tous les débours effectués par les ménages pour l'achat de biens et services de consommation. Les revenus en nature et le logement occupé en propriété comptent comme recettes et comme dépenses. Les biens achetés pendant la période de référence sont pris en compte. Pour les achats à crédit, ne sont retenus comme dépenses que les montants versés pendant la périodes de référence. Les achats d'articles d'occasion sont exclus. Les cotisations à la sécurité sociale déduites du revenu brut comptent comme dépenses de consommation. Sont encore retenus les primes versées pendant la période de référence au titre d'assurances sur des biens de consommation ou d'assurances-vie.

Mode de relevé des prix
Les prix de certains produits alimentaires de grande consommation sont notés chaque semaine ou chaque quinzaine par achat direct sur divers marchés. Les prix des autres biens et services sont relevés par des enquêteurs. Il s'agit dans tous les cas des prix réels payés par les consommateurs, impôts indirects compris. Les rabais, le prix des soldes, les achats d'occasion et les prix à l'importation ne sont pas pris en compte. Les prix fixés par les autorités ne sont pris en compte que si ce sont les prix réellement payés par les consommateurs.

Logement
Les données relatives au loyer sont relevées sur un échantillon de maisons, d'appartements et de chambres, à raison d'un sixième de l'échantillon par mois. Le calcul est effectué sur la base des moyennes arithmétiques pondérées. Il n'est pas tenu compte des logements occupés par leur propriétaire.

Spécification des variétés
Les variétés des biens et services de grande consommation font l'objet de spécifications portant sur la marque, la taille, le poids, l'unité, etc.

Substitution, changement de qualité, etc.
Lorsqu'un article disparaît, il est remplacé par un autre article aux caractéristiques comparables. Un article dont la qualité change est considéré comme un nouvel article donnant lieu à une correction effectuée à l'aide de la formule d'enchaînement.

Articles saisonniers
Les articles retenus dans le calcul de l'indice ont été choisis de manière à ce que la continuité des relevés de prix soit assurée toute l'année. Toutefois, lorsqu'un article n'est pas en vente pendant un mois donné, le relevé du mois précédent est maintenu.

Calcul
L'indice est calculé selon la formule de Laspeyres sous forme de moyenne arithmétique pondérée à base fixe, les coefficients de pondération correspondant à la période de base. L'indice de chacune des douze villes est calculé séparément, puis on calcule des indices régionaux et l'indice national en prenant comme coefficients de pondération les estimations de population de 1979.

Organisation et publication
Instituto Nacional de Estadística y Censos: «Indice de Precios al Consumidor, Area Urbana Nacional» (Quito).

ESPAGNE

Dénomination officielle
Indice de precios de consumo (Indice des prix à la consommation).

Portée
L'indice est calculé mensuellement et porte sur les familles composées d'au moins deux personnes disposant, à l'époque de l'enquête (avril 1980-mars 1981) d'un revenu compris entre 322 575 et 2 000 000 pesetas.

Base originale
1983 = 100.

Source des coefficients de pondération
Les coefficients de pondération et les articles sélectionnés ont été déterminés sur la base des résultats d'une enquête sur les dépenses des ménages menée entre avril 1980 et mars 1981 auprès d'un échantillon de 24 000 ménages dans l'ensemble du pays.

Pondération et composition

Groupes principaux	Nombre d'articles	Pondération	Nombre approximatif de relevés de prix
Alimentation et tabac	171	330	...
Habillement et chaussure	56	87	...
Logement	24	186	...
Ameublement, biens d'équipement ménager et services domestiques	56	74	...
Soins médicaux	18	24	...
Transports et communications	26	144	...
Instruction et loisirs	40	70	...
Autres biens et services	37	85	...
Total	428	1 000	146 000

Dépenses de consommation des ménages
Les dépenses de consommation entrant dans le calcul de l'indice se rapportent à tous les biens et services acquis par les ménages de référence pour leur consommation. Sont inclus les biens produits par les ménages pour leur propre consommation, les primes d'assurance et les impôts sur les véhicules. Sont exclus les impôts directs et indirects, les fournitures et matériels spéciaux à usage professionnel, les jeux de hasard, les soins vétérinaires, les intérêts payés sur des emprunts et les remboursements d'emprunts, les envois de fonds, les dons, etc.

Mode de relevé des prix
Les prix sont relevés par des enquêteurs sur les marchés, dans les supermarchés, dans d'autres points de vente au détail et auprès de prestataires de services, dans tout le pays. Pour les denrées périssables, les relevés sont effectués quatre fois par mois dans les grandes villes et deux fois par mois dans les autres. Pour les biens d'équipement, les relevés sont mensuels et pour les appareils électroménagers, ils sont trimestriels. Les prix, qui sont uniformes dans l'ensemble du pays (combustible, électricité, tabac, téléphone), sont tirés du «Boletin Oficial del Estado».

Logement
Les loyers sont relevés tous les mois pour un échantillon de 3 000 logements loués et 2 000 logements occupés par leur propriétaire. Les loyers protégés sont relevés annuellement et ceux du secteur libre mensuellement.

Spécification des variétés
Les spécifications dépendent de l'article et portent généralement sur la qualité, la marque et l'unité, mais non sur la date de fabrication.

Substitution, changement de qualité, etc.
Lorsqu'un article disparaît du marché ou que sa qualité change, on le remplace par un article analogue. De nouveaux articles ne sont inclus que lorsque l'indice est révisé.

Articles saisonniers
Il est tenu compte des fluctuations saisonnières des prix des fruits et légumes frais en variant les articles et leur coefficient de pondération à l'intérieur de «paniers» mensuels dont le coefficient de pondération d'ensemble demeure constant.

Calcul
L'indice est calculé selon la formule de Laspeyres sous forme

de moyenne arithmétique pondérée à base fixe, les coefficients de pondération correspondant à la période de base.

Dans le calcul de l'indice, les rapports des prix moyens sont calculés en divisant le prix moyen de la période courante par le prix moyen de la période de base. Tout d'abord, les prix moyens sont calculés sous forme de moyennes arithmétiques simples pour chaque unité primaire d'échantillonnage. Ensuite, ils sont pondérés en utilisant des coefficients de pondération de la population pour arriver à des prix moyens pour l'ensemble du pays.

Autres informations
Les groupes principaux sont publiés.

Organisation et publication
Instituto Nacional de Estadística: «Indice de Precios de Consumo - Boletín Informativo» (Madrid).

idem: «Indicadores de coyuntura».

idem: «Indice de precios de consumo, base 1983, Monografía Técnica» (Madrid, 1985).

ETATS-UNIS

Dénomination officielle
Consumer Price Index for All Urban Consumers (CPI-U). (Indice des prix à la consommation pour l'ensemble des consommateurs urbains CPI-U).

Portée
L'indice est calculé mensuellement et porte sur environ 80 pour cent de la population ne relevant pas d'une institution. Les résidents ruraux, les familles agricoles, les militaires et les personnes vivant dans des institutions sont exclus de l'indice.

Base originale
1982 - 84 = 100.

Source des coefficients de pondération
Les coefficients de pondération ont été déterminés sur la base des résultats d'une enquête sur les dépenses de consommation effectuée en 1982-84. Cette enquête était en deux parties; une enquête effectuée au moyen d'entretiens et l'autre au moyen de carnets de relevés. Environ 5 000 unités de consommation ont été contactées chaque année et pour chaque type d'enquête. Le concept d'unité de consommation est basée sur l'interdépendance économique dans une unité de logement et diffère donc des concepts de famille et de ménage. La pondération pour chaque article est une estimation de la dépense totale qu'effectue la population de référence pour cet article et est le produit obtenu à partir d'estimations des dépenses moyennes des unités de consommation et du nombre d'unités de consommation.

Pondération et composition

Groupes principaux	Nombre d'articles	Pondé-ration	Nombre approximatif de relevés de prix
Alimentation et boissons	100	17,627	44 102
Logement	97	41,544	(c) 18 864
Habillement, chaussure et entretien des vêtements	59	6,097	11 059
Transports	38	17,013	6 564
Soins médicaux	15	6,689	4 483
Loisirs	30	4,357	2 800
Autres biens et services	31	6,674	2 080
Total	(a) 370	(b) 100,000	89 952

Remarque: (a) Y compris 23 articles dont les prix ne sont pas relevés. (b) Importance relative décembre 1991. (c) Y compris 9 000 relevés pour l'habitation.

Dépenses de consommation des ménages
Les dépenses de consommation des ménages prises en compte dans le calcul de l'indice comprennent les biens et services achetés pour la consommation courante.

Mode de relevé des prix
Le choix des points de vente résulte de l'enquête sur les points d'achat effectuée chaque année dans environ un cinquième des régions urbaines comprises dans l'indice des prix à la consommation. Les unités de consommation sont enquêtées dans chacune des régions où les prix sont relevés. Les questions portent sur les achats d'articles spécifiques au cours d'une période donnée. Si un achat a été effectué, le nom et l'adresse du point de vente est relevé ainsi que le coût de la transaction. Le Bureau of Labor Statistics choisit un échantillon probabiliste de ces points de vente pour chaque catégorie de dépenses, en utilisant comme mesure de la taille de chaque point de vente les dépenses qui y sont effectuées. Ceci garantit un échantillon non biaisé des points de vente s'assurant ainsi que tous les types d'établissements sont représentés; ce système permet également l'estimation des variances et de l'erreur de l'échantillonnage.

Les prix de la plupart des articles et services sont recueillis par des enquêteurs du Bureau auprès d'environ 21 000 points de vente au détail et 6 000 unités de logements. Des enquêtes par correspondance sont utilisées pour obtenir les données relatives aux tarifs des services publics et aux prix de certains combustibles et autres articles. Les prix sont obtenus auprès de points de vente au détail et prestataires de service dans 85 centres urbains répartis dans l'ensemble du pays. Les prix des denrées alimentaires, du combustible et de quelques autres articles sont recueillis mensuellement dans ces 85 centres urbains. Ceux des autres articles et services sont relevés mensuellement dans les cinq plus grandes régions métropolitaines et tous les deux mois dans les autres régions. Le relevé des prix des denrées alimentaires est effectué pendant tout le mois. Les prix retenus pour le calcul de l'indice sont des prix réguliers au comptant, y compris tous les impôts directement associés à l'achat et à l'utilisation de ces articles.

Logement
Les données relatives au loyer proviennent de l'enquête sur les loyers. L'échantillon comprend environ 60 000 habitations classées en six listes. Chaque mois, les loyers d'une liste sont relevés par rotation afin que les mêmes habitations soient enquêtées tous les six mois. On applique une technique d'équivalence locative destinée à mesurer le coût des logements occupés par leur propriétaire. Le prix des matériaux utilisés par les locataires pour la réparation du logement est inclu ainsi que la valeur locative des logements de vacances occupés par leur propriétaire.

L'indice de l'habitation est ajusté afin de tenir compte du changement de qualité en raison du vieillissement du logement loué en utilisant la méthode de régression hédonique.

Spécification des variétés
Les articles à retenir pour les relevés de prix sont choisis par l'enquêteur lui-même dans chacun des points de vente de l'échantillon, en fonction des quantités (chiffrées en dollars) qui y sont vendues, c'est-à-dire selon la méthode de la probabilité proportionnelle à la taille (qui est ici la part du chiffre d'affaires). L'enquêteur rédige une description détaillée de l'article retenu en s'aidant d'une liste de contrôle, élaborée par des spécialistes, pour chaque article. C'est cette spécification propre au point de vente qui sert à identifier les articles à retenir pour les relevés de prix.

Substitution, changement de qualité, etc.
Lorsqu'il y a substitution, une correction est effectuée par un spécialiste pour tenir compte du changement de qualité. Quand cela s'avère impossible, la formule d'enchaînement est appliquée.

Articles saisonniers
Le prix des articles saisonniers disparus du marché est estimé en utilisant des procédures standard d'estimation.

Calcul
L'indice est calculé selon la formule de Laspeyres sous forme de moyenne arithmétique pondérée à base fixe, les coefficients de pondération correspondant à la période de base.

L'indice pour un article est obtenu en utilisant les rapports de prix pondérés de la période courante et de la période précédente. Les pondérations sont basées sur l'importance de l'article, du point de vente et de la région ainsi que sur le nombre des autres relevés de prix de l'échantillon.

L'indice pour l'ensemble des consommateurs urbains est une agrégation des 85 unités primaires de sondage où les prix sont relevés. Les pondérations reflètent la structure des dépenses courantes estimées à la période de base. Elles sont calculées pour chaque article dans chaque unité primaire de sondage et sont ensuite pondérées selon la population dans chacune de ces unités afin d'obtenir les pondérations par article pour l'ensemble des consommateurs urbains.

Organisation et publication
US Department of Labor, Bureau of Labor Statistics: «The CPI Detailed Report» (Washington, DC).

idem: «The Consumer Price Index: The 1987 Revision, Report 736»

idem: «The Consumer Price Index: BLS Handbook of Methods » Bulletin no 2285, chapitre 19.

ETHIOPIE (ADDIS-ABEBA)

Dénomination officielle
Retail Price Index for Addis Ababa (Indice des prix de détail à Addis-Abeba).

Portée
L'indice est calculé mensuellement et porte sur les ménages urbains ayant un revenu mensuel inférieur à 400 birrs éthiopiens en 1963.

Base originale
1963 = 100.

Source des coefficients de pondération
La valeur initiale des coefficients de pondération et le choix des articles résultent d'une enquête sur les dépenses des ménages menée à Addis-Abeba en 1963 sur un échantillon d'environ 600 ménages.

Pondération et composition

Groupes principaux	Nombre d'articles	Pondération	Nombre approximatif de relevés de prix
Alimentation et tabac	33	48,98	318
Loyer	...	...	...
Combustible et éclairage	4	10,23	42
Articles ménagers	3	4,37	33
Transports	3	4,52	30
Habillement et chaussure	6	6,71	30
Soins personnels et médicaux	11	2,64	87
Lecture et loisirs	5	2,57	25
Autres biens et services	9	5,43	36
Total	74	85,45	601

Dépenses de consommation des ménages
Les dépenses de consommation prises en compte dans le calcul de l'indice correspondent à tous les achats de biens et services effectués par les ménages de référence pour leur consommation. Elles comprennent aussi les assurances couvrant des biens de consommation déterminés et les redevances d'usage. En sont exclus l'impôt sur le revenu, les primes d'assurance-vie et l'épargne.

Mode de relevé des prix
Les prix sont relevés par le personnel permanent du Bureau central de statistique dans quelque 545 magasins de détail, marchés de plein air et établissements de services.

Les prix sont relevés chaque mois pour la plupart des articles. Pour les biens de consommation durables, habillement, transports et divers, ils le sont tous les trois mois.

Les prix retenus pour le calcul de l'indice sont les prix effectifs au détail. N'entrent en ligne de compte ni les soldes ni les rabais.

Logement
L'indice exclut les loyers.

Spécification des variétés
Tous les articles objets de l'enquête sur les prix à la consommation sont spécifiés en grand détail de façon à éviter des difficultés dans la collecte des données. Les spécifications comprennent le nom, la marque, l'unité employée, la couleur, l'état matériel, etc., de tous les articles compris dans l'échantillon.

Substitution, changement de qualité, etc.
Lorsqu'un article disparaît, il est remplacé par un article analogue ou bien on conserve le dernier prix relevé, jusqu'à la réapparition de l'article.

Articles saisonniers
Les prix de vente au détail du poisson, de la viande, de tous les fruits et légumes, des cahiers, crayons, parapluies et chaussures en caoutchouc subissent des variations saisonnières, dont on ne les corrige pas, pas plus qu'on ne calcule d'indice saisonnier.

Calcul
L'indice est calculé selon la formule de Laspeyres sous forme de moyenne arithmétique pondérée à base fixe, les coefficients de pondération correspondant à la période de base.

Organisation et publication
Central Statistical Office: «Statistical Abstract» (Addis-Abeba).

FIDJI

Dénomination officielle
Consumer Price Index (Indice des prix à la consommation).

Portée
L'indice est calculé mensuellement et porte sur les ménages urbains habitant les six principaux centres urbains de l'île.

Base originale
1985 = 100.

Source des coefficients de pondération
La valeur des coefficients de pondération et le choix des articles résultent d'une enquête sur les dépenses des ménages effectuée entre février 1983 et janvier 1984 auprès d'un échantillon de 4 402 ménages répartis dans l'ensemble de l'île de Fidji. L'indice porte sur 1 756 ménages habitant des zones urbaines. Les coefficients de pondération n'ont fait l'objet d'aucun ajustement visant à prendre en compte les changements de prix survenus entre l'époque de l'enquête et la période de base.

Pondération et composition

Groupes principaux	Nombre d'articles	Pondération	Nombre approximatif de relevés de prix
Alimentation	103	339,3	...
Boissons alcoolisées et tabac	7	63,8	...
Logement (loyer, taux d'intérêt, entretien)	9	186,1	...
Combustible et éclairage	3	48,7	...
Biens durables d'équipement ménager	36	75,6	...
Habillement et chaussure	32	63,1	...
Transports	15	112,9	...
Services	27	67,5	...
Divers	35	43,0	...
Total	267	1 000,0	...

Dépenses de consommation des ménages
Sont exclus l'impôt sur le revenu, les versements effectués aux caisses d'épargne et de retraite, les primes d'assurance vie, les sommes versées pour l'achat d'un logement et les intérêts hypothécaires, les cotisations sociales et les paris.

Mode de relevé des prix
Les prix sont relevés pendant les deux semaines du milieu de chaque mois auprès de centres situés dans la zone de Suva/Nausori et pendant la semaine du milieu du mois auprès des centres de Ba, Lautoka, Nadi et Labasa. En tant qu'indice fondé sur le même modèle de consommation qui s'applique à tous les résidents de Fidji, la zone Suva/Nausori est considérée comme représentative de la région Centre, celle de Labasa comme représentative de la région Nord et les centres situés à Ba, Lautoka et Nadi comme reflétant les changements de prix survenus dans la région Ouest. Pris conjointement, les changements de prix survenus dans ces zones sont considérés comme représentatifs des mouvements de prix survenus dans l'ensemble des zones urbaines de Fidji.

Les prix relevés pour la constitution de l'indice sont ceux pratiqués lors des transactions au comptant. Les enquêteurs effectuent une visite auprès de chaque centre et prennent note personnellement des prix et des pondérations des articles disponibles dans les magasins. Par exemple, lorsque certains prix ne sont pas affichés ou sont illisibles, les enquêteurs ont pour instruction d'obtenir directement l'information nécessaire auprès des dirigeants ou des responsables des supermarchés concernés. Les prix des articles «spéciaux» ou «en promotion» sont enregistrés lorsqu'ils sont pratiqués pour des articles de l'indice, sauf quand les prix ont été réduits pour cause d'endommagement et de manque de fraîcheur ou de détérioration des biens. Ces dernières conditions reflètent les changements de qualité de la marchandise et, pour cette raison, il importe que les variations de prix dues à des différences de qualité soient exclues de l'indice.

Les fonctionnaires du Bureau des Statistiques effectuent des visites personnelles auprès de chaque établissement pour enregistrer les prix et les informations relatives aux services imposés par le gouvernement et les organes statutaires sont obtenues directement auprès des sources compétentes. Une certaine constance est maintenue tous les mois pour visiter les établissements le même jour de la semaine et à la même heure, en particulier sur les marchés régionaux et municipaux où des variations considérables des prix peuvent survenir, par exemple, entre le matin et l'après-midi.

Aux fins d'évaluation des prix, les produits alimentaires sont répartis entre articles vendus sur les marchés municipaux et articles vendus en supermarchés. Dans les supermarchés, ces articles sont clairement définis en termes de taille et de marque et leurs prix sont affichés et lisibles. Cependant, avec les articles vendus sur les marchés, les fonctionnaires font usage de leurs propres instruments de mesure pour peser et attribuer un prix aux articles. D'une manière générale, trois échantillons d'un article sont prélevés sur le marché auprès de divers vendeurs et le prix moyen par unité est ensuite calculé par le Bureau. Les visites auprès des marchés sont effectuées le vendredi et le samedi, pendant la matinée, à des heures précises. Cette pratique a pour but de déterminer les prix normaux des biens périssables, lesquels se trouvent souvent détériorés vers la fin du jour de marché et généralement vendus à prix réduit.

Les prix du gaz de cuisine, du benzine blanc et du kérosène sont estimés à partir des établissements où ces produits sont habituellement mis en vente, alors que les tarifs de l'électricité sont, en raison de possibles modifications, contrôlés directement auprès de la Fiji Electric Authority, à intervalles réguliers.

Logement
Le loyer constitue la principale composante de cette rubrique. L'échantillon a été choisi parmi les logements en location sur lesquels portait l'enquête sur les dépenses. De ce fait, cet échantillon constitue un choix aléatoire de l'ensemble des logements en location occupés par des citoyens des Fidji en 1983. Les données relatives aux frais de location sont relevées mensuellement en même temps que les prix d'autres articles. Lors de chaque visite, il est demandé aux ménages si leur logement a subi une transformation: toute augmentation de loyer due à une telle transformation est alors ajustée au titre de changement de qualité. D'autres produits, tels les articles d'entretien, sont relevés suivant la méthode habituelle au moyen de visites mensuelles auprès des magasins fournisseurs de matériel.

Spécification des variétés
Après la sélection des articles de l'indice, il importait de décider la «marque» et les dimensions particulières d'un article déterminé qui devaient faire l'objet d'une évaluation. Lorsqu'un article particulier bénéficie d'un engouement manifeste, il est alors relativement aisé de le choisir parmi les détails relatifs aux dépenses et aux marques notifiées chaque semaine par les ménages durant l'enquête. Cependant, dans de nombreux cas, certains détails supplémentaires ont dû être obtenus auprès des distributeurs et responsables des supermarchés avant que les choix définitifs soient effectués. Les critères retenus pour inclure un article dans l'indice étaient les suivants: l'article concerné devait être représentatif, «bien se vendre» et se trouver généralement disponible dans les principaux centres commerciaux de Fidji.

Les spécifications relatives aux biens ménagers durables ont été élaborées à partir de modèles, de tailles et de matériaux de fabrication normalisés.

Substitution, changement de qualité, etc.
Lorsqu'un article n'est pas disponible à la vente, son prix est généralement conservé pendant trois mois, avant qu'un produit de substitution lui soit trouvé. On s'assure que ce dernier soit aussi semblable que possible à l'article original sur le plan de la qualité, de la taille et de la durée d'utilisation.

Articles saisonniers
Pour les articles saisonniers tels que les fruits et légumes frais, les prix de clôture de la saison précédente sont maintenus hors-saison.

Calcul
L'indice urbain national (relatif à la principale des îles Fidji) est calculé sous la forme d'une moyenne pondérée de trois indices régionaux (centre, ouest et nord de l'île). Chacun de ces indices régionaux est calculé selon la formule de Laspeyres sous forme de moyenne arithmétique pondérée à base fixe, les coefficients de pondération correspondant à la période février 1983 - janvier 1984. Les trois indices régionaux sont ensuite combinés, à raison des dépenses relatives de chaque région, pour constituer l'indice urbain national. Les parts des différentes régions sont les suivantes: 0,571 pour le centre, 0,361 pour l'ouest et 0,068 pour le nord.

Dans le calcul des indices par article, ont été utilisées les moyennes pondérées des rapports de prix entre la période en vigueur et la période de base.

Autres informations
Les principaux indices par sous-groupe sont publiés.

Organisation et publication
Bureau of Statistics, Suva: «Statistical News».
idem: «Methodological Report on the Consumer Price Index (Base average 12 months 1985 = 100)», Parliamentary Paper No. 22, 1988.

FINLANDE

Dénomination officielle
Consumer Price Index (Indice des prix à la consommation).

Portée
L'indice est calculé mensuellement et porte sur tous les ménages privés et tous les groupes de population du pays.

Base originale
1985 = 100.

Source des coefficients de pondération
La valeur des coefficients de pondération et le choix des articles résultent d'une enquête sur les dépenses des ménages effectuée en 1985. Portant sur tous les ménages privés et tous les groupes de population de l'ensemble du pays, l'enquête a duré un an. Au total 11 800 personnes appartenant à différents ménages de la population cible ont été sélectionnées sur la base d'un échantillon stratifié comprenant 25 strates. Sur ce total 8 200 ménages ont fourni des informations tout à fait acceptables. La probabilité de l'ensemble des réponses était de 69,5 pour cent. Les cas de non-réponse ont été les plus élevés pour les ménages d'une personne et dans les grandes villes. Pour certains articles, les données concernant la consommation ont été révisées en utilisant d'autres sources. Ces dépenses étaient relatives à la consommation d'alcool, de tabac, de confiseries et de boissons non alcoolisées. Le choix des articles était fondé principalement sur leur importance, leur représentativité, leur disponibilité et leur usage. La valeur pondérée d'un article ne définit pas toujours uniquement la contribution relative du dit article à la consommation. Elle peut représenter la valeur d'achat à la consommation combinée de plusieurs articles approximativement de même nature, dont les prix varient dans la même proportion et ne sont pas relevés.

Pondération et composition

Groupes principaux	Nombre d'articles	Pondération	Nombre approximatif de relevés de prix
Alimentation	111	19	...
Boissons et tabac	7	7	...
Habillement et chaussure	51	6	...
Logement, combustible et éclairage	9	19	...
Ameublement, équipement de ménage et services	70	7	...
Santé et soins médicaux	10	3	...
Transports et communications	34	17	...
Instruction et loisirs	57	9	...
Autres biens et services	54	13	...
Total	403	100	(a) 38 000

Remarque: (a) Les relevés de prix utilisés pour la mesure des articles de logement ne sont pas pris en compte dans le total des relevés de prix.

Dépenses de consommation des ménages
Dans son ensemble, la définition des dépenses de consommation utilisée pour les coefficients de pondération est pratiquement la même que dans l'enquête sur les ménages. Les dépenses de consommation s'écartent de l'enquête sur les ménages en ne prenant compte que des produits achetés. En d'autres termes, les coefficients de pondération de l'indice des prix à la consommation ne tiennent pas compte de la valeur des articles produits par les intéressés eux-mêmes tels que produits agricoles résultant de leur propre production, fruits à baie et champignons provenant de cueillettes etc.

En général, les dépenses de consommation sont enregistrées compte tenu de la notion d'achat. C'est ainsi que les articles achetés en régime de location-vente et à crédit (y compris les achats à crédit de produits durables) sont pris en compte dans les dépenses de consommation avant qu'ils ne soient payés (c'est-à-dire au moment de leur acquisition).

Dans les dépenses de consommation figurent la fourniture de biens et de services ainsi que la valeur des dons en nature.

Sont exclus des dépenses de consommation les dons et l'aide octroyés à d'autres ménages, tels que dons en espèces et en nature, journaux et revues, produits de consommation durables, voyages, indemnités d'entretien, paiements effectués directement à des ménages à titre de dédommagement.

Sont pris en compte dans les dépenses de consommation les biens et services reçus en tant que paiements en nature (sur la base d'un contrat d'emploi ou d'une rente viagère ou bien à titre d'assistance) ainsi que la valeur de biens reçus (par exemple logement, automobile, repas).

Les frais remboursables au titre de la loi sur l'assurance-maladie, de même que les dépenses en matière de voyages, médicaments, soins de santé et billets de loterie sont enregistrés sous forme de sommes nettes (c'est-à-dire après déduction des gains obtenus à la loterie et des remboursements).

Pour certains produits de consommation, les recettes provenant de la vente d'articles usagés ont été déduites de la valeur d'achat des nouveaux. Tel est le cas des appareils ménagers et des moyens de transport. Le paiement de certains articles assimilables à un transfert est considéré comme une dépense de consommation, étant donné qu'il a été effectué à titre volontaire. Au nombre de ces articles figurent les redevances et les amendes payées obligatoirement aux pouvoirs publics, les frais d'appartenance à des institutions à but non lucratif (églises, partis politiques, syndicats), les primes d'assurance et les paiements d'intérêts concernant les achats à crédit (soit primes d'assurance-vie et assurance-accident, primes d'assurance-voyage et de transport de marchandises, d'assurance routière, frais d'enregistrement et de permis, d'obtention de passeports et de visas, paiements d'amendes et autres versements de caractère obligatoire, adhésions à des syndicats, impôt ecclésiastique, dons, versements à des oeuvre caritatives etc, paiements d'intérêts sur prêts pour études et sur achats à crédit d'articles de consommation). De même que l'achat d'autres marchandises, les achats de marchandises usagées sont pris en compte dans les dépenses de consommation.

Sont exclus de ces dépenses l'impôt sur le revenu et autres dépenses directes, de même que les contributions aux fonds de pensions et aux régimes d'assurance sociale.

Le montant brut des primes d'assurance-automobile (responsabilité civile aux tiers obligatoire, et assurance du véhicule) est pris en compte.

Les bénéfices réalisés sur les changes, et ceux attribués au loyer des logements occupés en propriété, ne figurent pas dans les dépenses de consommation de l'indice.

Les primes d'assurance liées à des biens de consommation spécifiques sont prises en compte dans les dépenses de consommation. Dans les dépenses de consommation au titre de logements occupés en propriété sont compris les frais d'amortissement - usure, coûts d'entretien et autres frais fixes.

Mode de relevé des prix
Pour le choix des localités un échantillon aléatoire stratifié (stratification régionale) a été utilisé. Lors de la révision de l'IPC (1985 = 100) il n'a pas été procédé à la révision des échantillons; l'échantillon des localités et celui des points de vente proviennent de 1983.

Les centres dont la population est la plus élevée (agglomérations urbaines) des quatres principales régions de Finlande ont été utilisés en tant que principaux centres régionaux pour le relevé relatif aux localités. Les critères selon lesquels ces localités ont été choisies dans chacune des principales régions sont les suivants: importance de la population de la région, son revenu disponible, total de ses dépenses de consommation, total des dépenses de consommation dans cette région, l'adéquation des données concernant les prix en vue du calcul d'un indice fiable pour la région.

Dix-sept localités situées dans des centres régionaux ont été choisies. Les points de vente de ces localités ont été sélectionnés par l'enquêteur après consultation avec le personnel des Services chargés de l'Indice. Les prix des points de vente les plus importants et disposant de la plus forte clientèle ont été relevés et une attention particulière a été portée à la situation relative, dans la région, des points de vente de différents magasins de vente au détail et à la représentativité de différentes boutiques spécialisées. La sélection a porté sur environ 1 400 points de vente. Le relevé des prix des articles de l'indice a été effectué principalement à la suite des visites des points de vente par les enquêteurs. Par ailleurs, en ce qui concerne un petit nombre de produits alimentaires et d'autres biens périssables, les prix ont été relevés à partir des catalogues des points de vente concernés.

Les prix des produits alimentaires et autres biens périssables, des ustensiles de ménage, des produits de nettoyage et de lavage et autres fournitures de ménage sont relevés mensuellement. Les relevés ont lieu tous les deux mois pour les produits de consommation durables et certains types de vêtements; ils ont lieu une fois dans la saison pour certaines autres catégories de vêtements, les fruits de toutes sortes et les légumes; ils sont effectués tous les trimestres ou chaque fois que cela est nécessaire pour les services et autres articles.

Les relevés ont lieu entre le 11 et le 17 de chaque mois. Les enquêteurs ont été chargés de relever les prix sous une forme aléatoire dans le laps de temps spécifié, en évitant, par exemple, de répéter le relevé le même jour de la semaine.

Le relevé des prix a lieu: i) pour l'eau, le gaz et l'électricité, auprès des compagnies locales d'adduction d'eau et d'électricité; ii) pour les soins médicaux, auprès des services officiels des soins de santé, iii) pour l'éducation et la formation, respectivement auprès des universités et des organes de presse; iv) pour les transports et communications par demande d'informations centralisée auprès du Bureau central des statistiques au moyen d'appels téléphoniques, de consultation des barèmes officiels et de brochures ainsi que de visites rendues aux entreprises concernées.

Il est tenu compte essentiellement des prix de détail et de tout rabais normal sur le prix de détail dont chacun peut bénéficier. Les prix de solde normaux sont pris en compte, mais les rabais pour paiement au comptant et les achats en location-vente ou à crédit ne le sont pas. Les relevés de prix ne concernent que les articles neufs (les articles d'occasion n'entrent pas dans le calcul des coefficients de pondération).

Logement
Les loyers des appartements en location sont évalués en tenant compte des fluctuations de prix des loyers réellement payés. Tous les trimestres, le Bureau central des statistiques effectue une enquête sur les loyers. L'échantillon, sélectionné sur une base annuelle, comprend un total d'environ 24 000 logements en location. Il est demandé aux locataires de fournir des informations sur leur loyer en répondant à un questionnaire qui leur est adressé par la poste.

La fluctuation des prix des services concernant les appartements occupés en propriété est évaluée en tenant compte des fluctuations de prix des différents chapitres de prix, tels que frais d'entretien, intérêts et frais d'amortissement. Pour les maisons occupées en propriété, les frais d'entretien portent sur les réparations, le ramonage des cheminées, le ramassage des ordures, les redevances foncières, les primes d'assurances, l'eau, le nettoyage des rues. Les intérêts des prêts sur les logements, qu'il s'agisse de prêts conventionnels ou de prêts d'Etat à faible intérêt, sont évalués en fonction des fluctuations du taux d'intérêt nominal. Les fluctuations des amortissements sont prises en compte dans l'indice des prix du Bureau central des statistiques relatif aux appartements occupés en propriété.

En ce qui concerne ces appartements, les coûts d'entretien sont évalués en tenant compte des fluctuations des frais d'entretien et du coût des réparations. Les intérêts payés et les déductions au titre d'amortissements sont évalués de la même façon que pour les maisons occupées en propriété. La valeur des coefficients de pondération des différents chapitres de coûts des logements occupés en propriété résulte de l'enquête de 1985 du Bureau central des statistiques.

Spécification des variétés
Lors de l'établissement des spécifications détaillées des articles, il a été fait appel à la compétence de différents organismes (associations, organisations, sociétés commerciales, distributeurs, importateurs, fabricants et entreprises) de même qu'à celle du personnel des Services de l'IPC en ce qui concerne les articles concernés. L'OCDE a également été consultée en matière de comparaison des prix au niveau international.

Des spécifications détaillées (spécifications des qualités) ont été établies pour tous les articles dont les prix ont été relevés.

La spécification des articles (spécification des produits) indique les conditions auxquelles ils doivent répondre. L'enquêteur a fréquemment toute latitude pour procéder à la sélection finale des articles pour autant que ce choix ait lieu conformément aux directives en vigueur. Les spécifications des articles sont notamment les suivantes:
spécification détaillée de la qualité du produit; taille ou ordre de grandeur du produit; composition, matériau etc. du produit; pour certains articles, une liste de noms commerciaux acceptés dans le relevés des prix; pour certains articles, les instructions concernant le type d'empaquetage devant être utilisé. Dans quelques spécifications, le relevé de certains articles (principalement services, accessoires automobiles) a été limité à une marque, à un produit ou un service nettement spécifié.

Substitution, changement de qualité, etc.
Lorsque la qualité de certains articles change, les changements de prix qui ne sont dus qu'à un changement de qualité ne sont jamais pris en compte. Les changements de qualité portent sur les différences de matériau, de taille, de finition, de durée, ou sur les différences relatives à la force énergétique existant entre la qualité de l'ancien et du nouvel article. Les différences qui ne sont dues qu'au changement de mode ou au pays de fabrication du produit ne sont pas prises en compte en tant que changement de qualité du produit. L'évaluation du changement de qualité a toujours pour origine le service fourni au consommateur par l'ancien et le nouveau produit. Il en découle que du point de vue du consommateur, les changements des coûts de production ne reflètent pas nécessairement des changements de qualité.

Les articles mis chaque jour sur le marché ne sont guère soumis à des révisions en matière de changements de qualité, étant donné qu'ils sont vendus par unité: il s'agit, en d'autres termes, de prix au gramme ou au litre et non de prix à la pièce. Toute révision des changements de qualité de ces produits est effectuée par le Bureau central des statistiques.

En ce qui concerne l'habillement, les appareils électroménagers, ordinateurs familiaux et autres articles pour lesquels les relevés de prix sont assurés par un centre régional, le changement de qualité fait initialement l'objet de l'évaluation de l'enquêteur après consultation du vendeur sur la différence de qualité entre l'ancien et le nouvel article. La décision finale est prise par le Bureau central des statistiques qui assure un traitement uniforme aux changements de qualité qui ont lieu dans tout le pays.

Articles saisonniers
L'indice porte sur des produits qui ne sont mis en vente que pendant une partie de l'année. Au nombre des produits traditionnels mis en vente selon les saisons, on peut mentionner les pommes de terre nouvelles, et les fruits à baie. Il en est de même pour l'habillement, les équipements de sport, dont l'usage est prévu soit pour l'hiver, soit pour l'été. Les données relatives au prix des produits qui font l'objet de variations saisonnières sont relevées pendant les mois où ces produits sont mis en vente (ou achetés). Au cours des autres mois, leur prix se maintient au niveau du mois où ils ont été relevés pour la dernière fois. Il ne change que lorsqu'il est procédé de nouveau à un relevé de prix. Certains produits (les légumes frais par exemple) sont souvent vendus à des prix exceptionnels quand ils font leur apparition sur le marché ou lorsqu'on les en retire. Dans ce cas, il n'est procédé à aucun relevé de prix. On peut mentionner à cet égard les concombres produits sur place: leur prix ne figure pas dans le relevé du mois de mars.

Comme à tous les autres produits, le même coefficient de pondération est appliqué, tout au long de l'année, aux produits qui font l'objet de variations saisonnières.

Calcul
L'indice est calculé selon la formule de Laspeyres sous forme de moyenne arithmétique pondérée à base fixe, les coefficients de pondération correspondant à la période de base. Le rapport de prix pour chaque article est calculé en divisant le prix de la période en cours par le prix de la période de base.

Le rapport de prix d'un produit par zone importante est calculé en tant que moyenne arithmétique des rapports de prix des produits dont le prix est établi dans cette zone. Lors des calculs au niveau national, les rapports de prix des principales zones font l'objet d'une pondération qui tient compte de leurs coefficients de pondération respectifs (apports relatifs aux dépenses finales de consommation pour les principales zones).

L'indice est calculé en évaluant les indices des principales zones par rapport aux contributions relatives de ces principales zones aux dépenses finales de consommation. A l'intérieur de chacune des principales zones, il est procédé au calcul de l'indice par la pondération des rapports de prix des produits, compte tenu de leurs contributions relatives aux dépenses de consommation finales de la zone. Lorsqu'on ne dispose pas de données sur les prix de certains produits, les données du relevé précédent sont appliquées. Au cas où aucune donnée n'a jamais été relevée pour un produit, ce dernier est exclu de l'indice et n'exerce sur lui aucune incidence. Lorsque des données sont défectueuses, les enquêteurs s'efforcent d'obtenir des données correctes. En cas d'impossibilité, les données tenues pour correctes lors de la période précédente demeurent en vigueur.

Autres informations
L'indice est publié mensuellement au niveau des groupes principaux. L'indice général est également disponible selon les groupes de population suivants: exploitants agricoles à leur compte; toutes les personnes employées (direction et cadres salariés, autres employés salariés, ouvriers salariés); retraités; et en fonction des principales zones suivantes: agglomération d'Helsinki; autres régions du sud de la Finlande; centre de la Finlande; nord de la Finlande; ainsi que pour: les ménages d'une personne; les ménages sans enfant; les familles avec enfants. Il est également procédé au calcul de l'indice des prix nets et de l'indice du taux d'imposition.

Organisation et publication
Central Statistical Office of Finland: «Bulletin of Statistics» (Helsinki).

idem: «Consumer Price Index 1985 = 100», Studies No. 144, 1988.

FRANCE

Dénomination officielle
Indice des prix à la consommation des ménages urbains dont le chef est ouvrier ou employé.

Portée
L'indice est calculé mensuellement et porte sur les ménages urbains de toute taille dont le chef est ouvrier ou employé.

Base originale
1980 = 100.

Source des coefficients de pondération
Les coefficients de pondération sont révisés au début de chaque année civile sur la base des résultats d'enquêtes permanentes sur les dépenses des ménages effectuées auprès de 10 000 ménages et de données tirées des comptes des ménages dans le système de comptabilité nationale; les pondérations retenues pour le calcul des indices d'une année déterminée reposent sur les résultats de ces enquêtes pour l'avant-dernière année, résultats mis à jour jusqu'à décembre de l'année précédente. Le nombre de postes et les coefficients de pondération utilisés en 1992 sont les suivants:

Pondération et composition

Groupes principaux	Nombre d'articles	Pondération	Nombre approximatif de relevés de prix
Alimentation	91	22,67	...
Habillement, chaussure et linge de maison	59	8,36	...
Mobilier, ameublement, articles de ménage, produits d'entretien, tabac, etc.	82	25,64	...
Combustible et énergie	7	8,18	
Logement:			
Loyer	1	7,74	...
Eau	1	0,76	...
Entretien et réparations	3	1,22	...
Soins personnels et médicaux	12	6,14	...
Transports publics et réparations de véhicules	8	6,81	...
Autres services (y c. restaurants, etc.)	32	12,48	...
Total	296	100,00	180 000

Dépenses de consommation des ménages
Ne sont pas compris dans l'indice, les biens et services produits à la maison, les achats d'occasion, les services hospitaliers, les cotisations à la sécurité sociale, les primes d'assurance, les automobiles d'occasion, les transports maritimes et aériens, la location de voitures sans chauffeur, les services vétérinaires, les biens et services funéraires et les

services domestiques, mais les impôts indirects (TVA) sont compris dans l'indice.

Mode de relevé des prix
Les prix sont relevés par des enquêteurs auprès de 30 000 points de vente au détail et prestataires de services dans 108 agglomérations urbaines de plus de 2 000 habitants, mensuellement pour la plupart des biens et services, trimestriellement pour l'habillement et l'ameublement et deux fois par mois pour les produits frais. On ne retient pas les organismes de vente par correspondance. Les prix relevés sont ceux effectivement payés par les consommateurs.

Logement
Les loyers sont relevés à l'aide d'une enquête spéciale auprès des ménages pendant le premier mois du trimestre pour tous les types de logements. Les logements occupés par leur propriétaire sont exclus de l'indice.

Spécification des variétés
Les spécifications sont détaillées. Les enquêteurs choisissent dans chaque point de vente au détail les produits spécifiques pour les relevés de prix réguliers.

Substitution, changement de qualité, etc.
Si la qualité d'un article change, soit on le remplace par un article similaire en supposant qu'il n'y a pas de changement de prix, soit on mesure le changement de qualité et on le sépare du changement de prix. Les nouveaux articles ne sont pris en compte que lorsque leur vente devient importante.

Articles saisonniers
Il est tenu compte des fluctuations saisonnières des prix des denrées fraîches en variant les articles et leur coefficient de pondération à l'intérieur de «paniers» mensuels dont le coefficient de pondération d'ensemble demeure constant et en utilisant une moyenne mobile sur douze mois.

Calcul
L'indice est un indice-chaîne dont les pondérations sont révisées au début de chaque année civile. L'indice de chaque mois est calculé d'abord sur la base 100 en décembre de l'année précédente; l'indice ainsi obtenu est ensuite calculé, par raccord, sur la base 100 en 1980 (indice-chaîne de Laspeyres).

Autres informations
Des sous-groupes détaillés et des regroupements divers sont publiés ainsi que des estimations d'indices des prix à la consommation pour différentes catégories socio-professionnelles du chef du ménage (base 1970 = 100) et une série portant sur l'agglomération parisienne uniquement.

Organisation et publication
Institut national de la statistique et des études économiques: «Bulletin mensuel de statistique» (Paris).

idem: «Informations rapides».

idem: «Pour comprendre l'indice des prix».

GABON (LIBREVILLE 1)

Dénomination officielle
Indice des prix à la consommation - Africains.

Portée
L'indice est calculé mensuellement et porte sur les familles africaines résidant à Libreville et dont le chef est ouvrier ou employé (secteur public ou privé, y compris services domestiques).

Base originale
Juin 1975 = 100.

Source des coefficients de pondération
La valeur des coefficients de pondération et le choix des articles résultent d'une enquête sur les dépenses des ménages menée en 1968-69 à Libreville parmi 9 942 familles africaines dont le chef était ouvrier ou employé (secteur public ou privé, y compris services domestiques).

Dépenses de consommation des ménages
Les dépenses de consommation prises en compte dans le calcul de l'indice comprennent tous les biens et services importants achetés par les ménages de référence pour leur consommation. Elles excluent l'impôt sur le revenu, les dons et aumônes, les emprunts et remboursements, l'achat d'une maison et les dots.

Pondération et composition

Groupes principaux	Nombre d'articles	Pondération	Nombre approximatif de relevés de prix
Alimentation	57	547	...
Habillement et chaussure	9	175	...
Logement:			
Loyer et matériaux de construction	4	23	...
Combustible, éclairage, eau et savon	8	14	...
Equipement ménager	16	93	...
Soins personnels et médicaux	10	19	...
Transports	9	63	...
Loisirs et divers	12	66	...
Total	125	1 000	...

Mode de relevé des prix
Les prix sont relevés par des agents, durant la seconde moitié de chaque mois, dans des marchés choisis à cet effet, magasins de détail et autres points de vente.

Les prix retenus pour le calcul de l'indice sont les prix effectifs payés par les consommateurs.

Logement
Pas disponible.

Spécification des variétés
Les articles sont spécifiés par le nom, la marque, la qualité et l'unité employée.

Substitution, changement de qualité, etc.
Pas disponible.

Articles saisonniers
L'indice ne tient pas compte des fluctuations saisonnières des prix.

Calcul
L'indice est calculé selon la formule de Laspeyres sous forme de moyenne arithmétique pondérée à base fixe, les coefficients de pondération correspondant à la période 1968-69.

Organisation et publication
Présidence de la République, Direction générale de la statistique et des études économiques: «Bulletin mensuel de statistique» (Libreville).

Pour de plus amples détails d'ordre méthodologique, voir:

idem: «Changement de base de l'indice des prix à la consommation des ménages-types africains résidant à Libreville».

GABON (LIBREVILLE 2)

Dénomination officielle
Indice des prix à la consommation - Familles à revenu élevé.

Portée
L'indice est calculé mensuellement et porte sur les ménages africains dont le revenu mensuel dépassait 100 000 francs CFA et sur les ménages non africains des secteurs public et privé dont le revenu mensuel était inférieur à 100 000 francs CFA en mars et mai 1969. L'indice se rapporte à Libreville.

Base originale
Juin 1972 = 100.

Source des coefficients de pondération
La valeur des coefficients de pondération et le choix des articles résultent d'une enquête sur les dépenses des ménages menée entre mars et mai 1969 à Libreville sur un échantillon de 156 ménages à revenu élevé. Cet échantillon se composait de 20 ménages africains dont le chef disposait d'un revenu mensuel supérieur à 100 000 francs CFA à la date de l'enquête, de 59 ménages non africains du secteur public et de 77 ménages non africains du secteur privé dont le revenu mensuel était inférieur à 100 000 francs CFA.

Dépenses de consommation des ménages
Les dépenses de consommation prises en compte dans le calcul de l'indice correspondent aux achats de tous les biens et services effectués par les ménages de référence pour leur consommation. Elles excluent l'impôt sur le revenu, les dons et aumônes, emprunts et remboursements, achats de logements et loyers.

Mode de relevé des prix
Les prix de la plupart des articles sont relevés par des agents

Pondération et composition

Groupes principaux	Nombre d'articles	Pondération	Nombre approximatif de relevés de prix
Alimentation	84	511	...
Dépenses de ménage:			
Electricité, gaz et eau	3	56	...
Services domestiques	3	65	...
Produits d'entretien	7	21	...
Articles d'équipement du ménage et linge de maison	10	32	...
Habillement et chaussure	8	34	...
Hygiène et santé	10	35	...
Transports et communications	10	123	...
Divers	20	123	...
Total	155	1 000	...

vers le 25 de chaque mois dans de grands points de vente au détail, dans un marché et dans des établissements de services de Libreville. Les prix des aliments frais sont relevés chaque semaine.

Les prix retenus pour le calcul de l'indice sont les prix de détail effectifs.

Logement
Le loyer n'entre pas dans l'indice.

Spécification des variétés
Les variétés sont spécifiées par le nom, la marque, la qualité et l'unité employée.

Substitution, changement de qualité, etc.
Pas disponible.

Articles saisonniers
L'indice ne tient pas compte des fluctuations saisonnières des prix.

Calcul
L'indice est calculé selon la formule de Laspeyres sous forme de moyenne arithmétique pondérée à base fixe, les coefficients de pondération correspondant à la période mars - mai 1969.

Organisation et publication
Présidence de la République, Direction générale de la statistique et des études économiques: «Bulletin mensuel de statistique» (Libreville).

Pour de plus amples détails d'ordre méthodologique, voir:
Ministère délégué à la Présidence de la République chargé du Plan, du Développement et de l'Aménagement du territoire, Direction générale de la statistique et des études économiques: «Bulletin mensuel de statistique» (Libreville), no. 166-167, janv.-fév. 1973.

GAMBIE (BANJUL, KOMBO ST. MARY)

Dénomination officielle
Consumer Price Index (Indice des prix à la consommation).

Portée
L'indice est calculé mensuellement et porte sur le groupe des ménages à revenu modique, dont le revenu annuel, entre août 1968 et août 1969, ne dépassait pas 1 500 dalasis. Il se rapporte à Banjul, la capitale, et à Kombo St. Mary.

Base originale
1974 = 100.

Source des coefficients de pondération
La valeur des coefficients de pondération et le choix des articles résultent d'une enquête sur les dépenses des ménages menée d'août 1968 à août 1969 auprès de 618 ménages de Banjul. Les changements de prix survenus entre la période de l'enquête et la période de base (1974) n'ont pas été pris en compte dans la détermination des coefficients de pondération. Le critère de sélection des articles pour le relevé des prix consistait à retenir tous les articles de dépenses représentant au moins 0,5 pour cent du total.

Dépenses de consommation des ménages
Les dépenses de consommation prises en compte dans le calcul de l'indice correspondent aux achats de tous les biens et services importants effectués par les ménages de l'indice pour leur

Pondération et composition

Groupes principaux	Nombre d'articles	Pondération	Nombre approximatif de relevés de prix
Alimentation	52	580	...
Habillement, chaussure et linge de maison	12	175	...
Loyer	42	51	...
Combustible et éclairage	5	54	...
Divers (y c. soins personnels et médicaux, instruction, loisirs, tabac, etc.)	24	140	...
Total	135	1 000	...

consommation. En sont exclus les articles suivants: impôt sur le revenu, dons et aumônes, cérémonies religieuses ou autres (naissances, funérailles, mariages), emprunts, achats et entretien de véhicules automobiles, assurance-vie, crédit et épargne.

Mode de relevé des prix
Les relevés sont effectués par le personnel permanent de la Central Statistics Division dans quatre régions commerciales et auprès de 48 points de vente au détail et de prestataires de services à Banjul et à Kombo St. Mary. Les relevés sont effectués mensuellement pour la plupart des articles et deux fois par mois, par achat direct, pour certains articles présentant de fortes variations de prix. Les prix sont relevés une fois par mois pour les articles suivants: frais d'électricité, honoraires médicaux, coiffure, frais de scolarité, billets d'entrée dans les cinémas et pistes de danse, journaux, taxis et transports aériens, envois postaux aériens destinés à l'étranger, frais de blanchissage et de lavage.

Les prix retenus pour le calcul de l'indice sont les prix effectivement payés.

Logement
Les données relatives au loyer sont relevées en février, mai, août et novembre, auprès d'un échantillon de 42 logements en location. Cet échantillon est maintenu tel quel, excepté lors d'ajustements occasionnels.

Spécification des variétés
Une description détaillée de tous les articles est remise aux enquêteurs.

Substitution, changement de qualité, etc.
Lorsqu'un produit n'est plus en vente, il lui est substitué un produit analogue auquel on applique la formule d'enchaînement.

Articles saisonniers
Les fruits et légumes frais sont traités comme des articles saisonniers. Hors-saison, leurs coefficients de pondération sont répartis sur les autres articles du même groupe.

Calcul
L'indice est calculé selon la formule de Laspeyres sous forme de moyenne arithmétique pondérée à base fixe, les coefficients de pondération correspondant à la période août 1968 - août 1969.

Lors du calcul des indices par article, on utilise les rapports des prix de la période en cours et de la période de base.

Organisation et publication
Ministry of Economic Planning and Industrial Development, Central Statistics Division: «Consumer Price Index» (Banjul).

President's Office, Central Statistics Division: «Proposals for a new series of Consumer Price Index Numbers for Banjul and Kombo St. Mary» (Banjul, novembre 1973).

GHANA

Dénomination officielle
Consumer Price Index Numbers - National (Indices nationaux des prix à la consommation).

Portée
L'indice est calculé mensuellement et porte sur les ménages urbains et ruraux.

Base originale
1977 = 100.

Source des coefficients de pondération
La valeur des coefficients de pondération et le choix des articles résultent d'une enquête nationale sur les dépenses des ménages menée au cours de la période mars 1974-février 1975.

Lors de l'élaboration des coefficients de pondération, les dépenses portant sur des articles ne figurant pas dans l'indice ont été reportées sur les articles sélectionnés en tenant compte de la similitude de la nature des articles. C'est ainsi que le total des dépenses concernant les légumes a été reporté sur les légumes sélectionnés. Certaines dépenses ont été divisées en deux parties ou plus et reportées sur différents articles. Les dépenses concernant les repas préparés, par exemple, ont été divisées et réparties sur les principaux composants du repas.

Pondération et composition

Groupes principaux	Nombre d'articles	Pondération	Nombre approximatif de relevés de prix
Alimentation	71	49,2	...
Boissons et tabac	21	6,2	...
Habillement et chaussure	65	19,2	...
Loyer, combustible et éclairage	6	6,8	...
Mobilier, ameublement, équipement et dépenses de ménage	48	5,1	...
Soins médicaux et santé	8	1,8	...
Transports et communications	15	4,3	...
Instruction et loisirs	10	5,5	...
Divers	6	1,9	...
Total	250	100,0	...

Dépenses de consommation des ménages
Les dépenses de consommation prises en compte dans le calcul de l'indice correspondent aux achats de tous les biens et services importants effectués par les ménages de référence pour leur consommation. En sont exclus la valeur attribuée aux productions propres des ménages et consommées par eux, les intérêts, les taxes et redevances liées à l'usage de certains biens et services.

Mode de relevé des prix
Les prix sont relevés auprès de magasins de détail et de marchés sélectionnés de 9 centres urbains et de 30 centres ruraux. Les relevés sont effectués deux fois par mois à la date la plus proche du 8 et du 22 du mois. Les prix retenus pour le calcul de l'indice sont ceux que le public aurait dû payer le jour du relevé pour acquérir le bien ou le service demandé. Lorsque les articles sont en vente aux prix contrôlés dans les points de vente de l'échantillon, ces prix-là sont relevés et utilisés. Les enquêteurs sont équipés de balances qui leur permettent de convertir en poids standard les quantités vendues en vrac ou selon des mesures traditionnelles.

Logement
Les données relatives au loyer sont relevées sur un échantillon aléatoire de 300 logements de ménages urbains obtenu auprès des Municipal Assessment Registers (Registres de base d'imposition locale). Chaque mois, les loyers sont relevés sur un tiers de l'échantillon, de sorte que, par rotation, chaque logement de l'échantillon fait l'objet d'un relevé trimestriel. Tous les ménages occupent des logements en location. Ne sont pas retenus les logements occupés en propriété et les logements de fonction fournis par les employeurs. Les données relatives aux dépenses en eau et électricité sont également relevées si elles ne sont pas comprises dans le loyer.

Spécification des variétés
Selon l'importance de l'article, plus d'une variété est sélectionnée pour certains articles. Les articles sont spécifiés, mention étant faite de la taille, de l'unité de mesure et parfois de la marque.

Substitution, changement de qualité, etc.
Pas disponible.

Articles saisonniers
Pas disponible.

Calcul
L'indice est calculé selon la formule de Laspeyres sous forme de moyenne arithmétique pondérée à base fixe, les coefficients de pondération correspondant à la période mars 1974 - février 1975.

Les prix moyens des variétés sont des moyennes arithmétiques simples de tous les relevés de prix. Les rapports de prix pour chaque variété d'un article sont ensuite calculés en divisant le prix moyen de la période en cours par le prix moyen de la période de base. Si deux ou plusieurs variétés sont sélectionnées pour un article, une moyenne arithmétique simple des rapports de prix des variétés représente le rapport de prix de l'article.

Des indices urbains et ruraux de chaque région du pays sont tout d'abord calculés séparément. Ces indices sont ensuite combinés pour obtenir des indices nationaux urbains ou ruraux. L'indice national découle de la moyenne pondérée de ces indices, les pondérations utilisées étant les dépenses de consommation des ménages urbains et ruraux.

Autres informations
Le Bureau central de statistiques calcule et publie des indices séparés de prix à la consommation pour la ville d'Accra, les régions urbaines et rurales.

Organisation et publication
Central Bureau of Statistics: «Quarterly Digest of Statistics» (Accra).

idem: «Consumer Price Index Numbers, A new series» (octobre 1978).

GIBRALTAR

Dénomination officielle
Index of Retail Prices (Indice des prix de détail).

Portée
L'indice est calculé mensuellement pour l'alimentation et chaque trimestre pour les autres groupes. Il porte sur toutes les catégories de ménages résidant en permanence à Gibraltar.

Base originale
Octobre 1980 = 100.

Source des coefficients de pondération
La valeur des coefficients de pondération et le choix des articles résultent d'une enquête sur les dépenses des ménages menée entre février 1979 et mars 1980. Elle a porté sur un échantillon de 221 ménages.

Pondération et composition

Groupes principaux	Nombre d'articles	Pondération	Nombre approximatif de relevés de prix
Alimentation	104	330,67	...
Boissons et tabac	9	59,56	...
Habillement et chaussure	39	110,00	...
Articles ménagers durables	26	100,42	...
Loyer	12	125,90	...
Services	24	75,39	...
Transports et véhicules	17	133,29	...
Divers	44	64,77	...
Total	294	1 000,00	...

Dépenses de consommation des ménages
Les dépenses de consommation prises en compte dans le calcul de l'indice comprennent presque tous les biens et services importants que la population de référence acquiert pour les consommer. Elles excluent l'impôt sur le revenu et les autres impôts directs, les cotisations d'assurance sociale, l'épargne et les placements, les cotisations aux caisses de retraite et les paris.

Mode de relevé des prix
Les prix sont relevés par des agents durant les quelques jours qui précèdent et suivent le 1er du mois. Les prix des denrées alimentaires sont relevés dans une trentaine de points de vente au détail chaque mois. Le relevé pour les autres articles se fait chaque trimestre, dans un maximum de cinq points de vente différents pour chacun.

Les prix retenus pour le calcul de l'indice sont les prix effectivement demandés aux consommateurs.

Logement
Les données sur les loyers sont obtenues pour des immeubles appartenant à l'Etat et pour un échantillon d'une centaine de logements privés.

Spécification des variétés
Les articles sont spécifiés par le nom, la marque, la qualité et la taille.

Substitution, changement de qualité, etc.
Si un nouvel article en remplace un autre, son prix est relevé pendant trois mois et on en calcule le prix moyen de base.

Articles saisonniers
En général, la saison n'influe pas sur l'offre à Gibraltar.

Calcul
L'indice est calculé selon la formule de Laspeyres sous forme de moyenne arithmétique pondérée à base fixe, les coefficients de pondération correspondant à la période de base.

L'indice pour un article est obtenu en utilisant les rapports de prix de la période courante et de la période de base.

Organisation et publication
L'indice est calculé par l'Economic Planning and Statistics Office (Gibraltar).

Government Printer: «Gibraltar Gazette» (l'indice général est publié chaque trimestre et l'indice de l'alimentation chaque mois).

GRECE

Dénomination officielle
Consumer Price Index (Indice des prix à la consommation).

Portée
L'indice est calculé mensuellement et porte sur les centres urbains.

Base originale
1982 = 100.

Source des coefficients de pondération
Les coefficients de pondération et les articles sélectionnés ont été déterminés sur la base des résultats d'une enquête sur les dépenses des ménages effectuée en 1982 auprès d'un échantillon aléatoire de 3 725 ménages dans des centres urbains de 10 000 habitants ou plus. Toutefois, l'enquête porte également sur les régions semi-urbaines et rurales. Les pondérations des articles dont les prix ne sont pas relevés sont allouées aux articles qui les représentent.

Pondération et composition

Groupes principaux	Nombre d'articles	Pondération	Nombre approximatif de relevés de prix
Alimentation	134	324,4	...
Boissons alcoolisées et tabacs	8	36,5	...
Habillement et chaussure	58	128,3	...
Loyer (y compris combustible et éclairage)	11	130,6	...
Equipement ménager	65	85,5	...
Soins personnels et médicaux	34	62,5	...
Instruction et loisirs	37	87,4	...
Transports et communications	26	130,0	...
Autres biens et services	13	14,8	...
Total	386	1 000,0	...

Dépenses de consommation des ménages
Les dépenses de consommation prises en considération pour l'établissement de l'indice correspondent à toutes les dépenses monétaires (au comptant et à crédit) consacrées par les ménages à l'achat des biens et services destinés à leur consommation. Pour la santé et l'instruction, seules les dépenses effectivement payées par les consommateurs sont prises en compte. La valeur imputée des loyers, les impôts et les cotisations aux régimes d'assurance ne sont pas pris en compte.

Mode de relevé des prix
Les relevés sont effectués par des enquêteurs auprès de 1 016 points de vente au détail et prestataires de services dans 17 villes représentatives des changements de prix dans toutes les régions urbaines du pays (cinq villes pour certains articles d'habillement et biens durables). Pour les articles dont les prix sont fixés par l'Etat, les prix sont tirés des factures officielles. La fréquence des relevés dépend de la nature des articles; par exemple dans le cas des fruits frais, des légumes, de la viande, du poisson, etc., ils sont effectués une fois par semaine. Les prix des autres articles sont relevés tous les mois. Les relevés hebdomadaires sont effectués le mardi, les relevés mensuels sont faits de telle manière qu'ils couvrent le mois entier (par exemple les relevés pour la première période de cinq jours sont effectués dans le premier établissement, ceux de la deuxième période de cinq jours dans le deuxième établissement, etc.).

En général, les prix retenus dans le calcul de l'indice sont les prix réels au comptant. Il est tenu compte des rabais, mais non pas des «offres spéciales». Lorsque le prix d'un article diffère du prix officiel, c'est ce dernier qui est pris en compte.

Logement
Les données relatives au loyer sont obtenues deux fois par an à partir d'un échantillon aléatoire de 600 logements. Il est tenu compte des loyers mensuels effectivement versés. L'indice des loyers est obtenu en comparant les dépenses totales consacrées au loyer pendant le mois courant, avec les dépenses mensuelles moyennes correspondantes de l'année de référence. On ne tient pas compte du loyer imputé des logements occupés par leur propriétaire.

Spécification des variétés
Les spécifications des articles sont établies au moyen d'une étude de marché. Pour chaque article de l'indice, il est donné une spécification détaillée (par exemple caractéristiques techniques, marque, nom, poids, qualité, variété, etc.).

Substitution, changement de qualité, etc.
Lorsqu'un produit n'est plus disponible pour le calcul des prix, il est remplacé par un produit analogue. Il est tenu compte des changements de qualité entre l'ancien et le nouveau produit en appliquant à ce dernier un prix de référence fictif.

Articles saisonniers
Il est tenu compte des fluctuations saisonnières des prix des fruits et des légumes frais en variant la pondération de ces articles à l'intérieur de «paniers» mensuels dont le coefficient de pondération d'ensemble demeure constant. Les autres articles saisonniers, tels que les vêtements et chaussures d'été et d'hiver, sont pris en compte en conservant durant la basse saison les prix de clôture de la saison précédente.

Calcul
L'indice est calculé selon la formule de Laspeyres, sous forme de moyenne arithmétique pondérée à base fixe, les coefficients de pondération correspondant à la période de base.

Les rapports de prix pour chaque variété dans chaque point de vente sont d'abord calculés en divisant le prix moyen de la période courante par le prix moyen de la période de base. Puis, des moyennes arithmétiques simples de ces rapports de prix sont calculées pour chaque ville. Celles-ci sont ensuite pondérées en fonction des pondérations des villes pour obtenir les rapports de prix des variétés pour l'ensemble du pays. Enfin, des moyennes arithmétiques simples de ces rapports de prix sont calculées pour obtenir les indices, par article, pour l'ensemble du pays.

Autres informations
L'indice général et neuf groupes sont publiés mensuellement.

Une nouvelle série (base 1988 = 100) est maintenant calculée mais les informations méthodologiques relatives à cette série n'étaient pas disponibles au BIT lors de la publication du présent Volume.

Organisation et publication
National Statistical Service of Greece: «Monthly Statistical Bulletin» (Athènes).

idem: «Statistical Yearbook of Greece».

GRENADE

Dénomination officielle
Consumer Price Index (Indice des prix à la consommation).

Portée
L'indice est calculé mensuellement et porte sur tous les ménages de l'ensemble du pays.

Base originale
1987 = 100.

Source des coefficients de pondération
La valeur des coefficients de pondération et le choix des articles résultent d'une enquête sur les dépenses des ménages effectuée en 1987 auprès d'un échantillon aléatoire de 900 ménages de l'ensemble du pays. Les coefficients de pondération des articles non sélectionnés dans l'évaluation des prix ont été soit répartis parmi des articles similaires du même sous-groupe, soit regroupés au sein d'une autre catégorie, afin d'y être pris en compte par l'article le plus important.

Dépenses de consommation des ménages
Sont inclus les biens produits à domicile, les dons, les primes d'assurance-vie, les achats à crédit. Sont exclus l'impôt sur le revenu et autres impôts directs, le paiement des intérêts sur

Pondération et composition

Groupes principaux	Nombre d'articles	Pondération	Nombre approximatif de relevés de prix
Alimentation, Boissons alcoolisées et tabac:	149	...	569
Alimentation	...	38,7	...
Boissons alcoolisées et tabac	...	2,0	...
Habillement et chaussure	72	5,2	72
Loyer, Travaux ménagers:	20	...	30
Loyer	...	11,9	...
Travaux ménagers	...	5,4	...
Combustible et éclairage, Mobilier, ameublement et équipement ménager:	62	...	169
Combustible et éclairage	...	3,9	...
Mobilier, ameublement et équipement ménager	...	8,3	...
Transports	17	9,1	20
Soins personnels et de santé	30	8,6	139
Instruction, loisirs et lecture	24	4,6	30
Divers	10	2,3	10
Total	384	100,0	1 039

prêts et autres frais bancaires, le paiement des locations-ventes, les donations et contributions ecclésiastiques.

Mode de relevé des prix
La viande fraîche, le poisson, les fruits et légumes font l'objet d'un relevé hebdomadaire, le vendredi à St. Georges et le samedi à Grenville et Gouyave.

Les articles vendus en supermarché, l'habillement, les produits ménagers, le combustible, les produits d'éclairage et de soins personnels sont relevés mensuellement. Les données relatives aux loyers, les primes d'assurance, les frais de voyage, les dépenses relatives aux transports et aux loisirs et les frais divers sont relevés chaque trimestre.

Le prix des articles relevés mensuellement ou trimestriellement est obtenu pendant la dernière semaine du mois en cours, en suivant un ordre déterminé tous les jours, à compter du lundi, auprès des supermarchés, pharmacies, etc. Les agents du Département des Statistiques (Statistical Department) recueillent l'ensemble des prix au cours de visites sur le terrain, ou, dans certains cas, par téléphone (par exemple, honoraires des médecins, tarifs téléphoniques ou d'électricité). En ce qui concerne les marchés de fruits et légumes dont les unités de mesure diffèrent (par exemple, il est possible de compter par fagots, cageots, pièces), une balance de cuisine est utilisée afin de pouvoir disposer d'une unité de mesure normalisée.

Les prix de soldes sont utilisés s'ils deviennent permanents; si le prix d'un article retrouve son prix d'origine à la fin de sa période de solde, il n'est pas pris en compte. Les prix des locations-ventes et les prix d'escompte ne sont pas retenus. Le prix des articles d'occasion n'est pas évalué, car leur marché n'est pas officiel. Les prix à l'importation ne font l'objet d'aucun traitement particulier. Les prix utilisés sont ceux auxquels les consommateurs effectuent leurs achats dans les points de ventes précisés.

Logement
Les données relatives aux loyers sont relevées chaque trimestre auprès d'un échantillon de logements de deux et trois pièces. Les mêmes données sont également retenues pour prendre en compte les logements occupés par leur propriétaire. Les coefficients de pondération des logements occupés par leur propriétaire ont été combinés avec ceux des logements en location.

Spécification des variétés
L'enquête relative aux points d'achat faisait partie de l'enquête sur les dépenses des ménages, dans le cadre de laquelle les personnes interrogées étaient priées d'indiquer les magasins où elles effectuent leurs achats.

Le questionnaire a fourni un certain nombre d'informations sur la marque et le type de chaque article acheté. Ces informations ont permis de sélectionner les marques les plus connues afin d'évaluer leur prix dans chaque magasin retenu. Des visites ont été effectuées auprès de ces magasins, ce qui a permis d'obtenir des spécifications détaillées sur la qualité, la taille, le pays d'origine et la variété des produits concernés.

Substitution, changement de qualité, etc.
Les changements de qualité ne sont pas traités comme des augmentations de prix; en fait, le dernier prix des articles de qualité «ancienne» est maintenu à un niveau constant pendant trois mois, jusqu'à l'introduction d'un article de qualité nouvelle. Les nouveaux produits sont inclus dans le «panier» au moment où se déroule, tous les cinq ans environ, une nouvelle enquête sur les dépenses des ménages.

Si un type ou une qualité déterminés disparaissent du marché, le dernier prix de l'article spécifié est maintenu à un niveau constant pendant trois mois. Si l'article en question ne reparaît pas au bout du quatrième mois, un article similaire, dont le prix a été relevé pendant les trois derniers mois, est alors introduit dans l'indice.

Articles saisonniers
Si un article n'est pas disponible sur le marché pendant trois semaines par mois au minimum, il est alors considéré comme saisonnier.

Lorsqu'il n'y a pas de poisson frais sur le marché, on utilise l'évolution du prix de la viande fraîche.

Tous les articles compris dans le groupe des légumes frais et des féculents sont considérés comme saisonniers, à l'exception des oignons, des pommes de terre irlandaises, de l'ail, des bananes et du plantain. Les articles compris dans ce groupe reçoivent un traitement différent du poisson frais, étant donné qu'ils ne sont pas, en général, absents du marché pendant plus de trois mois. De ce fait, le traitement pratiqué consiste à maintenir le dernier prix disponible à un niveau constant jusqu'à ce que l'article en question reparaisse sur le marché.

Les fruits frais, à l'exception des bananes, sont considérés comme saisonniers. Il reçoivent le même traitement que les légumes frais, sauf les oranges et le raisin. Dans ces deux cas, le jus concentré est utilisé comme substitut.

Calcul
L'indice est calculé selon la formule de Laspeyres, sous forme de moyenne arithmétique pondérée à base fixe, les coefficients de pondération correspondant à la période de base.

La moyenne des prix est calculée en utilisant la moyenne arithmétique simple, les rapports étant obtenus en divisant le prix moyen de la période courante par le prix moyen de la période précédente.

Autres informations
Des indices détaillés par sous-groupe sont publiés.

Organisation et publication
Ministry of Finance. Statistical Department, «Annual Abstract of Statistics», (St. Georges).

Government Printer «Government Gazette».

GROENLAND

Dénomination officielle
Consumer Price Index for Greenland (Indice des prix à la consommation pour le Groenland).

Portée
L'indice est calculé deux fois par an et porte sur les ménages de résidents habitant les villes et lieux de peuplement du Groenland.

Base originale
Janvier 1981 = 100.

Source des coefficients de pondération
Les coefficients de pondération ont été déterminés sur la base des statistiques de 1985 sur l'approvisionnement en biens et services destinés à la consommation privée. Les sources provenaient des statistiques sur les importations, des ventes de la Greenland Trade Company et, pour ce qui est de la production intérieure de biens et de services, des informations recueillies en 1985 auprès d'un échantillon de 195 ménages privés. La pondération des loyers se fonde sur les informations fournies par le Ministère danois pour le Groenland et par l'administration locale, étant donné que 60 pour cent des logements en location sont la propriété des pouvoirs publics, Gouvernement autonome du Groenland et municipalités. Les coûts des logements occupés par leur propriétaire sont calculés de manière à obtenir l'équivalent de leurs loyers. Les coefficients de pondération des dépenses en matière d'énergie ont été déterminés à partir des données fournies par l'Organisation technique pour le Groenland. Les coefficients de pondération ont été ajustés afin de prendre en compte les changements de prix survenus

entre l'année de l'enquête et le mois de janvier 1987, lorsque l'application de nouveaux coefficients est entrée en vigueur.
Les articles dont les prix sont relevés et qui composent l'échantillon ont été adaptés aux changements survenus depuis la dernière révision, effectuée en 1977/78.

Pondération et composition

Groupes principaux	Nombre d'articles	Pondération	Nombre approximatif de relevés de prix
Alimentation	139	18,62	1 129
Boissons	20	11,44	84
Tabac	7	7,13	30
Loyer brut (logement)	5	10,01	23
Combustible et éclairage	7	5,40	7
Habillement et chaussure	50	7,69	332
Mobilier, appareils ménagers, etc.	64	9,21	279
Soins médicaux	6	0,29	18
Transports	11	4,86	32
Communications	4	3,28	11
Chasse à la trappe, pêche, etc.	16	2,99	56
Autres dépenses de loisirs	32	12,47	110
Biens et services divers	32	6,61	231
Total	393	100,00	(a) 2 342

Remarque: (a) A l'exception de l'enquête portant sur les loyers.

Dépenses de consommation des ménages
La consommation est définie comme étant la consommation privée totale de biens et de services au Groenland. Les revenus en nature sont exclus, de même que les impôts directs. Ne sont pas comptées les contributions à la sécurité sociale et aux fonds de pensions. Les soins de santé, entièrement à la charge de l'Etat et dispensés gratuitement, ne sont pas inclus dans le système de pondération. Sont incluses les primes d'assurance pour des biens spécifiques, telles que celles couvrant les maisons (incendie) ou les automobiles. Les autres assurances, souscriptions et dépenses du même genre, qui représentent environ 1,7 pour cent de la consommation totale, ne sont pas incluses. Un coefficient de pondération supplémentaire est attribué pour les logements possédés au Danemark.

Mode de relevé des prix
Les prix sont relevés essentiellement au moyen d'un questionnaire adressé par la poste et de barèmes officiels. Le prix des biens est obtenu deux fois l'an auprès de la Compagnie commerciale du Groenland (régie publique du Gouvernement autonome), de six sociétés en coopérative et d'environ 50 commerces privés de détail. Les tarifs publics pour l'eau, l'électricité, le chauffage, etc., sont fournis par l'Organisation technique et les municipalités. En ce qui concerne le prix des services, les tarifs sont obtenus auprès de sept municipalités, de l'Organisation technique, d'une compagnie d'assurance et de quelques autres organes.
Les données relatives aux prix se réfèrent aux premières semaines des mois de janvier et de juillet. Les prix retenus pour l'indice sont les prix normaux acquittés par n'importe quel particulier (c'est-à-dire les prix du marché).

Logement
Les chiffres retenus sont ceux des loyers bruts, y compris les charges relatives à l'eau et au ramassage des ordures. Etant donné que 60 pour cent des logements en location appartiennent au Gouvernement autonome du Groenland ou aux municipalités, les informations relatives à l'évolution des loyers sont recueillies auprès de l'administration. Les loyers des logements existants sont fixés une fois l'an, au mois d'octobre; en principe, un pourcentage général d'augmentation du tarif est fixé par mètre carré. Pour les nouveaux logements, un calcul supplémentaire est effectué, sur la base de l'augmentation des coûts de construction. Les coûts relatifs aux logements occupés par leur propriétaire ne font ordinairement l'objet d'aucune modification puisque les charges relatives à l'eau, au ramassage des ordures, etc., sont prises en compte séparément. Certaines informations complémentaires sur les logements neufs ou ayant fait l'objet d'une acquisition récente sont recueillies et entrent dans les calculs fondés sur l'augmentation des coûts de construction. Les frais d'entretien sont pris en compte séparément.

Spécification des variétés
Il existe des spécifications détaillées pour chaque article. Sont prises en compte la qualité, la marque, le type et la quantité.

Substitution, changement de qualité, etc.
Les nouveaux produits ne sont introduits dans le calcul de l'indice que s'ils remplacent des produits déjà existants. Les changements de qualité et la disparition du marché d'un certain type de qualité sont traités de la même manière en utilisant la méthode des «périodes de chevauchement».
Par exemple, si un appareil radio d'une marque et d'une qualité déterminées est disponible à la vente jusqu'en juillet 1984, le nouveau modèle qui le remplace aura, généralement, été introduit préalablement sur le marché. Cela signifie que le prix du nouveau modèle peut être lié à l'indice de l'ancien modèle pour juillet 1984.

Articles saisonniers
Il n'est pas tenu compte des fluctuations saisonnières. Les articles faisant l'objet de fluctuations saisonnières très importantes ne sont pas pris en considération pour l'établissement de l'indice.

Calcul
L'indice est calculé selon la formule de Laspeyres, sous forme de moyenne arithmétique pondérée à base fixe, les coefficients de pondération correspondant à 1985.

Autres informations
Des indices détaillés par sous-groupe sont publiés pour ces séries. Le Bureau des statistiques du Danemark («Danmarks Statistik») calcule également un indice des prix nets de taxes à l'importation, dénommé «Reguleringspristallet for Gronland». Cet indice est généralement utilisé aux fins d'indexation dans les contrats privés. Le même indice a précédemment été utilisé pour la réglementation des salaires, mais cette pratique a été interrompue.

Organisation et publication
Danmarks Statistik: «Nyt fra Danmarks Statistik» (Copenhague).

idem: «Statistiske Efterretninger» (serien om Faeroerne og Gronland) (Copenhague).

idem: «Statistik Aarbog».

idem: «Statistik tiaarsoversigt».

GUADELOUPE

Dénomination officielle
Indice des prix à la consommation des ménages en milieu urbain.

Portée
L'indice est calculé mensuellement et porte sur les ménages urbains.

Base originale
Avril 1978-mars 1979 = 100.

Source des coefficients de pondération
Les coefficients de pondération et les articles sélectionnés ont été déterminés sur la base des résultats d'une enquête sur les dépenses des ménages effectuée de septembre à décembre 1972 à Basse-Terre et Pointe-à-Pitre. Les résultats ont été extrapolés en estimant que la structure de consommation de 1972 à 1978 avait évolué de façon similaire en France et en Guadeloupe.

Pondération et composition

Groupes principaux	Nombre d'articles	Pondération	Nombre approximatif de relevés de prix
Alimentation	66	34,39	...
Restaurants	8	2,34	...
Habillement et chaussure	37	9,25	...
Logement:			
Loyer	1	10,06	...
Entretien et réparations	3	2,49	...
Mobilier, ameublement et articles d'équipement ménager	24	6,02	...
Combustible, éclairage et eau	5	5,72	...
Soins personnels et médicaux et services domestiques	14	6,80	...
Transports	19	16,34	...
Instruction et loisirs	21	6,59	...
Total	198	100,00	3 500

159

Dépenses de consommation des ménages
Seuls les achats directs de biens et services de consommation sont pris en compte. Sont exclues: les dépenses d'investissement destinées à maintenir ou accroître un patrimoine et les dépenses de transfert (impôts, cotisations sociales, etc.) qui couvrent des sommes prélevées sur les revenus de certains ménages pour être redistribué à d'autres soit directement (prestations sociales), soit sous forme de services fournis gratuitement aux ménages (services rendus par les administrations, enseignement, réseau routier, etc.)

Mode de relevé des prix
Les prix, pour la plupart des articles, sont relevés mensuellement par des enquêteurs, sur des marchés, auprès de points de vente au détail et prestataires de services à Basse-Terre et Pointe-à-Pitre. Les prix du poisson, des fruits et légumes frais sont recueillis chaque semaine. Lorsque pour la même denrée les prix officiels sont pratiqués en même temps que les prix du marché libre, on ne tient compte que des prix officiels, sauf dans le cas des transports en commun (taxis, autobus) où l'on calcule des prix médians à partir des prix du marché libre. L'indice est alors calculé à partir de ces prix médians. Les escomptes et rabais ne sont pas pris en compte. Les prix de soldes sont relevés comme s'ils étaient les prix régulièrement pratiqués.

Logement
Les données relatives au loyer sont obtenues deux fois par an pour 99 logements locatifs de tous types.

Spécification des variétés
Pour les variétés homogènes, les spécifications sont peu nombreuses et pour les variétés hétérogènes, les dimensions, la marque, le modèle etc. sont précisés.

Substitution, changement de qualité, etc.
Lorsqu'il y a parfaite identité des caractéristiques, le nouveau produit prend la place de l'ancien sans rupture de série. Lorsque le produit remplaçant diffère qualitativement du produit remplacé, il est procédé à un raccordement dont l'effet est de ne prendre en compte que la partie de la variation du prix qui est due à l'évolution normale des prix. Pour certains articles d'habillement, notamment pour les vêtements féminins, on définit les caractéristiques qualificatives les plus fréquemment rencontrées. Les prix de tous ces articles sont alors relevés et on utilise le prix médian pour le calcul de l'indice de ce sous-groupe.

Articles saisonniers
Il est tenu compte des fluctuations saisonnières des prix des fruits et légumes frais et du poisson en variant les articles et leur coefficient de pondération à l'intérieur de «paniers» mensuels dont le coefficient de pondération d'ensemble demeure constant.

Calcul
L'indice est calculé selon la formule de Laspeyres, sous forme de moyenne arithmétique pondérée à base fixe, les coefficients de pondération correspondant à la période de base.

Organisation et publication
INSEE, Service départemental de la Guadeloupe: «Bulletin de statistique» (Basse-Terre).
idem: «Les cahiers de l'INSEE - Dossier prix» (Basse-Terre, premier trimestre 1979).

GUAM

Dénomination officielle
Consumer Price Index (Indice des prix à la consommation).

Portée
L'indice est calculé chaque trimestre et se rapporte aux ménages appartenant à tous les groupes de revenus.

Base originale
1978 = 100.

Source des coefficients de pondération
Les coefficients de pondération et les articles sélectionnés ont été déterminés sur la base des résultats d'une enquête sur les dépenses de consommation effectuée en 1978 auprès d'un échantillon de 500 ménages représentant tous les groupes de revenus.

Pondération et composition

Groupes principaux	Nombre d'articles	Pondération	Nombre approximatif de relevés de prix
Alimentation	103	24,13	...
Logement	51	28,59	...
Habillement, chaussure et entretien des vêtements	44	10,61	...
Transports	15	17,98	...
Soins médicaux	13	4,75	...
Loisirs	15	5,07	...
Autres biens et services	18	8,87	...
Total	259	100,00	1 200

Dépenses de consommation des ménages
Les dépenses de consommation prises en compte dans le calcul de l'indice comprennent presque tous les biens et services achetés par les ménages de référence pour leur consommation, y compris les services médicaux et les articles de loisirs.

Mode de relevé des prix
Les prix sont relevés par des enquêteurs au cours du second mois de chaque trimestre auprès de quelque 120 épiceries, magasins départementaux et autres points de vente de détail et prestataires de services.

Logement
Les loyers sont relevés pour les logements comprenant une à trois chambres à coucher.

Spécification des variétés
Pas disponible.

Substitution, changement de qualité, etc.
Pas disponible.

Articles saisonniers
Les articles saisonniers ne sont pas compris dans l'indice.

Calcul
L'indice est calculé selon la formule de Laspeyres sous forme de moyenne arithmétique pondérée à base fixe, les coefficients de pondération correspondant à la période de base.
Le rapport de prix pour chaque article est calculé en divisant le prix moyen de la période courante par le prix moyen de la période de base.

Autres informations
Des sous-groupes détaillés sont publiés pour cet indice.

Organisation et publication
Department of Commerce, Economic Research Center, Cost of Living Office: «Quarterly Report on the Guam Consumer Price Index» (Agana).
idem: «The Guam Consumer Price Index: 1978 Market Basket and Expenditure Weight Adjustment».

GUATEMALA

Dénomination officielle
Indice de los precios al consumidor para la República de Guatemala - áreas urbanas (Indice des prix à la consommation de la République de Guatemala, régions urbaines).

Portée
L'indice est calculé mensuellement et porte sur tous les ménages urbains.

Base originale
Mars-avril 1983 = 100.

Source des coefficients de pondération
Le choix des articles et la valeur des coefficients de pondération résultent d'une enquête nationale sur les dépenses des ménages effectuée au cours de la période novembre 1979 - août 1981 auprès d'un échantillon de 4 800 ménages de la région urbaine centrale et de 2 678 ménages des autres régions urbaines du pays. Par «ménage» on entend deux personnes au moins qui vivent en commun dans un logement familial ou dans une partie de ce logement et consomment des aliments et autres biens au compte du même budget.

Dépenses de consommation des ménages
Pas disponible.

Pondération et composition
Ville de Guatemala

Groupes principaux	Nombre d'articles	Pondération	Nombre approximatif de relevés de prix
Alimentation	99	42,25	...
Loyer, eau, réparations et entretien	6	9,94	...
Combustible et éclairage	6	4,73	...
Mobilier, articles d'équipement ménager et services domestiques	24	7,82	...
Habillement et chaussure	30	10,07	...
Soins médicaux	7	2,71	...
Instruction	6	2,44	...
Transports et communications	17	11,59	...
Lecture et loisirs	7	4,20	...
Autres biens et services	11	4,25	...
Total	213	100,00	...
Autres régions urbaines			
Alimentation	91	57,27	...
Loyer, eau, réparations et entretien	5	4,74	...
Combustible et éclairage	5	7,92	...
Mobilier, articles d'équipement ménager et services domestiques	15	5,96	...
Habillement et chaussure	27	10,35	...
Soins médicaux	4	2,09	...
Instruction	4	0,98	...
Transports et communications	10	5,78	...
Lecture et loisirs	3	1,75	...
Autres biens et services	7	3,16	...
Total	171	100,00	...

Mode de relevé des prix
Les prix des produits alimentaires sont relevés chaque semaine dans les sept régions du pays. Les prix de l'ameublement, de l'habillement, de l'eau et du combustible sont obtenus mensuellement et ceux concernant les soins médicaux, l'instruction, la lecture, les loisirs et les transports et communications sont relevés tous les trimestres. Les prix sont relevés au moyen de questionnaires adressés par la poste aux marchés, supermarchés, points de vente au détail et prestataires de services des sept régions urbaines du pays.

Logement
Les données relatives au loyer sont obtenues tous les trimestres et portent su un total de 589 logements pour la ville de Guatemala et de 60 pour les autres régions. Dans le calcul de l'indice il n'est pas tenu compte des logements occupés en propriété.

Spécification des variétés
La spécification des variétés a lieu en fonction des habitudes des consommateurs et porte sur la variété, la qualité, la marque et l'unité employée.

Substitution, changement de qualité, etc.
Lorsqu'un article disparaît définitivement du marché on lui en substitue un autre ayant les mêmes caractéristiques. Les changements de qualité donnent lieu à certaines corrections effectuées à l'aide de la formule d'enchaînement.

Articles saisonniers
Pas disponible.

Calcul
L'indice est calculé selon la formule de Laspeyres, sous forme de moyenne arithmétique pondérée à base fixe, les coefficients de pondération correspondant à la période de base.

Le rapport de prix pour chaque article est calculé en divisant le prix moyen de la période courante par le prix moyen de la période de base.

Organisation et publication
Ministerio de Economía, Dirección General de Estadística: «Informador Estadístico» (Guatemala).

idem: «Anuario Estadístico».

idem: «Metodología de los índices de precios al consumidor para la República de Guatemala, base marzo-abril de 1983 = 100» (mars 1983).

GUYANA

Dénomination officielle
Urban Consumer Price Index (Indice des prix à la consommation urbain).

Portée
L'indice est calculé mensuellement et se réfère à Georgetown, New Amsterdam et Linden.

Base originale
1970 = 100.

Source des coefficients de pondération
Les coefficients de pondération et les articles sélectionnés ont été déterminés sur la base des résultats d'une enquête sur les dépenses des ménages effectuée en 1969-1970.

Pondération et composition

Groupes principaux	Nombre d'articles	Pondération	Nombre approximatif de relevés de prix
Alimentation et tabac	86	42,5	...
Habillement et chaussure	56	8,6	...
Logement:			
Combustible et éclairage	5	5,2	...
Loyer, eau et charges	5	21,4	...
Mobilier, ameublement, articles de ménage et services	7	2,9	...
Divers:			
Soins personnels et médicaux	21	7,2	...
Instruction et loisirs	15	6,4	...
Transports et communications	8	4,8	...
Autres biens et services	2	1,0	...
Total	205	100,0	

Dépenses de consommation des ménages
Pas disponible.

Mode de relevé des prix
Les prix pour la plupart des articles, sont relevés vers le 15 de chaque mois auprès d'environ 200 points de vente au détail, marchés et prestataires de services à Georgetown, New Amsterdam et Linden. Les prix pour certaines denrées alimentaires telles que poissons, fruits et légumes frais sont recueillis chaque semaine.

Logement
Pas disponible.

Spécification des variétés
Pas disponible.

Substitution, changement de qualité, etc.
Pas disponible.

Articles saisonniers
Pas disponible.

Calcul
L'indice est calculé selon la formule de Laspeyres, sous forme de moyenne arithmétique pondérée à base fixe, les coefficients de pondération correspondant à la période de base.

Organisation et publication
L'indice est calculé par le Ministry of Economic Development, Statistical Bureau (Georgetown).

Government Georgetown: «Official Gazette».

idem: «Household Consumer Expenditure Survey, 1969-1970, Part 1» (Georgetown).

GUYANE FRANCAISE (CAYENNE)

Dénomination officielle
Indice des prix à la consommation.

Portée
L'indice est calculé mensuellement et porte sur les ménages urbains à revenu modeste résidant à Cayenne.

Base originale
1980 = 100.

Source des coefficients de pondération
Les coefficients de pondération et les articles sélectionnés ont

été déterminés sur la base des résultats d'une enquête sur les dépenses des ménages effectuée en 1969 à Cayenne et Kourou.

Pondération et composition

Groupes principaux	Nombre d'articles	Pondération	Nombre approximatif de relevés de prix
Alimentation	...	50,0	...
Logement (y compris combustibles, éclairage et eau)	...	19,5	...
Habillement et chaussure	...	8,4	...
Hygiène, santé et services	...	7,6	...
Transports et communications	...	6,1	...
Education et loisirs	...	4,9	...
Autres services	...	3,5	...
Total		100,0	

Dépenses de consommation des ménages
Pas disponible.

Mode de relevé des prix
Les relevés de prix, dont la fréquence dépend de la nature des articles, sont effectués par des enquêteurs auprès de 46 points de vente au détail et 15 prestataires de services. Les prix des fruits et légumes sont recueillis chaque semaine et ceux des autres denrées alimentaires une fois par mois; les relevés pour les articles manufacturés et les services sont effectués trimestriellement. On ne tient pas compte des prix des soldes.

Logement
Les données relatives au loyer sont obtenues trimestriellement auprès d'une société spécialisée dans la location des logements (1 840 logements).

Spécification des variétés
L'INSEE a fourni pour chaque article une liste des variétés. Les enquêteurs choisissent la variété la mieux appropriée (c'est-à-dire celle qui se vend couramment et qui pourra être utilisée pour les relevés ultérieurs). La spécification du produit choisi porte sur la marque, la qualité, la taille, etc.

Substitution, changement de qualité, etc.
Lorsqu'un produit change de qualité, on le considère comme un nouveau produit qui entre dans le calcul de l'indice après plusieurs mois de présence sur le marché.

Articles saisonniers
Il est tenu compte des fluctuations saisonnières des prix de certains légumes en utilisant des moyennes mobiles pour le calcul de l'indice.

Calcul
L'indice est calculé selon la formule de Laspeyres, sous forme de moyenne arithmétique pondérée à base fixe, les coefficients de pondération correspondant à la période de base.

Organisation et publication
Institut national de la statistique et des études économiques, Service régional de la Guyane: «Bulletin mensuel de statistique» (Cayenne).

idem: «Annuaire de la Guyane».

HAITI

Dénomination officielle
Indice des prix à la consommation - Aire Métropolitaine.

Portée
L'indice est calculé mensuellement et porte sur les ménages urbains de l'aire métropolitaine.

Base originale
1980 = 100.

Source des coefficients de pondération
Les coefficients de pondération et les articles sélectionnés résultent d'une enquête sur les dépenses des ménages effectuée en 1976 auprès de ménages urbains et ruraux. Les dépenses de 747 ménages de deux personnes ou plus ayant un revenu familial annuel au moins égal à 250 gourdes ont servi à calculer les coefficients de pondération de l'indice.

L'indice se rapporte aux ménages urbains de l'aire métropolitaine de Port-au-Prince, Delmas, Carrefour et Pétion-Ville. Les pondérations n'ont pas été ajustées pour tenir compte de l'évolution des prix entre le moment de l'enquête et 1980.

Pondération et composition

Groupes principaux	Nombre d'articles	Pondération	Nombre approximatif de relevés de prix
Alimentation	27	64,48	...
Habillement et chaussure	15	3,16	...
Logement	6	11,71	...
Mobilier et ameublement	16	5,75	...
Services	13	14,90	...
Total	77	100,00	...

Dépenses de consommation des ménages
Les dépenses de consommation prises en compte dans le calcul de l'indice comprennent tous les biens et services achetés par les ménages de référence pour leur consommation. En sont exclus l'impôt sur le revenu, les dépôts d'épargne, les primes d'assurances, etc.

Mode de relevé des prix
Les prix sont relevés par des enquêteurs auprès d'un échantillon de points de vente au détail et prestataires de services. La fréquence des relevés de prix et le nombre de points de vente retenus dépendent de la nature de l'article. Les prix des denrées alimentaires sont relevés trois fois par semaine (mardi, jeudi et samedi) sur les trois grands marchés et auprès de supermarchés et épiceries sélectionnés. Les prix pour l'habillement, le mobilier, l'ameublement et les services sont relevés les première, deuxième et troisième semaines de chaque mois.

Logement
Les données relatives au loyer sont obtenues le premier mois de chaque trimestre à partir d'un échantillon de logements loués.

Spécification des variétés
Pas disponible.

Substitution, changement de qualité, etc.
Pas disponible.

Articles saisonniers
Pas disponible.

Calcul
L'indice est calculé selon la formule de Laspeyres sous forme de moyenne arithmétique pondérée à base fixe, les coefficients de pondération correspondant à 1976.

Les rapports de prix pour les variétés de chaque article sont calculés en divisant le prix moyen de la variété pour la période courante par son prix moyen de la période de base. Ensuite, des moyennes arithmétiques simples de ces indices sont utilisées pour obtenir des indices par article.

Organisation et publication
Département des finances et des affaires économiques, Institut haïtien de statistique: «Bulletin trimestriel de statistique» (Port-au-Prince).

Ministère du Plan, Institut haïtien de statistique et d'informatique, Division des statistiques générales: «Indices des prix à la consommation, base 100 en 1980» (Port-au-Prince, juin 1983).

HONDURAS

Dénomination officielle
Indice General de Precios al Consumidor (Indice général des prix à la consommation).

Portée
L'indice est calculé mensuellement et porte sur les familles de toutes les zones urbaines qui disposaient, au cours de la période 1978-79, d'un revenu compris entre 3 000 et 12 000 lempiras par an.

Base originale
1978 = 100.

Source des coefficients de pondération
Les coefficients de pondération et le choix des articles résultent d'une enquête nationale sur les dépenses des ménages urbains effectuée de janvier 1978 à août 1979 auprès de 5 328 ménages répartis entre 44 villes. L'échantillon retenu pour l'indice comprend 2 306 ménages urbains dont le revenu annuel se situait entre 3 000 et 12 000 lempiras au moment de l'enquête.

Pondération et composition

Groupes principaux	Nombre d'articles	Pondé-ration	Nombre approximatif de relevés de prix
Alimentation	64	41,214	7 968
Boissons et tabac	7	3,790	133
Logement:			
Loyer	1	13,202	164
Réparations	4	3,288	73
Dépenses de ménage (y compris combustible et éclairage)	19	9,611	190
Mobilier et articles d'équipement ménager	13	4,510	520
Habillement et chaussure	34	9,110	1 320
Soins personnels et médicaux	30	6,952	906
Transports	7	3,033	94
Instruction et loisirs	10	5,290	184
Total	189	100,000	11 552

Dépenses de consommation des ménages
Pas disponible.

Mode de relevé des prix
Les prix sont relevés par des enquêteurs auprès de marchés, points de vente au détail et prestataires de service dans 6 villes réparties dans l'ensemble du pays. Les relevés sont effectués le mardi de chaque semaine pour les produits alimentaires, annuellement pour l'instruction, tous les six mois pour les loyers, les services médicaux et les transports. Les prix d'environ 150 articles sont relevés vers le 15 de chaque mois.

Logement
Les données relatives au loyer sont obtenues deux fois par an auprès d'un échantillon de 164 logements occupés par des ménages à revenu moyen et comprenant salon, salle à manger, cuisine, et au moins deux chambres à coucher.

Spécification des variétés
Les relevés des produits se fondent sur une spécification rigoureuse de ces derniers.

Substitution, changement de qualité, etc.
Lorsqu'un produit disparaît du marché, il est remplacé par un autre article comparable aux fins de relevé de prix. Il n'est pas tenu compte des changements de qualité dans la spécification des articles.

Articles saisonniers
Les articles dont les prix sont soumis à des fluctuations saisonnières sont écartés de l'indice.

Calcul
L'indice est calculé selon la formule de Laspeyres sous forme de moyenne arithmétique pondérée à base fixe, les coefficients de pondération correspondant à la période de base.

Les prix moyens pour chaque article dans chaque ville correspondent aux moyennes arithmétiques simple des prix obtenus dans chacune d'entre elles. Ces prix moyens sont ensuite combinés en utilisant les pondérations des régions afin d'obtenir des prix moyens régionaux. Pour chaque article, les rapports des prix moyens régionaux sont ensuite calculés en divisant le prix moyen régional de la période courante par le prix moyen régional de la période de base.

L'indice national est une moyenne pondérée de cinq indices urbains régionaux (centre, nord, sud, est et ouest). Les pondérations utilisées sont proportionnelles à la structure des dépenses des régions conformément à l'enquête sur les dépenses des ménages.

Organisation et publication
Banco Central de Honduras, Departamento de Estudios Económicos: «Boletín Estadístico» (Tegucigalpa, D.C.).

idem: «Indice de Precios al Consumidor» (mensuel).

idem: «Honduras en Cifras» (annuel).

idem: «Indice General de Precios al Consumidor, Base 1978 = 100, Metodología y Series Cronológicas» (Novembre 1982).

HONG-KONG

Dénomination officielle
Consumer Price Index - A (Indice des prix à la consommation - A).

Portée
L'indice est calculé mensuellement et porte sur environ 50 pour cent des ménages urbains de Hong-kong, dont les dépenses étaient comprises entre 2 500 et 9 999 dollars par mois pendant la période allant d'octobre 1989 à septembre 1990.

Base originale
Octobre 1989 - septembre 1990 = 100.

Source des coefficients de pondération
Les coefficients de pondération résultent d'une enquête sur les dépenses des ménages effectuée entre octobre 1989 et septembre 1990. Cette enquête portait sur l'ensemble des ménages privés habitant les zones urbaines de Hong-kong, à l'exception des gens de mer, des collectivités et des ménages ruraux. Etaient également exclus les ménages bénéficiant de l'assistance publique et les ménages absents de Hong-kong pendant la période de référence de l'enquête. Pris conjointement, environ 4 850 ménages ont participé à l'enquête. La période de référence de 12 mois a été divisée en 26 cycles bimensuels. Chaque ménage participant a été prié de prendre part à l'un de ces cycles; pendant ces deux semaines, tous les membres du ménage âgés de 12 ans au moins devaient notifier toutes leurs dépenses dans des journaux spécialement conçus à ce propos. Les ménages ont également été priés de rappeler les dépenses qu'ils ont consacrées, au cours d'un trimestre de référence, à certains articles dont l'achat est peu fréquent (tels que les automobiles, les réfrigérateurs, les bijoux).

Les critères adoptés pour la sélection des articles aux fins du relevé des prix sont les suivants: (i) Le coefficient de pondération d'un article choisi ne doit pas être trop réduit, afin d'éviter qu'un changement significatif du prix moyen de l'article n'ait qu'un impact négligeable sur l'indice général; (ii) Au total, les articles doivent pratiquement représenter l'ensemble de la consommation des ménages couverts par l'Indice; (iii) le nombre d'articles sélectionnés doit être proche de celui de l'ancienne série de l'Indice, de manière à maintenir une certaine continuité entre l'ancienne et la nouvelle série. Les coefficients de pondération des articles non sélectionnés ont été répartis proportionnellement sur les articles sélectionnés du même groupe.

Pondération et composition

Groupes principaux	Nombre d'articles	Pondé-ration	Nombre approximatif de relevés de prix
Alimentation	387	41,2	...
Boissons alcoolisées et tabac (consommation à domicile)	16	2,45	...
Logement	26	20,56	...
Combustible et éclairage	5	3,18	...
Habillement et chaussure	113	4,56	...
Articles de ménage durables	110	4,92	...
Transports et véhicules	52	7,20	...
Services	104	10,05	...
Divers	147	5,88	...
Total	960	100,00	40 000

Dépenses de consommation des ménages
Les dépenses des ménages désignent les dépenses de consommation consacrées à l'acquisition de biens et services (y compris les paiements en nature). En sont exclus les frais d'affaires, les envois de fonds, les paris, l'impôt sur le revenu, les primes d'assurance-vie adressées aux fondations, les paiements hypothécaires relatifs au logement, les investissements sur les propriétés, valeurs mobilières et actions, et divers autres versements de type épargne. En général, les dépenses comprennent les paiements réels effectués pendant la période de référence pour l'acquisition de biens et services, sans qu'il importe de savoir si ces biens et services ont été acquis ou consommés au cours de cette période. Cependant, en ce qui concerne les paiements à crédit ou par carte de crédit, on a enregistré le montant des dépenses signées au cours de la période de référence, mais non le montant des dépenses destinées au paiement des intérêts échus pendant la même période. Certains cas particuliers sont traités comme suit:

Les revenus en nature ont été comptabilisés, pour les ménages, à la fois comme des revenus et comme des dépenses. Ils comprennent les logements fournis ou payés par les employeurs, les dépenses médicales et les frais de carburant remboursés par les employeurs, ainsi que tous les articles obtenus auprès des employeurs à des prix de concessionnaire. Le prix de détail total de ces articles a été comptabilisé au titre de dépenses et la différence entre le prix de détail et le prix de concessionnaire a été ajoutée au revenu. Les avantages à caractère marginal, tels que la viande, le transport, les soins médicaux gratuits n'ont pas été enregistrés en raison des difficultés pratiques que pose leur quantification.

En ce qui concerne les ménages occupant leur logement en propriété et qui ne paient donc aucun loyer, celui-ci a été estimé sur la base des prix habituels du marché. Ce loyer estimé est considéré à la fois comme un revenu et comme une dépense pour les ménages, à partir de l'approche fondée sur le loyer équivalent.

Pour les biens durables acquis par location-vente (avec des intérêts à payer), le prix total de l'article a été pris en compte en tant que dépense, et non le remboursement ou le versement des intérêts. En conséquence, pour les locations-ventes effectuées pendant la période de référence, les personnes interrogées ont été priées de rappeler le prix au comptant qui aurait été payé si l'article avait été acheté en un seul versement. De ce fait, les intérêts versés au cours de la période de référence pour les biens durables acquis auparavant n'ont pas été pris en compte.

Le paiement effectif des achats de biens d'occasion a été enregistré en tant que dépense. Tout article acquis par échange partiel a été enregistré par le montant net du paiement, auquel est ajouté le montant approximatif de l'échange partiel, s'il est possible de le quantifier. Les frais de patentes, les assurances couvrant des biens de consommation spécifiques, les soins médicaux ont été traités comme des biens de consommation courants. Les contributions à la sécurité sociale et aux fonds de pensions, l'impôt sur le revenu et les autres impôts directs, les primes d'assurance-vie n'ont pas été traités comme des dépenses de consommation. Les dons ont été traités comme des biens de consommation courants et ont été compris dans les dépenses des ménages.

Mode de relevé des prix
Les prix sont relevés auprès de points de vente sélectionnés situés dans les zones urbaines les plus peuplées qui ont été divisées en 12 districts de relevés. Pour l'essentiel, les prix sont relevés par des visites effectuées auprès de points de vente sélectionnés et, occasionnellement, par téléphone. Les prix sont relevés trois fois par semaine pour tous les aliments frais, à l'exception des fruits frais, de la viande de porc et de boeuf, des oeufs et du riz, articles dont le prix n'est relevé qu'une fois par semaine. Les autres articles font l'objet d'un relevé mensuel, bimestriel, trimestriel ou annuel. Pour certains articles, tels que les transports publics, les loyers des logements de propriété publique, les charges relatives à l'eau, l'essence et les combustibles, les frais d'immatriculation des véhicules, les changements de prix sont enregistrés chaque fois qu'ils se produisent.

Les prix utilisés dans l'indice sont les prix de détail effectivement payés par les consommateurs. Les prix réduits ne sont acceptables que pour les articles qui font périodiquement l'objet de soldes, sont de fabrication récente et en bonne condition, et sont disponibles à la vente en quantité raisonnable pour l'ensemble de la clientèle.

Logement
Les loyers des logements privés sont relevés au moyen d'une enquête mensuelle par sondage. Les données relatives aux loyers de tous les logements faisant partie de l'échantillon font l'objet d'un relevé portant à la fois sur le mois en cours et sur le mois précédent. Les logements sont ensuite post-stratifiés par zone d'appartements. Le loyer total payé par les ménages de chacune des strates est alors calculé pour le mois en cours comme pour le mois précédent, ainsi que son changement relatif. Ces «rapports de prix» correspondant à chacune des strates sont alors, par l'utilisation des différents coefficients de pondération déterminés au cours de l'enquête sur les dépenses des ménages de 1989/90, combinés afin d'obtenir un indice global avant d'être enchaînés à la période de base. Les changements survenus dans les loyers des logements subventionnés par les autorités sont pris en compte au moment où ils se produisent, sur la base des informations fournies par les organismes publics concernés. Pour ce qui est des logements occupés en propriété, on utilise la méthode de l'équivalence des loyers, par laquelle il est estimé que le coût du logement concerné évolue au même taux que le loyer des logements privés en location. Les rapports de loyers calculés pour chaque strate sont, comme indiqué ci-dessus, également agrégés par les coefficients de pondération correspondant aux logement occupés en propriété afin d'obtenir un indice mensuel.

Spécification des variétés
La méthode utilisée d'évaluation des prix, établie en fonction des magasins, stipule que les prix ne sont définis qu'au sens large. Cependant, des spécifications détaillées précisant la variété, la qualité, la fabrication, l'unité, sont enregistrées en conséquence pour chaque relevé de prix lors de l'enquête sur le terrain. Les enquêteurs demandent aux commerçants interrogés de préciser quelles sont les variétés, vendues au moment même dans leurs magasins, les plus prisées par les consommateurs (c'est-à-dire celles dont le volume des ventes est le plus important). Si les variétés les plus prisées pour le mois en cours sont les mêmes que celles des mois précédents, les prix du mois en cours sont relevés. Dans le cas contraire, quelques autres variétés davantage prisées sont sélectionnées pour le mois en cours et leurs prix sont collectés aux fins de raccordement, aussi bien pour le mois précédent que pour le mois en cours.

Substitution, changement de qualité, etc.
La méthode d'enchaînement est utilisée lorsque survient un changement dans la qualité d'un article. Les prix correspondant à la nouvelle qualité sont relevés durant deux mois consécutifs avant d'être introduits dans l'indice. Si un produit est entièrement nouveau et ne peut être classé sous aucune rubrique figurant dans la liste des articles dont le prix est relevé, son prix ne sera pas relevé pour le calcul de l'indice avant la révision suivante de ce dernier. D'autre part, si le produit ne représente qu'une nouvelle marque d'un produit déjà existant, on applique alors la méthode d'enchaînement. Si un article disparaît du marché, le prix d'un article similaire est relevé au titre de substitut.

Articles saisonniers
Les aliments frais saisonniers sont exclus de l'indice lorsqu'ils sont hors-saison, et leurs coefficients de pondération sont répartis sur les articles restants du même groupe. En ce qui concerne les denrées alimentaires non périssables, les prix de la dernière saison sont gardés tels quels jusqu'à la saison suivante.

Calcul
L'indice est calculé selon la formule de Laspeyres sous forme de moyenne arithmétique pondérée à base fixe, les coefficients de pondération correspondant à ceux de la période de base.

Deux méthodes sont appliquées pour le calcul de l'indice. Pour les articles homogènes, les rapports de prix sont calculés en divisant le prix moyen de la période en cours par celui de la période de base. Pour les autres articles, les rapports de prix sont calculés, pour chaque variété et chaque magasin, en divisant le prix moyen de la période en cours par celui de la période précédente. La moyenne de ces rapports est alors calculée pour obtenir les indices par article.

Autres informations
Outre le CPI (A), deux autres indices des prix à la consommation sont publiés tous les mois à Hong-kong. D'une part le Consumer Price Index (B) (CPI (B)), base 1989/90, qui est également calculé par le Census and Statistics Department du gouvernement de Hong-kong. Cet indice porte sur les ménages dont les dépenses étaient comprises entre 10 000 et 17 499 dollars de Hong-kong par mois pendant la période octobre 1989-septembre 1990, au cours de laquelle a été menée l'enquête sur les dépenses des ménages. Le second indice, le Hang Seng Consumer Price Index (Hang Seng CPI), est calculé par la Hang Seng Bank (organisation privé de Hong-kong) et porte sur les ménages habitant des logements privés dont les dépenses moyennes mensuelles étaient comprises entre 17 500 et 37 499 dollars de Hong-kong en 1989-90. En ce qui concerne la couverture des ménages, le CPI (B) couvre environ 30 pour cent des ménages urbains de Hong-kong, cette proportion étant de 10 pour cent pour l'indice Hang Seng.

Organisation et publication
Census and Statistics Department, Consumer Price Index Section: «Consumer Price Index Report» (Hong-kong).
idem: «Hong Kong Monthly Digest of Statistics» (Hong-kong).

HONGRIE

Dénomination officielle
Consumer Price Index (Indice des prix à la consommation).

Portée
L'indice est calculé mensuellement et porte sur la totalité du territoire et l'ensemble de la population.

Base originale
La période de base de l'indice employée dans les publications hongroises est le mois correspondant de l'année précédente, le mois précédent et décembre de l'année précédente. L'Office central hongrois de la statistique recalcule l'indice sur la base utilisée pour publication par le BIT.

Source des coefficients de pondération
Les coefficients de pondération et les articles sélectionnés ont été déterminés sur la base des résultats d'une enquête sur les dépenses des ménages et sont révisés périodiquement. L'enquête porte sur un échantillon de 8 000 ménages. Chaque ménage tient un carnet de relevé détaillé sur ses dépenses. Les dépenses relatives à certains articles, comme l'alcool, le tabac, la confiserie et les repas pris en dehors de la maison, sont corrigées à l'aide de données globales, car les chiffres indiqués sont généralement en dessous de la réalité.

Pondération et composition

Groupes principaux	Nombre d'articles	Pondération	Nombre approximatif de relevés de prix
Alimentation	49	28	27 100
Boissons et tabac	5	12	4 800
Combustible et éclairage	8	5	1 100
Habillement et chaussure	27	8	22 400
Services	34	15	13 200
Loyer	2	5	400
Autre	39	27	33 200
Total	164	100	102 200

Dépenses de consommation des ménages
Les dépenses de consommation entrant dans le calcul de l'indice portent sur la quasi totalité des biens et des services acquis par les ménages de référence. Elles comprennent la redevance de télévision, la réparation et le loyer imputé des logements occupés par leur propriétaire. En sont exclus les biens produits par les ménages pour leur consommation propre ou reçus gratuitement, les taxes sur les automobiles, les intérêts au titre du crédit à la consommation, les primes d'assurance vie et les impôts directs, les soins de santé gratuits et les achats d'articles d'occasion (excepté les automobiles d'occasion).

Mode de relevé des prix
Les prix d'environ 1 800 articles sont relevés par 145 enquêteurs auprès de points de vente choisis et des autorités locales. Les prix des fruits et légumes sont relevés sur des marchés et des points de vente. Les prix pratiqués à l'occasion de ventes spéciales sont pris en considération.

Logement
Pas disponible.

Spécification des variétés
Les articles sont choisis d'après leurs caractéristiques les plus marquantes. Pour chaque type d'article manufacturé spécifié on relève les prix de deux ou trois produits parmi les plus vendus, choisis en consultation avec le personnel de vente.

Substitution, changement de qualité, etc.
Lorsqu'une variété spécifique est sélectionnée, elle est maintenue aussi longtemps que possible. L'enquêteur est autorisé à substituer une variété à une autre dans les limites des spécifications. D'autres substitutions sont contrôlées centralement; aucun ajustement n'est fait sur la base d'un changement de qualité.

Articles saisonniers
Les indices mensuels sont calculés à partir de coefficients de pondération mensuels variables à l'intérieur d'un «panier» fixe, qui reflètent les fluctuations saisonnières de l'offre des denrées alimentaires saisonnières.

Calcul
On se sert des rapports des prix moyens de chaque article de référence sans tenir compte des observations manquantes. Il y a des coefficients de pondération annuels fixes pour chaque groupe social et chaque tranche de revenus.

Autres informations
Dans les publications nationales, l'indice est publié sur base 1980 = 100, l'année précédente = 100, le mois correspondant de l'année précédente = 100, le mois précédent = 100 et base décembre de l'année précédente = 100.

Organisation et publication
Központi Statisztikai Hivatal (Office central hongrois de la statistique): «Statisztikai Havi Közlemények» (Bulletin mensuel de statistiques) (Budapest).

idem: «Statisztikai Evkönyv» (Annuaire statistique).

idem: «Fogyasztói árindex fuzetek» (Livre de l'indice des prix à la consommation).

ILES CAIMANES

Dénomination officielle
Consumer Price Index (Indice des prix à la consommation).

Portée
L'indice est calculé quatre fois l'an, aux mois de mars, juin, septembre et décembre, et porte sur tous les ménages résidant à Grand Cayman et Cayman Brac.

Base originale
Septembre 1984 = 100.

Source des coefficients de pondération
La valeur des coefficients de pondération et le choix des articles résultent d'une enquête sur les dépenses des ménages menée entre avril 1983 et mars 1984 auprès de 234 ménages privés habitant les îles de Grand Cayman et Cayman Brac. A l'époque de l'enquête, les dépenses hebdomadaires moyennes par ménage s'élevaient à 440 dollars et la taille moyenne des ménages était de 3,52 personnes.

Pondération et composition

Groupes principaux	Nombre d'articles	Pondération	Nombre approximatif de relevés de prix
Alimentation	282	206,43	590
Boissons alcoolisées et tabac	56	31,46	133
Logement:			
Loyer	13	67,58	13
Intérêts hypothécaires	1	36,98	3
Réparations, entretien et assurances	70	27,90	83
Combustible, éclairage et eau	16	45,01	24
Habillement et chaussure	160	39,21	242
Mobilier, fournitures et équipement ménager	200	57,85	222
Transports et communications	59	178,64	84
Instruction	29	24,35	32
Soins médicaux	29	56,89	48
Loisirs	93	178,90	115
Biens et services personnels	82	48,76	130
Total	1 090	1000,00	1 719

Dépenses de consommation des ménages
Les assurances, ainsi que les biens de consommation et les dépenses de santé, sont compris dans les calculs. En sont exclus les frais professionnels, les dons et les revenus en nature utilisés par les ménages pour leur consommation.

Mode de relevé des prix
Les prix sont relevés quatre fois l'an, aux mois de mars, juin, septembre et décembre, auprès des supermarchés, des grands magasins et des entreprises de services à George Town et dans ses environs immédiats, ainsi que dans l'île de Cayman Brac. Pendant le mois où est effectué le relevé, les prix sont recueillis par les agents les mardi, mercredi et jeudi. L'office des statistiques centralise le relevé de certains prix à la suite de questions posées au téléphone ou de réponses à des questionnaires adressés par la poste, pour des articles tels que l'électricité, le gaz, l'eau, les soins médicaux, l'éducation, les transports et les communications. Le coût des remboursements d'emprunts est alloué aux dépenses importantes, comme les véhicules ou l'ameublement.

Pour tous les biens et services ayant fait l'objet d'une évaluation, les prix entrant dans le calcul de l'indice sont ceux effectivement pratiqués lors des transactions au comptant. Les frais relatifs au crédit en sont exclus. Il n'est pas tenu compte des réductions, à moins qu'elles ne soient consenties à l'ensemble du public. Il en va de même pour les prix figurant sur des listes, s'il s'avère qu'un magasin pratique un prix différent à la vente. Les prix des catalogues ne sont compris que lorsqu'ils représentent une véritable réduction de prix, et ne sont pas un moyen permettant d'écouler des marchandises usées, endommagées, défraîchies ou défectueuses.

Logement
Les maisons et appartements de 1, 2 et 3 chambres font l'objet d'une évaluation trimestrielle, qui inclut les logements appartenant à des particuliers de même que ceux appartenant à des collectivités. Le paiement des intérêts est pris en compte pour les logements occupés par leurs propriétaires.

Spécification des variétés
Etant donné que l'indice doit mesurer les changements de prix, les informations recueillies chaque trimestre concernent les mêmes biens et services, proposés en même quantité au même point de vente. Les articles dont les prix sont enregistrés doivent demeurer inchangés tant que l'indice reste en vigueur. Des spécifications approximatives sont indiquées pour l'habillement et l'ameublement lorsqu'il n'est pas possible d'apporter plus de précisions.

Substitution, changement de qualité, etc.
Lorsqu'un article n'est plus disponible pendant trois périodes consécutives, un nouvel article est introduit en calculant le prix du nouvel article par rapport à celui de l'ancien article afin d'estimer, par défaut, un prix de base pour le nouvel article. Les articles dont le prix est plus élevé en raison d'une qualité supérieure voient, en conséquence, leur prix réduit dans l'indice, sauf lorsque la quantité d'un article spécifique est augmentée sans que sa description soit modifiée. Les nouveaux produits ne sont pas relevés (sauf dans le cas décrit plus haut) et leur introduction doit attendre une révision de l'indice.

En ce qui concerne les articles manquants, des prix fictifs sont calculés sur la base des changements de prix relevés pour les mêmes articles en d'autres occasions. Si l'on ne dispose pas d'autre prix pour un article, on utilise la moyenne des changements de prix concernant le groupe à trois chiffres auquel appartient l'article en question. Mais, les statisticiens peuvent modifié ces différents prix fictifs à la suite de visites sur le terrain.

Articles saisonniers
Les fluctuations saisonnières des prix des articles ne font l'objet d'aucun ajustement.

Calcul
L'indice est calculé selon la formule de Laspeyres sous forme de moyenne arithmétique pondérée à base fixe, les coefficients de pondération correspondant à la période avril 1983 - mars 1984.

La moyenne des prix est calculée pour chaque groupe à cinq chiffres. Les moyennes pour Grand Cayman et Cayman Brac sont calculées séparément et pondérées en fonction des dépenses relatives des ménages.

Autres informations
L'indice est publié environ deux semaines après le mois de référence.

Des indices par sous-catégories sont publiés pour l'alimentation, les boissons alcoolisées et le tabac, le logement, l'habillement, les biens durables des ménages, les transports et communications, les frais scolaires et médicaux, les biens et services personnels.

Organisation et publication
Department of Finance and Development, Statistics Unit: «Annual Abstract of Statistics» (Grand Cayman).

idem: «Annual Report of the Cayman Islands».

idem: «Cayman Islands, A Guide to the new Consumer Price Index», février 1985.

ILES COOK (RAROTONGA)

Dénomination officielle
Retail Price Index (Indice des prix de détail).

Portée
L'indice est calculé trimestriellement et se rapporte aux ménages de salariés.

Base originale
Deuxième trimestre de 1967 = 100.

Source des coefficients de pondération
Les coefficients de pondération et les articles sélectionnés ont été déterminés sur la base des résultats d'une enquête sur les dépenses des ménages effectuée en mai 1967 auprès de ménages de salariés sélectionnés sur une base ad hoc (non compris les ouvriers agricoles) dont le chef de famille disposait, lors de l'enquête, d'un revenu moyen compris entre 4 livres et 20 livres par semaine (pour 156 budgets analysés, le chef de 99 ménages disposait d'un revenu compris entre 4 livres et 6 livres par semaine).

Pondération et composition

Groupes principaux	Nombre d'articles	Pondération	Nombre approximatif de relevés de prix
Alimentation	76	58,4	...
Tabac et alcool	5	6,8	...
Logement	11	3,1	...
Dépenses de ménage	51	9,6	...
Habillement et chaussure	48	12,4	...
Transports	10	5,7	...
Divers	36	4,0	...
Total	237	100,0	...

Dépenses de consommation des ménages
Pas disponible.

Mode de relevé des prix
Les prix sont relevés par des enquêteurs au cours de la troisième et de la quatrième semaine de février, mai, août et novembre, auprès de cinq principaux centres d'achats de Rarotonga.

Logement
Pas disponible.

Spécification des variétés
Pas disponible.

Substitution, changement de qualité, etc.
Pas disponible.

Articles saisonniers
Pas disponible.

Calcul
L'indice est calculé sous forme de moyenne arithmétique pondérée à base fixe, les coefficients de pondération correspondant à la période de base.

Autres informations
Une nouvelle série (base juin 1989 = 100) est maintenant calculée mais les informations méthodologiques relatives à cette série n'étaient pas disponibles au BIT lors de la publication du présent Volume.

Organisation et publication
Statistical Office: «Quarterly Statistical Bulletin» (Rarotonga).

Government of Cook Islands: «Rarotonga Retail Price Index» (Rarotonga, 1967).

ILES FALKLAND (MALVINAS) (STANLEY)

Dénomination officielle
Retail Price Index (Indice des prix de détail).

Portée
L'indice porte sur les familles d'ouvriers résidant à Stanley.

Base originale
1er janvier 1971 = 100.

Source des coefficients de pondération
Les coefficients de pondération et les articles sélectionnés ont été déterminés sur la base des résultats d'une enquête sur les dépenses des ménages effectuée en 1971 auprès de familles d'ouvriers (à l'exclusion des familles nombreuses) résidant à Stanley.

Dépenses de consommation des ménages
Pas disponible.

Mode de relevé des prix
Les prix sont relevés par des enquêteurs à la fin du dernier mois de chaque trimestre, auprès de trois points de vente au détail et prestataires de services à Stanley.

Pondération et composition

Groupes principaux	Nombre d'articles	Pondération	Nombre approximatif de relevés de prix
Alimentation	15	409	...
Boissons et tabac	6	94	...
Habillement et chaussure	64	128	...
Combustible et éclairage	2	45	...
Mobilier, ameublement et articles d'équipement ménager	24	54	...
Logement (intérêts hypothécaires, impôts locaux et réparations)	6	98	...
Produits d'entretien	7	28	...
Soins personnels et médicaux	7	30	...
Papeterie	2	27	...
Services	10	87	...
Total	143	1 000	...

Logement
Le loyer n'est retenu ni dans le calcul de l'indice ni dans la détermination des coefficients de pondération.

Spécification des variétés
Pas disponible.

Substitution, changement de qualité, etc.
Pas disponible.

Articles saisonniers
Les fluctuations saisonnières des prix ne font pas l'objet d'ajustement.

Calcul
L'indice est calculé selon la formule de Laspeyres, sous forme de moyenne arithmétique pondérée à base fixe, les coefficients de pondération correspondant à la période de base.

Autres informations
Une nouvelle série (base 1er juillet 1989 = 100) est maintenant calculée mais les informations méthodologiques relatives à cette série n'étaient pas disponibles au BIT lors de la publication du présent Volume.

Organisation et publication
Government Printing Office: «Falkland Island Gazette» (Stanley).

ILE DE MAN

Dénomination officielle
General Index of Retail Prices (Indice général des prix de détail).

Portée
L'indice est calculé mensuellement et porte sur tous les ménages privés, sauf les 3 à 4 pour cent formant le groupe supérieur de revenu et le groupe des assistés sociaux dont le revenu est le plus bas.

Base originale
Mars 1976 = 100.

Source des coefficients de pondération
La valeur des coefficients de pondération et le choix des articles résultent d'une enquête sur les dépenses des ménages menée en 1976 auprès d'un échantillon aléatoire de ménages.

Pondération et composition

Groupes principaux	Nombre d'articles	Pondération	Nombre approximatif de relevés de prix
Alimentation	...	244	...
Boissons alcoolisées	...	82	...
Tabac	...	53	...
Logement	...	104	...
Combustible et éclairage	...	90	...
Articles ménagers durables	...	66	...
Habillement et chaussure	...	72	...
Transports et véhicules	...	134	...
Biens divers	...	64	...
Services	...	59	...
Repas au dehors	...	32	...
Total	450	1 000	...

Dépenses de consommation des ménages
Les dépenses de consommation prises en compte dans le calcul de l'indice comprennent presque tous les biens et services qu'achète la population de l'indice. Elles excluent les cotisations aux caisses de retraite, l'impôt sur le revenu et autres impôts directs, les dons en espèces et les primes d'assurance vie.

Mode de relevé des prix
Les prix sont relevés dans une centaine de magasins de vente au détail et d'établissements de services par des enquêteurs, au moyen de questionnaires par correspondance ou d'enquêtes par téléphone. Le relevé a lieu chaque mois le mardi le plus proche du milieu du mois. Les prix retenus pour le calcul de l'indice sont les prix effectivement payés. N'entrent en ligne de compte ni les remises ni les rabais qui ne sont consentis qu'à certains acheteurs. Les soldes et occasions ne sont pris en considération que si l'article se présente dans la taille et la qualité ordinaires.

Logement
Les données sur les loyers s'obtiennent pour un petit nombre de logements représentatifs.

Spécification des variétés
Les articles sont spécifiés par le nom, la marque, la qualité, la taille, etc.

Substitution, changement de qualité, etc.
On tient compte, par un examen attentif, des changements que subissent des produits analogues afin de distinguer les purs renchérissements des augmentations de prix dues à des changements de qualité.

Articles saisonniers
Pour les fruits et légumes frais, un coefficient de pondération fixe pour l'ensemble du sous-groupe est réparti entre les coefficients de pondération des articles du sous-groupe qui varient chaque mois.

Calcul
L'indice est calculé selon la formule de Laspeyres sous forme de moyenne arithmétique pondérée à base fixe, les coefficients de pondération correspondant à la période de base.

Organisation et publication
Treasury's Economics Section: «Index of Retail Prices» (Douglas).
idem: «Digest of Economic and Social Statistics»

ILES SALOMON (HONIARA)

Dénomination officielle
Retail Price Index (Indice des prix de détail).

Portée
L'indice est calculé mensuellement et porte sur les ménages à Honiara dont le chef disposait d'un revenu annuel net inférieur à 4 000 dollars SI en 1977.

Base originale
Octobre - décembre 1977 = 100.

Source des coefficients de pondération
Les coefficients de pondération et les articles sélectionnés ont été déterminés sur la base des résultats d'une enquête sur les dépenses des ménages effectuée en octobre-novembre 1977 à Honiara, auprès de ménages dont le chef gagnait, lors de l'enquête, moins de 4 000 dollars SI nets par an.

Pondération et composition

Groupes principaux	Nombre d'articles	Pondération	Nombre approximatif de relevés de prix
Alimentation	76	47,0	...
Boissons et tabac	8	9,5	...
Habillement et chaussure	12	5,0	...
Transports	22	11,0	...
Logement (y compris loyer, combustible et éclairage, etc.)	14	15,5	...
Divers	33	12,0	...
Total	165	100,0	...

Dépenses de consommation des ménages
Pas disponible.

Mode de relevé des prix
Les prix sont relevés par des enquêteurs entre le 15 et le 20 de chaque mois sur des marchés, auprès de points de vente au

détail et de prestataires de services à Honiara. Les prix des fruits et légumes frais sont recueillis chaque semaine.

Logement
Les données relatives au loyer sont obtenues pour trois logements appartenant au gouvernement et quatre logements privés.

Spécification des variétés
Pas disponible.

Substitution, changement de qualité, etc.
Pas disponible.

Articles saisonniers
Il est tenu compte des fluctuations saisonnières des prix de certains articles, en maintenant, hors saison, le dernier prix de saison.

Calcul
L'indice est calculé selon la formule de Laspeyres, sous forme de moyenne arithmétique pondérée à base fixe, les coefficients de pondération correspondant à la période de base.

Autres informations
Une nouvelle série portant sur les ménages à Honiara ayant un revenu annuel provenant de toutes les sources, inférieur à 11 000 dollars SI en 1982 (base octobre - décembre 1984 = 100) est maintenant calculée mais les informations méthodologiques relatives à cette série n'étaient pas disponibles au BIT lors de la publication du présent Volume.

Organisation et publication
Ministry of Finance, Statistics Office: «Statistical Bulletin» (Honiara).

ILES VIERGES (BRITANNIQUES)

Dénomination officielle
Consumer Price Index (Indice des prix à la consommation).

Portée
L'indice est calculé mensuellement et porte sur les ménages à revenus moyens des Iles Vierges britanniques, disposant d'un revenu mensuel de 500 à 700 dollars des Etats-Unis en septembre 1983.

Base originale
Mars 1985 = 100.

Source des coefficients de pondération
La valeur des coefficients de pondération et le choix des articles résultent d'une enquête sur les dépenses des ménages effectuée en septembre 1983 auprès d'un échantillon de 105 ménages à revenus moyens, disposant d'un revenu mensuel de 500 à 700 dollars des Etats-Unis en septembre 1983. Les pondérations n'ont pas été ajustées pour tenir compte de l'évolution des prix entre le moment de l'enquête et mars 1985.

Pondération et composition

Groupes principaux	Nombre d'articles	Pondération	Nombre approximatif de relevés de prix
Alimentation et tabac	133	400	...
Logement	11	206	...
Mobilier et fournitures de ménage	24	62	...
Habillement et chaussure	23	115	...
Transports	12	114	...
Services	19	82	...
Divers	15	21	...
Total	237	1 000	...

Dépenses de consommation des ménages
Sont exclus les cotisations à la sécurité sociale, l'impôt sur le revenu et l'achat ou l'échange d'articles usagés.

Mode de relevé des prix
Les prix sont relevés par des enquêteurs dans 89 commerces de détail et autres établissements de Road Town, la capitale, et Virgin Gorda. Les relevés sont effectués mensuellement - le jeudi ou le vendredi le plus proche du 15 du mois - pour la plupart des articles. Ils le sont trimestriellement ou semestriellement pour les frais de poste et téléphone, l'électricité et les courses en taxi. Les prix entrant dans le calcul de l'indice sont les prix de détail réellement payés. Ne sont pas retenus le prix des soldes et des objets vendus au rabais.

Logement
Les données relatives aux loyers sont relevées trimestriellement pour des logement loués avec deux chambres à coucher.

Spécification des variétés
Les articles retenus font l'objet de spécifications détaillés fondées sur les résultats de l'enquête sur les dépenses des ménages. Elles portent le nom, la marque, la qualité et la taille.

Substitution, changement de qualité, etc.
Lorsqu'un produit disparaît du marché, on lui substitue un produit comparable.

Articles saisonniers
Ils ne font l'objet d'aucun traitement spécial.

Calcul
L'indice est calculé selon la formule de Laspeyres sous forme de moyenne arithmétique pondérée à base fixe, les coefficients de pondération correspondant à septembre 1983.

L'indice pour un article est obtenu en utilisant les rapports de prix de la période courante et de la période précédente.

Autres informations
Les indices des principaux sous-groupes sont publiés.

Organisation et publication
Chief Minister's Office, Development Planning Unit: «Consumer Price Index Report» (Road Town).

INDE (ENSEMBLE DU PAYS 1)

Dénomination officielle
Consumer Price Index for Agricultural Labourers (Indice des prix à la consommation pour les travailleurs agricoles).

Portée
L'indice est calculé mensuellement pour les ménages de travailleurs agricoles, c'est-à-dire pour les salariés employés à des travaux de production agricole et leur famille.

Base originale
Juillet 1960 - juin 1961 = 100.

Source des coefficients de pondération
La pondération a été établie d'après les dépenses de consommation obtenues lors de la deuxième enquête sur les travailleurs agricoles, effectuée d'août 1956 à août 1957 auprès de 7 800 ménages. Les coefficients de pondération ont été corrigés pour tenir compte de la variation des niveaux de prix entre 1956-57 et 1960-61. Les articles retenus pour le calcul de l'indice sont ceux qui occupent une place relativement importante dans les dépenses des ménages, dont la variation des prix est sensible, et qui sont représentatifs d'un groupe plus large de produits voisins. Les dépenses relatives à des articles qu'il n'a pas été possible de retenir ont été convenablement affectées à d'autres articles ou groupes d'articles.

Pondération et composition

Groupes principaux	Nombre d'articles	Pondération	Nombre approximatif de relevés de prix
Alimentation	37	78,1	...
Combustible et éclairage	4	8,0	...
Habillement, chaussure et literie	11	6,1	...
Divers	10	7,8	...
Total	62	100,0	...

Dépenses de consommation des ménages
Les dépenses de consommation prises en compte pour le calcul de l'indice ne visent que les biens et services occupant une place relativement importante dans les dépenses des ménages. Sont exclus les dépenses engagées pour des cérémonies et le coût de la remise en état des bâtiments et terrains.

Mode de relevé des prix
Le personnel du National Sample Survey relève mensuellement les prix de détail auprès des commerces et marchés des 422 villages constituant l'échantillon. Les relevés sont effectués le premier jour de marché ou le premier samedi de chaque mois. Lorsque les articles retenus pour l'indice peuvent être achetés dans les magasins contrôlés, leurs prix sont également relevés.

Logement
Les dépenses de loyer étant nulles ou négligeables, il n'en est pas tenu compte.

Spécification des variétés
Les articles retenus pour l'indice font l'objet de spécifications détaillées pour chacun des 422 villages de l'échantillon, ce sur la base de renseignements recueillis lors d'une enquête spéciale menée dans ces villages en juillet-septembre 1960.

Substitution, changement de qualité, etc.
Chaque fois que les caractéristiques d'un produit changent, on ajuste l'indice en conséquence, si cela est possible. On applique aussi, dans certains cas, la formule d'enchaînement.

Articles saisonniers
Les articles saisonniers n'ont pas été retenus dans l'indice.

Calcul
L'indice pour l'ensemble du pays est calculé sous forme de moyenne pondérée de plusieurs séries d'indices pour chacun des 15 Etats du pays (ou groupes de petits Etats ou territoires).
L'indice de chaque Etat est calculé selon la formule de Laspeyres, sous forme de moyenne arithmétique pondérée à base fixe, les coefficients de pondération correspondant à la période août 1956 - août 1957. Ces indices partiels sont ensuite pondérés et combinés pour former l'indice relatif à l'ensemble du pays, dont les coefficients de pondération sont les dépenses totales de consommation de la population de chaque Etat.

Organisation et publication
Ministry of Labour, Labour Bureau: «Indian Labour Journal» (Simla).
Ministry of Labour, Employment and Rehabilitation: «Indian Labour Journal» (Simla, décembre 1962 et octobre 1968).

INDE (ENSEMBLE DU PAYS 2)

Dénomination officielle
Consumer Price Index for Urban Non-Manual Employees (Indice des prix à la consommation pour les salariés non-manuels urbains).

Portée
L'indice est calculé mensuellement et porte sur les familles tirant la majeure partie de leurs revenus d'activités non manuelles exercées dans les secteurs non agricoles, et habitant 59 centres urbains sélectionnés.

Base originale
Avril 1984 - mars 1985 = 100.

Source des coefficients de pondération
Les coefficients de pondération et les articles choisis résultent d'une enquête sur les dépenses des ménages effectuée une année durant (juillet 1982 - juin 1983) auprès d'un échantillon de 45 000 ménages de travailleurs non manuels habitant 59 centres urbains sélectionnés. Les coefficients de pondération n'ont fait l'objet d'aucun ajustement visant à prendre en compte les changements de prix survenus entre l'époque de l'enquête et la période de base. Les coefficients correspondant aux articles exclus ont été attribués aux articles inclus dans le barème de pondération, généralement selon des critères de similitude des tendances observées dans l'évolution des prix. Dans les cas où les attributions à des articles spécifiques ne sont pas considérées comme appropriées, elles sont effectuées au niveau des sous-groupes.

Pondération et composition

Groupes principaux	Nombre d'articles (a)	Pondération (b)	Nombre approximatif de relevés de prix
Alimentation et tabac	...	...	...
Combustible et éclairage	...	...	...
Logement	...	...	...
Habillement, chaussure et literie	...	...	...
Divers	...	...	...
Total	...	...	167 540

Remarque: (a) Le nombre d'articles est compris entre 146 et 345 selon le centre considéré. (b) Les coefficients de pondération diffèrent d'un centre à l'autre.

Dépenses de consommation des ménages
Les sommes allouées à l'épargne et à l'investissement, comprenant les primes d'assurance-vie, les contributions aux fonds de pensions, le remboursement des dettes, les intérêts, les frais de litige, les impôts (y compris les taxes routières, municipales, etc.), les cotisations aux syndicats, les dépenses pour les cérémonies, les dons et oeuvres de bienfaisance, les envois de fonds aux personnes à charge, etc., ont été exclues du barème de pondération parce qu'elles ne constituent pas, en général, des dépenses de consommation. Bien que les envois de fonds, les dépenses pour les cérémonies, etc., puissent comporter une part de consommation, il est impossible de leur attribuer un prix car on ne peut les assimiler exclusivement à une quantité déterminée de biens et/ou de services.

Les revenus en nature (qu'ils soient obtenus à titre gratuit ou octroyés par l'employeur ou d'autres personnes) et les dons reçus ont été évalués aux prix prévalant sur le marché. Leur valeur a été enregistrée comme partie du revenu global et ils ont été également inclus dans les chapitres des dépenses correspondants. La valeur locative des logements occupés par leur propriétaire, ou cédés à titre gratuit par l'employeur ou d'autres personnes, a été évaluée sur la base du loyer des habitations en location d'un type équivalent et généralement pratiqué dans la localité concernée. Aucune distinction n'a été établie dans le traitement des biens durables par rapport à celui des denrées périssables. Cependant, étant donné que les achats de biens durables sont peu fréquents, les dépenses ont été enregistrées non seulement pour le mois de référence mais également pour l'année de référence.

Ainsi, les dépenses moyennes mensuelles, fondées sur les valeurs de l'année de référence, ont été utilisées dans le but d'obtenir les coefficients de pondération. Il n'y a pas eu de différence de traitement entre les achats de biens neufs et ceux de biens d'occasion. Les dépenses relatives aux soins de santé, comprenant l'achat de médicaments, le paiement des services médicaux et des soins de santé correspondants ainsi que les contributions aux régimes de santé, ont été inclus dans le barème de pondération.

Mode de relevé des prix
Le choix d'un échantillon de marchés et de magasins fréquentés par les familles composant l'indice a été effectué au moyen d'une enquête sur le terrain, menée en 1983 dans tous les centres urbains, en utilisant une combinaison appropriée de méthodes d'échantillonnage aléatoire et par choix raisonné.

Le prix de tous les articles est relevé mensuellement sur les marchés, dans les magasins contrôlés, les magasins à prix modéré, les coopératives de consommateurs (y compris les grands bazars), les autres points de vente au détail et les établissements de services. Ces relevés sont effectués par la Field Operations Division de la National Sample Survey Organisation, organisme permanent travaillant sur le terrain qui effectue des enquêtes à grande échelle et rassemble régulièrement des données statistiques.

Dans la mesure du possible, le relevé des prix relatifs aux différents groupes d'articles intervient à date fixe dans la semaine de l'enquête, de manière à ce que la comparaison entre deux relevés effectués sur le même point de vente ne soit pas faussée par les différences de calendrier. Le choix final des dates auxquelles doit avoir lieu le relevé des données relatives au prix d'un groupe particulier de biens est fixé en prenant en compte le volume des transactions effectuées chaque jour de la semaine.

Les prix relevés sont ceux payés pour les transactions effectivement réalisées. Les chiffres retenus comprennent les taxes sur les ventes et autres frais similaires généralement à la charge du consommateur, déduction faite des soldes et rabais habituellement consentis. Les prix illégaux (marché noir), la location-vente et le paiement des intérêts, les achats d'occasion et les transactions portant sur les biens usagés ne sont pas inclus dans le relevé des prix. Les prix à l'importation en tant que tels sont également exclus. Ces derniers entrent rarement, ou pas du tout, dans la consommation des familles composant l'indice. De surcroît, il n'existe pas de points de vente distincts où les articles d'importation sont disponibles périodiquement et en exclusivité.

Logement
Les données relatives aux loyers sont recueillies auprès d'un échantillon de logements en location au moyen d'une enquête permanente sur le loyer des habitations, menée tous les six mois. L'ensemble des logements en location ayant fait l'objet d'une visite aux fins de l'enquête détaillée sur les loyers, elle-même effectuée dans le cadre de l'enquête de 1982-83 sur les dépenses des ménages, a constitué le cadre fondamental de

l'enquête permanente sur les loyers. Le relevé des logements en question a été réparti uniformément sur la période de six mois allant de juin à décembre. Au niveau mensuel, cette répartition était la suivante: les logements visités entre juillet 1982 et janvier 1983 comptent pour le mois de juillet, ceux visités pendant la période août 1982 - février 1983 comptent pour le mois d'août, et ainsi de suite. A partir de la liste de logements affectés à chaque mois, et après que les logements aient été classés en quatre catégories en fonction du nombre de pièces, chacun des enquêteurs effectue le relevé d'un échantillon de 14 logements en location. Les données relatives aux loyers sont relevées tous les six mois auprès des logements inclus dans chaque échantillon mensuel. L'indice des loyers est calculé sur la base des données couvrant une période de six mois, afin de refléter leur évolution moyenne sur la moitié d'une année.

Outre les logements en location, les logements gratuits et occupés par leur propriétaire sont également inclus dans l'indice global des loyers. L'indice des loyers obtenu à partir des données concernant les logements en location est utilisé par défaut comme indice du loyer des logements occupés par leur propriétaire.

La méthode de calcul de l'indice consiste à établir la moyenne des loyers des six mois en cours par rapport aux six mois immédiatement antérieurs pour chacun des relevés de prix, et de calculer ensuite l'indice des loyers comme un indice chaîne. Des rapports moyens sont calculés pour chacune des quatre catégories mentionnées ci-dessus, puis combinés en utilisant la composition effective des logements en location et occupés par leur propriétaire, disponible d'après les résultats de l'enquête sur les dépenses de consommation des ménages, afin d'obtenir les rapports moyens globaux. L'indice pour les logements en location et ceux occupés par leur propriétaire est calculé comme un indice chaîne en utilisant l'indice des six mois précédents. L'indice pour les logements gratuits est fixé à 100. L'indice global des loyers est calculé sur la base d'un indice pour les logements gratuits et d'un indice pour les logements en location et pour ceux occupés par leur propriétaire, en tenant compte du pourcentage de ménages appartenant à la catégorie correspondante, ce pourcentage étant communiqué par l'enquête sur les dépenses de consommation des ménages.

Spécification des variétés
Des spécifications pour divers articles ont été établies avec suffisamment de précision en ce qui concerne la qualité, la variété et les autres caractéristiques physiques essentielles telles que la taille, les dimensions, le contenu matériel, etc., en gardant à l'esprit les conditions prévalant dans les différents centres, de manière à garantir l'absolue fiabilité de l'identification.

La détermination des spécifications pour chacun des articles jouissant d'une grande renommée auprès des familles composant l'indice a été effectuée en tenant compte d'une approche portant à la fois sur les marchés et sur les consommateurs. Les spécifications ainsi définies ont été signalées aux magasins sélectionnés pour faire l'objet d'un relevé régulier des prix.

Substitution, changement de qualité, etc.
Certaines procédures ont été établies pour les cas où l'on ne dispose pas, dans le mois en cours, de certains relevés de prix provenant des spécifications de magasins. Des relevés de prix de remplacement sont alors recueillis, soit auprès d'autres magasins, gardés en réserve pour la même spécification, soit à partir d'une spécification d'une réputation comparable. Les nouveaux relevés sont alors enchaînés anciens, au moyen des techniques habituelles d'enchaînage. Les changements de qualité et la disparition des produits anciens sont traités de la même manière, dans la mesure où le changement des spécifications permet de les refléter.

Articles saisonniers
La couverture des articles entrant dans l'indice des fruits et légumes varie chaque mois en fonction de leur disponibilité. La méthode adoptée pour appliquer des coefficients de pondération à ces articles saisonniers est la suivante:

Les coefficients de pondération du sous-groupe «fruits et légumes» sont calculés sur la base des dépenses moyennes mensuelles relatives à tous les articles des sous-groupes. Cependant, les coefficients de pondération pour chaque article et pour chaque mois sont calculés en répartissant la pondération des articles pour lesquels aucun prix n'a été attribué sur la pondération, au prorata, des articles pour lesquels un prix a été relevé.

Calcul
L'indice est calculé selon la formule de Laspeyres, sous forme de moyenne arithmétique pondérée à base fixe, les coefficients de pondération correspondant à la période juillet 1982 - juin 1983.

L'indice est directement calculé pour chacun des centres. L'indice pour l'ensemble de l'Inde est calculé en tant que moyenne pondérée des indices par centre, les coefficients de pondération étant fondés sur l'estimation de la consommation totale des ménages des différents centres, en utilisant les données fournies par le recensement de la population de 1981 et celles fournies par l'enquête sur les dépenses des ménages de 1982-83.

Autres informations
Les indices des prix à la consommation pour les travailleurs de l'industrie et de l'agriculture sont calculés par le Labour Bureau et publiés dans «l'Indian Labour Journal».

Organisation et publication
L'indice est calculé mensuellement par la Central Statistical Organisation (New Delhi) et publié dans le «Monthly Abstract of Statistics».

idem: «Statistical Abstract».

Labour Bureau (Simla): «Indian Labour Journal».

INDE (ENSEMBLE DU PAYS 3)

Dénomination officielle
Consumer Price Index for Industrial Workers (Indice des prix à la consommation pour les travailleurs de l'industrie).

Portée
L'indice est calculé mensuellement et porte sur les ménages d'ouvriers de 70 centres industriels répartis dans l'ensemble du pays.

Base originale
1982 = 100.

Source des coefficients de pondération
Les coefficients de pondération et le choix des articles résultent d'une enquête sur les dépenses des ménages effectuée une année durant (juillet 1982-juin 1983) auprès de 32 616 familles d'ouvriers habitant 70 centres urbains et travaillant dans sept secteurs industriels: manufactures, mines, plantations, chemins de fer, entreprises publiques de transport routier, sociétés de production et de distribution d'électricité, ports et bassins portuaires. Les coefficients de pondération n'ont pas été ajustés pour tenir compte de l'évolution des prix entre le moment de l'enquête et la période de base.

L'admission d'un article dans la composition de l'indice dépend de la moyenne des dépenses signalées par les familles de classe ouvrière par rapport aux dépenses totales de consommation. Elle dépend également du nombre de familles faisant état de leurs dépenses. Les coefficients de pondération des articles pour lesquels les dépenses sont négligeables se voient en général affectés à des articles assimilés du même sous-groupe.

Pondération et composition

Groupes principaux	Nombre d'articles	Pondération	Nombre approximatif de relevés de prix
Alimentation	106	57,00	...
Tabac, pan, supari, etc.	16	3,15	...
Logement	1	8,67	...
Combustible et éclairage	10	6,28	...
Habillement, chaussure et literie	39	8,54	...
Divers	88	16,36	...
Total	260	100,00	...

Dépenses de consommation des ménages
Les revenus en nature, les logements occupés par leur propriétaire, les dons, etc. ont été pris en compte par l'attribution d'une valeur imputée. En ce qui concerne les paiements à titre partiel, seuls ceux effectués au cours du mois de référence ont été pris en compte. L'achat des biens d'occasion et le commerce des biens usagés ont été exclus. Les dépenses consacrées à la sécurité sociale, aux fonds de pensions, aux patentes, aux assurances sur les biens, aux impôts directs, aux assurances-vie, aux envois de fonds, etc. ont été traitées comme des dépenses non-affectées à la consommation.

Mode de relevé des prix
Les agents de l'administration de l'Etat procèdent au relevé du

prix des différents biens et services, y compris l'électricité, le gaz, les soins médicaux, l'éducation, les transports et communications, par des inspections directes dans les marchés et les magasins de détail les plus fréquentés, les magasins contrôlés par les pouvoirs publics (à prix modérés) et les établissements de services. La fréquence du relevé est hebdomadaire pour les articles à prix instable. Les prix de certains articles, tels que les billets de cinéma, le mobilier, l'outillage, les appareils ménagers, les transports, l'habillement et les chaussures, etc. font l'objet d'un relevé mensuel car ils ne subissent pas de trop fréquentes modifications. Les loyers, les frais de scolarisation, le prix des fournitures scolaires sont relevés tous les six mois. Tous les prix sont recueillis au même moment, le jour fixé pour leur relevé. Les prix nets sont utilisés dans l'indice. Les prix du marché libre et les prix officiels (contrôlés) sont combinés dans les rapports des articles correspondant à la demande moyenne par l'intermédiaire de deux sources. Les prix du marché noir, la location-vente, l'achat de biens d'occasion et les prix à l'importation ne sont pas pris en compte dans le calcul de l'indice.

Logement
Les relevés relatifs aux logements en location, aux logements gratuits et à ceux occupés par leur propriétaire, sont effectués tous les six mois, en tenant compte des impôts, des réparations accessoires et des frais de blanchiment à la charge des habitants, mais à l'exclusion des charges telles que l'eau, l'électricité, le balayage, etc. L'indice des loyers est calculé selon la méthode des enchaînements à la période de base, qui consiste à comparer les modifications du loyer par rapport à la période précédente de six mois, et non à la période de base. Cette méthode tient compte d'une manière plus appropriée des dépréciations liées au logement. Les nouveaux logements ne sont pas inclus dans l'échantillon, car on estime que l'évolution de leur loyer ne différera pas de celle des logements anciens.

Dans le cas des habitations occupées par leur propriétaire, on utilise le montant des loyers de logements similaires. Si de tels logements sont introuvables sur le marché, l'indice des habitations occupées par leur propriétaire est considéré comme équivalent à celui des logements en location.

Spécification des variétés
Chaque article se voit attribuer une spécification déterminée, comprenant la variété, la qualité, la fabrication et la marque, le nombre, etc. Les spécifications sont élaborées sur la base des préférences locales, déterminées au moyen d'études de marché.

Substitution, changement de qualité, etc.
Lorsque la qualité prescrite pour un article n'est pas en vente, on lui substitue une autre variété de qualité comparable ou équivalente. L'ancienne variété est réintégrée dans l'indice si elle réapparaît sur le marché. Des corrections sont pratiquées pour tenir compte des différences de prix dues aux différences de qualité de l'article de substitution. Lorsque la qualité de ce dernier diffère de 100 pour cent (ou que la différence est difficile à évaluer), la série de prix du nouveau produit est rattachée à celle du produit remplacé.

Articles saisonniers
Au sein du groupe des produits alimentaires, les coefficients de pondération du sous-groupe des fruits et légumes ont été maintenus à un niveau constant. Cependant, pour divers articles, des pondérations différentes selon les mois ont été calculées en fonction de la disponibilité desdits articles. Les pondérations des articles qui ne sont pas disponibles au cours d'un mois donné sont appliquées à d'autres articles apparentés.

Calcul
L'indice est calculé chaque mois selon la formule de Laspeyres sous forme de moyenne arithmétique pondérée à base fixe, les coefficients de pondération correspondant à la période 1981-82. En général, une simple moyenne de tous les prix relevés dans le mois est établie pour chaque article. Une simple moyenne des rapports de prix est calculée pour les articles dont plus d'une variété est soumise à évaluation.

Tous les indices par centre font l'objet d'un calcul direct. Toutefois, l'indice pour l'ensemble du pays est calculé comme la moyenne pondérée de tous les indices par centre, ces derniers étant fondés sur le produit des dépenses moyennes de consommation par famille par le nombre de familles habitant chacun des centres en 1981-82.

Autres informations
Outre l'Indice des prix à la consommation pour les travailleurs de l'industrie, deux autres séries statistiques sont publiées en Inde: l'Indice des prix à la consommation pour les travailleurs agricoles et l'Indice des prix à la consommation pour les employés urbains. Le premier est calculé et publié par le Labour Bureau dans le cadre de sa publication mensuelle, «Indian Labour Journal». Le second est calculé et publié par la Central Statistical Organisation (New Delhi) dans la publication «Monthly abstract of Statistics».

Organisation et publication
Ministry of Labour, Labour Bureau: «Indian Labour Journal» (Simla) (pour toute information complémentaire d'ordre méthodologique, voir les numéros de novembre 1988 et janvier 1989)

idem: «Indian Labour Year Book - Annual.»

idem: «Pocket Book of Labour Statistics - Annual.»

idem: «Indian Labour Statistics - Annual.»

INDE (DELHI)

Dénomination officielle
Consumer Price Index for Industrial Workers (Indice des prix à la consommation pour les travailleurs de l'industrie).

Portée
L'indice est calculé mensuellement et porte sur les ménages d'ouvriers habitant Delhi.

Base originale
1982 = 100.

Source des coefficients de pondération
Les coefficients de pondération et le choix des articles résultent d'une enquête sur les dépenses des ménages effectuée une année durant (juillet 1982-juin 1983) auprès de 648 familles d'ouvriers habitant 70 centres urbains et travaillant dans sept secteurs industriels: manufactures, mines, plantations, chemins de fer, entreprises publiques de transport routier, sociétés de production et de distribution d'électricité, ports et bassins portuaires. L'indice porte sur des familles de travailleurs de l'industrie habitant Delhi. Les coefficients de pondération n'ont pas été ajustés pour tenir compte de l'évolution des prix entre le moment de l'enquête et la période de base. L'admission d'un article dans la composition de l'indice dépend de la moyenne des dépenses signalées par les familles de classe ouvrière par rapport aux dépenses totales de consommation. Elle dépend également du nombre de familles faisant état de leurs dépenses. Les coefficients de pondération des articles pour lesquels les dépenses allouées sont négligeables se voient en général affectés à des articles assimilés du même sous-groupe.

Pondération et composition

Groupes principaux	Nombre d'articles	Pondération	Nombre approximatif de relevés de prix
Alimentation	61	50,71	524
Tabac, pan, supari, etc.	8	2,35	56
Loyer	1	14,02	21
Combustible et éclairage	6	5,61	39
Habillement, chaussure et literie	15	12,53	31
Divers	39	14,78	143
Total	130	100,00	814

Dépenses de consommation des ménages
Les revenus en nature, les logements occupés par leur propriétaire, les dons, etc. ont été pris en compte par l'attribution d'une valeur imputée. En ce qui concerne les paiements à titre partiel, seuls ceux effectués au cours du mois de référence ont été pris en compte. L'achat des biens d'occasion et le commerce des biens usagés ont été exclus. Les dépenses consacrées à la sécurité sociale, aux fonds de pensions, aux patentes, aux assurances sur les biens, aux impôts directs, aux assurances-vie, aux envois de fonds, etc. ont été traitées comme des dépenses non affectées à la consommation.

Mode de relevé des prix
Les agents de l'administration de l'Etat procèdent au relevé du prix des différents biens et services, y compris l'électricité, le gaz, les soins médicaux, l'éducation, les transports et communications, par des inspections directes dans les marchés et les magasins de détail les plus fréquentés, les magasins contrôlés par les pouvoirs publics (à prix modérés) et les établissements de services. La fréquence du relevé est hebdomadaire pour les

articles à prix instable. Les prix de certains articles, tels que les billets de cinéma, le mobilier, l'outillage, les appareils ménagers, les transports, l'habillement et les chaussures, etc. font l'objet d'un relevé mensuel car ils ne subissent pas de trop fréquentes modifications. Les loyers, les frais de scolarisation, le prix des fournitures scolaires sont relevés tous les six mois. Tous les prix sont recueillis au même moment, le jour fixé pour leur relevé. Les prix nets sont utilisés dans l'indice. Les prix du marché libre et les prix officiels (contrôlés) sont combinés dans les rapports des articles correspondant à la demande moyenne par l'intermédiaire de deux sources. Les prix du marché noir, la location-vente, l'achat de biens d'occasion et les prix à l'importation ne sont pas pris en compte dans le calcul de l'indice.

Logement
Les relevés relatifs aux logements en location, aux logements gratuits et à ceux occupés par leur propriétaire, sont effectués tous les six mois, en tenant compte des impôts, des réparations accessoires et des frais de blanchiment à la charge des habitants, mais à l'exclusion de charges telles que l'eau, l'électricité, le balayage, etc. L'indice des loyers est calculé selon la méthode des enchaînements à la période de base, qui consiste à comparer les modifications du loyer par rapport à la période précédente de six mois, et non à la période de base. Cette méthode tient compte d'une manière plus appropriée des dépréciations liées au logement. Les nouveaux logements ne sont pas inclus dans l'échantillon, car on estime que l'évolution de leur loyer ne différera pas de celle des logements anciens.

Dans le cas des habitations occupées par leur propriétaire, on utilises les montants des loyers de logements similaires. Si de tels logements sont introuvables sur le marché, l'indice des habitations occupées par leur propriétaire est considéré comme équivalent à celui des logements en location.

Spécification des variétés
Chaque article se voit attribuer une spécification déterminée, comprenant la variété, la qualité, la fabrication et la marque, le nombre, etc. Les spécifications sont élaborées sur la base des préférences locales, déterminées au moyen d'études de marché.

Substitution, changement de qualité, etc.
Lorsque la qualité prescrite pour un article n'est pas en vente, on lui substitue une autre variété de qualité comparable ou équivalente. L'ancienne variété est réintégrée dans l'indice si elle réapparaît sur le marché. Des corrections sont pratiquées pour tenir compte des différences de prix dues aux différences de qualité de l'article de substitution. Lorsque la qualité de ce dernier diffère de 100 pour cent (ou que la différence est difficile à évaluer), la série de prix du nouveau produit est rattachée à celle du produit remplacé.

Articles saisonniers
Au sein du groupe des produits alimentaires, les coefficients de pondération du sous-groupe des fruits et légumes ont été maintenus à un niveau constant. Cependant, pour divers articles, des pondérations différentes selon les mois ont été calculées en fonction de la disponibilité desdits articles. Les pondérations des articles qui ne sont pas disponibles au cours d'un mois donné sont appliquées à d'autres articles apparentés.

Calcul
L'indice est calculé chaque mois selon la formule de Laspeyres sous forme de moyenne arithmétique pondérée à base fixe, les coefficients de pondération correspondant à la période 1981-82.

En général, une simple moyenne de tous les prix relevés dans le mois est établie pour chaque article. Une simple moyenne des rapports de prix est calculée pour les articles dont plus d'une variété est soumise à évaluation.

Tous les indices par centre font l'objet d'un calcul direct. Toutefois, l'indice pour l'ensemble du pays est calculé comme la moyenne pondérée de tous les indices par centre, ces derniers étant fondés sur le produit des dépenses moyennes de consommation par famille par le nombre de familles habitant chacun des centres en 1981-82.

Autres informations
Outre l'Indice des prix à la consommation pour les travailleurs de l'industrie, deux autres séries statistiques sont publiées en Inde: l'Indice des prix à la consommation pour les travailleurs agricoles et l'Indice des prix à la consommation pour les employés urbains. Le premier est calculé et publié par le Labour Bureau dans le cadre de sa publication mensuelle, «Indian Labour Journal». Le second est calculé et publié par le Central Statistical Organisation (New Delhi) dans la publication «Monthly abstract of Statistics».

Organisation et publication
Ministry of Labour, Labour Bureau: «Indian Labour Journal» (Simla) (pour toute information complémentaire d'ordre méthodologique, voir les numéros de novembre 1988 et janvier 1989)
idem: «Indian Labour Year Book - Annual.»
idem: «Pocket Book of Labour Statistics - Annual.»
idem: «Indian Labour Statistics - Annual.»

INDONESIE

Dénomination officielle
Combined Consumer Price Index of 27 capital cities of provinces (Indice combiné des prix à la consommation de 27 grandes villes de provinces).

Portée
L'indice est calculé mensuellement et porte sur les ménages privés habitant les zones urbaines de 27 grandes villes de provinces.

Base originale
Avril 1988 - mars 1989 = 100.

Source des coefficients de pondération
La valeur des coefficients de pondération et le choix des articles résultent d'une enquête sur le coût de la vie effectuée de juillet 1988 à juin 1989 dans 27 grandes villes de provinces. L'échantillon portait sur 35 000 ménages privés. N'étaient pas compris dans l'enquête les ménages d'une seule personne, ceux comptant plus de dix membres, les ménages vivant en institutions et ceux dont les membres sont analphabètes.

Pondération et composition
Pas disponible.

Dépenses de consommation des ménages
Les dépenses de consommation des ménages ont été prises en compte pour l'alimentation, les boissons, le tabac et les services, et la date de leur livraison pour le calcul des dépenses concernant les biens semi-durables et durables. L'estimation du loyer des logements occupés en propriété et à titre gratuit est calculée en estimant le loyer pratiqué au même moment. Le montant de l'estimation est classé en tant que revenu du ménage et aussi comme total de dépenses ayant la même valeur. Lorsque le ménage habite une maison de fonction (ou fournie par sa société) dont le loyer est inférieur à celui pratiqué sur le marché, la différence est classée dans la catégorie des revenus estimés et la valeur du loyer sur le marché est considérée en tant que dépense.

De même, les biens reçus sans frais et ceux achetés à bas prix sont estimés au prix du marché et classés dans les dépenses relatives à ces biens, tandis que la différence entre la valeur sur le marché et les bas prix constitue les revenus du ménage.

Les achats à crédit de biens et de services consommés au cours de la période de référence sont classés en tant que dépenses de consommation pour les biens et services concernés, de même que comme estimations du revenu, tandis que les paiements anticipés et les acomptes versés au cours de la période de référence sont classés dans la catégorie des dépenses effectuées à des fins autres que la consommation.

Les dépenses à des fins autres que la consommation ainsi que d'autres paiements sont: impôt sur le revenu, impôt sur le transfert de la propriété, de véhicules automobiles, impôts fonciers et immobiliers, taxes sur la propriété et redevances audio-visuelles, épargne, paiement des primes d'assurance, remboursement des dettes et intérêts, paiements anticipés pour l'achat de biens, prêts à des tiers, achat de biens immeubles (terrains, maisons, y compris réparations importantes) frais de participation à des fêtes, contribution à des manifestations religieuses/traditionnelles, pertes d'argent, etc.

Mode de relevé des prix
Les prix sont relevés par des agents des services centraux et locaux des statistiques auprès de magasins et points de vente au détail sélectionnés. La collecte des prix a lieu chaque semaine, chaque mois ou chaque trimestre. Elle est effectuée le mardi pour les relevés hebdomadaires, le 15 du mois pour les relevés mensuels, et du 10 au 20 pour les relevés trimestriels.

Les données relatives aux prix de l'électricité, du gaz, de l'eau et des communications sont extraites des barèmes officiels.

Les prix retenus pour le calcul de l'indice sont les prix de détail réellement payés par le consommateur.

Logement
Les prix sont relevés en mars et septembre de chaque année auprès de 16 types de logements, compte tenu de la qualité de leur construction et de leurs équipements. Les logements occupés en propriété sont compris dans les calculs des coefficients de pondération. Cependant, dans l'indice, les changements de prix sont calculés en tenant compte des matériaux de construction et des salaires des ouvriers du bâtiment.

Spécification des variétés
Chacun des articles entrant dans l'indice fait l'objet d'une spécification détaillée. Les spécifications décrivent la variété, la qualité et la marque.

Substitution, changement de qualité, etc.
Lorsqu'un changement se produit dans la qualité d'un article, il n'est remplacé par un article d'une autre qualité que si l'on dispose du prix de la période en cours et de celle qui l'a précédée.

Articles saisonniers
Il n'y a pas de changement de saison et c'est ainsi que l'ensemble des articles sont disponibles tout au long de l'année.

Calcul
L'indice est calculé selon la formule de Laspeyres, sous forme de moyenne arithmétique pondérée à base fixe, les coefficients de pondération correspondant à la période de base.

Le rapport de prix de chaque article est calculé en divisant le prix moyen de la période en cours par le prix moyen de la période précédente. Les prix moyens sont des moyennes arithmétiques simples.

On obtient les indices combinés en prenant la moyenne pondérée des indices de prix de chaque sous-groupe, puis de chaque groupe jusqu'à l'indice général.

L'indice est un agrégat de séries relatives aux différentes capitales de provinces. L'indice national résulte du calcul des séries concernant les villes, à la suite de l'utilisation, en tant que coefficient de pondération, du nombre des ménages habitant les agglomérations urbaines de chacune des villes.

Autres informations
Des indices distincts pour chacune des 27 grandes villes sont également calculés et publiés.

Organisation et publication
Central Bureau of Statistics: «Monthly Statistical Bulletin» (Djakarta).

IRAN, REP. ISLAMIQUE D'

Dénomination officielle
Consumer Price Index (Indice des prix à la consommation).

Portée
L'indice est calculé mensuellement et porte sur les familles urbaines dont les dépenses annuelles totales s'élevaient jusqu'à 4 700 000 rials en 1982-83.

Base originale
21 mars 1982 - 20 mars 1983 = 100.

Source des coefficients de pondération
La valeur des coefficients de pondération et le choix des articles résultent d'une enquête sur les dépenses des ménages effectuée au cours de la période mars 1982 - mars 1983. L'enquête portait sur 15 000 ménages urbains dont les dépenses annuelles ne dépassaient pas 4 700 000 rials.

Dépenses de consommation des ménages
Les dépenses de consommation prises en compte pour le calcul des coefficients de pondération correspondent à la valeur de tous les biens et services acquis par les ménages aux fins de consommation ou remis à d'autres ménages au cours de l'année de référence. Ces dépenses comprennent la valeur totale des biens durables, les achats à crédit lors de la période de l'achat, les revenus en nature (ne provenant pas d'autres ménages), les cotisations aux assurances sociales, les frais d'obtention de licence et patente, de soins de santé, d'assurance, les paiements de primes d'assurance-vie et les dons. Ne sont pas compris les remises de fonds, les impôts directs, les cotisations aux caisses de retraite et la valeur des articles produits et consommés par les ménages.

Pondération et composition

Groupes principaux	Nombre d'articles	Pondération	Nombre approximatif de relevés de prix
Alimentation, boissons et tabac	96	40,06	55 000
Autres groupes:	...	...	45 000
Habillement et chaussure	42	8,07	...
Logement, combustible et éclairage	25	26,20	...
Ameublement et dépenses de ménage	41	7,24	...
Soins médicaux	41	3,94	...
Transports et communications	22	8,14	...
Loisirs, instruction et lecture	16	1,60	...
Articles et services divers	20	4,75	...
Total	303	100,00	100 000

Mode de relevé des prix
Les prix de la plupart des articles sont relevés par des enquêteurs au cours des 25 premiers jours de chaque mois auprès de points de vente au détail, supermarchés et prestataires de services de 80 villes.

Le prix des articles vendus au rabais, en solde ou au marché noir n'est pas pris en compte. Dans le cas d'articles pour lesquels un prix officiel et un prix au marché libre existent, il est procédé au calcul d'un coefficient moyen de pondération. Les coefficients de pondération proviennent de la dernière enquête sur les dépenses des ménages.

Logement
Les données relatives au loyer sont obtenues tous les trimestres auprès d'un échantillon d'environ 7 000 logements. Un prix de loyer est attribué aux logements occupés en propriété, en partant de l'hypothèse selon laquelle le taux d'inflation les concernant correspond à celui de l'indice général.

Spécification des variétés
Les articles dont les prix sont à relever font l'objet de spécifications précisant la qualité, l'unité employée, la taille, etc.

Substitution, changement de qualité, etc.
On s'efforce d'obtenir tous les mois le prix d'articles de la même qualité; si cela n'est pas possible, le prix relevé est celui de l'article dont la qualité est la plus proche. Lorsque se produit un changement sensible dans la qualité d'un article, les qualités sont ajustées ou la méthode de l'enchaînement est utilisée.

Articles saisonniers
Lorsqu'un article saisonnier est absent du marché, un prix lui est attribué à partir de l'hypothèse selon laquelle il fait l'objet du même taux d'inflation que la moyenne pondérée d'autres articles du groupe.

Calcul
L'indice est calculé selon la formule de Laspeyres sous forme de moyenne arithmétique pondérée à base fixe, les coefficients de pondération correspondant à la période de base. La moyenne de prix compatibles est utilisée pour obtenir les rapports de prix de mois consécutifs. Il est procédé à l'ajustement nécessaire lorsque les prix sont défectueux. Les prix manquants sont remplacés par des prix d'articles en provenance d'autres villes du même ordre. Le calcul de l'indice est effectué directement sur une base régionale.

Autres informations
L'indice des principaux sous-groupes est publié. Aucune autre série ne fait l'objet de calcul au plan national.

Organisation et publication
Economic Statistics Department, Central Bank Markazi: «Economic Report and Balance Sheet» (Téhéran).

IRAQ

Dénomination officielle
Consumer Price Index (Indice des prix à la consommation).

Portée
L'indice est calculé mensuellement et porte sur tous les ménages urbains.

Base originale
1973 = 100.

Source des coefficients de pondération
La valeur des coefficients de pondération et le choix des articles résultent d'une enquête sur les dépenses des ménages menée dans les zones urbaines en 1971-72, sur un échantillon de tous les types de ménages.

Pondération et composition

Groupes principaux	Nombre d'articles	Pondération	Nombre approximatif de relevés de prix
Alimentation	80	49,73	...
Tabac et alcool	7	3,47	...
Habillement	73	8,20	...
Chaussure	9	1,77	...
Equipement ménager	37	5,01	...
Combustible	7	4,01	...
Produits d'entretiens et soins personnels	14	1,69	...
Instruction et loisirs	5	1,72	...
Logement et dépenses de ménage	2	15,62	...
Biens et services divers	2	8,78	...
Total	236	100,00	...

Dépenses de consommation des ménages
Pas disponible.

Mode de relevé des prix
Les prix sont relevés les 3, 9, 21 et 27 de chaque mois sur 10 grands marchés à Bagdad et sur deux grands marchés dans les autres centres urbains.

Logement
Les données relatives au logement sont relevées en mars et septembre de chaque année pour 143 habitations en location à Bagdad et 208 habitations dans les autres gouvernorats.

Spécification des variétés
Pas disponible

Substitution, changement de qualité, etc.
Pas disponible.

Articles saisonniers
Pas disponible.

Calcul
L'indice est calculé selon la formule de Laspeyres sous forme de moyenne arithmétique pondérée à base fixe, les coefficients de pondération correspondant à 1971-72.

Autres informations
Une nouvelle série (base 1988 = 100) est maintenant calculée mais les informations méthodologiques relatives à cette série n'étaient disponibles au BIT lors de la publication du présent Volume.

Organisation et publication
Ministry of Planning, Central Statistical Organisation: «Annual Abstract of Statistics» (Bagdad). Cette publication contient également des informations méthodologiques.

IRLANDE

Dénomination officielle
Consumer Price Index (Indice des prix à la consommation).

Portée
L'indice est calculé en février, mai, août et novembre. Il porte sur tous les ménages du pays sans distinction de taille ni de revenu.

Base originale
Mi-novembre 1989 = 100.

Source des coefficients de pondération
Le schéma de pondération est fondé sur les meilleures estimations disponibles des dépenses moyennes hebdomadaires consacrées par l'ensemble des ménages du pays à l'acquisition de biens et de services. Presque toutes ces estimations ont été obtenues à partir des résultats d'une enquête nationale sur les dépenses des ménages effectuée en 1987. L'enquête portait sur un échantillon national représentatif de 7 705 ménages privés de l'ensemble du pays. Le travail sur le terrain a débuté en février 1987 et a pris fin en avril 1988. Les estimations tirées de l'enquête, qui se réfèrent à l'année 1987, ont été actualisées à la mi-novembre 1989 en faisant usage des pourcentages relatifs aux changements, survenus entre-temps, des prix de chacun des articles compris dans la précédente série d'indices. Il n'a pas été possible de disposer d'informations appropriées sur les changements quantitatifs affectant le barème détaillé de la consommation des ménages durant cette période de deux ans; aucun ajustement n'a donc été effectué à ce propos.

Les dépenses correspondant aux variétés ne faisant l'objet d'aucune évaluation au sein de leur catégorie d'articles sont, soit ajoutées directement à la pondération de variétés équivalentes que l'on considère susceptibles de présenter la même évolution de prix, soit réparties proportionnellement sur l'ensemble des variétés pour lesquelles un prix est attribué.

Pondération et composition

Groupes principaux	Nombre d'articles	Pondération	Nombre approximatif de relevés de prix
Alimentation (y compris repas pris à l'extérieur)	50	25,7528	12 700
Boissons alcoolisées	3	11,7301	1 400
Tabac	3	3,3382	400
Logement:			
Loyer	1	1,5150	900
Intérêts hypothécaires	1	3,3864	2
Réparations, décoration, eau et assurance habitation	3	1,6098	400
Combustible et éclairage	7	5,9012	800
Habillement et chaussure	24	6,7229	4 300
Biens d'équipement ménager durables	13	4,7146	4 200
Autres biens (produits d'entretien, articles d'hygiène, de sport et de loisirs, etc.)	20	5,8502	5 400
Transports	13	13,7488	1 400
Services et dépenses assimilées	21	15,0850	5 600
Total	159	100,0000	39 000

Dépenses de consommation des ménages
L'indice porte sur tous les biens de consommation et les services auxquels les ménages privés affectent leurs dépenses.

Outre l'alimentation, les boissons, l'habillement, la chaussure, etc., l'indice comprend également, entre autres, les assurances relatives à l'habitation, les impôts et les assurances véhicules, les frais d'obtention du permis de conduire, les cotisations aux cercles, sociétés, associations et organisations syndicales, le paiement des intérêts hypothécaires et le remboursement des achats à crédit. Etant donné qu'il porte sur les prix, l'indice ne peut, dans la pratique, comprendre des biens et services dont le prix n'est pas établi ou ne peut être évalué. Pour cette raison, les biens de consommation suivants sont exclus: donations au culte ou à des oeuvres, rentes immobilières, prestations individuelles en espèces, billets de loterie et paris. De surcroît, l'indice étant fondé sur les dépenses des ménages, les articles suivants, qui ne constituent pas des achats de consommation, sont exclus: produits de la ferme ou du jardin faisant l'objet d'une autoconsommation par les ménages, prestations de la sécurité sociale et autres revenus en nature, loyer attribué aux logements occupés par leur propriétaire. Certaines autres dépenses sont également écartées de l'indice, même si elles affectent le coût de la vie et le budget de nombreux ménages: il s'agit des primes d'assurance-vie, des contributions aux fonds de pensions, des remboursements de prêts hypothécaires ou d'autres prêts à titre individuel, des dépenses en capital relatives à l'achat d'une habitation au comptant ou à la réalisation d'extensions ou de réparations structurelles de première importance, des autres formes d'épargne et d'investissement, des contributions à la sécurité sociale et des impôts sur le revenu.

Mode de relevé des prix
Les prix sont relevés trimestriellement le mardi le plus proche du milieu des mois de février, mai, août et novembre, auprès de quelque 3 000 points de vente au détail et prestataires de services répartis entre toutes les agglomérations de 10 000 habitants au minimum et un échantillon représentatif de villes de moindre dimension.

L'indice comprend au total 807 variétés différentes. En tout, 403 variétés font l'objet d'une évaluation au niveau local. Les variétés restantes concernent soit des entreprises prises isolément (par exemple, entreprises d'électricité, services de transport routier ou ferroviaire, frais postaux ou téléphoniques), soit des groupes de sociétés (gaz domestique, combustible, etc.), ou ne font pas nécessairement l'objet d'une évaluation exhaustive au niveau local (ainsi, les médecins, les dentistes, les opticiens, les abonnements périodiques). Ces dernières variétés sont directement évaluées par l'Office central des Statistiques au moyen d'enquêtes effectuées à cet effet par courrier ou par téléphone.

Les prix relevés sont ceux effectivement payés par les consommateurs lors des transactions au comptant. Les estimations, les moyennes ou les fourchettes de prix ne sont pas admises. Les relevés de prix comprennent les impôts indirects. Les frais relatifs aux achats à crédit ne sont pas pris en compte, pas plus que les rabais, sauf si ces derniers sont proposés à l'ensemble de la clientèle. Les prix des offres spéciales et des soldes sont retenus s'ils sont en vigueur le jour du relevé, mais les prix de liquidation des articles défraîchis, endommagés ou de qualité insuffisante ne sont pas acceptés. Les prix de catalogue ne comptent que s'ils sont réellement payés par le consommateur.

Les versements consécutifs à l'achat à crédit d'appareils ménagers, d'appareils électro-acoustiques, d'automobiles et de motocyclettes font l'objet d'un traitement particulier. Pour le paiement des intérêts et le remboursement des avances, on utilise des indicateurs de prix distincts fondés sur un ensemble fixe de contrats de location-vente ou de vente à crédit, contrats conclus à différentes dates. Des indicateurs de prix fondés sur les prix courants au comptant sont utilisés pour la pondération correspondant aux paiements initiaux effectués lors de la conclusion de nouveaux contrats.

Logement

L'indice porte sur les frais de logement effectivement supportés. Les changements dont a fait l'objet le coût des articles ménagers suivants sont pris en compte d'une manière spécifique: loyer des propriétés privées et des propriétés dépendant des autorités locales; frais des services dispensés par les autorités locales; primes d'assurance pour les logements (de toutes catégories); frais de réparation et de décoration (pour toutes catégories de logements); paiement des intérêts hypothécaires (pour les logements en régime d'hypothèque). Dans le cas des intérêts hypothécaires, leur versement brut (c'est-à-dire avant la déduction de l'impôt sur le revenu) est utilisé à la fois aux fins de pondération et d'évaluation. L'élément correspondant à l'amortissement du capital dans le remboursement des emprunts hypothécaires n'est pas pris en compte par le concept de dépenses des ménages tel que le considère l'indice, puisque ce dernier se réfère à l'acquisition d'un actif capitalisé pouvant faire l'objet d'une évaluation (à savoir le logement).

Les changements survenus dans le niveau moyen des loyers versés aux autorités locales par leurs locataires sont incorporés tous les trimestres dans l'indice. Les calculs sont fondés sur des informations détaillées concernant le nombre total et les loyers agrégés de cette catégorie de logements, informations obtenues directement auprès de chaque administration locale. Les modifications du loyer des logements en propriété privée sont également prises en compte trimestriellement. Une enquête directe spéciale sur les loyers est effectuée chaque trimestre par l'Office central des Statistiques dans la zone métropolitaine de Dublin et par des enquêteurs privés travaillant à temps partiel dans les petites villes de province. Des enquêtes à grande échelle et par correspondance sont également effectuées auprès de deux échantillons réduits de propriétaires et de locataires.

En ce qui concerne les logements occupés par leur propriétaire, c'est le coût effectif de l'habitat qui est pris en compte, et non une valeur locative imputée. L'évolution du coût des intérêts hypothécaires est mesurée à partir d'un ensemble fixe d'hypothèques d'âges, de montants et de taux d'intérêt divers, consenties par les mutuelles et les pouvoirs publics locaux. L'élément correspondant à l'amortissement du capital dans le remboursement des emprunts hypothécaires n'est pas pris en compte. Le prix de l'eau est relevé annuellement auprès des administrations locales.

L'indicateur du prix de l'assurance habitation est calculé à partir des tarifs normalisés des assurances, applicables aux logements privés et à leur mobilier, ainsi qu'à partir d'indices appropriés pour l'actualisation des valeurs. Les prix d'un échantillon représentatif de matériaux destinés à la réparation et à la décoration sont relevés trimestriellement au moyen d'une enquête par correspondance menée auprès d'un échantillon national de commerçants.

Spécification des variétés

Les méthodes d'évaluation des prix sont exclusivement fondées sur le principe selon lequel, pour chaque variété choisie, une même qualité, ou une même une marque doit être relevée, dans la mesure du possible, auprès du même magasin à chaque occasion. La spécification des variétés choisies revêt un caractère général et se présente sous la forme d'une gamme de produits (se différenciant par la marque, la qualité, la taille, etc.) parmi lesquels chacun des enquêteurs est libre, initialement (ou lorsqu'il s'agit d'opérer un remplacement), de choisir un produit particulier se prêtant à des relevés périodiques. Par exemple, lors de l'élaboration des séries statistiques actuelles, il a été procédé à la sélection de cinq variétés différentes, constituant la catégorie «jouets». L'une de ces variétés est représentée par une voiture en modèle réduit. Aucune spécification supplémentaire n'est établie, et les enquêteurs sont initialement libres de choisir, pour en effectuer le relevé périodique, n'importe lequel des différents types de voitures en modèle réduit disponibles au niveau local. Les seules contraintes qui s'appliquent au choix des enquêteurs précisent que le modèle choisi doit être de vente courante, se prêter à des relevés périodiques (autrement dit, l'article doit pouvoir être spécifié avec précision), et être susceptible de demeurer disponible à long terme. Une fois que le choix initial a été effectué, il est demandé à chaque enquêteur de relever le prix du même produit à chaque occasion. A cause de l'intervalle entre chaque enquête et de la possibilité de voir différents enquêteurs relever les données relatives aux mêmes articles, les formulaires des relevés de prix ont été spécialement conçus de manière à ce que les spécifications exactes de chaque produit sélectionné soient enregistrées. De cette façon, on est assuré que la même série d'articles a fait l'objet d'une évaluation lors de chaque enquête, ainsi qu'il l'a été précisé.

Conformément à ce règlement, les produits spécifiques relevés par les différents enquêteurs pour une variété déterminée ne sont pas les mêmes. La méthode utilisée permet de relever le prix d'une grande variété de marques et de qualités dans des lieux différents. Ainsi, étant donné qu'elles reflètent les goûts et les préférences locales, les données recueillies constituent une représentation des mouvements de prix de la variété en question bien meilleure que si une seule variété, définie d'une manière étroite, était relevée partout.

Substitution, changement de qualité, etc.

Des substitutions sont opérées au niveau local lorsqu'il y a discontinuité due à un changement de modèle ou de qualité ou lorsqu'un produit se raréfie ou n'est plus guère demandé. Il est alors prévu d'introduire des articles de remplacement bénéficiant d'une grande renommée.

Les formulaires de relevés de prix sont conçus de manière à ce que les spécifications détaillées des nouveaux produits puissent être introduites. Une discontinuité particulière affecte un seul formulaire, et le prix correspondant est exclu du calcul de l'indice jusqu'à ce que deux relevés consécutifs soient obtenus pour l'article de remplacement. Il est permis aux enquêteurs de remplacer par un nouvel article tout produit original dont l'approvisionnement a été réduit ou qui ne bénéficie plus d'une demande locale aussi importante que par le passé. Cependant, le prix d'un produit déterminé n'est utilisé dans le calcul de l'indice que lorsque deux relevés trimestriels consécutifs sont disponibles pour ce même produit.

Les changements affectant les points de vente sont également considérés comme des discontinuités: le prix des produits offerts dans le nouveau point de vente n'est retenu que lorsqu'il a pu être relevé plusieurs trimestres de suite. Les formulaires des relevés de prix sont conçus de manière à ce que chacun des magasins dans lequel s'effectue le relevé de chaque produit soit clairement défini. Si un point de vente déterminé ne peut plus être utilisé (par exemple, en cas de cessation d'activité ou d'un refus de coopérer, etc.) l'enquêteur le remplace par un magasin équivalent, bien connu et situé dans la même zone.

Un responsable de l'Office central des statistiques effectue des visites périodiques auprès des enquêteurs locaux afin d'assurer la cohésion de l'organisation des relevés. Les enquêteurs travaillant sur la zone métropolitaine de Dublin reçoivent leurs directives au siège même de l'Office.

Articles saisonniers

Le prix de certains aliments frais, tels que les oeufs, les fruits, les légumes, etc., subissent des fluctuations saisonnières à des degrés divers suivant l'importance de l'offre et de la demande sur le marché. Traditionnellement, on procède, dans le calcul de l'indice, à la correction des variations saisonnières des prix de trois articles, à savoir, les oeufs, les tomates et les pommes de terre. En effet, si l'on tient compte de leur coefficient de pondération, leurs variations saisonnières pourraient avoir un impact sensible sur l'indice. Une telle situation pouvant causer des difficultés excessives dans la détermination des tendances sous-jacentes de l'évolution des prix, les variations saisonnières des articles en question demeurent exclues de l'indice.

La correction est effectuée à l'aide de la méthode dite «X-11 Variant of the US Bureau of the Census (Method 11) Seasonal Adjustment Program».

L'indice comprend d'autres articles dont les prix connaissent des modifications périodiques, simplement parce que les dépenses sont engagées chaque année à la même époque. Il s'agit, par exemple, des frais scolaires ou universitaires, des cotisations annuelles à des cercles ou associations, etc. Les articles dont le prix est étroitement déterminé par les taxes (boissons et tabac) sont affectés de la même manière par les modifications du budget de l'Etat. Les changements de prix de ce type de produits et ceux d'autres articles présentant des contributions saisonnières particulières insignifiantes sont reflétées sans ajustement par l'indice. Pour cette raison, la saisonnalité n'est pas entièrement exclue de l'Indice des prix à la consommation.

Calcul

L'indice est calculé selon la formule de Laspeyres sous forme de moyenne arithmétique pondérée à base fixe, les coefficients de pondération correspondant à la période de base.

Il est d'abord procédé au calcul des moyennes nationales des prix relatifs à chaque variété de l'échantillon. Ce calcul s'effectue en deux phases. On calcule en premier lieu une moyenne arithmétique simple pour chaque strate correspondant à la dimension des villes; ces moyennes sont ensuite combinées en utilisant des coefficients de pondération proportionnels au chiffre des ventes au détail de chaque strate, obtenus lors du Recensement des Services effectué en 1987, afin d'obtenir des prix moyens valables pour l'ensemble du pays. Les grands magasins constituent une strate particulière, de manière à ce que leurs prix soient incorporés dans la moyenne nationale au moyen d'une pondération appropriée. Des moyennes nationales complémentaires sont calculées à nouveau pour le trimestre précédent en utilisant un ensemble approprié de relevés. Le rapport de ces moyennes nationales directement comparables permet d'obtenir le coût du «panier» permanent correspondant au trimestre en cours. Les indices d'évolution des prix peuvent alors être directement calculés pour tous les articles et toutes les combinaisons d'articles en divisant leur coût total du trimestre en cours par celui du trimestre de base.

Autres informations

Des indices spécifiques seront établis pour les dix groupes de biens dégagés dans les séries statistiques précédentes, à savoir: alimentation, boissons alcoolisées, tabac, habillement et chaussure, combustible et électricité, logement, biens ménagers durables, autres biens, transports, services et dépenses assimilées. Un indice complémentaire est également publié pour les produits énergétiques et porte sur le carburant, l'électricité, l'essence, l'huile pour moteur diesel, le gaz pour moteur (LPC) et le pétrole pour moteur. Afin qu'une certaine continuité soit assurée, chacune de ces séries sera publiée en prenant pour base initiale 100: mi-novembre 1982.

La prochaine mise à jour de l'Indice des prix à la consommation sera terminée en novembre 1996 sur la base des résultats d'une enquête à grande échelle sur les dépenses des ménages, qui sera effectuée en 1994.

Organisation et publication

Central Statistics Office: «Irish Statistical Bulletin» (Dublin).

idem: «Consumer Price Index - Introduction of Updated series - Base: Mid-November 1989 as 100».

ISLANDE (REYKJAVIK)

Dénomination officielle
Cost of Living Index (Indice du coût de la vie).

Portée
L'indice est calculé mensuellement et porte sur tous les types de ménages (y compris les fonctionnaires) habitant Reykjavik.

Base originale
Mai 1988 = 100.

Source des coefficients de pondération
L'enquête sur les dépenses des ménages sur laquelle est fondé le présent indice a été menée de juillet 1985 à juin 1986. Cette enquête a porté sur l'ensemble du pays. Les ménages ont été choisis par échantillon aléatoire à partir du Registre national, sans considérations liées à la taille, à la profession ou au domicile, mais en imposant, pour chacun d'eux, une limite d'âge de 70 ans au chef de famille.

Lorsque cette nouvelle base statistique a été adoptée, certains ajustements ont été effectués dans la pondération des dépenses des ménages pour prendre en compte le temps écoulé entre la période de l'enquête et le mois de mai 1988. Cet ajustement s'appliquait principalement aux augmentations de coûts survenues en matière de propriété, dans l'utilisation des voitures de passagers et dans les redevances audiovisuelles, suite à la création d'une chaîne de télévision privée, financée en partie au moyen des redevances versées par les téléspectateurs. Les coefficients de pondération des articles dont le prix n'a pas été établi sont reflétés par ceux des proches substituts parmi les articles ayant fait l'objet d'un relevé.

Pondération et composition

Groupes principaux	Nombre d'articles	Pondération	Nombre approximatif de relevés de prix
Alimentation	269	20,6	2 933
Boissons et tabac	32	4,4	245
Habillement et chaussure	75	7,9	327
Loyer, électricité et eau chaude pour le chauffage	59	16,2	59
Mobilier et biens d'équipement ménager	99	7,4	371
Soins médicaux	34	2,3	60
Transports et communications	46	18,9	158
Loisirs et instruction	100	11,0	179
Autres biens et services	80	11,3	358
Total	794	100,0	4 690

Dépenses de consommation des ménages

L'enquête sur les dépenses des ménages à partir de laquelle ont été calculés les coefficients de pondération visait à inclure, autant que possible, toutes les dépenses pouvant être envisagées. Les revenus en nature n'ont pas été traités dans les comptes des ménages mais, dans une certaine mesure, dans le cadre des rapports relatifs aux dépenses correspondant à l'année 1985; de ce fait, ils sont en partie reflétés par l'indice. La propriété immobilière est prise en compte, étant donné que le taux d'occupation des logements en propriété est, en Islande, estimé à plus de 80 pour cent. Les dépenses relatives à cette catégorie comprennent le paiement des intérêts, l'amortissement, les coûts d'entretien et d'assurance, l'impôt foncier, etc. Les achats à crédit de biens durables, les achats de biens d'occasion et de produits importés ont tous été pris en compte par l'enquête sur les dépenses des ménages et utilisés pour la détermination des pondérations originelles. Cependant, une fois adoptés, ces coefficients de pondération ont été tous spécifiés au titre de nouveaux achats et il n'est tenu compte ni des achats à crédit, ni des changements affectant les modalités du crédit à la consommation.

En Islande, les assurances sociales sont financées par le système fiscal, et les dépenses y relatives n'ont pas été comprises dans l'indice.

Les contributions aux fonds de pensions n'ont pas été prises en compte; en Islande, ces contributions sont constituées par la déduction obligatoire, à taux unique, des traitements et des salaires.

Les honoraires des patentes sont compris dans la mesure où ils ont été reflétés par l'enquête sur les dépenses de consommation des ménages. Il en va de même pour les primes d'assurances couvrant des biens de consommation spécifiques, les primes d'assurance-vie et les envois de fonds de différentes natures.

Les dépenses relatives aux soins de santé sont comprises dans la mesure où elles sont effectuées directement par les patients. L'impôt sur le revenu et les autres impôts directs ne sont pas compris.

Mode de relevé des prix

Les points de vente et autres sources fournissant les données relatives aux prix des biens et services ont été essentiellement sélectionnés afin d'obtenir, si possible, une distribution géographique des ventes dans la région de la capitale. Là où cela s'est avéré possible (en général pour les magasins d'alimentation), des coefficients de pondération ont été attribués aux points de vente sur la base d'une estimation de leurs chiffres d'affaires respectifs. Les prix sont obtenus auprès de 322 points de vente au détail et établissements de services.

Pour la plupart des chapitres de dépenses, les prix sont relevés lors de la première semaine de chaque mois. Pour certaines dépenses à caractère saisonnier (voyages de vacances à l'étranger, vacances familiales et loisirs, certains frais de scolarité concentrés au début de l'année scolaire) les prix sont relevés moins souvent et leur ajustement est moins fréquent.

Les informations relatives aux prix des biens et des services à caractère privé sont relevées directement auprès des vendeurs, soit au moyen de visites effectuées dans les points de vente par les enquêteurs, soit par téléphone - principalement en ce qui concerne certains services.

Les informations relatives aux coûts des services publics sont obtenues par contact direct avec les services concernés, ou bien au moyen des tarifs, règlements officiels, etc.

Les prix de l'électricité et de l'eau d'origine géothermique (chauffage central, eau chaude) sont calculés en tant que moyennes nationales. Le Bureau des Statistiques obtient ses informations auprès de la Régie nationale de l'Energie, laquelle relève les prix auprès de l'ensemble des services de production et de distribution d'électricité et de chauffage géothermique dans tout le pays. Les frais relatifs aux soins médicaux ne sont inclus dans l'indice que dans la mesure où leur paiement est directement effectué par les patients et les bénéficiaires; les informations y relatives se fondent principalement sur les tarifs officiels. Les prix des soins dentaires sont fondés sur les tarifs publiés par l'Association des dentistes.

Les informations sur le prix du matériel pédagogique sont obtenues à la fois par les enquêteurs et par contact direct avec les établissements concernés.

Les prix des transports et communications sont relevés à la fois à partir des tarifs officiels ou ayant été publiés, à la suite de contacts directs avec les établissements concernés.

Sur le terrain, les prix sont relevés par un personnel qualifié. Il est de règle que les mêmes personnes effectuent le travail sur le terrain auprès des différents types d'établissement. En d'autres termes, il s'agit d'agents déterminés qui relèvent les données relatives aux prix de l'alimentation, des boissons, de l'habillement, etc.

En principe, les prix réduits ne sont pas pris en compte, à l'exception des réductions consenties pour les paiements au comptant. Les prix officiels ne sont inclus que dans la mesure où ils représentent avec certitude les prix réellement pratiqués sur le marché. Si une différence survient entre les prix officiels ou réglementés et les prix du marché, les prix officiels sont toujours écartés. Aucune tentative n'est effectuée pour connaître les prix du marché noir; de toute manière, en Islande, ce marché concerne presque exclusivement des biens ou services à caractère illégal, tels que les stupéfiants, etc. Les prix des locations-ventes et les modalités du crédit ne sont pas traités. Tous les relevés de prix sont fondés sur les prix pratiqués au comptant. Les achats de biens d'occasion ne sont pas inclus. Les prix des biens importés sont simplement relevés auprès des points de vente concernés; les importations de biens effectuées directement par les consommateurs ne font l'objet d'aucune attention particulière, étant donné qu'elles ne constituent qu'une part réduite de l'ensemble des achats.

Logement
En raison du taux élevé, en Islande, de l'occupation des logements en propriété, le loyer n'est pas traité comme un article particulier.

La propriété du logement est prise en compte, étant donné que le taux d'occupation des logements en propriété est estimé comme étant supérieur à 80 pour cent. Les dépenses relatives à cette catégorie comprennent le paiement des intérêts, l'amortissement, l'entretien et les primes d'assurance, les taxes immobilières, etc.

Spécification des variétés
Aux fins du relevé des prix, les articles ont été choisis sur la base de l'enquête sur les dépenses des ménages, laquelle précisait en détail la fabrication, la marque, l'unité de mesure et la description de chaque article, sous réserve de certaines révisions motivées par le laps de temps écoulé entre l'époque de l'enquête et l'adoption de l'indice. Des spécifications détaillées existent pour chaque article, décrivant la variété, la fabrication, la marque, l'unité, etc., le choix étant effectué comme il est indiqué ci-dessus.

Substitution, changement de qualité, etc.
Les changements de qualité ne constituent pas un problème majeur, étant donné qu'une description détaillée par produit est effectuée. Si l'on estime que de tels changements constituent une cause de préoccupation, ils sont traités en modifiant la marque ou le type spécifié. L'apparition de nouveaux produits est censée figurer dans les enquêtes sur les dépenses des ménages menées à des intervalles minimums de cinq ans. Toutefois, les nouveaux produits sont introduits au fur et à mesure de leur apparition dans la mesure où ils remplacent entièrement les produits antérieurement relevés dans l'indice. La disparition de produits ayant précédemment été relevés dans l'indice est traitée au moyen de leur remplacement par leurs substituts les plus proches existant sur le marché.

Articles saisonniers
Aucun ajustement n'est effectué pour tenir compte des fluctuations saisonnières. Les prix de certains services saisonniers, principalement dans le secteur des loisirs, sont relevés à des dates prévues et sont considérés comme constants; ils ne font l'objet d'aucune modification jusqu'au relevé suivant.

Calcul
L'indice est calculé selon la formule de Laspeyres sous forme de moyenne arithmétique pondérée à base fixe, les coefficients de pondération correspondant à la période de base.

Des moyennes arithmétiques pondérées sont utilisées pour le calcul des moyennes de prix. Dans la plupart des cas, les chiffres des coefficients de pondération sont fondés sur des estimations de chiffres d'affaires ou de ventes. Les problèmes posés par des données manquantes ou erronées sont en général résolus par l'utilisation du changement moyen des prix des autres produits du même groupe ou sous-groupe.

Cependant, le calcul de l'indice est fondé sur les prix pratiqués dans la région de la capitale, à quelques exceptions près; les prix du combustible, du chauffage et de l'électricité sont calculés sous forme de moyennes s'appliquant à l'ensemble du pays. Les moyennes annuelles sont calculées sous forme de moyennes arithmétiques des calculs mensuels; les indices correspondant au début des mois allant de février à décembre disposent des mêmes pondérations, mais l'indice correspondant au début du mois de janvier ainsi qu'un indice spécial établi pour la fin du mois de décembre se voient attribuer une pondération égale à la moitié de celle des autres mois: cela équivaut plus ou moins à convertir les indices du début du mois en indices du milieu du mois.

Organisation et publication
Statistical Bureau of Iceland: «Hagtidindi» (Reykjavik).
Central Bank of Iceland: «Economic Statistics» (publication trimestrielle).

ISRAEL

Dénomination officielle
Consumer Price Index (Indice des prix à la consommation).

Portée
L'indice est calculé mensuellement et porte sur toutes les familles habitant les zones urbaines.

Base originale
1987 = 100.

Source des coefficients de pondération
La valeur des coefficients de pondération et le choix des articles résultent d'une enquête menée de juin 1986 à mai 1987 sur un échantillon représentatif d'environ 5 000 ménages composés d'un membre ou plus et vivant dans 104 zones urbaines. Certains ajustements ont été effectués sur les coefficients de pondération afin de prendre en compte les changements de prix survenus entre l'époque de l'enquête et la période de base.

Dépenses de consommation des ménages
Il est tenu compte de la valeur des biens et services acquis par les ménages, à l'exception des achats liés à l'investissement et à l'épargne (par exemple, l'acquisition d'un appartement, d'un véhicule, de valeurs, etc.). Les dépenses de consommation sont mesurées en calculant la somme des paiements versés par les ménages ou que ces derniers se sont engagés à verser. La consommation comprend les dépenses supplémentaires liées aux achats, si celles-ci sont payées au vendeur (par exemple, intérêts, commissions, tarifs de transport ou frais d'installation).

De même, la consommation comprend une estimation de la valeur des amortissements et autres intérêts affectant le capital investi dans l'achat d'un logement ou d'un véhicule ou, si ces derniers ne sont pas la propriété privée du ménage concerné, le coût de leur utilisation. En outre, sont inclus les intérêts re-

Pondération et composition

Groupes principaux	Nombre d'articles	Pondération	Nombre approximatif de relevés de prix
Alimentation (n.c. fruits et légumes)	270	16,51	7 000
Fruits et légumes	90	6,42	17 000
Logement	5	16,46	(a)
Entretien du ménage (y c. combustible et éclairage)	85	9,33	2 000
Mobilier, ameublement et articles d'équipement ménager	185	7,18	3 000
Habillement et chaussure	190	7,20	12 000
Santé	80	5,50	1 000
Instruction, culture et loisirs	260	12,01	3 000
Transports et taxes postales	85	15,25	1 000
Divers	110	4,14	1 000
Total	1 355	100,00	47 000

Remarque: (a) Voir plus bas sous le titre Logement.

latifs aux biens et services reçus des employeurs. En revanche, ne sont pas inclus le paiement des achats futurs (pour les biens non encore acquis), le remboursement des dettes pour des achats effectués dans le passé et les dépenses ayant fait l'objet d'une restitution. Sont également inclus dans la consommation l'achat des biens d'occasion, l'échange de biens usagés à titre de paiement partiel de nouveaux biens (dans ce dernier cas, seule la différence de valeur entre l'ancien et le nouveau bien est considérée comme consommation), les assurances couvrant des biens de consommation spécifiques et l'assurance-maladie. Sont exclues les dépenses liées aux impôts directs, à la sécurité sociale, aux fonds de pension, à l'assurance-vie, aux dons pécuniaires et aux loteries.

Mode de relevé des prix
Le choix des articles est effectué en fonction de la valeur des dépenses qui leur sont allouées d'après l'enquête sur les dépenses des ménages, et du nombre de variétés existantes pour chaque article. Les articles représentant plus de 0,1 pour cent des dépenses des ménages font l'objet d'un traitement spécifique. Les articles comptant pour moins de 0,1 pour cent ne sont traités séparément que dans le cas où aucun autre article approprié n'est disponible pour représenter leurs mouvements de prix. Les dépenses consacrées aux articles dont le prix n'a pas été établi sont transférées à des articles similaires, ce qui permet de mesurer, d'une manière appropriée, leurs mouvements de prix.

La taille des points de vente entrant dans l'échantillon est déterminée par la pondération du groupe d'articles proposés dans un point de vente donné, et par la variance des changements de prix de chaque article du groupe, dans les différents points de vente. Les localités ont été sélectionnées selon la méthode probabiliste, proportionnellement à leur taille au sein de chaque zone géographique. On entend par «taille» les dépenses de consommation totales des ménages de la localité en question. Les prix de la plupart des articles sont relevés mensuellement par des enquêteurs auprès de 1 300 points de vente. Pour l'électricité, le gaz, l'eau, les soins médicaux, l'instruction, les transports et communications, etc., les relevés sont effectués par correspondance à l'aide de questionnaires adressés par la poste, ou bien par téléphone, à partir de 600 sources différentes.

Les prix sont relevés par 20 enquêteurs, qui transmettent les données recueillies aux bureaux situés sur le terrain dans trois grandes villes, lesquels, à leur tour, transfèrent les données à l'office central de Jérusalem. Les prix de solde sont pris en compte s'ils sont proposés à tous les acheteurs. Les prix du marché sont utilisés, et non les tarifs officiels. Les articles sont évalués sur la base des achats effectués au comptant. Les voitures d'occasion et les logements occupés par leur propriétaire font l'objet d'une évaluation fondée sur les prix locaux.

Afin d'obtenir une moyenne mensuelle des prix de la plupart des articles relevés, les points de vente sont répartis en quatre groupes distincts, chaque groupe faisant l'objet d'une évaluation au cours d'une semaine différente.

Logement
Deux échantillons de logements en location comprenant des logements meublés ou non meublés, font l'objet d'une évaluation par mois alternés.

Les dépenses annuelles liées aux charges des habitations occupées par leur propriétaire sont calculées en tenant compte de la dépréciation qui se produit au cours des années, ainsi que des intérêts du capital investi dans l'achat du logement concerné.

L'indice actuellement en vigueur comprend tous les achats de logements, qu'il s'agisse d'habitations neuves ou d'occasion. Les prix sont calculés à partir des formulaires utilisés pour la perception des impôts sur les achats immobiliers, et sont obtenus auprès des services fiscaux. Les données concernent trois à quatre mille logements, répartis sur 25 localités urbaines, au cours d'une période trimestrielle. Les données relatives à la qualité des logements sont utilisées pour l'élaboration des analyses de régression, de manière à ce que l'indice ne reflète que les changements de prix.

Spécification des variétés
Des spécifications générales sont élaborées pour chaque article. Des spécifications détaillées pour chaque article (par exemple, marque, fabrication, qualité, etc.) sont choisies par les enquêteurs pour chaque point de vente, et les prix sont relevés mensuellement pour chacune des variétés.

Substitution, changement de qualité, etc.
Les changements de qualité importants et les substitutions sont pris en compte dans l'indice, de manière à ce que leur introduction n'affecte pas le niveau des prix. Les changements de qualité peu importants sont considérés comme des changements de prix. Les ajustements de qualité ne sont effectués que dans certains cas précis, lorsqu'il est possible de disposer de caractéristiques suffisantes et pouvant être mesurées.

Articles saisonniers
Les prix des articles saisonniers sont relevés aussi longtemps que ceux-ci sont présents sur le marché. Lorsqu'ils ne sont plus disponibles, leurs prix sont estimés sur la base des mouvements de prix d'articles similaires. Lorsqu'un article saisonnier réapparaît sur le marché, son prix est comparé à celui du dernier mois au cours duquel il était disponible. Avant 1988, des pondérations variables étaient utilisées pour les fruits et légumes frais.

Calcul
L'indice est calculé selon la formule de Laspeyres sous forme de moyenne arithmétique pondérée à base fixe, les coefficients de pondération correspondant à la période de base.
Pour chaque article, l'indice est calculé sur la base des rapports de prix. Lorsque, dans un point de vente particulier, aucun prix n'est disponible pour un article donné, ses mouvements de prix sont estimés en fonction des mouvements de prix survenus dans d'autres magasins. Si aucun prix n'est disponible dans aucun magasin pour l'article en question, ses mouvements de prix sont estimés d'après ceux d'articles similaires.

Autres informations
Outre l'indice relatif aux familles habitant en milieu urbain, il existe un calcul des mouvements de prix du «panier de la ménagère» pour 10 pour cent des ménages dont le revenu est le plus faible et 10 pour cent des ménages dont le revenu est le plus élevé.

Organisation et publication
Central Bureau of Statistics: «Monthly Bulletin of Statistics» (Jérusalem).
idem: «Price statistics Monthly» (en hébreu uniquement).
Les révisions de l'indice des prix à la consommation figurant dans «Price Statistics Monthly», janvier 1988 (en hébreu uniquement).

ITALIE

Dénomination officielle
Indice national des prix à la consommation.

Portée
L'indice est calculé mensuellement et porte sur tous les ménages des grandes villes de 93 provinces.

Base originale
1990 = 100.

Source des coefficients de pondération
Ils ont été établis à partir des modèles de consommation et de données des comptes nationaux pour les deux premiers trimestres de 1989 et les deux derniers de 1990.

Pondération et composition

Groupes principaux	Nombre d'articles	Pondération	Nombre approximatif de relevés de prix
Alimentation et tabac	250	22,78	200 000
Habillement et chaussure	57	10,83	20 000
Logement:	...	7,62	13 500
Loyer	1	...	...
Entretien et réparations	5	...	...
Combustible et éclairage	7	...	...
Autres groupes:	...	...	50 000
Mobilier et articles d'équipement ménager	76	10,58	...
Soins médicaux	137	6,74	...
Transports et communications	168	13,46	...
Instruction et loisirs	110	9,97	...
Autres biens et services	96	18,02	...
Total	907	100,00	283 500

Dépenses de consommation des ménages
Les dépenses de consommation prises en compte dans le calcul de l'indice ne comprennent pas l'impôt sur le revenu, les investissements et l'épargne, la consommation de biens produits dans le pays ni le loyer estimé des logements occupés en propriété.

Mode de relevé des prix
Les relevés sont effectués par des enquêteurs dans les chefs-lieux des 93 provinces, auprès d'environ 26 300 commerces et points de vente au détail (9 500 pour l'alimentation, 10 800 pour d'autres articles et 6 000 prestataires de services).

Les relevés pour les poissons, pommes de terre, fruits et légumes frais ont lieu le 5, le 15 et le 25 de chaque mois alors que ceux concernant les autres produits alimentaires, l'habillement et les services personnels sont effectués vers le 15 de chaque mois. Cependant, pour le calcul de l'indice, les prix retenus sont ceux du cinquième et du quinzième jour du mois en cours et du vingt-cinquième jour du mois précédent. Le relevé des prix des biens ménagers durables, ainsi que des coûts de certains services, s'effectue le 5 de chaque mois en février, mai, août et novembre. Les prix retenus pour le calcul de l'indice sont les prix normaux payés par le consommateur. Ne sont pas pris en compte dans le calcul les éléments suivants: prix de soldes, rabais, location-vente ou vente à crédit. Néanmoins, les prix de vente des articles alimentaires sont relevés s'ils couvrent au moins un mois.

Logement
Les données relatives aux loyers sont obtenues trimestriellement pour 13 500 habitations, le 5 de chaque mois en janvier, avril, juillet et octobre.

Spécification des variétés
Chaque article retenu fait l'objet d'une spécification détaillée. Celle-ci fournit la description complète de l'article, sa dénomination, sa marque, l'emballage, la quantité ou l'unité employée, etc.

Substitution, changement de qualité, etc.
Lorsqu'un produit n'est plus en vente, il lui en est substitué un autre, analogue, auquel on applique la formule de l'enchaînement.

Articles saisonniers
Sont traités comme tels les fruits, les légumes frais et les fleurs. La composition de l'indice pour les articles saisonniers s'obtient en utilisant le prix moyen de 75 pour cent des premiers articles relevés en tenant compte d'une liste faisant l'objet d'une échelle progressive de prix. Il est supposé que les articles saisonniers disponibles sur le marché peuvent être remplacés les uns par les autres. Les ajustements sont effectués en utilisant une moyenne mobile établie sur 13 mois (le mois en cours et les 12 mois antérieurs).

Calcul
L'indice est calculé selon la formule de Laspeyres sous forme de moyenne arithmétique pondérée à base fixe, les coefficients de pondération correspondant à la période de base.

Pour chaque article dans chaque ville, l'indice est constitué par la moyenne arithmétique simple de tous les indices de base du même article dans la même ville. L'indice moyen d'un article au niveau régional est la moyenne arithmétique pondérée de tous les indices obtenus dans cette région.

L'indice national représente la moyenne arithmétique pondérée d'indices relatifs à 20 régions, les coefficients de pondération utilisés étant proportionnels à la population (urbaine) de ces régions au 31 décembre 1989.

Autres informations
L'Istituto Nazionale di Statistica procède également au calcul et à la publication d'une série d'indices de prix à la consommation pour les ouvriers et les employés.

Organisation et publication
Istituto Nazionale di Statistica, «Bollettino mensile di statistica» (Rome).

JAMAIQUE

Dénomination officielle
Consumer Price Index (Indice des prix à la consommation).

Portée
L'indice est calculé mensuellement et porte sur les ménages des zones urbaines et rurales, dont le revenu annuel n'était pas supérieur à 24 mille dollars jamaïquains au moment de l'enquête.

Base originale
Janvier 1988 = 100.

Source des coefficients de pondération
La valeur des coefficients de pondération et le choix des articles résultent d'une enquête sur les dépenses des ménages effectuée en 1984 dans les zones urbaines et rurales auprès de ménages dont le revenu annuel n'était pas supérieur à 24 000 dollars jamaïquains au moment de l'enquête. Les sous-groupes qui représentaient moins de 0,50 pour cent des dépenses à l'intérieur d'un groupe dans toutes les régions n'ont pas été pris en compte et leurs coefficients de pondération ont été redistribués parmi les sous-groupes restants. Le même critère de sélection a été appliqué aux articles de chaque sous-groupe. Une exception a été faite pour les groupes «alimentation» et «boissons» où le minimum pour chaque article était de 0,40 pour cent.

Pondération et composition

Groupes principaux	Nombre d'articles	Pondération	Nombre approximatif de relevés de prix
Alimentation	...	55,63	...
Combustible et éclairage	...	7,35	...
Loyer et gestion du ménage	...	7,86	...
Mobilier et ameublement	...	2,83	...
Soins médicaux	...	6,97	...
Habillement et chaussure	...	5,07	...
Transports	...	6,44	...
Divers	...	7,85	...
Total	...	100,00	...

Dépenses de consommation des ménages
Pas disponible.

Mode de relevé des prix
Les prix de la plupart des articles sont relevés au cours du premier week-end de chaque mois auprès d'un nombre fixe de points de vente situés dans l'ensemble de l'île. Les honoraires de médecins et de dentistes sont relevés tous les trimestres, les frais scolaires et les primes d'assurance-maladie sont relevés annuellement. Les changements survenus dans les tarifs du téléphone, de l'eau et des autobus sont enregistrés lorsque le public en est informé. L'équipe d'enquêteurs sur le terrain de l'Institut est responsable du relevé des prix. Ceux-ci sont relevés auprès de différentes sources: supermarchés, grands magasins, magasins de chaussures, restaurants, stations-service, médecins et dentistes, clubs, établissements scolaires, coiffeurs pour hommes et femmes. Les prix de l'électricité et du téléphone par exemple sont relevés auprès des services pertinents, alors que les informations relatives au loyer sont obtenues à partir d'un échantillon de logements.

Les enquêteurs chargés du relevé des prix sur une base mensuelle pour tous les articles, à l'exception de quelques-uns tels que l'assurance-maladie et les frais scolaires qui sont enregistrés tous les trimestres, se rendent tous les mois dans tous les points de vente. Ceux dont les responsables répondent aux enquêtes sont situés dans des régions généralement utilisées pour le groupe cible et correspondent au type de magasins auquel il apporterait sa clientèle. Il convient de noter qu'il n'a pas été procédé à un choix aléatoire mais que l'échantillon a fait l'objet d'un choix raisonné en collaboration avec les enquêteurs travaillant sur le terrain qui, du fait de leur expérience, disposent d'une très bonne connaissance de la région considérée, et en raison des bonnes relations que la population cible entretient avec les magasins. Les points de vente sont choisis en fonction du volume des ventes. Le processus de sélection ne s'est pas limité aux établissements les plus importants: les petites épiceries et petits magasins où la population se livre à ses achats quand certains articles lui manquent figurent dans l'échantillon.

Les prix des articles défraîchis, endommagés après un long séjour en magasin ou souffrant d'imperfections ne sont pas pris en compte car ils s'éloignent des spécifications indiquées. Lorsque les groupes auxquels l'indice s'applique connaissent ouvertement des prix illégaux, ces prix doivent être pris en considération.

Logement
Les prix sont relevés chaque mois auprès d'un échantillon de logements de types déterminés compte tenu du nombre de chambres à coucher et autres pièces. Les paiements des ménages tels que paiements hypothécaires, remboursements et intérêts, de même que l'assurance des appartements, représentent le coût d'usage des logements occupés en propriété. En d'autres termes, les paiements en espèce devraient être utilisés à titre d'indicateur pour l'estimation du loyer. L'indice des prix utilisé pour parvenir à un quantum doit se fonder sur le loyer des catégories représentatives de logements.

Spécification des variétés
Les articles qui font l'objet de relevés de prix sont clairement spécifiés afin de faire en sorte que, chaque mois, les prix d'articles d'une qualité comparable soient établis.

Substitution, changement de qualité, etc.
Il se peut qu'on s'aperçoive qu'un bien ou un service disparaît pour faire place sur le marché à une nouvelle variété de biens et de services. Lorsqu'un chevauchement se produit en ce qui concerne l'observation des prix et qu'une différence est évidente en matière de qualité, la formule de l'enchaînement est utilisée. Dans cette méthode, il est procédé à l'estimation du prix pendant une période de base pour la nouvelle variété en utilisant les rapports de prix de la période en cours et de la période de base.

Cependant, lorsque la situation décrite ci-dessus se présente, les variétés, aussi bien anciennes que nouvelles, sont d'une qualité comparable; ainsi le nouveau prix sera donc relevé et la différence de prix traitée en tant qu'augmentation ou diminution selon le cas. Là où le consommateur n'a pas d'autre choix que celui de la nouvelle variété, la différence de prix sera considérée comme un changement de prix et non comme un paiement pour une qualité supérieure ou inférieure, même s'il existe une disparité en ce qui concerne l'article.

L'apparition de produits réellement nouveaux (c'est-à-dire des produits qui ne remplacent aucun article figurant à l'indice) qui entraîne des réajustements importants pour le budget du consommateur est rare. Si le cas se produit, une révision de l'indice est nécessaire.

Articles saisonniers
Les fluctuations saisonnières des prix des articles ne font l'objet d'aucun ajustement.

Calcul
L'indice est calculé selon la formule de Laspeyres sous forme de moyenne arithmétique pondérée à base fixe, les coefficients de pondération correspondant à l'année 1984.

On calcule le rapport des prix pour chaque article en divisant le prix moyen de la période en cours par le prix moyen de la période de base. La moyenne pondérée de trois indices régionaux est calculée pour obtenir l'indice de l'ensemble de l'île.

Organisation et publication
Statistical Institute of Jamaica: «Consumer Price Index Monthly Bulletin» (Kingston).
idem: «Consumer Price Index Monthly Report».
idem: «Consumer Price Index - Annual Review».

JAPON

Dénomination officielle
Consumer Price Index (Indice des prix à la consommation).

Portée
L'indice est calculé mensuellement et porte sur les ménages de l'ensemble du pays à l'exclusion des ménages d'une personne et de ceux qui vivent principalement de l'agriculture, de l'exploitation forestière ou de la pêche.

Base originale
1990 = 100.

Source des coefficients de pondération
Les coefficients de pondération proviennent des résultats d'une enquête sur les dépenses des ménages menée en 1990 auprès d'environ 8 000 ménages. En ce qui concerne les denrées alimentaires fraîches (poisson, fruits et légumes), les coefficients de pondération mensuels ont été calculés à partir des dépenses moyennes pour 1989 et 1990. Les articles de l'indice ont été choisis en tenant compte de l'importance relative de chacun d'entre eux dans l'ensemble des dépenses de consommation (en principe 0,01 pour cent au minimum), de la représentativité du mouvement des prix et de la continuité du relevé des prix. Les coefficients de pondération des articles dont le prix n'est pas relevé ont été attribués aux articles dont le prix a été relevé et qui les représentent.

Pondération et composition

Groupes principaux	Nombre d'articles	Pondération	Nombre approximatif de relevés de prix
Alimentation	215	3 140	...
Logement	23	1 478	...
Combustible, éclairage et eau	6	553	...
Mobilier et articles de ménage	60	444	...
Habillement et chaussure	84	860	...
Soins médicaux	23	312	...
Transports et communications	36	1 185	...
Instruction	13	466	...
Lecture et loisirs	69	1 115	...
Divers	32	446	...
Total	561	10 000	230 000

Dépenses de consommation des ménages
Les dépenses de consommation entrant dans le calcul de l'indice concernent les déboursements pour l'achat de biens et de services nécessaires à la vie quotidienne et comprennent la valeur locative des logements occupés par leur propriétaire. En sont exclus l'impôt sur le revenu, les primes d'assurance-vie, les cotisations à la sécurité sociale, l'épargne, les titres, les envois de fonds, les dons, les dépenses de culte et dépenses autres que celles portant sur la consommation.

Mode de relevé des prix
Les prix de la plupart des articles sont relevés par des enquêteurs à la suite de visites personnelles auprès de points de vente et de prestataires de services sélectionnés de 167 villes et villages. Pour certains services, tels que les transports et la poste, on utilise les barèmes officiels. Les prix sont relevés le mercredi, le jeudi et le vendredi de la semaine qui inclut le 12 du mois. Cependant, pour 42 denrées alimentaires fraîches comme le poisson, les fruits et les légumes, les relevés ont lieu trois fois par mois. Les frais scolaires font l'objet d'une enquête en avril et en septembre. Les prix entrant dans le calcul de l'indice sont les prix de détail réellement payés par les consommateurs le jour du relevé, à l'exclusion des prix réduits pour cause de promotion, liquidation, rabais ou soldes, des prix provisoirement anormaux, des prix de faveur pour achats en grand nombre, des prix des articles d'occasion, etc.

Logement
Sont pris en considération les loyers des logements privés et des logements appartenant aux pouvoirs publics. Pour les logements occupés par leur propriétaire, on utilise la valeur locative. Les données concernant les logements du secteur public sont communiquées tous les mois par les sociétés chargées de gérer ces logements. En ce qui concerne les logements privés, les loyers sont calculés en fonction de l'agencement et de la superficie à l'issue d'enquêtes mensuelles effectuées auprès de tous les ménages vivant dans les logements privés des quartiers de référence. La méthode d'équivalence en matière de loyer (valeur locative) est utilisée pour les logements occupés en propriété.

Spécification des variétés
Les caractéristiques des variétés sont spécifiées en détail (taille, qualité, marque et accessoires) pour que les produits suivis soient les mêmes tous les mois.

Substitution, changement de qualité, etc.
Lorsqu'un article de référence n'est plus disponible, il est remplacé par un article similaire. Si l'ancien et le nouvel article sont parfaitement identiques, la méthode de l'enchaînement direct est utilisée. Dans le cas contraire, les prix sont ajustés en fonction des différences de quantité ou de qualité.

Articles saisonniers
Les coefficients de pondération du sous-groupe des articles saisonniers (poissons frais, fruits et légumes frais) sont fixés pour l'année entière. Chaque article est pondéré en fonction de son importance relative, qui varie d'un mois à l'autre. En ce qui concerne les articles saisonniers autres que les aliments frais, on applique, hors saison, les prix moyens de la saison précédente.

Calcul
L'indice est calculé selon la formule de Laspeyres sous forme de moyenne arithmétique pondérée à base fixe, les coefficients de pondération correspondant à la période de base.

Les rapports de prix par article pour chaque commune sont calculés avant que soit établie leur moyenne par rapport au coefficient de pondération de chaque commune et la moyenne des rapports de prix par article pour l'ensemble du pays. La moyenne des rapports de prix pour l'ensemble du pays est ensuite établie en tenant compte des coefficients de pondération relatifs pour chaque article afin d'obtenir les indices des sous-groupes. De même, les indices des groupes principaux et l'indice général sont calculés à partir de l'indice du sous-groupe en utilisant les coefficients de pondération du groupe respectif.

Autres informations
Un «Indice général», dix «Indices des groupes principaux» et un «Indice des sous-groupes» sont calculés. Ces indices portent sur 72 zones, à savoir l'ensemble du pays, huit groupes de villes, 10 districts, 4 zones métropolitaines, 37 préfectures, Kawasaki-shi et Kitakyushu-shi. Il est procédé au calcul de l'indice du groupe «Biens et services» et de l'«Indice par articles» pour l'ensemble du pays et pour la zone de Ku de Tokyo. Un «Indice par type de ménage», un «Indice par caractéristiques des articles» et un «Indice calculé au moyen de la méthode de l'enchaînement» sont établis pour l'ensemble du pays.

Organisation et publication
Management and Coordination Agency, Statistics Bureau: «Monthly Report on the Consumer Price Index».
idem: «Annual Report on the Consumer Price Index».

JORDANIE

Dénomination officielle
Cost of Living Index (indice du coût de la vie).

Portée
L'indice est calculé mensuellement et porte sur tous les ménages urbains et ruraux du Royaume (rive orientale).

Base originale
1986 = 100.

Source des coefficients de pondération
La valeur des coefficients de pondération et le choix des articles résultent d'une enquête sur les dépenses des ménages, menée une année durant, en 1986/87, auprès de 2 537 ménages appartenant à tous les groupes de population habitant des zones urbaines et rurales.

Les articles ont été sélectionnés par échantillonnage, en fonction de leur importance relative.

Pondération et composition

Groupes principaux	Nombre d'articles	Pondération	Nombre approximatif de relevés de prix
Alimentation	141	41,170	1 870
Habillement et chaussure	65	7,454	1 394
Logement	55	28,092	1 445
Autres biens et services	47	23,284	2 244
Total	208	100,000	6 953

Dépenses de consommation des ménages
L'indice comprend toutes les dépenses effectuées par les ménages durant une année entière, ainsi que les revenus en nature ayant fait l'objet de la consommation des ménages. Une estimation de la valeur locative des logements occupés par leur propriétaire est également incluse.

Les achats à crédit de biens durables sont traités comme des dépenses. Les achats de biens d'occasion et l'échange de biens usagés à titre de paiement partiel pour de nouveaux biens n'ont pas été pris en considération. Les contributions à la sécurité sociale et aux fonds de pensions, le paiement des patentes, les primes d'assurances couvrant des biens de consommation spécifiques, les dépenses de santé, les impôts sur le revenu et autres impôts directs, le paiement des assurances-vie, les envois de fonds, les dons et autres déboursements similaires ont fait l'objet d'un traitement visant à les rendre conformes aux définitions établies pour les comptes nationaux.

Mode de relevé des prix
Les prix sont relevés chaque mois, par des agents enquêteurs, dans tous les chefs-lieu de province et de district de Jordanie, compte tenu de la densité de la population. Les points de vente sont choisis en fonction du nombre des articles composant le «panier» du marché, et ne doivent pas être situés à proximité des résidences de personnes à revenu très élevé. Dix points de vente sont sélectionnés pour chaque article. Les prix des fruits et légumes frais sont obtenus le jeudi, quatre fois par mois. Les prix des autres articles d'alimentation sont établis mensuellement, au cours de la première semaine. L'habillement fait l'objet de la même opération durant la deuxième semaine, les autres biens et services durant les troisième et quatrième semaines.

Les prix relevés sont ceux régulièrement pratiqués sur le marché, qu'ils soient ou non officiels. Les prix de soldes, de catalogue, du marché noir, des locations-ventes et des achats d'occasion ne sont pas pris en compte.

Logement
Les loyers sont relevés tous les six mois pour tous les types de logement. Les logements occupés par leur propriétaire sont exclus de l'indice.

Spécification des variétés
Les spécifications des articles faisant l'objet d'une évaluation sont obtenus auprès des commerçants et portent sur la variété, la qualité, la fabrication, la marque, l'unité, le pays d'origine, etc., du produit concerné.

Substitution, changement de qualité, etc.
Si un produit disparaît du marché, un produit analogue lui est substitué.

Articles saisonniers
Lorsqu'un article n'est plus de saison, son prix fait l'objet d'une estimation.

Calcul
L'indice est calculé selon la formule de Laspeyres sous forme de moyenne arithmétique pondérée à base fixe, les coefficients de pondération correspondant à la période de base.

Le prix moyen de chaque article lors du mois en cours est d'abord divisé par le prix correspondant de la période de base pour obtenir le rapport de prix.

La moyenne pondérée des prix dans chaque localité est multipliée par le coefficient de pondération de la localité concernée, en fonction de l'importance de sa population.

Organisation et publication
L'indice est calculé par le Department of Statistics (Amman).
Central Bank of Jordan: «Monthly Statistical Bulletin» (Amman).

KENYA (NAIROBI)

Dénomination officielle
Consumer Price Index - Lower Income Group (Indice des prix à la consommation - Ménages à revenu modeste).

Portée
L'indice est calculé mensuellement et porte sur les ménages vivant à Nairobi dont le revenu mensuel ne dépassait pas 1 999 shillings kenyans au cours de la période 1982-83.

Base originale
Février-mars 1986 = 100.

Source des coefficients de pondération
La valeur des coefficients de pondération et le choix des articles résultent d'une enquête sur les dépenses des ménages ef-

fectuée au cours de la période 1982-83 dans tous les centres urbains sur un échantillon de 1 648 ménages à revenus modeste, moyen et élevé. L'indice porte sur les ménages à revenu modeste vivant à Nairobi et disposant d'un revenu mensuel ne dépassant pas 1 999 shillings kenyans à l'époque de l'enquête. Aucune correction n'a été apportée aux coefficients de pondération pour prendre en compte les changements de prix survenus entre la période de l'enquête et février-mars 1986.

Pondération et composition

Groupes principaux	Nombre d'articles	Pondération	Nombre approximatif de relevés de prix
Alimentation	49	44,2	...
Boissons et tabac	11	2,1	...
Habillement et chaussure	34	5,0	...
Loyer	1	25,0	...
Combustible, éclairage et eau	4	3,1	...
Mobilier, ameublement, articles d'équipement ménager et dépenses de ménage	29	5,3	...
Santé et soins personnels	18	3,0	...
Transports et communications	15	4,1	...
Instruction et loisirs	15	6,2	...
Biens et services divers	10	2,0	...
Total	186	100,0	

Dépenses de consommation des ménages
Les dépenses de consommation prises en compte pour le calcul de l'indice correspondent aux achats des biens et services effectués par les ménages de référence pour leur consommation. Elles excluent l'impôt sur le revenu, les versements aux caisses de retraite, l'épargne, les primes d'assurance-vie, les achats de maison, les cotisations syndicales et les paris.

Mode de relevé des prix
Les prix sont relevés par les agents du Bureau de statistiques dans des marchés, supermarchés, points de vente au détail et établissements de services. Les prix des produits alimentaires sont estimés sur la base d'achats directs effectués au cours de la première semaine de chaque mois. Les prix des articles ménagers non durables sont obtenus au cours de la troisième semaine de chaque mois, alors que ceux des biens durables ainsi que ceux des services sont relevés tous les trimestres. Les prix retenus pour le calcul de l'indice sont les prix effectivement payés sur le marché par les ménages.

Logement
Les relevés des loyers ont lieu une fois par an. Pour les mois intermédiaires, on suppose que les loyers varient dans la même proportion que tous les autres articles de l'indice. Il est procédé au relevé de la valeur locative des logements occupés en propriété.

Spécification des variétés
Les spécifications des articles prennent en compte dans leur détail la vogue dont jouissent ces derniers et la continuité des séries de prix. Sont fournis le nom, la marque, la qualité et la taille.

Substitution, changement de qualité, etc.
Si un produit disparaît du marché, un autre lui est substitué. Le prix de l'ancien produit au cours de la période de base est corrigé en fonction de son rapport numérique au prix du nouveau. En cas de changement de qualité, l'article est traité comme s'il était nouveau et la même méthode est utilisée.

Articles saisonniers
Il est tenu compte des fluctuations saisonnières des prix des articles en utilisant des moyennes mensuelles mobiles.

Calcul
L'indice est calculé selon la formule de Laspeyres sous forme de moyenne arithmétique pondérée à base fixe, les coefficients de pondération correspondant à la période 1982-83.

L'indice pour un article est obtenu en utilisant les rapports de prix moyens de la période en cours et de la période de base. Les prix moyens sont les moyennes arithmétiques simples de tous les relevés de prix.

Autres informations
Outre l'indice des prix à la consommation des ménages à revenu modeste, le Bureau central de statistiques publie un indice des prix à la consommation pour les ménages à revenu moyen et pour les ménages à revenu élevé habitant Nairobi.

Organisation et publication
Ministry of Finance and Planning, Central Bureau of Statistics: «Kenya Statistical Digest» (Nairobi).
idem: «On current and revised Kenyan Consumer Price Indices».

KIRIBATI (TARAWA)

Dénomination officielle
Retail Price Index (Indice des prix de détail).

Portée
L'indice est calculé trimestriellement et porte sur les ménages urbains de Tarawa.

Base originale
Octobre-décembre 1975 = 100.

Source des coefficients de pondération
Les coefficients de pondération et les articles sélectionnés ont été déterminés sur la base des résultats d'une enquête sur les dépenses des ménages effectuée au cours d'une période de six semaines de fin août à début octobre 1975 auprès d'un échantillon de 61 ménages résidant dans les régions urbaines de Tarawa, et de diverses autres sources.

Pondération et composition

Groupes principaux	Nombre d'articles	Pondération	Nombre approximatif de relevés de prix
Alimentation	47	50,00	...
Boissons et tabac	8	14,00	...
Habillement et chaussure	15	8,00	...
Transports	15	8,00	...
Logement:			
Loyer	4	1,01	...
Combustible et éclairage	4	3,56	...
Entretien et équipement du ménage	13	2,93	...
Divers	22	12,50	...
Total	128	100,00	...

Dépenses de consommation des ménages
Pas disponible.

Mode de relevé des prix
Les prix sont relevés par des enquêteurs vers le 15 de chaque mois sur des marchés, auprès de points de vente au détail et de prestataires de services, situés dans trois centres principaux des régions urbaines de Tarawa.

Logement
Pas disponible.

Spécification des variétés
Pas disponible.

Substitution, changement de qualité, etc.
Pas disponible.

Articles saisonniers
Les fluctuations saisonnières des prix ne font pas l'objet d'ajustements.

Calcul
L'indice est calculé selon la formule de Laspeyres, sous forme de moyenne arithmétique pondérée à base fixe, les coefficients de pondération correspondant à la période de base.

Organisation et publication
Ministry of Finance, Statistical Unit: «Quarterly Digest of Statistics» (Tarawa).

KOWEIT

Dénomination officielle
Consumer Price Index Numbers (Indice des prix à la consommation).

Portée
L'indice est calculé mensuellement et porte sur tous les ménages privés, y compris ceux d'une personne.

Base originale
1978 = 100.

Source des coefficients de pondération
La valeur des coefficients de pondération et le choix des articles résultent de l'enquête sur le budget des ménages effectué en 1977-78.

Pondération et composition

Groupes principaux	Nombre d'articles	Pondération	Nombre approximatif de relevés de prix
Alimentation	192	357,09	2 484
Boissons et tabac	8	12,70	85
Habillement et chaussure	67	99,55	323
Logement	14	187,03	25
Biens et services ménagers	119	110,23	646
Transports et communications	73	152,91	105
Education et soins médicaux	55	25,49	365
Autres biens et services	72	55,00	291
Total	(a) 600	1 000.00	4 324

Remarque: (a) Variétés (représentant environ 260 articles).

Dépenses de consommation des ménages
Les dépenses de consommation prises en compte dans le calcul de l'indice correspondent aux achats de tous les biens et services importants effectués par les ménages de référence pour leur consommation. En sont exclus l'impôt sur le revenu, l'épargne et les placements et les dépenses à des fins autres que la consommation.

Mode de relevé des prix
Le relevé des prix est effectué auprès de points de vente au détail choisis pour leur fréquentation par les consommateurs. Le ministère du Commerce et de l'Industrie fournit lui-même les prix de tous les articles subventionnés.

Les prix sont recueillis par déplacement personnel d'enquêteurs, mensuellement pour la plupart des articles, deux fois par mois pour les fruits et légumes frais et trimestriellement pour les services. En ce qui concerne les services publics (transports, service postal, instruction, santé, etc.), l'indice est modifié en conséquence chaque fois que les tarifs en sont révisés.

Logement
Les données relatives au loyer proviennent de l'enquête annuelle sur les loyers qu'effectue l'Office central de la statistique.

Spécification des variétés
Chacun des articles compris dans le panier fait l'objet d'une spécification détaillée, qui en donne la description complète, le nom, la marque, le pays d'origine, le type d'emballage, la quantité ou l'unité, etc. Seules les spécifications importantes de chaque article sont retenues pour le calcul de l'indice.

Substitution, changement de qualité, etc.
Il n'est pas tenu compte des changements de qualité. Mais, pour en minimiser l'influence sur l'indice, on s'efforce de ne relever que les prix des variétés de produits pour lesquelles on disposait déjà d'un prix pendant l'année de base.

Articles saisonniers
Sont traités comme tels les fruits et légumes frais. Pour chacun des douze mois de l'année, on compose, avec ces produits, un panier de saison typique. On relève alors les prix de tous les articles qui s'y trouvent et on les compare avec ceux du même mois de l'année de base.

Calcul
L'indice est calculé selon la formule de Laspeyres sous forme de moyenne arithmétique pondérée à base fixe, les coefficients de pondération correspondant à la période de base.

Le rapport de prix pour chaque variété est calculé en divisant le prix de la période courante par le prix de la période de base. L'indice pour un article est ensuite calculé comme une moyenne des rapports de prix des variétés. Pour les articles subventionnés et les articles disponibles au marché libre, on obtient des rapports de prix à partir de moyennes pondérées, les pondérations étant proportionnelles à la quantité vendue au prix du marché contrôlé et du marché libre. Aussi, pour certains articles non subventionnés, des rapports de prix moyens pondérés sont calculés en attribuant des pondérations aux variétés importantes.

Autres informations
Des sous-groupes détaillés sont publiés pour 13 mois.

Organisation et publication
Ministry of Planning, Central Statistical Office: «Monthly Price Index Number» (Koweït).
idem: «Consumer Price Index Numbers, Revised Series 1978 = 100, Scope and method of construction» (Koweït).

LESOTHO

Dénomination officielle
Consumer Price Index for Low Income Households (Indice des prix à la consommation pour les ménages à revenu modique).

Portée
L'indice est calculé trimestriellement et porte sur tous les ménages urbains à revenu modique.

Base originale
Avril 1989 = 100.

Source des coefficients de pondération
La valeur des coefficients de pondération et le choix des articles résultent d'une enquête sur les dépenses des ménages menée entre octobre 1986 et septembre 1987 auprès de l'ensemble des groupes de population (à l'exception des institutions) dans toutes les zones géographiques du pays.

Dans le cadre de cette enquête, le choix des unités de l'échantillon était fondé sur un échantillon stratifié, prélevé en deux étapes à l'échelle nationale, portant sur 4 800 ménages ruraux et 2 880 ménages urbains. Le pays a fait l'objet d'un découpage effectué en fonction des districts et de quatre zones agro-écologiques, comprenant 24 strates dans les zones rurales, 14 dans les zones urbaines et 3 pour la seule ville de Maseru. Les quartiers urbains de Maseru ont été répartis en différentes strates de revenu (élevés, moyens ou modiques) d'après les caractéristiques externes des logements, afin d'apporter une amélioration supplémentaire à la conception de l'enquête. L'échantillonnage était proportionnel à la taille de chaque strate. Dans les zones urbaines, la tâche mensuelle optimale a été fixée à huit logements par enquêteur; dans les zones rurales, ce chiffre est de cinq logements.

L'indice porte sur les ménages à revenu modique, qui incluent ceux dont le revenu mensuel est inférieur à 200 malotis. Aucun ajustement n'a été effectué pour prendre en compte les changements de prix survenus entre la période de l'enquête et le mois d'avril 1989.

Les critères de sélection des articles étaient fonction des dépenses totales; des coefficients de pondération relatifs aux articles dont le prix n'a pas été établi ont été introduits dans les groupes et sous-groupes correspondants lorsque des agrégats élémentaires ont été constitués.

Pondération et composition

Groupes principaux	Nombre d'articles	Pondération	Nombre approximatif de relevés de prix
Alimentation et tabac	108	76,3	552
Habillement et chaussure	46	13,9	148
Loyer brut, combustible et éclairage	25	12,4	58
Mobilier, ameublement et dépenses de ménage	49	10,0	171
Transports et communications	16	3,9	32
Autres biens et services	48	7,1	139
Total	292	100,0	1 100

Dépenses de consommation des ménages
La définition des dépenses de consommation est la même que celle établie par la Comptabilité nationale. Cela signifie que les coefficients de pondération ont subi certains ajustements à partir de l'enquête sur les dépenses de consommation des ménages. La consommation en nature et les dépenses de consommation estimées pour les logements occupés par leur propriétaire ont été incluses dans les coefficients de pondération.

Mode de relevé des prix
Les prix sont relevés par des agents enquêteurs aux mois de janvier, avril, juillet et octobre auprès d'environ 170 points de vente au détail et établissements de services répartis dans six villes. A Maseru, les prix sont relevés du lundi au vendredi pendant la première semaine du mois où l'enquête est effectuée. Dans les autres villes, les relevés de prix ont lieu du lundi au vendredi pendant la troisième semaine du mois en question.

Les prix retenus pour le calcul de l'indice sont les prix effectivement payés. Les prix de soldes sont retenus s'ils sont proposés à l'ensemble du public et non uniquement à un groupe déterminé. La location-vente et le remboursements des prêts, les achats de biens d'occasion et les prix à l'importation n'entrent pas en ligne de compte.

Logement
Les relevés des loyers sont obtenus trimestriellement et comprennent les coûts de location, de réparation et de décoration. Les logements occupés par leur propriétaire sont évalués d'après les coûts de location des logements de type analogue.

Spécification des variétés
Les spécifications comprennent toutes précisions qui permettent aux différents enquêteurs d'obtenir des variétés presque identiques dans les différents points de vente. Par exemple, les spécifications portent sur le type, la variété, le nom, l'origine, la taille, la marque, l'emballage, etc. Cependant, l'enquêteur dispose d'une certaine liberté de choix en fonction de l'assortiment du point de vente concerné.

Substitution, changement de qualité, etc.
Les remplacements sont effectuées par des produits de qualité presque similaire. Si de nouveaux produits font leur apparition et connaissent un succès durable sur le marché, ils sont finalement introduits dans le groupe d'articles correspondant. Si un article disparaît du marché, de nouveaux articles de remplacement sont sélectionnés.

Articles saisonniers
Pour les articles saisonniers, tels que les fruits et légumes frais ne se trouvant pas sur le marché en dehors de la saison, on utilise, pour le calcul de l'indice, les derniers prix disponibles jusqu'à ce que de nouveaux prix soient obtenus.

Calcul
L'indice est calculé selon la formule de Laspeyres sous forme de moyenne arithmétique pondérée à base fixe, les coefficients de pondération correspondant à la période octobre 1986 - septembre 1987.

Les rapports de prix sont d'abord calculés pour chaque relevé, chaque variété et chaque article, en utilisant les rapports de prix pour la période courante et la période précédente.

Des indices pondérés sont calculés pour les sous-groupes, les groupes principaux et l'ensemble des articles rattachés à une période précédente = 100. Ils sont ensuite rattachés à la période avril 1989 = 100.

Autres informations
Un Indice des prix à la consommation est publié pour tous les groupes urbains et toutes les catégories de revenu, ainsi que des séries statistiques relatives aux catégories à revenu élevé habitant Maseru.

Organisation et publication
Bureau of Statistics: «Statistical Reports - Consumer Price Index» (Maseru).

idem: «Lesotho - Consumer Price Index».

LIBERIA (MONROVIA)

Dénomination officielle
Consumer Price Index (Indice des prix à la consommation).

Portée
L'indice est calculé mensuellement et porte sur les ménages d'ouvriers et d'employés de bureau composés d'au moins deux personnes et dont le revenu mensuel ne dépasse pas 250 dollars libériens au cours de la période octobre-décembre 1963. L'indice concerne la capitale, Monrovia.

Base originale
Septembre - novembre 1964 = 100.

Source des coefficients de pondération
La valeur des coefficients de pondération et le choix des articles résultent d'une enquête sur les dépenses des ménages effectuée au cours de la période octobre-décembre 1963 à Monrovia auprès d'un échantillon de ménages d'ouvriers et d'employés de bureau composés d'au moins deux personnes et disposant, lors de l'enquête, d'un revenu mensuel ne dépassant pas 250 dollars libériens. Les coefficients de pondération ont été ajustés en fonction des résultats d'une enquête sommaire sur les dépenses effectuées en juin 1964, afin de tenir compte du laps de temps qui s'est écoulé entre les deux périodes.

Pondération et composition

Groupes principaux	Nombre d'articles	Pondération	Nombre approximatif de relevés de prix
Alimentation	32	34,4	...
Boissons et tabac	6	5,7	...
Combustible et éclairage	3	5,0	...
Loyer	1	14,9	...
Habillement et chaussure	14	13,8	...
Articles d'équipement ménager et mobilier	7	6,1	...
Santé, soins personnels et services	9	11,4	...
Divers	7	8,7	...
Total	79	100,0	188

Dépenses de consommation des ménages
Les dépenses de consommation des ménages prises en compte dans le calcul de l'indice correspondent aux achats de tous les biens et services effectués par les ménages de référence pour leur consommation. Elles comprennent les redevances en matière de licence, le coût des prestations médicales et juridiques, les loisirs et d'autres services. En sont exclus les paiements en nature, les achats à crédit, les primes d'assurance-vie, l'assurance sur les biens ainsi que l'impôt sur les revenus et l'impôt immobilier.

Mode de relevé des prix
Les prix sont relevés par des enquêteurs auprès de 18 magasins, deux marchés et 14 prestataires de services. Les prix pour l'alimentation sont relevés deux fois par mois. Le relevé a lieu mensuellement pour les boissons et le tabac, les combustibles et l'éclairage, l'habillement, les articles d'équipement ménager et le mobilier, et annuellement pour les soins médicaux et les frais de scolarité.

Les articles vendus sous une forme non normalisée, par exemple par pile, à la pièce, en paquet, etc. sont pesés et font ensuite l'objet d'un ajustement afin que leur prix soit conforme au coefficient de pondération de la période de base. Les prix retenus pour le calcul de l'indice sont les prix de détail réellement payés par les consommateurs. Sont écartés les prix des articles au rabais, vendus en solde et les autres prix anormaux.

Logement
Les données relatives aux loyers sont relevées deux fois par an, en janvier et en juillet, pour une centaine d'habitations. Les logements occupés en propriété n'entrent pas dans le calcul de l'indice.

Spécification des variétés
Chaque article de l'indice est l'objet d'une spécification détaillée qui fait état de la marque, de la taille, de l'unité de quantité employée, de sa description, de la marque de fabrique, etc.

Substitution, changement de qualité, etc.
Lorsqu'un produit n'est plus disponible, un produit comparable lui est substitué et la méthode d'enchaînement est appliquée.

Articles saisonniers
Les fluctuations saisonnières des prix de certains articles sont prises en compte en maintenant, hors saison, les prix de clôture de la saison précédente.

Calcul
L'indice est calculé selon la formule de Laspeyres sous forme de moyenne arithmétique pondérée à base fixe, les coefficients de pondération correspondant à juin 1964.

L'indice pour un article est obtenu en utilisant les rapports de prix de la période courante et de la période de base. Les prix moyens sont des moyennes arithmétiques simples de tous les relevés de prix. Lorsque l'on ne dispose pas du prix d'un article, on utilise le prix obtenu précédemment pour le même article.

Organisation et publication
National Planning Agency, Bureau of Statistics: «Statistical Newsletter» (Monrovia).

idem: «Quarterly Statistical Bulletin».

idem: «Economic Survey of Liberia».

idem: «Results of the Study related to the Consumer Price Index for Monrovia», Methodological Series No. 1 (1964).

LUXEMBOURG

Dénomination officielle
Indice des prix à la consommation.

Portée
L'indice est calculé mensuellement et porte sur l'ensemble des ménages dans tout le pays, sauf ceux des travailleurs indépendants dans l'industrie et les services et des agriculteurs.

Base originale
1990 = 100.

Source des coefficients de pondération
Les coefficients de pondération ont été déterminés sur la base des résultats d'une enquête sur les dépenses des ménages menée entre avril 1986 et septembre 1987 et portant sur 2 764 ménages représentatifs de l'ensemble de la population. L'indice se rapporte à tous les ménages dans l'ensemble du pays, sauf ceux des travailleurs indépendants dans l'industrie et les services et des agriculteurs. Aucun ajustement n'a été apporté aux coefficients de pondération pour tenir compte de l'évolution des prix entre la période de l'enquête et 1990.
La sélection des articles est opérée en fonction de leur importance dans les budgets des ménages et de leur aptitude à se prêter à des observations de prix dans le temps.
Les coefficients de pondération des articles non retenus en raison de leur poids insuffisant dans les dépenses des ménages sont affectés à d'autres articles similaires. Les valeurs des articles non retenus pour des raisons politiques (élimination des cigarettes, des tabacs et des alcools forts et de certains services liés étroitement à l'échelle mobile des salaires) sont écartées avant détermination du total des dépenses de consommation prises en considération.

Pondération et composition

Groupes principaux	Nombre d'articles	Pondération	Nombre approximatif de relevés de prix
Alimentation	91	205,2	2 175
Habillement et chaussure	42	131,1	800
Logement, combustible, éclairage	11	137,0	600
Mobilier, ameublement et biens d'équipement ménager	39	100,8	700
Soins médicaux	27	81,9	300
Transports et communications	24	148,6	275
Instruction et loisirs	37	79,9	700
Autres biens et services	32	115,5	850
Total	303	100,0	6 400

Dépenses de consommation des ménages
En principe, le concept «dépenses» a été retenu, à quelques exceptions substantielles près. Selon cette notion, seules les sommes effectivement déboursées par les ménages durant la période d'observation ont été comptabilisées. Ni les biens autoconsommés, c'est-à-dire ceux produits par les ménages eux-mêmes, ni les loyers imputés des logements occupés par leurs propriétaires n'ont été pris en considération pour le calcul des pondérations.
On prend en considération la partie non remboursée des soins de santé et les cotisations patronales et salariales pour les prestations en nature dans le calcul de la pondération des dépenses de santé. Pour la détermination du coefficient de pondération afférent aux services d'assurances, il s'agit d'isoler, dans le prix de la prime, la partie qui correspond au prix payé pour l'achat du service d'assurance lui-même. La différence, sur une longue période, entre les primes émises et les charges pour sinistres constitue cette part représentant l'achat du service d'assurance. Le rapport sur dix ans entre cet écart et le total des primes émises est appliqué au montant des dépenses des ménages au titre des assurances. La dépense pour l'achat du service d'assurance ainsi calculée détermine la pondération du poste «assurance».

Mode de relevé des prix
Les prix sont relevés mensuellement par des enquêteurs auprès de supermarchés, de points de vente au détail et de prestataires de services dans la capitale et dans des localités représentatives des autres régions du pays. Les prix des fruits et légumes frais, des poissons et des fleurs sont observés trois fois par mois.

Les tarifs officiels sont obtenus auprès des autorités nationales ou communales compétentes pour leur fixation. Les prix de l'électricité, du gaz, de l'eau, des soins médicaux (prestations de médecins, de praticiens paramédicaux et services hospitaliers) et de certains articles du groupe «Transports et communications» (essence, chemin de fer, autobus, affranchissement de lettres, téléphone) sont fixés par voie de tarifs officiels. Le prix de transaction (prix total) est toujours pris en considération pour le calcul de l'indice, quelles que soient les modalités de paiement et les conditions de remboursement par des organismes de sécurité sociale (dépenses de santé).
L'instruction publique est gratuite. Dans la mesure où certains articles représentatifs peuvent ne pas être gratuits, le prix à payer par le consommateur est retenu pour le calcul de l'indice.
Les offres spéciales ou rabais sont pris en considération pour le calcul de l'indice à condition qu'ils bénéficient indistinctement à tous les consommateurs, qu'ils soient disponibles en nombre significatif et pendant une durée dépassant un mois et que le produit réponde aux mêmes caractéristiques que précédemment.
Les prix des soldes ne sont pas pris en considération pour le calcul de l'indice étant donné que leur durée, strictement limitée par voie réglementaire, ne dépasse pas 15 jours et que les autres conditions requises pour les offres spéciales ne sont pas toutes remplies. Les prix sont relevés tels qu'ils sont pratiqués à la date de référence de l'indice, c'est-à-dire au premier du mois, quelles que soient les modalités de paiement arrangées entre le vendeur et l'acheteur. Les achats d'occasion et reprises d'articles usagés ne sont pas pris en considération dans l'indice.
Les prix retenus sont ceux observés au stade de la consommation finale des ménages; des prix intermédiaires éventuels ne sont pas pris en considération.

Logement
Le loyer observé est le prix payé par le locataire pour l'occupation du logement loué vide, abstraction faite des frais et charges annexes (loyer net). Les logements retenus sont dans une large proportion représentatifs de l'ensemble de la population. Aucun type de logement n'est exclu à priori. Le loyer est relevé auprès des locataires deux fois par année, 1/6 de l'échantillon étant observé à tour de rôle mensuellement. Les loyers sont relevés par voie d'enquête téléphonique et, exceptionnellement, par voie d'enquête postale. L'indice du loyer (deux positions séparées, à savoir loyer appartement et loyer maison) est égal à la moyenne arithmétique des indices particuliers calculés pour chaque logement retenu dans les deux échantillons en question.
Les logements occupés par leurs propriétaires ne sont pas pris en compte dans l'indice (notion dépense).

Spécification des variétés
Les spécifications sont détaillées en ce qui concerne les variétés, les marques et les modèles; elles dépendent uniquement du STATEC et ont un caractère confidentiel.

Substitution, changement de qualité, etc.
En cas de changement de qualité, deux hypothèses sont envisagées:
- les caractéristiques essentielles du produit ne sont pas modifiées, les changements n'ont qu'un caractère accessoire: la variation de prix qui peut accompagner ce changement de qualité se répercute sur l'indice sans ajustement;
- le changement de qualité porte sur les caractéristiques essentielles du produit, il a un caractère significatif: la contrepartie de l'amélioration qualitative dans le prix est neutralisée.

En pratique, les changements de qualité sont accompagnés de variations de prix et il s'agit d'examiner si la variation de prix correspond entièrement ou partiellement au changement de qualité. Il est alors procédé, selon le cas, à des raccords statistiques intégraux ou partiels.
Le panier des biens et services sera révisé à l'avenir tous les cinq ans. A l'intérieur de cette période, le principe de sa composition constante est respecté. Si néanmoins un nouveau produit fait son apparition et s'impose de façon telle qu'il n'est pas possible de l'ignorer, il est intégré à l'indice par la voie du raccord statistique en tant que variété représentative d'un article de la liste réglementaire.
En cas de disparition d'un type ou d'une qualité donnés du marché, il est remplacé, de préférence dans le même point de

vente, par un autre produit qui répond à des caractéristiques semblables. Si la nouvelle variété appartient à la même marque et fournit au consommateur les mêmes satisfactions, elle est intégrée à l'indice avec prise en compte d'une éventuelle variation de prix parallèle. Si la nouvelle variété possède des caractéristiques essentielles différentes (y compris au niveau du service de vente ou après-vente) ou si elle émane d'une autre marque, elle est intégrée à l'indice en tant que remplaçant avec raccord statistique.

Articles saisonniers
Les fruits et légumes frais constituent deux articles à pondération fixe; les paniers représentatifs de chacun de ces deux articles ont une composition mensuelle variable, y compris les pondérations des différentes variétés retenues. On procède, pour ces deux articles, au calcul d'une moyenne mobile sur 12 mois.

Les autres articles saisonniers qui ne sont pas offerts pendant toute l'année sont maintenus, en dehors de leur saison, à l'indice avec le dernier prix observé dans l'attente de leur réapparition sur le marché.

Calcul
L'indice est calculé selon la formule de Laspeyres sous forme de moyenne arithmétique pondérée à base fixe (1990), les coefficients de pondération correspondant à 1986-87. L'indice pour un article est obtenu en utilisant les rapports de prix de la période courante et de la période de base.

Autres informations
L'indice général, les indices de groupes, les principaux indices de sous-groupes et les indices de quelques articles importants sont publiés mensuellement. Tous les indices de sous-groupes et d'articles sont par ailleurs accessibles au public, sur demande.

Organisation et publication
L'indice est calculé et publié mensuellement par le Service central de la statistique et des études économiques dans «Indicateurs rapides du STATEC, série A1, Indice des prix à la consommation» (Luxembourg).

idem: «Cahier économique du STATEC no. 81, Le nouvel indice des prix à la consommation, Réforme de 1990/91».

idem: «Note de conjoncture» (trimestrielle).

idem: «Annuaire statistique».

MACAO

Dénomination officielle
Indice de Preços no Consumidor (Indice des prix à la consommation).

Portée
L'indice est calculé mensuellement et porte sur les ménages dont les dépenses mensuelles moyennes, s'élèvent à 3 313 patacas. La zone géographique couvre la péninsule de Macao (à l'exclusion des deux îles Taipa et Coloane).

Base originale
Octobre 1982 - septembre 1983 = 100.

Source des coefficients de pondération
La valeur des coefficients de pondération et le choix des articles ont été déterminés à partir d'une enquête sur les ménages effectuée sur une année en 1981-82 auprès d'un échantillon aléatoire de 1 560 ménages, la période de référence des données relatives aux dépenses de chaque ménage ayant été de deux semaines. Il n'a été procédé à aucun ajustement des coefficients de pondération pour prendre en compte les changements de prix survenus entre la période de l'enquête et la période de base.

Les critères et la méthode adoptés pour sélectionner les articles pour lesquels un relevé des prix est effectué se fondent sur les coefficients de pondération des articles résultant de l'enquête sur les dépenses des ménages. De même, la faveur dont l'article jouit sur le marché pourrait faire l'objet d'un relevé périodique et constant. En ce qui concerne les coefficients de pondération des articles pour lesquels aucun prix n'est relevé, ils sont redistribués entre les articles voisins, au moyen d'une attribution directe ou proportionnelle.

Dépenses de consommation des ménages
Afin de définir les dépenses de consommation utilisées pour l'obtention des coefficients de pondération, il convient de tenir

Pondération et composition

Groupes principaux	Nombre d'articles	Pondération	Nombre approximatif de relevés de prix
Alimentation	72	42,03	...
Boissons alcoolisées et tabac	4	2,22	...
Logement	-	-	-
Combustibles et éclairage	4	4,78	...
Dépenses de ménage	8	1,63	...
Habillement et chaussure	29	7,25	...
Biens durables	26	2,91	...
Articles divers	29	4,97	...
Transport	17	4,88	...
Services	35	8,14	...
Total	224	78,81	...

compte de toutes les dépenses des ménages en achats de biens et de services. Etant donné que ces dépenses sont payées au moment de l'achat, il s'ensuit que toutes les consommations effectuées par le ménage au cours du cycle ont été relevées.

Les achats à crédit n'ont été considérés comme dépenses que si leur paiement a été effectué au cours du cycle. Il a été tenu compte, au prix du marché, de la valeur des biens et services dont ont bénéficié les ménages en tant que revenus en nature. Un loyer fictif a été imputé aux logements occupés en propriété et à ceux dont bénéficient gratuitement des ménages. Il n'est pas tenu compte de l'impôt sur le revenu et autres impôts directs, hypothèques, investissements, paris, contributions aux fonds de pension, assurance-vie, etc.

Mode de relevé des prix
Les relevés sont effectués par des enquêteurs ou au moyen de questionnaires adressés par la poste aux marchés, points de vente au détail et prestataires de services dans les cinq localités. Le prix des aliments frais est obtenu chaque jour et toutes les semaines, celui des produits alimentaires chaque mois. Tous les jours, au début de la matinée, des enquêteurs procèdent au relevé des prix des aliments frais sur le marché, puis à celui des prix d'autres biens et services, en fonction du temps dont ils disposent. Le prix des boissons alcoolisées, du tabac, de la chaussure, des biens durables, des produits divers est obtenu tous les deux mois et celui des autres articles tous les trois ou six mois.

Cependant, une action immédiate est prise en cas de changement soudain du prix d'articles tels que le gaz, l'électricité, l'eau, les journaux, etc.

Le prix des articles vendus en solde et avec un rabais ne dépassant pas 20 pour cent est relevé et utilisé dans le calcul de l'indice.

Le prix des achats au marché noir, des articles en location-vente ou achetés à crédit, des articles d'occasion, celui de la reprise d'articles usagés et le paiement partiel de nouveaux articles ne sont pas pris en compte.

Les prix effectivement payés par les consommateurs procédant à l'acquisition de biens et de services aux fins de consommation sont utilisés.

Logement
Le loyer est exclu du calcul de l'indice.

Spécification des variétés
Chaque article fait l'objet de spécifications détaillées en fonction, par exemple, de leur variété, de la qualité, du lieu d'origine, de la marque, de l'unité, de la taille, de l'emballage, etc.

Les prix sont relevés chaque mois en tenant compte des mêmes spécifications.

Substitution, changement de qualité, etc.
En cas de changement de qualité ou de disparition du marché d'un article d'un type ou d'une qualité déterminés, les méthodes appliquées sont les suivantes: substitution directe en utilisant l'enchaînement entre l'article ancien (variété précédente) et l'article de remplacement (nouvelle variété) ou en recalculant le rapport du prix imputé dans le sous-groupe existant.

Articles saisonniers
Il existe deux sortes d'habillement: habillement d'été et habillement d'hiver. En été, le prix des vêtements d'été est relevé alors qu'une valeur constante est attribuée au prix des vêtements d'hiver, et il en est de même en hiver pour les vêtements d'été.

Calcul
L'indice est calculé selon la formule de Laspeyres sous forme de moyenne arithmétique pondérée à base fixe, les coefficients de pondération correspondant à la période 1981-82.

Autres informations
Des sous-groupes tels qu'alimentation, logement, combustible et éclairage, boissons alcoolisées et tabacs, habillement et chaussure, biens durables, biens divers, transport et véhicules et services, sont publiés.

Organisation et publication
Dirrecçao de Servicios de Estatistica e Censos: «Indice de Peços no Consumidor» (Macao).
idem: «Metodologia do Indice de Preços no Consumidor».

MADAGASCAR (ANTANANARIVO)

Dénomination officielle
Indice des prix de détail à la consommation familiale malgache.

Portée
L'indice est calculé mensuellement et porte sur les ménages malgaches à Antananarivo.

Base originale
Août 1971 - juillet 1972 = 100.

Source des coefficients de pondération
Les coefficients de pondération et les articles sélectionnés ont été déterminés sur la base des résultats d'une enquête sur les dépenses des ménages effectuée de mars 1968 à février 1969 auprès de ménages malgaches (toutes tailles et catégories) à Antananarivo.
Les articles retenus dans le calcul de l'indice sont tous les articles ayant une valeur marchande à laquelle on peut assigner une unité et une qualité bien déterminées et dont l'observation des prix dans le temps est facile. Ces articles ont une part relative à la dépense totale supérieure ou égale à 0,05 pour cent pour l'indice en milieu Malagasy.

Pondération et composition

Groupes principaux	Nombre d'articles	Pondération	Nombre approximatif de relevés de prix
Alimentation	60	603,5	3 636
Combustible et éclairage	8	91,4	140
Habillement et chaussure	15	85,5	144
Biens d'équipement ménager	3	4,1	56
Produits d'entretien	5	20,3	292
Soins personnels et médicaux	20	38,6	988
Services domestiques	1	18,2	1
Divers	19	138,4	390
Total	131	1 000,0	5 647

Dépenses de consommation des ménages
L'autoconsommation est prise en compte dans le calcul des coefficients de pondération. On ne tient pas compte des dépenses relatives au loyer ni des logements occupés par leur propriétaire.
Sont également exclues les dépenses pour: les biens durables, l'instruction, les assurances autres que pour véhicules, cotisations, cadeaux, impôts, taxes, amendes, transferts, objets personnels et les dépenses diverses.
Les salaires versés pour les services domestiques (sans tenir compte des avantages en nature), les dépenses de fonctionnement et les assurances des véhicules particuliers sont inclus.

Mode de relevé des prix
L'observation des prix est limitée à un certain nombre de magasins, choisis de telle façon qu'ils correspondent à la population couverte par l'indice et reflètent l'importance de la population de référence qui y achète. Ces magasins sont choisis empiriquement en tenant compte de l'emplacement, du type ou de la catégorie du magasin et de la répartition de la population de référence. Le nombre et la répartition des magasins différent suivant le groupe de produits.
Les prix des denrées alimentaires et des produits d'entretien sont relevés dans 20 magasins du centre ville et des quartiers dont la population Malagasy est assez importante.
Les prix de certaines denrées alimentaires telles que volailles, fruits et légumes frais sont obtenus la première, deuxième et quatrième semaines du mois par achat direct de ces articles par des enquêteurs sur deux grands marchés publics hebdomadaires. Les prix des autres articles sont relevés au moyen de questionnaires envoyés mensuellement à environ 40 magasins de détail et prestataires de services.
Les données relatives aux services domestiques sont obtenues une fois par an par une enquête spéciale menée auprès d'un échantillon de ménages. La liste de ces ménages est mise à jour tous les ans à partir de la liste des employeurs fournie par la Caisse Nationale de Prévoyance Sociale.

Logement
Les dépenses relatives au loyer ne sont retenues ni dans le calcul de l'indice ni dans la détermination des coefficients de pondération.

Spécification des variétés
Les articles sont spécifiés et définis par les termes les plus connus par les commerçants et les acheteurs, ayant une influence sur le prix (genre, qualité, dimension, poids, pays d'origine, etc.). La méthode d'acquisition des articles est aussi un des éléments qui entrent dans la spécification de l'article, et elle est précisée à partir du comportement des ménages de référence. Pour les articles qui ne présentent pas d'homogénéité, surtout les produits manufacturés, la définition retenue n'est pas rigoureuse mais chaque magasin est obligé de suivre le prix de la même variété d'article.

Substitution, changement de qualité, etc.
Si un magasin ferme ou change d'activité, on cherche un magasin comparable à lui substituer, si possible dans le même quartier.
Si un article disparaît du marché et s'il n'est pas possible de trouver un article équivalent à celui qui a disparu, mais qu'un article similaire est déjà introduit dans le calcul de l'indice, on affecte le coefficient de l'article disparu à l'article similaire. Dans le cas où un article similaire n'est pas introduit dans le panier et qu'il n'est pas possible de trouver un article de remplacement, son coefficient est réparti entre les différents articles du même groupe.
Dans la plupart des cas, la disparition d'un article mène à l'apparition d'un nouvel article. En général, il est donc possible de relever parallèlement pendant un certain temps, les prix de ces deux articles et la différence de qualité et de prix est évaluée afin que l'enchaînement ne cache pas la différence réelle de prix. Le nouvel article n'est incorporé dans le calcul de l'indice qu'au moment où son volume de vente devient assez important.

Articles saisonniers
Il est tenu compte des fluctuations saisonnières du prix des fruits et légumes frais en variant la pondération mensuelle des articles du sous-groupe, dont la pondération d'ensemble demeure constante.

Calcul
L'indice est calculé selon la formule de Laspeyres, sous forme de moyenne arithmétique pondérée à base fixe, les coefficients de pondération correspondant à la période mars 1968 - février 1969.

Organisation et publication
Ministère des Finances, Direction générale de la Banque de données de l'Etat: «Bulletin mensuel de statistique» (Antananarivo).
idem: «Situation économique».
Direction générale du gouvernement, Direction de l'Institut national de la statistique et de la recherche économique: «L'établissement des nouveaux indices des prix de détail à la consommation familiale à Tananarive, base août 1971 à juillet 1972 = 100» (Antananarivo).

MADAGASCAR (ANTANANARIVO, EUROPEENS)

Dénomination officielle
Indice des prix de détail à la consommation familiale européenne.

Portée
L'indice est calculé mensuellement et porte sur les familles européennes à Antananarivo.

Base originale
Août 1971 - juillet 1972 = 100.

Source des coefficients de pondération
Les coefficients de pondération et les articles sélectionnés ont été déterminés sur la base des résultats d'une enquête sur les dépenses des ménages effectuée de mai à juin 1969 auprès de familles européennes (toutes tailles et catégories) à Antananarivo.
Les articles retenus dans le calcul de l'indice sont tous les articles ayant une valeur marchande à laquelle on peut assigner une unité et une qualité bien déterminées et dont l'observation des prix dans le temps est facile. Ces articles ont une part relative à la dépense totale supérieure ou égale à 0,03 pour cent pour l'indice en milieu Européen.

Pondération et composition

Groupes principaux	Nombre d'articles	Pondération	Nombre approximatif de relevés de prix (a)
Alimentation	105	451,6	7 110
Combustible et éclairage	5	60,8	20
Habillement et chaussure	20	76,2	508
Biens d'équipement ménager	5	6,4	324
Produits d'entretien	12	29,7	804
Soins personnels et médicaux	24	67,6	1 576
Services domestiques	3	112,6	36
Divers	25	195,1	475
Total	199	1 000,0	10 853

Remarque: (a) Nombre de relevés annuels.

Dépenses de consommation des ménages
L'autoconsommation est prise en compte dans le calcul des coefficients de pondération. On ne tient pas compte des dépenses relatives au loyer ni des logements occupés par leur propriétaire.
Sont également exclues les dépenses pour: les biens durables, l'instruction, les assurances autres que pour véhicules, les cotisations, cadeaux, impôts, taxes, amendes, transferts, objets personnels et les dépenses diverses.
Les salaires versés pour les services domestiques (sans tenir compte des avantages en nature), les dépenses de fonctionnement et les assurances des véhicules particuliers sont inclus.

Mode de relevé des prix
L'observation des prix est limitée à un certain nombre de magasins, choisis de telle façon qu'ils correspondent à la population couverte par l'indice et reflètent l'importance de la population de référence qui y achète. Ces magasins sont choisis empiriquement en tenant compte de l'emplacement, du type ou de la catégorie du magasin et de la répartition de la population de référence. Le nombre et la répartition des magasins diffèrent suivant le groupe de produits.
Les prix des denrées alimentaires et des produits d'entretien sont relevés dans les magasins à rayons multiples et dans les grandes épiceries du centre de la ville ou des quartiers à forte population européenne (23 magasins).
Les prix de certaines denrées alimentaires telles que fruits et légumes frais sont obtenus tous les six jours par achat direct de ces articles par des enquêteurs sur le grand marché public. Les prix des autres articles sont relevés au moyen de questionnaires envoyés mensuellement à quelque 43 magasins de détail et prestataires de services.
Les données relatives aux services domestiques sont obtenues une fois par an par une enquête spéciale menée auprès d'un échantillon de ménages. La liste de ces ménages est mise à jour tous les ans à partir de la liste des employeurs fournie par la Caisse Nationale de Prévoyance Sociale.

Logement
Les dépenses relatives au loyer ne sont retenues ni dans le calcul de l'indice ni dans la détermination des coefficients de pondération.

Spécification des variétés
Les articles sont spécifiés et définis par les termes les plus connus par les commerçants et les acheteurs, ayant une influence sur le prix (genre, qualité, dimension, poids, pays d'origine, etc.). La méthode d'acquisition des articles est aussi un des éléments qui entrent dans la spécification de l'article, et elle est précisée à partir du comportement des ménages de référence. Pour les articles qui ne présentent pas d'homogénéité, surtout les produits manufacturés, la définition retenue n'est pas rigoureuse mais chaque magasin est obligé de suivre le prix de la même variété d'article.

Substitution, changement de qualité, etc.
Si un magasin ferme ou change d'activité, on cherche un magasin comparable à lui substituer, si possible dans le même quartier.
Si un article disparaît du marché et s'il n'est pas possible de trouver un article équivalent à celui qui a disparu, mais qu'un article similaire est déjà introduit dans le calcul de l'indice, on affecte le coefficient de l'article disparu à l'article similaire. Dans le cas où un article similaire n'est pas introduit dans le panier et qu'il n'est pas possible de trouver un article de remplacement, son coefficient est réparti entre les différents articles du même groupe.
Dans la plupart des cas, la disparition d'un article mène à l'apparition d'un nouvel article. En général, il est donc possible de relever parallèlement pendant un certain temps, les prix de ces deux articles et la différence de qualité et de prix est évaluée afin que l'enchaînement ne cache pas la différence réelle de prix. Le nouvel article n'est incorporé dans le calcul de l'indice qu'au moment où son volume de vente devient assez important.

Articles saisonniers
Il est tenu compte des fluctuations saisonnières du prix des fruits et légumes frais en variant la pondération mensuelle des articles du sous-groupe, dont la pondération d'ensemble demeure constante.

Calcul
L'indice est calculé selon la formule de Laspeyres, sous forme de moyenne arithmétique pondérée à base fixe, les coefficients de pondération correspondant à la période mai-juin 1969.

Organisation et publication
Ministère des Finances, Direction générale de la Banque de données de l'Etat: «Bulletin mensuel de statistique» (Antananarivo).

idem: «Situation économique».

Direction générale du gouvernement, Direction de l'Institut national de la statistique et de la recherche économique: «L'établissement des nouveaux indices des prix de détail à la consommation familiale à Tananarive, base août 1971 à juillet 1972 = 100» (Antananarivo).

MALAISIE

Dénomination officielle
Consumer Price Index (Indice des prix à la consommation).

Portée
L'indice est calculé mensuellement et porte sur tous les ménages privés des régions urbaines et rurales.

Base originale
1980 = 100.

Source des coefficients de pondération
La valeur des coefficients de pondération et le choix des articles résultent de deux enquêtes sur les dépenses des ménages, l'une effectuée en Malaisie péninsulaire au mois de décembre 1980 auprès d'environ 3 000 ménages privés, l'autre effectuée au Sabah et au Sarawak six mois durant, de mai à octobre 1982, auprès du même nombre de ménages privés. Les coefficients de pondération n'ont fait l'objet d'aucun ajustement pour prendre en compte l'évolution des prix entre l'année de l'enquête et l'année de base, bien que les chiffres relatifs aux dépenses aient été ajustés pour la Malaisie péninsulaire afin de refléter la situation de 1982. Des articles dont les coefficients de pondération sont relativement importants sont choisis pour les relevés de prix. Pour calculer le rapport de prix des articles disposant d'une pondération, mais pour lesquels il n'est pas possible d'effectuer de relevé de prix, on utilise le rapport de prix pondéré d'autres articles du même groupe ou du même sous-groupe. Les coefficients de pondération des articles non sélectionnés sont redistribués parmi les articles du même groupe ayant fait l'objet d'une sélection.

Dépenses de consommation des ménages
Le relevé des données relatives aux dépenses a été effectué par la méthode tenant compte des acquisitions, selon laquelle l'enregistrement des dépenses consacrées par les ménages à l'achat de biens et de services doit être effectué en même temps que les transactions. Il a été considéré que les biens acquis en location-vente ont été achetés au moment de la signature du contrat, ou, en l'absence de contrat, au moment où les biens ont été mis à la disposition de l'acheteur. En outre le

Pondération et composition

Groupes principaux	Nombre d'articles	Pondération	Nombre approximatif de relevés de prix
Alimentation	468	36,9	32 539
Boissons et tabac	42	4,7	2 026
Habillement et chaussure	96	4,8	2 053
Loyer brut, combustible et éclairage	46	18,7	1 017
Mobilier, ameublement, équipement et dépenses ménagères	170	5,8	5 676
Soins médicaux	64	1,2	2 010
Transports et communications	119	16,0	499
Loisirs, instruction et services culturels	105	6,4	863
Biens et services divers	139	5,5	5 414
Total	1 249	100,0	52 097

concept de dépenses des ménages utilisé par l'enquête comprend aussi bien les articles ayant fait l'objet d'un achat que ceux produits à des fins d'autoconsommation ou utilisés dans la consommation finale. Le loyer fictif des logements occupés par leur propriétaire, la consommation provenant de la production propre ou de provisions, les biens et services fournis aux employés gratuitement ou à prix réduit ainsi que les biens perçus en tant que rétributions en nature ont été inclus dans l'estimation des dépenses des ménages. Les acquisitions par les ménages de biens et de services auprès d'organismes gouvernementaux (y compris les frais encourus auprès des hôpitaux publics) ont également été considérées comme des dépenses de consommation s'il a été possible d'établir clairement un lien entre le paiement et l'acquisition des biens et services concernés, et si la décision de payer pour ces derniers a été prise volontairement. L'impôt sur le revenu, les contributions à la sécurité sociale, le paiement des compensations, les frais d'arbitrage et les amendes, les envois de fonds à l'intention d'autres ménages, les sommes investies ou prêtées, le remboursement des prêts, les apports à l'épargne, les sommes perdues au jeu, les subventions et les dons, ainsi que les services culturels et de loisirs fournis gratuitement à l'ensemble du public par le gouvernement, n'ont pas été considérés comme faisant partie des dépenses de consommation des ménages.

Mode de relevé des prix
Les prix de toutes les catégories de biens et services sont relevés vers le milieu de chaque mois par des agents enquêteurs auprès d'environ 6 800 marchés, points de vente au détail et établissements de services répartis sur plus de 103 Centres de relevés (localités) répartis dans toute la Malaisie.

Les prix de soldes sont pris en compte comme des prix de vente normaux. Les prix de catalogue sont pris en compte si les articles concernés sont vendus en quantité suffisante. Certains articles sont soumis au contrôle de la Loi sur l'Approvisionnement (Supplies Act) et, bien souvent, leurs prix recommandés font l'objet d'une vaste publicité. Ces articles peuvent être vendus au prix du marché libre. Les critères pour le relevé de leurs prix exigent que les transactions soient effectuées aux prix de vente normaux. Toutefois, si l'intéressé notifie un prix «officiel» au titre du prix normal, c'est ce prix qui est retenu. Les prix du marché noir n'entrent pas en ligne de compte. Seuls les prix payés au comptant sont pris en considération, alors que sont exclus les prix des locations-ventes et les transactions effectuées à crédit. Les achats de biens d'occasion ne sont pas relevés. Le relevé des prix des produits importés tient compte des taxes à l'importation et des taxes sur les ventes.

Logement
L'enquête relative aux loyers est effectuée une fois par trimestre, aux mois de janvier, avril, juillet et octobre. Les enquêteurs locaux effectuent la visite d'un échantillon de logements en location. Le loyer total par type de logement est d'abord calculé puis il est enchaîné au loyer relatif précédent en fonction de l'indice par type de logement. L'indice enchaîné par type de logement est ensuite pondéré selon la proportion de chaque type pour d'obtenir l'indice du loyer.

Les logements occupés par leur propriétaire ne sont pas inclus dans l'indice.

Spécification des variétés
Les spécifications ont été élaborées en utilisant les spécifications des produits obtenues auprès des fabricants et des industriels. Les spécifications sont soit détaillées, soit générales. Pour les articles faisant l'objet de spécifications détaillées, la description comprend la marque, la qualité, l'unité, la fabrication, etc. Pour les autres articles faisant l'objet de spécifications générales, des descriptions générales sont formulées et les marques spécifiques au magasin doivent être choisies.

Substitution, changement de qualité, etc.
Aucune tentative n'a été effectuée pour quantifier les changements de qualité correspondant aux changements de modèles pour des appareils électriques, des véhicules à moteur et autres articles tels que les vêtements. Les nouveaux produits ne sont rattachés à l'indice que s'ils sont pris comme substituts. Si un type, ou une qualité donnée, disparaît du marché, un substitut analogue est relevé et rattaché à l'indice.

Articles saisonniers
Pour les articles présentant de fortes fluctuations saisonnières, les prix courants ne sont utilisés que durant les mois de la saison. En dehors de la saison, le calcul de l'indice des prix des produits est fondé sur les prix moyens de la saison précédente.

Calcul
L'indice est calculé selon la formule de Laspeyres sous forme de moyenne arithmétique pondérée à base fixe, les coefficients de pondération correspondant à la période de base.

Le rapport de prix de chaque article pour chaque centre régional de relevé de prix est calculé en divisant, pour chaque centre, le prix moyen par le prix de référence. Ces rapports de prix sont pondérés par les coefficients de pondération des centres pour fixer les rapports de prix des articles, qui sont, à leur tour, pondérés par les coefficients de pondération des articles pour établir les indices des sous-groupes et l'indice général. Les prix trop faibles ou trop élevés dont l'origine n'est pas justifiée sont éliminés, les prix antérieurs étant retenus. Les prix manquants sont également insérés. Les prix dont l'origine n'est pas justifiée font l'objet d'une étude et une action est alors entreprise pour les accepter ou les rejeter.

Sur le plan régional, l'indice est calculé directement. Toutefois, au niveau de l'ensemble de la Malaisie, l'indice est calculé comme un indice composite, prenant en considération la proportion des dépenses dans chacune des trois régions du pays.

Autres informations
Les indices des neuf groupes les plus importants ainsi que les sous-groupes de l'indice des produits alimentaires sont publiés. Sont également disponibles les indices classant les produits en Biens durables, Biens semi-durables, Biens périssables et Services.

Organisation et publication
Department of Statistics: «Consumer Price Index for Malaysia» (Kuala Lumpur). Cette publication comprend également une brève description de la méthodologie utilisée.

MALAWI (BLANTYRE 1)

Dénomination officielle
Retail Price Index for Low Income Group Families (Indice des prix de détail - familles à revenu modique).

Portée
L'indice est calculé mensuellement et porte sur les ménages de Blantyre dont les dépenses mensuelles étaient inférieurs à 100 kwacha au cours de la période 1979-80.

Base originale
1980 = 100.

Source des coefficients de pondération
La valeur des coefficients de pondération et le choix des articles résultent d'une enquête sur les dépenses des ménages urbains effectuée en 1979-80 auprès de 4 000 ménages répartis dans les villes de Blantyre, Lilongwe, Zomba et Mzuzu. L'indice porte sur des familles à revenu modique dont les dépenses mensuelles étaient inférieures à 100 kwacha durant la période de l'enquête.

Dépenses de consommation des ménages
Les dépenses de consommation prises en compte dans le calcul de l'indice portent sur toutes les dépenses en espèces que les ménages effectuent pour se procurer des biens et des services destinés à leur consommation et comprennent le remboursement des prêts. Les revenus en nature et la valeur locative des logements occupés par leur propriétaire sont exclus.

Mode de relevé des prix
Les prix sont relevés par des enquêteurs sur des marchés, au-

Pondération et composition

Groupes principaux	Nombre d'articles	Pondération	Nombre approximatif de relevés de prix
Alimentation	34	500	102
Boissons et tabac	7	39	21
Habillement et chaussure	24	154	72
Logement	14	108	42
Dépenses de ménage	7	86	21
Transports	8	48	8
Divers	14	65	42
Total	108	1 000	308

près de points de vente au détail et de prestataires de services à Blantyre. Les prix des articles vendus sur les marchés sont relevés trois fois par mois, ceux de tous les autres articles le mardi ou le vendredi le plus proche du 15 de chaque mois. Les prix pour les fruits, légumes et poissons frais sont déterminés par achat direct sur les marchés. Les prix retenus pour le calcul de l'indice sont les prix normaux payés par tout le monde. Les prix de solde, avec escompte ou rabais, sont exclus.

Logement
Les dépenses relatives au loyer et au coût des logements occupés par leur propriétaire ne sont pris en compte ni dans le calcul de l'indice, ni dans la détermination des coefficients de pondération.

Spécification des variétés
Les articles dont les prix sont à relever font l'objet de spécifications détaillées portant sur la variété, la qualité, la fabrication, la marque et l'unité employée.

Substitution, changement de qualité, etc.
Lorsqu'un produit n'est plus disponible, un produit comparable lui est substitué et la formule d'enchaînement est appliquée.

Articles saisonniers
Dans la période où ils ne sont pas de saison, les prix des articles saisonniers sont estimés.

Calcul
L'indice est calculé selon la formule de Laspeyres sous forme de moyenne arithmétique pondérée à base fixe, les coefficients de pondération correspondant à la période de 1979-80.
Pour calculer les prix moyens, on relève au moins trois prix pour chaque article.

Autres informations
L'Office national des statistiques calcule et publie également des séries concernant les ménages à revenus moyen et élevé résidant à Blantyre et Lilongwe et les ménages à revenus modique et moyen habitant Zomba et Mzuzu. De plus, les séries relatives à Blantyre et Lilongwe sont combinées de manière à établir un indice composite ayant pour base les deux villes.

Organisation et publication
National Statistical Office: «Monthly Statistical Bulletin» (Zomba).

MALAWI (BLANTYRE 2)

Dénomination officielle
Retail Price Index for High-Income Group Families (Indice des prix de détail - familles à revenu élevé).

Portée
L'indice est calculé mensuellement et porte sur les ménages de Blantyre dont les dépenses mensuelles s'élevaient à 400 kwacha et plus au cours de la période 1979-1980.

Base originale
1980 = 100.

Source des coefficients de pondération
La valeur des coefficients de pondération et le choix des articles résultent d'une enquête sur les dépenses des ménages effectuée en 1979-80. L'enquête portait sur 400 ménages résidant à Blantyre et dont les dépenses mensuelles étaient de 400 kwacha et plus durant la période de l'enquête.

Dépenses de consommation des ménages
Les dépenses de consommation prises en compte dans le calcul de l'indice visent toutes les dépenses en espèces que les mé-

Pondération et composition

Groupes principaux	Nombre d'articles	Pondération	Nombre approximatif de relevés de prix
Alimentation	49	203	147
Boissons et tabac	14	76	42
Habillement et chaussure	27	71	81
Logement	26	130	78
Dépenses de ménage	12	108	36
Transports	19	253	19
Divers	26	159	78
Total	173	1 000	481

nages effectuent pour se procurer des biens et des services destinés à leur consommation et comprennent le remboursement des prêts. Sont exclus les revenus en nature et la valeur locative des logements occupés par leur propriétaire.

Mode de relevé des prix
Les prix sont relevés par des enquêteurs sur des marchés, auprès de points de vente au détail et prestataires de services de Blantyre. Pour la plupart des articles, les prix sont relevés le mardi ou le vendredi le plus proche du 15 de chaque mois. Les prix des articles alimentaires importants sont obtenus trois fois par mois par achat direct sur deux marchés. Les données sur la rémunération des services domestiques sont obtenues d'une enquête annuelle. Les données pour les autres services sont obtenues auprès des établissements de services appropriés. Les prix retenus pour le calcul de l'indice sont les prix normaux payés par tout le monde. Les prix de solde, avec escompte ou rabais, sont exclus.

Logement
Les dépenses relatives au loyer et au coût des logements occupés par leur propriétaire ne sont pris en compte ni dans le calcul de l'indice, ni dans la détermination des coefficients de pondération.

Spécification des variétés
Les articles dont les prix sont à relever font l'objet de spécifications détaillées portant sur la variété, la qualité, la fabrication, la marque et l'unité employée.

Substitution, changement de qualité, etc.
Lorsqu'un produit n'est plus disponible, un produit comparable lui est substitué et la formule d'enchaînement est appliquée.

Articles saisonniers
Dans la période où ils ne sont pas de saison, les prix des articles saisonniers sont estimés.

Calcul
L'indice est calculé selon la formule de Laspeyres sous forme de moyenne arithmétique pondérée à base fixe, les coefficients de pondération correspondant à la période 1979-80.
Pour calculer les prix moyens, on relève au moins trois prix pour chaque article.

Autres informations
L'Office national des statistiques calcule et publie également des séries concernant les ménages à revenus modique et moyen habitant Blantyre et Lilongwe et les ménages à revenus modique et moyen habitant Zomba et Mzuzu. De plus, les séries relatives à Blantyre et Lilongwe sont combinées de manière à établir un indice composite ayant pour base les deux villes.

Organisation et publication
National Statistical Office: «Monthly Statistical Bulletin» (Zomba).

MALI (BAMAKO)

Dénomination officielle
Indice des prix du groupe «Alimentation» (marchés de Bamako).

Portée
L'indice est calculé mensuellement et porte sur les ménages d'au moins quatre personnes à Bamako.

Base originale
1 juillet 1962-1 juillet 1963 = 100.

Source des coefficients de pondération
Les coefficients de pondération ont été estimés sur la base des

résultats d'une enquête pilote sur les dépenses des ménages effectuée à Bamako en mars 1963, auprès de ménages composés de quatre membres au moins, et d'après des comparaisons des coefficients de pondération utilisés dans le calcul d'indices d'autres pays africains à structures de consommation similaires.

Pondération et composition

Groupes principaux	Nombre d'articles	Pondération	Nombre approximatif de relevés de prix
Alimentation:			
Farineux et féculents	4	33,9	...
Condiments	5	8,0	...
Légumes et fruits frais	5	9,1	...
Viande et poissons	5	38,1	...
Lait, corps gras, divers	5	10,9	...
Total	24	100,0	...

Dépenses de consommation des ménages
Pas disponible.

Mode de relevé des prix
Les prix sont relevés trois ou quatre fois par mois par des enquêteurs, sur neuf marchés à Bamako.

Logement
Pas disponible.

Spécification des variétés
Pas disponible.

Substitution, changement de qualité, etc.
Pas disponible.

Articles saisonniers
Les variations saisonnières du prix de ces articles ne font l'objet d'aucun ajustement.

Calcul
L'indice est calculé selon la formule de Laspeyres, sous forme de moyenne arithmétique pondérée à base fixe, les coefficients de pondération correspondant à mars 1963.

Autres informations
Depuis 1988, un indice national des prix à la consommation (base juillet 1986 - juin 1987 = 100) est calculé, qui porte sur les villes de Kayes, Sikasso et Bamako. Cette série est publiée dans l'Annuaire et le Bulletin des statistiques du travail mais les informations méthodologiques correspondantes n'étaient pas disponibles au BIT lors de la publication du présent Volume.

Organisation et publication
Ministère du Plan, Direction nationale de la statistique et de l'informatique: «Bulletin mensuel de statistique» (Bamako).

MALTE

Dénomination officielle
Retail Price Index (Indice des prix de détail).

Portée
L'indice est calculé mensuellement et porte sur les ménages de salariés.

Base originale
1983 = 100.

Source des coefficients de pondération
La valeur des coefficients de pondération et le choix des articles résultent d'une enquête sur les dépenses des ménages effectuée en 1983. L'enquête portait sur des ménages de salariés de deux à six personnes ne comprenant pas plus de deux membres travaillant à plein temps, le revenu du chef de ménage se situant entre 23 et 40 livres par semaine. Les ménages de cadres, de travailleurs à leur propre compte et de retraités étaient exclus de cette enquête.

Dépenses de consommation des ménages
Les frais de permis de conduire et les primes d'assurance-automobile sont exclus.

Mode de relevé des prix
Les prix de la plupart des articles sont relevés une fois par mois par des enquêteurs auprès de points de vente au détail et de prestataires de services répartis sur 13 localités. Les relevés sont effectués trois fois par mois pour les fruits, légumes, viande et poissons frais. Les prix retenus pour le calcul de l'indice sont les prix réellement payés par les acheteurs.

Pondération et composition

Groupes principaux	Nombre d'articles	Pondération	Nombre approximatif de relevés de prix
Alimentation	90	41,91	...
Boissons et tabac	13	9,46	...
Habillement et chaussure	37	10,57	...
Logement:			
Loyer	2	1,90	...
Eau et charges	2	0,25	...
Entretien et réparations	5	1,82	...
Combustible et éclairage	5	3,14	...
Mobilier, ameublement et articles d'équipement ménager	29	6,15	...
Transports et communications	13	9,93	...
Soins personnels et médicaux	33	5,55	...
Instruction et loisirs	31	4,92	...
Autres biens et services	14	4,40	...
Total	274	100,00	...

Logement
Les données relatives aux loyers sont obtenues d'une enquête annuelle portant sur un échantillon de 400 ménages vivant dans des logements en location. Il n'est pas tenu compte, dans l'indice, des logements occupés en propriété.

Spécification des variétés
Pas disponible.

Substitution, changement de qualité, etc.
Lorsque la qualité d'un article change ou qu'un nouvel article fait son apparition sur le marché, une nouvelle série de prix est établie.

Articles saisonniers
Il est tenu compte des fluctuations saisonnières des prix de certains articles en variant les coefficients mensuels de pondération de ces articles, les coefficients de pondération des groupes auxquels ils appartiennent demeurant constants.

Calcul
L'indice est calculé selon la formule de Laspeyres, sous forme de moyenne arithmétique pondérée à base fixe, les coefficients de pondération correspondant à la période de base.
L'indice national est la moyenne des treize localités.

Autres informations
Des indices par sous-groupes sont publiés pour l'alimentation, les boissons et tabacs, l'habillement et la chaussure, le logement, le combustible et l'éclairage, l'ameublement et les articles d'équipement ménager, les transports et communications, les soins personnels et médicaux, l'instruction et les loisirs, ainsi que les autres biens et services.
Une nouvelle série (base 1991 = 100) est maintenant calculée mais les informations méthodologiques relatives à cette série n'étaient pas disponibles au BIT lors de la publication du présent Volume.

Organisation et publication
Central Office of Statistics: «Quarterly Digest of Statistics» (La Valette).
idem: «Annual Abstract of Statistics».
idem: «Report on Proposals for a New Index of Retail Prices - 1984».

MAROC

Dénomination officielle
Indice du coût de la vie.

Portée
L'indice est calculé mensuellement et porte sur les familles à revenu modique résidant dans huit principales villes du pays.

Base originale
Mai 1972 - avril 1973 = 100.

Source des coefficients de pondération
Les coefficients de pondération et les articles sélectionnés ont été déterminés sur la base des résultats d'une enquête sur les dépenses des ménages effectuée en 1970-71 auprès de familles à revenu modique résidant dans huit principales villes du pays.

Pondération et composition

Groupes principaux	Nombre d'articles	Pondération	Nombre approximatif de relevés de prix
Alimentation	83	54,0	...
Tabac	1	1,9	...
Logement:			
Loyer	1	5,8	...
Entretien et réparations	2	1,2	...
Combustible, éclairage et eau	7	3,0	...
Mobilier et linge de maison	14	2,1	...
Equipement ménager	21	1,5	...
Habillement et chaussure	34	8,5	...
Produits d'entretien, hygiène et soins médicaux	19	5,5	...
Transports et communications	12	6,9	...
Instruction, loisirs et divers	16	9,6	...
Total	210	100,0	...

Dépenses de consommation des ménages
Pas disponible.

Mode de relevé des prix
Les prix sont relevés par des agents enquêteurs auprès de points de vente au détail et prestataires de services situés dans huit principales villes du pays. La fréquence des relevés dépend de la variabilité des prix des articles.

Logement
Les données relatives au loyer sont obtenues trimestriellement à partir d'un échantillon de logements de trois ou quatre pièces situés dans les quartiers de prix modérés.

Spécification des variétés
Les spécifications décrivent la qualité et la marque.

Substitution, changement de qualité, etc.
Lorsqu'un article n'est pas disponible sur le marché pendant un certain temps, le dernier prix est reporté si les produits similaires au produit manquant n'ont pas enregistré une variation de prix importante. Dans le cas contraire, le prix du produit manquant est estimé en se basant sur les variations de prix des produits similaires. Si un article a définitivement disparu, il est remplacé par un article similaire, et à défaut, par un article de qualité différente. Un coefficient de raccord est alors appliqué basé soit sur les prix observés à la même période et correspondant aux deux produits (le produit disparu et celui nouvellement retenu), soit sur la comparaison des coûts à la production, soit sur la recherche de l'égale satisfaction du consommateur, soit, enfin, sur l'élaboration d'un modèle économétrique visant à déterminer les différences de qualités.

Articles saisonniers
Il est tenu compte des fluctuations saisonnières des prix des fruits et légumes frais en variant la composition mensuelle des articles du sous-groupe, dont le coefficient de pondération d'ensemble demeure constant, et en utilisant, pour le calcul de l'indice final, une moyenne mobile calculée sur trois mois.

Calcul
L'indice est calculé selon la formule de Laspeyres, sous forme de moyenne arithmétique pondérée à base fixe, les coefficients de pondération correspondant à la période 1970-71.

Autres informations
Des indices séparés sont également publiés pour les villes de Casablanca, Rabat, Fès, Tétouan, Kénitra, Marrakech, Oujda et Agadir.

Organisation et publication
Premier Ministre, Secrétariat d'Etat au plan et au développement régional, Direction de la Statistique: «Bulletin mensuel de statistiques» (Rabat).

idem: «Bulletin méthodologique trimestriel», nouvelle série, no. 3 (Rabat).

MARTINIQUE

Dénomination officielle
Indice des prix à la consommation.

Portée
L'indice est calculé mensuellement et porte sur les ménages urbains de condition moyenne dont le chef est ouvrier ou employé du secteur privé ou public non agricole, à l'exclusion des forces armées.

Base originale
1979 = 100.

Source des coefficients de pondération
Les coefficients de pondération sont fondés sur des données de plusieurs sources, telles que les fichiers administratifs ou les statistiques de la production et du commerce, complétées par des données sur les dépenses de consommation des ménages en France et à la Réunion.

Pondération et composition

Groupes principaux	Nombre d'articles	Pondération	Nombre approximatif de relevés de prix
Alimentation	57	31,66	...
Habillement et chaussure	24	8,79	...
Logement:			
Combustible et éclairage	4	4,33	...
Loyer	1	9,96	...
Mobilier, biens d'équipement ménager, entretien et autres services	25	10,83	...
Soins personnel et médicaux	12	8,58	...
Transports	12	16,44	...
Instruction et loisirs	31	9,41	...
Total	166	100,00	...

Dépenses de consommation des ménages
Les dépenses de consommation entrant dans le calcul de l'indice comprennent tous les biens et services importants acquis par les ménages de référence pour leur propre consommation, y compris les services domestiques et administratifs. Elles excluent les impôts directs, les dépenses de construction considérées comme un investissement, les biens produits par les ménages pour leur propre consommation, la valeur locative des logements occupés par leur propriétaire, les achats d'articles d'occasion, les cotisations sociales et les primes d'assurance.

Mode de relevé des prix
Les prix sont relevés par des enquêteurs auprès de 277 points de vente au détail, marchés et prestataires de services dans deux grandes agglomérations urbaines, Fort-de-France et Schoelcher. Les relevés sont mensuels pour la plupart des articles. Les prix pour le poisson, les fruits et légumes frais sont relevés deux fois par mois dans les magasins de détail, et une fois par semaine sur les marchés. Les prix pour d'autres articles font l'objet de relevés trimestriels.

Les prix entrant dans le calcul de l'indice sont les prix au détail effectivement payés.

Logement
Les données relatives au loyer sont relevées tous les six mois pour un échantillon de 144 logements loués, à Fort-de-France et Schoelcher.

Spécification des variétés
Les spécifications ne sont pas détaillées. Les enquêteurs choisissent dans chaque point de vente au détail les produits les plus vendus, dont ils relèvent régulièrement les prix.

Substitution, changement de qualité, etc.
Lorsqu'un article n'est plus disponible, il est remplacé par un autre article d'une qualité sensiblement équivalente. Si, toutefois, la différence de qualité est trop grande, on apporte les ajustements nécessaires dans la mesure du possible.

Articles saisonniers
Il est tenu compte des fluctuations saisonnières des prix du poisson frais et des fruits et légumes frais en variant les articles et leur coefficient de pondération à l'intérieur de «paniers» mensuels dont le coefficient de pondération d'ensemble demeure constant.

Calcul
L'indice est calculé selon la formule de Laspeyres sous forme de moyenne arithmétique pondérée à base fixe.

L'indice pour un article est obtenu en utilisant les rapports de prix de la période courante et de la période de base. Pour la plupart des articles, on se sert des rapports des prix moyens alors que pour les articles ayant des variétés hétérogènes, on calcule les moyennes des rapports de prix.

Autres informations
Des sous-groupes détaillés sont publiés pour cette série.

Organisation et publication
Institut national de la statistique et des études économiques,

Service régional de la Martinique: «Bulletin statistique de la Martinique» (Fort-de-France).
idem: «Sélection mensuelle de statistiques».
INSEE, Service interrégional Antilles - Guyane: «L'indice des prix de la Martinique, base 100 en 1979; méthodes, bilan 1979-1984 et perspectives», Dossiers Antilles - Guyane, no. 10 (Fort-de-France, juin 1985).

MAURICE

Dénomination officielle
Consumer Price Index (Indice des prix à la consommation).

Portée
L'indice est calculé mensuellement et porte sur toutes les catégories de ménages, tous les groupes de population et l'ensemble des zones géographiques.

Base originale
Juillet 1986 - juin 1987 = 100.

Source des coefficients de pondération
La valeur des coefficients de pondération et le choix des articles résultent d'une enquête sur les dépenses des ménages menée de juillet 1986 à juin 1987 sur la base d'un échantillon. Cet échantillon a été prélevé de telle sorte que toutes les catégories de ménages, tous les groupes de population et l'ensemble des zones géographiques de Maurice soient représentés parmi les 4 320 ménages sélectionnés.
En conséquence, les articles sont choisis à partir des résultats de l'enquête. Ils doivent faire l'objet d'achats fréquents de la part des ménages mauriciens, être habituellement disponibles dans les magasins et sur les marchés pour qu'il soit possible d'en relever le prix, et être disponibles plusieurs années durant afin d'assurer une certaine continuité de leur relevé. Les coefficients de pondération des articles non sélectionnés sont simplement redistribués parmi les articles identiques du même sous-groupe.

Pondération et composition

Groupes principaux	Nombre d'articles	Pondération	Nombre approximatif de relevés de prix
Alimentation et boissons	76	419	1 964
Boissons alcoolisées et tabac	6	72	138
Habillement et chaussure	37	84	275
Logement et dépenses ménagères	53	135	525
(dont loyer brut)	(3)	(24)	(180)
Soins médicaux et dépenses de santé	10	30	136
Transports et communications	11	93	94
Loisirs, distractions, instruction et services culturels	20	60	158
Biens et services divers	25	50	251
Total	241	1 000	3 566

Dépenses de consommation des ménages
Les biens et services acquis gratuitement ou produits à des fins d'autoconsommation sont évalués aux prix du marché prévalant au moment de leur enregistrement par l'enquête sur les dépenses des ménages. Les articles qui ont été exclus lors de la détermination des coefficients de pondération sont les suivants: biens et services fournis gratuitement par les pouvoirs publics (tels que les services médicaux, les médicaments, la scolarisation et les manuels scolaires), loyers imputés des logements occupés par leur propriétaire, contributions aux assurances sociales et aux fonds de pension, impôt sur le revenu et autres impôts directs, remboursement des dettes, dépenses consacrées aux paris et aux jeux de hasard, primes d'assurance-vie, dons en espèces et envois de fonds. Les honoraires concernant les patentes liées aux activités privées des ménages et les assurances sur des biens de consommation spécifiques sont inclus.

Mode de relevé des prix
Une enquête sur les points d'achat a été effectuée dans le cadre de l'enquête de 1986-87 sur les dépenses des ménages.
Le choix des localités pour le relevé des prix a été effectué non seulement pour que soient représentées à la fois les régions urbaines et rurales, mais également en fonction de l'importance de ces mêmes localités comme centres commerciaux. En ce qui concerne les zones urbaines, les cinq régions disposant d'un conseil municipal (Port-Louis, Rose Hill, Quatre Bornes, Vacoas et Curepipe) ont toutes été sélectionnées. Dans les régions rurales, un village de première importance au moins a été sélectionné pour le Nord, le Sud, l'Est, l'Ouest et le Centre de l'île.
Le relevé des prix est effectué par le personnel de l'Office central des Statistiques.
Lorsque les localités et les points de vente sont sélectionnés, les statisticiens repèrent les différents articles et variétés disponibles dans les magasins de chaque localité. De même, la plupart des biens et services composant le «panier» sont relevés dans toutes les localités.
Les prix des denrées périssables tels que les fruits et légumes frais, la viande et le poisson font l'objet d'un relevé hebdomadaire sur les marchés, effectué un jour déterminé de la semaine.
Les prix des autres biens et services sont relevés mensuellement dans toutes les localités entre le 12 et le 18 de chaque mois.
Pour les prix de l'électricité, de l'eau, des billets d'autobus et du téléphone, les statisticiens se réfèrent aux tarifs officiels.
Sont pris en considération les prix du marché libre effectivement payés par les consommateurs. Le prix des soldes et des catalogues sont pris en compte mais les ventes de caractère irrégulier, telles que les liquidations, sont ignorées.
Il n'est pas tenu compte des prix du marché noir, ni des échéances des locations-vente ou des crédits, ni des achats de biens d'occasion, ni de l'échange de biens usagés et des paiements partiels de nouveaux biens, ni des prix à l'importation.

Logement
Le terme de «loyer» désigne le prix effectivement payé par les locataires, non compris les frais relatifs à l'électricité, à l'eau et au système d'évacuation des eaux usées.
L'indice des loyers est calculé trimestriellement pour les mois de mars, juin, septembre et décembre dans le cadre d'une enquête portant sur 180 ménages disposant d'un logement en location. Sur les 4 320 ménages couverts par l'enquête de 1986-87, 785 habitaient des logements en location. L'échantillon de 180 ménages a été prélevé sur les 785 ménages en question, en tenant compte systématiquement de la région concernée et du montant du loyer. L'enquête sur les logements en location est entreprise sur la base d'un questionnaire conçu spécialement à cet effet.
Les logements occupés par leur propriétaire ne sont pas pris en compte par l'indice. Les données relatives aux taux et aux dépenses consacrées à l'entretien et aux réparations des logements ont été rassemblées dans le cadre de l'enquête, puis incluses dans l'indice.

Spécification des variétés
Pour chaque article, un échantillon représentatif de variétés et d'indicateurs est constitué, puis leur prix est établi en fonction des disponibilités du marché. Des spécifications concernant la qualité, la fabrication, la marque, l'unité, etc. sont alors élaborées pour chaque article ou variété dans chaque point de vente de chacune des localités.

Substitution, changement de qualité, etc.
Il s'avère difficile de quantifier les changements de qualité. Les changements d'ordre secondaire ne sont pas pris en compte. Lorsque survient un changement substantiel, l'ancien produit est considéré comme ayant disparu. Il est alors remplacé par le produit de nouvelle qualité, qui est rattaché à l'indice.
Lorsque de nouveaux produits apparaissent sur le marché, leurs prix sont relevés afin d'être utilisés ultérieurement, s'il y a lieu de réviser le «panier» de biens et services, ou s'il est nécessaire d'opérer un remplacement à la suite de la disparition définitive d'un produit du marché.
Lorsqu'un produit n'est plus disponible, il est remplacé par le produit qui lui ressemble le plus sur le marché. Le prix de base (fictif) de ce substitut est calculé de manière à ce que son rapport de prix courant soit le même que celui du produit remplacé.

Articles saisonniers
Les fluctuations saisonnières des légumes frais sont prises en compte en modifiant mensuellement les articles composant ce sous-groupe, tout en conservant les mêmes coefficients de pondération d'ensemble. L'indice pour les légumes compare le coût du panier du mois courant à celui du même mois de l'année de base.

Calcul
L'indice est calculé selon la formule de Laspeyres sous forme

de moyenne arithmétique pondérée à base fixe, les coefficients de pondération correspondant à la période de base.

Les prix moyens ne sont calculés que pour les fruits et légumes frais, le poisson frais et la viande, et relevés dans différents magasins. Ces prix moyens constituent la moyenne arithmétique simple de tous les relevés de prix effectués.

Les rapports de prix sont calculés en divisant les prix courants par les prix de base. Si différentes variétés sont utilisées pour un article, le rapport de prix est calculé pour chaque variété et des moyennes pondérées des rapports de prix sont calculées pour obtenir les indices par article.

Une fois relevés, les prix font l'objet d'un examen approfondi à différents niveaux, afin d'éviter un relevé erroné. Au cas où certaines données font défaut, on utilise le prix du mois précédent.

Organisation et publication
Central Statistical Office: «Annual Digest of Statistics» (Rose Hill).

Ministry of Finance: «Government Gazette of Mauritius» (Rose Hill).

MEXIQUE

Dénomination officielle
Indice nacional de precios al consumidor (Indice national des prix à la consommation).

Portée
L'indice est calculé chaque mois et porte sur tous les consommateurs urbains du pays.

Base originale
1978 = 100.

Source des coefficients de pondération
Les coefficients de pondération et les articles sélectionnés ont été déterminés principalement sur la base des résultats d'une enquête nationale sur les revenus et les dépenses effectuée en 1977.

Pondération et composition

Groupes principaux	Nombre d'articles	Pondération	Nombre approximatif de relevés de prix
Alimentation et tabac	141	37,39	60 000
Habillement et chaussure	45	9,88	40 000
Logement	6	17,77	20 000
Mobilier, ameublement et articles de ménage	34	6,21	5 000
Soins personnels et médicaux	28	5,81	4 000
Transports	17	11,25	4 000
Instruction et loisirs	23	5,75	5 000
Autres services	8	5,94	2 000
Total	302	100,00	140 000

Dépenses de consommation des ménages
Pas disponible.

Mode de relevé des prix
Les prix des denrées alimentaires et du tabac sont relevés chaque semaine. Les prix des autres articles sont obtenus chaque quinzaine. Les prix utilisés pour le calcul de l'indice sont ceux effectivement payés par les consommateurs: prix nets et au comptant (y compris les impôts, les charges et les rabais, si ces derniers étaient en vigueur au moins plus de la moitié des jours compris dans la période des relevés de prix).

Logement
Les données relatives au loyer des maisons dans les 35 villes comprises dans l'indice, sont obtenues pour environ 10 milles logements visités directement par les enquêteurs.

Spécification des variétés
Pas disponible.

Substitution, changement de qualité, etc.
Si la spécification d'un produit change, la méthode d'enchaînement est adoptée. Si un article disparaît du marché, il est remplacé par un article analogue en utilisant la méthode d'enchaînement et, si besoin est, on procède à un ajustement de la qualité de façon à respecter le principe de la qualité constante.

Articles saisonniers
Il est tenu compte des fluctuations saisonnières des prix de certains articles en maintenant, hors saison, le dernier prix de saison.

Calcul
L'indice est calculé selon la formule de Laspeyres sous forme de moyenne arithmétique pondérée à base fixe, les coefficients de pondération correspondant à 1977.

Des rapports de prix pour chaque variété dans chaque magasin sont d'abord calculés en divisant le prix moyen de la période courante par le prix moyen de la période de base. Une moyenne arithmétique simple des rapports de prix des variétés représentant un article est alors calculée afin d'obtenir un indice d'un article.

Des indices séparés sont calculés pour 35 villes. L'indice national est une moyenne pondérée d'indices des 35 villes, les pondérations étant proportionnelles à la structure des dépenses de consommation de chaque ville.

Organisation et publication
Banco de México, Dirección de Investigación Económica: «Indices de precios» (Mexico).

MONTSERRAT

Dénomination officielle
Consumer Price Index (Indice des prix à la consommation).

Portée
L'indice est calculé mensuellement et porte sur l'ensemble de la population.

Base originale
Septembre 1982 = 100.

Source des coefficients de pondération
La valeur des coefficients de pondération et le choix des articles résultent d'une enquête sur les dépenses des ménages, menée en 1980 pendant deux semaines auprès d'un échantillon aléatoire de 400 ménages. Les coefficients de pondération n'ont pas été ajustés pour tenir compte de l'évolution des prix entre 1980 et 1982. Les pondérations des articles non compris dans l'indice ont été réparties sur les articles compris dans l'indice.

Pondération et composition

Groupes principaux	Nombre d'articles	Pondération	Nombre approximatif de relevés de prix
Alimentation	73	495	...
Boissons alcoolisées et tabac	9	46	...
Biens d'équipement ménager	37	102	...
Gaz, électricité et eau	3	18	...
Loyer	3	7	...
Habillement et chaussure	43	179	...
Services et autres	34	153	...
Total	202	1 000	...

Dépenses de consommation des ménages
Elles comprennent la taxe d'immatriculation et les primes d'assurance des véhicules automobiles. En sont exclus l'impôt sur le revenu, les cotisations à la sécurité sociale et aux caisses de retraite, les envois de fonds, les dons et dépenses assimilées.

Mode de relevé des prix
Les prix sont relevés le 15 de chaque mois par des enquêteurs sur un échantillon de points de vente au détail et de prestataires de services à Plymouth.

Les prix retenus dans le calcul de l'indice sont les prix de détail payés par les acheteurs. Les rabais et le prix des soldes ne sont pas pris en compte.

Logement
Les données relatives au loyer sont relevées mensuellement pour trois types de logements meublés. Les logements occupés par leur propriétaire ne sont pas inclus dans l'indice.

Spécification des variétés
Les articles dont les prix sont relevés font l'objet de spécifications portant sur la marque, la qualité, l'unité employée, la taille, etc.

Substitution, changement de qualité, etc.
Il n'est pas tenu compte des changements de qualité.

Articles saisonniers
Il n'est pas tenu compte des fluctuations saisonnières des prix des articles.

Calcul
L'indice est calculé selon la formule de Laspeyres sous forme de moyenne arithmétique pondérée à base fixe, les coefficients de pondération correspondant à 1980.

Organisation et publication
Government of Montserrat, Statistics Office: «Montserrat Statistics Digest» (Plymouth).
idem: «Cost of Living Report».

MYANMAR (YANGON)

Dénomination officielle
Consumer Price Index at Yangon (Indice des prix à la consommation à Yangon).

Portée
L'indice est calculé mensuellement et porte sur tous les ménages quel que soit leur revenu en 1978. Il concerne la capitale Yangon.

Base originale
1978 = 100.

Source des coefficients de pondération
La valeur des coefficients de pondération et le choix des articles résultent d'une enquête sur les dépenses des ménages menée en 1978 dans 24 communes de la division de Yangon. L'enquête a porté sur 1 200 ménages.

Pondération et composition

Groupes principaux	Nombre d'articles	Pondération	Nombre approximatif de relevés de prix
Alimentation	43	64,42	...
Tabac	2	3,74	...
Loyer et réparations	3	3,82	...
Combustible et éclairage	6	7,84	...
Habillement et chaussure	9	8,04	...
Divers	17	12,14	...
Total	80	100,00	...

Dépenses de consommation des ménages
Les dépenses de consommation prises en compte dans le calcul de l'indice correspondent aux achats de tous les biens et services importants effectués par les ménages de référence pour leur consommation. Elles excluent l'impôt sur le revenu, les assurances-vie, les dons et les dépenses consacrées à des cérémonies.

Mode de relevé des prix
Les prix sont relevés dans des marchés choisis de la zone gérée par la Commission d'urbanisation de Yangon.
Les prix de détail sont relevés chaque jour, sauf ceux des articles contrôlés qui le sont chaque mois. Pour les frais de scolarité et de transport, les relevés se font chaque année auprès des établissements de services appropriés.

Logement
Les pondérations ont été obtenues à partir de l'enquête sur les dépenses des ménages effectuée en 1978. L'indice du loyer est maintenu stable à 100.

Spécification des variétés
Les articles sont spécifiés par la qualité, la marque, le nom, la taille et l'unité employée, etc.

Substitution, changement de qualité, etc.
Si un produit disparaît du marché, il est remplacé par un produit analogue, et on révise le prix de l'année de base de l'ancien produit.

Articles saisonniers
A ces articles, tels que fruits et légumes frais, des ajustements sont apportés pour éliminer les fluctuations saisonnières.

Calcul
L'indice est calculé selon la formule de Laspeyres sous forme de moyenne arithmétique pondérée à base fixe, les coefficients de pondération correspondant à la période de base.

Autres informations
Une nouvelle série pour Yangon (base 1986 = 100) est maintenant calculée mais les informations méthodologiques relatives à cette série n'étaient pas disponibles au BIT lors de la publication du présent Volume.

Organisation et publication
Central Statistical Organisation, Yangon: «Selected Monthly Economic Indicators» (Yangon).
idem: «Statistical Yearbook».
idem: «Statistical Abstracts».

NEPAL

Dénomination officielle
National Urban Consumer Price Index (Indice national urbain des prix à la consommation).

Portée
L'indice est calculé mensuellement et porte sur les ménages privés habitant 13 régions urbaines du pays.

Base originale
Mi-juillet 1983 - mi-juillet 1984 = 100.

Source des coefficients de pondération
La valeur des coefficients de pondération et le choix des articles découlent d'une enquête sur les dépenses des ménages effectuée entre la mi-mars 1984 et la mi-février 1985 auprès de 1 161 ménages privés habitant les zones urbaines. L'indice est conçu de manière à porter sur tous les ménages non institutionnels habitant les zones urbaines du pays, à l'exception des cas suivants: ménages composés d'une seule personne, ménages composés de plus de dix personnes, ménages dont les dépenses de consommation sont inférieures à 450 Rs ou supérieures à 3 500 Rs, ménages tirant plus de 50 pour cent du montant de leurs dépenses de consommation de la production à domicile ou de ressources autres que celle du marché. L'indice porte sur 13 régions urbaines du Népal.

Pondération et composition

Groupes principaux	Nombre d'articles	Pondération	Nombre approximatif de relevés de prix
Alimentation	...	62,63	...
Habillement	...	10,09	...
Chaussure	...	1,72	...
Logement (y c. combustible, électricité et eau)	...	12,66	...
Transports et communications	...	2,13	...
Soins personnels et médicaux	...	4,59	...
Instruction, lecture et loisirs	...	4,14	...
Tabac	...	2,04	...
Total	...	100,00	...

Dépenses de consommation des ménages
Elles incluent la valeur totale des biens et services acquis par les ménages, celle des biens produits à domicile, acquis à titre gratuit ou en guise de versement partiel du salaire (puis faisant l'objet d'une consommation), y compris la valeur estimée du loyer des logements occupés par leur propriétaire et occupés gratuitement. En revanche, sont exclus les impôts directs, les dons et contributions, les primes d'assurance, les frais professionnels, le remboursement des dettes de consommation, l'achat de billets de loterie et les pertes d'argent liquide, ainsi que les dépenses liées aux mariages, aux frais de justice, etc.

Mode de relevé des prix
Les prix sont relevés par des enquêteurs qui se rendent personnellement auprès d'environ 700 commerces de détail et prestataires de services.
Les relevés sont effectués une fois par semaine pour les fruits et légumes frais, deux fois par mois pour le poisson frais, le lait et les produits laitiers, etc., une fois par mois pour l'habillement, les combustibles, etc., une fois par trimestre pour tous les autres articles, à l'exception des frais de scolarité, des honoraires médicaux et des dépenses relatives à l'électricité et à l'eau, qui font l'objet de relevés annuels.
Les prix retenus pour le calcul de l'indice sont ceux que toute personne aurait à payer le jour du relevé pour se procurer l'article ou le service en question, taxes indirectes comprises.
Les enquêteurs effectuent le relevé des prix auprès des points de vente au détail sur la base des paiements en liquide. Si un bien donné n'est pas disponible sur le marché libre, on relève alors également le prix prévalant sur le marché noir.

Logement
Les données relatives aux loyer sont relevées annuellement au moyen d'une enquête sur les loyers portant sur 448 ménages. Les logements occupés par leur propriétaire ne sont pas pris en compte par l'indice.

Spécification des variétés
Plusieurs études de marché ont été effectuées dans les différentes villes de l'échantillon, principalement pour déterminer les points de vente et les spécifications des articles devant faire l'objet d'un relevé de prix. Dans chaque point de vente de l'échantillon, chacun de ces articles a fait l'objet d'une spécification portant sur la taille, le poids, les matières employées, les soins portés à la fabrication et d'autres caractéristiques d'ordre qualitatif ou quantitatif.

Substitution, changement de qualité, etc.
Lorsqu'un article donné disparaît du marché, une substitution appropriée est opérée et l'indice est corrigé pour tenir compte du changement de qualité.

Articles saisonniers
Lorsque des articles saisonniers tels que le poisson, les fruits et les légumes frais ne sont pas en vente hors saison, on retient pour le calcul de l'indice les derniers prix en vigueur aussi longtemps que l'on ne dispose pas de nouveaux prix.

Calcul
L'indice est calculé selon la formule de Laspeyres sous forme de moyenne arithmétique pondérée à base fixe, les coefficients de pondération correspondant à la période de base.

L'indice national des prix urbains s'obtient en effectuant la combinaison des trois indices régionaux, pondérés à l'aide de coefficients proportionnels à la population urbaine de chaque région.

Autres informations
Des indices séparés sont publiés pour les trois régions urbaines: Urban Consumer Price Index for Kathmandu (Indice des prix à la consommation urbaine pour Katmandou), Urban Consumer Price Index for Hills (Indice des prix à la consommation urbaine pour Hills), Urban Consumer Price Index for Terai (Indice des prix à la consommation urbaine pour Terai).

Organisation et publication
Nepal Rastra Bank, Research Department: «Main Economic Indicators».

idem: «Quaterly Economic Bulletin» (Katmandou).

NICARAGUA (MANAGUA)

Dénomination officielle
Indice de los precios al consumidor (Indice des prix à la consommation).

Portée
L'indice est calculé mensuellement et porte sur les ménages de la zone métropolitaine de Managua qui disposaient, en mai-octobre 1972, d'un revenu mensuel allant de 400 à 7 000 córdobas.

Base originale
Décembre 1974 = 100.

Source des coefficients de pondération
La valeur des coefficients de pondération et le choix des articles résultent d'une enquête sur les dépenses des ménages menée à Managua de mai à octobre 1972 auprès d'un échantillon de 330 ménages tiré du recensement de la population et du logement d'avril 1971.

Dépenses de consommation des ménages
Les dépenses de consommation prises en compte dans le calcul de l'indice correspondent à la quasi-totalité des achats de biens et services importants effectués par les ménages de référence pour leur consommation. Elles comprennent aussi la valeur des biens et services reçus à titre de revenu en nature et les biens que le ménage produit et consomme à la maison.

Mode de relevé des prix
Les prix des fruits et légumes frais sont obtenus entre le mardi et le vendredi de chaque semaine, par achat direct. Ceux d'autres biens et services sont relevés mensuellement par des enquêteurs entre le mardi et le vendredi de la semaine comprenant le 15 du mois, ce sur un échantillon de marchés, de points de vente au détail et de prestataires de services.

Pondération et composition

Groupes principaux	Nombre d'articles	Pondération	Nombre approximatif de relevés de prix
Alimentation et tabac	81	43,07	...
Habillement et chaussure	36	6,62	...
Logement (y c. loyer, combustible, éclairage, réparations, mobilier, dépenses de ménage, etc.)	34	24,74	...
Dépenses diverses:	31		
Soins personnels et médicaux	...	7,61	...
Instruction et loisirs	...	6,13	...
Transports	...	11,61	...
Assurances personnelles	...	0,22	...
Total	182	100,00	...

Les prix retenus dans le calcul de l'indice sont les prix normalement payés par le public. Les rabais et le prix des soldes ne sont pas pris en compte.

Logement
Les données relatives au loyer sont relevées sur 33 logements répartis entre les différents quartiers de la ville.

Spécification des variétés
Les articles dont les prix sont à relever font l'objet de spécifications suffisamment larges pour rendre possibles les substitutions.

Substitution, changement de qualité, etc.
Lorsqu'un produit disparaît du marché, il lui est substitué un produit analogue et la formule d'enchaînement est appliquée.

Articles saisonniers
Les articles saisonniers sont supposés connaître, lorsqu'ils ne sont pas de saison, les mêmes variations de prix que les autres articles de leur sous-groupe. Lorsqu'un article saisonnier réapparaît sur le marché, on calcule le rapport du nouveau prix au dernier prix relevé.

Calcul
L'indice est calculé selon la formule de Laspeyres sous forme de moyenne arithmétique pondérée à base fixe, les coefficients de pondération correspondant à la période mai-oct. 1972.

Le rapport de prix pour chaque article est calculé en divisant le prix moyen de la période courante par le prix moyen de la période précédente.

Autres informations
Une nouvelle série (base octobre-décembre 1987 = 100) est maintenant calculée mais les informations méthodologiques relatives à cette série n'étaient pas disponibles au BIT lors de la publication du présent Volume.

Organisation et publication
Oficina Ejecutiva de Encuestas y Censos: «Indice General de Precios al Consumidor de la Ciudad de Managua» (Managua).

NIGER (NIAMEY, AFRICAINS)

Dénomination officielle
Indice des prix à la consommation familiale africaine.

Portée
L'indice est calculé mensuellement et porte sur les familles africaines à Niamey.

Base originale
Juillet 1962 - juin 1963 = 100.

Source des coefficients de pondération
Les coefficients de pondération et les articles sélectionnés ont été déterminés sur la base des résultats d'une enquête sur les dépenses des ménages effectuée à Niamey de mars 1961 à avril 1962 auprès de 317 ménages africains.

Dépenses de consommation des ménages
Pas disponible.

Mode de relevé des prix
Les prix des denrées alimentaires, de même que ceux d'autres articles sont relevés par des enquêteurs deux fois par mois dans cinq magasins de détail et quatre fois par mois sur un marché. Les données concernant certains services publics sont obtenues mensuellement à partir des tarifs officiels.

Pondération et composition

Groupes principaux	Nombre d'articles	Pondération	Nombre approximatif de relevés de prix
Alimentation	42	45	...
Habillement et chaussure	9	10	...
Dépenses de ménage (y compris combustible, éclairage et eau)	9	18	...
Divers	16	27	...
Total	76	100	...

Logement
Les dépenses relatives au loyer ne sont retenues ni dans le calcul de l'indice ni dans la détermination des coefficients de pondération.

Spécification des variétés
Pas disponible.

Substitution, changement de qualité, etc.
Pas disponible.

Articles saisonniers
Les prix des articles soumis à des fluctuations saisonnières sont relevés toute l'année. Les prix moyens de ces articles sont utilisés pour le calcul de l'indice.

Calcul
L'indice est calculé selon la formule de Laspeyres, sous forme de moyenne arithmétique pondérée à base fixe, les coefficients de pondération correspondant à la période mars 1961 - avril 1962.

Organisation et publication
Ministère du développement et de la coopération, Direction de la statistique: «Bulletin de statistique» (Niamey).

NIGER (NIAMEY, EUROPEENS)

Dénomination officielle
Indice des prix à la consommation familiale européenne.

Portée
L'indice est calculé mensuellement et porte sur les familles européennes à Niamey.

Base originale
15 novembre - 15 décembre 1964 = 100.

Source des coefficients de pondération
Les coefficients de pondération et les articles sélectionnés ont été déterminés sur la base des résultats d'une enquête sur les dépenses des ménages effectuée à Niamey du 15 novembre au 15 décembre 1964 au moyen de questionnaires envoyés à un échantillon de ménages de fonctionnaires français de la coopération technique.

Pondération et composition

Groupes principaux	Nombre d'articles	Pondération	Nombre approximatif de relevés de prix
Alimentation	78	46,1	...
Electricité, gaz et eau	3	11,1	...
Produits d'entretien	10	2,5	...
Habillement, chaussure et linge de maison	12	6,0	...
Services domestiques	2	8,2	...
Divers	28	26,1	...
Total	133	100,0	...

Dépenses de consommation des ménages
Pas disponible.

Mode de relevé des prix
Les prix des denrées alimentaires, de même que ceux d'autres articles, sont relevés par des enquêteurs deux fois par mois dans cinq magasins de détail et quatre fois par mois sur un marché. Les données concernant certains services publics sont obtenues mensuellement à partir des tarifs officiels.

Logement
Les dépenses relatives au loyer ne sont retenues ni dans le calcul de l'indice ni dans la détermination des coefficients de pondération.

Spécification des variétés
Pas disponible.

Substitution, changement de qualité, etc.
Pas disponible.

Articles saisonniers
Les prix des articles soumis à des fluctuations saisonnières sont relevés toute l'année. Les prix moyens de ces articles sont utilisés pour le calcul de l'indice.

Calcul
L'indice est calculé selon la formule de Laspeyres, sous forme de moyenne arithmétique pondérée à base fixe, les coefficients de pondération correspondant à la période de base.

Organisation et publication
Ministère du développement et de la coopération, Direction de la statistique: «Bulletin de statistique» (Niamey).

NIGERIA 1

Dénomination officielle
Urban Consumer Price Index - All Income Groups (Indice des prix à la consommation urbaine - toutes catégories de revenu).

Portée
L'indice est calculé mensuellement et porte sur les ménages des régions urbaines appartenant à toutes les catégories de revenu.

Base originale
1975 = 100.

Source des coefficients de pondération
La valeur des coefficients de pondération et le choix des articles résultent d'une enquête sur les dépenses des ménages menée en 1974-75 dans les régions urbaines et rurales, auprès des ménages de toutes les catégories de revenu.

Pondération et composition
Pas disponible.

Dépenses de consommation des ménages
Pas disponible.

Mode de relevé des prix
Les prix sont relevés par des enquêteurs sur les marchés et auprès des commerces locaux. La fréquence des relevés dépend de la variabilité du prix des articles: elle est quotidienne pour les produits alimentaires et mensuelle pour les autres articles.

Les prix retenus pour le calcul de l'indice sont les prix de détail effectivement payés.

Logement
Pas disponible.

Spécification des variétés
Les articles dont les prix sont à relever font l'objet de spécifications portant sur le nom, la marque, la qualité et la taille

Substitution, changement de qualité, etc.
Lorsqu'un produit n'est plus en vente, un produit semblable lui est substitué et la formule d'enchaînement appliquée dans les calculs. En cas d'impossibilité, le dernier prix enregistré est répété.

Articles saisonniers
Les prix des articles saisonniers, comme les fruits et légumes frais, ne sont pris en compte que lorsqu'ils existent, pendant la saison desdits articles.

Calcul
L'indice est calculé selon la formule de Laspeyres sous forme de moyenne arithmétique pondérée à base fixe, les coefficients de pondération correspondant à la période 1974-75.

Des indices séparés sont d'abord calculés pour les revenus modiques, moyens et élevés dans chaque centre. Le rapport de prix pour chaque article d'un centre est calculé en divisant le prix moyen de la période courante par le prix moyen de la période de base. Les indices des régions urbaines sont combinés afin d'obtenir l'indice pour toutes les catégories de revenus dans les régions urbaines.

Autres informations
Une nouvelle série pour les régions urbaines (base septembre 1985 = 100) est maintenant calculée mais les informations

méthodologiques correspondantes n'étaient pas disponibles au BIT lors de la publication du présent Volume.

Organisation et publication
Federal Office of Statistics: «Retail Prices in Selected Centres and Consumer Price Indices» (Lagos).
Pour de plus amples détails d'ordre méthodologique, voir:
idem: «Retail Prices in Selected Centres and Consumer Price Indices» (mars 1978).

NIGERIA 2

Dénomination officielle
Composite Consumer Price Index - Rural and Urban Areas (Indice composite des prix à la consommation - régions rurales et urbaines).

Portée
L'indice est calculé mensuellement et porte sur les ménages de tous les catégories de revenu des régions urbaines et rurales.

Base originale
1975 = 100.

Source des coefficients de pondération
La valeur des coefficients de pondération et le choix des articles résultent d'une enquête nationale sur les dépenses familiales menée en 1974-75 dans les régions urbaines et rurales, auprès des ménages de toutes les catégories de revenu.

Pondération et composition
Pas disponible.

Dépenses de consommation des ménages
Pas disponible.

Mode de relevé des prix
Les prix sont relevés par des enquêteurs sur les marchés et auprès des commerces locaux. La fréquence des relevés dépend de la variabilité du prix des articles: elle est quotidienne pour les produits alimentaires et mensuelle pour les autres articles.
Les prix retenus pour le calcul de l'indice sont les prix de détail effectivement payés.

Logement
Pas disponible.

Spécification des variétés
Les articles dont les prix sont à retenir font l'objet de spécifications portant sur le nom, la qualité et la taille.

Substitution, changement de qualité, etc.
Lorsqu'un produit n'est plus en vente, un produit semblable lui est substitué et la formule d'enchaînement appliquée dans les calculs. En cas d'impossibilité, le dernier prix enregistré est répété.

Articles saisonniers
Les prix des articles saisonniers, comme les fruits et légumes frais, ne sont pris en compte que lorsqu'ils existent, pendant la saison desdits articles.

Calcul
L'indice est calculé selon la formule de Laspeyres sous forme de moyenne arithmétique pondérée à base fixe, les coefficients de pondération correspondant à la période de 1974-75.
Des indices séparés sont d'abord calculés pour les revenus modiques, moyens et élevés dans chaque centre. Le rapport de prix pour chaque article d'un centre est calculé en divisant le prix moyen de la période courante par le prix moyen de la période de base.
L'indice national est une moyenne arithmétique pondérée d'indices se rapportant aux régions urbaines et rurales, et aux revenus modiques, moyens et élevés. Les pondérations utilisées sont proportionnelles à la population des régions concernées.

Autres informations
Une nouvelle série pour les régions urbaines et rurales (base septembre 1985 = 100) est maintenant calculée mais les informations méthodologiques correspondantes n'étaient pas disponibles au BIT lors de la publication du présent Volume.

Organisation et publication
Federal Office of Statistics: «Retail Prices in Selected Centres and Consumer Price Indices» (Lagos).
Pour de plus amples détails d'ordre méthodologique, voir :
idem: «Retail Prices in Selected Centres and Consumer Price Indices», mars 1978.

NIOUE

Dénomination officielle
Retail Price Index (Indice des prix de détail).

Portée
L'indice est calculé trimestriellement et porte sur tous les ménages des zones urbaines (ville d'Alofi) disposant d'un revenu moyen.

Base originale
Trimestre de mars 1982 = 100.

Source des coefficients de pondération
La valeur des coefficients de pondération et le choix des articles ont été déterminés en 1981 après consultation de plusieurs sources: statistiques du commerce, opinion des trois principaux commerçants, comptes nationaux et compléments d'information fournis par diverses administrations publiques.

Pondération et composition

Groupes principaux	Nombre d'articles	Pondération	Nombre approximatif de relevés de prix
Alimentation	59	430	...
Boissons alcoolisées et tabac	6	115	...
Logement	9	50	...
Dépense de ménage	26	130	...
Habillement et chaussure	13	50	...
Transports	12	175	...
Divers	12	50	...
Total	137	1 000	...

Dépenses de consommation des ménages
Les dépenses de consommation prises en compte pour le calcul de l'indice visent presque tous les biens et services importants acquis en vue de leur consommation. En sont exclus l'achat de logements neufs, le coût des transports aériens à l'arrivée ou au départ définitifs de Nioué, les dons et donations.

Mode de relevé des prix
Les relevés sont effectués vers le milieu de chaque trimestre par des enquêteurs qui se rendent auprès des points de vente au détail et des prestataires de services. Les prix relevés sont ceux que paient réellement les consommateurs.

Logement
Pas disponible.

Spécification des variétés
Les articles dont le prix est à relever font l'objet de spécifications portant sur le nom, la marque, la taille, la qualité, etc.

Substitution, changement de qualité, etc.
Lorsqu'un produit disparaît du marché, il lui est substitué un produit analogue ou un produit de son groupe.

Articles saisonniers
Pas disponible.

Calcul
L'indice est calculé selon la formule de Laspeyres sous forme de moyenne arithmétique pondérée à base fixe, les coefficients de pondération correspondant à la période de base.
L'indice pour un article est obtenu en utilisant les rapports de prix de la période courante et de la période de base.

Autres informations
Une nouvelle série (base janvier - mars 1990 = 100) est maintenant calculée mais les informations méthodologiques relatives à cette série n'étaient pas disponibles au BIT lors de la publication du présent Volume.

Organisation et publication
L'indice est calculé par la Statistics Unit, Development Planning Office (Alofi).
Treasurer Department: «Quarterly Abstract of Statistics» (Alofi).

NORVEGE

Dénomination officielle
Consumer Price Index (Indice des prix à la consommation).

Portée
L'indice est calculé mensuellement et porte sur tous les ménages privés du pays.

Base originale
1979 = 100.

Source des coefficients de pondération
La valeur des coefficients de pondération s'obtient en faisant la moyenne de la part des dépenses d'après les enquêtes sur les dépenses des ménages menées les trois années précédentes. Depuis août 1991, les coefficients proviennent des enquêtes de 1988, 1989 et 1990. Les articles choisis sont constamment révisés. Les pondérations ci-dessous se réfèrent à la période août 1991 à juillet 1992.

Pondération et composition

Groupes principaux	Nombre d'articles	Pondération	Nombre approximatif de relevés de prix
Alimentation	241	152,1	27 910
Boissons et tabac	45	36,0	1 360
Habillement et chaussure	89	67,4	3 910
Logement (y c. réparations et entretien)	29	215,4	1 930
Combustible et éclairage	5	47,5	130
Mobilier, ameublement et articles d'équipement ménager	113	81,5	5 180
Soins médicaux et hygiène	25	23,3	120
Transports et communications	105	199,0	1 460
Instruction et loisirs	62	98,3	760
Biens et services divers	66	81,1	2 020
Total	780	1 001.6	44 780

Dépenses de consommation des ménages
Les dépenses de consommation prises en compte dans le calcul de l'indice comprennent les biens et services achetés pour la consommation par la population de référence. Pour les biens durables, elles correspondent à l'écart entre la valeur de l'achat de biens neufs et celle de la vente de biens d'occasion. En outre, sont inclus le coût de la location-vente, la valeur de l'autoconsommation et les dons reçus. En sont exclus l'impôt direct, l'épargne et les placements, les prêts personnels, les primes d'assurance vie, les cotisations à des caisses de retraite et les dons effectués.

Mode de relevé des prix
Les prix sont relevés par des enquêteurs dans environ 1 400 magasins de vente au détail et établissements de services choisis à cet effet. La plupart des prix sont obtenus le 15 de chaque mois. Les prix retenus pour le calcul de l'indice sont les prix normaux payés par tout acheteur.

Logement
Les données sur les loyers sont relevées chaque trimestre pour environ 1 800 logements.

Spécification des variétés
Les spécifications des articles relevés sont détaillées et indiquent la marque, le nom, la taille, etc.

Substitution, changement de qualité, etc.
Lorsqu'un article disparaît du marché, il lui est substitué un article analogue.

Articles saisonniers
Il est tenu compte des fluctuations saisonnières des prix de certains fruits, légumes et poissons frais en utilisant, hors saison, la moyenne des prix de la saison précédente.

Calcul
Depuis août 1982, il s'agit d'un indice à enchaînement annuel, utilisant la formule de Laspeyres, dont les coefficients de pondération changent en août de chaque année. On calcule d'abord l'indice de chaque mois, pour chaque article, dans chaque région, en tant que changement de prix de la moyenne arithmétique non pondérée de tous les prix d'un article. Le niveau moyen des prix du mois de juillet précédent est égalé à 100. L'indice mensuel d'un article pour l'ensemble du pays est calculé en pondérant le changement de prix dans les différentes régions, compte tenu de leur part relative dans le chiffre d'affaires du pays.

Organisation et publication
Statistisk sentralbyrä (Central Bureau of Statistics): «Statistisk Mänedshefte» (Monthly Bulletin of Statistics) (Oslo).

NOUVELLE-CALEDONIE (NOUMEA)

Dénomination officielle
Indice des prix de détail à la consommation.

Portée
L'indice est calculé mensuellement et se rapporte aux ménages d'ouvriers et employés urbains des secteurs privé et public (non compris les ouvriers agricoles).

Base originale
Août 1975 = 100.

Source des coefficients de pondération
Les coefficients de pondération et les articles sélectionnés ont été déterminés sur la base des résultats d'une enquête sur les dépenses des ménages effectuée en 1968-69 auprès de ménages de différentes catégories sociales et groupes ethniques, en régions urbaine, minière et rurale (à l'exception des Mélanésiens résidant en région rurale). Les pondérations se rapportent aux ouvriers et employés des secteurs privé et public (non compris les ouvriers agricoles). Les pondérations de 1975 ont été obtenues par extrapolation fondée sur l'évolution des prix entre 1969 et fin 1974.

Pondération et composition

Groupes principaux	Nombre d'articles	Pondération	Nombre approximatif de relevés de prix
Alimentation	245	37,00	...
Produits manufacturés:			
Habillement, chaussure et linge de ménage	114	7,00	...
Combustible et éclairage	4	7,00	...
Ameublement, équipement de ménage et articles divers	174	20,50	...
Services:			
Loyer, eau, entretien	14	15,70	...
Soins personnels et médicaux	24	3,30	...
Transports et communications	29	5,25	...
Instruction et loisirs	10	1,15	...
Repas au dehors	6	2,00	...
Divers	20	1,10	...
Total	640	100,00	5 500

Dépenses de consommation des ménages
Toutes les dépenses monétaires effectivement à la charge des ménages sont incluses. Les logements mis à disposition, les logements en propriété, les dons en nature, les cotisations sociales, les impôts et taxes directs ainsi que l'autoconsommation sont exclus.

Mode de relevé des prix
Les prix sont relevés entre le 2 et le 25 de chaque mois par des enquêteurs auprès d'environ 250 commerces ou prestataires de services, dans la commune de Nouméa. Les prix pour l'électricité (relevé d'une consommation type deux fois l'an), l'eau, le gaz, les transports, les soins médicaux, etc., sont ceux fixés par tarifs ou conventions. Les soldes ne sont pas pris en compte.

Logement
Les données relatives au loyer sont fournies par 10 agences de location de Nouméa et portent sur environ 80 logements (principalement des logements HLM).

Spécification des variétés
Les spécifications des variétés sont détaillées pour chaque article, décrivant la variété, la qualité, fabrication, marque, unité, etc.

Substitution, changement de qualité, etc.
Si un article disparaît du marché, il est remplacé par un article similaire et la méthode d'enchaînement est utilisée. Lors d'un changement de qualité on applique également la méthode d'enchaînement.

Articles saisonniers
Il est tenu compte des fluctuations saisonnières des prix des fruits et légumes frais en maintenant, hors saison, le dernier prix de saison et en utilisant une moyenne mobile calculée sur les 12 derniers mois.

Calcul
L'indice est calculé selon la formule de Laspeyres sous forme de moyenne arithmétique pondérée à base fixe, les coefficients de pondération correspondant à la période de base.

Organisation et publication
Direction territoriale de la statistique et des études économiques: «Indice des prix de détail, Nouvelle-Calédonie»(Nouméa).

NOUVELLE-ZELANDE

Dénomination officielle
Consumer Price Index (Indice des prix à la consommation).

Portée
L'indice est calculé trimestriellement et porte sur tous les ménages privés résidant en Nouvelle-Zélande. Aucune discrimination n'est pratiquée sur le plan de la localisation géographique, des niveaux de revenu ou des classifications professionnelles.

Base originale
Octobre - décembre 1988 = 1000.

Source des coefficients de pondération
La première source de données utilisée dans le calcul des coefficients de pondération provient de l'enquête sur les dépenses des ménages effectuée par le Department of Statistics. Cette enquête continue fournit des informations exhaustives et détaillées sur les dépenses effectuées par les ménages privés dans toute la Nouvelle-Zélande. La taille de l'échantillon est, lors des années où s'effectuent les enquêtes de révision de l'Indice, d'environ 4 500 ménages.

Les résultats ont été complétés à l'aide d'autres sources, telles que les statistiques de production et du commerce, les enquêtes sur les ménages et d'autres sources publiques ou privées. Le barème de pondération de l'indice actuellement en vigueur est fondé sur les dépenses d'achats de biens et de services effectuées par les ménages privés dans les 12 mois précédant le 31 mars 1988. Le chiffre des dépenses relatives à cette période est alors révisé à la hausse, de manière à correspondre au niveau des prix du trimestre comprenant le mois de décembre 1988, en utilisant les mouvements de prix des articles appropriés de l'Indice. La population visée par l'enquête comprend l'ensemble des ménages privés résidant en Nouvelle-Zélande et habitant les deux îles principales du pays, à l'exception des zones rurales très éloignées. Par ménages résidant en Nouvelle-Zélande on entend ceux dont le chef habite le pays depuis 12 mois au minimum. Entrent dans cette définition 95 pour cent de la population totale.

Pondération et composition

Groupes principaux	Nombre d'articles	Pondération	Nombre approximatif de relevés de prix (a)
Alimentation	94	18,35	...
Logement:			
Loyer	2	4,20	...
Coût de l'habitat en propriété	22	19,31	...
Opérations ménagères:			
Combustible et éclairage	3	2,77	...
Mobilier et ameublement	44	6,82	...
Equipements, communications et services ménagers	27	6,20	...
Habillement et chaussure	54	5,34	...
Transports	24	15,39	...
Divers:			
Boissons alcoolisées et tabac	8	9,72	...
Soins personnels et médicaux	42	4,90	...
Loisirs, instruction et frais de crédit	32	7,00	...
Total	**352**	**100,00**	**150 000**

Remarque: (a) Aucune liste présentant le nombre des relevés de prix pour chaque article n'est disponible.

Dépenses de consommation des ménages
L'indice des prix à la consommation a été conçu pour constituer une mesure statistique de l'évolution du niveau des prix des biens et services effectivement acquis en Nouvelle-Zélande par des ménages privés néo-zélandais. En conséquence, la consommation provenant de l'autoproduction, les biens acquis au titre de revenus en nature et les biens et services fournis gratuitement se trouvent en dehors du champ de l'indice. L'impôt sur le revenu (qui ne constitue pas le paiement d'un service dont la qualité peut être mesurée et contrôlée sous forme statistique) ainsi que les articles constituant plutôt de l'épargne et des investissements que des dépenses sont également considérés comme non couverts par l'indice.

Sont exclus certains types de dépenses, non parce qu'ils se trouvent en dehors du domaine théoriquement couvert par l'indice, mais parce que leurs mouvements de prix ne peuvent être mesurés de façon satisfaisante et ne peuvent pas davantage être établis d'une manière appropriée par les mouvements de prix d'autres produits apparentés ou associés qui pourraient faire l'objet d'une évaluation. C'est le cas, par exemple, des oeuvres d'art, des sommes versées à titre d'amendes, des dons à titre caritatif, des frais d'approvisionnement et de l'entretien des animaux familiers.

Pour déterminer la pondération des logements occupés par leur propriétaire, l'indice actuellement en vigueur utilise une approche fondée sur les engagements de dépenses. Selon cette approche, la pondération des dépenses assignées à la propriété immobilière est représentée par la valeur brute des dépenses encourues par la population composant l'indice lors de l'acquisition et de la construction de logements au cours de l'année de référence, compensée par les bénéfices tirés de la vente des logements.

En Nouvelle-Zélande, les ménages attachent une grande importance à la sécurité de la jouissance de leur logement. On considère donc que l'achat et la construction des logements doivent être pris en compte si l'indice a pour objet de fournir une mesure adéquate de l'expérience effective des ménages en matière de déboursement.

La pondération des autres biens durables est également déterminée au moyen d'une approche fondée sur les engagements de dépenses. Conformément à cette approche, le coût intégral d'un bien durable est pris en compte lors de l'achat, quel que soit le moment du paiement effectif ou de la consommation réelle. Les frais liés au crédit pour les achats de biens durables constituent une rubrique distincte au sein de la même section de l'indice.

La pondération de la plupart des dépenses consacrées à l'achat de biens d'occasion est ajoutée à celle des biens neufs de la même catégorie. Seuls les prix des articles neufs font l'objet d'un relevé, étant donné que l'on considère que les mouvements de prix des articles d'occasion sont similaires, exception faite pour les automobiles d'occasion et les logements préalablement occupés, qui constituent des rubriques distinctes de l'indice.

Lors du calcul des coefficients de pondération, la valeur des ventes d'importation et apparentées est déterminée en tant que bénéfice net sur les achats de produits équivalents.

Le paiement des primes d'assurance-vie et les contributions aux fonds de pension sont exclus parce qu'ils sont plus liés à l'épargne qu'aux dépenses. Le remboursement des logements et des hypothèques, le paiement des primes d'assurance couvrant le mobilier et les véhicules sont inclus dans l'indice en tant que rubriques distinctes.

Les droits à payer pour l'obtention de patentes et les dépenses pour les soins de santé sont inclus dans l'indice.

Mode de relevé des prix
Les prix sont relevés auprès de 15 centres différents.

a) Les points de vente situés dans les centres commerciaux suburbains font le plus souvent partie de l'échantillon des magasins auprès desquels sont relevés les prix de produits d'épicerie, alimentaires et non alimentaires. Les prix des autres produits sont principalement relevés dans les districts commerciaux centraux des zones urbaines, afin de réduire les coûts de déplacement des enquêteurs. Certains points de ventes des zones commerciales suburbaines les plus importantes font également l'objet d'une enquête. Cependant, étant donné que la plupart des points de vente au détail des zones suburbaines sont des filiales de magasins implantés en centre-ville et pratiquant les mêmes prix, on ne considère généralement pas qu'il soit nécessaire de procéder à un relevé à grande échelle des prix proposés en zone suburbaine.

b) Lorsque les prix des articles sont relevés par les enquêteurs, le choix des points de vente est habituellement effectué au moyen de méthodes d'échantillonnage non aléatoires. Les prix sont relevés auprès d'un échantillon représentatif des points de vente les plus fréquentés par la population de l'indice. Le même coefficient de pondération est attribué aux prix de chaque magasin dont la moyenne est ensuite calculée.

Pour un certain nombre d'enquêtes effectuées par la poste, comme celles relatives aux loyers et aux honoraires d'avocats, une méthode d'échantillonnage probabiliste est utilisée en vue du choix des points de vente.

Le prix des fruits et légumes frais est relevé tous les vendredis dans les 15 zones urbaines principales. Tous les autres articles alimentaires font l'objet d'un relevé vers le 15 de chaque mois dans les mêmes zones urbaines.

Les prix des articles de l'intitulé «Fournitures ménagères» de l'indice sont également, à l'exception des équipements de jardinage, relevés mensuellement, de même que ceux des journaux, de l'électricité, du gaz, des cigarettes et du tabac, de l'alcool et des tarifs aériens nationaux. Le prix de l'essence est relevé deux fois par mois. Tous ces prix sont également relevés dans les 15 zones urbaines sus-mentionnées.

Le relevé des prix des autres articles de l'indice, effectué par les équipes départementales locales, est effectué une fois par trimestre. Le jour de l'enquête se situe vers le 15 du mois intermédiaire de chaque trimestre.

Dans la plupart des cas, les relevés établis pour le compte de l'Indice des prix à la consommation sont effectués au moyen de visites directes auprès des points de vente au détail par des équipes locales départementales travaillant à plein temps. Les enquêteurs proviennent des quatre zones urbaines principales.

Pour certains articles, les prix affichés en rayon peuvent s'avérer inappropriés ou impossibles à obtenir. Certains matériaux d'entretien ménager, tondeuses à moteur, tapis et meubles tapissés, par exemple, entrent parfois dans cette catégorie. Dans de tels cas, les enquêteurs relèvent les prix de catalogue.

Des enquêtes menées trimestriellement par correspondance sont effectuées pour les articles suivants de l'Indice: loyers, dépenses liées à l'acquisition et au financement des logements en propriété, contrats d'entretien des logements, charbon et bois de chauffage, déménagement du mobilier des ménages, primes d'assurances pour les habitations, les véhicules à moteur, les soins médicaux et de santé, frais de prescription, frais de téléphone, de cartes de crédit, coûts des logements de vacances, tarifs d'autobus et de chemin de fer pour les transports urbains, suburbains et de longue distance, tarifs des transports maritimes, frais de taxis, prix des automobiles usagées, immatriculation des véhicules à moteur, cotisations aux automobile-clubs, frais d'auto-école, billets de cinéma et de théâtre, billets d'entrée à des manifestations et événements sportifs, inscriptions aux associations sportives, cotisations aux syndicats, frais de vétérinaire, leçons de musique, frais de scolarité pour l'enseignement primaire, secondaire et supérieur, frais de jardins d'enfants et de soins aux enfants, abonnements à des revues.

Les prix réels des «tickets» sont relevés aux fins de calcul de l'indice. Dans la mesure où ils constituent une réduction du prix du «ticket» des articles relevés, les prix de soldes sont également inclus. Les prix officieux de soldes, négociés à titre individuel, ne sont pas reflétés par l'indice. Les prix de catalogue, habituellement enregistrés au cours des relevés de prix, sont inclus dans l'indice. Il n'existe aucune distinction entre les prix du marché libre et les prix officiels. Pour des raisons techniques, les transactions à caractère illégal ne sont pas couvertes par l'indice. Les frais de crédit pour l'acquisition d'automobiles neuves ou usagées et les frais des locations-ventes (autres que celles des véhicules à moteur), sont inclus dans le présent indice dans la même section que l'article considéré. La méthode d'évaluation des frais de crédit consiste à comparer les changements du taux d'intérêt relatif au prêt avec les changements survenus dans le prix des articles pour lesquels le même prêt a été accordé. A l'exception des automobiles usagées et des biens d'occasion, seuls les prix des nouveaux articles sont relevés. Dans la mesure où ils affectent le prix des articles couverts par l'enquête, les changements survenus dans les prix à l'importation sont inclus dans l'indice. Les facteurs déterminant le nombre de relevés de prix sont les suivants:

a) Le degré de similitude des mouvements de prix des articles au sein d'un groupe particulier. Si les articles en question présentent des mouvements de prix semblables, il est alors possible de calculer un indicateur de changement de prix approprié à partir d'un nombre relativement réduit de relevés de prix.

b) L'importance globale et le poids relatif des articles au sein du même groupe. D'une manière générale, plus un groupe est important, plus le nombre d'articles dont le prix est à relever sera grand.

c) Lorsque prévaut un seul prix national pour un article donné, un seul relevé de prix est requis.

Logement

Les types de logements répertoriés par loyers sont les suivants: maisons et appartements des sociétés immobilières, maisons et appartements appartenant aux autorités locales, maisons privées, appartements privés. Le nombre de pièces concerne tous les types de pièces, à l'exception des salles de bains, des toilettes séparées et des buanderies. Tous les logements sont considérés comme non meublés. Dans le cas des logements privés et appartenant aux autorités locales, le relevé des prix est effectué au moyen d'une enquête trimestrielle menée par la poste auprès des propriétaires. Un relevé complet est obtenu pour les loyers des logements des sociétés immobilières.

Maisons et appartements occupés en partie et au préalable: Pour préparer les informations concernant le prix de vente des propriétés, on utilise les données relatives aux ventes des maisons, appartements et logements occupés en partie, répertoriés chaque trimestre par l'agence gouvernementale d'expertise, Valuation New Zealand.

Construction des logements: Le changement trimestriel du coût de construction des logements (maisons et appartements) est mesuré en utilisant les données obtenues auprès d'un échantillon représentatif de constructeurs, lesquels fournissent les prix permettant d'élaborer les spécifications en matière de logements.

Achats de maison et d'appartements nouvellement construits: Les séries relatives aux constructions de logements sont combinées avec les mouvements des prix fractionnés pour obtenir l'indicateur de changement du prix d'achat des maisons et appartements nouvellement construits.

Intérêt hypothécaire: Cet indice par articles s'applique au coût d'emprunt du montant moyen nécessaire pour compléter le financement d'un achat immobilier; ce montant doit être le même que celui requis pendant la période de base de l'indice général. Cette méthode est dite «de réévaluation simple». En conséquence, le calcul des modifications des intérêts hypothécaires requiert le produit de deux indicateurs distincts, à savoir:

a) le changement du taux d'intérêt moyen payé sur les hypothèques immobilières, et

b) le changement du prix des propriétés immobilières elles-mêmes.

Ce dernier indicateur constitue une mesure de prix appropriée, qui garantit que le pouvoir d'achat (ou la valeur réelle des emprunts destinés au financement) demeure inchangé (d'une qualité constante).

Pour l'ensemble de la population constituée par les ménages privés, les taux d'intérêts moyens payés sur les hypothèques immobilières devant être remboursées sont obtenus à partir de l'enquête sur les dépenses des ménages effectuée par le Département. Le contrôle de qualité du profil hypothécaire, dont les taux d'intérêt sont mesurés dans le cadre de l'enquête, est réalisé au moyen d'une classification des hypothèques de l'échantillon en fonction de leurs échéances, un coefficient de pondération fixe étant attribué à chacune des différentes classes de l'indice. Cette pratique est fondée sur le principe selon lequel, à tout moment, l'utilité d'une hypothèque est déterminée avant tout par le montant engagé et par le solde correspondant à l'époque du prêt.

Honoraires des notaires et agents immobiliers: Depuis que la pratique des barèmes d'honoraires a été abandonnée, le Department of Statistics effectue par correspondance des enquêtes trimestrielles relatives aux honoraires des agents immobiliers et des notaires. Un échantillon aléatoire est prélevé pour chaque groupe. Les honoraires des notaires et agents immobiliers sont affectés par la valeur des propriétés faisant l'objet de transactions. En conséquence, un changement du niveau moyen des honoraires payés pour un panier déterminé de propriétés peut se produire, soit à cause d'une modification des honoraires eux-mêmes, soit en raison d'un changement du prix des propriétés concernées. Les questionnaires relèvent les honoraires pratiqués sur les transactions relatives aux propriétés dont les prix de vente sont spécifiés. Ces prix font l'objet d'un ajustement trimestriel pour tenir compte des modifications survenues dans les prix des propriétés préalablement occupées.

Spécification des variétés
Lorsque l'indicateur de changement de prix le plus approprié est un article disponible au niveau national pour un article déterminé, une spécification détaillée et précise est alors donnée sur un questionnaire d'enquête élaboré au préalable. Lorsque différentes marques, tailles, qualités, etc., d'un article déterminé peuvent être vendues dans les points de vente de différentes régions, la spécification est laissée «ouverte» à ce stade. Dans ce cas, les détails des spécifications sont établis et fixés pour chaque point de vente particulier. Cette méthode permet de relever le prix, dans chaque point de vente, de l'article le plus approprié en fonction de la demande des consommateurs.

Substitution, changement de qualité, etc.
Lorsque survient un changement de qualité, une évaluation est effectuée sur la valeur (exprimée en dollars) de la différence de qualité existant entre l'ancien et le nouveau modèle. Le prix du produit concerné est alors ajusté en conséquence. Lors des révisions, de nouveaux produits sont introduits dans l'indice avec les chiffres des dépenses correspondants, à condition que l'on puisse vérifier qu'il s'agit de produits devenus largement disponibles, qu'ils occuperont probablement une place persistante dans le budget des ménages et que leurs structures de prix ont été établies déduction faite des primes élevées sanctionnant la nouveauté ou la rareté. Dans la mesure du possible, la même quantité et la même qualité d'un produit donné sont relevées à chaque période, de façon à ce que seul le «changement de prix pur» soit incorporé dans l'indice. La substitution d'un produit déterminé de l'indice est rendue nécessaire lorsque le produit en question disparaît du marché ou lorsque, de par son évolution, son prix n'est plus représentatif du groupe de produits auxquels il est rattaché. Un ajustement de qualité est effectué dès lors que l'article de remplacement est considéré comme différent de l'article substitué, à quelque degré que ce soit, sur le plan qualitatif comme sur le plan quantitatif. En pratique, ce procédé consiste à évaluer la valeur en dollars de la différence existant entre les deux articles, puis à calculer un facteur de graduation, qui sera appliqué au relevé de prix de l'article de remplacement. Le facteur de graduation, appelé «coefficient du relevé», permet d'ajuster le prix du «nouvel» article à celui qui sera imputé, même s'il s'agit d'un article de même qualité que celle de l'«ancien» article.

Au cas où des données manqueraient, on reporte le prix correspondant à la période précédente. Si les données ne sont toujours pas disponibles après un laps de temps déterminé à l'avance, une substitution est opérée pour l'article concerné.

Articles saisonniers
Un traitement spécial est appliqué au sous-groupe des fruits et légumes frais pour tenir compte des fluctuations saisonnières des prix et de l'approvisionnement. Si les prix ne sont pas disponibles pour la saison en cours, un report des prix de la saison précédente est opéré pour les articles suivants: inscriptions aux associations sportives saisonnières, billets d'entrée aux manifestations sportives saisonnières, repas à base de salade, huîtres, plantes d'intérieur et fleurs, articles d'habillement à caractère saisonnier. S'ils sont disponibles, les prix des transports aériens internationaux de haute et basse saison sont relevés lors de chaque période.

Calcul
L'indice est calculé selon la formule de Laspeyres sous forme de moyenne arithmétique pondérée à base fixe, les coefficients de pondération correspondant à la période de base.

Les prix utilisés dans le calcul de l'Indice (15 zones urbaines prises conjointement) constituent des moyennes, pondérées en fonction de la population, des prix arithmétiques moyens relevés dans les zones en question. Les coefficients de pondération de la population représentent la population totale estimée de chaque zone urbaine combinée avec celle des zones environnantes relevant des autorités locales rattachées aux zones urbaines sus-mentionnées. Les coefficients de pondération sont obtenus à partir du Recensement de population le plus récent (1986) et ajustés pour tenir compte des changements survenus depuis lors au sein de la population.

Autres informations
Des indices séparés en fonction des groupes et sous-groupes d'articles sont publiés trimestriellement en ce qui concerne:
a) chacune des trois zones urbaines les plus importantes (Auckland, Wellington et Christchurch);
b) les trois zones urbaines les plus importantes prises conjointement;
c) l'ensemble des zones urbaines de North Island et l'ensemble des zones urbaines de South Island;
d) l'ensemble de la Nouvelle-Zélande (15 zones urbaines principales et secondaires prises conjointement).

Des indices par groupes d'articles sont également publiés, mais uniquement pour les 15 zones urbaines prises conjointement.

En outre, en ce qui concerne les produits alimentaires, des indices par groupes, sous-groupes et sections sont publiés mensuellement pour les régions géographiques mentionnées ci-dessus.

Organisation et publication
Department of Statistics: «Key Statistics» (mensuel) (Wellington).
idem: «News Release» (trimestriel).
idem: «Hot off the Press» (bulletin d'informations).
idem: «New Zealand Official Year Book».

OUGANDA (KAMPALA)

Dénomination officielle
Consumer Price Index (Indice des prix à la consommation).

Portée
L'indice est calculé mensuellement et porte sur tous les ménages dont le montant mensuel des dépenses est inférieur ou égal à 100 000 shillings, et habitant Kampala et Entebbe.

Base originale
Décembre 1988 = 100.

Source des coefficients de pondération
La valeur des coefficients de pondération et le choix des articles résultent d'une enquête sur les dépenses des ménages effectuée entre avril 1989 et avril 1990 auprès des ménages à revenu modeste ou moyen dont les dépenses mensuelles sont inférieures ou égales à 100 000 shillings.

Les critères utilisés pour le choix des articles dont le prix doit être relevé sont les suivants: le coefficient de pondération de l'article choisi doit être élevé dans le cadre de l'enquête; l'article choisi doit être commun à de nombreux ménages de l'enquête; enfin, l'article choisi doit être disponible en qualité et quantité spécifiques dans des lieux déterminés. Cependant, en raison des ressources limitées du Statistics Department, certains articles sélectionnés ne font l'objet d'aucun relevé de prix, même s'ils présentent les caractéristiques décrites ci-dessus. Dans ce cas, les coefficients de pondération de deux articles ou plus sont combinés, si l'on estime que l'un d'entre eux ne disparaîtra pas trop rapidement du marché; ces articles ont été sélectionnés pour représenter les autres à l'aide de coefficients combinés. Les articles ont été combinés de manière à ce que leurs mouvements de prix présentent les mêmes tendances et afin que leur utilisation finale soit la même.

Pondération et composition

Groupes principaux	Nombre d'articles	Pondération	Nombre approximatif de relevés de prix
Alimentation	29	50,8	...
Boissons et tabac	7	6,3	...
Combustible et éclairage	3	7,3	...
Transports	9	5,9	...
Habillement et chaussure	12	5,5	...
Divers	14	8,5	...
Services (y c. loyer, instruction et loisirs)	15	15,7	...
Total	89	100.00	...

Dépenses de consommation des ménages
Données non disponibles.

Mode de relevé des prix
Six marchés ont été retenus pour les villes de Kampala et d'Entebbe. Aucune méthode scientifique n'a été utilisée pour le choix de ces centres commerciaux. Les critères utilisés ont été la taille et la répartition géographique de ces marchés.

Dans chacun de ces six marchés, ont été relevés les prix des denrées alimentaires, des boissons et du tabac, du combustible et de l'énergie, de l'habillement et de la chaussure. Les cliniques et hôpitaux fournissent les prix des médicaments et des produits pharmaceutiques ainsi que les tarifs de consultation. Ces établissements ont été sélectionnés en fonction de leur taux de fréquentation et de leur répartition géographique. Les écoles primaires et secondaires transmettent les frais relatifs à l'instruction et ont été choisies en fonction du nombre d'élèves ou d'étudiants qui les fréquentent et de leur situation. Les compagnies de transports et les groupes généralement responsables de la plus grande part de cette activité fournissent les informations concernant les changements des tarifs.

Les prix de tous les articles sont relevés mensuellement, à l'exception des frais d'instruction, relevés tous les quatre mois, c'est-à-dire à l'occasion de chaque terme académique. Il convient de noter que les relevés de prix correspondent au milieu du mois en question et que les fruits et légumes ne font l'objet d'aucun traitement spécifique.

Les prix des articles dont la mesure n'est pas normalisée, en particulier ceux vendus en vrac et ceux dont la présentation ne correspond à aucune pondération normalisée, sont obtenus par achat direct. Néanmoins, en ce qui concerne les articles dont les prix sont trop élevés pour les moyens financiers du Statistics Department, les prix sont obtenus à la suite d'entretiens ou par notification.

Les données relatives aux services sont obtenues au moyen de questionnaires adressés par correspondance.

Quatre personnes travaillent habituellement au relevé des prix, et disposent des mêmes crédits pour chaque marché, de deux barèmes de pondération et d'une liste des articles devant être relevés. L'achat de la plupart des articles fait l'objet de négociations, puis d'une pondération, tandis que les prix des autres articles sont simplement notifiés.

Les prix effectifs, réellement payés par le consommateur, sont pris en considération, sans qu'aucune attention particulière ne soit accordée aux prix de soldes ou de catalogue. De ce fait, les prix du marché noir sont pris en compte comme prix à la consommation.

Logement
Les loyers sont relevés pour des appartement sélectionnés, résidences de jeunes gens, appartements et bungalows, de manière à ce que l'ensemble des catégories sociales soient représentées.

Spécification des variétés
Les spécifications précisent la quantité, la qualité et la localisation des points de vente.

Substitution, changement de qualité, etc.
Lorsqu'un article subit un changement considérable du point de vue de la qualité, l'article de nouvelle qualité est considéré comme un article différent et comme un proche substitut de l'ancien article. Lorsqu'un nouveau produit apparaît dans l'indice, son prix est relevé mais il n'est pas introduit sur le marché tant que l'on ne dispose pas de données suffisantes. Lorsqu'un article disparaît du marché, les prix correspondant au mois précédent sont utilisés pour une période d'environ deux mois; cependant, si une telle situation se prolonge, l'article en question est remplacé par un proche substitut.

Articles saisonniers
Bien que les relevés des prix à la consommation comprennent ceux des articles saisonniers, aucun ajustement n'a été effectué pour prendre en compte les fluctuations saisonnières.

Calcul
L'indice est calculé selon la formule de Laspeyres sous forme de moyenne arithmétique pondérée à base fixe, les coefficients de pondération correspondant à la période de base.

Lors du calcul des indices par article, on utilise les rapports de prix de la période courante et de la période précédente.

Autres informations
L'indice est révisé sur la base des calculs finals de l'enquête sur les dépenses des ménages

Organisation et publication
Ministry of Planning and Economic Development, Statistics Department: «Key Economic Indicators» (Entebbe).

idem: «Statistical Bulletin No. CPI/1 Consumer Price Index Kampala (jusqu'en septembre 1990)», Entebbe, octobre 1990.

PAKISTAN

Dénomination officielle
Combined Consumer Price Index (Indice combiné des prix à la consommation).

Portée
L'indice est calculé mensuellement et porte sur les salariés de l'industrie, du commerce et de la fonction publique, répartis en quatre classes de revenus: jusqu'à 1 000 roupies, 1 001-2 500 roupies, 2 501-4 500 roupies, et 4 501 roupies et plus par mois. Il porte sur 25 grands centres urbains.

Base originale
Juillet 1980 - juin 1981 = 100.

Source des coefficients de pondération
Le système de pondération résulte de l'enquête sur les dépenses des ménages effectuée en 1982 dans 46 centres urbains y compris 25 centres urbains principaux, auprès d'un échantillon de 26 864 ménages. Les articles retenus pour le calcul de l'indice l'ont été du fait qu'ils sont représentatifs des goûts, des habitudes et des coutumes des habitants, qu'ils sont faciles à reconnaître et à décrire et qu'ils ont peu de chances de présenter des changements de qualité.

Pondération et composition

Groupes principaux	Nombre d'articles	Pondération	Nombre approximatif de relevés de prix
Alimentation et tabac	176	49,90	...
Habillement et chaussure	73	6,68	...
Loyer	1	17,76	...
Combustible et éclairage	15	5,62	...
Mobilier et équipement de ménage	38	2,34	...
Transports et communications	44	6,20	...
Instruction et loisirs	44	3,50	...
Produits d'entretien et soins personnels	45	5,56	...
Divers	28	2,44	...
Total	464	100,00	(a) ...

Remarque: (a) Environ quatre par article (effectués dans des commerces différents) et par zone commerçante.

Dépenses de consommation des ménages
Les dépenses de consommation prises en compte dans le calcul de l'indice correspondent aux achats de tous les biens et services importants effectués par les ménages de référence pour leur consommation. En sont exclus les dépenses à des fins autres que la consommation, les achats de logements, le paiement d'intérêts, les achats de bijouterie et toutes les formes d'actif et de passif.

Mode de relevé des prix
Le personnel de terrain du Federal Bureau of Statistics assure le relevé des prix sur des marchés, auprès d'un échantillon de commerces de détail et de prestataires de services dans 46 centres urbains y compris 25 villes principales. Les prix sont relevés au moyen de quatre formulaires. Les prix des biens de consommation de base et des denrées alimentaires périssables (viande, poisson, oeufs, légumes, etc.) sont relevés le troisième mardi de chaque mois; ceux des autres articles sont relevés mensuellement.

Les prix retenus pour le calcul de l'indice sont ceux auxquels détaillants et prestataires de services vendent leurs biens et services directement aux consommateurs.

Logement
On ne dispose pas de données courantes relatives au loyer pour l'ensemble du pays; c'est l'évolution des prix des matériaux de construction qui sert d'indicateur de tendance des loyers.

Spécification des variétés
La spécification de la plupart des articles retenus est effectuée par la Division statistique du Bureau fédéral de la statistique. Lorsqu'il n'est pas possible, pour certains articles, d'établir de spécification, c'est la meilleure qualité locale qui est adoptée.

Substitution, changement de qualité, etc.
La Division statistique examine toutes les propositions que lui font ses enquêteurs sur le terrain en vue de substituer un nouvel article à un produit qui n'est pas disponible du tout ou qui n'est pas conforme à la spécification ou à la qualité préétablie. L'article de substitution, une fois accepté, est introduit dans l'indice à l'aide de la formule d'enchaînement.

Articles saisonniers
Les prix de ces articles varient dans de très larges limites selon qu'ils sont vendus en saison ou hors saison. On a fait le nécessaire pour éliminer des calculs l'effet de telles variations en considérant comme nul le prix de ces articles lorsqu'ils ne sont pas de saison.

Calcul
L'indice est calculé selon la formule de Laspeyres sous forme de moyenne arithmétique pondérée à base fixe, les coefficients de pondération correspondant à 1982.

Des systèmes de pondération propres à chaque ville, fournis par l'enquête sur les revenus et les dépenses de ménages, ont servi à calculer des indices par ville pour les trois catégories de travailleurs et les quatre classes de revenu.

L'indice national est obtenu en utilisant un ensemble de pondérations combinées qui ne tient pas compte de la distinction entre les villes, les catégories professionnelles et les groupes de revenus.

Organisation et publication
Federal Bureau of Statistics, Statistics Division: «Monthly Statistical Bulletin» (Karachi).

idem: «Pakistan Key Economic Indicators».

idem: «Consumer Price Index Numbers of Pakistan 1980-81 = 100».

PANAMA (VILLE DE PANAMA)

Dénomination officielle
Indice de precios al consumidor (Indice des prix à la consommation).

Portée
L'indice est calculé mensuellement et porte sur tous les ménages privés de la ville de Panama, quels que soient leurs revenus.

Base originale
1987 = 100.

Source des coefficients de pondération
La valeur des coefficients de pondération et le choix des articles résultent d'une enquête sur les dépenses effectuée en 1983-84 dans la ville de Panama sur un échantillon de 1 070 ménages de différents niveaux de revenus.

Les ménages avaient été sélectionnés sur la base d'un échantillon aléatoire stratifié constitué à partir d'une liste de logements établie selon le recensement de la population de 1980, complétée par la liste des immeubles construits après la date du recensement, le logement ayant constitué l'unité de sélection et le ménage l'unité observée. Pour effectuer l'enquête, la technique de l'interview direct des ménages a été utilisée et les données ont été relevées au moyen d'un formulaire mensuel qui traitait en détail des dépenses et recettes des familles et d'un bloc-notes qui a servi à l'obtention des dépenses et recettes quotidiennes pendant une semaine. Les coefficients de pondération n'ont pas été ajustés pour tenir compte des changements de prix survenus entre la période de l'enquête et 1987.

Pondération et composition

Groupes principaux	Nombre d'articles	Pondération	Nombre approximatif de relevés de prix
Alimentation	101	34,9	81
Habillement et chaussure	38	5,1	34
Loyer, combustible et éclairage (1)	4	12,6	5
Mobilier, ameublement, articles de ménage et entretien	37	8,4	43
Soins personnels et médicaux	11	3,5	21
Transports et communications	10	15,1	24
Instruction et loisirs	20	11,7	41
Autres biens et services	23	8,7	26
Total	244	100,0	275

Remarque: (1) Non compris 109 logements dont le loyer est relevé, répartis dans tous les quartiers de la ville de Panama.

Dépenses de consommation des ménages
Elles couvrent les dépenses nettes une fois déduites les ventes de biens d'occasion effectuées par les ménages et la valeur sur le marché de ces biens usagés remis en tant que paiement partiel pour l'acquisition de biens neufs.

En sont exclues les cotisations à la sécurité sociale et aux caisses de retraite, les assurances relatives à certains biens de consommation, l'impôt sur le revenu et autres impôts directs. Dans le calcul de la pondération de l'indice, il est tenu compte des paiements effectués au titre d'assurance-vie, virements, dons et dépenses assimilées.

Mode de relevé des prix
Le relevé périodique des prix est effectué par des visites directes d'enquêteurs du Bureau des Statistiques aux établissements sélectionnés, au moyen de formulaires établis à cet effet. Les agents qui se consacrent à cette tâche font l'objet d'une formation spéciale afin d'effectuer leur travail avec précision dans le temps imparti.

Les relevés de prix ont lieu tous les mois, à l'exception de ceux portant sur le loyer, l'entretien, la coiffure, la manucure, les voyages aériens et les compagnies d'assurances qui ont lieu tous les trois mois, et des dépenses relatives aux employés de maison et à l'instruction dont le relevé a lieu tous les six mois. Les relevés de prix, d'articles et de services, à l'exception de ceux du marché, sont effectués au cours des trois premières semaines de chaque mois, et ceux du marché ont lieu le mardi et le jeudi de la deuxième semaine du mois.

Les prix de liquidation ne sont pas pris en compte pour le calcul de l'indice. En ce qui concerne les prix de solde, ils sont inclus si ils conservent cette qualité pendant plusieurs semaines, si les articles sont en bon état et s'ils font partie des stocks réguliers du magasin.

Logement
Les relevés des loyers sont effectués trimestriellement auprès de 109 logements. Il n'est pas tenu compte des logements occupés en propriété.

Spécification des variétés
Lorsque les articles et services ont été sélectionnés, il est procédé à l'obtention de la spécification définie comme la description détaillée des caractéristiques physiques d'un bien ou d'un service, considérées comme facteurs déterminants pour l'établissement des prix, par exemple, la qualité, la taille, le mode de fabrication, le modèle, le style, etc. Les spécifications portent sur les précisions généralement demandées par les acheteurs et que fournissent les vendeurs. L'identification des articles a pour objet de faire en sorte que seul l'indice indique les changements de prix.

Pour faciliter le relevé des prix à partir des descriptions établies, il est fait usage d'un manuel qui tient compte de l'article et des spécifications requises pour ce relevé. Il convient évidemment de tenir compte du fait que tous les articles inclus dans l'indice ne requièrent pas le même degré d'exactitude en matière de définition.

Substitution, changement de qualité, etc.
Lorsque des changements se produisent dans la spécification d'un article, la substitution a lieu de la manière suivante: a) par comparaison directe des prix: cette méthode est utilisée lorsque l'article de remplacement correspond plus ou moins à la qualité de l'article épuisé, mais n'est pas de la même marque. Dans ce cas, il est procédé à la comparaison directe des prix des deux marques et, le cas échéant, le changement de prix est reflété dans l'indice; b) par rapport d'enchaînements: par cette méthode, le nouvel article peut avoir la même utilité ou le même objet, mais différer quant à la qualité, même quand le prix demeure égal; ces changements ne se produisent pas subitement et un moment arrive où les deux catégories d'articles se trouvent en même temps sur le marché. Il est alors procédé simultanément au relevé des prix des deux articles et, lorsqu'on dispose des prix du nouvel article au cours de deux périodes consécutives, l'article de remplacement est enchaîné à l'indice de façon à ce que la différence de prix entre les deux catégories d'articles n'apparaisse pas dans l'indice. On y parvient en comparant le prix de l'article de remplacement au prix de l'article qu'il remplace, relevé au cours de la période précédente, et en appliquant le rapport de prix de celui-ci au prix pondéré de l'article qui n'est plus sur le marché.

Articles saisonniers
Pendant les périodes où l'on ne peut obtenir les prix d'un article saisonnier, le rapport de prix correspondant aux articles du même sous-groupe disponibles tout au long de l'année lui est appliqué. Ce rapport est obtenu en divisant la somme des prix pondérés du trimestre considéré par le total des prix pondérés de la période précédente. Il est procédé à l'évaluation du coût de l'article saisonnier en multipliant le coût de la période précédente par le rapport de prix estimé de la période considérée.

Calcul
L'indice est calculé selon la formule de Laspeyres sous forme

de moyenne arithmétique pondérée à base fixe, les coefficients de pondération correspondant à 1983-84.
Le rapport de prix pour chaque article est calculé en divisant le prix moyen de la période en cours par le prix moyen de la période précédente.

Autres informations
Des sous-groupes détaillés sont publiés pour l'indice actuel.

Organisation et publication
Dirección de Estadísticas y Censos: «Estadística Panameña» (Panama, mars, juin, septembre et décembre).

PAPOUASIE-NOUVELLE-GUINEE

Dénomination officielle
Consumer Price Index (Indice des prix à la consommation).

Portée
L'indice est calculé trimestriellement et porte sur les ménages d'ouvriers des zones urbaines. Un ménage d'ouvrier est, par définition, un ménage dont au moins la moitié du revenu provient de salaires et de traitements. Le terme «urbain» s'applique ici aux zones comptant 2 000 habitants ou plus en 1977.

Base originale
1977 = 100.

Source des coefficients de pondération
La valeur des coefficients de pondération et le choix des articles résultent d'une enquête sur les dépenses des ménages menée entre septembre 1975 et février 1976 sur 501 ménages d'ouvriers vivant dans six zones urbaines d'au moins 2 000 habitants en 1977. Les résultats ont été corrigés de l'évolution des prix entre la période de l'enquête et 1977. Les critères ci-après ont été appliqués pour le choix des articles à prendre en compte dans l'indice: (i) ces articles doivent correspondre à une dépense d'au moins 0,05 pour cent du total; (ii) ils doivent être représentatifs du groupe d'articles apparentés dans lequel ils sont rangés; (iii) ils doivent se prêter à des relevés de prix réguliers.

Pondération et composition

Groupes principaux	Nombre d'articles	Pondération	Nombre approximatif de relevés de prix
Alimentation	51	40,89	...
Boissons et tabac	7	20,00	...
Habillement et chaussure	16	6,17	...
Loyer, combustible et éclairage	4	7,19	...
Equipement et dépenses de ménages	15	5,28	...
Transports et communications	11	12,96	...
Biens et services divers	20	7,51	...
Total	124	100,00	...

Dépenses de consommation des ménages
Les dépenses de consommation prises dans le calcul de l'indice visent tous les biens et services que la population de l'indice acquiert pour les consommer. En sont exclus les dépenses de jeu, les cotisations aux caisses de retraite, l'épargne, les dons en espèces, les primes d'assurance vie et l'impôt sur le revenu.

Mode de relevé des prix
Les prix, obtenus sur place par les enquêteurs ou par correspondance à l'aide de questionnaires expédiés par la poste, proviennent de quelque 240 points de vente répartis entre les six zones urbaines. Les relevés sont effectués chaque semaine sur les marchés pour les fruits et légumes frais et les noix d'arec; mensuellement pour les autres produits alimentaires, l'épicerie, les boissons et les tabacs; annuellement pour les dépenses de scolarité; trimestriellement pour tous les autres biens et services. Les relevés ont lieu vers le 15 de chaque mois sauf pour les fruits et légumes frais, dont les prix sont obtenus le vendredi ou le samedi de chaque semaine. Les prix retenus pour le calcul de l'indice sont les prix demandés aux consommateurs le jour du relevé. Les rabais et les prix de solde ne sont retenus que s'ils correspondent à un volume de vente appréciable.

Logement
Les données relatives au loyer sont recueillies pour des logements en location comprenant une à quatre chambres à coucher.

Spécification des variétés
Les articles dont les prix sont à relever font l'objet de spécifications portant sur la marque, la fabrication, la qualité, la taille, l'unité, etc.

Substitution, changement de qualité, etc.
Des ajustements spéciaux sont prévus afin que les prix retenus ne présentent que des variations «pures», indépendantes du changement de la qualité ou de la quantité d'une spécification.

Articles saisonniers
Aucun ajustement n'est appliqué pour tenir compte des fluctuations saisonnières.

Calcul
L'indice se présente comme la moyenne pondérée de six séries d'indices relatifs respectivement à Port Moresby, Lae, Rabaul, Madang, Goroka et Kieta/Arawa/Panguna. Chacun de ces indices est calculé selon la formule de Laspeyres sous forme de moyenne arithmétique pondérée à base fixe, les coefficients de pondération correspondant à la période de base; ils sont ensuite pondérés à l'aide de coefficients proportionnels à la population urbaine des villes considérées, ce qui permet d'obtenir l'indice combiné valable pour l'ensemble des six zones urbaines.

Autres informations
Des indices séparés pour les six régions urbaines sont également publiés.

Organisation et publication
National Statistical Office: «Statistical Bulletin, Consumer Price Index» (Port Moresby).
idem: «Statistical Bulletin, Consumer Price Indexes», trimestres se terminant en mars et en juin 1979.
idem: «Technical Note, No. 4, Consumer Price Indexes (Base year 1977), April 1980.».

PARAGUAY (ASUNCION)

Dénomination officielle
Indice de precios del consumo (Indice des Prix à la Consommation).

Portée
L'indice est calculé mensuellement et porte sur les familles de tous les niveaux sociaux et économiques de l'agglomération d'Asunción.

Base originale
1980 = 100.

Source des coefficients de pondération
La valeur des coefficients de pondération et le choix des articles sélectionnés se fondent sur les résultats d'une enquête sur les dépenses des ménages effectuée de septembre 1978 à septembre 1979 auprès d'un échantillon de 1.591 familles urbaines d'ouvriers, d'employés, de cadres et de retraités, célibataires ou mariés avec ou sans enfants. L'enquête exclut les personnes qui vivent dans les types d'établissements suivants: casernes (armée ou police), hôpitaux, couvents et autres lieux assimilés. Le nombre moyen de personnes par famille était de 4,7. L'indice porte sur les familles de tous les niveaux sociaux et économiques de l'agglomération d'Asunción. La présélection des articles se fonde sur le montant des dépenses et le nombre des familles.

Pondération et composition

Groupes principaux	Nombre d'articles	Pondération	Nombre approximatif de relevés de prix
Alimentation et tabac	146	36,98	1 937
Logement:			725
Loyer	1	15,47	...
Combustible et éclairage	13	6,37	...
Mobilier et articles d'équipement ménager	44	4,67	...
Produits d'entretien	11	1,21	...
Habillement et chaussures	99	8,99	972
Divers	231	26,30	2 074
Total	545	100,00	5 708

Dépenses de consommation des ménages
Non disponibles.

Mode de relevé des prix
Pour calculer la variation de l'indice des prix, on relève en moyenne 5 700 prix différents par mois. On choisit les magasins les plus fréquentés par les familles et on y ajoute d'autres centres d'achat représentatifs. On établit ensuite une moyenne de dix sources pour chaque article vendu dans les différents points de vente (marchés, magasins et supermarchés). La périodicité d'enregistrement des prix à Asunción est la suivante: chaque semaine pour les principaux articles d'alimentation; chaque mois pour les autres articles d'alimentation, le logement et les articles divers; tous les deux mois pour l'habillement et les articles connexes. Les relevés de prix sont effectués par des fonctionnaires de la Banco Central del Paraguay bien au fait des techniques d'établissement des systèmes d'indices.

Lorsque les rabais sont une pratique courante de l'établissement commercial enquêté et que tous les clients sans exception en bénéficient, on en tient compte dans le calcul de l'évolution du prix par rapport aux prix de la période précédente assortis d'un rabais correspondant.

Les prix affichés sont enregistrés normalement lorsque le ou les établissements commerciaux n'accordent pas à tous les clients de rabais sur les articles faisant l'objet de l'enquête. Ils servent au calcul de l'évolution des prix par rapport aux prix affichés de la période précédente.

Pour les articles qui ont un prix officiel et qui sont commercialisés sur le marché libre à un prix différent de celui fixé par les pouvoirs publics, on retient le prix du marché libre parce que c'est lui qui détermine la somme effectivement dépensée par le consommateur.

Les prix au marché noir ne sont pas enregistrés parce que les produits qui y sont proposés ne sont pas censés exister légalement.

On tient compte seulement des achats au comptant, et non des achats à tempérament ou à crédit.

Les achats d'articles d'occasion et la remise de biens usagés en paiement de biens neufs sont calculés en monnaie nationale et au prix auquel peut prétendre le vendeur. Autrement dit, on retient le prix versé par le consommateur pour l'achat du produit.

Logement
Pour ce qui est des articles compris dans la rubrique «loyer», il convient de noter que le sous-groupe logements occupés par leur propriétaire et logements en location n'inclut que les logements en location. L'échantillon ayant servi à l'enregistrement du prix des logements en location se compose de 200 unités réparties en quatre groupes de 50 unités chacun, situés dans des quartiers différents d'Asunción. Chacune des unités appartenant à l'un des quatre groupes de logements fait l'objet d'une enquête tous les quatre mois et à tour de rôle. Par exemple, le groupe I, qui se compose de 50 logements situés dans le quartier A, est relevé en janvier. Les prix enregistrés servent au calcul de l'évolution des prix par rapport à ceux enregistrés en septembre de l'année précédente, tandis que les trois autres groupes restent constants. Le groupe 2, qui se compose de 50 logements situés dans le quartier B, est relevé en février. On compare les prix relevés à ceux de la période précédente, c'est-à-dire octobre, tandis que les autres groupes restent constants. En mars on relève les prix du troisième groupe qui se compose de 50 logements situés dans le quartier C, et on les compare à ceux enregistrés en novembre de l'année précédente, tandis que les autres groupes restent constants. En avril, on relève les prix du quatrième groupe, qui se compose de 50 logements situés dans le quartier D et on les compare à ceux du mois de décembre précédent tandis que les trois autres groupes restent constants.

Spécification des variétés
Les données utilisées pour établir les spécifications des articles indiquent la variété, la qualité et l'unité de mesure retenues pour le calcul de l'évolution des prix. Selon le produit, on indique également la marque, la provenance, le poids et les dimensions.

Substitution, changement de qualité, etc.
Quand un produit disparaît du marché, on estime son prix relatif en se fondant sur celui des autres éléments du groupe auquel il appartient; pour ce qui est de la qualité, on peut le remplacer par un autre produit similaire sans comparer les prix au moment de la substitution.

Articles saisonniers
On considère comme constants le prix et la pondération des articles saisonniers pendant les périodes d'enquête où ils sont absents du marché; pendant les périodes où ils sont en vente, on relève leur prix que l'on compare au prix antérieur considéré comme constant. Cette méthode vise à ne pas fausser encore d'avantage les pondérations.

Calcul
On calcule l'indice selon la formule de Laspeyres modifiée selon un volume de consommation fixe et des pondérations mobiles. L'indice de chaque produit est obtenu en utilisant les rapports de prix de la période courante et de la période précédente.

Autres informations
La Banco Central del Paraguay établit parallèlement un autre indice des prix à la consommation, qui porte sur les familles d'ouvriers de l'agglomération d'Asunción.

Organisation et publication
Banco Central del Paraguay: «Folleto Explicativo del Indice de Precios del Consumo, Año 1980», juin 1988.

idem: «Boletín Estadístico».

idem: «Revista Ñemú Renda».

Dirección General de Estadística y Censos, Presidencia de la República: «Anuario Estadístico».

PAYS-BAS

Dénomination officielle
Price Index Numbers of Final Consumption Expenditure (Indice des prix de dépenses à la consommation finale).

Portée
L'indice est calculé mensuellement. Il porte sur les ménages d'ouvriers et d'employés sans enfants ou avec enfants vivant dans ces ménages mais sans revenu propre, disposant en 1985 d'un revenu familial situé en deçà de la limite salariale imposée pour l'assurance-maladie obligatoire. L'indice porte sur l'ensemble du pays.

Base originale
1985 = 100.

Source des coefficients de pondération
La valeur des coefficients de pondération et le choix des articles résultent d'une enquête sur les dépenses des ménages effectuée en 1985 auprès d'un échantillon de 962 ménages.

Pondération et composition

Groupes principaux	Nombre d'articles	Pondération	Nombre approximatif de relevés de prix
Alimentation	234	21,3	...
Habillement et chaussure	120	6,8	...
Soins médicaux	5	11,4	...
Biens d'équipement ménager	60	6,6	...
Loyer, combustible et éclairage	41	27,2	...
Transports et communications	49	11,4	...
Instruction et loisirs	103	8,4	...
Autres biens et services	78	6,9	...
Total	690	100,0	(a) ...

Remarque: (a) Au total, 100 000 prix en moyenne sont relevés chaque mois (non compris les données relatives aux loyers qui sont relevées chaque fois que ceux-ci font l'objet d'un relèvement général).

Dépenses de consommation des ménages
Les dépenses de consommation des ménages prises en compte dans le calcul de l'indice comprennent tous les biens et services de consommation pour lesquels les ménages privés engagent des dépenses, notamment dans les secteurs suivants: commerces, grands magasins et autres fournisseurs, prestations de mécaniciens et d'artisans, hôtels, restaurants et cafés, transports et loisirs, les honoraires des médecins et spécialistes, le coût des services hospitaliers et des produits pharmaceutiques, services médicaux et domestiques, frais administratifs liés à l'assurance vie et aux caisses de retraite, biens d'équipement tels que meubles, récepteurs radio, etc. En sont exclus les transferts effectués volontairement par les ménages à des institutions sans but lucratif, les transferts effectués entre ménages, les transferts obligatoires effectués par les ménages aux pouvoirs publics et aux organismes d'assurance sociale, l'épargne sous forme de primes d'assurance vie ou de cotisations à des caisses de retraite.

Mode de relevé des prix
Les prix sont relevés mensuellement le jeudi de la semaine du 15 du mois, auprès d'un échantillon de points de vente dans lequel figurent vendeurs de marchés et de rues, éventaires mobiles, grands magasins, petits, moyens et grands commerces de détail, grossistes et prestataires de services de 100 municipalités d'au moins 10 000 habitants. Sont relevées des données permettant de mesurer l'évolution des prix d'environ 1 200 articles. Pour une partie de ceux-ci (dans laquelle n'entrent pas les loyers), représentant environ 38 pour cent de la pondération totale, les relevés sont effectués au moyen d'enquêtes par correspondance. Les prix relevés sont ceux payés effectivement par les consommateurs, y compris les taxes indirectes. Le prix des soldes n'est pris en compte que lorsque les consommateurs peuvent en profiter sans difficulté et lorsque les soldes en question durent au moins une semaine. Les rabais en espèces consentis au moment de l'achat sont déduits. Les prix de l'électricité, du gaz et de l'eau sont relevés auprès des compagnies responsables.

Logement
Les données relatives aux loyers sont, pour une large part, relevées par correspondance auprès des propriétaires ou des gérants. Pour environ 3 pour cent des logements en location, lorsque l'enquête par correspondance se révèle impossible, ces données sont relevées par les enquêteurs auprès des locataires. L'enquête sur les loyers touche 482 des 702 municipalités des Pays-Bas. L'achat, par des personnes privées, d'habitations destinées à être occupées en propriété n'entre pas dans l'indice, mais la prestation que constitue ce mode d'habitat est réputée faire partie de la consommation des ménages. Il est chiffré par une valeur locative qui correspond au loyer payé par les locataires d'habitations comparables.

Spécification des variétés
Tous les biens et services font l'objet de descriptions qualitatives très précises portant notamment sur le poids, le nombre, la marque, la taille, la matière (pour l'habillement), etc.

Substitution, changement de qualité, etc.
Les produits nouveaux sont insérés dans le système de pondération lors du prochain changement d'année de base. Lorsqu'un article disparaît du marché, il lui est substitué un article analogue, auquel on applique la formule d'enchaînement.

Articles saisonniers
Les coefficients de pondération des groupes comprenant les pommes de terre, légumes et fruits frais, fleurs et plantes d'appartement sont invariables d'un mois à l'autre. Les pondérations à l'intérieur de ces groupes ne sont pas calculées sur la seule année de base, mais constituent une moyenne établie sur plusieurs années, dont l'année de base est la dernière. Pour l'habillement et la chaussure de saison, deux paniers sont constitués, dont l'un est pris en compte pour les mois d'hiver et l'autre pour les mois d'été. En mars et en septembre, les deux paniers figurent dans le système de pondération, chacun avec la moitié de son coefficient.

Calcul
L'indice est calculé selon la formule de Laspeyres sous forme de moyenne arithmétique pondérée à base fixe, les coefficients de pondération correspondant à la période de base.
Le rapport de prix pour chaque article est calculé en divisant le prix moyen de la période courante par le prix moyen de la période de base.

Organisation et publication
Centraal Bureau voor de Statistiek (Bureau central de la statistique): «Maandstatistiek van de prijzen» (Bulletin mensuel des statistiques de prix) (Voorburg).
idem: «Statistisch bulletin» (Bulletin statistique).

PEROU (LIMA)

Dénomination officielle
Indice de precios al consumidor (Indice des prix à la consommation).

Portée
L'indice est calculé mensuellement et porte sur les ménages urbains dont le chef est un employé ou un ouvrier disposant d'un revenu moyen. Sont exclus les ménages d'une personne et ceux dont le revenu par personne est bas ou très élevé.

Base originale
1979 = 100.

Source des coefficients de pondération
La valeur des coefficients de pondération et le choix des articles résultent d'une enquête sur les dépenses des ménages effectuée durant douze mois, de septembre 1977 à août 1978, sur 1 985 ménages de la zone métropolitaine de Lima.
Pour le choix des articles, les critères suivants ont été appliqués: leur importance relative au sein de leur sous-groupe, leur représentativité à l'égard des variations de prix d'un ensemble de produits similaires, la possibilité d'en relever les prix régulièrement. La valeur des dépenses correspondant aux articles écartés du «panier familial» a été ajoutée de deux manières à celle des article retenus: a) soit par imputation directe, c'est-à-dire par affectation des dépenses de l'article écarté à celles d'un article retenu, doté de caractéristiques suffisamment comparables et susceptible de lui être substitué; b) soit par imputation indirecte, c'est-à-dire par répartition proportionnelle entre tous les articles retenus du sous-groupe.

Pondération et composition

Groupes principaux	Nombre d'articles	Pondération	Nombre approximatif de relevés de prix
Alimentation et tabac	75	38,09	23 386
Habillement et chaussure	11	7,33	1 323
Loyer, combustibles et électricité	8	15,57	1 424
Mobilier, articles d'équipement ménager	36	6,98	1 589
Soins personnels et médicaux	8	2,64	417
Transports et communications	10	9,83	272
Instruction et loisirs	12	7,40	592
Autres biens et services	13	12,16	997
Total	173	100,00	30 000

Dépenses de consommation des ménages
On entend par consommation des ménages celle qui vise les biens et services destinés à satisfaire les besoins de la famille, à l'exclusion des achats d'habitations et de terrains et de toutes les dépenses génératrices de revenu ou de rentes pour le ménage. Cette consommation des ménages comprend l'autoconsommation, c'est-à-dire les biens et services, évalués aux prix du marché, que ses membres produisent pour les consommer. Les dépenses des ménages comprennent donc, par exemple, la valeur locative des habitations occupées par leur propriétaire. Ne sont retenus, par ailleurs, que les dépenses exemptes de double comptage, c'est-à-dire que, par exemple, les primes d'assurance automobile ne sont retenues que si les frais de réparation du véhicule assuré ne le sont pas.

Mode de relevé des prix
S'agissant du choix des marchés de détail à visiter, l'Institut national de la statistique en a effectué un recensement, puis en a extrait les plus importants par le nombre des points de vente et des vendeurs ambulants installés à proximité, réalisant ainsi un échantillon de 33 marchés et quatre supermarchés. Quant aux établissements commerciaux et prestataires de services, on a opéré une sélection à partir d'un inventaire des avenues ou zones commerçantes de chaque quartier, en prenant comme critères le bon vouloir du commerçant et l'importance de son assortiment. Ont été aussi retenues les grandes chaînes de supermarchés. Les prix utilisés dans le calcul de l'indice sont ceux-là même que paient les chefs de famille au marché ou la plupart des consommateurs dans les établissements. Les prix sont relevés par des enquêteurs auprès des marchés, points de vente au détail et prestataires de services.

Les relevés sont effectués chaque semaine pour les articles dont les prix varient beaucoup, comme les produits frais (légumes, fruits, poisson), ou pour ceux dont les prix varient peu, mais qui sont commercialisés dans les halles (riz, sucre, graisses et huiles comestibles, etc.); mensuellement pour les articles dont les prix sont plus stables comme les céréales, l'habillement, les meubles, etc.; et semestriellement pour les loyers, les taxes urbaines et municipales. Les tarifs des services publics sont obtenus occasionnellement. Certains prix s'obtiennent par achat direct sur les marchés.

Logement
Les montants des loyers sont relevés auprès des ménages saisis dans l'enquête et sont maintenus fixes.

Spécification des variétés
La sélection d'une variété donnée pour représenter une rubrique dépend de son importance à l'intérieur de cette rubrique,

de la facilité avec laquelle on peut la définir et obtenir un relevé de prix, et de la stabilité dans le temps des articles qui répondent à la définition ainsi posée.

Les articles choisis aux fins d'une enquête sur les dépenses des ménages ne sont pas toujours dotés de caractéristiques bien définies, portant spécification de la marque, de la taille, etc. Pour constituer leurs premiers échantillons de prix à relever, les enquêteurs se sont donc rendus auprès des établissements sélectionnés à cet effet. Munis de la liste des articles de l'enquête, ils y ont noté avec précision les caractéristiques des produits dont ils devaient relever le prix: nom, marque, modèle, taille ou poids, etc. Dans la mesure du possible, ils se sont enquis auprès du commerçant du nom de la variété la plus vendue correspondant à la définition de l'article noté. L'échantillon ainsi constitué fait ensuite l'objet d'un contrôle centralisé destiné à assurer que les prix relevés correspondent exactement aux produits de l'échantillon.

Substitution, changement de qualité, etc.
Pour diverses raisons - caractère saisonnier de l'article, absence d'informateur, disparition de l'article -, il est parfois impossible de relever certains prix. L'Institut national de la statistique résoud ainsi cette difficulté: lorsque la variété est homogène, on calcule un prix moyen pour la période à partir de celles des données qui ont été effectivement relevées pendant ladite période. Lorsque la variété est hétérogène, on applique un prix relevé antérieurement. Il convient en effet de «prolonger» temporairement le prix d'un article si on est sûr que celui-ci réapparaîtra dans un avenir proche. Mais si au bout de trois mois, l'article n'a pas réapparu, il faut absolument lui nommer un substitut.

Articles saisonniers
Voir le paragraphe ci-dessus.

Calcul
L'indice est calculé selon la formule de Laspeyres sous forme de moyenne arithmétique pondérée à base fixe, les coefficients de pondération correspondant à la période septembre 1977 - août 1978.

L'indice pour un article est obtenu en utilisant les rapports de prix de la période courante et de la période précédente. Pour les articles ayant des spécifications homogènes, on calcule les rapports de prix moyens et pour les articles ayant des spécifications hétérogènes, des moyennes des rapports de prix sont utilisées. Dans les deux cas, on calcule des moyennes arithmétiques simples.

Autres informations
Une nouvelle série (base 1990 = 100) est maintenant calculée mais les informations méthodologiques relatives à cette série n'étaient pas disponibles au BIT lors de la publication du présent Volume.

Organisation et publication
Instituto Nacional de Estadística: «Indices de Precios al Consumidor de Lima Metropolitana» (Lima).

idem: «Indices de Precios al Consumidor de Lima Metropolitana, Metodología, Diciembre 1980» (Lima).

PHILIPPINES

Dénomination officielle
Consumer Price Index for All-Income Households in the Philippines (Indice des prix à la consommation pour les ménages de tous les groupes de revenu).

Portée
L'indice est calculé mensuellement et porte sur tous les ménages (urbains et ruraux) de 72 provinces des 13 régions du pays.

Base originale
1988 = 100.

Source des coefficients de pondération
Les coefficients de pondération ont été déterminés sur la base des résultats d'une enquête sur les dépenses des ménages effectuée en 1988 auprès d'un échantillon de 19 000 ménages. Les articles et services sélectionnés pour des relevés de prix réguliers, ainsi que les points de vente où ces services sont régulièrement achetés, sont tirés d'une enquête sur les articles et points de vente effectuée en 1985 auprès d'un échantillon de 19 000 ménages. Cette approche assure la représentativité d'articles communément consommés par les ménages.

Pondération et composition

Groupes principaux	Nombre d'articles	Pondération	Nombre approximatif de relevés de prix
Alimentation et tabac	198	58,5	...
Habillement et chaussure	106	4,3	...
Logement et réparations	34	13,3	...
Combustible, éclairage et eau	15	5,4	...
Services	98	10,9	...
Divers	111	7,6	...
Total	562	100,0	(a) ...

Remarque: (a) Chaque produit ou service fait en général l'objet de six relevés de prix.

Dépenses de consommation des ménages
Les dépenses de consommation prises en compte dans le calcul de l'indice ne visent que celles destinées à la consommation des ménages. En sont exclus les taxes d'habitation, l'impôt foncier et l'impôt sur le revenu, les dons et les aides accordés à autrui, les primes d'assurance vie, les cotisations à l'assurance maladie et accidents et aux caisses de retraite et de sécurité sociale, la valeur des services rendus par un membre de la famille à un autre membre de la famille, et les dépenses à des fins autres que la consommation. Sont retenues certaines dépenses à caractère non pécuniaire: la valeur de l'autoproduction alimentaire consommée, les paiements en nature effectués par la famille et la valeur locative estimée des logements occupés en propriété ou gratuitement.

Mode de relevé des prix
Les prix proviennent d'une enquête effectuée dans 72 capitales provinciales et environ 744 municipalités du pays. Le choix de ces dernières s'est fait en fonction de la disponibilité sur leurs marchés des produits et autres articles de l'indice. Les points de vente retenus l'ont été à cause de l'importance de leur chiffre d'affaires, de la stabilité et de l'assortiment de leurs stocks, de leur caractère plus ou moins permanent, de la collaboration qu'offre le commerçant, de leur commodité et de leur facilité d'accès. Le relevé des prix s'effectue auprès du Bureau of Agricultural Statistics pour les denrées alimentaires agricoles non transformées, et auprès du National Statistics Office pour les denrées alimentaires transformées, les boissons, le tabac, les transports, les services et tous les autres articles non alimentaires.

Les relevés sont effectués par des enquêteurs qui se déplacent en personne. Dans la région métropolitaine de Manille, les prix sont relevés le lundi, le mercredi et le vendredi de chaque semaine pour les articles alimentaires non transformés, le vendredi ou samedi de chaque semaine pour les articles alimentaires transformés, les boissons et le tabac. Les prix de tous les autres articles sont relevés deux fois par mois.

Seuls les prix prédominants du marché sont retenus dans le calcul de l'indice. N'entrent en ligne de compte ni les rabais ni les articles soldés.

Logement
Les données relatives aux loyers sont relevées mensuellement auprès des locataires. Les logements occupés par leur propriétaire ne sont pas compris.

Spécification des variétés
Les articles entrant dans l'indice font l'objet de spécifications très détaillées portant sur les éléments suivants: catégorie, marque, nom, taille, nombre, qualité, composition, poids et unité de mesure.

Substitution, changement de qualité, etc.
Les articles du panier restent les mêmes tant que l'année de base n'est pas modifiée. Toutefois, en cas de disparition d'un article sur le marché, on opère une substitution dans les conditions suivantes: (a) l'article de substitution doit être de la même qualité ou presque que l'article disparu; (b) l'article de substitution doit se situer dans la même catégorie ou au même niveau de prix que l'article disparu.

Articles saisonniers
Ils ne font l'objet d'aucun traitement spécial. En général, tous les articles du panier sont disponibles toute l'année.

Calcul
L'indice est calculé selon la formule de Laspeyres sous forme de moyenne arithmétique pondérée à base fixe, les coefficients de pondération correspondant à la période de base.

L'indice est un agrégat des indices provinciaux: ceux-ci sont d'abord combinés pour donner des indices régionaux, puis agrégés pour donner l'indice pour l'ensemble des Philippines. Tous ces indices sont pondérés.

Autres informations
Les indices sont publiés pour le mois courant et le mois précédent, pour les groupes principaux et pour les différentes régions du pays.

Organisation et publication
National Statistics Office: «Monthly Statistical Bulletin» (Manille).
idem: «Quarterly Journal of Philippine Statistics»
idem: «Philippine Yearbook»

POLOGNE

Dénomination officielle
Indice des prix à la consommation.

Portée
L'indice est calculé mensuellement et couvre plus de 90 pour cent de la population.

Base originale
La période de base de l'indice qui est utilisée dans les publications nationales est la période correspondante de l'année précédente considérée comme 100. L'Office central de la statistique de Pologne ramène ces indices à la base utilisée par le BIT dans ses publications.

Source des coefficients de pondération
Le système de pondération découle d'une enquête sur les dépenses des ménages.

Pondération et composition

Groupes principaux	Nombre d'articles	Pondération	Nombre approximatif de relevés de prix
Alimentation	390	41,8	...
Boissons alcoolisées	40	5,9	...
Produits autres qu'alimentaires	800	32,2	...
Services	220	20,1	...
Total	1 450	100,0	...

Dépenses de consommation des ménages
Pas disponible.

Mode de relevé des prix
Les prix sont relevés par les agents des services statistiques dans 307 régions comprenant 281 villes, au cours de la période allant du 1er au 25 de chaque mois. Les prix sont relevés dans 27 556 points de vente dont 45 pour cent sont des commerces de détail, 5 pour cent des établissements de restauration et 50 pour cent des prestataires de services. Les prix des produits alimentaires sont relevés trois fois par mois et ceux des produits non alimentaires, condiments, boissons alcoolisées et tabac deux fois par mois.

Logement
Pas disponible.

Spécification des variétés
Pas disponible.

Substitution, changement de qualité, etc.
Pas disponible.

Articles saisonniers
Les fluctuations saisonnières des prix des pommes de terre, des légumes et des fruits sont prises en compte en modifiant mensuellement les coefficients de pondération des produits appartenant à des groupes dont les coefficients sont constants.

Calcul
L'indice est calculé selon la formule de Laspeyres, sous forme de moyenne arithmétique pondérée à coefficient de pondération fixe.
Pour chaque article, un indice de prix individuel est calculé pour la période en cours, par rapport au prix moyen d'une période de base. Chacun des indices de prix d'un article déterminé, à l'échelle nationale, est calculé en tant que moyenne géométrique des indices de prix spécifiques de l'article dans chacune des régions respectives. Pour chaque groupe élémentaire, il est procédé au calcul d'un indice par groupe en tant que moyenne géométrique des indices de prix de chaque article d'un groupe déterminé (si le groupe ne comprend qu'un article, il s'agit de l'indice de prix de cet article).
Les indices des groupes des biens de consommation et services respectifs sont alors calculés. L'indice des prix définitif est alors obtenu par des agrégations et des pondérations successives.

Autres informations
L'Office central de la statistique publie également des indices de prix établis pour quatre groupes socio-économiques de la population: (1) salariés, (2) agriculteurs, (3) travailleurs agricoles et (4) retraités et bénéficiaires de pensions.

Organisation et publication
Glowny Urzad, Statystycznz (Office central de la statistique): «Bulletin statistique» (Varsovie).

POLYNESIE FRANCAISE

Dénomination officielle
Indice des prix de détail à la consommation familiale.

Portée
L'indice est calculé mensuellement et se rapporte aux ménages de toutes catégories résidant dans l'ensemble de la Polynésie française.

Base originale
Décembre 1980 = 100.

Source des coefficients de pondération
Les coefficients de pondération et les articles sélectionnés ont été déterminés sur la base des résultats d'une enquête nationale sur les dépenses des ménages, complétés par des statistiques d'importation. L'enquête a été effectuée au cours d'une période de trois mois et demi durant le second semestre de 1979, auprès d'un échantillon de 836 ménages de toutes catégories.

Pondération et composition

Groupes principaux	Nombre d'articles	Pondération	Nombre approximatif de relevés de prix
Alimentation	79	3 650	4 107
Produits manufacturés:			
Habillement, chaussure et linge de maison	28	900	362
Mobilier, ameublement et articles d'équipement ménager	25	922	508
Produits d'entretien	13	522	785
Véhicules	6	916	87
Articles de loisirs et de lecture	18	699	375
Combustible et éclairage	5	862	6
Tabac et autres	6	279	60
Services:			
Loyer, eau	2	445	25
Entretien et réparations	4	148	34
Soins personnels et médicaux	5	101	32
Transports et communications	11	390	46
Instruction, loisirs, autres	14	166	130
Total	216	10 000	6 557

Dépenses de consommation des ménages
Il a été tenu compte des biens produits par le ménage. Les achats d'occasion et le coût supplémentaire représenté par les achats à crédit sont exclus ainsi que les cotisations à la sécurité sociale, mais les primes d'assurance auto-moto sont incluses.

Mode de relevé des prix
Les prix pour la plupart des articles sont relevés mensuellement soit par des enquêteurs, soit au moyen d'enquêtes par téléphone, auprès de 326 points de vente au détail et prestataires de service. Les prix des denrées alimentaires et des produits manufacturés de grande consommation sont obtenus dans l'ensemble des 13 communes des Iles de Tahiti et de Moorea. Les prix des autres articles et services sont relevés dans la zone urbaine de l'île de Tahiti (Papeete, Faaa, Pirae, Arue). Les prix observés comprennent les impôts indirects.

Logement
Les données relatives au loyer sont obtenues quatre fois par an pour 22 logements.

Spécification des variétés
Une liste de 2 180 spécifications est utilisée pour le relevé des prix. Celles-ci sont très détaillées et indiquent le type, marque, poids, qualité et pays d'origine.

Substitution, changement de qualité, etc.
Lorsqu'un article disparaît du marché, il est remplacé par un article analogue et la méthode d'enchaînement est utilisée. On ne tient pas compte des changements mineurs de qualité. Si le changement de qualité est important, on utilise la méthode d'enchaînement.

Articles saisonniers
Les prix des fruits et légumes frais et du poisson sont relevés toutes les semaines sur les marchés de Papeete et Pirae et mensuellement dans les autres points de vente. On utilise une moyenne mobile de 12 mois pour le calcul final de l'indice.

Calcul
L'indice est calculé selon la formule de Laspeyres sous forme de moyenne arithmétique pondérée à base fixe, les coefficients de pondération correspondant à la période de base.

Autres informations
Une nouvelle série (base décembre 1988 = 100) est maintenant calculée mais les informations méthodologiques relatives à cette série n'étaient pas disponibles au BIT lors de la publication du présent Volume.

Organisation et publication
Institut territorial de la statistique: «Te Avei'a» (Papeete).
idem: «Journal officiel de la Polynésie française».

PORTO RICO

Dénomination officielle
Consumer Price Index for All Families (Indice des prix à la consommation pour toutes les familles).

Portée
L'indice est calculé mensuellement et porte sur tous les ménages urbains, dont ceux d'ouvriers, d'employés, de travailleurs indépendants, de retraités et de chômeurs. En sont exclus les familles d'agriculteurs, le personnel militaire et les pensionnaires d'institutions.

Base originale
1967 = 100.

Source des coefficients de pondération
La valeur des coefficients de pondération et le choix des articles résultent d'une enquête sur les dépenses des ménages effectuée en 1977 et portant sur 2 017 ménages (1 360 ménages urbains et 657 ménages ruraux). La pondération se fonde sur le budget des ménages urbains. Les articles retenus pour le calcul de l'indice l'ont été en raison de leur importance relative dans ce budget. Les coefficients de pondération ont été ajustés pour prendre en compte les changements de prix survenus entre la période de l'enquête et l'année 1979.

Pondération et composition

Groupes principaux	Nombre d'articles	Pondération	Nombre approximatif de relevés de prix (a)
Alimentation	110	30,40	366
Logement:			
Loyer	1	2,00	(b)
Dépenses de logement dans les hôtels	1	0,71	25
Logements occupés par leur propriétaire	4	7,02	27
Mobilier et dépenses de ménage	42	9,46	172
Combustible et éclairage	5	5,11	8
Habillement et chaussure	37	10,00	310
Transports	12	17,20	318
Soins médicaux	19	5,10	165
Instruction et loisirs	11	4,60	38
Autres biens et services	16	8,40	71
Total	258	100,00	1 500

Remarque: (a) Nombre d'établissements. (b) 2 000 logements loués.

Dépenses de consommation des ménages
Les dépenses de consommation prises en compte pour le calcul de l'indice visent tous les biens et services que la population de référence acquiert pour sa consommation. Elles comprennent les primes d'assurance couvrant un bien ou un service spécifique (véhicules, assurances des locataires ou propriétaires et intérêts des emprunts hypothécaires). En sont exclus les primes d'assurance-vie, l'impôt sur le revenu et l'impôt sur la propriété personnelle.

Mode de relevé des prix
Les prix sont relevés sur un échantillon de 1 500 commerces de détail et prestataires de services de 11 municipalités. Les relevés sont effectués mensuellement pour la plupart des services et tous les trimestres pour les dépenses ci-après: logement, services juridiques, cordonnerie, plomberie, coiffure, soins médicaux, transports, etc. Les prix retenus pour le calcul de l'indice sont les prix payés régulièrement par le public. Les prix des articles soldés sont également relevés.

Logement
Les dépenses de logement proprement dites comprennent le loyer, la location de logements en hôtel et les dépenses de logement de l'habitat en propriété. Les données relatives au loyer sont relevées trimestriellement sur un échantillon de 2 343 habitations en location. Pour l'habitat en propriété, les données relevées concernent les intérêts sur les emprunts hypothécaires, les réparations et l'entretien.

Spécification des variétés
Les articles dont les prix sont à relever sont décrits dans leurs grandes lignes. Pour représenter un article donné on peut choisir des marques différentes d'un point de vente à l'autre, mais, dans un point de vente donné, le relevé de prix doit porter sur la même marque mois après mois. Pour ce qui est de l'article lui-même, il est choisi en fonction des informations fournies sur le chiffre d'affaires.

Substitution, changement de qualité, etc.
Lorsqu'un article n'est plus disponible, il est remplacé par un article analogue.

Articles saisonniers
Très peu d'articles saisonniers sont inclus dans l'indice. Les prix de certains fruits frais sont relevés en saison, lorsqu'ils sont disponibles, et ne font l'objet d'aucun ajustement.

Calcul
L'indice est calculé selon la formule de Laspeyres, sous forme de moyenne arithmétique pondérée à base fixe, les coefficients de pondération correspondant à l'année 1979. L'indice a fait l'objet d'un enchaînement en décembre 1979, la base 1967 = 100.

Le rapport de prix pour chaque article est calculé en divisant le prix moyen de la période en cours par le prix moyen de la période précédente. Le prix moyen d'un article est la moyenne arithmétique simple de tous les relevés de prix obtenus pour cet article.

Autres informations
Un indice des prix pour les familles d'ouvriers (base 1967 = 100) est également établi et publié.

Organisation et publication
Departamento del Trabajo y recursos humanos: «Indice de precios al consumidor para todas las familias en Puerto Rico» (San Juan).
idem: «Importancia relativa de los bienes y servicios de consumo en el índice de precios al consumidor para todas las familias en Puerto Rico» (juin 1980).
idem: «Artículos y servicios cuyos precios se recopilan para el índice de precios al consumidor de todas las familias y el revisado de familias obreras en Puerto Rico» (septembre 1980).

PORTUGAL

Dénomination officielle
Indice de preços no consumidor - series A - Continente General (Indice des prix à la consommation - série A - Continent Général).

Portée
L'indice est calculé mensuellement et porte sur l'ensemble des ménages urbains et ruraux.

Base originale
1983 = 100.

Source des coefficients de pondération
Les coefficients de pondération et les articles sélectionnés ont été déterminés sur la base des résultats d'une enquête sur les dépenses des ménages effectuée de mars 1980 à février 1981

auprès d'un échantillon aléatoire de 8 000 ménages. Les pondérations ont été ajustées pour tenir compte de l'évolution des prix entre la période de l'enquête et 1983.

Pondération et composition

Groupes principaux	Nombre d'articles	Pondération	Nombre approximatif de relevés de prix
Alimentation	188	4 606	11 461
Habillement et chaussure	73	1 014	5 980
Loyer	...	(515)	...
Logement	75	1 261	3 876
Soins médicaux	69	263	748
Transports et communications	41	1 382	847
Instruction et loisirs	29	412	1 195
Tabac	5	128	62
Autres biens et services	31	419	1 286
Total	511	10 000	25 455

Dépenses de consommation des ménages
Les biens produits par les ménages pour leur propre consommation et le revenu en nature sont inclus. Sont exclus les impôts directs, les contributions ou les cotisations, excepté lorsque l'on peut les considérer comme paiement d'un service, comme par exemple les redevances de télévision ou de radio.

Mode de relevé des prix
Les prix des denrées alimentaires, du tabac et des produits d'utilisation courante sont relevés mensuellement, lors de la dernière semaine complète du mois. Les prix des autres articles ou services sont recueillis trimestriellement, en constituant trois échantillons fragmentés pour lesquels on relève les prix mensuellement à tour de rôle. Les données relatives à l'instruction sont obtenues annuellement, et les tarifs des biens et services fixés officiellement sont recueillis lorsqu'il y a modification des tarifs. Les prix sont relevés auprès de 4 800 marchés, supermarchés, points de vente au détail et prestataires de services dans 25 agglomérations. Les prix relevés sont ceux directement payés dans le point de vente. On ne tient pas compte des prix spéciaux et des prix de promotion.

Logement
Les dépenses relatives au loyer ne sont pas prises en compte pour le calcul mensuel de l'indice, bien que ce poste figure dans la détermination des coefficients de pondération. Les données relatives au loyer sont relevées par rotation au cours des deuxième et troisième trimestres de chaque année pour 32 000 logements. L'indice du loyer est incorporé une fois par année dans l'indice annuel.

Spécification des variétés
Les caractéristiques des biens et services sont décrites le plus complètement possible en ce qui concerne la qualité et les autres caractéristiques physiques afin que les mêmes articles soient relevés dans tous les établissements.

Substitution, changement de qualité, etc.
Lorsqu'il y a un changement de quantité, on calcule un coefficient d'ajustement proportionnel. Lors d'un changement de qualité on estime le prix au moyen d'un coefficient de qualité. Si un article change de quantité et de qualité simultanément on utilise une méthode économétrique. Lorsqu'un nouvel article est introduit dans l'indice, on estime le prix de base en se référant à l'évolution des prix d'articles similaires.

Articles saisonniers
Il est tenu compte des fluctuations saisonnières des prix des fruits et légumes frais en variant les articles et leur coefficient de pondération à l'intérieur de paniers mensuels dont le coefficient de pondération d'ensemble demeure constant et en utilisant une moyenne mobile de 12 mois pour le calcul final de l'indice.

Calcul
L'indice est calculé selon la formule de Laspeyres, sous forme de moyenne arithmétique pondérée à base fixe, les coefficients de pondération correspondant à la période de base.
Le rapport de prix pour chaque article est calculé en divisant le prix moyen de la période courante par le prix moyen de la période de base. L'indice général pour le continent est une moyenne arithmétique pondérée d'indices relatifs à la population de chaque agglomération selon le recensement de 1981.

Autres informations
La série «A»: Continent Général publiée par le BIT exclut le loyer; la moyenne annuelle y compris le loyer est publiée par l'Instituto Nacional de Estatística dans «Anuário Estatístico», Lisbonne. La série «B» se réfère à la population urbaine de Lisbonne et à celle de Porto. Une nouvelle série pour le continent et une série nationale (base 1991 = 100) sont maintenant calculées mais les informations méthodologiques relatives à ces séries n'étaient pas disponibles au BIT lors de la publication du présent Volume.

Organisation et publication
Instituto Nacional de Estatística: «Anuário Estatístico», Lisbonne.

QATAR

Dénomination officielle
Consumer Price Index Number (Indice des prix à la consommation)

Portée
L'indice est calculé mensuellement et porte sur tous les ménages, ressortissants ou non du Qatar.

Base originale
1988 = 100.

Source des coefficients de pondération
Les coefficients de pondération et les articles sélectionnés ont été déterminés sur la base des résultats d'une enquête sur les dépenses des ménages effectuée en 1988 dans l'Etat du Qatar auprès d'un échantillon de ménages, ressortissants ou non du Qatar.

Pondération et composition

Groupes principaux	Nombre d'articles	Pondération	Nombre approximatif de relevés de prix
Alimentation et tabac	...	286,8	...
Habillement et chaussure	...	106,3	...
Logement:			
Loyer	...	78,5	...
Entretien	...	23,2	...
Combustible, électricité et eau	...	22,3	...
Mobilier et ameublement	...	125,8	...
Transports et communications	...	193,3	...
Soins médicaux	...	12,3	...
Instruction et loisirs	...	76,4	...
Divers biens et services	...	75,1	...
Total	...	1 000,0	...

Dépenses de consommation des ménages
Pas disponible.

Mode de relevé des prix
Pas disponible.

Logement
Pas disponible.

Spécification des variétés
Pas disponible.

Substitution, changement de qualité, etc.
Pas disponible.

Articles saisonniers
Pas disponible.

Calcul
L'indice est calculé selon la formule de Laspeyres sous forme de moyenne arithmétique pondérée à base fixe, les coefficients de pondération correspondant à la période de base.

Organisation et publication
Central Statistical Organisation: «Annual Statistical Abstract».
idem: «Monthly Survey on Retail and Consumer Prices».

REUNION

Dénomination officielle
Indice des prix à la consommation des ménages urbains de condition moyenne.

Portée
L'indice est calculé mensuellement et se rapporte aux ménages de Saint-Denis de toute taille et de condition moyenne, dont le chef est ouvrier ou employé des secteurs privé ou public.

Base originale
1978 = 100.

Source des coefficients de pondération
La valeur des coefficients de pondération et le choix des articles résultent d'une enquête sur les dépenses des ménages effectuée en 1986 et 1987 couvrant toute la population de la Réunion. Seule la consommation des ménages urbains dont le chef est ouvrier ou employé a été retenue pour déterminer les coefficients de pondération.

Pondération et composition

Groupes principaux	Nombre d'articles	Pondération	Nombre approximatif de relevés de prix
Alimentation	87	27,93	...
Habillement et chaussure	49	8,60	...
Combustible et éclairage	6	7,16	...
Loyer	1	6,27	...
Autres produits manufacturés (biens d'équipement de ménage, produits d'entretien, etc.)	75	35,32	...
Autres services (transports, hygiène et soins médicaux, etc.)	50	14,72	...
Total	268	100,00	8 000

Dépenses de consommation des ménages
Les dépenses de consommation prises en compte dans le calcul de l'indice correspondent à la quasi-totalité des achats de biens et services importants effectués par les ménages de référence pour leur consommation. Elles comprennent les soins médicaux et les réparations de véhicules pour la valeur réellement payée par les ménages ainsi que les primes d'assurances automobiles. Elles excluent les impôts directs, les dépenses de construction considérées comme investissement, l'autoconsommation (valeur des services des logements occupés par leur propriétaire et produits alimentaires provenant des jardins et élevages familiaux), les avantages en nature perçus par les ménages qui sont aussi des dépenses qui ne seraient pas de consommation au sens des comptes économiques.

Mode de relevé des prix
Les prix sont relevés par des enquêteurs de l'INSEE-Direction Régionale de la Réunion, auprès de 224 points de vente au détail et prestataires de service à Saint-Denis. Les prix sont ceux réellement pratiqués et ne tiennent pas compte des soldes. Les prix pour la viande, les oeufs, les fruits et légumes frais sont relevés chaque semaine; les prix pour les loyers sont recueillis trimestriellement et ceux de tous les autres biens et services mensuellement.

Les points de vente ont été déterminés en tenant compte des divers quartiers de l'agglomération de Saint-Denis, des différentes formes de commerce: supermarchés, commerçants indépendants, marchés, etc., et des habitudes d'achat des consommateurs.

Logement
Les données relatives au loyer sont obtenues à partir d'une enquête trimestrielle portant sur un échantillon de 284 logements en location.

Spécification des variétés
La liste des variétés peut changer en fonction des modifications qui interviendraient dans les habitudes de consommation, lesquelles peuvent être plus fréquentes dans le domaine alimentaire. Le choix se fait en fonction de leur représentativité dans le cadre des 268 postes de dépenses.

Substitution, changement de qualité, etc.
Trois méthodes sont utilisées quand il y a modification, mutation, disparition ou apparition de produits sur le marché: (i) lorsque le nouveau produit ne diffère de l'ancien que par la quantité, on considère que les prix sont proportionnels aux quantités; (ii) si cette hypothèse est trop hasardeuse, on substitue un produit voisin en admettant que le nouveau produit, s'il avait existé à la période de base, aurait subi la même évolution de prix que le produit défaillant; (iii) en dernier lieu, l'enquêteur apprécie sur place la différence de prix par rapport au changement de qualité.

Articles saisonniers
Il est tenu compte des fluctuations saisonnières des fruits et légumes frais en variant la composition mensuelle des articles du sous-groupe, dont le coefficient de pondération d'ensemble demeure constant. L'indice compare le coût du panier du mois courant à celui du mois correspondant de l'année de base. Le prix de base pour une variété est celui de la moyenne annuelle pondérée de l'année précédente qu'on applique pour chaque mois.

Calcul
Depuis janvier 1990, l'indice est un indice-chaîne dont les pondérations sont révisées chaque année civile. L'indice de chaque mois est calculé d'abord sur la base 100 en décembre de l'année précédente; l'indice ainsi obtenu est ensuite calculé, par raccord, à la base 100 en 1978 (indice-chaîne de Laspeyres).

L'indice pour un article est obtenu en utilisant des rapports de prix de la période courante et de la période de base. Des rapports de prix moyens sont calculés pour des articles ayant des variétés homogènes, et des moyennes des rapports de prix sont utilisées pour les articles comportant des variétés hétérogènes.

Organisation et publication
INSEE, Direction Régionale de la Réunion: «Bulletin de statistiques» (Saint-Denis).

idem: «L'indice des prix à la consommation des ménages urbains de condition moyenne» (document no. 33, octobre 1980).

ROUMANIE

Dénomination officielle
Indice des prix à la consommation de la population.

Portée
L'indice est calculé mensuellement et porte sur les ménages dont le chef est employé, agriculteur ou retraité dans l'ensemble du pays.

Base originale
Octobre 1990 = 100.

Source des coefficients de pondération
Les coefficients de pondération et les articles sélectionnés ont été déterminés sur la base des résultats d'une enquête sur les dépenses des ménages effectuée de janvier à décembre 1990 auprès de 5 900 ménages d'employés, 2 700 ménages d'agriculteurs et 400 ménages de retraités.

Pondération et composition

Groupes principaux	Nombre d'articles	Pondération	Nombre approximatif de relevés de prix
Alimentation	79	40,5	...
Produits non alimentaires	111	40,3	...
Services	51	19,2	...
Total	241	100,0	...

Dépenses de consommation des ménages
Les dépenses de consommation des ménages utilisées pour établir les coefficients se réfèrent aux articles et services acquis des secteurs public, coopératif, privé ou mixte. Il n'est pas tenu compte de l'autoconsommation des biens et services produits par les ménages, les loyers imputés pour les logements occupés par leur propriétaire, les impôts, taxes, amendes, jeux de fortune, intérêts payés pour les crédits, les cotisations à la sécurité sociale, les emprunts et les remises de fonds.

Mode de relevé des prix
Les prix sont relevés par des enquêteurs sur des marchés et foires, auprès de points de vente au détail, de coopératives et de prestataires de services. Les prix des denrées alimentaires sont relevés sur les marchés les 5, 15 et 25 de chaque mois. Les données concernant le loyer, l'électricité, le gaz, l'eau, le chauffage, les postes, les télécommunications et les abonnements de transports sont des tarifs officiels et sont obtenus une fois par mois. On tient compte des rabais, des prix du marché libre pour les articles ayant aussi un prix officiel et des prix à l'importation lorsque le volume des ventes est important.

Logement
Les données relatives au loyer sont obtenues mensuellement pour des logements propriété d'état. Les logements occupés par leur propriétaire ne sont pas pris en compte dans l'indice.

Spécification des variétés
Les spécifications sont détaillées et décrivent les caractéristiques techniques etc.

Substitution, changement de qualité, etc.
Lorsqu'un article change de qualité, disparaît ou si un nouvel article apparaît sur le marché, un prix de base est estimé en tenant compte de l'évolution des prix des articles du même sous-groupe.

Articles saisonniers
Pour les articles saisonniers tels que fruits, légumes et laine, on utilise des paniers mensuels dont les coefficients de pondération d'ensemble demeurent constants.

Calcul
L'indice est calculé selon la formule de Laspeyres sous forme de moyenne arithmétique pondérée à base fixe, les coefficients de pondération correspondant à la période de base. L'indice pour un article est obtenu en utilisant les rapports de prix de la période courante et de la période de base. Les prix moyens sont des moyennes arithmétiques simples de tous les relevés de prix.

Organisation et publication
Commission nationale de statistique, Division des statistiques des prix et tarifs: «Bulletin statistique des prix» (Bucarest).
idem: «La méthodologie de construction de l'indice des prix à la consommation de la population».

ROYAUME-UNI

Dénomination officielle
Retail Prices Index (Indice des prix de détail).

Portée
L'indice est calculé mensuellement et porte sur les biens et services acquis par tous les ménages, à l'exception de ceux qui se situent dans la tranche de 4 pour cent la plus élevée de la distribution du revenu, et des ménages de retraités dont au minimum les trois quarts du revenu proviennent de prestations de l'Etat. L'indice couvre l'ensemble du Royaume-Uni.

Base originale
Janvier 1987 = 100.

Source des coefficients de pondération
La valeur des coefficients de pondération et le choix des articles sont révisés au début de février de chaque année. Les derniers résultats disponibles de l'enquête sur les dépenses des ménages sont utilisés à cet effet. En général, les données relatives à l'année prenant fin en juin de l'année précédente sont utilisées pour calculer les coefficients de pondération devant être appliqués à partir de février de l'année suivante. Il est procédé à des ajustements afin de tenir compte du laps de temps qui s'écoule lors de la mise en application des nouveaux coefficients de pondération à partir de l'hypothèse selon laquelle les dépenses de certaines catégories de biens et services auront changé conformément au mouvement des prix les concernant (il n'est tenu compte d'aucune augmentation ou diminution du volume de consommation).

L'enquête couvre tous les types de ménages privés du Royaume-Uni. Il s'agit d'une enquête permanente portant sur plus de 7 000 ménages effectuée au cours d'une année, sélectionnés de telle manière que chaque ménage dispose d'une chance égale de figurer dans l'enquête. Chaque ménage procède au relevé des dépenses qu'il effectue sur une période de deux semaines et fournit également des informations portant sur une période plus étendue en ce qui concerne des paiements relativement peu fréquents.

Le nombre d'articles et les coefficients de pondération utilisés en 1992 sont présentés dans le tableau.

Dépenses de consommation des ménages
Les dépenses de consommation comprennent les revenus en nature, les coûts de la propriété immobilière, la reprise d'articles usagés et le paiement partiel de nouveaux articles, les honoraires pour l'obtention de patentes, le paiement de primes d'assurances lié à des biens de consommation spécifiques et les soins de santé. Sont exclus l'impôt sur le revenu et autres impôts directs, les primes d'assurance-vie, les envois de fonds, les dons et versements analogues, la cotisation aux assurances sociales et aux fonds de retraite, l'épargne ainsi que les investissements et frais de crédit.

Mode de relevé des prix
Les 180 localités où il est procédé à des relevés de prix sont choisies comme constituant un échantillon représentatif de l'en-

Pondération et composition

Groupes principaux	Nombre d'articles	Pondération	Nombre approximatif de relevés de prix
Alimentation	127	152	...
Repas pris au dehors	4	47	...
Boissons alcooliques	9	80	...
Tabacs	4	36	...
Logement:			
Loyer	2	35	...
Paiement des intérêts hypothécaires, des logements occupés en propriété, assurance-logements, etc.	2	72	...
Réparation et entretien	12	25	...
Impôts et eau	4	40	...
Combustible et éclairage	11	47	...
Biens durables et services	57	125	...
Habillement et chaussure	66	59	...
Transports et véhicules	17	163	...
Biens divers	69	75	...
Services	10	44	...
Total	394	1 000	130 000

semble du pays. Dans chaque zone, un enquêteur familiarisé avec le commerce local jouit d'une grande latitude dans le choix des points de vente types, et dispose de directives étendues en vue d'assurer la représentation appropriée de chaque type de points de vente.

- Les prix sont relevés mensuellement pour tous les biens et la plupart des services.
- L'indice porte sur un seul jour chaque mois (généralement, mais pas forcément, le deuxième mardi du mois). Le jour où il est procédé au relevé des prix, la plupart des points de vente au détail utilisés à cet effet reçoivent la visite des agents du Central Statistical Office. Pour des grandes chaînes de supermarchés dont tous les points de vente pratiquent les mêmes prix, les agents obtiennent des listes de prix auprès du siège. En ce qui concerne l'électricité, le gaz, les tarifs des transports publics, téléphoniques et postaux, les informations sont obtenues auprès du siège de l'organisme intéressé.
- Une organisation existe déjà sur le terrain à d'autres fins. C'est ainsi que des données peuvent être obtenues auprès des Unemployment Benefit Offices (Bureaux de prestations de chômage) qui envoient chaque mois les formulaires à un point central.
- Les prix utilisés pour l'indice sont nets d'escompte à condition que les articles soient mis à la disposition de tous les clients potentiels, et/ou que le vendeur en assure le financement.
- Les prix de soldes sont considérés comme des réductions à moins qu'il ne s'agisse d'articles d'une qualité inférieure à celle d'articles dont les prix ont été préalablement relevés.
- Il n'est pas tenu compte des articles achetés en location-vente et à crédit.
- L'indice couvre, en principe, les articles d'occasion et les prix de reprise d'articles. Cependant, dans la pratique, les seuls prix d'occasion utilisés concernent les automobiles.
- Aucune distinction n'est établie en ce qui concerne les articles d'importation.
- Les articles à prix fixe (par exemple journaux, frais postaux, etc.) font l'objet de relevés séparés obtenus auprès d'un point central.
- Des relevés portant sur des articles à prix variables sont effectués auprès de nombreux points de vente au détail sur l'ensemble du Royaume-Uni - 130 000 prix environ figurent sur une liste qui couvrant 600 articles. Le nombre des estimations des articles spécifiques est en général conforme à leur coefficient de pondération spécifique.

Logement
L'indice porte sur tous les types de logements pouvant être habituellement loués. Dans la plupart des cas, ils sont la propriété des pouvoirs publics locaux qui ne procèdent à la révision de leur loyer qu'en avril et en octobre-novembre, les informations pertinentes étant rassemblées à ce moment au moyen d'enquêtes par correspondance. L'indicateur de prix est constitué par le loyer moyen sans qu'il soit tenu compte d'aucune déduction ou allocation. Les paiements d'intérêts hypothécaires figurent dans l'indice en tant qu'indicateurs pour les frais de logement (autres qu'impôts, réparation, etc. qui fi-

gurent séparément) des personnes qui les occupent en propriété.

Spécification des variétés
Les spécifications varient entre les produits et selon les années. Certaines marques et spécifications figurent généralement dans l'indice. Les enquêteurs locaux choisissent la marque d'un article déterminé, le plus représentatif dans chacun des points de vente où ils se rendent.

Substitution, changement de qualité, etc.
Les enquêteurs ont la possibilité de notifier les changements qui surviennent dans la qualité des articles. Il est tenu compte de ces changements dans la mesure du possible lors de l'élaboration de l'indice. Il est procédé chaque année à un nouvel examen des articles afin de prendre en compte les changements survenus dans les goûts et l'attitude des consommateurs.

Articles saisonniers
Les prix des articles saisonniers sont relevés lorsqu'ils sont disponibles. En général, les coefficients de pondération des articles saisonniers ne subissent pas de variations d'un mois à l'autre. Néanmoins, les coefficients de pondération relatifs des différentes variétés de fruits et de légumes frais varient au cours de l'année (dans les limites d'un coefficient de pondération total fixé pour les fruits et légumes frais) de manière à tenir compte des structures de consommation.

Calcul
L'indice est un indice-chaîne selon la formule de Laspeyres, avec enchaînement annuel en janvier. Les indices relatifs à chacune des variétés de fruits et de légumes frais sont combinés en utilisant une formule de type Paasche. Selon l'article, il est procédé au calcul de moyennes de prix ou de rapports de prix. Les prix manquants ou inutilisables sont remplacés par des estimations fondées sur l'hypothèse selon laquelle les prix réels auront changé en même temps que ceux des articles sur lesquels des données fiables ont été relevées autre part. L'indice est calculé directement.

Autres informations
Depuis 1989, le Central Statistical Office est responsable de la collecte des données relatives aux prix courants et du calcul de l'indice.
Un «Tax and Price Index» (Indice des taxes et des prix) est également calculé et publié par le Central Statistical Office.

Organisation et publication
Central Statistical Office: «Monthly Digest of Statistics» (Londres).
Department of Employment: «Employment Gazette».
idem: «A short guide to the Retail Price Index», publié en août 1987 comme numéro du «Employment Gazette».

RWANDA (KIGALI)

Dénomination officielle
Indice des prix à la consommation.

Portée
L'indice est calculé mensuellement et porte sur les ménages de salariés des secteurs public, para-public et privé de la circonscription urbaine de Kigali.

Base originale
Mars-juin 1982 = 100.

Source des coefficients de pondération
Les coefficients de pondération et les articles sélectionnés ont été déterminés sur la base des résultats d'une enquête sur les dépenses des ménages effectuée de mars à juin 1982 auprès de salariés des secteurs public, para-public et privé de la circonscription urbaine de Kigali, dont le revenu mensuel se situait entre 5 000 et 100 000 Francs rwandais lors de l'enquête.

Dépenses de consommation des ménages
Les dépenses de consommation comprennent: les dépenses monétaires de consommation, les cadeaux donnés en nature, les biens échangés par troc et l'autoconsommation (c'est-à-dire la production du ménage pour sa propre consommation). Cette dernière a été prise en compte de façon indirecte parce qu'elle ne pouvait pas être isolée à la fin de l'enquête, le but de celle-ci n'étant pas de déterminer la consommation finale des ménages mais les coefficients de pondération des divers produits de l'indice.

Pondération et composition

Groupes principaux	Nombre d'articles	Pondération	Nombre approximatif de relevés de prix
Tous produits:			
Alimentation	105	34,90	...
Boissons et tabac	22	9,30	...
Habillement et chaussure	71	11,35	...
Entretien ménager	36	8,40	...
Soins médicaux	37	1,70	...
Autres soins et hygiène	55	3,55	...
Logement	59	13,20	...
Transports	20	10,30	...
Distractions et loisirs	12	1,20	...
Divers	24	6,10	...
Total	441	100,00	...

Les revenus en nature ont été pris en compte dans la comptabilisation du revenu global des ménages enquêtés et concernent notamment le logement gratuit, l'électricité et l'eau gratuites et le transport gratuit.

Les logements en propriété, la reprise de biens usagés et les arrhes pour l'achat de biens neufs n'ont pas été pris en compte lors de l'enquête. De même les impôts sur le revenu et autres impôts directs ainsi que les cotisations d'assurances sociales et de caisses de pensions, bien que constituant des charges des ménages n'ont pas été pris en compte car ce ne sont pas des achats de consommation et il est en outre difficile, sinon impossible, d'y discerner des prix. Les versements au titre d'assurances sur la vie ont été exclus de l'indice à défaut de considérer le service des assurances pour éviter des doubles comptes. Au niveau des soins médicaux, les frais d'hospitalisation ne figurent pas dans l'indice mensuel des prix à la consommation en raison du manque d'information rapide sur les prix correspondants; seuls les coûts des consultations médicales auprès des services médicaux public et privé (de même que les médicaments les plus couramment consommés) ont été pris en compte lors de l'enquête. L'envoi de fonds, dons et versements similaires n'ont pas été pris en compte puisque ne donnant pas lieu à des prix. Les achats de biens durables, les achats à crédit et les achats d'occasion ont été pris en compte dans les dépenses de consommation des ménages enquêtés.

Mode de relevé des prix
Les prix sont relevés deux fois par mois par des enquêteurs auprès de tous les marchés et les points de vente au détail les plus représentatifs de la circonscription urbaine de Kigali. Les prix retenus dans le calcul de l'indice sont les prix effectivement payés par les consommateurs.
Les tarifs concernant l'électricité, le gaz, l'eau, les consultations médicales, les frais de scolarité et les frais de transports et communications sont fixés par le Gouvernement et relevés lorsque les prix changent.

Logement
Les données relatives au loyer sont obtenues chaque mois pour quatre logements loués dont deux logements à deux chambres sans électricité et deux logements à deux chambres avec électricité. Les logements occupés par leur propriétaire ne sont pas pris en compte.

Spécification des variétés
Les spécifications portent sur les articles importés, mixtes ou locaux. Les produits mixtes désignent les produits traités localement mais à composante importée (matières premières importées).

Substitution, changement de qualité, etc.
Lorsque le produit qui subit un changement de qualité peut être considéré comme nouveau et s'il fait disparaître l'ancien produit, on inclut le nouveau produit dans les relevés et on calcule un prix de base fictif en lui appliquant le pourcentage d'augmentation de l'ancien produit.

Articles saisonniers
Lorsqu'un article saisonnier n'est pas disponible sur le marché, son prix est maintenu pendant trois mois au maximum.

Calcul
L'indice est calculé selon la formule de Laspeyres sous forme de moyenne arithmétique pondérée à base fixe, les coefficients de pondération correspondant à la période de base.

Organisation et publication
Banque Nationale du Rwanda: «Bulletin de la Banque Nationale du Rwanda» (Kigali).
idem: «Rapport annuel sur l'évolution économique et monétaire du Rwanda».

SAINTE-HELENE

Dénomination officielle
Retail Price Index (Indice des prix de détail).

Portée
L'indice est calculé tous les trimestres et porte sur tous les ménages habitant l'ensemble de l'île.

Base originale
Novembre 1987 = 100.

Source des coefficients de pondération
La valeur des coefficients de pondération et le choix des articles résultent d'une enquête sur les dépenses des ménages effectuée en deux étapes: la première a été menée en octobre-novembre 1987 auprès d'un échantillon de 84 ménages, la seconde en avril-mai 1988 auprès d'un échantillon de 94 ménages. Les dépenses moyennes hebdomadaires par ménage étaient d'environ 74 livres à l'époque de l'enquête. Les résultats ont été contrôlés à l'aide de données provenant des statistiques relatives aux importations afin de corriger les coefficients de pondération.

Pondération et composition

Groupes principaux	Nombre d'articles	Pondération	Nombre approximatif de relevés de prix
Alimentation	75	44,6	75
Alcool et tabac	7	10,1	7
Logement (y c. loyers et intérêts)	3	5,6	3
Combustible et éclairage	5	5,1	5
Habillement et chaussures	15	5,8	15
Articles de ménage	13	7,3	13
Transports	10	11,6	10
Biens divers	15	7,9	15
Services	6	2,0	6
Total	149	100,0	149

Dépenses de consommation des ménages
Sont inclus les frais d'examen du permis de conduire, les primes d'assurance pour les automobiles ainsi que le remboursement des prêts immobiliers. En revanche, les primes d'assurance-vie sont exclues de l'indice.

Mode de relevé des prix
Les prix sont relevés par deux agents de l'Economic and Statistics Unit opérant pendant deux jours ouvrables, auprès de sept points de vente situés à Jamestown, aux alentours du 20 des mois de février, mai, août et novembre. L'approvisionnement de Sainte-Hélène dépend de l'arrivée du navire de liaison, qui a lieu toutes les six semaines environ. Si les prix sont relevés avant l'arrivée du navire (moins d'une semaine), la date du relevé est reportée au moment où les biens sont disponibles sur le marché. Les prix soumis au contrôle des autorités, tels ceux de l'eau et de l'électricité, ainsi que les impôts fonciers et les prix de certains matériaux de construction sont obtenus au moyen d'appels téléphoniques effectués auprès des services gouvernementaux. Les prix de soldes et de décompte sont pris en considération.

Logement
Les loyers hebdomadaires des logements de trois pièces en propriété publique sont relevés tous les trimestres. Les logements occupés par leur propriétaire ne font l'objet d'aucun traitement spécifique.

Spécification des variétés
Les spécifications portent sur le type, la taille, la marque et le point d'achat des articles. Les formulaires de relevé des prix restent en vigueur une année durant, ce qui permet de déterminer aisément les écarts de grande importance.

Substitution, changement de qualité, etc.
Lorsqu'un article n'est plus disponible sur le marché, un article similaire lui est substitué.

Articles saisonniers
Les prix du marché ne font l'objet d'aucun ajustement.

Calcul
L'indice est calculé selon la formule de Laspeyres sous forme de moyenne arithmétique pondérée à base fixe, les coefficients de pondération correspondant à la période de base.

Autres informations
Des indices par sous-groupe sont publiés pour l'alimentation, l'alcool et le tabac, le combustible et l'éclairage, l'habillement, les articles de ménage, le transport, les biens et services divers. Un indice pour les revenus modestes est également calculé, mais non publié.

Organisation et publication
Economic and Statistics Unit: «Quarterly Statistical Review» (Jamestown).
idem: «Statistical News».

SAINTE-LUCIE

Dénomination officielle
Consumer Price Index (Indice des prix à la consommation).

Portée
L'indice est calculé mensuellement et porte sur les ménages situés en zones urbaine, suburbaine et rurale.

Base originale
Avril 1984 = 100.

Source des coefficients de pondération
Les coefficients de pondération ont été déterminés sur la base des résultats d'enquêtes relatives aux dépenses des ménages, effectuées au cours de la période de septembre à novembre 1982 dans la zone administrative de Castries, capitale de Sainte-Lucie, auprès d'un échantillon de 170 ménages urbains, 157 ménages suburbains et 154 ménages ruraux. Il n'a été procédé à aucun ajustement des coefficients de pondération visant à prendre en compte les changements de prix survenus entre la période de l'enquête et la période de base.

Pondération et composition

Groupes principaux	Nombre d'articles	Pondération	Nombre approximatif de relevés de prix
Alimentation	77	467,51	...
Boissons et tabac	5	28,17	...
Habillement et chaussure	16	64,97	...
Logement	7	135,34	...
Combustible et éclairage	4	44,95	...
Mobilier et dépenses de ménage	11	57,71	...
Soins médicaux	6	22,78	...
Transports et communications	10	63,48	...
Loisirs	6	32,36	...
Divers	26	82,73	...
Total	168	1 000,00	...

Dépenses de consommation des ménages
Le système de classification est conforme à celui du SCN en matière de dépenses de consommation finale des ménages.

Mode de relevé des prix
Des enquêteurs procèdent mensuellement, le deuxième mardi de chaque mois, au relevé des prix auprès de supermarchés, de points de vente au détail et de prestataires de services.

Les tarifs de l'électricité sont obtenus au moyen de questionnaires adressés par la poste. Les tarifs du téléphone et de l'eau sont relevés à la suite d'appels téléphoniques et ceux des autres services au moyen de visites personnelles. Le relevé du prix, de la marque, de la qualité, de l'unité, etc., des différents articles, est obtenu par les enquêteurs de l'Office des Statistiques auprès de points de vente au détail. Les prix de ces «articles du panier» ont été relevés pendant quatre mois et les points de vente sélectionnés ont été choisis à partir de ces données.

Logement
Les données relatives au loyer des maisons sont relevées tous les six mois. Il n'est pas tenu compte dans l'indice des logements occupés en propriété.

Spécification des variétés
Chaque article fait l'objet de spécifications détaillées en ce qui concerne l'unité, la marque, la qualité etc.

Substitution, changement de qualité, etc.
Lorsqu'un article disparaît du marché, il est remplacé par un

autre article. Le coefficient de pondération demeure le même mais le prix de base est ajusté.

Articles saisonniers
Les articles saisonniers ne sont pas inclus dans l'indice.

Calcul
L'indice est calculé selon la formule de Laspeyres sous forme de moyenne arithmétique pondérée à base fixe, les coefficients de pondération correspondant à la période septembre-novembre 1982.

Autres informations
L'indice est calculé par le Government Statistical Department, Castries.

Organisation et publication
Government Printer: «The St. Lucia Gazette» (Castries).

SAINT-MARIN

Dénomination officielle
Consumer Price Index (Indice des prix à la consommation).

Portée
L'indice est calculé mensuellement et porte sur les ménages d'ouvriers et d'employés habitant Saint-Marin.

Base originale
1985 = 100.

Source des coefficients de pondération
La valeur des coefficients de pondération résulte des données sur les structures de consommation et les comptes nationaux pour 1984 en Italie, corrigées à l'usage des ménages de Saint-Marin. Les articles qui font l'objet d'un relevé de prix sont ceux consommés par la majorité des ménages.

Pondération et composition

Groupes principaux	Nombre d'articles	Pondération	Nombre approximatif de relevés de prix
Alimentation et tabac	86	30,92	...
Habillement et chaussure	38	8,67	...
Loyer, entretien et réparations	3	4,97	...
Combustible et éclairage	5	4,72	...
Autres biens et services	150	50,72	...
Total	282	100,00	...

Dépenses de consommation des ménages
Sont exclus des dépenses de consommation prises en compte dans le calcul de l'indice, l'impôt sur le revenu, les investissements et l'épargne, la production aux fins de consommation des ménages ou la valeur locative des logements occupés en propriété.

Mode de relevé des prix
Les prix sont relevés le 15 de chaque mois à la suite de l'envoi d'un questionnaire à 50 points de vente au détail et prestataires de services répartis sur l'ensemble du territoire en tenant compte du nombre d'habitants. Les tarifs officiels fixés par le gouvernement sont pris en compte pour certains articles et services. Les prix retenus pour le calcul de l'indice sont les prix réellement payés par les consommateurs. Les prix de soldes et les rabais, les achats en location-vente ou à crédit et l'acquisition d'articles d'occasion ne sont pas pris en compte dans l'indice.

Logement
Le prix des loyers est obtenu deux fois par an auprès de 47 logements privés en location.

Spécification des variétés
Des spécifications détaillées sont fournies pour chaque article du panier. Les spécifications donnent une description complète de l'article: nom ou marque de fabrique, empaquetage, quantité ou unité employée, etc.

Substitution, changement de qualité, etc.
Lorsqu'un article n'est pas disponible, il est remplacé par un autre article similaire et la formule d'enchaînement est utilisée.

Articles saisonniers
Les fruits et légumes frais sont pris en compte en tant qu'articles saisonniers. Pour chacun des 12 mois de l'année, un panier type d'articles saisonniers est établi pour ces articles.

Calcul
L'indice est calculé selon la formule de Laspeyres sous forme de moyenne arithmétique pondérée à base fixe, les coefficients de pondération correspondant à 1984.

Le rapport de prix pour chaque article est calculé en divisant le prix moyen de la période en cours par le prix moyen de la période précédente.

Autres informations
Des indices détaillés portant sur les sous-groupes sont publiés.

Organisation et publication
Centro Elaborazione dati e statistica: «Bollettino di statistica» (San Marino).

SAINT-VINCENT-ET-GRENADINES (ST. VINCENT)

Dénomination officielle
Index of Retail Prices (Indice des prix de détail).

Portée
L'indice est calculé mensuellement et porte sur l'ensemble de la population de Saint-Vincent.

Base originale
Janvier 1981 = 100.

Source des coefficients de pondération
Les coefficients de pondération et les articles sélectionnés ont été déterminés sur la base des résultats d'une enquête sur les dépenses des ménages effectuée pendant six mois à partir de novembre 1975 dans la région urbaine et les régions rurales de Saint-Vincent. L'enquête portait sur 164 ménages de tous les groupes de revenus. La taille moyenne du ménage était de 5,84 personnes.

Pondération et composition

Groupes principaux	Nombre d'articles	Pondération	Nombre approximatif de relevés de prix
Alimentation	88	597,9	...
Autres groupes:	130	402,1	...
Habillement et chaussure	...	...	...
Logement, combustible et éclairage	...	...	...
Mobilier et articles de ménage	...	...	...
Soins médicaux	...	...	...
Transports et communications	...	...	...
Instruction et loisirs	...	...	...
Divers	...	...	...
Total	218	1 000,0	...

Dépenses de consommation des ménages
Pas disponible.

Mode de relevé des prix
Les prix sont relevés par des enquêteurs le second mardi de chaque mois sur les marchés, dans les supermarchés, points de vente au détail et prestataires de service.

Logement
Le loyer concerne une maison non meublée de trois chambres à coucher située dans la capitale, et une maison non meublée de trois chambres à coucher située dans la région rurale. Les logements occupés par leur propriétaire ne sont pas inclus dans l'indice.

Spécification des variétés
Pas disponible.

Substitution, changement de qualité, etc.
Pas disponible.

Articles saisonniers
Pas disponible.

Calcul
L'indice est calculé selon la formule de Laspeyres sous forme de moyenne arithmétique pondérée à base fixe, les coefficients de pondération correspondant à 1975-76.

L'indice pour un article est obtenu en utilisant les rapports de prix de la période courante et de la période de base.

Organisation et publication
Central Planning Division, Statistical Office: «Annual Digest of Statistics» (Kingstown).

idem: «Retail Price Bulletin».

SAMOA

Dénomination officielle
Consumer Price Index (Indice des prix à la consommation).

Portée
L'indice est calculé mensuellement et porte sur les ménages samoans de tout le pays.

Base originale
1980 = 100.

Source des coefficients de pondération
La valeur des coefficients de pondération et le choix des articles résultent d'une enquête sur les revenus et les dépenses des ménages menée d'août 1976 à juillet 1977 sur 1 560 ménages répartis dans l'ensemble du pays. Les coefficients n'ont pas été ajustés pour tenir compte de l'évolution des prix entre la période de l'enquête et 1980.

Pondération et composition

Groupes principaux	Nombre d'articles	Pondération	Nombre approximatif de relevés de prix
Alimentation	55	588	1 016
Habillement et chaussure	16	42	168
Logement:			
Matériaux de construction	7	14	67
Ustensiles de cuisine	7	26	96
Linge de maison	7	11	48
Combustible et éclairage	5	50	24
Autres	7	19	48
Transports et communications	9	90	37
Divers	24	160	96
Total	137	1 000	1 600

Dépenses de consommation des ménages
Les dépenses de consommation prises en compte dans le calcul de l'indice visent tous les biens et services que la population de l'indice acquiert pour sa consommation. Les biens et services produits par le ménage lui-même et ceux qu'il reçoit à titre de revenu en nature pour sa propre consommation sont exclus.

Mode de relevé des prix
Les prix sont relevés par des fonctionnaires du Département de la statistique, auprès d'un échantillon de commerces de détail, de marchés et de prestataires de services. Dix magasins importants ont été retenus dans la zone urbaine d'Apia, sept dans le reste d'Upolu, six à Satelologa et sept dans le reste de Savaii. Les mouvements des prix dans les zones rurales étant similaires à ceux de la zone urbaine, les relevés des prix sont maintenant limités à la zone urbaine seulement.

La plupart des relevés sont effectués mensuellement vers le milieu du mois. Pour les légumes, fruits, noix et poisson frais, ils ont lieu chaque vendredi de la semaine dans la zone urbaine d'Apia. Les prix retenus pour le calcul de l'indice sont les prix de détail réellement payés par les acheteurs. Le prix des soldes et les rabais ne sont pas pris en compte.

Logement
Les loyers sont exclus de l'indice. L'indice du logement porte sur les articles ci-après: matériaux de construction et meubles, ustensiles de cuisine, linge, combustibles et éclairage et autres.

Spécification des variétés
Les articles dont les prix sont à relever font l'objet de spécifications détaillées portant sur le nom, la marque, la qualité et la taille.

Substitution, changement de qualité, etc.
Lorsqu'un produit disparaît du marché, il est remplacé par un produit analogue. Les changements de qualité font l'objet, dans la mesure du possible, de corrections destinées à en rapporter le prix à la qualité originale.

Articles saisonniers
Pour les articles saisonniers comme les fruits et légumes, qui ne sont pas vendus hors saison, l'indice est calculé sur le dernier prix affiché tant que n'apparaissent pas les nouveaux prix.

Calcul
L'indice est calculé selon la formule de Laspeyres sous forme de moyenne arithmétique pondérée à base fixe, les coefficients de pondération correspondant à la période août 1976-juillet 1977.

Le rapport de prix pour chaque article est calculé en divisant le prix moyen de la période courante par le prix moyen de la période de base. Les prix moyens sont des moyennes arithmétiques simples de tous les relevés de prix.

Organisation et publication
Department of Statistics: «Quarterly Statistical Bulletin» (Apia).
idem: «Annual Abstract».
idem: «Monthly C.P.I. Release»
idem: «Report on the revised Consumer Price Index for Western Samoa, 1980 = 100».

SAMOA AMERICAINES (PAGO-PAGO)

Dénomination officielle
Retail Price Index (Indice des prix de détail).

Portée
Pas disponible.

Base originale
Janvier - mars 1974 = 100.

Source des coefficients de pondération
Les coefficients de pondération utilisés pour le calcul de l'indice ont été déterminés sur la base de statistiques sur les importations.

Pondération et composition
Pas disponible.

Dépenses de consommation des ménages
Pas disponible.

Mode de relevé des prix
Les prix sont relevés trimestriellement par des enquêteurs auprès de sept supermarchés.

Logement
Pas disponible.

Spécification des variétés
Pas disponible.

Substitution, changement de qualité, etc.
Pas disponible.

Articles saisonniers
Il est tenu compte des fluctuations saisonnières des prix de certains articles en maintenant, hors saison, le dernier prix de saison.

Calcul
L'indice est calculé selon la formule de Laspeyres, sous forme de moyenne arithmétique pondérée à base fixe, les coefficients de pondération correspondant à la période de base.

Autres informations
Une nouvelle série (base octobre-décembre 1982 = 100) est maintenue calculée mais les informations méthodologiques relatives à cette série n'étaient pas disponibles au BIT lors de la publication du présent Volume.

Organisation et publication
L'indice est calculé par: Economic and Planning Office (Fagatogo).

SENEGAL (DAKAR)

Dénomination officielle
Indice des prix à la consommation.

Portée
L'indice est calculé mensuellement et porte sur les ménages sénégalais à Dakar disposant d'un revenu mensuel inférieur à 100 000 francs CFA en 1960-1961.

Base originale
1967 = 100.

Source des coefficients de pondération
Les coefficients de pondération et les articles sélectionnés ont été déterminés sur la base des résultats d'une enquête sur les

dépenses des ménages effectuée à Dakar en 1960-1961 auprès de ménages sénégalais ayant, lors de l'enquête, un revenu mensuel inférieur à 100 000 francs CFA.

Pondération et composition

Groupes principaux	Nombre d'articles	Pondération	Nombre approximatif de relevés de prix
Alimentation	71	56,0	...
Habillement et chaussure	22	11,9	...
Logement:			
Loyer et réparations	5	8,7	...
Combustible, éclairage et eau	5	5,8	...
Equipement ménager	7	1,7	...
Soins personnels et médicaux et produits d'entretien	14	4,0	...
Transports	9	5,4	...
Education, loisirs, tabac, services domestiques, etc.	18	6,5	...
Total	151	100,0	...

Dépenses de consommation des ménages
Pas disponible.

Mode de relevé des prix
Les prix des denrées alimentaires sont relevés chaque semaine, par des enquêteurs, auprès de points de vente au détail et sur six marchés à Dakar. Les prix des autres articles sont relevés au cours de la deuxième quinzaine de chaque mois. Les données relatives aux services sont obtenues à partir des tarifs officiels. Il n'est pas tenu compte des prix des soldes.

Logement
Les données relatives au loyer sont recueillies auprès d'une importante société immobilière pour des logements récents de deux pièces.

Spécification des variétés
Les spécifications décrivent la variété, la qualité, la fabrication, la marque, l'unité, etc.

Substitution, changement de qualité, etc.
Lorsqu'un article disparaît du marché, son prix est reporté pendant trois mois au maximum. Passé ce délai, l'article est remplacé par un article similaire en calculant un prix fictif pour la période de base.

Articles saisonniers
Il est tenu compte des fluctuations saisonnières de certains prix en maintenant, hors saison, les derniers prix de saison.

Calcul
L'indice est calculé selon la formule de Laspeyres, sous forme de moyenne arithmétique pondérée à base fixe, les coefficients de pondération correspondant à la période 1960-61.

Organisation et publication
Ministère de l'Economie, des Finances et du Plan, Direction de la prévision et de la statistique: «Note mensuelle sur les indices des prix de détail» (Dakar).

SEYCHELLES

Dénomination officielle
Retail Price Index (Indice des prix de détail).

Portée
L'indice est calculé mensuellement et porte sur des ménages appartenant à tous les groupes de revenu dans l'ensemble du pays.

Base originale
Mars 1986 = 100.

Source des coefficients de pondération
Les coefficients de pondération et les articles sélectionnés ont été déterminés sur la base des résultats d'une enquête sur les dépenses des ménages, menée entre le 8 août 1983 et le 5 août 1984, auprès d'un échantillon de 969 ménages appartenant à tous les groupes de revenu, résidant dans les îles de Mahé, Praslin et la Digue. Les dépenses de tous les membres des ménages ont été relevées sur une période de deux semaines et des informations ont été fournies sur les principaux achats effectués au cours des trois mois précédents. Les coefficients de pondération n'ont pas été ajustés pour tenir compte de l'évolution des prix entre la période de l'enquête et 1986.

Pondération et composition

Groupes principaux	Nombre d'articles	Pondération	Nombre approximatif de relevés de prix
Poisson frais	1	5,16	...
Autres denrées alimentaires	90	28,90	...
Boissons alcoolisées et tabac	9	18,74	...
Habillement et chaussure	15	8,57	...
Loyer, coût de construction	3	11,20	...
Combustible, éclairage et eau	7	7,44	...
Articles de ménage	14	5,86	...
Soins personnels	16	1,63	...
Transports et communications	14	7,63	...
Autres services et loisirs	16	4,87	...
Total	185	100,00	...

Dépenses de consommation des ménages
Les dépenses de consommation prises en compte dans le calcul de l'indice correspondent à la quasi-totalité des achats de biens et services effectués par les ménages de référence pour leur consommation. Elles comprennent les primes d'assurance sur les automobiles, les redevances et la valeur locative des logements occupés par leur propriétaire. En sont exclus l'épargne et les placements, ainsi que l'impôt sur le revenu et les autres impôts directs.

Mode de relevé des prix
Les prix de la plupart des articles sont relevés tous les mois par des enquêteurs auprès de 22 points de vente au détail et marchés, à Mahé et Praslin. Les données relatives aux services sont obtenues auprès de leurs prestataires. Les prix sont ceux en vigueur au cours de la semaine incluant le 15 de chaque mois. Les prix des poissons sont déterminés cinq fois par semaine par achat direct. Les prix des fruits et des légumes sont relevés une fois par semaine.
Les prix entrant dans le calcul de l'indice sont ceux qui sont effectivement demandés aux consommateurs. On se sert aussi des prix officiels fixés par le gouvernement des Seychelles pour des produits comme les fruits et les légumes.

Logement
Les loyers sont relevés tous les trois mois, par roulement, sur un échantillon de 180 logements, dont 20 pour cent de logements publics et 80 pour cent de logements privés.

Spécification des variétés
Les spécifications des articles de référence portent sur la variété, la qualité, l'emballage, le fabricant, la marque et l'unité.

Substitution, changement de qualité, etc.
Si un produit n'est plus disponible, il est remplacé par un produit analogue, auquel on applique la formule d'enchaînement.

Articles saisonniers
Le seul article saisonnier est le poisson, dont le prix ne fait l'objet d'aucun ajustement.

Calcul
L'indice est calculé selon la formule de Laspeyres sous forme de moyenne arithmétique pondérée à base fixe, les coefficients de pondération correspondant à la période comprise entre le 8 août 1983 et le 5 août 1984.
Les rapports de prix sont d'abord calculés par articles et points de vente avant qu'il soit procédé au calcul de la moyenne.

Organisation et publication
Ministry of Finance, Statistics Division: «Monthly Statistical Bulletin - Retail Price Index» (Victoria).

SIERRA LEONE (FREETOWN)

Dénomination officielle
Consumer Price Index for Low Income Families (Indice des prix à la consommation - familles à revenu modeste).

Portée
L'indice est calculé mensuellement et porte sur les ménages à revenu modeste de Freetown, y compris sa banlieue, dont les dépenses mensuelles moyennes totales ne dépassaient pas 100 leones en 1976-77.

Base originale
1978 = 100.

Source des coefficients de pondération
La valeur des coefficients de pondération et le choix des articles résultent d'une enquête sur les dépenses des ménages menée au cours de la période avril 1976 - juillet 1977 auprès de 576 ménages privés de Freetown, y compris sa banlieue, dont les dépenses mensuelles moyennes ne dépassaient pas 100 leones en 1976-77. Les coefficients de pondération ont été corrigés pour tenir compte des changements de prix survenus entre la période de l'enquête et 1978.

Pondération et composition

Groupes principaux	Nombre d'articles	Pondération	Nombre approximatif de relevés de prix
Alimentation	62	63,1	...
Tabac et noix de kola	5	3,8	...
Logement:			
Loyer	1	9,2	...
Charges municipales et réparations	4	0,3	...
Combustible et éclairage	6	6,9	...
Meubles, ameublement et équipement ménager	18	1,8	...
Habillement et chaussure	31	5,4	...
Biens et services divers:			
Soins personnels	10	1,4	...
Soins médicaux	11	1,6	...
Produits d'entretien	6	1,9	...
Loisirs	4	0,2	...
Lecture et instruction	5	0,6	...
Transports et communications	7	3,5	...
Autres dépenses	2	0,3	...
Total	172	100,0	

Dépenses de consommation des ménages
Pas disponible.

Mode de relevé des prix
Les prix de la plupart des articles sont relevés par des enquêteurs auprès de points de vente au détail, mais les prix des denrées alimentaires sont relevés sur trois grands marchés publics. La fréquence des relevés peut être hebdomadaire, mensuelle ou trimestrielle selon la variabilité des prix de l'article considéré; elle est hebdomadaire pour la plupart des denrées alimentaires.

Logement
Les données relatives au loyer sont obtenues trimestriellement pour 91 logements; les taux dus pour des services communaux sont relevés annuellement.

Spécification des variétés
Les articles dont le prix est relevé font l'objet de spécifications détaillées, compte tenu de leur succès auprès du public. Ces spécifications portent sur la marque, la fabrication, la qualité et la taille.

Substitution, changement de qualité, etc.
Lorsqu'un article n'est plus disponible, il est remplacé par un article similaire et la méthode d'enchaînement est utilisée.

Articles saisonniers
En dehors de leur saison, les prix des fruits et légumes frais sont censés suivre l'évolution des prix des autres articles du même sous-groupe.

Calcul
L'indice est calculé selon la formule de Laspeyres sous forme de moyenne arithmétique pondérée à base fixe, les coefficients de pondération correspondant à la période de base.

L'indice pour un article est obtenu en utilisant les rapports de prix de la période en cours et de la période précédente.

Organisation et publication
Central Statistics Office: «Statistical Bulletin» (Freetown).

idem: «Technical Report on Revision of Consumer Price Index for Freetown with base 1978 = 100» (août 1984).

Government Printing Department: «The Sierra Leone Gazette».

SINGAPOUR

Dénomination officielle
Consumer Price Index (Indice des prix à la consommation).

Portée
L'indice est calculé tous les mois et porte sur les ménages dont les dépenses mensuelles se situaient entre 500 et 4 999 dollars singapouriens en 1987-1988.

Base originale
Septembre 1987 - août 1988 = 100.

Source des coefficients de pondération
La valeur des coefficients de pondération et le choix des articles résultent d'une enquête sur les dépenses des ménages effectuée entre septembre 1987 et août 1988.

La structure des dépenses des ménages dont les dépenses mensuelles varient entre 500 et 4 999 dollars de Singapour a été utilisée pour l'obtention du barème de pondération. Ce groupe de ménages représente 90 pour cent du nombre total des ménages de l'échantillon.

L'enquête porte sur l'ensemble du pays et a été effectuée sur un échantillon représentatif de tous les ménages privés composés d'au moins deux personnes et habitant l'île principale de Singapour. En revanche, les ménages composés d'une personne et les ménages de ressortissants étrangers ont été exclus du champ d'investigation. L'enquête, qui a fait appel à des entretiens individuels, s'est étendue sur une période de douze mois, du mois de septembre 1987 au mois d'août 1988. Les chiffres relatifs au premier groupe de ménages ont pour période de référence le mois de septembre 1987, et ceux relatifs au dernier groupe le mois d'août 1988. Pour les analyses et calculs finaux, il a été fait appel aux dossiers d'inscription de 5 742 ménages.

Les critères de sélection des articles sont les suivants: importance relative, mouvement du prix équivalent à celui d'articles semblables ou apparentés et faculté de se prêter aux évaluations (c'est-à-dire leur disponibilité aux fins de relevés périodiques). Bien qu'exclus des relevés, les articles relativement peu importants, qui ne sont pas disponibles en grande quantité, ou dont les spécifications ne sont pas normalisées, sont néanmoins représentés indirectement par les articles similaires ou apparentés qui ont été sélectionnés, leurs parts dans les dépenses totales ayant été attribuées à ces derniers.

Pondération et composition

Groupes principaux	Nombre d'articles	Pondération	Nombre approximatif de relevés de prix
Alimentation	272	3 977	8 424
Habillement et chaussure	65	570	382
Logement:	71	1 717	1 011
Logement loué	4	110	224
Logement occupé par le propriétaire	7	603	382
Réparations et entretien	4	226	34
Combustible et éclairage	8	456	42
Biens d'équipement ménager durables	48	322	329
Transports et communications	38	1 450	255
Divers:	147	2 286	1 904
Instruction	34	500	322
Santé	22	249	403
Loisirs et spectacles	15	295	110
Boissons alcoolisées et tabac	12	282	175
Autres biens et services	64	960	894
Total	593	10 000	11 976

Dépenses de consommation des ménages
Les chiffres des dépenses de consommation utilisés dans le calcul des coefficients de pondération sont ceux des paiements effectués par les ménages pour l'acquisition de biens et de services pendant le mois de l'enquête. Les montants des articles achetés à crédit ont été enregistrés le jour de leur acquisition. Pour les articles ou biens provenant d'une épicerie ou d'une ferme en propriété, le montant affecté au prix courant du marché est enregistré au chapitre des dépenses. En ce qui concerne les dépenses de grande ampleur mais de faible fréquence, comme les achats de biens de consommation durables, les voyages d'agrément, les importants travaux de réparation et de rénovation du logement, les ménages ont été invités à enregistrer le montant des dépenses effectuées au cours des 12 mois précédant l'enquête; le douzième de ce montant étant alors inscrit au chapitre des dépenses correspondant au mois de l'enquête. Pour l'échange de biens usagés et le paiement partiel de nouveaux biens, le paiement net (c'est-à-dire la différence entre le prix du nouvel article et la valeur d'échange) est utilisé. La même méthode est appliquée aux achats de biens d'occasion. Sont exclus les contributions au Central Provident Fund (Fonds central de Prévoyance) ainsi que les autres paiements hors-consommation tels l'impôt sur le revenu, le remboursement d'emprunts, les frais relatifs aux propriétés, aux

actions et valeurs mobilières. Les dons ne sont pas davantage inclus. Les frais des patentes, les primes d'assurance-logement et d'assurance-santé sont considérés comme des dépenses de consommation, et leur paiement a été inclus dans l'indice.

Mode de relevé des prix
La fréquence des relevés varie en fonction de l'évolution des prix des articles. Les articles dont le prix présente de fréquentes fluctuations, tels les biens alimentaires périssables, sont relevés trois fois par semaine auprès des points de vente du marché. Les prix des provisions et les frais divers, dont les fluctuations ne sont pas aussi fréquentes que pour les biens alimentaires périssables, sont relevés une fois par semaine. Les prix présentant une plus grande stabilité, tels ceux relatifs à l'habillement, aux produits textiles, à la coiffure, à la confection des vêtements, à la vaisselle et à l'ameublement, sont relevés une fois par mois. Les modifications des tarifs du Mass Rapid Transit, des autobus et des taxis, des billets d'entrée aux cinémas, des frais relatifs au paiement des services publics, des frais de maintenance et d'entretien des appartements, des tarifs des services médicaux publics et des frais de scolarisation sont introduites dans l'indice au fur et à mesure de leur révision.

Les prix des biens alimentaires périssables sont relevés tous les mardis, jeudis et vendredis. Ceux des provisions et des accessoires sont relevés tous les mercredis de chaque semaine. Les prix des relevés effectués mensuellement correspondent à ceux du 15 de chaque mois.

Les informations relatives aux lieux habituellement fréquentés par les consommateurs pour leurs achats d'articles divers, de provisions et de vêtements ont été obtenues auprès des personnes ayant répondu à l'enquête sur les dépenses des ménages. Ces informations ont servi de guide pour le choix des points de vente, et ont été complétées par d'autres sources, comme l'enquête du Département sur les commerces de gros et de détail, dont les résultats ont permis d'établir une liste des principaux points de vente pour chaque type de produit. En ce qui concerne les produits alimentaires, les points de vente sélectionnés sont généralement situés dans les zones à forte densité de population, en particulier les grands ensembles de logements en propriété publique. Les prix des articles non alimentaires, tels le prêt-à-porter et les chaussures, l'ameublement, l'équipement et les appareils ménagers ont été principalement relevés auprès des centres commerciaux où se trouvent concentrés un grand nombre de détaillants spécialisés dans les articles en question.

Les prix des articles alimentaires périssables sont essentiellement relevés au moyen de visites effectuées directement auprès des marchés et des magasins de provisions et de vaisselle tandis que les prix des autres articles sont obtenus au moyen de questionnaires adressés par courrier. Les tarifs relatifs à l'électricité, au gaz et à l'eau sont obtenus directement auprès du Bureau des services publics. Le prix des soins de santé (frais d'hospitalisation et honoraires médicaux) est relevé au moyen de questionnaires adressés par correspondance aux d'hôpitaux et cliniques aussi biens publics que privés. Les frais d'instruction, tous niveaux confondus, sont obtenus directement auprès du Ministère de l'Education, des établissements d'enseignement supérieur et d'autres établissements privés. Les prix des transports et communications (automobiles, motocyclettes, essence et autres articles liés à la circulation) sont obtenus auprès des détaillants respectifs. Les tarifs des transports routiers publics, des autobus et du métro sont transmis par le Singapore Bus Services et Mass Rapid Transit Corporation. Les tarifs des transports aériens sont obtenus auprès des bureaux de certaines compagnies sélectionnées à cet effet. Les tarifs postaux et téléphoniques sont recueillis auprès de Singapore Telecom.

Six enquêteurs visitent à tout moment les points de vente sélectionnés. Quatre enquêteurs se rendent sur les marchés tous les mardis, jeudis et vendredis pour relever les prix du poisson, des légumes, de la viande, des fruits, etc. Chaque mercredi, ces mêmes enquêteurs ont pour tâche de visiter les magasins de provisions afin d'y relever les prix des denrées non périssables et de divers produits. D'autres relevés de prix requérant des visites directes, tels ceux concernant les textiles, les aliments précuisinés, l'habillement féminin, etc., sont effectués le lundi.

Les prix de soldes et les autres prix pratiqués à l'occasion de promotions des ventes sont ignorés. Les prix de tels articles ne sont pas utilisés dans le calcul de l'indice ou des prix moyens. Les prix de catalogue sont utilisés lorsqu'ils constituent des réductions authentiques et largement pratiquées; en d'autres termes, lorsqu'ils deviennent prédominants. En ce qui concerne les intérêts des locations-ventes et des crédits, seuls sont relevés les prix pratiqués à l'occasion des transactions habituelles au comptant.

Pour chaque article, le nombre des relevés de prix dépend de son importance relative, de l'élasticité de son prix et de l'existence d'un contrôle de la part d'un organisme central.

Logement
Les chiffres relatifs aux loyers sont les seuls à être inclus dans le chapitre correspondant. Les loyers des appartements de propriété publique, des appartements privés, des maisons de campagne, des maisons jumelées et en terrasse ainsi que des locaux commerciaux sont relevés une fois par trimestre, en janvier, avril, juillet et octobre. Les ménages choisis sont divisés en deux groupes, chacun ne faisant l'objet que d'une enquête tous les six mois: le premier groupe en janvier et en juillet, le deuxième en avril et en octobre. Il n'est pas nécessaire que des enquêtes soient effectuées plus fréquemment auprès des mêmes ménages, étant donné que la plupart des logements en location sont régis par des contrats prévoyant un loyer fixe durant une ou deux années. Des questionnaires sont envoyés par courrier aux ménages sélectionnés, pour le relevé des données relatives aux loyers; les ménages sont priés de remplir les questionnaires et de préciser le montant du loyer en vigueur, celui versé six mois auparavant, la durée du bail signé entre locataire et propriétaire ainsi que des précisions relatives, le cas échéant, à l'ameublement et aux biens d'équipement durables. Au sein de l'indice, différents coefficients de pondération sont attribués aux loyers des différents types d'habitations. Pour chaque type d'appartement ou de maison, l'indice est calculé en utilisant la moyenne des rapports de prix, fondés sur le chiffres des loyers relevés. Les divers indices correspondant aux différents types de logements sont alors pondérés pour obtenir l'indice global des loyers.

En ce qui concerne les habitations occupées par leur propriétaire, on utilise la méthode de l'équivalence des loyers. Le loyer qu'aurait à verser le propriétaire au cas où il serait locataire est estimé par les experts des services publics. L'estimation des loyers de l'échantillon des logements occupés par leur propriétaire est obtenue tous les trimestres auprès de la Valuation and Assessment Division de l'Inland Revenue Department.

Spécification des variétés
Pour s'assurer que les changements de prix ne soient pas provoqués par des changements de qualité, des spécifications détaillées des articles sont établies afin d'aider les enquêteurs travaillant sur le terrain ou les propriétaires des magasins de détail. Sont précisés la marque, la qualité, les matériaux, la taille, l'unité de mesure et le pays d'origine de chacun des articles, afin de les distinguer clairement d'autres produits équivalents. Ces spécifications détaillées ont d'abord été obtenues lors des enquêtes sur le terrain. Pour les articles de lingerie féminine, sujets aux fluctuations de la mode, outre les spécifications habituellement requises, (conception du modèle, numéro de confection, tissu utilisé, motifs d'impression - couleur unie ou motifs floraux - tailles et couleurs disponibles) les enquêteurs répertorient les patrons des différents modèles, afin de permettre à l'équipe du bureau des statistiques de déterminer si les articles concernés doivent être pris en compte.

Substitution, changement de qualité, etc.
Changement de qualité: pour autant qu'on puisse quantifier l'ampleur du changement de qualité, les prix sont, dans la mesure du possible, ajustés en conséquence. Cependant, lorsqu'un changement de qualité ne peut être évalué, on tente de «remplacer» l'ancien article par un nouveau lorsque les deux articles sont disponibles simultanément pendant un certain laps de temps.

Apparition de nouveaux produits: une méthode d'assemblage est utilisée.

Disparition de certains types ou qualités: le personnel du bureau des statistiques est habituellement informé à l'avance, soit par les enquêteurs travaillant sur le terrain, soit par les personnes répondant aux questionnaires. Avant la disparition d'un article du marché, le prix de celui qui s'en rapproche le plus est en général obtenu pour la période au cours de laquelle l'ancien et le nouvel article sont disponibles en même temps, afin de rendre possible l'utilisation des techniques d'assemblage des séries de prix. Si un article disparaît soudainement, on considère, généralement, que son prix demeure inchangé durant le mois en cours, tandis que la recherche d'un proche substitut est immédiatement entreprise.

Articles saisonniers
La plupart des articles composant le panier de l'Indice des prix à la consommation sont des articles non saisonniers. En d'autres termes, leurs prix sont habituellement connus en permanence. Les articles saisonniers d'importance sont peu nombreux.

Calcul
L'indice est calculé selon la formule de Laspeyres sous forme de moyenne arithmétique pondérée à base fixe, les coefficients de pondération correspondant à la période de base.
Des moyennes de prix sont calculées pour chacune des différentes marques en additionnant les prix obtenus et en divisant leur somme par le nombre total des relevés. Les rapports de prix sont calculés en divisant le prix du mois de référence par celui de l'année de base correspondante (prix moyen de la période septembre 1987 - août 1988). Les prix manquants font l'objet de différents traitements compte tenu des motifs de leur absence. Si le prix d'une marque déterminée d'un point de vente particulier n'est pas disponible, aucun changement n'est comptabilisé pour le mois concerné. Les prix manquants qui résultent de la disparition d'un article sont rattachés au prix d'un proche substitut. Les données de prix erronées ou sujettes à caution font généralement l'objet d'un éclaircissement et d'une nouvelle confirmation, en accord avec les personnes répondant à l'enquête.

Autres informations
Les principaux composants des groupes et sous-groupes font l'objet de publication.

Organisation et publication
Department of Statistics: «Consumer Price Index, Singapore» - rapport mensuel de l'Indice;
idem: «Monthly Digest of Statistics» - publication mensuelle; Les indices mensuels par groupes et sous-groupes sont publiés pour les 24 derniers mois.
idem: «Yearbook of Statistics» - publication annuelle; publication des indices annuels des dix dernières années.
idem: «The consumer price index, Singapore, based on Household Expenditure Survey 1987/88».

SOUDAN

Dénomination officielle
Retail Price Index (Indice des prix de détail).

Portée
L'indice est calculé mensuellement et porte sur les ménages de six personnes disposant en 1967-68 d'un revenu annuel compris entre 300 et 500 livres soudanaises.

Base originale
Janvier 1970 = 100.

Source des coefficients de pondération
La valeur des coefficients de pondération et le choix des articles résultent d'une enquête sur les dépenses des ménages menée en 1967-68 à Khartoum, Khartoum Nord et Omdurman auprès d'un échantillon aléatoire de 1 500 ménages de six personnes, disposant d'un revenu annuel compris entre 300 et 500 livres soudanaises.

Pondération et composition

Groupes principaux	Nombre d'articles	Pondération	Nombre approximatif de relevés de prix
Alimentation et tabac	31	66,5	...
Logement:			
Loyer, combustible, éclairage et eau	5	12,4	...
Habillement et chaussure	22	5,9	...
Divers	12	15,2	...
Total	70	100,0	...

Dépenses de consommation des ménages
Pas disponible.

Mode de relevé des prix
Les prix sont relevés auprès des magasins de détail et prestataires de services retenus à cet effet à Khartoum, Khartoum Nord et Omdurman. Les relevés sont effectués par des enquêteurs tous les jeudis pour la plupart des articles. Les prix de l'électricité et du gaz, les frais de scolarité et les tarifs des transport s'obtiennent auprès des administrations. Le coût des services médicaux est calculé à partir des honoraires des médecins et du prix d'un produit médical choisi.
Les prix retenus pour le calcul de l'indice sont les prix normalement payés. Le prix des soldes et les rabais sont écartés.

Logement
Les données de base relatives au loyer proviennent d'une enquête entreprise en décembre 1969. Comme ils ne changent pas souvent, les loyers ne sont relevés qu'occasionnellement.

Spécification des variétés
Pas disponible.

Substitution, changement de qualité, etc.
Pas disponible.

Articles saisonniers
Les prix relevés sont des prix courants qui ne font pas l'objet d'ajustements pour fluctuations saisonnières.

Calcul
L'indice est calculé selon la formule de Laspeyres sous forme de moyenne arithmétique pondérée à base fixe, les coefficients de pondération correspondant à la période 1967-68.
L'indice pour un article est obtenu en utilisant les rapports de prix moyens de la période courante et de la période de base. Les prix moyens sont des moyennes arithmétiques simples de prix obtenus dans les trois villes.

Autres informations
Des séries nouvelles pour les familles à revenus modiques, moyens et élevés (base janvier 1988 = 100) sont maintenant calculées mais les informations méthodologiques relatives à ces séries n'étaient pas disponibles au BIT lors de la publication du présent Volume.

Organisation et publication
L'indice est calculé par le Department of Statistics (Khartoum). Les chiffres que publie le Bureau international du Travail proviennent directement de cet organisme et ne figurent pas dans les publications nationales.

SRI LANKA (COLOMBO)

Dénomination officielle
Consumer Price Index (Indice des prix à la consommation).

Portée
L'indice est calculé mensuellement et porte sur les familles de travailleurs manuels à Colombo.

Base originale
1952 = 100.

Source des coefficients de pondération
La valeur des coefficients de pondération et le choix des articles résultent d'une enquête sur les dépenses des ménages menée en 1949-50. L'enquête a porté sur 455 ménages de travailleurs manuels à Colombo. Les données de dépenses de consommation qui en proviennent ont été réévaluées aux prix de 1959, pour obtenir les coefficients de pondération.

Pondération et composition

Groupes principaux	Nombre d'articles	Pondération	Nombre approximatif de relevés de prix
Alimentation	94	61,9	...
Combustible et éclairage	4	4,3	...
Loyer	1	5,7	...
Habillement, chaussure et linge de maison	63	9,4	...
Divers	57	18,7	...
Total	219	100,0	...

Dépenses de consommation des ménages
Les dépenses de consommation prises en compte dans le calcul de l'indice correspondent aux achats de tous les biens et services effectués par les ménages de référence pour leur consommation. Elles excluent les primes d'assurance vie et d'assurance immobilière, l'impôt sur le revenu et sur les biens personnels.

Mode de relevé des prix
Les prix sont relevés chaque semaine par des enquêteurs du

Département du recensement et de la statistique dans des magasins de vente au détail et autres établissements choisis à cet effet sur les sept marchés principaux à Colombo. Pour la plupart des denrées alimentaires, ils s'obtiennent par achat direct.

Pour les articles vendus aussi bien sur le marché libre que dans les coopératives, on calcule une moyenne des prix en les pondérant par des coefficients proportionnels aux quantités estimatives vendues dans les deux catégories de magasins.

Les prix retenus pour le calcul de l'indice sont ceux effectivement payés. On tient compte des rabais et des prix de soldes. La location-vente et la vente à crédit, les achats d'occasion et la reprise d'articles usagés ne sont pas retenus.

Logement
Les données relatives aux loyers sont relevées tous les trois mois pour 148 logements ouvriers sur les registres d'imposition locale des municipalités. La notion de valeur locative imputée s'applique pour les logements occupés en propriété.

Spécification des variétés
Chacun des articles entrant dans l'indice fait l'objet d'une spécification détaillée: description complète, marque, pays d'origine, qualité et unité employée.

Substitution, changement de qualité, etc.
Si un produit manque, on le remplace par un produit analogue, et la méthode d'enchaînement est appliquée.

Articles saisonniers
Sont considérés comme tels les fruits et légumes frais. Leurs prix sont relevés en saison. Hors saison, on conserve les prix de clôture de la saison précédente.

Calcul
L'indice est calculé selon la formule de Laspeyres sous forme de moyenne arithmétique pondérée à base fixe, les coefficients de pondération correspondant aux dépenses de consommation de 1949-50, réévaluées aux prix de 1959.

Organisation et publication
L'indice est calculé par le Department of Census and Statistics (Colombo).

Department of Government Printing: «The Gazette of the Republic of Sri Lanka» (Colombo).

Government Publications Bureau: «A New Consumers' Price Index», Sessional Paper VI, 1953 (Colombo).

idem: «Report of Committee to Revise the Cost of Living Index», Sessional Paper XI, 1959 (Colombo).

SUEDE

Dénomination officielle
Consumer Price Index (Indice des prix à la consommation).

Portée
L'indice est calculé mensuellement et porte sur toute la population du pays, aussi bien urbaine que rurale.

Base originale
1980 = 100.

Source des coefficients de pondération
La valeur des coefficients de pondération et le choix des articles sont révisés au début de chaque année. Les coefficients de pondération des groupes principaux sont établis à partir du système des comptes nationaux suédois: statistiques trimestrielles pour les trois premiers trimestres de l'année précédente, complétées par une estimation pour le quatrième trimestre. A l'intérieur des groupes, la valeur des coefficients résulte des sources les plus récentes, telles que, pour l'alimentation par exemple, les enquêtes et évaluations effectuées par le Conseil national suédois des marchés agricoles. Pour d'autres articles, la valeur des coefficients de pondération résulte de la dernière enquête sur les dépenses des ménages, laquelle porte sur l'ensemble des dépenses des ménages privés suédois effectuées une année durant.

Dépenses de consommation des ménages
Les dépenses de consommation prises en compte dans le calcul des coefficients de pondération comprennent l'ensemble des dépenses consacrées par les ménages à l'acquisition de biens et services provenant du secteur privé. Il s'agit de l'ensemble des sommes versées par les ménages, y compris celles consacrées à l'acquisition de certains biens d'équipement (à l'exception des terrains, des résidences principales en propriété et des résidences secondaires).

Sont compris les coûts liés à l'acquisition de logements en propriété privée. Les achats à crédit de biens de consommation durables sont enregistrés au moment de la livraison de ces derniers. Les achats de biens d'occasion, l'échange de biens usagés et à titre de paiement partiel pour de nouveaux biens ne sont pas inclus dans l'indice. Sont également exclues les transactions de caractère financier, telles que les primes d'assurance-vie, les cotisations aux assurances sociales, l'impôt sur le revenu et autres impôts directs. Les dons sont enregistrés en tant que dépenses de consommation effectuées par le donateur pour l'acquisition des biens et services concernés; l'enregistrement a lieu au moment de leur acquisition. Les revenus en nature ne constituent qu'une faible part de la consommation privée suédoise. La valeur des revenus en nature n'est estimée pour les biens alimentaires qu'à partir des enquêtes publiées périodiquement par l'Office national suédois du Commerce agricole dans le cadre de ses statistiques sur l'alimentation.

Pondération et composition

Groupes principaux	Nombre d'articles	Pondération	Nombre approximatif de relevés de prix
Alimentation	(1) 25 + 770	172	18 000
Boissons alcoolisées	(a) (1) 15	32	(a) 500
Tabac	(1) 25	21	1 200
Habillement	27	62	900-1 800
Chaussure	10	13	650
Logement, combustible et électricité		270	(b)
Mobilier et articles d'équipement ménager	(1) 39 + 60	65	3 300
Transports et communications	22	175	(2) 800
Loisirs, distractions et services culturels	50 + 20	98	2 100
Divers	(1) 33 + 30	92	(3) 2 800
Total	...	1 000	...

Remarque: (a) et (b) Voir ci-après. (1) Variétés spécifiées de l'échantillon. (2) A l'exception des relevés et des calculs de prix relatifs aux voyages. (3) A l'exception des calculs relatifs aux soins médicaux et dentaires ainsi qu'aux médicaments.

(a) Pratiquement tous les articles et variétés sont pris en compte pour le vin, les liqueurs et les bières à haute teneur d'alcool (coefficient de pondération 28). (b) Voir texte ci-dessous.

Mode de relevé des prix
Les prix sont relevés par des enquêteurs vers le 15 de chaque mois sur un échantillon aléatoire d'environ 900 commerces de détail et établissements de services. L'ensemble des enquêtes par entretiens menés à l'échelle nationale (y compris les relevés de prix) sont effectuées par l'intermédiaire d'un organisme général, composé d'environ 200 personnes. Le siège central de cet organisme est établi au bureau du SCB et son personnel d'encadrement demeure en contact avec les enquêteurs par téléphone, par courrier, et au moyen de conférences périodiques. Les prix des denrées alimentaires (à l'exception de certains aliments frais, tels que le pain, le poisson, les légumes et les fruits) et d'autres produits d'usage quotidien sont relevés mensuellement à partir des listes des prix pratiqués par un échantillon aléatoire d'environ 60 magasins. Une fois par an, au mois de décembre, les prix des produits concernés sont relevés par des enquêteurs auprès des magasins en question. Ces prix ne sont utilisés que pour le calcul du coefficient d'enchaînement à long terme (voir ci-dessous). Les questionnaires sont adressés par la poste dans le cas des loyers et des tarifs relatifs à l'électricité et à l'eau. Les renseignements sont fournis par téléphone pour l'essence et les automobiles. Les données relatives aux soins médicaux, aux transports et aux communications sont obtenues à partir des tarifs officiels. Les prix utilisés dans l'indice représentent les prix régulièrement payés par le public dans son ensemble. Les impôts indirects sont pris en compte dans les prix. Les remises sur les paiements effectués au comptant font l'objet d'une déduction. Les prix résultant d'une négociation effectuée au moment du relevé des prix sont enregistrés. Les prix du marché noir sont inapplicables. Seuls les prix au comptant sont enregistrés, les intérêts des locations-ventes et des crédits n'étant pas pris en compte. Sont également exclus les achats de biens d'occasion et l'échange de biens usagés et à titre de paiement partiel de nouveaux biens, ainsi que les achats directs de produits d'importation par les ménages.

Logement
Les enquêtes sur les loyers sont menées auprès d'un échantillon de 1 000 logements en location, et sont effectuées quatre fois par an, aux mois de janvier, avril, juillet et octobre, ou au moment de l'entrée en vigueur des loyers négociés. Les charges relatives au chauffage sont comprises dans l'enregistrement des loyers. Un échantillon d'appartements nouvellement construits est introduit tour à tour dans les calculs de l'indice des loyers. Un indice relatif aux logements occupés par leur propriétaire est calculé en fonction de l'évolution mensuelle des coûts. Les calculs des coûts comprennent l'ensemble des frais habituels de logement, tels que les frais liés aux intérêts, les primes d'assurance pour les maisons, les charges relatives à l'eau, au ramassage des déchets, au ramonage, l'impôt sur la propriété immobilière, le chauffage, l'électricité et les réparations ménagères, ainsi que les amortissements. Les coûts liés aux intérêts sont calculés sur la base du montant total du capital défini en fonction du prix d'achat (par le propriétaire actuel). Les subventions de l'Etat sur les intérêts font l'objet d'une déduction.

Spécification des variétés
Dans la mesure des possibilités pratiques, les définitions des articles font l'objet de spécifications. L'enquêteur doit spécifier très soigneusement chaque article dont le prix est à relever, afin que le même article ou service puisse être relevé de nouveau par un nouvel enquêteur. Des spécifications détaillées, comprenant le numéro des articles, sont énoncées pour certains produits alimentaires et d'autres biens faisant l'objet d'un achat quotidien.

Substitution, changement de qualité, etc.
Les changements de qualité sont évalués, autant que possible, au moment du relevé des prix. A qualité égale, seule la différence de prix est prise en compte. En principe, les substitutions ne sont pas autorisées pour certains produits alimentaires et d'autres biens faisant l'objet d'un achat quotidien. Pour l'habillement, les substitutions ne sont effectuées qu'entre des articles de qualité équivalente, conformément à certains critères. Les nouveaux produits sont habituellement introduits à l'occasion de l'examen annuel du choix des articles. Si possible, les types ou qualités appelés à disparaître sont remplacés. En cas d'impossibilité, une non-réponse est notifiée.

Articles saisonniers
Les prix des vêtements d'hiver ne sont relevés que durant la période septembre - mars. Les derniers prix enregistrés sont alors utilisés pour le calcul de l'indice en dehors de la saison hivernale, pendant la période avril - août. Les prix de certains articles (pommes de terre, légumes, fruits) font l'objet d'une correction des variations saisonnières. Les prix de ces articles se voient affecter des coefficients saisonniers fondés sur les prix de saison des trois années précédentes.

Calcul
Il s'agit d'un indice chaîne à enchaînements annuels, la pondération étant remaniée avec chaque enchaînement. Ces enchaînements sont de deux types: à court terme et à long terme (pour chacun, la période de base est le mois de décembre de l'année précédente). L'enchaînement à court terme est pratiqué chaque mois, de janvier à décembre. L'enchaînement à long terme est annuel et se pratique d'un mois de décembre sur l'autre.

L'enchaînement mensuel est d'abord calculé sous la forme d'une moyenne arithmétique de prix relatifs d'articles avec, comme base (100), les prix du mois de décembre précédent. Le résultat obtenu est alors enchaîné sur le mois de décembre de chaque année antérieure, de manière à remonter jusqu'en 1980.

Autres informations
Un indice des prix nets est également calculé. Il s'agit d'un indice dans lequel les biens de consommation ont fait l'objet d'une déduction du montant des impôts indirects, qui constituent des coûts supplémentaires aux différentes phases de la production des biens de consommation finale. Les prix sont également ajustés par la prise en compte de certaines subventions.

Les «statistiques fondamentales» (Basic Amount Statistics) sont utilisées pour procéder à l'ajustement des pensions minimales, des pensions complémentaires, des bourses d'études du gouvernement, de certaines rentes viagères et des allocations d'entretien.

Organisation et publication
Statistics Sweden: «Statistika meddelanden», serie P14 och P15 (Comptes rendus statistiques, séries P14 à P15) (Stockholm).

idem: «Allmän Manadsstatistik» (Recueil mensuel de statistiques suédoises).

Sveriges officiella Statistik, Statistika central byrån: «Konsumentpriser och index beräkningar 1989» (Stockholm, 1990).

SUISSE

Dénomination officielle
Indice suisse des prix à la consommation.

Portée
L'indice est calculé mensuellement et porte sur les ménages de salariés dans l'ensemble du pays.

Base originale
Décembre 1982 = 100.

Source des coefficients de pondération
Les coefficients de pondération et les articles sélectionnés ont été déterminés sur la base des résultats d'une enquête sur les dépenses des ménages effectuée en 1981 auprès d'un échantillon de 442 ménages de salariés dans l'ensemble du pays. Les données relatives aux revenus et dépenses ont été relevées mensuellement auprès de chaque ménage de l'échantillon au cours d'une période de 12 mois. Les pondérations ont été ajustées pour tenir compte de l'évolution des prix entre le milieu de 1981 et le milieu de 1982.

Pondération et composition

Groupes principaux	Nombre d'articles	Pondération	Nombre approximatif de relevés de prix
Alimentation	127	21	73 300
Boissons et tabac	22	5	27 700
Habillement et chaussure	56	7	61 800
Loyer	15	18	107 000
Combustible et éclairage	13	5	2 600
Equipement et entretien du ménage	35	6	24 800
Transports et communications	58	14	5 300
Santé et soins personnels	54	8	12 300
Instruction et loisirs	33	16	19 500
Total	413	100	334 300

Dépenses de consommation des ménages
Les dépenses de consommation prises en compte dans le calcul de l'indice comprennent les biens et services achetés par les ménages de salariés. Les impôts indirects, les primes d'assurance relatives à l'utilisation de véhicules à moteur, les redevances radio et télévision sont inclus. Les dépenses de consommation non comprises dans le calcul de l'indice concernent des articles et services tels que cotisations versées à des sociétés, cadeaux, amendes, intérêts d'emprunts, voyages d'affaires, effets personnels tels que bijoux, montres, sacs, etc.

Mode de relevé des prix
Les prix sont relevés auprès de points de vente au détail et de prestataires de services, soit par les enquêteurs des autorités communales, soit au moyen d'enquêtes par correspondance. Le choix d'un point de vente se fait sur la base de son impact économique sur le plan local. Les prix de la plupart des denrées alimentaires, du chauffage, de l'éclairage et de l'essence sont recueillis au cours de la première quinzaine de chaque mois dans 48 villes (communes). Les prix des autres articles et services sont relevés trimestriellement. On tient compte des prix des actions au moment de l'enquête.

Logement
Les données relatives au loyer sont obtenues en mai et novembre de chaque année dans 85 communes pour 100 000 appartements de une à cinq chambres. Les différents genres d'appartements (anciens, nouveaux et ceux construits depuis le dernier relevé) entrent dans le calcul de l'indice en proportion de leur part au nombre total d'appartements.

Spécification des variétés
Chaque enquêteur peut choisir pour chaque article les spécifications les plus importantes du point de vue du chiffre d'affaires réalisé et adapter au besoin son choix au fur et à mesure de l'évolution du marché.

Substitution, changement de qualité, etc.
On ne tient pas compte des modifications mineures de qualité. Lors d'une modification importante de la qualité d'un article, on utilise la formule d'enchaînement. Lorsqu'un article n'est plus en vente et que le consommateur se voit contraint d'acheter un article de substitution, le prix de cet article est utilisé pour le calcul de l'indice.

Articles saisonniers
Il est tenu compte des fluctuations saisonnières des prix des fruits et légumes frais en variant les articles et leur coefficient de pondération à l'intérieur de «paniers» mensuels dont le coefficient de pondération d'ensemble demeure constant.

Calcul
L'indice est calculé selon la formule de Laspeyres sous forme de moyenne arithmétique pondérée à base fixe, les coefficients de pondération correspondant à la période de base.

Des indices séparés sont d'abord calculés pour chaque prix dans chaque point de vente en utilisant les moyennes des rapports de prix de la période courante et de la période de base. L'indice national est la moyenne arithmétique pondérée d'indices relatifs à différents types de points de vente et de communes.

Autres informations
Un nouvel indice des prix à la consommation est actuellement en préparation et paraîtra prochainement. Des sous-groupes très détaillés sont publiés pour l'indice actuel ainsi que des indices séparés pour 48 communes.

Organisation et publication
Département fédéral de l'intérieur, Office fédéral de la statistique: «L'indice suisse des prix à la consommation» (Berne).
idem: «Communiqué de presse».

Département fédéral de l'économie publique, Office fédéral de l'industrie, des arts et métiers et du travail: «La vie économique», fév. 1983, et le 89e numéro spécial, 1977, de «L'indice suisse des prix à la consommation».

SURINAME (PARAMARIBO)

Dénomination officielle
Consumer Price Index (Indice des prix à la consommation).

Portée
L'indice est calculé mensuellement et porte sur les ménages d'ouvriers et d'employés ayant disposé d'un revenu annuel ne dépassant pas 6 000 florins au cours de la période avril 1968 - mars 1969. L'indice concerne la capitale, Paramaribo.

Base originale
Avril 1968 - mars 1969 = 100.

Source des coefficients de pondération
La valeur des coefficients de pondération et le choix des articles résultent d'une enquête sur les dépenses des ménages menée à Paramaribo et aux environs, d'avril 1968 à mars 1969. L'enquête portait sur 592 ménages d'ouvriers et d'employés composés d'au moins trois personnes et disposant, à l'époque de l'enquête, d'un revenu annuel ne dépassant pas 6 000 florins. Deux critères ont présidé au choix des articles: ils doivent représenter une certaine importance dans la consommation des ménages et être acquis par la majorité de ceux-ci.

Pondération et composition

Groupes principaux	Nombre d'articles	Pondération	Nombre approximatif de relevés de prix
Alimentation	92	39,9	1 252
Logement:			
Loyer, eau et électricité	3	9,5	3
Combustible	4	1,9	20
Mobilier, ameublement et produits d'entretien	36	12,3	400
Habillement et chaussure	48	11,0	252
Autres:			
Soins personnels et médicaux	23	6,2	251
Transports	5	9,5	10
Tabac	2	1,3	46
Instruction et loisirs	16	8,4	104
Total	229	100,0	2 338

Dépenses de consommation des ménages
Les dépenses de consommation prises en compte dans le calcul de l'indice correspondent aux achats de tous les biens et services importants effectués par les ménages de référence pour leur consommation. Elles comprennent la valeur des biens et services reçus par le ménage à titre de revenu en nature et les biens qu'il produit et consomme à domicile. En sont exclus les éléments suivants: impôts sur le revenu, cotisations à la sécurité sociale, remboursements des emprunts, primes d'assurance, dons et cotisations, paris et dépenses de jeu, grosses réparations effectuées sur le logement et remboursement du principal des emprunts hypothécaires, autres placements, épargne et intérêts versés sur les emprunts personnels.

Mode de relevé des prix
Les prix sont relevés par une équipe d'enquêteurs auprès d'un échantillon de 125 commerces de détail et prestataires de services de Paramaribo et ses environs. Après 1969, il a été procédé à la sélection de nouveaux points de vente et à la normalisation de plusieurs biens et services. Les enquêtes effectuées auprès de 150 à 200 ménages par mois permettent de relever les prix des marchandises en faible quantité sur le marché et de celles vendues au marché noir. Les enquêteurs ont suivi les prix de la plupart des articles, entre le 1er et le 30 de chaque mois. Les prix des fruits et légumes frais sont relevés trois jours par semaine (lundi, mercredi et vendredi) au marché central et sur les marchés de légumes de Paramaribo et de ses environs. Quatorze relevés de prix par article sont effectués chaque jour.

Logement
L'indice du logement porte sur le loyer, l'eau et l'électricité, les combustibles, les meubles, les objets d'ameublement et les produits d'entretien. Les données relatives aux loyers sont relevées au rythme de 20 par mois, sur 60 logements loués du secteur privé.

Spécification des variétés
Chacun des articles retenus pour le calcul de l'indice fait l'objet d'une spécification détaillée qui en donne la description complète, le nom, la marque, le mode d'emballage, la qualité, l'unité employée, etc.

Substitution, changement de qualité, etc.
Si un article disparaît du marché, il est remplacé par un article similaire.

Articles saisonniers
Les articles saisonniers ne sont pas compris dans l'indice.

Calcul
L'indice est calculé selon la formule de Laspeyres sous forme de moyenne arithmétique pondérée à base fixe, les coefficients de pondération correspondant à la période de base.

Organisation et publication
Algemeen Bureau voor de Statistiek: «Prijsindexcijfers van de Gezinsconsumptie» (Paramaribo).
Stichting Planbureau: «Basis Budget Van Consumptieve Huishouduitgaven in Paramaribo en Omgeving 1968-69» (Paramaribo).

SWAZILAND (MBABANE-MANZINI)

Dénomination officielle
Retail Price Index «B» (Indice des prix de détail «B»).

Portée
L'indice est calculé mensuellement et porte sur les ménages de salariés à revenu modique, résidant à Mbabane et Manzini et disposant d'un revenu annuel d'environ 1 000 emalangeni en 1977.

Base originale
Janvier 1967 = 100.

Source des coefficients de pondération
Ils ont été établis à partir des statistiques concernant les budgets des ménages à revenu modique du Kenya, de la Rhodésie, du Royaume-Uni et de la République sud-africaine.

Dépenses de consommation des ménages
Pas disponible.

Mode de relevé des prix
Les prix sont relevés dans quatre marchés et auprès de points de vente et de prestataires de services de Mbabane et de Manzini. Ils le sont par un fonctionnaire titulaire de l'Office cen-

Pondération et composition

Groupes principaux	Nombre d'articles	Pondération	Nombre approximatif de relevés de prix
Alimentation:			
Fruits et légumes	5	4,5	...
Autres produits alimentaires	19	57,5	...
Boissons et tabac	3	12,0	...
Combustible et éclairage	4	6,0	...
Habillement et chaussure	9	10,0	...
Autres articles	8	10,0	...
Total	48	100,0	...

tral de la statistique pour tous les articles autres que les fruits et légumes, lesquels sont couverts par des contractuels.

Les relevés sont effectués le mardi de chaque semaine pour les fruits et légumes frais, et vers le 15 de chaque mois pour les autres produits. Les données relatives à l'instruction, aux transports et aux soins médicaux sont obtenues par téléphone.

Les prix retenus pour le calcul de l'indice sont les prix de détail réellement payés par les acheteurs.

Logement
Les loyers ne figurent pas dans l'indice et ne sont pas non plus pris en compte dans la détermination des coefficients de pondération.

Spécification des variétés
Les biens et services dont les prix sont relevés font l'objet de spécifications précises quant à la taille, le nom, la marque, la quantité et la qualité.

Substitution, changement de qualité, etc.
Lorsqu'un produit n'est plus en vente, on lui substitue un autre produit de qualité sensiblement égale et on applique la formule d'enchaînement.

Articles saisonniers
Pas disponible.

Calcul
L'indice est calculé selon la formule de Laspeyres sous forme de moyenne arithmétique pondérée à base fixe, les coefficients de pondération correspondant à la période de base.

L'indice pour un article est généralement obtenu en utilisant les rapports de prix de la période courante et de la période de base, sauf pour l'habillement et les articles textiles, pour lesquels les rapports de prix de la période courante et de la période précédente sont utilisés. Pour calculer les prix moyens, on utilise les prix relevés aux magasins dans différentes localités, pondérés selon le chiffre d'affaires du commerce de détail.

Autres informations
Des séries nouvelles pour les familles à revenus modiques, moyens et élevés (base septembre 1988 = 100) sont maintenant calculées mais les informations méthodologiques correspoondantes n'étaient pas disponibles au BIT lors de la publication du présent Volume.

Organisation et publication
Central Statistical Office: «Swaziland Statistical News» (Mbabane).

REPUBLIQUE ARABE SYRIENNE (DAMAS)

Dénomination officielle
Retail Price Index (Indice des prix de détail).

Portée
L'indice est calculé mensuellement et porte sur les ménages privés à Damas.

Base originale
1970 = 100.

Source des coefficients de pondération
La valeur des coefficients de pondération et le choix des articles résultent d'une enquête sur les dépenses des ménages menée en 1971-72.

Dépenses de consommation des ménages
Les dépenses de consommation prises en compte dans le calcul

Pondération et composition

Groupes principaux	Nombre d'articles	Pondération	Nombre approximatif de relevés de prix
Alimentation et tabac	74	488,2	...
Combustible et éclairage	5	45,6	...
Loyer	1	177,3	...
Mobilier et articles d'équipement ménager	8	18,4	...
Produits d'entretien	4	11,8	...
Biens de consommation durables	5	11,4	...
Linge de maison	4	9,5	...
Habillement et chaussure	17	90,6	...
Transports	6	38,1	...
Soins personnels et médicaux	19	78,4	...
Instruction et loisirs	7	30,7	...
Total	150	1 000.0	...

de l'indice comprennent presque tous les biens et services importants achetés par les ménages de référence.

Mode de relevé des prix
Les prix sont relevés par des agents dans des points de vente au détail et établissements de services choisis à cet effet. Ils le sont chaque semaine pour les fruits et légumes et chaque mois pour les autres articles.

Les prix retenus pour le calcul de l'indice sont les prix effectivement payés.

Logement
Les données sur les loyers sont obtenues pour des logements loués meublés et non meublés. Les logements occupés par leur propriétaire ne sont pas compris.

Spécification des variétés
Les variétés sont spécifiées par la qualité, le nom, la marque, l'unité employée, etc.

Substitution, changement de qualité, etc.
On n'opère pas de substitution et, si un article disparaît, son prix et son coefficient de pondération sont omis dans l'indice.

Articles saisonniers
Leurs prix sont relevés en saison. Ils sont omis hors saison dans l'indice.

Calcul
L'indice est calculé selon la formule de Laspeyres sous forme de moyenne arithmétique pondérée à base fixe, les coefficients de pondération correspondant à la période 1971-72.

Autres informations
Des moyennes annuelles sont publiées pour Alep et pour Damas, pour tous les groupes et sous-groupes.

Organisation et publication
Office of the Prime Minister, Central Bureau of Statistics: «Statistical Abstract» (Damas).

TANZANIE (TANGANYIKA)

Dénomination officielle
National Consumer Price Index (Indice national des prix à la consommation).

Portée
L'indice est calculé trimestriellement et porte sur tous les types de ménages et groupes de population dans 20 régions urbaines de la Tanzanie continentale.

Base originale
1977 = 100.

Source des coefficients de pondération
Les coefficients de pondération et les articles sélectionnés ont été déterminés sur la base des résultats d'une enquête sur les dépenses des ménages effectuée pendant un an entre septembre 1976 et novembre 1977. L'enquête a porté sur un échantillon de 6 042 ménages. Les articles dont les prix sont relevés représentent une part appréciable des dépenses des ménages. Les pondérations des articles dont les prix ne sont pas relevés sont exclues.

Dépenses de consommation des ménages
Les dépenses de consommation des ménages prises en compte dans le calcul de l'indice comprennent tous les biens et services importants acquis par la population de référence. En sont

Pondération et composition

Groupes principaux	Nombre d'articles	Pondération	Nombre approximatif de relevés de prix
Alimentation	44	64,2	...
Boissons et tabac	5	2,5	...
Loyer	1	4,9	...
Combustible, éclairage et eau	6	7,6	...
Habillement et chaussure	21	9,9	...
Mobilier et articles de ménage	18	1,4	...
Dépenses de ménage	9	3,4	...
Soins personnels et médicaux	9	1,3	...
Loisirs	5	0,7	...
Transports	12	4,1	...
Total	130	100,0	...

exclus les impôts et amendes, les dépenses de jeux, les transferts d'argent, les dons, l'épargne, les placements, les primes d'assurance vie et les frais encourus pour l'acquisition d'une épouse.

Mode de relevé des prix
Les prix sont relevés en mars, juin, septembre et décembre sur des marchés, auprès de points de vente au détail et de prestataires de service de 20 régions urbaines. Il n'a pas été effectué d'enquête sur les points d'achat, soit que les points d'achat aient tous été couverts, s'il y en a peu, soit qu' au moins 50 pour cent d'entre eux aient été couverts, s'il y en a beaucoup. Les prix des articles relevés sur des marchés, tels que fruits, légumes, céréales et légumineuses, sont obtenus par achat direct. D'autres prix sont recueillis au moyen d'enquêtes par correspondance dans des magasins. Les tarifs pour l'électricité, l'eau et les communications sont les tarifs officiels. Les prix utilisés dans le calcul de l'indice sont les prix du marché libre payés par les consommateurs. On ne tient pas compte des prix de soldes et des rabais. Les prix du marché noir sont relevés si les articles sont disponibles pour tous les consommateurs.

Logement
Les données relatives au loyer sont obtenues trimestriellement au moyen d'enquêtes par correspondance pour au moins 30 logements occupés par des familles à revenu modique, 30 logements occupés par des familles à revenu moyen et 30 logements occupés par des familles à revenu élevé dans chaque ville. Les logements occupés par leur propriétaire sont exclus de l'indice.

Spécification des variétés
Les articles retenus pour les relevés de prix font l'objet de spécifications portant sur la variété, la qualité, le nom, la marque, l'unité, etc.

Substitution, changement de qualité, etc.
Si un article disparaît du marché ou si la qualité d'un article change, il est remplacé par un article analogue.

Articles saisonniers
Les prix des articles saisonniers sont relevés uniquement lorsque ceux-ci sont disponibles en saison.

Calcul
L'indice est calculé selon la formule de Laspeyres sous forme de moyenne arithmétique pondérée à base fixe, les coefficients de pondération correspondant à la période de base. L'indice pour un article est obtenu en utilisant les rapports de prix de la période courante et de la période de base. L'indice national est une moyenne pondérée d'indices de 20 villes, les pondérations utilisées étant proportionnelles à la population de chaque ville.

Organisation et publication
Ministry of Finance, Planning and Economic Affairs, Bureau of Statistics: «Quarterly Statistical Bulletin» (Dar-es-Salaam).
Pour de plus amples détails d'ordre méthodologique, voir: Ministry of Economic Affairs and Development Planning, Bureau of Statistics: «National Consumer Price Index» (octobre 1974).

TCHAD (N'DJAMENA)

Dénomination officielle
Indice des prix à la consommation.

Portée
L'indice est calculé mensuellement et porte sur des ménages de salariés des secteurs public et privé résidant à N'Djamena.

Base originale
Février 1988 = 100.

Source des coefficients de pondération
Les coefficients de pondération et les articles sélectionnés ont été déterminés sur la base des résultats d'une enquête sur les dépenses des ménages effectuée en 1972 à N'Djamena. L'enquête portait sur les ménages de salariés non célibataires des secteurs public et privé ayant un salaire compris entre 5 000 et 20 000 francs CFA au moment de l'enquête. Les coefficients de pondération ont été ajustés pour tenir compte de l'évolution des prix entre le moment de l'enquête et février 1988.

Pondération et composition

Groupes principaux	Nombre d'articles	Pondération	Nombre approximatif de relevés de prix
Alimentation	67	5 902	...
Habillement	13	959	...
Equipement ménager	18	277	...
Hygiène et soins médicaux	16	401	...
Combustible et éclairage	4	437	...
Matériaux de construction	10	403	...
Véhicules	8	491	...
Tabac	4	59	...
Services relatifs au logement	2	770	...
Services personnels	4	93	...
Autres services (y compris transports et voyages)	9	208	...
Total	155	10 000	...

Dépenses de consommation des ménages
L'indice des prix à la consommation ne couvre que les catégories de dépenses pour lesquelles la somme payée résulte d'un prix (réel ou fictif) appliqué à une quantité et, parmi ces catégories, celles qui correspondent à la consommation des ménages.

Elle inclut l'autofourniture et l'autoconsommation (surtout des produits agricoles). Ces biens et services sont valorisés en leur affectant des prix fictifs ou conventionnels (prix sur le marché le plus proche de consommation).

Le loyer et les petites réparations faites dans le logement (consolidation des murs en pisé avec du ciment) font partie des dépenses de consommation mais non pas l'achat d'une maison-même payée par mensualités - ni l'ajout d'une pièce supplémentaire qui représente une épargne des ménages.

Les impôts directs, les diverses cotisations, les jeux d'argent ne sont pas des consommations. En revanche, les impôts indirects inclus dans les prix payés par les consommateurs sont couverts par l'indice des prix à la consommation.

Dans de nombreux ménages, certains membres de la famille possèdent ou gèrent une entreprise individuelle: agricole, industrielle, artisanale ou commerciale. Les approvisionnements dans le cadre de cette activité sont évidemment à exclure des dépenses pour la consommation finale des ménages.

Sont aussi exclus de l'indice mensuel les dépenses pour lesquelles, soit l'information rapide sur les prix manque, soit les prix observables ne sont pas toujours conformes à la définition stricte de l'article retenu.

Mode de relevé des prix
Les prix sont relevés par des enquêteurs deux fois par mois sur les deux principaux marchés de N'Djamena. Les prix des produits vendus en vrac (vente au «tas» dont le volume varie suivant les saisons avec un prix constant) ne sont déterminables qu'après achat et pesée des produits ramenés au kilo. Pour certains articles dont les prix varient très lentement, les relevés n'ont lieu qu'une ou deux fois par an (loyer par exemple). Les prix relevés sont des prix d'offre pratiqués dans les points de vente retenus, toutes taxes comprises.

Le prix d'offre (prix proposé par le commerçant ou l'artisan) diffère du prix moyen effectivement payé par les ménagères. La différence entre ces deux prix est variable: faible dans le secteur de l'ameublement, de la confection, des articles ménagers; mais certainement assez considérable dans le domaine de l'alimentation. L'évolution concordante des deux types de prix est supposée exister pour les céréales et les postes non alimentaires de l'indice.

Logement
Pas disponible.

Spécification des variétés
Chacun des 155 articles figure directement dans l'indice alors que, très souvent, l'on rencontre pour un poste de l'indice plusieurs articles c'est-à-dire une variété d'articles soit homogènes, soit hétérogènes.

Dans le cas des variétés homogènes, on constate généralement que les prix sont peu dispersés. Un prix moyen calculé comme une moyenne des prix observés dans chacun des points de vente-échantillon a un sens. L'indice de la variété à N'djamena est alors égal au rapport des prix moyens de cette variété entre les deux périodes. Néanmoins, l'indice actuel retient même dans ce cas la moyenne arithmétique simple des indices élémentaires.

Dans le cas des variétés hétérogènes, les produits peuvent différer les uns des autres ou être très disparates. Ces produits ne sont pas forcément substituables pour le consommateur. La notion de prix moyen n'a pas de sens. On peut néanmoins pour chaque produit - par exemple trois types de pantalons - calculer un indice élémentaire égal au rapport du prix du produit dans un point de vente à la période de base. L'indice de la variété à N'djamena est alors égal à la moyenne arithmétique simple des indices élémentaires.

Substitution, changement de qualité, etc.
L'introduction dans l'indice d'un produit dont le prix à la période de base ne pouvait pas être ou n'était pas observé ne pose pas de problème pour des produits appartenant à des variétés homogènes puisque la notion de prix moyen dans une telle variété est valable. Le problème concerne surtout les variétés hétérogènes.

Plusieurs méthodes sont offertes: a) l'article de l'indice des prix n'existe plus et on le remplace par un autre existant déjà sur le marché à la période de référence; b) le prix du nouvel article peut être estimé à partir d'une proportionnalité calculée à partir d'une variable quantitative (méthode de la règle de trois); c) le prix est lié à plusieurs caractéristiques du produit: on peut, pour simplifier, privilégier l'une des caractéristiques et être ainsi ramené au problème précédent. Mais il est possible, en introduisant une formule dite «économétrique», de passer des caractéristiques à la valeur du produit; c'est la méthode des régressions. Au moment de son intégration dans l'indice le nouveau produit est censé «remplacer» en totalité ou partiellement un ou plusieurs produits figurant dans l'indice. Ceci revient à intégrer, par l'intermédiaire de la création d'une variété, le nouveau produit dans un poste déjà existant.

Articles saisonniers
Pas disponible.

Calcul
L'indice est calculé selon la formule de Laspeyres sous forme de moyenne arithmétique pondérée à base fixe, les coefficients de pondération correspondant à 1972.

Organisation et publication
Direction de la statistique, des études économiques et démographiques: «Evolution des prix à la consommation dans la ville de N'Djamena».

idem: «Indice des prix à la consommation 1983-1989», février 1990.

TCHECOSLOVAQUIE

Dénomination officielle
Consumer Price Index (Indice des prix à la consommation).

Portée
L'indice est calculé mensuellement et porte sur toute la population de la Tchécoslovaquie.

Base originale
Janvier 1989 = 100.

Source des coefficients de pondération
La valeur des coefficients de pondération et le choix des articles ont été déterminés sur la base du chiffre d'affaires du commerce de détail. La pondération se réfère à l'année 1989.

Dépenses de consommation des ménages
L'indice comprend toutes les dépenses des ménages dans les magasins d'Etat, coopératives et magasins privés pour l'achat de produits alimentaires et d'articles manufacturés. Il comprend également les dépenses dans les restaurants et les cantines publiques, ainsi que les dépenses pour divers services, y

Pondération et composition

Groupes principaux	Nombre d'articles	Pondération	Nombre approximatif de relevés de prix
Alimentation	239	297,64	...
Cantines	79	105,63	...
Biens industriels:	500	450,77	...
Habillement	150	101,86	...
Chaussure et maroquinerie	52	28,69	...
Autres (y c. combustible)	248	320,22	...
Services (y c. loyer, transports et communications)	233	145,96	...
Total	1 051	1 000,00	...

compris les honoraires pour frais administratifs, notariaux, honoraires d'avocats, de caractère judiciaire et local, de même que les assurances pour les biens et pour les personnes physiques.

Mode de relevé des prix
Les articles choisis pour le relevé des prix doivent faire l'objet d'achats fréquents de la part des consommateurs, représenter une part importante dans les dépenses de ces derniers, et être typiquement représentatifs de certaines catégories de biens.

Les prix font l'objet d'un relevé mensuel, effectué le 15 du mois par des statisticiens de chaque région, auprès de magasins et d'établissements de services sélectionnés dans tous les districts de la République Tchèque et de la République Slovaque.

Pour certains articles dont le prix est resté fixe plusieurs années durant, les prix sont enregistrés au début de chaque année par l'office chargé de l'enquête.

Si un changement de prix survient en cours d'année, l'équipe notifie le nouveau prix dans un délai de cinq jours. Par exemple, les prix de l'électricité, du gaz, de l'eau, des transports et des communications sont les mêmes pour l'ensemble du pays et leur étude est centralisée.

Les prix des fruits et légumes font l'objet d'un relevé trimensuel, le 1er, le 10 et le 20 de chaque mois.

Les soins de santé et médicaux, ainsi que l'enseignement, sont dispensés gratuitement. Les données concernant les honoraires relatifs à certains services particuliers, tels que les cours de langue et de musique, peuvent être obtenues auprès des établissements qui les dispensent.

L'indice est fondé sur celui des biens achetés à leur valeur réelle dans des établissements d'Etat, coopératives ou commerces privés (le prix des articles d'occasion n'est pas inclus dans l'indice).

Logement
Les données concernant les loyers sont déterminées à partir du taux unitaire par mètre carré et compte tenu du prix des équipements ménagers de base (par exemple, cuisinières, espaces réservés au combustible, aux denrées alimentaires, au matériel sanitaire, à l'adduction d'eau et d'électricité, au système d'évacuation des eaux usées, aux salles de bains, aux éléments de cuisine, toilettes, chauffage central, matériel de nettoyage, aux ascenseurs).

Les données relatives aux loyers sont obtenues pour des habitations de dimensions différentes: studios d'une seule pièce, appartements d'une pièce avec cuisine, de deux pièces avec cuisine, de trois pièces avec cuisine. Les taux d'utilisation des appartements ont été fixés d'une manière centralisée (par décret de l'organe central). La possibilité de mener des enquêtes décentralisées sur les loyers est actuellement à l'étude.

L'évolution du coût des logements occupés par leur propriétaire est présente dans l'indice, qui fait état de la tendance observée dans le prix des matériaux de construction et le coût de la main-d'oeuvre employée dans la construction et l'entretien des logements.

Spécification des variétés
Des spécifications détaillées sont établies pour les biens et les services et portent sur la taille, la fabrication, la marque, la quantité, la qualité, etc. La description en fonction de la qualité a été établie avec l'aide de spécialistes du commerce.

Substitution, changement de qualité, etc.
Lorsqu'un produit cesse d'être disponible, il est remplacé par un autre de qualité approximativement égale. Si la qualité ne peut être directement comparée, des corrections sont apportées, sur avis des spécialistes d'organismes commerciaux. Il est de règle que les différences insignifiantes en matière de

qualité (liées à la mode, par exemple) ne soient pas prises en compte.
Articles saisonniers
Les fruits et légumes frais ne sont pas toujours mis en vente chaque mois. Il est procédé, tous les mois, à la composition d'un «panier» distinct, comprenant les variétés mises en vente au cours du mois considéré. Pour les différentes variétés de fruits et légumes, les coefficients de pondération des paniers se fondent sur la moyenne des années de la période 1985 à 1989. L'indice du sous-groupe des fruits et légumes est alors calculé à l'aide de coefficients de pondération constants, déterminés en fonction de leur importance dans les dépenses totales de consommation.
Calcul
L'indice est calculé selon la formule de Laspeyres, sous forme de moyenne arithmétique pondérée à base fixe, les coefficients de pondération correspondant à la période de base.

A partir des prix calculés dans les déclarations fournies par les établissements, on calcule la moyenne arithmétique simple. Des indices séparés sont calculés pour la République Tchèque et la République Slovaque. L'indice pour l'ensemble du pays représente la moyenne de ces deux indices.
Autres informations
Un «Indice du coût de la vie» est également calculé et publié pour les principales catégories sociales des ménages, pour les ménages à revenu faible et élevé, et pour les ménages comptant 1, 2 et 3 enfants.
Organisation et publication
Federal Statistical Office, Czech Statistical Office and Slovak Statistical Office: «Statistical Information». - Evolution des indices de prix dans le domaine de la consommation et de la production (informations mensuelles rapides). - Evolution des indices de prix à la consommation (informations mensuelles).

idem: «Statistical Yearbook».

idem: «Figures for everybody».

THAILANDE

Dénomination officielle
General Consumer Price Index (Indice général des prix à la consommation).
Portée
L'indice est calculé mensuellement et porte sur les familles habitant les zones urbaines de l'ensemble du pays, familles composées de deux à dix personnes et dépensant en 1986 entre 4 000 et 10 000 bahts par mois.
Base originale
1986 = 100.
Source des coefficients de pondération
La valeur des coefficients de pondération et le choix des articles résultent d'une enquête socio-économique sur les ménages menée en 1986 dans l'ensemble du pays sur un échantillon de tous les ménages privés non institutionnels. Les articles ont été retenus en fonction de leur importance relative dans le budget des ménages, de la mesure dans laquelle l'évolution de leurs prix est représentative de celle d'un groupe plus large, de la variabilité des changements de prix au sein du groupe dans lequel ils sont classés, de la mesure dans laquelle il est possible de les identifier en toute sécurité par spécification, et de la probabilité de les voir gagner en importance relative par accroissement de la demande. Les demandes correspondant à des articles dont les prix ne sont pas relevés, mais qui ressemblent, par leurs caractéristiques physiques et leur usage, à d'autres articles dont les prix sont relevés, ont été ajoutées aux dépenses relatives à ces derniers. Les dépenses correspondant à d'autres articles à prix non relevés d'un sous-groupe donné sont réparties proportionnellement au sein du sous-groupe. Toutes les dépenses diverses n'entrant dans aucun sous-groupe ont été réparties proportionnellement entre tous les articles donnant lieu à un relevé de prix. Le nombre d'articles et les coefficients de pondération utilisés depuis 1991 sont présentés dans le tableau.
Dépenses de consommation des ménages
Les dépenses de consommation prises en compte dans le calcul de l'indice correspondent aux achats de biens et services, à la valeur des biens et services acquis à titre de paiement partiel, acquis gratuitement et produits à domicile, ainsi qu'à la valeur

Pondération et composition

Groupes principaux	Nombre d'articles	Pondération	Nombre approximatif de relevés de prix
Alimentation	...	40,38	...
Logement:			
Loyer	...	24,76	...
Mobilier et articles de ménage	...	4,77	...
Habillement et chaussures	...	5,13	...
Soins personnels et médicaux	...	8,94	...
Transports et communications	...	11,69	...
Loisirs et instruction	...	4,33	...
Tabac et boissons alcoolisées	...	100,00	...

locative des logements occupés par leur propriétaire. En sont exclus les impôts directs versés à l'Etat, les cotisations et dons en espèces, les primes d'assurance, les billets de loterie et autres dépenses liées aux jeux de hasard, l'intérêt des emprunts, les titres et toutes les formes d'actifs et de passifs.
Mode de relevé des prix
Les prix sont relevés par des agents auprès des centres commerciaux, des points de vente au détail et des établissements de services situés dans les zones urbaines. Les prix des produits alimentaires sont relevés une fois par semaine auprès d'au moins quatre points de vente au détail de chaque zone commerciale. Pour les autres articles, les relevés ont lieu pendant la semaine comprenant le 15 du mois. Les tarifs du téléphone, de l'électricité et de l'eau, des hôpitaux, etc., sont obtenus auprès des administrations. Les prix retenus pour le calcul de l'indice sont ceux que toute personne aurait à payer le jour du relevé.
Logement
La valeur locative des logements occupés par leur propriétaire est ajoutée aux dépenses servant à pondérer les loyers. L'évolution du prix des loyers se mesure aux changements affectant d'une période à l'autre les loyers moyens payés par les locataires. Ces loyers sont relevés trimestriellement sur un échantillon d'environ 335 locataires.
Spécification des variétés
Les spécifications décrivent la variété, la qualité, la fabrication, la marque, etc.
Substitution, changement de qualité, etc.
En cas de modification des caractéristiques d'un produit, on applique la méthode d'enchaînement. Lorsqu'un article disparaît du marché, il est remplacé par un article similaire.
Articles saisonniers
Il n'est pas tenu compte, en principe, des fluctuations saisonnières du prix de ces articles. On élimine cependant certains d'entre eux en maintenant, lorsqu'ils ne sont pas de saison, les prix de clôture de la saison précédente.
Calcul
L'indice est calculé selon la formule de Laspeyres sous forme de moyenne arithmétique pondérée à base fixe, les coefficients de pondération correspondant à la période de base.

Dans la pratique cependant, l'indice est calculé par enchaînement mensuel des pondérations de base et des prix relatifs de deux périodes consécutives: avec cette méthode, on obtient l'indice du mois courant en mettant à jour celui du mois précédent.

L'indice national est un agrégé des séries nationales, pondérés par le poids démographique de chaque région.
Organisation et publication
L'indice est calculé mensuellement par le Ministry of Commerce, Department of Business Economics, Price Index Division (Bangkok).

idem: «Monthly Report Consumers Price Index». Office of the Prime Minister, National Statistical Office: «Bulletin of Statistics» (Bangkok).

TOGO (LOME)

Dénomination officielle
Indice des prix à la consommation.
Portée
L'indice est calculé mensuellement et porte sur les ménages privés africains à Lomé.

Base originale
1963 = 100.

Source des coefficients de pondération
Les coefficients de pondération et les articles sélectionnés ont été déterminés sur la base des résultats d'une enquête sur les dépenses des ménages effectuée de juin 1964 à juin 1965 à Lomé auprès de ménages privés africains.

Pondération et composition

Groupes principaux	Nombre d'articles	Pondération	Nombre approximatif de relevés de prix
Alimentation	53	47,9	...
Boissons alcooliques, tabac et kola	12	10,6	...
Combustible, éclairage et eau	6	5,3	...
Equipement ménager et produits d'entretien	13	2,8	
Logement:			
Loyer	1	2,9	...
Réparations	7	3,9	...
Habillement et chaussure	16	7,7	...
Transports	4	3,5	...
Services	9	3,1	...
Divers	30	12,3	...
Total	151	100,0	...

Dépenses de consommation des ménages
Pas disponible.

Mode de relevé des prix
Les prix, pour l'ensemble des articles, sont relevés par des enquêteurs sur le marché local, dans les principaux magasins et auprès de certains prestataires de services. Les prix sont recueillis deux fois par semaine pour les denrées alimentaires du pays; les prix des autres articles sont obtenus une fois par mois.

Logement
Les données relatives au loyer sont obtenues à partir de relevés des contributions directes.

Spécification des variétés
Pas disponible.

Substitution, changement de qualité, etc.
Pas disponible.

Articles saisonniers
Pas disponible.

Calcul
L'indice est calculé selon la formule de Laspeyres, sous forme de moyenne arithmétique pondérée à base fixe, les coefficients de pondération correspondant à la période juin 1964 - juin 1965.

Organisation et publication
Ministère du Plan, Direction de la statistique: «Bulletin mensuel de statistique» (Lomé).
Ministère des Finances, de l'Economie et du Plan, Direction de la statistique: «Prix-Indices des prix et coût de la vie à Lomé - Indice des prix à la consommation familiale à Lomé, base 100 en 1963».

TONGA

Dénomination officielle
Consumer Price Index (Indice des prix à la consommation).

Portée
L'indice est calculé trimestriellement et porte sur tous les ménages d'ouvriers de Tongatapu.

Base originale
1984 = 100.

Source des coefficients de pondération
La valeur des coefficients de pondération et le choix des articles résultent d'une enquête sur les dépenses des ménages menée à Tongatapu en 1984.
La valeur des coefficients de pondération des articles qui ne sont pas pris en compte dans l'indice est affectée de deux manières différentes aux articles qui y sont inclus:
- lorsqu'un article exclu est très proche d'un article inclus, le coefficient de l'article y figurant représente la dépense relative à chacun des articles dont il est fait mention en tant qu'articles voisins. Ainsi, le coefficient de pondération de l'orange représente également les dépenses en oranges amères, cédrats, citrons et mandarines.
- dans la plupart des autres cas, c'est-à-dire lorsqu'un article exclu ne peut être raisonnablement considéré comme similaire à tout autre article inclus, le coefficient de pondération de l'article exclu est réparti sur un certain nombre d'articles inclus ou parmi tous les articles d'un sous-groupe ou d'un groupe entier. Par exemple, le coefficient de pondération des aspirateurs, dont il n'est pas tenu compte dans l'indice, est réparti sur toute une série d'appareils ménagers.

Dans quelques cas, lorsqu'il n'est pas possible de répartir le coefficient de pondération sur d'autres articles, sur un sous-groupe ou un groupe, la dépense est exclue complètement des calculs des coefficients de pondération. L'effet est le même que si ce coefficient avait été réparti sur tous les articles de l'ensemble de l'indice, c'est-à-dire qu'il ne modifie le coefficient de pondération d'aucun des articles inclus.

Pondération et composition

Groupes principaux	Nombre d'articles	Pondération	Nombre approximatif de relevés de prix
Alimentation	104	49,308	5
Logement	34	10,458	5
Biens d'équipement ménager	60	13,316	5
Habillement et chaussure	40	5,623	5
Transports	15	5,771	3
Tabacs, boissons alcoolisées et Kava	6	6,987	5
Autres biens et services	48	8,537	4
Total	307	100,000	32

Dépenses de consommation des ménages
Les dépenses de consommation prises en compte dans le calcul de l'indice excluent l'impôt sur le revenu, les loyers, l'entretien des maisons en propriété, l'épargne et les achats à des fins commerciales.

Mode de relevé des prix
Les prix sont relevés à Nuku'alofa et dans d'autres centres de l'île de Tongatapu au cours de la période la plus proche de la moitié du mois intermédiaire de chaque trimestre, c'est-à-dire à mi-février, mi-mai, mi-août et mi-novembre. Il est évidemment nécessaire de répartir le relevé sur une période en raison, tout simplement, de la charge de travail qu'entraînent les visites personnelles. Dans le cas des fruits et légumes frais dont les prix accusent fréquemment de fortes variations sur de brèves périodes, le relevé a lieu toutes les quinzaines du trimestre afin d'obtenir une meilleure représentation des prix moyens au cours du trimestre.
Lors du choix des points de vente pour les relevés de prix, le choix porte en premier lieu sur les principaux commerces étant donné l'importance de leur part dans l'ensemble des ventes et la gamme étendue des articles qu'ils vendent. Ce choix est complété par un échantillon de points de vente de moindre importance et de différents types, afin de s'assurer d'une prise en compte équilibrée de tous les articles. Par exemple, lors du relevé d'articles tels que produits alimentaires en conserve, quelques petits magasins de quartier sont choisis à l'intérieur et à l'extérieur de Nuku'alofa, de même que les grands supermarchés de Nuku'alofa. Les prix sont relevés non seulement auprès de magasins de détail mais aussi auprès d'une grande variété de commerces qui se livrent à la vente de biens de consommation et de services au public. Ceci inclut des marchés de fruits et légumes, des restaurants, des hôtels, des véhicules à moteur et stations-service, de l'électricité, des services de taxis et d'autobus, des entreprises de construction et différentes sortes de commerçants, des postes et téléphones etc. Presque toutes les données relatives aux prix de détail sont relevées à la suite de visites personnelles d'agents du service des statistiques aux magasins et commerces concernés.

L'indice des prix à la consommation mesure les changements des prix effectifs des transactions, c'est-à-dire les prix payés effectivement par les consommateurs lorsqu'ils se livrent à l'achat de biens ou de services. Il prend en compte tous les rabais, offres spéciales, etc., pour autant qu'ils portent sur des biens et services spécifiés et qui sont mis à la disposition de tous les acheteurs. Il ne tient pas compte des rabais pour articles endommagés ou détériorés, effectués par les magasins, ni des prix spéciaux pour les articles en fin de stock. Dans l'IPC sont comprises les taxes sur les ventes au détail, qui constituent un élément des prix effectivement payés par les consommateurs. Ainsi, tout changement du taux de la taxe sur le chiffre d'affaires affecte le mouvement de l'indice des prix à la consommation.

Logement
Le loyer n'entre pas dans l'indice.

Spécification des variétés
Après avoir déterminé la liste des articles devant être inclus dans l'indice, il convient de spécifier d'une façon précise les biens et services dont les prix doivent être établis périodiquement aux fins de relevés des chiffres de l'indice. Des articles décrits en tant que «thé», ou «chemise d'homme», ou «bicyclette», ou «frais de taxi» sont suffisamment définis pour le calcul des coefficients de pondération, mais leur description n'est pas assez détaillée pour permettre l'établissement de prix cohérents. Dans le cas du «thé», il est nécessaire de préciser s'il s'agit de thé en sac ou en paquet, quelle est la taille du paquet, etc. Dans le cas d'une chemise d'homme il convient de préciser s'il s'agit d'une chemise à manches longues ou à manches courtes, le type de tissu, etc. Dans le cas d'une bicyclette, il est nécessaire d'en préciser le modèle et la dimension, et d'indiquer les accessoires qu'elle comprend, etc. Dans le cas de frais de taxi, le relevé doit préciser la longueur du trajet effectué.

En conséquence, pour tout article compris dans l'indice, des spécifications détaillées sont fournies pour orienter les agents chargés des relevés afin qu'ils puissent obtenir le prix de biens et services comparables pour chaque trimestre successif. Dans certains cas, il n'est fait mention que d'une seule spécification par article inclus dans l'indice, mais, dans d'autres cas, l'article fait l'objet de deux ou plusieurs spécifications.

Substitution, changement de qualité, etc.
Lorsqu'on s'aperçoit qu'un article sélectionné est temporairement épuisé, la pratique habituelle consiste à utiliser le dernier relevé de prix où l'article figure, jusqu'à ce que cet article soit de nouveau disponible. Dans certains cas, si un article est absent du marché pendant plusieurs trimestres successifs (mais que l'on s'attend à ce qu'il soit de nouveau disponible dans un avenir proche), on peut lui attribuer un prix sur la base des changements survenus dans les prix d'articles analogues dont on prévoit un changement qui les rendra similaires à l'article épuisé. Lorsque l'absence d'un article devient permanente, la pratique habituelle est de le remplacer par un article du même genre. S'il s'agit d'un nouveau modèle, il remplace dans l'indice l'ancien article. Si rien ne remplace directement l'article disparu, un autre article similaire est choisi pour le remplacer. Dans l'un ou l'autre cas le nouvel article doit être introduit dans l'indice de telle manière que toute différence de prix des deux articles n'affecte pas le niveau de l'indice. On y parvient en enchaînant les deux prix. S'il arrive que l'ancien et le nouvel article soient disponibles en même temps, il est procédé directement au raccordement. Cependant, si l'ancien article a disparu du marché sans avertissement et qu'un nouvel article doit être choisi, le processus n'est pas aussi simple. Il est alors souhaitable, en principe, d'obtenir des informations complémentaires avant de tenter de raccorder les deux séries de prix; dans l'idéal, il serait bon d'obtenir, pour le nouvel article, le prix de l'ancien article au cours de la dernière période où il a été disponible.

Toutefois, dans la pratique, cela est souvent impossible et l'on doit procéder au raccordement en partant de l'hypothèse selon laquelle le dernier prix de l'ancien article et le premier prix du nouveau représentent un rapport de prix approprié entre les deux articles.

Articles saisonniers
Lorsqu'un article saisonnier, par exemple fruit ou légume, n'est pas disponible au cours de certains trimestres, il est procédé à la répartition de son coefficient de pondération sur d'autres articles similaires jusqu'à ce qu'il soit de nouveau disponible. Cette méthode a le même effet que l'attribution de prix aux articles manquants.

Calcul
L'indice est calculé selon la formule de Laspeyres sous forme de moyenne arithmétique pondérée à base fixe, les coefficients de pondération correspondant à la période de base.

En ce qui concerne les articles dont les prix sont relevés auprès de plus d'un point de vente, ou pour ceux qui, comme les fruits ou légumes frais, font l'objet de relevés de prix plus d'une fois par trimestre, il est procédé en premier lieu au calcul du prix moyen de l'article au cours du trimestre. Le prix de chaque article au cours du trimestre en cours est ensuite comparé au prix du même article pour l'année de base, aux fins du calcul d'un «rapport de prix».

Organisation et publication
Statistics Departement: «The Annual Statistical Abstract» (Nuku'alofa).
idem: «Consumer Price Index.»

TRINITE-ET-TOBAGO

Dénomination officielle
Index of Retail Prices (Indice des prix de détail).

Portée
L'indice est calculé mensuellement et porte sur des ménages disposant en 1976 d'un revenu mensuel compris entre 100 et 800 dollars de Trinité-et-Tobago.

Base originale
Septembre 1982 = 100.

Source des coefficients de pondération
Les coefficients de pondération résultent d'une enquête sur les dépenses des ménages menée en 1975-76 auprès d'un échantillon de 2 493 ménages, dont 1 681 ménages disposaient d'un revenu mensuel compris entre 100 et 800 dollars de Trinité-et-Tobago en 1976. Les pondérations n'ont pas été ajustées pour tenir compte de l'évolution des prix entre le moment de l'enquête et septembre 1982. Ont été retenus pour le calcul de l'indice les articles affectés d'un coefficient de pondération au moins égal à 1 pour 1000.

Pondération et composition

Groupes principaux	Nombre d'articles	Pondération	Nombre approximatif de relevés de prix
Alimentation	94	351	...
Repas au dehors	4	15	...
Boissons alcoolisées et tabac	6	47	...
Combustible et éclairage	5	26	...
Loyer et eau	5	126	...
Entretien et réparations	11	12	...
Mobilier et articles ménagers	44	84	...
Services	5	14	...
Habillement et chaussure	45	189	...
Transports	13	86	...
Instruction	6	25	...
Fournitures médicales	8	25	...
Total	246	1 000	(a)

Remarque: (a) Trois par article dans la mesure du possible.

Dépenses de consommation des ménages
Les dépenses de consommation prises en compte dans le calcul de l'indice correspondent aux achats de tous les biens et services effectués par les ménages de référence pour leur consommation, y compris les primes d'assurance et les intérêts des emprunts hypothécaires. Les revenus en nature sont pris en compte s'ils sont reçus régulièrement. Les dons et les redevances liés à l'usage de certains biens et services entrent aussi dans l'indice. On n'exclut pas l'impôt sur le revenu et autres impôts directs, les cotisations à la sécurité sociale et aux caisses de retraite, les primes d'assurance couvrant un objet de consommation particulier, les cotisations aux caisses maladie et les primes d'assurance vie.

Mode de relevé des prix
Les prix des biens et des services sont relevés sur un échantillon de quelque 375 points de vente. Les localités retenues l'ont été en raison de l'importance des dépenses qui y sont engagées et de leur population, tandis que le choix des points de vente résulte de l'expérience des enquêteurs locaux. Les prix sont relevés sous la responsabilité du chef du Census and Surveys Office (Office du recensement et des enquêtes) par neuf agents locaux qui se rendent périodiquement auprès des points de vente choisis pour y procéder aux relevés nécessaires. Ceux-ci sont effectués deux fois par mois pour les légumes, les fruits et la viande; une fois par mois pour l'alimentation, les boissons et le tabac. Les données relatives à l'habillement, les réparations et l'entretien du logement, les repas pris en dehors, le loyer, les articles de ménage, les services, les transports et les soins médicaux sont obtenues trimestriellement. Les prix du combustible et de l'éclairage sont recueillis soit mensuellement, soit trimestriellement et ceux

de l'instruction, semi-annuellement. Les relevés commencent le deuxième mercredi du mois et se poursuivent pendant une semaine.

Les prix retenus dans le calcul de l'indice sont ceux que toute personne aurait à payer le jour du relevé pour se procurer les bien et services correspondants. Le prix des soldes n'est pris en compte que si les articles soldés représentent une part importante des ventes pendant la période de référence. Les prix du marché noir le sont si le détaillant en fait état. Rabais, opérations de location-vente ou de vente à crédit et achats d'articles d'occasion ne sont pas retenus.

Logement
Les données relatives aux loyers sont relevées trimestriellement sur un échantillon de logements comprenant d'une à trois chambres à coucher. Le total des loyers relevés pendant la période courante dans une zone de prix donnée est rapporté au total des loyers relevés pendant la période de base dans la même zone. Les indices de zone ainsi obtenus sont pondérés par les coefficients de zone et combinés pour former l'indice global des loyers.

La valeur locative nette des logements occupés par leur propriétaire, estimée par application d'un certain pourcentage à leur valeur vénale, a été ajoutée à la valeur des loyers véritables pour constituer le coefficient de pondération de l'article «loyer». Mais seul le montant des loyers des logements en location a été pris en compte pour le calcul de l'indice lui-même.

Spécification des variétés
Les variétés retenues pour les relevés de prix font l'objet de spécifications quant à la marque, la qualité, l'unité, etc.

Substitution, changement de qualité, etc.
Lorsque les caractéristiques des produits subissent des modifications, les prix de l'année de base sont modifiés en conséquence. Les articles périmés ou disparus du marché sont remplacés par des articles de substitution appropriés.

Articles saisonniers
Les produits alimentaires frais à caractère saisonnier sont, une fois la saison terminée, retirés de l'indice et leurs coefficients de pondération sont répartis entre les autres articles du même groupe.

Calcul
L'indice est calculé selon la formule de Laspeyres sous forme de moyenne arithmétique pondérée à base fixe, les coefficients de pondération correspondant à la période de base.

Les prix moyens des articles dans chaque région sont des moyennes arithmétiques simples des relevés de prix obtenus. Des rapports de prix séparés pour les articles dans chaque région sont ensuite calculés en divisant les prix moyens de la période courante par les prix moyens de la période précédente. Ces rapports de prix sont ensuite pondérés en utilisant des pondérations régionales afin d'obtenir des rapports de prix nationaux, les pondérations étant proportionnelles à la population et aux données relatives aux ventes au détail dans les régions concernées.

Organisation et publication
Central Statistical Office: «The Index of Retail Prices 1982 - Statistical Studies and Papers», No. 10, 1984 (Port of Spain).

Government Printing: «Gazette of Trinidad and Tobago» (Port of Spain).

TUNISIE

Dénomination officielle
Indice spécifique des prix à la consommation.

Portée
L'indice est calculé mensuellement et porte sur les ménages urbains de salariés dont les dépenses annuelles étaient comprises entre 160 et 250 dinars par personne en 1980.

Base originale
1983 = 100.

Source des coefficients de pondération
Les coefficients de pondération et les articles sélectionnés ont été déterminés sur la base des résultats d'une enquête sur les dépenses des ménages effectuée en 1980. Les coefficients de pondération n'ont pas été ajustés pour tenir compte de l'évolution des prix entre le moment de l'enquête et 1983.

Pondération et composition

Groupes principaux	Nombre d'articles	Pondération	Nombre approximatif de relevés de prix
Alimentation	164	503	25 000
Logement:			
Loyer et charges	2	33	64
Combustible et éclairage	16	62	512
Mobilier, équipement et entretien du ménage	60	78	1 924
Soins personnels et médicaux et produits d'entretien	127	56	4 064
Transports	25	54	800
Habillement et chaussure	91	101	2 910
Instruction, loisirs et divers	69	113	2 210
Total	554	1 000	37 484

Dépenses de consommation des ménages
Les dépenses de consommation des ménages prises en compte dans le calcul de l'indice correspondent aux biens et services couramment achetés par la population urbaine et comprennent les achats à crédit qui sont comptabilisés en totalité. En sont exclus, le revenu en nature, les biens produits par les ménages pour leur propre consommation, la valeur locative des logements occupés par leur propriétaire, l'acompte pour l'achat de biens neufs, l'achat du logement et de terrains, les cotisations aux assurances sociales et caisses de pension et les primes d'assurance vie, le coût des patentes, les assurances liées à des biens de consommation particuliers (excepté l'assurance de voiture particulière), les impôts, les envois de fonds, les dons et les versements similaires.

Mode de relevé des prix
Les prix sont relevés par des enquêteurs sur des marchés et auprès de points de vente au détail et prestataires de services répartis dans les 16 villes les plus importantes du pays. Le choix des points de vente a été fait d'une façon raisonnée. Les points de vente sélectionnés dans les villes représentent toutes les formes de commerce et sont choisis judicieusement dans chaque type de quartier (Medina, quartier moderne et quartier périphérique). Les relevés de prix se font systématiquement dans toutes les grandes surfaces, sur 55 marchés, dans 322 épiceries et 240 magasins d'habillement et auprès de 785 prestataires de services. Les tarifs publics sont observés directement dans les administrations concernées. L'enquête des prix se fait par contact direct par l'intermédiaire d'enquêteurs affectés en permanence à cette fin. Pratiquement, il y a un enquêteur par localité à l'exception de Tunis et Sfax où l'on a affecté respectivement trois et deux agents en raison de l'importance de ces deux villes. Les prix pour la plupart des articles sont recueillis une fois par mois et par point de vente, sauf ceux des fruits, légumes et poissons frais qui le sont tous les jours sur les marchés. Cette cadence d'observation permet d'obtenir en fin de chaque mois deux à trois prix par variété et par mois. L'étalement des observations au cours du mois dépend du planning des visites des points de vente. Dans le cas des produits frais, les moyennes journalières des prix sont généralement les observations des prix faites le matin (de 10h à 12h) sur les marchés. Les ventes de soldes, les rabais, la location-vente, les ventes à crédit ne sont pas pris en compte.

Logement
Les données relatives au loyer sont obtenues tous les six mois auprès d'un échantillon de 2 000 locataires d'appartements, villas et maisons arabes. Le loyer comprend le prix mensuel du loyer et, le cas échéant, les charges. Le calcul de l'indice loyer tient compte de l'importance de chaque type de logement.

Les logements occupés par leurs propriétaires ne sont pas considérés dans l'indice.

Spécification des variétés
Afin de suivre dans le temps le prix du même objet ou du même service à qualité égale de sorte que les changements éventuels de prix soient des variations pures de prix, les variétés sont déterminées par les enquêteurs dans chaque point de vente et indiquent la marque, le volume, le poids, etc.

Substitution, changement de qualité, etc.
Il se peut que des variétés observées depuis un certain temps viennent à disparaître dans un point de vente ou du marché. Il faut signaler que la disparition d'un produit est considérée comme temporaire tant qu'elle ne dépasse pas les six mois, au delà de cette échéance la disparition devient définitive et l'on procède alors à un remplacement.

La méthode de substitution diffère selon la nature de la variété. Dans le cas de variétés hétérogènes, l'enquêteur procède au remplacement selon le point de vente et change le prix de base de l'article dans le magasin au cas où il y a une différence appréciable de qualité.

Dans le cas de variétés homogènes, si la variété de remplacement est assimilable à celle disparue (différence de marque seulement), l'enquêteur est autorisé à faire la substitution sans modification de prix de base.

Articles saisonniers
Les produits frais tels que fruits, légumes et poissons se caractérisent non seulement par la grande fréquence de changement des prix, mais aussi par la variation du volume de la production selon les saisons. De ce fait ces produits ne sont pas traités comme les autres variétés ordinaires contenues dans le panier de l'indice.

L'indice pour un produit frais est obtenu en utilisant les rapports de prix du mois courant et du même mois de la période de base. Ces indices sont ensuite pondérés et des moyennes mobiles sont utilisées pour le calcul final de l'indice.

Calcul
L'indice est calculé selon la formule de Laspeyres sous forme de moyenne arithmétique pondérée à base fixe, les coefficients de pondération correspondant à 1980.

D'abord on calcule des prix moyens simples par localité dans le cas des variétés homogènes ou des indices moyens simples par localité dans le cas des variétés hétérogènes. Pour passer de la localité à la région on utilise comme pondération la population urbaine de chaque localité appartenant à la région. Pour passer du régional au national on utilise les pondérations régionales selon la structure des dépenses de consommation de chaque région.

Autres informations
Des sous-groupes détaillés sont publiés dans le «Bulletin mensuel de statistique», ainsi qu'un autre indice national: «Indice général des prix à la consommation familiale» (base 1983 = 100).

Organisation et publication
Institut national de la statistique: «Bulletin mensuel de statistique» (Tunis).

idem: «Annuaire statistique de la Tunisie».

idem: «Economie Tunisienne en chiffres».

TURQUIE

Dénomination officielle
Urban Areas Consumer Price Index (Indice des prix à la consommation pour les zones urbaines).

Portée
L'indice est calculé tous les mois et porte sur les ménages urbains disposant en 1987 d'un revenu mensuel moyen compris entre 50 000 et un million de livres turques, et habitant les cinq régions urbaines principales du pays: Egée et Marmara, Méditerranée, Anatolie centrale, Mer Noire et Anatolie de l'Est et du Sud-Est.

Base originale
1987 = 100.

Source des coefficients de pondération
La valeur des coefficients de pondération et le choix des articles résultent d'une enquête sur les dépenses des ménages, menée entre janvier et décembre 1987 auprès de 14 424 ménages appartenant à l'ensemble des groupes socio-économiques d'un échantillon de 16 villes et de 50 localités de plus de 20 000 habitants, représentant les cinq régions urbaines principales mentionnées ci-dessus.

Les articles faisant l'objet d'une consommation habituelle de la part des ménages ont été choisis pour entrer dans le calcul de l'indice. Dans chaque groupe, les articles ont été classés par ordre décroissant en fonction de leur part dans la consommation totale, et leur valeur cumulée a été prise en compte. Les articles constituant 85 à 90 pour cent de la consommation totale de leur groupe ont été sélectionnés pour représenter celui-ci dans l'indice. Ce rapport est de 100 pour cent pour certains groupes et de 60 à 65 pour cent pour d'autres.

Dépenses de consommation des ménages
Les montants réels et estimés relatifs à la consommation ont

Pondération et composition

Groupes principaux	Nombre d'articles	Pondération	Nombre approximatif de relevés de prix
Alimentation	132	34,88	36 451
Habillement et chaussure	62	12,80	18 727
Mobilier, ameublement et équipement ménager	53	11,24	11 199
Soins personnels et médicaux	29	3,44	4 470
Transports et communications	23	6,48	1 278
Instruction et loisirs	33	5,01	3 748
Logement:	...	26,15	4 397
Loyer	2	...	...
Combustible et éclairage	8	...	...
Réparations et entretien	5	...	...
Total	347	100,00	80 270

servi de base au calcul des coefficients de pondération (revenus en nature utilisés pour la consommation des ménages, loyers estimés pour les logements occupés par leur propriétaire).

La consommation est assimilée à l'«achat», c'est-à-dire à l'entrée en possession, par un ménage, d'un bien donné. Dans la plupart des cas, les dates de livraison des biens ont été prises en compte, contrairement aux délais. A l'exception des achats à tempérament, l'achat est considéré comme accompli lorsque le bien entre en possession du ménage. Dans le cas des achats à tempérament, on considère l'achat comme effectué au moment de la livraison du bien. Dans le cas des «revenus en nature», la prise en compte est effectuée au moment où le bien entre en possession du ménage.

Mode de relevé des prix
Les prix sont relevés dans 33 zones de peuplement par le personnel de la Division des Statistiques et de l'Indice des Prix du SIS d'Ankara et par les équipes des agences régionales du SIS.

Les prix des biens ne présentant pas de différences par régions sont relevés à partir du centre, dans le but d'éviter les erreurs pouvant survenir des relevés établis séparément et pour ne pas surcharger les agences régionales. (Par exemple: hôpitaux d'Etat, lignes aériennes, services postaux, journaux, téléphone, encyclopédies, manuels scolaires publiés par le ministère de l'Education, frais d'inscription à l'Université, médicaments, électricité, biens dont la vente est régie par un monopole, etc.).

Dans le cadre du relevé des prix courants mensuels, il a été décidé de relever les prix deux fois par mois pour l'ensemble des biens, à l'exception des fruits et légumes frais, afin de pouvoir obtenir tous les changements de prix possibles. Ces prix sont relevés lors des semaines comprenant le 10 et le 20 de chaque mois. Etant donné que les fruits et légumes frais présentent une plus grande variabilité que les autres biens, leurs prix sont relevés une fois par semaine, c'est à dire quatre fois par mois.

Les prix retenus pour le calcul de l'indice sont les prix normalement payés par le public. Il n'est pas tenu compte des frais de crédit et des rabais, mais les prix des soldes pour les articles d'habillement et les tissus sont pris en considération.

Logement
Les loyers font l'objet d'une évaluation, qu'il s'agisse des loyers réels ou des loyers estimés pour les ménages. De ce fait, l'indice reflète non seulement les loyers payés par les locataires, mais également ceux des ménages propriétaires de leur logement.

Dans chaque localité, les logements dont les loyers doivent être enregistrés sont choisis en prenant en considération les structures socio-économiques et les caractéristiques d'habitation des districts compris dans les échantillons de l'enquête de 1987 sur les dépenses des ménages, où résident des ménages disposant d'un revenu mensuel moyen compris entre 50 000 et un million de livres turques.

Spécification des variétés
Les 347 articles utilisés dans le calcul de l'indice ont été décrits pour chaque zone de peuplement et, lorsque cela s'est avéré nécessaire, ont fait l'objet d'une nouvelle description détaillée en fonction des établissements. La description des articles est si précise que, même si les prix sont relevés par différents enquêteurs, le prix d'un même article sera relevé de façon précise.

Substitution, changement de qualité, etc.
Lorsqu'un produit spécifique n'est plus disponible, il est remplacé par un article similaire, ou bien son coefficient de pondération est ajouté à cet article similaire ou réparti sur l'ensemble du sous-groupe. Les nouveaux produits sont inclus dans le barème de pondération lors du prochain changement de l'année de base.

Articles saisonniers
Des coefficients de pondération, variables selon les mois, sont utilisés pour les articles dont la consommation présente des fluctuations saisonnières. Il s'agit des fruits frais, des fruits secs, des légumes, du poisson et de la volaille. Des coefficients de pondération variables sont utilisés pour ces articles; en effet, un article entrant dans l'indice pour les quelques mois où il est de saison cède la place à un autre article lors de la saison suivante, et n'est pas consommé en même quantité tous les mois.
Les coefficients de pondération ont été analysés pour chaque article. La réduction du coefficient de pondération, à cause de la sous-consommation d'un fruit ou d'un légume précoce, ainsi que l'augmentation du même coefficient en cas de surconsommation, font chaque mois l'objet d'études et de contrôles.

Calcul
L'indice est calculé selon la formule de Laspeyres sous forme de moyenne arithmétique pondérée à base fixe, les coefficients de pondération correspondant à la période de base.
L'indice des prix à la consommation des régions urbaines est calculé sous forme de moyenne pondérée de l'indice des cinq régions urbaines, les coefficients de pondération étant constitués par la consommation totale de chaque région.

Autres informations
L'indice des prix à la consommation est en général remis à jour tous les cinq ans pour prendre en compte les changements structurels.
Des indices séparés sont publiés pour les cinq principales régions urbaines et pour 16 villes, ainsi que pour certains sous-groupes précis.
Les indices sont publiés dans le Press Bulletin le 4 du premier mois postérieur à leur calcul.

Organisation et publication
State Institute of Statistics: «Aylik Istatistik Bulteni» (Monthly Bulletin of Statistics) (Ankara).
idem: «Wholesale and Consumer Price Indexes Monthly Bulletin» (janvier, février, mars 1990).

URUGUAY (MONTEVIDEO)

Dénomination officielle
Indice de los precios del consumo (Indice des prix à la consommation).

Portée
L'indice est calculé mensuellement et porte sur des ménages à revenu moyen résidant à Montevideo.

Base originale
Décembre 1985 = 100.

Source des coefficients de pondération
Les coefficients de pondération et les articles sélectionnés ont été déterminés sur la base des résultats d'une enquête sur les dépenses des ménages effectuée entre septembre 1982 et août 1983 à Montevideo auprès d'un échantillon de 1 946 ménages à revenu moyen. Les pondérations ont été ajustées pour tenir compte de l'évolution des prix entre le moment de l'enquête et décembre 1985.

Dépenses de consommation des ménages
Les dépenses de consommation prises en compte dans le calcul de l'indice comprennent tous les achats de biens et de services destinés à la consommation pendant la période de référence, y compris la consommation de biens produits par les ménages eux-mêmes et les revenus perçus en nature. L'acquisition de biens durables autres que les maisons occupées par leur propriétaire est mesurée d'après les versements faits pendant la période de référence. Les dons, impôts directs, impôts municipaux et autres dépenses telles que les redevances liées à l'usage de biens ou de services sont aussi pris en compte. Sont exclus de l'indice: les virements, les impôts sur le revenu et autres impôts directs, l'épargne et les jeux d'argent.

Pondération et composition

Groupes principaux	Nombre d'articles	Pondération	Nombre approximatif de relevés de prix
Alimentation	84	39,91	...
Habillement et chaussure	50	7,02	...
Logement	16	17,58	...
Mobilier, articles de ménage et produits d'entretien	19	6,36	...
Soins médicaux	11	9,26	...
Transports et communications	9	10,38	...
Loisirs	11	3,10	...
Instruction	8	1,30	...
Autres dépenses (y compris soins personnels et tabac)	13	5,09	...
Total	221	100,00	...

Mode de relevé des prix
Les prix sont relevés auprès de 400 points de vente au détail, marchés et prestataires de services à Montevideo. La collecte des données relatives aux prix est faite, pour la plupart des articles, par des agents qui se rendent périodiquement en des points de vente sélectionnés. Pour les articles vendus sur les marchés, les prix sont relevés chaque semaine. Dans le cas des articles dont les prix sont fixés centralement (tels que le lait, le pain, les redevances pour l'électricité, les tarifs des transports publics), les prix sont obtenus directement auprès des autorités ou des prestataires de services compétents, quand des changements se produisent.
Les prix retenus dans le calcul de l'indice sont ceux que toute personne aurait à payer le jour du relevé pour se procurer les biens ou services correspondants.

Logement
Les données relatives au loyer sont relevées auprès de 12 agences de location de logements sélectionnées. Pour les logements occupés par leur propriétaire, les informations sont obtenues auprès de la banque hypothécaire de l'Uruguay.

Spécification des variétés
Les spécifications des variétés dont les prix sont à relever donnent de façon détaillée la marque, la description, l'unité employée et la taille.

Substitution, changement de qualité, etc.
Si un article disparaît d'un point de vente, son prix est imputé sur la base des articles disponibles dans d'autres points de vente.

Articles saisonniers
Il est tenu compte des fluctuations saisonnières des prix des fruits et légumes frais en variant les articles et leur coefficient de pondération à l'intérieur de «paniers» mensuels dont le coefficient de pondération d'ensemble demeure constant.

Calcul
L'indice est calculé selon la formule de Laspeyres, sous forme de moyenne arithmétique pondérée à base fixe, les coefficients de pondération correspondant à la période de base.
Le rapport de prix pour chaque article est calculé en divisant le prix moyen de la période courante par le prix moyen de la période de base.

Organisation et publication
Dirección General de Estadística y Censos: «Boletín mensual» (Montevideo).
idem: «Indice de los precios del consumo, Metodología, Base Diciembre 1985».

VANUATU

Dénomination officielle
Consumer Price Index - Low Income Group Families (Indice des prix à la consommation, familles à revenu modeste).

Portée
L'indice est calculé trimestriellement et porte sur les familles à revenu modeste des zones urbaines, dont le chef disposait en 1975 d'un revenu mensuel inférieur à 20 000 francs NH.

Base originale
Janvier - mars 1976 = 100.

Source des coefficients de pondération
La valeur des coefficients de pondération et le choix des articles résultent d'une enquête sur les dépenses des ménages menée au premier trimestre de 1975 sur 220 ménages de Vila et de Santo (Luganville).

Pondération et composition

Groupes principaux	Nombre d'articles	Pondération	Nombre approximatif de relevés de prix
Alimentation	...	45,8	...
Boissons et tabac	...	10,1	...
Habillement et chaussure	...	14,1	...
Loyer, combustible, éclairage et eau	...	2,2	...
Mobilier, ameublement, articles et services ménagers	...	8,0	...
Transports et communications	...	9,8	...
Santé, instruction et loisirs	...	10,0	...
Total	...	100,0	...

Dépenses de consommation des ménages
Les dépenses de consommation prises en compte dans le calcul de l'indice portent sur tous les biens et services importants que la population de l'indice acquiert pour sa consommation. En sont exclus l'impôt sur le revenu, les placements, l'épargne et les emprunts personnels.

Mode de relevé des prix
Les prix sont relevés vers le 15 de chaque mois à Santo et vers le milieu de chaque trimestre à Vila, auprès d'un échantillon de points de vente au détail et de prestataires de services. Les prix retenus sont ceux que paient normalement les consommateurs.

Logement
Pas disponible.

Spécification des variétés
Les articles dont les prix sont à relever font l'objet de spécifications portant sur le nom, la marque, la qualité et la taille.

Substitution, changement de qualité, etc.
Lorsqu'un produit manque à un point de vente donné, un produit analogue lui est substitué dans l'indice.

Articles saisonniers
Pas disponible.

Calcul
L'indice est calculé selon la formule de Laspeyres sous forme de moyenne arithmétique pondérée à base fixe, les coefficients de pondération correspondant au premier trimestre de 1975.

L'indice pour un article est obtenu en utilisant les rapports de prix de la période courante et de la période précédente.

Autres informations
Une nouvelle série portant sur tous les ménages de la zone urbaine de Vanuatu (base janvier-mars 1990 = 100) est maintenant calculée mais les informations méthodologiques relatives à cette série n'étaient pas disponibles au BIT lors de la publication du présent Volume.

Organisation et publication
National Planning and Statistics Office: «Statistical Bulletin» (Port Vila).

VENEZUELA (CARACAS)

Dénomination officielle
Indice de precios al consumidor para el área metropolitana de Caracas (Indice des prix à la consommation pour la zone métropolitaine de Caracas).

Portée
L'indice est calculé mensuellement et porte sur toutes les familles vivant dans la zone métropolitaine de Caracas.

Base originale
1984 = 100.

Source des coefficients de pondération
Les coefficients de pondération et les articles sélectionnés ont été déterminés sur la base des résultats d'une enquête sur les dépenses des ménages effectuée pendant 12 mois, du 1er novembre 1974 au 31 octobre 1975 et se rapportant à tous les types de ménages dans la zone métropolitaine de Caracas. Les articles ont été choisis pour le relevé des prix lorsqu'ils représentaient plus de 1 pour cent des dépenses totales des ménages. Les fluctuations des prix des articles non retenus sont attribuées aux articles dont les prix ont été relevés et qui les représentent. Les pondérations n'ont pas été ajustés pour tenir compte de l'évolution des prix entre le moment de l'enquête et 1984.

Pondération et composition

Groupes principaux	Nombre d'articles	Pondération	Nombre approximatif de relevés de prix
Alimentation et tabac	180	30,83	...
Dépenses de ménage (logement, combustibles et éclairage, ameublement, etc.)	59	29,64	...
Habillement et chaussure	72	9,33	...
Divers	64	30,20	...
Total	375	100,00	...

Dépenses de consommation des ménages
Les dépenses de consommation prises en compte dans le calcul de l'indice comprennent tous les biens et services achetés pour la consommation par la population de référence. Elles comprennent aussi la consommation de biens cultivés et produits à domicile et les revenus perçus en nature, les cotisations à la sécurité sociale et aux caisses de retraite, les paiements fait aux autorités municipales en rapport avec l'usage de biens ou de services, c'est-à-dire les droits d'immatriculation de voitures automobiles, les redevances, etc.

Mode de relevé des prix
Les prix sont obtenus mensuellement par des enquêteurs auprès de 1 136 points de vente sélectionnés comprenant des marchés, supermarchés, magasins de détail et prestataires de services. Les échantillons sont répartis uniformément sur tout le mois. Pour les fruits frais, les prix sont relevés trois fois auprès de chaque point de vente sélectionné afin d'obtenir un prix moyen par point de vente. Les tarifs officiels sont retenus pour l'électricité, le gaz et l'eau et des enquêtes spéciales sont effectuées pour les soins médicaux, l'instruction, les transports et communications.

Les prix retenus dans le calcul de l'indice sont les prix réels réglés en espèces. Les prix des biens d'occasion et ceux du marché noir ne sont pas pris en considération.

Logement
Les données relatives au loyer sont obtenues mensuellement auprès d'un échantillon de logements loués (maisons et appartements). L'échantillon est réparti sur 12 mois et les enquêteurs se rendent dans environ 200 logements loués chaque mois. Il n'est pas tenu compte des logements occupés par leur propriétaire.

Spécification des variétés
Les spécifications des articles dont le prix doit être relevé sont données en détail et portent sur la marque, la description, l'unité employée et la taille, etc.

Substitution, changement de qualité, etc.
Un article dont la qualité a changé est considéré comme nouveau. Quand ce nouvel article est retenu, il est inclus dans l'indice au titre de variété du sous-groupe examiné. Quand un article disparaît du marché, on le remplace par un article similaire.

Articles saisonniers
Il n'est pas tenu compte dans le calcul de l'indice des fluctuations saisonnières des prix.

Calcul
L'indice est calculé selon la formule de Laspeyres, sous forme de moyenne arithmétique pondérée à base fixe, les coefficients de pondération correspondant à la période 1er novembre 1974 - 31 octobre 1975.

En calculant l'indice des articles, on utilise des rapports de prix, pour chaque variété dans chaque point de vente, de la période courante et de la période précédente. On calcule les moyennes arithmétiques simples de ces rapports de prix pour établir les indices des articles.

Organisation et publication
Banco Central de Venezuela, Departamento de Estadísticas de Precios: «Boletín mensual» (Caracas).

YEMEN (ADEN)

Dénomination officielle
Retail Price Index (Indice des prix de détail).

Portée
L'indice est calculé annuellement et porte sur les ménages habitant Aden.

Base originale
1969 = 100.

Source des coefficients de pondération
La valeur des coefficients de pondération et le choix des articles résultent d'une enquête sur les dépenses des ménages de fonctionnaires du gouvernement. Les coefficients de pondération ont été révisés ultérieurement pour tenir compte des changements survenus dans la structure des dépenses.

Pondération et composition

Groupes principaux	Nombre d'articles	Pondération	Nombre approximatif de relevés de prix
Alimentation	48	508	...
Combustible, éclairage et eau	6	39	...
Loyer	5	60	...
Habillement et chaussure	24	90	...
Articles de ménage	13	40	...
Khat, tabac et boissons	3	100	...
Autres dépenses (soins de santé, soins personnels, transports, culture et loisirs)	24	163	...
Total	123	1 000	...

Dépenses de consommation des ménages
Pas disponible.

Mode de relevé des prix
Les prix sont relevés régulièrement tous les mois, les lundis et mardis de la deuxième semaine, à Aden.

Logement
Pas disponible.

Spécification des variétés
Afin que les prix puissent être comparables dans le temps, la qualité et la quantité des articles et des services ont été soigneusement définies.

Substitution, changement de qualité, etc.
Pas disponible.

Articles saisonniers
Pas disponible.

Calcul
L'indice est calculé selon la formule de Laspeyres sous forme de moyenne arithmétique pondérée à base fixe, les coefficients de pondération correspondant à la période de base.

Organisation et publication
Central Statistical Organisation: «Statistical Yearbook» (Aden).

YOUGOSLAVIE

Dénomination officielle
Cost of Living Index (Indice du coût de la vie).

Portée
L'indice est calculé mensuellement et porte sur les familles d'ouvriers et d'employés.

Base originale
Les indices paraissant dans les publications nationales sont calculés sur la base des changements par rapport aux prix moyens de l'année précédente; par conséquent, la base de l'indice varie chaque année civile.

Source des coefficients de pondération
Les coefficients de pondération et les articles sélectionnés sont déterminés sur la base des résultats d'une enquête permanente sur les revenus et dépenses effectuée dans plus de 50 grandes villes et auprès de plus de 2 000 ménages d'ouvriers et d'employés (comprenant deux adultes et un ou deux enfants ou personnes à charge). Les coefficients de pondération pour 1979 sont présentés dans le tableau suivant.

Pondération et composition

Groupes principaux	Nombre d'articles	Pondération	Nombre approximatif de relevés de prix
Alimentation	94	45,84	...
Boissons et tabac	8	4,92	...
Logement:			
Loyer	1	3,60	...
Entretien et eau	4	2,74	...
Combustible et éclairage	9	5,62	...
Habillement et chaussure	54	12,37	...
Biens et services ménagers	36	6,88	...
Soins personnels	17	3,58	...
Instruction et loisirs	18	5,54	...
Transports et communications	9	8,91	...
Total	260	100,00	...

Dépenses de consommation des ménages
Pas disponible.

Mode de relevé des prix
Pour la plupart des articles, les prix sont relevés chaque mois par des enquêteurs auprès d'environ 3 500 points de vente au détail répartis dans 53 villes; ceux des produits agricoles sont recueillis chaque quinzaine.

Logement
Les données relatives au loyer sont obtenues à partir de huit catégories types de logements dans chacune des 53 villes.

Spécification des variétés
Pas disponible.

Substitution, changement de qualité, etc.
Pas disponible.

Articles saisonniers
Il est tenu compte des fluctuations saisonnières des prix des fruits et légumes frais en variant la composition mensuelle des articles à l'intérieur d'un groupe dont le coefficient de pondération d'ensemble demeure constant.

Calcul
L'indice est calculé selon la formule de Laspeyres, sous forme de moyenne arithmétique pondérée à base fixe, les coefficients de pondération correspondant à la période de base. L'indice est obtenu au moyen de pondérations successives des moyennes arithmétiques des prix, les pondérations utilisées étant estimées sur la base des chiffres de vente des articles dans les différentes villes ou républiques où les prix sont recueillis et sur la base de la structure des dépenses des familles couverts par l'enquête permanente.

Organisation et publication
Institut fédéral de la statistique: «Indeks» (Belgrade).
idem: «Metodoloski Materyali», nos. 122, 168 et 233.

ZAMBIE

Dénomination officielle
Consumer Price Index for Low Income Group Families (Indice des prix à la consommation des familles à revenu modique).

Portée
L'indice est calculé mensuellement et porte sur les ménages urbains disposant d'un revenu mensuel ne dépassant pas 100 kwachas en 1974-75. L'indice reflète les variations de prix à Lusaka, Kabwe, Livingstone et dans la Copperbelt.

Base originale
1975 = 100 et 1985 = 100.

Source des coefficients de pondération
La valeur des coefficients de pondération et le choix des articles résultent d'une enquête sur les dépenses des ménages menée pour la période mars 1974 - mars 1975 à Lusaka, Ndola et Kitwe. L'indice porte sur les ménages urbains qui disposaient d'un revenu mensuel inférieur à 100 kwachas à l'époque de l'enquête.

Dépenses de consommation des ménages
En sont exclus les primes d'assurance-vie, l'impôt sur le revenu et les impôts sur les biens personnels.

Mode de relevé des prix
Une enquête sur les prix est effectuée vers le 10 de chaque mois par des fonctionnaires de l'Office central des statistiques,

Pondération et composition

Groupes principaux	Nombre d'articles	Pondération	Nombre approximatif de relevés de prix
Alimentation et tabac	74	680	459
Habillement et chaussure	40	99	268
Combustible et éclairage	25	106	87
Articles ménagers, ameublement	25	44	208
Soins médicaux	36	3	98
Transports et communications	11	22	16
Instruction et loisirs	10	9	43
Autres biens et services	63	37	244
Total	284	1 000	1 423

qui visitent un échantillon de points de vente à Lusaka, alors que des questionnaires sont envoyés par la poste à des points de vente et prestataires de services des autres villes. Les prix sont relevés à la suite d'achats directs. Pour des articles tels que l'eau, le gaz, l'électricité, les transports et communications, les tarifs officiels sont utilisés.

Le relevé des prix des fruits et légumes frais a lieu deux fois par mois au marché central de la ville.

Les prix retenus pour le calcul de l'indice sont ceux que les consommateurs payent effectivement. Les rabais et prix de soldes sont également pris en compte.

Logement
Les loyers et le coût des logements occupés en propriété n'entrent pas dans l'indice.

Spécification des variétés
Chacun des articles dont les prix sont à relever fait l'objet d'une spécification portant sur la taille, l'unité, la marque et la qualité.

Substitution, changement de qualité, etc.
Les changements de qualité font l'objet d'une estimation sur la base d'articles de substitution similaires. Les articles de remplacement ne sont introduits que lorsqu'ils prennent suffisamment d'importance sur le marché.

Articles saisonniers
Les fluctuations saisonnières des prix ne font l'objet d'aucun ajustement.

Calcul
L'indice est calculé selon la formule de Laspeyres sous forme de moyenne arithmétique pondérée à base fixe, les coefficients de pondération correspondant à la période mars 1974 - mars 1975.

L'indice pour un article est obtenu en utilisant les rapports de prix moyens de la période en cours et de la période de base. Les prix moyens sont des moyennes arithmétiques simples des prix relevés.

Autres informations
Il est également procédé au calcul d'un indice des prix à la consommation des familles à revenu élevé (base 1975 = 100).

Organisation et publication
Central Statistical Office: «Monthly Digest of Statistics» (Lusaka).

idem: «Studies in Official Statistics - No. 3, Methods and Procedures used in Compiling Price Statistics».

ZIMBABWE

Dénomination officielle
Consumer Price Index for Lower Income Urban Families (Indice des prix à la consommation des familles urbaines à revenu modique).

Portée
L'indice est calculé mensuellement et porte sur les ménages africains; les ménages dont le chef est à la retraite, au chômage, ou travaille à son compte sont exclus, de même que les ménages dont le revenu était supérieur à 250 dollars par mois à l'époque de l'enquête. L'indice porte sur les quatre centres urbains suivants: Harare, Bulawayo, Mutare et Gweru.

Base originale
1980 = 100.

Source des coefficients de pondération
La valeur des coefficients de pondération et le choix des articles résultent de l'enquête sur les dépenses des ménages effectuée en 1978-79. L'enquête portait sur 250 ménages de Harare et 233 ménages de Bulawayo. Les données n'ont pas été ajustées pour tenir compte de l'évolution des prix entre la période de l'enquête et la période de base.

Pondération et composition

Groupes principaux	Nombre d'articles	Pondération	Nombre approximatif de relevés de prix
Alimentation	27	54,9	1 466
Boissons et tabac	5	5,4	156
Habillement et chaussure	25	6,6	496
Loyer, combustible et éclairage	4	18,4	87
Equipement ménager	23	4,6	741
Transports	19	4,7	34
Divers	21	5,4	295
Total	124	100,0	3 275

Dépenses de consommation des ménages
La consommation de biens et de services reçus à titre de revenu en nature n'est pas prise en compte. Elle exclut les impôts directs et l'épargne (primes d'assurance-vie et cotisations aux caisses de retraite) ainsi que les sommes dépensées aux jeux et en dons.

Mode de relevé des prix
Les prix sont relevés mensuellement auprès d'un échantillon de commerces de détail et prestataires de services des banlieues à forte densité de population de Harare, Bulawayo, Mutare et Gweru. L'indice couvre également les points de vente du centre des villes.

Les relevés sont effectués par correspondance pour la plupart. A Bulawayo, Mutare et Gweru, les questionnaires sont distribués et rassemblés par des fonctionnaires du Département des services communautaires. Dans ces centres, les relevés de prix pour les fruits et légumes sont effectués trimestriellement par les enquêteurs sur les marchés. A Harare, une partie des relevés de prix pour des articles tels que les fruits et légumes vendus sur le marché sont rassemblés par le personnel de la section des prix du Central Statistical Office.

Les prix retenus pour l'indice sont ceux qu'aurait à payer tout consommateur à la date de référence. Les relevés de prix se réfèrent au huitième jour de chaque mois. Les prix des soldes et rabais ne sont pas pris en compte.

Logement
Les données relatives au loyer sont relevées à partir d'une enquête trimestrielle sur les logements. L'indice du loyer se rapporte au loyer y compris les dépenses pour l'eau et l'assainissement payées pour divers types de logements municipaux. Les frais de réparation de logement sont exclus du groupe principal «Loyer», mais sont compris dans le groupe «Divers».

Spécification des variétés
Pour certains articles, principalement les produits d'épicerie, la marque et la taille sont spécifiées dans les formulaires de relevés de compte. Pour les autres articles, le questionnaire adressé par le Central Statistical Office comporte des descriptions assez larges. Si, d'un point de vente à l'autre, la marque choisie pour représenter un article peut varier, les relevés effectués dans un point de vente donné doivent porter sur la même marque mois après mois. Dans une gamme donnée, les articles à prix moyen les plus vendus sont ceux qu'il convient de choisir.

Substitution, changement de qualité, etc.
Lorsqu'un article est provisoirement épuisé, son dernier prix est maintenu dans le relevé jusqu'à ce qu'il soit de nouveau disponible, ou bien un article de remplacement est introduit, la formule d'enchaînement étant utilisée.

Articles saisonniers
Seuls les fruits et légumes sont traités comme articles saisonniers. Il est tenu compte des variations saisonnières en dotant ces articles d'une structure de pondération qui varie de mois en mois, le coefficient de pondération globale du groupe fruits et légumes restant fixe.

Calcul
L'indice est calculé selon la formule de Laspeyres sous forme de moyenne arithmétique pondérée dont la base est décembre

1981. Les indices des groupes sont ensuite convertis à la base 1980 = 100 en utilisant certains facteurs de conversion.

Afin d'obtenir les indices par article, on utilise des rapports de prix de la période en cours et de la période précédente. Pour la plupart des articles, il est procédé au calcul des rapports de prix moyens et pour quelques autres articles tels que les pièces de rechange pour voitures, à celui des moyennes des rapports de prix.

Des indices séparés sont calculés dans chacune des quatre villes; ces indices sont ensuite pondérés selon la population de chaque ville afin d'obtenir l'indice national. Les pondérations appliquées à chaque ville sont les suivantes: Harare 56, Bulawayo 32, Gweru 6 et Mutare 6.

Autres informations
Le Central Statistical Office publie également un Indice des prix à la consommation des familles urbaines à revenu élevé (base 1980 = 100). En outre, un indice portant sur tous les articles à l'exclusion des contributions indirectes est également publié pour les familles urbaines à revenu modique aussi bien qu'élevé.

Organisation et publication
Central Statistical Office: «Quarterly Digest of Statistics» (Harare).

idem: «Monthly Supplement to the Digest of Statistics».

INTRODUCCION

El presente volumen 1 de *Fuentes y métodos: estadísticas del trabajo* ofrece una descripción metodológica de las principales características de las series nacionales de índices de precios del consumo, publicadas por la OIT en las ediciones de 1992 del *Anuario de Estadísticas del Trabajo* y del *Boletín de Estadísticas del Trabajo*, y es una versión revisada, ampliada y actualizada de la segunda edición de *Fuentes y métodos estadísticos*, aparecida en 1987.

En él se describen 171 series de índices de precios del consumo referentes a 157 países. La mayoría de estas descripciones fueron preparadas a partir de las respuestas oficiales de las oficinas nacionales de estadísticas a un cuestionario específicamente concebido, o bien a partir de publicaciones nacionales sobre los índices de precios del consumo, o bien de una combinación de ambas fuentes. En ciertos casos, las descripciones presentadas pueden referirse solamente a nuevas series publicadas en el *Boletín*, dado a que no se dispone de promedios anuales para publicación en el *Anuario*.

Este volumen tiene dos objetivos fundamentales: (i) ofrecer información básica sobre las fuentes y los métodos utilizados en cada país, en cada una de las series de índices de precios del consumo publicadas por la OIT con el propósito de acrecentar su utilidad para diferentes fines, y ii) señalar las diferencias existentes entre las series nacionales en lo que se refiere a su alcance, cobertura, fuentes de los datos, definiciones, clasificaciones, tratamiento de determinados problemas especiales y la fórmula utilizada para su cómputo. Las descripciones se han estructurado y se presentan según 14 encabezamientos genéricos para las diferentes características con el fin de facilitar la comparación. Estos encabezamientos son los siguientes:

Denominación oficial
La denominación del índice de precios del consumo figura en la lengua que utiliza el país para su correspondencia oficial con la OIT, acompañada, si es necesario, de su traducción al español.

Alcance
Se informa sobre la periodicidad de la serie (mensual, trimestral, semestral o anual), los tipos de hogares analizados, según su encuadre en una categoría dada de ingresos o gastos, u hogares de un tamaño determinado; los grupos de población, que pueden referirse a la población en su conjunto o a grupos socioeconómicos determinados, tales como obreros, empleados, etc., y las áreas geográficas, tales como todo el país, los centros urbanos, la capital, y ciudades o grupos de ciudades específicos.

Base oficial
Se considera el año o período de base utilizado por las oficinas del país para el cálculo del índice y su presentación en las publicaciones nacionales.

Fuente de la ponderación
Se indican la fuente o fuentes de las ponderaciones utilizadas para el índice y el período de referencia, por ejemplo, encuestas sobre los gastos de los hogares, cuentas nacionales, etc. Si el período de referencia para las ponderaciones difiere del período de base del índice, se describen los ajustes introducidos en las ponderaciones para tener en cuenta las diferencias de precios entre los dos períodos.

Cuando las ponderaciones se han obtenido a partir de una encuesta sobre los gastos de los hogares, se facilita información sobre las zonas geográficas, los tipos de hogares y los grupos de población cubiertos, la duración de la encuesta, el período de referencia de los datos sobre los gastos y el tamaño de la muestra. Cuando las ponderaciones se han obtenido a partir de las cuentas nacionales o de otras fuentes, se ofrecen, siempre que sea posible, los métodos de obtención de las mismas. Asimismo, se describen los criterios y el método seguidos para la selección de los artículos del índice o para el tratamiento de los artículos de precio no fijado (atribución de ponderaciones).

Ponderaciones y composición
El número de artículos y las ponderaciones utilizados para el cálculo del índice se presentan por grupos de gastos. Un "artículo" significa aquí el grupo más pequeño de mercancías o servicios para los cuales se hace una ponderación específica. Por ejemplo, la carne de vaca podría ser un artículo representado por varias variedades como filete, solomillo, etc. para las cuales no se dispone de ponderaciones independientes. Los principales son: alimentación, combustible y luz, vestido, vivienda y varios. Cuando las clasificaciones no se ajustan a estos grupos mencionados, se da la clasificación utilizada por el país. Cuando ello es posible, se indica el número aproximado de cotizaciones de precios utilizadas para el cálculo del índice.

Gastos de consumo de los hogares
Los gastos de consumo de los hogares se definen generalmente como los efectuados por los hogares en bienes de consumo y servicios. Esta expresión puede referirse a las compras en sí o al consumo propiamente dicho. En las descripciones se explica, cuando ello es posible, el tratamiento que reciben los bienes producidos en el hogar para el consumo propio, la propiedad de la vivienda, los productos duraderos, las adquisiciones a crédito, las adquisiciones de segunda mano, las cotizaciones al seguro social y a cajas de pensiones, los pagos en concepto de disfrute de licencias, los seguros relacionados con determinados bienes de consumo, la asistencia médica, impuestos sobre la renta y otros impuestos directos, pagos por seguros de vida, remesas de dinero, regalos y desembolsos similares.

Método de recolección de los datos
El método utilizado para seleccionar localidades y puntos de venta; la frecuencia con que se recogen los precios de diferentes categorías de bienes y servicios; el trato que se da a los descuentos, precios de rebaja, precios de mercado negro, condiciones de alquiler, de compra o de crédito, adquisiciones de segunda mano, precios de importación, impuestos indirectos; los métodos de recolección de precios para diferentes tipos de artículos (visitas a los puntos de venta, cuestionarios enviados por correo, tarifas oficiales, compras) y las técnicas especiales utilizadas para recoger los precios relativos a artículos tales como electricidad, gas y agua, asistencia médica, educación o transportes y comunicaciones.

Vivienda
Se describen los métodos utilizados para la obtención de datos sobre alquileres, así como el tratamiento que reciben las viviendas ocupadas por sus propietarios. Cuando se dispone de información, también se indica el tratamiento que se da a desembolsos tales como impuestos municipales a la vivienda, seguros, intereses hipotecarios, reparaciones, etc., y la frecuencia y método de recolección de los datos.

Especificación de las variedades
Las especificaciones son los criterios utilizados para describir de una manera precisa la variedad correspondiente a un precio. Estos criterios podrían referirse a la calidad, fabricación, marca, unidad, etc. Cuando no existen especificaciones detalladas y claras, se indican los procedimientos utilizados para distinguir variedades.

Sustitución, cambio de calidad, etc.
La aparición de un nuevo producto en el mercado, la desaparición de un artículo o las variaciones en la calidad afectan al índice. Los métodos que utilizan los países para afrontar estos problemas se describen brevemente.

Artículos estacionales
Los precios de ciertos productos, tales como las frutas y verduras frescas, varían según la época del año. Se indican brevemente diversos procedimientos utilizados para calcular esta influencia estacional.

Cálculo
Normalmente se ponderan los precios de los diferentes artículos incluidos en el cálculo del índice, para tener en cuenta la importancia relativa de cada artículo con respecto al gasto de consumo total. En la mayoría de los países, los índices se calculan según una forma derivada tal como los promedios aritméticos ponderados de las relaciones de precio para un número determinado de artículos representativos entre el período que se considera y el período de base, recurriendo a una de las formas de la fórmula de Laspeyres. En las descripciones se explica el método exacto utilizado por los países, cuando es conocido.

Unos cuantos países utilizan un índice encadenado de Laspeyres con eslabones anuales o la fórmula de Paasche para el cálculo de sus índices. Cuando ese es el caso, así se indica en las descripciones.

Se describen los métodos de cálculo de los precios medios y de los relativos de precios, y se indica si el índice se calcula directamente o como una agregación de índices locales o regionales.

Informaciones complementarias
Se presentan las informaciones complementarias de que se dispone sobre la publicación, por países y por los subgrupos diversos del índice o sobre el cálculo de series relativas a otros grupos de población o de ingresos y sobre otras áreas geográficas.

Organización y publicación
Aquí se citan las organizaciones estadísticas responsables del cálculo y de la publicación del índice así como de los títulos de las publicaciones nacionales actuales más importantes en que aparecen los índices y quienes las publican. También se indican, siempre que es posible, los títulos y las fuentes de las publicaciones nacionales que incluyen descripciones metodológicas detalladas.

Lista de los cuadros publicados por la OIT
A. *Anuario de Estadísticas del Trabajo:*
Precios del consumo:
  23 Indices generales
  24 Indices generales, excluida la habitación
  25 Indices de la alimentación
  26 Indices del combustible y alumbrado
  27 Indices del vestido
  28 Indices del alquiler

B. *Boletín de Estadísticas del Trabajo:*
  9A Indices generales
  9B Indices de la alimentación

Observaciones
Dado que el período de base original de las series varía de un país a otro, se ha adoptado un período de base uniforme para la presentación de los datos en las publicaciones de la OIT. Desde 1986, este período de base ha sido el año 1980. (Cuando sólo se dispone de datos para períodos posteriores a este año, se elige como período de base para la presentación de los índices el primer año civil del que existen datos que aparecen en cursiva.) Esta operación no supone ningún cambio en el sistema de ponderación utilizado para el cálculo de las series.

Signos y símbolos utilizados
.   No se aplica
...   No disponible
-     Nula o inferior a la mitad de la unidad empleada
(a)   Nota al pie de página

En los cuadros, los decimales se separan por medio de un punto.

ALEMANIA 1

Nota: La descripción se refiere al territorio de la República Federal de Alemania antes del 3.10.1990.

Denominación oficial
Preisindex für die Lebenshaltung aller privaten Haushalte (Indice de precios del consumo para el conjunto de hogares privados).

Alcance
La compilación del índice es mensual y abarca todos los hogares privados de residentes alemanes, pero no los hogares colectivos.

Base oficial
1985 = 100.

Fuente de la ponderación
La selección de los artículos y la determinación de los coeficientes de ponderación se basaron en una encuesta de 1983 sobre los gastos de los hogares, que abarcó unos 55 000 hogares privados, de uno o más miembros, con ingresos mensuales netos de hasta 25 000 DM. Las ponderaciones se actualizaron a 1985 mediante la encuesta de ese año sobre el presupuesto de unos 1 000 hogares privados seleccionados. El índice se refiere a hogares con un tamaño medio de 2,3 personas y un gasto de consumo medio de 3 105 DM en 1985. La ponderación de los artículos sin precio registrado se distribuyen entre los demás artículos.

Ponderaciones y composición

Grupos principales	Número de artículos	Ponderación	Número aproximado de cotizaciones de precio
Alimentación y tabaco	186	229,89	116 000
Vestido y calzado	77	69,47	31 000
Alquiler	5	177,77	13 000
Combustible y luz	18	72,52	4 000
Muebles y otros enseres del hogar	138	72,21	37 000
Transportes y comunicaciones	81	144,03	14 000
Asistencia médica y personal	55	40,99	15 000
Educación y distracciones	147	83,71	29 000
Bienes y servicios varios	44	109,41	41 000
Total	751	1 000,00	300 000

Gastos de consumo de los hogares
Los gastos de consumo de los hogares utilizados para la ponderación comprenden la vivienda propia, los honorarios profesionales, los seguros de bienes de consumo específicos, los regalos y otros desembolsos similares. Se excluyen las contribuciones a seguros de vida, sociales y de vejez, así como ingresos en especie, adquisiciones a crédito, compras de artículos de segunda mano, impuesto a la renta y otros impuestos directos.

Método de recolección de los datos
Los investigadores recogen los precios aproximadamente a mediados de cada mes, en unos 15 000 puntos de venta al por menor y establecimientos de servicios de 118 municipios.

Los precios uniformes para todo el país (como libros y revistas, tarifas postales y aéreas, excursiones "todo incluido" y primas de seguros) se determinan en forma central, a intervalos regulares o cuando se modifican. Los precios considerados a los efectos del índice son los que pagan los consumidores en ese momento y no los de lista o catálogo; comprenden impuestos al valor añadido, gravámenes indirectos (como los del petróleo o el tabaco) y otros recargos obligatorios (como los de compensación de la energía eléctrica y la contribución debida por almacenamiento de derivados del petróleo). Sólo se recogen los precios rebajados de ordinario, pero no los de liquidación u otros descuentos.

Vivienda
Los datos sobre el alquiler se obtienen trimestralmente de todas las viviendas de la muestra (11 000). Sin embargo, para mostrar las variaciones mensuales, todos los meses sólo se incluye en el índice un tercio de las viviendas (aproximadamente 3 700).

En la ponderación también se toman en cuenta las viviendas ocupadas por sus propietarios; cuyas variaciones de alquiler se representa por la evolución de los precios.

Especificación de las variedades
Las descripciones de cada uno de los servicios y bienes abarcados por la encuesta es tan amplia que se pueden determinar, para cada unidad informante, las variedades de la mayor parte de su giro comercial. El investigador debe consignar la descripción exacta de cada uno de los bienes y servicios (marca, artículo, número, cantidad, etc.) para permitir así las comprobaciones y garantizar la comparabilidad a través del tiempo.

Sustitución, cambio de calidad, etc.
Cuando varían las características que determinan un precio, se efectúan cálculos o estimaciones, en colaboración con los expertos pertinentes, para eliminar toda modificación de precio no auténtica. Se sustituye un artículo por otro cuando el antiguo aún conserva importancia en el mercado y el nuevo ya ha alcanzado la suficiente; en tal caso se sigue un procedimiento de enlace simple entre las series de los precios antiguos y nuevos.

Artículos estacionales
No se incluyen en el índice los precios de artículos que sólo se pueden conseguir en el mercado durante un período breve. En vez, se toma en cuenta el monto total de las fluctuaciones de precio de los artículos que se ofrecen durante todo el año.

Cálculo
El índice se calcula según la fórmula de Laspeyres, como un promedio aritmético ponderado de base fija, cuyos coeficientes de ponderación corresponden al período de base.

En primer lugar se calcula la media no ponderada de los precios por municipio y por "Land" (región); para calcular los índices de artículos se utiliza la media de los precios relativos del período en curso y del período de base. Se ponderan luego los índices regionales, correspondientes a los once "Länder", en función de la población de cada uno de ellos y, por último, se combinan para obtener el índice nacional.

Informaciones complementarias
Se calculan series separadas para (a) hogares de 4 personas de funcionarios públicos y asalariados con ingresos elevados; (b) de 4 personas de obreros y asalariados con ingresos medios; (c) de 2 personas titulares de una pensión o prestaciones de la seguridad social, con bajos ingresos; (d) con un hijo menor de 18 años.

Organización y publicación
Statistisches Bundesamt: "Wirtschaft und Statistik" (Wiesbaden).

idem: "Eilbericht und Monatsbericht der Fachserie 17, Reihe 7, Preise und Preisindizes für die Lebenshaltung".

idem: "Wirtschaft und Statistik" (Nos. 7/84 y 1/90), contiene detalles metodológicos más amplios.

ALEMANIA 2

Denominación oficial
Preisindex für die Lebenshaltung aller Arbeitnehmerhaushalte (Indice de precios del consumo de todos los hogares de empleados).

Alcance
El índice se compila mensualmente y abarca todos los hogares de empleados de los 5 nuevos "Länder" y Berlín (este).

Base oficial
1989 = 100.

Fuente de la ponderación
La determinación de los coeficientes de ponderación y la selección de los artículos se basaron en los resultados de una encuesta de gastos de los hogares realizada en los 5 nuevos "Länder", incluido Berlin (este). La recolección mensual de los datos tuvo lugar de enero a diciembre de 1989 y abarcó una muestra representativa de 2 600 hogares, con un tamaño medio de 2,87 personas.

Ponderaciones y composición

Grupos principales	Número de artículos	Ponderación aproximado	Número de cotizaciones de precio
Alimentación y tabaco	187	385,9	19 000
Vestido y calzado	79	134,1	10 000
Alquiler, combustible y luz	30	55,1	8 000
Muebles, equipos y funcionamiento del hogar	138	119,1	15 000
Asistencia médica y aseo personal	47	29,7	7 000
Transporte y comunicaciones	68	124,0	7 500
Educación, recreación y distracciones (excl. servicios de hoteles y restaurantes)	145	90,4	11 500
Artículos y servicios personales del alojamiento lucrativo y otros bienes	44	61,7	4 000
Total	738	1 000,0	82 000

Nota: (a) Véase a bajo.

(a) Para precios no fijados a nivel central, el número de cotizaciones para cada artículo es, por lo general, el siguiente: en ciudades con más de 20 mil habitantes: 4; en ciudades con 20 a 100 mil habitantes: 6; en ciudades con más de 100 mil habitantes: 8. Son excepciones los alquileres: seleccionados por sociedad de viviendas; los precios regulados (uniformes): una cotización única.

Gastos de consumo de los hogares
Para obtener los coeficientes de ponderación se registran los gastos de los hogares privados para pagar bienes, servicios, contribuciones a seguros de bienes e impuestos a los vehículos automóviles. En este sentido, no se cuentan como "gastos" las contribuciones pagadas a seguros sociales o de vejez. Sólo se incluyen los gastos de salud a cargo de personas privadas pues la mayor parte de éstos (visitas médicas, hospitalización, productos farmacéuticos recetados y otras curas, aplicaciones y aparatos clínicos) corren a cargo del seguro público de salud y, por lo tanto, no integran la ponderación. Los impuestos a los ingresos y otras cargas fiscales directas no se consideran como gastos de consumo, salvo el impuesto a los vehículos automóviles, que integran la ponderación. Se han excluido los ingresos en especie, las transferencias de dinero, donaciones, contribuciones y desembolsos similares. En cuanto a las compras a plazo o a crédito y los alquileres con opción de compra, se registra el precio total en el momento del registro de la adquisición. Se incluyen las compras y las ventas de bienes usados que, sin embargo, no figuran por separado en el índice. También se incluyen las tasas administrativas y las contribuciones a los seguros de bienes (vivienda, ajuar y otros objetos) y de automóviles.

Método de recolección de los datos
Se seleccionó una muestra representativa de 80 comunidades o ciudades de la encuesta. Cuando la recolección de precios es directa, los informantes de las comunidades de la encuesta se seleccionan en función de la importancia de su giro comercial, estimado por personal competente. Los investigadores registran directamente los precios en los puntos de información, aproximadamente a mediados de cada mes. Para algunos artículos (como los servicios de electricidad, gas y agua) se recurre a las tarifas publicadas por las empresas respectivas y para otros, como los alquileres, a cuestionarios. Se registran a nivel central las tarifas oficiales uniformes en vigor (como las del correo y las del transporte ferroviario de pasajeros). En los puntos de información los investigadores registran tanto los precios normales del momento como los comprables del mes anterior y luego cada uno de ellos se expande a efectos de obtener los precios medios de las comunidades, es decir la media aritmética simple entre los precios de un mes y los precios comparables del mes anterior. No se registran los descuentos y rebajas ni se investigan los precios del mercado negro, los alquileres con opción de compra, ni las compras a crédito o a plazos.

Vivienda
Se obtienen cotizaciones de alquiler para seis clases distintas de viviendas. Los datos no registrados a nivel central se obtienen a intervalos mensuales merced a documentos especiales de encuesta y se incluyen en el índice como promedios o relativos. No se abarcan las viviendas ocupadas por sus propietarios en cuanto tales.

Especificación de las variedades
La descripción de los artículos cuyos precios se registran es bastante poco específica. Se indica la calidad y la unidad de medida, pero no la marca. El encargado de la recolección de precios elige las mercancías específicas según su volumen de venta, en colaboración con el informante.

Sustitución, cambio de calidad, etc.
Cuando se produce un cambio de calidad se registra el precio comparable del mes anterior y, mediante el cociente entre el precio del momento y el del último mes se ajusta el precio de base. Cuando desaparece del mercado una variedad o artículo cuyo precio se venía registrando, se selecciona uno nuevo y se evalúa la diferencia de calidad con el antiguo y, basándose en esta evaluación, se calcula un precio comparable para el mes precedente.

Artículos estacionales
Los precios de los artículos estacionales se registran como todos los demás y se incluyen en el cálculo mensual del índice sin ajustes.

Cálculo
El índice se calcula según la fórmula de Laspeyres como un promedio aritmético ponderado de base fija, cuyos coeficientes de ponderación corresponden al período de base.

Los promedios y relativos de precio de cada "Land" se calculan recurriendo a una media aritmética simple; los del territorio de los cinco nuevos "Länder" en su conjunto se ponderar por el número de habitantes del "Land" respectivo. Los promedios anuales del índice principal y de los índices de grupo se calculan recurriendo a la media aritmética simple de los índices mensuales.

Informaciones complementarias
Los índices se publican por grandes grupos, junto con los índices para otros tipos de hogares. Se prevé publicar índices ajustados al procedimiento seguido en la República Federal (territorio anterior al 3 de octubre de 1990) a partir del segundo semestre de 1991. Cabe suponer que se procederá a una revisión del índice cuando se introduzca un nuevo año de base (1991) para toda Alemania. Actualmente se calcula una nueva serie (base julio de 1990-junio de 1991 = 100), pero en el mo-

mento de publicar el presente Volumen, la OIT no disponía de informaciones metodológicas sobre esta serie.

Organización y publicación
La compilación del índice está a cargo de la Oficina Federal de Estadísticas; Servicio de Berlín, Alexanderplatz, y su publicación de la Administración Federal de Estadísticas: "Eilbericht und Monatsbericht der Fachserie 17, Reihe 7, Preise und Preisindizes für die Lebenshaltung" (Wiesbaden).

ANGOLA (LUANDA)

Denominación oficial
Indice de Preços no Consumidor da Cidade de Luanda (Indice de Precios del Consumo - Luanda).

Alcance
El índice se compila mensualmente y abarca todos los hogares de la zona urbana de Luanda.

Base oficial
Diciembre de 1990 = 100.

Fuente de la ponderación
La determinación de los coeficientes de ponderación y la selección de los artículos se basaron en los resultados de una encuesta sobre los gastos de los hogares realizada por el UNICEF y el Instituto Nacional de Estadística en 16 distritos de Luanda entre febrero y abril 1990. La ponderación de los artículos no seleccionados para el registro de precios se distribuyeron entre los artículos similares del mismo subgrupo.

Ponderaciones y composición

Grupos principales	Número de artículos	Ponderación	Número aproximado de cotizaciones de precio
Alimentación y tabaco	85	74,07	4 200
Vestido y calzado	10	5,48	450
Vivienda (incl. combustible y luz)	6	5,47	200
Muebles, bienes, reparación y mantenimiento del hogar	26	4,67	1 065
Asistencia médica	5	1,81	110
Transporte y comunicaciones	7	3,92	35
Educación y recreación	11	2,69	250
Otros bienes y servicios	10	1,89	410
Total	160	100,00	6 720

Gastos de consumo de los hogares
Los gastos considerados para la ponderación son los efectuados en adquirir bienes y servicios durante el período de la encuesta, salvo en inversiones, transferencias, compra o reparaciones importantes de casas, gastos comerciales, etc.

Método de recolección de los datos
Los precios se registran en 81 mercados, puntos de venta al por menor y establecimientos de servicios seleccionados en Luanda. Los precios se registran en forma diaria (alimentos), semanal o mensual (periódicos, combustibles, energía eléctrica). Hasta diciembre de 1991 también se investigaron los precios de los artículos subvencionados vendidos a los trabajadores mediante carta de racionamiento, así como los precios del mercado libre. Los precios registrados son los que pagan realmente los consumidores.

Vivienda
No disponible.

Especificación de las variedades
Para los artículos heterogéneos se especifica su marca, calidad, modelo, tamaño, unidad de medida, etc., para asegurar que siempre se registren los precios de los mismos artículos. Los artículos homogéneos no necesitan tantas especificaciones (por ejemplo, kilogramo de azúcar blanca).

Sustitución, cambio de calidad, etc.
Cuando ya no se puede conseguir un producto se le sustituye por otro con características similares y se enlazan los precios.

Artículos estacionales
Las ponderaciones de los artículos estacionales son de poca importancia y abarcan mangos, piñas y naranjas. Las fluctuaciones estacionales de los precios de estos artículos se toman en consideración manteniendo, fuera de temporada, los últimos precios de la temporada precedente.

Cálculo
El índice se calcula según la fórmula de Laspeyres como un promedio aritmético ponderado de base fija, cuyos coeficientes de ponderación corresponden al período febrero - abril de 1990. Para calcular los índices de artículos específicos, se utilizan los relativos de precio del período en curso y del período de base. Se calculan relativos de los promedios de precio para artículos con variedades homogéneas y promedios de relativos de precio para los que comprenden variedades heterogéneas.

Informaciones complementarias
También se publica información detallada sobre los índices de grupos y subgrupos según los precios de mercado controlados y libres.

Organización y publicación
Instituto Nacional de Estadística: "Indice de Preços no Consumidor da Cidade de Luanda" (Luanda).
idem: "Metodologia de Indice de Preços no Consumidor de Luanda", Serie A: Metodologia No. 1 (noviembre de 1991).

ANTIGUA Y BARBUDA

Denominación oficial
Cost of Living Index (Indice del costo de la vida).

Alcance
El índice se calcula mensualmente y abarca los hogares de clase media, cuyos ingresos mensuales se situaban, en 1974 entre 350 y 550 dólares; y cuya composición era de 4 a 5 miembros (por lo menos tres adultos).

Base oficial
1 de enero de 1969 = 100.

Fuente de la ponderación
La selección de los artículos y la determinación de los coeficientes de ponderación han sido obtenidos sobre la base de una "canasta tipo" mensual determinada a partir de estudios efectuados en 1974 sobre la estructura de consumo de una sección tangencial de hogares de distinta composición numérica y de ingresos diferentes.

Ponderaciones y composición

Grupos principales	Número de artículos	Ponderación	Número aproximado de cotizaciones de precio
Alimentación	43	46,5	...
Alquiler, combustible y luz	4	28,8	...
Vestido y calzado	4	7,5	...
Transportes	1	10,0	...
Aseo personal y asistencia médica	9	7,2	...
Total	61	100,0	...

Gastos de consumo de los hogares
No disponible.

Método de recolección de los datos
Los precios durante el período de 1969 a 1973 han sido determinados el 1 de enero y el 1 de julio de cada año, a partir de fuentes diferentes. A partir de 1974, los precios se registran trimestralmente.

Vivienda
No disponible.

Especificación de las variedades
No disponible.

Sustitución, cambio de calidad, etc.
No disponible.

Artículos estacionales
No disponible.

Cálculo
El índice se calcula conforme a la fórmula de Laspeyres como un promedio aritmético ponderado de base fija, cuyos coeficientes de ponderación corresponden al período de base.

Informaciones complementarias
No disponible.

Organización y publicación
Ministry of Planning, Development and External Affairs, Statistics Division: "Cost of Living Index" (Antigua).

idem: "Cost of Living Index 1969-74" (Antigua), Vol. I.

ANTILLAS NEERLANDESAS

Denominación oficial
Consumer Price Index (Indice de precios del consumo).

Alcance
El índice se calcula mensualmente y abarca el conjunto de la población de Curaçao y Bonaire.

Base oficial
Diciembre de 1984 = 100.

Fuente de la ponderación
La selección de los artículos y la determinación de los coeficientes de ponderación se basaron en los resultados de una encuesta sobre los gastos de los hogares efectuada en 1981 sobre una muestra del conjunto de la población de Curaçao y Bonaire.

Ponderaciones y composición

Grupos principales	Número de artículos	Ponde-ración	Número aproximado de cotizaciones de precio
Alimentación	9	22,07	...
Bebidas y tabaco	2	2,32	...
Vestido y calzado	2	8,68	...
Vivienda (incl. alquiler, combustible y electricidad y gastos para el hogar)	5	18,76	...
Moblaje y accesorios para el hogar	7	9,96	...
Asistencia médica	1	2,16	...
Transportes y comunicaciones	4	19,45	...
Educación y distracciones	5	5,95	...
Otros (incl. aseo personal, seguridad y otros bienes y servicios)	3	10,65	...
Total	(a) 38	100,00	...

Nota: (a) Número de sub-grupos.

Gastos de consumo de los hogares
No disponible.

Método de recolección de los datos
Los precios se recogen en puntos de venta al por menor y establecimientos de servicios.

Vivienda
No disponible.

Especificación de las variedades
No disponible.

Sustitución, cambio de calidad, etc.
No disponible.

Artículos estacionales
No disponible.

Cálculo
El índice se calcula conforme a la fórmula de Laspeyres como un promedio aritmético ponderado de base fija, cuyos coeficientes de ponderación corresponden a 1981.

Informaciones complementarias
Actualmente se calcula una nueva serie (base octubre de 1990 = 100), pero en el momento de publicar el presente Volumen la OIT no disponía de informaciones metodológicas sobre esta serie.

Organización y publicación
Central Bureau of Statistics: "Statistical Monthly Bulletin" (Willemstad).

ARABIA SAUDITA 1

Denominación oficial
Cost of Living Index - All Cities Index (Indice del Costo de la Vida - todas las ciudades).

Alcance
El índice se compila mensualmente y abarca hogares sauditas y no sauditas en las diez ciudades siguientes: Riyadh, Jeddah, Damman, Abha, Buraydah, Makkah, Medinah, Taif, Hofhuf y Tabuk.

Base oficial
1988 = 100.

Fuente de la ponderación
La determinación de los coeficientes de ponderación y la selección de los artículos se basaron en los resultados de la encuesta de 1985-86 sobre los gastos de los hogares, realizada durante todo un año. El período de referencia de los gastos mensuales informados sobre cualquier hogar fue un mes. La encuesta se realizó en 15 ciudades del Reino, las 10 antes mencionadas y otras cinco más pequeñas, y todas las regiones geográficas estuvieron representadas en ella, pues el diseño muestral fue por regiones, en las cuales se seleccionaron los hogares específicos en forma aleatoria. Inicialmente se entrevistó un total aproximado de 15 000 hogares.

Los coeficientes de ponderación utilizados en el Indice del Costo de la Vida combinaron coste (basado en los datos sobre el gasto doméstico) y población. No se utilizó ningún dato de la contabilidad nacional.

Los artículos del Indice del Costo de la Vida (ICV) se seleccionaron mediante métodos de probabilidad proporcional al tamaño (PPT), así como por procedimientos aleatorios para los artículos no seleccionados por los métodos PPT. En la muestra de artículos se incluyeron más de 200 en total. Las ponderaciones de los artículos no seleccionados se calculan mensualmente por el movimiento del grupo en el cual caen los "artículos sin precio registrado".

Ponderaciones y composición

Grupos principales	Número de artículos	Ponde-ración	Número aproximado de cotizaciones de precio
Alimentación	87	32,62	6 090
Vivienda (incl. combustible, luz y agua)	7	19,69	353
Vestido y calzado	29	8,40	725
Muebles y moblaje	36	9,38	900
Asistencia médica	7	1,24	175
Transporte y comunicaciones	8	17,30	200
Educación y recreación	15	2,95	375
Otros gastos	13	8,42	275
Total	202	100,00	(a) 9 093

Nota: (a) Véase abajo.

(a) El número de cotizaciones de precio para cada artículo se determina por apreciación fundada en la experiencia adquirida. Se registran siete cotizaciones de precio para cada componente de la alimentación y cinco para los demás artículos. La volatilidad de los precios de la alimentación explican ese mayor número de cotizaciones.

Gastos de consumo de los hogares
No incluyen impuestos, seguros ni casas ocupadas por sus propietarios.

Método de recolección de los datos
La selección de tiendas y otros puntos de venta al por menor se basó en los resultados de una encuesta sobre los puntos de venta al por menor. El Departamento Central de Estadísticas se encarga de la recolección mensual, en cada una de las ciudades, de las siete cotizaciones de precio para cada artículo alimenticio. Los demás artículos se registran en forma bimensual, la mitad de ellos en cada mes. Para estos artículos se registran cinco cotizaciones, salvo si se trata de precios fijados o controlados por el gobierno, como los servicios de electricidad, teléfono, gasolina, etc., que se registran sólo cuando tiene lugar una modificación, que es anunciada por los periódicos. Las cotizaciones de la asistencia médica se obtienen mediante visitas personales a consultorios y hospitales, las de la educación de una muestra de institutos de enseñanza de cada una de las diez ciudades del ICV, las del transporte mediante visitas a compañías aéreas, de autobuses, etc. Las tarifas aéreas que se registran comprenden tanto los vuelos nacionales como los internacionales. Para las tarifas telefónicas también se utiliza una combinación de la tasa básica del servicio y de las llamadas a larga distancia.

La recolección de los precios está a cargo de personal formado que, por lo general, obtiene los datos mediante visitas personales. Los precios se registran al azar entre el 1ro. y el 20 del mes. Se recomienda a los encargados que cada mes visiten los puntos de venta aproximadamente en la misma fecha y de esta forma algunos serán visitados alrededor del día 5 y otros alrededor del 20 y el que sea visitado alrededor del 5 no lo será el mes siguiente en fecha cercana al 20.

Los investigadores también han recibido instrucciones para averiguar el precio más corriente de los artículos. Si habitualmente se hacen descuentos, se registra el precio rebajado. Los precios de liquidación se registran de la misma forma que los demás, y será en la etapa de cálculo que el artículo mostrará una disminución de su precio ordinario anterior.

En cuanto a los precios de mercado libre de los artículos que también tienen precios oficiales, cabe explicar que en el Reino se subsidian varios productos alimenticios (precios oficiales) y no se dan precios más bajos que éstos. En el Reino no existen precios de mercado negro.

Los alquileres con opción de compra y las ventas a crédito no se aplican en Arabia Saudita (ningún artículo figura en el índice).

Compra y comercio de bienes de segunda mano, entrega de objetos usados como pago parcial de la compra de otros nuevos: no se cotizan los precios de bienes de segunda mano. Los encargados de la recolección reciben instrucciones para registrar los precios de mercancías recientes ofrecidas en cantidades vendibles.

Los precios de importación se tratan como los demás. En Arabia Saudita muchos artículos son importados. Los encargados de la recolección identifican el país de origen.

Vivienda

Los investigadores completan un formulario detallado de alquileres donde se consigna si el alquiler comprende o no servicios y si la vivienda tiene o no aire acondicionado, etc. Se cotizan tanto los alquileres de villas como de apartamentos. La muestra de alquileres de cada ciudad se divide en seis grupos, cada uno de los cuales se investiga una vez por semestre. Un sexto del movimiento de las cotizaciones de alquiler de cada ciudad se aplica a la ponderación coste-población del alquiler. Una vez combinadas las ponderaciones de las 10 ciudades, se calcula el índice de alquileres para todo el Reino. Los valores locativos de las casas ocupadas por sus propietarios no se registran para el componente vivienda del índice.

Especificación de las variedades

El Departamento Central de Estadísticas cuenta con especificaciones detalladas de todos los artículos del ICV que exigen que el investigador anote la variedad, modelo, factura, marca, número de serie, país de origen, etc., de tal forma que en el siguiente período de recolección se registren los precios del mismo artículo o de uno comparable.

Sustitución, cambio de calidad, etc.

Cambios de calidad: cuando se registra el precio de un artículo cuyo tamaño o ponderación difiere del anterior, se ajusta la ponderación del artículo anterior para permitir una comparación adecuada. Dada la carencia de datos necesarios para poder ajustar la mayoría de los cambios de calidad, no se han hecho esfuerzos para ajustarlos y el nuevo artículo no se enlaza al índice. Aparición de nuevos productos: el ICV se revisa cada cinco años. Los precios de los nuevos productos que aparecen en el mercado entre dos revisiones no se registran pero pueden ser recogidos en la siguiente encuesta de los gastos de consumo. Si el nuevo producto que se ofrece en el mercado sustituye un artículo cuyo precio se viene registrando el investigador no lo sustituirá, salvo que ya no sea posible encontrar el artículo con precio registrado y que sea el sustituto más próximo disponible.

Desaparición del mercado de una determinada clase de calidad: suele ocurrir en algunas ocasiones y, en tales casos, se comienza por imputar simplemente la ponderación del artículo por el movimiento de ese grupo. Cuando se adquiere la certeza de que el artículo no volverá a venderse ni almacenarse, se instruye al centro de computación para que se combinen los coeficientes de ponderación de ese artículo con los que no tienen precio registrado. Esta categoría de artículos sin precio registrado también se calcula por el movimiento de precios de ese grupo específico.

Artículos estacionales

Los precios de los artículos estacionales se registran mientras dura su oferta. Por ejemplo, ciertas frutas o legumbres abundan en ciertos períodos del año y sus precios lógicamente bajan. Por el contrario la disminución de la oferta aumenta los precios. Si los encargados de la recolección no pueden registrar el precio de un determinado artículo, anotan en el formulario de precios que no es posible encontrar el artículo y dejan de registrar su precio hasta que se ofrezca nuevamente en el mercado.

Cálculo

El índice se calcula según la fórmula de Laspeyres como un promedio aritmético ponderado de base fija, cuyos coeficientes de ponderación corresponden al período de base.

Para calcular los índices de precios de los artículos se utilizan los relativos de los promedios de precios del período corriente y del anterior. El índice para todas las ciudades es una combinación de las diez UPM (unidades primarias de muestreo). En cada UPM se determina una ponderación de cada artículo que refleje la estimación de los gastos actuales de la canasta del período de base. Para combinar las ponderaciones de artículos se utiliza la población de cada UPM, para obtener así los coeficientes de ponderación finales para todas las ciudades.

Informaciones complementarias

Se publican índices detallados de subgrupo y también de ciudades. El Departamento Central de Estadísticas también publica un Indice de Ingresos Medios.

Organización y publicación

Ministry of Finance and National Economy, Central Department of Statistics: "The Statistical Indicator" (Riyadh).

idem: "Statistical Yearbook".

idem: "Cost of Living Index".

ARABIA SAUDITA 2

Denominación oficial

Cost of Living Index - Middle Income Index (Indice del Costo de la Vida - Hogares con Ingresos Medios).

Alcance

El índice se compila mensualmente y abarca hogares con ingresos medios que oscilan entre 2 500 y 10 000 riyals en las diez ciudades siguientes: Riyadh, Jeddah, Damman, Abha, Buraydah, Makkah, Medinah, Taif, Hofhuf y Tabuk.

Base oficial

1988 = 100.

Fuente de la ponderación

La determinación de los coeficientes de ponderación y la selección de los artículos se basaron en los resultados de una encuesta sobre los gastos de los hogares realizada durante todo un año entre 1985 y 1986. El período de referencia de todo gasto mensual de los hogares fue de un mes. La encuesta se realizó en 15 ciudades del Reino, las 10 antes mencionadas y otras cinco más pequeñas, y todas las regiones geográficas estuvieron representadas en ella. El diseño de muestreo de los hogares fue el de una muestra de áreas en las cuales los hogares específicos se seleccionaron en forma aleatoria. Inicialmente se entrevistó un total aproximado de 15 000 hogares.

Los coeficientes de ponderación utilizados en el Indice del Costo de la Vida fueron una combinación de costo (basado en los datos sobre el gasto doméstico) y población. No se utilizó ningún dato de la contabilidad nacional.

Los artículos del Indice del Costo de la Vida (ICV) se seleccionaron mediante métodos de probabilidad proporcional al tamaño (PPT), así como por procedimientos aleatorios para los artículos no seleccionados por los métodos PPT. En la muestra de artículos se incluyeron más de 200 artículos en total. Las ponderaciones de los artículos no seleccionados se atribuyen mensualmente por el movimiento del grupo en el cual caen los "artículos no apreciados".

Gastos de consumo de los hogares

No incluyen impuestos, seguros ni casas ocupadas por sus propietarios.

Método de recolección de los datos

La selección de tiendas y otros puntos de venta al por menor se basó en los resultados de una encuesta sobre los puntos de venta al por menor. El Departamento Central de Estadísticas se encarga de la recolección mensual, en cada una de las ciudades, de las siete cotizaciones de precio para cada artículo alimenticio. Los demás artículos se registran en forma bimensual, la mitad de ellos en cada mes. Para estos artículos se registran cinco cotizaciones, salvo si se trata de precios fijados o controlados por el gobierno, como los servicios de electricidad, teléfono, gasolina, etc., que se registran sólo cuando tiene lugar una modificación, que es anunciada por los periódicos. Las cotizaciones de la asistencia médica se obtienen mediante visitas personales a consultorios y hospitales, las de la

Ponderaciones y composición

Grupos principales	Número de artículos	Ponderación aproximado	Número de cotizaciones de precio
Alimentación	85	37,66	5 950
Vivienda (incl. combustible, luz y agua)	8	21,11	353
Vestido y calzado	26	7,93	650
Muebles y moblaje	31	7,42	750
Asistencia médica	7	1,13	175
Transporte y comunicaciones	9	15,08	225
Educación y recreación	15	2,01	350
Otros gastos	13	7,66	300
Total	194	100,00	(a) 8 753

Nota: (a) Véase abajo.

(a) El número de cotizaciones de precio para cada artículo se determina por apreciación fundada en la experiencia adquirida. Se registran siete cotizaciones de precio para cada componente de la alimentación y cinco para los demás artículos. La volatilidad de los precios de la alimentación explican ese mayor número de cotizaciones.

educación de una muestra de institutos de enseñanza de cada una de las diez ciudades del ICV, las del transporte mediante visitas a compañías aéreas, de autobuses, etc. Las tarifas aéreas que se registran comprenden tanto los vuelos nacionales como los internacionales. Para las tarifas telefónicas también se utiliza una combinación de la tasa básica del servicio y de las llamadas a larga distancia.

La recolección de los precios está a cargo de personal formado que, por lo general, obtiene los datos mediantes visitas personales. Los precios se registran al azar entre el 1ro. y el 20 del mes. Se recomienda a los encargados que cada mes visiten los puntos de venta aproximadamente en la misma fecha y de esta forma algunos serán visitados alrededor del día 5 y otros alrededor del 20 y el que sea visitado alrededor del 5 no lo será el mes siguiente en fecha cercana al 20.

Los investigadores también han recibido instrucciones para averiguar el precio más corriente de los artículos. Si habitualmente se hacen descuentos, se registra el precio rebajado. Los precios de liquidación se registran de la misma forma que los demás, y será en la etapa de cálculo que el artículo mostrará una disminución de su precio ordinario anterior.

En cuanto a los precios de mercado libre de los artículos que también tienen precios oficiales, cabe explicar que en el Reino se subsidian varios productos alimenticios (precios oficiales) y no se dan precios más bajos que éstos. En el Reino no existen precios de mercado negro.

Los alquileres con opción de compra y las ventas a crédito no se aplican en Arabia Saudita (ningún artículo figura en el índice).

Compra y comercio de bienes de segunda mano, entrega de objetos usados como pago parcial de la compra de otros nuevos: no se cotizan los precios de bienes de segunda mano. Los encargados de la recolección reciben instrucciones para registrar los precios de mercancías recientes ofrecidas en cantidades vendibles.

Los precios de importación se tratan como los demás. En Arabia Saudita muchos artículos son importados. Los encargados de la recolección identifican el país de origen.

Vivienda

Los investigadores completan un formulario detallado de alquileres donde se consigna si el alquiler comprende o no servicios y si la vivienda tiene o no aire acondicionado, etc. Se cotizan tanto los alquileres de villas como de apartamentos. La muestra de alquileres de cada ciudad se divide en seis grupos, cada uno de los cuales se investiga una vez por semestre. Un sexto del movimiento de las cotizaciones de alquiler de cada ciudad se aplica a la ponderación coste-población del alquiler. Una vez combinadas las ponderaciones de las 10 ciudades, se calcula el índice de alquileres para todo el Reino. Los valores locativos de las casas ocupadas por sus propietarios no se registran para el componente vivienda del índice.

Especificación de las variedades

El Departamento Central de Estadísticas cuenta con especificaciones detalladas de todos los artículos del ICV que exigen que el investigador anote la variedad, modelo, factura, marca, número de serie, país de origen, etc., de tal forma que en el siguiente período de recolección se registren los precios del mismo artículo o de uno comparable.

Sustitución, cambio de calidad, etc.

Cambios de calidad: cuando se registra el precio de un artículo cuyo tamaño o ponderación difiere del anterior, se ajusta la ponderación del artículo anterior para permitir una comparación adecuada. Dada la carencia de datos necesarios para poder ajustar la mayoría de los cambios de calidad, no se han hecho esfuerzos para ajustarlos y el nuevo artículo se enlaza al índice.

Aparición de nuevos productos: el ICV se revisa cada cinco años. Los precios de los nuevos productos que aparecen en el mercado entre dos revisiones no se registran pero pueden ser recogidos en la siguiente encuesta de los gastos de consumo. Si el nuevo producto que se ofrece en el mercado sustituye un artículo cuyo precio se viene registrando el investigador no lo sustituirá, salvo que ya no sea posible encontrar el artículo con precio registrado y que sea el sustituto más próximo disponible.

Desaparición del mercado de una determinada clase de calidad: suele ocurrir en algunas ocasiones y, en tales casos, se comienza por imputar simplemente la ponderación del artículo por el movimiento de ese grupo. Cuando se adquiere la certeza de que el artículo no volverá a venderse ni almacenarse, se instruye al centro de computación para que se combinen los coeficientes de ponderación de ese artículo con los que no tienen precio registrado. Esta categoría de artículos sin precio registrado también se calcula por el movimiento de precios de ese grupo específico.

Artículos estacionales

Los precios de los artículos estacionales se registran mientras dura su oferta. Por ejemplo, ciertas frutas y legumbres abundan en ciertos períodos del año y sus precios lógicamente bajan. Por el contrario la disminución de la oferta aumenta los precios. Si los encargados de la recolección no pueden registrar el precio de un determinado artículo, anotan en el formulario de precios que no es posible encontrar el artículo y dejan de registrar su precio hasta que se ofrezca nuevamente en el mercado.

Cálculo

El índice se calcula según la fórmula de Laspeyres como un promedio aritmético ponderado de base fija, cuyos coeficientes de ponderación corresponden al período de base.

Para calcular los índices de precios de los artículos se utilizan los relativos de los promedios de precios del período corriente y del anterior. El índice para todas las ciudades es una combinación de las diez UPM (unidades primarias de muestreo). En cada UPM se determina una ponderación de cada artículo que refleje la estimación de los gastos actuales de la canasta del período de base. Para combinar las ponderaciones de artículos se utiliza la población de cada UPM, para obtener así los coeficientes de ponderación finales para todas las ciudades.

Informaciones complementarias

Se publican índices detallados de subgrupo y también de ciudades. El Departamento Central de Estadísticas también publica un Índice de todas las ciudades.

Organización y publicación

Ministry of Finance and National Economy, Central Department of Statistics: "The Statistical Indicator" (Riyadh).

idem: "Statistical Yearbook".

idem: "Cost of Living Index".

ARGELIA (ARGEL)

Denominación oficial

Indice des prix à la consommation (Indice de precios del consumo).

Alcance

El índice se calcula mensualmente y abarca todos los hogares de Argel, independientemente de su dimensión y de las categorías socioprofesionales.

Base oficial

1982 = 100.

Fuente de la ponderación

Los coeficientes de ponderación se determinan sobre la base de los resultados de una encuesta nacional relativa a los gastos de los hogares realizada entre marzo de 1979 y marzo de 1980 con una muestra de 8 208 hogares repartidos en todo el territorio argelino con arreglo a seis sectores de vivienda, cinco zonas económicas y 20 categorías socioprofesionales. El índice abarca todos los hogares de la ciudad de Argel (con exclusión de los solteros), independientemente de su dimensión y de las categorías socioprofesionales. Los artículos seleccionados lo han sido con arreglo a una recopilación de las variedades y servicios consumidos por los hogares que se realizó en 1982. El índice se compone de 712 variedades seleccionadas con base en criterios como gastos anuales, frecuencia de los gastos y utilidad. Las ponderaciones de las variedades se calculan con base en los gastos anuales en 1979, según figuran en la encuesta nacional sobre el consumo de los hogares. La tasa de cobertura del índice (en términos de gastos de consumo) es de 93 por ciento.

Ponderaciones y composición

Grupos principales	Número de artículos	Ponderación	Número aproximado de cotizaciones de precio
Alimentación	56	522,4	9 919
Vestido y calzado	59	70,6	709
Vivienda, combustible, y luz	9	72,5	95
Moblaje	43	55,0	152
Asistencia médica	26	26,5	6
Transportes y comunicaciones	20	96,1	47
Educación y distracciones	20	42,3	28
Otros bienes y servicios	23	84,6	128
Total	256	1 000,0	11 084

Gastos de consumo de los hogares
Los gastos de consumo elegidos para establecer los coeficientes de ponderación comprenden los bienes y servicios recopilados en la encuesta sobre los gastos de los hogares. Se excluyen los gastos de inversión, la vivienda propia, las cuotas del seguro social y de las cajas de pensiones, las patentes, los impuestos sobre la renta y demás impuestos directos, los pagos por concepto de seguro de vida, los envíos de fondos donativos y pagos análogos.

Método de recolección de los datos
Investigadores proceden periódicamente a una recolección de los precios en diez sectores geográficos de la ciudad de Argel con arreglo a una muestra de diez puntos de venta (públicos y privados), de conformidad con un programa de encuesta establecido para cada grupo de bienes y servicios. Se trata de precios declarados o publicados. Se consideran mensualmente unas 450 variedades y se analizan 11 000 precios por mes. En especial, los precios de las frutas y verduras frescas así como del pescado fresco se recogen tres veces por semana en diez puntos de venta (mercados) públicos y privados; los de la carne, las aves de corral y los huevos dos veces por mes en 36 puntos de venta públicos y privados. Los precios de las prendas de vestir se recogen cada cuatro meses. Los datos relativos al agua, la electricidad, el gas, la enseñanza, los transportes y las comunicaciones se acopian anualmente y los relativos a gastos médicos dos veces por año.

Vivienda
Los investigadores recogen anualmente los precios de los alquileres y de los gastos de comunidad para las viviendas de tres habitaciones con cocina y cuarto de baño en los organismos encargados de la administración de inmuebles en el sector público y en los hogares para el sector privado. El índice para el grupo "alquileres" se obtiene combinando el índice del sector público y el índice del sector privado. Se excluyen del cálculo del índice las viviendas ocupadas por su propietario.

Especificación de las variedades
Se realizó en 1982 una recopilación de las variedades de bienes y servicios consumidos por los hogares. Se analizan sobre esta base unas 2 000 variedades (especificación, definición del artículo, cálculo del precio medio, etc.) con miras a la composición del índice. Cada artículo contiene especificaciones detalladas y describe la variedad, la calidad, la elaboración, la marca, la unidad, etc.

Sustitución, cambio de calidad, etc.
No se toman en cuenta en el cálculo del índice el cambio de calidad de un artículo ni la aparición de un nuevo artículo en el mercado.

Artículos estacionales
Las frutas y verduras frescas, en razón del carácter estacional de su comercialización, son objeto de un trato especial: se calcula un índice bruto con base en una canasta mensual de plena temporada y éste compara los precios (mensuales) de la misma canasta en el mes en curso y el correspondiente mes del año de referencia (1982). Se calculan mensualmente los precios de base de las variedades de la canasta, así como las ponderaciones. La comparación de los índices brutos correspondientes a meses con nombres diferentes no indican exclusivamente la variación (relativa) de los precios, sino la relación entre las variaciones de precio para cada mes.

Cálculo
El índice se calcula según la fórmula de Laspeyres, como un promedio aritmético ponderado de base fija, cuyos coeficientes de ponderación corresponden a 1979.

Informaciones complementarias
En la actualidad, un índice nacional se calcula sobre la base de la recolección de precios en una muestra de 18 ciudades y aldeas. Ese índice nacional se elabora mensualmente desde enero de 1989.

Organización y publicación
Office national des statistiques: "Statistiques" (trimestral) (Alger).
idem: "Données statistiques" (mensual).

ARGENTINA (BUENOS AIRES)

Denominación oficial
Indice de precios al Consumidor.

Alcance
El índice se calcula mensualmente y abarca conjunto de hogares particulares residentes en la Capital Federal y los 19 partidos que comprenden el Gran Buenos Aires, excluyendo al 5% de los hogares que corresponden a los de mayor ingreso familiar per cápita y a los unipersonales debido a que estos últimos poseen estructuras de consumo particulares que difieren de los restantes.

Base oficial
1988 = 100.

Fuente de la ponderación
La selección de los artículos y la determinación de los coeficientes de ponderación se basaron en los resultados de una encuesta sobre los gastos de los hogares realizada entre julio de 1985 y junio de 1986 en el aglomerado urbano de Gran Buenos Aires, sobre una muestra de 2 745 unidades de gasto. Una unidad de gasto a los fines de la encuesta, se definió como constituida por una o varias personas, ligadas o no por relaciones de parentesco, que participan en la formación y utilización de un mismo presupuesto, compartiendo el suministro de alimentos y habitando la misma vivienda.

Se seleccionaron los bienes y servicios adquiridos por los hogares que tuvieran ponderación significativa dentro de cada subgrupo. Se tuvo en cuenta también que fueran vendidos y adquiridos con cierto grado de regularidad y en suficiente cantidad de modo de poder obtener cotizaciones de precios con un nivel de precisión adecuada.

Las ponderaciones correspondientes a los demás bienes y servicios del subgrupo se asignaron por afinidad, o proporcionalmente dentro del subgrupo. Dos bienes o servicios se consideran afines si son sustitutos entre sí y si su evolución de precios es similar. Entonces, la ponderación perteneciente a un artículo no seleccionado pero afín a uno seleccionado, se asignó a este artículo seleccionado, mientras que la ponderación correspondiente a los demás se repartió proporcionalmente dentro del subgrupo.

Gastos de consumo de los hogares
Los gastos de consumo comprenden los gastos monetarios realizados por los miembros del hogar en bienes y servicios para su consumo individual o para el consumo del conjunto del hogar; los bienes y servicios producidos por el hogar para su propio consumo (autoconsumo alimentario y autosuministro); los bienes y servicios recibidos como remuneración en especie por miembros del hogar. Se registraron en gastos de vivienda los correspondientes a reparación y mantenimiento de la vivienda propia.

Método de recolección de los datos
La muestra de puntos de venta correspondiente a áreas residenciales se realizó en dos etapas; en la primera se seleccionaron 130 radios censales (46 en Capital Federal y 84 en los partidos que integran el Gran Buenos Aires) como conglome-

Ponderaciones y composición

Grupos principales	Número de artículos	Ponderación aproximada	Número de cotizaciones de precio
Alimentación	205	40,1	72 500
Vestido y calzado	111	9,4	7 900
Vivienda:			
Alquiler	1	2,3	400
Reparaciones y conservación	13	2,0	800
Combustible, luz y servicios sanitarios	5	4,2	200
Enseres para el hogar	84	8,6	12 300
Asistencia médica	31	7,2	1 600
Transportes y comunicaciones	23	11,4	800
Educación y distracciones	61	8,9	4 800
Bienes y servicios varios	23	5,9	4 700
Total	557	100,0	106 000

rados de puntos de venta. En la segunda etapa se seleccionó, en cada una de estas áreas, un punto de venta de cada clase (almacén, carnicería, mercería, rotisería, artículos de limpieza, ferretería, farmacia, peluquería, papelería, etcétera) en los cuales se relevan precios dos veces por mes.

En relación a los centros comerciales, se eligieron 47 centros distribuidos, 21 en Capital Federal y 26 en los partidos del Gran Buenos Aires. Del conjunto total de puntos de venta pertenecientes a estos centros se seleccionaron 140 submuestras de negocios, visitando cada una de ellas una vez por mes.

Para la determinación del número de informantes de cada variedad, se tuvo en cuenta la cobertura geográfica del índice y la variabilidad del precio. Está previsto que la muestra de puntos de venta sea objeto de revisión periódica con el fin de incorporar las nuevas formas de comercialización y los posibles cambios que se produzcan en la distribución geográfica de los negocios.

Los precios de los bienes y servicios se relevan todos los días hábiles del mes. O sea, la muestra de puntos de venta para un bien o servicio determinado se distribuye entre los días hábiles del mes. No se incluyen por lo tanto, los sábados, domingos y días feriados. La mayor parte de los precios se releva por medio de la entrevista directa. Se utiliza el teléfono únicamente para algunos servicios que no presentan cambio de calidad frecuente, y tienen alta tasa de respuesta a la encuesta telefónica. En el caso de servicios cuyos precios son fijados por el estado (luz, gas por red, servicios sanitarios, transporte público, etc.), se consideran dentro del mes los días de vigencia del precio. El precio relevado para los distintos bienes y servicios es el precio de contado.

Vivienda

El tratamiento especial de alquiler reside en que los informantes no son los negocios, que en este caso serían los locadores o dueños de las viviendas, sino los propios consumidores, o sea los inquilinos. Para recoger los precios se recurre a una muestra de viviendas alquiladas. Esta muestra se renueva por cuartos cada trimestre con el fin de no producir cansancio en el informante por una parte, y por otra captar el momento de la renovación del contrato. El tamaño de la muestra total es de 624 viviendas que se dividen en 6 grupos de rotación de 104 viviendas cada uno; observando cada mes el valor locativo de 416 viviendas.

Dentro de las numerosas variantes que presenta el mercado de alquileres, se toman precios de las viviendas alquiladas que reúnen las siguientes condiciones: vivienda familiar habitada; alquilada sin muebles; casas, departamentos, hoteles de residencia permanente e inquilinatos; alquileres pagados en moneda nacional; viviendas en donde el alquiler pueda discriminarse de los servicios; y alquiladas sin mediar relaciones laborales. Además del monto del alquiler se recogen otros datos sobre la vivienda y sobre el contrato que permiten controlar el valor declarado y detectar el momento en que se producen cambios de calidad en la vivienda.

Especificación de las variedades

Para una especificación precisa de los bienes y servicios de la "canasta familiar" es necesario describir en detalle todas las características que determinan la existencia de precios diferentes en un mismo momento, y los límites entre los cuales los cambios de estas características se imputarán, por razones prácticas, a variaciones de precios. Para cada informante de precios, un detalle mayor de la variedad suele ser necesario (marca, modelo, tamaño, etcétera) con el fin de asegurar la comparabilidad en las observaciones sucesivas de precios.

Para la especificación de los bienes se optó por dos tipos de definiciones. La primera, denominada variedad homogénea, corresponde al caso en que el producto cotizado en los distintos puntos de venta es equivalente, permitiendo calcular un precio medio significativo (manteca, asado, huevos, naranja, acelga, jabón en pan, etcétera). La segunda, denominada variedad heterogénea, corresponde a una especificación incompleta, de forma tal que la descripción del producto deberá cerrarse en cada punto de venta. La utilización de variedades heterogéneas es de gran utilidad en el caso, por ejemplo, de vestimenta, por presentar heterogeneidad entre negocios y variación con la moda (zapatos, vestido, televisor, escuela, alquiler, etcétera).

Sustitución, cambio de calidad, etc.

El método para tratar los cambios de calidad así como también los cambios de informantes y la sustitución de bienes, cuando existe solapamiento de observaciones de precios, es asumir que la relación entre los precios refleja la relación entre las calidades y, en consecuencia, el encadenamiento es posible. Cuando no existe solapamiento de observaciones de precios pero es factible realizar una comparación de calidad, se ajusta por calidad el precio de la nueva variedad para que sea comparable con la anterior.

Artículos estacionales

Cuando un bien estacional desaparece temporariamente del mercado, el cálculo del relativo de precio se realiza bajo la hipótesis de que el movimiento del precio del bien desaparecido hubiera sido similar al cambio registrado en el precio de los bienes semejantes.

La denominación de bienes estacionales corresponde al conjunto de bienes o servicios donde la cantidad consumida y los precios muestran variación intra-anual significativa. En general se trata de fluctuaciones de oferta (verduras, fruta, etcétera) o de demanda (prendas de vestir de invierno, de verano, etcétera) que pueden llevar a la desaparición temporaria del bien.

Cálculo

El índice se calcula mediante la fórmula de Laspeyres como un promedio aritmético ponderado de base fija, cuyos coeficientes de ponderación corresponden al período de julio de 1985 - junio de 1986.

Se estiman los índices de cada agregado elemental (nivel mínimo de detalle del gasto para el cual las ponderaciones son constantes) utilizando una muestra de precios de un grupo determinado de bienes o servicios a partir de un conjunto establecido de puntos de venta.

La forma de calcular el relativo de precio de un bien depende de si se lo considera una variedad homogénea o heterogénea. En el caso de las variedades homogéneas es el relativo del precio medio de un período respecto al precio medio del período anterior. Para las variedades heterogéneas es el promedio de los relativos de precios de los distintos puntos de venta.

Se asignan ponderaciones a los supermercados, almacenes departamentales y otros puntos de venta al por menor según la importancia del volumen de venta. Estas ponderaciones se utilizan para calcular las relaciones de precios medios o medios de la relaciones de precios.

Informaciones complementarias

Se publican sub-grupos detallados (134). El índice se publica el tercer día hábil del mes siguiente al que corresponde el índice por medio de una "Información de prensa".

Organización y publicación

Instituto Nacional de Estadística y Censos: "Estadística mensual" (Buenos Aires).

idem: "Indice de precios al consumidor, Revisión base 1988 = 100, Síntesis metodológica".

AUSTRALIA

Denominación oficial

Consumer Price Index (Indice de precios del consumo).

Alcance

La compilación del índice es trimestral y abarca todos los hogares de asalariados metropolitanos. Se han definido como hogares de asalariados los que obtienen por lo menos los tres cuartos de sus ingresos totales de pago de salarios y sueldos, pero excluyendo el 10 por ciento más alto (en términos de ingresos). El término "metropolitano" se refiere a las ocho ciudades capitales de los estados y territorios de Australia.

Base oficial
Año que termina en junio de 1981 = 100.

Fuente de la ponderación
Las ponderaciones actuales se basan en la encuesta sobre gastos del hogar de 1984, complementada con informaciones procedentes de otras estadísticas, tales como las obtenidas de instituciones financieras y por medio de la encuesta sobre seguridad social de 1986. La selección de los artículos, para investigar sus precios, se realiza en función de la importancia cuantitativa en los gastos de los hogares metropolitanos y de la posibilidad de relacionar sus precios con una mercancía o un servicio identificable y específico y de registrarlos para una calidad constante. Se considera que las fluctuaciones de los precios de los artículos no seleccionados se pueden representar por las de los artículos cuyos precios se registran, se adjudica la ponderación del artículo no evaluado a la del artículo que lo representa.

Ponderaciones y composición

Grupos principales	Número de artículos (a)	Ponderación	Número aproximado de cotizaciones de precio (b)
Alimentación	34	19,0	27 000
Tabaco y alcohol	4	8,2	11 200
Vestido y calzado	14	6,9	5 500
Vivienda:			
Alquiler de viviendas de propiedad privada	1	4,1	8 200
Alquiler de viviendas de propiedad del gobierno	1	0,4	5 600
Vivienda propia (coste de los intereses hipotecarios, contribuciones municipales, reparaciones, mantenimiento y seguros)	4	9,6	22 000
Equipo y gastos del hogar:			
Combustible y luz	3	2,4	100
Accesorios para el hogar	1	1,5	900
Moblaje y alfombras	2	4,1	1 200
Ropa blanca	2	0,7	600
Otros bienes y servicios para el hogar	14	5,7	3 000
Comunicaciones	2	1,5	200
Crédito del consumo	1	2,5	200
Aseo personal y asistencia médica	6	5,6	3 800
Transportes	7	17,0	5 600
Distracciones y educación	11	10,8	5 500
Total	107	100,0	100 600

Nota: (a) Véase a bajo. (b) Por trimestre.

(a) Estas cifras representan el número de "clases de gastos" y no los diferentes artículos cuyos precios se registran. Cada clase de gasto consta de una selección de "artículos" similares; por ejemplo, las cuatro clases de gasto del grupo relativo al tabaco y alcohol son: cerveza; vino; licor, cigarrillos y tabaco. Cada una de estas clases abarca una serie de variedades de bebidas alcohólicas o de productos de tabaco.

Gastos de consumo de los hogares
A los fines del índice, los gastos de consumo son los que corresponden a los realizados en el momento en artículos y servicios destinados al consumo durante el período que sirve de base para las ponderaciones. Se excluyen los gastos ficticios, las contribuciones a fondos privados de jubilaciones y pensiones, los impuestos a la renta de las personas físicas y otras cargas fiscales directas, los pagos de seguro de vida, los giros y regalos, las joyas, los servicios legales, las cuotas de participación o suscripciones a clubes y sindicatos y los gastos de juego. Se incluyen los ingresos en especie, el coste de los intereses hipotecarios, los recargos por créditos a los consumidores, los servicios de óptica, el registro de automóviles y los pagos necesarios para obtener una licencia, los seguros vinculados con bienes de consumo específicos, el cuidado de la salud y las contribuciones a los gobiernos locales y cargas anexas.

Método de recolección de los datos
La selección de las localidades y de los puntos de venta se efectúa sobre la base de las informaciones recogidas por el censo de la población, de los datos sobre el comercio minorista obtenidos por el personal especializado que se encarga de la recolección y del conocimiento local del terreno que tienen esos funcionarios. No se ha efectuado ninguna encuesta sobre los puntos de venta. Para la recolección de precios se consultan aproximadamente 5 500 informantes de las ocho ciudades y se recogen alrededor de 100 000 cotizaciones cada trimestre de supermercados, grandes almacenes, zapaterías, restaurantes, proveedores domiciliarios, otros puntos de venta al por menor, establecimientos de servicios, etc. Para renglones tales como las tarifas de los ferrocarriles, los servicios de electricidad y otros similares, los precios se obtienen directamente de las autoridades pertinentes. La recolección de precios es semanal en el caso de las frutas y las verduras frescas, quincenal para el pescado fresco y mensual para la carne fresca, el pan, los cigarrillos y el tabaco, las bebidas alcohólicas embotelladas y el petróleo. Para algunos artículos importantes, los precios se recogen al final del trimestre y se registran las fechas de las modificaciones de los precios para poder calcular los precios medios a lo largo de un trimestre. Para los demás artículos, los precios se registran cada tres meses, con la excepción de las contribuciones de los municipios y las cargas, la vestimenta de estación y las cortadoras de césped, cuyos precios son recopilados anualmente. Los precios utilizados en el índice son los que cualquier persona tendría que pagar el día en que se registran esos precios para adquirir los bienes o utilizar los servicios determinados, incluyendo los impuestos a las ventas y los indirectos. Los precios de las liquidaciones, los descuentos y otras rebajas "especiales" se reflejan en el índice siempre que los artículos ofrecidos sean de calidad normal y se vendan en cantidades razonables. No existe una fecha determinada para el registro general de precios. Su recopilación se distribuye a lo largo del trimestre.

Vivienda
Los datos referentes al alquiler se recogen trimestralmente y se basan en una extensa muestra de viviendas de propiedad privada y estatal. Los costos de las viviendas ocupadas por sus propietarios se representan por los gastos reales en concepto de reparaciones y mantenimiento, por las contribuciones municipales, por los seguros y por el coste de los intereses hipotecarios.

Especificación de las variedades
La selección de las variedades particulares de los artículos cuyos precios se deben registrar, se realiza tras analizar los datos de los fabricantes, importadores y minoristas. Las marcas y las variedades corresponden generalmente a las de mayor volumen de venta. Con la base de esos datos, se elaboran especificaciones detalladas para cada artículo evaluado y se incluyen detalles tales como la marca, el modelo, el tamaño, el país de fabricación y toda información necesaria para registrar los precios a calidad constante en el tiempo.

Sustitución, cambio de calidad, etc.
Cada vez que se revisa el índice, aproximadamente cada cuatro o cinco años, se introducen productos totalmente nuevos. Las nuevas variedades de los productos que permanecen en el índice sólo se introducen si revisten importancia para los gastos de los consumidores de productos de esa categoría. Cuando desaparece del mercado un determinado tipo de calidad, se lo elimina del índice y, si corresponde, se lo reemplaza por un sustitutivo utilizando el procedimiento de enlace. Con respecto a los cambios de calidad, las principales técnicas utilizadas son: i) la estimación directa del valor del cambio de calidad, con el correspondiente ajuste del precio del artículo afectado; ii) el enlace con las nuevas especificaciones.

Artículos estacionales
Con respecto a las frutas y las verduras frescas, la recolección de los precios se extiende a los artículos estacionales que no pueden obtenerse durante todo el año. En los períodos en los que no se dispone de determinados artículos estacionales, los precios se atribuyen basándose en las modificaciones de los precios de los artículos de que se dispone. Con respecto a las prendas de vestir de estación, los precios se recogen una vez por año en el trimestre que interesa. Para los restantes trimestres del año, los precios se mantienen sin variaciones. No se hacen ajustes para las fluctuaciones estacionales de los precios de los artículos.

Cálculo
El índice se calcula trimestralmente, conforme a la fórmula de cadena de Laspeyres, con un coeficiente de ponderación de base fija. Las modificaciones en la estructura y composición de los coeficientes de ponderación se realizan cada cinco años aproximadamente. El índice nacional se calcula como promedio ponderado de los números índices de las ocho ciudades capitales, cuyos coeficientes de ponderación corresponden al nú-

mero de hogares del grupo de población del índice en cada ciudad.

Informaciones complementarias
Un nuevo índice de precios del consumo (base año que termina en junio de 1990 = 100) está preparándose y aparecerá próximamente.

Organización y publicación
Australian Bureau of Statistics: "Consumer Price Index", Cataloque No. 6401.0, de publicación trimestral (Canberra, ACT).
Los precios vigentes de una selección de artículos que figuran en el Consumer Price Index se publican en "Average Retail Prices of Selected Items, Eight Capital Cities", Catalogue No. 6403.0.
idem: "A Guide to the Consumer Price Index", cat. No. 6440.0, 1987.
idem: "Review of the Consumer Price Index", cat. No. 6450.0.
idem: "The Australian Consumer Price Index; Concepts, Sources and Methods", cat. No. 6461.0.

AUSTRIA

Denominación oficial
Consumer Price Index (Indice de precios del consumo).

Alcance
La compilación del índice es mensual y de alcance nacional, abarcando todos los hogares sin limitación de ingresos o tamaño.

Base oficial
1986 = 100.

Fuente de la ponderación
La selección de los artículos y la determinación de los coeficientes de ponderación se basaron en los resultados de una encuesta sobre los gastos de los hogares efectuada durante un mes, entre marzo de 1984 y febrero de 1985, que abarcó 6 599 hogares representative toda la población. En el momento de la encuesta, los gastos mensuales medios por hogar eran de 20 390 Schilling y la composición del hogar medio de 2,7 personas. Los coeficientes de ponderación se revisaron basándose en datos de la contabilidad nacional.

Ponderaciones y composición

Grupos principales	Número de artículos	Ponderación	Número aproximado de cotizaciones de precio
Alimentación	149	23 268	...
Tabaco	79	2 512	...
Alquiler (incl. gastos de reparación y conservación)	28	13 056	...
Combustible y luz	13	5 405	...
Accesorios para el hogar	41	7 582	...
Vestido y calzado	50	10 694	...
Productos de conservación y limpieza	9	1 402	...
Aseo personal y asistencia médica	31	6 006	...
Educación y distacciones	85	14 302	...
Transportes y comunicaciones	130	15 773	...
Total	615	100 000	50 000

Gastos de consumo de los hogares
A los fines del índice, los gastos de consumo comprenden todo desembolso de dinero de los hogares en bienes y servicios destinados al consumo. Se incluye el valor al consumo de los productos caseros para el consumo del hogar. No se incluyen las contribuciones a la seguridad social y a fondos de pensión, el compra de la vivienda, los impuestos a la renta de las personas físicas y otras cargas fiscales, ni los giros y regalos.

Método de recolección de los datos
Los investigadores recogen los precios los segundos miércoles de cada mes. Los precios de 328 artículos se obtienen centralizadamente y los de 287 artículos se obtienen regionalmente, en 20 ciudades, en puntos de venta al por menor, áreas fijas de mercado y establecimientos de servicios que representan sitios habituales de compras. Los precios utilizados en el cálculo del índice son los que regularmente pagan los consumidores. No se toman en consideración las rebajas y los descuentos.

Vivienda
Las cotizaciones del alquiler se obtienen por medio de los resultados trimestrales de un microcenso de viviendas, alquiladas y propias. Para facilitar las comparaciones de costos de vivienda, en los cálculos se toma como base el metro cuadrado. Las modificaciones en las cotizaciones de alquiler señaladas de un trimestre a otro se distribuyen proporcionalmente en los tres próximos meses.

Especificación de las variedades
La descripción de las variedades es de naturaleza general a fin de permitir que el recolector de precios elija, para el normal registro de precios, el tipo, la calidad, la cantidad, etc., del artículo en cada uno de los puntos de venta al por menor que representa el mayor volumen de venta.

Sustitución, cambio de calidad, etc.
Si se modifica la calidad de un artículo, se modifica el precio de base conforme al valor del porcentaje de cambio entre el mes anterior y el corriente.

Articulos estacionales
Se tienen en cuenta las fluctuaciones estacionales de los precios de las frutas y verduras frescas, variando la composición mensual de los artículos del subgrupo, cuyos coeficientes de ponderación permanecen, en conjunto, constantes.

Cálculo
El índice se calcula conforme a la fórmula de Laspeyres como un promedio aritmético ponderado de base fija, cuyos coeficientes de ponderación corresponden al período de base. El índice para un artículo se obtiene utilizando los medios de las relaciones de precios del período corriente y del período de base. El índice nacional representa el promedio aritmético ponderado de los índices relativos a 20 ciudades, y los coeficientes de ponderación están en proporción a la población de cada ciudad según el censo de población de 1981.

Informaciones complementarias
No disponible.

Organización y publicación
Oesterreichisches Statistisches Zentralamt: "Statistische Nachrichten" (Viena).
idem: "Verbraucherpreisindex, Revision 1986", Beiträge zur österreichischen Statistik, Heft 853, 1987.

BAHAMAS

Denominación oficial
Retail Price Index for New Providence (Indice de precios al por menor de Nueva Providencia).

Alcance
El índice se compila mensualmente y abarca todos los hogares privados de Nueva Providencia.

Base oficial
Marzo - abril de 1987 = 100.

Fuente de la ponderación
La determinación de los coeficientes de ponderación y la selección de los artículos se basaron en los resultados de una encuesta, realizada en 1983, sobre los gastos de una muestra representativa de hogares de toda la isla de Nueva Providencia, salvo sus puntas extremas occidental y oriental. Los artículos que representan más del 0,001 por ciento del total del gasto doméstico se seleccionaron para formar parte de la canasta. Se combinaron los coeficientes de ponderación de los artículos no seleccionados y la suma se adjudicó a la categoría "otros" de ese grupo de artículos. No se ajustaron las ponderaciones en función de las variaciones de precio registradas entre el período de base y la encuesta.

Gastos de consumo de los hogares
Comprenden la adquisición de la casa, los seguros e impuestos de bienes inmobiliarios y los seguros de accidentes, salud y vida asociados a la actividad profesional. Se han excluido los seguros de vida ordinarios, ahorros, adquisiciones de existencias y acciones, la parte de los pagos hipotecarios que corresponden al capital y la amortización de préstamos bancarios.

Método de recolección de los datos
Los investigadores registran la mayoría de los precios, en forma personal o por teléfono, en 208 puntos de venta al por menor y establecimientos de servicios; los costos de los servi-

Ponderaciones y composición

Grupos principales	Número de artículos	Ponderación	Número aproximado de cotizaciones de precio
Alimentación	98	17,196	1 332
Vestido y calzado	20	6,647	294
Vivienda:			
Alquiler	2	5,213	39
Valor locativo neto de la casa propia	3	13,435	7
Combustible y luz	3	3.992	3
Mantenimiento y reparaciones	4	2.965	12
Muebles, moblaje, equipos y funcionamiento del hogar	28	9,527	296
Asistencia médica	8	3,263	118
Transporte y comunicaciones	17	22,094	151
Educación y recreación	25	12.792	221
Varios	15	2,878	287
Total	223	100,000	2 760

cios médicos y seguros se obtienen mediante cuestionarios enviados por correo. Las cotizaciones se establecen en forma mensual o trimestral y se refieren por lo general a las dos primeras semanas del mes. Los precios o tarifas de todas las mercancías y servicios incluidos en el índice son los que se pagan al contado y en efectivo. Se excluyen los recargos adicionales por créditos y se ignoran las rebajas, así como los precios de venta si el minorista, normalmente, no los practica; no se toman en consideración las reducciones de precio temporales.

Vivienda
Se incluyen tanto viviendas alquiladas con muebles como sin ellos. Pueden tener uno o dos dormitorios. Las cotizaciones de alquiler se obtienen de 32 viviendas alquiladas sin muebles y 7 alquiladas con muebles, mediante visitas personales o llamadas telefónicas. Para determinar el valor locativo neto de la casa propia se toman en cuenta el valor de adquisición de la casa y los seguros e impuestos inmobiliarios.

Especificación de las variedades
A efectos de seleccionar las especificaciones de los artículos se examina, con los dependientes de tienda, las marcas o tamaños de un artículo que son las más vendidas.

Sustitución, cambio de calidad, etc.
Si la modificación del precio de un artículo obedece a un cambio de calidad, se modifica el precio de base para anular la variación de precio. Si un artículo desaparece del mercado se le puede sustituir por otro nuevo y tanto el precio de éste como del "antiguo" se registrarán durante los meses que se superponen para garantizar que en el mes de la sustitución sólo se registren variaciones de precio. Si la desaparición es temporal, se mantiene el último precio registrado hasta que el artículo vuelva a ofrecerse en el mercado. No obstante si la desaparición del artículo dura un cierto tiempo, como por ejemplo 3 meses, es necesario proceder a una sustitución.

Artículos estacionales
Los artículos estacionales no tienen un trato especial en el índice.

Cálculo
El índice se calcula según la fórmula de Laspeyres como un promedio aritmético ponderado de base fija, cuyos coeficientes de ponderación corresponden a 1983. El relativo de precio de cada artículo se calcula dividiendo el precio medio del período en curso por el precio medio del período de base. El precio medio de un artículo es la media aritmética simple de los precios obtenidos para ese artículo.

Informaciones complementarias
El Departamento de Estadísticas también publica un Indice de Precios al por menor de Gran Bahama (base: marzo de 1974 = 100). Sin embargo, para representar al Indice Nacional se utiliza el Indice de Precios al por menor de Nueva Providencia.

Organización y publicación
Ministry of Finance, Department of Statistics: "Retail Price Index" (Nassau).
idem: "Quarterly Statistical Summary".
idem: "Annual Review of Retail Prices".
idem: "An explanation of the Retail Price Index".
idem: "The Revised Index for New Providence".

BANGLADESH (DHAKA)

Denominación oficial
Middle-Class Cost of Living Index for Government Employees in Dhaka City. (Indice del costo de la vida para empleados del gobierno de clase media en la ciudad de Dhaka).

Alcance
El índice se compila mensualmente y abarca hogares de clase media de empleados gubernamentales en la ciudad de Dhaka.

Base oficial
1973 - 1974 = 100.

Fuente de la ponderación
La selección de los artículos y la determinación de los coeficientes de ponderación se basaron en los resultados de una encuesta sobre los gastos de los hogares efectuada en 1973-74. La encuesta abarcó hogares de todos los grupos de ingresos, mientras que el índice se refiere a hogares de la clase media de Dhaka cuyos ingresos mensuales en el momento de la encuesta oscilaban entre 300 y 999 Taka.

Ponderaciones y composición

Grupos principales	Número de artículos	Ponderación	Número aproximado de cotizaciones de precio
Alimentación	77	62,74	...
Combustible y luz	5	7,50	...
Vivienda y accesorios para el hogar	24	11,85	...
Vestido y calzado	25	6,20	...
Varios	57	11,71	...
Total	188	100,00	...

Gastos de consumo de los hogares
No disponible.

Método de recolección de los datos
Los precios se recogen en mercados, tiendas al por menor y establecimientos de servicios por investigadores en forma semanal, quincenal, mensual y trimestral. La frecuencia de la recolección depende de la naturaleza de los artículos. Los precios de los servicios de electricidad, gas, asistencia médica, educación y transportes se recogen en los establecimientos pertinentes. Los precios utilizados en el índice son los del mercado libre para todos los artículos, salvo el arroz en cuyo precio se tienen en cuenta tanto los precios libres como los controlados.

Vivienda
Las cotizaciones del alquiler se obtienen de una muestra de 10 viviendas.

Especificación de las variedades
No disponible.

Sustitución, cambio de calidad, etc.
Cuando ya no es posible encontrar un producto, se lo substituye por otro de calidad aproximadamente igual y se utiliza el método de enlace.

Artículos estacionales
Se consideran como tales las frutas y verduras frescas. Los precios de esos artículos se registran durante la estación en que se pueden conseguir. Fuera de temporada se mantienen los precios de clausura de la estación precedente.

Cálculo
El índice se calcula conforme a la fórmula de Laspeyres como un promedio aritmético ponderado de base fija, cuyos coeficientes de ponderación corresponden al período de base.

Informaciones complementarias
La Oficina de Estadísticas de Bangladesh calcula también series para hogares de la clase media de Khulna y Chittangong, así como para hogares con bajos y altos ingresos de Dhaka.

Organización y publicación
Bangladesh Bureau of Statistics, Dhaka: "Monthly Statistical Bulletin of Bangladesh" (Dhaka).

BARBADOS

Denominación oficial
Index of Retail Prices (Indice de Precios al por Menor).

Alcance
El índice se compila mensualmente y abarca todo el país. Se excluyen del índice los hogares que mensualmente disponen de ingresos de 2 000 dólares de Barbados o más.

Base oficial
Marzo de 1980 = 100.

Fuente de la ponderación
La determinación de los coeficientes de ponderación y la selección de los artículos se basaron en los resultados de una encuesta sobre los gastos de los hogares realizada durante el período 1 de abril de 1978 - 31 de marzo de 1979. La muestra comprendió 1 200 hogares. Los artículos se seleccionaron en función de la proporción en que contribuyen al total de los gastos de los hogares. Los artículos cuya contribución se consideró insignificante o bien fueron dejados completamente de lado o bien se agruparon con otros artículos afines y se incluyeron como un artículo de grupo.

Ponderaciones y composición

Grupos principales	Número de artículos	Ponderación	Número aproximado de cotizaciones de precio
Alimentación	62	43,2	257
Bebidas alcohólicas y tabaco	7	8,4	36
Vivienda	9	13,1	26
Combustible y luz	5	6,2	9
Gastos y artículos del hogar	24	9,6	96
Vestido y calzado	21	5,1	99
Transportes	13	4,6	30
Asistencia médica y aseo personal	19	6,0	69
Educación, recreación y varios	8	3,8	36
Total	168	100,0	658

Gastos de consumo de los hogares
Incluyen los bienes consumidos por los hogares, los productos caseros para uso propio, la vivienda propia, las compras a crédito. Las contribuciones a la seguridad social y los pagos obligatorios a fondos de pensión no se consideran gastos de consumo de los hogares, ni tampoco los impuestos a los ingresos.

Método de recolección de los datos
Personal sobre el terreno del Servicio Estadístico ("Statistical Service") registra los precios en 85 tiendas y establecimientos minoristas seleccionados. La mayoría de los precios se registran mensualmente, el miércoles más próximo a la mitad del mes. Los precios de frutas, legumbres y pescado se registran todos los viernes del mes. La recolección de los precios de las tarifas de los servicios de teléfono, agua, lavado, peluquería, autobuses y taxis se realiza trimestralmente, en el segundo mes de cada trimestre.

Los precios que se usan en el índice son los que pagan regularmente las personas del público en general. Las rebajas sólo se consideran cuando se ofrecen a todos los compradores. No se toman en consideración las reducciones de precio para grupos especiales de clientes.

Vivienda
Los datos referentes al alquiler se recogen únicamente para las casas de propiedad del gobierno. Las modificaciones de los alquileres se registran cuando así lo informan las autoridades.

Especificación de las variedades
Los artículos cuyos precios se debe registrar han de tener especificaciones claras y precisas, tales como la marca, unidad, calidad y cantidad.

Sustitución, cambio de calidad, etc.
Cuando no se puede encontrar un producto se lo sustituye por otro que tenga aproximadamente la misma calidad, utilizándose el método de enlace.

Artículos estacionales
El principal artículo estacional es el pescado local.

Cálculo
El índice se calcula según la fórmula de Laspeyres como un promedio aritmético ponderado de base fija, cuyos coeficientes de ponderación corresponden al período de base.
El relativo de precio para cada artículo se obtiene dividiendo la suma de los precios registrados en el período en curso por la suma de los precios registrados en el período anterior. El precio promedio de un artículo es la media aritmética simple de los precios obtenidos para ese artículo.

Organización y publicación
Statistical Service: "Monthly Digest of Statistics" (Bridgetown).
idem: "The Barbados Economic Report".
idem: "Monthly Statistical Bulletin".
idem: "Economic and Financial Statistics".

BELGICA

Denominación oficial
Indice des prix à la consommation (Indice de Precios del Consumo).

Alcance
El índice se compila mensualmente y abarca todos los hogares medios del país.

Base oficial
1988 = 100.

Fuente de la ponderación
La determinación de los coeficientes de ponderación y la selección de los artículos se basaron en los resultados de una encuesta sobre los gastos de los hogares realizada entre mayo de 1987 y mayo de 1988 que abarcó a 3 315 hogares de obreros, empleados, trabajadores independientes y personas no económicamente activaos.

Ponderaciones y composición

Grupos principales	Número de artículos	Ponderación	Número aproximado de cotizaciones de precio (a)
Alimentación	157	18,985	58 900
Tabaco	4	1,130	1 200
Vestido y calzado	46	8,580	9 600
Vivienda:			
Alquiler	2	7,175	-
Reparaciones, mantenimiento y agua	10	6,155	-
Combustible y luz	20	6,070	-
Muebles y equipo del hogar	54	7,850	12 500
Asistencia médica	17	4,900	2 100
Transportes y comunicaciones	33	16,495	2 600
Educación y recreación	39	8,355	5 900
Otros bienes y servicios	47	14,305	7 300
Total	429	100,000	102 300

Nota: (a) Número de cotizaciones efectuadas por los investigadores exteriores, excluídas las cotizaciones efectuadas por el Servicio central.

Gastos de consumo de los hogares
Los gastos que se toman en cuenta a efectos del índice comprenden casi todos los bienes y servicios para el consumo de los hogares. También comprenden los valores estimados de los productos caseros (recogidos o elaborados) y de los recibidos como ingresos en especie.

Método de recolección de los datos
Los investigadores registran la mayoría de los precios en puntos de venta al por menor y establecimientos de servicios de 65 localidades de todo el país. Los precios de casi todos los artículos se registran entre el primero y el 20 de cada mes.

Los precios que se registran comprenden todas las cargas fiscales que gravan las compras al contado de los consumidores que no gozan de ninguna condición particular. Las reducciones de precio se toman en consideración desde el primer día de la oferta promocional, si ésta dura por lo menos un día, siempre que los productos rebajados sean de buena calidad y disponibles en cantidades suficientes. Los precios de los artículos en liquidación no se toman en cuenta.

Vivienda
Se obtienen las cotizaciones de alquiler de viviendas sociales y no sociales de las once provincias del país. El alquiler de las viviendas sociales se obtiene de varias sociedades autorizadas de viviendas sociales: el de las viviendas no sociales a partir

de una muestra de 1,521 departamentos y casas de diferente tamaño. Todos los meses se renueva la muestra para introducir dos viviendas nuevas en sustitución de dos antiguas y reflejar así la renovación del parque inmobiliario.

Especificación de las variedades
Las especificaciones se refieren más concretamente a la selección de unidades utilizadas. En la mayoría de los casos, las definiciones tienen la flexibilidad suficiente como para permitir eventuales modificaciones, pero la rigidez necesaria para garantizar la continuidad de los precios registrados.

Sustitución, cambio de calidad, etc.
Los investigadores pueden sustituir un artículo que ha desaparecido del mercado, a reserva de la autorización del servicio central y sujetos a la observancia de la siguientes directrices: el negocio sustituido y el sustitutivo deben ser de la misma clase y un producto determinado se debe sustituir por otro equivalente del mismo negocio o por el mismo producto de otro negocio.

Para ciertos artículos específicos para los cuales se han constituido muestras, como vehículos automóviles, alquileres no sociales, seguros de responsabilidad civil para vehículos automóviles y seguros de vida (responsabilidad civil familiar), el nuevo artículo se escoge de una lista establecida de antemano y en función de criterios precisos. El nuevo artículo se introduce en el índice medio alcanzado por los otros artículos del mismo subgrupo. Un aumento con respecto al mes anterior se toma en cuenta atribuyendo al artículo desaparecido la misma evolución que el índice medio de los otros artículos del mismo subgrupo.

Artículos estacionales
Se investigan las fluctuaciones estacionales de los precios de las frutas, legumbres y flores frescas variando la composición mensual de los artículos del subgrupo pero manteniendo constante su ponderación global. Los índices de ciertos artículos y servicios estacionales se calculan en relación con el mes correspondiente del período de base, siendo los precios de base el resultado de la media aritmética de los precios registrados en los meses correspondientes de 1987, 1988 y 1989.

Cálculo
El índice se calcula según la fórmula de Laspeyres como un promedio aritmético ponderado de base fija, cuyos coeficientes de ponderación corresponden al período de base.

Se calculan índices separados para 65 localidades. Las relaciones de precio para cada artículo y para cada localidad se obtienen dividiendo el promedio de precios del período en curso por el promedio de precios del período de base. Los promedios de precios son medias aritméticas simples de todos los precios registrados. Se ponderan luego los índices de las 65 localidades para obtener el índice nacional, utilizándose coeficientes proporcionales a la población de cada localidad según los datos sobre la población el primero de enero de 1988.

Informaciones complementarias
También se publica el índice general con bases 1981 = 100, julio de 1974 - junio de 1975 = 100 y 1971 = 100.

Organización y publicación
Ministère des Affaires économiques, Institut national de statistique: "Bulletin de statistique" (Bruselas).

idem: "Communiqué hebdomadaire".

Ministère des Affaires économiques, Administration du commerce, Service de l'indice: "Le nouvel indice des prix à la consommation; base 1988 = 100" (Bruselas, 1991).

BELICE

Denominación oficial
Consumer Price Index (Indice de Precios del Consumo).

Alcance
El índice se compila trimestralmente y abarca todo el país.

Base oficial
Febrero de 1980 = 100.

Fuente de la ponderación
La determinación de los coeficientes de ponderación y la selección de los artículos se basaron en los resultados de una encuesta, realizada en 1980, sobre los gastos de los hogares de Belice. La encuesta comprendió 1 800 hogares, urbanos y rurales.

Ponderaciones y composición
Corozola

Grupos principales	Número de artículos	Ponderación	Número aproximado de cotizaciones de precio
Alimentación	39	386	...
Productos de limpieza	5	33	...
Asistencia médica y aseo personal	9	71	...
Vestido y calzado	14	152	...
Alquiler, combustible y luz	5	47	...
Muebles, moblaje y equipo del hogar	12	107	...
Transportes	8	89	...
Varios	15	115	...
Total	107	1 000	...

Orange Walk

Grupos principales	Número de artículos	Ponderación	Número aproximado
Alimentación	39	378	...
Productos de limpieza	5	26	...
Asistencia médica y aseo personal	9	65	...
Vestido y calzado	14	117	...
Alquiler, combustible y luz	5	62	...
Muebles, moblaje y equipo del hogar	12	127	...
Transportes	8	106	...
Varios	15	119	...
Total	107	1 000	...

Belice

Grupos principales	Número de artículos	Ponderación	Número aproximado
Alimentación	39	394	...
Productos de limpieza	5	27	...
Asistencia médica y aseo personal	9	48	...
Vestido y calzado	14	116	...
Alquiler, combustible y luz	5	122	...
Muebles, moblaje y equipo del hogar	12	104	...
Transportes	8	60	...
Varios	15	129	...
Total	107	1 000	...

Cayo

Grupos principales	Número de artículos	Ponderación	Número aproximado
Alimentación	39	376	...
Productos de limpieza	5	30	...
Asistencia médica y aseo personal	9	46	...
Vestido y calzado	14	128	...
Alquiler, combustible y luz	5	85	...
Muebles, moblaje y equipo del hogar	12	127	...
Transportes	8	85	...
Varios	15	123	...
Total	107	1 000	...

Stan Creek

Grupos principales	Número de artículos	Ponderación	Número aproximado
Alimentación	39	481	...
Productos de limpieza	5	28	...
Asistencia médica y aseo personal	9	47	...
Vestido y calzado	14	121	...
Alquiler, combustible y luz	5	79	...
Muebles, moblaje y equipo del hogar	12	85	...
Transportes	8	28	...
Varios	15	131	...
Total	107	1 000	...

Toledo

Grupos principales	Número de artículos	Ponderación	Número aproximado
Alimentación	39	396	...
Productos de limpieza	5	39	...
Asistencia médica y aseo personal	9	53	...
Vestido y calzado	14	201	...
Alquiler, combustible y luz	5	40	...
Muebles, moblaje y equipo del hogar	12	102	...
Transportes	8	43	...
Varios	15	126	...
Total	107	1 000	...

Gastos de consumo de los hogares
No disponible.

Método de recolección de los datos
Los precios se registran durante tres semanas de febrero, mayo, agosto y noviembre, en mercados, puntos de venta al por menor y establecimientos de servicios de seis distritos.

Vivienda
No disponible.

Especificación de las variedades
No se utilizan especificaciones detalladas.

Sustitución, cambio de calidad, etc.
Cuando un artículo desaparece del mercado se mantiene el precio que tenía el trimestre anterior.

Artículos estacionales
No disponible.

Cálculo
El índice se calcula según la fórmula de Laspeyres como un promedio aritmético ponderado de base fija, cuyos coeficientes de ponderación corresponden al período de base.

En primer lugar se calculan índices separados de cada uno de los seis distritos. El Índice Nacional es un promedio ponderado de los números índices de los seis distritos, cuyos coeficientes de ponderación son proporcionales a la población de cada uno de ellos.

Organización y publicación
Ministry of Economic Development, Central Statistical Office: "Belize Consumer Price Index (trimestral)" (Belmopan).

BERMUDAS

Denominación oficial
Consumer Price Index (Indice de precios del consumo).

Alcance
El índice se compila mensualmente y abarca aproximadamente el 87 por ciento de todos los hogares de las Bermudas cuyos ingresos semanales oscilaban entre 200 y 1.499 dólares de Bermudas (B$) en 1982.

Base oficial
Enero de 1985 = 100.

Fuente de la ponderación
La determinación de los coeficientes de ponderación y la selección de los artículos se basaron en los resultados de una encuesta sobre los gastos de los hogares realizada en 1982. La encuesta comprendió unos 750 hogares que en el momento de la encuesta tenían ingresos semanales comprendidos entre 200 y 1.499 B$. No se ajustaron los coeficientes de ponderación para tomar en cuenta las modificaciones de precio ocurridas entre la encuesta y el período de base.

Ponderaciones y composición

Grupos principales	Número de artículos	Ponderación	Número aproximado de cotizaciones de precio
Alimentación	111	181	2 000
Alquiler	1	218	420
Vestido y calzado	37	60	200
Bebidas alcohólicas y tabaco	4	26	80
Combustible y luz	2	45	2
Muebles, moblaje, equipo y gastos del hogar	52	147	450
Transportes, viajes al extranjero	15	171	85
Educación, recreación y lecturas	17	84	115
Asistencia médica y aseo personal	9	68	400
Total	248	1 000	3 752

Gastos de consumo de los hogares
A los efectos del índice comprenden todas las adquisiciones de los hogares para el consumo, al contado o a crédito, más las contribuciones periódicas que en esos momentos se efectuaban a instituciones tales como compañías de seguros u organismos de seguridad social. Se incluyen las viviendas ocupadas por sus propietarios pero no los impuestos a los ingresos y otras cargas fiscales directas, los ahorros e inversiones, la devolución de préstamos y los regalos.

Método de recolección de los datos
Los precios se obtienen mediante entrevistas personales de los funcionarios del Departamento de Estadísticas realizadas a diversos puntos de venta y verificadas en cada uno de ellos, de ser necesario, por el personal de supervisión. Los precios de alimentos, artículos para el hogar, tabaco y bebidas alcohólicas, productos de aseo personal, medicamentos adquiridos sin prescripción facultativa y suministros médicos se recopilan mensualmente en once de los mayores supermercados del país. Se llevan a cabo encuestas trimestrales de los precios que suelen variar con más lentitud, como los de automóviles, motocicletas, vestidos y calzados, electrodomésticos, medicamentos que exigen prescripción médica, etc. El registro de los precios de matrículas escolares, primas de seguros de automóviles y seguros de enfermedad, así como las tasas de los permisos de circulación y conducción de automóviles, es anual. De resultar necesario, se modifica la frecuencia de la recolección de los precios que experimenten un rápida evolución, con la finalidad de mantenerlos al día.

Vivienda
Para las casas ocupadas por sus propietarios se estima como alquiler un valor anual equivalente que se incluye en el cálculo de los coeficientes de ponderación del componente vivienda del conjunto de los artículos del índice. No obstante, a los efectos del registro de los precios, las modificaciones de las cotizaciones del alquiler se basan simplemente en las fluctuaciones de mercado del alquiler mensual de una muestra representativa de casas alquiladas. No se observan los gastos concretos que sean específicos de las viviendas ocupadas por sus propietarios, tales como tipos de intereses hipotecarios, costes de reparaciones y seguros, ni gastos indicativos como la depreciación.

Especificación de las variedades
En cada uno de los puntos de venta de la muestra se seleccionan determinadas variedades para investigar sus precios. Para su recolección periódica se seleccionan las marcas, clases y volúmenes (tamaños vendibles) más populares, con asesoramiento del administrador o gerente del punto de venta.

Sustitución, cambio de calidad, etc.
Cuando cambia la calidad de un artículo se recurre al método de enlaces.

Artículos estacionales
Las fluctuaciones estacionales de los precios no son objeto de ajuste.

Cálculo
El índice se calcula según la fórmula de Laspeyres como un promedio aritmético ponderado de base fija, cuyos coeficientes de ponderación corresponden a 1982.

Organización y publicación
Ministry of Finance, Department of Statistics: "Bermuda Annual Digest" (Hamilton).
idem: "Bermuda Quarterly Digest of Statistics".
idem: "Retail Price Index Reference Paper" (abril de 1986).

BOLIVIA (LA PAZ)

Denominación oficial
Indice de Precios al Consumidor.

Alcance
El índice se compila mensualmente y abarca las familias de obreros y empleados de ingresos bajos y medios de la Paz.

Base oficial
1966 = 100.

Fuente de la ponderación
La selección de los artículos y la determinación de los coeficientes de ponderación se basaron en los resultados de una encuesta sobre los gastos de los hogares efectuada en la Paz, desde fines de 1964 hasta fines de 1965, de una muestra aleatoria de alrededor 800 familias de obreros y empleados de ingresos bajos y medios.

Ponderaciones y composición

Grupos principales	Número de artículos	Ponderación	Número aproximado de cotizaciones de precio
Alimentación	66	51,30	...
Vivienda:			
Alquiler	1	7,41	...
Impuestos sobre los bienes raices	1	1,25	...
Combustible y luz	2	5,03	...
Gastos del hogar	32	5,18	...
Vestido y calzado	32	12,10	...
Varios	27	17,73	...
Total	161	100,00	...

Gastos de consumo de los hogares
No se incluyen los ahorros, las inversiones, los impuestos sobre la renta y otros impuestos directos.

Método de recolección de los datos
Los precios son recogidos por investigadores en 1 200 puntos de venta y establecimientos de servicio, con una frecuencia que varía según la naturaleza de los artículos, llegando a ser sema-

nal, mensual, y anual. Los artículos alimenticios y los del grupo "Vivienda" se recogen semanalmente.

Informaciones sobre combustible y jabón de lavar ropa se obtienen semanalmente, y sobre la luz en forma mensual.

Los precios utilizados para el cálculo del índice son los que se pagan en el momento en los puntos de venta seleccionados. No se tienen en cuenta los precios de los descuentos.

Vivienda
Los datos referentes al alquiler se obtienen mensualmente de una muestra de 100 viviendas. No se tienen en cuenta las viviendas ocupadas por su propietario.

Especificación de las variedades
Las especificaciones de los productos cuyos precios se deben registrar comprenden la marca de fábrica, el tamaño, la unidad, la calidad, el volumen y el peso.

Sustitución, cambio de calidad, etc.
Cuando un artículo desaparece del mercado se sustituye por otro similar, manteniendo su ponderación.

Artículos estacionales
Los precios fuera de temporada siguen el movimiento de los precios de los demás artículos incluidos en el mismo subgrupo.

Cálculo
El índice se calcula según la fórmula de Laspeyres como un promedio aritmético ponderado de base fija, cuyos coeficientes de ponderación corresponden al período de 1964-65.

El índice para un artículo se obtiene utilizando las relaciones de precios del período corriente y del período precedente.

Informaciones complementarias
Tanto en la publicación mensual como en la anual se publican los índices General, por Grupos y Subgrupos, y variación e incidencia del índice respecto al mes anterior.

Organización y publicación
Instituto Nacional de Estadística, Departamento de Estadísticas Económicas, División de Precios: "Indice de Precios al Consumidor", Boletín mensual (La Paz).

idem: "Indice de Precios al Consumidor", Anuario.

BOTSWANA

Denominación oficial
National Cost of Living Index (Indice nacional del costo de la vida).

Alcance
La compilación del índice es mensual y abarca todos los hogares, rurales y urbanos.

Base oficial
Septiembre de 1985 = 100.

Fuente de la ponderación
La selección de los artículos y la determinación de los coeficientes de ponderación se basan en los resultados de una encuesta sobre los gastos de los hogares, que se realizó entre fines de 1978 y los tres primeros trimestres de 1979, cuya muestra abarcó 915 hogares urbanos y 1 221 rurales, ubicados en las cuatro ciudades principales y en las 13 aldeas que, al realizarse el censo de 1971, contaban con más de 3 000 habitantes. Si bien se ha revisado el número de artículos y las ponderaciones, no se han ajustado los coeficientes de ponderación para tomar en cuenta los cambios de precio entre el período de la encuesta y septiembre de 1985.

Al seleccionar los artículos del índice, se trató de que en cada subgrupo figurara tanto la totalidad de los artículos más importantes, como una selección de los menos importantes para representar a todos los demás artículos de ese subgrupo. En consecuencia, muchos de los artículos del índice se eligieron por ser representativos de una amplia gama de bienes de consumo y no por su importancia intrínseca.

Gastos de consumo de los hogares
A los efectos del índice, comprenden tanto los efectuados al contado como a crédito para adquirir bienes nuevos o de segunda mano. Se excluyen los ingresos en especie, la producción casera para el consumo del propio hogar, los pagos de seguros de vida, pensiones y contribuciones a la seguridad social.

Ponderaciones y composición

Grupos principales	Número de artículos (a)	Ponderación	Número aproximado de cotizaciones de precio
Alimentación	48	36,65	2 970
Bebidas y tabaco	7	3,43	270
Vestido y calzado	13	10,84	717
Alquiler, combustible, luz y agua	16	13,07	239
Enseres y gastos del hogar	24	13,70	1 069
Asistencia médica	6	1,30	127
Transportes y comunicaciones	18	10,54	129
Bienes y servicios varios	20	10,46	582
Total	152	100,00	6 103

Nota: (a) Si bien para compilar el índice no se utilizan directamente las ponderaciones nacionales se las incluye a título de referencia.

Método de recolección de los datos
Cada mes se recogen los precios en establecimientos de venta al por menor representativos, ubicados en una selección de ciudades y aldeas de todo el país, en particular, cuatro zonas urbanas, ocho aldeas grandes y cinco pequeñas.

Todas las clases de establecimientos (grandes, medianos y pequeños) están representados en la recolección de precios, a cuyo efecto se visitan en total unos 300 establecimientos minoristas por mes. La recolección de precios está a cargo de funcionarios de la Oficina Central de Estadísticas de Gaborone, quienes visitan todas las regiones indicadas durante las dos primeras semanas de cada mes. El total de las cotizaciones de precio registradas cada mes es de aproximadamente 6 100.

Las remuneraciones del servicio doméstico se recogen cada tres meses en Gaborone. Algunos precios se obtienen mediante llamadas telefónicas. También se registran los precios que tienen una cotización oficial cuando se producen descuentos, rebajas por liquidación y precios de mercado libre.

Las compras al contado son las únicas que se toman en consideración.

La recolección de los precios se lleva a cabo de conformidad con la ley de estadísticas de 1976, que obliga a las personas encuestadas a comunicar los datos que se les preguntan y exige al mismo tiempo a la Oficina Central de Estadísticas que mantenga el carácter confidencial estricto de los datos y no los revele a ninguna persona, organización o dependencia oficial ajena a dicha Oficina.

Vivienda
Las cotizaciones del alquiler se obtienen de la "Botswana Housing Corporation" y de una encuesta trimestral de la Oficina Central de Estadísticas sobre el precio promedio de los alquileres de viviendas de una habitación, pagados por arrendatarios privados de Gaborone. Las variaciones de alquiler que se produzcan en Gaborone indican las que, muy probablemente, se producen en el resto del país. Las viviendas ocupadas por sus propietarios se representan mediante el interés pagadero por el terreno y la amortización de préstamos para materiales de construcción.

Especificación de las variedades
Se utilizan tanto especificaciones detalladas como especificaciones amplias. Las detalladas comprenden descripciones de la marca, factura, calidad, número, etc. Las amplias dan una descripción general de los artículos que se deben seleccionar en un negocio específico.

Sustitución, cambio de calidad, etc.
Durante todas las series de un índice, en principio las descripciones no varían, salvo si se debe modificar algún componente, en cuyo caso la descripción del artículo se modificará en consecuencia. A tal efecto, se atribuye un nuevo precio de base al artículo de sustitución, suponiéndose que desde septiembre de 1985 ha tenido la misma tasa de aumento que el artículo sustituido.

En virtud de este procedimiento, si un comercio no tiene existencias de mantequilla de 250 gramos, no se utiliza el precio de los paquetes de medio quilo, pues no resulta indispensable contar con los precios de todos los artículos en la totalidad de los establecimientos. En vez se hace el promedio de todos los precios registrados por 250 gramos de mantequilla en todos los establecimientos de la misma zona y se compara ese promedio con el precio de base correspondiente a ese artículo en la misma zona. Al mes siguiente, la misma descripción del artículo (250 g. de mantequilla) aparece en el cuestionario para dicho establecimiento. Se presume que disminuirán así los errores causados por atribuir precios a artículos que no corresponden exactamente a la descripción de los mismos.

Artículos estacionales
No son objeto de ningún tratamiento especial.

Cálculo
El índice se calcula según la fórmula de Laspeyres, como un promedio aritmético ponderado con base fija, cuyos coeficientes de ponderación corresponden al período 1978-1979.

En primer lugar se calcula el precio relativo de cada artículo dividiendo el precio medio del período en curso por el precio medio del período de base. Luego, con los precios relativos así obtenidos se calculan índices separados para grupos de hogares con ingresos elevados, medianos y bajos de las zonas urbanas y de las aldeas, grandes y pequeñas, de las regiones rurales.

Los índices que comprenden todos los grupos de ingresos de las zonas urbanas se calculan como promedios ponderados de los tres índices por grupos de ingreso, tomando en cuenta la media de los gastos de consumo de las regiones urbanas. El índice nacional es el promedio ponderado de los índices urbanos y rurales, utilizando como coeficiente de ponderación la población de las regiones urbanas y rurales.

Informaciones complementarias
Se publican índices de subgrupos principales. También se publican índices generales separados para las zonas urbanas y las regiones rurales.

Actualmente se calculan nuevas series para zonas urbanas, regiones rurales y todo el país (base noviembre de 1991 = 100), pero en el momento de publicar el presente Volumen, la OIT no disponía de informaciones metodológicas sobre estas nuevas series.

Organización y publicación
Central Statistics Office: "Statistical Bulletin" (Gaborone), (trimestral).

idem: "Cost of living index 1985", noviembre de 1985.

idem: "Consumer Price Statistics".

BRASIL

Denominación oficial
Indice de Preços ao Consumidor Amplo (IPCA)(Indice de Precios del Consumo).

Alcance
El índice se compila mensualmente y abarca todos los hogares de asalariados de las zonas urbanas del país con remuneraciones que oscilan entre uno y 40 salarios mínimos.

Base oficial
Diciembre de 1990 = 100.

Fuente de la ponderación
La determinación de los coeficientes de ponderación y la selección de los artículos se basaron en los resultados de una encuesta nacional sobre los gastos de los hogares realizada entre agosto de 1974 y agosto de 1975. La muestra de esta encuesta comprendió 55.000 hogares, de una a cinco personas, ubicados en todas las regiones metropolitanas del país. Los coeficientes de ponderación se actualizaron con los resultados de una encuesta sobre los gastos de los hogares realizada entre marzo de 1987 y febrero de 1988. No se ajustaron los coeficientes de ponderación para tomar en cuenta las modificaciones de precio ocurridas entre el período de la encuesta y el período de base.

Ponderaciones y composición
No disponible.

Gastos de consumo de los hogares
Se excluyen de las ponderaciones los gastos que significan un incremento de las economías, como por ejemplo la adquisición de casas, teléfonos, etc. También se excluyen los impuestos directos y los que gravan la propiedad inmueble, además de intereses, seguros, cancelación de deudas, cartas de crédito, amortización de préstamos y compras de materiales de construcción para mejora de viviendas. También se excluyen los gastos relativos a nacimientos, bautismos, bodas, carnavales y Navidad, etc. En las ponderaciones no se toman en consideración las viviendas ocupadas por sus propietarios.

Los bienes durables se consideran como los demás artículos y se incluyen en los gastos efectuados durante los 12 meses del período de referencia. Las compras a crédito se consideran como pagos efectuados durante el período de referencia de la encuesta. Se incluyen en los coeficientes de ponderación las adquisiciones de vehículos de segunda mano. Se excluyen las primas de los seguros de vida.

Método de recolección de los datos
Según el artículo de que se trate, los investigadores recogen los precios en forma mensual, trimestral o anual, en determinados puntos de venta al por menor y establecimientos de servicios de todas las zonas urbanas del país. No se envían cuestionarios por correo. Las modificaciones de cierta tarifas fijadas por el Estado, como las de la electricidad, el agua, el gas, los transportes y las comunicaciones se registran en cuanto entran en vigor. Los datos sobre costes de la asistencia médica se registran cada dos meses. Se toman en consideración los descuentos y las rebajas. Todos los precios registrados son los que deben pagar los consumidores.

Vivienda
Una encuesta nacional de viviendas permite obtener una muestra de viviendas, que se divide en doce para investigar una parte cada mes En los coeficientes de ponderación no se incluyen las viviendas ocupadas por sus propietarios.

Especificación de las variedades
Para las mayor parte de los artículos, las especificaciones son detalladas y describen la marca, envasado, tamaño, calidad, unidad de medida, etc. Para algunos otros, que no es posible detallar tanto, las especificaciones no los describen completamente.

Sustitución, cambio de calidad, etc.
No se toma en consideración el cambio de calidad de los artículos. Los nuevos productos que aparecen en el mercado se introducen cuando se revisan las especificaciones. En casos de desaparición temporal del mercado se atribuyen precios en función del movimiento de precios de los artículos restantes del mismo subgrupo.

Artículos estacionales
Para tomar en cuenta las variaciones estacionales del precio de artículos tales como tubérculos, frutas y legumbres frescas, se utilizan artículos y ponderaciones mensuales. Para calcular el índice de artículos estacionales se utiliza la fórmula de Paasche.

Cálculo
El índice se calcula según la fórmula de Laspeyres como un promedio aritmético ponderado de base fija, cuyos coeficientes de ponderación corresponden al período entre marzo de 1987 y marzo de 1988.

Para compilar los índices se utilizan los promedios de los relativos de precio del período en curso y del precedente.

Para obtener el índice nacional, se determinan en primer lugar los índices de las regiones metropolitanas, que luego se combinan, correspondiendo las ponderaciones utilizadas al gasto total estimado de cada región metropolitana en ese momento.

Informaciones complementarias
Al "Instituto Brasileiro de Geografia e Estatística" (IBGE), calcula también un Indice Nacional de los Precios del Consumo (INPC) y un Indice de Precios del Consumo (IPC) que se refiere a hogares que perciben entre uno y ocho salarios mínimos.

Organización y publicación
"Fundaçao Instituto Brasileiro de Geografia e Estatística" (IBGE): "Indicadores" (Río de Janeiro).

idem: "Sistema Nacional de Indices de Preços ao Consumidor, Métodos de Cálculo", 1984.

idem: "Estructura Básica de Ponderaçoes", 1983.

idem: "Guia de campo para a Pesquisa de Especificaçao de Produtos e Serviços", Janeiro 1980.

idem: "Métodos para o Trabalho de Campo", 1983.

idem: "Manual de Implantaçao", November 1979.

idem: "Para compreender o INPC", 1981.

BRASIL (SAO PAULO)

Denominación oficial
Indice de Preços ao Consumidor (Indice de precios del consumo).

Alcance
El índice se calcula mensualmente y abarca los hogares que disponían de un ingreso mensual entre 451 y 1 353 cruzeiros en 1971.

Base oficial
Diciembre del año precedente = 100.

Fuente de la ponderación
La selección de los artículos y la determinación de los coeficientes de ponderación se basaron en los resultados de una encuesta piloto entre familias de ingresos medios efectuada en mayo y junio de 1971 en São Paulo por el Instituto de Investigaciones Economicas (Instituto de Pesquisas Econômicas) de la Universidad de São Paulo.

Ponderaciones y composición

Grupos principales	Número de artículos	Ponderación	Número aproximado de cotizaciones de precio
Alimentación	143	435,3	...
Vivienda:			
Alquiler	1	86,3	...
Combustible, luz, agua, reparaciones, impuestos municipales, servicio doméstico, etc.	18	117,7	...
Productos de limpieza	12	22,9	...
Vestido y calzado	7	64,0	...
Gastos personales:			
Bebidas y tabaco	11	54,3	...
Servicios personales	6	16,1	...
Educación y distracciones	8	21,2	...
Salud y aseo personal	17	21,9	...
Otros gastos	4	22,7	...
Transportes	10	62,8	...
Asistencia médica	7	52,8	...
Educación	4	22,0	...
Total	248	1 000,0	

Gastos de consumo de los hogares
No disponible.

Método de recolección de los datos
Los precios son recogidos por investigadores cada día para los artículos alimenticios y mensualmente para los otros artículos, en 1 251 puntos de venta al por menor y establecimientos de servicios en São Paulo.

Vivienda
No disponible.

Especificación de las variedades
No disponible.

Sustitución, cambio de calidad, etc.
No disponible.

Artículos estacionales
No disponible.

Cálculo
El índice es un índice en cadena (es decir, en vez de comparar los precios recogidos el mes de referencia con los del período de base, se los compara con los del mes precedente) calculado según una fórmula equivalente a la del promedio aritmético ponderado de base fija.

Organización y publicación
Universidade de São Paulo, Instituto de Pesquisas Econômicas: "Indice de Preços ao Consumidor" (São Paulo).
idem: "O actual Indice de Preços ao Consumidor - Custo de Vida da classe de renda familiar modal do Município de São Paulo", Relatório Preliminar No. 2.

BRUNEI DARUSSALAM

Denominación oficial
Consumer Price Index for Brunei Darussalam (Indice de precios del consumo para Brunéi Darussalam).

Alcance
El índice se compila mensualmente y abarca hogares de empleados del gobierno cuyos ingresos oscilaban en 1977 entre 300 y 2 099 dólares de Brunéi.

Base oficial
1977 = 100.

Fuente de la ponderación
La selección de los artículos y la determinación de los coeficientes de ponderación se basaron en los resultados de una encuesta sobre los gastos de los hogares efectuada en 1977. La encuesta se limitó a los empleados del gobierno. La estructura de la ponderación se basó en los hogares cuyos gastos mensuales oscilaban entre 300 y 2 099 dólares de Brunéi en 1977.

Ponderaciones y composición

Grupos principales	Número de artículos	Ponderación	Número aproximado de cotizaciones de precio
Alimentación	42	4 507	...
Vestido y calzado	8	614	...
Vivienda:			
Alquiler	1	181	...
Reparaciones menores y mantenimiento	1	83	...
Combustible y servicios:			
Agua, electricidad y gas	1	215	...
Otros gastos de combustible y luz	1	20	...
Moblaje, equipo y gastos del hogar	8	831	...
Transportes y comunicaciones	6	1 718	...
Educación, distracciones, servicios culturales y de educación	8	893	...
Bienes y servicios varios	8	938	...
Total	84	10 000	...

Gastos de consumo de los hogares
A los fines del índice, los gastos de consumo comprenden la mayor parte de los bienes y servicios consumidos o utilizados por la población de referencia. Se excluyen los gastos en terreno y edificios, las primas de los seguros de vida, los ahorros y los impuestos a la renta de las personas físicas.

Método de recolección de los datos
Los precios se recogen en tiendas de venta al por menor seleccionadas y establecimientos del distrito Brunéi-Muara que incluye la capital Bandar Seri Begawan. La información sobre los precios para todos los artículos se recogen mediante visitas personales a los comerciantes, que realizan los funcionarios de la Statistics Division, Economic Planning Unit, y por medio de llamadas telefónicas.

Los precios del pescado fresco, de las verduras y las frutas frescas se recogen todos los sábados, mientras que los precios de los demás artículos se recogen todos los meses en una fecha fija.

Los precios utilizados en el índice son los que se pagan en el momento de las transacciones al contado. No se incluyen los recargos extraordinarios por créditos ni los descuentos, salvo que se ofrezcan con carácter general a todos los compradores. Las rebajas se toman en consideración si alcanzan al artículo especificado y satisfacen los requisitos de comparabilidad.

Vivienda
La información sobre los alquileres se obtiene mensualmente en edificios con viviendas de dos dormitorios.

Especificación de las variedades
Las especificaciones de los artículos cuyos precios se han de fijar establecen su marca de fábrica, unidad, calidad y tamaño.

Sustitución, cambio de calidad, etc.
Cuando un artículo dado desaparece del mercado se substituye su precio por el del más similar que pueda conseguirse.

Artículos estacionales
Los artículos alimenticios frescos de temporada no se incluyen en el índice fuera de temporada, distribuyéndose sus coeficientes de ponderación entre los demás del mismo grupo.

Cálculo
El índice se calcula conforme a la fórmula de Laspeyres como un promedio aritmético ponderado de base fija, cuyos coeficientes de ponderación corresponden al período de base.

El índice para un artículo se obtiene utilizando las relaciones de precios del período corriente y del período de base. El promedio aritmético simple de las relaciones de precios de todas las variedades de un artículo da el índice por un artículo.

Informaciones complementarias
No disponible.

Organización y publicación
State Secretariat, Economic Planning Unit, Statistics Division: "Brunei Statistical Yearbook" (Bandar Seri Begawan).

idem: "Consumer Price Index for Brunei, Base Year 1977 = 100" (Bandar Seri Begawan, enero de 1980).

BULGARIA

Denominación oficial
Indice des prix de détail d'Etat (Indice de precios al por menor del Estado).

Alcance
No disponible.

Base oficial
1960 = 100.

Fuente de la ponderación
Los coeficientes de ponderación se calculan sobre la base del valor y de la cantidad de los bienes y servicios vendidos o suministrados a la comunidad, valores que se determinan mediante informaciones obtenidas de las estadísticas del comercio al por menor y de datos relativos a los gastos de los hogares.

Ponderaciones y composición
No disponible.

Gastos de consumo de los hogares
No disponible.

Método de recolección de los datos
Los precios de la mayoría de los artículos son establecidos por las autoridades; son uniformes en todo el país, salvo algunos artículos cuyo precio se fija por región. Los precios de las frutas y las verduras frescas se recogen los días 5, 15 y 25 de cada mes en puntos de venta (comercios del Estado) distribuidos en más de 90 ciudades.

Vivienda
Los datos referentes al alquiler se refieren a las viviendas de una o más habitaciones.

Especificación de las variedades
No disponible.

Sustitución, cambio de calidad, etc.
No disponible.

Artículos estacionales
No disponible.

Cálculo
El índice es un índice-cadena que se calcula y eslabona anualmente mediante la fórmula de Paasche.

Informaciones complementarias
Actualmente se calcula una nueva serie, pero en el momento de publicar el presente volumen la OIT no disponía ni de informaciones metodológicas ni de datos sobre esta serie.

Organización y publicación
Central Statistical Office of the Council of Ministers: "Statistical Yearbook of the People's Republic of Bulgaria" (Sofia).

BURKINA FASO (OUAGADOUGOU)

Denominación oficial
Indice des prix à la consommation africaine (Indice de precios del consumo para los hogares africanos).

Alcance
El índice se calcula mensualmente, se publica trimestralmente y abarca los hogares de ingresos módicos de Ouagadougou.

Base oficial
Julio de 1981 - junio 1982 = 100.

Fuente de la ponderación
Los coeficientes de ponderación y los artículos seleccionados se basaron en los resultados de una encuesta sobre los gastos de los hogares efectuada en Ouagadougou durante los doce meses de 1980 y abarcó una muestra de 54 hogares con un ingreso mensual comprendido entre 15 000 y 20 000 francos CFA durante la encuesta y un tamaño medio de estos hogares de 4,54 miembros.

Ponderaciones y composición

Grupos principales	Número de artículos	Ponderación	Número aproximado de cotizaciones de precio
Alimentación	48	4 766	...
Vestido y calzado	8	441	...
Alquiler y costo de construcción	5	515	...
Combustible, luz y agua	5	1 368	...
Accesorios para el hogar	13	303	...
Higiene y asistencia médica	8	518	...
Transportes y comunicaciones	8	1 858	...
Educación y recreación	4	231	...
Total	99	10 000	...

Gastos de consumo de los hogares
Los gastos de consumo de los hogares comprenden todos los desembolsos efectuados por los hogares para el consumo. No se tienen en cuenta los bienes y servicios percibidos como ingresos en especie y consumidos por el hogar, las contribuciones a las cajas de pensión y a la seguridad social, y pagos de licencias.

Método de recolección de los datos
Los precios se recogen por investigadores en el mercado central, en puntos de venta al por menor y establecimientos de servicios en Ouagadougou. Los precios de los artículos alimenticios y de las bebidas se obtienen tres veces al mes (de las cuales una vez por el sistema de compra). Los artículos cuyos precios no varían con frecuencia se recogen trimestralmente.

Vivienda
Los datos referentes al alquiler se obtienen mensualmente. El costo de las viviendas ocupadas por el propietario se representa por el precio de los materiales de construcción.

Especificación de las variedades
La especificación de los artículos cuyos precios se han de registrar se dan en detalle.

Sustitución, cambio de calidad, etc.
Cuando un artículo desaparece del mercado se mantiene el último precio durante seis meses; despues se lo sustituye por uno similar.

Artículos estacionales
Se tienen en cuenta las fluctuaciones estacionales de los precios de ciertos artículos alimenticios frescos, omitiendo del cálculo del índice estos artículos cuando están fuera de temporada; los coeficientes de ponderación que les conciernen se asignan a artículos de sustitución.

Cálculo
El índice se calcula conforme a la fórmula de Laspeyres como un promedio aritmético ponderado de base fija cuyos coeficientes de ponderación corresponden a 1980.

Informaciones complementarias
No disponible.

Organización y publicación
Institut national de la statistique et de la démographie, Direction des études démographiques; Service des prix: "Indice des prix à la consommation africaine" (Ouagadougou).

idem: "Bulletin d'information statistique et économique".

BURUNDI (BUJUMBURA)

Denominación oficial
Indice des prix à la consommation des ménages de Bujumbura

(Indice de precios del consumo para los hogares de Bujumburá).

Alcance
La compilación del índice es mensual y abarca todos los hogares de Bujumburá.

Base oficial
Enero de 1980 = 100.

Fuente de la ponderación
La selección de los artículos y la determinación de los coeficientes de ponderación se basan en los resultados de una encuesta de 1978-1979 sobre los gastos de los hogares, que abarcó a una muestra de hogares de Bujumburá. Para preparar el índice se tomaron en cuenta una selección de 130 artículos con mayores coeficientes de ponderación.

Ponderaciones y composición

Grupos principales	Número de artículos	Ponderación	Número aproximado de cotizaciones de precio
Alimentación	61	55,31	...
Vestido y calzado	19	13,21	...
Vivienda y gastos del hogar	23	16,70	...
Transporte y diversiones	8	10,80	...
Asistencia médica y varios	19	3,98	...
Total	130	100,00	...

Gastos de consumo de los hogares
Los gastos de consumo considerados para la ponderación corresponden a la adquisición de toda clase de bienes y servicios que han efectuado los hogares de referencia para su propio consumo.

Los gastos de consumo excluyen los impuestos a los ingresos, las cotizaciones sociales, las inversiones y todos suerte de los seguros. También excluyen las cotizaciones a cajas o fondos de pensión, viviendas ocupadas por sus propietarios pues sólo se toman en cuenta las alquiladas, arras y entregas de bienes usados como pago parcial de otros nuevos, patentes, transferencias de fondos, donaciones y desembolsos similares, así como todos los impuestos y seguros.

Por el contrario se incluyen los ingresos en especie, las compras de artículos de ocasión, los bienes durables, la atención médica y las compras a crédito (sólo se incluye la parte amortizada correspondiente al período de la encuesta).

Método de recolección de los datos
La recopilación de precios está a cargo de investigadores que los registran en unos 34 comercios minoristas, mercados y prestatarios de servicios seleccionados. Los precios de ciertos artículos alimenticios (como los farináceos y feculentos, el pescado y las frutas y legumbres), además de ciertas prendas de vestir, se recogen cuatro veces por semana; los demás artículos, una vez por semana. Los precios de los artículos alimenticios vendidos en los mercados se obtienen pesando estos artículos.

Vivienda
Las cotizaciones de alquiler que se registran corresponden a viviendas alquiladas de dos habitaciones, con luz eléctrica y piso cimentado. De las ocupadas por sus propietarios, sólo se incluyen en el índice los gastos de su reparación y mantenimiento.

Especificación de las variedades
Se especifica en forma detallada la marca, nombre, calidad y cantidad de los artículos cuyo precio se debe registrar.

Sustitución, cambio de calidad, etc.
Cuando un determinado artículo se deja de vender, se le sustituye por otro similar.

Artículos estacionales
Esta clase de artículos, como las frutas y legumbres frescas, que no tienen mayor importancia en el índice, no son objeto de ningún ajuste.

Cálculo
El índice se calcula según la fórmula de Laspeyres, como un promedio aritmético ponderado con base fija, cuyos coeficientes de ponderación corresponden al período 1978-1979.

Para calcular los índices de los artículos se recurre a las relaciones de precios medios. El índice anual es la media de los índices de los doce meses.

Informaciones complementarias
Actualmente se está realizando en Bujumburá una encuesta para actualizar la base del índice de precios del consumo.

Organización y publicación
Institut de statistique et d'études économiques, (ISTEEBU): "Bulletin mensuel des prix" (Bujumburá).
idem: "Annuaire statistique".
idem: "Bulletin trimestriel".

CABO VERDE (PRAYA)

Denominación oficial
Indice de preços no consumidor (Indice de precios del consumo).

Alcance
El índice se calcula trimestralmente y abarca toda la población.

Base oficial
1983 = 100.

Fuente de la ponderación
La selección de los artículos y la determinación de los coeficientes de ponderación se basaron en los resultados de una encuesta sobre los gastos familiares efectuada en 1983 en Praia.

Ponderaciones y composición

Grupos principales	Número de artículos	Ponderación	Número aproximado de cotizaciones de precio
Alimentación y tabaco	83	...	...
Vestido y calzado	40	...	...
Combustible, electricidad y agua	4	...	...
Mobiliario y equipo de hogares	9	...	...
Higiene y aseo personal	5	...	...
Transportes y comunicaciones	4	...	...
Total	145	...	...

Gastos de consumo de los hogares
No disponible.

Método de recolección de los datos
Los precios se recogen en puntos de venta al por menor y establecimientos de servicios en Praia.

Vivienda
Los gastos de alquiler no se tienen en cuenta en el índice.

Especificación de las variedades
No disponible.

Sustitución, cambio de calidad, etc.
No disponible.

Artículos estacionales
No disponible.

Cálculo
El índice se calcula mediante la fórmula de Laspeyres como un promedio aritmético ponderado de base fija, cuyos coeficientes de ponderación corresponden al período de base.

Informaciones complementarias
Se calcula igualmente un índice para St. Vicente.

Organización y publicación
Direcçao-General de Estatistica: "Indices de preços no consumidor, Praia 1984-1986", Enero de 1987, Praia.

CAMERUN (YAUNDE, AFRICANOS)

Denominación oficial
Indice des prix de détail à la consommation des familles de condition moyenne - Familles originaires (Indice de precios al por menor del consumo de las familias de ingresos medios - familias camerunesas).

Alcance
El índice se calcula mensualmente y abarca todos los hogares de la clase media, con un presupuesto aproximado de 21 900 francos CFA, y de una composición media de 4,15 unidades de consumo en 1964-65.

Base oficial
1968 = 100.

Fuente de la ponderación
La selección de los artículos y la determinación de los coeficientes de ponderación se basaron en los resultados de una encuesta sobre los gastos de los hogares efectuada en Yaundé en 1964-65 y que abarcó a 764 hogares de cameruneses representativos del conjunto de consumidores urbanos.

Ponderaciones y composición

Grupos principales	Número de artículos	Ponderación	Número aproximado de cotizaciones de precio
Alimentación	50	336	...
Bebidas y tabaco	11	103	...
Alquiler, combustible, luz, agua y servicios domésticos	7	75	...
Moblaje y accesorios para el hogar	16	71	...
Vestido y calzado	13	163	...
Transportes	8	105	...
Aseo personal y asistencia médica	13	50	...
Distracciones	4	51	...
Servicios y varios	10	46	...
Total	132	1 000	...

Gastos de consumo de los hogares
No disponible.

Método de recolección de los datos
Los precios de la mayoría de los artículos se recogen una vez por mes por investigadores o mediante encuestas por correspondencia en aproximadamente 60 puntos de venta al por menor y establecimientos de servicios o a partir de la documentación oficial para los precios fijados por el Gobierno. Ciertos artículos alimenticios son, además, objeto de compra por parte de los investigadores el 5, 15 y 25 de cada mes en tres mercados públicos.

Vivienda
Los datos referentes al alquiler provienen de los resultados de una encuesta efectuada en una importante sociedad inmobiliaria.

Especificación de las variedades
No disponible.

Sustitución, cambio de calidad, etc.
No disponible.

Artículos estacionales
Se tienen en cuenta las fluctuaciones estacionales de los precios de ciertas frutas omitiendo del cálculo del índice estos artículos cuando están fuera de temporada; los diferentes coeficientes de ponderación que les conciernen se asignan a artículos de substitución.

Cálculo
El índice se calcula conforme a la fórmula de Laspeyres como un promedio aritmético ponderado de base fija, cuyos coeficientes de ponderación corresponden al período 1964-65.

Organización y publicación
Direction de la statistique et de la comptabilité nationale: "Bulletin mensuel de statistique" (Yaoundé).

CAMERUN (YAUNDE, EUROPEOS)

Denominación oficial
Indice des prix de détail à la consommation familiale - Familles "non-originaires" (Indice de precios al por menor del consumo de las familias "no originarias").

Alcance
El índice se calcula mensualmente y abarca todos los hogares europeos de más de una persona en Yaundé.

Base oficial
Mayo de 1966 = 100.

Fuente de la ponderación
La selección de los artículos y la determinación de los coeficientes de ponderación se basaron en los resultados de una encuesta sobre los gastos de los hogares efectuada en Yaundé de marzo a julio de 1965 entre 91 hogares europeos de más de una persona.

Ponderaciones y composición

Grupos principales	Número de artículos	Ponderación	Número aproximado de cotizaciones de precio
Alimentación	50	373	...
Bebidas y tabaco	13	133	...
Gastos del hogar (servicio doméstico, agua, gas, electricidad y accesorios para el hogar)	13	193	...
Vestido y calzado	6	36	...
Transportes	7	65	...
Distracciones	5	59	...
Aseo personal y asistencia médica	9	35	...
Servicios y varios	10	106	...
Total	113	1 000	...

Gastos de consumo de los hogares
No disponible.

Método de recolección de los datos
Los precios de los artículos alimenticios se recogen dos o tres veces al mes por investigadores en los comercios al por menor; por lo que se refiere a los demás artículos, los precios se recogen mediante cuestionarios que se envían mensualmente a diferentes puntos de venta al por menor y establecimientos de servicios. El importe de los salarios del personal del servicio doméstico se basa en los salarios mínimos fijados por las autoridades gubernamentales.

Vivienda
Los gastos de alquiler no se tienen en cuenta ni en el cálculo del índice ni en la determinación de los coeficientes de ponderación.

Especificación de las variedades
No disponible.

Sustitución, cambio de calidad, etc.
No disponible.

Artículos estacionales
No disponible.

Cálculo
El índice se calcula conforme a la fórmula de Laspeyres como un promedio aritmético ponderado de base fija, cuyos coeficientes de ponderación corresponden al período marzo - julio de 1965.

Organización y publicación
Direction de la statistique et de la comptabilité nationale: "Bulletin mensuel de statistique" (Yaoundé).

CANADA

Denominación oficial
Consumer Price Index (Indice de Precios del Consumo).

Alcance
El índice se compila mensualmente y abarca todos los hogares privados, de familias o individuos, que viven en centros urbanos de 30 000 habitantes o más.

Base oficial
1986 = 100.

Fuente de la ponderación
La determinación de los coeficientes de ponderación y la selección de los artículos se basaron en las encuestas sobre los gastos de los hogares y sobre los gastos de alimentos de los hogares, ambas de 1986. Estos datos corresponden al costo de la canasta según los precios de 1986.

Gastos de consumo de los hogares
A los efectos del índice, sólo se toman en cuenta los bienes y servicios cuyos precios pueden relacionarse con cantidades o calidades específicas. En consecuencia no se incluyen los bienes y servicios que el Estado proporciona a la población, pues el monto individual de los impuestos que los sufragan no se relaciona con la cantidad o calidad concreta de los bienes y servicios públicos recibidos.

Es necesario distinguir entre los seguros para sólo incluir en el índice aquéllos que se pueden relacionar con bienes o servicios determinados, como es el caso de los seguros de casas y automóviles, cuyos contratos garantizan la sustitución o restau-

Ponderaciones y composición

Grupos principales	Número de artículos	Ponderación	Número aproximado de cotizaciones de precio
Alimentación	213	18,05	550 000
Vivienda:			
Alojamientos alquilados	3	7,75	170 000
Casa propia (incl. reparación y mantenimiento)	10	12,72	5 000
Otros alojamientos	5	1,38	1 000
Agua, combustible y electricidad	5	3,82	1 400
Otros gastos del hogar	44	5,77	23 000
Moblaje y equipo del hogar	67	4,88	15 000
Vestido y calzado	91	8,69	50 000
Transporte	30	18,29	33 000
Asistencia médica y aseo personal	35	4,20	62 000
Recreación, lectura y educación	95	8,84	35 000
Tabaco y bebidas alcohólicas	10	5,60	21 000
Total	608	100,00	(a) 966 400

Nota: (a) Número anual de cotizaciones.

ración de bienes concretos. Lo contrario sucede con los seguros de vida o incapacidad física pues los pagos estipulados en sus contratos representan un poder adquisitivo futuro que no se puede relacionar con ninguna cantidad o conjunto concreto de bienes o servicios. Los servicios prestados a la población por el sistema de seguro de salud tampoco se incluyen pues sus primas no reflejan el valor real de los servicios prestados ni una proporción constante de este valor. También se excluyen los servicios de salud pagados directamente al médico o al hospital pues su monto depende, en diverso grado, de las subvenciones que el Estado acuerde a la asistencia médica. Por el contrario se suelen incluir en el índice actual los gastos en prótesis, medicamentos y asistencia odontológica pues se pueden relacionar con frecuencia a cantidades o calidades determinadas de bienes o servicios.

Los impuestos a la propiedad inmobiliaria constituyen una excepción. En efecto, aun cuando los propietarios no obtengan una contrapartida directa de bienes o servicios de estos impuestos, se les incluye en el índice por considerarlos parte integrante de los gastos de la vivienda propia.

Método de recolección de los datos

La selección de ciudades y puntos de venta para el registro de precios se basa en la apreciación de datos de diversas fuentes, comprendidos los que proporcionan las Oficinas Regionales de Estadísticas del Canadá sobre la situación del mercado. Para la alimentación se registran tanto los precios de las cadenas comerciales como de las tiendas independientes; los precios de las prendas de vestir y del ajuar doméstico se registran en tiendas de ramos generales o en comercios especializados y los de automóviles y sus repuestos en garages y comercios del ramo. El diseño de muestreo permite abarcar principalmente los negocios minoristas con un importante volumen de ventas. Los precios de ciertos artículos, tales como las tarifas de autobuses, ferrocarriles y aviones, servicios de agua, gas y teléfonos, así como las cargas impositivas que gravan la propiedad, se obtienen de las autoridades provinciales, regionales o locales pertinentes.

La frecuencia de la recolección de los precios depende de la naturaleza de la mercancía. Los bienes y servicios cuyos precios se modifican con menos frecuencia exigen una recolección también menos frecuente. Los precios de los artículos alimenticios y de la gasolina, por ejemplo, se registran dos veces por mes, mientras que para la mayoría de los demás artículos la recolección de precios se hace una sola vez al mes. Tal es el caso de los electrodomésticos, vestidos, productos farmacéuticos, artículos de aseo personal y tabaco, bebidas alcohólicas, alquileres, intereses hipotecarios y casas nuevas. Las demás mercancías se caracterizan por una modificación menos frecuente de sus precios que, en consecuencia, se registran a intervalos de más de un mes. Los precios de muebles y electrodomésticos se registran seis veces por año, los de automóviles, aseo personal, vestidos y periódicos cada tres meses y las tasas del registro de automóviles y de los impuestos a la propiedad una vez al año.

No obstante, se realizan registros adicionales de los precios de las mercancías que hayan tenido variaciones ostensibles en el correr de su plazo normal de registro y cuando es necesario se modifica el calendario originalmente previsto para la recolección.

Para cada mes del índice el registro de los precios de la mayor parte de las mercancías se cumple en un plazo de cuatro semanas, a partir del día 20 del mes anterior y hasta mediados del mes en cuestión, aproximadamente.

Vivienda

El registro de las cotizaciones del alquiler se basa en la encuesta sobre la fuerza de trabajo del Canadá, cuya muestra comprende unos 54 000 viviendas, propias y alquiladas, de todo el país. Como término medio 14 000 de ellas son viviendas alquiladas de los centros urbanos abarcados por el índice. Cuando la vivienda de una determinada localidad ingresa en la muestra, los datos se recopilan por un período de seis meses consecutivos, pues el diseño de muestreo determina la rotación de un sexto de la muestra cada seis meses. Los datos sobre las cotizaciones del alquiler se refieren a viviendas alquiladas y son sus arrendatarios quienes las comunican. El tratamiento de los datos sobre la vivienda propia permite apreciar las repercusiones que tienen las modificaciones de los precios en una selección de gastos específicos de los propietarios.

Entre estos gastos se incluyen: reparaciones, impuestos a la propiedad, amortización de las partes de la vivienda ocupada por sus propietarios que se supone necesario renovar, pagos de seguros e intereses hipotecarios de la casa propia.

Especificación de las variedades

La especificación de una mercancía da sus características detalladas e informaciones tales como cantidad estándar, unidad de medida, frecuencia del registro de precios y otras instrucciones para los investigadores. Con frecuencia una misma descripción detallada sirve para todos los puntos de venta de registro de precios, pero en otros casos lo dicho no es posible y corresponde a los investigadores decidir, siguiendo ciertas directrices, las mercancías particulares cuyos precios se han de registrar en puntos de venta específicos. La selección puede variar según los puntos de venta pero debe permanecer inalterada con respecto a un punto de venta determinado mientras se mantengan, los fundamentos previstos de representatividad y oferta continua de las mercancías elegidas.

Sustitución, cambio de calidad, etc.

Cuando ciertos puntos de venta no poseen en sus existencias determinadas mercancías se toman medidas especiales: si los precios de mercancías, semejantes se registran en otros puntos de venta del mismo estrato de centro urbano, se imputa a la mercancía que falta un precio derivado de la observación de los precios registrados en esos otros puntos de venta o bien se mantiene el último precio registrado en el punto de venta en cuestión (salvo que sea un precio rebajado de liquidación, en cuyo caso el precio que se mantiene es el último normal registrado). Sin embargo si un artículo no estacional no figura en las existencias de un determinado punto de venta por más de dos períodos consecutivos, su precio no se utiliza para el cómputo del índice y esa mercancía se sustituye por otra similar existente en el mismo punto de venta o, de ser necesario, por la misma mercancía (o similar) de otro punto de venta.

Con frecuencia es posible registrar en el mismo momento tanto los precios de la variedad inicial como los de la sustitutiva. En tales casos la razón entre ambos precios puede utilizarse como factor de ajuste de precio por cambio de calidad. La misma técnica también se utiliza cuando en la muestra se sustituye un determinado punto de venta por otro. Esta técnica, alguna veces calificada como de empalme, se funda implícitamente en el supuesto de que la diferencia entre los precios de mercado de dos mercancías o de dos puntos de venta en un mismo momento se debe exclusivamente a diferencias cualitativas entre esas dos mercancías o entre los servicios prestados por dos puntos de venta.

Algunas veces es posible efectuar ajustes de calidad de los precios registrados en forma explícita, es decir apreciar la diferencia de valor entre la variedades (nueva y sustituida) debida a una diferencia de calidad entre ambas. Cuando los cambios son relativamente menores, la apreciación puede basarse sea en un análisis de costos, sea en la comparación de los respectivos precios de mercado al por menor de los equipos o servicios añadidos o suprimidos.

Artículos estacionales

La oferta de algunas mercancías está sujeta a variaciones estacionales. Tal es el caso de varias frutas y legumbres frescas (como las fresas y el maíz) de las que sólo se dispone en abundancia durante unos pocos días o semanas al año. La demanda de otras mercancías varía según la estación, como la de muchas prendas de vestir (por ej. bañadores y abrigos de invierno) y la mayor parte de los artículos deportivos y equipos de recreo (por ej. bicicletas o equipos de esquí nórdico).

Para los artículos estacionales la nueva práctica utilizada consiste en extrapolar los precios de los bienes de temporada del índice según el movimiento de los precios registrados sin solución de continuidad para otras mercancías del mismo grupo. Por ejemplo, el índice de precios de abrigos femeninos de invierno correspondiente a febrero resultará de la multiplicación del índice de enero por la razón entre los índices de febrero y de enero para el grupo prendas de vestir femeninas. Este grupo, así como los demás que se utilizan para imputar precios a los artículos estacionales, excluye todo agrupamiento básico de artículos con precios estacionales registrados. A nivel de punto de venta los precios se imputan por relación, mientras que se hacen imputaciones de grupo para los índices de precio a nivel de grupo de base. Siempre que sea posible el grupo que sirve de base para la imputación es el inmediatamente superior al del producto en cuestión en la clasificación primaria. Si en el grupo superior de dicha clasificación no existen bienes con precios registrados en forma continua, se recurre a su vez al de nivel contiguo más alto.

Cálculo
El índice se calcula según la fórmula de Laspeyres como un promedio aritmético ponderado de base fija, cuyos coeficientes de ponderación corresponden al período de base.

En primer lugar se obtiene el promedio mensual de los precios de cada mercancía en cada estrato de centro urbano. Los índices de precio de un mes a otro se calculan luego como razones entre los correspondientes promedios de precio de un mes y del anterior. Los índices de precios con otra base que el mes anterior no se calculan directamente por comparación de los promedios de precio mas por multiplicación de los índices de todos los meses siguientes al de base hasta el mes dado. Si un grupo de base está representado por más de un artículo cuyo precio se registra, se calculan en primer lugar los índices de precio de cada uno de esos artículos y su promedio ponderado constituye la estimación del movimiento de los precios de ese grupo de base.

El índice nacional del Canadá puede calcularse como índice de precios de las mercaderías de una canasta fija relacionada con la estructura nacional de la canasta de 1986 o como promedio aritmético ponderado de la totalidad de los índices de precio de los 82 centros urbanos.

Informaciones complementarias
Con la introducción de la canasta de 1986, el Indice de Precios del Consumo comprende 82 centros urbanos agrupados en 34 estratos de centro urbano y 10 provincias. Sin embargo sólo se publican índices de los precios del consumo para los 18 centros urbanos siguientes: St. John's, Charlottetown-Summerside, Halifax, Saint John, Québec, Montréal, Ottawa, Toronto, Thunder Bay, Winnipeg, Regina, Saskatoon, Edmonton, Calgary, Vancouver, Victoria, Whitehorse et Yellowknife.

Organización y publicación
Statistics Canada, Prices Division: "The Consumer Price Index" (Ottawa), Monthly Catalogue No. 62-001, mensual, bilingüe (inglés y francés).

idem: "The Consumer Price Index reference paper: Updating based on 1986 expenditures", Catalogue No. 62-553, bilingüe (inglés y francés).

REP. CENTROAFRICANA (BANGUI)

Denominación oficial
Indice des prix à la consommation (Indice de Precios del Consumo).

Alcance
El índice se compila mensualmente y abarca hogares urbanos cuyo jefe es obrero o empleado residente en Bangui.

Base oficial
1981 = 100.

Fuente de la ponderación
La determinación de los coeficientes de ponderación y la selección de los artículos se basaron en los resultados de una encuesta realizada en 1975-76. La encuesta abarcó a todo el país y las áreas son repartidos según seis sectores geográficos importantes del país. La muestra comprendió 1 530 unidades presupuestarais. El índice, por su parte, se refiere a los hogares de residentes en Bangui. No se ajustaron los coeficientes de ponderación para tomar en cuenta las modificaciones de precio ocurridas entre el período de la encuesta y 1981.

Ponderaciones y composición

Grupos principales	Número de artículos	Ponderación	Número aproximado de cotizaciones de precio
Alimentación	76	705	585
Vestido y calzado	14	85	30
Productos manufacturados	43	76	61
Combustible y luz	7	73	43
Servicios	20	61	33
Total	160	1 000	752

Gastos de consumo de los hogares
A los efectos del cálculo del índice comprenden todos los bienes y servicios consumidos por los hogares de referencia. Se excluyen el impuesto a los ingresos, las contribuciones a la seguridad social, los intereses pagados por deudas, las primas de seguros, la adquisición o construcción de inmuebles, las compras de mobiliario, los gastos importantes para el mantenimiento de inmuebles y los bienes producidos por los hogares para su propio consumo.

Método de recolección de los datos
La recolección de precios está a cargo de encuestadores especializados que los registran en una muestra representativa de 37 puntos de venta al por menor (grandes tiendas y pequeños comercios) para los productos manufacturados y en cuatro mercados para los géneros alimenticios. La recolección de precios de los productos manufacturados tiene lugar durante la segunda semana de cada mes y la de productos alimenticios durante la primera y la segunda. Si en el mercado no se exhiben los precios de venta, éstos se obtienen consultando al vendedor y pesando los artículos en cuestión. Las tarifas de la electricidad, la gasolina y el gas, que son oficiales, se solicitan a las autoridades pertinentes.

Vivienda
Los datos sobre alquileres se obtienen una vez por mes, para viviendas de tres habitaciones.

Especificación de las variedades
Existen especificaciones detalladas para cada artículo. Los productos se venden por unidades tales como montones o puñados, cubos, manojos o gavillas, saquillos o paquetes, unidades o piezas, litros, kilogramos, etc.

Sustitución, cambio de calidad, etc.
Si en el período en curso un investigador no encuentra un artículo que había sido seleccionado en el período de base, se le recomienda que, para mantener la representatividad del muestreo, elija otro similar o parecido y vuelva a calcular un precio de base ficticio.

Artículos estacionales
No son objeto de ningún ajuste.

Cálculo
El índice se calcula según la fórmula de Laspeyres como un promedio aritmético ponderado de base fija, cuyos coeficientes de ponderación corresponden al período 1975-76.

El precio promedio es igual a la media aritmética simple de los precios registrados en los distintos puntos de venta.

Informaciones complementarias
La División de Estadística calcula igualmente un índice de los precios del consumo para las familias con asistencia técnica.

Organización y publicación
Direction de la statistique et des études économiques: "Lettres mensuelles de la statistique" (Bangui).

idem: "Bulletin trimestriel".

idem: "Annuaire statistique".

COLOMBIA

Denominación oficial
Indice de Precios al Consumidor - familias de ingresos bajos.

Alcance
El índice se calcula mensualmente y abarca las familias urbanas de ingresos bajos.

Base oficial
Diciembre de 1988 = 100.

Fuente de la ponderación
La selección de los artículos y la determinación de los coeficientes de ponderación se basaron en los resultados de la encuesta sobre los gastos de los hogares efectuada entre marzo 1984 y febrero 1985, y referida a los hogares particulares, que sirvió de base en la delimitación del estrato de referencia del índice. Por ello, el índice de precios debe definir un grupo social lo más amplio posible y suficientemente homogéneo en sus hábitos de consumo, a partir del cual se pueda establecer el estrato de referencia del IPC.

Como resultado de este estudio, la población de referencia quedó definida por el conjunto de hogares particulares ubicados en el área urbana de 13 ciudades; se excluyeron los hogares unipersonales y los hogares colectivos, por tener estructuras de consumo muy particulares. También se excluyeron los hogares con ingresos muy altos por la gran dispersión que presentan en sus hábitos de consumo. Estos representan el 5 por ciento del total de hogares encuestados en cada ciudad.

Para la selección de los artículos, se tuvieron en cuenta los siguientes criterios: Primero, el peso relativo del gasto en el artículo: 5 por ciento o más dentro del grupo. Segundo, la frecuencia observada de adquisición: que fuera adquirido por más del 30 por ciento de los hogares. Tercero, la factibilidad de identificación o sea la posibilidad práctica de realizar la observación de precios-cantidad.

No se efectuaron reajustes de los coeficientes de ponderación para tener en cuenta las variaciones de precios entre 1984-85 y 1988.

Ponderaciones y composición

Grupos principales	Número de artículos	Ponderación	Número aproximado de cotizaciones de precio
Alimentación	77	42,58	2 540
Vivienda:			7 341
Alquiler	1	19,35	...
Combustible, luz y agua	5	4,82	...
Moblaje, productos de limpieza, ropa blanca	28	7,14	...
Vestido	24	8,16	1 715
Asistencia médica	13	3,30	1 037
Educación y recreación	18	4,79	990
Transportes y comunicaciones	12	4,03	420
Otros	16	5,84	1 039
Total	194	100,00	15 082

Gastos de consumo de los hogares
Sólo se incluye dentro del gasto lo que corresponde a la adquisición de bienes y servicios de consumo final. Por lo tanto, se excluyen del índice los gastos correspondientes a operaciones financieras, pagos de deudas, intereses de tarjetas de crédito, pago de impuestos, multas, etc.

Una vez excluídos estos gastos - investigados por la Encuesta de Ingresos y Gastos - que no correspondían al concepto de gastos de consumo, se procedió a reagrupar los gastos restantes en categorías más significativas para la estructura del índice de precios. La reagrupación se hizo de acuerdo con su función de producción.

El ingreso en especie se imputa como gasto del respectivo bien y/o servicio, la vivienda propia se imputa a la ponderación de arrendamientos, pero sólo se le hace seguimiento de precios a los arriendos. Los bienes usados se registran como cualquier otra adquisición; la encuesta investigó la cuota a la seguridad social como una deducción al ingreso.

Método de recolección de los datos
Los precios son recogidos por investigadores en puntos de venta al por menor y establecimientos de servicios.

Además de los establecimientos especializados en la venta al por menor de bienes y servicios, hay otro tipo de fuentes para el Indice de Precios al Consumidor, como las viviendas que conforman la muestra para el subgrupo de arrendamientos. En ellas se pregunta directamente al inquilino el valor que paga por concepto del arrendamiento de la casa de habitación.

Otras fuentes de información son las empresas públicas municipales, en las cuales se obtienen las tarifas a aplicar en el cálculo de los índices de los servicios residenciales de acueducto, alcantarillado, energía eléctrica y teléfono. También lo son las alcaldías, que suministran los decretos mediante los cuales se establecen las tarifas del transporte urbano de pasajeros.

Los precios de los alimentos se investigan con una periodicidad inferior a la mensual. El mes, se divide entre períodos iguales, visitando en cada período un tercio de las fuentes de información. Aunque las fuentes se visitan mensualmente, los precios se obtienen en tres períodos a lo largo del mes.

Se recogen mensualmente artículos como los servicios públicos (acueducto y alcantarillado, energía eléctrica y teléfono) y pasajes en avión, dado que presentan mensualmente variación en sus tarifas y precios.

En relación con la visita a los establecimientos que suministran la información, y no obstante que se recojan precios en todos los meses del año, existen las siguientes periodicidades supramensuales:

- Bimestral, para artículos de limpieza del hogar, medicamentos, artículos para el aseo personal.

- Trimestral, para vestuario, muebles, aparatos domésticos, útiles escolares.

- Anual, para matrículas, pensiones y textos escolares.

Estas periodicidades fueron establecidas así en atención a la relativa variabilidad de los precios de los bienes y servicios, a través del tiempo.

Para algunos artículos de la canasta, se recogen los precios en el período en que ocurre la variación. Ellos son: gas, gas de cocina, gasolina para automotor, loterías y cine, entre otros.

Los precios observados o recogidos son los que paga el consumidor por un bien o servicio que se encuentra para la venta al por menor y de contado, en el momento en que el recolector de datos realiza la visita al establecimiento fuente.

Vivienda
Los datos referentes al alquiler son recogidos cada cuatro meses, pero se reporta mensualmente en el índice las variaciones de precios de 1/4 de la muestra y el resto se incluye sin variación.

Como alquiler de la vivienda sólo se incluye el valor del vivienda privada. La recolección se hace por entrevista directa y cada mes se investiga 1/4 de la muestra, su periodicidad es cuatrimestral.

La vivienda propia no se investiga.

Especificación de las variedades
Seleccionados los artículos, se procedió a definir sus calidades, como variedades que se deben cotizar periódicamente para cada uno de los artículos. Para lograr este objetivo, se desarrolló un estudio en las 13 ciudades consideradas para el índice en enero de 1987; se investigaron, las especificaciones detalladas de los artículos definidos. Se estableció como condición indispensable que los artículos escogidos a nivel de cada uno de los subgrupos, cumplieran con los siguientes criterios adicionales de selección:

- Cada artículo debe tener una evolución de precios similar a la de los demás artículos del subgrupo,

- Deben ser consumidos habitualmente por los hogares del estrato socioeconómico respectivo,

- Deben garantías razonables de permanencia en el mercado,

- Deben ser fácilmente observables.

Sustitución, cambio de calidad, etc.
Cuando no es posible continuar registrando el precio de la especificación que se venía tomando, o cuando es necesario reemplazar el establecimiento fuente, se recurre al procedimiento "cambio de referencia": este es un recurso que invalida las variaciones de precios que resultan de cambiar la especificación del artículo o la fuente de información. Sin embargo, para los subgrupos de vestuario, en los que ocurren numerosas movilidades en las referencias y en general, en las especificaciones, cada novedad que se presenta en la recolección, es objeto de análisis con el fin de tomar una decisión respecto a la validez de la variación de precios registrada.

Artículos estacionales
No se le da ningún tratamiento especial a los bienes estacionales.

Cálculo
El índice por cada ciudad se calcula mediante la fórmula de

Laspeyres como un promedio aritmético ponderado de base fija, cuyos coeficientes de ponderación corresponden a marzo de 1984 - febrero de 1985.
El índice de un agregado (subgrupo, grupos, ciudad, nacional) es una media ponderada de los índices elementales: las ponderaciones usadas en el cálculo del índice corresponden a las estructuras derivadas de los gastos de los hogares e ingresos bajos en los distintos conjuntos espaciales (13 ciudades).

Informaciones complementarias
Otros índices son calculados por familias urbanas de ingresos medios (empleados) y total nacional (ingresos bajos y medios) así como por 13 ciudades separadas (total, ingresos bajos, ingresos medios).
Se publican subgrupos detallados.

Organización y publicación
Departamento Administrativo Nacional de Estadística: "Boletín Mensual de Estadística" (Bogotá).
idem: "Boletín Mensual de Estadística" (Bogotá) núm. 433, abril de 1989 (para más amplios detalles metodológicos).

COMUNIDAD DE ESTADOS INDEPENDIENTES

Denominación oficial
General Consumer Price Index (Indice general de precios del consumo).

Alcance
El índice se compila trimestralmente y abarca todas las familias rurales y urbanas de todos los Estados miembros de la Comunidad de Estados Independientes (CEI).

Base oficial
En las publicaciones nacionales el período de base que se utiliza por lo general es un año = 100.

Fuente de la ponderación
La determinación de los coeficientes de ponderación se basó en los resultados de una encuesta sobre los gastos familiares, realizada durante todo el año 1989. La muestra comprendió unas 90 000 familias de los Estados miembros de la CEI que vivían en regiones rurales o en zonas urbanas. No se ajustaron los coeficientes de ponderación para tomar en cuenta las diferencias de precio entre el momento de la encuesta y el período de base.

Ponderaciones y composición

Grupos principales	Número de artículos	Ponderación	Número aproximado de cotizaciones de precio
Alimentación	58	35,168	...
Bebidas alcohólicas	4	9,620	...
Vestido y calzado	27	22,616	...
Muebles, moblaje y equipos domésticos	11	11,805	...
Productos de limpieza y aseo personal, asistencia médica, tabaco, combustible, etc.	9	7,070	...
Servicios:			
Reparación, mantenimiento, recreación	11	6,462	...
Transportes y comunicaciones	2	3,346	...
Alquiler y tasas	1	3,418	...
Otros servicios	1	0,496	...
Total	124	100,000	...

Gastos de consumo de los hogares
Se incluyen todos los gastos destinados al consumo, comprendidos los regalos. Se excluyen toda clase de impuestos y contribuciones, primas de seguros, ingresos en especie y valor locativo de las viviendas ocupadas por sus propietarios.

Método de recolección de los datos
Investigadores estadísticos registran los precios en aproximadamente 100 000 puntos de venta al por menor y establecimientos de servicios ubicados en todos los Estados miembros de la Comunidad de Estados Independientes (CEI). La selección de las localidades y los puntos de venta se basó en datos sobre el volumen y estructura del giro comercial. El registro de los precios tiene lugar los 7 o 10 últimos días de cada mes. Los datos sobre tarifas de la asistencia médica, servicios comunales y transportes y comunicaciones se obtienen un día determinado del mes. Se tienen en cuenta las transacciones y precios especulativos del mercado negro registrándolos a fines de cada trimestre. No obstante, no se toman totalmente en consideración la interferencia en los promedios de precio que deriva de la escasez de artículos vendidos a precios más accesibles y más bajos fijados por los puntos de venta de los Estados.

Vivienda
No disponible.

Especificación de las variedades
Se dan especificaciones detalladas de cada artículo, describiéndo las materias primas, calidad y características fundamentales del producto.

Sustitución, cambio de calidad, etc.
Los cambios de calidad se estiman durante la recolección de precios en los puntos de venta. Los precios de las calidades nuevas se ajustan recurriendo a un factor de enlace.

Artículos estacionales
No se ajustan las fluctuaciones estacionales de los precios.

Cálculo
El índice se calcula según la fórmula de Laspeyres como un promedio aritmético ponderado de base fija, cuyos coeficientes de ponderación corresponden a 1989.
El Indice General de la Comunidad de Estados Independientes es un agregado de los índices locales de los Estados miembros de la CEI y las ponderaciones corresponden a la estructura del empleo, los niveles de ingreso y el volumen general de las ventas de mercancías.

Informaciones complementarias
En varios Estados miembros se calcula además un IPC para hogares con presupuestos que alcanzan el nivel de subsistencia mínimo y que comprenden un conjunto estándar de bienes y servicios.
En el momento de publicar el presente volumen, las cifras de la serie de los índices de los precios del consumo descrita más arriba no estaban aun disponibles en la OIT.

Organización y publicación
Comité de Estadísticas: "Narodnoe Khozyaistvo" (Economía Nacional).
idem: "Sotsialnoe Razvitie" (Desarrollo Social).
idem: "Boletín Estadístico" (Números especiales).

CONGO (BRAZZAVILLE, AFRICANOS)

Denominación oficial
Indice des prix à la consommation familiale africaine (Indice de Precios del Consumo Familiar Africano).

Alcance
El índice se compila mensualmente y abarca hogares africanos de Brazzaville.

Base oficial
Diciembre de 1977 = 100.

Fuente de la ponderación
La determinación de los coeficientes de ponderación y la selección de los artículos se basaron en los resultados de una encuesta sobre los gastos de hogares africanos de Brazzaville, realizada entre julio de 1976 y julio de 1977, que abarcó 100 hogares, de todas las categorías sociales.

Ponderaciones y composición

Grupos principales	Número de artículos	Ponderación	Número aproximado de cotizaciones de precio
Alimentación	70	58.6	1 035
Bebidas y tabaco	10	3,4	59
Vestido, calzado y ropa de casa	12	6,9	11
Vivienda, construcción	17	10,1	17
Combustible, luz y agua	8	5,7	16
Higiene y asistencia médica	15	3,8	47
Transportes y recreación	12	8,6	14
Varios	13	2,9	23
Total	157	100,0	1 222

Gastos de consumo de los hogares
Comprenden los pagos en especie y el consumo de la propia producción. Se excluye el impuesto a los ingresos.
Método de recolección de los datos
Los investigadores registran los precios de la mayoría de los artículos una vez por mes en distintos negocios minoristas y de servicio de los mercados. Los precios de los alimentos frescos se obtienen en los mercados 18 veces por mes. Los datos relativos a la electricidad, el agua, los transportes, la asistencia médica y las diversiones se registran cada tres meses. No se consideran las rebajas ni los precios de liquidación.
Vivienda
Los datos sobre las cotizaciones de alquiler se obtienen en forma trimestral de una muestra de 14 viviendas de cuatro habitaciones, con luz eléctrica y un grifo de agua corriente en la parcela, ubicadas en barrios centrales. No se toman en consideración las viviendas propias.
Especificación de las variedades
Son muy detalladas.
Sustitución, cambio de calidad, etc.
Cuando desaparece un artículo del mercado, se registra el último precio durante tres meses como máximo y luego se consigna el precio de un artículo similar, aplicándose un factor de corrección a los efectos del cálculo.
Artículos estacionales
Cuando la desaparición de un artículo del mercado es temporal, se repite el último precio registrado o se le sustituye por el de otro artículo similar.
Cálculo
El índice se calcula según la fórmula de Laspeyres como un promedio aritmético ponderado de base fija, cuyos coeficientes de ponderación corresponden al período entre julio de 1976 y julio de 1977.
El índice de cada artículo se obtiene recurriendo a las relaciones proporcionales entre los precios del período en curso y los del período de base. Los promedios de precios son las medias aritméticas simples de todos los precios registrados.
Organización y publicación
Centre National de la statistique et des études économiques: "Bulletin mensuel des statistiques" (Brazzaville).
idem: "Annuaire statistique du Congo".

CONGO (BRAZZAVILLE, EUROPEOS)

Denominación oficial
Indice des prix à la consommation familiale européenne (Indice de Precios del Consumo Familiar Europeo).
Alcance
El índice se compila mensualmente y abarca hogares europeos de Brazzaville.
Base oficial
Enero de 1964 = 100.
Fuente de la ponderación
La determinación de los coeficientes de ponderación y la selección de los artículos se basaron en los resultados de una encuesta sobre los gastos de los hogares efectuada de febrero a marzo de 1963 mediante cuestionarios enviados a un cierto número de hogares de europeos de Brazzaville.
Ponderaciones y composición

Grupos principales	Número de artículos	Ponderación	Número aproximado de cotizaciones de precio
Alimentación	71	51,6	112
Artículos y gastos del hogar	18	6,9	24
Asistencia médica	5	3,1	10
Vestido, calzado y ropa de casa	13	7,7	15
Combustible, luz y agua	3	5,4	4
Servicios domésticos	5	6,7	5
Varios	20	18,6	21
Total	135	100,0	191

Gastos de consumo de los hogares
Comprenden los pagos en especie y el consumo de la propia producción. Se excluye el impuesto a los ingresos.
Método de recolección de los datos
Los investigadores registran los precios de la mayoría de los artículos una vez por mes en distintos puntos de venta al por menor y establecimientos de servicio. Los precios de los alimentos frescos se obtienen en los mercados dos veces por mes. Los datos relativos a la electricidad, el agua, los transportes, la asistencia médica y las diversiones se registran cada tres meses. No se consideran las rebajas ni los precios de liquidación.
Vivienda
No se consideran los gastos de vivienda ni en la compilación del índice ni en la determinación de los coeficientes de ponderación.
Especificación de las variedades
Son muy detalladas.
Sustitución, cambio de calidad, etc.
Cuando desaparece un artículo del mercado, se registra el último precio durante tres meses como máximo y luego se consigna el precio de un artículo similar, aplicándose un factor de corrección a los efectos del cálculo.
Artículos estacionales
Cuando la desaparición de un artículo del mercado es temporal, se repite el último precio registrado o se le sustituye por el de otro artículo similar.
Cálculo
El índice se calcula según la fórmula de Laspeyres como un promedio aritmético ponderado de base fija, cuyos coeficientes de ponderación corresponden al período de febrero a marzo de 1963.
El índice de cada artículo se obtiene recurriendo a las relaciones proporcionales entre los precios del período en curso y los del período de base. Los promedios de precios son las medias aritméticas simples de todos los precios registrados.
Organización y publicación
Centre National de la statistique et des études économiques: "Bulletin mensuel des statistiques" (Brazzaville).
idem: "Annuaire statistique du Congo".

REPUBLICA DE COREA

Denominación oficial
All cities Consumer Price Index (Indice de Precios del Consumo - todas las ciudades).
Alcance
El índice se compila mensualmente y abarca hogares urbanos de obreros y empleados.
Base oficial
1985 = 100.
Fuente de la ponderación
La determinación de los coeficientes de ponderación y la selección de los artículos se basaron en los resultados de una encuesta sobre los gastos de los hogares realizada durante el año 1985 en 50 ciudades y que abarcó unos 3 700 hogares privados, excluidos los de una persona, de extranjeros, de pescadores o rurales, pues sus ingresos y gastos son de difícil determinación. El índice se refiere tan sólo a los hogares de obreros y empleados. Se seleccionaron los artículos que representaban más de 1/10 000 del total de los gastos de los hogares, formaban parte de géneros homogéneos de mercancías y se ofrecían en forma permanente. Sin embargo, aun cuando representen menos de 1/10 000 del total de los gastos, también se seleccionan los artículos importantes con consumo en aumento. Las ponderaciones de los artículos sin un precio registrado se esparcen entre otros similares o se distribuyen en forma proporcional dentro de grupos similares.
Gastos de consumo de los hogares
Comprenden regalos y desembolsos similares, compras a crédito de bienes durables, compras y trueques de bienes de segunda mano y su entrega como pago parcial de otros nuevos, seguros asociados con bienes de consumo específicos y tasas de permisos o concesiones.

Ponderaciones y composición

Grupos principales	Número de artículos	Ponderación	Número aproximado de cotizaciones de precio
Alimentación	380,2	153	...
Vivienda	129,8	17	...
Combustible, luz y agua	76,1	9	...
Muebles y enseres domésticos	49,5	57	...
Vestido y calzado	77,7	45	...
Asistencia médica	69,3	26	...
Educación, lectura y recreación	114,7	59	...
Transporte y comunicaciones	64,6	16	...
Varios	38,1	29	...
Total	1000,0	411	...

Se excluyen los gastos que no son de consumo, tales como: impuestos a los ingresos y otras cargas fiscales directas, contribuciones al seguro social o fondos de pensión, remesas, cuidado de la salud; desembolsos distintos de los gastos de consumo, como por ejemplo pagos de seguros de vida; valor locativo de la vivienda propia e ingresos en especie.

Método de recolección de los datos
El principal método adoptado es la entrevista personal, pero se recurre a llamadas telefónicas para los precios únicos predominantes (36 artículos relacionados con los servicios de electricidad, agua y gas, la asistencia médica, la educación, los transportes y comunicaciones, etc.).

La mayor parte de los precios se registran tres veces por mes (los días 5, 15 y 25) en unos 2 600 puntos de venta al por menor y establecimientos de servicios de once ciudades. Constituyen excepciones a esta práctica los alquileres, cuyas cotizaciones se registran un vez al mes, los billetes de teatro y las matrículas escolares, que se registran trimestralmente.

Si alguna de las fechas de referencia para la recolección, que son los días 5, 15, y 25 de cada mes, cae en domingo se le sustituye por el día anterior, o dos días si se trata de otros feriados. En el caso particular de las frutas y legumbres frescas, dadas las fluctuaciones de sus precios, la recolección tiene lugar a determinadas horas. Se excluyen los precios con descuentos y rebajas de liquidación, del mercado negro, de compras a crédito o a plazos y de objetos de segunda mano.

Vivienda
Mensualmente se investigan unos 2 500 hogares de las muestras de la encuesta de gastos de los hogares y de la encuesta de la población económicamente activa para obtener datos sobre los alquileres. Se excluye del índice el coste de la vivienda ocupada por sus propietarios.

Especificación de las variedades
Por lo general se especifica en detalle la variedad, precios y marcas de los artículos, tomando también en cuenta el volumen de sus ventas.

Sustitución, cambio de calidad, etc.
Cuando se produce un cambio de calidad importante se aplica la siguiente fórmula de distribución de sus coeficientes de ponderación:

$$P'o = Po \times (P't/Pt)$$

siendo P'o el precio de la mejora de calidad en el período de base hipotético, Po el precio de la calidad original en el período de base, P't el precio de la mejora de calidad en el momento de la sustitución y, Pt el precio de la calidad original en el momento de la sustitución.

Si en el mercado se ofrece un producto nuevo, el empalme (o encadenamiento) se hará dentro del subgrupo al que pertenece:

$$P'o = (P't/I) \times 100$$

siendo P'o el precio del nuevo artículo en el período de base hipotético, P't el precio del nuevo artículo en el momento del encadenamiento, I el índice de subgrupo al que pertenece el nuevo artículo.

Cuando ha desaparecido del mercado una calidad determinada de artículo y no es posible encontrar sustitutivo, la ponderación se vuelve a distribuir entre los restantes artículos del mismo subgrupo.

Artículos estacionales
A los efectos de la compilación del índice, los últimos precios registrados de artículos estacionales tales como las frutas y legumbres frescas se mantienen en el índice fuera de temporada hasta que se puedan registrar de nuevo sus precios.

Cálculo
El índice se calcula según la fórmula de Laspeyres como un promedio aritmético ponderado de base fija, cuyos coeficientes de ponderación corresponden al período de base.

Los relativos de precios para cada artículo en cada ciudad se calculan dividiendo el precio medio del período corriente por el precio medio del período de base. Los precios medios son los promedios simples de los precios obtenidos en cada ciudad. Los índices para los artículos para once ciudades se ponderan luego para obtener un índice para los artículos para todas las ciudades.

Informaciones complementarias
Se publican subíndices de artículos principales.

Organización y publicación
National Bureau of Statistics, Economic Planning Board, Bureau of Statistics: "Monthly Statistics of Korea" (Seúl).

idem: "Annual Report of the Price Survey" (para mayor información metodológica).

COSTA RICA (SAN JOSE)

Denominación oficial
Indice de precios para los consumidores de ingresos medios y bajos del área metropolitana de San José.

Alcance
El índice se calcula mensualmente y abarca las familias de ingresos medios y bajos que viven en el área metropolitana de San José.

Base oficial
1975 = 100.

Fuente de la ponderación
La selección de los artículos y la determinación de los coeficientes de ponderación se basaron en los resultados de una encuesta sobre los gastos de los hogares efectuada en 1974, durante 52 semanas, en el área metropolitana de San José, que abarcó una muestra de 1 633 familias con ingresos medios o bajos, es decir, ingresos mensuales no mayores de 5 499 colones en 1974. Se introdujeron reajustes en los coeficientes de ponderación para tener en cuenta los cambios de precios entre el período de la encuesta y 1975.

Ponderaciones y composición

Grupos principales	Número de artículos	Ponderación	Número aproximado de cotizaciones de precio
Alimentación	59	40,76	1 845
Vivienda:			
Alquiler	1	12,30	106
Combustible, luz y teléfono	7	6,62	13
Producto de limpieza, moblaje y accesorios para el hogar	24	8,19	510
Vestido y calzado	34	10,02	336
Varios:			
Aseo personal y asistencia médica	20	6,39	390
Educación y distracciones	10	9,23	92
Transportes	3	6,50	28
Total	158	100,00	3 320

Gastos de consumo de los hogares
Los gastos de consumo de los hogares se refieren a los bienes y servicios consumidos en la época de referencia. De las compras a plazos se consideran únicamente la cantidad pagada durante el período de referencia. Se excluye el valor de un artículo usado cuando entrada para adquirir uno nuevo y solo se tomó en cuenta lo efectivamente pagado. Se excluyen la propiedad del hogar, las cotizaciones a los seguros sociales y las contribuciones a cajas de pensiones. Se tiene en cuenta el consumo procedente de ingresos en especie.

Método de recolección de los datos
Los precios de la mayoría de los artículos son recogidos mensualmente por investigadores en puntos de venta al por menor y establecimientos de servicios. Los precios de las frutas y las verduras frescas son recogidos dos veces por semana. Se excluyen las rebajas, los precios de saldo, los precios en el mercado negro y las compras de segunda mano.

Vivienda
Los datos referentes al alquiler se obtienen cada tres meses. No se tienen en cuenta las viviendas ocupadas por su propietario.

Especificación de las variedades
Las especificaciones para cada artículo indican las características principales como calidad, peso, presentación, etc.

Sustitución, cambio de calidad, etc.
El cambio de calidad de un artículo o la aparición de un nuevo artículo en el mercado sólo se tiene en cuenta cuando se dispone de los precios correspondientes a dos meses consecutivos.

Artículos estacionales
No se toma en cuenta la estacionalidad. Las cantidades permanecen fijas a lo largo de todo el año.

Cálculo
El índice se calcula según la fórmula de Laspeyres, como un promedio aritmético ponderado de base fija, cuyos coeficientes de ponderación corresponden a 1975.

Informaciones complementarias
Se publican subíndices a nivel de subgrupo y se ponen a disposición del público a nivel de artículo.
En 1987-88 se llevó a cabo la Encuesta de Ingresos y Gastos a los Hogares con el propósito de actualizar la base del Indice.

Organización y publicación
Dirección General de Estadísticas y Censos: "Indices de precios para los consumidores de ingresos medios y bajos del área metropolitana de San José" (San José).

COTE D'IVOIRE (ABIDJAN, AFRICANOS)

Denominación oficial
Indice des prix à la consommation (Africains) (Indice de precios del consumo - Africanos).

Alcance
El índice se calcula mensualmente y abarca las familias africanas de obreros y empleados compuestas de cuatro o cinco personas; se omiten las familias con más de tres adultos y con más de un obrero o empleado.

Base oficial
Febrero de 1960 = 100.

Fuente de la ponderación
La selección de los artículos y la determinación de los coeficientes de ponderación se basaron en los resultados de una encuesta sobre los gastos de los hogares efectuada en Abidjan en agosto-septiembre de 1956 entre familias africanas de obreros y empleados compuestas de cuatro o cinco personas; la encuesta omitió las familias con más de tres adultos y con más de un asalariado.

Ponderaciones y composición

Grupos principales	Número de artículos	Ponderación	Número aproximado de cotizaciones de precio
Alimentación	47	51,1	...
Alquiler	2	11,6	...
Combustible, luz, agua y jabón	6	8,1	...
Vestido y calzado	12	8,4	...
Artículos del hogar	13	7,3	...
Servicios	9	8,5	...
Varios	11	5,0	...
Total	100	100,0	...

Gastos de consumo de los hogares
No disponible.

Método de recolección de los datos
Los precios de los artículos alimenticios, del combustible y de algunos otros artículos, se recogen diariamente en cuatro grandes mercados. Los datos referentes a los restantes artículos y servicios se recogen mensualmente.

Vivienda
Los datos referentes al alquiler se refieren a los apartamentos de tres habitaciones y de alquiler barato.

Especificación de las variedades
No disponible.

Sustitución, cambio de calidad, etc.
No disponible.

Artículos estacionales
No disponible.

Cálculo
El índice se calcula conforme a la fórmula de Laspeyres como un promedio aritmético ponderado de base fija, cuyos coeficientes de ponderación corresponden al período agosto - septiembre de 1956.

Informaciones complementarias
Actualmente se calcula una nueva serie relativa a hogares africanos de Abidjan cuyo jefe es obrero, empleado calificado o artesano tradicional (base agosto de 1984 - julio de 1985 = 100), pero en el momento de publicar el presente Volumen la OIT no disponía de informaciones metodológicas sobre esta serie.

Organización y publicación
Ministère de l'Economie et des Finances, Direction de la statistique: "Bulletin mensuel de statistique" (Abidjan).

COTE D'IVOIRE (ABIDJAN, EUROPEOS)

Denominación oficial
Indice des prix à la consommation - européens (Indice de precios del consumo (europeos).

Alcance
El índice se calcula mensualmente y abarca las familias europeas compuestas de dos o más personas en Abidjan.

Base oficial
1960 = 100.

Fuente de la ponderación
La selección de los artículos y la determinación de los coeficientes de ponderación se basaron en los resultados de una encuesta sobre los gastos de los hogares efectuada en Abidjan en junio de 1961, entre las familias europeas compuestas de dos o más personas.

Ponderaciones y composición

Grupos principales	Número de artículos	Ponderación	Número aproximado de cotizaciones de precio
Alimentación	57	50	...
Combustible, luz y agua	5	4	...
Vestido, calzado, ropa blanca y accesorios varios para el hogar	28	8	...
Productos de limpieza, aseo personal y asistencia médica	22	10	...
Servicio doméstico	2	8	...
Varios	26	20	...
Total	140	100	...

Gastos de consumo de los hogares
No disponible.

Método de recolección de los datos
Los precios de todos los artículos se recogen por agentes en cinco mercados, cuatro grandes almacenes y determinados establecimientos de servicios. Los precios de los artículos alimenticios del país, los artículos del subgrupo "Combustible" y los de algunos otros artículos se recogen diariamente, y los precios de los artículos alimenticios importados se recogen semanalmente; los precios de los demás artículos se recogen a fines de cada mes.

Vivienda
Los gastos de alquiler no se tienen en cuenta ni en el cálculo del índice ni en la determinación de los coeficientes de ponderación.

Especificación de las variedades
No disponible.

Sustitución, cambio de calidad, etc.
No disponible.

Artículos estacionales
No disponible.

Cálculo
El índice se calcula conforme a la fórmula de Laspeyres como un promedio aritmético ponderado de base fija, cuyos coeficientes de ponderación corresponden a junio de 1961.

Organización y publicación
Ministère de l'Economie et des Finances, Direction de la statistique: "Bulletin mensuel de statistique" (Abidjan).
Ministère des Finances, des Affaires économiques et du Plan, Direction de la statistique: Supplément trimestriel del "Bulletin mensuel de statistique" (Abidjan) Etudes et rapports Núm. 3, 1962.

CHAD (N'DJAMENA)

Denominación oficial
Indice des prix à la consommation (Indice de Precios del Consumo).

Alcance
El índice se compila mensualmente y abarca hogares de asalariados de los sectores público y privado de N'Djamena.

Base oficial
Febrero de 1988 = 100.

Fuente de la ponderación
La determinación de los coeficientes de ponderación y la selección de los artículos se basaron en los resultados de una encuesta sobre los gastos de los hogares realizada el año 1972 en N'Djamena. La encuesta comprendió hogares con más de un miembro, cuyos miembros eran asalariados de los sectores público y privado y cuyos salarios oscilaban entre 5 000 y 20 000 francos CFA en el momento de la encuesta. Se ajustaron los coeficientes de ponderación para tomar en cuenta las modificaciones de precio ocurridas entre el momento de la encuesta y febrero de 1988.

Ponderaciones y composición

Grupos principales	Número de artículos	Ponderación	Número aproximado de cotizaciones de precio
Alimentación	67	5 902	...
Vestido	13	959	...
Ajuar doméstico	18	277	...
Asistencia médica y aseo personal	16	401	...
Combustible y luz	4	437	...
Materiales de construcción	10	403	...
Vehículos	8	491	...
Tabaco	4	59	...
Servicios relativos a la vivienda	2	770	...
Servicios personales	4	93	...
Otros servicios (incl. transportes y viajes)	9	208	...
Total	155	10 000	...

Gastos de consumo de los hogares
El índice sólo abarca las categorías de gastos en las cuales la suma pagada resulta de un precio (real o ficticio) aplicado a una cantidad y, entre esas categorías, las que corresponden a un consumo de los hogares.
Comprende el consumo de la producción y existencias propias (sobre todo de productos agrícolas). Estos bienes y servicios se evalúan atribuyéndoles precios ficticios o convencionales (precios del mercado más próximo al lugar del consumo).
El alquiler y las reparaciones menores de la vivienda (consolidación de muros de adobe con cemento) forman parte del consumo, pero no la compra de una casa, aun cuando se pague a plazos, ni la construcción de una habitación adicional, pues son formas de ahorro de los hogares.
No se consideran como consumo los impuestos directos, las diversas contribuciones y los juegos de azar por dinero. Por el contrario, se incluyen en el índice los impuestos directos incluidos en los precios que pagan los consumidores.
En muchos hogares uno de sus miembros posee o dirige una empresa particular, agrícola, industrial, artesanal o comercial, cuyo aprovisionamiento se debe lógicamente excluir de los gastos para el consumo final de los hogares.
También se excluyen del índice mensual los gastos en artículos cuyos precios no se han podido determinar, ni siquiera en forma rápida, o no corresponden a la definición estricta del artículo seleccionado.

Método de recolección de los datos
Los investigadores registran los precios dos veces por mes en los dos mercados principales de N'Djamena. Los precios de los productos vendidos a granel (ventas "por montones" cuyo volumen varía según las estaciones pero su precio es constante) se establecen luego de haberlos comprado, pesado y expresado el peso en kilogramos. Los precios más estables, como los alquileres, se registran sólo una o dos ves al año. Los precios registrados son los de oferta practicados en los puntos de venta seleccionados, comprendidos los impuestos.
El precio de oferta, es decir el pedido por los comerciantes y artesanos, difiere del precio medio efectivamente pagado por los hogares. La variación entre ambos es naturalmente variable: escasa en el sector del mobiliario, la confección y los electrodomésticos, es mucho más considerable en la alimentación. Se supone que la evolución concordante de ambos tipos de precio también existe para los cereales y los artículos no alimenticios del índice.

Vivienda
No disponible.

Especificación de las variedades
Cada uno de los 155 artículos figura directamente en el índice; en la práctica, cada artículo del índice puede abarcar con frecuencia varios artículos, es decir una variedad de artículos tanto homogéneos como heterogéneos.
Se ha podido comprobar que, por lo general, la dispersión de precios de los artículos homogéneos es escasa. En tal caso tiene sentido calcular el promedio de los precios registrados en cada uno de los puntos de venta de la muestra como media de precios y, por lo tanto, el índice de esa variedad en N'Djamena será igual a la relación de los promedios de precios entre ambos períodos. No obstante, aún para este caso, el índice actual utiliza la media aritmética simple de los índices parciales.
Para las variedades heterogéneas, los productos pueden presentar algunas diferencias entre sí o ser totalmente distintos. Estos productos no son siempre sustituibles para el consumidor. La noción de precio promedio no tiene sentido. Sin embargo se puede calcular para cada producto (por ejemplo tres clases de pantalones) un índice parcial igual a la relación entre el precio del producto en un punto de venta y el precio del período de base. El índice de la variedad en N'Djamena será entonces igual a la media aritmética simple de los índices parciales.

Sustitución, cambio de calidad, etc.
La introducción en el índice de un producto cuyo precio no había sido o no había podido ser registrado en el período de base no plantea problemas si los productos pertenecen a categorías homogéneas pues la noción de precio promedio es válida. El problema se plantea sobre todo con respecto a las variedades heterogéneas.
Varios métodos son posibles: a) el artículo del índice de precios ya no existe y se le sustituye por otro que existía en el mercado durante el período de referencia; b) el precio del nuevo artículo puede estimarse a partir de una proporción calculada a partir de una variable cuantitativa (método de la regla de tres); c) el precio se relaciona con varias características del producto y en tal caso, para simplificar, se puede dar la preferencia a una de las características, lo que replantea el problema anterior. Pero también es posible, recurriendo a una fórmula llamada "econométrica", pasar de las características al valor del producto: es el método de las regresiones. En el momento de su integración al índice se supone que el nuevo producto "sustituye" total o parcialmente uno o varios productos que figuran en el índice. Es decir que el nuevo producto se integra en un renglón ya existente mediante la creación de una variedad.

Artículos estacionales
No disponible.

Cálculo
El índice se calcula según la fórmula de Laspeyres como un promedio aritmético ponderado de base fija, cuyos coeficientes de ponderación corresponden a 1972.

Organización y publicación
Direction de la statistique, des études économiques et démographiques: "Evolution des prix à la consommation dans la ville de N'Djamena".

idem: "Indice des prix à la consommation 1983-1989", febrero de 1990.

CHECOSLOVAQUIA

Denominación oficial
Consumer Price Index (Indice de precios del consumo).

Alcance
La compilación del índice es mensual y abarca toda la población de Checoslovaquia.

Base oficial
Enero de 1989 = 100.

Fuente de la ponderación
La selección de los artículos y la determinación de los coeficientes de ponderación se basaron en el giro del comercio al por menor. Las ponderaciones se refieren a 1989.

Ponderaciones y composición

Grupos principales	Número de artículos	Ponderación	Número aproximado de cotizaciones de precio
Alimentación	239	297,64	...
Abastecimiento público de comidas	79	105,63	...
Bienes de producción industrial:	500	450,77	...
Vestido	150	101,86	...
Calzado y cuero	52	28,69	...
Otros (combustible comprendido)	248	320,22	...
Servicios: alquiler comprendido y transporte y comunicaciones	233	145,96	...
Total	1 051	1 000,00	...

Gastos de consumo de los hogares
Todos los gastos en metálico efectuados por los hogares en comercios estatales, cooperativos o privados para adquirir productos alimenticios o bienes de producción industrial, los gastos de restaurante y cantinas públicas, así como los de servicios, comprendidos los de carácter administrativo y notarial, de abogado y judiciales, los pagos de tasas locales y los seguros (de personas y de bienes).

Método de recolección de los datos
Los artículos seleccionados para la recolección de los precios deben ser los que pagan los consumidores en el momento y tienen importancia desde el punto de vista del consumo, además de ser típicamente representativos de ciertos grupos de mercancías.

Los días 15 de cada mes civil, los estadísticos regionales recogen los precios en los puntos de venta y establecimientos de prestación de servicios seleccionados en todos los distritos de las Repúblicas Checa y Eslovaca.

Los precios de ciertos artículos que no varían durante varios años, se registran según lo informado al comienzo de cada año por el organismo correspondiente. Si en el correr del año se produce un cambio, el organismo pertinente debe comunicar el nuevo precio en el término de cinco días. Por ejemplo, los precios de la electricidad, el agua, el gas, los transportes y las comunicaciones son uniformes para todo el país y se investigan a nivel central. Los precios de las frutas y legumbres se determinan tres veces por mes, los días 1, 10 y 20.

Los servicios de salud y educación son gratuitos. El monto de las tasas o matrículas que corresponde pagar en algunos casos, como ser para cursos lingüísticos y musicales, se obtiene del establecimiento de educación respectivo.

El índice se basa en los precios que se pagan en los comercios estatales, cooperativos o privados por el valor total de las mercancías (no se incluyen en el índice los precios de artículos de segunda mano).

Vivienda
Los alquileres se obtienen en función de tasas de ocupación de las viviendas (espacio en metros cuadrados) y las tasas de equipamiento básico del hogar (por ejemplo hornillos, capacidad del depósito de combustibles, conservación de víveres, instalaciones sanitarias, electricidad, agua corriente y saneamiento, cuartos de baño, tipo de cocina, despachos, calefacción central, limpieza, ascensor).

Los alquileres de viviendas, según su distinto tamaño, se obtienen con el siguiente detalle: una habitación (estudio), una habitación y cocina, dos habitaciones y cocina, tres habitaciones y cocina. El monto del alquiler según las tasas de ocupación de las viviendas se fija en forma centralizada (por decreto del organismo central competente). Se está preparando una encuesta de alquileres descentralizada.

El aumento de los gastos de los hogares que viven en casa propia se reflejan en el índice como la tendencia del costo de los materiales, obras y mantenimiento de la construcción.

Especificación de las variedades
La especificación de cada uno de los servicios y bienes es detallada y abarca, por ejemplo, marca, tamaño, factura, cantidad, calidad, etc. Las descripciones de calidades se realiza con asesoramiento de especialistas comerciales.

Sustitución, cambio de calidad, etc.
Cuando ya no es posible encontrar un determinado artículo se le substituye por otro de calidad similar. Si la calidad no es comparable, se efectúan ajustes de calidad, con el asesoramiento de especialistas de organizaciones comerciales. Sin embargo, por regla general, no se toman en consideración las diferencias de calidad insignificantes, como por ejemplo las modas.

Artículos estacionales
Como las frutas y legumbres frecas no suelen venderse todo el año, se preparan canastas mensuales separadas en las cuales se seleccionan las variedades que de ordinario se venden en el mes de que se trata. Las ponderaciones de cada una de las variedades de frutas y legumbres incluidas en esas canastas, se basan en la media de los años 1985-1989. Se calcula luego el índice para el subgrupo de frutas y legumbres con la ayuda de coeficientes de ponderación constantes, expresados como porcentaje del gasto de consumo total.

Cálculo
El índice se calcula según la fórmula de Laspeyres, como un promedio aritmético ponderado con base fija, cuyos coeficientes de ponderación corresponden al período de base.

Los precios registrados en cada puesto informante se compilan como promedios aritméticos no ponderados. Se elaboran índices separados para la República Checa y para la República Eslovaca. El índice para todo el país es la media de dichos índices.

Informaciones complementarias
También se calcula y publica un "Cost of Living Index" de los hogares, según los principales grupos sociales, los ingresos elevados o bajos y según tengan uno, dos o tres hijos.

Organización y publicación
Federal Statistical Office, Czech Statistical Office y Slovak Statistical Office: "Statistical Information" - Development of price indices in consumer and production sphere (quick monthly information) - Development of consumer price indices (monthly information).

idem: "Statistical Yearbook".

idem: "Figures for Everybody".

CHILE (SANTIAGO)

Denominación oficial
Indice de precios al consumidor.

Alcance
El índice se calcula mensualmente y abarca todos los hogares privados de la ciudad de Santiago y sus alrededores.

Base oficial
Abril de 1989 = 100.

Fuente de la ponderación
La selección de los artículos y la determinación de los coeficientes de ponderación se basaron en los resultados de una encuesta sobre los gastos de los hogares efectuada entre diciembre de 1987 y noviembre de 1988 en el Gran Santiago, sobre una muestra de alrededor 5 500 familias de todos los grupos sociales. El criterio fundamental para determinar los bienes y servicios a ser incluidos en la canasta fue el de seleccionar todos aquellos productos cuya importancia individual dentro del gasto total de los hogares fuese igual o superior a una magnitud de 0,0325 pormil.

Adicionalmente, si la importancia de un subrupo de bienes o servicios resultaba igual o superior a 0,0325 pormil pero ningún artículo del mismo alcanzaba ese porcentaje, se eligió aquel(llos) bien(es) que tuviese(n) la mayor ponderación. Una vez seleccionados los bienes o servicios que representan a un subgrupo, se procedió, como norma general, a distribuir proporcionalmente la ponderación total del subrupo entre dichos bienes. Por su parte, para el caso de subgrupos no seleccionados, su ponderación se repartió proporcionalmente entre los bienes seleccionados dentro del grupo al cual pertenecía dicho subrupo.

Ponderaciones y composición

Grupos principales	Número de artículos	Ponderación aproximado	Número de cotizaciones de precio
Alimentación	137	32,98	...
Vivienda:			
Alquiler y reparaciones	11	9,89	...
Combustible, luz y agua	6	6,40	...
Moblaje y accesorios para el hogar etc.	53	9,11	...
Vestido y calzado	64	8,44	...
Transportes y comunicaciones	19	16,96	...
Otros:			
Asistencia médica y aseo personal	32	5,15	...
Educación y distracciones	35	6,90	...
Tabaco	1	1,81	...
Varios	10	2,37	...
Total	368	100,00	...

Gastos de consumo de los hogares
Se consideró bienes de consumo a todos los bienes y servicios adquiridos por los hogares, con excepción de los inmuebles (sitios, viviendas y otros) y de los activos mobiliarios (acciones, bonos, letras hipotecarias, etc.). Comprenden las primas de los seguros de vida, giros, regalos y pagos de seguros relacionados con bienes de consumo (viviendas, vehículos). No comprenden los beneficios recibidos en especie, el valor de las viviendas ocupadas por sus propietarios, las contribuciones a fondos de seguridad social y de pensiones, los impuestos a la renta y demás impuestos directos. En el caso de las compras a crédito, se toma en consideración el gasto del momento, efectuado en el período de referencia.

Método de recolección de los datos
Los precios son recogidos por investigadores, en aproximadamente 3 700 puntos de venta al por menor y establecimientos de servicios en las 28 áreas que abarca la ciudad de Santiago y sus alrededores (Gran Santiago). Los precios de los artículos alimenticios se recogen semanalmente; los de los grupos vivienda, vestido, y varios, mensualmente y, los de la asistencia médica, trimestralmente.

El trabajo de distribución de la muestra total de fuentes de información, determinada para cada producto, entre las distintas comunas y sectores geográficos del Gran Santiago, considerando los distintos tipos de establecimientos en que puedan adquirirse los diferentes artículos, se apoyó en dos encuestas complementarias. La primera fue una encuesta de empadronamiento de más de 6 000 establecimientos de comercio al por menor. En ella se procedió a detectar en todas las comunas del Gran Santiago los establecimientos más representativos en cuanto a ventas para los distintos productos y a realizar una tipología de dichos establecimientos en relación con la disponibilidad de bienes, subgrupos, grupos o agrupaciones de bienes para la venta.

La segunda fue una encuesta denominada de "puntos de compra", aplicada sobre una muestra de alrededor de 1 000 hogares particulares. Esta encuesta, que también tuvo una representación comunal, estuvo orientada a detectar las comunas y los tipos de establecimientos que tienen una mayor frecuencia e importancia dentro de los gastos realizados por los hogares del Gran Santiago.

Vivienda
Los datos referentes al alquiler se obtienen trimestralmente.

Especificación de las variedades
En forma paralela a la determinación de la canasta, se procedió a detallar, con el máximo de precisión que fue posible, los bienes y servicios específicos que serían objeto del seguimiento de precios. Este trabajo consistió en la definición de la calidad, forma, tamaño, peso, marca y expresión concreta de los artículos seleccionados. Para tal efecto, se tuvo en cuenta información proveniente de la propia encuesta de los gastos de los hogares, estudios de mercado y trabajos metodológicos afines realizados recientemente para el Gran Santiago y la experiencia acumulada por el INE en labores de seguimiento de precios.

Sustitución, cambio de calidad, etc.
Si un artículo desaparece del mercado se lo substituye por otro similar y se utiliza el método de enlace. Si no existe un artículo similar, el coeficiente de ponderación se redistribuye entre los artículos restantes del mismo subgrupo. Cuando se trata de un cambio cualitativo, se aplica el método de enlace.

Artículos estacionales
No se incluyen en el índice.

Cálculo
El índice se calcula conforme a la fórmula de Laspeyres como un promedio aritmético ponderado de base fija, cuyos coeficientes de ponderación corresponden al período de base.

La relación de precio para cada artículo se calcula dividiendo el precio medio del período corriente por el precio medio del período de base. Los precios medios son promedios aritméticos simples de precios obtenidos de diferentes puntos de venta.

Informaciones complementarias
Se publican subíndices para: Alimentación, Vivienda, Vestuario, Transportes y Comunicaciones, Otros.

Organización y publicación
Instituto Nacional de Estadísticas: "Indice de Precios al Consumidor" (Santiago).
idem: "Informativo Estadístico".
idem: "Indice de Precios al Consumidor, Base Abril 1989 = 100, Aspectos Metodológicos".

CHINA

Denominación oficial
Overall Staff and Workers' Cost of Living Index. (Indice general del costo de la vida para empleados y obreros).

Alcance
El índice se calcula anualmente y abarca empleados y obreros en todo el país.

Base oficial
1950 = 100.

Fuente de la ponderación
El valor actual de las ventas y las adquisiciones basadas en precios diferentes se toma como coeficientes de ponderación para calcular el índice general.

Ponderaciones y composición
No disponible.

Gastos de consumo de los hogares
No disponible.

Método de recolección de los datos
Los precios se recogen en 140 ciudades y en 230 centros urbanos provinciales y abarcan las listas de precios oficiales de los departamentos comerciales de propiedad del estado, los precios del mercado libre, los precios negociados y los precios de compra de los excedentes agrícolas y productos secundarios. Los precios se recogen para 450 artículos de mercancías en las ciudades y para 400 artículos en los centros urbanos provinciales.

Vivienda
No disponible.

Especificación de las variedades
Se adopta el precio de una mercancía característica de cada artículo.

Sustitución, cambio de calidad, etc.
No disponible.

Artículos estacionales
No disponible.

Cálculo
No disponible.

Informaciones complementarias
El índice se publica igualmente por regiones y sobre la base del año precedente = 100. Otros índices se calculan para residentes y para agricultores, así como por regiones.

Organización y publicación
State Statistical Bureau: "Statistical Yearbook" (Beijing).

CHIPRE

Denominación oficial
Retail Price Index (Indice de precios al por menor).

Alcance
La compilación del índice es mensual y abarca todos los hogares privados, con ingresos anuales netos que oscilaban entre 3 000 y 8 000 libras de Chipre en 1984-85, ubicados en zonas urbanas.

Base oficial
1986 = 100.

Fuente de la ponderación
La selección de los artículos y la determinación de los coeficientes de ponderación se basan en los resultados de una encuesta sobre los gastos de los hogares, que se realizó entre marzo de 1984 y febrero de 1985, a una muestra aleatoria de hogares ubicados en las regiones controladas por el gobierno del país. En dicha encuesta estuvieron representadas todas las clases de hogares rurales y urbanos. Sin embargo, siguiendo las recomendaciones del Comité Asesor, para calcular los coeficientes de ponderación sólo se tomaron en cuenta los hogares de las zonas urbanas cuyos ingresos anuales oscilaban entre 3 000 y 8 000 libras de Chipre. Este grupo comprende el 56,9 por ciento de todos los hogares urbanos y excluye al mismo tiempo el 22,9 por ciento de los hogares con ingresos muy bajos y el 20,2 de aquéllos con ingresos más elevados. Se excluyeron de la muestra los hogares de extranjeros y los colectivos, tales como hospitales, casas de ancianos, etc.

La enumeración comprendió en total 3 759 hogares (2 363 urbanos y 1 396 rurales) que representaban el 2,5 por ciento del total de hogares, pero para el cálculo de los coeficientes de ponderación el número se redujo a 1 346 hogares, es decir los de zonas urbanas con ingresos situados entre 3 000 y 8 000 libras de Chipre. Se ajustaron los coeficientes de ponderación para tomar en cuenta los cambios de precio entre el período de la encuesta y 1986. El método seguido para efectuar los ajustes se basó en el aumento promedio de precios registrados en los 12 meses de 1986.

Ponderaciones y composición

Grupos principales	Número de artículos	Ponderación	Número aproximado de cotizaciones de precio
Alimentación	98	3 206	2 226
Bebidas alcohólicas y tabaco	4	301	24
Bienes durables y suministros del hogar	52	679	342
Vestido y calzado	42	958	252
Transporte y comunicaciones	36	1 930	76
Alquiler y alojamiento	5	1 530	232
Combustible y luz	4	208	9
Bienes y servicios varios	72	1 188	397
Total	313	10 000	3 558

Gastos de consumo de los hogares
Los gastos de consumo utilizados para obtener los coeficientes de ponderación corresponden a la clasificación del gasto de consumo final de los hogares de la SNA, con las modificaciones siguientes: a) no se incluyen en el cálculo de las ponderaciones los gastos en loterías, juegos de cartas por dinero, apuestas a los caballos, etc.; b) se incluyen en el cálculo de la ponderación los gastos en permisos de circulación y permisos de conducción de vehículos a motor.

Se incluyen como gasto los artículos de producción propia, cuyos precios se evalúan al por mayor. Se fija un alquiler ficticio para las viviendas ocupadas por sus propietarios y es esta estimación la que entra en los índices de ponderación. Los bienes durables adquiridos a crédito se consideran como compras normales, tomándose en cuenta su precio total.

Los bienes de segunda mano también se toman en consideración por su precio de compra. El comercio de bienes usados sólo se considera en la compra de coches. Solo la diferencia neta entre los precios del coche usado y del nuevo se utilizó en el cálculo del gasto en automóviles.

Las contribuciones a la seguridad social y fondos de pensión o jubilación se excluyen de los gastos considerados para la ponderación. Se incluyen los seguros de bienes de consumo específicos. Los gastos de salud sólo se incluyen cuando los paga directamente un miembro del hogar. El impuesto a la renta y otros impuestos directos, los pagos de los seguros de vida y las transferencias de dinero a otros hogares también se excluyen. No obstante, se incluyen las compras de regalos para otros hogares.

Método de recolección de los datos
Para la recopilación de precios, los criterios de selección de los artículos son: su disponibilidad en el mercado al por menor, la proporción que representan en los gastos y las especificaciones de calidad, unidad de medida, variedad y otras que puedan disponerse. Para los artículos cuyos precios no se registran su ponderación es una proporción adecuada a la de artículos similares de cuyos precios se disponen.

Como no se efectuó ninguna encuesta previa de los lugares de compra, los puntos donde se obtuvieron los precios se seleccionaron en forma empírica para poder contar con una muestra representativa de los negocios en donde la población del índice efectúa sus compras. Los puestos seleccionados se limitaron a tres grandes ciudades: Nicosia, Limassol y Larnaca y, en cada una de éstas, los enumeradores del Departamento de Investigación y Estadísticas, debidamente formados, obtuvieron los precios de dos puntos de venta para cada tipo de mercancía o servicio.

La frecuencia de la recolección de precios varía según el artículo de que se trata. Los precios de las frutas y legumbres frescas se obtienen una vez por semana (los jueves) en mercados municipales, mientras que los de otros artículos se recogen una vez por mes (el jueves más próximo al día 15). Los datos sobre precios controlados (combustibles, electricidad, teléfono, agua, etc.) se obtienen de las facturas de las organizaciones correspondientes.

Los precios son los efectivamente pagados en el momento. A partir de 1991 se toman en cuenta las rebajas, descuentos, liquidaciones y ofertas especiales de estación. Estas se celebran actualmente dos veces al año, en febrero y en agosto/septiembre, y están sometidas a una reglamentación legal que entró en vigor en 1991. No se toman en consideración las operaciones del mercado negro ni los créditos. Los precios de importación se reflejan en los precios al por menor respectivos.

Vivienda
Las cotizaciones de alquiler se obtienen en forma bimensual de 200 hogares, mediante cuestionarios enviados por correo y visitas personales a los que no respondieron. Una selección aleatoria de Nicosia (98), Limassol (70) y Larnaca (32) permitió obtener esta muestra de 200 hogares. El número seleccionado para cada ciudad se basó en su población respectiva. La selección de la muestra se limitó a los hogares urbanos con un alquiler mensual situado entre 30 y 100 libras de Chipre, según la encuesta de gastos de los hogares. Este grupo representa el 77,5 por ciento del total de casas urbanas alquiladas y excluye el 19,4 por ciento con alquileres muy bajos y el 3,2 por ciento muy elevados.

Para elaborar el índice de alquileres: se calcula en primer lugar el alquiler medio por vivienda en cada ciudad y luego el alquiler medio nacional se obtiene utilizando los mismos coeficientes de ponderación que para todos los demás artículos del índice (es decir, 5 para Nicosia, 3 para Limassol y 2 para Larnaca). Por último, el relativo se calcula dividiendo el alquiler medio nacional del momento por el índice de alquileres del mes anterior, obteniéndose así el índice del mes en curso.

La vivienda propia se toma en cuenta para calcular el coeficiente general de ponderación de los alquileres estableciendo un alquiler ficticio. Para calcular el índice de alquileres sólo se toman en consideración los alquileres realmente pagados y no los ficticios, pues se considera que estos últimos tendrán una evolución similar.

Especificación de las variedades
Se especifican en forma detallada los bienes y servicios, describiéndose, por ejemplo, la marca, factura, tamaño, cantidad, calidad, presentación comercial y otras características que permitan evitar las variaciones de precio que obedezcan a diferencias de calidad, método de envasado, modelo, etc. Normalmente la especificación es la misma para todos los puntos de venta, pero en los pocos casos en que esta uniformidad no es posible, los artículos pertinentes se definen en forma separada. De un mes a otro, los investigadores deben utilizar la misma variedad o informar el cambio que se produzca.

Sustitución, cambio de calidad, etc.
Cuando cambia la calidad, los artículos afectados se substi-

tuyen de tal forma que el precio relativo no varíe. Sólo se introducen productos nuevos cuando se revisan las ponderaciones, cada cinco años aproximadamente. Si una determinada calidad desaparece del mercado, se la sustituye por otra similar disponible, manteniéndose invariable el precio relativo. Si la calidad de los productos, nuevo y antiguo, no pueden compararse en forma directa, se efectúa un ajuste de calidad.

La sustitución se hace mediante un enlace de los precios del artículo nuevo y del antiguo, atribuyéndose un nuevo precio de base hipotético al artículo sustituido. Para este procedimiento es necesario obtener tanto los precios del mes en curso como los del mes anterior.

Artículos estacionales
Las frutas y legumbres frescas se consideran artículos estacionales. Para superar el problema de las fluctuaciones estacionales, se prepara una canastas mensual separada con los datos obtenidos sobre los precios de frutas y legumbres en todos los mercados municipales al por mayor. Las ponderaciones de cada una de las variedades de frutas y legumbres incluidas en dicha canastas es proporcional al valor total de su venta en los mercados al por mayor durante tres años. En efecto, los precios correspondientes a los años 1983, 1984 y 1985 se calculan combinando primero las cantidades respectivas de cada artículo y multiplicándolas luego por los precios al por menor que prevalecieron en el mercado durante el año de base (1986).

Cabe señalar que al calcular los índices de frutas y legumbres frescas, el total de los coeficientes de ponderación se mantiene constante, pero la variedad de los artículos y sus ponderaciones respectivas varían de un mes a otro según su disponibilidad. En el caso de artículos que no se venden durante todo el año, como estufas, prendas y calzados de verano o de invierno, flores y pescado fresco, etc., los últimos precios registrados se repiten durante los meses en que no se venden dichos artículos.

Cálculo
El índice se calcula según la fórmula de Laspeyres, como un promedio aritmético ponderado con base fija, cuyos coeficientes de ponderación corresponden al período de base.

El índice se compila directamente a nivel nacional. Se calcula un índice ponderado para las tres ciudades con estos coeficientes de ponderación: 5 para Nicosía, 3 para Limassol y 2 para Larnaca, que reflejan aproximadamente la relación entre sus respectivas poblaciones. El precio relativo se calcula dividiendo el precio medio del mes corriente por el precio medio del mes anterior y multiplicando el resultado por el precio relativo del mes precedente.

Informaciones complementarias
También se publican índices de subgrupos principales y subíndices según el origen de las mercancías o servicios.

Organización y publicación
Ministry of Finance, Department of Statistics and Research: "Monthly Economic Indicators".

idem: "Economic Report".

idem: "Statistical Abstract".

idem: "Labour Statistics".

idem: "Methodology of the Retail Price Index", Series I, Report 4; noviembre de 1988 (Nicosía).

DINAMARCA

Denominación oficial
Consumer Price Index (Indice de precios del consumo).

Alcance
El índice se compila mensualmente y abarca todo el consumo privado del territorio danés.

Base oficial
1980 = 100.

Fuente de la ponderación
Los coeficientes de ponderación se basaron en las estadísticas de la contabilidad nacional de 1987. El gasto total del consumo final de los hogares se divide en la contabilidad nacional en 63 grupos. El desglose del gasto dentro de esos grupos se basa en las informaciones más detalladas obtenidas de una encuesta sobre los gastos de los hogares efectuada en 1981. Esta encuesta abarcaba una muestra de 2 232 hogares privados. Se ajustaron las ponderaciones a la evolución de los precios entre 1987 y enero de 1991. Cuando el gasto para un artículo era insignificante la ponderación se redistribuyó entre los artículos seleccionados del mismo subgrupo. El gasto total se distribuyó así entre los artículos seleccionados antes de calcular los coeficientes de ponderación relativos.

Ponderaciones y composición

Grupos principales	Número de artículos	Ponderación	Número aproximado de cotizaciones de precio
Alimentación	152	14,45	14 000
Bebidas y tabaco	21	6,63	900
Alquiler y gastos de conservación	13	21,46	(a) 150
Combustible y luz	8	6,99	200
Vestido y calzado	60	5,71	1 300
Accesorios para el hogar	90	6,51	2 350
Asistencia médica	12	1,79	(b) 100
Transportes y comunicaciones	64	17,19	700
Educación y distracciones	64	9,47	1 800
Otros bienes y servicios	47	9,80	500
Total	531	100,00	22 000

Nota: (a) Gastos de conservación únicamente, excl. las encuestas semestrales sobre alquileres de una muestra de 4 200 viviendas alquiladas. (b) Excl. una encuesta especial de medicamentos abarcados por el conjunto de productos.

Gastos de consumo de los hogares
El concepto de gasto del consumo de los hogares en la contabilidad nacional de Dinamarca equivale al del consumo final en el mercado interno.

Método de recolección de los datos
Los precios son recogidos cada mes en aproximadamente 1 700 almacenes privados y filiales locales de empresas con cadena de tiendas y en 270 establecimientos, organizaciones comerciales, etc.

Los precios para 71 artículos, principalmente la alimentación y las bebidas, son recogidos por entrevistadores en alrededor de 480 puntos de venta al por menor en 34 municipalidades. Para otros productos alimenticios, accesorios no duraderos para el hogar, artículos para el aseo personal, etc., los precios se recogen en empresas nacionales o regionales con cadena de tiendas, ya sea basándose en las listas de precios o en la información directa a través de un cuestionario. Para los artículos restantes, los precios se recogen mediante una encuesta mensual por correspondencia, que abarca un número variable de tiendas distribuidas por todo el país.

Los precios utilizados en el índice son los precios reales pagados por cualquier persona. Los precios rebajados se toman en consideración cuando la calidad y la cantidad del producto están de acuerdo con las especificaciones.

Vivienda
Los datos sobre alquileres se obtienen en abril y en octubre de cada año, basándose en 4 200 viviendas alquiladas de todo el país. El cálculo del promedio de los alquileres incluye las viviendas nuevas, que tienen un estándard más alto que la media. Toda solución al problema de diferencia de calidad que a este respecto se plantee comportará algo de arbitrario pues dependerá del momento en que se investiguen los alquileres. En Dinamarca se sigue el criterio de medir el alquiler de las nuevas viviendas en relación con las construidas en los últimos 3 años. Es decir que la influencia de los pisos nuevos en el cálculo es similar a la que tendría un índice separado para las viviendas nuevas, consideradas como un artículo separado. El coeficiente de ponderación para el alquiler también incluye el alquiler imputado para las viviendas ocupadas por el propietario. El cálculo del alquiler imputado para estas viviendas se basa en las informaciones sobre los alquileres de los apartamentos alquilados.

Especificación de las variedades
Para 345 artículos incluidos en la encuesta por correspondencia, se facilitan especificaciones detalladas según la marca de fábrica, el tamaño, la unidad y el modelo, etc. En varios casos, la selección de la marca y el modelo se deja a los distintos comerciantes y, una vez seleccionados se incluyen en el cuestionario. En cuanto a los artículos incluidos en la recolección de los precios por las municipalidades locales, las especificaciones son menos estrictas y se dejan a la selección de los entrevis-

tadores, los cuales tienen que utilizar cada mes la misma variedad o comunicar un cambio de tipo cuando se produzca.

Sustitución, cambio de calidad, etc.
Cuando ya no se dispone de un producto, se substituye por el producto similar o el coeficiente de ponderación se añade a otro artículo o se distribuye dentro del subgrupo. Los cambios de calidad en los productos se examinan consultando a los comerciantes o a los fabricantes o importadores. Si se puede estimar el cambio de precio como consecuencia del cambio de calidad, se hace una corrección. En caso contrario, el precio del producto substitutivo no se incluirá en el cálculo hasta que se disponga de un precio para dos meses seguidos. Para los automóviles, los ajustes por los cambios introducidos en un modelo se basan en la opinión de la organización de consumidores y del importador o productor.

Artículos estacionales
Para el pescado (bacalao y platija), la fruta fresca (manzanas, naranjas o uva) y las verduras frescas, los precios están sujetos a ajustes estacionales.

Cálculo
El índice se calcula según la fórmula de Laspeyres, como un promedio aritmético ponderado de base fija, cuyos coeficientes de ponderación corresponden a enero de 1991.

Los índices de artículo son calculados utilizando relativos de precios medios para muchos artículos y medias de relativos de precios por los otros. Estos precios medios así como los medios de relativos de precios son promedios aritméticos simples o ponderados según la naturaleza de los precios recogidos. Los coeficientes de ponderación utilizados en los promedios son el número de habitantes de las áreas urbanas o los derivados de las estadísticas de giro del comercio al por menor.

Informaciones complementarias
Además del Indice de precios del consumo, se publica un índice que excluye impuestos y subsidios: el "Nettoprisindekset" (Indice de precios netos).

Organización y publicación
Danmarks Statistik: "Statistiske Efterretninger" (Copenhague).
idem: "Nyt fra Danmarks Statistik" (newsletter).
idem: "Statistik Manedsoversigt".
idem: "Statistikservice: Prisstatistik".
idem: "Statistik Arbog".
idem: "Statistiske Efterretninger, Indkomst, forbrug og priser", no. 8, 1991.

DOMINICA

Denominación oficial
Retail Price Index (Indice de precios al por menor).

Alcance
El índice se calcula mensualmente y abarca todos los hogares privados del país.

Base oficial
Abril de 1964 = 100.

Fuente de la ponderación
La selección de los artículos y la determinación de los coeficientes de ponderación se basaron en los resultados de una encuesta sobre los gastos de los hogares efectuada en 1961, que abarcó a una muestra aleatoria de 232 hogares representativos de toda la población.

Ponderaciones y composición

Grupos principales	Número de artículos	Ponderación	Número aproximado de cotizaciones de precio
Alimentación	51	56,9	...
Bebidas alcohólicas y tabaco	5	8,3	...
Vivienda:			
Alquiler	1	3,7	...
Mantenimiento y reparación	1	5,2	...
Combustible y luz	3	5,4	...
Artículos para el hogar y varios	11	4,6	...
Vestido y calzado	12	9,5	...
Servicios	13	6,4	...
Total	97	100,0	...

Gastos de consumo de los hogares
No disponible.

Método de recolección de los datos
Los precios son recogidos por agentes en el curso de la tercera semana de cada mes en tres almacenes, un mercado y establecimientos de servicios en Roseau.

Vivienda
Los datos referentes al alquiler se obtienen cada mes y corresponden a un tipo de vivienda que comprende dos dormitorios.

Especificación de las variedades
No disponible.

Sustitución, cambio de calidad, etc.
No disponible.

Artículos estacionales
No se tienen en cuenta las fluctuaciones estacionales de los precios.

Cálculo
El índice se calcula conforme a la fórmula de Laspeyres como un promedio aritmético ponderado de base fija, cuyos coeficientes de ponderación corresponden al período de base.

Informaciones complementarias
Actualmente se calcula una nueva serie (base julio de 1984 = 100), pero en el momento de publicar el presente Volumen la OIT no disponía de informaciones metodológicas sobre esta serie.

Organización y publicación
Department of Economic Development and Planning, Statistical Division: "Annual Statistical Digest" (Roseau).

REPUBLICA DOMINICANA

Denominación oficial
Indice nacional de precios al consumidor.

Alcance
El índice se calcula mensualmente en todo el país y abarca las familias cuyos ingresos mensuales se situa entre 50 y 600 pesos en 1976/77.

Base oficial
Mayo de 1976 - abril de 1977 = 100.

Fuente de la ponderación
La selección de los artículos y la determinación de los coeficientes de ponderación se basaron en los resultados de una encuesta sobre los gastos de los hogares efectuada entre mayo de 1976 y abril de 1977 y que abarcó una muestra de 4 457 hogares multipersonales representativos de toda la población, cuyos ingresos mensuales se situa entre 50 y 600 pesos en el momento de la encuesta.

Ponderaciones y composición

Grupos principales	Número de artículos	Ponderación	Número aproximado de cotizaciones de precio
Alimentación y tabaco	46	...	...
Vivienda:			
Alquiler y costo de reparación	2	...	...
Combustible, luz, agua y teléfono	7	...	...
Moblaje y artículos para el hogar	8	...	...
Productos de limpieza etc.	9	...	...
Vestido y calzado	33	...	...
Varios:			
Aseo personal y asistencia médica	17	...	...
Educación y distracciones	6	...	...
Transportes y comunicaciones	2	...	...
Total	130	...	...

Gastos de consumo de los hogares
En el cálculo del índice, los gastos del consumo comprenden todos los bienes y servicios adquiridos para el consumo por la población de referencia. Se incluyen ciertos gastos relativos a los impuestos directos, regalos, contribuciones, tasas postales y pagos hipotecarios para las viviendas ocupadas por el propietario.

Método de recolección de los datos
La periodicidad con que debe recabarse la información varía según el tipo de producto. Para los artículos del grupo "Ali-

mentos, bebidas y tabaco", la recolección en general será diaria o semanal, según el tipo de artículos y la localidad. Para los grupos "Vivienda", "Prendas de vestir" y "Diversos", la recolección será semanal o mensual. En conjunto, 4 300 establecimientos son visitados por el recolector. No se toman los precios de baratillos.

Vivienda
Los datos referentes al alquiler se obtienen de 604 habitaciones (cinco alquileres por semana). Se tienen en cuenta el valor imputado del alquiler, el costo de reparación, el pago de hipotecas, la cuota mensual (incluyendo seguros).

Especificación de las variedades
Para cada artículo específico se anotará: nombre más conocido en el lugar, marca o clase, tamaño, peso, etc. Se dipone para cada ciudad y zona rural de una lista de las fuentes de información y de las especificaciones para cada artículo.

Sustitución, cambio de calidad, etc.
En el cálculo del índice se tienen en cuenta los cambios de calidad por empalme.

Artículos estacionales
Las fluctuaciones estacionales de los precios no son objeto de ajuste.

Cálculo
El índice se calcula según la fórmula de Laspeyres, como un promedio aritmético ponderado de base fija, cuyos coeficientes de ponderación corresponden al período de base.

La relación del precio para cada artículo se calcula dividiendo el precio medio del período corriente por el precio medio del período precedente. Los índices separados son calculados para las áreas urbanas y rurales de cada área principal del país. Después estos índices son ponderados para obtener índices urbanos e índices rurales separados para el conjunto del país. Los índices urbanos y rurales son finalmente ponderados para obtener el índice nacional. Las ponderaciones son proporcionales a los gastos de consumo de las áreas abarcadas.

Informaciones complementarias
Actualmente se calcula una nueva serie (base julio de 1984 = 100), pero en el momento de publicar el presente Volumen la OIT no disponía de informaciones metodológicas sobre esta serie.

Organización y publicación
Banco Central de la República Dominicana: "Boletín Mensual" (Santo Domingo).

idem: "Metodología para el Cálculo del Indice de Precios al Consumidor en la República Dominicana", 1982 (Santo Domingo).

ECUADOR

Denominación oficial
Indice de precios al consumidor - área urbana nacional.

Alcance
El índice se calcula mensualmente y abarca familias de ingresos medios y bajos que viven en áreas urbanas.

Base oficial
Mayo de 1978 - abril de 1979 = 100.

Fuente de la ponderación
La selección de los artículos y la determinación de los coeficientes de ponderación se basaron en los resultados de una encuesta sobre los gastos de los hogares efectuada entre julio de 1975 y junio de 1976 en 12 ciudades con más de 10 000 habitantes. La encuesta, que duró 52 semanas, se efectuó entre familias de ingresos medios y bajos. La estructura de la ponderación fue ajustada en previsión de los cambios de precio ocurridos entre 1976 y 1978-79.

Gastos de consumo de los hogares
Los gastos del consumo comprenden todos los desembolsos efectuados por los hogares para adquirir artículos de consumo y servicios. Se contabilizan como ingresos y como gastos los ingresos en especies y las viviendas ocupadas por sus propietarios. Los artículos no perecederos, adquiridos durante el período de referencia, también han sido tomados en consideración. En el caso de adquisiciones a crédito, sólo se han incluido las sumas pagadas durante el período de referencia. Se excluyen las compras de artículos de segunda mano.

Ponderaciones y composición

Grupos principales	Número de artículos	Ponderación	Número aproximado de cotizaciones de precio
Alimentación	18	396,0	2 413
Vivienda:			
Alquiler	1	161,0	1 400
Combustible y luz	1	29,6	47
Moblaje y accesorios para el hogar	6	56,0	332
Vestido y calzado	5	107,7	1 060
Varios	8	249,7	1 354
Total	(a) 39	1 000,0	6 606

Nota: (a) Número de subgrupos. Según las ciudades, entre 150 y 170 artículos.

Los impuestos relacionados con la seguridad social, que se descuentan del ingreso bruto, se consideran como gastos de consumo. También se incluyen los pagos efectuados durante el período de referencia relativos a seguros de artículos de consumo y a seguros de vida.

Método de recolección de los datos
Los precios de ciertos artículos alimenticios de gran consumo se determinan semanalmente, o cada dos semanas, mediante compra directa en diversos mercados. Los precios para los demás artículos y servicios son recogidos por investigadores y, en todos los casos, se refieren a los que pagan en el momento los consumidores, comprendiendo los impuestos indirectos pero excluyendo los descuentos, las rebajas, las compras de artículos de segunda mano y los precios de importación. Los precios fijados por las autoridades sólo se toman en consideración si son los que realmente pagan los consumidores.

Vivienda
Las cotizaciones del alquiler se obtienen de una muestra de casas, apartamentos y habitaciones. Cada mes se investiga un sexto de la muestra. El cálculo se efectúa en base del promedio aritmético ponderado. No se tienen en cuenta las viviendas ocupadas por sus propietarios.

Especificación de las variedades
Se especifican las variedades de los bienes y servicios de mayor consumo, describiéndose la marca, dimensiones, peso, unidad, etc.

Sustitución, cambio de calidad, etc.
Si un producto desaparece del mercado se lo substituye por otro de características similares. En caso de cambio de calidad, el producto se considera como nuevo y se efectúan los ajustes utilizando el método de enlace.

Artículos estacionales
La selección de los artículos incluidos en el índice se realizó para asegurar la continuidad de la recolección de los precios a lo largo del año; no obstante, en el caso de los artículos que no pueden encontrarse durante ciertos meses en el mercado se mantienen las cotizaciones de precio del mes anterior.

Cálculo
El índice se calcula conforme a la fórmula de Laspeyres como un promedio aritmético ponderado de base fija, cuyos coeficientes de ponderación corresponden al período de base.

El índice para cada una de las 12 ciudades se calcula en forma separada, según la fórmula de Laspeyres; los índices regionales y el índice nacional se calculan utilizando coeficientes de ponderación de la población estimada en 1979.

Informaciones complementarias
No disponible.

Organización y publicación
Instituto Nacional de Estadistica y Censos: "Indice de Precios al Consumidor Area Urbana Nacional" (Quito).

EGIPTO

Denominación oficial
Consumer Price Index - All Urban Population (Indice de precios del consumo: toda la población urbana).

Alcance
El índice se compila mensualmente y abarca todos los hogares

de las zonas urbanas del país, sin limitación de ingresos o tamaño.

Base oficial
Julio de 1986 - junio de 1987 = 100.

Fuente de la ponderación
La determinación de los coeficientes de ponderación y la selección de los artículos se basaron en los resultados de una encuesta sobre los gastos de los hogares realizada en 1981-82, cuya muestra comprendió 17 000 hogares. Los artículos se incluyeron en el índice en función de su importancia relativa. Las ponderaciones de los artículos no incluidos se adjudicaron por afijación, sea al artículo más semejante que tenga la misma tendencia de precios, sea entre los demás artículos del mismo grupo. No se ajustaron los coeficientes de ponderación para tomar en cuenta las modificaciones de precio ocurridas entre el período de base y el de la encuesta.

Gastos de consumo de los hogares
A los efectos del índice se les define como los gastos efectivamente realizados en bienes y servicios de consumo durante el período de referencia. No se incluyen los impuestos a los ingresos y otras cargas fiscales directas, los pagos de seguros de vida, las transferencias de dinero internas o externas, los pagos de mercancías recibidas fuera del período de referencia, los regalos y obras de caridad.

Método de recolección de los datos
La recolección de la mayoría de los precios es mensual y está a cargo de las oficinas estadísticas regionales. Los precios de los servicios y de algunas manufacturas se registran en forma trimestral. Para cada mercancía y servicio informan por lo menos tres puntos de venta de cada una de las 26 ciudades. De los 402 productos y servicios, los precios de unos 190 artículos se registran en forma centralizada, por división de los precios. Sólo se registran en el índice los precios pagados en efectivo y al contado. Se toman en consideración los precios controlados de productos racionados.

Vivienda
El índice de alquileres se calcula periódicamente merced a las viviendas nuevas y demolidas, pues las autoridades mantienen constantes los alquileres de las viviendas antiguas.

Especificación de las variedades
No disponible.

Sustitución, cambio de calidad, etc.
Cuando ya no se ofrece un artículo en el mercado se le sustituye por otro similar. El ajuste del precio de base del artículo antiguo está a cargo de expertos para tomar en cuenta el cambio de calidad.

Artículos estacionales
Se consideran artículos estacionales las frutas y legumbres frescas. Fuera de estación las ponderaciones de estas mercancías se asignan al resto de los artículos del mismo grupo.

Cálculo
El índice de toda la población urbana se compila como un promedio ponderado de los seis índices correspondientes a El Cairo, Alejandría, la zona del Canal, Alto Egipto, Bajo Egipto y los territorios fronterizos. El índice de cada ciudad o grupo de ciudades se calcula según la fórmula de Laspeyres como un promedio ponderado de relativos. Estos índices se ponderan luego según la población de cada ciudad o grupo de ciudades. Para obtener el índice de toda la población urbana se aplican los siguientes coeficientes de ponderación: 28,6 por ciento para El Cairo, 13,8 por ciento para Alejandría, 4,7 por ciento para la zona del Canal, 25,5 por ciento para el Alto Egipto, 25,9 por ciento para el Bajo Egipto y 1,4 por ciento para los territorios fronterizos.

Informaciones complementarias
Se publican índices separados para El Cairo, Alejandría, la zona del Canal, Alto Egipto, Bajo Egipto y los territorios fronterizos, así como un índice de toda la población rural e índices separados para el Alto y el Bajo Egipto. Para todas estas series se publican subgrupos detallados.

Organización y publicación
Central Agency for Public Mobilisation and Statistics: "Monthly Bulletin of Consumer Price Index", El Cairo.

Ponderaciones y composición
Alto Egipto

Grupos principales	Número de artículos	Ponderación	Número aproximado de cotizaciones de precio
Alimentación	141	576,2	...
Alquiler y agua	4	77,4	...
Combustible y luz	9	38,3	...
Muebles, productos de limpieza y servicio doméstico	55	48,7	...
Vestido y calzado	92	106,5	...
Asistencia médica	42	23,9	...
Transporte y comunicaciones	14	29,9	...
Educación y recreación	29	27,4	...
Varios	16	71,7	...
Total	402	1 000,0	...

Bajo Egipto

Grupos principales	Número de artículos	Ponderación	Número aproximado
Alimentación	141	575,5	...
Alquiler y agua	4	72,0	...
Combustible y luz	9	37,6	...
Muebles, productos de limpieza y servicio doméstico	55	44,1	...
Vestido y calzado	92	116,5	...
Asistencia médica	42	26,8	...
Transporte y comunicaciones	14	34,1	...
Educación y recreación	29	25,0	...
Varios	16	68,4	...
Total	402	1 000,0	...

Ciudades del Canal

Grupos principales	Número de artículos	Ponderación	Número aproximado
Alimentación	141	567,2	...
Alquiler y agua	4	64,8	...
Combustible y luz	9	36,0	...
Muebles, productos de limpieza y servicio doméstico	55	59,9	...
Vestido y calzado	92	106,5	...
Asistencia médica	42	23,1	...
Transporte y comunicaciones	14	45,5	...
Educación y recreación	29	30,0	...
Varios	16	67,0	...
Total	402	1 000,0	...

Alexandria

Grupos principales	Número de artículos	Ponderación	Número aproximado
Alimentación	141	559	...
Alquiler y agua	4	59	...
Combustible y luz	9	41	...
Muebles, productos de limpieza y servicio doméstico	55	47	...
Vestido y calzado	92	101	...
Asistencia médica	42	26	...
Transporte y comunicaciones	14	63	...
Educación y recreación	29	32	...
Varios	16	72	...
Total	402	1 000	...

El Cairo

Grupos principales	Número de artículos	Ponderación	Número aproximado
Alimentación	141	520	...
Alquiler y agua	4	59	...
Combustible y luz	9	34	...
Muebles, productos de limpieza y servicio doméstico	55	58	...
Vestido y calzado	92	107	...
Asistencia médica	42	32	...
Transporte y comunicaciones	14	67	...
Educación y recreación	29	45	...
Varios	16	78	...
Total	402	1 000	...

Territorios fronterizos

Grupos principales	Número de artículos	Ponderación	Número aproximado
Alimentación	141	583,8	...
Alquiler y agua	4	81,6	...
Combustible y luz	9	40,7	...
Muebles, productos de limpieza y servicio doméstico	55	34,3	...
Vestido y calzado	92	122,3	...
Asistencia médica	42	12,9	...
Transporte y comunicaciones	14	42,9	...
Educación y recreación	29	23,6	...
Varios	16	57,9	...
Total	402	1 000,0	...

EL SALVADOR

Denominación oficial
Indice de precios al consumidor.

Alcance
El índice se calcula mensualmente y abarca todos los hogares urbanos de ingresos medios.

Base oficial
Diciembre de 1978 = 100.

Fuente de la ponderación
La selección de los artículos y la determinación de los coeficientes de ponderación se basaron en los resultados de una encuesta sobre los gastos de los hogares efectuada entre agosto de 1976 y julio de 1977 y que abarcó 1 819 hogares urbanos y 1 408 rurales. Los coeficientes de ponderación se refieren a familias urbanas de ingresos medios.

Ponderaciones y composición

Grupos principales	Número de artículos	Ponderación	Número aproximado de cotizaciones de precio
Alimentación	56	42,78	...
Vestido y calzado	30	8,38	...
Vivienda:			
Alquiler	1	11,70	...
Agua, teléfono y servicios domésticos	3	2,97	...
Combustible y luz	7	3,87	...
Utensilios del hogar y ropa blanca	9	1,27	...
Accesorios para el hogar	11	6,01	...
Productos de limpieza	4	1,23	...
Varios:			
Asistencia médica	7	2,54	...
Aseo personal	12	2,12	...
Educación y distracciones	10	8,69	...
Transportes y comunicaciones	7	7,76	...
Tabaco	1	0,68	...
Total	158	100,00	...

Gastos de consumo de los hogares
No disponible.

Método de recolección de los datos
Los precios de la mayoría de los artículos y servicios son recogidos por investigadores, la semana que comprende el día 15 de cada mes, en el área metropolitana de San Salvador, en Santa Ana y en San Miguel. La determinación de algunos precios de cantidades inciertas se realiza mediante compra directa. Los precios de las frutas y verduras frescas se recogen la primera y la tercera semana de cada mes, los de la vestimenta cada dos meses y en forma trimestral los del moblaje, equipo para el hogar, y tarifas de servicios médicos y dentales.

Vivienda
Los datos referentes al alquiler se obtienen en marzo y septiembre de cada año en 50 viviendas alquiladas. No se tienen en cuenta las viviendas ocupadas por sus propietarios.

Especificación de las variedades
Se mantiene el carácter confidencial de las especificaciones, cuyos detalles toman en consideración la calidad, marca, modelo, etc.

Sustitución, cambio de calidad, etc.
Si se produce un cambio en la especificación de un artículo, se lo considera como nuevo y su precio respectivo se calcula tras haberlo registrado dos veces, permaneciendo sin modificaciones el coeficiente de ponderación asignado al nuevo artículo. En el caso de un artículo completamente nuevo, una encuesta especial demostrará su importancia relativa, redistribuyéndose los coeficientes de ponderación entre los restantes artículos de ese subgrupo.

Artículos estacionales
Si un artículo desaparece temporariamente del mercado se lo considera como estacional, presumiéndose que su precio varía en la misma proporción que los demás del mismo subgrupo.

Cálculo
El índice se calcula conforme a la fórmula de Laspeyres como un promedio aritmético ponderado de base fija, cuyos coeficientes de ponderación corresponden al período de base. La relación de precio para cada artículo es calculado dividiendo el precio medio del período en curso por el precio medio del período precedente. Los precios medios son promedios aritméticos simples.

Organización y publicación
Ministerio de Economía, Dirección General de Estadística y Censos: "Boletín Estadístico" (San Salvador).

Ministerio de Planificación y Coordinación del Desarrollo Económico y Social, Unidad Investigaciones Muestrales: "Metodología para la construcción del índice de precios al consumidor, base diciembre 1978 = 100" (San Salvador, nov. 1978).

ESPAÑA

Denominación oficial
Indice de precios de consumo.

Alcance
El índice se calcula mensualmente y comprende familias compuestas de dos o más personas cuyos ingresos oscilaron entre 322 575 y 2 000 000 de pesetas en el momento de la encuesta (abril de 1980 a marzo de 1981).

Base oficial
1983 = 100.

Fuente de la ponderación
La selección de los artículos y la determinación de los coeficientes de ponderación se basaron en los resultados de una encuesta sobre los gastos de los hogares realizada entre abril de 1980 y marzo de 1981, que abarcó una muestra de 24 000 hogares en todo el país.

Ponderaciones y composición

Grupos principales	Número de artículos	Ponderación	Número aproximado de cotizaciones de precio
Alimentación	171	330	...
Vestido y calzado	56	87	...
Vivienda	24	186	...
Moblaje, accesorios para el hogar y servicios domésticos	56	74	...
Asistencia médica	18	24	...
Transportes y comunicaciones	26	144	...
Educación y distracciones	40	70	...
Otros bienes y servicios	37	85	...
Total	428	1 000	146 000

Gastos de consumo de los hogares
A los fines del índice, los gastos de consumo comprenden todos los bienes y servicios adquiridos por la población del índice. Comprenden los productos caseros de consumo, los pagos de primas de seguros y los impuestos a los automóviles. Se excluyen los impuestos indirectos y los directos, materiales especiales y gastos relativos a las actividades profesionales y juegos de azar, los cuidados veterinarios, amortizaciones de préstamos, remisiones, regalos y pagos similares.

Método de recolección de los datos
Los precios son recopilados por investigadores en áreas de mercados, supermercados y otros puntos de venta y establecimientos de servicios en todo el país. Los precios de los artículos alimenticios perecederos se recogen cuatro veces por mes en ciertas ciudades importantes y dos veces al mes en las demás ciudades. Los precios de los artículos duraderos se obtienen una vez por mes y los del equipo para el hogar y electrodomésticos trimestralmente. Los precios que son uniformes para todo el país se extraen del Boletín Oficial del Estado para los combustibles, el tabaco y los servicios de electricidad y teléfonos.

Vivienda
Las cotizaciones de los alquileres se recogen mensualmente por medio de una muestra de 3 000 viviendas alquiladas y 2 000 viviendas ocupadas por sus propietarios. Los alquileres protegidos se recogen una vez al año y los libres una vez por mes.

Especificación de las variedades
Las especificaciones de las variedades varían según los artículos. Por lo general, en la descripción se toma en cuenta la calidad, marca y unidad, pero no la fecha de fabricación o manufactura.

Sustitución, cambio de calidad, etc.
Si un artículo desaparece del mercado o cambia su calidad, se lo sustituye por otro similar. Los artículos nuevos se introducen cuando se revisa el índice.

Artículos estacionales
Las fluctuaciones estacionales del precio de las frutas y las verduras frescas se toman en cuenta variando los artículos y sus coeficientes de ponderación dentro de canastas mensuales, cuyos coeficientes de ponderación de grupo son constantes.

Cálculo
El índice se calcula conforme a la fórmula de Laspeyres, como un promedio aritmético ponderado de base fija, cuyos coeficientes de ponderación corresponden al período de base. Las relaciones de los precios medios para cada artículo se calculan dividiendo el precio medio del período corriente por el precio medio del período de base. En un principio, los precios medios se calculan como promedios aritméticos simples para cada muestra primaria de unidades de área. Esos precios medios se ponderan luego utilizando ponderaciones relativas de la población para determinar los precios medios para todo el país.

Informaciones complementarias
Se publican los grupos principales.

Organización y publicación
Instituto Nacional de Estadística: "Indice de precios de consumo - Boletín Informativo" (Madrid).
idem: "Indicadores de coyuntura"
idem: "Indice de precios de consumo, base 1983, Monografía Técnica" (Madrid, 1985).

ESTADOS UNIDOS

Denominación oficial
Consumer Price Index for All Urban Consumers (CPI-U). (Indice de precios del consumo para la totalidad de los consumidores urbanos (CPI-U)).

Alcance
El índice se calcula mensualmente y abarca aproximadamente a un 80 por ciento de la población total que no vive en instituciones. Quedan excluidos del índice los residentes rurales, todas las familias agrícolas, los militares y las personas que viven en instituciones.

Base oficial
1982-84 = 100.

Fuente de la ponderación
Las ponderaciones se han determinado basándose en los resultados de una encuesta sobre los gastos de consumo efectuada en 1982-84, que estuvo subdividida en dos encuestas separadas: una realizada por medio de entrevistas y otra con auxilio de dietarios. Cada año y para cada tipo de encuesta se contactaron unas 5 000 unidades de consumo. El concepto de unidad de consumo se basa en las interdependencias económicas existentes dentro de una unidad de vivienda, y difiere por tanto de los conceptos de familia y de hogar. La ponderación de los gastos para cada artículo es una estimación de los gastos totales que efectúa la población de referencia para dicho artículo y se obtiene multiplicando estimaciones de los gastos medios de las unidades de consumo por el número de unidades de consumo.

Ponderaciones y composición

Grupos principales	Número de artículos	Ponderación	Número aproximado de cotizaciones de precio
Alimentación y bebidas	100	17,627	44 102
Vivienda	97	41,544	(c) 18 864
Vestido, calzado y mantenimiento	59	6,097	11 059
Transportes	38	17,013	6 564
Asistencia médica	15	6,689	4 483
Distracciones	30	4,357	2 800
Otros bienes y servicios	31	6,674	2 080
Total	(a) 370	(b) 100,000	89 952

Nota: (a) Incluidos 23 artículos cuyos precios no se han registrado. (b) Importancia relativa diciembre de 1991. (c) Incluidos 9 000 registros de habitación.

Gastos de consumo de los hogares
Los gastos de consumo de los hogares que se toman en cuenta para el cálculo del índice incluyen todos los bienes y servicios adquiridos por la población para el consumo cotidiano.

Método de recolección de los datos
La muestra de puntos de venta se selecciona basándose en los resultados de una encuesta sobre los puntos de compra efectuada cada año en un quinto aproximadamente de las áreas urbanas incluidas en el índice de precios de consumo. Se efectúan entrevistas a unidades de consumo en cada una de las áreas en las que se registran precios. Se les pide información sobre compras de artículos de categorías específicas durante un período de referencia prescrito. Si se ha efectuado una compra, se registran el nombre y dirección del punto de venta y el costo de la transacción. El Oficina de Estadísticas del Trabajo elige entonces una muestra probabilística de esos puntos de venta para cada categoría de gastos, utilizando como medida del tamaño de cada punto de venta los gastos efectuados en él. Ello garantiza una muestra objetiva de los puntos de venta en la que están representados todos los tipos de establecimientos; este sistema permite también estimar las varianzas erráticas y el error de muestreo.

Los precios de la mayoría de los bienes y servicios se obtienen de visitas personales de investigadores del Bureau a unos 21 000 puntos de venta al por menor y 6 000 unidades de vivienda. Para obtener las tarifas de servicios públicos y los precios de algunos combustibles y de ciertos artículos se envían cuestionarios por correspondencia. Los precios se toman de puntos de venta al por menor y establecimientos de servicios de 85 áreas urbanas repartidas en todo el país. Los precios de los artículos alimenticios, del combustible y de algunos otros artículos se registran mensualmente en todas estas 85 áreas urbanas. Los precios de otros artículos y servicios se obtienen mensualmente en las cinco áreas metropolitanas más grandes, y bimensualmente en las demás. Los precios de los artículos alimenticios se registran durante todo el mes. Los precios utilizados en el cálculo del índice son los precios ordinarios al contado, incluidos todos los impuestos directamente asociados a la compra y utilización de los artículos.

Vivienda
Las informaciones relativas al alquiler se recogen de la encuesta sobre alquileres. La muestra abarca unas 60 000 unidades de vivienda, que se dividen en seis grupos. Cada mes se registran los alquileres de un grupo; la rotación de los grupos hace que cada seis meses se registren los alquileres de las mismas unidades de vivienda. Para evaluar el costo de las viviendas ocupadas por sus propietarios se aplica el método de valor imputado del alquiler. Están incluidos los precios de los materiales adquiridos por los inquilinos para reparar su vivienda y la renta de los apartamentos de vacaciones utilizados por sus propietarios. Mediante el método de regresión hedónica se ajusta el índice de alojamiento para tener en cuenta el cambio de calidad causado por el envejecimiento de la vivienda alquilada.

Especificación de las variedades
Dentro de cada punto de venta de la muestra el propio investigador selecciona determinados artículos con miras al registro de sus precios, en proporción al volumen de ventas (evaluado en dólares) realizadas en el mismo, es decir, según el método de probabilidad proporcional al tamaño (cuya medida viene dada por el porcentaje de ventas). El investigador prepara una descripción detallada del artículo seleccionado utilizando una lista de control elaborada por especialistas para cada artículo. Esta especificación concreta sobre el punto de venta sirve para identificar el artículo cuyo precio debe registrarse.

Sustitución, cambio de calidad, etc.
Cuando hay una sustitución, un especialista efectúa la corrección necesaria para tener en cuenta el cambio de calidad. Cuando esta corrección no es posible se recurre al método de enlace.

Artículos estacionales
El precio de los artículos estacionales que no se encuentran en el mercado se evalúa utilizando procedimientos normalizados de estimación.

Cálculo
El índice se calcula conforme a la fórmula de Laspeyres como un promedio aritmético ponderado de base fija, cuyos coeficientes de ponderación corresponden al período de base. El índice de cada artículo se obtiene utilizando las relaciones de precios

ponderados del período en curso y del período precedente. Las ponderaciones se basan en la importancia del artículo, del punto de venta y del área, y en el número de los demás registros de precios de la muestra. El índice par la totalidad de los consumidores urbanos es una agregación de las 85 unidades primarias de muestreo donde se han registrado los precios. Para cada artículo en cada unidad primaria de muestreo se calculan ponderaciones que reflejan los gastos corrientes estimados para la canasta de la compra durante el período de base. Las canastas de la compra se ponderan entonces utilizando la población de cada una de estas unidades para obtener las ponderaciones por artículo para la totalidad de los consumidores urbanos.

Organización y publicación
US Department of Labor, Bureau of Labor Statistics: "The CPI Detailed Report"(Washington, D.C.).

idem: "The Consumer Price Index: The 1987 Revision, Report 736".

idem: "The Consumer Price Index: BLS Handbook of Methods " Bulletin No 2285, capítulo 19.

ETIOPIA (ADDIS ABEBA)

Denominación oficial
Retail Price Index for Addis Ababa (Indice de precios al por menor para Addis Abeba).

Alcance
El índice se compila mensualmente y abarca los hogares urbanos cuyos ingresos mensuales fueron inferiores a 400 Birr de Etiopía en 1963.

Base oficial
1963 = 100.

Fuente de la ponderación
La selección de los artículos y la determinación de los coeficientes de ponderación se basaron en los resultados de una encuesta sobre los gastos de los hogares, efectuada en Addis Abeba en 1963, con una muestra de unos 600 hogares.

Ponderaciones y composición

Grupos principales	Número de artículos	Ponderación	Número aproximado de cotizaciones de precio
Alimentación y tabaco	33	48,98	318
Alquiler	...	...	...
Combustible y luz	4	10,23	42
Artículos para el hogar	3	4,37	33
Transportes	3	4,52	30
Vestido y calzado	6	6,71	30
Aseo personal y asistencia médica	11	2,64	87
Lectura y distracciones	5	2,57	25
Otros bienes y servicios	9	5,43	36
Total	74	85,45	601

Gastos de consumo de los hogares
A los fines del índice, los gastos del consumo comprenden todos los bienes y servicios adquiridos para el consumo por la población cubierta por el índice. También comprenden los seguros relacionados con bienes de consumo específico y el pago de las autorizaciones. Se excluyen los impuestos a la renta de las personas físicas, los pagos de seguros de vida y los ahorros.

Método de recolección de los datos
Los precios son recogidos por funcionarios permanentes de la Oficina Central de Estadística en unos 545 comercios al por menor, mercados libres y establecimientos de servicios.

Para la mayor parte de los artículos, la recolección de precios es mensual. En el caso de artículos de consumo durables, vestidos, transportes y bienes varios, los precios se recogen cada tres meses.

Los precios utilizados para el cálculo del índice son los precios al por menor que se pagan en el momento. No se toman en consideración las rebajas y los descuentos.

Vivienda
El índice no incluye el alquiler.

Especificación de las variedades
Todos los artículos comprendidos en la encuesta sobre los precios de consumo se especifican con gran detalle para evitar complicaciones en la recolección de los datos. La especificación describe la factura, marca, unidad, color, estado físico, etc. de todos los artículos incluidos en la muestra.

Sustitución, cambio de calidad, etc.
Cuando un artículo desaparece del mercado, o bien se lo substituye por uno similar, o bien se mantiene el último precio hasta que vuelva a aparecer en el mercado.

Artículos estacionales
Los precios al por menor del pescado, la carne, y todo tipo de verduras y frutas, cuadernos de ejercicios, lápices, paraguas y botas de goma presentan variaciones estacionales, pero no se confecciona un índice estacional, ni tampoco se utiliza un procedimiento especial para esos artículos.

Cálculo
El índice se calcula conforme a la fórmula de Laspeyres como un promedio aritmético ponderado de base fija, cuyos coeficientes de ponderación corresponden al período de base.

Organización y publicación
Central Statistical Office: "Statistical Abstract" (Addis Abeba).

FIJI

Denominación oficial
Consumer Price Index (Indice de Precios del Consumo).

Alcance
El índice se compila mensualmente y abarca hogares de los seis centros urbanos más importantes de la isla.

Base oficial
1985 = 100.

Fuente de la ponderación
La determinación de los coeficientes de ponderación y la selección de los artículos se basaron en los resultados de una encuesta sobre los gastos de los hogares, realizada entre febrero de 1983 y enero de 1984, con una muestra de 4 402 hogares diseminados en todo Fiji. Por su parte el índice se refiere a 1 756 hogares de zonas urbanas. No se ajustaron los coeficientes de ponderación para tomar en cuenta la evolución de los precios entre la encuesta y el período de base.

Ponderaciones y composición

Grupos principales	Número de artículos	Ponderación	Número aproximado de cotizaciones de precio
Alimentación	103	339,3	...
Bebidas alcohólicas y tabaco	7	63,8	...
Vivienda (alquiler, tasas, mantenimiento)	9	186,1	...
Combustible y luz	3	48,7	...
Bienes domésticos durables	36	75,6	...
Vestido y calzado	32	63,1	...
Transporte	15	112,9	...
Servicios	27	67,5	...
Varios	35	43,0	...
Total	267	1 000,0	...

Gastos de consumo de los hogares
Se excluyen los pagos de impuestos a los ingresos, fondos de ahorro y pensión, seguros de vida, compras de casas e intereses hipotecarios, cuotas de afiliación sindical y deudas de juego.

Método de recolección de los datos
La recolección de precios en los centros comerciales de la región Suva-Nausori tiene lugar en las dos semanas centrales de cada mes y en la semana central para los de Ba, Lautoka, Nadi y Labasa. Como el fundamento del índice es la estructura del consumo de todos los residentes urbanos de Fiji, se estimó que la región de Suva-Nausori era representativa de la evolución de los precios en los centros comerciales urbanos de la parte central de la isla, Labasa de la septentrional y Ba, Lautoka y Nadi de la región occidental. Se considera que el conjunto de las fluctuaciones de los precios en estas regiones representan adecuadamente el movimiento de los precios en todas las zonas urbanas de Fiji.

Los precios del índice corresponden a transacciones al contado y en efectivo. Los encargados de la recolección visitan personalmente cada uno de los centros y anotan los precios y ponderaciones de los artículos ofrecidos. Cuando los precios no están marcados o son ilegibles los investigadores tienen instrucciones de averiguarlos pidiendo informaciones directamente a los administradores o dependientes de los supermercados. Se registran los precios de "liquidación" o de "ofertas especiales" de los artículos del índice, salvo que la reducción de precio obedezca a un defecto, mancha o cualquier otra forma de deterioro de los productos, pues constituyen un cambio de la calidad de la mercancía y es importante que las variaciones de precio relacionadas con estos cambios no se incluyan en el índice.

Los funcionarios de la Oficina de Estadísticas visitan personalmente cada uno de los establecimientos seleccionados para registrar los precios y se obtienen directamente de las autoridades públicas competentes los datos sobre cargas fiscales y recargos impuestos por el Estado. La regularidad del día y la hora de las visitas se mantiene de un mes a otro, en especial en los mercados municipales, donde pueden producirse diferencias considerables de los precios según sea, por ejemplo, la mañana o la tarde.

A los efectos de la recolección de precios, los productos alimenticios se dividen en artículos de mercados y artículos de supermercados. El tamaño y la marca de estos últimos están claramente definidos y sus precios legibles en tarjetas. Pero la ponderación y cotización de los productos de los mercados está a cargo de los investigadores, que suelen llevar consigo sus propias escalas de medida. En general se anotan tres muestras de un mismo artículo en diversos puestos de mercado y el precio promedio de la unidad ponderada se calcula ulteriormente en la oficina. Las visitas a los mercados se hacen los viernes y los sábados a determinadas horas de la mañana para obtener los precios normales de productos perecederos que, con frecuencia, se deterioran al fin de la jornada y se venden a menos precio.

Los precios del gas, la gasolina o bencina blanca y el queroseno de uso doméstico se obtienen de los establecimientos que habitualmente los suministran, mientras que toda posible modificación de las tarifas de los servicios de electricidad se averiguan periódicamente en la Administración Eléctrica de Fiji.

Vivienda
El principal componente de esta sección del índice es el alquiler. De las casas alquiladas abarcadas por la encuesta de gastos, se eligió una muestra que, por lo tanto, representa una selección aleatoria de la totalidad de las casas alquiladas y ocupadas por ciudadanos de Fiji en 1983. Los datos sobre las cargas anexas se registran mensualmente junto con los precios de los demás artículos. En cada visita a los hogares se pregunta por toda eventual mejora de la vivienda y el consiguiente aumento de alquiler que, en tal caso, se ajusta como cambio de calidad. Los precios de otros artículos, como los de mantenimiento, se investigan de la manera habitual, visitando los respectivos comercios todos los meses.

Especificación de las variedades
Una vez seleccionados los artículos, decidir cuál "marca" particular y que tamaño de envasado o cuáles "marcas" de un determinado artículo han de ser objeto de la recolección de precios mereció una atenta reflexión. Los productos que gozan de una popularidad indiscutible se pueden identificar fácilmente por los detalles que sobre el consumo y la marca preferidos registraron los hogares en las relaciones semanales de los gastos diarios utilizadas durante la encuesta. No obstante, en muchos casos se han obtenido detalles suplementarios de los distribuidores o de los dependientes de supermercados antes de adoptar una decisión definitiva al respecto. Los motivos determinantes para incluir un artículo en el índice son que sea representativo, se "venda bien" y se ofrezca normalmente en los principales centros de todo el país. Las especificaciones de los bienes domésticos durables se ajustan a los modelos, tamaños y materiales estándar.

Sustitución, cambio de calidad, etc.
Si no es posible encontrar un artículo, el precio se repite durante tres meses y luego se elige un sustitutivo. Se trata de que estos últimos se asemejen lo más posible al original en cuanto a su calidad, tamaño y utilización.

Artículos estacionales
Fuera de temporada, se mantienen los precios de la estación anterior de los artículos estacionales tales como frutas y legumbres frescas.

Cálculo
El índice nacional urbano (para la isla principal de Fiji) se calcula como un promedio ponderado de los tres índices correspondientes a las regiones central, meridional y oriental. Cada índice regional se calcula según la fórmula de Laspeyres como un promedio aritmético ponderado de base fija, cuyos coeficientes de ponderación corresponden al período entre febrero de 1983 y enero de 1984. Para formar el índice nacional urbano se combinan los tres índices regionales en forma proporcional al gasto de consumo de cada región, siendo las proporciones de 0,571 para la central, 0,361 para la occidental y 0,068 para la septentrional.

Para calcular los índices por artículo se recurre al promedio ponderado de los precios relativos entre el período en curso y el de base.

Informaciones complementarias
Se publican subíndices para los grandes subgrupos.

Organización y publicación
Bureau of Statistics, Suva: "Statistical News".

idem: "Methodological Report on the Consumer Price Index (Base average 12 months 1985 = 100)", Documento Parlamentario No. 22, de 1988.

FILIPINAS

Denominación oficial
Consumer Price Index for All-Income Households in the Philippines (Indice de precios del consumo de todos los hogares de Filipinas).

Alcance
La compilación del índice es mensual y abarca todos los hogares (urbanos y rurales) de 72 provincias de las 13 regiones del país.

Base oficial
1988 = 100.

Fuente de la ponderación
La determinación de los coeficientes de ponderación se basaron en los resultados de una encuesta sobre los gastos de los hogares efectuada en 1988 a una muestra de 19 000 hogares. La selección de los artículos y servicios cuyos precios se han de registrar periódicamente, así como los puntos de venta en donde dichos artículos se compran se basan en una encuesta de puntos de venta realizada en 1985 a una muestra de 19 000 hogares. Este procedimiento permite asegurar la representatividad de los artículos que de ordinario consumen los hogares que figuran en el índice.

Ponderaciones y composición

Grupos principales	Número de artículos	Ponderación	Número aproximado de cotizaciones de precio
Alimentación y tabaco	198	58,5	...
Vestido y calzado	106	4,3	...
Vivienda y reparaciones	34	13,3	...
Combustible, luz y agua	15	5,4	...
Servicios	98	10,9	...
Varios	111	7,6	...
Total	562	100,0	(a) ...

Nota: (a) Por lo general se han tomado seis cotizaciones de precio para cada mercancía o servicio.

Gastos de consumo de los hogares
A los fines del índice, los gastos de consumo abarcan solamente los necesarios para el consumo familiar. Se excluyen los impuestos que gravan la residencia, los bienes inmobiliarios y las rentas de las personas físicas; los regalos, contribuciones y asistencia a terceros; los seguros de accidentes y de salud; las primas de retiro o de seguridad social, el valor de los servicios prestados por un familiar a otro miembro de la familia y desembolsos que no se consideran como gastos indispensables del consumo familiar. Comprenden el valor de los artículos que no implican un desembolso en efectivo, como el de los productos alimenticios producidos por quienes los consumen, los pagos en especie efectuados por la familia y el valor locativo ficticio de las viviendas propias o de las casas cuyos moradores no pagan alquiler.

Método de recolección de los datos
Los precios se recogen mediante una encuesta de precios llevada a cabo en 72 capitales de provincia y unos 744 municipios del país. La selección de los municipios se basó en la disponibilidad de mercancías y servicios ofrecidos. Los puntos de venta fueron seleccionados sobre la base de su volumen de ventas o giro comercial, la cantidad y variedad de las mercancías almacenadas, la estabilidad del punto de venta, la disposición a cooperar del comerciante y la conveniencia y accesibilidad del punto de venta. Los precios de los artículos alimenticios agrícolas no industrializados los recoge la Oficina de Estadísticas Agrícolas, los precios de los artículos alimenticios procesados, las bebidas y el tabaco, las informaciones relativas a los precios de los transportes, los servicios y todos los demás artículos no alimenticios, los obtiene la Oficina Nacional de Censos y Estadísticas.

Los precios se obtienen mediante entrevistas personales. Los precios de los alimentos no industrializados de Manila metropolitana se registran los lunes, miércoles y viernes de cada semana, mientras que los de todos los artículos de alimentos procesados, las bebidas y el tabaco se recogen todas las semanas, el viernes o el sábado. Todos los precios de los demás artículos se determinan dos veces por mes. A los efectos del índice, sólo se recogen los precios de mercado predominantes. No se recogen las rebajas ni se cotizan los precios de los artículos con descuento.

Vivienda
Las cotizaciones de alquileres se recogen mensualmente. Todos los datos relativos a los alquileres son suministrados por los arrendatarios ocupantes. No se incluyen las viviendas ocupadas por sus propietarios.

Especificación de las variedades
Las especificaciones de los artículos cuyos precios han de fijarse se consignan con gran detalle e incluyen el grado, el nombre o marca, el tamaño, la calidad, confección, contenido, peso y unidad de medida.

Sustitución, cambio de calidad, etc.
Los artículos que componen la canasta no se modifican hasta que no se haya cambiado la base anual. Sin embargo, si un artículo desaparece del mercado se efectúa una sustitución sobre las bases siguientes:

a) el sustitutivo debe ser igual, al menos en su calidad;
b) el sustitutivo debe tener el mismo orden de precios.

Artículos estacionales
Los artículos de temporada no reciben un trato especial. Por lo general, todos los artículos comprendidos en la canasta se obtienen durante todo el año.

Cálculo
El índice se calcula según la fórmula de Laspeyres como un promedio aritmético ponderado de base fija, cuyos coeficientes de ponderación corresponden al período de base.

El índice es el resultado de una combinación de los índices provinciales; los índices provinciales se combinan en primer término para obtener los índices regionales cuya combinación permite a su vez obtener el índice de las Filipinas. Todos esos índices son ponderados.

Informaciones complementarias
Se publican índices por grupos principales y por diferentes regiones del país y abarcan el mes en curso y el precedente.

Organización y publicación
National Statistics Office: "Monthly Statistical Bulletin" (Manila).
"Quarterly Journal of Philippine Statistics"
"Philippine Yearbook"

FINLANDIA

Denominación oficial
Consumer Price Index (Indice de Precios del Consumo).

Alcance
El índice se compila mensualmente y abarca el conjunto de hogares privados y grupos de población de todo el país.

Base oficial
1985 = 100.

Fuente de la ponderación
La determinación de los coeficientes de ponderación y la selección de los artículos se basaron en una encuesta sobre los gastos de los hogares en 1985. La encuesta comprendió el conjunto de hogares privados y grupos de población de todo el país. La encuesta duró un año y abarcó 11 800 personas de los hogares investigados seleccionadas mediante un muestreo de 25 estratos geográficos. Como 8 200 hogares dieron informaciones plenamente satisfactorias; la tasa global de respuesta fue de un 69,5 por ciento. El mayor porcentaje de no respuesta correspondió a los hogares de una sola persona y a los de grandes ciudades. Se utilizaron otras fuentes para obtener datos sobre el consumo de ciertas mercancías, en especial: bebidas alcohólicas, tabaco, dulces, loterías y bebidas no alcohólicas. La selección de los artículos se fundó principalmente en su importancia, carácter representativo, disponibilidad y difusión. El coeficiente de ponderación atribuido a un artículo no siempre refleja su contribución relativa al consumo de ese artículo sino el valor de consumo combinado de varios otros artículos cuyos precios no se registran pero cuya naturaleza y movimiento de precios son similares.

Ponderaciones y composición

Grupos principales	Número de artículos	Ponderación	Número aproximado de cotizaciones de precio
Alimentación	111	19	...
Bebidas y tabaco	7	7	...
Vestido y calzado	51	6	...
Vivienda, combustible y luz	9	19	...
Muebles, moblaje, equipo y servicios del hogar	70	7	...
Salud y cuidados médicos	10	3	...
Transporte y comunicaciones	34	17	...
Pasatiempos, recreación y cultura	57	9	...
Otros bienes y servicios	54	13	...
Total	403	100	(a) 38 000

Nota: (a) El total de las cotizaciones de precio no comprende el número de cotizaciones utilizadas para medir los elementos del artículo vivienda.

Gastos de consumo de los hogares
Salvo unas pocas excepciones, el concepto de gastos de consumo seguido para los coeficientes de ponderación fue prácticamente el de la encuesta: como en ésta los gastos de consumo de los hogares sólo comprenden las compras, es decir que en las ponderaciones del IPC no se incluye el valor de la producción propia, como ciertos productos de la huerta doméstica o la recolección de bayas y setas, etc.

Como por lo general los gastos de consumo se registran siguiendo el criterio de adquisición en el momento, las compras efectuadas mediante sistemas de alquiler con opción de compra, a plazos o a crédito (aún la compra a crédito de bienes durables) se incluyen entre los gastos de consumo antes del pago, es decir en el momento de su adquisición. Se incluyen como gastos de consumo el valor de los bienes y servicios, así como los regalos que se reciben. Se excluyen los regalos y la asistencia dada a otros hogares, en efectivo o en especie, los diarios y otras publicaciones periódicas, los bienes durables de consumo, los viajes, los pagos de asignaciones de subsistencia y el resarcimiento de daños pagados directamente a los hogares. Se incluyen entre los gastos de consumo los bienes y servicios recibidos en especie (en virtud del contrato de empleo o renta vitalicia o a título de asistencia) y el valor de los regalos recibidos (por ejemplo, una vivienda, un vehículo automóvil, comidas). Los gastos reembolsables en virtud de la legislación sobre el seguro de enfermedad, tales como viajes, medicamentos y servicios de asistencia médica, así como los gastos de lotería, se registran por su monto neto, es decir luego de deducir los reembolsos recibidos y los premios ganados. Para ciertas mercancías, como electrodomésticos y equipos de transporte, el valor de los ingresos correspondientes a la venta de bienes usados se deduce del precio de compra de los nuevos. Se consideran como de consumo ciertos gastos similares a las transferencias al contado por el carácter voluntario de los pagos. Tales gastos comprenden las tasas y multas obligatorias de las autoridades públicas, las cuotas a instituciones benévolas (como iglesias, partidos políticos y sindicatos), las indemnizaciones de las compañías de seguros y los intereses de los créditos de consumo (por ejemplo, primas de seguros de vida y accidente, primas de seguros de viaje, transporte de cosas o responsabilidad civil, tasas de permisos o registros, pasaportes y visados, multas y otras contribuciones obligatorias análogas, cuotas a organizaciones del mercado de trabajo, diezmos eclesiásticos, ofrendas, limosnas y contribuciones similares, intereses de los préstamos de estudio y de consumo). Las compras de bienes usados se incluyen entre los gastos de consumo de la misma forma que las demás compras. Además de las contribuciones a fondos de pensión o de seguridad social, se excluyen los impuestos a los ingresos y otras cargas fiscales directas. Se registra el monto neto de los seguros de automóviles (tanto el obligatorio por daños a terceros, como de vehículos). Los gastos de consumo del IPC no comprenden los cambios de divisas ni los alquileres ficticios de la vivienda propia. Se incluyen como gastos de consumo los seguros relacionados con bienes de consumo específicos. De los gastos de la vivienda propia, se consideran como consumo la depreciación causada por el envejecimiento o el uso, el mantenimiento y otros gastos fijos.

Método de recolección de los datos

Las localidades se seleccionaron mediante una muestra aleatoria estratificada (por regiones). Cuando se revisó la base del IPC (1985 = 100), no se hizo lo mismo con las muestras y, en consecuencia, tanto los datos sobre las localidades como sobre los de puntos de venta tienen como base el año 1983.

La recolección de datos regionales se concentra en los centros de mayor población (zonas urbanas) de las cuatro regiones principales de Finlandia. El número de localidades de cada región se determinó por la importancia de su población, los ingresos conocidos de la misma y el total de los gastos de consumo de la región, así como por la adecuación del número de datos de precio para poder computar un índice regional fiable.

Como centros regionales se seleccionaron 17 localidades, en las cuales los encuestadores, en consulta con el personal del IPC, seleccionaron los puntos de venta, incluyéndose los más grandes y populares, prestando especial atención a la ubicación regional de los comercios pertenecientes a cadenas de venta al por menor y al grado de representatividad de las diversas tiendas de especialidades. Los puntos de venta seleccionados fueron unos 1 400.

Los precios de los artículos del IPC se obtienen principalmente mediante entrevistas personales, pero para una porción reducida de alimentos y otros productos perecederos los datos se obtienen de la lista de precios del punto de venta investigado.

Para los alimentos y otros productos perecederos, el ajuar, los productos de limpieza, lavado y otros artículos domésticos, los precios se registran todos los meses; los de bienes de consumo durables y ciertas vestimentas cada dos meses o según la estación para otras clases de prendas de vestir, frutas, legumbres y bayas y trimestralmente, o cuando sea necesario, las tarifas de los servicios y los precios de otros artículos.

Los precios se registran entre el 11 y el 17 de cada mes. Los investigadores tienen instrucciones de registrar los precios al azar dentro del período asignado evitando de hacerlo siempre el mismo día de la semana, por ejemplo.

Los precios de: i) las tarifas de electricidad, agua y gas se obtienen de las dependencias municipales encargadas de esos servicios; ii) la asistencia médica, de las autoridades públicas de salud; iii) la educación y la formación, de las universidades y la prensa; iv) transportes y comunicaciones los obtiene centralmente la Oficina Central de Estadísticas por teléfono o consultando listas de precios, tarifas oficiales y folletos, o por visitas a las empresas en cuestión.

El principio rector es registrar los precios al por menor y toda rebaja normal que se ofrezca a todo el público.

Los precios de liquidaciones normales se toman en consideración pero no los descuentos por pago al contado, opciones de compra ni ventas a plazo.

Sólo se registran los precios de los productos nuevos (se estima el precio neto de las compras de bienes de segunda mano cuando se determinan los coeficientes de ponderación).

Vivienda

Para las viviendas alquiladas, los movimientos de las cotizaciones de alquiler se miden por el movimiento de los alquileres realmente pagados. La Oficina Central de Estadísticas realiza cuatro veces al año un encuesta de alquileres que, en un año, abarca unas 24 000 viviendas alquiladas. Las informaciones sobre los alquileres se obtienen mediante cuestionarios enviados por correo a los inquilinos.

El movimiento del precio de las viviendas que ocupan sus propietarios se mide por los movimientos de precio de los componentes del artículo vivienda tales como el mantenimiento, los intereses y la depreciación.

Para la vivienda propia, el mantenimiento comprende los gastos de reparación, limpieza de chimeneas, eliminación de residuos, alquiler del terreno, primas de seguros, tasas de agua y vialidad. Los intereses de préstamos para la vivienda, sean convencionales u oficiales (con tipos de interés más bajos), se miden por el movimiento de los tipos de interés nominal. El índice de precios para apartamentos propios que no sean nuevos, de la Oficina Central de Estadísticas, permite medir el movimiento de precios correspondiente a la depreciación.

Los costes de mantenimiento del apartamento propio se miden por el movimiento de las cargas de mantenimiento y el coste de las reparaciones. Los gastos ocasionados por los intereses y las deducciones por causa de depreciación se miden de la misma forma que para la vivienda propia. Los coeficientes de ponderación de los distintos gastos de los propietarios de su vivienda provienen de una encuesta de hogares realizada por la Oficina Central de Estadísticas en 1985.

Especificación de las variedades

La preparación de especificaciones detalladas de los artículos cuyos precios se deben registrar exigió consultar a varios organismos con experiencia (asociaciones, organizaciones, comercios, distribuidores, importadores, fabricantes y empresas) y al personal del IPC con competencia técnica para asesorar en las diversas materias de interés. También se consultaron comparaciones internacionales de precios (OCDE). Para todos los artículos del IPC se prepararon especificaciones de calidad detalladas. Las especificaciones de los artículos (productos) establecen los requisitos que deben satisfacer. En muchos casos el investigador puede elegir libremente el artículo cuyo precio registrará en definitiva, siempre que la selección se haga de conformidad con el conjunto de las directrices establecidas. Las especificaciones de los artículos incluyen:

- especificaciones detalladas de la calidad del producto
- tamaño u orden de tamaño del producto
- composición, materiales, etc. del producto
- para algunos artículos, una lista de marcas aceptadas para la recolección de precios
- para algunos artículos, instrucciones relativas al tipo de envasado.

En algunas especificaciones la recolección de precios se ha limitado a una sola marca, producto o servicio (principalmente servicios, coches, repuestos de coches).

Sustitución, cambio de calidad, etc.

Cuando se modifica la calidad de un producto se elimina sistemáticamente toda modificación de precio que se deba exclusivamente a un cambio de calidad. Los cambios de calidad obedecen por lo general a diferencias de materiales, tamaño, terminado, duración, potencia, etc., entre el producto nuevo y el anterior. Para evaluar los cambios de calidad siempre se comienza por el servicio que representa para los consumidores el nuevo producto con respecto al antiguo. Por lo tanto, desde este punto de vista del consumidor, las modificaciones de los costes de producción no indican necesariamente un cambio de calidad.

Los bienes de consumo diario sólo son objeto de unos poco ajustes por cambios de calidad pues sus precios se registran por unidades de medida, tales como gramos o litros, y no por artículo. La Oficina Central de Estadísticas se encarga de todos los ajustes por cambio de calidad de dichas mercancías.

Con respecto a prendas de vestir, electrodomésticos, aparatos electrónicos del hogar y otras mercancías cuyos precios registra un centro regional, la primera evaluación de un cambio de calidad está a cargo del entrevistador estadístico, que consulta con el vendedor las diferencias de calidad entre la mercancía anterior y la nueva. La decisión final corresponde a la Oficina Central de Estadísticas, que asegura así un tratamiento uniforme de todos los cambios de calidad del país.

Artículos estacionales

Se excluyen del IPC las mercancías que sólo se ofrecen a la venta una parte del año. Los productos tradicionales estacionales son las patatas y las bayas frescas. Comparables a estas mercancías son las prendas de vestir, equipos de deportes, etc., que se usan exclusivamente en invierno o en verano. Los datos sobre los precios de mercancías que varían según la temporada se registran durante el período en que se venden. En los demás meses se mantienen los últimos precios de temporada hasta que se vuelvan a registrar de nuevo. Algunos productos (como las legumbres frescas) se venden a precios excepcionales cuando se introducen por primera vez en el mercado o cuando se retiran de él. No se registran los precios en estas circumstances. El caso de los pepinos de uso doméstico es ejemplar: sus precios no se incluyen en el registro del mes de marzo. Las mercancías con variaciones estacionales de precio, al igual que todas las demás, tienen el mismo coeficiente de ponderación durante todo el año.

Cálculo
El índice se calcula según la fórmula de Laspeyres como un promedio aritmético ponderado de base fija, cuyos coeficientes de ponderación corresponden al período de base.

Los relativos de precio de cada artículo se calculan dividiendo el precio corriente por el precio de base.

Los relativos de precio de una mercancía por región principal se calculan como promedio (media aritmética) de los precios relativos de los productos cuyos precios se han registrado en la región. En los cálculos de nivel nacional se ponderan los relativos de precio de las regiones principales por los coeficientes respectivos (contribuciones relativas a los gastos de consumo final) de cada región principal.

El IPC se computa ponderando los índices de las regiones principales por las contribuciones relativas de las regiones principales respectivas al gasto de consumo final. Dentro de cada región principal el índice se computa ponderando los relativos de precio de las mercancías por sus contribuciones relativas al gasto de consumo final de la región.

Cuando falta un dato se considera vigente el obtenido en el anterior período de investigación. Cuando no se ha registrado ningún dato para un determinado producto, se le excluye del índice pues dicho producto no tiene en él ninguna influencia. Los datos erróneos se tratan de corregir mediante entrevistas de los investigadores o, cuando no es posible, manteniendo el último dato obtenido que se estima correcto.

Informaciones complementarias
El IPC se publica mensualmente a nivel de grupo principal. El índice general también se facilita según los grupos sociales siguientes: campesinos por cuenta propia; todos los asalariados (personal de dirección y niveles superiores, otras categorías de empleados, obreros); jubilados; para las principales regiones metropolitanas: región metropolitana de Helsinki; resto de la región meridional de Finlandia; Finlandia central; Finlandia meridional; y para: hogares unipersonales; hogares de una pareja sin hijos; hogares de familias con hijos. También se calcula un Indice de Precios Netos y un Indice de Tasas de Imposición Fiscal.

Organización y publicación
Central Statistical Office of Finland: "Bulletin of Statistics" (Helsinki).

idem: "Consumer Price Index 1985 = 100", Studies No. 144, 1988.

FRANCIA

Denominación oficial
Indice des prix à la consommation des ménages urbains dont le chef est ouvrier ou employé (Indice de precios del consumo para hogares urbanos cuyo cabeza de familia sea obrero o empleado).

Alcance
El índice se compila mensualmente y abarca hogares urbanos de todo tamaño cuyo cabeza de familia sea obrero o empleado.

Base oficial
1980 = 100.

Fuente de la ponderación
Los coeficientes de ponderación se revisan al comienzo de cada año civil con base en los resultados de encuestas familiares de carácter continuo realizadas en 10 000 hogares y los datos extraídos de las cuentas de los hogares obtenidos del sistema de cuentas nacionales; los coeficientes de ponderación utilizados para calcular los índices de un año dado se basan en los resultados de encuestas efectuadas dos años antes y actualizadas en función de la evolución relativa de los precios hasta diciembre del año precedente. El número de artículos y los coeficientes de ponderación utilizados en 1992 figuran en el cuadro abajo.

Gastos de consumo de los hogares
Están excluidos del índice los bienes y servicios producidos en el hogar, las compras de segunda mano, los servicios hospitalarios, las cotizaciones a la seguridad social, las primas de

Ponderaciones y composición

Grupos principales	Número de artículos	Ponderación	Número aproximado de cotizaciones de precio
Alimentación	91	22,67	...
Vestido, calzado y ropa blanca	59	8,36	...
Moblaje, artículos para el hogar, productos de limpieza, tabaco, etc	82	25,64	...
Combustible y luz	7	8,18	...
Vivienda:			
Alquiler	1	7,74	...
Agua	1	0,76	...
Reparaciones y conservación	3	1,22	...
Aseo personal y asistencia médica	12	6,14	...
Transportes públicos y mantenimiento de vehículos	8	6,81	...
Otros servicios (incl. restaurantes, etc.)	32	12,48	...
Total	296	100,00	180 000

seguros, los automóviles de ocasión, los transportes marítimos y aéreos, el alquiler de coches sin chófer, los servicios de veterinaria, los bienes y servicios funerarios y los servicios domésticos, pero se incluyen en el índice los impuestos indirectos (TVA).

Método de recolección de los datos
Los precios son recogidos por agentes en 30 000 puntos de venta al por menor y establecimientos de servicios de 108 centros urbanos de más de 2 000 habitantes, mensualmente para la mayoría de los bienes y servicios, trimestralmente para los vestidos y los artículos destinados al hogar y dos veces al mes para los productos frescos. No se toman en consideración los organismos de venta por correspondencia. Los precios registrados son los que efectivamente pagan los consumidores.

Vivienda
Los datos referentes al alquiler se obtienen por una encuesta especial de hogares de inquilinos durante el primer mes de cada trimestre de todo tipo de viviendas. Están excluidas del índice las viviendas ocupadas por su propietario.

Especificación de las variedades
Las especificaciones son detalladas. Los agentes eligen en cada punto de venta al por menor los productos específicos para la recolección regular de sus precios.

Sustitución, cambio de calidad, etc.
Cuando cambia la calidad de un artículo, o bien se sustituye éste por otro similar suponiendo que no hay variación en el precio, o bien se mide el cambio de calidad y se separa del cambio de precio. Los artículos nuevos no se toman en consideración mientras sus ventas no alcancen un volumen importante.

Artículos estacionales
Se tienen en cuenta las fluctuaciones estacionales de los precios de los productos frescos variando los artículos y las ponderaciones de los mismos dentro de "canastas" mensuales con ponderaciones de grupo constantes y utilizando un promedio móvil a lo largo de doce meses.

Cálculo
El índice es un índice-cadena cuyos coeficientes de ponderación se revisan al comienzo de cada año civil. El índice mensual se calcula primero con base de diciembre del año precedente igual a 100. Los índices así obtenidos se encadenan entonces con base 1980 = 100 (índice-cadena de Laspeyres).

Informaciones complementarias
Se publican subgrupos detallados y agrupaciones diversas, así como estimaciones de índices de los precios del consumo para las diversas categorías socioprofesionales de los cabezas de familia (con base 1970 = 100) y una serie que abarca sólo la aglomeración de París.

Organización y publicación
Institut national de la statistique et des études économiques: "Bulletin mensuel de statistique" (París).

idem: "Informations rapides".

idem: "Pour comprendre l'indice des prix".

GABON (LIBREVILLE 1)

Denominación oficial
Indice des prix à la consommation - Africains (Indice de precios del consumo - Africanos).

Alcance
El índice se compila mensualmente y abarca las familias africanas de Libreville cuyo jefe de familia es un obrero o empleado del sector público o privado, incluyendo el servicio doméstico.

Base oficial
Junio de 1975 = 100.

Fuente de la ponderación
La selección de los artículos y la determinación de los coeficientes de ponderación se basaron en los resultados de una encuesta sobre los gastos de los hogares efectuada en 1968-69 en Libreville y que abarcó a 9 942 familias africanas cuyo jefe era obrero o empleado (sector público o privado, incluidos los servicios domésticos).

Ponderaciones y composición

Grupos principales	Número de artículos	Ponderación	Número aproximado de cotizaciones de precio
Alimentación	57	547	...
Vestido y calzado	9	175	...
Vivienda:			
Alquiler y materiales de construcción	4	23	...
Combustible, luz, agua y jabón	8	14	...
Accesorios para el hogar	16	93	...
Aseo personal y asistencia médica	10	19	...
Transportes	9	63	...
Distracciones y varios	12	66	...
Total	125	1 000	...

Gastos de consumo de los hogares
A los fines del índice, los gastos de consumo comprenden todos los bienes y servicios adquiridos para el consumo por la población cubierta por el índice. Comprende los impuestos a la renta de las personas físicas, los regalos y las obras de caridad, los préstamos y reembolsos, la adquisición de casas y las dotes.

Método de recolección de los datos
Los precios son recogidos por investigadores durante la segunda mitad de cada mes, en mercados seleccionados y otros puntos comerciales de venta.
Los precios utilizados en el índice son los precios al por menor que pagan en el momento los consumidores.

Vivienda
No disponible.

Especificación de las variedades
En la especificación de los artículos se establece la marca, factura, calidad y unidad.

Sustitución, cambio de calidad, etc.
No disponible.

Artículos estacionales
Las fluctuaciones de precios estacionales no se toman en consideración en el índice.

Cálculo
El índice se calcula conforme a la fórmula de Laspeyres como un promedio aritmético ponderado de base fija, cuyos coeficientes de ponderación corresponden al período 1968-69.

Organización y publicación
Présidence de la République, Direction générale de la statistique et des études économiques: "Bulletin mensuel de statistique" (Libreville).
Para más amplios detalles metodológicos, véase:
idem: "Changement de base de l'indice des prix à la consommation des ménages type africain résidant à Libreville".

GABON (LIBREVILLE 2)

Denominación oficial
Indice des prix à la consommation - Familles à revenu élevé (Indice de precios de consumo - Familias de ingresos elevados).

Alcance
El índice se compila mensualmente y abarca hogares africanos cuyos ingresos mensuales eran superiores a 100 000 francos CFA y a los hogares no africanos del sector público y privado con ingresos mensuales inferiores a 100 000 CFA en marzo y mayo de 1969. El índice se refiere a la ciudad de Libreville.

Base oficial
Junio de 1972 = 100.

Fuente de la ponderación
La selección de los artículos y la determinación de los coeficientes de ponderación se basaron en los resultados de una encuesta sobre los gastos de los hogares efectuada entre marzo y mayo de 1969 en Libreville, que abarcó una muestra de 156 hogares de ingresos elevados. La muestra se compuso de 20 hogares africanos con un ingreso mensual del jefe del hogar superior a 100 000 francos CFA en el momento de la encuesta, de 59 hogares no africanos del sector público y de 77 hogares no africanos del sector privado con un ingreso mensual inferior a 100 000 francos CFA.

Ponderaciones y composición

Grupos principales	Número de artículos	Ponderación	Número aproximado de cotizaciones de precio
Alimentación	84	511	...
Gastos del hogar:			
Electricidad, gas y agua	3	56	...
Servicio doméstico	3	65	...
Productos de limpieza	7	21	...
Accesorios para el hogar y ropa blanca	10	32	...
Vestido y calzado	8	34	...
Higiene y salud	10	35	...
Transportes y comunicaciones	10	123	...
Varios	20	123	...
Total	155	1 000	...

Gastos de consumo de los hogares
A los fines del índice, los gastos del consumo comprenden todos los bienes y servicios adquiridos para el consumo por la población cubierta por el índice. Se excluyen los impuestos a las rentas de las personas físicas, los regalos y las obras de caridad, los préstamos y reembolsos, la adquisición de casas y los alquileres.

Método de recolección de los datos
Los precios para la mayor parte de los artículos son recogidos por investigadores en fechas próximas al 25 de cada mes, en los principales puestos de venta al por menor, en un mercado y en establecimientos de servicios de Libreville. Los precios de los artículos alimenticios frescos se determinan semanalmente.
Los precios utilizados en el índice son los precios al por menor pagados en el momento.

Vivienda
En el índice no se incluye el alquiler.

Especificación de las variedades
Las especificaciones se dan en términos de marca, factura, calidad y unidad.

Sustitución, cambio de calidad, etc.
No disponible.

Artículos estacionales
En el índice no se toman en consideración las fluctuaciones estacionales de los precios.

Cálculo
El índice se calcula conforme a la fórmula de Laspeyres como un promedio aritmético ponderado de base fija, cuyos coeficientes de ponderación corresponden al período de marzo a mayo de 1969.

Organización y publicación
Présidence de la République, Direction générale de la

statistique et des études économiques: "Bulletin mensuel de statistique" (Libreville).

Para más amplios detalles metodológicos, véase:

Ministère délégué à la Présidence de la République chargé du plan, du développement et de l'aménagement du territoire, Direction de la statistique et des études économiques: "Bulletin mensuel de statistique" (Libreville) núm. 166-167, enero - febrero de 1973.

GAMBIA (BANJUL, KOMBO ST. MARY)

Denominación oficial
Consumer Price Index (Indice de Precios del Consumo).

Alcance
El índice se compila mensualmente y abarca los hogares de ingresos bajos, es decir que no superaban 1 500 dalasis por año entre agosto de 1968 y agosto de 1969. El índice se refiere a la capital, Banjul, y a Kombo St. Mary.

Base oficial
1974 = 100.

Fuente de la ponderación
La determinación de los coeficientes de ponderación y la selección de los artículos se basaron en los resultados de una encuesta sobre los gastos de los hogares realizada de agosto de 1968 a agosto de 1969. La encuesta abarcó 618 hogares de Banjul. En los coeficientes de ponderación no se tomaron en cuenta las modificaciones de precio ocurridas entre la encuesta y el período de base. Se seleccionaron los artículos de la canasta del índice que representaban el 0,5 por ciento o más del total de los gastos de la "canasta del mercado".

Ponderaciones y composición

Grupos principales	Número de artículos	Ponderación	Número aproximado de cotizaciones de precio
Alimentación	52	580	...
Vestido, calzado y lencería	12	175	...
Alquiler	42	51	...
Combustible y luz	5	54	...
Varios (incl. asistencia médica y aseo personal, educación, recreación, tabaco, etc.)	24	140	...
Total	135	1 000	...

Gastos de consumo de los hogares
A los efectos del índice, se consideran todos los bienes y servicios adquiridos para el consumo por la población de referencia. Se excluyen los impuestos a los ingresos; regalos y limosnas; ceremonias religiosas o no, tales como nacimientos, funerales y bodas; préstamos; adquisición y mantenimiento de vehículos automóviles para uso comercial; seguros de vida, créditos y ahorros.

Método de recolección de los datos
La recolección está a cargo de personal permanente de la División Central de Estadísticas, que registra los precios en cuatro zonas de mercado, 48 puntos de venta al por menor y establecimientos de servicio de Banjul y Kombo St. Mary.

Para la mayoría de los artículos la recolección de precios es mensual, pero si tienen grandes fluctuaciones el registro se efectúa cada 15 días mediante compra directa. Para artículos tales como la electricidad, asistencia médica, peluquería, matrículas escolares, cines, bailes, periódicos, taxis, correo aéreo al extranjero, y lavandería, la recolección es mensual. Los precios utilizados en el índice son los que se pagan en el momento.

Vivienda
Los datos sobre los alquileres se obtienen de 42 viviendas alquiladas en febrero, mayo, agosto y noviembre. La muestra se mantiene fija, salvo ajustes ocasionales.

Especificación de las variedades
Los investigadores cuentan con una descripción detallada de cada mercancía cuyos precios deben registrar.

Sustitución, cambio de calidad, etc.
Cuando cesa la oferta de un producto en el mercado se le sustituye por otro similar y se aplica el método de enlace.

Artículos estacionales
Las frutas y legumbres frescas se consideran artículos estacionales. Fuera de temporada las ponderaciones de estos artículos se asignan a los restantes del mismo grupo.

Cálculo
El índice se calcula según la fórmula de Laspeyres como un promedio aritmético ponderado de base fija, cuyos coeficientes de ponderación corresponden al período de agosto 1968 a agosto 1969.

Para calcular los índices de artículo se utilizan los relativos de precio del período en curso y del período de base.

Informaciones complementarias
No disponible.

Organización y publicación
Ministry of Economic Planning and Industrial Development, Central Statistics Division: "Consumer Price Index" (Banjul).

President's Office, Central Statistics Division: "Proposals for a new serie of Consumer Price Index Numbers for Banjul and Kombo St. Mary" (Banjul, nov. de 1973).

GHANA

Denominación oficial
Consumer Price Index Numbers (National).
(Indice de precios del consumo (Nacional).

Alcance
El índice se compila mensualmente y abarca hogares urbanos y rurales.

Base oficial
1977 = 100.

Fuente de la ponderación
La selección de los artículos y la determinación de los coeficientes de ponderación se basaron en los resultados de una encuesta nacional sobre los gastos de los hogares efectuada durante el período entre marzo de 1974 y febrero de 1975. A efectos de la ponderación, los gastos en artículos no incluidos en el índice, se han atribuído a los artículos seleccionados tomando en consideración la similitud entre los artículos. Por ejemplo, el gasto total en verduras se atribuye a las verduras seleccionadas. Algunos gastos se han dividido en dos o más partes para adjudicarlas a artículos diferentes. Por ejemplo, los gastos en comidas preparadas se han dividido y distribuído según el número de componentes principales de dicha comida.

Ponderaciones y composición

Grupos principales	Número de artículos	Ponderación	Número aproximado de cotizaciones de precio
Alimentación	71	49,2	...
Bebidas y tabaco	21	6,2	...
Vestido y calzado	65	19,2	...
Alquiler, combustible y luz	6	6,8	...
Moblaje, muebles, equipo y gastos de funcionamiento del hogar	48	5,1	...
Asistencia médica	8	1,8	...
Transportes y comunicaciones	15	4,3	...
Educación y distracciones	10	5,5	...
Varios	6	1,9	...
Total	250	100,0	...

Gastos de consumo de los hogares
A los fines del índice, los gastos del consumo comprenden todos los bienes y servicios importantes adquiridos para el consumo por la población del índice. Se excluyen el valor de los artículos de consumo de los hogares producidos por ellos mismos, los pagos de intereses, licencias, etc.

Método de recolección de los datos
Los precios se obtienen de tiendas al por menor y mercados seleccionados de nueve centros urbanos y 30 rurales. Los precios se registran dos veces por mes, lo más próximo posible a los días 8 y 22. Los precios del índice son los que cualquier persona del público tendría que pagar el día del registro de precios, para adquirir el artículo o el servicio determinado. Se

informan y utilizan los precios controlados de los artículos, siempre que se los pueda conseguir en los puntos de venta seleccionados. Los investigadores disponen de escalas de conversión de medidas que les permiten expresar en unidades corrientes las cantidades vendidas por medidas tradicionales o montones.

Vivienda
Los datos referentes al alquiler se obtienen a partir de una muestra aleatoria de 300 hogares elegidos entre los que figuran en los registros municipales de tasación. Todos los meses se recogen los alquileres de un tercio de la muestra. Se abarca así, por rotación, a cada uno de los hogares de la muestra una vez cada tres meses. Todos los hogares que componen la muestra ocupan viviendas alquiladas. Se excluyen las viviendas ocupadas por sus propietarios y los alojamientos suministrados por los empleadores. También se recogen los datos relativos a la electricidad y al agua, si esas cargas no están incluidas en el alquiler.

Especificación de las variedades
Para algunos artículos se selecciona más de una variedad, según sea la importancia del artículo en cuestión. La especificación de cada artículo se da en función de su tamaño, unidad y, en algunos casos, marca de fábrica.

Sustitución, cambio de calidad, etc.
No disponible.

Artículos estacionales
No disponible.

Cálculo
El índice se calcula conforme a la fórmula de Laspeyres como un promedio aritmético ponderado de base fija, cuyos coeficientes de ponderación corresponden al período de marzo de 1974 a febrero de 1975. Los precios medios de las variedades son promedios aritméticos simples de todos los precios recogidos. Después, la relación del precio para cada variedad de un artículo es calculada dividiendo el precio medio del período corriente por el precio medio del período de base. Si dos o más variedades están seleccionadas para un artículo, un promedio aritmético simple de las relaciones de precios de las variedades representan la relación del precio del artículo.
Primero, se calculan índices rurales y urbanos separados para cada área del país son primeramente calculados. Después, estos índices son combinados para obtener índices nacionales urbanos o rurales. El índice nacional es el promedio ponderado de estos índices, las ponderaciones utilizadas son los gastos del consumo de los hogares urbanos y rurales.

Informaciones complementarias
La Oficina Central de Estadísticas calcula y publica índices separados de los precios del consumo para el área urbana de Accra, las zonas urbanas y las regiones rurales.

Organización y publicación
Central Bureau of Statistics: "Quarterly Digest of Statistics" (Accra).
Para más amplios detalles metodológicos, véase:
idem: "Consumer Price Index Numbers". A new series (Accra, octubre de 1978).

GIBRALTAR

Denominación oficial
Index of Retail Prices (Indice de precios al por menor).

Alcance
El índice se compila mensualmente para el grupo de los alimentos y trimestralmente para los demás. El índice se refiere a todos los tipos de hogares de residentes permanentes en Gibraltar.

Base oficial
Octubre de 1980 = 100.

Fuente de la ponderación
La selección de los artículos y la determinación de los coeficientes de ponderación se basaron en los resultados de una encuesta sobre los gastos de los hogares efectuada entre febrero de 1979 y marzo de 1980. La encuesta abarcó unos 221 hogares.

Gastos de consumo de los hogares
A los fines del índice, los gastos del consumo comprenden casi

Ponderaciones y composición

Grupos principales	Número de artículos	Ponderación	Número aproximado de cotizaciones de precio
Alimentación	104	330,67	...
Bebidas y tabaco	9	59,56	...
Vestido y calzado	39	110,00	...
Artículos durables del hogar	26	100,42	...
Alquiler	12	125,90	...
Servicios	24	75,39	...
Transportes y vehículos	17	133,29	...
Varios	44	64,77	...
Total	294	1 000,00	...

todos los bienes y servicios importantes adquiridos para el consumo por la población de referencia. Se excluyen los impuestos a la renta de las personas físicas y otros impuestos directos, las contribuciones a la seguridad social, los ahorros y las inversiones, las contribuciones a fondos de pensión y las apuestas.

Método de recolección de los datos
Los precios son recogidos por agentes durante algunos de los días que preceden y siguen, en forma inmediata, al primero de cada mes. Los precios de los artículos alimenticios se recogen en 30 puntos de venta al por menor todos los meses.
La recolección de precios de los demás artículos es trimestral y se realiza en cinco puntos de venta diferentes, como máximo cinco para cada artículo.
Los precios que se utilizan para calcular el índice son los que debe pagar el consumidor en el momento.

Vivienda
Los gastos referentes al alquiler se obtienen en relación con viviendas pertenecientes al gobierno y de una muestra de cerca de 100 viviendas privadas.

Especificación de las variedades
Las especificaciones de los artículos que han de justipreciarse se dan en términos de tipo, factura, calidad, tamaño, etc.

Sustitución, cambio de calidad, etc.
Si en el índice se sustituye un artículo nuevo, su precio se recoge durante tres meses, calculándose un precio medio de base.

Artículos estacionales
Por lo general la temporada no afecta la posibilidad de conseguir artículos en Gibraltar.

Cálculo
El índice se calcula conforme a la fórmula de Laspeyres como un promedio aritmético ponderado de base fija, cuyos coeficientes de ponderación corresponden al período de base.
El índice para un artículo se obtiene utilizando las relaciones de precios del período corriente y del período de base.

Informaciones complementarias
No disponible.

Organización y publicación
El índice se compila por la Economic Planning and Statistics Office (Gibraltar).
Government Printer: "Gibraltar Gazette". (El índice para todos los artículos se publica trimestralmente y el del grupo de los alimentos, mensualmente).

GRANADA

Denominación oficial
Consumer Price Index (Indice de precios al consumo).

Alcance
El índice se compila mensualmente y abarca todos los hogares del país.

Base oficial
1987 = 100.

Fuente de la ponderación
La selección de los artículos y la determinación de los coeficientes de ponderación se basaron en una encuesta de 1987 sobre los gastos de una muestra aleatoria de 900 hogares de todo el país. Los coeficientes de ponderación de los artículos

no seleccionados, o bien se distribuyeron entre los artículos similares del mismo subgrupo o bien se agruparon todos en una única categoría distinta, representada por el artículo más importante de la categoría distinta.

Ponderaciones y composición

Grupos principales	Número de artículos	Ponderación	Número aproximado de cotizaciones de precio
Alimentación, Bebidas alcohólicas y tabaco:	149	...	569
Alimentación	...	38,7	...
Bebidas alcohólicas y tabaco	...	2,0	...
Vestido y calzado	72	5,2	72
Alquiler, gastos del hogar:	20	...	30
Alquiler	...	11,9	...
Gastos del hogar	...	5,4	...
Combustible y luz, muebles, moblaje y equipo del hogar:	62	...	169
Combustible y luz	...	3,9	...
Muebles, moblaje y equipo del hogar	...	8,3	...
Transporte	17	9,1	20
Asistencia médica y aseo personal	30	8,6	139
Educación, recreación y lectura	24	4,6	30
Artículos y servicios varios	10	2,3	10
Total	384	100,0	1 039

Gastos de consumo de los hogares
Comprenden los bienes de fabricación casera, regalos, seguros de vida y compras a crédito. Se excluyen los impuestos a la renta y otros impuestos directos, los intereses de los préstamos y las comisiones bancarias, los pagos por compras a plazo, las donaciones y las contribuciones eclesiásticas.

Método de recolección de los datos
Los precios de la carne, el pescado, las frutas y legumbres frescas se recogen todas las semanas, los viernes en St. Georges y los sábados en Grenville y Gouyave.

Los productos que se venden en supermercados, las prendas de vestir, los artículos del hogar, los combustibles, la luz y los artículos de aseo personal se obtienen todos los meses. Las cotizaciones de alquiler, seguros, gastos de viaje, medios de transporte, diversiones y otros artículos y servicios varios se determinan en forma trimestral.

Los precios de los artículos que se registran mensual o trimestralmente se recogen durante la última semana del mes en curso, siguiendo un orden establecido de antemano, y que comienza los lunes con los supermercados, farmacias, etc. De la recolección se encargan funcionarios del Departamento de Estadísticas, mediante visitas personales o, en algunos casos, llamadas telefónicas cuando, por ejemplo, deben determinarse honorarios médicos, tarifas eléctricas, etc. En los mercados de frutas y legumbres donde se vende por cantidades variables (como manojos, cucharadas o unidades) se utiliza una escala graduada de cocina para contar con una unidad de medida uniforme.

Los precios rebajados se utilizan si se mantienen, pero no si vuelven a su monto original al final del período de rebajas. No se toman en consideración las compras a plazo ni los descuentos. No se registra el precio de los artículos usados, pues no existe un mercado organizado de bienes de segunda mano. Los artículos de importación no reciben ningún tratamiento especial. Se consignan los precios que pagan los consumidores en los puntos de venta establecidos.

Vivienda
Las cotizaciones de alquiler se obtienen trimestralmente de una muestra de viviendas de dos y tres habitaciones. Estas cotizaciones también se utilizan para representar los gastos que, por este concepto, tienen los hogares que viven en casa propia. Los coeficientes de ponderación correspondientes a esta categoría se combinan con los de las viviendas alquiladas.

Especificación de las variedades
La investigación de los puntos de venta se incluyó en la encuesta sobre los gastos de los hogares mediante una pregunta sobre el lugar en que se hacían las compras.

El cuestionario contiene informaciones sobre la marca y la clase de cada uno de los artículos comprados, de los cuales se seleccionan los más populares para investigar sus precios en los puntos de venta elegidos. Mediante las visitas realizadas a los puntos de venta se obtuvieron especificaciones detalladas, incluyendo calidad, tamaño, país de origen y variedad de los artículos.

Sustitución, cambio de calidad, etc.
El cambio de calidad no se trata como aumento de precio, por el contrario se mantiene el último precio de las variedades "antiguas" durante tres meses sin alteración y luego se introduce el artículo con una nueva calidad.

Los productos nuevos se incluyen en la canasta cuando se realiza una encuesta, aproximadamente cada cinco años.

También cuando desaparece del mercado determinado tipo o calidad de artículo, se mantiene inalterado durante tres meses el último precio del artículo especificado y si éste no vuelve a aparecer en el cuarto mes, se introduce en el índice un artículo similar cuyo precio se haya recogido durante los últimos tres meses.

Artículos estacionales
Se consideran estacionales los artículos que no se ofrecen en el mercado por un mínimo de tres semanas al mes.

Cuando no se encuentra pescado fresco en el mercado, se utilizan las fluctuaciones de precio de la carne fresca.

Todos los artículos de los grupos de legumbres frescas y alimentos feculentos se consideran estacionales, salvo cebollas, patatas blancas, ajos, plátanos y llantén. Esta clase de artículos no se trata como el pescado fresco pues no suelen estar ausentes del mercado más de tres meses y por lo tanto se mantienen sin variaciones sus últimos precios registrados hasta que reaparezcan en el mercado.

Salvo los plátanos, se considera estacional toda la fruta fresca, que se trata de la misma manera que las legumbres frescas, con excepción de naranjas y pomelos. Como substitutivos de estos últimos se utilizan sus zumos concentrados.

Cálculo
El índice se calcula según la fórmula de Laspeyres, como un promedio aritmético ponderado con base fija, cuyos coeficientes de ponderación corresponden al período de base.

Para obtener el promedio de los precios se utiliza el método aritmético simple, resultando los precios relativos de la división del precio medio del período en curso por el precio medio del período precedente.

Informaciones complementarias
Se publican índices de subgrupos detallados.

Organización y publicación
Ministry of Finance; Statistical Department: "Annual Abstract of Statistics", (St. Georges).

Imprenta Nacional: Gaceta Oficial ("Government Gazette").

GRECIA

Denominación oficial
Consumer Price Index (Indice de precios del consumo).

Alcance
El índice se compila mensualmente y se refiere a los centros urbanos.

Base oficial
1982 = 100.

Fuente de la ponderación
La selección de los artículos y la determinación de los coeficientes de ponderación se basaron en los resultados de la encuesta sobre los gastos de los hogares efectuada en 1982 y que abarcó una muestra aleatoria de 3 725 hogares en los centros urbanos de 10 000 habitantes o más. Sin embargo, la encuesta también abarcaba las áreas semiurbanas y rurales. Los coeficientes de ponderación de los artículos no seleccionados se atribuyen a los artículos que los representan y que están incluidos en el registro de precios.

Gastos de consumo de los hogares
El gasto del consumo para compilar el índice se refiere a todos los gastos monetarios (al contado o a crédito) de los hogares en bienes y servicios destinados al consumo. Para la salud y la educación, únicamente se tienen en cuenta los gastos realmente pagados por los consumidores. Se excluyen los alquileres imputados, los impuestos directos y las contribuciones para fondos de seguros.

Método de recolección de los datos
Los precios son recogidos por investigadores en 1 016 puntos de venta al por menor y establecimientos de servicios en 17 ciudades que se consideran representativas de los cambios de

Ponderaciones y composición

Grupos principales	Número de artículos	Ponde-ración	Número aproximado de cotizaciones de precio
Alimentación	134	324,4	...
Bebidas alcohólicas y tabaco	8	36,5	...
Vestido y calzado	58	128,3	...
Vivienda (incl. combustible y luz)	11	130,6	...
Accesorios para el hogar	65	85,5	...
Aseo personal y asistencia médica	34	62,5	...
Educación y distracciones	37	87,4	...
Transportes y comunicaciones	26	130,0	...
Otros bienes y servicios	13	14,8	...
Total	386	1 000,0	...

precios de todas las zonas urbanas del país (5 ciudades para ciertos artículos de vestido y los bienes durables). Para los artículos cuyos precios son fijados por el Estado, los precios se obtienen de las facturas oficiales. La frecuencia de la recolección de los precios varía según la naturaleza de los artículos y, por ejemplo, los de las frutas frescas, verduras, carne, pescado, etc. se recogen una vez por semana. Los precios de los otros artículos se recogen mensualmente. Los precios semanales corresponden al martes y los precios mensuales se recogen de forma que se refieran a todo el mes (por ejemplo, el primer período de cinco días en el primer establecimiento, el segundo período de cinco días en el segundo establecimiento, etc.).

Generalmente, los precios utilizados en el índice son los "precios al contado" reales. Se toman en consideración los descuentos pero no los precios de "ofertas especiales". Cuando el precio de un determinado artículo discrepa del oficial, se tiene en cuenta este último.

Vivienda
Los datos referentes al alquiler de una muestra aleatoria de 600 viviendas se obtienen dos veces al año. Se toman en consideración los alquileres mensuales realmente pagados. El índice de alquiler se obtiene del gasto total de alquiler del mes en curso comparado con el correspondiente gasto medio mensual del año fijado como base. No se tiene en cuenta el alquiler atribuido a las viviendas ocupadas por sus propietarios.

Especificación de las variedades
Las especificaciones de los artículos se consiguieron por medio de una investigación del mercado. Para cada artículo del índice, se facilita una especificación detallada (por ejemplo, características técnicas, fabricación, marca, peso, calidad, variedad, etc.).

Sustitución, cambio de calidad, etc.
Cuando ya no se dispone de un determinado producto para poder fijar su precio, se substituye por un producto similar. Los cambios de calidad en los productos antiguos y nuevos se tienen en cuenta utilizando un precio de base ficticio para el nuevo producto.

Artículos estacionales
Se tienen en cuenta las fluctuaciones estacionales de los precios de las frutas y verduras frescas variando los coeficientes de ponderación de los artículos comprendidos en una "canasta" mensual cuyo coeficiente de ponderación global permanece constante. Los otros artículos estacionales, tales como el vestido y el calzado de verano y de invierno, se tienen en cuenta manteniendo cuando están fuera de temporada los precios finales de la estación anterior.

Cálculo
El índice se calcula según la fórmula de Laspeyres, como un promedio aritmético ponderado de base fija, cuyos coeficientes de ponderación corresponden al período de base.

Las relaciones de precios para cada variedad en cada almacen son primeramente calculadas dividiendo el precio medio del período corriente por el precio medio del período de base. Después, promedios aritméticos simples de estas relaciones de precios son calculadas para cada ciudad. Estas son ponderadas según la importancia de las ciudades para obtener relaciones de precios de las variedades para el conjunto del país. Se calculan promedios aritméticos simples de estas relaciones de precios, para obtener los índices por artículo para el conjunto del país.

Informaciones complementarias
Se publican mensualmente un índice general y nueve índices de grupos.

Actualmente se calcula una nueva serie (base 1988 = 100), pero en el momento de publicar el presente Volumen la OIT no disponía de informaciones metodológicas sobre esta serie.

Organización y publicación
National Statistical Service of Greece: "Monthly Statistical Bulletin" (Atenas).

idem: "Statistical Yearbook of Greece".

GROENLANDIA

Denominación oficial
Consumer Price Index for Greenland (Indice de precios al consumo en Groenlandia).

Alcance
La compilación del índice es bianual y abarca todos los hogares que residen en ciudades y asentamientos de Groenlandia.

Base oficial
Enero de 1981 = 100.

Fuente de la ponderación
Los coeficientes de ponderación se basaron en las estadísticas de gastos en bienes y servicios de los hogares del año 1985. Las fuentes fueron las estadísticas de importaciones, las ventas de la Compañía Comercial de Groenlandia y, para la producción y los servicios interiores, una muestra de 195 hogares privados investigados en 1985. Las ponderaciones de los alquileres se basaron en datos del Ministerio danés para Groenlandia y de la administración local, pues el 60 por ciento de las viviendas alquiladas son de propiedad pública, del dominio nacional de Groenlandia o de propiedad municipal. Para la vivienda propia se fija un alquiler ficticio equivalente. A efectos de su ponderación, los precios relacionados con la energía se obtienen de la Organización Técnica de Groenlandia. Se ajustaron las ponderaciones para tomar en cuenta las variaciones de precios ocurridas entre el año de la encuesta y enero de 1987, fecha en que se aplicaron por primera vez los nuevos coeficientes de ponderación.

Se ajustó la muestra de artículos con precio determinado en función de las modificaciones ocurridas desde la última revisión (1977-78).

Ponderaciones y composición

Grupos principales	Número de artículos	Ponde-ración	Número aproximado de cotizaciones de precio
Alimentación	139	18,62	1 129
Bebidas	20	11,44	84
Tabaco	7	7,13	30
Alquiler bruto (vivienda)	5	10,01	23
Combustible y luz	7	5,40	7
Vestido y calzado	50	7,69	332
Muebles, equipo del hogar, etc.	64	9,21	279
Asistencia médica	6	0,29	18
Transporte	11	4,86	32
Comunicaciones	4	3,28	11
Caza, pesca, etc.	16	2,99	56
Otros pasatiempos y recreaciones	32	12,47	110
Artículos y servicios varios	32	6,61	231
Total	393	100,00	(a) 2 342

Nota: (a) Excluída la encuesta de alquileres.

Gastos de consumo de los hogares
Se considera el consumo privado total de bienes y servicios de Groenlandia.

No se incluyen los ingresos en especie. Se excluyen los impuestos directos. No existen contribuciones de seguridad social ni cotizaciones a fondos de pensión. En las ponderaciones no se incluye la asistencia médica, que es totalmente pública y gratuita. Se incluyen las primas de seguros específicos, como los de incendio y coches. No se incluyen otros seguros, suscripciones y desembolsos similares. Abarcan alrededor del 1,7 por ciento del consumo total. Los propietarios de viviendas en Dinamarca reciben un coeficiente de ponderación adicional.

Método de recolección de los datos
Consiste principalmente en cuestionarios enviados por correo y

tarifas oficiales. Los precios de las mercancías se obtienen de la Compañía Comercial de Groenlandia (propiedad del dominio público de Groenlandia), de seis sociedades cooperativas y de unos 50 minoristas privados. Para los servicios de electricidad, agua, calefacción, etc., las tarifas públicas se obtienen de la Organización Técnica de Groenlandia y de los municipios. Las tarifas de los servicios las comunican siete municipios, la Organización Técnica de Groenlandia, una compañía de seguros y unos pocos organismos más.

Las informaciones sobre los precios se refieren a la primera semana de enero y de julio. Los precios que se toman en consideración son los pagados normalmente por cualquier persona del público (es decir los precios de mercado).

Vivienda
Se considera el gasto bruto de vivienda que, además del alquiler, comprende los recargos por agua y recolección de residuos. Como el 60 por ciento de las viviendas alquiladas son propiedad de los municipios o del dominio nacional de Groenlandia, los datos sobre la evolución de los precios se obtiene de fuentes administrativas. Los alquileres de las viviendas existentes se regulan una vez al año (en octubre), normalmente como un aumento de carácter general del precio del metro cuadrado. Para las nuevas viviendas se hace un cálculo complementario basado en el aumento de los costos de construcción. Para los propietarios que habitan en sus propias viviendas, los gastos normalmente no tienen modificaciones, pues las sumas pagadas por agua, recolección de desperdicios, etc., se tratan por separado. Se recopilan informaciones complementarias sobre las viviendas nuevas o compradas, que forman parte del cálculo fundado en el aumento de los costos de la construcción. Los gastos de mantenimiento se consideran como artículos separados.

Especificación de las variedades
Existen especificaciones detalladas para cada artículo, que comprenden la marca, factura, cantidad y calidad.

Sustitución, cambio de calidad, etc.
En el índice sólo se introducen artículos nuevos cuando existen productos de sustitución. Los cambios de la calidad y la desaparición de determinados tipos o calidades de productos se tratan de la misma forma, es decir que se emplea el método llamado de "superposición de períodos". Por ejemplo si un aparato de radio de una determinada clase y calidad se ha vendido hasta julio de 1984, el nuevo modelo que le sustituye tendrá que haberse introducirdo ya normalmente en el mercado. Esto significa que el precio del modelo nuevo se puede enlazar con el precio del modelo anterior correspondiente al índice de julio de 1984.

Artículos estacionales
No se da un tratamiento especial a esta clase de artículos. Los que presentan fluctuaciones estacionales de precio muy acentuadas no se incluyen en el índice.

Cálculo
El índice se calcula según la fórmula de Laspeyres, como un promedio aritmético ponderado con base fija, cuyos coeficientes de ponderación corresponden a 1985.

Informaciones complementarias
Para esta serie se publican índices de subgrupos detallados. La Oficina de Estadísticas de Dinamarca también calcula un índice de precios netos de derechos de importación con el título de "Reguleringspristallet for Gronland". Este índice se ha utilizado por lo general para regular los salarios y las remuneraciones hasta que se abandonó esta práctica.

Organización y publicación
Danmarks Statistik: "Nyt fra Danmarks Statistik" (Copenhague).

idem: "Statistike Efterretninger" (Serien om Faeroerne og Gronland) (Copenhague).

idem: "Statistik Aarbog".

idem: "Statistik tiaarsoversigt".

GUADALUPE

Denominación oficial
Indice des prix à la consommation des ménages en milieu urbain (Indice de Precios del Consumo - Hogares urbanos).

Alcance
El índice se compila mensualmente y abarca hogares urbanos.

Base oficial
Abril de 1978 - marzo de 1979 = 100.

Fuente de la ponderación
La determinación de los coeficientes de ponderación y la selección de los artículos se basaron en los resultados de una encuesta sobre los gastos de los hogares realizada de septiembre a diciembre de 1972 en Basse-Terre y Pointe-à-Pitre. Se procedió a una extrapolación de los resultados, por estimarse que de 1972 a 1978 la estructura del consumo había tenido una evolución similar en Francia y en Guadalupe.

Ponderaciones y composición

Grupos principales	Número de artículos	Ponderación	Número aproximado de cotizaciones de precio
Alimentación	66	34,39	...
Restaurantes	8	2,34	...
Vestido y calzado	37	9,25	...
Vivienda:			
Alquiler	1	10,06	...
Mantenimiento y reparaciones	3	2,49	...
Muebles, moblaje y equipo del hogar	24	6,02	...
Combustible, luz y agua	5	5,72	...
Asistencia médica, aseo personal y servicios domésticos	14	6,80	...
Transportes	19	16,34	...
Educación y diversiones	21	6,59	...
Total	198	100,00	3 500

Gastos de consumo de los hogares
Sólo se toman en cuenta las compras directas de bienes y servicios de consumo. Se excluyen los gastos para mantener o aumentar el patrimonio (inversiones) y las transferencias (impuestos, cotizaciones sociales, etc.) que comprenden las retenciones de los ingresos de algunos hogares que se atribuyen a otros, sea en forma directa (prestaciones sociales), sea en la forma indirecta de servicios gratuitos (como los que prestan las administraciones o la enseñanza, las redes viales, etc.).

Método de recolección de los datos
Los investigadores registran mensualmente los precios de la mayor parte de los artículos en mercados, puntos de venta al por menor y establecimientos de servicios de Basse-Terre y Point-à-Pitre. Los precios del pescado, frutas y legumbres frescas se registran todas las semanas. Cuando los artículos con precios oficiales se cotizan también en el mercado libre, se tienen en cuenta los precios oficiales, salvo las tarifas de los transportes en común (taxi, autobús), o se calcula la mediana de los precios a partir de la cotizaciones del mercado libre y, en ese caso, el índice se calcula a partir de esos precios medios. No se consideran los descuentos ni las rebajas. Los precios especiales de liquidación se registran como si fueran los normalmente exigidos.

Vivienda
Las cotizaciones del alquiler se obtienen dos veces por año de 99 viviendas alquiladas de toda clase.

Especificación de las variedades
Para las variedades homogéneas las especificaciones son poco numerosas y para las heterogéneas se precisa la marca, el modelo, las dimensiones, etc.

Sustitución, cambio de calidad, etc.
Cuando las características del nuevo producto coinciden perfectamente con las del antiguo, la sustitución no implica una ruptura de la serie. Cuando el producto de sustitución difiere cualitativamente del sustituido, se procede a un enlace para no tomar en cuenta ninguna variación de precio que resulte de la evolución normal de los precios. Para ciertas prendas de vestir, en especial los vestidos femeninos, se definen las características cualitativas más frecuentes. Los precios de todos esos artículos se registran entonces y se utiliza la media de los precios para calcular el índice correspondiente a ese subgrupo.

Artículos estacionales
Se toman en cuenta las variaciones estacionales de los precios de las frutas y las legumbres frescas, así como del pescado, variando los coeficientes de ponderación dentro de "canastas" mensuales con coeficientes globales de ponderación invariables.

Cálculo
El índice se calcula según la fórmula de Laspeyres como un promedio aritmético ponderado de base fija, cuyos coeficientes de ponderación corresponden al período de base.

Informaciones complementarias
No disponible.

Organización y publicación
INSEE, Service départemental de la Guadeloupe: "Bulletin de statistique" (Basse Terre).

idem: "Les cahiers de l'INSEE - Dossier prix" (Basse-Terre, primer trimestre de 1979).

GUAM

Denominación oficial
Consumer Price Index (Indice de precios del consumo).

Alcance
El índice se compila cada tres meses y abarca hogares que representan todos los grupos de ingresos.

Base oficial
1978 = 100.

Fuente de la ponderación
La selección de los artículos y la determinación de los coeficientes de ponderación se basaron en los resultados de una encuesta sobre los gastos de consumo efectuada en 1978 y que abarcó una muestra de 500 hogares que representaban todos los grupos de ingresos.

Ponderaciones y composición

Grupos principales	Número de artículos	Ponderación	Número aproximado de cotizaciones de precio
Alimentación	103	24,13	...
Vivienda	51	28,59	...
Vestido, calzado y gastos de mantenimiento	44	10,61	...
Transportes	15	17,98	...
Asistencia médica	13	4,75	...
Distracciones	15	5,07	...
Otros bienes y servicios	18	8,87	...
Total	259	100,00	1 200

Gastos de consumo de los hogares
A los fines del índice, los gastos del consumo comprenden casi todos los bienes y servicios adquiridos para el consumo por los hogares de referencia, incluidos la asistencia médica y los artículos de entretenimiento.

Método de recolección de los datos
Los precios son recogidos por investigadores durante el segundo mes de cada trimestre en epicerías, almacenes departamentales y otros puntos de venta al por menor y establecimientos de servicios.

Vivienda
Los datos sobre el alquiler se refieren a viviendas con uno y hasta tres dormitorios.

Especificación de las variedades
No disponible.

Sustitución, cambio de calidad, etc.
No disponible.

Artículos estacionales
En el índice no están incluidos los artículos de temporada.

Cálculo
El índice se calcula según la fórmula de Laspeyres, como un promedio aritmético ponderado de base fija, cuyos coeficientes de ponderación corresponden al período de base.

La relación del precio para cada artículo se calcula dividiendo el precio medio del período corriente por el precio medio del período de base.

Informaciones complementarias
Se publican sub-grupos detallados.

Organización y publicación
Department of Commerce, Economic Research Center, Cost of Living Office: "Quarterly Report on the Guam Consumer Price Index" (Agana).

idem: "The Guam Consumer Price Index: 1978 Market Basket and Expenditure Weight Adjustment".

GUATEMALA

Denominación oficial
Indice de precios al consumidor para la República de Guatemala - áreas urbanas.

Alcance
El cálculo del índice es mensual y abarca todos los hogares urbanos.

Base oficial
Marzo - Abril de 1983 = 100.

Fuente de la ponderación
La selección de los artículos y la determinación de los coeficientes de ponderación se basaron en los resultados de una encuesta nacional sobre los gastos de los hogares efectuada durante el período de Noviembre de 1979 a Agosto de 1981 sobre una muestra de 4 800 hogares del area urbana central y de 2 678 hogares de las otras áreas urbanas del país. El hogar es el conjunto de dos o más personas que ocupan en común una vivienda familiar o parte de ella y consumen alimentos y otros bienes con cargo a un mismo presupuesto.

Ponderaciones y composición
Cuidad de Guatemala

Grupos principales	Número de artículos	Ponderación	Número aproximado de cotizaciones de precio
Alimentación	99	42,25	...
Alquiler, agua, reparación y conservación	6	9,94	...
Combustible y luz	6	4,73	...
Moblaje, accesorios para el hogar y servicios domésticos	24	7,82	...
Vestido y calzado	30	10,07	...
Asistencia médica	7	2,71	...
Educación	6	2,44	...
Transportes y comunicaciones	17	11,59	...
Lectura y distracciones	7	4,20	...
Otros bienes y servicios	11	4,25	...
Total	213	100,00	...

Resto urbano

Alimentación	91	57,27	...
Alquiler, agua, reparación y conservación	5	4,74	...
Combustible y luz	5	7,92	...
Moblaje, accesorios para el hogar y servicios domésticos	15	5,96	...
Vestido y calzado	27	10,35	...
Asistencia médica	4	2,09	...
Educación	4	0,98	...
Transportes y comunicaciones	10	5,78	...
Lectura y distracciones	3	1,75	...
Otros bienes y servicios	7	3,16	...
Total	171	100,00	...

Gastos de consumo de los hogares
No disponible.

Método de recolección de los datos
Los precios de los artículos alimenticios son recogidos semanalmente en las siete regiones del país. Los precios del amueblamiento, vestido, agua, combustible son obtenidos mensualmente y los de la asistencia médica, educación, lectura, recreación, transportes y comunicaciones se recogen trimestralmente. Los precios se recogen mediante cuestionarios por correspondencia en mercados, super-mercados, puntos de venta al por menor y establecimientos de servicios en las siete regiones urbanas del país.

Vivienda
Los datos referentes al alquiler se obtienen trimestralmente con un total de 589 cotizaciones para la ciudad de Guatemala y 60 cotizaciones para las otras regiones. No se tienen en cuenta las viviendas ocupadas por los propietarios en el tratamiento del índice.

Especificación de las variedades
Las especificaciones de las variedades se basan en los hábitos de los consumidores y se toman en consideración la variedad, calidad, marca y unidad.

Sustitución, cambio de calidad, etc.
Si un artículo desaparece definitivamente del mercado, se lo substituye por otro que tenga iguales características. Si se produce un cambio de calidad, se efectúan los ajustes necesarios utilizando el método de enlace.

Artículos estacionales
No disponible.

Cálculo
El índice se calcula según la fórmula de Laspeyres, como un promedio aritmético ponderado de base fija, cuyos coeficientes de ponderación corresponden al período de base.

La relación del precio para cada artículo es calculada dividiendo el precio medio del período corriente por el precio medio del período de base.

Informaciones complementarias
No disponible.

Organización y publicación
Ministerio de Economía, Dirección General de Estadística: "Informador Estadístico" (Guatemala).

idem: "Anuario Estadístico".

idem: "Metodología de los índices de precios al consumidor para la República de Guatemala, base marzo-abril de 1983 = 100, (marzo de 1983)".

GUAYANA FRANCESA (CAYENA)

Denominación oficial
Indice des prix à la consommation (Indice de precios del consumo).

Alcance
El índice se calcula mensualmente y abarca los hogares urbanos de ingresos módicos de Cayena.

Base oficial
1980 = 100.

Fuente de la ponderación
La selección de los artículos y la determinación de los coeficientes de ponderación se basaron en los resultados de una encuesta sobre los gastos de los hogares efectuada en 1969 en Cayena y Kourou.

Ponderaciones y composición

Grupos principales	Número de artículos	Ponderación	Número aproximado de cotizaciones de precio
Alimentación	...	50,0	...
Vivienda (incl. combustible, luz y agua)	...	19,5	...
Vestido y calzado	...	8,4	...
Higiene, salud y servicios	...	7,6	...
Transportes y comunicaciones	...	6,1	...
Educación y distracciones	...	4,9	...
Otros servicios	...	3,5	...
Total	...	100,0	...

Gastos de consumo de los hogares
No disponible.

Método de recolección de los datos
Los precios son recogidos por agentes encuestadores en 46 puntos de venta al por menor y en 15 establecimientos de servicios. La frecuencia de la recolección depende de la naturaleza de los artículos. Los precios de las frutas y verduras se obtienen cada semana; los de otros artículos alimenticios una vez por mes, y los de artículos manufacturados y de servicios cada tres meses. No se toman en cuenta los precios de las liquidaciones o rebajas.

Vivienda
Los datos referentes al alquiler se obtienen trimestralmente de una sociedad especializada en el alquiler de viviendas (1 840 viviendas).

Especificación de las variedades
El INSEE ha facilitado una lista de variedades para cada producto. Los encuestadores seleccionan la variedad más adecuada (es decir, de venta corriente y disponible para futuras recolecciones de precios). A partir de allí se registra la especificación del producto seleccionado en términos de marca, modelo, calidad y tamaño, etc.

Sustitución, cambio de calidad, etc.
Cuando un artículo cambia de calidad se le considera como un artículo nuevo y se le introduce en el cómputo del índice una vez que ha estado presente en el mercado durante varios meses.

Artículos estacionales
Se tienen en cuenta las fluctuaciones estacionales de los precios de ciertas verduras calculando promedios móviles para el cómputo del índice.

Cálculo
El índice se calcula conforme a la fórmula de Laspeyres, como un promedio aritmético ponderado de base fija, cuyos coeficientes de ponderación corresponden al período de base.

Informaciones complementarias
No disponible.

Organización y publicación
INSEE, Service régional de la Guyane: "Bulletin Mensuel de Statistique" (Cayena).

idem: "Annuaire de la Guyane".

GUYANA

Denominación oficial
Urban Consumer Price Index (Indice de precios del consumo urbano).

Alcance
El índice se calcula mensualmente y abarca Georgetown, Nueva Amsterdam y Linden.

Base oficial
1970 = 100.

Fuente de la ponderación
La selección de los artículos y la determinación de los coeficientes de ponderación se basaron en los resultados de una encuesta sobre los gastos de los hogares efectuada en 1969-70.

Ponderaciones y composición

Grupos principales	Número de artículos	Ponderación	Número aproximado de cotizaciones de precio
Alimentación y tabaco	86	42,5	...
Vestido y calzado	56	8,6	...
Vivienda:			
Combustible y luz	5	5,2	...
Alquiler, agua y tasas	5	21,4	...
Moblaje, artículos para el hogar y servicios	7	2,9	...
Varios:			
Aseo personal y asistencia médica	21	7,2	...
Educación y distracciones	15	6,4	...
Transportes y comunicaciones	8	4,8	...
Otros bienes y servicios	2	1,0	...
Total	205	100,0	

Gastos de consumo de los hogares
No disponible.

Método de recolección de los datos
Los precios de la mayoría de los artículos se recogen alrededor del 15 de cada mes en cerca de 200 puntos de venta al por menor, mercados y establecimientos de servicios en Georgetown, Nueva Amsterdam y Linden. Los precios de ciertos artículos alimenticios tales como pescado, frutas y verduras frescas se recogen cada semana.

Vivienda
No disponible.

Especificación de las variedades
No disponible.

Sustitución, cambio de calidad, etc.
No disponible.

Artículos estacionales
No disponible.

Cálculo
El índice se calcula conforme a la fórmula de Laspeyres como un promedio aritmético ponderado de base fija, cuyos coeficientes de ponderación corresponden al período de base.

HAITI

Denominación oficial
Indice des prix à la consommation - Aire Métropolitaine (Indice de Precios del Consumo - área metropolitana).

Alcance
El índice se compila mensualmente y abarca hogares urbanos del área metropolitana.

Base oficial
1980 = 100.

Fuente de la ponderación
La determinación de los coeficientes de ponderación y la selección de los artículos se basaron en los resultados de una encuesta, realizada en 1976, sobre los gastos de los hogares urbanos y rurales. Los gastos de 747 hogares, de dos o más personas y con ingresos familiares de por lo menos 250 gourdes por año, sirvieron para calcular los coeficientes de ponderación del índice.

El índice se refiere a los hogares urbanos del área metropolitana de Puerto Príncipe, Delmas, Carrefour y Pétion-Ville. No se ajustaron los coeficientes de ponderación para tomar en cuenta la evolución de precios ocurrida entre el período de la encuesta y 1980.

Ponderaciones y composición

Grupos principales	Número de artículos	Ponderación	Número aproximado de cotizaciones de precio
Alimentación	27	64,48	...
Vestido y calzado	15	3,16	...
Vivienda	6	11,71	...
Muebles y moblaje del hogar	16	5,75	...
Servicios	13	14,90	...
Total	77	100,00	...

Gastos de consumo de los hogares
A los efectos del índice comprenden todos los bienes y servicios adquiridos por los hogares de referencia para su propio consumo. Se excluyen los impuestos a los ingresos, los depósitos de ahorro, las primas de los seguros, etc.

Método de recolección de los datos
Los investigadores registran los precios en una muestra de tiendas minoristas y establecimientos de servicios. La frecuencia del registro de precios y el número de puntos de venta seleccionados dependen de la naturaleza del artículo. Los precios de los productos alimenticios se registran tres veces por semana (martes, jueves y sábado) en tres grandes mercados y en supermercados y tiendas seleccionados. Los precios del vestido, ajuar doméstico y servicios se registran la primera, segunda y tercer semana de cada mes.

Vivienda
Los datos sobre las cotizaciones del alquiler se obtienen durante el primer mes de cada trimestre, de una muestra de viviendas alquiladas.

Especificación de las variedades
No disponible.

Sustitución, cambio de calidad, etc.
No disponible.

Artículos estacionales
No disponible.

Cálculo
El índice se calcula según la fórmula de Laspeyres como un promedio aritmético ponderado de base fija, cuyos coeficientes de ponderación corresponden a 1976.

Los relativos de precio de las variedades de cada artículo se obtienen dividiendo el promedio de los precios registrados en el período en curso por el correspondiente al período de base. Luego, los índices por artículos se obtienen mediante las medias aritméticas simples de dichos relativos.

Informaciones complementarias
No disponible.

Organización y publicación
Département des finances et des affaires économiques, Institut haïtien de statistique: "Bulletin trimestriel de statistique" (Port-au-Prince).

Ministère du Plan, Institut haïtien de statistique et d'informatique, Division des statistiques générales: "Indices des prix à la consommation, base 100 en 1980" (Port-au-Prince, juin 1983).

HONDURAS

Denominación oficial
Indice General de Precios al Consumidor.

Alcance
El índice se calcula mensualmente y abarca familias de todas las áreas urbanas con ingresos comprendidos entre 3 000 y 12 000 lempiras por año en el período 1978-79.

Base oficial
1978 = 100.

Fuente de la ponderación
La selección de los artículos y la determinación de los coeficientes de ponderación se basaron en los resultados de una encuesta sobre los gastos de los hogares urbanos, de alcance nacional, efectuada entre enero de 1978 y agosto de 1979, que abarcó 5 328 hogares en 44 ciudades. La muestra para el índice abarcó 2 306 hogares urbanos de ingresos comprendidos entre 3 000 y 12 000 lempiras por año en el momento de la encuesta.

Ponderaciones y composición

Grupos principales	Número de artículos	Ponderación	Número aproximado de cotizaciones de precio
Alimentación	64	41,214	7 968
Bebidas y tabaco	7	3,790	133
Vivienda:			
Alquiler	1	13,202	164
Reparaciones	4	3,288	73
Gastos del hogar (incl. combustible y luz)	19	9,611	190
Moblaje y accesorios para el hogar	13	4,510	520
Vestido y calzado	34	9,110	1 320
Aseo personal y asistencia médica	30	6,952	906
Transportes	7	3,033	94
Educación y distracciones	10	5,290	184
Total	189	100,000	11 552

Gastos de consumo de los hogares
No disponible.

Método de recolección de los datos
Los precios son recogidos por investigadores en mercados, puntos de venta al por menor y establecimientos de servicios en seis ciudades distribuidas en todo el país. Los precios de los artículos alimenticios se recogen todas las semanas, los días martes; los servicios de educación se recogen una vez por año; el alquiler, los servicios médicos y el transporte se recogen cada seis meses. Los precios de unos 150 artículos se recogen alrededor del día 15 de cada mes.

Vivienda
Las cotizaciones de alquiler se obtienen dos veces por año de una muestra de 164 viviendas, ocupadas por familias de ingresos medios que comprenden sala, comedor, cocina y por lo menos dos dormitorios.

Especificación de las variedades
Los productos investigados se fundamentan en una especificación rigurosa.

Sustitución, cambio de calidad, etc.
Si un artículo desaparece del mercado, para registrar su precio se le substituye por un producto similar. No se toman en consi-

deración los cambios de calidad en las especificaciones de los artículos.

Artículos estacionales
Los artículos sujetos a fluctuaciones estacionales de precio no se incluyen en el índice.

Cálculo
El índice se calcula conforme a la fórmula de Laspeyres como un promedio aritmético ponderado de base fija, cuyos coeficientes de ponderación corresponden al período de base. Los precios medios para cada artículo en cada ciudad son los promedios aritméticos simples de precios obtenidos en cada ciudad. Estos precios medios se combinan utilizando las ponderaciones de las áreas para obtener los precios medios regionales. Después, para cada artículo las relaciones de precios medios regionales se calculan dividiendo el precio medio del área del período corriente por el precio medio del área del período de base. El índice nacional es un promedio ponderado de cinco índices urbanos regionales (centro, norte, sur, este y oeste). Las ponderaciones utilizadas son proporcionales a la estructura de los gastos de las áreas según la encuesta sobre los gastos de los hogares.

Informaciones complementarias
No disponible.

Organización y publicación
Banco Central de Honduras, Departamento de Estudios Económicos: "Boletín Estadístico" (Tegucigalpa, D.C.).
idem: "Indice de Precios al Consumidor" (mensual).
idem: "Honduras en Cifras" (anual).
idem: "Indice general de Precios al Consumidor, Base 1978 = 100, Metodología y Series Cronológicas" (noviembre de 1982).

HONG KONG

Denominación oficial
Consumer Price Index (A) (Indice de Precios del Consumo - A).

Alcance
El índice se compila mensualmente y abarca aproximadamente el 50 por ciento de los hogares urbanos de Hong Kong, cuyos ingresos mensuales oscilaban entre $ 2 500 y $ 9 999 entre octubre de 1989 y septiembre de 1990.

Base oficial
Octubre de 1989 - septiembre de 1990 = 100.

Fuente de la ponderación
La determinación de los coeficientes de ponderación se basó en los resultados de una encuesta sobre los gastos de los hogares realizada de octubre de 1989 a septiembre de 1990 y que abarcó todos los hogares urbanos de Hong Kong que no eran colectivos, rurales o de pescadores. También se excluyeron los hogares que recibían asistencia pública y aquéllos cuyos miembros estaban ausentes de Hong Kong durante el período de referencia de la encuesta. En total ésta abarcó unos 4 850 hogares. Los 12 meses del período de referencia se dividieron en 26 ciclos bisemanales. A los hogares que deseaban colaborar con la encuesta se les pidió que, durante uno de los ciclos, todos los miembros del hogar de 12 años y más anotaran, en libros diarios especialmente concebidos al efecto, todos sus gastos durante la quincena de referencia. También se les solicitó que consignaran las compras poco frecuentes (como coches, refrigeradores y joyas) que recordaban haber hecho durante un trimestre de referencia. La selección de los artículos para la recolección de precios se basó en: (i) que la ponderación del artículo tuviera entidad suficiente como para que un aumento importante de su precio promedio repercutiera en forma apreciable en el conjunto del Indice de Precios del Consumo (IPC); (ii) que el conjunto de los artículos representen la estructura general de todo el consumo de los hogares abarcados por el IPC; (iii) que el número de artículos seleccionados se aproxime al de las series anteriores del IPC para mantener la continuidad. Los coeficientes de ponderación de los artículos no seleccionados se distribuyeron en forma proporcional entre los seleccionados de un mismo grupo.

Gastos de consumo de los hogares
Se refieren a los gastos (comprendidos los pagos en especie) para adquirir bienes y servicios con finalidades de consumo y por lo tanto no comprenden los gastos comerciales, remesas, apuestas de juego, pago de impuestos, inversiones en existen-

Ponderaciones y composición

Grupos principales	Número de artículos	Ponderación	Número aproximado de cotizaciones de precio
Alimentación	387	41,2	...
Bebidas alcohólicas y tabaco (para consumo doméstico)	16	2,45	...
Vivienda	26	20,56	...
Combustible y luz	5	3,18	...
Vestido y calzado	113	4,56	...
Bienes durables del hogar	110	4,92	...
Transporte y vehículos	52	7,20	...
Servicios	104	10,05	...
Varios	147	5,88	...
Total	960	100,00	40 000

cias, bienes inmuebles o acciones, ni otros gastos diversos efectuados con finalidad de ahorro. Por lo general los gastos se refieren a los pagos al contado de bienes o servicios efectuados durante el período de referencia, independientemente de si esos bienes o servicios se recibieron o consumieron en dicho período. Sin embargo los pagos con tarjetas u órdenes de crédito se registraron por las sumas suscritas durante el período de referencia, pero no los montos de los gastos abonados mediante órdenes de pago recibidas durante ese período. Algunos casos especiales se tratan de la forma siguiente:

Los ingresos en especie se consideran como ingresos y como gastos de los hogares y comprenden el alojamiento gratuito o subvencionado que proporcionan los empleadores, los gastos de asistencia médica y petróleo reembolsados por los empleadores y cualquier contribución pagada por artículos obtenidos de los empleadores a precios especiales. El total del precio al por menor de estos artículos se registró como gasto de consumo y la diferencia entre ese precio y el especial se añadió al ingreso. Los complementos de la remuneración, tales como prestación gratuita de comidas, transporte y asistencia médica no se registraron por la dificultad de cuantificarlos.

Para las viviendas ocupadas sin pago de alquiler se fija un valor locativo fijo basado en las cotizaciones normales del mercado. Este alquiler ficticio se consideró tanto como ingreso que como gasto de los hogares, según el criterio de equivalencia del alquiler.

Con respecto a los bienes durables adquiridos a plazos (ventas a crédito o a plazos y alquileres con opción de compra), se registra el valor total de los artículos en el momento de la compra y no las mensualidades o cantidades pagadas a cuenta. Por tal motivo el informante debe recordar el precio al contado que hubiera debido pagar por los bienes que adquirió mediante alquiler con opción de compra durante el período de referencia. Por el mismo motivo, no se incluyen los gastos efectuados durante el período de referencia por mercancías adquiridas a plazo pero no recibidas en dicho período.

Se registran como gastos de consumo las compras de segunda mano pagadas al contado. Toda compra pagada mediante entrega a cuenta se registró por el monto total del pago en metálico más el valor estimado del objeto, cuando es cuantificable. Los gastos en permisos o autorizaciones, seguros de bienes de consumo específicos y asistencia médica se han considerado como gastos de consumo corrientes, pero no los pagos de contribuciones a la seguridad social o fondos de pensión, impuestos a los ingresos y otras cargas fiscales directas y seguros de vida. Por su parte las remesas, regalos y desembolsos similares o las contribuciones en efectivo a otros hogares no se trataron como gastos de consumo normales. Los regalos se trataron como bienes normales de consumo y se incluyeron entre los gastos de los hogares.

Método de recolección de los datos
A efectos de la recolección en los puntos de venta seleccionados, las zonas urbanas más pobladas se dividen en 12 distritos. Los precios se registran por lo general mediante visitas personales y, algunas veces, por teléfono. La recolección de alimentos frescos se realiza tres veces por semana, salvo fruta, carne de cerdo o vaca, huevos y arroz, cuyos precios se registran semanalmente. Los demás precios se registran en forma mensual, trimestral o anual. Para artículos tales como transporte, alquiler de casas de propiedad pública, servicio de agua, petróleo, aceite y permisos de conducir vehículos, los precios sólo se registran cuando se modifican.

Los precios utilizados en el índice son los del comercio minorista, por transacciones pagadas al contado y en efectivo. Los precios con descuento sólo se aceptan cuando se trata de ventas con rebajas (o liquidaciones), que tienen lugar en forma periódica, de mercancías actuales y en buenas condiciones, ofrecidas en cantidades razonables a todos los consumidores.

Vivienda
Las cotizaciones de alquiler se obtienen todos los meses mediante encuesta a una muestra de viviendas privadas. Se registran los alquileres de todas las viviendas de la muestra, tanto los del mes en curso como los anteriores. Las viviendas se estratifican posteriormente por superficie. Se establece luego el total de los alquileres de cada estrato, tanto del mes en curso como anteriores y se calcula la modificación relativa. Para obtener un índice combinado, estos "relativos de alquiler" de los estratos se unen y ponderan por un conjunto de coeficientes establecidos en la encuesta de gastos de los hogares de 1989-90, procediéndose luego a su enlace con el período de base. Las modificaciones de los alquileres de viviendas con subvenciones públicas se registran cuando tienen lugar, de acuerdo con las informaciones obtenidas de las autoridades competentes. Se supone que los costes de las viviendas ocupadas por sus propietarios siguen la evolución general de los alquileres (criterio de valor locativo equivalente). Los relativos de alquiler calculados para cada estrato, según lo antedicho, también se combinan con las ponderaciones de las casas ocupadas por sus propietarios para obtener así el índice mensual.

Especificación de las variedades
Como la recolección de precios es específica para cada tienda, la especificación de los artículos es necesariamente general. Sin embargo, durante la visita sobre el terreno, se registran para cada artículo especificaciones detalladas de su variedad, calidad, factura, marca, unidad o cantidad. Se pregunta a los entrevistados de los puntos de venta seleccionados de la muestra cuáles variedades prefieren en ese momento los clientes de ese punto de venta (es decir las más vendidas). Si estas variedades son las mismas que las de meses anteriores se registran sus precios de ese momento, pero en caso contrario se eligen otras variedades populares y se registran tanto sus precios de ese mes como los de meses anteriores a efectos de su empalme.

Sustitución, cambio de calidad, etc.
Para los cambios de calidad se utiliza el método del empalme. Antes de su incorporación al IPC los precios se registran durante dos meses consecutivos.

Cuando un producto totalmente nuevo no puede equipararse en ninguno de los artículos cuyos precios se deben registrar, su precio no se registrará hasta la próxima revisión del IPC. Pero si el producto en cuestión es tan sólo una nueva marca de un artículo existente, se aplica el método de encadenamiento. Cuando un producto desaparece del mercado, se recoge el precio de un sustituto similar.

Artículos estacionales
Fuera de temporada, se omiten del índice los precios de los alimentos frescos distribuyéndose sus coeficientes de ponderación entre los demás artículos del mismo grupo. Para los demás artículos estacionales, el precio se mantiene constante hasta la próxima temporada.

Cálculo
El índice se calcula según la fórmula de Laspeyres como un promedio aritmético ponderado de base fija, cuyos coeficientes de ponderación corresponden al período de base.

Para compilar índices de artículos se siguen dos métodos: los relativos de precio de los artículos homogéneos se calculan dividiendo el precio medio del período corriente por el precio medio del período de base; para los demás artículos los relativos de precio se calculan para cada variedad de cada uno de los puntos de venta dividiendo el precio medio del período corriente por el precio medio del período de base y a su vez, para obtener el índice por artículos, se calcula el promedio de esos relativos.

Informaciones complementarias
Además del IPC-A, todos los meses se publican en Hong Kong dos otros índices de los precios del consumo. El IPC-B, que es un índice de precios del consumo con base en 1989-90 compilado por el Departamento de Censos y Estadísticas del Gobierno de Hong Kong, para hogares que gastaban entre $ 10 000 y $ 17 499 por mes entre octubre de 1989 y septiembre de 1990, período que coincide con el de la encuesta sobre los gastos de los hogares de 1989-90. El otro índice es el IPC Hang Seng, banco privado de Hong Kong, compilado para hogares que habitan en viviendas privadas con un promedio mensual de gastos que se situaba entre $ 17 500 y $ 37 499 en 1989-90. En relación a su alcance, el IPC-B abarca un 30 por ciento de los hogares urbanos de Hong Kong y el IPC Hang Seng un 10 por ciento.

Organización y publicación
Census and Statistics Department, Consumer Price Index Section: "Consumer Price Index Report" (Hong Kong).
idem: "Hong Kong Monthly Digest of Statistics" (Hong Kong).

HUNGRIA

Denominación oficial
Indice des prix à la consommation (Indice de precios del consumo).

Alcance
El índice se compila mensualmente y abarca todo el país y toda la población.

Base oficial
En las publicaciones nacionales, el período de base del índice es el mes respectivo del año anterior, el mes precedente y diciembre del año anterior igualado a 100. La Oficina Central de Estadística de Hungría armoniza estos índices sobre la base utilizada en las publicaciones de la OIT.

Fuente de la ponderación
La selección de los artículos y la determinación de los coeficientes de ponderación se basan en los resultados de encuestas sobre los gastos de los hogares que se revisan periódicamente. La muestra de la encuesta abarca unos 8 000 hogares. Cada hogar establece un diario con información detallada sobre sus gastos. La insuficiencia de datos acerca de gastos para ciertos artículos, incluido el alcohol, el tabaco, la repostería y las comidas fuera del hogar, se compensa con la utilización de macrodatos.

Ponderaciones y composición

Grupos principales	Número de artículos	Ponderación	Número aproximado de cotizaciones de precio
Alimentación	49	28	27 100
Bebidas y tabaco	5	12	4 800
Combustible y luz	8	5	1 100
Vestido y calzado	27	8	22 400
Servicios	34	15	13 200
Alquiler	2	5	400
Otros	39	27	33 200
Total	164	100	102 200

Gastos de consumo de los hogares
A los efectos del índice, los gastos del consumo comprenden casi todos los bienes y servicios adquiridos por la población de referencia. Se incluyen el impuesto por el uso de la televisión y los alquileres ficticios de las viviendas ocupadas por sus propietarios. Se excluyen los consumos en especie, de producción propia o recibidos gratuitamente, las matrículas de automóvil, el impuesto sobre el crédito del consumidor, los seguros de vida y los impuestos directos, así como los servicios gratuitos de salud y las compras y ventas de artículos de segunda mano, salvo los vehículos automóviles.

Método de recolección de los datos
145 recolectores de precios registran los precios de unos 1 800 artículos individuales en puntos de venta seleccionados y en organismos públicos.

Los precios de las frutas y verduras se obtienen en mercados y puntos de venta seleccionados. Se tienen en consideración los precios de rebajas y liquidaciones especiales.

Vivienda
No disponible.

Especificación de las variedades
Cada artículo se selecciona en función de sus rasgos más distintivos. Dentro de cada especificación de artículos manufacturados, los precios se compilan en dos o tres de los tipos de mayor venta elegidas en previa consulta con el personal de ventas.

Sustitución, cambio de calidad, etc.
Una vez elegida una especificación se la mantiene el mayor tiempo posible. Sin embargo el investigador encargado de la recolección de precios está facultado para sustituir variedades dentro de los límites de la especificación de que se trata. Las demás sustituciones son objeto de un control central; no se hacen ajustes por cambios de calidad.

Artículos estacionales
Para su cálculo mensual se utilizan coeficientes variables de ponderación que reflejan los cambios estacionales respecto de su disponibilidad en el marco de una "canasta" de alimentos estacionales.

Cálculo
Se utilizan los precios medios relativos calculados para cada artículo especificado, haciendo caso omiso de las observaciones de que no se dispone. Se han establecido coeficientes anuales fijos de ponderación para cada grupo social y cada grupo de ingresos.

Informaciones complementarias
En las publicaciones nacionales, el índice se publica sobre la base 1980 = 100, año precedente = 100, mes correspondiente del año precedente = 100, mes precedente = 100 y diciembre del año anterior = 100.

Organización y publicación
Központi Statiszikai Hivatal (Oficina Central de Estadística): "Statiszikai Havi Közlemények" (Boletín mensual de estadística) (Budapest).
idem: "Statiszikai Evkönyv" (Anuario estadístico).
idem: "Fogyasztói árindex fuzetek" (Folleto sobre los índices de los precios del consumo).

INDIA (TODO EL PAIS 1)

Denominación oficial
Consumer Price Index for Agricultural Labourers (Indice de precios del consumo para trabajadores agrícolas).

Alcance
El índice se compila mensualmente y abarca hogares de trabajadores agrícolas, es decir los asalariados que trabajan en los cultivos y la producción agrícola, y sus dependientes.

Base oficial
Julio de 1960 - junio de 1961 = 100.

Fuente de la ponderación
La selección de los artículos y la determinación de los coeficientes de ponderación se basaron en los resultados de una encuesta sobre los gastos de los hogares efectuada de agosto de 1956 a agosto de 1957, y que abarcó unas 7 800 familias. No se modificaron los coeficientes de ponderación en función de las diferencias en los niveles de precios entre 1956-57 y 1960-61. Los artículos seleccionados en el índice son los relativamente importantes para los gastos de los hogares y los que tienen una corriente de precios determinada, siendo representativos de un mayor grupo de artículos afines. Los gastos en artículos y servicios que no se pueden incluir en el índice fueron imputados convenientemente a otros artículos o grupos según los casos.

Ponderaciones y composición

Grupos principales	Número de artículos	Ponderación	Número aproximado de cotizaciones de precio
Alimentación	37	78,1	...
Combustible y luz	4	8,0	...
Vestido, calzado y ropa blanca	11	6,1	...
Varios	10	7,8	...
Total	62	100,0	...

Gastos de consumo de los hogares
A los fines del índice, los gastos del consumo comprenden sólo los bienes y servicios de relativa entidad para los gastos de los hogares. No se incluyen los gastos en ceremonias ni los costos de la reparación de edificios ni de terrenos.

Método de recolección de los datos
El personal de la National Sample Survey, trabajando en el terreno, recopila mensualmente los precios al por menor en tiendas y mercados de una muestra de 422 aldeas. La fecha de la recolección de precios es el primer día de mercado o el primer sábado de cada mes. Siempre que se puedan encontrar los artículos seleccionados en los "emporios" (tiendas que venden a precio fijo y razonable) se utilizan sus cotizaciones de precio.

Vivienda
Se han excluido los gastos de alquiler, por ser nulos o insignificantes.

Especificación de las variedades
Se establecieron con detalle las especificaciones de los artículos cuyos precios se deberían registrar para cada una de las 422 aldeas de la muestra, basándose en las informaciones recogidas durante la encuesta especial llevada a cabo en ellas de julio a septiembre de 1960.

Sustitución, cambio de calidad, etc.
Siempre que se alteren las características de los productos, se realizan, si es posible, ajustes de calidad. También se utiliza en algunos casos el método de enlace.

Artículos estacionales
No se incluyen en el índice.

Cálculo
El índice para todo el país se calcula como un promedio ponderado de las distintas series de índices para los trabajadores agrícolas de 15 Estados distintos del país (incluyendo grupos de pequeños Estados y Territorios de la Unión).
El índice para cada Estado se calcula, conforme a la fórmula de Laspeyres, como un promedio aritmético ponderado de base fija, cuyos coeficientes de ponderación corresponden al período de agosto de 1956-agosto de 1957. Esos índices son a su vez ponderados para obtener el índice nacional, cuyos coeficientes de ponderación corresponden al conjunto de los gastos de consumo de los grupos de población de cada Estado.

Informaciones complementarias
No disponible.

Organización y publicación
Ministry of Labour, Labour Bureau: "Indian Labour Journal" (Simla).
Ministry of Labour, Employment and Rehabilitation: "Indian Labour Journal" (Simla, dic. de 1962 y oct. de 1968).

INDIA (TODO EL PAIS 2)

Denominación oficial
Consumer Price Index for Urban Non-manual Employees (Indice de precios del consumo para empleados urbanos no manuales).

Alcance
El índice se compila mensualmente y comprende hogares de 59 centros urbanos seleccionados cuyos principales ingresos provienen de trabajos no agrícolas.

Base oficial
Abril de 1984 - marzo de 1985 = 100.

Fuente de la ponderación
La selección de los artículos y la determinación de los coeficientes de ponderación se basaron en una encuesta por muestra sobre los gastos de 45 000 hogares de empleados intelectuales de 59 centros urbanos seleccionados, que se llevó a cabo durante un año, de julio de 1982 a junio de 1983. No se ajustaron las ponderaciones para tomar en cuenta las modificaciones de precio ocurridas entre el momento de la encuesta y el período de base. Los coeficientes de ponderación de los artículos no seleccionados se atribuyen, por un procedimiento de imputación, a los incluidos en el diagrama de ponderación, basándose por lo general en la similitud de las tendencias de sus precios. Cuando no se ha estimado conveniente efectuar la atribución a cualquier artículo específico, se ha procedido a hacerlo a nivel de subgrupo.

Gastos de consumo de los hogares
Se han excluido del diagrama de la ponderación los gastos en ahorros e inversiones, incluidos seguros de vida, contribuciones de pensión, amortización de deudas, intereses, gastos judiciales e impuestos (comprendidas los impuestos de vialidad, municipales, etc.), cotizaciones sindicales, ceremonias, etc., regalos y limosnas, remesas a dependientes, etc., pues la mayoría de estos gastos no son de consumo, y aún cuando los desembolsos para ceremonias y las remesas a dependientes, etc., puedan contener algún elemento de consumo, no es posi-

Ponderaciones y composición

Grupos principales	Número de artículos (a)	Ponderación (b)	Número aproximado de cotizaciones de precio
Alimentación y tabaco	...	...	...
Combustible y luz	...	...	...
Vivienda	...	...	...
Vestido, calzado y ropa de cama	...	...	...
Artículos y servicios varios	...	...	...
Total			167 540

Nota: (a) Según los centros, el número de artículos varía entre 146 y 345. (b) Las ponderaciones de cada centro son distintas.

ble investigarlos por separado pues no se relacionan exclusivamente con una mercancía dada o con un servicio cuantificable.

Los bienes recibidos en especie, en forma gratuita o cedidos por el empleador u otras personas y los regalos se evaluaron al precio corriente de mercado y se registraron como parte del ingreso, incluyéndose también en la clase de gasto respectiva.

Para la vivienda propia y las gratuitas o cedidas por el empleador u otras personas, se supusieron alquileres tomando como base las cotizaciones de alquiler predominantes en la localidad para viviendas similares. No se dio a los bienes durables trato distinto que a los perecederos. Sin embargo, dado que la compra de bienes durables es menos frecuente, los gastos no sólo se registraron en el mes de referencia sino también en todo el año de referencia y se utilizó el gasto medio mensual derivado de los valores del año de referencia para obtener los coeficientes de ponderación. Tampoco se trataron en forma distinta las compras de bienes nuevos o de segunda mano.

Se incluyeron en el diagrama de la ponderación los gastos para el cuidado de la salud, consistentes en medicamentos, servicios de asistencia médica y relacionados, así como las contribuciones a sistemas de salud.

Método de recolección de los datos

Una encuesta de mercado realizada durante 1983 en cada uno de los centros urbanos, que utilizó una combinación adecuada de métodos de muestreo aleatorios y determinados, permitió seleccionar una muestra de mercados y puestos de venta populares entre las familias del índice.

Los precios de todos los artículos se recogen mensualmente en mercados, comercios controlados, negocios con precios equitativos, tiendas de cooperativas de consumidores (comprendidos los superbazares) y otros puntos de venta o prestación de servicios. La recolección está a cargo de la División de actividades locales de la Organización Nacional de Encuestas por Muestra, que es una organización permanente que se ocupa, en el plano local, de realizar encuestas en gran escala y recopilar periódicamente datos estadísticos.

La recopilación de los precios correspondientes a los distintos grupos de mercancías se efectúa en fechas fijas y, en lo posible, dentro de una semana para que la comparación entre dos cotizaciones del mismo puesto no resulte viciada por la diferencia entre las fechas. La selección actual de las fechas para registrar los precios de un grupo dado de mercancías se funda en el volumen de las transacciones en cada uno de los días de la semana.

Se consignan los precios del momento. Comprenden los impuestos a las ventas y otros recargos que pagan habitualmente los consumidores, así como los descuentos o rebajas que de ordinario se les conceden. Los precios "ilegales" (mercado negro), las compras a plazo o a crédito y las compras de objetos de segunda mano, así como el comercio de objetos usados, no se incluyen en la recopilación de precios. Tampoco se incluyen los precios de importación en cuanto tales. Estos bienes de importación nunca, o muy rara vez, se incluyen en el consumo de los hogares del índice; tampoco existen puntos que los vendan en forma exclusiva y permanente.

Vivienda

Los datos relativos a las cotizaciones de alquiler se obtienen de una muestra de viviendas alquiladas, mediante una encuesta continua de alquileres de casas de habitación que se realiza cada seis meses. Todas las viviendas sondeadas para la encuesta detallada sobre alquileres de casas, incluida en la encuesta sobre gastos de los hogares de 1982-1983, constituyen el marco básico de la encuesta continua de alquileres de habitación. Estas viviendas se distribuyeron uniformemente durante los seis meses que van de julio a diciembre de la siguiente forma: las viviendas sondeadas entre julio de 1982 y enero de 1983 se atribuyeron al mes de julio; las sondeadas entre agosto de 1982 y febrero de 1983 se atribuyeron al mes de agosto, y así sucesivamente. De la lista de viviendas correspondientes a un mes se extrajo una muestra de 14 viviendas por investigador, después de haber estratificado las viviendas en cuatro, según su número de habitaciones. Los datos sobre alquileres se obtienen cada seis meses de una muestra de las viviendas asignadas a los diferentes meses de un semestre. El índice de alquiler se compila con los datos semestrales obtenidos sobre el alquiler de casas para poder representar así la media semestral de las variaciones del alquiler.

En el índice general de alquileres se incluyen, además de las viviendas alquiladas, las propias y las gratuitas. El índice de alquileres elaborado con los datos sobre casas alquiladas se utiliza como valor representativo de las propias en el índice de alquileres.

Para elaborar el índice, se promedian los alquileres relativos de los últimos seis meses por los del período de seis meses inmediatamente anterior para cada una de las cotizaciones de alquiler y se obtiene así un índice de alquileres en cadena. Los alquileres relativos medios se obtienen para cada uno de los estratos y los cuatro promedios resultantes se combinan según la composición actual de las viviendas propias o según los resultados disponibles de la encuesta sobre el gasto de los hogares, para derivar la media general de los alquileres relativos. El índice de alquileres para las viviendas propias y alquiladas se elabora como un índice en cadena, que se basa en el índice de alquileres de los seis meses previos. Para las viviendas ocupadas en forma gratuita, el índice se fija en 100 y el índice general de alquileres de casas se elabora tomando como base un índice para las viviendas gratuitas y otro índice para las propias y las alquiladas, utilizando la proporción de hogares de la categoría respectiva según las informaciones de la encuesta sobre el gasto de los hogares.

Especificación de las variedades

Los diversos artículos se especifican con detalles sobre su calidad, variedad y otras características físicas fundamentales tales como tamaño, dimensión, contenido material, etc., teniendo presentes las condiciones imperantes en cada centro para evitar toda ambigüedad de identificación.

La especificación de cada mercancía de consumo popular entre los hogares del índice se determinó siguiendo los criterios del mercado y del consumidor. Las especificaciones así determinadas se utilizaron para seleccionar los puntos para el registro periódico de precios.

Sustitución, cambio de calidad, etc.

Se han establecido procedimientos para los casos en que no se dispone en el mes de una cotización particular, del precio correspondiente a las especificaciones de los puestos de venta. En tales casos se reúnen precios sustitutivos, sea de los de puestos de venta de reserva para artículos con la misma especificación, sea de especificaciones comparables a nivel popular, enlazando las nuevas cotizaciones y las antiguas mediante las técnicas habituales. Los cambios de calidad y la desaparición de productos del mercado se tratan de igual manera, en la medida en que reflejen las modificaciones producidas.

Artículos estacionales

El índice abarca todos los meses un número distinto de frutas y legumbres, según la oferta. Para los coeficientes de ponderación de los artículos estacionales, los que corresponden a los subgrupos "frutas" y "legumbres" se obtienen tomando como base el promedio mensual del gasto de todos los artículos de los subgrupos. No obstante, las ponderaciones individuales de los artículos cuyos precios se dispongan durante varios meses, se obtienen distribuyendo a prorata las ponderaciones de los artículos sin precio registrado entre los que tienen precio registrado.

Cálculo

El índice se calcula según la fórmula de Laspeyres, como un promedio aritmético ponderado con base fija, cuyos coeficientes de ponderación corresponden al período julio de 1982 - junio de 1983.

El índice se compila directamente para cada uno de los centros. El índice para todo el país se calcula como promedio ponderado de los índices de centro, basándose los coeficientes de ponderación en el total estimado de los gastos de consumo de los distintos centros, tomando como base los datos del censo de población de 1981 y de la encuesta sobre los gastos de los hogares de 1982-1983.

Informaciones complementarias
La Oficina del Trabajo ("Labour Bureau") compila índices de precios del consumo de hogares de trabajadores de la industria y de peones rurales, que se publican en el periódico laboral de la India titulado "Indian Labour Journal".

Organización y publicación
La "Central Statistical Organisation" de Nueva Delhi compila y publica el índice en: "Monthly Abstract of Statistics".
idem: "Statistical Abstract".
Labour Bureau, Simla: "Indian Labour Journal".

INDIA (TODO EL PAIS 3)

Denominación oficial
Consumer Price Index for Industrial Workers (Indice de precios del consumo para trabajadores industriales).

Alcance
El índice se compila mensualmente y comprende hogares de trabajadores de la industria ubicados en 70 centros industriales de todo el país.

Base oficial
1982 = 100.

Fuente de la ponderación
La selección de los artículos y la determinación de los coeficientes de ponderación se basaron en una encuesta realizada durante un año, 1981-1982, sobre los gastos de una muestra de 32 616 hogares de trabajadores de siete sectores industriales, a saber, las fábricas, las minas, las plantaciones, los ferrocarriles, las empresas de transporte de personas por carretera en vehículos automotores, las plantas generadoras y establecimientos de distribución de energía, los puertos y muelles de 70 centros industriales. No se ajustaron las ponderaciones para tomar en cuenta las modificaciones de precios ocurridas entre el momento de la encuesta y el período de base.

La inclusión de artículos en las canastas de gastos familiares consideradas en el índice dependió del gasto medio que comunicaron los hogares de trabajadores en comparación con el total de los gastos de consumo y el número de hogares que informaron sobre sus gastos. Los precios de los artículos que según los hogares informantes representaban una proporción insignificante de los gastos se atribuyeron generalmente, por un procedimiento de imputación, a otros gastos en artículos afines del mismo subgrupo.

Ponderaciones y composición

Grupos principales	Número de artículos	Ponderación	Número aproximado de cotizaciones de precio
Alimentación	106	57,00	...
Tabaco, pan, supari, etc.	16	3,15	...
Vivienda	1	8,67	...
Combustible y luz	10	6,28	...
Vestido, calzado y ropa blanca	39	8,54	...
Artículos y servicios varios	88	16,36	...
Total	260	100,00	...

Gastos de consumo de los hogares
Se han atribuido valores ficticios a los ingresos en especie, la vivienda propia, los regalos, etc. Los pagos parciales sólo se consideraron por la parte efectivamente pagada durante el mes de referencia. Se han excluido la compra de artículos de segunda mano y el comercio de bienes usados. No se trataron como gastos de consumo los pagos de cotizaciones a la seguridad social, fondos de pensión, patentes y matrículas, seguros de bienes, impuestos directos, seguros de vida, remesas de dinero, etc.

Método de recolección de los datos
La recopilación de precios de los diversos bienes y servicios (comprendidos los de electricidad, gas, asistencia médica, educación, transporte y comunicaciones), está a cargo de los funcionarios públicos de cada Estado de la Unión, que les registran en los mercados y puestos de venta al por menor más populares, así como en los comercios controlados (precios equitativos) y establecimientos de servicios. Los precios más inestables se registran todas las semanas. Los de otros artículos, como cines, muebles, utensilios, electrodomésticos, transporte, prendas de vestir y calzar, etc., se registran una vez al mes, pues no varían con demasiada frecuencia. Las cotizaciones de precio de ciertos artículos, como alquileres, matrículas de enseñanza y textos de estudio se registran una vez por semestre. En todos los casos se consignan los precios del momento en el mismo lugar de venta. En el índice se utilizan los precios netos; los del mercado libre y los oficiales (controlados por el Estado) se combinan en la razón del promedio de los suministros necesarios establecido a través de dos fuentes. Para compilar el índice no se consideran los precios del mercado negro, las compras a plazo o de objetos de segunda mano, ni los precios de importación.

Vivienda
Los datos relativos a las cotizaciones de alquiler se obtienen cada seis meses con respecto a viviendas alquiladas, propias o gratuitas e incluyen los gastos en impuestos y reparaciones menores o blanqueo, que generalmente corren a cargo de los ocupantes, pero no los de agua corriente, electricidad, barrendeo y cargas similares. El índice de alquileres sigue el método de base de cadena que compara los movimientos de las cotizaciones de alquiler con las del semestre anterior y no con las del período de base, permitiendo así establecer mejor la depreciación de las viviendas. No se incluyen en la muestra las nuevas viviendas por estimarse que el movimiento relativo de los alquileres de las casas nuevas no difiere mucho con respecto al conjunto de las antiguas.

Para las viviendas ocupadas por sus propietarios, se registra el alquiler de una vivienda comparable. Si no existe en el mercado ninguna casa con características comparables se supone, a los efectos del índice, que tienen la misma cotización que las viviendas alquiladas.

Especificación de las variedades
Se ha fijado para cada artículo una especificación detallada, que comprende la variedad, calidad, marca o factura, cantidad, etc. Las especificaciones se han basado en las preferencias locales, determinadas mediante investigaciones de mercado.

Sustitución, cambio de calidad, etc.
Cuando no es posible encontrar un artículo de determinada calidad, se le sustituye por otro, de calidad similar o comparable. Si la variedad anterior vuelve a aparecer en el mercado, se reintroduce su precio. Se realizan ajustes por las diferencias de precio que obedezcan a diferencias de calidad del sustituto. Cuando la diferencia de calidad del sustituto elegido es mayor de 100 por ciento, o cuando la diferencia es difícil de evaluar, el precio del nuevo producto se enlaza con las cotizaciones del producto sustituido.

Artículos estacionales
Las ponderaciones del subgrupo legumbres y frutas se han mantenido constantes dentro del grupo de los alimentos, pero todos los meses se calculan coeficientes variables para los distintos artículos, según su disponibilidad. Las ponderaciones de los artículos no disponibles en un determinado mes se imputan a los artículos similares.

Cálculo
El índice se calcula según la fórmula de Laspeyres, como un promedio aritmético ponderado con base fija, cuyos coeficientes de ponderación corresponden al período 1981-1982. Para cada artículo se utiliza por lo general un promedio simple de todos los precios registrados en un mes. Cuando para un solo artículo se hayan registrado los precios de más de una calidad, se atribuye a ese artículo el promedio simple de los precios relativos. Los índices de los centros, en su totalidad, se compilan directamente, pero el índice para todo el país es un promedio ponderado de todos los índices de centro, basándose las ponderaciones de estos últimos en el producto del gasto de consumo medio por hogar y el número de hogares de cada centro en 1981-1982.

Informaciones complementarias
Además de los índices de los precios de consumo para hogares de trabajadores industriales, se están publicando para la India otras dos series: los índices de los precios del consumo para hogares de peones agrícolas y los índices de los precios del consumo para hogares de asalariados urbanos no manuales. La compilación de la primera serie está a cargo de la Oficina del Trabajo, que lo publica mensualmente en su "Indian Labour Journal", mientras que la segunda serie la compila la Organización Central de Estadísticas de Nueva Delhi, que la publica en "Monthly Abstract of Statistics" (Nueva Delhi).

Organización y publicación
Ministry of Labour, Labour Bureau: "Indian Labour Journal" (Simla) (para mas amplias informaciones metodológicas, véanse los números de nov. de 1988 y enero de 1989).
idem: "Indian Labour Year Book - Annual".
idem: "Pocket Book of Labour Statistics - Annual".
idem: "Indian Labour Statistics - Annual".

INDIA (DELHI)

Denominación oficial
Consumer Price Index for Industrial Workers (Indice de precios del consumo para trabajadores industriales).

Alcance
El índice se compila mensualmente y comprende hogares de trabajadores industriales de Delhi.

Base oficial
1982 = 100.

Fuente de la ponderación
La selección de los artículos y la determinación de los coeficientes de ponderación se basaron en una encuesta sobre los gastos de 648 hogares de asalariados no manuales de 7 sectores de la economía, a saber, las fábricas, las minas, las plantaciones, los ferrocarriles, las empresas de transporte público en vehículos automotores, las fábricas y establecimientos de distribución de energía, los puertos y muelles de 70 centros industriales. El índice se refiere a los hogares de trabajadores de la industria que viven en Delhi. No se ajustaron las ponderaciones para tomar en cuenta las modificaciones de precios ocurridas entre el momento de la encuesta y el período de base. La inclusión de artículos en las canastas del índice dependió del gasto medio comunicado por los hogares de trabajadores comparado con el total de los gastos de consumo y el número de hogares que informaron sobre sus gastos. Los precios de los artículos que, según lo informado por los hogares, representaban una proporción insignificante de los gastos se atribuyeron por lo general a los artículos afines del mismo subgrupo.

Ponderaciones y composición

Grupos principales	Número de artículos	Ponderación	Número aproximado de cotizaciones de precio
Alimentación	61	50,71	524
Tabaco, pan, supari, etc.	8	2,35	56
Vivienda	1	14,02	21
Combustible y luz	6	5,61	39
Vestido, calzado y ropa blanca	15	12,53	31
Artículos y servicios varios	39	14,78	143
Total	130	100,00	814

Gastos de consumo de los hogares
Se han supuesto valores ficticios a los ingresos en especie, la vivienda propia, los regalos, etc. Los pagos parciales sólo se consideraron por la parte efectivamente pagada durante el mes de referencia. Se ha excluido la compra de artículos de segunda mano y el comercio de bienes usados. No se trataron como gastos de consumo los efectuados en pagar cotizaciones a la seguridad social, fondos de pensión, patentes y matrículas, seguros de bienes, impuestos directos, seguros de vida, remesas de dinero, etc.

Método de recolección de los datos
La recopilación de precios de los diversos bienes y servicios (comprendidos los de electricidad, gas, asistencia médica, educación, transporte y comunicaciones), está a cargo de los funcionarios públicos de cada Estado de la Unión, que los registran en los mercados y puestos de venta al por menor más populares, así como en los comercios con controlados (precios equitativos) y establecimientos de servicios. Los precios más inestables se registran todas las semanas. Los de otros artículos, como cines, muebles, utensilios, electrodomésticos, transporte, prendas de vestir y calzar, etc., se registran una vez al mes, pues no varían con demasiada frecuencia. Las cotizaciones de precio de ciertos artículos, como alquileres, matrículas de enseñanza y textos de estudio se registran una vez por semestre. En todos los casos se consignan los precios del momento en el mismo lugar de venta. En el índice se utilizan los precios netos; los del mercado libre y los oficiales (controlados por el Estado) se combinan en la razón del promedio de los suministros necesarios establecido a través de dos fuentes. Para compilar el índice no se consideran los precios del mercado negro, las compras a plazo o de objetos de segunda mano, ni los precios de importación.

Vivienda
Los datos relativos a las cotizaciones de alquiler se obtienen cada seis meses con respecto a viviendas alquiladas, propias o gratuitas, e incluyen los gastos en impuestos y reparaciones menores o blanqueo, que generalmente corren a cargo de los ocupantes, pero no los de agua corriente, electricidad, barrendeo y cargas similares. El índice de alquileres sigue el método de base de cadena que compara los movimientos de las cotizaciones de alquiler con las del semestre anterior y no con las del período de base, permitiendo así establecer mejor la depreciación de las viviendas. No se incluyen en la muestra las nuevas viviendas por estimarse que el movimiento relativo de los alquileres de las casas nuevas no difiere mucho con respecto al conjunto de las antiguas.
Para las viviendas ocupadas por sus propietarios, se registra el alquiler de una vivienda comparable. Si no existe en el mercado ninguna casa con características comparables se supone, a los efectos del índice, que tienen la misma cotización que las viviendas alquiladas.

Especificación de las variedades
Se ha fijado para cada artículo una especificación detallada, que comprende la variedad, calidad, marca o factura, cantidad, etc. Las especificaciones se han basado en las preferencias locales, determinadas mediante investigaciones de mercado.

Sustitución, cambio de calidad, etc.
Cuando no es posible encontrar un artículo de determinada calidad, se le sustituye por otro, de calidad similar o comparable. Si la variedad anterior vuelve a aparecer en el mercado, se reintroduce su precio. Se realizan ajustes por las diferencias de precio que obedezcan a diferencias de calidad del sustituto. Cuando la diferencia de calidad del sustituto elegido es mayor de 100 por ciento, o cuando la diferencia es difícil de evaluar, el precio del nuevo producto se enlaza con las cotizaciones del producto sustituido.

Artículos estacionales
Las ponderaciones del subgrupo legumbres y frutas se han mantenido constantes dentro del grupo de los alimentos, pero todos los meses se calculan coeficientes variables para los distintos artículos, según su disponibilidad. Las ponderaciones de los artículos no disponibles en un determinado mes se imputan a los artículos similares.

Cálculo
El índice se calcula según la fórmula de Laspeyres, como un promedio aritmético ponderado con base fija, cuyos coeficientes de ponderación corresponden al período 1981-1982. Para cada artículo se utiliza por lo general un promedio simple de todos los precios registrados en un mes. Cuando para un solo artículo se hayan registrado los precios de más de una calidad, se atribuye a ese artículo el promedio simple de los precios relativos. Los índices de los centros, en su totalidad, se compilan directamente, pero el índice para todo el país es un promedio ponderado de todos los índices de centro, basándose las ponderaciones de estos últimos en el producto del gasto de consumo medio por hogar y el número de hogares de cada centro en 1981-1982.

Informaciones complementarias
Además de los índices de los precios de consumo para hogares de trabajadores industriales, se están publicando para la India otras dos series: los índices de los precios del consumo para hogares de peones agrícolas y los índices de los precios del consumo para hogares de asalariados urbanos no manuales. La compilación de la primera serie está a cargo de la Oficina del Trabajo, que lo publica mensualmente en su "Indian Labour Journal", mientras que la segunda serie la compila la Organización Central de Estadísticas de Nueva Delhi, que la publica en "Monthly Abstract of Statistics" (Nueva Delhi).

Organización y publicación
Ministry of Labour, Labour Bureau: "Indian Labour Journal" (Simla; para mas amplias informaciones metodológicas, véanse los números de nov. de 1988 y enero de 1989).
idem: "Indian Labour Year Book - Annual".
idem: "Pocket Book of Labour Statistics - Annual".

idem: "Indian Labour Statistics - Annual".

INDONESIA

Denominación oficial
Combined Consumer Price Index of 27 capital cities of provinces (Indice de Precios del Consumo, combinado para 27 capitales de provincia).

Alcance
La compilación del índice es mensual y abarca hogares privados urbanos de 27 capitales de provincia.

Base oficial
abril de 1988 - marzo de 1989 = 100.

Fuente de la ponderación
La determinación de los coeficientes de ponderación y la selección de los artículos se basaron en los resultados de una encuesta sobre el costo de la vida, realizada de abril de 1988 a marzo de 1989 en 27 ciudades capitales de provincia. La muestra abarcó 35 000 hogares privados, excluyéndose de la encuesta los de una sola persona o más de diez, los institucionales y los compuestos por analfabetos.

Ponderaciones y composición
No disponible.

Gastos de consumo de los hogares
Se siguió el criterio del consumo para calcular el gasto en alimentación, bebidas, tabaco y servicios, y el de la entrega para toda clase de bienes semidurables y durables.

El valor locativo de las viviendas, propias y gratuitas, corresponde a las cotizaciones de alquiler predominantes en ese momento. Su monto se clasifica como ingreso del hogar y también, por igual valor, como gasto. Si el hogar ocupa una vivienda oficial o una vivienda de una compañía con un alquiler menor que el de mercado, el monto de la diferencia se considera como ingreso y el valor de mercado como gasto. También para los bienes recibidos en forma gratuita o los adquiridos a menor precio que el de mercado se clasifican como gastos de los hogares por su valor de mercado y como ingresos por la diferencia entre dicho valor y el precio rebajado.

Las compras a crédito o a plazos de bienes y servicios consumidos durante el período de referencia se consideran como gastos de consumo de esos artículos y también como ingresos, pero cuando sólo se considera la totalidad de las cuotas y anticipos pagados durante el período de referencia, tales desembolsos no se clasifican como gastos de consumo.

Gastos y otros pagos que no son de consumo: impuestos a ingresos y vehículos, transferencias de propiedad, tasas de radio y televisión, ahorros, seguros, amortización de deudas, pagos anticipado de compras, préstamos a terceros, adquisición de inmuebles (tierras y casas, comprendidas las reparaciones mayores), fiestas, ceremonias religiosas y tradicionales, pérdidas de dinero en efectivo, etc.

Método de recolección de los datos
El personal estadístico, local y nacional, se encarga de registrar los precios de las tiendas minoristas y los establecimientos seleccionados. La recolección de precios puede ser semanal, mensual o trimestral. En el primer caso el día de la recolección es el jueves, en el segundo el 15 del mes y del 10 al 20 si el registro es trimestral.

Los datos sobre los servicios de electricidad, gas, agua y comunicaciones se basan en las tarifas oficiales.

Para calcular el índice se utilizan los precios al por menor que pagan los consumidores en el momento.

Vivienda
Las cotizaciones de los alquileres de 16 clases de viviendas diferenciadas por el tipo de construcción e instalaciones se registran en marzo y septiembre de cada año. Las viviendas ocupadas por sus propietarios se toman en consideración para el cálculo de los coeficientes de ponderación, pero en el índice los movimientos de precio se determinan a partir del coste de los materiales y salarios de la construcción.

Especificación de las variedades
Existen especificaciones detalladas de la variedad, calidad y marca de cada uno de los artículos del índice.

Sustitución, cambio de calidad, etc.
Cuando cambia la calidad de un artículo sólo se le introduce cuando se dispone de los precios del período en curso y del anterior.

Artículos estacionales
No existen cambios de estación y por lo tanto todos los artículos pueden conseguirse a lo largo del año.

Cálculo
El índice se calcula según la fórmula de Laspeyres como un promedio aritmético ponderado de base fija, cuyos coeficientes de ponderación corresponden al período de base.

El precio relativo de cada artículo se calcula dividiendo el precio medio del período corriente por el precio medio del período precedente. Los medios de precios son medias aritméticas simples.

El cálculo de los índices de precios ponderados de cada subgrupo, gran grupo y de todos los artículos permite obtener el Indice Combinado.

El Indice es una combinación de las series de las capitales de provincia. El Indice Nacional se obtiene a partir de las series de ciudades, para cuyo cálculo se utiliza como coeficiente de ponderación el número de hogares de las áreas urbanas de cada ciudad.

Informaciones complementarias
También se calculan y publican índices para cada una de las 27 capitales.

Organización y publicación
Central Bureau of Statistics: "Monthly Statistical Bulletin" (Jakarta).

IRAN, REP. ISLAMICA DEL

Denominación oficial
Consumer Price Index (Indice de Precios del Consumo).

Alcance
El índice se compila mensualmente y abarca hogares urbanos que en 1982-1983 tenían un gasto anual de hasta 4 700 000 rials.

Base oficial
21 de marzo de 1982 - 20 de marzo de 1983 = 100.

Fuente de la ponderación
La determinación de los coeficientes de ponderación y la selección de los artículos se basaron en los resultados de una encuesta sobre los gastos de los hogares realizada entre marzo de 1982 y marzo de 1983. La encuesta abarcó 15 000 hogares urbanos cuyos gastos anuales no superaron los 4 700 000 rials.

Ponderaciones y composición

Grupos principales	Número de artículos	Ponderación	Número aproximado de cotizaciones de precio
Alimentación, bebidas y tabaco	96	40,06	55 000
Otros grupos:	...	...	45 000
Vestido y calzado	42	8,07	...
Vivienda, combustible y energía eléctrica	25	26,20	...
Moblaje y gastos del hogar	41	7,24	...
Asistencia médica	41	3,94	...
Transportes y comunicaciones	22	8,14	...
Recreación, educación y lectura	16	1,60	...
Diversos bienes y servicios	20	4,75	...
Total	303	100,00	100 000

Gastos de consumo de los hogares
Para obtener los coeficientes de ponderación se consideran los valores monetarios de todos los bienes y servicios adquiridos durante el año de base por los hogares, para el consumo propio o para darlos a otros hogares. Comprenden el valor total de los bienes durables adquiridos a crédito en el momento de la compra, los ingresos en especie (no recibidos de otros hogares), las contribuciones a fondos de pensiones o de seguridad social, las tasas de licencias y permisos, la asistencia médica, los seguros, los pagos del seguro de vida y los gastos en regalos. Se excluyen las remesas, los impuestos directos, las contribuciones jubilatorias y el valor de los bienes de producción y consumo caseros.

Método de recolección de los datos
Los investigadores registran los precios de la mayoría de los

artículos los 25 primeros días de cada mes, en puntos de venta al por menor, supermercados y establecimientos de servicios de 80 ciudades. Las rebajas, precios de liquidación y precios del mercado negro no se toman en consideración. Para los productos con precio oficial y cotización libre en el mercado se calcula un promedio ponderado de los precios. Los coeficientes de ponderación se basan en la última encuesta sobre los gastos de consumo de los hogares.

Vivienda
Las cotizaciones del alquiler se obtienen trimestralmente de una muestra de aproximadamente 7 000 viviendas. Para calcular el valor locativo equivalente de la vivienda propia se supone que ha tenido la misma tasa de inflación que el índice general.

Especificación de las variedades
Se especifica la calidad, unidad y tamaño, etc., de los artículos cuyos precios se deben registrar.

Sustitución, cambio de calidad, etc.
Se trata de registrar siempre los precios de artículos de la misma calidad o, de no ser posible, de la calidad más cercana. Si el cambio de calidad es importante, se procede a un ajuste de calidad o se recurre al método de enlace.

Artículos estacionales
Fuera de temporada, los precios de los artículos estacionales se calculan suponiendo que han tenido la misma tasa de inflación que el promedio ponderado de los demás artículos del grupo.

Cálculo
El índice se calcula según la fórmula de Laspeyres como un promedio aritmético ponderado de base fija, cuyos coeficientes de ponderación corresponden al período de base.
El promedio de los precios sirve para derivar los relativos de precio de los meses consecutivos. Se hacen los ajustes necesarios de los precios erróneos. Los precios que faltan se sustituyen por otros de ciudades similares. El índice se computa directamente sobre la base de región.

Informaciones complementarias
Se publican índices de los principales subgrupos. No se calculan otras series nacionales.

Organización y publicación
Economic Statistics Department, Central Bank Markazi: "Economic Report and Balance Sheet" (Teherán).

IRAQ

Denominación oficial
Consumer Price Index (Indice de precios del consumo).

Alcance
El índice se compila mensualmente y se refiere a todos los hogares urbanos.

Base oficial
1973 = 100.

Fuente de la ponderación
La selección de los artículos y la determinación de los coeficientes de ponderación se basaron en los resultados de una encuesta sobre los gastos de los hogares efectuada en 1971-72, en áreas urbanas, que abarcó una muestra de todos los tipos de hogares.

Ponderaciones y composición

Grupos principales	Número de artículos	Ponderación	Número aproximado de cotizaciones de precio
Alimentación	80	49,73	...
Tabaco y alcohol	7	3,47	...
Vestido	73	8,20	...
Calzado	9	1,77	...
Accesorios para el hogar	37	5,01	...
Combustible	7	4,01	...
Productos de limpieza y aseo persona	14	1,69	...
Educación y distracciones	5	1,72	...
Vivienda y gastos del hogar	2	15,62	...
Bienes y servicios varios	2	8,78	...
Total	236	100,00	...

Gastos de consumo de los hogares
No disponible.

Método de recolección de los datos
Los precios se recogen los días 3, 9, 21 y 27 de cada mes en los diez mercados principales de Bagdad y en los dos mercados principales de los demás centros urbanos.

Vivienda
Las cotizaciones de alquiler se obtienen en marzo y en septiembre de cada año en 143 viviendas alquiladas de Bagdad y en 208 casas alquiladas de otras gobernaciones.

Especificación de las variedades
No disponible.

Sustitución, cambio de calidad, etc.
No disponible.

Artículos estacionales
No disponible.

Cálculo
El índice se calcula conforme a la fórmula de Laspeyres como un promedio aritmético ponderado de base fija. Los coeficientes de ponderación corresponden a 1971-72.

Informaciones complementarias
Actualmente se calcula una nueva serie (base 1988 = 100), pero en el momento de publicar el presente volumen la OIT no disponía de informaciones metodológicas sobre esta serie.

Organización y publicación
Ministry of Planning, Central Statistical Organisation: "Annual Abstract of Statistics" (Bagdad). Esta publicación también contiene detalles metodológicos.

IRLANDA

Denominación oficial
Consumer Price Index (Indice de Precios del Consumo: IPC).

Alcance
El índice se compila en febrero, mayo, agosto y noviembre. Abarca todos los hogares privados del país, sin limitaciones por motivos de tamaño o ingreso.

Base oficial
Mediados de noviembre de 1989 = 100.

Fuente de la ponderación
Para determinar los coeficientes de ponderación se utilizaron las estimaciones disponibles más recientes sobre el promedio semanal de gastos de todos los hogares del país en bienes de consumo o servicios. Prácticamente la totalidad de estas estimaciones provienen de los resultados de una encuesta nacional en gran escala, realizada específicamente con esta finalidad durante 1987, que sondeó una muestra nacional representativa de 7 705 hogares privados de todo el país. El trabajo de campo comenzó en febrero de 1987 y finalizó en abril de 1988. A efectos de su actualización, las estimaciones de esta encuesta, que se referían al año civil de 1987, se ajustaron para referirse a la mitad de noviembre de 1989 en función del promedio de las variaciones de precio que tuvieron cada uno de los artículos del antiguo índice entre 1987 y mediados de 1989. No se pudieron obtener informaciones precisas sobre cambios cuantitativos de la estructura detallada o del consumo de los hogares durante esos dos años y no se hicieron ajustes a ese respecto.
Los gastos en variedades no cotizadas de una categoría de artículos, sea se añadieron directamente al coeficiente de ponderación de variedades similares con una misma tendencia estimada de precios, sea se distribuyeron proporcionalmente entre todas las variedades con precio registrado.

Gastos de consumo de los hogares
El índice abarca todos los gastos efectuados por los hogares para adquirir bienes de consumo u obtener prestaciones de servicios. Además de los gastos en alimentación, bebidas, vestido y calzado, etc., también se incluyen los de seguros de la casa, permisos de conducir, cotizaciones a clubes, sociedades, asociaciones y sindicatos, pagos periódicos de intereses hipotecarios y compras a crédito. Por su propia naturaleza el IPC no puede abarcar los bienes o servicios que carecen de precio o cuya determinación es imposible. Por tal motivo se excluyen los gastos de los hogares en contribuciones eclesiásticas y obras de caridad, alquiler de terrenos, prestaciones personales en efectivo, apuestas y loterías. Por otra parte, como el IPC se funda en el concepto de gastos del consumo de los hogares, se excluyen también los artículos de consumo no comprados, tales

Ponderaciones y composición

Grupos principales	Número de artículos	Ponderación	Número aproximado de cotizaciones de precio
Alimentación (incl. comidas fuera del hogar)	50	25,7528	12 700
Bebidas alcohólicas	3	11,7301	1 400
Tabaco	3	3,3382	400
Vivienda:			
Alquiler	1	1,5150	900
Intereses hipotecarios	1	3,3864	2
Reparación, decoración, agua y seguros de la casa	3	1,6098	400
Combustible y luz	7	5,9012	800
Vestido y calzado	24	6,7229	4 300
Artículos domésticos durables	13	4,7146	4 200
Otros artículos (productos de limpieza e higiene, deportes y distracción, etc.)	20	5,8502	5 400
Transporte	13	13,7488	1 400
Servicios y gastos conexos	21	15,0850	5 600
Total	159	100,0000	39 000

como los productos del propio huerto o jardín para consumo del mismo hogar, las prestaciones y otros pagos en especie de la seguridad social y el valor locativo ficticio de la vivienda propia. Pese a que afectan el nivel de vida y el presupuesto de muchos hogares, también se excluyen del índice: primas de seguros de vida, contribuciones a fondos de pensión, amortizaciones del capital de préstamos hipotecarios u otros préstamos personales, inversiones de capital en efectivo para comprar casas o hacerles modificaciones o reparaciones importantes, otras formas de ahorro e inversión, pagos de contribuciones a la seguridad social y del impuesto a la renta.

Método de recolección de los datos

La recolección trimestral de precios tiene lugar los martes más próximos a la mitad de febrero, mayo, agosto y noviembre en unos 3 000 puntos de venta al por menor y establecimientos de servicios de todas las ciudades con 10 000 o más habitantes y de una muestra representativa de centros urbanos más pequeños.

El total de las variedades apreciadas es de 807, determinándose locamente el precio de 403. La diferencia corresponde sea a las variedades de una sola empresa (como las de electricidad, transporte por carretera o ferrocarril, correos y teléfonos) o de un pequeño grupo de empresas (como las de gas, combustible, etc. de uso doméstico), sea a variedades cuya cotización no es necesario determinar en el plano local, como los honorarios de médicos, dentistas u optometristas y las subscripciones periódicas. Estos precios los registra directamente la Oficina Central de Estadísticas (OCE) mediante encuestas especiales realizadas por correo o por teléfono.

Los precios registrados son los que pagan en efectivo los consumidores en el momento de la transacción. No se aceptan promedios, estimaciones o gamas de precios. Las cotizaciones de precio comprenden los impuestos directos. No se consideran los recargos por créditos ni las rebajas, salvo si se conceden a todo el público. Se aceptan los precios de liquidaciones y ofertas especiales si se practican el día del registro de precios, pero no las rebajas de mercancías averiadas, defectuosas o de calidad inferior a la estándar. Los precios de lista sólo se consideran cuando se exigen en ese momento al consumidor.

Se distinguen los pagos de las adquisiciones a plazo de aparatos electrodomésticos y acústicos, automóviles y bicicletas. Para los acuerdos de ventas a crédito con plazos variables se utilizan indicadores de precio diferentes para el pago de intereses y para el reembolso de anticipos, basados en un sistema fijo de compras a plazo o de alquiler con opción de compra. Los indicadores de los precios actuales al contado se utilizan para ponderar los pagos iniciales de nuevos acuerdos.

Vivienda

El IPC abarca los gastos de vivienda del momento. Se toman especialmente en cuenta las modificaciones de costo de los siguientes elementos: alquileres privados y de la autoridad local, tarifas de los servicios públicos locales, seguros de la casa (todas las viviendas), reparación y decoración (todas las viviendas), pago de intereses hipotecarios (vivienda propia hipotecada). El importe bruto (es decir, antes de deducir el impuesto a la renta) de los intereses hipotecarios se emplea para determinar tanto los coeficientes de ponderación como las cotizaciones de precio. La parte de los pagos hipotecarios correspondiente a la amortización del capital no se incluye en la definición de gasto del hogar del índice, pues se relaciona con la adquisición de valores de activo fijo, en este caso la propiedad de la vivienda.

Las modificaciones del nivel medio de los alquileres locales se incorporan al índice todos los trimestres. Los cálculos se basan en los detalles de todas esas viviendas y en los agregados de los alquileres obtenidos directamente de cada administración local. También todos los trimestres se investiga la modificación de los alquileres ficticios establecidos para las viviendas propias. Todos los trimestres funcionarios de la OCE realizan directamente un sondeo especial sobre los alquileres de la región de Dublín, mientras que investigadores privados, contratados a tiempo parcial para la recolección de precios, hacen un sondeo similar en la pequeñas ciudades de provincia. También se realizan dos encuestas permanentes por correo dirigidas, respectivamente, a pequeños grupos de propietarios y de arrendatarios.

Se abarcan los gastos de vivienda que efectivamente tienen los propietarios que viven en ella, es decir que no se consideran los alquileres ficticios. Las fluctuaciones del costo de los intereses hipotecarios se basan en las características fijas del conjunto de hipotecas de distinto plazo, monto y tipo de interés de la empresa constructora y de la autoridad local. No se incluye la parte correspondiente a la amortización del capital de los préstamos hipotecarios. Los detalles relativos a las tarifas de los servicios de agua se obtienen todos los años de la autoridad local pertinente.

El indicador de precios para los seguros de casas se basa en las tasas corrientes de los seguros de viviendas privadas y sus enseres, como en los apropiados índices de actualización de su valor. Los precios de una selección representativa de materiales de reparación y decoración del hogar se obtienen mediante una encuesta que todos los trimestres se envía por correo a una lista nacional de comerciantes.

Especificación de las variedades

Los procedimientos de registro se ajustan estrictamente al principio de que, en lo posible, los precios de los artículos de una variedad seleccionada de igual calidad o marca deben registrarse siempre en el mismo negocio. Las especificaciones de cada variedad seleccionada son generales y describen una línea de productos (es decir, marcas, tamaños, calidades, etc., particulares) entre los cuales cada investigador tiene la facultad de elegir uno, inicialmente o en casos de sustitución, para registrar periódicamente su precio. Así por ejemplo, en la categoría "juguetes" de la serie actual se han seleccionado cinco variedades distintas, una de las cuales es un modelo reducido de coche. Como no se dan especificaciones complementarias, los investigadores pueden en principio seleccionar libremente cualquiera de los modelos de coches reducidos disponibles locamente para investigar periódicamente su precio, con la única restricción de que el modelo elegido tenga una demanda popular, se pueda fijar su precio en forma periódica (es decir que sea posible especificarlo con precisión) y tenga probabilidades de mantenerse largo tiempo en el mercado. A partir de la elección inicial, en todas las ocasiones sucesivas, los investigadores deben registrar los precios de los mismos productos. Dado el lapso que puede transcurrir entre una ocasión y otra, así como la posibilidad de que en la investigación participen personas distintas, se elaboraron folletos especiales con la especificación exacta de cada uno de los productos seleccionados, para garantizar que en cada ocasión se cotizan los precios del mismo conjunto de artículos.

En virtud de estas disposiciones, los productos específicos de una determinada variedad cuyos precios registran los distintos investigadores no son en cada caso los mismos. El método permite que se recojan los precios de una amplia variedad de marcas y calidades en sitios distintos que reflejan los gustos y preferencias locales, además de presentar las fluctuaciones de precio en mejor forma que si siempre se registraran los precios de una sola e idéntica variedad, definida con un sentido restringido.

Sustitución, cambio de calidad, etc.

En casos de discontinuidad por cambios de modelo o calidad, escasez de la oferta o pérdida de popularidad, se realizan sustituciones a nivel local y se introducen artículos populares sustitutivos.

Los folletos de precios permiten especificar detalladamente todo nuevo producto que se introduzca. Cada discontinuidad particular se limita a un sólo folleto, excluyéndose de los cálculos del índice la cotización pertinente hasta que se obtengan dos nuevas cotizaciones de precio sucesivas del producto sustitutivo. Los encargados de registrar los precios también tienen facultades para sustituir los artículos originalmente seleccionados cuya oferta haya disminuido o que ya no gocen de una demanda popular en el plano local. Sin embargo el precio de un determinado artículo sólo se utiliza para compilar el índice cuando se dispone de dos cotizaciones trimestrales sucesivas.

También se considera como discontinuidad toda modificación ocurrida en el negocio encuestado y los precios de los productos afectados no entran en el cálculo del índice hasta obtener dos cotizaciones trimestrales sucesivas en el mismo negocio. Los folletos de precios permiten identificar claramente el negocio en donde se registran los precios de cada producto. Si en un determinado momento ya no es posible investigar los precios en un negocio dado (por cese de su actividad comercial o negativa a seguir cooperando, etc.) el encargado de la recolección lo sustituye por otro negocio similar de la misma zona.

Un funcionario de la OCE visita periódicamente a todos los investigadores de precios de las provincias para asegurarse del adecuado cumplimiento de las disposiciones adoptadas en materia de registro de precios. La OCE se encarga de dar formación e instrucciones a los funcionarios responsables de la encuesta de precios de Dublín.

Artículos estacionales
Los precios de algunos productos alimenticios frescos, como huevos, legumbres, frutas, etc., fluctúan con mayor o menor intensidad según las variaciones estacionales de la oferta y la demanda. Tradicionalmente, en el IPC sólo se ajustan las variaciones estacionales del precio de huevos, patatas y tomates por la evidente repercusión de su peso en el índice. Como esta forma de proceder puede dificultar indebidamente la determinación de las tendencias subyacentes de los precios, se continúan excluyendo del índice las fluctuaciones estacionales de los precios de esos artículos, que se ajustan mediante la variante X-11 del Método 11 del Programa de Ajustes Estacionales de la Oficina de Censos de los Estados Unidos.

Existen otros artículos en el índice cuyos precios tienden a variar regularmente en el mismo período cada año, simplemente porque se pagan anualmente durante ese período. Ejemplo de dichos artículos son las notas de colegio y universidad, subscripciones anuales a clubes y asociaciones. Los artículos con cargas impositivas elevadas (alcohol y tabaco) también se ven afectados de esta manera ante un cambio en el presupuesto. Los cambios en los precios de estos artículos particulares y de otros artículos cuya contribución estacional es insignificante, se reflejan en el IPC, sin ajuste. Es por esta razón que la estacionalidad no se excluye totalmente del IPC.

Cálculo
El índice se calcula según la fórmula de Laspeyres como un promedio aritmético ponderado de base fija, cuyos coeficientes de ponderación corresponden al período de base.

Se calculan en primer lugar los promedios nacionales del precio de cada una de las variedades de la muestra. Estos promedios se obtienen en dos etapas. En la primera se calculan los promedios aritméticos simples de los precios dentro de los estratos por tamaño de los centros urbanos; estos promedios por estrato se combinan en una etapa ulterior con las ponderaciones de los estratos de ventas al por menor, obtenidas del Censo de Servicios de 1987, para obtener así promedios nacionales de precios. Se forma un estrato separado con los grandes almacenes para que sus precios se puedan incorporar al promedio nacional con la ponderación adecuada. Se vuelven a calcular promedios nacionales complementarios de los precios correspondientes al trimestre precedente utilizando conjuntos equiparables de cotizaciones. La razón entre estos promedios nacionales comparables de precios expresa la fluctuación trimestral estimada de los precios y permite actualizar el costo de la misma cantidad de cada una de las variedades del índice correspondiente al trimestre anterior y obtener así el costo constante de la canasta para el trimestre en curso. De esta forma se pueden obtener directamente índices de las variaciones de precio de todos los artículos, o de cualquier combinación de los mismos, dividiendo su costo total del momento por su costo respectivo en el trimestre tomado como base.

Informaciones complementarias
Se continuarán compilando índices separados para los diez grupos siguientes de mercancías de la serie anterior: alimentos, bebidas alcohólicas, tabaco, vestido o calzado, combustibles y luz, mobiliario y accesorios para el hogar, bienes domésticos durables, otros bienes, transportes, servicios y gastos conexos. También se publica un índice adicional para artículos relacionados con la energía que abarca: combustible, alumbrado, petróleo, diesel de motor, gas (LPG) o gasolina de motor. A efectos de su continuidad, la publicación de cada una de estas series continuará tomando mediados de noviembre como base 100.

La próxima actualización del IPC, que ha de completarse en noviembre de 1996, se basará en los resultados de una encuesta en gran escala sobre los gastos de los hogares prevista para 1994.

Organización y publicación
Central Statistical Office (Oficina Central de Estadísticas: OFC): "Irish Statistical Bulletin" (Dublin).

idem: "Consumer Price Index - Introduction of Updated series - Base: Mid-November 1989 as 100".

ISLANDIA (REYKIAVIK)

Denominación oficial
Cost of Living Index (Indice del Costo de la Vida).

Alcance
El índice se compila mensualmente y abarca toda clase de hogares (comprendidos los de funcionarios públicos) de Reykiavik.

Base oficial
Mayo de 1988 = 100.

Fuente de la ponderación
El presente Indice del Costo de la Vida (ICV) se basa en una encuesta sobre los gastos de los hogares realizada de julio de 1985 a junio de 1986. Los hogares se seleccionaron por muestreo aleatorio simple del Registro Nacional sin consideración de tamaño, ocupación o domicilio, salvo los 70 años de edad del jefe de familia.

Al adoptarse la nueva base se ajustaron los coeficientes de ponderación de los gastos de los hogares para tomar en consideración los cambios producidos entre el período de la encuesta y mayo de 1988. Este ajuste responde fundamentalmente al aumento de la propiedad individual y de la utilización de automóviles y canales de televisión parcialmente financiados por los usuarios. Las ponderaciones de los artículos sin precio registrado las reflejan los sustitutivos con precio registrado más similares.

Ponderaciones y composición

Grupos principales	Número de artículos	Ponderación	Número aproximado de cotizaciones de precio
Alimentación	269	20,6	2 933
Bebidas alcohólicas y tabaco	32	4,4	245
Vestido y calzado	75	7,9	327
Alquiler, electricidad y agua caliente para calefacción	59	16,2	59
Muebles y enseres del hogar	99	7,4	371
Asistencia médica	34	2,3	60
Transporte y comunicaciones	46	18,9	158
Recreación y educación	100	11,0	179
Otros bienes y servicios	80	11,3	358
Total	794	100,0	4 690

Gastos de consumo de los hogares
El propósito de la encuesta en que se basa la ponderación era abarcar todos los aspectos posibles de los gastos de los hogares. Los gastos en especie no se incluyeron en las cuentas de los hogares de la encuesta pero en cierta medida se reflejaron en los informes de gastos correspondientes al año 1985 y por consiguiente, en forma parcial, en el índice. Se incluye la casa propia pues se estima que en Islandia el 80 por ciento de las viviendas están ocupadas por sus propietarios. Los gastos de esta categoría incluyen los intereses, la depreciación, el mantenimiento y los seguros, los impuestos a los bienes inmuebles, etc. El ámbito de la encuesta sobre los gastos domésticos comprendió la adquisición a crédito o a plazos de bienes durables, la de bienes de segunda mano y su entrega a cuenta y todos ellos sirvieron para determinar los coeficientes de ponderación originales. Sin embargo, una vez adoptadas estas ponderaciones, todas ellas se consideraron sin excepción como nuevas compras y no se tomaron en cuenta las compras a crédito ni las condiciones crediticias acordadas a los consu-

midores. La seguridad social de Islandia se financia con cargo al régimen fiscal y no se incluye en el índice. Tampoco se incluyen las contribuciones a fondos de pensión, que en Islandia son obligatorias y se deducen de los salarios o retribuciones. El pago de licencias, permisos o autorizaciones se incluyen en la medida en que se hayan reflejado en los gastos domésticos de la encuesta en relación con bienes de consumo específicos, seguros de vida y remesas de diverso orden. Sólo se incluyen los gastos de salud costeados directamente por los pacientes. No se incluyen los impuestos a los ingresos y otras cargas fiscales directas.

Método de recolección de los datos
Los puntos de venta y otras fuentes de información sobre los precios de bienes y servicios se seleccionan principalmente con la intención de obtener una distribución geográfica homogénea dentro de la capital y su región. En su caso, también se han adjudicado coeficientes de ponderación a los puntos de venta (en especial del ramo de la alimentación) fundándose en la estimación de su volumen de ventas. Los precios se registran en 322 puntos de venta al por menor y establecimientos de prestación de servicios. La recolección de la gran mayoría de los precios tiene lugar la primera semana de cada mes. Pero el registro o ajuste es menos frecuente con respecto a ciertos gastos de temporada (vacaciones en el extranjero o en el país, recreaciones, gastos de educación que se concentran al comienzo del año escolar). Las informaciones sobre los precios de los bienes y servicios privados se obtiene directamente de los proveedores, sea mediante visitas personales de los investigadores, sea - principalmente para los servicios - por llamadas telefónicas. Las informaciones sobre el costo de los servicios públicos se obtienen directamente de los servicios pertinentes o de las tarifas, los decretos oficiales y otros documentos similares. El coste de los servicios de electricidad y agua geotérmica (para calefacción o "corriente") se calcula como promedio nacional de sus tarifas. El Organismo Nacional de la Energía, que reúne los precios de todos los servicios de electricidad y calefacción geotérmica prestados en el país, comunica a la Oficina de Estadísticas los datos que ésta le pide.

En el índice sólo se incluyen los gastos de atención médica que corren exclusivamente a cargo de los pacientes o beneficiarios. Estas informaciones se basan principalmente en las tarifas oficiales; los de la asistencia odontológica, por su parte, en los aranceles de honorarios establecidos por la Asociación de Dentistas.

Los datos relacionados con los gastos de educación se obtienen tanto de su registro por parte de los investigadores como por comunicación directa de los establecimientos pertinentes.

Los precios del transporte y las comunicaciones se obtienen por el registro de los investigadores o de las tarifas oficiales, publicadas o comunicadas directamente por los establecimientos pertinentes.

La recolección de precios sobre el terreno está a cargo de personal debidamente formado y, en general, son las mismas personas las que se encargan de las labores sobre el terreno para cada clase de establecimiento, es decir que son siempre los mismos investigadores los que se encargan de la recolección de los precios de la alimentación, bebidas, vestidos, etc.

En principio los descuentos no se toman en consideración, salvo los de pagos al contado. Las rebajas de liquidación no se investigan. Los precios oficiales sólo se incluyen en la medida en que sean precios de mercado reales. Cuando los precios oficiales o controlados y los de mercado difieren siempre se descartan los oficiales. Hasta ahora no se ha tratado de investigar los precios del mercado negro, que en Islandia se limita casi exclusivamente a objetos o servicios fuera del comercio legal, como los narcóticos, etc. Las compras a crédito y los alquileres con opción de compra no se toman en consideración. Todas las cotizaciones de precio se basan en los precios pagados al contado y en efectivo. No se incluyen las compras de artículos de segunda mano. Los precios de mercancías importadas se recogen, como las demás, en los puntos de venta; la importación directa por parte del público consumidor no se investiga en forma especial pues sólo representa una fracción de las compras.

Vivienda
Dada la alta proporción de propietarios, el alquiler de la vivienda no se considera como un artículo. Se estima que en Islandia las viviendas ocupadas por sus propietarios constituyen más del 80 por ciento. Para esta categoría los gastos comprenden intereses, depreciación, mantenimiento, seguros, impuestos a los bienes raíces, etc.

Especificación de las variedades
La selección de los artículos para la recolección de precios se basó en la encuesta sobre los gastos de los hogares, que especificó todo detalle relativo a la factura, marca, unidad o cantidad y descripción de las mercaderías. Se hicieron algunos ajustes para actualizar dichas especificaciones dado el lapso transcurrido entre la encuesta y la fecha adoptada como base del índice para el cual, como se ha indicado, se especifican la variedad, factura, marca, unidad, etc. de cada artículo seleccionado.

Sustitución, cambio de calidad, etc.
Los cambios de calidad no presentan mayores problemas dada la cuidadosa descripción de los productos. Si se estima que algunos de ellos pueden plantear problemas se procede a una sustitución de la marca o clase en cuestión. Cuando aparecen productos nuevos se supone que se reflejarán en los gastos familiares que se investigan en la encuesta que tiene lugar cada cinco años, como máximo. Sin embargo se incorporan al índice los productos nuevos que sustituyen totalmente a otros cuyos precios se venían registrando en el mercado. Los productos con precios registrados que desaparecen se les sustituye en el índice por los más similares que se ofrezcan en el mercado.

Artículos estacionales
No se ajustan los precios de los artículos estacionales. En muy pocos casos los de ciertos servicios de temporada, principalmente de carácter recreativo, se registran en puntos determinados de antemano y, fuera de temporada, los precios se mantienen constantes y sin ajustes.

Cálculo
El índice se calcula según la fórmula de Laspeyres como un promedio aritmético ponderado de base fija, cuyos coeficientes de ponderación corresponden al período de base. Los promedios de precios se calculan como promedios aritméticos ponderados. En la mayoría de los casos la ponderación se basa en la estimación del giro comercial o volumen de las ventas. Para los precios faltantes o incorrectos se recurre al movimiento promedial de los precios de otros artículos del mismo grupo o subgrupo.

El cómputo del índice se basa sin embargo en los precios de la capital y su región, salvo los de combustibles, calefacción y luz, que se expresan como porcentajes de los precios vigentes en todo el país. Los porcentajes anuales se calculan como una media aritmética en la cual cada uno de los índices para el comienzo de cada mes, de febrero a diciembre, tienen iguales ponderaciones, pero el índice de enero y el especial estimado para diciembre tienen coeficientes de ponderación que son la mitad de los correspondientes a los demás meses, lo que equivale, poco más o menos, a convertir los índices de principios de mes en índices de mediados de mes.

Informaciones complementarias
No disponible.

Organización y publicación
Statistical Bureau of Iceland: "Hagtidindi" (Reykiavik).

Central Bank of Iceland: "Economic Statistics" (trimestral).

ISLAS CAIMAN

Denominación oficial
Consumer Price Index (Indice de precios del consumo).

Alcance
El índice se compila cuatro veces al año, los meses de marzo, junio, septiembre y diciembre. Abarca todos los hogares de residentes en Gran Caimán y Caimán Brac.

Base oficial
Septiembre de 1984 = 100.

Fuente de la ponderación
La selección de los artículos y la determinación de los coeficientes de ponderación se basaron en una encuesta realizada entre abril de 1983 y marzo de 1984 sobre los gastos de una muestra de 234 hogares privados de residentes en Gran Caimán y Caimán Brac. El promedio semanal de los gastos de cada hogar en el momento de la encuesta era de 440 dólares y su tamaño medio de 3,52 personas.

Gastos de consumo de los hogares
Se incluyen los seguros relacionados con bienes de consumo y

Ponderaciones y composición

Grupos principales	Número de artículos	Ponderación	Número aproximado de cotizaciones de precio
Alimentación	282	206,43	590
Bebidas alcohólicas y tabaco	56	31,46	133
Vivienda:			
Alquiler	13	67,58	13
Intereses hipotecarios	1	36,98	3
Reparación, mantenimiento y seguros de la casa	70	27,90	83
Combustible, luz y agua	16	45,01	24
Vestido y calzado	160	39,21	242
Muebles, moblaje y equipo doméstico	200	57,85	222
Transportes y comunicaciones	59	178,68	84
Educación	29	24,35	32
Asistencia médica	29	56,89	48
Distracciones	93	178,90	115
Objetos personales y servicios	82	48,76	130
Total	1 090	1000,00	1 719

el costo de la asistencia médica, pero no los gastos comerciales, regalos y productos para el consumo del propio hogar.

Método de recolección de los datos
Los precios se recogen cuatro veces al año, en marzo, junio, septiembre y diciembre, registrándolos en los supermercados, puntos de venta al por menor y establecimientos de prestación de servicios más importantes de George Town, de sus alrededores y de la isla de Caimán Brac. La recolección de los precios está a cargo de investigadores que los registran durante un mes, los días martes, miércoles o jueves. La recolección centralizada de algunas cotizaciones está a cargo del Servicio de Estadísticas que, mediante llamadas telefónicas o cuestionarios enviados por correo, investiga por ejemplo las tarifas de los servicios de electricidad, gas o agua, los honorarios médicos, las matrículas de educación y las tarifas de los servicios de transporte y comunicaciones. Las amortizaciones de préstamos se atribuyen a los gastos de consumo que los originan, tales como la adquisición de vehículos o muebles. Los precios de todos los bienes y servicios que se utilizan para compilar el índice son los que se pagan en ese momento al contado. Se excluyen los recargos por créditos y las rebajas que no se hagan a todo el público. Tampoco se consideran los precios de lista si el negocio vende a un precio distinto. Los precios de liquidación sólo se incluyen cuando significan una rebaja real de precios y no sirven para promover la venta de artículos caducos, dañados, sucios o defectuosos.

Vivienda
Todos los trimestres se registran las cotizaciones de alquiler de casas y apartamentos de uno, dos y tres dormitorios. También se toman en consideración ciertas viviendas ocupadas por sus propietarios y algunas de propiedad estatal. El pago de intereses sólo se considera en el caso de viviendas ocupadas por sus propietarios.

Especificación de las variedades
Como el índice mide las fluctuaciones de los precios, los datos registrados todos los trimestres corresponden estrictamente a bienes y servicios idénticos que, en igual cantidad, se ofrecen en un mismo punto de venta. Los artículos cuyos precios se registran deben mantenerse constantes durante todo el período del índice. Para los vestidos y los muebles, donde no es posible una gran precisión, se utilizan especificaciones más flexibles.

Sustitución, cambio de calidad, etc.
Cuando un artículo desaparece del mercado por tres períodos consecutivos se enlaza uno nuevo cuyo precio de base sustitutivo se estima mediante la razón entre los precios del artículo nuevo y del antiguo. En el índice se descuentan los aumentos de precio debidos a una mejor calidad, pero no los debidos a un aumento de cantidad que no modifique la descripción del producto. Fuera de los casos antes indicados, los precios de los productos nuevos no se recogen mientras la base del índice no cambie.

Los precios de sustitución de los artículos que desaparecen del mercado se estiman utilizando los precios que se recogen actualmente para ese artículo. Cuando no se dispone de ninguna cotización para un determinado artículo se utiliza la media de los cambios de precio registrados para el grupo de artículos de esa clase con clave de tres dígitos. En sus inspecciones los estadísticos pueden modificar dichas estimaciones.

Artículos estacionales
No se ajustan las variaciones de precio de estos artículos.

Cálculo
El índice se calcula según la fórmula de Laspeyres como un promedio aritmético ponderado de base fija, cuyos coeficientes de ponderación corresponden al período abril de 1983 - marzo de 1984.

Se obtienen promedios de precios dentro de cada una de las divisiones del índice con clave de cinco dígitos. Los promedios correspondientes a Gran Caimán y Caimán Brac se calculan en forma separada y se ponderan juntos en proporción al gasto relativo de los hogares.

Informaciones complementarias
El índice se publica aproximadamente a mediados del mes siguiente al de referencia.

Se publican los siguientes índices de subgrupo: alimentación, bebidas alcohólicas, tabaco, vivienda, vestido y calzado, equipo doméstico durable, transporte y comunicaciones, educación y asistencia médica, enseres personales y servicios.

Organización y publicación
Department of Finance and Development, Statistics Unit (Servicio de Estadísticas del Ministerio de Finanzas y desarrollo): "Annual Abstract of Statistics" (Gran Caimán).

idem: "Annual Report of the Cayman Islands".

idem: "Cayman Islands, A Guide to the new Consumer Price Index", febrero de 1985.

ISLAS COOK (RAROTONGA)

Denominación oficial
Retail Price Index (Indice de precios al por menor).

Alcance
El índice se calcula trimestralmente y abarca los hogares de asalariados.

Base oficial
Segundo trimestre de 1967 = 100.

Fuente de la ponderación
La selección de los artículos y la determinación de los coeficientes de ponderación se basaron en los resultados de la encuesta sobre los gastos de los hogares efectuada en mayo de 1967 en hogares de asalariados seleccionados sobre una base ad hoc (excluidos los obreros agrícolas) en donde el ingreso medio del cabeza de familia comprendía entre 4 y 20 libras por semana en el momento de la encuesta (de los 156 hogares analizados, en 99 el cabeza de familia contaba con un ingreso de 4 a 6 libras por semana).

Ponderaciones y composición

Grupos principales	Número de artículos	Ponderación	Número aproximado de cotizaciones de precio
Alimentación	76	58,4	...
Tabaco y alcohol	5	6,8	...
Vivienda	11	3,1	...
Gastos del hogar	51	9,6	...
Vestido y calzado	48	12,4	...
Transportes	10	5,7	...
Varios	36	4,0	...
Total	237	100,0	...

Gastos de consumo de los hogares
No disponible.

Método de recolección de los datos
Los precios se recogen la tercera y la cuarta semana de febrero, mayo, agosto y noviembre en cinco principales centros de ventas en Rarotonga.

Vivienda
No disponible.

Especificación de las variedades
No disponible.

Sustitución, cambio de calidad, etc.
No disponible.

Artículos estacionales
No disponible.

Cálculo
El índice se calcula conforme a la fórmula de Laspeyres como un promedio aritmético ponderado de base fija, cuyos coeficientes de ponderación corresponden al período de base.

Informaciones complementarias
Actualmente se calcula una nueva serie (base junio de 1989 = 100), pero en el momento de publicar el presente volumen la OIT no disponía de informaciones metodológicas sobre esta serie.

Organización y publicación
Statistical Office: "Quarterly Statistical Bulletin" (Rarotonga).
Government of Cook Islands: "Rarotonga Retail Price Index" (Rarotonga, 1967).

ISLAS MALVINAS (FALKLAND) (STANLEY)

Denominación oficial
Retail Price Index (Indice de precios al por menor).

Alcance
El índice abarca las familias de obreros en Stanley.

Base oficial
Primero de enero de 1971 = 100.

Fuente de la ponderación
La selección de los artículos y la determinación de los coeficientes de ponderación se basaron en los resultados de una encuesta sobre los gastos de los hogares efectuada en 1971, que abarcó a familias de obreros (salvo las familias numerosas).

Ponderaciones y composición

Grupos principales	Número de artículos	Ponderación aproximado	Número de cotizaciones de precio
Alimentación	15	409	...
Bebidas y tabaco	6	94	...
Vestido y calzado	64	128	...
Combustible y luz	2	45	...
Moblaje y accesorios para el hogar	24	54	...
Vivienda (intereses hipotecarios, contribuciones locales y reparaciones)	6	98	...
Productos de limpieza	7	28	...
Aseo personal y asistencia médica	7	30	...
Papelería	2	27	...
Servicios	10	87	...
Total	143	1 000	...

Gastos de consumo de los hogares
No disponible.

Método de recolección de los datos
Los precios son recogidos por investigadores al final del último mes de cada trimestre, en tres puntos de venta al por menor y establecimientos de servicios de Stanley.

Vivienda
Los gastos del alquiler no se tienen en cuenta ni en el cálculo del índice ni en la determinación de los coeficientes de ponderación.

Especificación de las variedades
No disponible.

Sustitución, cambio de calidad, etc.
No disponible.

Artículos estacionales
Las fluctuaciones estacionales de los precios no son objeto de ajuste.

Cálculo
El índice se calcula conforme a la fórmula de Laspeyres como un promedio aritmético ponderado de base fija, cuyos coeficientes de ponderación corresponden al período de base.

Informaciones complementarias
Actualmente se calcula una nueva serie (base primero de julio de 1989 = 100) pero en el momento de publicar el presente volumen la OIT no disponía de informaciones metodológicas sobre esta serie.

Organización y publicación
Government Printing Office: "The Falkland Island Gazette" (Stanley).

ISLA DE MAN

Denominación oficial
General Index of Retail Prices (Indice general de precios al por menor).

Alcance
El índice se compila mensualmente y abarca todos los hogares privados, excluyendo unos 3-4 por ciento correspondiente al grupo de ingresos más elevados y a la categoría de menores ingresos que reciben asistencia social.

Base oficial
Marzo de 1976 = 100.

Fuente de la ponderación
La selección de los artículos y la determinación de los coeficientes de ponderación se basaron en los resultados de una encuesta sobre los gastos de los hogares efectuada en 1976 que abarcó una muestra aleatoria de hogares.

Ponderaciones y composición

Grupos principales	Número de artículos	Ponderación aproximado	Número de cotizaciones de precio
Alimentación	...	244	...
Bebidas alcohólicas	...	82	...
Tabaco	...	53	...
Vivienda	...	104	...
Combustible y luz	...	90	...
Bienes perdurables para el hogar	...	66	...
Vestido y calzado	...	72	...
Transportes y vehículos	...	134	...
Bienes varios	...	64	...
Servicios	...	59	...
Comidas fuera del hogar	...	32	...
Total	450	1 000	...

Gastos de consumo de los hogares
A los fines del índice, los gastos del consumo comprenden todos los bienes y servicios adquiridos para el consumo por la población de referencia. Excluyen las contribuciones efectuadas a fondos de pensión, los impuestos a la renta de las personas físicas y otros impuestos directos, y los pagos de los seguros de vida.

Método de recolección de los datos
Los precios se recogen en unos 100 puntos de venta al por menor y establecimientos de servicios. Los encuestadores utilizan cuestionarios por correspondencia o encuestas por teléfono. La recolección de precios es mensual y se efectúa el día martes más próximo a mediados de mes.

Los precios utilizados para el cálculo del índice son los que se pagan en el momento.

Las reducciones y los descuentos de que gozan sólo algunas personas del público no se toman en cuenta. Los precios de liquidación, las ofertas especiales y similares sólo se toman en consideración si el producto en cuestión tiene la calidad y el tamaño usuales.

Vivienda
Los datos referentes al alquiler se obtienen de un pequeño número de viviendas representativas.

Especificación de las variedades
Las especificaciones de los artículos cuyos precios han de registrarse se dan en términos de tipo, calidad y tamaño, etc.

Sustitución, cambio de calidad, etc.
Se toman en consideración los cambios ocurridos en productos similares para distinguir un aumento genuino de precio del derivado de los cambios de calidad; se utiliza un criterio racional para identificarlos.

Artículos estacionales
En el caso de las frutas y las verduras frescas, se distribuye un porcentaje de ponderación fijo para el subgrupo entre los por-

centajes de ponderación de los artículos cuyos precios varían mensualmente.
Informaciones complementarias
No disponible.
Cálculo
El índice se calcula conforme a la fórmula de Laspeyres como un promedio aritmético ponderado de base fija, cuyos coeficientes de ponderación corresponden al período de base.
Organización y publicación
Treasury's Economics Section: "Index of Retail Prices" (Douglas).
idem: "Digest of Economic and Social Statistics"

ISLAS SALOMON (HONIARA)

Denominación oficial
Retail Price Index (Indice de precios al por menor).
Alcance
El índice se calcula mensualmente y abarca los hogares de Honiara cuyos ingresos anuales del jefe eran menores de 4 000 dólares SI en 1977.
Base oficial
Octubre - diciembre de 1970 = 100.
Fuente de la ponderación
La selección de los artículos y la determinación de los coeficientes de ponderación se basaron en los resultados de una encuesta sobre los gastos de los hogares efectuada en octubre-noviembre de 1977 en Honiara, que abarcó los hogares en donde los ingresos anuales del jefe eran menores de 4 000 dólares SI netos en el momento de la encuesta.
Ponderaciones y composición

Grupos principales	Número de artículos	Ponde-ración	Número aproximado de cotizaciones de precio
Alimentación	76	47,0	...
Bebidas y tabaco	8	9,5	...
Vestido y calzado	12	5,0	...
Transportes	22	11,0	...
Vivienda (incl. alquiler, combustible y luz, etc.)	14	15,5	...
Varios	33	12,0	...
Total	165	100,0	...

Gastos de consumo de los hogares
No disponible.
Método de recolección de los datos
Los precios son recogidos por investigadores entre el día 15 y 20 de cada mes en mercados, puntos de venta al por menor y establecimientos de servicios en Honiara. Los precios de las frutas y las verduras frescas se recogen cada semana.
Vivienda
Los datos referentes al alquiler se obtienen de tres viviendas pertenecientes al Gobierno y cuatro viviendas privadas.
Especificación de las variedades
No disponible.
Sustitución, cambio de calidad, etc.
No disponible.
Artículos estacionales
Se tienen en cuenta las fluctuaciones estacionales de ciertos artículos; fuera de temporada se mantiene el último precio de la temporada.
Cálculo
El índice se calcula conforme a la fórmula de Laspeyres como un promedio aritmético ponderado de base fija, cuyos coeficientes de ponderación corresponden al período de agosto de 1976 - julio de 1977.
El relativo de precio para cada artículo se calcula dividiendo el precio medio del período corriente por el precio medio del período de base. Los precios medios son la promedia aritmética simple de todos los precios disponibles.
Informaciones complementarias
Actualmente se calcula una nueva serie relativa a los hogares de Honiara cuyos ingresos anuales procedentes de todas las fuentes eran menores de 11 000 dólares SI en 1982 (base octubre-diciembre de 1984 = 100), pero en el momento de publicar el presente Volumen la OIT no disponía de informaciones metodológicas sobre esta serie.
Organización y publicación
Ministry of Finance, Statistical Office: "Statistical Bulletin" (Honiara).

ISLAS VIRGENES (BRITANICAS)

Denominación oficial
Consumer Price Index (Indice de precios del consumo).
Alcance
La compilación del índice es mensual y abarca los hogares de ingresos medios que oscilan entre 500 y 700 dólares de los Estados Unidos por mes de las Islas Vírgenes Británicas.
Base oficial
Marzo de 1985 = 100.
Fuente de la ponderación
La selección de los artículos y la determinación de los coeficientes de ponderación se basaron en los resultados de una encuesta sobre los gastos de los hogares efectuada en septiembre de 1983. La encuesta abarcó una muestra de 105 hogares de familias con ingresos medios que se situaban entre 500 y 700 dólares de los Estados Unidos por mes en septiembre de 1983. No se introdujeron reajustes en los coeficientes de ponderación para tener en consideración los cambios de precio entre el período de la encuesta y marzo de 1985.
Ponderaciones y composición

Grupos principales	Número de artículos	Ponde-ración	Número aproximado de cotizaciones de precio
Alimentación y tabaco	133	400	...
Vivienda	11	206	...
Moblaje y equipo para el hogar	24	62	...
Vestido y calzado	23	115	...
Transportes	12	114	...
Servicios	19	82	...
Varios	15	21	...
Total	237	1 000	...

Gastos de consumo de los hogares
Se excluyen las contribuciones a la seguridad social, los impuestos directos, las adquisiciones de bienes de segunda mano y el comercio de mercancías usadas.
Método de recolección de los datos
Los datos de los precios se recogen por investigadores en 89 tiendas al por menor y establecimientos seleccionados en la capital, Road Town y Virgin Gorda. El precio de la mayor parte de los artículos se registra mensualmente el jueves y viernes más cercano del día 15 de cada mes. Los precios se recogen cada tres meses y cada seis meses para teléfonos, franqueo postal, servicios de electricidad y recorridos en taxi. Los precios utilizados para calcular el índice son los que en el momento se pagan al por menor. No se toman en consideración las rebajas y los descuentos.
Vivienda
Los datos referentes al alquiler se recogen trimestralmente en viviendas alquiladas con dos dormitorios.
Especificación de las variedades
Las especificaciones de los artículos cuyos precios se han de registrar se dan en detalles, según los resultados de las encuestas sobre los gastos del hogar. Las especificaciones se dan en términos de marca, factura, calidad y tamaño.
Sustitución, cambio de calidad, etc.
Cuando un producto desaparece del mercado, se lo substituye por uno similar.
Artículos estacionales
Los artículos estacionales no reciben un trato especial.
Cálculo
El índice se calcula conforme a la fórmula de Laspeyres como un promedio aritmético ponderado de base fija, cuyos coeficientes de ponderación corresponden a septiembre de 1983.

El índice para un artículo se obtiene utilizando las relaciones de precios del período corriente y del período precedente.

Informaciones complementarias
Se publican los subgrupos principales.

Organización y publicación
Chief Minister's Office, Development Planning Unit: "Consumer Price Index Report" (Road Town).

ISRAEL

Denominación oficial
Consumer Price Index (Indice de precios del consumo).

Alcance
El índice se compila mensualmente y abarca todos los hogares de las zonas urbanas.

Base oficial
1987 = 100.

Fuente de la ponderación
La determinación de los coeficientes de ponderación y la selección de los artículos se basaron en los resultados de una encuesta sobre los gastos de los hogares realizada entre junio de 1986 y mayo de 1987. La muestra representativa de esta encuesta comprendió unos 5 000 hogares, de una persona o más, ubicados en 104 zonas urbanas. Se ajustaron los coeficientes de ponderación para tomar en cuenta las modificaciones de precio ocurridas entre el período de base y el de la encuesta.

Ponderaciones y composición

Grupos principales	Número de artículos	Ponderación	Número aproximado de cotizaciones de precio
Alimentación (salvo frutas y legumbres)	270	16,51	7 000
Frutas y legumbres	90	6,42	17 000
Vivienda	5	16,46	(a)
Mantenimiento del hogar (incl. combustible y luz)	85	9,33	2 000
Moblaje y accesorios para el hogar	185	7,18	3 000
Vestido y calzado	190	7,20	12 000
Salud	80	5,50	1 000
Educación, cultura y recreación	260	12,01	3 000
Tarifas postales y de transporte	85	15,25	1 000
Varios	110	4,14	1 000
Total	1 355	100,00	47 000

Nota: (a) Véase más adelante Vivienda.

Gastos de consumo de los hogares
Comprenden el valor de mercancías y servicios adquiridos por los hogares que no representen ahorro o inversión, como la compra de pisos, vehículos, existencias, etc. El consumo se mide por la suma de los pagos que el hogar se ha obligado a hacer o que ya ha efectuado. Se incluyen los gastos pagables al vendedor, tales como intereses, comisiones, fletes o costos de instalación.

Los gastos de consumo también comprenden los valores estimados de la depreciación y el interés que devengaría el capital invertido en una vivienda o vehículo, así como el valor de uso de viviendas o vehículos que no sean propiedad del hogar ni se hayan pagado. Del mismo modo comprenden el valor de las mercancías y los servicios recibidos de los empleadores. No se consideran gastos de consumo los pagos a cuenta de compras futuras (bienes aún no recibidos), la amortización de deudas contraídas en ocasión de compras anteriores ni las devoluciones. Se incluyen entre los gastos de consumo las compras de artículos de segunda mano y la diferencia de valor entre los objetos usados que se entregan a cuenta del pago de otros nuevos, así como los seguros relacionados con bienes de consumo específicos y con la salud. Se excluyen los pagos de impuestos directos, contribuciones a la seguridad social y fondos de pensión, seguros de vida, regalos en metálico y loterías.

Método de recolección de los datos
Los artículos se seleccionan en función del valor de consumo que representan en la encuesta sobre los gastos de los hogares y del número de sus variedades disponibles. Los artículos que representan más del 0,1 por ciento del consumo de los hogares se registran por separado; los que representan menos del 0,1 por ciento sólo se cotizan en forma separada si no se dispone de otros artículos que representen adecuadamente el movimiento de sus precios. Los gastos en artículos cuyos precios no se registran se atribuyen a otros similares, que representen cabalmente sus movimientos de precio.

El tamaño de la muestra de puntos de venta se determina según los coeficientes de ponderación del grupo de artículos de cada punto de venta y por la variancia entre las fluctuaciones de precio de cada uno de los artículos del grupo en los distintos puntos de venta. La probabilidad de muestreo de las localidades es proporcional a su tamaño dentro de un estrato geográfico, definiéndose el tamaño como el total de los gastos de los hogares de una localidad. Los investigadores recogen mensualmente los precios de la mayoría de los artículos en 1 300 puntos de venta. Para los servicios de electricidad, gas, agua, asistencia médica, educación, transportes y comunicaciones, etc., sus tarifas se obtienen de 600 fuentes, por correo o por teléfono.

Los veinte encargados de la recolección de precios los transmiten a las oficinas locales, ubicadas en las tres grandes ciudades, que a su vez los comunican al Servicio Central de Jerusalén. Sólo se registran los descuentos acordados a todos los compradores y las rebajas de liquidación cuando corresponde. Se utilizan los precios de mercado y no los oficiales. Los precios que se registran son los que se pagan en el momento. Los valores atribuidos a coches usados y casas ocupadas por sus propietarios se determinan en función de los precios locales vigentes.

A efectos de obtener un promedio mensual, los puntos de venta donde se registran los precios de la mayoría de los artículos se dividen en cuatro grupos, cada uno de los cuales se investiga en una semana distinta.

Vivienda
Se investigan en meses alternados dos grupos de viviendas alquiladas, con o sin muebles.

En el cálculo del gasto anual del propietario que ocupa su vivienda se incluyen la depreciación de la propiedad por el transcurso del tiempo y los intereses que devengaría el capital invertido en la vivienda.

En el índice actual se determinan tanto los precios de las viviendas nuevas como de las antiguas cuya propiedad cambia de mano, mediante formularios de impuestos a las ventas que facilitan las autoridades fiscales. Los datos sobre unas 3 000 o 4 000 viviendas divididas en 25 localidades urbanas se refieren a un determinado trimestre del año. Los datos relativos a la calidad de las viviendas se utilizan en la elaboración de análisis regresivos para que el índice sólo refleje variaciones de precio.

Especificación de las variedades
Para cada artículo se preparan especificaciones generales. Las especificaciones detalladas de cada artículo (como marca, factura, calidad, etc.) las eligen los investigadores en cada punto de venta, registrándose mensualmente los precios de una misma variedad específica.

Sustitución, cambio de calidad, etc.
En el índice se enlaza un gran número de cambios de calidad y sustituciones para evitar que su introducción afecte al nivel de los precios. Los cambios de calidad pequeños se consideran como cambio de precio y sólo se hacen ajustes por cambio de calidad cuando se cuenta con características suficientes como para permitir su medida.

Artículos estacionales
Los precios de los artículos estacionales se registran mientras se ofrezcan en el mercado; cuando desaparecen del mismo se estiman en base a las fluctuaciones de precio de artículos similares. Cuando el artículo estacional vuelve a aparecer, se compara su precio actual con la última cotización mensual disponible. Antes de 1988 se utilizaban coeficientes de ponderación variables para las frutas y las legumbres frescas.

Cálculo
El índice se calcula según la fórmula de Laspeyres, como un promedio aritmético ponderado de base fija, cuyos coeficientes de ponderación corresponden al período de base.

El índice de cada artículo se calcula por sus relativos de precio. Cuando en un punto de venta no se dispone de ningún precio para un artículo, las variaciones de precio se estiman en función de las variaciones registradas en otros puntos de venta. Si en ninguno de los puntos de venta se dispone de precios, las variaciones del precio de ese artículo siguen las que han tenido artículos similares.

Informaciones complementarias
Además del índice relativo a todos los hogares urbanos se calculan las fluctuaciones de precio de las "canastas" correspondientes a los hogares de los deciles de ingresos inferior y superior.

Organización y publicación
Central Bureau of Statistics (Servicio Central de Estadísticas): "Monthly Bulletin of Statistics" (Jerusalén).
idem: "Price Statistics Monthly" (sólo en hebreo).
Revisión del Consumer Price Index, publicada en "Price Statistics Monthly" (sólo en hebreo).

ITALIA

Denominación oficial
National Consumer Price Index (Indice Nacional de Precios del Consumo).

Alcance
El índice se compila mensualmente y abarca todos los hogares de las principales ciudades de 93 provincias.

Base oficial
1990 = 100.

Fuente de la ponderación
Los coeficientes de ponderación se han determinado en función de las características de la estructura del consumo y de datos de la contabilidad nacional correspondientes a los dos primeros trimestres de 1989 y los dos últimos de 1990.

Ponderaciones y composición

Grupos principales	Número de artículos	Ponderación	Número aproximado de cotizaciones de precio
Alimentación y tabaco	250	22,78	200 000
Vestido y calzado	57	10,83	20 000
Vivienda:	...	7,62	13 500
Alquiler	1	...	...
Mantenimiento y reparaciones	5	...	...
Combustible y luz	7	...	...
Otros grupos:	...	...	50 000
Muebles y utensilios del hogar	76	10,58	...
Asistencia médica	137	6,74	...
Transporte y comunicaciones	168	13,46	...
Educación y recreación	110	9,97	...
Otros bienes y servicios	96	18,02	...
Total	907	100,00	283 500

Gastos de consumo de los hogares
A los efectos del índice no comprenden impuestos, inversiones, ahorros, consumo de la producción propia ni valor locativo de las viviendas ocupadas por sus propietarios.

Método de recolección de los datos
Los investigadores registran los precios practicados por 26 300 comercios minoristas (9 500 de productos alimenticios y 10 800 de otros bienes) y 6 000 establecimiento de prestacíon de servicios de las capitales de 93 provincias.

La recolección de los precios del pescado fresco, las patatas y las frutas y legumbres tiene lugar los días 5, 15 y 25 de cada mes, mientras que los demás productos alimenticios, las vestimentas y los servicios personales se registran alrededor del 15 de cada mes. Sin embargo, para el cálculo del índice, se toman en consideración los precios de los días 5 y 15 del mes en curso y del 25 del mes anterior. La recolección de los precios de bienes domésticos durables, así como el coste de ciertos servicios, tiene lugar el día 5 de los meses de febrero, mayo, agosto y noviembre. Para compilar el índice sólo se utilizan los precios normales que pagan los consumidores y a tal efecto no se toman en cuenta los precios de liquidaciones, rebajas, alquileres con opción de compra, ventas a plazo y a crédito, compras de artículos de segunda mano, salvo para la alimentación si las rebajas se mantienen, por lo menos, un mes.

Vivienda
Se registran en forma trimestral, es decir los días 5 de los meses de enero, abril, julio y octubre, las cotizaciones del alquiler de 13 500 viviendas.

Especificación de las variedades
Para cada uno de los artículos de la canasta de compra se dan especificaciones detalladas, que consisten en una descripción completa del artículo, su marca de fábrica, denominación o marca registrada, clase de envasado, cantidad o unidad, etc.

Sustitución, cambio de calidad, etc.
Cuando cesa la oferta de un producto se le sustituye por otro similar y para los cómputos se recurre al método de enlaces.

Artículos estacionales
Las frutas, legumbres y flores frescas se consideran artículos estacionales. Para éstos el índice compuesto se obtiene mediante del precio promedio del primer 75 por ciento de los artículos que figuran por orden ascendente en una lista de precios registrados. Se supone que los artículos estacionales que se ofrecen en el mercado pueden sustituirse entre sí. Para los ajustes se utiliza un promedio móvil de 13 meses (el mes en curso y los 12 anteriores).

Cálculo
El índice se calcula según la fórmula de Laspeyres como un promedio aritmético ponderado de base fija, cuyos coeficientes de ponderación corresponden al período de base.

Los índices por artículo para cada ciudad son un promedio aritmético simple de todos los índices básicos de cada artículo de esa ciudad. Cada índice promedio de los artículos de una región dada se pondera por el promedio aritmético de todos los índices de esa región que se han obtenido. El índice nacional representa el promedio aritmético de los índices de 20 regiones, ponderado en proporción a la población urbana de esas regiones el 31 de diciembre de 1989.

Informaciones complementarias
El Instituto Nacional de Estadística también calcula y publica las series del Indice de Precios del Consumo de Obreros y Empleados.

Organización y publicación
Instituto Nacional di Statistica: "Bollettino mensile di statistica" (Roma).

JAMAICA

Denominación oficial
Consumer Price Index (Indice de Precios del Consumo).

Alcance
El índice se compila mensualmente y abarca hogares rurales y urbanos cuyos ingresos anuales eran de $ 24 000 o menos en el momento de la encuesta.

Base oficial
Enero de 1988 = 100.

Fuente de la ponderación
La determinación de los coeficientes de ponderación y la selección de los artículos se basaron en los resultados de una encuesta sobre los gastos de los hogares rurales y urbanos con ingresos de $ 24 000 o menos, realizada en 1984. Se excluyeron los subgrupos que representaban menos del 0,50 por ciento del consumo, distribuyéndose sus coeficientes de ponderación entre los subgrupos restantes. El mismo criterio se siguió para seleccionar los artículos dentro de cada subgrupo. Se hizo una excepción para la alimentación y las bebidas, cuyo porcentaje mínimo de consumo se fijó en 0,40 por ciento.

Ponderaciones y composición

Grupos principales	Número de artículos	Ponderación	Número aproximado de cotizaciones de precio
Alimentación	...	55,63	...
Combustible y suministros del hogar	...	7,35	...
Alquiler y funcionamiento del hogar	...	7,86	...
Muebles y moblaje	...	2,83	...
Asistencia médica	...	6,97	...
Vestido y calzado	...	5,07	...
Transporte	...	6,44	...
Varios	...	7,85	...
Total	...	100,00	...

Gastos de consumo de los hogares
No disponible.

Método de recolección de los datos
La recolección de precios de la mayoría de los artículos tiene lugar el primer fin de semana da cada mes en un conjunto fijo de puntos de venta, distribuidos en toda la isla. Los honorarios

de médicos y dentistas se registran en forma trimestral, las matrículas de estudios en cada período escolar y los seguros de salud en forma anual. Las modificaciones de las tarifas de teléfonos, agua y autobuses se registran cuando se comunican. El equipo del Instituto de Estadísticas que trabaja sobre el terreno se encarga de la recolección de los precios en diversos lugares, tales como supermercados, tiendas de ramos generales, zapateras y peluquerías. Ciertas tarifas, como las eléctricas y telefónicas, se obtienen de las autoridades pertinentes, mientras que los alquileres de una muestra de viviendas.

Los encargados de la recolección, en sus visitas mensuales a los puntos de venta, registran los precios de todos los artículos salvo uno pocos, como los seguros de salud y las matrículas escolares, que se registran en forma trimestral. Los puntos de venta visitados se encuentran en sitios generalmente concurridos por los consumidores abarcados por el índice y presentan las características típicas de los negocios que pueden gozar de la preferencia de la clientela. Cabe señalar que para el muestreo no se utilizó ningún método aleatorio sino de selección juicio y se contó con la colaboración de funcionarios sobre el terreno de experiencia y perfecto conocimiento de la región abarcada y las tiendas preferidas por el público del índice. Los puntos de venta se seleccionaron en función del volumen de sus ventas, pero la selección no se limitó a los grandes establecimientos, incluyéndose también los pequeños negocios de comestibles u otras tiendas ubicadas en comunidades donde las personas compran los productos que necesitan.

No se toman en cuenta los precios de mercancías averiadas, manchadas o con desperfectos, por no ajustarse a ninguna especificación concreta. En cuanto a los precios "ilegales", sólo se toman en consideración si se cobran abiertamente a todos los grupos de consumidores abarcados por el índice.

Vivienda
Las cotizaciones de alquiler se obtienen todos los meses de una muestra de viviendas, clasificadas por el número de dormitorios y otras habitaciones. Ciertos pagos, como hipotecas, amortizaciones y reembolsos de intereses, además de los seguros de la casa, representan el valor locativo de las vivienda propia ocupada por sus dueños. En otras palabras, se pueden utilizar los pagos en efectivo como representativos del valor estimado del alquiler. El índice de precios que se debe utilizar como cuantum final será el alquiler de las clases representativas de la vivienda.

Especificación de las variedades
Se especifican claramente los artículos cuyos precios se deben registrar para que así todos los meses los precios registrados correspondan a artículos de calidad comparable.

Sustitución, cambio de calidad, etc.
Cuando se observa que la oferta de una mercancía o servicio comienza a disminuir y que entra en el mercado una variedad nueva, la observación de los precios se duplica y, de hacerse evidente una diferencia de calidad, se efectúan los enlaces pertinentes. En virtud de este procedimiento se puede atribuir un precio de base a la variedad nueva recurriendo a los relativos de precio del período en curso y del período de base.

Sin embargo, cuando la calidad de ambas variedades, antigua y nueva, son comparables o equivalentes, se registra el precio del artículo nuevo y la diferencia con el antiguo se trata como un aumento o una disminución, según corresponda. Cuando el consumidor no tiene oportunidad de elegir y está obligado a aceptar el producto nuevo, la diferencia de precio se trata como una modificación del mismo y no como pago de una calidad distinta, inferior o superior, aun cuando tal diferencia exista.

La aparición de productos realmente nuevos, es decir que tengan repercusiones importantes en el presupuesto de los consumidores, es poco frecuente, pero cuando ocurre es necesario revisar el índice.

Artículos estacionales
No se ajustan las fluctuaciones de precios que tienen carácter estacional.

Cálculo
El índice se calcula según la fórmula de Laspeyres como un promedio aritmético ponderado de base fija, cuyos coeficientes de ponderación corresponden a 1984.

El precio relativo de cada artículo se obtiene dividiendo el precio medio del período corriente por el precio medio del período de base. Para obtener el índice de toda la isla se calcula un promedio ponderado de los tres índices regionales.

Organización y publicación
Statistical Institute of Jamaica: "Consumer Price Index Monthly Bulletin" (Kingston).

idem: "Consumer Price Index Monthly Report".

idem: "Consumer Price Index - Annual Review".

JAPON

Denominación oficial
Consumer Price Index (Indice de Precios del Consumo).

Alcance
El índice se compila mensualmente y abarca todos los hogares del país, con excepción de los constituídos por una sola persona y de los que se dedican principalmente a la agricultura, la silvicultura y la pesca.

Base oficial
1990 = 100.

Fuente de la ponderación
La ponderación se basó en los resultados de una encuesta sobre los gastos de los hogares realizada en 1990, cuya muestra comprendió unos 8 000 hogares. Los coeficientes mensuales de ponderación de los alimentos frescos (pescado, fruta, legumbres) se obtuvieron de los datos sobre el promedio de gastos de 1989 y 1990. La selección de los artículos se fundó en la proporción en que contribuyen al total de los gastos de los hogares (en principio, importancia relativa de 0,01 por ciento o más), el carácter representativo del movimiento de sus precios y la continuidad de su registro. Las ponderaciones de los artículos para los que no se recolectaron precios se atribuyeron a los artículos con precios que los representaban.

Ponderaciones y composición

Grupos principales	Número de artículos	Ponderación	Número aproximado de cotizaciones de precio
Alimentación	215	3 140	...
Vivienda	23	1 478	...
Combustible, luz y agua	6	553	...
Muebles y utensilios del hogar	60	444	...
Vestido y calzado	84	860	...
Asistencia médica	23	312	...
Transportes y comunicaciones	36	1 185	...
Educación	13	466	...
Lectura y recreación	69	1 115	...
Varios	32	446	...
Total	561	10 000	230 000

Gastos de consumo de los hogares
Se relacionan con los desembolsos efectuados para comprar u obtener los bienes y servicios necesarios para la vida de todos los días y comprenden el valor locativo atribuido a la vivienda propia. No comprenden los impuestos a los ingresos, seguros de vida, pagos de seguridad social, ahorros, garantías, giros, regalos, contribuciones religiosos y otros gastos que no se consideran de consumo.

Método de recolección de los datos
Para la mayor parte de los artículos los precios se obtienen mediante visitas personales a los puntos de venta y establecimientos de servicio seleccionados en 167 ciudades, pueblos y aldeas. Para el transporte, los servicios postales y artículos similares se recurre a las tarifas oficiales. El registro de los precios tiene lugar los miércoles, jueves o viernes de la semana que comprende el día 12 de cada mes; para 42 artículos frescos, tales como pescado, frutas y legumbres frescos, los precios se registran tres veces por mes. Las matrículas escolares se investigan en abril y septiembre. Los precios que se usan en el índice son los que pagan al por menor los consumidores el día del registro. Se excluyen las reducciones de precio debidas a acuerdos, compensaciones, liquidaciones, rebajas temporales, bonificaciones por compras en cantidad y los precios de los artículos de segunda mano y similares.

Vivienda
Las cotizaciones registradas se refieren a los alquileres de casas y habitaciones de propiedad privada o pública. Los datos de estas últimas se obtienen mensualmente de las administraciones pertinentes.

Las cotizaciones del alquiler de las viviendas privadas, según su estructura y superficie, se obtienen mediante una encuesta mensual que abarca todos los hogares que alquilan viviendas privadas en los distritos de la muestra. Para las viviendas ocupadas por sus propietarios se utiliza el criterio de valor locativo, es decir que se estiman los gastos de vivienda como un alquiler ficticio.

Especificación de las variedades
Las especificaciones de las variedades se establecen en forma detallada con arreglo a criterios de tamaño, calidad, marca, accesorios y similares que permitan que se investiguen los mismos artículos todos meses de manera constante.

Sustitución, cambio de calidad, etc.
Cuando no es posible encontrar un producto seleccionado, se le sustituye por otro similar a efectos del registro de precios. Cuando el antiguo y el nuevo son idénticos, se utiliza el método de enlace directo. En caso contrario se ajustan los precios para tomar en cuenta las diferencias de calidad o cantidad.

Artículos estacionales
Para estos artículos, tales como frutas, legumbres y pescado frescos, la ponderación del subgrupo son fijos durante todo el año. La ponderación de cada artículo de este subgrupo se determina en función de su importancia relativa, que varía de un mes a otro. Para los artículos estacionales distintos de los alimentos frescos, se mantienen, fuera de estación, los precios medios de la última temporada.

Cálculo
El índice se calcula según la fórmula de Laspeyres como un promedio aritmético ponderado de base fija, cuyos coeficientes de ponderación corresponden al período de base.

En primer lugar se calculan para cada localidad los relativos de precio de cada artículo y luego su promedio ponderado por los coeficientes correspondientes a cada municipio permite obtener los promedios de los relativos de precio de cada artículo para todo el país. Por su parte, los promedios de los relativos de precio para todo el país se ponderan por los respectivos coeficientes de artículo para obtener índices de subgrupo. Los índices de grandes grupos y el índice general se obtienen en forma similar, a partir del índice de subgrupo y recurriendo a los respectivos coeficientes de ponderación de grupo.

Informaciones complementarias
El "Indice General", el "Indice de los 10 grupos principales" y el "Indice de Subgrupos" se compilan para 72 regiones, es decir todo el país, ocho grupos urbanos, diez distritos, cuatro áreas metropolitanas, 47 ciudades sedes de gobierno prefectural, Kawasaki-shi y Kitakyushu-shi. El "Indice de bienes y servicios" y el "Indice por artículo" se compilan para todo el país y el área Ku de Tokio. El "Indice por tipos de hogares", el "Indice por características de artículos" y el "Indice calculado utilzando el metodo de encadenamiento" se compilan para todo el país.

Organización y publicación
Management and Coordination Agency, Statistics Bureau: "Monthly Report on the Consumer Price Index".
idem: "Annual Report on the Consumer Price Index".

JORDANIA

Denominación oficial
Cost of Living Index (Indice del costo de la vida).

Alcance
El índice se compila mensualmente y abarca todos los hogares urbanos y rurales del Reino (ribera oriental).

Base oficial
1986 = 100.

Fuente de la ponderación
La determinación de los coeficientes de ponderación y la selección de los artículos se basaron en los resultados de una encuesta sobre los gastos de los hogares, cuya muestra abarcó 2 357 hogares urbanos y rurales de todos los grupos de población. Los artículos se eligieron mediante técnicas de muestreo en función de su importancia relativa.

Gastos de consumo de los hogares
Incluyen el total de los gastos de los hogares durante un año completo y los ingresos en especie para el propio consumo. También se incluyen los valores estimados como alquiler para

Ponderaciones y composición

Grupos principales	Número de artículos	Ponderación	Número aproximado de cotizaciones de precio
Alimentación	141	41,170	1 870
Vestido y calzado	65	7,454	1 394
Vivienda	55	28,092	1 445
Otros bienes y servicios	47	23,284	2 244
Total	208	100,000	6 953

las viviendas ocupadas por sus propietarios. Se trata como gasto la adquisición a crédito de bienes durables. No se toman en consideración las compras de segunda mano, el comercio de objetos usados o su entrega como pago parcial de la compra de otros nuevos. Los pagos de contribuciones a la seguridad social y fondos de pensión, patentes, seguros relacionados con bienes de consumo específicos, atención médica, impuestos a los ingresos y otras cargas fiscales directas, seguros de vida y regalos u otros desembolsos similares se han tratado de conformidad con las definiciones de la contabilidad nacional.

Método de recolección de los datos
La recolección de precios es mensual y está a cargo de investigadores que los registran en todas las capitales y distritos de Jordania tomando en consideración su densidad demográfica. Los puntos de venta se seleccionan según el número de artículos que contiene la canasta del mercado y no deben estar ubicados en las cercanías de zonas donde residen hogares con ingresos muy elevados. Para cada artículo se seleccionan diez puntos de venta. Los precios de las legumbres y frutas frescas se registran los martes, cuatro veces al mes. Los precios de los demás productos alimenticios se recogen durante la primera semana de cada mes; los del vestido y calzado la segunda, y los de todos los demás bienes y servicios la tercera y cuarta semanas.

Vivienda
Las cotizaciones de alquiler para toda clase de viviendas se registran cada seis meses. Se excluyen del índice las viviendas ocupadas por sus propietarios.

Especificación de las variedades
Las especificaciones detalladas de los artículos se obtienen de los comerciantes y comprenden la variedad, calidad, marca, factura, cantidad, país de origen, etc.

Sustitución, cambio de calidad, etc.
Si un artículo desaparece del mercado se le sustituye por otro similar.

Artículos estacionales
Mediante un procedimiento de imputación se obtienen los precios de los artículos que no son de temporada.

Cálculo
El índice se calcula según la fórmula de Laspeyres como un promedio aritmético ponderado de base fija, cuyos coeficientes de ponderación corresponden al período de base.

El promedio de los precios ponderados de cada localidad se multiplica por el coeficiente de ponderación que corresponde a la localidad según su población.

Organización y publicación
La compilación del índice está a cargo del "Department of Statistics" (Departamento de Estadísticas), (Amán).
Central Bank of Jordan: "Monthly Statistical Bulletin" (Amán).

KENYA (NAIROBI)

Denominación oficial
Consumer Price Index - Lower Income Group (Indice de Precios del Consumo - grupo de ingresos módicos).

Alcance
El índice se compila mensualmente y abarca hogares de Nairobi que en 1982-83 no superaban 1 999 chelines kenyanos de ingreso mensual.

Base oficial
Febrero - marzo de 1986 = 100.

Fuente de la ponderación
La determinación de los coeficientes de ponderación y la selec-

ción de los artículos se basaron en los resultados de una encuesta de 1982-1983 sobre los gastos de los hogares de todos los centros urbanos. La muestra comprendió 1 648 hogares de los grupos de ingresos bajos, medios y altos. Por su parte el índice se refiere a los hogares del grupo de ingresos módicos de Nairobi, es decir los hogares cuyos ingresos mensuales no superaban en la época de la encuesta la suma de 1 999 chelines de Kenya. No se ajustaron los coeficientes de ponderación para tomar en cuenta la diferencia de los precios entre el período de la encuesta y febrero-marzo de 1986.

Ponderaciones y composición

Grupos principales	Número de artículos	Ponderación	Número aproximado de cotizaciones de precio
Alimentación	49	44,2	...
Bebidas y tabaco	11	2,1	...
Vestido y calzado	34	5,0	...
Alquiler	1	25,0	...
Combustible, luz y agua	4	3,1	...
Muebles, moblaje, equipo y gastos del hogar	29	5,3	...
Asistencia médica y aseo personal	18	3,0	...
Transportes y comunicaciones	15	4,1	...
Educación, cultura y recreación	15	6,2	...
Bienes y servicios varios	10	2,0	...
Total	186	100,0	...

Gastos de consumo de los hogares
A los efectos del índice comprenden los bienes y servicios adquiridos para el consumo por la población de referencia. No se incluyen el impuesto a la renta, pagos a fondos de pensión, ahorros, primas de seguros de vida, adquisición de viviendas, cotizaciones a sindicatos y pagos de apuestas.

Método de recolección de los datos
Los investigadores registran los precios en mercados, supermercados, comercios minoristas y establecimientos de servicios. Los precios de los alimentos se obtienen mediante compra directa todos los meses, durante la primer semana. Los bienes domésticos no durables se registran durante la tercera semana de cada mes y los durables, así como los servicios, todos los trimestres. Los precios del índice son los que pagan los hogares en el momento.

Vivienda
Las cotizaciones del alquiler se obtienen una vez por año. Se supone que durante los meses entre un registro y otro las cotizaciones varían de la misma manera que los demás artículos del índice. Se incluye el valor locativo asignado a la vivienda propia.

Especificación de las variedades
Las especificaciones de los artículos cuyos precios se han de registrar son detalladas, toman en cuenta su popularidad y la continuidad de las series de precios, y comprenden la marca, factura, calidad y tamaño.

Sustitución, cambio de calidad, etc.
Cuando ya no se ofrece un producto en el mercado se le sustituye por otro. El precio del período de base del artículo antiguo se ajusta según la razón entre los precios del artículo antiguo y del sustitutivo. Cuando se da un cambio de calidad se procede como si se tratara de un artículo nuevo y se sigue el mismo método.

Artículos estacionales
Las fluctuaciones de precio de los artículos estacionales se toman en cuenta mediante promedios mensuales móviles.

Cálculo
El índice se calcula según la fórmula de Laspeyres como un promedio aritmético ponderado de base fija, cuyos coeficientes de ponderación corresponden al período 1982-1983.
Los relativos de los promedios de precio del período en curso y del período de base se utilizan para calcular índices de artículo. Los promedios de precio son medias aritméticas simples de todas las cotizaciones obtenidas.

Informaciones complementarias
Junto con el índice para hogares del grupo de ingresos bajos, la Oficina Central de Estadísticas de Nairobi publica también un índice para hogares de los grupos de ingresoso medios y elevados de Nairobi.

Organización y publicación
Ministry of Finance and Planning, Central Bureau of Statistics: "Kenya Statistical Digest" (Nairobi).

idem: "On current and revised Kenyan Consumer Price Indices".

KIRIBATI (TARAWA)

Denominación oficial
Retail Price Index (Indice de precios al por menor).

Alcance
El índice se calcula trimestralmente y abarca los hogares de las áreas urbanas de Tarawa.

Base oficial
Octubre-diciembre de 1975 = 100.

Fuente de la ponderación
La selección de los artículos y la determinación de los coeficientes de ponderación se basaron en los resultados de una encuesta sobre los gastos de los hogares efectuada en el curso de un período de seis semanas, de fin de agosto a principios de octubre de 1975, que abarcó una muestra de 61 hogares de residentes en las áreas urbanas de Tarawa, y en diversas fuentes.

Ponderaciones y composición

Grupos principales	Número de artículos	Ponderación	Número aproximado de cotizaciones de precio
Alimentación	47	50,00	...
Bebidas y tabaco	8	14,00	...
Vestido y calzado	15	8,00	...
Transportes	15	8,00	...
Vivienda:			
Alquiler	4	1,01	...
Combustible y luz	4	3,56	...
Mantenimiento y artículos para el hogar	13	2,93	...
Varios	22	12,50	...
Total	128	100,00	...

Gastos de consumo de los hogares
No disponible.

Método de recolección de los datos
Los precios son recogidos por agentes alrededor del día 15 de cada mes, en mercados, puntos de venta al por menor y establecimientos de servicios situados en tres centros principales de las áreas urbanas de Tarawa.

Vivienda
No disponible.

Especificación de las variedades
No disponible.

Sustitución, cambio de calidad, etc.
No disponible.

Artículos estacionales
Las fluctuaciones estacionales de los precios no son objeto de ajuste.

Cálculo
El índice se calcula conforme a la fórmula de Laspeyres como un promedio aritmético ponderado de base fija, cuyos coeficientes de ponderación corresponden al período de base.

Informaciones complementarias
No disponible.

Organización y publicación
Ministry of Finance, Statistical Unit: "Quarterly Digest of Statistics" (Tarawa).

KUWAIT

Denominación oficial
Consumer Price Index Numbers (Indice de precios del consumo).

Alcance
La compilación del índice es mensual y comprende a todos los hogares privados, incluso los de una sola persona.

Base oficial
1978 = 100.

Fuente de la ponderación
La selección de los artículos y la determinación de los coeficientes de ponderación se basaron en los resultados de una encuesta sobre los gastos de los hogares efectuada en 1977-78.

Ponderaciones y composición

Grupos principales	Número de artículos	Ponderación	Número aproximado de cotizaciones de precio
Alimentación	192	357,09	2 484
Bebidas y tabaco	8	12,70	85
Vestido y calzado	67	99,55	323
Vivienda	14	187,03	25
Bienes y servicios del hogar	119	110,23	646
Transportes y comunicaciones	73	152,91	105
Educación y asistencia médica	55	25,49	365
Otros bienes y servicios	72	55,00	291
Total	(a) 600	1 000,00	4 324

Nota: (a) Variedades (que representan alrededor de 260 artículos).

Gastos de consumo de los hogares
A los fines del índice, los gastos del consumo comprenden todos los bienes y servicios adquiridos para el consumo por la población de referencia. Se excluyen los impuestos a la renta de las personas físicas, las inversiones, los ahorros y todos los demás gastos que no sean de consumo.

Método de recolección de los datos
Los datos de los precios se obtienen en puntos de venta al por menor importantes que han sido elegidos en función de su grado de aceptación entre los consumidores. El Ministerio de Comercio e Industria brinda las cotizaciones de precios de todos los artículos subvencionados.

Los precios se recogen mediante visitas personales, efectuadas por funcionarios formados, que las realizan mensualmente para la mayor parte de los artículos, dos veces por mes para las frutas y las verduras frescas y trimestralmente para los servicios. Para los servicios suministrados por los organismos de gobierno, como los de transporte, salud, educación, correos, etc., se efectúan los cambios necesarios cuando se revisan las tarifas.

Vivienda
La encuesta anual de alquileres de casas, que lleva a cabo la Oficina Central de Estadística, establece las cotizaciones del alquiler.

Especificación de las variedades
Se brindan especificaciones detalladas para cada uno de los artículos del consumo que forman la "canasta" de mercado. Una "especificación" describe en forma completa el producto mencionando su nombre o marca de fábrica, país de origen, tipo de embalaje, cantidad o unidad, etc. En el cálculo del índice de precios, sólo se incluyen las especificaciones importantes.

Sustitución, cambio de calidad, etc.
Los cambios de calidad no han sido tomados en cuenta, pero se ha hecho todo lo posible para asegurar cotizaciones de precio para la misma variedad para la cual se obtuvieron precios en el año de base, para reducir al mínimo la influencia de los cambios de calidad en los precios del índice.

Artículos estacionales
Las frutas y las verduras frescas se consideran como artículos de temporada. Para cada uno de los 12 meses se confeccionó una "canasta" típica de frutas y verduras frescas de estación que se venden en el mercado. Los precios se recogen para todos los artículos de la "canasta" y se comparan con los precios que tenían en el mes correspondiente del año de base.

Cálculo
El índice se calcula conforme a la fórmula de Laspeyres como un promedio aritmético ponderado de base fija, cuyos coeficientes de ponderación corresponden al período de base.

La relación del precio para cada variedad se calcula dividiendo el precio del período corriente por el precio del período de base. El índice para un artículo es calculado como las relaciones de precios de variedades. Para los artículos subvencionados y los disponibles en los mercados libres, se obtienen las relaciones de precios a partir de promedios ponderados, las ponderaciones son proporcionales a la cantidad vendida a precio de mercado controlado y en el mercado libre. Para ciertos artículos no subvencionados, las relaciones de precios medios ponderados son calculados aplicando las ponderaciones a las importantes variedades.

Informaciones complementarias
Se publican subgrupos detallados para 13 meses.

Organización y publicación
Ministry Planning, Central Statistical Office: "Monthly Price Index Number" (Kuwait).

idem: "Consumer Price Index Number Revised Series 1978 = 100, Scope and Method of Construction" (Kuwait).

LESOTHO

Denominación oficial
Consumer Price Index for Low Income Households (Indice de precios del consumo de hogares con ingresos bajos).

Alcance
El índice se compila trimestralmente y abarca todos los hogares urbanos con ingresos bajos.

Base oficial
Abril de 1989 = 100.

Fuente de la ponderación
La determinación de los coeficientes de ponderación y la selección de los artículos se basaron en los resultados de una encuesta nacional sobre gastos de los hogares, con una muestra bietápica estratificada que abarcó 4 800 hogares rurales y 2 880 rurales de todo el país. La muestra nacional se dividió en distritos y cuatro regiones agroecológicas, con 24 estratos para las regiones rurales y 14 para las zonas urbanas, 3 sólo para Maseru. En la aglomeración urbana de Maseru los suburbios se afijaron entre los estratos de ingresos elevados, medios y bajos con la finalidad de mejorar el diseño de muestreo, que era proporcional al tamaño de cada estrato. Considerando el volumen de trabajo óptimo de los investigadores, se seleccionaron ocho hogares por mes en las zonas urbanas y cinco en las regiones rurales. Los hogares con ingresos bajos del índice son los que tienen ingresos mensuales inferiores a 200 maloti. No se ajustaron las variaciones de precio ocurridas entre el período de la encuesta y abril de 1989. Los artículos se seleccionaron según el criterio del gasto total; al hacerse los agregados de base se repartieron entre los grupos y subgrupos los coeficientes de ponderación de los artículos sin precio registrado.

Ponderaciones y composición

Grupos principales	Número de artículos	Ponderación	Número aproximado de cotizaciones de precio
Alimentación y tabaco	108	76,3	552
Vestido y calzado	46	13,9	148
Alquiler bruto, combustible y luz	25	12,4	58
Muebles, moblaje y funcionamiento del hogar	49	10,0	171
Transporte y comunicaciones	16	3,9	32
Otros bienes y servicios	48	7,1	139
Total	292	100,0	1 100

Gastos de consumo de los hogares
Como los gastos de consumo se definen de conformidad con la contabilidad nacional, se han hecho algunos pocos ajustes de las ponderaciones de la encuesta sobre los gastos de los hogares. Los coeficientes de ponderación incluyen los valores atribuidos a los productos en especie y las viviendas ocupadas por sus propietarios.

Método de recolección de los datos
En enero, abril, julio y octubre, los investigadores registran los precios en unos 170 puntos de venta al por menor y establecimientos de servicios diseminados en seis ciudades. Los precios de Maseru se determinan la primer semana (de lunes a viernes) del mes correspondiente. Los precios del índice son los que se pagan en el momento. Sólo se registran los descuentos y las rebajas que se ofrecen a todos los compradores y no tan sólo a un grupo determinado. No se utilizan los precios de alquileres con opción de compra y ventas a plazo o a crédito, ni los precios de objetos usados y de importación.

Vivienda
Todos los trimestres se registran las cotizaciones de los alquileres, que incluyen los recargos y gastos de reparación y nueva decoración de la casa. Las cotizaciones de las viviendas ocupadas por sus propietarios se estiman por los alquileres vigentes para viviendas similares.

Especificación de las variedades
Las especificaciones incluyen todas las características que permitan a los distintos investigadores registrar los precios de variedades prácticamente idénticas en los distintos puntos de venta y comprenden, por ejemplo, clase, variedad, nombre, origen, tamaño, marca, envasado, etc. Sin embargo, los investigadores pueden elegir libremente dentro del surtido del punto de venta seleccionado.

Sustitución, cambio de calidad, etc.
Las sustituciones se realizan recurriendo a artículos que tengan prácticamente la misma calidad. Cuando aparecen productos nuevos con demanda popular probada, sus precios se distribuyen entre los artículos o grupos correspondientes. A su vez, cuando desaparecen productos del mercado se seleccionan nuevos productos como sustitutos.

Artículos estacionales
Para compilar el índice, los precios de artículos estacionales, como frutas y legumbres fescas que no están disponibles en el mercado durante ciertas temporadas, se continúan utilizando los ultimos precios registrados hasta que dichos artículos reaparezcan en el mercado.

Cálculo
El índice se calcula según la fórmula de Laspeyres como un promedio aritmético ponderado de base fija, cuyos coeficientes de ponderación corresponden al período octubre de 1986 - septiembre de 1987.

Los relativos de precio se calculan primero para cada cotización, utilizándose para cada variedad y artículo los relativos del período corriente y del precedente.

Se calculan índices ponderados de subgrupos, grupos principales y todos los artículos con cotizaciones anteriores al período de base, que luego se actualizan tomando como base 100 el mes de abril de 1989.

Informaciones complementarias
Además de los índices de los precios del consumo de hogares con ingresos bajos, también se publican series de índices para hogares de ingresos elevados de Maseru.

Organización y publicación
Bureau of Statistics: "Statistical Reports - Consumer Price Index" (Maseru).

idem: "Lesotho - Consumer Price Index".

LIBERIA (MONROVIA)

Denominación oficial
Consumer Price Index (Indice de Precios del Consumo).

Alcance
El índice se compila mensualmente y abarca todos los hogares de trabajadores y empleados de oficina compuestos por dos o más personas cuyos ingresos mensuales no excedían 250 dólares entre octubre y diciembre de 1963. El índice se refiere a la ciudad capital, Monrovia.

Base oficial
Septiembre - noviembre de 1964 = 100.

Fuente de la ponderación
La determinación de los coeficientes de ponderación y la selección de los artículos se basaron en los resultados de una encuesta sobre los gastos de los hogares realizada en Monrovia de octubre a diciembre de 1963 a una muestra de hogares de trabajadores y de empleados de oficina cuyos ingresos no excedían los 250 dólares por mes en el momento de dicha encuesta. Se ajustaron los coeficientes de ponderación según los resultados de una encuesta restringida sobre los gastos de los hogares que se efectuó en junio de 1964 para tomar en cuenta las modificaciones ocurridas entre ambos períodos.

Gastos de consumo de los hogares
Son, a los efectos del índice, todos los bienes y servicios adquiridos para el consumo por la población del índice e incluyen las tasas de permisos y autorizaciones, los servicios de salud y jurídicos, recreo y otros servicios. No se incluyen los seguros de vida o de bienes ni los impuestos al ingreso o a bienes personales.

Ponderaciones y composición

Grupos principales	Número de artículos	Ponderación	Número aproximado de cotizaciones de precio
Alimentación	32	34,4	...
Bebidas y tabaco	6	5,7	...
Combustible y luz	3	5,0	...
Alquiler	1	14,9	...
Vestido y calzado	14	13,8	...
Bienes y muebles del hogar	7	6,1	...
Asistencia médica, aseo personal y servicios	9	11,4	...
Varios	7	8,7	...
Total	79	100,0	188

Método de recolección de los datos
Los investigadores registran los precios en 18 tiendas, dos mercados y 14 establecimientos de servicios. Los precios de los alimentos se registran dos veces por mes y una los de bebidas y tabaco, combustible y luz, vestidos, bienes y muebles del hogar. Las tarifas de la asistencia médica y las matrículas escolares se registran una vez al año. Se ponderan los precios de los artículos vendidos a granel, como montones, pilas, unidades, ramas, etc., y luego se ajustan al coeficiente de ponderación del período de base.

Para el índice se utilizan los precios al por menor que pagan los consumidores en el momento. No se toman en consideración los descuentos, ventas rebajadas y otros precios anormales.

Vivienda
Las cotizaciones del alquiler de unas 100 viviendas se registran dos veces por año, en enero y julio. En el índice no se incluyen las viviendas ocupadas por sus propietarios.

Especificación de las variedades
Para cada artículo del índice se dan especificaciones detalladas, que dan una descripción completa del artículo, su marca, tamaño, unidad o cantidad material, marca de fábrica registrada, etc.

Sustitución, cambio de calidad, etc.
Cuando deja de ofrecerse un artículo en el mercado, se le sustituye por otro similar y se utiliza el método de enlace.

Artículos estacionales
Las fluctuaciones estacionales de los precios de ciertos artículos se toman en cuenta manteniendo fuera de estación los últimos precios de la temporada anterior.

Cálculo
El índice se calcula según la fórmula de Laspeyres como un promedio aritmético ponderado de base fija, cuyos coeficientes de ponderación corresponden a junio de 1964.

Para el cálculo de los índices por artículo, se utilizan los relativos del promedio de precios del período en curso. Los promedios de precio son medias aritméticas simples de todos los precios obtenidos. Si falta el precio de un artículo, se utiliza el precio anteriormente registrado para el mismo artículo.

Organización y publicación
National Planning Agency, Bureau of Statistics: "Statistical Newsletter" (Monrovia).

idem: "Quarterly Statistical Bulletin".

idem: "Economic Survey of Liberia".

idem: "Results of the Study related to the Consumer Price Index for Monrovia", Serie metodológica No. 1 (1964).

LUXEMBURGO

Denominación oficial
Indice des prix à la consommation (Indice de Precios del Consumo).

Alcance
El índice se compila mensualmente y abarca todos los hogares del país, salvo los de independientes en la industria y servicios y los de los agricultores.

Base oficial
1990 = 100.

Fuente de la ponderación
La determinación de los coeficientes de ponderación y la selección de los artículos se basaron en los resultados de una encuesta sobre los gastos de los hogares realizada entre abril de 1986 y septiembre de 1987, que comprendió 2 764 hogares representativos del conjunto de la población. El índice se refiere a todos los hogares del país, salvo los de agricultores e independientes en la industria y los servicios. No se ajustaron los coeficientes de ponderación para tomar en cuenta las modificaciones de precio ocurridas entre el período de la encuesta y 1990.

Los artículos se seleccionaron en función de su importancia para el presupuesto de los hogares y para poder observar la evolución de sus precios en el tiempo.

Los coeficientes de ponderación de los artículos no seleccionados, por no representar una proporción importante del gasto de los hogares, se atribuyen a otros artículos similares. El valor de los artículos descartados por razones de política (cigarrillos, tabacos y bebidas alcohólicas fuertes, así como ciertos servicios ligados directamente a la fijación de la escala móvil de los salarios) se dejan de lado antes de determinar el total de los gastos del consumo tomados en consideración.

Ponderaciones y composición

Grupos principales	Número de artículos	Ponderación	Número aproximado de cotizaciones de precio
Alimentación	91	205,2	2 175
Vestido y calzado	42	131,1	800
Vivienda, combustible y luz	11	137,0	600
Muebles, moblaje y equipos del hogar	39	100,8	700
Asistencia médica	27	81,9	300
Transporte y comunicaciones	24	148,6	275
Educación y recreación	37	79,9	700
Otros bienes y servicios	32	115,5	850
Total	303	100,0	6 400

Gastos de consumo de los hogares
Con muy pocas excepciones importantes, se ha adoptado en principio el concepto de "gasto", es decir considerar sólo los desembolsos efectivamente realizados por los hogares durante el período de observación. Ni el consumo de la producción o existencias propias ni los alquileres ficticios de las viviendas ocupadas por sus propietarios intervienen en la determinación de los coeficientes de ponderación.

En la ponderación de los gastos de salud se consideran los gastos de la atención médica no reembolsados y las cotizaciones patronales y salariales para prestaciones en especie. En la ponderación de los seguros, se trata de separar la parte de la prima que corresponde al precio del servicio de seguros en sí. La diferencia, a largo plazo, entre las primas establecidas y los recargos por siniestros constituye esa parte que representa sólo la adquisición del servicio del seguro. La relación entre esta diferencia y el total de las primas establecidas en un lapso de 10 años se aplica al monto de los gastos de los hogares por concepto de seguros. Los gastos por la adquisición del servicio de los seguros así calculados constituye la ponderación de la partida "seguros".

Método de recolección de los datos
Todos los meses los investigadores registran los precios en supermercados, puntos de venta al por menor y establecimientos de servicios de la capital y otras localidades representativas de las demás regiones del país. Los precios de las frutas y legumbres frescas, del pescado y las flores se registran tres veces por mes.

Las tarifas oficiales se obtienen de los organismos nacionales o comunales con facultades para fijarlas. Las de los servicios de electricidad, gas y agua, atención médica (que comprende las prestaciones de médicos, practicantes de profesiones paramédicas y los servicios hospitalarios) y ciertos elementos de los transportes y las comunicaciones (que comprenden gasolina, ferrocarriles, autobuses, franqueo de cartas, teléfonos) se registran de conformidad con las tarifas oficiales. Para compilar el índice se toman siempre en consideración los precios (totales) de las transacciones, independientemente de las formas de pago y condiciones de que puedan establecer los organismos de asistencia social para el reembolso de los gastos de salud.

La instrucción pública es gratuita. En la medida en que ciertos artículos representativos pueden no serlo, se toma en cuenta el precio que deben pagar por ellos los consumidores.

Las rebajas y ofertas especiales sólo se consideran si se ofrecen a todos los consumidores, en cantidades importantes, durante más de mes, y si el artículo rebajado presenta las mismas características que antes de esa rebaja.

En los cálculos del índice no se consideran los precios de liquidación, que por disposición reglamentaria no pueden durar más de 15 días, pues no llenan los demás requisitos de las ofertas especiales.

Los precios se registran tal como se practican en la fecha de referencia del índice, es decir a comienzos de mes, cualesquiera sean las modalidades de pago convenidas entre el vendedor y el comprador.

No se toman en consideración las compras de los artículos de segunda mano y su entrega a título de pago parcial.

Los precios de los artículos registrados corresponden a los del consumo final de los hogares, sin considerar los eventuales precios de la intermediación.

Vivienda
Se investigan los alquileres que pagan los locatarios por viviendas sin muebles, haciendo abstracción de los gastos y recargos anexos, es decir el "alquiler neto". Se han elegido los alojamientos que representan el conjunto de la población, sin excluirse a priori ninguna clase de vivienda. La recolección de las cotizaciones del alquiler tiene lugar dos veces por año, investigándose cada mes un sexto de la muestra. Los precios se obtienen merced a entrevistas telefónicas o, excepcionalmente, por correo. El índice de los alquileres (que se divide en alquileres de apartamentos y alquileres de casas) es igual a la media aritmética de los índices particulares calculados para cada vivienda de los dos muestreos mencionados. Para compilar el índice no se toman en cuenta las viviendas ocupadas por sus propietarios (noción de gasto).

Especificación de las variedades
Las especificaciones, que son detalladas en cuanto a las variedades, marcas y modelos, dependen exclusivamente del STATEC (Servicio Central de Estadística y Estudios Económicos) y tienen carácter confidencial.

Sustitución, cambio de calidad, etc.
Para los cambios de calidad se prevén dos situaciones: que las características esenciales del producto no se alteran y el cambio en el precio se refleja en el índice sin ajuste; o que el cambio de calidad implica modificaciones importantes de las características esenciales del producto: en cuyo caso se neutraliza en los precios la parte correspondiente a la mejora cualitativa. En la práctica los cambios de calidad se acompañan de variaciones del precio y se trata de investigar si corresponden exclusivamente a un cambio de calidad o no y, según sea el caso, los enlaces estadísticos consiguientes serán parciales o totales.

Se prevé que en el futuro la canasta de bienes y servicios se revisará cada cinco años, manteniéndose constante durante todo ese período el principio de su composición. Si no obstante resulta imposible ignorar la aparición de un nuevo producto, se le integra en el índice recurriendo al método de encadenamiento o empalme estadístico, siempre que la variedad sea representativa de un artículo que figura en la canasta.

En caso de desaparición de una determinada calidad o género, se procede a su sustitución, de preferencia en el mismo punto de venta, por otro producto con características semejantes. Si la nueva variedad pertenece a la misma marca y satisface por igual a los consumidores, se la incluye en el índice tomando en cuenta su eventual aumento de precio.

Si las características de la nueva variedad son fundamentalmente distintas (comprendidos los servicios de venta y posteriores) o si es de otra marca, se la incluirá en el índice como sustitutivo, con enlace estadístico.

Artículos estacionales
Las frutas y las legumbres frescas son artículos con ponderación fija, pero las canastas de cada uno de ellos tiene una composición mensual diferente, así como los coeficientes de ponderación correspondientes a las variedades elegidas. Para ambos artículos se calcula una media móvil de sus precios durante 12 meses.

Para los demás artículos estacionales no ofrecidos durante todo el año, se mantienen en el índice sus últimas cotizaciones

mientras estén fuera de temporada y hasta que vuelvan al mercado.
Cálculo
El índice se calcula según la fórmula de Laspeyres como un promedio aritmético ponderado de base fija (1990), cuyos coeficientes de ponderación corresponden al período 1986-87. El índice de producto se obtiene mediante los relativos de precio del período en curso y del período de base.
Informaciones complementarias
El índice general y los índices de grupo, así como los principales índices de subgrupo y de ciertos artículos importantes se publican en forma mensual. Los índices de subgrupo y de artículo están a disposición del público que los solicite.
Organización y publicación
El STATEC (Service central de la statistique et des études économiques) calcula y publica mensualmente el índice en: "Indicateurs rapides du STATEC, série A1, Indice des prix à la consommation" (Luxemburgo).

idem: "Cahier économique du STATEC no. 81, Le nouvel indice des prix à la consommation, Réforme de 1990/91".

idem: "Note de conjoncture" (trimestral).

idem: "Annuaire statistique".

MACAO

Denominación oficial
Indice de Preços no Consumidor (Indice de Precios del Consumo).
Alcance
El índice se compila mensualmente y abarca los hogares con un promedio mensual de gastos de 3 313 pataca, situados en la península de Macao, con excepción de las islas Taipa y Coloane.
Base oficial
Octubre de 1982 - septiembre de 1983 = 100.
Fuente de la ponderación
La determinación de los coeficientes de ponderación y la selección de los artículos se basaron en los resultados de una encuesta sobre los gastos de los hogares (EGH) realizada durante un año, entre 1982 y 1983, con una muestra aleatoria de 1 560 hogares y un período de referencia de dos semanas para los datos sobre los gastos de cada hogar. No se ajustaron los coeficientes de ponderación para tomar en cuenta las modificaciones de precio ocurridas entre el período de base y el de la encuesta.

Los criterios y métodos para seleccionar los artículos cuyos precios se deben registrar se basan en la ponderación de los artículos de la EGH, así como en la popularidad de los artículos que se ofrecen en el mercado y la facilidad de registrar sus precios en forma periódica e ininterrumpida. En cuanto a las ponderaciones de los artículos no seleccionados, sus ponderaciones se distribuyen entre los artículos similares, tanto en forma directa como proporcional.

Ponderaciones y composición

Grupos principales	Número de artículos	Ponderación	Número aproximado de cotizaciones de precio
Alimentación	72	42,03	...
Bebidas alcohólicas y tabaco	4	2,22	...
Alquiler	-	-	-
Gastos del hogar	4	4,78	...
Combustible y luz	8	1,63	...
Vestido y calzado	29	7,25	...
Bienes durables	26	2,91	...
Bienes varios	29	4,97	...
Transporte	17	4,88	...
Servicios	35	8,14	...
Total	224	78,81	...

Gastos de consumo de los hogares
La definición de los gastos de consumo a efectos de la ponderación comprende todos los efectuados por los hogares para adquirir bienes y servicios. Como las cotizaciones de estos gastos corresponden al momento en que se realizan, se registran todos los pagos hechos por los hogares durante el ciclo del registro de los precios. Las compras a crédito o a plazos sólo se consideran si se pagan durante dicho ciclo. El valor de todos los bienes y servicios recibidos por los hogares en especie corresponde a su cotización en el mercado. El valor locativo de las viviendas ocupadas por sus propietarios y de las gratuitas se estimó en forma ficticia. Se excluyen los impuestos a los ingresos y otros impuestos directos, las inversiones, apuestas de juego, contribuciones a fondos de pensión, los seguros de vida, etc.

Método de recolección de los datos
Consisten en visitas personales de los investigadores o en cuestionarios enviados por correo a mercadillos, puntos de venta al por menor y establecimientos de precios fijos de cinco localidades. Los precios de los alimentos frescos se registran todos los días o una vez por semana y mensualmente los de los demás productos alimenticios. Por consiguiente los investigadores registran diariamente en los mercados, a primeras horas de la mañana, los precios de los alimentos frescos y, según un programa establecido de antemano, las cotizaciones de los demás productos alimenticios, que se registran una vez al mes. Cada dos meses se obtienen los precios de las bebidas alcohólicas y el tabaco, los vestidos y el calzado, los bienes durables y otros bienes varios y cada tres o seis meses los precios de los artículos restantes. Sin embargo se toman medidas inmediatas si se produce una modificación repentina del precio de ciertos artículos, como el gas, el agua, la electricidad, los periódicos, etc. Para el cálculo del índice sólo se registran y utilizan los descuentos y precios de liquidación que no excedan el 20%. Los precios del mercado negro y los de compras a crédito o a plazos, los de bienes usados y su entrega como pago parcial para adquirir otros nuevos no se toman en consideración. Se utilizan los precios que los consumidores pagan en el momento de adquirir los bienes o servicios que piensan consumir.

Vivienda
Para el cálculo del índice se excluye el alquiler.

Especificación de las variedades
Para cada artículo existen especificaciones detalladas de, por ejemplo, la variedad, calidad, origen, marca, unidad, tamaño, envasado, etc. Todos los meses se registran los precios de artículos que tienen la misma especificación.

Sustitución, cambio de calidad, etc.
Los cambios de calidad o la desaparición del mercado de una determinada calidad o clase de artículo se tratan sea por sustitución directa, estableciendo enlaces entre el artículo antiguo (variedad anterior) y el sustitutivo (nueva variedad), sea volviendo a calcular el relativo de precio e incluyéndolo en el subgrupo existente.

Artículos estacionales
Las prendas de vestir se dividen en vestimentas de verano y de invierno. Durante el verano se registran los precios de las prendas de vestir correspondientes a esa estación y se mantienen inalterados los precios de las de invierno y en esta estación, mutatis mutandis, se procede de la misma manera.

Cálculo
El índice se calcula según la fórmula de Laspeyres como un promedio aritmético ponderado de base fija, cuyos coeficientes de ponderación corresponden al período 1981-1982.

Informaciones complementarias
Se publican índices de subgrupos para la alimentación, bebidas alcohólicas y tabaco, vestido y calzado, bienes durables y varios, transporte, vehículos y servicios.

Organización y publicación
Direcçao de Serviços de Estadística e Censos: "Indice de Preços no Consumidor" (Macau).

idem: "Metodologia do Indice de Preços no Consumidor".

MADAGASCAR (ANTANANARIVO)

Denominación oficial
Indice des prix de détail à la consommation familiale malgache (Indice de Precios al Por Menor del Consumo para las familias malgaches).

Alcance
El índice se compila mensualmente y abarca hogares de familias malgaches de Antananarivo.

Base oficial
Agosto de 1971 - julio de 1972 = 100.

Fuente de la ponderación
La determinación de los coeficientes de ponderación y la selección de los artículos se basaron en los resultados de una encuesta sobre los gastos de los hogares realizada de marzo de 1968 a febrero de 1969 a hogares malgaches (de todo tamaño y categoría) de Antananarivo.

Los artículos seleccionados para el cómputo del índice son los que, teniendo un valor comercial, se les puede asignar una unidad y una calidad bien determinadas y cuyos precios se pueden registrar con facilidad a través del tiempo. La parte relativa del total de gastos que estos artículos representan es igual o superior a 0,05 por ciento para el índice malgache.

Ponderaciones y composición

Grupos principales	Número de artículos	Ponderación	Número aproximado de cotizaciones de precio
Alimentación	60	603,5	3 636
Combustible y luz	8	91,4	140
Vestido y calzado	15	85,5	144
Accesorios para el hogar	3	4,1	56
Productos de mantenimiento	5	20,3	292
Asistencia médica y aseo personal	20	38,6	988
Servicios domésticos	1	18,2	1
Varios	19	138,4	390
Total	131	1 000,0	5 647

Gastos de consumo de los hogares
En el cálculo de los coeficientes de ponderación no entran los gastos relativos al alquiler y a la vivienda propia pero sí la producción para el propio consumo. También se excluyen los gastos en bienes durables, instrucción, recreo, seguros que no sean de vehículos, cotizaciones, regalos, impuestos, tasas, multas, transferencias, objetos personales y gastos varios. Pero se incluyen los salarios pagados por servicios domésticos (excluyendo los complementos en especie), los gastos de funcionamiento y los seguros de vehículos particulares.

Método de recolección de los datos
La observación de los precios se limita a un cierto número de comercios elegidos de tal forma que su clientela corresponda a la población abarcada por el índice y refleje su importancia.

La selección de dichos comercios es empírica, teniendo en cuenta la ubicación, clase o categoría comercial y distribución de la población de referencia. El número y distribución de los comercios seleccionados varía según los grupos de productos.

Los precios de los productos alimenticios y de mantenimiento se registran en 20 comercios del centro de la ciudad y de barrios con muy importante población malgache.

Los precios de ciertos géneros alimenticios como las aves, frutas y legumbres frescas, se obtienen la primera, segunda y cuarta semanas del mes mediante compra directa de los investigadores en dos importantes mercados públicos semanarios; los de otros artículos por cuestionarios que se envían todos los meses a 40 comercios minoristas y establecimientos de prestación de servicios.

Los datos sobre los servicios domésticos se obtienen una vez por mes, mediante una encuesta especial a una muestra de hogares, cuya lista se actualiza todos los años a partir de la lista de empleadores de la Caja Nacional de Previsión Social (Caisse Nationale de Prévoyance Sociale).

Vivienda
Los gastos relativos al alquiler no se consideran en los cálculos del índice ni de los coeficientes de ponderación.

Especificación de las variedades
Los artículos se especifican y definen utilizando los términos más corrientemente empleados por comerciantes y compradores para referirse a los factores que influyen en los precios, como género, calidad, dimensión, peso, país de origen, etc. Para especificar un artículo también se considera el método de adquisición, precisado a partir del comportamiento de los hogares de referencia. Para los artículos que no son homogéneos, sobre todo las manufacturas, la definición empleada no es rigurosa, pero cada negocio tiene la obligación de registrar siempre los precios de la misma variedad.

Sustitución, cambio de calidad, etc.
Si un negocio cierra o cambia de actividad se busca un negocio comparable para sustituirlo, de ser posible en el mismo barrio. Al artículo que desaparece del mercado sin que pueda encontrarse un equivalente, se le asigna el coeficiente de ponderación de otro artículo similar ya incluido en el cálculo del índice. Cuando no se ha incluido en la canasta un artículo similar y es imposible encontrar un artículo de sustitución, su coeficiente se reparte entre los distintos artículos del mismo grupo. Como en la mayor parte de los casos la desaparición de un artículo coincide con la aparición de otro nuevo, por lo general es posible registrar paralelamente, durante un cierto lapso, los precios de ambos artículos, evaluándose la diferencia de calidad y precios para que el empalme no oculte la diferencia real de precios. El nuevo artículo no se incorpora a los cálculos del índice hasta que tenga un volumen de ventas de cierta importancia.

Artículos estacionales
Se tienen en cuenta las fluctuaciones estacionales del precio de las frutas y legumbres frescas variando los coeficientes de la ponderación mensual de los artículos del subgrupo, pero manteniendo invariable la ponderación global.

Cálculo
El índice se calcula según la fórmula de Laspeyres como un promedio aritmético ponderado de base fija, cuyos coeficientes de ponderación corresponden al período de marzo de 1968 a febrero de 1969.

Organización y publicación
Ministère des Finances, Direction générale de la Banque de données de l'Etat: "Bulletin mensuel de statistique" (Antananarivo).

idem: "Situation économique".

idem: Direction générale du gouvernement, Direction de l'Institut national de la statistique et de la recherche économique: "L'établissement des nouveaux indices des prix de détail à la consommation familiale à Tananarive, base août 1971 à juillet 1972 = 100" (Antananarivo).

MADAGASCAR (ANTANANARIVO, EUROPEOS)

Denominación oficial
Indice des prix de détail à la consommation familiale européène (Indice de Precios al Por Menor del Consumo para las familias europeas).

Alcance
El índice se compila mensualmente y abarca hogares de familias europeas de Antananarivo.

Base oficial
Agosto de 1971 - julio de 1972 = 100.

Fuente de la ponderación
La determinación de los coeficientes de ponderación y la selección de los artículos se basaron en los resultados de una encuesta sobre los gastos de los hogares realizada de mayo a junio de 1969 a hogares europeos (de todo tamaño y categoría) de Antananarivo.

Los artículos seleccionados para el cómputo del índice son los que, teniendo un valor comercial, se les puede asignar una unidad y una calidad bien determinadas y cuyos precios se pueden registrar con facilidad a través del tiempo. La parte relativa del total de gastos que estos artículos representan es igual o superior a 0,03 por ciento para el índice europeo.

Gastos de consumo de los hogares
En los cálculos de los coeficientes de ponderación entra la producción para el propio consumo, pero no los gastos relativos al alquiler y la vivienda propia. También se excluyen los gastos en bienes durables, instrucción, recreo, seguros que no sean de vehículos, cotizaciones, regalos, impuestos, tasas, multas, transferencias, objetos personales y gastos varios. Pero se incluyen los salarios pagados por servicios domésticos (excluyendo los complementos en especie), los gastos corrientes y los seguros de vehículos particulares.

Método de recolección de los datos
La observación de los precios se limita a un cierto número de comercios elegidos de tal forma que su clientela corresponda a la población abarcada por el índice y refleje su importancia. La selección de dichos comercios es empírica, teniendo en cuenta

Ponderaciones y composición

Grupos principales	Número de artículos	Ponderación	Número aproximado de cotizaciones de precio (a)
Alimentación	105	451,6	7 110
Combustible y luz	5	60,8	20
Vestido y calzado	20	76,2	508
Accesorios para el hogar	5	6,4	324
Productos de mantenimiento	12	29,7	804
Asistencia médica y aseo personal	24	67,6	1 576
Servicios domésticos	3	112,6	36
Varios	25	195,1	475
Total	199	1 000,0	10 853

Nota: (a) Número de cotizaciones anuales.

la ubicación, clase o categoría comercial y distribución de la población de referencia. El número y distribución de los comercios seleccionados varía según los grupos de productos. Los precios de los productos alimenticios y de mantenimiento se registran en 23 supermercados y grandes espicerías del centro de la ciudad y de barrios con muy importante población europea. Los precios de ciertos artículos alimenticios como las frutas y legumbres frescas, se obtienen cada seis días mediante compra directa de los investigadores en el principal mercado público; los de otros artículos por cuestionarios que se envían todos los meses a 43 comercios minoristas y establecimientos de prestación de servicios. Los datos sobre los servicios domésticos se obtienen una vez por año, mediante una encuesta especial a una muestra de hogares, cuya lista se actualiza todos los años a partir de la lista de empleadores de la Caja Nacional de Previsión Social (Caisse Nationale de Prévoyance Sociale).

Vivienda
Los gastos relativos al alquiler no se consideran en los cálculos del índice ni de los coeficientes de ponderación.

Especificación de las variedades
Los artículos se especifican y definen utilizando los términos más corrientemente empleados por comerciantes y compradores para referirse a los factores que influyen en los precios, como tipo, calidad, dimensión, peso, país de origen, etc. Para especificar un artículo también se considera el método de adquisición, precisado a partir del comportamiento de los hogares de referencia. Para los artículos que no son homogéneos, sobre todo las manufacturas, la definición empleada no es rigurosa, pero cada negocio tiene la obligación de registrar siempre los precios de la misma variedad.

Sustitución, cambio de calidad, etc.
Si un negocio cierra o cambia de actividad se busca un negocio comaprable para sustituirlo, de ser posible en el mismo barrio. Al artículo que desaparece del mercado sin que pueda encontrarse un equivalente, se le asigna el coeficiente de ponderación de otro artículo similar ya incluido en el cálculo del índice. Cuando no se ha incluido en la canasta un artículo similar y es imposible encontrar un artículo de sustitución, su coeficiente se reparte entre los distintos artículos del mismo grupo. Como en la mayor parte de los casos la desaparición de un artículo coincide con la aparición de otro nuevo, por lo general es posible registrar paralelamente, durante un cierto lapso, los precios de ambos artículos, evaluándose la diferencia de calidad y precios para que el empalme no oculte la diferencia real de precios. El nuevo artículo no se incorpora a los cálculos del índice hasta que tenga un volumen de ventas de cierta importancia.

Artículos estacionales
Se tienen en cuenta las fluctuaciones estacionales del precio de las frutas y legumbres frescas variando los coeficientes de la ponderación mensual de los artículos del subgrupo, pero manteniendo invariable la ponderación global.

Cálculo
El índice se calcula según la fórmula de Laspeyres como un promedio aritmético ponderado de base fija, cuyos coeficientes de ponderación corresponden al período marzo de 1968 - febrero de 1969.

Organización y publicación
Ministère des Finances, Direction générale de la Banque de données de l'Etat: "Bulletin mensuel de statistique" (Antananarivo).

idem: "Situation économique".

idem: Direction générale du gouvernement, Direction de l'Institut national de la statistique et de la recherche économique: "L'établissement des nouveaux indices des prix de détail à la consommation familiale à Tananarive, base août 1971 à juillet 1972 = 100" (Antananarivo).

MALASIA

Denominación oficial
Consumer Price Index (Indice de precios del consumo).

Alcance
El índice se calcula mensualmente y abarca todos los hogares de las zonas urbanas.

Base oficial
1980 = 100.

Fuente de la ponderación
La determinación de los coeficientes de ponderación y la selección de los artículos se basaron en los resultados de dos encuestas sobre gastos de los hogares, una para Malasia peninsular realizada en diciembre de 1980 que abarcó unos 3 000 hogares privados, y otra para Sabah y Sarawak que duró seis meses (de mayo a octubre de 1982) y abarcó unos 3 000 hogares privados. No se ajustaron los coeficientes de ponderación para tomar en cuenta las modificaciones de precio ocurridas entre el período de base y las fechas de las encuestas, pero se ajustaron las proporciones de los gastos de consumo de Malasia peninsular para reflejar la situación existente en 1982.

Para la recolección de precios se seleccionan los artículos con coeficientes de ponderación más elevados. Para los artículos que tiene coeficientes de ponderación pero cuyos precios no se pueden registrar se utilizan los relativos ponderados del precio de otros artículos del mismo grupo o subgrupo, para obtener el relativo de precio del artículo en cuestión. Los coeficientes de ponderación de los artículos no seleccionados se redistribuyen entre los artículos seleccionados del mismo grupo.

Ponderaciones y composición

Grupos principales	Número de artículos	Ponderación	Número aproximado de cotizaciones de precio
Alimentación	468	36,9	32 539
Bebidas y tabaco	42	4,7	2 026
Vestido y calzado	96	4,8	2 053
Alquiler bruto, combustible y luz	46	18,7	1 017
Muebles, moblaje, equipos y mantenimiento del hogar	170	5,8	5 676
Asistencia médica	64	1,2	2 010
Transporte y comunicaciones	119	16,0	499
Servicios de recreación, educación y cultura	105	6,4	863
Otros bienes y servicios diversos	139	5,5	5 414
Total	1 249	100,0	52 097

Gastos de consumo de los hogares
Para la recolección de datos se ha seguido el criterio de adquisición, es decir que los gastos en mercancías y servicios deben registrarse en el sitio y con el monto del momento de su realización. Los bienes alquilados con opción de compra se consideran adquiridos en la fecha de la firma del contrato o, en su defecto, en la fecha de entrega. El concepto de consumo doméstico de bienes y servicios abarca tanto los adquiridos como los producidos por el hogar para el consumo propio. En la estimación del consumo se incluyen los valores del alquiler atribuido a las viviendas ocupadas por sus propietarios, la producción o existencias propias consumidas, los bienes y servicios proporcionados por los empleadores en forma gratuita o a precios rebajados, los salarios pagados en especie y los regalos. Los bienes o servicios que el Estado vende o presta a los hogares (comprendidas las tarifas vigentes en los hospitales públicos) también se consideran como gastos de consumo siempre que exista una clara relación entre las sumas pagadas y los bienes o servicios obtenidos a cambio y que la decisión de hacer esos gastos sea voluntaria. Por el contrario, no se consideran como gastos de consumo el pago de impuestos a los ingresos, contribuciones al seguro social, compensaciones,

tasas y aportaciones a otros hogares que tengan carácter obligatorio, ni los gastos en inversiones, préstamos, amortización de créditos, aumento del ahorro, pago de deudas de juego, prestaciones y donaciones en efectivo, ni tampoco los servicios públicos y gratuitos de cultura y recreación.

Método de recolección de los datos
La recolección de los precios de todos los artículos y servicios está a cargo de investigadores y tiene lugar a mediados de cada mes en unos 6 800 mercados, puntos de venta al por menor y establecimientos de servicios, distribuidos en 103 centros de recolección de precios (localidades) de toda Malasia.

Los precios con descuento se consideran como si fueran los normales de venta; los de liquidación sólo se toman en cuenta si los artículos se venden en cantidades suficientes. Los artículos controlados en virtud de la "Supplies Act" (ley de suministros) tiene precios recomendados que reciben amplia difusión, pero también es posible que se vendan al precio de venta normal y por lo tanto si se responde al investigador que el precio "oficial" de un artículo se considera como su precio de venta normal, es éste precio el que se registra. No se investigan los precios del mercado negro. Sólo se consideran los precios al contado, pero no los de compra a plazo o a crédito ni los alquileres con opción de compra. No se registran los precios de bienes de segunda mano. En cuanto a los artículos de importación los precios incluyen los recargos por derechos de importación e impuestos a las ventas.

Vivienda
Las encuestas sobre los alquileres se realizan los trimestres de enero, abril, julio y octubre. Los agentes de campo sondean un grupo de hogares de inquilinos. En primer término se calculan totales de alquileres por clase de vivienda y se enlazan con los relativos anteriores, obteniéndose así un índice en cadena de alquileres por clase de vivienda. En segundo término se pondera ese índice en cadena por los coeficientes de las clases de vivienda y se obtiene así el índice de los alquileres. En el índice no se incluyen las viviendas ocupadas por sus propietarios.

Especificación de las variedades
Las especificaciones de los artículos se basan en las que comunican fabricantes y productores. Se utilizan tanto especificaciones generales como detalladas. Estas últimas comprenden marca, grado, unidad, factura, calidad, etc. Las generales son descripciones amplias de artículos entre los cuales se eligen marcas específicas de una tienda.

Sustitución, cambio de calidad, etc.
No se ha intentado cuantificar los cambios de calidad que implican los nuevos modelos de aparatos eléctricos, vehículos de motor y otros productos tales como las prendas de vestir. Sólo se enlazan en el índice los productos nuevos ni se trata de sustitutivos. Cuando una variedad o calidad determinada desaparece del mercado se registra la más próxima y se enlazan los precios.

Artículos estacionales
Se registran los precios de los artículos con fluctuaciones estacionales importantes durante los meses en que se ofrecen en el mercado. Fuera de estación, los precios del índice se estiman tomando como base la media de los precios de la última temporada.

Cálculo
El índice se calcula según la fórmula de Laspeyres como un promedio aritmético ponderado de base fija, cuyos coeficientes de ponderación corresponden al período de base. El relativo de precio para cada artículo de cada uno de los centros de recolección se calcula dividiendo el precio medio de cada centro por el precio de base. Estos relativos se ponderan por los coeficientes de los centros para obtener los relativos de precio de los artículos, que a su vez se ponderan por los coeficientes de los artículos para obtener los índices de subgrupo y el índice general. Se suprimen los precios injustificadamente elevados o bajos, insertándose los precios anteriores. También se insertan los precios que faltan. Se investigan los precios injustificados antes de decidir sobre su aceptación o rechazo. A nivel regional el índice se compila en forma directa. Pero el índice a nivel con clave de tres dígitos para toda Malasia se compila como un índice compuesto que considera la proporción de los gastos de las tres regiones.

Informaciones complementarias
Se publican los índices de los nueve grandes grupos y los subgrupos de la alimentación. También se pueden solicitar índices para la reclasificación de los bienes en durables, semidurables, no durables y servicios.

Organización y publicación
Department of Statistics (Departamento de Estadísticas): "Consumer Price Index for Malaysia" (Kuala Lumpur). En esta publicación también se ofrece una breve descripción metodológica.

MALAWI (BLANTYRE 1)

Denominación oficial
Retail Price Index for Low-Income Group Families (Indice de precios al por menor - familias de ingresos bajos).

Alcance
El índice se compila mensualmente y abarca hogares de Blantyre cuyo gastos mensuales eran inferiores a 100 kwacha en 1979-80.

Base oficial
1980 = 100.

Fuente de la ponderación
La selección de los artículos y la determinación de los coeficientes de ponderación se basaron en los resultados de una encuesta sobre los gastos de los hogares urbanos efectuada en 1979-80, que abarcó 4 000 hogares diseminados en las ciudades de Blantyre, Zomba y Mzuzu. El índice por su parte se refiere a hogares del grupo de ingresos bajos, que tenían un gasto mensual inferior a 100 Kwachas en el período de la encuesta.

Ponderaciones y composición

Grupos principales	Número de artículos	Ponderación	Número aproximado de cotizaciones de precio
Alimentación	34	500	102
Bebidas y tabaco	7	39	21
Vestido y calzado	24	154	72
Vivienda	14	108	42
Gastos del hogar	7	86	21
Transportes	8	48	8
Varios	14	65	42
Total	108	1 000	308

Gastos de consumo de los hogares
A los fines del índice, los gastos del consumo comprenden todos los bienes y servicios adquiridos para el consumo por la población de referencia incluido el reembolso de préstamos. Se excluyen los ingresos en especie y el valor locativo asignado a la vivienda propia.

Método de recolección de los datos
Los precios son recogidos por investigadores en mercados, puntos de venta al por menor y establecimientos de servicios de Blantyre. Los precios de los artículos vendidos en los mercados se obtienen tres veces al mes, los de los otros artículos se recogen los martes o viernes más próximos al día 15 de cada mes. Los precios de las frutas, verduras y pescado fresco son obtenidos por el sistema de compra en los mercados. Los precios utilizados para calcular el índice son los que paga normalmente cualquier persona del público. Los precios de saldos, descuentos y rebajas se excluyen.

Vivienda
Los gastos de alquiler y el costo de las viviendas ocupadas por los propietarios no se tienen en cuenta, ni en el cálculo del índice ni en la determinación de los coeficientes de ponderación.

Especificación de las variedades
Las especificaciones de los artículos cuyos precios se han de registrar dan la variedad, calidad, factura, marca y unidad.

Sustitución, cambio de calidad, etc.
Cuando ya no se consigue un producto en el mercado se lo substituye por uno similar y se utiliza el método de enlace.

Artículos estacionales
Los precios de los artículos de estación se estiman durante el período fuera de temporada.

Cálculo
El índice se calcula conforme a la fórmula de Laspeyres como un promedio aritmético ponderado de base fija, cuyos coeficientes de ponderación corresponden al período de 1979 a 1980.

Para calcular los precios medios, por lo menos tres precios son recogidos para cada artículo.

Informaciones complementarias
La Oficina Nacional de Estadística compila y publica también series para hogares de los grupos de ingresos medios y altos de Blantyre y Lilongwe, así como para grupos de ingresos bajos y medios de Zomba y Mzuzu. Además se combinan los índices de Blantyre y de Lilongwe para formar un índice compuesto de ambas ciudades.

Organización y publicación
National Statistical Office: "Monthly Statistical Bulletin" (Zomba).

MALAWI (BLANTYRE 2)

Denominación oficial
Retail Price Index for High-Income Group Families (Indice de precios al por menor - familias de ingresos elevados).

Alcance
El índice se compila mensualmente y abarca hogares de Blantyre cuyo gastos mensuales eran de 400 kwacha o más en 1979-80.

Base oficial
1980 = 100.

Fuente de la ponderación
La selección de los artículos y la determinación de los coeficientes de ponderación se basaron en los resultados de una encuesta sobre los gastos de los hogares efectuada en 1979-80 en Blantyre sobre 400 hogares cuyos gastos eran de 400 Kwachas o más durante el período de la encuesta.

Ponderaciones y composición

Grupos principales	Número de artículos	Ponde- ración	Número aproximado de coti- zaciones de precio
Alimentación	49	203	147
Bebidas y tabaco	14	76	42
Vestido y calzado	27	71	81
Vivienda	26	130	78
Gastos del hogar	12	108	36
Transportes	19	253	19
Varios	26	159	78
Total	173	1 000	481

Gastos de consumo de los hogares
A los fines del índice, los gastos del consumo comprenden todos los bienes y servicios adquiridos para el consumo por la población de referencia incluido el reembolso de préstamos. Se excluyen los ingresos en especie y el valor locativo asignado a la vivienda propia.

Método de recolección de los datos
Los precios con recogidos por investigadores en mercados, puntos de venta al por menor y establecimientos de servicios de Blantyre. Los precios de la mayoría de los artículos se recogen los martes o viernes más próximos al día 15 de cada mes. Los precios de los artículos alimenticios importantes se obienen por el sistema de compra en dos mercados, tres veces por mes. Los datos sobre la remuneración del servicio doméstico se obtienen de una encuesta anual; los de otros servicios se averiguan en los establecimientos correspondientes. Los precios utilizados para calcular el índice son los que paga normalmente cualquier persona del público. Los precios de saldos, descuentos y rebajas se excluyen.

Vivienda
Los gastos de alquiler y el costo de las viviendas ocupadas por los propietarios no se tienen en cuenta, ni en el cálculo del índice ni en la determinación de los coeficientes de ponderación.

Especificación de las variedades
Las especificaciones de los artículos cuyos precios se han de registrar dan la variedad, calidad, factura, marca y unidad.

Sustitución, cambio de calidad, etc.
Cuando ya no se consigue un producto en el mercado se lo substituye por uno similar y se utiliza el método de enlace.

Artículos estacionales
Los precios de los artículos de estación se estiman durante el período fuera de temporada.

Cálculo
El índice se calcula conforme a la fórmula de Laspeyres como un promedio aritmético ponderado de base fija, cuyos coeficientes de ponderación corresponden al período de 1979 a 1980.

Para calcular los precios medios, por lo menos tres precios son recogidos para cada artículo.

Informaciones complementarias
La Oficina Nacional de Estadística compila y publica también series para hogares de los grupos de ingresos bajos y medios de Blantyre y Lilongwe, así como para grupos de ingresos bajos y medios de Zomba y Mzuzu. Además se combinan los índices de Blantyre y de Lilongwe para formar un índice compuesto de ambas cuidades.

Organización y publicación
National Statistical Office: "Monthly Statistical Bulletin" (Zomba).

MALI (BAMAKO)

Denominación oficial
Indice des prix du groupe "Alimentation" (marchés de Bamako) - (Indice de precios del grupo alimentación - mercados de Bamako).

Alcance
El índice se calcula mensualmente y abarca los hogares de 4 personas por lo menos en Bamako.

Base oficial
1 de julio de 1962 - 1 de julio de 1963 = 100.

Fuente de la ponderación
La selección de los artículos y la determinación de los coeficientes de ponderación se basaron en los resultados de una encuesta piloto sobre los gastos de los hogares efectuada en marzo de 1963 en Bamako y que abarcó hogares de 4 personas por lo menos y según comparaciones de los coeficientes de ponderación utilizados en el cálculo de índices de otros países africanos con estructuras de consumo similares.

Ponderaciones y composición

Grupos principales	Número de artículos	Ponde- ración	Número aproximado de coti- zaciones de precio
Alimentación:			
Farináceos y feculentos	4	33,9	...
Condimentos	5	8,0	...
Verduras y frutas frescas	5	9,1	...
Carne y pescado	5	38,1	...
Leche, grasos, varios	5	10,9	...
Total	24	100,0	...

Gastos de consumo de los hogares
No disponible.

Método de recolección de los datos
Los precios son recogidos 3 o 4 veces por mes, por agentes en 9 mercados en Bamako.

Vivienda
No disponible.

Especificación de las variedades
No disponible.

Sustitución, cambio de calidad, etc.
No disponible.

Artículos estacionales
Las fluctuaciones estacionales de los precios no son objeto de ajuste.

Cálculo
El índice se calcula conforme a la fórmula de Laspeyres como un promedio aritmético ponderado de base fija, cuyos coeficientes de ponderación corresponden a marzo de 1963.

Informaciones complementarias
Desde 1988 se calcula un índice nacional de precios del consumo (base julio de 1986 - junio 1987 = 100), sobre las ciudades de Kayes, Sikasso y Bamako. Esta serie se publica en

el Anuario y Boletín de estadísticas del Trabajo, pero en el momento de publicar el presente Volumen la OIT no disponía de informaciones metodológicas sobre esta serie.

Organización y publicación
Ministère du Plan, Direction nationale de la statistique et de l'informatique: "Bulletin mensuel de statistique" (Bamako).

MALTA

Denominación oficial
Retail Price Index (Indice de Precios al por Menor).

Alcance
El índice se compila mensualmente y abarca hogares de empleados.

Base oficial
1983 = 100.

Fuente de la ponderación
La determinación de los coeficientes de ponderación y la selección de los artículos se basaron en los resultados de una encuesta sobre los gastos de los hogares realizada en 1983. La encuesta abarcó hogares de empleados que comprendían entre dos y seis miembros, de los cuales trabajaban a tiempo completo un máximo de dos y cuyo jefe tenía entre 23 y 40 libras de ingreso semanal. Se excluyeron los hogares de profesionales, trabajadores por cuenta propia y jubilados.

Ponderaciones y composición

Grupos principales	Número de artículos	Ponderación	Número aproximado de cotizaciones de precio
Alimentación	90	41,91	...
Bebidas y tabaco	13	9,46	...
Vestido y calzado	37	10,57	...
Vivienda:			
Alquiler	2	1,90	...
Agua	2	0,25	...
Mantenimiento y reparaciones	5	1,82	...
Combustible y luz	5	3,14	...
Muebles, moblaje y equipo del hogar	29	6,15	...
Transporte y comunicaciones	13	9,93	...
Asistencia médica y aseo personal	33	5,55	...
Educación y recreación	31	4,92	...
Otros bienes y servicios	14	4,40	...
Total	274	100,00	...

Gastos de consumo de los hogares
Se excluyen las tasas de permisos de conducir y las primas de seguros de vehículos automóviles.

Método de recolección de los datos
Los investigadores registran los precios de la mayoría de los artículos una vez por mes en los puntos de venta al por menor y establecimientos de servicios de 13 localidades. Los precios de las frutas, legumbres, carnes y pescados frescos se determinan tres veces al mes. Los precios para calcular el índice son los que se pagan en el momento.

Vivienda
Las cotizaciones de alquiler se obtienen mediante una encuesta anual a 400 hogares que viven en casas alquiladas. En el índice no se consideran las viviendas ocupadas por sus propietarios.

Especificación de las variedades
No disponible.

Sustitución, cambio de calidad, etc.
Cuando cambia la calidad de un producto o aparece en el mercado un nuevo artículo se establece una nueva serie de precios.

Artículos estacionales
Para tomar en cuenta las fluctuaciones estacionales de los precios de ciertos artículos se varían mensualmente los coeficientes de ponderación dentro de los grupos cuyas ponderaciones son constantes.

Cálculo
El índice se calcula según la fórmula de Laspeyres como un promedio aritmético ponderado de base fija, cuyos coeficientes de ponderación corresponden al período de base. El índice nacional es un promedio de las 13 localidades.

Informaciones complementarias
Se publican índices de subgrupo para: alimentación, bebidas alcohólicas y tabaco, vestido y calzado, vivienda, combustible y energía eléctrica, muebles, moblaje y equipo del hogar, transporte y comunicaciones, asistencia médica y aseo personal, educación y recreación, otros bienes y servicios. Actualmente se calcula una nueva serie con base 1991 = 100, pero en el momento de publicar el presente volumen la OIT no disponía de informaciones metodológicas sobre esta serie.

Organización y publicación
Central Office of Statistics: "Quarterly Digest of Statistics" (Valletta).
idem: "Annual Abstract of Statistics".
idem: "Report on Proposals for a New Index of Retail Prices - 1984".

MARRUECOS

Denominación oficial
Indice du coût de la vie (Indice del costo de la vida).

Alcance
El índice se calcula mensualmente y abarca los hogares de ingresos bajos residentes en las 8 ciudades más importantes del país.

Base oficial
Mayo de 1972 - abril de 1973 = 100.

Fuente de la ponderación
La selección de los artículos y la determinación de los coeficientes de ponderación se basaron en los resultados de una encuesta sobre los gastos de los hogares efectuada en 1970-71 y que abarcó hogares de ingresos bajos residentes en las 8 ciudades más importantes del país.

Ponderaciones y composición

Grupos principales	Número de artículos	Ponderación	Número aproximado de cotizaciones de precio
Alimentación	83	54,0	...
Tabaco	1	1,9	...
Vivienda:			
Alquiler	1	5,8	...
Reparaciones y conservación	2	1,2	...
Combustible, luz y agua	7	3,0	...
Moblaje y ropa blanca	14	2,1	...
Accesorios para el hogar	21	1,5	...
Vestido y calzado	34	8,5	...
Productos de limpieza, aseo personal y asistencia médica	19	5,5	...
Transportes y comunicaciones	12	6,9	...
Educación, distracciones y varios	16	9,6	...
Total	210	100,0	...

Gastos de consumo de los hogares
No disponible.

Método de recolección de los datos
Los precios son recogidos por investigadores en puntos de venta al por menor y establecimientos de servicios en las 8 ciudades más importantes del país. La frecuencia con la que se recogen depende de la variabilidad de los precios de dichos artículos.

Vivienda
Las cotizaciones del alquiler se obtienen trimestralmente de una muestra de viviendas de tres o cuatro habitaciones, situadas en barrios modestos.

Especificación de las variedades
Las especificaciones describen la calidad y la marca.

Sustitución, cambio de calidad, etc.
Cuando un artículo desaparece del mercado durante un cierto tiempo, se repite su último precio registrado siempre que otros productos similares no hayan tenido variaciones de precio importantes. En tal caso el precio del producto desaparecido se estima en base a las variaciones de precio de los productos similares. Si la desaparación de artículo es definitiva, se le reemplaza por otro similar o, en su caso, por uno de calidad diferente. Se aplica entonces un coeficiente de enlace que se basa sea en los precios observados en el mismo período que

corresponden a los dos productos (el desaparecido y el de reciente incorporación), sea en la comparación de los costos de producción, sea en la búsqueda del producto que de una satisfacción igual al consumidor, sea, en fin, en la elaboración de un modelo econométrico que permita determinar las diferencias cualitativas.

Artículos estacionales
Se tienen en cuenta las fluctuaciones estacionales de los precios de las frutas y verduras frescas variando la composición mensual de los artículos del subgrupo, cuyo conjunto de coeficientes de ponderación permanece constante, y utilizando, para el cálculo del índice final, un promedio móvil de 3 meses.

Cálculo
El índice se calcula conforme a la fórmula de Laspeyres como un promedio aritmético ponderado de base fija, cuyos coeficientes de ponderación corresponden al período 1970-71.

Organización y publicación
Premier Ministre, Secrétariat d'Etat au plan et au développement régional, Direction de la statistique: "Bulletin mensuel de statistique" (Rabat).

idem: "Bulletin méthodologique trimestriel", nouvelle série no. 3, (Rabat).

MARTINICA

Denominación oficial
Indice des prix à la consommation (Indice de precios del consumo).

Alcance
El índice se compila mensualmente y abarca los hogares urbanos de gastos e ingresos medios; incluye solamente los hogares cuyo jefe es un obrero o un empleado a sueldo en los sectores público o privado no agrícolas, con exclusión de las fuerzas armadas.

Base oficial
1979 = 100.

Fuente de la ponderación
Los coeficientes de ponderación se calculan en base a los datos recogidos en diversas fuentes, tales como expedientes administrativos, estadísticas de la producción y del commercio, junto con las normas privadas de gastos de consumo en Francia y la Reunión.

Ponderaciones y composición

Grupos principales	Número de artículos	Ponderación	Número aproximado de cotizaciones de precio
Alimentación	57	31,66	...
Vestido y calzado	24	8,79	...
Vivienda:			
Combustible y luz	4	4,33	...
Alquiler	1	9,96	...
Mobiliario, accesorios para el hogar, mantenimiento y otros servicios	25	10,83	...
Aseo personal y asistencia médica	12	8,58	...
Transportes	12	16,44	...
Educación y distracciones	31	9,41	...
Total	166	100,00	...

Gastos de consumo de los hogares
A los efectos del índice, los gastos de consumo comprenden todos los bienes y servicios importantes adquiridos para su consumo por la población de referencia, incluidos los gastos de los servicios domésticos y administrativos. Se excluyen los impuestos directos, el costo de la construcción considerada como inversión, los bienes de producción doméstica consumidos en los mismos hogares, el valor de las viviendas ocupadas por su propietario, las adquisiciones de segunda mano, las contribuciones a la seguridad social y las primas de seguro.

Método de recolección de los datos
Los precios son recogidos por investigadores en 277 puntos de venta al por menor, mercados y en establecimientos de servicios en dos zonas urbanas principales: Fort-de-France y Schoelcher. Los precios se recogen mensualmente para la mayor parte de los artículos. Los precios de los alimentos frescos, a saber, el pescado, las frutas y las verduras se calculan dos veces por mes en tiendas de venta al por menor y semanalmente en los centros de mercado. En el caso de ciertos artículos, los precios sólo se calculan cada tres meses.

Los precios utilizados para el cálculo del índice son los precios de venta al por menor pagados generalmente.

Vivienda
Las cotizaciones relativas al alquiler se recogen cada seis meses en una muestra de 144 viviendas alquiladas en Fort-de-France y Schoelcher.

Especificación de las variedades
Las especificaciones se establecen en general. La persona encargada de anotar los precios selecciona en cada punto de venta el artículo de mayor difusión para establecer su lista.

Sustitución, cambio de calidad, etc.
Si ya no se puede encontrar un artículo, se lo sustituye por otro de calidad aproximadamente similar. Si la calidad del producto de sustitución no puede compararse directamente con el producto anterior, siempre que es posible se procede a reajustes por concepto de calidad.

Artículos estacionales
Se tienen en cuenta las fluctuaciones estacionales de los precios de los productos frescos como el pescado, la fruta y la verdura variando los artículos y las ponderaciones de los mismos dentro de canastas mensuales con ponderaciones de grupo constantes.

Cálculo
El índice se calcula conforme a la fórmula de Laspeyres como un promedio aritmético ponderado de base fija.

El índice para un artículo se obtiene utilizando las relaciones de precios del período corriente y del período de base. Se calculan relaciones de precios medios para la mayor parte de los artículos y, respecto de las variedades heterogéneas, se calculan los medios de las relaciones de precios.

Informaciones complementarias
Esta serie publica sub-grupos detallados.

Organización y publicación
INSEE, Service régional de la Martinique: "Bulletin statistique de la Martinique" (Fort-de-France).

idem: "Sélection mensuelle de statistiques".

INSEE, Service Interregional Antilles-Guyane; les dossiers Antilles-Guyane: "L'indice des prix de la Martinique, base 100 en 1979; Méthodes, bilan 1979-1984 et perspectives", núm. 10 (Fort-de-France, junio de 1985).

MAURICIO

Denominación oficial
Consumer Price Index (Indice de precios del consumo).

Alcance
El índice se calcula mensualmente y abarca todo tipo de hogares, grupos de población y regiones geográficas.

Base oficial
Julio de 1986 - junio de 1987 = 100.

Fuente de la ponderación
La determinación de los coeficientes de ponderación y la selección de los artículos se basaron en los resultados de una encuesta realizada entre julio de 1986 y junio de 1987 a una muestra representativa de 4 320 hogares de todo tipo, grupo de población y región geográfica de Mauricio.

Ponderaciones y composición

Grupos principales	Número de artículos	Ponderación	Número aproximado de cotizaciones de precio
Alimentación y bebidas	76	419	1 964
Bebidas alcohólicas y tabaco	6	72	138
Vestido y calzado	37	84	275
Vivienda y mantenimiento del hogar	53	135	525
(del cual alquiler bruto)	(3)	(24)	(180)
Asistencia médica y gastos de salud	10	30	136
Transporte y comunicaciones	11	93	94
Servicios de recreación, diversión, educación y cultura	20	60	158
Artículos y servicios varios	25	50	251
Total	241	1 000	3 566

Gastos de consumo de los hogares
Comprenden el valor de los bienes y servicios que los hogares obtienen gratuitamente o producen para el consumo propio al precio de venta predominate en el mercado al realizarse la encuesta. Se han excluído los bienes y servicios cuya ponderación predominante es la provisión gratuita por el Estado, tales como asistencia médica, productos farmacéuticos, educación y libros, alquileres estimados de las viviendas ocupadas por sus propietarios, contribuciones a seguros sociales y fondos de pensión, impuestos a los ingresos y otras cargas fiscales directas, amortización de deudas, apuestas y juegos de azar, regalos y remesas en metálico. Se incluyen las cuotas de permisos que se relacionan con las actividades de los hogares privados y los seguros de bienes de consumo específicos.

Método de recolección de los datos
Durante la encuesta de gastos de los hogares de 1986-87 también se efectuó una encuesta de puntos de venta. Las localidades seleccionadas para recopilar los precios se eligieron no sólo por ser representativas tanto de las regiones urbanas como de las rurales sino también por su importancia como centros comerciales. Para las zonas urbanas se seleccionaron las administradas por cinco consejos municipales (Port-Louis, Rose Hill, Quatre Bornes, Vacoas y Curepipe), mientras que para las regiones rurales se seleccionó por lo menos un centro urbano importante de las regiones septentrional, meridional, oriental, occidental y central de Mauricio. La recolección de los precios está a cargo del personal de la Oficina Central de Estadísticas. Terminada la selección de localidades y puntos de venta, los investigadores identifican los distintos artículos y variedades disponibles en los puntos de venta de cada localidad, para que en cada una de ellas se registren así los precios de la mayor parte de los bienes y servicios de la canasta. Los precios de productos perecederos, como legumbres, frutas, carne y pescado frescos, se registran en los mercados todas las semanas, un día determinado. Los precios de los demás bienes y servicios se registran mensualmente en todas las localidades, entre los días 12 y 18. Para los servicios de electricidad, agua, teléfono y trayectos de autobús se utilizan las tarifas oficiales. Los precios son los del mercado libre que pagan los consumidores en el momento. Se toman en consideración los descuentos y las rebajas siempre que no sean irregulares, tales como los precios de liquidación. No se toman en cuenta los precios del mercado negro, alquileres con opción de compra, ventas a crédito, compras de artículos de segunda mano, comercio de objetos usados o entrega de éstos como pago parcial para adquirir otros nuevos, ni los de importación.

Vivienda
En el "alquiler" se incluyen las sumas que por tal concepto pagan efectivamente los inquilinos, sin las cargas adicionales de electricidad, agua y alcantarillado. El índice de alquileres se compila los trimestres de marzo, junio, septiembre y diciembre a partir de una encuesta de 180 hogares de inquilinos. De los 4 320 hogares abarcados por la encuesta de 1986-87 sobre gastos de los hogares, 785 eran inquilinos. Los 180 hogares de la muestra de alquileres se seleccionaron en forma sistemática de los 785 antes mencionados en función de la región y del monto del alquiler. Esta encuesta de viviendas alquiladas utiliza un cuestionario especialmente diseñado para tal propósito. En el índice no se toman en consideración las viviendas ocupadas por sus propietarios. Los datos sobre los gastos de mantenimiento y reparación se obtienen de la encuesta y se incluyen en el índice.

Especificación de las variedades
Para cada artículo se selecciona una muestra representativa de variedades o indicadores y se registran los precios de los que se ofrecen en el mercado. Se elaboran especificaciones detalladas relativas a la calidad, factura, marca, cantidad, etc., de todo artículo o variedad de cada punto de venta de cada una de las localidades.

Sustitución, cambio de calidad, etc.
Los cambios de calidad son difíciles de cuantificar y no se toman en cuenta los de escasa importancia. Cuando son importantes, se supone que el producto más antiguo ha desaparecido del mercado y se le sustituye por el que ha cambiado de calidad, con el enlace consiguiente. Cuando aparecen en el mercado nuevos productos, sus precios se registran para utilizarlos en el futuro, sea al revisar la canasta de bienes y servicios, sea cuando se deban sustituir productos desaparecidos del mercado en forma permanente. Cuando desaparece un producto, se le sustituye por el producto más similar que se ofrezca en el mercado. El precio de base (ficticio) de dicho sustitutivo se calcula de tal forma que el relativo del precio actual del sustitutivo sea el mismo que el del producto que se reemplaza.

Artículos estacionales
Se toman en cuenta las fluctuaciones estacionales de las legumbres frescas modificando mensualmente los artículos de ese subgrupo pero manteniendo constantes los coeficientes de ponderación del conjunto. El índice de las legumbres compara los precios de la canasta del mes en curso con los correspondientes al mismo mes del año de base.

Cálculo
El índice se calcula según la fórmula de Laspeyres como un promedio aritmético ponderado de base fija, cuyos coeficientes de ponderación corresponden al período de base. Sólo se calculan promedios de los precios de las legumbres, frutas, carne y pescado frescos registrados en distintos puntos de venta. Los promedios de precio son medias aritméticas simples de todas las cotizaciones de precio obtenidas. Los relativos de precio se calculan dividiendo los precios vigentes por los precios de base. Si un artículo comprende variedades distintas, para cada una de ellas se calcula un relativo de precio y los promedios ponderados de estos relativos de precio permiten obtener los índices de esas variedades. Terminada la recolección, los precios se examinan minuciosamente a varios niveles para eliminar las informaciones defectuosas. Cuando faltan datos se utilizan los precios del mes anterior.

Organización y publicación
Central Statistical Office (Oficina Central de Estadísticas): "Annual Digest of Statistics" (Rose Hill).
Ministry of Finance (Ministerio de Finanzas): "Government Gazette of Mauritius" (Rose Hill).

MEXICO

Denominación oficial
Indice nacional de precios al consumidor.

Alcance
El índice se calcula mensualmente y abarca todos los consumidores urbanos del país.

Base oficial
1978 = 100.

Fuente de la ponderación
La selección de los artículos y la determinación de los coeficientes de ponderación se basaron en los resultados de la encuesta nacional de ingresos y gastos, realizada en 1977.

Ponderaciones y composición

Grupos principales	Número de artículos	Ponderación	Número aproximado de cotizaciones de precio
Alimentación y tabaco	141	37,39	60 000
Vestido y calzado	45	9,88	40 000
Vivienda	6	17,77	20 000
Muebles, aparatos y accesorios domésticos	34	6,21	5 000
Aseo personal y asistencia médica	28	5,81	4 000
Transportes	17	11,25	4 000
Educación y distracciones	23	5,75	5 000
Otros servicios	8	5,94	2 000
Total	302	100,00	140 000

Gastos de consumo de los hogares
No disponible.

Método de recolección de los datos
Los precios de los artículos alimenticios y el tabaco se recogen semanalmente; los precios del resto de los otros artículos son recogidos quincenalmente. Los precios que se utilizan para el cálculo del índice son los que pagan los consumidores: netos y al contado (incluyendo impuestos, comisiones y descuentos, cuando estos últimos están vigentes al menos más de la mitad de los días que comprende el período de la medición).

Vivienda
Los datos referentes al alquiler de casa-habitación en las 35 ciudades comprendidas en el índice se obtienen en aproximadamente 10 mil viviendas que visitan directamente los investigadores de precios.

Especificación de las variedades
No disponible.

Sustitución, cambio de calidad, etc.
Si cambia la especificación de un producto, se adopta el método de enlace. Si un artículo desaparece del mercado, es reemplazado por un artículo similar recurriendo al método de enlace y, de ser necesario, se hace un reajuste de calidad a fin de asegurar la vigencia del principo de calidad constante.

Artículos estacionales
Se tienen en cuenta las fluctuaciones estacionales de los precios de ciertos artículos manteniendo, fuera de temporada, el último precio de la temporada.

Cálculo
El índice se calcula mediante la fórmula de Laspeyres como un promedio aritmético ponderado de base fija, cuyos coeficientes de ponderaciones corresponden a 1977.

Las relaciones de los precios de cada variedad en cada almacén se calculan primeramente dividiendo el precio medio del período corriente por el precio medio del período de base. Se calcula un promedio aritmético simple de las relaciones de precios de las variedades que representan un artículo para obtener un índice del artículo. Se calculan índices separados para 35 ciudades. El índice nacional es un promedio ponderado de los índices en las 35 ciudades; las ponderaciones son proporcionales a la estructura de los gastos del consumo de cada ciudad.

Organización y publicación
Banco de México, Dirección de Investigación Económica: "Indices de precios" (México).

MONTSERRAT

Denominación oficial
Consumer Price Index (Indice de Precios del Consumo).

Alcance
El índice se compila mensualmente y se refiere al conjunto de la población.

Base oficial
Septiembre de 1982 = 100.

Fuente de la ponderación
La determinación de los coeficientes de ponderación y la selección de los artículos se basaron en una encuesta sobre los gastos de los hogares realizada durante dos semanas de 1980, con una muestra aleatoria de 400 hogares. No se ajustaron los coeficientes de ponderación para tomar en cuenta las modificaciones de precio ocurridas entre 1980 y 1982. Las ponderaciones de los artículos no incluidos en el índice se redistribuyeron entre los incluidos.

Ponderaciones y composición

Grupos principales	Número de artículos	Ponderación	Número aproximado de cotizaciones de precio
Alimentación	73	495	...
Bebidas alcohólicas y tabaco	9	46	...
Artículos del hogar	37	102	...
Gas, electricidad y agua	3	18	...
Alquiler	3	7	...
Vestido y calzado	43	179	...
Servicios y otros	34	153	...
Total	202	1 000	...

Gastos de consumo de los hogares
Comprenden las tasas de los permisos y patentes de automóviles y seguros de los mismos. Se excluyen el impuesto a los ingresos, las contribuciones a fondos de pensiones o de seguro social, giros, regalos y desembolsos similares.

Método de recolección de los datos
Los investigadores registran los precios el 15 de cada mes en los puntos de venta al por menor y establecimientos de servicio seleccionados de Plymouth.
Los precios utilizados para el cálculo del índice son los precios al por menor efectivamente pagados. No se toman en cuenta descuentos ni rebajas.

Vivienda
Las cotizaciones del alquiler se obtienen de tres tipos de viviendas amuebladas arrendadas. La vivienda propia no se incluye en el índice.

Especificación de las variedades
Se establecen con arreglo a criterios de marca de fábrica, factura, calidad, unidad y tamaño de los artículos cuyo precio se deben registrar.

Sustitución, cambio de calidad, etc.
No se toman en cuenta los cambios de calidad.

Artículos estacionales
No se toman en cuenta las fluctuaciones estacionales de los precios de los artículos.

Cálculo
El índice se calcula según la fórmula de Laspeyres como un promedio aritmético ponderado de base fija, cuyos coeficientes de ponderación corresponden a 1980.

Organización y publicación
Government of Montserrat, Statistics Office: "Montserrat Statistical Digest" (Plymouth).
idem: "Cost of living report".

MYANMAR (YANGON)

Denominación oficial
Consumer Price Index at Yangon (Indice de precios del consumo en Yangon).

Alcance
La compilación del índice es mensual y abarca todos los hogares con ingresos varios en 1978. El índice se refiere a la capital del país, Yangon.

Base oficial
1978 = 100.

Fuente de la ponderación
La selección de los artículos y la determinación de los coeficientes de ponderación se basaron en los resultados de una encuesta sobre los gastos de los hogares efectuada en 1978 y que abarcó 24 municipios de Yangon. La encuesta abarcó 1 200 hogares.

Ponderaciones y composición

Grupos principales	Número de artículos	Ponderación	Número aproximado de cotizaciones de precio
Alimentación	43	64,42	...
Tabaco	2	3,74	...
Alquiler y reparaciones	3	3,82	...
Combustible y luz	6	7,84	...
Vestido y calzado	9	8,04	...
Varios	17	12,14	...
Total	80	100,00	...

Gastos de consumo de los hogares
A los fines del índice, los gastos del consumo comprenden todos los bienes y servicios adquiridos para el consumo por la población. No incluyen los impuestos a los ingresos, los seguros de vida, los regalos y los gastos destinados a ceremonias.

Método de recolección de los datos
Los precios se recogen en mercados seleccionados de la región administrada por el Yangon City Development Committee.
Los precios al por menor de las mercancías se recogen diariamente, mientras que los precios controlados se obtienen una vez por mes. Los costos de las matrículas escolares y del transporte se obtiene de los establecimientos de servicios apropiados una vez por año.

Vivienda
Las ponderaciones se han obtenido de la encuesta sobre los gastos de hogares efectuada en 1978. El índice del alquiler se mantiene estable a 100.

Especificación de las variedades
La especificación de los artículos cuyos precios han de registrarse se dan en términos de calidad, marca, tamaño y unidad, etc.

Sustitución, cambio de calidad, etc.
Si no se puede conseguir un producto en el mercado se substituye por otro similar y se modifica el precio de base anual del antiguo producto.

Artículos estacionales
Para artículos estacionales tales como las frutas y las verduras frescas, se realizan ajustes para eliminar las fluctuaciones estacionales.

Cálculo
El índice se calcula conforme a la fórmula de Laspeyres como un promedio aritmético ponderado de base fija, cuyos coeficientes de ponderación corresponden al período de base.

Informaciones complementarias
Actualmente se calcula una nueva serie relativa a Yangon (base 1986 = 100), pero en el momento de publicar el presente volumen la OIT no disponía de informaciones metodológicas sobre esta serie.

Organización y publicación
Central Statistical Organization: "Selected Monthly Economic Indicators" (Yangon).
idem: "Statistical Yearbook".
idem: "Statistical Abstracts".

NEPAL

Denominación oficial
National Urban Consumer Price Index (Indice urbano nacional de precios del consumo).

Alcance
El índice se compila mensualmente y abarca los hogares privados de 13 zonas urbanas del país.

Base oficial
1983 (mediados de julio) - 1984 (mediados de julio) = 100.

Fuente de la ponderación
La determinación de los coeficientes de ponderación y la selección de los artículos se basaron en los resultados de una encuesta sobre gastos de los hogares, realizada entre mediados de marzo de 1984 y mediados de febrero de 1985, con una muestra de 1 161 hogares privados ubicados en zonas urbanas. El diseño del índice abarca todos los hogares privados no institucionales de las zonas urbanas del país, salvo los de una persona o los de más de diez y aquéllos cuyos gastos de consumo eran, en total, inferiores a 450 rupias nepalesas o superiores a 3 500, así como los que obtenían más del 50 por ciento du su consumo de la producción propia o de fuentes ajenas al mercado. El índice abarca 13 zonas urbanas del país.

Ponderaciones y composición

Grupos principales	Número de artículos	Ponderación	Número aproximado de cotizaciones de precio
Alimentación	...	62,63	...
Vestido	...	10,09	...
Calzado	...	1,72	...
Vivienda (incl. combustible, luz y agua)	...	12,66	...
Transporte y comunicaciones	...	2,13	...
Cuidados médicos y personales	...	4,59	...
Educación, lectura y recreaciones	...	4,14	...
Tabaco	...	2,04	...
Total	...	100,00	...

Gastos de consumo de los hogares
Comprenden el total de bienes y servicios adquiridos, los de producción casera propia y los recibidos gratuitamente o como parte en especie del salario para su consumo, así como el alquiler ficticio de las viviendas gratuitas u ocupadas por sus propietarios. Se excluyen los impuestos directos, regalos y contribuciones, primas de seguros, gastos profesionales, deudas de los consumidores, billetes de lotería y pérdidas de dinero. También se excluyen los gastos de bodas, judiciales, etc.

Método de recolección de los datos
Los precios se registran mediante visitas personales efectuadas a unos 700 comercios minoristas y establecimientos de servicios. Los precios de las legumbres y frutas frescas se registran semanalmente, los del pescado, la leche y los productos lácteos, etc. frescos cada 15 días y los de vestidos, combustibles, etc. en forma mensual. Los precios de todos los demás artículos se registran trimestralmente, salvo las matrículas de la enseñanza, los honorarios médicos y las tarifas de los servicios de electricidad y agua, que se registran en forma anual. Los precios del índice son los que paga el público el día del registro para adquirir u obtener los bienes o servicios de que se trata, comprendidos los impuestos que gravan las ventas o el consumo. Los investigadores registran los precios que se pagan al contado en los puntos de venta. Para los productos que no se ofrecen en el mercado libre, se registran los practicados en el mercado negro.

Vivienda
Los datos sobre los alquileres se registran anualmente por conducto de una encuesta sobre alquileres de viviendas que abarca unos 448 hogares. El índice no toma en consideración las viviendas ocupadas por sus propietarios.

Especificación de las variedades
En cada una de las ciudades de la muestra se efectuaron encuestas principalmente para seleccionar los puntos de venta y las especificaciones para el registro de precios. Cada uno de los artículos cuyos precios se registran en cada uno de los centros seleccionados se describen especificando tamaño, peso, composición, factura y otras características cuantitativas y cualitativas.

Sustitución, cambio de calidad, etc.
Si cesa la oferta de un determinado artículo en el mercado, se efectúa la sustitución apropiada y se hacen ajustes en el índice por cambio de calidad.

Artículos estacionales
Para calcular el índice se utilizan los últimos precios disponibles de los artículos estacionales, tales como las frutas y legumbres frescas, mientras no se ofrezcan en el mercado por no ser la temporada y hasta que se vuelva a disponer de sus nuevos precios.

Cálculo
El índice se calcula según la fórmula de Laspeyres como un promedio aritmético ponderado de base fija, cuyos coeficientes de ponderación corresponden al período de base. Para obtener el índice urbano nacional se combinan los tres índices regionales utilizando los coeficientes de ponderación regionales basados en el total de la población urbana de cada región.

Informaciones complementarias
Se publican índices urbanos de los precios del consumo para las tres regiones siguientes: Katmandú, Hills y Terai.

Organización y publicación
Nepal Rastra Bank, Research Department (Banco Rastra de Nepal, Departamento de Investigación): "Main Economic Indicators".
idem: "Quarterly Economic Bulletin", (Katmandú).

NICARAGUA (MANAGUA)

Denominación oficial
Indice de precios al consumidor.

Alcance
El índice se compila mensualmente y abarca hogares del área metropolitana de Managua cuyos ingresos mensuales oscilaban entre 400 y 7 000 córdobas de mayo a octubre de 1972.

Base oficial
Diciembre de 1974 = 100.

Fuente de la ponderación
La selección de los artículos y la determinación de los coeficientes de ponderación se basaron en los resultados de una encuesta sobre los gastos de los hogares efectuada en Managua durante el período mayo - octubre de 1972 y que abarcó una muestra de 330 familias escogidas en base al Censo de población y vivienda de abril de 1971.

Gastos de consumo de los hogares
A los fines del índice, los gastos del consumo comprenden todos los bienes y servicios adquiridos para el consumo por la población de referencia. Incluye el valor de los artículos y los servicios recibidos como ingresos en especie y los productos caseros de consumo familiar.

Método de recolección de los datos
Los precios de las verduras y frutas frescas se determinan en-

Ponderaciones y composición

Grupos principales	Número de artículos	Ponderación	Número aproximado de cotizaciones de precio
Alimentación y tabaco	81	43,07	...
Vestido y calzado	36	6,62	...
Vivienda (incl. alquiler, combustible, luz, reparaciones, moblaje, gastos del hogar, etc.)	34	24,74	...
Gastos varios:	31		
Aseo personal y asistencia médica	...	7,61	...
Educación y distracciones	...	6,13	...
Transporte	...	11,61	...
Seguros personales	...	0,22	...
Total	182	100,00	...

tre el martes y el viernes de cada semana mediante compra directa. Los precios de los demás artículos y servicios los recogen los investigadores mensualmente, entre el martes y el viernes de la semana que comprende el día 15 de cada mes, en mercados seleccionados, puntos de venta al por menor y establecimientos de servicios.

Los precios utilizados para el cálculo del índice son los precios que se pagan normalmente. No se toman en consideración los descuentos y las rebajas.

Vivienda
Las cotizaciones del alquiler se obtienen de 33 viviendas distribuidas en las diferentes áreas de la ciudad.

Especificación de las variedades
Las especificaciones de los artículos a los que se ha de fijar precio se dan en forma general, para poder efectuar sustituciones.

Sustitución, cambio de calidad, etc.
Cuando un producto desaparece del mercado se lo sustituye por otro similar y se utiliza el método de enlace.

Artículos estacionales
Para estos artículos, se supone que los precios fuera de temporada siguen el movimiento de los precios de los otros artículos del mismo subgrupo. Cuando reaparece un artículo estacional en el mercado la razón del precio se efectúa estableciendo la relación entre el nuevo precio y el último que se ha registrado.

Cálculo
El índice se calcula conforme a la fórmula de Laspeyres como un promedio aritmético ponderado de base fija, cuyos coeficientes de ponderación corresponden al período de mayo-octubre de 1972. La relación de precio para cada artículo se calcula dividiendo el precio medio del período corriente por el precio medio del período precedente.

Informaciones complementarias
Actualmente se calcula una nueva serie (base octubre - diciembre de 1987 = 100), pero en el momento de publicar el presente Volumen la OIT no disponía de informaciones metodológicas sobre esta serie.

Organización y publicación
Oficina Ejecutiva de Encuestas y Censos: "Indice General de Precios al Consumidor de la Ciudad de Managua" (Managua).

NIGER (NIAMEY, AFRICANOS)

Denominación oficial
Indice des prix à la consommation familiale africaine (Indice de precios del consumo - familias africanas).

Alcance
El índice se calcula mensualmente y abarca los hogares africanos en Niamey.

Base oficial
Julio de 1962 - junio de 1963 = 100.

Fuente de la ponderación
La selección de los artículos y la determinación de los coeficientes de ponderación se basaron en los resultados de una encuesta sobre los gastos de los hogares efectuada en Niamey de marzo de 1961 a abril de 1962, entre 317 hogares africanos.

Ponderaciones y composición

Grupos principales	Número de artículos	Ponderación	Número aproximado de cotizaciones de precio
Alimentación	42	45	...
Vestido y calzado	9	10	...
Gastos del hogar (incl. combustible, luz y agua)	9	18	...
Varios	16	27	...
Total	76	100	...

Gastos de consumo de los hogares
No disponible.

Método de recolección de los datos
Los precios de los artículos alimenticios así como los de otros artículos, son recogidos por agentes dos veces por mes en cinco almacenes al por menor y cuatro veces por mes en un mercado. Los datos referentes a determinados servicios públicos se obtienen mensualmente de las tarifas oficiales.

Vivienda
Los gastos de alquiler no se tienen en cuenta ni en el cálculo del índice ni en la determinación de los coeficientes de ponderación.

Especificación de las variedades
No disponible.

Sustitución, cambio de calidad, etc.
No disponible.

Artículos estacionales
Los precios de artículos con fluctuaciones estacionales se registran todo el año. Para el cálculo del índice se utilizan los promedios de los precios de dichos artículos.

Cálculo
El índice se calcula conforme a la fórmula de Laspeyres como un promedio aritmético ponderado de base fija, cuyos coeficientes de ponderación corresponden al período marzo de 1961 - abril de 1962.

Informaciones complementarias
No disponible.

Organización y publicación
Ministère du développement et de la coopération, Direction de la statistique: "Bulletin de statistique" (Niamey).

NIGER (NIAMEY, EUROPEOS)

Denominación oficial
Indice des prix à la consommation familiale européenne (Indice de precios del consumo - familias europeas).

Alcance
El índice se calcula mensualmente y abarca las familias europeas en Niamey.

Base oficial
15 de noviembre - 15 de diciembre de 1964 = 100.

Fuente de la ponderación
La selección de los artículos y la determinación de los coeficientes de ponderación se basaron en los resultados de una encuesta sobre los gastos de los hogares efectuada en Niamey del 15 de noviembre al 15 de diciembre de 1964 mediante cuestionarios enviados a una muestra de hogares de funcionarios franceses de la Cooperación Técnica.

Ponderaciones y composición

Grupos principales	Número de artículos	Ponderación	Número aproximado de cotizaciones de precio
Alimentación	78	46,1	...
Electricidad, gas y agua	3	11,1	...
Productos de limpieza	10	2,5	...
Vestido, calzado y ropa blanca	12	6,0	...
Servicio doméstico	2	8,2	...
Varios	28	26,1	...
Total	133	100,0	...

Gastos de consumo de los hogares
No disponible.

Método de recolección de los datos
Los precios de los artículos alimenticios, así como los de otros artículos, son recogidos por agentes dos veces por mes en cinco comercios al por menor y cuatro veces por mes en un mercado. Los datos referentes a determinados servicios públicos se obtienen mensualmente de las tarifas oficiales.

Vivienda
Los gastos de alquiler no se tienen en cuenta ni en el cálculo del índice ni en la determinación de los coeficientes de ponderación.

Especificación de las variedades
No disponible.

Sustitución, cambio de calidad, etc.
No disponible.

Artículos estacionales
Los precios de artículos con fluctuaciones estacionales se registran todo el año. Para el cálculo del índice se utilizan los promedios de los precios de dichos artículos.

Cálculo
El índice se calcula conforme a la fórmula de Laspeyres como un promedio aritmético ponderado de base fija, cuyos coeficientes de ponderación corresponden al período de base.

Organización y publicación
Ministère du développement et de la coopération, Direction de la statistique: " Bulletin de statistique" (Niamey).

NIGERIA 1

Denominación oficial
Urban Consumer Price Index - All Income Groups (Indice de precios del consumo - Areas urbanas - Conjunto de los grupos de ingreso).

Alcance
El índice se compila mensualmente y abarca hogares de todos los grupos de ingresos en áreas urbanas.

Base oficial
1975 = 100.

Fuente de la ponderación
La selección de los artículos y la determinación de los coeficientes de ponderación se basaron en los resultados de una encuesta sobre los gastos de los hogares efectuada en 1974-75 en áreas urbanas, sobre hogares de todos los grupos de ingresos.

Ponderaciones y composición
No disponible.

Gastos de consumo de los hogares
No disponible.

Método de recolección de los datos
Los precios son recogidos por agentes en mercados y almacenes al por menor. La frecuencia de su recolección se escalona desde el registro diario de los precios de los alimentos hasta la recolección mensual de otros artículos, dependiendo de la variabilidad de los precios.
En el cálculo del índice se utilizan los precios al por menor que se pagan en el momento.

Vivienda
No disponible.

Especificación de las variedades
Las especificaciones de los artículos cuyos precios se han de registrar se dan en términos de marca, factura, calidad y tamaño.

Sustitución, cambio de calidad, etc.
Cuando no se consigue un producto se lo substituye por otro similar al original y, para el cálculo, se utiliza el método de enlace. Si ello no es posible, se repite el último precio registrado del artículo.

Artículos estacionales
Los artículos estacionales, como las frutas y verduras frescas, sólo se justiprecian durante su temporada.

Cálculo
El índice se calcula conforme a la fórmula de Laspeyres como un promedio aritmético ponderado de base fija, cuyos coeficientes de ponderación corresponden al período 1974-75.
Los índices separados son primeramente calculados para los grupos de ingresos módicos, medios y elevados en cada centro. La relación de precio por cada artículo en un centro es calculada dividiendo el precio medio del período corriente por el precio medio del período de base. Los índices para los centros urbanos están combinados para obtener el índice de todos los grupos de ingresos y áreas urbanas.

Informaciones complementarias
Actualmente se calcula una nueva serie relativa a las regiones urbanas (base septiembre de 1985 = 100), pero en el momento de publicar el presente Volumen la OIT no disponía de informaciones metodológicas sobre esta serie.

Organización y publicación
Federal Office of Statistics: "Retail Prices in selected centres and consumer price indices" (Lagos).
Para más amplios detalles metodológicos, véase:
idem: "Retail prices in selected centres and consumer price indices" (marzo de 1978).

NIGERIA 2

Denominación oficial
Composite Consumer Price Index - Rural and Urban Areas (Indice de precios del consumo - Conjunto de los grupos de ingresos - Areas urbanas y rurales).

Alcance
El índice se compila mensualmente y abarca hogares de todos los grupos de ingresos en áreas urbanas y rurales.

Base oficial
1975 = 100.

Fuente de la ponderación
La selección de los artículos y la determinación de los coeficientes de ponderación se basaron en los resultados de una encuesta sobre los gastos de los hogares efectuada en 1974-75 en áreas rurales y urbanas, que abarcó a hogares de todos los grupos de ingresos.

Ponderaciones y composición
No disponible.

Gastos de consumo de los hogares
No disponible.

Método de recolección de los datos
Los precios son recogidos por agentes en mercados y almacenes al por menor. La frecuencia de su recolección depende de su variabilidad, escalonándose entre la recolección diaria para los precios de los alimentos y la mensual para los otros artículos.
En el cálculo del índice se utilizan los precios al por menor que se pagan en el momento.

Vivienda
No disponible.

Especificación de las variedades
Las especificaciones de los artículos cuyos precios se han de registrar se dan en términos de marca, factura, calidad y tamaño.

Sustitución, cambio de calidad, etc.
Cuando no se consigue un producto se lo substituye por otro similar al original y, para el cálculo, se utiliza el método de enlace. Si ello no es posible, se repite el último precio registrado del artículo.

Artículos estacionales
Los artículos estacionales, como las frutas y verduras frescas, sólo se justiprecian durante su temporada.

Cálculo
El índice se calcula conforme a la fórmula de Laspeyres como un promedio aritmético ponderado de base fija, cuyos coeficientes de ponderación corresponden al período 1974-75.
Los índices separados son primeramente calculados para los grupos de ingresos módicos, medios y elevados en cado centro. La relación de precio por cada artículo en un centro se cal-

cula dividiendo el precio medio del período corriente por el precio medio del período de base.

El índice nacional es el promedio aritmético ponderado de los índices sobre áreas urbanas y rurales y sobre los grupos de ingresos módicos, medios y elevados. Las ponderaciones son proporcionales a la población de las áreas cubiertas.

Informaciones complementarias
Actualmente se calcula una nueva serie relativa a las regiones urbanas y rurales (base septiembre de 1985 = 100), pero en el momento de publicar el presente Volumen la OIT no disponía de informaciones metodológicas sobre esta serie.

Organización y publicación
Federal Office of Statistics: "Retail prices in selected centres and consumer price indices" (Lagos).

Para más amplios detalles metodológicos, véase:
idem: "Retail prices in selected centres and consumer price indices" (marzo de 1978).

NIUE

Denominación oficial
Retail Price Index (Indice de precios al por menor).

Alcance
El índice se calcula trimestralmente y abarca todos los hogares de medianos ingresos en el área urbana (ciudad de Alofi).

Base oficial
Primer trimestre de 1982 = 100.

Fuente de la ponderación
Los coeficientes de ponderación y los artículos seleccionados provienen de varias fuentes, durante 1981, que incluyen estadísticas comerciales, asesoramientos de las tres tiendas principales, cuentas oficiales y otros datos adicionales de las autoridades gubernamentales.

Ponderaciones y composición

Grupos principales	Número de artículos	Ponderación	Número aproximado de cotizaciones de precio
Alimentación	59	430	...
Bebidas alcohólicas y tabaco	6	115	...
Vivienda	9	50	...
Gastos del hogar	26	130	...
Vestido y calzado	13	50	...
Transportes	12	175	...
Varios	12	50	...
Total	137	1 000	...

Gastos de consumo de los hogares
A los fines del índice, los gastos del consumo comprenden todos los bienes y servicios adquiridos para el consumo por la población de referencia. No comprenden la adquisición de casas nuevas, las tarifas de los viajes aéreos de llegada o salida permanente de Niue, los regalos y las donaciones.

Método de recolección de los datos
Los precios se recogen a mediados de cada trimestre por investigadores en puntos de venta al por menor y establecimientos de servicios. Los precios que se recogen son los que pagan los consumidores en el momento.

Vivienda
No disponible.

Especificación de las variedades
Las especificaciones de los artículos cuyos precios han de registrarse establecen marca, factura, tamaño y calidad, etc.

Sustitución, cambio de calidad, etc.
Cuando ya no se puede encontrar un producto se lo sustituye por otro similar o por otro del mismo subgrupo.

Artículos estacionales
No disponible.

Cálculo
El índice se calcula según la fórmula de Laspeyres, como un promedio aritmético ponderado de base fija, cuyos coeficientes de ponderación corresponden al período de base.

El índice para un artículo se obtiene utilizando las relaciones de precios del período corriente y del período de base.

Informaciones complementarias
Actualmente se calcula una nueva serie (base enero - marzo de 1990 = 100), pero en el momento de publicar el presente Volumen la OIT no disponía de informaciones metodológicas sobre esta serie.

Organización y publicación
El índice se calcula por el Development Planning Office, Statistics Unit (Alofi).

Treasurer Department: "Quarterly Abstract of Statistics" (Alofi).

NORUEGA

Denominación oficial
Consumer Price Index (Indice de precios del consumo).

Alcance
El índice se compila mensualmente y abarca todos los hogares privados del país.

Base oficial
1979 = 100.

Fuente de la ponderación
Los coeficientes de ponderación se determinan como el promedio de las cuotas de gastos obtenidas de las encuestas sobre gastos realizadas durante los últimos tres años. Desde agosto de 1991, la determinación de los coeficientes de ponderación se basa en los resultados obtenidos por las encuestas de 1988, 1989 y 1990. La selección de los artículos se revisa en forma continua. Los que figuran a continuación se refieren al período de agosto de 1991 a julio de 1992.

Ponderaciones y composición

Grupos principales	Número de artículos	Ponderación	Número aproximado de cotizaciones de precio
Alimentación	241	152,1	27 910
Bebidas y tabaco	45	36,0	1 360
Vestido y calzado	89	67,4	3 910
Vivienda (incl. mantenimiento y reparación)	29	215,4	1 930
Combustible y luz	5	47,5	130
Moblaje y accesorios para el hogar	113	81,5	5 180
Asistencia médica e higiene	25	23,3	120
Transportes y comunicaciones	105	199,0	1 460
Educación, distracciones	62	98,3	760
Bienes y servicios varios	66	81,1	2 020
Total	780	1 001.6	44 780

Gastos de consumo de los hogares
A los fines del índice, los gastos del consumo comprenden todos los bienes y servicios adquiridos para el consumo por la población de referencia. En cuanto a los bienes durables, los gastos de consumo corresponden a la diferencia entre lo gastado en adquirir los "nuevos" bienes y lo percibido por la venta de los "antiguos". Se incluyen los pagos de las compras a plazo. También se incluyen los productos caseros y los regalos recibidos. Se excluyen los impuestos directos, los ahorros e inversiones, los préstamos personales, las primas de los seguros de vida, las contribuciones a fondos de pensión y los desembolsos hechos en regalos.

Método de recolección de los datos
Los investigadores recogen los precios en una selección de 1 400 establecimientos de servicios y tiendas minoristas. Los precios de la mayor parte de los artículos se recogen el día 15 de cada mes. Los precios utilizados en el índice son los que paga normalmente cualquier persona del público.

Vivienda
Los datos referentes al alquiler se recogen trimestralmente en unas 1 800 viviendas.

Especificación de las variedades
Las especificaciones de los artículos cuyos precios se han de registrar detallan marca, factura, tamaño, etc.

Sustitución, cambio de calidad, etc.
Si un producto no se puede conseguir en los puntos de venta, se lo sustituye por otro similar al original.

Artículos estacionales
Se tienen en cuenta las fluctuaciones estacionales de los pre-

cios de algunas frutas, verduras y pescado fresco, utilizando durante el período fuera de estación los precios medios de la estación precedente.

Cálculo
Desde agosto de 1982 el índice se calcula según la fórmula de índices en cadena de Laspeyres con enlaces anuales. Los coeficientes de ponderación se modifican todos los años en agosto. El índice mensual se calcula en primer lugar para cada artículo en una sola región y según la medida en que el precio difiera de la media aritmética no ponderada de la totalidad de los precios del artículo. Como base igualada a 100 se toma el nivel promedio de los precios del mes de julio precedente. El índice mensual de los precios de un artículo en todo el país se calcula ponderando las modificaciones de precio de la diversas regiones, según su cuota relativa en la modificación general de precios del país.

Organización y publicación
Statistisk Sentralbyrå (Central Bureau of Statistics): "Statistisk Månedshefte (Monthly Bulletin of Statistics)" (Oslo).

NUEVA CALEDONIA (NUMEA)

Denominación oficial
Indice des prix de détail à la consommation (Indice de precios al por menor).

Alcance
El índice se calcula mensualmente y abarca hogares urbanos de obreros y empleados de los sectores público y privado (excluyendo los trabajadores del sector agrícola).

Base oficial
Agosto de 1975 = 100.

Fuente de la ponderación
La selección de los artículos y la determinación de los coeficientes de ponderación se basaron en los resultados de una encuesta sobre los gastos de los hogares efectuada en 1968-69 sobre hogares de diferentes categorías sociales y grupos étnicos en áreas urbanas, mineras y rurales (excluidos los melanesios residentes en áreas rurales). Los coeficientes de ponderación abarcan a los obreros y empleados de los sectores público y privado (excluyendo los trabajadores del sector agrícola). Los coeficientes de ponderación de 1975 se han obtenido por extrapolación basada en la evolución de los precios entre 1969 y fines de 1974.

Ponderaciones y composición

Grupos principales	Número de artículos	Ponderación	Número aproximado de cotizaciones de precio
Alimentación	245	37,00	...
Productos manufacturados:			
Vestido, calzado y ropa blanca	114	7,00	...
Combustible y luz	4	7,00	...
Moblaje, accesorios para el hogar y artículos varios	174	20,50	...
Servicios:			
Alquiler, agua y conservación	14	15,70	...
Aseo personal y asistencia médica	24	3,30	...
Transportes y comunicaciones	29	5,25	...
Educación y distracciones	10	1,15	...
Comidas tomadas fuera del hogar	6	2,00	...
Varios	20	1,10	...
Total	640	100,00	5 500

Gastos de consumo de los hogares
Se han incluido todos los gastos monetarios que se encuentran efectivamente a cargo de los hogares. Las viviendas puestas a disposición, las viviendas propias, los ingresos en especies, las cotizaciones sociales, los impuestos y tasas directas así como el autoconsumo están excluidos.

Método de recolección de los datos
Los precios son recogidos por agentes entre los días 2 y 25 de cada mes, en alrededor de 250 puntos de venta al por menor y establecimientos de servicios de Numea. Los precios para la electricidad (recolección semestral de un consumo tipo), el agua, el gas, los transportes y la asistencia médica, etc., son los fijados por tarifas o convenciones. No se toman en consideración los precios de las liquidaciones.

Vivienda
Las cotizaciones del alquiler se obtienen de diez agencias de locación de Numea y se refieren a unas 80 viviendas (fundamentalmente viviendas subvencionadas).

Especificación de las variedades
Se especifican en detalle las variedades de cada artículo, describiendo su variedad, calidad, factura, marca, unidad, etc.

Sustitución, cambio de calidad, etc.
Si un producto desaparece del mercado se lo sustituye por uno similar, utilizándose el método de enlace. También para los cambios de calidad se emplea el método de enlace.

Artículos estacionales
Se tienen en cuenta las fluctuaciones estacionales de las frutas y las verduras frescas, manteniendo fuera de temporada, el último precio de la temporada y utilizando una media móvil de 12 meses.

Cálculo
El índice se calcula según la fórmula de Laspeyres, como un promedio aritmético ponderado de base fija, cuyos coeficientes de ponderación corresponden al período de base.

Informaciones complementarias
No disponible.

Organización y publicación
Direction territoriale de la statistique et des études économiques: "Indice des Prix de Détail, Nouvelle Caledonie" (Noumea).

NUEVA ZELANDIA

Denominación oficial
Consumer Price Index (Indice de Precios del Consumo: IPC).

Alcance
El índice se compila trimestralmente y abarca todos los hogares privados de residentes de Nueva Zelandia. No se hacen exclusiones por ubicación geográfica, niveles de ingreso o calificaciones profesionales.

Base oficial
Octubre - diciembre de 1988 = 100.

Fuente de la ponderación
La determinación de los coeficientes de ponderación de los gastos de los hogares se basa principalmente en la encuesta permanente del Departamento de Estadísticas que permite contar con informaciones globales y detalladas sobre los gastos de consumo de los hogares privados de toda Nueva Zelandia. En un año de revisión del IPC el tamaño de la muestra es de aproximadamente 4 500 hogares.

Los resultados de la encuesta se completan con informaciones de otras fuentes, tales como las estadísticas de comercio y producción, de viviendas y datos de origen público o privado. El sistema actual de ponderación del índice se basa en el consumo de bienes y servicios de los hogares privados durante el año que finalizó el 31 de marzo de 1988. Los gastos de consumo de este período se amplían luego al nivel de precios correspondiente al trimestre de diciembre de 1988, utilizando los movimientos de precio de las mercancías pertinentes del IPC. Por su alcance demográfico, la encuesta abarca todas las personas que viven en un hogar privado de las dos principales islas de Nueva Zelandia (salvo regiones rurales muy remotas). En el índice se consideran como hogares de residentes en Nueva Zelandia aquéllos cuyo jefe ha vivido en Nueva Zelandia un mínimo de 12 meses. El 95 por ciento de la población total está comprendida en esta definición. Las ponderaciones de los gastos correspondientes a todos los artículos del índice se distribuyen (por afijación) entre todas las mercancías con precio registrado, sea a una o más mercancías en forma directa (porcentajes), sea a pro-rata entre dos o más mercancías (mencionándose ocasionalmente la sección, subgrupo o grupo), sea por una combinación de ambos métodos.

Gastos de consumo de los hogares
Por su diseño, el índice permite medir estadísticamente la variación de los niveles de precio de los bienes y servicios realmente pagados por los hogares privados de Nueva Zelandia. En consecuencia se excluyen de los artículos del índice la producción para el consumo propio, los ingresos en especie y los bienes y servicios gratuitos. También se consideran fuera del ámbito del índice el impuesto a los ingresos (por no ser el pago

Ponderaciones y composición

Grupos principales	Número de artículos	Ponderación aproximado	Número de cotizaciones de precio (a)
Alimentación	94	18,35	...
Vivienda:			
Alquiler	2	4,20	...
Costos de la vivienda propia	22	19,31	...
Gastos del hogar:			
Combustible y luz	3	2,77	...
Muebles y moblaje	44	6,82	...
Suministros, comunicación y servicios del hogar	27	6,20	...
Vestido y calzado	54	5,34	...
Transporte	24	15,39	...
Varios:			
Bebidas alcohólicas y tabaco	8	9,72	...
Asistencia médica y aseo personal	42	4,90	...
Gastos de educación, recreación y créditos	32	7,00	...
Total	352	100,00	150 000

Nota: (a) no se dispone de ninguna lista con el número de cotizaciones de precio para cada artículo del índice.

de un servicio cuya calidad pueda ser objeto de medida o control estadístico) y los artículos que representan más formas de ahorro o inversión que gastos de consumo.

Pese a estar dentro del marco conceptual del índice, se excluyen ciertos objetos de consumo porque no es posible medir adecuadamente el movimiento de sus precios ni éstos resultan debidamente indicados por los movimientos de precio de cualquier otro artículo o mercancía con precio determinable, como por ejemplo las obras de arte, multas de los tribunales, donaciones de caridad, cría de animales y perros.

En el presente índice se sigue un criterio de objeto del gasto para ponderar las viviendas ocupadas por sus propietarios. En virtud de este criterio los coeficientes de ponderación de la vivienda propia corresponden al gasto bruto que ha tenido la población del índice para adquirir o construir viviendas durante el año de referencia, compensado por el producto de las casas vendidas.

En Nueva Zelandia los propietarios otorgan gran valor a la seguridad de la tenencia de sus casas y por lo tanto se considera que la compra y construcción de viviendas deben figurar en el índice si se desea que éste sea una medida pertinente de la situación actual de los precios que pagan realmente los hogares.

El criterio antedicho también se aplica para ponderar otros bienes durables. Por tal motivo se toma en cuenta el precio total pagado por un bien durable en el momento de su compra, independientemente de si el pago se efectúa al contado o si la mercancía se consume de inmediato. Los recargos por créditos para adquirir bienes durables constituyen una mercancía distinta dentro de la misma sección del régimen.

Los coeficientes de ponderación de la mayoría de los gastos en bienes de segunda mano se añaden a los de bienes nuevos de la misma clase. Sólo se encuestan los precios de las mercancías nuevas, suponiéndose que las fluctuaciones de precio de los bienes de segunda mano será similar. Constituyen excepciones los coches usados y las casas previamente ocupadas, que son mercancías separadas dentro del régimen.

El valor de los objetos usados entregados como pago parcial y transacciones similares se separa de las compras de mercancías equivalentes cuando se calculan los coeficientes de ponderación del gasto.

Se excluyen los pagos de seguros de vida y contribuciones a fondos de pensión o vejez por representar formas de inversión y no consumos. La amortización de hipotecas, los seguros de vehículos automotores y del ajuar doméstico se incluyen como mercancías separadas en el régimen del índice.

En el régimen del índice se incluyen los tasas de patentes y permisos, así como los honorarios de los servicios médicos.

Método de recolección de los datos

Se realizan encuestas de precios en 15 centros comerciales:

a) los puntos de venta situados en centros comerciales suburbanos se incluyen por lo general en la muestra de puntos de venta del índice donde se encuestan los precios de ultramarinos comestibles y no comestibles. Los precios de los demás artículos se registran principalmente en los distritos comerciales del centro urbano para reducir los gastos de viaje de los principales suburbios, pero como la mayoría de éstos son sucursales de comercios del centro y practican los mismos precios, en general no se considera necesario que el registro de precios en la periferia tenga un alcance amplio.

b) cuando la investigación de los precios de una mercancía está a cargo de un encuestador, los puntos de venta se seleccionan en el momento actual mediante métodos de muestreo con selección dirigida. Por lo general los precios se encuestan en los puntos de venta de una muestra representativa de los que prefieren los consumidores del índice.

El muestreo de probabilidad se reserva para seleccionar los objetos de investigación de las diversas encuestas que se realizan por correo, tales como los alquileres y los honorarios de notarios o asesores jurídicos.

Los precios de las legumbres y frutas frescas se registran todos los viernes, en los 15 áreas urbanas del centro y de la periferia. Los precios de todos los demás alimentos se investigan el día 15 (u otra fecha próxima) en las mismas 15 regiones urbanas. Los precios de las mercancías de la sección "suministros, comunicación y servicios del hogar" del índice, salvo jardinería, también se investigan todos los meses, como es el caso de periódicos, gas, electricidad, cigarrillos y tabaco, bebidas alcohólicas y vuelos internos. Los precios del petróleo se investigan dos veces por mes. Los precios de todas estas mercancías también se encuestan en las 15 áreas urbanas. Los precios de las demás mercancías del índice encuestados por el personal departamental sobre el terreno se registran todos los trimestres, el día 15 de los meses intermedios, o en la fecha más próxima posible. Las encuestas de precios del IPC realizan normalmente visitas a los puntos de venta al por menor del personal departamental que trabaja sobre el terreno a tiempo completo. Las sedes de estos entrevistadores se encuentran en las cuatro áreas urbanas principales.

Para determinadas mercancías, como ciertos materiales para el mantenimiento del hogar, motores de cortadoras de césped, alfombras y muebles tapizados, pueden faltar los precios de escaparate o no ser apropiados; en tales casos el entrevistador recurre a los precios de lista.

Se realizan encuestas trimestrales por correo de los precios y tarifas de: alquileres de viviendas; gastos de compra y financiación de la casa propia; costos contractuales de los trabajos de mantenimiento del hogar; carbón y leña; mudanza de muebles; seguros de viviendas, ajuar doméstico, automotores y salud; asistencia médica; medicamentos; teléfono; cartas de crédito; vacaciones; trayectos urbanos, suburbanos y de larga distancia de autobuses y ferrocarriles; viajes marítimos; recorridos en taxi; coches usados; registro de vehículos automóviles; cuotas de afiliación a sociedades automovilísticas; escuelas de conducción de vehículos; cines y teatros, acontecimientos deportivos y de otra índole; cuotas a clubes deportivos; cotizaciones sindicales; veterinario; conservatorios y escuelas de música, instrucción primaria, secundaria y terciaria; jardines de párvulos y guarderías; abonos a revistas.

Generalmente, para el cálculo del índice, se suelen encuestar los precios "marcados" (en etiquetas). Los descuentos se incluyen sólo si non una rebaja efectiva de los precios "marcados", pero no si son negociados sin más formalidades que el regateo u otorgados a determinadas categorías de clientes. Se incluyen en el índice las rebajas registradas durante las encuestas sobre el curso normal de los precios. No se distingue entre precios oficiales y de mercado. Por razones técnicas, el índice no abarca las transacciones ilícitas. Los gastos de los créditos para adquirir coches (usados o nuevos) y los alquileres con opción de compra (salvo de vehículos automotores) se incluyen en la misma sección que el artículo respectivo del índice actual. El método para determinar el precio de los recargos por créditos implica una combinación compuesta de las fluctuaciones de los tipos de interés aplicables a los préstamos y de las modificaciones de precios de las mercancías para las cuales se han concedido los créditos. Salvo para coches usados y viviendas con un propietario anterior, sólo se encuestan los precios de mercancías nuevas. En la medida en que influyan en el precio de las mercancías encuestadas, se incluyen en el índice las modificaciones de los precios de importación.

Los factores que determinan el número de cotizaciones de precio son:

a) la similitud de los movientos de precio de las mercancías de un determinado grupo. Cuanto más similares sean estos movimientos, menor será, relativamente, el número de mercancías cuyos precios se deben encuestar para obtener un indicador adecuado de la fluctuación de los precios;

b) la importancia global y relativa de las mercancías agrupadas. En términos generales puede decirse que cuanto más importante sea la agrupación, tanto mayor será el número de mercancías investigadas;

c) para los precios nacionales únicos, sólo se requiere una cotización.

Vivienda

Los datos sobre el alquiler comprenden casa y pisos de las siguientes categorías de propiedad: cooperativa, municipal y privada. Como número de habitaciones las únicas que no se cuentan son los cuartos de baño y lavabos separados y los lavaderos. La totalidad de las viviendas investigadas se alquilan sin muebles. Los datos sobre las viviendas de propiedad privada o municipal se obtienen de los propietarios mediante una encuesta trimestral por correo. Del organismo de viviendas cooperativas se obtiene un censo completo de sus alquileres.

Habitaciones, casas y pisos previamente ocupados: las fecha de venta de casas, pisos y habitaciones previamente ocupadas las registra cada tres meses "Valuation New Zealand" (organismo oficial de evaluación de Nueva Zelandia), se utilizan para aportar datos sobre el coste de la propiedad.

Construcción de viviendas: la evolución trimestral del coste de la construcción de viviendas (casa y pisos) se mide merced a los datos de la encuesta a una muestra de constructores, sobre los precios vigentes para un conjunto de proyectos de casas con especificaciones determinadas.

La compra de casas y pisos nuevos: la serie de los costes de la construcción de viviendas se combina con los movimientos de precio de la sección para obtener el indicador de las modificaciones del precio de compra de casas y pisos nuevos.

Intereses hipotecarios: este artículo del índice se refiere al coste de tomar en préstamo el mismo promedio real del monto de dinero necesario para ayudar a financiar la compra de una vivienda que en el período de base del índice. Este método se le describe como "revaluación simple". Por lo tanto, el cálculo de las fluctuaciones de precio de los intereses hipotecarios supone la obtención de dos indicadores distintos, a saber:

a) la modificación del tipo medio de interés que se paga por los préstamos hipotecarios en vigor;

b) la modificación del precio de la propiedad de la vivienda misma, que es la medida de precio adecuada para asegurar que el poder adquisitivo (o el valor real del dinero tomado en préstamo) se mantiene invariable (calidad constante).

El promedio de los tipos de interés de los préstamos hipotecarios exigibles para el conjunto de los hogares privados se obtiene de la encuesta del gasto de los hogares del Departamento. El control de calidad del perfil de las hipotecas y los tipos de interés que se miden en la encuesta de hogares se obtienen mediante una estratificación por plazos de la muestra de las hipotecas, teniendo cada estrato un coeficiente de ponderación fijado en el índice. Esta forma de proceder se funda en la hipótesis de que la utilidad de una hipoteca depende fundamentalmente del monto del préstamo y del plazo para amortizarlo.

Tarifas de las agencias inmobiliarias y de las transferencias de propiedad: como la escala de tarifas ya no se usa, el Departamento de Estadísticas ha realizado una encuesta por correo entre las agencias inmobiliarias y los notarios encargados del registro de las transferencias de propiedad. Para cada uno de estos grupos se utiliza una selección de muestreo aleatorio. El valor de las transacciones inmobiliarias afecta a estos grupos. Una modificación del promedio que se paga como tarifa por las transferencias de propiedad de una canasta fija puede obedecer tanto a una modificación de las tarifas como a un variación del nivel de precios de la propiedad o a ambas cosas. Los cuestionarios averiguan las tarifas de transacciones relacionadas con propiedades cuyo precio de venta o de compra se especifica. Estos precios se ajustan todos los trimestres en función de las modificaciones de precio de las propiedades previamente ocupadas.

Especificación de las variedades

Cuando el indicador más adecuado de las fluctuaciones del precio de una mercancía particular es un artículo disponible en el plano nacional, en el cuestionario impreso de la encuesta de precios se inscribe una especificación detallada y precisa. Cuando en las distintas regiones los puntos de venta venden marcas, tamaños y calidades diferentes de una mercancía, se deja "abierta" la especificación en esta etapa. En cada punto de venta se precisan los detalles de estas especificaciones "abiertas", que quedan así establecidos en forma permanente para ese punto de venta. Esta forma de proceder permite asegurar que en cada punto de venta se investigan los precios de los artículos más apropiados en función de la demanda de los consumidores.

Sustitución, cambio de calidad, etc.

Cuando se produce un cambio de calidad se estima el valor en dólares de la diferencia de calidad entre el modelo antiguo y el nuevo, ajustándose los precios en consecuencia. Las nuevas mercancías, con un consumo importante, se añaden al régimen del índice cuando se procede a su revisión, siempre que haya sido posible apreciar la amplitud de su oferta, las probabilidades de que los hogares continúen consumiéndolas y determinar su precio característico, es decir cuando ha pasado el período de aumentos o rebajas que provoca la novedad. En lo posible, los precios de las mercancías siempre se registran para una misma cantidad e igual calidad, de manera que el índice incorpore sólo la "variación genuina de precio".

Las sustituciones son necesarias cuando una mercancía desaparece del mercado o sus precios fluctúan en forma atípica con respecto al grupo que esa mercancía representa. Se realizan ajustes de calidad toda vez que se estime que la mercancía sustituida difiere cuantitativa o cualitativamente de la anterior, en cualquier grado que sea. En la práctica se estima en dólares el valor de la diferencia entre ambas mercancías y se calcula en consecuencia una escala que se aplica a los precios de la mercancía de sustitución cuyas cotizaciones se investigan. Dicha escala, conocida como "cotización ponderada", reajusta el precio de la mercancía "nueva" al precio que hubiese correspondido a la mercancía "antigua" de haber tenido la misma calidad. Cuando faltan datos sobre una mercancía, se recurre a los precios del período anterior. Si transcurrido un plazo fijado de antemano aún no se dispone de los datos necesarios, se sustituye la mercancía en cuestión.

Artículos estacionales

Se da un tratamiento especial al subgrupo de las frutas y legumbres frescas para tener en cuenta las fluctuaciones estacionales de su oferta y precio. Las afiliaciones a clubes deportivos de temporada, las cuotas de admisión a espectáculos deportivos de temporada, el costo de las ensaladas, ostras, plantas comestibles y flores, así como el de prendas de vestir de temporada que no puedan encontrarse en un período determinado, se cotizan según los precios registrados en el período anterior. Los recargos y rebajas de temporada de las tarifas aéreas se investigan en cada período de cotización en que ocurran.

Cálculo

El índice se calcula según la fórmula de Laspeyres como un promedio aritmético ponderado de base fija, cuyos coeficientes de ponderación corresponden al período de base. Los precios que se utilizan para el cálculo del IPC (15 áreas urbanas combinadas) son promedios ponderados de población de los promedios aritméticos de los precios registrados en las 15 áreas urbanas investigadas. Los coeficientes de ponderación de la población representan el total de la población estimada de cada área urbana y los municipios adyacentes asignados. Las ponderaciones se basan en el último Censo de Población (1986), ajustándose los coeficientes para tomar en cuenta la ulterior evolución demográfica.

Informaciones complementarias

Se publican trimestralmente índices separados de grupos y subgrupos de mercancías para:

a) cada uno de las tres áreas urbanas más importantes (Auckland, Wellington y Christchurch);

b) las tres áreas urbanas más importantes combinadas;

c) todas las áreas urbanas de North Island combinadas con todas las áreas urbanas de South Island;

d) el conjunto de Nueva Zelandia (15 áreas urbanas más o menos importantes combinadas).

También se publican índices de secciones de mercancías, pero sólo para las 15 áreas urbanas combinadas. Además de los alimentos, se publican mensualmente índices de grupos, subgrupos y secciones para los mismos agrupamientos regionales antes mencionados.

Organización y publicación
Department of Statistics (Departamento de Estadísticas): "Key Statistics" (mensual) (Wellington).
idem: "News Release" (trimestral).
idem: "Hot off the Press" (Boletín de informaciones).
idem: "New Zealand Official Year Book".

PAISES BAJOS

Denominación oficial
Price Index Numbers of Final Consumption Expenditure (Indice de precios del consumo final).

Alcance
El índice se calcula mensualmente y abarca hogares de obreros y empleados formados por pareja sin hijos o con hijos que no tienen ingresos, con ingresos familiares en 1985 inferiores al límite fijado para el seguro de salud obligatorio. El índice abarca todo el país.

Base oficial
1985 = 100.

Fuente de la ponderación
La selección de los artículos y la determinación de los coeficientes de ponderación se basaron en los resultados de una encuesta sobre los gastos de los hogares efectuada en 1985 entre un muestra de 962 hogares.

Ponderaciones y composición

Grupos principales	Número de artículos	Ponderación	Número aproximado de cotizaciones de precio
Alimentación	234	21,3	...
Vestido y calzado	120	6,8	...
Asistencia médica	5	11,4	...
Artículos del hogar	60	6,6	...
Alquiler, combustible y luz	41	27,2	...
Transportes y comunicaciones	49	11,4	...
Educación y distracciones	103	8,4	...
Otros bienes y servicios	78	6,9	...
Total	690	100,0	(a) ...

Nota: (a) Todos los meses se recoge un promedio de 100 000 precios (no se incluyen los alquileres, cuyas cotizaciones se recogen cada vez que se produce un aumento en ese rubro).

Gastos de consumo de los hogares
A los fines del índice, los gastos del consumo comprenden todos los bienes y servicios adquiridos para el consumo por los hogares, incluyendo las compras en tiendas, grandes almacenes y otros proveedores, los pagos de servicios mecánicos o artesanales, los gastos de hotel, restaurantes, cafés, transportes, diversiones, los honorarios de médicos y especialistas, hospitales y productos farmacéuticos, servicios médicos y domésticos, los costes administrativos de seguros de vida y fondos de pensiones, los gastos en bienes durables como el moblaje, aparatos de radio, etc. Se excluyen las transferencias voluntarias hechas por las familias a instituciones sin fines de lucro, las transferencias dentro del sector familiar, las transferencias obligatorias de los hogares a instituciones de seguridad social y de gobierno, los ahorros efectuados bajo la forma de pagos de primas de seguros de vida y pensiones.

Método de recolección de los datos
Los precios se recogen mensualmente el martes de la semana que contiene el día 15 de cada mes en puntos de venta seleccionados, incluso mercados y vendedores callejeros, tiendas móviles, grandes almacenes y puntos de venta al por menor grandes, medianos y pequeños, así como mayoristas y servicios comerciales ubicados en 100 municipalidades de más de 10 000 habitantes.

Los datos recogidos se refieren a la evolución de los precios de unos 1 200 artículos. Para algunos de estos (salvo los alquileres de casas) que representan en conjunto un 38 por ciento de la ponderación total, los precios se recogen mediante cuestionarios enviados por correo. Los precios registrados son los que pagan en el momento los consumidores, incluso los impuestos indirectos. Los precios de liquidaciones sólo se toman en consideración cuando aprovechan a los consumidores sin mayores dificultades y cuando esas liquidaciones duran por lo menos una semana. Se deducen las rebajas en efectivo efectuadas en el momento de la compra. Los precios de la electricidad, el gas y el agua se recogen de las compañías que prestan esos servicios.

Vivienda
Una amplia proporción de los datos referentes al alquiler se recogen mediante encuestas enviadas por correo a los propietarios o administradores de casas. Para el caso de un 3 por ciento aproximadamente de las casas alquiladas, en donde la encuesta postal no es factible, los datos se recogen por investigadores que los obtienen de los inquilinos. Las encuestas sobre alquileres se realizan en 482 municipalidades, sobre un total de 702 municipios de los Países Bajos.

La adquisición de viviendas por particulares para vivir en ellas no se incluye en el índice, pero los servicios derivados de esas viviendas se evalúan mediante un alquiler ficticio determinado en función de los alquileres de casas comparables.

Especificación de las variedades
Existe una descripción de calidades muy precisa para todos los artículos y servicios. Se presta atención al peso, número, factura, tamaño, materiales (para vestidos), etc.

Sustitución, cambio de calidad, etc.
Los nuevos productos se incluyen en el sistema de ponderación en el próximo cambio del año de base. Cuando un artículo desaparece, se lo sustituye por otro similar y se emplea el método de enlace.

Artículos estacionales
Los coeficientes de ponderación de los grupos referentes a las patatas, las frutas y las verduras frescas, las flores y las plantas de interior se asignan con un mismo monto todos los meses. Los coeficientes de ponderación a lo dentro de esos grupos de artículos no se basan en el año de base sino en una media calculada a lo largo de varios años, y se toma el último como año de base.

Para los vestidos y calzado estacionales, se componen dos "canasta", una que se toma en consideración durante los meses de invierno y otra durante los meses de verano. En los meses de marzo y septiembre ambas "canasta" se incluyen en el sistema de ponderación, cada una por la mitad de su ponderación.

Cálculo
El índice se calcula según la fórmula de Laspeyres, como un promedio aritmético ponderado de base fija, cuyos coeficientes de ponderación corresponden al período de base.

La relación del precio para cada artículo se calcula dividiendo el precio medio del período corriente por el precio medio del período de base.

Informaciones complementarias
No disponible.

Organización y publicación
Centraal Bureau voor de Statistiek (Central Bureau of Statistics): "Maandstatistiek van de prijzen" (Voorburg).
idem: "Statistisch bulletin".

PAKISTAN

Denominación oficial
Combined Consumer Price Index (Indice combinado de precios del consumo).

Alcance
El índice se compila mensualmente y abarca los empleados gubernamentales, comerciales e industriales cuyos ingresos mensuales están comprendidos en uno de los cuatro grupos siguientes: hasta 1 000 rupias; de 1 001 a 2 500 rupias; de 2 501 a 4 500 rupias; y más de 4 500 rupias. El índice abarca 25 importantes centros urbanos.

Base oficial
Julio de 1980 - junio de 1981 = 100.

Fuente de la ponderación
La selección de los artículos y la determinación de los coeficientes de ponderación se basaron en los resultados de una encuesta sobre los gastos de los hogares efectuada en 1982 en 46 centros urbanos, incluidos 25 principales centros urbanos, y

que abarcó una muestra de 26 864 hogares. La selección de los artículos del índice se efectuó considerando que eran los más representativos del gusto, los hábitos y las costumbres de la población, que eran fácilmente reconocibles y de simple descripción y que no era probable que su calidad se modificara.

Ponderaciones y composición

Grupos principales	Número de artículos	Ponderación	Número aproximado de cotizaciones de precio
Alimentación y tabaco	176	49,90	...
Vestido y calzado	73	6,68	...
Alquiler	1	17,76	...
Combustible y luz	15	5,62	...
Mobiliario y accesorios para el hogar	38	2,34	...
Transportes y comunicaciones	44	6,20	...
Educación y distracciones	44	3,50	...
Productos de limpieza y aseo personal	45	5,56	...
Varios	28	2,44	...
Total	464	100,00	(a) ...

Nota: (a) Para cada uno de los artículos se han recabado unas cuatro cotizaciones en las distintas tiendas de cada una de las áreas de venta.

Gastos de consumo de los hogares
A los fines del índice, los gastos del consumo comprenden todos los bienes y servicios adquiridos para el consumo por la población del índice. No comprenden los gastos que no son de consumo, la adquisición de casas, el pago de intereses, las joyas y toda forma de valores, títulos y acciones.

Método de recolección de los datos
Personal de la Oficina Federal de Estadísticas, trabajando en el terreno, se encarga de recoger los precios en mercados, puntos de venta al por menor y establecimientos de servicios seleccionados en 46 centros urbanos incluidos 25 principales ciudades. La recolección de precios se consigna en cuatro registros. Los precios de los bienes de consumo básicos y de las mercancías perecederas, como la carne, el pescado, los huevos, las verduras, etc., se recogen el tercer martes de cada mes. Los precios de los demás artículos se recogen mensualmente. Los precios que se utilizan en el índice son los que minoristas y establecimientos de servicios practican cuando ofrecen sus servicios o venden los artículos a los consumidores en forma directa.

Vivienda
No se dispone de datos relativos a los alquileres actuales para todo el país y las modificaciones de precio de los artículos de construcción se utilizan como indicadores de las tendencias de los alquileres.

Especificación de las variedades
La mayor parte de las especificaciones de los artículos con precio registrado fueron definidas por la División Estadística de la Oficina Federal de Estadísticas. Cuando no se han podido establecer especificaciones para ciertos artículos, se ha utilizado la variedad local de mejor calidad.

Sustitución, cambio de calidad, etc.
La División Estadística examina todas las propuestas de substitución hechas por el personal de campo cuando un artículo desaparece completamente del mercado o cuando no se lo puede conseguir en la forma o la unidad especificadas. Si la utilización del producto substitutivo ha sido aceptada, se introduce en el índice mediante el método de enlace.

Artículos estacionales
Esta clase de artículo presenta una amplia gama de variaciones de precio según se trate del período "de temporada" o del de "fuera de temporada". Para evitar esas acentuadas fluctuaciones de precio, se han hecho arreglos en la programación del cálculo de esos índices, manteniendo en "cero" los precios de esos artículos fuera de la temporada.

Cálculo
El índice se calcula conforme a la fórmula de Laspeyres como un promedio aritmético ponderado de base fija, cuyos coeficientes de ponderación corresponden a 1982.

Los coeficientes de ponderación relacionados con las ciudades, y que fueron proporcionados por la encuesta sobre los ingresos y gastos de los hogares, se utilizaron para calcular los índices de las ciudades para tres categorías de asalariados y cuatro grupos de ingreso.

El índice nacional es obtenido utilizando un conjunto de ponderaciones combinadas que no tiene en cuenta la distición entre las ciudades, categorías profesionales y grupos de ingresos.

Organización y publicación
Federal Bureau of Statistics, Statistics Division: "Monthly Statistical Bulletin" (Karachi).
idem: "Pakistan Key Economic Indicators".
idem: "Consumer Price Index Numbers of Pakistan 1980-81 = 100".

PANAMA (CIUDAD DE PANAMA)

Denominación oficial
Indice de precios al consumidor.

Alcance
El índice se compila mensualmente y se refiere a todos los hogares privados, con distintos niveles de ingreso, de la ciudad de Panamá.

Base oficial
1987 = 100.

Fuente de la ponderación
La selección de los artículos y la determinación de los coeficientes de ponderación se basaron en los resultados de una encuesta sobre los gastos de los hogares efectuada en 1983-84 en la ciudad de Panamá, que abarcó una muestra de 1 070 familias de diferentes niveles de ingreso. Las familias fueron seleccionadas mediante una muestra estratificada al azar, cuyo marco lo constituyó un listado de viviendas reportadas en el Censo de Población de 1980, complementado con la lista de edificios construídos después del Censo. La unidad de selección la constituyó la vivienda y la unidad de observación la familia. Para realizar la encuesta se utilizó la técnica de la entrevista directa a las familias y los datos se recolectaron mediante un formulario mensual que contempla en detalle los gastos e ingresos de las familias y una libreta de apuntes diarios, la cual se utilizó para obtener los gastos e ingresos diarios durante una semana.

No se introdujeron reajustes en los coeficientes de ponderación para tener en consideración los cambios de precio entre el período de el encuesta y 1987.

Ponderaciones y composición

Grupos principales	Número de artículos	Ponderación	Número aproximado de cotizaciones de precio
Alimentación	101	34,9	81
Vestido y calzado	38	5,1	34
Alquiler, combustible y luz (1)	4	12,6	5
Moblaje, accesorios y cuidados del hogar	37	8,4	43
Aseo personal y asistencia médica	11	3,5	21
Transportes y comunicaciones	10	15,1	24
Educación y distracciones	20	11,7	41
Otros bienes y servicios	23	8,7	26
Total	244	100,0	275

Nota: (1) Excluye: 109 viviendas distribuidas en todos los distritos de la ciudad de Panamá donde se cotizan precios de alquiler.

Gastos de consumo de los hogares
La definición utilizada se refiere al gasto neto, deducidas las ventas de bienes de segunda mano efectuadas por las familias y el valor de mercado equivalente para aquellos bienes usados entregados como pago parcial para la adquisición de bienes nuevos. No se incluyeron cotizaciones al seguro social y a los fondos de pensión, seguro relacionado con determinados bienes de consumo, impuestos sobre la renta y otros impuestos directos. Se consideran en la ponderación del cálculo del índice los pagos a títulos de seguro de vida, giros, donaciones y desembolsos similares.

Método de recolección de los datos
La recolección periódica de los precios se hace a través de visitas directas a los establecimientos seleccionados, por personal de la oficina mediante formularios diseñados para tal fin. El personal dedicado a esta labor recibe un adiestramiento especial para efectuar dicho trabajo con exactitud y en el tiempo en que se requiere.

Los precios se investigan mensualmente excepto para el alquiler, mantenimiento, peinado de cabello, manicura, viajes en avión y compañías de seguro, los cuales se investigan trimestralmente, ni para el servicio domestico y educación, cuya recolección es anual.

Los datos de precios de bienes y servicios excepto aquellos se obtiene en el mercado, se obtienen en las tres primeras semanas de cada mes y los de mercado se realizan los martes y jueves de la segunda semana.

Para los efectos del cálculo del índice no se toman en consideración los precios de liquidación. En cuanto a los precios de baratillo, se incluyen solamente si permanecen en esa condición por varias semanas y si los artículos están en buenas condiciones y forman parte de la existencia regular del almacén.

Vivienda
Las cotizaciones de alquileres se obtienen trimestralmente de 109 viviendas. No se tienen en cuenta las viviendas ocupadas por su propietario.

Especificación de las variedades
Una vez seleccionados los artículos y servicios se procedió a la obtención de la especificación que se define como la descripción detallada de las características físicas que identifican un bien o servicio las cuales son factores determinantes para establecer los precios como son por ejemplo: calidad, tamaño, tipo de fabricación, modelo, estilo, etc. Las especificaciones comprenden las indicaciones que suelen generalmente solicitar los compradores y que suministran los vendedores. El propósito de identificar los artículos es el de asegurar que solamente el índice muestre cambios en los precios.

Para facilitar la recolección de los precios con base a las descripciones establecidas, se dispone de un manual que considera el artículo y las especificaciones que se requieren para el trabajo. Desde luego, hay que tomar en cuenta que no todos los artículos incluidos en el índice requieren el mismo grado de exactitud en su definición.

Sustitución, cambio de calidad, etc.
Cuando ocurren cambios en la especificación de un artículo se efectúan las substituciones de las siguientes maneras: (a) comparación directa de los precios. Se usa cuando el artículo sustituto es más o menos de la misma calidad del artículo eliminado, pero de diferente marca; en estos casos los precios de las dos marcas se comparan directamente y el cambio de precio, si lo hay, se refleja en el índice: (b) Eslabones relativos. Mediante este método el nuevo artículo puede tener la misma utilidad o propósito pero diferir en calidad aún cuando el precio se mantenga igual; estos cambios no ocurren de repente y llega un momento en que las dos clases de artículos están en el mercado. En estos casos se cotizan los dos artículos a un mismo tiempo y cuando se tienen los precios del nuevo artículo durante dos períodos consecutivos, el artículo sustituto se encadena al índice de manera que la diferencia de precios entre las dos clases de artículos no se refleja en el índice. Esto se hace comparando el precio del artículo sustituto con el precio del mismo artículo en el período anterior y aplicando el relativo de éste al precio ponderado del artículo anterior eliminado.

Artículos estacionales
En los períodos en que no se pueden obtener precios del artículo estacional se le aplica el relativo de precios correspondiente a los artículos del mismo subgrupo disponibles durante todo el año, el cual se obtiene al dividir la suma de los precios ponderados en el trimestre de estudio entre el total de precios ponderados en el período anterior. El costo del artículo estacional se estima multiplicando el costo del período anterior por el relativo de precios estimado para el período de estudio.

Cálculo
El índice se calcula conforme a la fórmula de Laspeyres como un promedio aritmético ponderado de base fija, cuyos coeficientes de ponderación corresponden a 1983-84.

La relación del precio para cada artículo se calcula dividiendo el precio medio del período corriente por el precio medio del período precedente.

Informaciones complementarias
Se publican subgrupos detallados para la serie actual.

Organización y publicación
Dirección de Estadística y Censos: "Estadística Panameña" (Panamá, marzo, junio, septiembre, diciembre).

PAPUA NUEVA GUINEA

Denominación oficial
Consumer Price Index (Indice de precios del consumo).

Alcance
El índice se compila trimestralmente y se refiere a hogares de obreros en regiones urbanas. Se define un hogar obrero como el que recibe por lo menos el 50 por ciento de sus ingresos del pago de un salario o remuneración. "Urbano", en este contexto, significa las regiones cuya población, en 1977, era de 2 000 habitantes o más.

Base oficial
1977 = 100.

Fuente de la ponderación
La selección de los artículos y la determinación de los coeficientes de ponderación se basaron en los resultados de una encuesta sobre los gastos de los hogares efectuada ente septiembre de 1975 y febrero de 1976, que abarcó a 501 hogares de asalariados residentes en 6 áreas urbanas de 2 000 o más habitantes en 1977. Los resultados fueron ajustados en función de los cambios de precio ocurridos entre el período de la encuesta y 1977. Para seleccionar los artículos del índice se aplicaron los siguientes criterios: i) artículos cuyos gastos no representaban un porcentaje inferior al 0,05 del gasto total; ii) su representatividad con respecto al grupo mayor de artículos afines al que pertenecía y iii) facilidad para recoger los precios en forma regular.

Ponderaciones y composición

Grupos principales	Número de artículos	Ponderación	Número aproximado de cotizaciones de precio
Alimentación	51	40,89	...
Bebidas y tabaco	7	20,00	...
Vestido y calzado	16	6,17	...
Alquiler, combustible y luz	4	7,19	...
Equipo y gastos del hogar	15	5,28	...
Transportes y comunicaciones	11	12,96	...
Bienes y servicios varios	20	7,51	...
Total	124	100,00	...

Gastos de consumo de los hogares
A los fines del índice, los gastos del consumo comprenden todos los bienes y servicios adquiridos para el consumo por la población de referencia. No comprenden los gastos de juego, las jubilaciones, los ahorros, los regalos en dinero, los seguros de vida y los impuestos a la renta de las personas físicas.

Método de recolección de los datos
Los investigadores obtienen los precios en aproximadamente 240 puntos de venta distintos de seis áreas urbanas, directamente o por medio de cuestionarios enviados por correo.

Los precios de las frutas y las verduras frescas y de la areca se recogen semanalmente en los mercados. Los precios para los demás alimentos y las provisiones no alimentarias, las bebidas y el tabaco, se recogen mensualmente; las informaciones relativas a la matrícula de los institutos de enseñanza se recogen anualmente; para todos los demás artículos y servicios los precios se recogen trimestralmente.

La recolección de precios se efectúa alrededor del día 15 de cada mes, salvo para las frutas y las verduras frescas que es semanal (viernes o sábado).

Los precios utilizados para calcular el índice son los que los consumidores deben pagar el día en que se registran los precios. Los descuentos y las rebajas se utilizan para ventas de volumen importante.

Vivienda
Los datos referentes al alquiler se obtienen en viviendas alquiladas, de uno a cuatro dormitorios.

Especificación de las variedades
Las especificaciones de los artículos cuyos precios han de registrarse se dan en términos de marca, factura, calidad, tamaño y unidad, etc.

Sustitución, cambio de calidad, etc.
Se efectúan ajustes especiales para asegurar que los precios utilizados reflejen exclusivamente los cambios de precio y no

otras modificaciones, como los cambios en la calidad o la cantidad de las especificaciones.

Artículos estacionales
Las fluctuaciones estacionales de los precios no son objeto de ajuste.

Cálculo
El índice se calcula como un promedio ponderado de 6 series distintas de índices que corresponden, respectivamente, a Port Moresby, Lae, Rabaul, Madang, Groka y Kieta/Arawa/Panguna. Cada índice se calcula según la fórmula de Laspeyres, como un promedio aritmético ponderado de base fija, cuyos coeficientes de ponderación corresponden el período de base, que se ponderan a su vez para obtener un índice combinado para las seis áreas urbanas, cuyos coeficientes de ponderación son proporcionales a la población urbana de las ciudades abarcadas.

Informaciones complementarias
Se publican igualmente índices separados para las 6 áreas urbanas.

Organización y publicación
National Statistical Office: "Statistical Bulletin, Consumer Price Indexes" (Port Moresby).

idem: "Statistical Bulletin, Consumer Price Indexes", primer trimestre de 1979, segundo trimestre de 1979.

idem: "Technical Note No.4, Consumer Price Indexes (Base Year 1977), Abril de 1980.".

PARAGUAY (ASUNCION)

Denominación oficial
Indice de precios del consumo.

Alcance
El índice se calcula mensualmente y abarca las familias de cualquier nivel social o económico en el área del Gran Asunción.

Base oficial
1980 = 100.

Fuente de la ponderación
La selección de los artículos y la determinación de los coeficientes de ponderación se basaron en los resultados de una encuesta sobre los gastos de los hogares efectuada de septiembre de 1978 a septiembre de 1979 y que abarcó a una muestra de 1 591 familias urbanas de obreros, empleados, profesionales, jubilados, solteros, casados, con familia o sin ella. No incluye personas que viven en instalaciones militares y policiales, hospitales, conventos y otras similares. El número promedio de personas por familia era de 4.7 personas. El índice abarca las familias de cualquier nivel social o económico en el área del Gran Asunción, la pre-selección de artículos tomó como base el monto de los gastos y el número de familias.

Ponderaciones y composición

Grupos principales	Número de artículos	Ponderación	Número aproximado de cotizaciones de precio
Alimentación y tabaco	146	36,98	1 937
Vivienda:			725
Alquiler	1	15,47	...
Combustible y luz	13	6,37	...
Moblaje y accesorios para el hogar	44	4,67	...
Productos de limpieza	11	1,21	...
Vestido y calzado	99	8,99	972
Varios	231	26,30	2 074
Total	545	100,00	5 708

Gastos de consumo de los hogares
No disponibles.

Método de recolección de los datos
Para calcular la variación del índice de precios se recolectan un promedio de 5 700 precios por mes. Los puntos de venta se seleccionan conforme a la ubicación de los negocios de donde con más frecuencia las familias adquieren mercaderías, agregándose otros centros de compras representativos. Se estableció un promedio de diez puntos de venta por cada artículo comercializado en puestos de ventas, mercados, almacenes y supermercados. La periodicidad de la recolección de precios en Asunción es como sigue: los precios de los principales artículos de alimentación se obtienen cada semana; otros artículos de alimentación, gastos de vivienda y gastos varios, cada mes; artículos de vestir y otros gastos conexos, cada dos meses. La encuesta de precios está a cargo de funcionarios del Banco Central del Paraguay entrenados en procesamiento técnico de elaboración de sistemas de índices.

Los descuentos se toman en cuenta toda vez que este sistema de comercialización sea una norma del establecimiento comercial y sean beneficiarios del mismo todos los clientes sin ningún tipo de excepción, e intervienen en el cálculo del relativo de precio comparándose con el precio del período anterior con el descuento correspondiente.

Normalmente, se recolectan los precios de venta siempre y cuando el o los establecimientos comerciales no otorguen descuentos sobre los artículos encuestados a todos los clientes. Intervienen en el cálculo del relativo de precio comparándose con el precio de venta del período anterior.

En el caso de los artículos que tienen precios oficiales y son comercializados en el mercado libre a un precio diferente al estipulado por el Gobierno, se recolectan los precios del mercado libre, ya que es esta la cantidad de dinero abonada por el consumidor al realizar la compra.

Los precios del mercado negro no son recolectados, ya que los artículos ofrecidos legalmente no existen.

La compras a plazo o a crédito no se toman en cuenta y se utilizan solamente las compras al contado.

Las compras de artículos de segunda mano y la entrega de bienes usados como parte de pago de otros nuevos son tomados en moneda nacional y a la cotización que los oferentes estan en condiciones de vender. En otras palabras, se captan los precios que el consumidor paga por la adquisición de un producto.

Vivienda
En cuanto a los artículos incluidos bajo a la rúbrica alquiler de la vivienda, cabe consignar que el subgrupo vivienda propia y alquilada está constituido por un solo artículo que es el de vivienda alquilada. La muestra para la recolección de precios de viviendas alquiladas está constituida por 200 unidades y está dividida en cuatro grupos de 50 unidades ubicadas en distintos barrios de Asunción. Cada una de las unidades que componen uno de los cuatro grupos de alquileres es visitada cada cuatro meses en forma secuencial. Por ejemplo; el grupo 1 está constituido por 50 alquileres en el Barrio A y se recolecta en el mes de enero. Estos precios recolectados intervienen en el cálculo del relativo de precio comparándose con los precios recolectados en el mes de septiembre del período anterior, mientras los otros tres grupos permanecen constantes. El grupo 2 está constituido por otras 50 unidades de alquileres situadas en el Barrio B y se recolectan precios en el mes de febrero. Estos precios captados se comparan con los precios del período anterior, es decir, octubre, mientras los demás grupos permanecen constantes. En el mes de marzo, se recolectan los precios del tercer grupo constituido por 50 alquileres situados en el Barrio C y se comparan con los recolectados en el mes de noviembre anterior, mientras los demás permanecen constantes. En el mes de abril, se recolectan los precios del cuarto grupo constituidos por 50 alquileres en el Barrio D y sus precios se comparan con los del mes de diciembre anterior, manteniéndose constantes los tres grupos restantes.

Especificación de las variedades
Los datos utilizados para elaborar las especificaciones de los artículos describen la variedad, la calidad y la unidad de medida tabulada para el cálculo del relativo de precio. Dependiendo del producto de que se trate, incluye además marca y procedencia determinada, peso y tamaño.

Sustitución, cambio de calidad, etc.
En cuanto a la desaparición de un tipo determinado de producto del mercado, se estima el relativo de precio del mismo por los demás componentes del estrato a que pertenece, y en cuanto a la calidad, se puede sustituir por otro similar sin comparar los precios en el momento de la sustitución.

Artículos estacionales
Los precios de los artículos estacionales, así como sus ponderaciones, se mantienen constantes en los períodos de recolección en que no se encuentran en el mercado y en los períodos de aparición se recolectan comparándose los precios recolectados con los anteriormente constantes. Este procedimiento se utiliza a fin de no distorsionar en demasía las ya distorsionadas ponderaciones.

Cálculo
El índice se calcula según la formula de Laspeyres modificada con un volumen de consumo fijo y ponderaciones móviles. El índice para cada producto se obtiene utilizando las relaciones de precios del período corriente y del último período de recolección.

Informaciones complementarias
El Banco Central del Paraguay elabora paralelamente otro Indice de Precios de Consumo que abarca las familias obreras en el Gran Asunción.

Organización y publicación
Banco Central del Paraguay: "Folleto Explicativo del Indice de Precios del Consumo, Año 1980", Junio de 1988.

idem: "Boletín Estadístico".

idem: "Revista Ñemú Renda".

Dirección General de Estadística y Censos, Presidencia de la República: "Anuario Estadístico".

PERU (LIMA)

Denominación oficial
Indice de precios al consumidor.

Alcance
El índice se calcula mensualmente y abarca los hogares urbanos cuyo jefe es obrero y/o empleado con ingreso medio. Se excluyeron a los hogares cuyo ingreso per capita fue demasiado bajo o muy alto y a los hogares unipersonales.

Base oficial
1979 = 100.

Fuente de la ponderación
La selección de los artículos y la determinación de los coeficientes de ponderación se basaron en los resultados de una encuesta sobre los gastos de los hogares efectuada durante 12 meses entre septiembre de 1977 y agosto de 1978, sobre 1 985 hogares en Lima Metropolitana.

La selección de los artículos se hizo de acuerdo con los siguientes criterios: mayor importancia relativa dentro de cada subgrupo de consumo, aptitud para representar los movimientos de precios de un conjunto de productos similares, seguimientos de sus precios. El valor del gasto de los artículos no incluidos en la canasta familiar se agregó al de los seleccionados de dos maneras: a) por imputación directa, asignando a otro de características bastante similares y que puede ser substituto; b) por imputación indirecta, distribuyéndolo proporcionalmente entre los restantes artículos considerados del subgrupo.

Ponderaciones y composición

Grupos principales	Número de artículos	Ponderación	Número aproximado de cotizaciones de precio
Alimentación y tabaco	75	38,09	23 386
Vestido y calzado	11	7,33	1 323
Alquiler, combustible y electricidad	8	15,57	1 424
Moblaje, accesorios para el hogar, productos de limpieza, etc.	36	6,98	1 589
Aseo personal y asistencia médica	8	2.64	417
Transportes y comunicaciones	10	9,83	272
Educación y distracciones	12	7,40	592
Otros bienes y servicios	13	12,16	997
Total	173	100,00	30 000

Gastos de consumo de los hogares
Se define al consumo del hogar como la parte del gasto en bienes y servicios destinados a satisfacer las necesidades de la familia excluyéndose de este concepto las adquisiciones de viviendas, terrenos y todos aquellos desembolsos capaces de originar ingresos al hogar o proporcionar rentas. Se incluye dentro del consumo del hogar el autoconsumo, es decir, la parte de bienes o servicios producidos por los miembros del hogar para ser consumidos por estos y valorizados a precio de mercado. Así, por ejemplo, se debe incluir en el gasto del hogar el alquiler imputado de aquellos hogares que ocupan su propia vivienda. Se consideran también todos aquellos gastos que no impliquen una doble cuenta, como por ejemplo el gasto de seguro de automóvil siempre y cuando no se incluyan gastos de reparación de vehículos asegurados.

Método de recolección de los datos
Para la selección de una muestra de mercados, el Instituto Nacional de Estadística realizó un censo de cuyos resultados se escogió los de mayor importancia en función del número de "puestos de venta" y del número de vendedores ambulantes habidos a su alrededor. La muestra quedó constituida por 33 mercados y 4 automercados. La selección de establecimientos comerciales y de servicios, se realizó identificando las "avenidas o zonas comerciales" de cada distrito, y tomando en cuenta la disposición del informante a colaborar y el buen surtido de productos de su establecimiento. Además se han considerado las grandes cadenas de supermercados. Los precios utilizados en el cálculo del índice son los mismos que paga el ama de casa en el mercado o el que realiza la mayoría de los consumidores en los establecimientos. Los precios son recogidos por agentes en mercados, puntos de venta al por menor y establecimientos de servicios.

Los precios para los artículos que tienen precios muy dispersos, como es el caso de los productos frescos (hortalizas, tubérculos, frutas, pescado, verduras) y otros, cuyos precios son poco dispersos, que se comercializan en mercados de abastos (arroz, azúcar, grasas y aceites comestibles, etc.) son recogidos semanalmente. Para artículos de precios menos fluctuantes, como son los cereales, indumentaria, muebles, etc., los precios se recogen mensualmente y los de los alquileres de vivienda, precios urbanos y gabelas municipales semestralmente. Las tarifas de servicios públicos se obtienen ocasionalmente. Ciertos precios se obtienen por compra directa en los mercados.

Vivienda
En el caso de los alquileres de vivienda, las observaciones se realizan en aquellos hogares captados en la encuesta de hogares y se mantienen fijas.

Especificación de las variedades
La selección de una variedad dada para conformar un artículo depende de su importancia en el interior del artículo, la facilidad para definirla y ubicarla y la estabilidad en el tiempo de los artículos que responden a esta definición y que se van a observar.

Los artículos seleccionados de las encuestas de hogares no siempre aparecen con las características bien definidas, es decir con especificaciones de marca, tamaño, etc. A efectos de constituir las muestras iniciales de observación, los agentes visitaron los establecimientos de la muestra de informantes. Con la relación de los artículos previamente seleccionados, se anotaron en detalle las características de los productos a recopilar: nombre, marca, modelo, tamaño o peso, etc. En lo posible se solicitó al comerciante el nombre del artículo más vendido correspondiente a la definición de la variedad anotada. La muestra así constituida debe ser controlada en forma centralizada para asegurar que los precios recopilados correspondan exactamente a aquellos que figuran en la muestra.

Sustitución, cambio de calidad, etc.
Algunas veces no es posible recoger todos los precios por diversas razones: estacionalidad, ausencia del informante, ausencia del artículo por discontinuidad. El Instituto Nacional de Estadística soluciona estas dificultades de la manera siguiente: cuando la variedad es homogénea, se calculan los precios promedios para cada período a partir de los datos efectivamente recopilados en este período. Cuando la variedad es heterogénea, se generalizan los precios anotados anteriormente. Es necesario prolongar temporalmente un precio si se está seguro de volver a encontrar el artículo en el futuro próximo. Si al fin de tres meses no se ha vuelto a encontrar de nuevo el producto observado, es absolutamente necesario reemplazarlo.

Artículos estacionales
No disponible.

Cálculo
El índice se calcula conforme a la fórmula de Laspeyres como un promedio aritmético ponderado de base fija, cuyos coeficientes de ponderación corresponden al período de septiembre de 1977 - agosto de 1978. El índice para un artículo es obtenido utilizando las relaciones de precios del período corriente y del período precedente. Para los artículos con especificaciones homogéneas se calculan las relaciones de precios medios y para los artículos heterogéneos se utilizan los medios de las relaciones de precios. En los dos casos, se calculan promedios aritméticos simples.

Informaciones complementarias
Actualmente se calcula una nueva serie (base 1990 = 100), pero en el momento de publicar el presente Volumen la OIT no disponía de informaciones metodológicas sobre esta serie.

Organización y publicación
Instituto Nacional de Estadística: "Indice de Precios al Consumidor de Lima Metropolitana" (Lima).

idem: "Indice de Precios al Consumidor de Lima Metropolitana, Metodología, diciembre 1980" (Lima).

POLINESIA FRANCESA

Denominación oficial
Indice des prix de détail à la consommation familiale (Indice de precios del consumo familiar).

Alcance
El índice se calcula mensualmente y abarca hogares de todas las categorías sociales en todo el territorio.

Base oficial
Diciembre de 1980 = 100.

Fuente de la ponderación
La selección de los artículos y la determinación de los coeficientes de ponderación se basaron en los resultados de una encuesta sobre los gastos de los hogares, de alcance nacional, y en las estadísticas sobre las importaciones que los complementan. La encuesta se realizó durante tres meses y medio, durante la segunda mitad de 1979, y abarcó a una muestra de 836 hogares de todas las categorías sociales.

Ponderaciones y composición

Grupos principales	Número de artículos	Ponderación	Número aproximado de cotizaciones de precio
Alimentación	79	3 650	4 107
Artículos manufacturados:			
Vestido, calzado y ropa blanca	28	900	362
Moblaje y accesorios para el hogar	25	922	508
Productos de limpieza	13	522	785
Vehículos	6	916	87
Educación y lectura	18	699	375
Combustible y luz	5	862	6
Tabaco y otros	6	279	60
Servicios:			
Alquiler, agua	2	445	25
Reparaciones y mantenimiento	4	148	34
Aseo personal y asistencia médica	5	101	32
Transportes y comunicaciones	11	390	46
Educación, distracciones, otros	14	166	130
Total	216	10 000	6 557

Gastos de consumo de los hogares
A los fines del índice, los gastos del consumo incluyen los bienes y servicios producidos por los hogares para autoconsumo. Se excluyen las compras de segunda mano, el costo adicional de las compras a plazos y las contribuciones a la seguridad social; pero se incluyen las primas de los seguros relacionados con la utilización de vehículos automotores.

Método de recolección de los datos
Los precios de la mayor parte de los artículos se recogen mensualmente por investigadores o por medio de llamadas telefónicas a 326 puntos de venta al por menor y establecimientos de servicios. Los precios de los géneros alimentarios y los de los productos manufacturados de gran consumo se recogen en las 13 localidades de las islas de Tahití y Moorea. Los precios de los demás artículos y servicios se recogen en las áreas urbanas de Tahití (Papeete, Faa, Pirae, Arne). Los precios incluyen los impuestos indirectos.

Vivienda
Las cotizaciones de alquiler se obtienen cuatro veces por año, para 22 viviendas.

Especificación de las variedades
Para la colección de los precios se utiliza una lista de 2 180 especificaciones muy detalladas que se refieren a tipo, marca, peso, calidad y país de origen.

Sustitución, cambio de calidad, etc.
Si un producto desaparece del mercado se lo sustituye por otro similar y se usa el método de enlace. No se consideran los cambios de calidad menores; para los importantes se utiliza también el método de enlace.

Artículos estacionales
Los precios de las frutas, verduras y pescado frescos se determinan semanalmente en los mercados de Papeete y Pirae, y mensualmente en los demás puntos de venta al por menor. Para el cálculo final del índice se emplea un promedio móvil de 12 meses.

Cálculo
El índice se calcula según la fórmula de Laspeyres, como un promedio aritmético ponderado de base fija, cuyos coeficientes de ponderación corresponden al período de base.

Informaciones complementarias
Actualmente se calcula una nueva serie (base diciembre de 1988 = 100), pero en el momento de publicar el presente Volumen la OIT no disponía de informaciones metodológicas sobre esta serie.

Organización y publicación
Institut Territorial de la Statistique: "Te Aveiʼa" (Papeete).

idem: "Journal Officiel de la Polynésie Française".

POLONIA

Denominación oficial
Consumer Price Index (Indice de Precios del Consumo).

Alcance
El índice se compila mensualmente y abarca más del 90 por ciento de la población.

Base oficial
El período de base del índice utilizado en las publicaciones nacionales es el período correspondiente del año anterior, tomado como = 100. La Oficina Central de Estadística de Polonia enlaza esos índices retrocediendo hasta llegar al año utilizado como base para la publicación de la OIT.

Fuente de la ponderación
El sistema de la ponderación se basa en una encuesta sobre los gastos de los hogares.

Ponderaciones y composición

Grupos principales	Número de artículos	Ponderación	Número aproximado de cotizaciones de precio
Alimentación	390	41,8	...
Bebidas alcohólicas	40	5,9	...
Artículos no alimenticios	800	32,2	...
Servicios	220	20,1	...
Total	1 450	100,0	...

Gastos de consumo de los hogares
No disponible.

Método de recolección de los datos
La recolección de los precios, que tiene lugar entre el primero y el 25 de cada mes, está a cargo de personal de las oficinas estadísticas de 307 regiones en 281 ciudades. Los precios se investigan en 27 556 puntos de venta de los cuales el 45 por ciento son minoristas, el 5 por ciento abastecedores de alimentos y comidas, correspondiendo el 50 por ciento restante a establecimientos de prestación de servicios. Los precios de los productos alimenticios se obtienen tres veces por mes y los de artículos no alimenticios, bebidas alcohólicas y tabaco, dos veces por mes.

Vivienda
No disponible.

Especificación de las variedades
No disponible.

Sustitución, cambio de calidad, etc.
No disponible.

Artículos estacionales
Las fluctuaciones estacionales de los precios de patatas, frutas y legumbres se toman en cuenta modificando mensualmente los coeficientes de ponderación de esa clase de artículos dentro de un grupo cuya ponderación es constante.

Cálculo
El índice se calcula según la fórmula de Laspeyres como un promedio aritmético ponderado de base fija.
En primer lugar se calcula un índice individual de los precios de cada artículo para el período en curso, tomando como término de comparación la media de los precios de ese artículo durante un período de base. Los índices individuales a escala nacional se calculan como una media geométrica de los índices individuales de los precios de cada artículo en las regiones respectivas. Para cada grupo primario se calcula luego un índice de grupo como una media geométrica de los índices individuales de precio de los artículos que forman el grupo en cuestión (si un grupo comprende un artículo solo, su índice será el del grupo).
Se calculan entonces los índices de los grupos de bienes de consumo y de servicios respectivos. A su vez, el índice final de los precios se obtiene mediante agregaciones y ponderaciones sucesivas.

Informaciones complementarias
La Oficina Central de Estadísticas también publica índices de precio compilados para estas cuatro categorías socioeconómicas de la población: 1) empleados, 2) agricultores, 3) trabajadores agrícolas y, 4) jubilados y pensionistas.

Organización y publicación
Glowny Urzad, Statistycznz (Oficina Central de Estadísticas): "Statistical Bulletin" (Varsovia).

PORTUGAL

Denominación oficial
Indice de preços no consumidor - Serie A - Continente General (Indice de Precios del Consumo - serie general).

Alcance
El índice se compila mensualmente y abarca el conjunto de los hogares, urbanos y rurales.

Base oficial
1983 = 100.

Fuente de la ponderación
La determinación de los coeficientes de ponderación y la selección de los artículos se basaron en los resultados de una encuesta sobre los gastos de los hogares realizada de marzo de 1980 a febrero de 1981 a una muestra aleatoria de 8 000 hogares. Las ponderaciones se ajustaron para tomar en cuenta la evolución de los precios entre el período de la encuesta y 1983.

Ponderaciones y composición

Grupos principales	Número de artículos	Ponderación	Número aproximado de cotizaciones de precio
Alimentación	188	4 606	11 461
Vestido y calzado	73	1 014	5 980
Alquiler	...	(515)	...
Alojamiento	75	1 261	3 876
Asistencia médica	69	263	748
Transporte y comunicaciones	41	1 382	847
Educación y recreación	29	412	1 195
Tabaco	5	128	62
Otros bienes y servicios	31	419	1 286
Total	511	10 000	25 455

Gastos de consumo de los hogares
Comprenden los bienes producidos por los hogares para su propio consumo y los ingresos en especie. Se excluyen los impuestos directos y toda contribución o cotización que no sea pago de un servicio, como los permisos de radio y televisión.

Método de recolección de los datos
Los precios de la alimentación, el tabaco y los productos de uso diario se registran en la última semana completa de cada mes. Los precios de los demás productos y servicios se registran en forma trimestral y rotativa, dividiéndose la tarea en tres para poder registrar un tercio cada mes. Los datos sobre la educación se obtienen una vez al año y las tarifas de bienes y servicios fijadas en forma oficial cuando se modifican. Los precios se registran en 4 800 mercados, supermercados, puntos de venta al por menor y establecimientos de servicios de 25 aglomeraciones. Se registran los precios que se pagan directamente en el comercio. No se toman en consideración los precios de liquidaciones y promociones diversas.

Vivienda
Si bien en la ponderación figura el alquiler, no se le toma en cuenta para calcular el índice mensual. Los alquileres de 32 000 viviendas se registran en forma rotativa durante el segundo y tercer trimestre de cada año. El índice de las cotizaciones del alquiler se incorpora una vez por año al índice anual.

Especificación de las variedades
Se describen lo más completamente posible las calidades y otras características físicas de los bienes y servicios, para registrar siempre los precios de los mismos artículos en todos los establecimientos.

Sustitución, cambio de calidad, etc.
Para los cambios cuantitativos se calcula un coeficiente de ajuste proporcional; para los cambios de calidad el precio se estima mediante un coeficiente de calidad. Cuando los cambios afectan a la vez la cantidad y la calidad de los productos se utiliza un método econométrico. Cuando se introduce en el índice un artículo nuevo, su precio de base se estima en función del movimiento de los precios de artículos similares.

Artículos estacionales
Las fluctuaciones estacionales de los precios de las frutas y las legumbres frescas se toman en consideración variando los artículos y las ponderaciones de las canastas mensuales (cuyo coeficiente global de ponderación permanece invariable) y se utiliza un promedio móvil de 12 meses para el cálculo final del índice.

Cálculo
El índice se calcula según la fórmula de Laspeyres como un promedio aritmético ponderado de base fija, cuyos coeficientes de ponderación corresponden al período de base.
La relación de los precios de cada artículo se calcula dividiendo el precio medio correspondiente al período en curso por el precio medio del período de base. El índice general para la parte continental del país es una media aritmética ponderada de los índices relativos a la población de cada aglomeración, según los datos del censo de 1981.

Informaciones complementarias
La serie general "A", que publica la OIT, no incluye el alquiler; la media anual que comprende el alquiler se publica en el "Anuário estadístico" del Instituto Nacional de Estadística en Lisboa. La serie "B" se refiere a la población urbana de Lisboa y Oporto. Actualmente se calcula una nueva serie relativa al continente y una serie nacional (base 1991 = 100), pero en el momento de publicar el presente volumen la OIT no dispone de informaciones metodológicas sobre estas series.

Organización y publicación
Instituto nacional de estadística: "Anuário estadístico" (Lisboa).
idem: "Boletín mensal de estadística".

PUERTO RICO

Denominación oficial
Consumer Price Index for All Families (Indice de Precios del Consumo de toda las familias).

Alcance
El índice se compila mensualmente y abarca todos los hogares urbanos, comprendidos los de obreros y empleados, trabajadores por cuenta propia, pensionistas y personas desocupadas. Se excluyen los hogares de granjeros, personal militar y personas que viven en instituciones.

Base oficial
1967 = 100.

Fuente de la ponderación
La determinación de los coeficientes de ponderación y la selección de los artículos se basaron en los resultados de una encuesta sobre los gastos de los hogares realizada en 1977. La muestra comprendió 2 017 hogares (1 360 urbanos y 657 rurales). Las ponderaciones se basaron en la estructura del consumo de los hogares urbanos y la selección de los artículos incluídos en el índice en su importancia relativa. Se ajustaron los coeficientes de ponderación para tomar en cuenta las modificaciones de precio ocurridas entre el período de la encuesta y 1979.

Ponderaciones y composición

Grupos principales	Número de artículos	Ponderación	Número aproximado de cotizaciones de precio (a)
Alimentación	110	30,40	366
Vivienda:			
Alquiler	1	2,00	(b)
Gastos de vivienda en hoteles	1	0,71	25
Casa propia	4	7,02	27
Moblaje y gastos del hogar	42	9,46	172
Combustible y luz	5	5,11	8
Vestido y calzado	37	10,00	310
Transportes	12	17,20	318
Asistencia médica	19	5,10	165
Educación y recreación	11	4,60	38
Otros bienes y servicios	16	8,40	71
Total	258	100,00	1 500

Nota: (a) Número de establecimientos. (b) 2 000 viviendas alquiladas.

Gastos de consumo de los hogares
A los efectos del índice comprenden todos los bienes y servicios adquiridos para el consumo por la población de referencia. Se incluyen los gastos en seguros, cuando pueden asociarse a un artículo o servicio determinado (como los de vehículos o de casas pagados por los inquilinos o los propietarios), e intereses hipotecarios. Se excluyen los seguros personales de vida, los impuestos a los ingresos y los que gravan la propiedad individual.

Método de recolección de los datos
Los investigadores registran los precios en unos 1 500 puestos de venta al por menor y establecimientos seleccionados de 11 municipios.

Los precios de la mayoría de los artículos se registran mensualmente. Las tarifas de los servicios de alojamiento, asistencia jurídica, reparación de calzado, fontanería, peluquería, asistencia médica, transporte y similares se obtienen trimestralmente.

Los precios que se usan en el índice son los que paga regularmente cualquier persona del público. Se registran precios de rebajas.

Vivienda
El artículo vivienda comprende los gastos de alquiler, hotel y casa propia. Las cotizaciones del alquiler se obtienen trimestralmente de 2 343 viviendas alquiladas. Para la casa propia se registran los gastos de los intereses hipotecarios, las reparaciones y el mantenimiento.

Especificación de las variedades
Se dan amplias descripciones de los artículos cuyos precios se deben registrar. Para representar un artículo se pueden utilizar marcas distintas en los diferentes puntos de venta siempre que mes tras mes se registren los precios de la misma marca. La selección de los artículos específicos cuyos precios se han de registrar se basan en los datos sobre su volumen de ventas.

Sustitución, cambio de calidad, etc.
Cuando ya no se puede encontrar un producto se lo sustituye por otro similar.

Artículos estacionales
Muy pocos artículos estacionales se incluyen en el índice. Los precios de las frutas y verduras frescas se registran en la temporada que les es propia y no se hacen ajustes por este concepto.

Cálculo
El índice se calcula según la fórmula de Laspeyres como un promedio aritmético ponderado de base fija, cuyos coeficientes de ponderación corresponden a 1979. En diciembre de 1979 el índice se enlazó a la base 1967 = 100.

Los relativos de precio para cada artículo se calculan dividiendo el promedio de los precios del período en curso por el promedio de los precios del período precedente. El precio promedio de un artículo es una media aritmética simple de todas las cotizaciones de precio obtenidas para ese artículo.

Informaciones complementarias
También se calcula y publica un Indice de precios del consumo de hogares de obreros (base 1967 = 100).

Organización y publicación
Departamento del Trabajo y recursos humanos: "Indice de precios al consumidor para todas las familias en Puerto Rico" (San Juan).

idem: "Importancia Relativa de los bienes y servicios de consumo en el índice de precios al consumidor para todas las familias en Puerto Rico" (Junio de 1980).

idem: "Articulos y servicios cuyos precios se recopilan para el índice de precios al consumidor de todas las familias y el revisado de familias obreras en Puerto Rico" (septiembre de 1980).

QATAR

Denominación oficial
Consumer Price Index Number (Indice de precios del consumo).

Alcance
El indice se calcula mensualmente y abarca hogares de nacionales y no nacionales de Qatar.

Base oficial
1988 = 100.

Fuente de la ponderación
La selección de los artículos y la determinación de los coeficientes de ponderación se basaron en los resultados de una encuesta sobre los gastos de los hogares efectuada en 1988 a hogares de nacionales y no nacionales de Qatar.

Ponderaciones y composición

Grupos principales	Número de artículos	Ponderación	Número aproximado de cotizaciones de precio
Alimentación y tabaco	...	286,8	...
Vestido y calzado	...	106,3	...
Vivienda:			
Alquiler	...	78,5	...
Mantenimiento	...	23,2	...
Combustible, electricidad y agua	...	22,3	...
Muebles y moblaje	...	125,8	...
Transportes y comunicaciones	...	193,3	...
Asistencia médica	...	12,3	...
Educación y distracciones	...	76,4	...
Varios bienes y servicios	...	75,1	...
Total	...	1 000,0	...

Gastos de consumo de los hogares
No disponible.

Método de recolección de los datos
No disponible.

Vivienda
No disponible.

Especificación de las variedades
No disponible.

Sustitución, cambio de calidad, etc.
No disponible.

Articulos estacionales
No disponible.

Cálculo
El índice se calcula conforme a la fórmula de Laspeyres como un promedio aritmético ponderado de base fija, cuyos coeficientes de ponderación corresponden al período de base.

Organización y publicación
Central Statistical Organisation: "Annual Statistical Abstract".

idem: "Monthly Survey on Retail and Consumer Index".

REINO UNIDO

Denominación oficial
Retail Price Index (Indice de Precios al por Menor).

Alcance
El índice se compila mensualmente y se refiere a los bienes y servicios adquiridos por todos los hogares, salvo el cuatro por ciento que representa los que tienen ingresos más elevados y los de jubilados que perciben por lo menos las tres cuartas partes de sus ingresos del Estado. El índice abarca todo el Reino Unido.

Base oficial
Enero de 1987 = 100.

Fuente de la ponderación
La determinación de los coeficientes de ponderación y la selección de los artículos se revisan a comienzos de febrero de cada año, en función de los últimos datos disponibles de la encuesta sobre los gastos de los hogares. Las informaciones correspondientes al año finalizado en el último mes de junio sirven para calcular los coeficientes de ponderación que se utilizarán a partir de febrero del año siguiente. Los coeficientes de ponderación se ajustan para tomar en cuenta el lapso transcurrido hasta el momento en que se aplican los nuevos coeficientes de ponderación, suponiéndose que los gastos en determinadas categorías de bienes y servicios habrán tenido modificaciones acordes con el movimiento de los precios (sin ningún aumento o disminución del volumen del consumo).

La encuesta, que comprende toda clase de hogares privados del Reino Unido, tiene carácter continuo y en el curso de un año abarca más de 7 000, seleccionados de tal forma que cada uno de ellos tenga las mismas posibilidades de selección. Cada hogar registra los gastos efectuados durante dos semanas e informa también sobre los menos frecuentes que puedan haber realizado en un período más largo. Los artículos y las ponderaciones utilizadas en 1992 son las siguientes:

Ponderaciones y composición

Grupos principales	Número de artículos	Ponderación	Número aproximado de cotizaciones de precio
Alimentación	127	152	...
Comidas fuera del hogar	4	47	...
Bebidas alcohólicas	9	80	...
Tabaco	4	36	...
Vivienda:			
Alquiler	2	35	...
Ocupantes propietarios: intereses y pagos hipotecarios, seguros domésticos, etc.	2	72	...
Reparaciones y mantenimiento	12	25	...
Tasas municipales y agua	4	40	...
Combustible y luz	11	47	...
Bienes domésticos durables y servicios	57	125	...
Vestido y calzado	66	59	...
Transporte y vehículos	17	163	...
Artículos varios	69	75	...
Servicios	10	44	...
Total	394	1 000	130 000

Gastos de consumo de los hogares
Comprenden los ingresos en especie, los costos de la casa propia, la entrega de bienes usados como pago parcial de otros nuevos, las matrículas de la enseñanza, los seguros de bienes de consumo específicos y la asistencia médica. Se excluyen los impuestos sobre los ingresos y otros de carácter directo, las primas de seguros de vida, las remesas, regalos y desembolsos similares, las contribuciones a fondos de seguridad social o de pensiones, los ahorros e inversiones y los recargos por créditos.

Método de recolección de los datos
Las 180 localidades donde se registran los precios se seleccionan de tal forma que constituyan una muestra representativa de todo el país. En la zona correspondiente a cada localidad el encargado de la recolección de precios, familiarizado con las condiciones locales de la compra, tiene amplias facultades para elegir los puntos de venta más característicos, siguiendo directrices generales para garantizar que cada clase de punto de venta tenga adecuada representación.

- Para todos los bienes y la mayoría de los artículos, los precios se registran en forma mensual.
- El índice se refiere a un día determinado del mes (normalmente, pero no siempre, el segundo martes).
- El día de la recolección los investigadores de la Oficina Central de Estadísticas visitan la mayoría de los puntos de venta. Para algunas grandes cadenas de supermercados, que venden al mismo precio en todas sus dependencias, la Oficina obtiene una lista de precios a nivel central. Para tarifas tales como las de la electricidad, el gas, los transportes en común y los servicios telefónicos y postales, las informaciones se obtienen de las oficinas centrales pertinentes.
- Actualmente existe una organización sobre el terreno para distintos propósitos. La recolección de los datos está a cargo de las oficinas encargadas de las prestaciones de desempleo, que envían todos los meses los cuestionarios a un punto de reunión central de los datos.
- En el índice sólo figuran los precios netos y no los descuentos, salvo si se ofrecen a todos los clientes potenciales o corren a cargo del vendedor o ambas cosas.
- Los precios de liquidación se consideran reducciones de precio, salvo que correspondan a mercancías de calidad inferior a las registradas en anteriores recolecciones de precios.
- Se ignoran los precios de los alquileres con opción de compra y las ventas a crédito.
- Si bien en principio se investiga el valor de los artículos usados y de los entregados a cuenta, en la práctica sólo se registran los precios de los vehículos automóviles de segunda mano.
- Los bienes de importación no se distinguen en forma separada. Las cotizaciones de artículos con precios fijos, tales como periódicos, franqueo, etc., se registran una sola vez en forma centralizada.
- Las cotizaciones de artículos con precios variables se registran en muchos puntos de venta al menudeo en todo el Reino Unido: unas 130 000 cotizaciones para 600 artículos. El número apropiado de cotizaciones se relaciona en general con la ponderación de los artículos.

Vivienda
El índice abarca todas las clases de vivienda que normalmente se alquilan. En su mayor parte son de propiedad municipal, cuyas autoridades sólo modifican los alquileres en abril y en octubre-noviembre de cada año. En dichas ocasiones las informaciones se obtienen por encuesta postal. El indicador de precios es el promedio de los alquileres exigidos, sin deducir las rebajas o subsidios que se puedan conceder. Los pagos hipotecarios se incluyen en el índice para representar los costes de las casas ocupadas por sus propietarios que no sean abarcados por separado, tales como las tasas, reparaciones, etc.

Especificación de las variedades
Varían según los productos y de año en año. Actualmente se incluyen ciertas designaciones y especificaciones de marcas comerciales. El encargado de la recolección de precios en el plano local elige entre los artículos especificados la marca más representativa en cada uno de los puntos de venta que visita.

Sustitución, cambio de calidad, etc.
Los encargados de registrar los precios tienen oportunidad de comunicar los cambios de calidad. En la medida de lo posible, tales cambios se toman en consideración cuando se prepara el índice. Los artículos se revisan todos los años para reflejar las modificaciones de los hábitos y preferencias de los consumidores.

Artículos estacionales
Se registran los precios de los artículos estacionales disponibles. Por lo general las ponderaciones de estos artículos no varían según los meses, pero sí las ponderaciones de las distintas variedades de frutas y legumbres frescas para reflejar las distintas características del consumo a lo largo del año, aun cuando para el total de las frutas y legumbres frescas se mantiene un coeficiente de ponderación fijo.

Cálculo
El índice es un índice en cadena de Laspeyres, con enlaces anuales de enero a enero. Los índices de cada una de las variedades de frutas y legumbres frescas se combinan mediante una fórmula de tipo Paasche. Según el artículo se calculan promedios o relativos de precio. Las cotizaciones que faltan o los precios inutilizables se sustituyen por valores ficticios, partiendo del supuesto que los precios del momento tendrán la misma evolución que los registrados validamente en otra parte. El cálculo del índice es directo.

Informaciones complementarias
Desde 1989 la Oficina Central de Estadísticas se encarga de recopilar los precios actuales y calcular el índice.

También calcula y publica un "Tax and price index" (Indice de Precios e Impuestos).

Organización y publicación
Central Statistical Office: "Monthly Digest of Statistics" (London).

Department of Employment: "Employment Gazette".

idem: "A short guide to the Retail Price Index", publicada en la edición de agosto de 1987 del "Employment Gazette".

REUNION

Denominación oficial
Indice des prix à la consommation des ménages urbains de condition moyenne (Indice de precios del consumo para hogares urbanos de ingresos medios).

Alcance
El cálculo del índice es mensual y abarca hogares de todo tamaño con ingresos medios, ubicados en Saint Denis, cuyo jefe es un obrero o empleado en el sector público o en el privado.

Base oficial
1978 = 100.

Fuente de la ponderación
La selección de los artículos y la determinación de los coeficientes de ponderación se basaron en los resultados de una encuesta sobre los gastos de los hogares efectuada en 1986-87, que abarcó toda la población de la Reunión. Para determinar los coeficientes de ponderación sólo se ha considerado el consumo de hogares urbanos cuyo jefe es un obrero o un empleado.

Ponderaciones y composición

Grupos principales	Número de artículos	Ponderación	Número aproximado de cotizaciones de precio
Alimentación	87	27,93	...
Vestido y calzado	49	8,60	...
Combustible y luz	6	7,16	...
Alquiler	1	6,27	...
Otros productos manufacturados (moblaje y otros artículos para el hogar, productos de limpieza, etc.)	75	35,32	...
Otros servicios (transportes, aseo personal y asistencia médica, etc.)	50	14,72	...
Total	268	100,00	8 000

Gastos de consumo de los hogares
A los fines del índice, los gastos del consumo comprenden todos los bienes y servicios adquiridos para el consumo por la población de referencia. Comprende la asistencia médica, la reparación de vehículos evaluada según el costo que en el momento representen para el hogar, así como los primas de los seguros de coches. Se excluyen los impuestos directos, los costos de edificación que sean una inversión, los productos caseros consumidos en el hogar, el valor de las viviendas ocupadas por sus propietarios y los beneficios recibidos en especie que no constituyan gastos de consumo en términos de contabilidad económica.

Método de recolección de los datos
Los datos relativos a los precios son recogidos por agentes del "INSEE - Direction Régionale de la Réunion", que trabajan en el terreno, en 224 puestos de venta al por menor y establecimientos de servicios de Saint Denis.

Los precios son los que se pagan en el momento, sin tomar en consideración las rebajas. Los precios de la carne, los huevos, las frutas y las verduras frescas se recogen semanalmente. Los datos de alquiler se recogen cada tres meses y los de los demás bienes y servicios mensualmente.

En la selección de los puntos de venta se considera la existencia de diferentes áreas dentro de la ciudad de Saint-Denis, de distintos tipos de comercio como por ejemplo, los supermercados, los negocios independientes, los mercados, etc., y los varios hábitos de compra de los consumidores.

Vivienda
Los datos relativos al alquiler se obtienen cada tres meses mediante una encuesta trimestral cuya muestra comprende 284 viviendas alquiladas.

Especificación de las variedades
La lista de las variedades se modifica para tomar en consideración todo cambio en los hábitos del consumo, que pueden ser frecuentes en el caso de los alimentos. Los artículos se seleccionan si son representativos de algunas de las 268 categorías de gastos.

Sustitución, cambio de calidad, etc.
Se utilizan tres métodos para tomar en consideración los cambios de cantidad o de calidad en los artículos a los que se fija precio, la desaparición de productos antiguos o la aparición de nuevos: i) para los nuevos productos que difieren del antiguo sólo en términos cuantitativos, los precios se ajustan en forma proporcional; ii) si esta última es una hipótesis débil, se lo substituye por un producto similar, presumiéndose que el nuevo producto tuvo en el pasado la misma evolución de precio que el antiguo; por último, iii) los agentes estiman en el terreno las diferencias de precios respecto al cambio de calidad.

Artículos estacionales
Se toman en consideración las fluctuaciones estacionales de los precios de las frutas y las verduras frescas, variando mensualmente los artículos en ese subgrupo pero manteniendo constante el porcentaje de ponderación global. El índice compara el costo de la "canasta" para el mes en curso con el mismo mes del año base. El precio de base de una variedad es el promedio anual ponderado del año precedente que se aplica a cada mes.

Cálculo
Desde enero de 1990, el índice es un Indice-cadena cuyos coeficientes de ponderación se revisan cada año civil. El índice mensual se calcula primero con base de diciembre del año precedente igual a 100. Los índices así obtenidos se encadenan entonces con base 1978 = 100 (índice-cadena de Laspeyres).

El índice para un artículo se obtiene utilizando las relaciones de precios del período corriente y del período de base. Para artículos con variedades homogéneas, se calculan las relaciones de precios medios y para artículos con variedades heterogéneas, se utilizan promedios de relaciones de precios.

Informaciones complementarias
No disponible.

Organización y publicación
INSEE, Service Départemental de la Réunion: "Bulletin de statistique" (Saint Denis).

idem: "L'indice des prix à la consommation des ménages urbains de condition moyenne", document no. 33 (octubre de 1980).

RUMANIA

Denominación oficial
Indice des prix à la consommation de la population (Indice de Precios del Consumo de la Población).

Alcance
El índice se compila mensualmente y abarca todos los hogares del país cuyo jefe sea empleado, jubilado o agricultor.

Base oficial
Octubre de 1990 = 100.

Fuente de la ponderación
La determinación de los coeficientes de ponderación y la selección de los artículos se basaron en los resultados de una encuesta sobre los gastos de los hogares realizada de enero a diciembre de 1990 a 5 900 hogares de empleados, 2 700 de agricultores y 400 de jubilados.

Ponderaciones y composición

Grupos principales	Número de artículos	Ponderación	Número aproximado de cotizaciones de precio
Alimentación	79	40,5	...
Productos no alimenticios	111	40,3	...
Servicios	51	19,2	...
Total	241	100,0	...

Gastos de consumo de los hogares
Se refieren a las adquisiciones de artículos y servicios del sector público, cooperativo, privado o mixto. No se tuvieron en cuenta el consumo propio de los bienes y servicios producidos o prestados por los hogares, el valor locativo de la vivienda propia, los impuestos, tasas y multas, los juegos de azar, los intereses de los créditos, las contribuciones a la seguridad social, los préstamos y remesas de fondos.

Método de recolección de los datos
Los investigadores registran los precios en los puntos de venta al por menor de los mercados y las ferias, las cooperativas y los establecimientos de prestación de servicios. Los precios de los alimentos se registran en los mercados los días 5, 15 y 25 de cada mes. El alquiler, los servicios de electricidad, gas, agua, calefacción, correos y telecomunicaciones, y los abonos del transporte son tarifas oficiales y se obtienen una vez por mes. Se toman en consideración las rebajas, las cotizaciones del mercado libre de artículos que también tienen precio oficial, así como los precios de importación de mercancías con un importante volumen de ventas.

Vivienda
Los datos sobre los alquileres de las viviendas estatales se obtienen todos los meses. En el índice no se toman en consideración las viviendas ocupadas por sus propietarios.

Especificación de las variedades
Las especificaciones son detalladas y describen las características técnicas, etc.

Sustitución, cambio de calidad, etc.
En casos de cambio de calidad y desaparición o aparición de artículos del mercado se estima un precio de base teniendo en cuenta la evolución de los precios de los artículos del mismo subgrupo.

Artículos estacionales
Para los precios de artículos estacionales tales como las frutas y legumbres frescas se utilizan canastas mensuales cuyos coeficientes de ponderación de conjunto permanecen invariables.

Cálculo
El índice se calcula según la fórmula de Laspeyres como un promedio aritmético ponderado de base fija, cuyos coeficientes de ponderación corresponden al período de base.

Los índices de artículo se obtienen como relaciones de precio entre el período en curso y el período de base. Los promedios de precio son medias aritméticas simples de todos los precios registrados.

Organización y publicación
Commission nationale de statistique, Division des statistiques des prix et tarifs: "Bulletin statistique des prix" (Bucarest).

idem: "La méthodologie de construction de l'indice des prix à la consommation de la population".

RWANDA (KIGALI)

Denominación oficial
Indice des prix à la consommation (Indice de Precios del Consumo).

Alcance
El índice se compila mensualmente y abarca hogares de asalariados de los sectores público, parapúblico y privado de la circunscripción urbana de Kigali.

Base oficial
Marzo - junio de 1982 = 100.

Fuente de la ponderación
La determinación de los coeficientes de ponderación y la selección de los artículos se basaron en los resultados de una encuesta sobre los gastos de los hogares realizada de marzo a junio de 1982 a asalariados de los sectores público, parapúblico y privado de la circunscripción urbana de Kigali, cuyos ingresos mensuales se situaban entre 5 000 y 100 000 francos en el momento de la encuesta.

Gastos de consumo de los hogares
Comprenden: gastos monetarios de consumo, regalos dados en especie, bienes intercambiados por trueque, autoconsumo, es decir la producción casera para el consumo del propio hogar. Este consumo se le ha tenido en cuenta en forma indirecta pues no se le pudo aislar al final de la encuesta, cuya finalidad no era determinar el consumo final de los hogares sino los coeficientes de ponderación de los diversos productos del índice. Los ingresos en especie se han tomado en cuenta al contabilizar el ingreso total de los hogares investigados y se relacionan principalmente con el alojamiento gratuito, los servicios de agua y electricidad gratuitos y el transporte gratuito.

En la encuesta no se tomaron en consideración el alojamiento en casa propia, los bienes usados entregados a cuenta y las arras para la compra de bienes nuevos. Tampoco los impuestos a los ingresos y otras cargas fiscales directas, ni las cotizaciones a cajas de pensión y sistemas de seguridad social, pese a constituir desembolsos de los hogares, por no tratarse de compras de consumo y ser difícil o imposible determinar sus precios. Los pagos de seguros de vida se han excluido del índice para evitar cuentas dobles, faltando la determinación del monto de la parte que corresponde al servicio de los seguros. Con respecto a la asistencia médica, no figuran en el índice mensual de los precios del consumo los gastos de hospitalización por falta de datos actuales sobre los precios correspondientes. Los costos de las consultas médicas en los servicios públicos y privados, así como los precios de los medicamentos más corrientes, sólo se consideraron en la encuesta. El envío de fondos, donaciones y desembolsos similares no se tomaron en consideración por no ser precios. La adquisición de bienes durables, las compras a crédito y las de bienes de ocasión se tomaron en cuenta entre los gastos de consumo de los hogares encuestados.

Ponderaciones y composición

Grupos principales	Número de artículos	Ponderación aproximada	Número de cotizaciones de precio
Totalidad de los productos:			
Alimentación	105	34,90	...
Bebidas y tabaco	22	9,30	...
Vestido y calzado	71	11,35	...
Gastos del hogar	36	8,40	...
Asistencia médica	37	1,70	...
Otra asistencia y aseo	55	3,55	...
Vivienda	59	13,20	...
Transportes	20	10,30	...
Distracción y recreaciones	12	1,20	...
Varios	24	6,10	...
Total	441	100,00	...

Método de recolección de los datos
Los investigadores registran los precios dos veces por mes en todos los mercados y puntos de venta al por menor más representativos de la circunscripción urbana de Kigali. Los precios seleccionados para el cómputo del índice son los efectivamente pagados por los consumidores. Las tarifas de la electricidad, agua y gas, consultas médicas, enseñanza, transportes y comunicaciones las fija el Gobierno y se registran toda vez que se modifican.

Vivienda
Todos los meses se obtienen las cotizaciones del alquiler de cuatro viviendas alquiladas de dos habitaciones, dos de ellas con luz eléctrica y dos sin electricidad. No se toman en consideración las viviendas ocupadas por sus propietarios.

Especificación de las variedades
Las especificaciones se refieren a los artículos importados, mixtos o locales. Por productos mixtos se entiende los terminados en el país pero con componentes extranjeros (materias primas importadas).

Sustitución, cambio de calidad, etc.
El cambio repentino de la calidad de un producto puede equipararse a la aparición de un producto nuevo y si desplaza a otro anterior se incluye el nuevo producto en la lista de artículos cuyos precios se deben registrar, calculándose un precio de base hipotético en función del porcentaje de aumento del producto anterior.

Artículos estacionales
Fuera de temporada, mientras no pueden conseguirse en el mercado, los precios de los artículos estacionales se mantienen durante tres meses como máximo.

Cálculo
El índice se calcula según la fórmula de Laspeyres como un promedio aritmético ponderado de base fija, cuyos coeficientes de ponderación corresponden al período de base.

Organización y publicación
Banque Nationale du Rwanda: "Bulletin de la Banque Nationale du Rwanda" (Kigali).

idem: "Rapport annuel sur l'évolution économique et monétaire du Rwanda".

SAMOA

Denominación oficial
Consumer Price Index (Indice de precios del consumo).

Alcance
La compilación del índice es mensual y abarca hogares de nacionales de Samoa, en todo el país.

Base oficial
1980 = 100.

Fuente de la ponderación
La selección de los artículos y la determinación de los coeficientes de ponderación se basaron en los resultados de una encuesta sobre los gastos de los hogares efectuada entre agosto de 1976 y julio de 1977. La encuesta abarcó 1 560 hogares de todo el país. No se han efectuado ajustes para tomar en cuenta los cambios de precio entre el período de la encuesta y 1980.

Ponderaciones y composición

Grupos principales	Número de artículos	Ponderación	Número aproximado de cotizaciones de precio
Alimentación	55	588	1 016
Vestido y calzado	16	42	168
Vivienda:			
Materiales de construcción	7	14	67
Utensilios de cocina	7	26	96
Ropa blanca	7	11	48
Combustible y luz	5	50	24
Otros	7	19	48
Transportes y comunicaciones	9	90	37
Varios	24	160	96
Total	137	1 000	1 600

Gastos de consumo de los hogares
A los fines del índice, los gastos del consumo comprenden todos los bienes y servicios adquiridos para el consumo por la población de referencia. Se excluyen los artículos y servicios recibidos como ingresos en especie para el consumo del hogar.

Método de recolección de los datos
La recolección de precios está a cargo de funcionarios del Departamento de Estadísticas, que los recaban en comercios minoristas seleccionados, mercados y establecimientos de servicios. Para el área urbana de Apia se eligieron diez tiendas principales, siete para el resto de Upopu, seis para Satelologa y siete para el resto de Savaii. Los movimientos de los precios en las regiones rurales son similares a los de las regiones urbanas y por tal motivo la recolección de precios se limita actualmente a la región urbana. La mayoría de los precios se recogen mensualmente, a mediados de mes. Para las frutas y las verduras frescas, nueces y pescado frescos, los precios se recogen todas las semanas, los días viernes, en el área urbana de Apia. Los precios utilizados para el cálculo del índice son los que se pagan al por menor en el momento. No se toman en cuenta las rebajas y los descuentos.

Vivienda
El alquiler se excluye del índice. La sección del índice destinada a la vivienda comprende los materiales de construcción y muebles, utensilios de cocina, ropa de casa, combustible y luz y otros artículos.

Especificación de las variedades
Las especificaciones de los artículos cuyos precios se registran se dan con detalles que comprenden su marca, factura, calidad y tamaño.

Sustitución, cambio de calidad, etc.
Cuando un producto desaparece del mercado se lo sustituye por otro similar. Los cambios de calidad se ajustan lo más posible a la calidad requerida del original.

Artículos estacionales
En el caso de artículos tales como las frutas y las verduras frescas que no pueden encontrarse en los mercados fuera de temporada, para el cálculo del índice se utilizan los últimos precios que se han obtenido, hasta que se puedan obtener los nuevos.

Cálculo
El índice se calcula conforme a la fórmula de Laspeyres como un promedio aritmético ponderado de base fija, cuyos coeficientes de ponderación corresponden al de período agosto de 1976 a julio de 1977.

EL relativo de precio para cada artículo se calcula dividiendo el precios medio del período en curso por el precio medio del período de base. Los precios medios son la media aritmética simple de todos los precios registrados.

Informaciones complementarias
No disponible.

Organización y publicación
Department of Statistics: "Quarterly Statistical Bulletin" (Apia).
idem: "The Annual Abstracts".
idem: "Monthly C.P.I. Release".
idem: "Report on the revised Consumer Price Index for Western Samoa, 1980 = 100".

SAMOA AMERICANA (PAGO-PAGO)

Denominación oficial
Retail Price Index (Indice de precios al por menor).

Alcance
No disponible.

Base oficial
Enero-marzo de 1974 = 100.

Fuente de la ponderación
Los coeficientes de ponderación utilizados para el cálculo del índice se basaron en los resultados de estadísticas sobre las importaciones.

Ponderaciones y composición
No disponible.

Gastos de consumo de los hogares
No disponible.

Método de recolección de los datos
Los precios son recogidos por investigadores trimestralmente en siete supermercados.

Vivienda
No disponible.

Especificación de las variedades
No disponible.

Sustitución, cambio de calidad, etc.
No disponible.

Artículos estacionales
Se tienen en cuenta las fluctuaciones estacionales de los precios de ciertos artículos, manteniendo, fuera de temporada, el último precio de la temporada.

Cálculo
El índice se calcula conforme a la fórmula de Laspeyres como un promedio aritmético ponderado de base fija, cuyos coeficientes de ponderación corresponden al período de base.

Informaciones complementarias
Actualmente se calcula una nueva serie (base octubre - diciembre de 1982 = 100), pero en el momento de publicar el presente volumen la OIT no disponía de informaciones metodológicas sobre esta serie.

Organización y publicación
El cálculo del índice lo efectúa el Economic and Planning Office (Fagotogo).

SAN MARINO

Denominación oficial
Consumer Price Index (Indice de Precios del Consumo).

Alcance
El índice se compila mensualmente y abarca todos los hogares de obreros y empleados de San Marino.

Base oficial
1985 = 100.

Fuente de la ponderación
La determinación de los coeficientes de ponderación y la selección de los artículos se basaron en las características del consumo y los datos de la contabilidad nacional italianas de 1984, ajustados a los hogares de San Marino. Para el registro de precios se seleccionaron los artículos consumidos por la mayoría de los hogares.

Ponderaciones y composición

Grupos principales	Número de artículos	Ponderación	Número aproximado de cotizaciones de precio
Alimentación y tabaco	86	30,92	...
Vestido y calzado	38	8,67	...
Alquiler, mantenimiento y reparaciones	3	4,97	...
Combustible y luz	5	4,72	...
Otros bienes y servicios	150	50,72	...
Total	282	100,00	...

Gastos de consumo de los hogares
A los efectos del índice no comprenden el impuesto a la renta, inversiones y ahorros, consumo de la producción propia ni el valor locativo de la vivienda propia.

Método de recolección de los datos
Los precios se registran el 15 de cada mes mediante cuestionarios enviado por correo a 50 minoristas y establecimientos de servicios de todo el país, distribuidos según el número de habitantes. También se registran las tarifas oficiales de ciertos artículos y servicios. Los precios utilizados para el cómputo del índice son los que normalmente pagan los consumidores. Los precios de liquidación, rebajas, alquileres con opción de compra, adquisiciones a crédito y de bienes de segunda mano no se toman en cuenta en el índice.

Vivienda
Las cotizaciones de alquiler se obtienen dos veces por año, para 47 viviendas privadas alquiladas.

Especificación de las variedades
Se dan especificaciones detalladas para cada artículo de la canasta. Cada especificación da una descripción completa del artículo, su marca, nombre o marca registrada, clase de envasado, cantidad o unidad, etc.

Sustitución, cambio de calidad, etc.
Cuando un artículo desaparece del mercado se le sustituye por otro similar y se aplica el método de enlace.

Artículos estacionales
Las frutas y las legumbres frescas se consideran artículos estacionales, para los cuales se estructura una canasta en cada uno de los 12 meses del año.

Cálculo
El índice se calcula según la fórmula de Laspeyres como un promedio aritmético ponderado de base fija, cuyos coeficientes de ponderación corresponden a 1984. Los relativos de precio para cada artículo se obtienen dividiendo el promedio de los precios del período en curso por el promedio de los precios del período precedente.

Informaciones complementarias
Se publican índices detallados de subgrupo.

Organización y publicación
Centro Elaborazione dati e statistica: "Bolletino di statistica" (San Marino).

SAN VICENTE Y LAS GRANADINAS (ST. VINCENT)

Denominación oficial
Index of Retail Prices (Indice de precios al por menor).

Alcance
El índice se compila mensualmente y abarca toda la población de San Vicente.

Base oficial
Enero de 1981 = 100.

Fuente de la ponderación
La selección de los artículos y la determinación de los coeficientes de ponderación se basaron en los resultados de una encuesta sobre los gastos de los hogares efectuada durante seis meses a partir de noviembre de 1975 en la zona urbana y las areas rurales de San Vicente. La encuesta abarca 164 hogares de todos los grupos de ingresos. El índice se refiere a un tamaño medio de hogares de 5.84 personas.

Ponderaciones y composición

Grupos principales	Número de artículos	Ponderación	Número aproximado de cotizaciones de precio
Alimentación	88	597,9	...
Otros grupos:	130	402,1	...
Vestido y calzado	...	...	...
Vivienda, combustible y luz	...	...	...
Mobiliario y articulos del hogar	...	...	...
Asistencia médica	...	...	...
Transportes y comunicaciones	...	...	...
Educación y distracciones	...	...	...
Varios	...	...	...
Total	218	1 000,0	...

Gastos de consumo de los hogares
No disponible.

Método de recolección de los datos
Los precios se recogen el segundo martes de cada mes, por investigadores en mercados, supermercados, puntos de venta al por menor y establecimientos de servicios.

Vivienda
El alquiler comprende una casa desamueblada con tres dormitorios en la capital y una casa desamueblada con tres dormitorios en el area rural. No se incluye en el índice las viviendas ocupadas por sus propietarios.

Especificación de las variedades
No disponible.

Sustitución, cambio de calidad, etc.
No disponible.

Articulos estacionales
No disponible.

Cálculo
El índice se calcula conforme a la fórmula de Laspeyres como un promedio aritmético ponderado de base fija cuyos coeficientes de ponderación corresponden a 1975-76.

El índice para un artículo es obtenido utilizando las relaciones de precios del período en curso y del período de base.

Organización y publicación
Central Planning Division, Statistical Office: "Annual Digest of Statistics" (Kingstown).
idem: "Retail Price Bulletin".

SANTA ELENA

Denominación oficial
Retail Price Index (Indice de precios al por menor).

Alcance
El índice se compila trimestralmente y abarca todos los hogares de la isla.

Base oficial
Noviembre de 1987 = 100.

Fuente de la ponderación
La determinación de los coeficientes de ponderación y la selección de los artículos se basaron en los resultados de una encuesta sobre los gastos de los hogares realizada en dos etapas, una en octubre-noviembre de 1987, con una muestra de 84 hogares, y otra en abril-mayo de 1988, con una muestra de 94 hogares. En la época de la encuesta el promedio mensual del gasto era de 74 libras por hogar. Los resultados se compararon con los datos de las estadísticas sobre las importaciones para corregir los coeficientes de ponderación.

Gastos de consumo de los hogares
Comprenden las tasas de los permisos de conducir y seguros de coches, así como las amortizaciones de préstamos para la vivienda e impuestos a los terrenos, pero no las primas de los seguros de vida.

Ponderaciones y composición

Grupos principales	Número de artículos	Ponderación	Número aproximado de cotizaciones de precio
Alimentación	75	44,6	75
Bebidas alcohólicas y tabaco	7	10,1	7
Vivienda (incl. alquiler y cargas)	3	5,6	3
Combustible y luz	5	5,1	5
Vestido y calzado	15	5,8	15
Artículos del hogar	13	7,3	13
Transporte	10	11,6	10
Artículos varios	15	7,9	15
Servicios	6	2,0	6
Total	149	100,0	149

Método de recolección de los datos
Dos funcionarios del Servicio de Economía y Estadísticas registran los precios de siete puntos de venta de Jamestown en los meses de febrero, mayo, agosto y noviembre, durante dos días hábiles próximos al 20.

Para su aprovisionamiento Santa Helena depende del barco que llega a la isla aproximadamente cada seis semanas. Si la fecha para la recolección de precios se sitúa poco antes (en la semana) de la llegada del barco, se la posterga hasta que los artículos se ofrezcan en el mercado. Los precios controlados como los del agua, la electricidad, los impuestos a la propiedad y ciertos materiales de construcción se preguntan por teléfono a las oficinas públicas pertinentes. Se toman en consideración las rebajas y los precios de liquidación.

Vivienda
Cada tres meses se obtienen las cotizaciones de los alquileres semanales de las viviendas con tres habitaciones de propiedad pública. Las viviendas ocupadas por sus propietarios no se tratan en forma explícita.

Especificación de las variedades
Las especificaciones comprenden la clase o modelo, el tamaño, la marca y el lugar de adquisición. Como las hojas de la recolección de precios abarcan un período de un año, se pueden descubrir con facilidad las desviaciones netas.

Sustitución, cambio de calidad, etc.
Cuando ya no se ofrece un artículo en el mercado se le sustituye por otro similar.

Artículos estacionales
No se hacen ajustes a los precios del mercado.

Cálculo
El índice se calcula según la fórmula de Laspeyres como un promedio aritmético ponderado de base fija, cuyos coeficientes de ponderación corresponden al período de base.

Informaciones complementarias
Se publican índices de subgrupo para: alimentación, bebidas alcohólicas y tabaco, vivienda, combustible y luz, vestido, artículos del hogar, transporte, artículos varios y servicios. También se compila, pero no se publica, un índice de hogares de bajos ingresos.

Organización y publicación
Economic and Statistics Unit (Servicio de Economía y Estadísticas): "Quarterly Statistical Review" (Jamestown).
idem: "Statistical News".

SANTA LUCIA

Denominación oficial
Consumer Price Index (Indice de Precios del Consumo).

Alcance
El índice se compila mensualmente y abarca hogares de las zonas urbanas, suburbanas y rurales.

Base oficial
Abril de 1984 = 100.

Fuente de la ponderación
La determinación de los coeficientes de ponderación y la selección de los artículos se basaron en los resultados de una encuesta sobre los gastos de los hogares realizada de septiembre a noviembre de 1982 en la zona administrativa de la capital (Castries), a una muestra de 170 hogares urbanos, 157 suburbanos y 154 rurales. No se ajustaron los coeficientes de ponderación para tomar en cuenta las modificaciones de precio ocurridas entre la encuesta y el período de base.

Ponderaciones y composición

Grupos principales	Número de artículos	Ponderación	Número aproximado de cotizaciones de precio
Alimentación	77	467,51	...
Bebidas y tabaco	5	28,17	...
Vestido y calzado	16	64,97	...
Vivienda	7	135,34	...
Combustible y luz	4	44,95	...
Muebles y funcionamiento del hogar	11	57,71	...
Asistencia médica	6	22,78	...
Transporte y comunicaciones	10	63,48	...
Recreación	6	32,36	...
Varios	26	82,73	...
Total	168	1 000,00	

Gastos de consumo de los hogares
El sistema de clasificación se ajusta a la clasificación del SNA de los gastos de consumo final de los hogares.

Método de recolección de los datos
Los investigadores registran los precios todos los segundos jueves de cada mes en supermercados, puntos de venta al por menor y establecimientos de servicios. Las tarifas de electricidad se obtienen mediante cuestionarios enviados por correo; las de teléfono y agua por entrevistas telefónicas y los demás servicios mediante visitas personales. Los funcionarios de la Oficina Estadística obtienen en todos los puntos de venta al por menor los precios, marcas, calidad, unidades, etc. de los artículos. Los precios de los que forman la canasta se registraron durante un período de cuatro meses y a partir de los datos así recopilados se seleccionaron los puntos de venta.

Vivienda
Las cotizaciones de alquiler de las viviendas se registran cada seis meses. En el índice no se toman en cuenta las ocupadas por sus propietarios.

Especificación de las variedades
Se especifica en forma detallada la unidad, marca, calidad, etc. de cada uno de los artículos.

Sustitución, cambio de calidad, etc.
Cuando un artículo desaparece del mercado se selecciona otro, manteniéndose la misma ponderación pero con ajuste del precio de base.

Artículos estacionales
No se les incluye en el índice.

Cálculo
El índice se calcula según la fórmula de Laspeyres como un promedio aritmético ponderado de base fija, cuyos coeficientes de ponderación corresponden al período de septiembre a noviembre de 1982.

Informaciones complementarias
El cálculo de índice está a cargo del "Government Statistical Department" (Castries).

Organización y publicación
Government Printer: "The St. Lucia Gazette" (Castries).

SENEGAL (DAKAR)

Denominación oficial
Indice des prix à la consommation (Indice de precios del consumo).

Alcance
El índice se calcula mensualmente y abarca los hogares senegaleses en Dakar con un ingreso mensual inferior a 100 000 francos CFA en 1960-61.

Base oficial
1967 = 100.

Fuente de la ponderación
La selección de los artículos y la determinación de los coeficientes de ponderación se basaron en los resultados de una encuesta sobre los gastos de los hogares efectuada en Dakar

en 1960-61 en los hogares senegaleses con un ingreso mensual inferior a 100 000 francos CFA en el momento de la encuesta.

Ponderaciones y composición

Grupos principales	Número de artículos	Ponderación aproximado	Número de cotizaciones de precio
Alimentación	71	56,0	...
Vestido y calzado	22	11,9	...
Vivienda:			
Alquiler y reparaciones	5	8,7	...
Combustible, luz y agua	5	5,8	...
Accesorios para el hogar	7	1,7	...
Aseo personal, asistencia médica y productos de limpieza	14	4,0	...
Transportes	9	5,4	...
Educación, distracciones, tabaco, servicio doméstico, etc.	18	6,5	...
Total	151	100,0	...

Gastos de consumo de los hogares
No disponible.

Método de recolección de los datos
Los precios de los artículos alimenticios son recogidos cada semana por investigadores en puntos de venta al por menor y 6 mercados en Dakar. Los precios de los otros artículos se recogen durante la segunda quincena de cada mes. Los datos referentes a los servicios se obtienen de las tarifas oficiales. No se toman en cuenta los precios de liquidación.

Vivienda
Los datos referentes a los gastos de alquiler provienen de una importante sociedad inmobiliaria para viviendas recientes de dos habitaciones.

Especificación de las variedades
Las especificaciones describen la variedad, calidad, fabricación, marca, unidad, etc.

Sustitución, cambio de calidad, etc.
Cuando desaparece un artículo del mercado, se mantiene el último precio registrado durante un plazo de tres meses como máximo. Pasado ese lapso se le reemplaza por un artículo similar, estimando la variación de su precio en relación con las variaciones de los precios de los demás artículos del mismo subgrupo.

Artículos estacionales
Se tienen en cuenta las fluctuaciones estacionales de los precios de ciertos artículos manteniendo, fuera de temporada, los últimos precios de la temporada precedente.

Cálculo
El índice se calcula conforme a la fórmula de Laspeyres como un promedio aritmético ponderado de base fija, cuyos coeficientes de ponderación corresponden al período de 1960-61.

Informaciones complementarias
No disponible.

Organización y publicación
Ministère de l'Économie, des Finances et du Plan, Direction de la prévision et de la statistique: "Note mensuelle sur les indices des prix de détail" (Dakar).

SEYCHELLES

Denominación oficial
Retail Price Index (Indice de precios al por menor).

Alcance
El índice se calcula mensualmente y se refiere a todo el país y a todos los grupos de ingresos.

Base oficial
Marzo de 1986 = 100.

Fuente de la ponderación
La selección de los artículos y la determinación de los coeficientes de ponderación se basaron en los resultados de una encuesta sobre los gastos de los hogares efectuada entre el 8 de agosto de 1983 y el 5 de agosto de 1984 en las islas de Mahe, Praslin y La Digue, a una muestra de 969 hogares de todos los grupos de ingresos. Los gastos de todos los miembros de los hogares se registraron durante dos semanas y se obtuvieron datos sobre casi todas las adquisiciones importantes de los tres meses anteriores. No se introdujeron reajustes en los coeficientes de ponderación para tener en consideración los cambios de precio entre el período de la encuesta y 1986.

Ponderaciones y composición

Grupos principales	Número de artículos	Ponderación aproximado	Número de cotizaciones de precio
Pescado fresco	1	5,16	...
Otros artículos alimenticios	90	28,90	...
Bebidas alcohólicas y tabaco	9	18,74	...
Vestido y calzado	15	8,57	...
Alquiler, costo de construcción	3	11,20	...
Combustible, luz y agua	7	7,44	...
Artículos para el hogar	14	5,86	...
Aseo personal	16	1,63	...
Transportes y comunicaciones	14	7,63	...
Otros servicios y distracciones	16	4,87	...
Total	185	100,00	...

Gastos de consumo de los hogares
A los fines del índice, los gastos del consumo comprenden todos los bienes y servicios adquiridos para el consumo por la población de referencia. Comprenden los seguros de automóvil, los pagos de licencia y los alquileres imputados de las viviendas ocupadas por sus propietarios. Se excluyen los ahorros, las inversiones y los impuestos a los ingresos y otras cargas fiscales directas.

Método de recolección de los datos
Los precios de la mayor parte de los artículos se recogen mensualmente por investigadores en 22 puntos de venta y mercados en Mahe y Praslin. Los precios de los servicios provienen de sus abastecedores. Los precios corresponden a la semana que comprende el día 15 del mes. Los precios del pescado se recogen por medio de compras directas cinco veces por semana. Los precios de la fruta y de la verdura se recogen una vez por semana.

Los precios utilizados para el cálculo del índice son los que pagan los consumidores. También se utilizan para el cálculo del índice los precios oficiales fijados por el Gobierno de Seychelles para artículos como la fruta y la verdura.

Vivienda
Los datos relativos al alquiler se recogen cada tres meses por rotación, a una muestra de 180 hogares, que comprenden un 20 por ciento de viviendas del Estado y 80 por ciento de viviendas privadas.

Especificación de las variedades
Las especificaciones de los artículos cuyos precios se han de registrar se establecen en términos de calidad, empaque, elaboración, marca y unidad.

Sustitución, cambio de calidad, etc.
Si un producto deja de poder conseguirse, se lo sustituye por otro similar al original, y se emplea para el cálculo el método de enlace.

Artículos estacionales
El único artículo estacional es el pescado y no se efectúa ninguna clase de ajustes.

Cálculo
El índice se calcula conforme a la fórmula de Laspeyres como un promedio aritmético ponderado de base fija cuyos coeficientes de ponderación corresponden al período transcurrido entre el 8 de agosto de 1983 y el 5 de agosto de 1984.

Los relativos de precio se calculan en primer lugar por artículo y punto de venta, calculándose en segundo lugar el promedio.

Organización y publicación
Ministry of Finance, Statistics Division: "Monthly Statistical Bulletin-Retail Price Index" (Victoria).

SIERRA LEONA (FREETOWN)

Denominación oficial
Consumer Price Index (Indice de precios del consumo).

Alcance
El índice se compila trimestralmente y abarca las familias que

viven en Freetown, incluido el Gran Freetown, cuyo gasto total medio no superaba los 100 leones mensuales en 1976 y 1977.

Base oficial
1978 = 100.

Fuente de la ponderación
La selección de los artículos y la determinación de los coeficientes de ponderación se basaron en los resultados de una encuesta efectuada entre abril de 1976 y julio de 1977 que abarcó a los hogares privados de Freetown, comprendido la Gran Freetown, cuyos gastos promedio no excedían 100 leones por mes en 1976-77. Las ponderaciones se ajustaron a la evolución de los precios ocurrida entre el período de la encuesta y 1978.

Ponderaciones y composición

Grupos principales	Número de artículos	Ponderación	Número aproximado de cotizaciones de precio
Alimentación	62	63,1	...
Tabaco y nuez de cola	5	3,8	...
Vivienda:			
Alquiler	1	9,2	...
Tasas municipales y reparaciones	4	0,3	...
Combustible y luz	6	6,9	...
Moblaje y artículos para el hogar	18	1,8	...
Vestido y calzado	31	5,4	...
Bienes y servicios varios:			
Aseo personal	10	1,4	...
Asistencia médica	11	1,6	...
Productos de limpieza	6	1,9	...
Distracciones	4	0,2	...
Lectura y educación	5	0,6	...
Transportes y comunicaciones	7	3,5	...
Otros gastos	2	0,3	...
Total	172	100,0	

Gastos de consumo de los hogares
No disponible.

Método de recolección de los datos
Los precios de la mayoría de los artículos son recogidos por investigadores en puntos de venta al por menor; los precios de los artículos alimenticios se recogen en los tres mayores mercados públicos. La recolección puede ser semanal, mensual o trimestral, dependiendo su frecuencia de la variabilidad de los precios de cada uno de los artículos. Los precios de los artículos alimenticios se registran en su mayor parte semanalmente.

Vivienda
Los datos relativos al alquiler se obtienen trimestralmente en 91 viviendas; las contribuciones por servicios municipales se obtienen anualmente.

Especificación de las variedades
Los artículos cuyos precios se han de registrar se especifican en detalle, considerando su popularidad. Las especificaciones establecen la marca, factura, calidad y tamaño.

Sustitución, cambio de calidad, etc.
Cuando ya no es posible encontrar un artículo se le sustituye por otro similar y se emplea el método de enlace.

Artículos estacionales
Para las frutas y las verduras frescas, se presume que sus precios fuera de temporada siguen el movimiento de precios de los demás artículos incluidos en el mismo subgrupo.

Cálculo
El índice se calcula conforme a la fórmula de Laspeyres como un promedio aritmético ponderado de base fija, cuyos coeficientes de ponderación corresponden al período de base.

El índice para un artículo es obtenido utilizando las relaciones de precios del período actual y del período precedente.

Organización y publicación
Central Statistics Office: "Statistical Bulletin" (Freetown).

idem: "Technical Report on Revision of Consumer Price Index for Freetown with base 1978 = 100" (agosto de 1984).

Government Printing Department: "The Sierra Leone Gazette" (Freetown).

SINGAPUR

Denominación oficial
Consumer Price Index (Indice de precios del consumo).

Alcance
El índice se compila mensualmente y abarca hogares cuyos gastos mensuales oscilaban entre 500 y 4 999 dólares de Singapur (S$) en el período 1987-88.

Base oficial
Septiembre de 1987 - agosto de 1988 = 100.

Fuente de la ponderación
La determinación de los coeficientes de ponderación y la selección de los artículos se basaron en los resultados de una encuesta sobre los gastos de los hogares realizada entre septiembre de 1987 y agosto de 1988.

La estructura del consumo de los hogares con un gasto mensual situado entre 500 y 4 999 S$ determinó las características de la ponderación. Este grupo de hogares constituyó más del 90 por ciento del total encuestado.

La muestra, que abarcó todo el país, era representativa de la totalidad de los hogares con un mínimo de dos personas de la isla principal de Singapur. La encuesta no abarcó los hogares de una sola persona ni los de residentes extranjeros. Las entrevistas personales de la encuesta sobre los gastos de los hogares se desarrollaron durante 12 meses, de septiembre de 1987 a agosto de 1988. El primer grupo de hogares se encuestó en el primer mes del período de referencia, septiembre de 1987, y el último en agosto de 1988. Los análisis y gráficos definitivos se basaron en los datos obtenidos de 5 742 hogares.

Los artículos se seleccionaron en función de su importancia relativa, de que el movimiento de sus precios fuera característico de artículos similares o afines y de la facilidad para encontrarlos a efectos del registro periódico de sus precios. Los artículos cuyos precios no se registran por ser relativamente insignificantes o no tener un número suficiente de unidades o especificaciones estandarizadas, están sin embargo representados en forma indirecta por los artículos similares o afines seleccionados, a quienes se atribuye la parte que los primeros representan en el total del consumo.

Ponderaciones y composición

Grupos principales	Número de artículos	Ponderación	Número aproximado de cotizaciones de precio
Alimentación	272	3 977	8 424
Vestido y calzado	65	570	382
Vivienda:	71	1 717	1 011
Alquilada	4	110	224
Propia	7	603	382
Reparaciones y mantenimiento	4	226	34
Combustible y luz	8	456	42
Bienes domésticos durables	48	322	329
Transporte y comunicaciones	38	1 450	255
Varios:	147	2 286	1 904
Educación	34	500	322
Salud	22	249	403
Cultura y recreación	15	295	110
Bebidas alcohólicas y tabaco	12	282	175
Otros bienes y servicios	64	960	894
Total	593	10 000	11 976

Gastos de consumo de los hogares
La ponderación se refiere a los pagos efectuados por los hogares durante el mes de la encuesta para obtener bienes y servicios. Los precios de los artículos comprados a crédito son los del día de su adquisición; los de artículos consumidos por los hogares de su propia tienda o granja, el valor de las cantidades de esos consumos, estimado al precio de mercado del momento. Para los gastos más importantes, pero menos frecuentes, como la compra de bienes durables, los viajes de vacaciones y las reparaciones o renovaciones inmobiliarias mayores, se pide a los interesados, mediante recordatorio, que anoten el total de esos gastos durante 12 meses, el último de los cuales coincide con el de la encuesta, registrándose como gasto de ese mes la duocécima parte de dicho valor. Con respecto a la entrega de objetos usados o pagos parciales para comprar otros nuevos, se toma en cuenta el pago neto, es decir la diferencia entre lo pagado por el nuevo objeto y el valor del

entregado. De la misma forma se procede con respecto a las compras de artículos de segunda mano. Se excluyen las contribuciones al "Central Provident Fund" (Fondo Central de Previsión Social) y otros gastos en bienes que no son de consumo como impuestos a los ingresos, amortización de préstamos, inmuebles, existencias y acciones. Tampoco no incluyen los regalos. Se consideran como gastos de consumo las tasas para obtener permisos, los seguros de la casa y la asistencia médica, registrándose los últimos pagos efectuados por tales conceptos.

Método de recolección de los datos
La frecuencia del registro de las cotizaciones varía según las características de las fluctuaciones de precio de los artículos. Para los que cambian con frecuencia, como los alimentos perecederos, los precios se registran tres veces por semana en los puestos del mercado; los precios de otras provisiones que no varían con tanta frecuencia, una vez por semana. Los que presentan aún mayor estabilidad de precios, como vestidos, textiles, peluquería, sastrería, muebles y adornos, se actualizan una vez por mes. Para artículos tales como el "Mass Rapid Transit" (Empresa de transporte público rápido), autobuses y taxis, cines, auxilios, mantenimiento y conservación de pisos, asistencia médica oficial y matrículas escolares, las modificaciones de sus tarifas se incorporan al índice cuando tienen lugar.

Los precios de los bienes perecederos se registran semanalmente los martes, jueves y viernes, los de otras provisiones los miércoles. Los precios que se registran una vez por mes suelen referirse al día 15.

Las informaciones sobre los lugares donde los consumidores prefieren comprar artículos tales como provisiones y prendas de vestir se obtuvieron de las respuestas dadas por los entrevistados en la encuesta sobre el consumo de los hogares, que además sirvieron como orientación para seleccionar los puntos de venta. Dichas informaciones se han completado con datos de la encuesta sobre el comercio mayorista y minorista y de la encuesta sobre servicios del Departamento de Estadísticas, que permitieron preparar una lista de los grandes puntos de venta por clase de mercancía. Para la alimentación por lo general se eligen los puntos de venta situados en sitios densamente poblados, en particular los grandes conglomerados de viviendas públicas. Para los artículos no alimentarios, tales como vestimentas y calzados de confección, muebles, equipos y aparatos domésticos, los precios se registran principalmente en los centros comerciales que concentran gran cantidad de minoristas especializados en los artículos respectivos.

En principio los precios de los artículos alimenticios perecederos y otros ultramarinos se obtienen mediante visitas personales a mercados y tiendas, mientras que para los demás artículos se utilizan cuestionarios enviados por correo. Las tarifas de los servicios de electricidad, agua y gas se obtienen directamente del organismo público pertinente. La asistencia médica (tarifas hospitalarias y honorarios médicos) se obtienen mediante cuestionarios enviados por correo a hospitales y clínicas, privadas o públicas. Las matrículas para todos los niveles de la educación se piden directamente al Ministerio de Educación y a instituciones de enseñanza universitaria u otros institutos privados. Los precios relativos al transporte y las comunicaciones (costo de coches, motos, gasolina y otros gastos de la circulación) se obtienen de los respectivos comerciantes al por menor. Las tarifas del transporte por carretera, recorridos de autobuses y metropolitanos las comunica la Empresa de transporte público rápido y el Servicio de autobuses de Singapur; las del transporte aéreo se obtienen de las oficinas de venta de compañías aéreas seleccionadas; las postales y el alquiler de aparatos telefónicos de la compañía "Telecom" de Singapur.

En cada ocasión seis investigadores de campo visitan los puntos de venta seleccionados. Cuatro de ellos concurren a los mercados los martes, jueves y viernes para recabar los precios del pescado, legumbres, carnes, frutas, etc. Los miércoles los dedican a visitar las tiendas de ultramarinos para recabar los precios de productos deshidratados y secos. Otros artículos que requieren visitas personales, como alimentos cocinados, vestidos femeninos, etc., se recaban los lunes. Los descuentos y otras rebajas promocionales no se toman en consideración ni se utilizan para compilar el índice o calcular promedios de precio. Las rebajas se incluyen cuando son reducciones de precio genuinas y generales que, por lo tanto, se vuelven precios predominantes. En cuanto a las compras a crédito o a plazo y los alquileres con opción de compra, cabe recordar que sólo se consideran los precios normales de las transacciones al contado. El número de cotizaciones de precio de un artículo depende de su importancia relativa, la volatilidad de su precio o si está sujeto al control de un organismo central.

Vivienda
Bajo este título sólo se considera el alquiler. Los alquileres de pisos públicos, privados, bungalows, casas adosadas y en terraza, así como las viviendas anexas a locales comerciales se registran trimestralmente en enero, abril, julio y octubre. Las viviendas seleccionadas se dividen en dos grupos, cada uno de los cuales se investiga sólo una vez cada seis meses, es decir que un grupo se investiga en enero y julio y el otro en abril y octubre de cada año. Una frecuencia mayor no es necesaria pues la mayoría de los inquilinos tienen contratos que fijan el alquiler por uno o dos años. Para la recolección de los datos se envían cuestionarios por correo a un número seleccionado de hogares para que los completen, declarando el monto actual del alquiler, el de los seis últimos meses, la duración del contrato firmado con el propietario y detalles sobre los muebles o bienes durables que puedan estar incluidos. En el índice de precios del consumo, los alquileres de las distintas clases de pisos y casas tienen coeficientes de ponderación diferentes. Para viviendas de la misma clase se calcula un índice como promedio de los relativos de precio de los alquileres registrados. Estos índices se ponderan luego para obtener el índice general de alquileres. Para las viviendas ocupadas por sus propietarios se sigue el método del valor locativo equivalente, o sea la evaluación del alquiler que debería pagar el propietario si fuera inquilino, que está a cargo de tasadores públicos. Los alquileres ficticios de una muestra de viviendas ocupadas por sus propietarios se obtienen trimestralmente de la División de Evaluación y Tasación del Departamento de Ingresos Interiores.

Especificación de las variedades
Para garantizar que las variaciones de precio no obedecen a cambios de calidad, se ayuda a los investigadores de campo y a los minoristas proporcionándoles especificaciones detalladas de los artículos, tales como marca, calidad, materiales, tamaño, unidad de medida y país de origen, que permiten distinguir un determinado artículo de los similares de una misma descripción genérica. Estas especificaciones genéricas se obtienen previamente, en los sondeos sobre el terreno. Para los vestidos femeninos, sujetos a la evolución de la moda, los investigadores sobre el terreno, además de las precisiones corrientes, como número del diseño o modelo, clase de tejido, estampado (liso o floreado), tallas y colores disponibles, esbozan también las características que permiten al personal de la oficina elegir los artículos más apropiados para la recolección de precios.

Sustitución, cambio de calidad, etc.
Cuando pueden cuantificarse los cambios de calidad, los precios se ajustan en la medida de lo posible, pero cuando no es posible evaluar el cambio de calidad, se trata de "reemplazar" el viejo artículo por uno nuevo, durante el período en que ambos están aún en oferta.

Para los productos nuevos, se utiliza el procedimiento encadenamiento (enlace). Por lo general la Oficina es informada con antelación por los encuestadores de campo o los entrevistados de la desaparición de una calidad o clase de productos y, antes de que el artículo "viejo" desaparezca totalmente del mercado se obtienen los precios del sustitutivo más similar durante el período común de oferta para permitir el encadenamiento o empalme de las series de precios. Si la desaparición es repentina, se supone que los precios no se han modificado durante el mes y se toman de inmediato medidas para encontrar el sustitutivo más próximo.

Artículos estacionales
Como la mayoría de los artículos seleccionados en la canasta del índice de precios del consumo no son estacionales, sus cotizaciones se pueden obtener generalmente en todo momento. Existen unos pocos artículos estacionales de importancia.

Cálculo
El índice se calcula según la fórmula de Laspeyres como un promedio aritmético ponderado de base fija, cuyos coeficientes de ponderación corresponden al período de base. Para cada marca se calculan promedios de precios, sumando los registrados y dividiendo el resultado por el número total de cotizaciones. Los relativos de precio se calculan dividiendo el precio del mes de referencia por el correspondiente al año de base (promedio de septiembre de 1987 - agosto de 1988). Los precios que faltan reciben un tratamiento diferente, según sea

la razón de su "falta". Si no se puede obtener el precio de una marca determinada en un punto de venta dado, se presume que su precio no ha variado durante el mes. Los precios que faltan por haber cesado la oferta del producto se enlazarán con los precios del sustitutivo más próximo. Si se trata de errores en los datos o de precios dudosos, se pide a los agentes que los vuelvan a confirmar.

Informaciones complementarias
Se publican amplios componentes a niveles de grupo y de subgrupo.

Organización y publicación
Department of Statistics (Departamento de Estadísticas): "Consumer Price Index, Singapore" (Indice de precios del consumo de Singapur); informe mensual del IPC.
idem: "Monthly Digest of Statistics"; publicación mensual, con índices mensuales a nivel de grupo y subgrupo de los últimos 24 meses.
idem: "Yearbook of Statistics"; publicación anual, se publican índices anuales de los últimos 10 años.
idem: "The Consumer Price Index, Singapore, based on Household Expenditure Survey 1987-88".

REPUBLICA ARABE SIRIA (DAMASCO)

Denominación oficial
Retail Price Index (Indice de precios al por menor).

Alcance
El índice se compila mensualmente y abarca hogares privados de Damasco.

Base oficial
1970 = 100

Fuente de la ponderación
La selección de los artículos y la determinación de los coeficientes de ponderación se basaron en los resultados de una encuesta sobre los gastos de los hogares efectuada en 1971-72.

Ponderaciones y composición

Grupos principales	Número de artículos	Ponderación	Número aproximado de cotizaciones de precio
Alimentación y tabaco	74	488,2	...
Combustible y luz	5	45,6	...
Alquiler	1	177,3	...
Moblaje y accesorios para el hogar	8	18,4	...
Productos de limpieza	4	11,8	...
Bienes durables	5	11,4	...
Ropa blanca	4	9,5	...
Vestido y calzado	17	90,6	...
Transportes	6	38,1	...
Aseo personal y asistencia médica	19	78,4	...
Educación y distracciones	7	30,7	...
Total	150	1 000,0	...

Gastos de consumo de los hogares
A los efectos del índice, los gastos de consumo comprenden casi todos los bienes y servicios importantes adquiridos por la población de referencia.

Método de recolección de los datos
Los precios son recogidos por investigadores en puestos de venta al por menor y en establecimientos de servicios. Los precios de las frutas y verduras se recogen semanalmente y los de los demás artículos mensualmente.
Los precios utilizados para calcular el índice son los que se pagan en el momento.

Vivienda
Los datos relativos al alquiler se recogen para viviendas alquiladas, con o sin muebles. No se incluyen las viviendas ocupadas por su propietario.

Especificación de las variedades
Las especificaciones de los artículos que se han de justipreciar se brindan en términos de calidad, factura, marca, unidad, etc.

Sustitución, cambio de calidad, etc.
No se efectúan sustituciones y si algún artículo desaparece del mercado tanto su precio como su ponderación se omiten en el índice.

Artículos estacionales
Los precios de los artículos estacionales se fijan en el período en que se consiguen; fuera de temporada se omiten del índice.

Cálculo
El índice se calcula según la fórmula de Laspeyres, como un promedio aritmético ponderado de base fija, cuyos coeficientes de ponderación corresponden al período de 1971-72.

Informaciones complementarias
Se publican promedios anuales por Aleppo y Damasco para todos los grupos y subgrupos.

Organización y publicación
Office of the Prime Minister, Central Bureau of Statistics: "Statistical Abstract" (Damasco).

SRI LANKA (COLOMBO)

Denominación oficial
Consumer Price Index (Indice de precios del consumo).

Alcance
El índice se compila mensualmente y abarca familias de trabajadores manuales de Colombo.

Base oficial
1952 = 100.

Fuente de la ponderación
La selección de los artículos y la determinación de los coeficientes de ponderación se basaron en los resultados de una encuesta sobre los gastos de los hogares efectuada en 1949-50. La encuesta abarcó 455 familias de trabajadores manuales de Colombo. Para determinar los coeficientes de ponderación, los datos sobre los gastos de consumo obtenidos a través de esta encuesta fueron ajustados al nivel de los precios en 1959.

Ponderaciones y composición

Grupos principales	Número de artículos	Ponderación	Número aproximado de cotizaciones de precio
Alimentación	94	61,9	...
Combustible y luz	4	4,3	...
Alquiler	1	5,7	...
Vestido, calzado y ropa blanca	63	9,4	...
Varios	57	18,7	...
Total	219	100,0	...

Gastos de consumo de los hogares
A los fines del índice, los gastos del consumo comprenden todos los bienes y servicios adquiridos para el consumo por la población de referencia. No comprenden los seguros de vida, los seguros de bienes, los impuestos que gravan las rentas y la propiedad de las personas físicas.

Método de recolección de los datos
Los precios son recogidos semanalmente por investigadores del Departamento de Censos y Estadísticas en puntos de venta al por menor y en establecimientos seleccionados en siete principales mercados de Colombo. Los precios, para la mayor parte de los artículos alimenticios, se determinan mediante compra directa.

Se registran los precios de los artículos vendidos en mercados abiertos y en cooperativas. Se calcula un promedio ponderado de los precios asignando los porcentajes de ponderación en función del número estimado de ventas efectuadas en los dos grupos de tiendas.

Los precios utilizados en el índice son los que se pagan en el momento. Se utilizan los descuentos y los precios rebajados. Las compras a plazo o a crédito, las compras de artículos de segunda mano y la entrega de bienes usados no se tienen en cuenta.

Vivienda
Los datos correspondientes al alquiler de viviendas se obtienen cada tres meses en los registros municipales para 148 hogares de trabajadores. Para la vivienda propia se fija un alquiler ficticio.

Especificación de las variedades
Para cada uno de los artículos incluidos en el índice se brindan

especificaciones detalladas. Una "especificación" describe en forma completa el producto, su marca, país de origen, calidad y unidad.

Sustitución, cambio de calidad, etc.
Si no es posible encontrar un producto, se lo substituye por uno similar y, para el cálculo se utiliza el método de enlace.

Artículos estacionales
Se consideran como tales las frutas y las verduras frescas. Los precios de estos artículos se fijan durante la estación en que se pueden conseguir. Fuera de temporada, se mantienen los precios vigentes al clausurarse la estación precedente.

Cálculo
El índice se calcula conforme a la fórmula de Laspeyres como un promedio aritmético ponderado de base fija, cuyos coeficientes de ponderación corresponden a los gastos de consumo de 1949-50, ajustados al nivel de los precios de 1959.

Organización y publicación
El índice de precios del consumo se compila por el Departamento de Censos y Estadísticas (Colombo).
Department of Government Printing: "The Gazette of the Republic of Sri Lanka" (Colombo).
Government Publications Bureau: "A New Consumers' Price Index", Sessional Paper VI, 1953 (Colombo).
idem: "Report of Committee to Revise the Cost of Living Index", Sessional Paper XI, 1959 (Colombo).

SUDAFRICA

Denominación oficial
Consumer Price Index (Indice de Precios del Consumo).

Alcance
El índice se compila mensualmente y abarca todos los grupos de población en 12 regiones urbanas.

Base oficial
1985 = 100.

Fuente de la ponderación
La determinación de los coeficientes de ponderación y la selección de los artículos se basaron en una encuesta sobre los gastos de los hogares realizada en noviembre de 1985.

Ponderaciones y composición

Grupos principales	Número de artículos	Ponderación aproximado	Número de cotizaciones de precio
Alimentación	88	22,72	...
Bebidas, bebidas alcohólicas y tabaco	8	2,84	...
Vestido y calzado	55	5,98	...
Vivienda:			
Alquiler	2	5,88	...
Gastos de la vivienda propia	7	13,91	...
Otros (incl. agua)	3	1,41	...
Combustible y luz	6	2,44	...
Muebles y moblaje del hogar	29	4,72	...
Gastos del hogar	14	3,77	...
Asistencia médica	5	2,56	...
Transportes y comunicaciones	21	18,93	...
Educación y recreación	21	4,96	...
Aseo personal	12	3,08	...
Varios	14	6,77	...
Total	285	100,00	...

Gastos de consumo de los hogares
Comprenden las tasas de permisos de circulación y registro, los intereses de préstamos y los recargos bancarios, las primas de seguros de vida, los actos de donación, las anualidades, los seguros de deudas hipotecarias, las cuotas de afiliación a sindicatos, asociaciones de personal y organizaciones profesionales, los costes judiciales y otros costes de servicios profesionales. A los efectos del índice no se toman en cuenta ciertos gastos, como los efectuados para pagar los impuestos a la renta o las contribuciones a fondos de pensión o previsión social.

Método de recolección de los datos
Los precios se obtienen mediante cuestionarios enviados por correo a una muestra representativa de puntos de venta al por menor y establecimientos de servicios de las distintas regiones o de otras organizaciones, asociaciones u organismos públicos.

Los precios de frutas y legumbres se obtienen de la División de Investigación del Comercio Agrícola del Departamento de Economía y Comercio Agrícola, que los registra todas las semanas.

Vivienda
Las cotizaciones del alquiler de casas y pisos se obtienen de una encuesta anual del Departamento de Estadísticas. Entre los gastos de la vivienda propia figuran los pagos de intereses, tasas de evaluación, servicios sanitarios, recolección de residuos, seguros, reparación y mantenimiento de edificios, y otros gastos a cargo de los propietarios.

Especificación de las variedades
No disponible.

Sustitución, cambio de calidad, etc.
No disponible.

Artículos estacionales
No se ajustan las fluctuaciones estacionales de los precios.

Cálculo
El índice se calcula según la fórmula de Laspeyres como un promedio aritmético ponderado de base fija, cuyos coeficientes de ponderación corresponden a 1985.
El índice se calcula como un promedio ponderado de los índices que corresponden a las 12 regiones urbanas.

Informaciones complementarias
También se publican series separadas para hogares de los grupos de ingresos elevados, medios y bajos, para todos los artículos salvo la vivienda, para todos los artículos salvo la alimentación, para subgrupos detallados y para cada una de las 12 regiones urbanas.
También se publica un índice de precios del consumo con ajustes estacionales y un índice de precios del consumo de los pensionistas de las regiones urbanas.
Actualmente existe una nueva serie (con base 1990 = 100), pero en el momento de publicar este volumen la OIT no dispone de las informaciones metodológicas relativas a esta serie.

Organización y publicación
Central Statistical Service: "Bulletin of Statistics" (Pretoria).

SUDAN

Denominación oficial
Retail Price Index (Indice de precios al por menor).

Alcance
El índice se compila mensualmente y abarca hogares de seis personas y con ingresos anuales que oscilaban entre 300 y 500 libras sudanesas en 1967-68.

Base oficial
Enero de 1970 = 100.

Fuente de la ponderación
La selección de los artículos y la determinación de los coeficientes de ponderación se basaron en los resultados de una encuesta sobre los gastos de los hogares efectuada en 1967-68 en Khartoum, Khartoum Septentrional y Omdurman, que abarcó una muestra aleatoria de 1 500 hogares compuestos de seis miembros cuyos ingresos anuales se situaban entre 300 y 500 libras sudanesas.

Ponderaciones y composición

Grupos principales	Número de artículos	Ponderación aproximado	Número de cotizaciones de precio
Alimentación y tabaco	31	66,5	...
Vivienda:			
Alquiler, combustible, luz y agua	5	12,4	...
Vestido y calzado	22	5,9	...
Varios	12	15,2	...
Total	70	100,0	...

Gastos de consumo de los hogares
No disponible.

Método de recolección de los datos
Los precios son recogidos en puntos de venta al por menor seleccionados y establecimientos de servicios de Khartoum, Khartoum septentrional y Omdurman. Para la mayor parte de los artículos, la recolección de precios es efectuada por agen-

tes todos los jueves. Las autoridades suministran los datos relativos a la electricidad, gas, educación y transportes. El costo de la asistencia médica se basa en los honorarios de los doctores y en el precio de un producto farmacéutico seleccionado.

Los precios utilizados para calcular el índice son los que se pagan normalmente. Las rebajas y descuentos no se toman en consideración.

Vivienda
Las cotizaciones básicas del alquiler se obtuvieron de una encuesta emprendida en 1969. Las encuestas sobre los alquileres sólo se realizan ocasionalmente, pues los alquileres no varían con frecuencia.

Especificación de las variedades
No disponible.

Sustitución, cambio de calidad, etc.
No disponible.

Artículos estacionales
Los precios recogidos son precios corrientes. Las fluctuaciones estacionales de los precios no son objeto de ajuste.

Cálculo
El índice se calcula conforme a la fórmula de Laspeyres como un promedio aritmético ponderado de base fija, cuyos coeficientes de ponderación corresponden al período 1967-68.

El índice para un artículo se obtiene utilizando las relaciones de precios medios del período corriente y del período de base. Los precios medios son promedios aritméticos simples de los precios recogidos en las tres ciudades.

Informaciones complementarias
Actualmente se calcula una nueva serie relativa a las familias de ingresos módicos, medios y elevados (base enero de 1988 = 100), pero en el momento de publicar el presente Volumen la OIT no disponía de informaciones metodológicas sobre esta serie.

Organización y publicación
El índice se compila por el Department of Statistics (Khartoum). Las cifras que publica la Oficina Internacional del Trabajo se reciben directamente del "Department of Statistics" (Khartoum). No aparecen en las publicaciones nacionales.

SUECIA

Denominación oficial
Konsumentprisindex (Indice de precios del consumo).

Alcance
El índice se compila mensualmente y abarca toda la población del país, tanto urbana como rural.

Base oficial
1980 = 100.

Fuente de la ponderación
Las ponderaciones y los artículos seleccionados se revisan a comienzos de cada año. Las ponderaciones se basan en el Sistema de Contabilidad Nacional de Suecia: estadísticas trimestrales para los tres primeros trimestres del año precedente que se completan con una estimación del cuarto trimestre. Las ponderaciones dentro de los grupos se basan en las fuentes más recientes, por ejemplo, respecto a los alimentos, en las encuestas y estimaciones de la "Swedish National Agricultural Market Board" (Junta Nacional del Mercado Agrícola de Suecia). Respecto a otros artículos las ponderaciones se basan en la última encuesta sobre los gastos de los hogares. La utilizada en el presente abarca todos los gastos de los hogares privados de Suecia durante un año.

Gastos de consumo de los hogares
Los gastos de consumo en que se basan las ponderaciones incluyen todos los bienes y servicios del sector privado consumidos por los hogares privados, o sea pagados por ellos, comprendiendo también los gastos en ciertos bienes de capital (excepto terrenos, vivienda propia principal y residencia secundaria, como granja o quinta para fines de semana). Se incluye el gasto de consumo correspondiente a la vivienda propia. Los precios de los bienes durables y de las compras a crédito o a plazos se registran en el momento de la entrega. Las compras de segunda mano, el comercio de objetos usados y su entrega como pago parcial no se incluyen en el índice. Se excluyen también las transacciones financieras, como los seguros de vida y otros seguros sociales, los impuestos al ingreso y otros directos. Los regalos se registran como consumo de los bienes y servicios dados por el donante con el precio que tenían en el momento de la compra. Los ingresos en especie sólo representan una parte pequeña del consumo privado sueco y su valor sólo se estima para la alimentación, a partir de encuestas publicadas periódicamente por la "Swedish National Agricultural Market Board" en sus estadísticas de alimentación.

Ponderaciones y composición

Grupos principales	Número de artículos	Ponderación	Número aproximado de cotizaciones de precio
Alimentación	(1) 25 + 770	172	18 000
Bebidas alcohólicas	(a) (1) 15	32	(a) 500
Tabaco	(1) 25	21	1 200
Vestido	27	62	900-1 800
Calzado	10	13	650
Vivienda, combustible y electricidad	(b)	270	(b)
Muebles y equipo domésticos	(1) 39 + 60	65	3 300
Transporte y comunicaciones	22	175	(2) 800
Servicios de educación, cultura y recreación	50 + 20	98	2 100
Varios	(1) 33 + 30	92	(3) 2 800
Total	...	1 000	...

Nota: (a) y (b) Véase abajo. (1) Variedades especificadas para una muestra. (2) Excluyendo cotizaciones y cálculos de precio de los viajes. (3) Excluyendo cálculos de la asistencia médica, servicios odontológicos y medicamentos.

(a) Abarca prácticamente todos los artículos/variedades de vino, alcoholes y cervezas fuertes (ponderación 28). (b) Véase texto más adelante.

Método de recolección de los datos
Los investigadores registran los precios alrededor del 15 de cada mes de una muestra aleatoria de unos 900 puntos de venta al por menor y establecimientos de servicios. Una organización general de entrevistadores, de unas 200 personas, se encarga de las entrevistas en todo el país y de la recolección de precios. Los supervisores permanecen en la Oficina Central de Estadísticas, la SCB, manteniéndose en contacto con los entrevistadores por teléfono, cartas y llamadas intermitentes. Los precios de los productos alimenticios (excepto ciertos alimentos frescos como pan, pescado, legumbres y frutas) y de otras mercancías de todos los días se obtienen de las listas de precios aplicados por una muestra aleatoria de aproximadamente 60 tiendas. Una vez al año, en diciembre, los investigadores obtienen los precios de estas mercancías en las tiendas. Estos precios sólo se usan para calcular el enlace de largo plazo (véase más adelante).

Los cuestionarios enviados por correo se usan para las cotizaciones del alquiler, la electricidad y el agua; las entrevistas telefónicas para la gasolina y los coches, mientras que los datos sobre el costo de la asistencia médica, el transporte y las comunicaciones corresponden a las tarifas oficiales.

Los precios del índice son los regulares, que paga cualquier miembro del público, con los impuestos indirectos incluidos. Se deducen los descuentos por pago al contado. Se registran los precios regateados durante el período de la recolección de precios. Los precios del mercado negro son irrelevantes. Sólo se registran los precios al contado y, por lo tanto, no se incluyen los alquileres con opción de compra ni las compras a crédito o plazos. Se excluyen también las compras de segunda mano, el trueque de bienes usados o su entrega a título de pago parcial, así como las compras de importación directa de los hogares.

Vivienda
Las encuestas de alquiler se realizan cuatro veces al año, en enero, abril, julio y octubre o cuando los alquileres negociados entran en vigor, a una muestra de 1 000 viviendas alquiladas. Los costos de calefacción se incluyen en el total registrado como alquiler. Una muestra de apartamentos de reciente construcción se incluye sucesivamente en los cálculos del índice de alquiler. Se calcula un índice de viviendas ocupadas por sus propietarios de acuerdo a la evolución de los costos de cada mes, comprendiendo todos los gastos corrientes, tales como intereses, seguros domésticos, agua, recolección de residuos, limpieza de chimeneas, impuestos a los bienes raíces, calefacción, electricidad y reparaciones, así como la depreciación. Los intereses se calculan sobre el monto total del capital definido en términos de precio de compra (por el propietario actual). Se deducen las prestaciones del Estado que subsidian intereses.

Especificación de las variedades
Las definiciones de los artículos contienen todas las especificaciones que sean prácticas. El recolector debe especificar cada artículo cuyo precio debe registrar de tal forma que el mismo artículo o servicio pueda ser apreciado la próxima vez incluso por otro recolector. Para ciertos alimentos y otros bienes comprados diariamente, las especificaciones se dan en detalle, incluyendo el número de artículo.

Sustitución, cambio de calidad, etc.
Los cambios de calidad se juzgan en lo posible en la etapa de la recolección de precios. Sólo se registra la diferencia de precio equivalente a la de calidad. Para ciertos alimentos y mercancías de todos los días la sustitución normalmente no se permite. Para el vestido, las sustituciones sólo se hacen entre artículos con calidad equivalente de acuerdo con ciertos criterios. Los productos nuevos se suelen introducir en conexión con el examen anual de la selección de artículos. En lo posible, se trata de reemplazar toda clase o calidad que desaparece. Alternativamente, se informa la no respuesta.

Artículos estacionales
Los precios de las vestimentas invernales sólo se registran de septiembre a marzo. El último precio registrado se usa luego en los cálculos del índice fuera de temporada, de abril a agosto. Los precios de ciertos artículos (patatas, legumbres y frutas) se ajustan en función de sus variaciones estacionales. Para los precios de estos artículos se calculan cocientes estacionales basados en los precios de temporada de los tres años previos.

Cálculo
El índice es en cadena, con enlaces anuales, cambiándose las ponderaciones para cada enlace. Se usan dos tipos diferentes de enlaces (cada enlace con diciembre del año precedente = 100), a saber, un enlace de corto plazo y un enlace de largo plazo.

El enlace de corto plazo se utiliza para cada uno de los meses de enero a diciembre. El enlace de largo plazo se usa sólo para enlaces anuales de diciembre a diciembre.

El enlace mensual se calcula primeramente como un promedio aritmético ponderado de los distintos relativos de precio de los artículos con precio registrado, tomándose como base 100 el mes de diciembre anterior. Estos resultados se encadenan hacia atrás mediante enlaces de largo plazo, de diciembre a diciembre de cada año precedente a 1980.

Informaciones complementarias
También se calcula un índice de precios netos, que es un índice en el cual se deducen del monto de los precios de bienes de consumo los impuestos indirectos que en las diferentes etapas de la producción concurren al coste de la producción final de dichos bienes. Los precios también se ajustan por inclusión de ciertos subsidios.

Las estadísticas de "Montos Básicos" se usan para ajustar las pensiones de base y las complementarias, los préstamos de estudio financiados por el gobierno, ciertas anualidades de vida y las prestaciones de subsistencia.

Organización y publicación
Statistics Sweden (Oficina de Estadísticas de Suecia): "Statistiska meddelanden", series P14 y P15 (Informes Estadísticos) (Estocolmo).

idem: "Allmän Manadsstatistik" (Compendio mensual de estadísticas suecas).

Sveriges officiella Statistik, Statistika central byrån (Oficina Central de Estadísticas, Estadísticas Oficiales de Suecia): "Konsumentpriser och index beräkningar 1989" (Estocolmo, 1990).

SUIZA

Denominación oficial
Indice suisse des prix à la consommation (Indice de precios del consumo).

Alcance
El índice se calcula mensualmente y abarca hogares de asalariados de todo el país.

Base oficial
Diciembre de 1982 = 100.

Fuente de la ponderación
La selección de los artículos y la determinación de los coeficientes de ponderación se basaron en los resultados de una encuesta sobre los gastos de los hogares efectuada en 1981, que abarcó una muestra de 422 hogares de asalariados en todo el país. Los datos relativos a los ingresos y a los gastos han sido recogidos mensualmente en cada uno de los hogares de la muestra durante 12 meses. La estructura de los coeficientes de ponderación se ajustó a las modificaciones de precio ocurridas entre mediados de 1981 y mediados de 1982.

Ponderaciones y composición

Grupos principales	Número de artículos	Ponderación	Número aproximado de cotizaciones de precio
Alimentación	127	21	73 300
Bebidas y tabaco	22	5	27 700
Vestido y calzado	56	7	61 800
Alquiler	15	18	107 000
Combustible y luz	13	5	2 600
Accesorios y mantenimiento del hogar	35	6	24 800
Transportes y comunicaciones	58	14	5 300
Salud y aseo personal	54	8	12 300
Educación y distracciones	33	16	19 500
Total	413	100	334 300

Gastos de consumo de los hogares
A los fines del índice, los gastos del consumo comprenden todos los bienes y servicios adquiridos para el consumo por la población de referencia. Se incluyen los impuestos indirectos, las primas de los seguros relacionados con la utilización de vehículos automotores, y los permisos de radio y televisión.

Los gastos de consumo no incluidos en la compilación del índice son los referentes a ciertos artículos como las contribuciones a sociedades, regalos, multas, intereses de préstamos, viajes de negocios y efectos personales tales como joyas, relojes, bolsos, etc.

Método de recolección de los datos
La recolección de precios está a cargo de investigadores de las autoridades locales o se efectúa por medio de cuestionarios enviados por correo a puntos de venta al por menor y establecimientos de servicios. El criterio para elegir los puntos de venta es el de su importancia económica local. Los precios para la mayor parte de los artículos alimenticios, los combustibles y la luz se fijan durante las dos primeras semanas de cada mes en 48 ciudades (localidades). Los precios para los demás artículos se recogen trimestralmente. Se toman en consideración los precios especiales en el momento de la encuesta.

Vivienda
Las cotizaciones del alquiler se obtienen en mayo y noviembre de cada año, en 85 localidades de 100 000 apartamentos de una a cinco habitaciones. Las diferentes clases de apartamentos (viejos, nuevos, y construidos desde la última cotización) entran en el cálculo del índice en proporción a su número respectivo.

Especificación de las variedades
Cada investigador puede elegir para cada artículo las especificaciones más importantes, en términos de volumen comercial, y adaptar su selección progresivamente según la evolución del mercado.

Sustitución, cambio de calidad, etc.
No se toman en consideración los pequeños cambios de calidad. Cuando un artículo sufre cambios importantes de calidad se lo considera como nuevo y se emplea el método de enlace. Si un artículo desaparece del mercado, y el consumidor está obligado a adquirir el sustitutivo, los precios de este último son los que se utilizan para el cálculo del índice.

Artículos estacionales
Las fluctuaciones estacionales de precios de las frutas y las verduras frescas se toman en consideración mediante artículos y coeficientes de ponderación variables dentro de "canastas" mensuales cuyos coeficientes de ponderación de grupo permanecen constantes.

Cálculo
El índice se calcula según la fórmula de Laspeyres, como un promedio aritmético ponderado de base fija, cuyos coeficientes de ponderación corresponden al período de base.

Primeramente, se calculan índices separados para cada precio en cada punto de venta, utilizando los medios de las relaciones de precios del período corriente y del período de base. El índice nacional representa el promedio aritmético ponderado de los índices relativos a diferentes tipos de puntos de venta y de municipios.

Informaciones complementarias
Un nuevo índice de precios del consumo está preparándose y aparecerá próximamente. Subgrupos detallados se publican para el índice actual así como índices separados para 48 localidades.

Organización y publicación
Département fédéral de l'intérieur, Office fédéral de la statistique: "L'indice suisse des prix à la consommation" (Berne).
idem: "Communiqué de presse".
Département fédéral de l'économie publique, Office fédéral de l'industrie, des arts et métiers et du travail: "La vie économique", feb. de 1983.
idem: "La vie économique, l'indice suisse des prix à la consommation", 89è numéro spécial, 1977.

SURINAME (PARAMARIBO)

Denominación oficial
Consumer Price Index (Indice de precios del consumo).

Alcance
El índice se compila mensualmente y abarca hogares de empleados y obreros cuyos ingresos anuales no superaban 6 000 florines entre abril de 1968 y marzo de 1969. El índice se refiere a la capital, Paramaribo.

Base oficial
Abril de 1968 - marzo de 1969 = 100.

Fuente de la ponderación
La selección de los artículos y la determinación de los coeficientes de ponderación se basaron en los resultados de una encuesta sobre los gastos de los hogares efectuada entre abril de 1968 y marzo de 1969 en Paramaribo y sus alrededores. La encuesta abarcó a 592 hogares de obreros y empleados compuestos de tres o más personas y cuyos ingresos anuales no excedían 6 000 florines en el momento de la encuesta. Los artículos del índice fueron seleccionados en base a dos criterios: su importancia en el consumo del hogar y su adquisición por la mayoría de los hogares.

Ponderaciones y composición

Grupos principales	Número de artículos	Ponderación	Número aproximado de cotizaciones de precio
Alimentación	92	39,9	1 252
Vivienda:			
Alquiler, agua y electricidad	3	9,5	3
Combustible	4	1,9	20
Moblaje y productos de limpieza	36	12,3	400
Vestido y calzado	48	11,0	252
Otros:			
Aseo personal y asistencia médica	23	6,2	251
Transporte	5	9,5	10
Tabaco	2	1,3	46
Educación y distracciones	16	8,4	104
Total	229	100,0	2 338

Gastos de consumo de los hogares
A los fines del índice, los gastos del consumo comprenden todos los bienes y servicios adquiridos o recibidos para el consumo por la población de referencia. Se incluyen ingresos en especie y productos caseros consumidos por los hogares. Se excluyen impuestos a los ingresos, contribuciones a la seguridad social, reembolsos de préstamos, primas de seguros, regalos y contribuciones, apuestas y gastos de juego, costes de las mejoras importantes de la casa y amortización del capital de hipotecas, otras inversiones, ahorros e intereses de deudas personales.

Método de recolección de los datos
Los precios son recogidos por un equipo de entrevistadores en 125 tiendas al por menor y establecimientos de servicios de Paramaribo y sus alrededores. Después de 1969, se eligieron nuevos puntos de venta y se normalizaron diversos bienes y servicios. Los precios de mercancías escasas y los precios del mercado negro se registran mediante entrevistas de los investigadores a unos 150 a 200 hogares por mes. En las entrevistas se registran y siguen los precios de la mayor parte de los artículos del mes en curso, entre el primero y el 30. Los precios de frutas y verduras frescas se registran tres veces por semana (los lunes, miércoles y viernes) en el Mercado Central y en los "mercados de verdura" de Paramaribo y alrededores, registrándose 14 cotizaciones de precios por día.

Vivienda
El índice de la vivienda se compone de alquiler, agua y electricidad, combustible, muebles, equipo y productos de limpieza. Los datos referentes al alquiler se recogen en 60 viviendas privadas alquiladas, cubriéndose 20 viviendas por mes.

Especificación de las variedades
Para cada uno de los artículos incluidos en el índice se dan especificaciones detalladas. Una "especificación" brinda una descripción completa del artículo, su nombre o su marca de fábrica, tipo de embalaje, calidad, unidad, etc.

Sustitución, cambio de calidad, etc.
Cuando un artículo desaparece del mercado se lo substituye por otro similar.

Artículos estacionales
No se les incluye en el índice.

Cálculo
El índice se calcula conforme a la fórmula de Laspeyres como un promedio aritmético ponderado de base fija, cuyos coeficientes de ponderación corresponden al período de base.

Informaciones complementarias
No disponible.

Organización y publicación
Algemeen Bureau voor de Statistiek: "Prijsindexcijfers van de Gezinsconsumptie" (Paramaribo).
Stichting Planbureau: "Basis Budget Van Consumptieve Huishouduitgaven in Paramaribo en Omgeving 1968-69" (Paramaribo).

SWAZILANDIA (MBABANE-MANZINI)

Denominación oficial
Retail Price Index "B" (Indice de precios al por menor "B").

Alcance
El índice se compila mensualmente y se refiere a hogares de asalariados con escasos ingresos que viven en Mbabane y en Manzini, cuyos ingresos mensuales alcanzaban aproximadamente 1 000 emalangeni en 1977.

Base oficial
Enero de 1967 = 100.

Fuente de la ponderación
La determinación de los coeficientes de ponderación se basó en los datos relativos a los gastos de las familias de escasos salarios de Kenya, Rodesia, Reino Unido y Sudáfrica.

Ponderaciones y composición

Grupos principales	Número de artículos	Ponderación	Número aproximado de cotizaciones de precio
Alimentación:			
Frutas y verduras	5	4,5	...
Otros productos alimenticios	19	57,5	...
Bebidas y tabaco	3	12,0	...
Combustible y luz	4	6,0	...
Vestido y calzado	9	10,0	...
Otros artículos	8	10,0	...
Total	48	100,0	...

Gastos de consumo de los hogares
No disponible.

Método de recolección de los datos
Los precios se obtienen en cuatro mercados y en puestos de venta al por menor y establecimientos de servicios, situados en Mbabane y Manzini. La recolección de precios está a cargo de miembros del personal permanente de la Central Statistical Office para todos los artículos, salvo la de frutas y verduras que está a cargo de investigadores.

Los precios de las frutas y verduras frescas se registran todas las semanas, los días martes, y los demás precios alrededor del día 15 de cada mes. Los datos sobre los precios de la educación, los transportes y la asistencia médica se recogen mediante llamadas telefónicas.

Los precios utilizados en el índice son los precios al por menor que se pagan en el momento.

Vivienda
El alquiler no se incluye en el índice ni se toma en consideración para determinar los coeficientes de ponderación.

Especificación de las variedades
Los artículos y los servicios cuyos precios se han de registrar se especifican en detalles tales como tamaño, factura, marca, cantidad y calidad.

Sustitución, cambio de calidad, etc.
Cuando ya no se puede conseguir un producto se lo sustituye por otro que sea de calidad aproximadamente igual utilizándose el método de enlace.

Artículos estacionales
No disponible.

Cálculo
El índice se calcula conforme a la fórmula de Laspeyres como un promedio aritmético ponderado de base fija, cuyos coeficientes de ponderación corresponden al período de base.

El índice para un artículo es generalmente obtenido utilizando las relaciones de precios del período corriente y del período de base, salvo para el vestido y artículos de textiles para los cuales se utilizan las relaciones de precios del período corriente y del período precedente. Para calcular precios medios, los precios de almacén de diferentes localidades son ponderados según el giro del comercio al por menor.

Informaciones complementarias
Actualmente se calcula una nueva serie relativa a las familias de ingresos módicos, medios y elevados (base septiembre de 1988 = 100), pero en el momento de publicar el presente volumen la OIT no disponía de informaciones metodológicas sobre esta serie.

Organización y publicación
Central Statistical Office: "Swaziland Statistical News" (Mbabane).

TAILANDIA

Denominación oficial
General Consumer Price Index (Indice General de Precios del Consumo).

Alcance
La compilación del índice es mensual y abarca hogares urbanos de dos a diez personas de todo el país, cuyos gastos mensuales oscilaban entre 4 000 y 10 000 bahts en 1986.

Base oficial
1986 = 100.

Fuente de la ponderación
La determinación de los coeficientes de ponderación y la selección de los artículos se basaron en los resultados de una encuesta socioeconómica, realizada en 1986 en todo el país, con una muestra representativa de todos los hogares privados, no institucionales. Los artículos se seleccionaron en función de su importancia relativa en el conjunto del consumo, su grado de representatividad de los movimientos de precio de un grupo más amplio de artículos, la variabilidad de sus precios dentro del grupo en el que se le ha clasificado, de que las especificaciones permitan identificarlo en forma fiable y las previsiones de aumento de su demanda e importancia relativa en el futuro. Los gastos en artículos sin precio registrado se añadieron a los gastos en artículos con precio registrado que tienen características físicas y uso similares. Los gastos en otros artículos sin precio registrado de subgrupos específicos se distribuyeron proporcionalmente en cada subgrupo. Todos los gastos varios no comprendidos en un subgrupo se distribuyeron proporcionalmente entre todos los gastos en artículos con precio determinado. Los artículos y coeficientes de ponderación que se utilizan desde 1991 figuran en el cuadro abajo.

Gastos de consumo de los hogares
A efectos del índice comprenden la adquisición de bienes y servicios, el valor de los bienes y servicios recibidos en especie como parte de la remuneración o a título gratuito, la producción doméstica y el valor locativo de la vivienda propia. Se excluyen los impuestos directos pagados al Estado, los regalos en efectivo y las contribuciones, primas de seguros, compra de billetes de lotería y otras formas de juego, los intereses de deudas y acciones, así como toda forma de operaciones financieras o de capitalización.

Ponderaciones y composición

Grupos principales	Número de artículos	Ponderación	Número aproximado de cotizaciones de precio
Alimentación	...	40,38	...
Vivienda:			
Alojamiento	...	24,76	...
Muebles y electrodomésticos	...	4,77	...
Vestido y calzado	...	5,13	...
Asistencia médica y aseo personal	...	8,94	...
Transporte y comunicaciones	...	11,69	...
Recreación y educación	...	4,33	...
Tabaco y bebidas alcohólicas	...	100,00	...

Método de recolección de los datos
Los investigadores proceden a la recolección de precios en mercados, puntos de venta al por menor y establecimientos de servicios de las zonas urbanas. Los precios de los alimentos se registran semanalmente en cuatro puntos de venta al por menor de cada zona de mercado como mínimo, los demás precios la semana que comprende el día 15 del mes. Las tarifas de los servicios de teléfonos, electricidad, agua, y de los hospitales, etc., se obtienen de organismos oficiales. Los precios registrados para el índice son los que debe pagar cualquier persona del público el día de la recolección.

Vivienda
El valor locativo de las viviendas ocupadas por sus propietarios se añade a los coeficientes de ponderación del alquiler. El promedio de las modificaciones de los alquileres de un período a otro permiten medir el movimiento de los precios. Estos se obtienen cada tres meses de una muestra de unos 355 inquilinos.

Especificación de las variedades
Las especificaciones describen la variedad, calidad, factura, marca, etc.

Sustitución, cambio de calidad, etc.
Toda vez que se modifican las características de un producto se utiliza el método de enlaces. Cuando un artículo desaparece del mercado se le sustituye por otro similar.

Artículos estacionales
Por lo general no se toman en cuenta las fluctuaciones de precio de los artículos estacionales. Sin embargo para algunos artículos se mantienen, fuera de estación, los precios que tenían al fin de la temporada anterior.

Cálculo
El índice se calcula según la fórmula de Laspeyres como un promedio aritmético ponderado de base fija, cuyos coeficientes de ponderación corresponden al período de base. Sin embargo en la práctica actual el índice se compila como un índice mensual en cadena de las ponderaciones de base y los relativos de precio correspondientes a dos períodos consecutivos, lo que permite obtener el índice del mes en curso actualizando el del mes anterior. El índice nacional es una combinación de las series regionales ponderadas por los coeficientes demográficos de cada región.

Informaciones complementarias
No disponible.

Organización y publicación
La compilación mensual del índice está a cargo del Ministry of Business Economics, Price Index Division (Ministerio de Comercio, Departamento de Asuntos Económicos, División del Indice de Precios) (Bangkok).

idem: "Monthly Report Consumers Price Index".

Office of the Prime Minister, National Statistical Office (Despacho del Primer Ministro, Oficina Estadística Nacional): "Bulletin of Statistics" (Bangkok).

TANZANIA (TANGAÑIKA)

Denominación oficial
National Consumer Price Index (Indice nacional de precios del consumo).

Alcance
El índice se calcula trimestralmente y abarca todos los tipos de hogares y grupos de población en 20 áreas urbanas de la Tanzanía continental.

Base oficial
1977 = 100.

Fuente de la ponderación
Los coeficientes de ponderación y los artículos seleccionados se basaron en los resultados de una encuesta sobre los gastos de los hogares efectuada durante un año entre septiembre de 1976 y noviembre de 1977, que abarcó una muestra de 6 042 hogares. Los artículos cuyos precios se registran tienen ponderaciones importantes. Las ponderaciones de los artículos cuyos precios no se registran quedan excluidas.

Ponderaciones y composición

Grupos principales	Número de artículos	Ponderación	Número aproximado de cotizaciones de precio
Alimentación	44	64,2	...
Bebidas y tabaco	5	2,5	...
Alquiler	1	4,9	...
Combustible, luz y agua	6	7,6	...
Vestido y calzado	21	9,9	...
Mobiliario y accesorios para el hogar	18	1,4	...
Gastos del hogar	9	3,4	...
Aseo personal y asistencia médica	9	1,3	...
Distracciones	5	0,7	...
Transportes	12	4,1	...
Total	130	100,0	...

Gastos de consumo de los hogares
A los fines del índice, los gastos de consumo de los hogares comprenden casi todos los bienes y servicios importantes adquiridos para el consumo por la población de referencia. Están excluidos impuestos y multas, gastos de juego, transferencias de dinero, donaciones, ahorros e inversiones, primas de seguros de vida y gastos de adquisición de una esposa.

Método de recolección de los datos
Los precios se registran en marzo, junio, septiembre y diciembre en mercados, puntos de venta al por menor y establecimientos de servicios en 20 áreas urbanas. No se efectuó ninguna encuesta sobre los puntos de compra, sea porque todos ellos han sido cubiertos, si sólo hay pocos, sea porque han sido cubiertos por lo menos el 50 por ciento de los mismos, si hay muchos. Los precios de los artículos procedentes de mercados, como frutas, verduras, cereales y leguminosas, se recogen por compra directa. Algunos precios se han obtenido mediante cuestionarios por correspondencia enviados a tiendas o almacenes. Las tarifas de la electricidad, el agua y las comunicaciones son las oficiales. Los precios utilizados para el cálculo del índice son los precios ordinarios del mercado libre pagados por los consumidores. No se tienen en cuenta los precios de liquidación y de rebajas. Se registran los precios del mercado negro si los artículos están disponibles para todos los consumidores.

Vivienda
Los datos referentes al alquiler se obtienen trimestralmente mediante cuestionarios por correspondencia enviados por lo menos a 30 viviendas ocupadas por familias con ingresos módicos, a 30 viviendas ocupadas por familias con ingresos medios y a 30 viviendas ocupadas por familias con ingresos elevados, en cada ciudad. Las viviendas ocupadas por su propietario se excluyen del índice.

Especificación de las variedades
Los artículos cuyos precios se registran se especifican en cuanto a variedad, calidad, factura, marca, unidad, etc.

Sustitución, cambio de calidad, etc.
Si un artículo desaparece del mercado o la calidad de un artículo cambia, se le sustituye por otro análogo.

Artículos estacionales
Los precios de los artículos estacionales sólo se recogen si estos últimos estan disponibles en el mercado.

Cálculo
El índice se calcula conforme a la fórmula de Laspeyres como un promedio aritmético ponderado de base fija, cuyos coeficientes de ponderación corresponden al período de base. El índice para un artículo se obtiene utilizando las relaciones de precios del período corriente y del período de base. El índice nacional es un promedio ponderado de los índices de 20 ciudades, las ponderaciones utilizadas son proporcionales a la población de cada ciudad.

Informaciones complementarias
No disponible.

Organización y publicación
Ministry of Finance, Planning and Economic Affairs, Bureau of Statistics: "Quarterly Statistical Bulletin" (Dar-es-Salaam).

Para más amplios detalles metodológicos, véase:

Ministry of Economic Affairs and Development Planning, Bureau of Statistics: "National Consumer Price Index" (Octubre de 1974).

TOGO (LOME)

Denominación oficial
Indice des prix à la consommation (Indice de precios del consumo).

Alcance
El índice se calcula mensualmente y abarca únicamente hogares privados africanos en Lomé.

Base oficial
1963 = 100.

Fuente de la ponderación
La selección de los artículos y la determinación de los coeficientes de ponderación se basaron en los resultados de una encuesta sobre los gastos de los hogares efectuada en Lomé entre junio de 1964 y junio de 1965, que abarcó únicamente a hogares privados africanos.

Ponderaciones y composición

Grupos principales	Número de artículos	Ponderación	Número aproximado de cotizaciones de precio
Alimentación	53	47,9	...
Bebidas alcohólicas, tabaco y cola	12	10,6	...
Combustible, luz y agua	6	5,3	...
Accesorios para el hogar y productos de limpieza	13	2,8	...
Vivienda:			
Alquiler	1	2,9	...
Reparaciones	7	3,9	...
Vestido y calzado	16	7,7	...
Transportes	4	3,5	...
Servicios	9	3,1	...
Varios	30	12,3	...
Total	151	100,0	...

Gastos de consumo de los hogares
No disponible.

Método de recolección de los datos
Los precios de los artículos son recogidos por investigadores en el mercado local, en los principales almacenes y en determinados establecimientos de servicios. Los precios de los artículos alimenticios locales se recogen dos veces por semana, y los de los demás artículos se obtienen una vez por mes.

Vivienda
Las cotizaciones de alquiler se obtienen de los registros de contribuciones directas.

Especificación de las variedades
No disponible.

Sustitución, cambio de calidad, etc.
No disponible.

Artículos estacionales
No disponible.

Cálculo
El índice se calcula conforme a la fórmula de Laspeyres como un promedio aritmético ponderado de base fija, cuyos coeficientes de ponderación corresponden al período junio de 1964 - junio de 1965.

Informaciones complementarias
No disponible.

Organización y publicación
Ministère du Plan, Direction de la statistique: "Bulletin mensuel de statistique" (Lomé).

Ministère des Finances, de l'Economie et du Plan, Direction de la statistique: "Prix-Indices des prix et coût de la vie à Lomé -Indices des prix à la consommation familiale à Lomé, Base 100 en 1963" (Lomé).

TONGA

Denominación oficial
Consumer Price Index (Indice de Precios del Consumo).

Alcance
La compilación del índice es trimestral y abarca todos los hogares de asalariados de Tongatapú.

Base oficial
1984 = 100.

Fuente de la ponderación
La determinación de los coeficientes de ponderación y la selección de los artículos se basaron en los resultados de una encuesta sobre los gastos de los hogares realizada en Tongatapú en 1984. Para adjudicar a los artículos del índice las ponderaciones de los no incluidos en él se siguieron dos procedimientos distintos:

- cuando el artículo excluído guarda una estrecha relación con alguno del índice, a éste se añaden directamente los coeficientes de ponderación, lo que significa que las ponderaciones de los artículos del índice representan los gastos de ambos artículos, que se califican como "afines". Por ejemplo, la ponderación atribuida al artículo "naranjas" representa también los gastos en naranjas amargas, cidras, limones, mandarinas.
- en la mayoría de los demás casos, es decir cuando el artículo excluído no se puede considerar "afín" de ninguno de los del índice, los coeficientes de ponderación de los artículos excluídos se distribuyen entre varios de los incluidos o entre todos los de un mismo grupo o subgrupo. Por ejemplo, la ponderación de las aspiradoras domésticas excluidas del índice se distribuye entre los diversos electrodomésticos.

En los pocos casos en que la ponderación de un artículo excluído no se puede atribuir a otros artículos, grupo o subgrupo del índice, el gasto correspondiente se excluye totalmente del cálculo de la ponderación.

Estos procedimientos tienen el mismo efecto que si la ponderación se distribuyera entre todos los artículos del entero CPI: no alteran las ponderaciones relativas de ninguno de los artículos incluidos.

Ponderaciones y composición

Grupos principales	Número de artículos	Ponderación	Número aproximado de cotizaciones de precio
Alimentación	104	49,308	5
Vivienda	34	10,458	5
Bienes del hogar	60	13,316	5
Vestido y calzado	40	5,623	5
Transportes	15	5,771	3
Tabaco, bebidas alcohólicas y Kava	6	6,987	5
Otros bienes y servicios	48	8,537	4
Total	307	100,000	32

Gastos de consumo de los hogares
A los efectos del índice se excluyen los gastos en impuestos, alquileres, ahorros para la vivienda propia y compras comerciales.

Método de recolección de los datos
Los precios se registran en la fecha más cercana posible a la mitad del segundo mes de cada trimestre, es decir a mediados de febrero, mayo, agosto y noviembre, en Nuku'alofa y otros centros de la isla Tongatapú. Por supuesto es necesario escalonar la recolección a lo largo de un período debido al volumen de trabajo que, simplemente, exigen las visitas personales. Los precios de las frutas y legumbres frescas, que en lapsos breves suelen tener grandes alzas y bajas, se registran cada 15 días para poder reflejar mejor el promedio de sus precios durante el trimestre.

Para seleccionar los puntos de venta donde se registrarán los precios, se eligenante todo los grandes comercios, por la importancia y diversidad de su volumen de ventas, que se completan con una muestra de puntos de venta más pequeños, de variado tipo, para garantizar una cobertura equilibrada de todos los artículos. Así, para abarcar adecuadamente los precios de alimentos enlatados se seleccionan algunas pequeñas tiendas de barrio, dentro o fuera de Nuku'alofa, así como los grandes supermercados de Nuku'alofa. Los precios no sólo se obtienen en comercios minoristas sino también en una amplia gama de negocios que venden bienes de consumo y servicios al público, tales como mercados de frutas y hortalizas, restaurantes y hoteles, concesionarios de automóviles y gasolineras, autoridad responsable de la energía eléctrica, compañías de taxis y autobuses, empresas de construcción y oficios diversos, autoridades encargadas de correos y teléfonos, etc. Los funcionarios del Departamento de Estadísticas obtienen casi todos los datos sobre precios al por menor mediante visitas personales a las tiendas y otros negocios pertinentes. Las medidas del CPI expresan los precios en el momento de las transacciones, es decir el precio real que pagan los consumidores cuando adquieren los bienes o servicios. Se toman en cuenta toda suerte de descuentos, ofertas especiales, etc., en la medida en que se apliquen a bienes y servicios determinados y se ofrezcan a toda la clientela, pero no se consideran los precios rebajados por manchas o averías ni los especiales que se relacionan únicamente con la liquidación de unas pocas existencias. Los precios comprenden el impuesto a las ventas al por menor pues integra el precio que deben pagar los consumidores y, por lo tanto, toda modificación de la tasa del impuesto a las ventas afectará el movimiento de los precios del CPI.

Vivienda
El alquiler no se incluye como artículo del índice.

Especificación de las variedades
Tras determinar la lista de artículos a incluir en el índice se debe definir con precisión los bienes y servicios cuyos precios se registrarán regularmente para compilar los índices. Las descripciones tales como "té", "camisa de hombre", "bicicleta" o "trayecto de taxi" son suficientes para calcular los coeficientes de ponderación pero les faltan los detalles necesarios para dar coherencia al registro de precios. Si se trata de registrar el precio del "té" se debe precisar si es envasado o en saquillos, el tamaño de los paquetes y así sucesivamente. Para "camisa de hombre", se debe especificar si de mangas largas o cortas, la clase de materiales, etc.; para "bicicleta", el tipo y tamaño, los accesorios que comprende, etc.; si se trata de recorridos de taxi, la distancia que corresponde al precio del viaje que se registra.

En consecuencia se dan pautas a los investigadores, mediante especificaciones detalladas por escrito de cada artículo del índice, para que a lo largo de los trimestres sucesivos registren siempre los precios de bienes y servicios que sean comparables. En algunos casos, para un artículo del índice sólo se registra el precio de una especificación, pero en otros se registran los precios de dos o más especificaciones del mismo artículo.

Sustitución, cambio de calidad, etc.
Cuando cesa temporalmente la oferta de un artículo, la práctica habitual consiste en mantener el último precio registrado hasta que se reanude la oferta. En algunos casos, si la ausencia del mercado dura varios trimestres sucesivos - pero se espera su reaparición en un futuro próximo -, se puede estimar un precio hipotético basándose en las modificaciones de precio de otros artículos muy afines cuyos precios cabe suponer que fluctúan en forma similar. Cuando la desaparición del producto se vuelve definitiva, el procedimiento habitual consiste en reemplazarlo por un artículo similar. Si un nuevo modelo le sustituye, también se le sustituye en el índice. Si nada reemplaza el artículo desaparecido se elige otro similar como sustitutivo. En ambos casos el nuevo artículo se debe introducir en el índice de tal manera que toda diferencia de precio entre los dos artículos no afecte el nivel del índice y a tal efecto se recurre al enlace de ambos precios. Si ocurre que el artículo nuevo y el

antiguo se pueden conseguir al mismo tiempo, el encadenamiento es directo.

Pero el procedimiento no es tan sencillo cuando la desaparción del artículo antiguo es repentina y aún no se ha elegido otro nuevo, en cuyo caso es preferible contar con más informaciones antes de intentar el encadenamiento de las dos series de precios, pues lo ideal sería obtener un precio para el nuevo artículo durante el último período de oferta del antiguo, pero como en la práctica no siempre es posible, se debe suponer que el último precio del artículo antiguo y el primero del nuevo guardan una adecuada relación.

Artículos estacionales
Las ponderaciones de los artículos estacionales, como ciertas frutas y legumbres, en los trimestres fuera de temporada, se redistribuyen entre los demás artículos similares hasta que se reanude su oferta. Este procedimiento tiene los mismos efectos que la atribución de los precios faltantes.

Cálculo
El índice se calcula según la fórmula de Laspeyres como un promedio aritmético ponderado de base fija, cuyos coeficientes de ponderación corresponden al período de base.

Cuando los precios de los artículos se registran en más de un punto de venta o más de una vez por trimestre (frutas y legumbres frescas), es necesario calcular primero el precio promedio de esos artículos para el trimestre. Luego, para calcular un "precio relativo", se compara el promedio de los precios del trimestre de cada artículo con los precios del año de base de los mismos artículos.

Organización y publicación
Statistics Department: "The Annual Statistical Abstract" (Nuku'alofa).

idem: "Consumer Price Index".

TRINIDAD Y TABAGO

Denominación oficial
Index of Retail Prices (Indice de precios al por menor).

Alcance
El índice se compila mensualmente y abarca hogares con ingresos mensuales que en 1976 se situaban entre 100 y 800 dólares de Trinidad y Tabago.

Base oficial
Septiembre de 1982 = 100.

Fuente de la ponderación
La selección de los artículos y la determinación de los coeficientes de ponderación se basaron en los resultados de una encuesta sobre los gastos de los hogares efectuada en 1975-76, que abarcó unos 2 493 hogares de los cuales 1 681 hogares cuyos ingresos mensuales se situaban entre 100 y 800 dólares de Trinidad y Tabago en 1976. No se introdujeron reajustes en los coeficientes de ponderación para tener en consideración los cambios de precio entre el período de la encuesta y septiembre de 1982. Los artículos cuyos coeficientes de ponderación igualaban o superaban 1 por 1 000 fueron seleccionados para su inclusión en el índice.

Ponderaciones y composición

Grupos principales	Número de artículos	Ponderación	Número aproximado de cotizaciones de precio
Alimentación	94	351	...
Comidas tomadas fuera del hogar	4	15	...
Bebidas alcohólicas y tabaco	6	47	...
Combustible y luz	5	26	...
Alquiler y agua	5	126	...
Reparaciones y conservación	11	12	...
Moblaje y accesorios para el hogar	44	84	...
Servicios	5	14	...
Vestido y calzado	45	189	...
Transportes	13	86	...
Educación	6	25	...
Medicinas	8	25	...
Total	246	1 000	(a) ...

Nota: (a) Cuando se pueden obtener, se recogen tres cotizaciones de precio para cada artículo.

Gastos de consumo de los hogares
A los fines del índice, los gastos del consumo comprenden todos los bienes y servicios adquiridos para el consumo por la población de referencia, incluyendo los seguros y los intereses hipotecarios relacionados con la vivienda. Los ingresos en especie se incluyen como tales si se reciben en forma regular. También se incluyen los regalos y el pago de las licencias. Por el contrario están excluidos del índice los impuestos a los ingresos y otros impuestos directos, las contribuciones a fondos de seguridad social de pensiones, los seguros relacionados con bienes de consumo específicos, la atención médica y los pagos de los seguros de vida.

Método de recolección de los datos
Los precios para los bienes y servicios se obtienen en unos 375 puntos de venta seleccionados. Las localidades han sido seleccionadas en función de su población y gasto; los puntos de venta han sido seleccionados en función del conocimiento de los investigadores que trabajan en el terreno. La recolección de los datos relativos a los precios es de responsabilidad del Jefe de la "Oficina de Censos y Encuestas" que tiene a sus órdenes nueve funcionarios que visitan periódicamente los puntos de venta seleccionados y recogen los datos necesarios en el terreno. Los precios de las verduras, frutas y carne se recogen dos veces por mes. En el caso de los demás alimentos, bebida y tabaco, los precios se recogen mensualmente y, para vestimentas, reparación y mantenimiento del hogar, las comidas tomadas fuera del hogar, los alquileres, los equipos para el hogar, los servicios y los servicios de transporte y médicos, la recolección es trimestral. Los datos sobre los precios de combustible y luz se recogen mensualmente o trimestralmente y los de la educación cada seis meses. La recolección de precios comienza el segundo miércoles del mes y continúa durante una semana.

Los precios utilizados en el índice son los que cualquier persona debería pagar, el día de la fijación de su precio, para adquirir los bienes y servicios especificados.

Se excluyen las rebajas, salvo que constituyan una gran proporción de las ventas durante el período de referencia. Los precios del mercado negro se toman en consideración si se cotizan por los minoristas. No se incluyen los descuentos, las compras a plazo o a crédito, ni las adquisiciones de artículos de segunda mano.

Vivienda
Los datos sobre el alquiler se obtienen trimestralmente en viviendas seleccionadas cuya capacidad oscila entre uno y tres dormitorios. La totalidad de los datos actuales del alquiler de un área particular se expresa como relativo del total de los datos sobre el alquiler de base del área respectiva. Los relativos del área se combinan en un relativo final utilizando los coeficientes de ponderación de áreas.

Para las viviendas ocupadas por sus propietarios se ha obtenido un valor estimado de arriendo neto, tomando un porcentaje del valor de mercado de cada vivienda y sumándolo al alquiler pagado, extrayendo los coeficientes de ponderación del artículo (alquiler pagado). Pero para calcular el índice sólo se manejan los datos referentes a viviendas alquiladas.

Especificación de las variedades
Para las variedades seleccionadas en el registro de precios existen especificaciones detalladas de la marca, calidad, unidad, etc.

Sustitución, cambio de calidad, etc.
Siempre que se alteren las características de los productos, se efectúan ajustes de los precios del año de base. Los artículos obsoletos y los que han desaparecido del mercado se sustituyen por los nuevos que sean adecuados.

Artículos estacionales
Los artículos alimenticios frescos de estación no se incluyen en el índice fuera de su período de temporada y sus coeficientes de ponderación se distribuyen entre los demás artículos del mismo grupo.

Cálculo
El índice se calcula conforme a la fórmula de Laspeyres como un promedio aritmético ponderado de base fija, cuyos coeficientes de ponderación corresponden al período de base. Los precios medios de los artículos en cada área son los promedios aritméticos simples de los precios obtenidos. Después las relaciones de precios separados para los artículos en cada área se calculan dividiendo los precios medios del período corriente por los precios medios del período precedente. Después estas

relaciones de precios son ponderadas utilizando las ponderaciones regionales para obtener las relaciones de precios nacionales. Las ponderaciones son proporcionales a la población y a los datos relativos a la venta al por menor en las áreas alcanzadas.

Informaciones complementarias
No disponible.

Organización y publicación
Central Statistical Office: "The Index of Retail Prices 1982 - Statistical Studies and Papers", No.10, 1984 (Port of Spain).

Government Printing: "Gazette of Trinidad and Tobago", (Port of Spain).

TUNEZ

Denominación oficial
Indice spécifique des prix à la consommation (Indice específico de precios del consumo).

Alcance
El índice se calcula mensualmente y abarca los hogares urbanos de asalariados cuyos gastos anuales oscilaban entre 160 y 250 dinares por persona en 1980.

Base oficial
1983 = 100.

Fuente de la ponderación
Los coeficientes de ponderación y los artículos seleccionados se han determinado sobre la base de los resultados de una encuesta relativa a los gastos de los hogares realizada en 1980. No se han ajustado los coeficientes de ponderación para tener en cuenta la evolución de los precios entre el momento de la encuesta y 1983.

Ponderaciones y composición

Grupos principales	Número de artículos	Ponderación	Número aproximado de cotizaciones de precio
Alimentación	164	503	25 000
Vivienda:			
Alquiler y cargas	2	33	64
Combustible, luz y agua	16	62	512
Moblaje, accesorios para el hogar y conservación	60	78	1 924
Aseo personal, asistencia médica y productos de limpieza	127	56	4 064
Transportes	25	54	800
Vestido y calzado	91	101	2 910
Educación, distracciones y varios	69	113	2 210
Total	554	1 000	37 484

Gastos de consumo de los hogares
Los gastos de consumo de los hogares que se toman en cuenta en el cálculo del índice corresponden a los bienes y servicios adquiridos habitualmente por la población urbana y comprenden las compras a crédito que se contabilizan en su totalidad. Se excluyen los ingresos en especie, el consumo de bienes producidos en el hogar, el valor de los alquileres de las viviendas ocupadas por su propietario, el anticipo para la compra de bienes nuevos, la compra de viviendas y solares, las cuotas del seguro social y de las cajas de pensiones y las primas de seguro de vida, los gastos de patente, los seguros relacionados con bienes de consumo específicos (con exclusión del seguro privado de automóvil), los impuestos, los envíos de fondos, los donativos y los pagos análogos.

Método de recolección de los datos
Los precios son recogidos por investigadores en puntos de venta al por menor y establecimientos de servicios en las 16 ciudades más importantes del país. La selección de los puntos de venta no se determina aleatoriamente. Los puntos de venta seleccionados en las ciudades representan todas las formas de comercio y se determinan oportunamente en cada categoría de barrio (Medina, barrio moderno y barrio periférico). Las cotizaciones de precio se realizan sistemáticamente en todas las grandes superficies, en 55 mercados, 322 tiendas de comestibles y 240 tiendas de vestido, así como en 785 establecimientos de servicios. Las tarifas públicas se recogen directamente en las correspondientes administraciones. La encuesta sobre los precios se realiza por contacto directo por medio de investigadores encargados con carácter permanente de esta tarea.

En la práctica, hay un investigador por localidad con exclusión de Túnez y Sfax, en que hay, respectivamente, tres y dos investigadores, en razón de la importancia de estas dos ciudades. Los precios de la mayor parte de los artículos se recogen una vez por mes y punto de venta, salvo los días de mercado. Este ritmo de observación permite obtener al fin de cada mes dos o tres precios por variedad y por mes. El escalonamiento de las observaciones durante el mes depende del programa de visitas a los puntos de venta. En el caso de productos frescos, los promedios diarios de los precios se establecen generalmente con base en observaciones de los precios realizadas por la mañana (de las 10 a las 12) en los mercados. No se toman en cuenta los descuentos, las rebajas, los contratos de compra-alquiler, y las ventas a plazos.

Vivienda
Los datos relativos al alquiler se obtienen semestralmente con una muestra de aproximadamente 2 000 inquilinos de apartamentos, casas particulares y casas árabes. El alquiler comprende el precio mensual del mismo y, cuando procede, los gastos de comunidad. En el cálculo del índice de alquileres se toma en cuenta la importancia de cada categoría de vivienda.

Se excluyen del índice las viviendas ocupadas por sus propietarios.

Especificación de las variedades
Con el fin de seguir la evolución en el tiempo de los precios de un mismo objeto o de un mismo servicio de igual calidad, de manera que los cambios eventuales en los precios se deban exclusivamente a variaciones en los precios, los investigadores determinan las variedades en cada punto de venta e indican su marca, volumen, peso, etc.

Sustitución, cambio de calidad, etc.
Ocurre que variedades investigadas durante cierto tiempo desaparezcan en un punto de venta o en el mercado. Conviene advertir que la desaparición de un producto se considera como temporal mientras no exceda de seis meses, a partir de lo cual la desaparición se considera como definitiva y se procede entonces a una sustitución.

El método de sustitución varía según la naturaleza y la variedad. En el caso de variedades heterogéneas, el investigador procede a la sustitución según el punto de venta y cambia el precio de base del artículo en la tienda cuando hay una diferencia notable en la calidad.

En el caso de variedades homogéneas, cuando la variedad es sustituible y asimilable a la que ha desaparecido (diferencias de marca solamente), el investigador está facultado para proceder a la sustitución sin modificación del precio de base.

Artículos estacionales
Los precios de productos frescos como frutas, verduras y pescado se caracterizan por una alta frecuencia de cambio, así como por una variación del volumen de producción según las temporadas. Habida cuenta de ello, estos productos no se desglosan como las demás variedades ordinarias de la canasta del índice.

El índice para un producto fresco se obtiene utilizando las relaciones de precio entre el mes de la encuesta y la del mismo mes en el período de base. Estos índices se ponderan luego y se utilizan promedios móviles para el cálculo final del índice.

Cálculo
El índice se calcula según la fórmula de Laspeyres, como un promedio aritmético ponderado de base fija, cuyos coeficientes de ponderación corresponden a 1980.

Se calculan primero precios medios sencillos por localidad para las variedades homogéneas o índices medios sencillos por localidad para variedades heterogéneas. Para pasar de la localidad a la región, se utiliza como factor de ponderación la población urbana de cada localidad perteneciente a la región. Para pasar del nivel regional al nacional, se utilizan los coeficientes de ponderación regional con arreglo a la estructura de los gastos de consumo de cada región.

Informaciones complementarias
Se publican subgrupos detallados en el "Bulletin mensuel de statistique" así como otro índice nacional: "Indice général des prix à la consommation familiale" (base 1983 = 100).

Organización y publicación
Institut national de la statistique: "Bulletin mensuel de statistique" (Túnez).

idem: "Annuaire statistique de la Tunisie".

TURQUIA

Denominación oficial
Urban Areas Consumer Price Index (Indice Urbano de Precios del Consumo).

Alcance
El índice se compila mensualmente y abarca los hogares de las cinco grandes regiones urbanas del país (Egeo y Mármara, Mediterráneo, Anatolia central, Mar Negro y Anatolia sudoriental), cuyos ingresos mensuales medios oscilaban en 1987 entre 50 000 y 1 000 000 libras turcas.

Base oficial
1987 = 100.

Fuente de la ponderación
La determinación de los coeficientes de ponderación y la selección de los artículos se basaron en los resultados de una encuesta sobre los gastos de los hogares realizada entre enero y diciembre de 1987 a 14 424 hogares de todos los grupos socioeconómicos de una muestra de 50 zonas pobladas por más de 20 000 habitantes, representativa de las cinco grandes regiones del país antes mencionadas, y 16 ciudades. Para compilar el índice se seleccionaron los artículos de consumo doméstico más corriente. En cada grupo los artículos se dispusieron en orden descendente según la parte que representaban en el total del consumo y se consideraron sus valores acumulados. Los que representaban entre el 85 y el 90 por ciento del consumo total en el grupo se seleccionaron para representar lo en el índice. Dicha proporción llegó a ser del 100 por ciento en algunos grupos y alrededor del 60 o 65 por ciento en otros.

Ponderaciones y composición

Grupos principales	Número de artículos	Ponderación	Número aproximado de cotizaciones de precio
Alimentación	132	34,88	36 451
Vestido y calzado	62	12,80	18 727
Muebles, moblaje y equipo del hogar	53	11,24	11 199
Asistencia médica y aseo personal	29	3,44	4 470
Transporte y comunicaciones	23	6,48	1 278
Educación y recreación	33	5,01	3 748
Vivienda:	...	26,15	4 397
Alquiler	2	...	...
Combustible y luz	8	...	...
Reparaciones y mantenimiento	5	...	...
Total	347	100,00	80 270

Gastos de consumo de los hogares
El cálculo de las ponderaciones se basó en el valor real de los artículos de consumo, o en el valor atribuido (ingresos en especie para consumo del hogar, alquiler ficticio de la vivienda propia). El consumo se considera como "adquisición", es decir bienes o servicios que pasan a manos de un hogar. En la mayor parte de los casos se considera el momento de la compra, ignorándose los plazos de entrega. Salvo para compras diferidas, la adquisición se realiza cuando el bien pasa a ser posesión del hogar. Para las compras diferidas la adquisición se realiza en la fecha de entrega. Los ingresos en especie se consideran adquiridos cuando entran en posesión del hogar.

Método de recolección de los datos
La recolección de precios, en 33 zonas pobladas, está a cargo de personal de la División de índices y estadísticas de precios del Instituto Estatal de Estadísticas (SIS) de Ankara y sus oficinas regionales. Los precios de bienes que no varían según las regiones se registran a nivel central para evitar los errores que puede provocar una recolección separada y aliviar la carga de trabajo de las oficinas regionales. Tal es el caso, por ejemplo, de hospitales públicos, compañías aéreas, servicios postales y telefónicos, periódicos, enciclopedias, libros de texto publicados por el Ministerio de Educación, matrículas universitarias, medicamentos, servicios de electricidad y bienes de monopolios. Se ha decidido registrar dos veces por mes, durante las semanas que comprenden respectivamente los días 10 y 20, los precios de todos los artículos que no sean frutas y legumbres frescas, con la finalidad de registrar todas las posibles modificaciones de precio. Dado que las cotizaciones de legumbres y frutas frescas son más fluctuantes, su recolección es semanal, es decir cuatro veces por mes. Los precios utilizados en el índice son los que habitualmente paga cualquier persona del público. Los recargos por créditos y las rebajas no se toman en consideración pero sí los precios de las liquidaciones de prendas de vestir y tejidos.

Vivienda
Los alquileres de los hogares comprenden tanto los reales como los ficticios. En consecuencia el índice refleja no sólo las cotizaciones de alquiler que pagan los inquilinos sino también las que corresponden a quienes residen en casa propia. En cada zona poblada, las viviendas para la recolección de las cotizaciones de alquiler se eligieron en función de la estructura socioeconómica y las características de las casas de los distritos comprendidos en el muestreo de la encuesta de 1987 sobre el gasto de los hogares con un promedio mensual de ingresos que oscilaba entre 50 000 y 1 000 000 libras turcas.

Especificación de las variedades
En cada una de las zonas pobladas se definieron los 347 artículos utilizados para compilar el índice y, de ser necesario, se volvieron a definir en forma detallada para cada zona. El detalle de las definiciones permite que personas distintas puedan registrar debidamente los precios del mismo artículo.

Sustitución, cambio de calidad, etc.
Cuando ya no es posible encontrar un artículo en el mercado, bien se le sustituye por otro similar, bien se añaden los coeficientes de su ponderación a un artículo similar o se les distribuyen en el subgrupo. Los productos nuevos se incluyen en el sistema de ponderación en el próximo cambio del año tomado como base.

Artículos estacionales
Para los artículos con fluctuaciones estacionales de su consumo, cada mes se utilizan coeficientes de ponderación variables.

La fruta, seca o fresca, las legumbres, el pescado y las aves son artículos cuyo consumo presenta variaciones mensuales. Para estos artículos se utilizan coeficientes de ponderación variables porque un artículo que ingresa en el índice durante los pocos meses de una temporada deja su lugar a otro en la próxima estación y no se consumen en la misma cantidad todos los meses. Las ponderaciones se analizan en función de los artículos. La disminución de los coeficientes de ponderación de una fruta o legumbre dado un consumo escaso y, a su vez, el aumento de dichos coeficientes cuando el aumenta a cuando bajan los precios, se estudian y controlan todos los meses.

Cálculo
El índice se calcula según la fórmula de Laspeyres como un promedio aritmético ponderado de base fija, cuyos coeficientes de ponderación corresponden al período de base. El índice de precios del consumo en zonas urbanas se calcula como un promedio ponderado del índice de las cinco regiones urbanas, tomándose como ponderación el total del consumo de cada región.

Informaciones complementarias
Por lo general el índice de precios del consumo se actualiza cada cinco años para plasmar la evolución estructural. Se publican índices separados para las cinco grandes regiones urbanas y para las 16 ciudades, así como índices detallados de subgrupo. Los índices se publican en el "Press Bulletin" (Boletín de Prensa), el cuarto del mes siguiente a su compilación.

Organización y publicación
State Institute of Statistics (Instituto Estatal de Estadísticas): "Aylik Istatistik Bulteni" (Boletín Mensual de Estadísticas) (Ankara).

idem: "Wholesale and Consumer Price Indexes Monthly Bulletin"; (enero, febrero, marzo de 1990).

UGANDA (KAMPALA)

Denominación oficial
Consumer Price Index (Indice de Precios del Consumo).

Alcance
El índice se compila mensualmente y abarca todos los hogares de Kampala y Entebbe con gastos mensuales de 100 000 chelines (Shillings) o menos.

Base oficial
Diciembre de 1988 = 100.

Fuente de la ponderación
La determinación de los coeficientes de ponderación y la selec-

ción de los artículos se basaron en los resultados de una encuesta, realizada entre abril de 1989 y abril de 1990, sobre los gastos de los hogares con ingresos bajos o medianos cuyos gastos, en esos momentos, no superaban 100 000 Shillings por mes. Los artículos para la recolección de precios se seleccionaron en función de la importancia de su ponderación en la encuesta, su popularidad entre los hogares de la encuesta y el tener una calidad, cantidad y ubicación específicas. Por falta de recursos no se registraron los precios de algunos artículos seleccionados, pese a tener todas las características mencionadas. En tales casos, se combinaron los coeficientes de ponderación de dos o más artículos, salvo el que se supone con menos posibilidades de desaparecer del mercado, que se selecciona para representar a los otros con ponderaciones combinadas de tal forma que sus movimientos de precio tengan igual tendencia y uso final.

Ponderaciones y composición

Grupos principales	Número de artículos	Ponderación	Número aproximado de cotizaciones de precio
Alimentación	29	50,8	...
Bebidas alcohólicas y tabaco	7	6,3	...
Combustible y luz	3	7,3	...
Transporte	9	5,9	...
Vestido y calzado	12	5,5	...
Varios	14	8,5	...
Servicios (incl. alquiler, educación y salud)	15	15,7	...
Total	89	100.00	...

Gastos de consumo de los hogares
No disponible.

Método de recolección de los datos
Se seleccionaron seis mercados de las ciudades de Kampala y de Entebbe en función de su tamaño y distribución geográfica, sin emplearse ningún otro método científico. En cada uno de esos seis mercados se registraron los precios de los siguientes artículos: alimentación, bebidas y tabaco, combustible y energía eléctrica, vestidos y calzado. Los hospitales y clínicas, seleccionados por su número de pacientes y distribución geográfica, comunican los precios de los medicamentos y honorarios de las consultas médicas. A su vez los institutos de enseñanza, primaria y secundaria, seleccionados por su número de estudiantes o alumnos y ubicación, comunican el costo de las matrículas escolares. Las informaciones sobre las tarifas del transporte y sus modificaciones se obtienen de las compañias y grupos responsables del grueso de esta actividad. La recolección de precios de todos los artículos es mensual, salvo para la educación que se realiza cada cuatro meses, es decir una vez por período académico. Cabe señalar que los precios registrados se refieren a la mitad del mes en cuestión y que no se da un tratamiento especial a las frutas y legumbres. Los precios de los artículos sin patrón de medida uniforme, en especial los que suelen vender los colmados por montones u otras medidas indeterminadas se registran mediante compra directa. Sin embargo los artículos cuyo precio es demasiado elevado para el presupuesto del Departamento de Estadísticas se obtienen mediante entrevistas o por simple estimación de su costo. Los datos sobre los servicios se obtienen mediante cuestionarios enviados por correo. En la recolección de precios suelen participar cuatro personas que disponen de la misma cantidad de dinero para cada mercado, dos escalas de pesos y una lista de los artículos cuyos precios se debe registrar. La mayor parte de los artículos se adquieren mediante regateo, ponderándose luego sus precios, mientras que otros son una simple estimación. Se registran los precios reales que el consumidor paga en el momento, sin considerar descuentos ni rebajas de liquidación, y por lo tanto los precios del mercado negro se consideran como precios del consumo.

Vivienda
Las cotizaciones de alquiler se obtienen de apartamentos, dormitorios de varones, pisos y "bungalows" seleccionados de tal forma que resulten representados todos los grupos sociales.

Especificación de las variedades
Se describen la cantidad, calidad y ubicación del punto de venta.

Sustitución, cambio de calidad, etc.
Toda vez que un cambio importante afecta la calidad de un producto se le considera como un artículo nuevo que, por su similitud, sustituye al antiguo. Cuando una mercancía nueva aparece en el mercado, se registra su precio, pero no se le introduce en el índice hasta poder disponer de datos suficientes. Cuando una mercancía desaparece del mercado se repiten durante uno o dos meses los precios anteriores y si la situación persiste se la sustituye por otra similar.

Artículos estacionales
Si bien los precios del consumo incluyen artículos estacionales, hasta la fecha no se han hecho ajustes para tomar en consideración los efectos de carácter estacional.

Cálculo
El índice se calcula según la fórmula de Laspeyres como un promedio aritmético ponderado de base fija, cuyos coeficientes de ponderación corresponden al período de base. Para compilar índices del artículo, se utilizan relativos de precio del período corriente y del período precedente.

Informaciones complementarias
La próxima revisión del índice tomará como base los cálculos finales de la encuesta sobre el gasto de los hogares.

Organización y publicación
Ministerio de Planificación y Desarrollo Economico, Departamento de Estadísticas: "Key Economic Indicators" (Entebbe).

idem: "Statistical Bulletin No. CPI/1 Consumer Price Index Kampala (to September 1990)", Entebbe, octubre de 1990.

URUGUAY (MONTEVIDEO)

Denominación oficial
Indice de precios del consumo.

Alcance
El índice se calcula mensualmente y abarca el grupo de hogares de ingresos medios de Montevideo.

Base oficial
Diciembre de 1985 = 100.

Fuente de la ponderación
La selección de los artículos y la determinación de los coeficientes de ponderación se basaron en los resultados de una encuesta sobre los gastos de los hogares realizada en Montevideo de septiembre de 1982 a agosto de 1983 entre una muestra de 1 946 hogares de ingresos medios. Se introdujeron reajustes en los coeficientes de ponderación para tener en consideración los cambios de precio entre el período de la encuesta y diciembre de 1985.

Ponderaciones y composición

Grupos principales	Número de artículos	Ponderación	Número aproximado de cotizaciones de precio
Alimentación	84	39,91	...
Vestido y calzado	50	7,02	...
Vivienda	16	17,58	...
Mobiliario, artículos para el hogar y productos de limpieza	19	6,36	...
Asistencia médica	11	9,26	...
Transportes y comunicaciones	9	10,38	...
Distracciones	11	3,10	...
Educación	8	1,30	...
Otros gastos (incl. aseo personal y tabaco)	13	5,09	...
Total	221	100,00	...

Gastos de consumo de los hogares
A los efectos del índice, los gastos de consumo comprenden la adquisición de bienes y servicios para el consumo durante el período de referencia, incluidos el consumo de artículos de producción propia y los ingresos recibidos en especies. La adquisición de bienes duraderos, diferentes a las viviendas ocupadas por propietarios, se calcula sobre la base de pagos realizados sucesivamente durante el período de referencia. También se incluyen los regalos, impuestos indirectos, tasas municipales y otros gastos relativos a la utilización de bienes y servicios tales como licencias. Se excluyen del índice las transferencias monetarias, los impuestos sobre la renta y otros impuestos directos, los ahorros y el juego.

Método de recolección de los datos
Los precios se recogen en más de 400 puntos de venta minorista, mercados y establecimientos de servicios de Montevideo. La recolección de datos sobre precios para la

mayoría de los artículos corre a cargo de agentes encuestadores que visitan periódicamente los puntos de venta seleccionados. En cuanto a los artículos vendidos en mercados, los precios se verifican semanalmente. En el caso de artículos cuyos precios se fijan oficialmente (tales como leche, pan, electricidad, transportes públicos), los precios se obtienen directamente de las autoridades competentes y/o de las compañías de servicios cuando se produce algún cambio al respecto.

Los precios utilizados en el índice son los que cualquier persona tendría que pagar en el día de la recolección para adquirir el bien o servicio especificado.

Vivienda
Los datos sobre el alquiler se recopilan mensualmente en 12 agencias seleccionadas de alquiler de viviendas. En cuanto a las viviendas ocupadas por los propietarios, la información se obtiene del Banco Hipotecario del Uruguay.

Especificación de las variedades
Las especificaciones de las variedades cuyos precios se han de consignar facilitan detalles sobre la marca, descripción, unidad y tamaño.

Sustitución, cambio de calidad, etc.
Si un artículo desaparece de un punto de venta, su precio es imputado sobre la base de artículos disponibles en otros puntos de venta.

Artículos estacionales
Se tienen en cuenta las fluctuaciones estacionales de los precios de las frutas y de las verduras frescas variando los artículos y los coeficientes de ponderación mensuales de estos artículos cuyos coeficientes de ponderación permanecen, en conjunto, constantes.

Cálculo
El índice se calcula conforme a la fórmula de Laspeyres como un promedio aritmético ponderado de base fija, cuyos coeficientes de ponderación corresponden al período de base.

La relación del precio para cada artículo se calcula dividiendo el precio medio del período corriente por el precio medio del período de base.

Organización y publicación
Dirección General de Estadística y Censos: "Boletín mensual" (Montevideo).

idem: "Indice de precios del consumo, Metodología, Base diciembre 1985".

VANUATU

Denominación oficial
Consumer Price Index - Low Income Group Families (Indice de precios del consumo - familias de ingresos módicos).

Alcance
El índice se calcula trimestralmente y abarca familias del grupo de bajos ingresos que viven en áreas urbanas, cuyo jefe de familia percibía menos de 20 000 FNH en 1975.

Base oficial
Enero - marzo de 1976 = 100.

Fuente de la ponderación
La selección de los artículos y la determinación de los coeficientes de ponderación se basaron en los resultados de una encuesta sobre los gastos de los hogares efectuada durante el primer trimestre de 1975 entre 220 hogares en Vila y en Santo (Luganville).

Ponderaciones y composición

Grupos principales	Número de artículos	Ponderación	Número aproximado de cotizaciones de precio
Alimentación	...	45,8	...
Bebidas y tabaco	...	10,1	...
Vestido y calzado	...	14,1	...
Alquiler, combustible, luz y agua	...	2,2	...
Moblaje, artículos y servicios para el hogar	...	8,0	...
Transportes y comunicaciones	...	9,8	...
Salud, educación y distracciones	...	10,0	...
Total	...	100,0	...

Gastos de consumo de los hogares
A los fines del índice, los gastos del consumo comprenden todos los bienes y servicios adquiridos para el consumo por la población de referencia. Se excluyen los impuestos a los ingresos, inversiones, ahorros y préstamos personales.

Método de recolección de los datos
Los precios se recogen alrededor de mediados de mes en Santo y a mediados de cada trimestre en Vila, en puntos de venta al por menor seleccionados y en establecimientos de servicios. En el cálculo del índice se utilizan los precios que pagan normalmente los consumidores.

Vivienda
No disponible.

Especificación de las variedades
Las especificaciones de los artículos cuyos precios se han de registrar establecen la marca, factura, calidad y tamaño.

Sustitución, cambio de calidad, etc.
Si no se encuentra un producto en un punto de venta se lo sustituye en el índice por otro que sea similar.

Artículos estacionales
No disponible.

Cálculo
El índice se calcula según la fórmula de Laspeyres, como un promedio aritmético ponderado de base fija, cuyos coeficientes de ponderación corresponden al primer trimestre de 1975.

El índice para un artículo se obtiene utilizando las relaciones de precios del período corriente y del período precedente.

Informaciones complementarias
Actualmente se calcula una nueva serie relativa a todos los hogares de la zona urbana de Vanuatu (base enero-marzo de 1990 = 100), pero en el momento de publicar el presente Volumen la OIT no disponía de informaciones metodológicas sobre esta serie.

Organización y publicación
National Planning and Statistics Office: "Statistical Bulletin" (Port Vila).

VENEZUELA (CARACAS)

Denominación oficial
Indice de precios al consumidor para el área metropolitana de Caracas.

Alcance
El índice se calcula mensualmente, y abarca todas las familias que viven en el área metropolitana de Caracas.

Base oficial
1984 = 100.

Fuente de la ponderación
La selección de los artículos y la determinación de los coeficientes de ponderación se basaron en los resultados de una encuesta sobre los gastos de los hogares, realizada durante 12 meses, del primero de noviembre de 1974 al 31 de octubre de 1975, que abarcó todos los hogares del área metropolitana de Caracas. Para la recolección de precios se seleccionaron los productos que representaban más de 1 por ciento del total de los gastos del hogar. Los movimientos de precios de los productos no seleccionados se consideran en función de aquéllos más representativos cuyo precio se haya recogido. No se introdujeron reajustes en los coeficientes de ponderación para tener en consideración los cambios de precio entre el período de la encuesta y 1984.

Ponderaciones y composición

Grupos principales	Número de artículos	Ponderación	Número aproximado de cotizaciones de precio
Alimentación y tabaco	180	30,83	...
Gastos del hogar (vivienda, combustible y luz, moblaje, etc.)	59	29,64	...
Vestido y calzado	72	9,33	...
Varios	64	30,20	...
Total	375	100,00	...

Gastos de consumo de los hogares
Los gastos de consumo a efectos del índice abarcan todos los bienes y servicios adquiridos para el consumo por la población comprendida en el índice. Incluyen asimismo el consumo de artículos cultivados y producidos en el hogar, así como los ingresos en especies, las cotizaciones a la seguridad social y fondos de pensiones, tasas pagadas a las autoridades municipales por utilización de bienes y servicios, por ejemplo, tasas por matriculación de vehículos, tasas por licencias, etc.

Método de recolección de los datos
Los precios los recogen mensualmente agentes encuestadores en 1 136 puntos de venta seleccionados, incluidas zonas comerciales, supermercados, almacenes minoristas y establecimientos de servicios. Las muestras se distribuyen uniformemente a lo largo del mes. En cuanto a las frutas frescas, se recogen los precios tres veces en cada punto de venta seleccionado para obtener un precio medio para cada una de ellas. Se recurre a las tarifas oficiales para la electricidad, gas y agua, y se llevan a cabo encuestas especiales para la asistencia médica, enseñanza, transporte y comunicaciones.

Los precios utilizados en el cálculo del índice son los precios reales practicados en transacciones al contado. No se tienen en cuenta los precios de los artículos de segunda mano ni los del mercado negro.

Vivienda
Los datos sobre alquileres se obtienen mensualmente de una muestra de viviendas alquiladas (casas y apartamentos). La muestra se distribuye en un período de 12 meses, y en cada uno de ellos se visitan aproximadamente unas 200 viviendas alquiladas. No se tienen en cuenta las viviendas ocupadas por los propietarios.

Especificación de las variedades
Las especificaciones de los artículos cuyos precios se han de registrar figuran con detalles sobre la marca, descripción, unidad y tamaño, etc.

Sustitución, cambio de calidad, etc.
Si cambia la calidad de un artículo, se considera como artículo nuevo; cuando éste tiene que entrar en línea de cuenta, se incluye en el índice como variedad del subgrupo estudiado. Cuando un artículo desaparece del mercado se sustituye por otro similar.

Artículos estacionales
En el cálculo del índice no se tienen en cuenta las fluctuaciones estacionales en los precios de los artículos.

Cálculo
El índice se calcula según la fórmula de Laspeyres, como un promedio aritmético ponderado de base fija, cuyos coeficientes de ponderación corresponden al período del primero de noviembre de 1974 al 31 de octubre de 1975.

El índice para un artículo se obtiene utilizando las relaciones de precios de cada variedad en cada punto de venta del período corriente y del período precedente. Para obtener los índices por artículos se calculan los promedios aritméticos simples de estas relaciones de precios.

Organización y publicación
Banco Central de Venezuela, Departamento de Estadísticas de Precios: "Boletín mensual" (Caracas).

YEMEN (ADEN)

Denominación oficial
Consumer Price Index (Índice de Precios del Consumo).

Alcance
El índice se compila mensualmente y abarca hogares de Adén.

Base oficial
1969 = 100.

Fuente de la ponderación
La determinación de los coeficientes de ponderación y la selección de los artículos se basaron en los resultados de una encuesta sobre los gastos de los hogares de empleados del gobierno. Posteriormente se ajustaron los coeficientes de ponderación para tomar en cuenta los cambios de la estructura del consumo.

Gastos de consumo de los hogares
No disponible.

Ponderaciones y composición

Grupos principales	Número de artículos	Ponderación	Número aproximado de cotizaciones de precio
Alimentación	48	508	...
Combustible, luz y agua	6	39	...
Alquiler	5	60	...
Vestido y calzado	24	90	...
Accesorios del hogar	13	40	...
Qat, tabaco y bebidas alcohólicas	3	100	...
Otros gastos (salud, aseo personal, transportes, cultura y recreación)	24	163	...
Total	123	1 000	...

Método de recolección de los datos
Los precios se registran regularmente en Adén, los lunes y martes de la segunda semana de cada mes.

Vivienda
No disponible.

Especificación de las variedades
Para asegurar que los precios sean comprables en el tiempo, se han definido cuidadosamente la calidad y cantidad de los bienes y los servicios.

Sustitución, cambio de calidad, etc.
No disponible.

Artículos estacionales
No disponible.

Cálculo
El índice se calcula según la fórmula de Laspeyres como un promedio aritmético ponderado de base fija, cuyos coeficientes de ponderación corresponden al período de base.

Organización y publicación
Central Statistical Organisation: "Statistical Yearbook" (Adén).

YUGOSLAVIA

Denominación oficial
Cost of Living Index (Índice del costo de la vida).

Alcance
El índice se calcula mensualmente y abarca las familias de obreros y empleados.

Base oficial
Los índices que figuran en las publicaciones nacionales se calculan de acuerdo con los precios medios all año precedente; la base de publicación del índice queda así modificada cada año civil.

Fuente de la ponderación
La selección de los artículos y la determinación de los coeficientes de ponderación se basaron en los resultados de una encuesta permanente sobre los ingresos y gastos familiares realizada en más de 50 grandes ciudades y que abarca más de 2 000 familias de obreros y empleados (compuestas de dos adultos y uno o dos menores de 18 años). Los coeficientes de ponderacion son los siguientes:

Ponderaciones y composición

Grupos principales	Número de artículos	Ponderación	Número aproximado de cotizaciones de precio
Alimentación	94	45,84	...
Bebidas y tabaco	8	4,92	...
Vivienda:			
Alquiler	1	3,60	...
Conservación y agua	4	2,74	...
Combustible y luz	9	5,62	...
Vestido y calzado	54	12,37	...
Bienes y servicios del hogar	36	6,88	...
Aseo personal	17	3,58	...
Educación y distracciones	18	5,54	...
Transportes y comunicaciones	9	8,91	...
Total	260	100,00	...

Gastos de consumo de los hogares
No disponible.

Método de recolección de los datos
Los precios de la mayoría de los artículos son recogidos mensualmente por investigadores en unos 3 500 puntos de venta al por menor de 53 ciudades; los de los productos agrícolas se recogen cada quincena.

Vivienda
Los datos referentes al alquiler se obtienen a partir de ocho categorías de vivienda en cada una de las 53 ciudades.

Especificación de las variedades
No disponible.

Sustitución, cambio de calidad, etc.
No disponible.

Artículos estacionales
Se tienen en cuenta las fluctuaciones estacionales de los precios de las frutas y las verduras frescas variando la composición mensual de los artículos del subgrupo cuyos coeficientes de ponderación permanecen, en conjunto constantes.

Cálculo
El índice se calcula conforme a la fórmula de Laspeyres como un promedio aritmético ponderado de base fija, cuyos coeficientes de ponderación corresponden al período de base. El índice se obtiene por ponderaciones sucesivas de los promedios aritméticos de los precios, los coeficientes de ponderacion utilizados se basan tanto en el valor total de la venta de los artículos en las diferentes ciudades o repúblicas en donde se recogen los precios, como en la estructura de los gastos de las familias cubiertas por la encuesta permanente.

Organización y publicación
Federal Statistical Institute: "Indeks" (Belgrado).
idem: "Metodoloski materijali" núms. 122, 168 y 233.

ZAMBIA

Denominación oficial
Consumer Price Index for Low-Income Group Families (Indice de Precios del Consumo para las familias de ingresos bajos).

Alcance
El índice se compila mensualmente y abarca hogares urbanos cuyos ingresos mensuales eran inferiores a 100 kwachas en 1974-1975. El índice refleja las modificaciones de los precios en Lusaka, el Copperbelt (cinturón del cobre), Kabwe y Livingstone.

Base oficial
1975 = 100 y 1985 = 100.

Fuente de la ponderación
La determinación de los coeficientes de ponderación y la selección de los artículos se basaron en los resultados de una encuesta sobre los gastos de los hogares realizada de marzo de 1974 a marzo de 1975 en Lusaka, Ndola y Kitwe. El índice se refiere a hogares urbanos que en la época de la encuesta tenía ingresos mensuales inferiores a 100 kwachas.

Ponderaciones y composición

Grupos principales	Número de artículos	Ponderación	Número aproximado de cotizaciones de precio
Alimentación y tabaco	74	680	459
Vestido y calzado	40	99	268
Combustible y luz	25	106	87
Bienes y moblaje del hogar	25	44	208
Asistencia médica	36	3	98
Transportes y comunicaciones	11	22	16
Educación y recreación	10	9	43
Otros bienes y servicios	63	37	244
Total	284	1 000	1 423

Gastos de consumo de los hogares
Se excluyen los seguros de vida y los impuestos a los ingresos y a las propiedades individuales.

Método de recolección de los datos
Todos los meses, alrededor del día diez, funcionarios de la Oficina Central de Estadística realizan una encuesta de precios que en Lusaka se obtienen mediante visitas personales a los puntos de venta seleccionados, mientras que en las demás ciudades se envían cuestionarios por correo a los puntos de venta y establecimientos de servicios. Algunos precios se investigan mediante compra directa y se recurre a las tarifas oficiales para artículos tales como electricidad, gas, agua, transportes y comunicaciones. Los precios de las frutas y legumbres frescas se registran dos veces por mes en el mercado urbano central. Los precios utilizados para el cálculo del índice son los que pagan en ese momento los consumidores. También se toman en cuenta los descuentos, rebajas y precios de liquidación.

Vivienda
No se incluyen en el índice las cotizaciones del alquiler ni los gastos de la vivienda propia.

Especificación de las variedades
Se especifica el tamaño, unidad, marca y calidad de cada artículo cuyo precio se debe registrar.

Sustitución, cambio de calidad, etc.
Se estiman los cambios de calidad tomando como base sustitutivos estrechamente relacionados. Sólo se introducen los artículos de sustitución cuando adquieren una importancia de mercado suficiente.

Artículos estacionales
No se ajustan las fluctuaciones de precio de los artículos estacionales.

Cálculo
El índice se calcula según la fórmula de Laspeyres como un promedio aritmético ponderado de base fija, cuyos coeficientes de ponderación corresponden al período de marzo de 1974 a marzo de 1975.

Para el cómputo de los índices de artículo se utilizan los relativos de los promedios de precios del período en curso y del período de base. Los promedios de precio son promedios aritméticos simples de las cotizaciones de precio.

Informaciones complementarias
También se compila un Indice de Precios del Consumo de hogares de ingresos elevados (base: 1975 = 100).

Organización y publicación
Central Statistical Office: "Monthly Digest of Statistics" (Lusaka).
idem: "Studies in Official Statistics - No. 3, Methods and Procedures used in Compiling Price Statistics".

ZIMBABWE

Denominación oficial
Consumer Price Index for Lower Income Urban Families (Indice de Precios del Consumo, Hogares de Ingresos Bajos).

Alcance
El índice se compila mensualmente y se refiere a hogares africanos, salvo aquellos cuyo jefe es jubilado, desocupado o independiente y los que tenían ingresos mensuales superiores a 250 dólares de Zimbabwe ($ Z) en el momento de la encuesta. El índice abarca cuatro zonas urbanas: Harare, Bulawayo, Mutare y Gweru.

Base oficial
1980 = 100.

Fuente de la ponderación
La determinación de los coeficientes de ponderación y la selección de los artículos se basaron en los resultados de una encuesta sobre los gastos de los hogares realizada en 1978-1979 que abarcó 250 hogares de Harare y 233 de Bulawayo. No se ajustaron los coeficientes de ponderación para tomar en cuenta las modificaciones de precio ocurridas entre el período de la encuesta y el período de base.

Ponderaciones y composición

Grupos principales	Número de artículos	Ponderación	Número aproximado de cotizaciones de precio
Alimentación	27	54,9	1 466
Bebidas y tabaco	5	5,4	156
Vestido y calzado	25	6,6	496
Alquiler, combustible y luz	4	18,4	87
Artículos del hogar	23	4,6	741
Transportes	19	4,7	34
Varios	21	5,4	295
Total	124	100,0	3 275

Gastos de consumo de los hogares
No se toma en cuenta el consumo de bienes y servicios recibidos como ingresos en especie. Se excluyen los impuestos directos y los ahorros tales como primas de seguros de vida y pagos a fondos de pensión, así como apuestas de juego y donativos.

Método de recolección de los datos
Los precios se registran mensualmente en tiendas minoristas y establecimientos seleccionados de los suburbios densamente poblados de Harare, Bulawayo, Mutare y Gweru, pero también en puntos de venta del centro de las ciudades.

La recolección se realiza principalmente mediante cuestionarios enviados por correo. En Bulawayo, Mutare y Gweru los cuestionarios los envían y reciben funcionarios del Departamento de Servicios Comunitarios. En esos sitios los datos sobre precios de frutas y legumbres se registran trimestralmente mediante visitas a los mercados. En Harare el registro de los precios de algunos artículos, como frutas y legumbres que se venden en los mercados, está a cargo del personal de la sección de precios de la Oficina Central de Estadística.

Los precios del índice son los que pagan efectivamente las personas de público el día del registro. No se toman en cuenta descuentos, rebajas ni precios del mercado negro.

Vivienda
Las cotizaciones del alquiler se registran mediante una encuesta semestral de viviendas. El índice de alquileres se basa en las sumas que pagan los arrendatarios de diversas clases de viviendas municipales, comprendidos los recargos de agua y recolección de residuos. Los gastos de reparación de las viviendas se excluyen del grupo principal "alquiler" pero se incluyen en el grupo "varios".

Especificación de las variedades
Para algunos artículos, principalmente de la alimentación, la marca y el tamaño se especifican en los formularios especiales del registro. De los demás artículos se dan descripciones generales en los cuestionarios de la Oficina Central de Estadística. Para representar un artículo se pueden utilizar marcas distintas en los diferentes puntos de venta siempre que mes tras mes se registren los precios de la misma marca. De una línea o gama de productos se elige el que tenga el mejor precio medio de venta.

Sustitución, cambio de calidad, etc.
Cuando temporalmente no se disponga de un artículo en existencia se mantiene el último precio registrado hasta que se le pueda conseguir de nuevo o se introduce un artículo de sustitución y se utiliza el método de enlace de los precios.

Artículos estacionales
Sólo se tratan como artículos estacionales las frutas y las legumbres. La estructura de la ponderación utilizada varía todos los meses para tomar en cuenta las fluctuaciones estacionales, pero el coeficiente total de frutas y legumbres se mantiene constante.

Cálculo
El índice se calcula según la fórmula de Laspeyres como un promedio aritmético ponderado de base fija, cuyos coeficientes de ponderación corresponden a diciembre de 1981. Los índices de grupo se ajustan luego a la base 1980 = 100 utilizando factores de conversión determinados.

Para el cómputo de los índices por artículo se utilizan los relativos de precio del período en curso y del anterior. Para la mayoría de los artículos se calculan relativos de precios medios y para los artículos nuevos, tales como repuestos de coches, promedios de los relativos de precio.

Los índices separados se calculan primero para cada una de las cuatro ciudades y luego esos índices se ponderan por la población de cada una de ellas para obtener el índice nacional. Los coeficientes de ponderación aplicados a las ciudades son: 56 para Harare, 32 para Bulawayo, 6 para Gweru y 6 para Mutare.

Informaciones complementarias
La Oficina Central de Estadística también publica un Indice de los precios del consumo de hogares urbanos con ingresos elevados (base 1980 = 100). Se elabora además un índice de precios de todos los artículos, excluídos los impuestos a las ventas y al consumo, tanto para los hogares urbanos con ingresos módicos como para los con ingresos elevados.

Organización y publicación
Central Statistical Office: "Quarterly Digest of Statistics" (Harare).

idem: "Monthly Supplement to the Digest of Statistics".